THE
ABC-CLIO
COMPANION TO

American Reconstruction, 1862–1877

A satirical cartoon of Benjamin F. Butler portrays the controversial figure as a self-serving politician.

THE
ABC-CLIO
COMPANION TO

American Reconstruction, 1862–1877

William L. Richter

ABC-CLIO

Santa Barbara, California
Denver, Colorado
Oxford, England

All illustrations courtesy of the Library of Congress

Illustration research by Susan Hormuth

Library of Congress Cataloging-in-Publication Data

Richter, William L. (William Lee), 1942–
 The ABC-CLIO companion to American reconstruction, 1862–1877 / William L. Richter.
  p. cm. — (ABC-CLIO companions to key issues in American history and life)
  Includes bibliographical references and index.
 1. Reconstruction. 2. United States—History—1849-1877.
I. Title. II. Series.
E668.R53 1996 973.8—dc21 96-46616

ISBN 0-87436-851-0

02 01 00 99 98 97 96 95   10 9 8 7 6 5 4 3 2 1

ABC-CLIO, Inc.
130 Cremona Drive, P.O. Box 1911
Santa Barbara, California 93116-1911

This book is printed on acid-free paper ∞.
Manufactured in the United States of America

To Charles B. Dew
who proved to me that American history did not begin at
Fort Sumter and end at Appomattox

ABC-CLIO Companions to Key Issues in American History and Life

Contents

Preface

Reconstruction. "Spell the word one way, with a small *r*, and it has good American purposefulness; for it means a putting together, a rebuilding, a rehabilitation. Spell it another way, with a capital *R*, and it becomes for many a malediction; and for others a forgotten, unreached, and needful goal; and for still others a vaguely unclean memory." So wrote Hodding Carter II, noted Southern newspaperman turned historian, in 1959.[1] In one of the best definitions of the historical era that traditionally spans the years from 1865 to 1877, he skillfully reduced 120 years of historical controversy into two short sentences.

Unlike Carter, people who lived at the time generally defined the term in a strict political and constitutional sense. To them Reconstruction referred to the status of the 11 secessionist states that had made up the defunct Confederacy. (The Rebels had also claimed Kentucky and Missouri and had 13 stars on their flags to indicate this, but the North refused to recognize such shenanigans and claimed them, too—an assertion made fact by military occupation.) Now that the North had won the war, how were these wayward 11 to be brought back into the Union? What political terms, conditions, or constitutional changes must they stipulate to? Everyone agreed that their 1865 status was not "normal," whether they had legally seceded or not. Something had to be done

to normalize the nation once again. But there was no agreement as to what would make the Union whole in fact as well as in name.

The idea that there was an era called "Civil War" and another named "Reconstruction" is an artificial device employed by historians. Reconstruction began as a germ in the Northern mind well before the Civil War made it a necessity. The earliest rumblings came in the 1830s in the struggle over freedom of thought that closed the mind of the Old South to the intellectual questioning that had been the Jeffersonian ideal.[2] They were also evident in the antislavery philosophy that fueled the Liberty party (1840–1844) and the Free Soil party (1848–1852), third political parties that questioned the existence of a different society south of the Mason-Dixon line and presaged the Republican party's protest of the extension of slavery into Kansas in 1854. At the time, the two major political parties had been the Jacksonian Democrats and the Whigs. But as the quarrel about slavery intensified, the Whigs lost out, their Northern brethren eventually drifting into the Republican ranks via the Know-Nothing party, while the Southern branch took a similar route to the Democrats. By 1860, the latter was the country's only national party, the Republicans being restricted to Northern support. When the Democrats broke up in 1860 over the perfidy represented by the presidential candidacy of Senator Stephen A. Douglas of Illinois, who was renowned for talking about slavery out of both sides of his mouth (as revealed by a relatively unknown opponent in the 1858 senatorial race, Abraham Lincoln), the stage was set for war.

The Northern voters who coalesced around the Republican banner in 1860 held two ideals in politics. The heart of Republican ideology was "free labor." Emphasized again and again by party orators, this meant the idea of a good, hard-working, moral society that was not merely against the institution of slavery but in favor of the capitalistic ideal of promoting an expanding industrial revolution. The main tenet was the dignity of labor. It reflected the Protestant Ethic of the Reformation, the Puritan ideal of hard work brought here by Calvinist dissenters, primarily from England, in the seventeenth century. One worked hard, went the notion, to serve God better. Embodied in this concept were honesty, frugality, diligence, punctuality, and sobriety.[3]

But there was more. Free labor meant that by hard, honest work one had the right to advance oneself economically in any field one chose. It reflected the inordinate American ideal of improving one's life and the life of one's children—to escape the social station of one's birth. Free labor was an opportunity to stop being a wage earner and become an entrepreneur—a wage payer. But the only place in the United States that Northerners saw this happening was above the Mason-Dixon line, the border between Pennsylvania and Maryland, north of slavery. Never mind that Southerners saw the same opportunity through agriculture, westward movement, and the purchase of slave labor. To the Yankees progress meant the extension of their way of life to the exclusion of the plantation economy. They believed that slavery stifled this dream and that to allow it to expand any farther westward would destroy opportunity for all the "little" Americans, nonslaveholders North and South.

Implicit in the free labor ideal was the second belief of Republicans, a critique of Southern society. Yankees maintained that the South failed to cherish the proper values of economic opportunity, social mobility, and political democracy. They saw the South as stagnant and blamed slavery for the region's stagnation. After all, slavery was essentially all that differentiated North from South to the casual Yankee observer. Because of the stifling effect of slavery on Southern society, thought the Yankees, the South lacked canals, railroads, public schools, charities, commerce, cities, farms that grew other than staple (cash) crops, and a rapidly increasing immigrant population. (Never mind that historians have shown all of this to be false—that the South was actually the richer section with its wealth in land and slaves.[4]) None of this was seen in the North as the fault of African Americans. It was the white planters who exploited blacks through the "peculiar institution," slavery. If freed, blacks would work harder for themselves rather than for others and become part of the American Dream, thus vastly increasing the wealth of the nation.

Worst of all for the national future was the Northern fear that slavery and free labor could not exist side by side. Slave labor would always undercut free labor costs. It also degraded all labor. Yankees pointed to the "poor white trash," the essence of every novel on the South to this day, as "proof." No one could improve oneself if even a single slave were present. The whole area would be doomed to second-class social, economic, and political development. Hence limiting slavery's spread was essential to get a grip on the perceived problem of the South. Slavery had to be kept confined to where it was, said Northerners. The ultimate elimination of slavery would be best for South, North, the whole nation. The South needed reconstruction through Northern immigration to revitalize the population and its benighted institutions and to show them the new way of the industrial state. The North represented progress; the South was decadence incarnate.[5]

Of course, the real problem with Reconstruction was its hidden meaning beyond the stated Republican prewar critique, the implications hinted at in the definition given by Hodding Carter. These gave the era its complexity and feeling of hollowness that exists even today. Central to the whole Reconstruction program were African Americans, in bondage to whites for the better part of 250 years. President Abraham Lincoln had declared them to be "freedmen," in the gender-bound language of the day. His wartime Emancipation Proclamation, however, was of dubious enough legality to prompt a constitutional amendment to guarantee its lofty goal. But more insidious questions arose among the white body politic. Were black people human beings in the full sense of the term? Even some of Lincoln's Republican party, especially from the Old Northwest, asserted African Americans' alleged innate biological inferiority. Their Democratic opponents seemed convinced of it. Other Republicans, generally from New England or areas influenced by New England mores, such as Ohio's Western Reserve, saw the freedmen as equal in all respects to white Americans.[6]

If blacks were free and equal, did they not need to be made citizens formally to enjoy the full rights of Americans? After all, the U.S. Supreme Court in the 1857 case *Dred Scott v. Sanford* had specifically declared them not citizens, whether slave or free.[7] All Republicans agreed that some African American rights had to be guaranteed on the federal level, but which ones? Obviously the ex-slaves had to be protected against exploitation by their former masters. This pointed to a guarantee of civil rights secured to all citizens, such as equal status in courts, the right to sue and be sued, the right to sit on juries and be tried by juries of their peers, and the enjoyment of equal protection of the law in and out of court.

But what about political rights? These were the exclusive domain of the states in 1865 and included not only the right to vote but access to public education and public accommodations. For the federal government to interfere here would mark a revolutionary step in state and federal relations. And what about social rights, the entrance to one's home and business, employment,

private associations and clubs, and private schools? These had traditionally been the prerogative of individuals and outside the scope of government on any level. They would prove even tougher to obtain than political rights.

With respect to obtaining government-protected rights, African Americans faced an onus of implied inferiority in the eyes of many. This bothered many Americans then as now.[8] But Radical Republicans, those who saw the full scope of the problem and wished to act to solve it immediately without conditions, maintained that society was responsible for the inferior position of blacks as slaves and must act now to redress the imbalance and allow the freedmen to advance along with all other Americans. Racism, however, prevented many whites, North and South, from confronting this seemingly obvious solution. So did something else. The North (as did the South) tended to fuse the concept of liberty with stable institutional structures. The secession of the South proved that these institutional structures were in disarray. The result was a vast experimentation in constitutional theory to crush the rebellion. But once the crisis had passed, the North opted for ordered liberty rather than the uncertainties of revolutionary change. Hence the very forces that made the struggle for equal justice possible also were the sources of its defeat.[9]

Along with the racial and order issues was the question of who would serve in public office and control state policies and politics. If the racial angle is taken out of consideration, the problem was essentially one of what to do with former Confederate leaders. Technically these men had committed treason, although the capture of so many Northern soldiers early in the civil conflict led the Lincoln government to recognize the Rebels as quasi-belligerents and accord them rights as prisoners of war, rather than hanging them en masse. The generous peace terms, typified by those granted to Gen. Robert E. Lee's surrendering army at Appomattox Court House—which permitted officers and men to go home and remain undisturbed so long as they kept their paroles—compounded the dilemma.

Northerners were willing enough to forgive the Rebels and accede to the principle of self-government as the cornerstone of U.S. government, but they found the ready access of leaders of the rebellion to public office repugnant. Could the population of any state be prevented, legally or constitutionally, from making a "mistake" in its choice of rulers? There were loyal men who had refused to support secession in every Southern state, men far preferable than ex-Rebels for public trust. But how did one find these voters? In the 1860s the standard practice was loyalty oaths, but to be eligible to vote, should one never have supported the Confederacy in thought or deed, or was a promise of future loyalty good enough? Either way, it was difficult to know whether the oaths were taken in good faith. Nonetheless, every Northern plan of Reconstruction contained some form of exclusion for Confederates, especially high-ranking ones, in its text.[10]

It all boiled down to one question: what made a loyal American? Was a simple pledge of future allegiance adequate, or did one have to promise to adhere to the tenets of an imposed (and possibly despised) program? The North wanted some sign that the South had lost the war. The Northern soldiers had seen their Rebel counterparts in the field surrender their flags and stack their weapons. The real problem, though, concerned the civilians. Northern politicians and voters wanted a sign of submission from the Southern politicians and civilians who had not been in the fighting line. But Southerners heretofore had been a part of the U.S. success story, despite the contradictions between slavery and freedom implicit in the antebellum South. Americans had not lost a war before, and Southerners were not about to beg forgiveness for doing what their forefathers had done, albeit more successfully, against the British in 1776.[11] Americans did not know how to lose gracefully, and until the United States' 1975 defeat in Vietnam, the experience of losing a war and suffering enemy occupation was what made Southerners as Americans unique; it galled them

for generations. In reality, of course, it was the North that was unique; the South shared its history of lost wars with most other nations of the world.[12]

So all the South was willing to promise was to be loyal in the future. There was to be no sign of surrender for the civilians back home; General Lee and his men were not marched to the Capitol in chains. In the end no one was hanged for rebellion, not even Confederate president Jefferson Davis. It was hard to try someone for treason against the United States when the Confederacy had been treated as a belligerent, in effect a separate country, for four long years.[13] The only miscreant hanged was a so-called war criminal, Maj. Henry Wirtz, commandant of the infamous Andersonville prison, primarily for his insensitive handling of prisoners. But to purists he was a Swiss, who spoke English with a German accent, not a "real" American secessionist. In sum, the North had to be satisfied with labeling the conflict the "War of the Rebellion" and letting it go at that.[14]

A great irony of the Reconstruction period concerned the fact that under the old (pre–Civil War) Constitution, three-fifths of all slaves had been counted for the purposes of taxation and representation. Now that African Americans were free, all of them would be counted as whole persons. In other words, the South was actually to be rewarded for losing the war by receiving more congressional representatives. Republican majorities would drop from a wartime 98 to a postwar 40 in the House of Representatives and from 28 to 6 in the Senate. This meant that the South could return to its old prewar game of obstructing Northern economic desires in league with its Northern Democratic allies. The entire Republican economic program enacted during the war, when most Democrats were leading the Southern armies in gray, was threatened with repeal. This sizable program included the transcontinental railroad and other internal improvements, land grant agricultural and mechanical colleges, the national banking system, the homestead law, and high tariffs to protect Northern industry.

The North, business and labor alike, wanted somehow to guarantee this economic progress as a condition of Southern readmission, but the Republicans' position was endangered by the very Constitution they fought to maintain. Although the war had stretched its fabric close to rending, the limited Constitution could nonetheless protect the Rebel South from receiving its just desserts, as the North saw it. The Founding Fathers had not foreseen a Civil War. Indeed, many of the Constitution's framers had purposely compromised their desires in favor of Southern concerns on slavery to get the document approved in 1787, something their Civil War progeny later refused to do.[15] Now Northerners questioned the adequacy of this fundamental law and proposed its alleged shortcomings as the true cause of the war and Reconstruction. The Constitution would have to be amended and updated to reflect the effects of the war. The result was a gaggle of theories as to the status of the South and what it must do to get back into the Union on equal terms with the nonsecessionist states. Was the South composed of states with constitutional guarantees, or was it made up of territories with fewer rights or even conquered provinces with no rights? Only full-fledged states have a say in amending the Constitution. If the Southern states were less than equal in status, how could they be forced to show their good faith in the surrender by voting to free the slaves (as specified in the Thirteenth Amendment), make them citizens with civil rights and equal privileges and immunities under the law (Fourteenth Amendment), and prevent discrimination by race for the vote (Fifteenth Amendment)?

In another bit of irony, the very position on states' rights that fostered secession in 1861 supported an immediate readmission of Southern states into the Union in 1865. Of course, the North was not about to allow any state that had seceded to return to the Union with full rights as if there had been no war. There would be conditions placed on the former Confederacy, and those stipulations would precede any readmission. After all, the Constitution also said that Congress had the right to ensure a republican (the political theory, not the party, although many Republicans saw little difference) form of government in each state, a right confirmed by the U.S. Supreme Court in *Luther v. Borden* (1849). And if the North was not about to forsake its victory in war, neither was the Republican party. If the South came into the Union with its representation increased by African Americans counted as whole persons, let these same blacks vote, reasoned Republican leaders. There was no question as to the loyalty of blacks during the war. African Americans had sabotaged the Rebel war effort, fled slavery to the protection of Northern armies, labored on military fortifications, and joined the conquering host, contributing 180,000 soldiers to the North's cause.[16] African Americans would have to receive the vote as a condition of readmission, to counter the increased representation of the South in Congress. This obviated any chance for gradual, staged development of black political rights, desired by conservatives on both sides. It was an immediate moral, legal, and political necessity to preserve the Northern victory and ensure the ascendancy of the Republican party through the black vote in the South.

The role of the Republican party was crucial to Reconstruction. The party's greatest novelty was not its economic solidarity—it was composed at that time of small businessmen and farmers, as well as legitimate tycoons and less honorable "Robber Barons." Rather, its uniqueness in U.S. history was its unity on Reconstruction issues. Never before had a party produced so many two-thirds votes to override a president's numerous vetoes. President Andrew Johnson vetoed seven bills and saw only one veto sustained (the initial 1866 renewal of the Freedmen's Bureau), and this by merely one vote. The party also won a whopping endorsement in the 1866 election that allowed it to return to Washington with a two-thirds vote in both houses of Congress and complete its Reconstruction program.[17]

The Republican party was also unusual in that a large group of its members were men of principle, known as Radicals. They saw the war as blood atonement for decades of national immorality in condoning slavery. (A lot of more moderate men, such as President Lincoln, also thought the same thing.) They believed that only when the president issued the Emancipation Proclamation did the war turn in favor of the North. The Radicals had a pronounced, dramatic sense of moving the nation forward into the future and avoiding the mistakes of the past. In particular they advocated human rights. Yet they had a quirk in their political thought. Although they believed in the will of the people as sovereign, they often moved to enshrine their program beyond the will of the people through constitutional amendments—almost as if they really did not trust the average American. They wished to punish the South for its past sins and guarantee the black vote and, through that vote, black civil rights.

Most Republicans, however, were Moderates. They supported some rights and some suffrage for African Americans, as well as some punishment for the white South. Events, particularly the struggle between Congress and the presidency, would drive them into the Radical ranks and guarantee a more complete Reconstruction.

Finally, there were some Conservative Republicans who basically were for readmission of the South with few rights guaranteed for blacks. These men often represented marginal districts with strong Democratic opposition, which forced them to be particularly circumspect on racial matters to win local elections.[18]

These branches of the Republican party were held together by ideology on Reconstruction issues. They wanted the South to consent to their program for the future, with its elements of an end to slavery and the slaveholder and the establishment of industry and free labor. This made the Republicans highly unusual in U.S. history—the party believed in more than merely getting elected. It also made the party more reluctant to compromise than most U.S. political groups. Although President Lincoln declared upon his 1864 inauguration that he wished "malice toward none and charity for all," the truth was that wartime Republican propaganda had sown deep into white Northern minds the evils of Southern political domination and slavery as an institution. After all, the South had controlled the federal government through the presidency (only 5 of the first 15 presidents had been from the North, and none had received two terms, as so many of the Southern candidates had), through patronage, and through an even vote in the U.S. Senate. These factors were generally referred to as the Slave Power Conspiracy and partly explained why the North could end slavery and still allow racial discrimination.[19] Thus the South had to be not only defeated on the battlefield but reformed and remade in the image of the North. This was to be accomplished by addressing three major Reconstruction issues: Who would govern the South at home? Who would govern the reformed nation at large? And what was to be the status of African Americans in U.S. society? There was to be a lot of reconstruction in Reconstruction.

Notes

1. Hodding Carter, *The Angry Scar: The Story of Reconstruction* (Garden City, NY: Doubleday, 1959), 11.

2. Clement Eaton, *The Freedom of Thought Struggle in the Old South*, enlarged ed. (New York: Harper & Row, 1964); Theodore C. Smith, *The Liberty and Free Soil Parties in the Northwest* (New York: Long-mans, Green & Co., 1897); Louis Filler, *The Crusade against Slavery, 1830–1860* (New York: Harper & Row, 1960); Frederick J. Blue, *The Free Soilers: Third Party Politics, 1848–1854* (Urbana: University of Illinois Press, 1973).

3. For these ideas and how they came to North America, see, for example, Perry

Miller, *The New England Mind: From Colony to Province* (Cambridge, Mass.: Harvard University Press, 1952); and Ralph Barton Perry, *Puritanism and Democracy* (New York: Vanguard Press, 1944). The South embodied these ideals more than one might think; see Perry Miller, "The Religious Impulse in the Founding of Virginia: Religion and Society in the Early Literature," *William and Mary Quarterly*, 3d series, 5 (1948): 492–522.

4. Hugh G. J. Aitken (ed.), *Did Slavery Pay?* (Boston: Houghton Mifflin, 1971).

5. Eric Foner, *Free Soil, Free Labor, Free Men: The Ideology of the Republican Party before the Civil War* (New York: Oxford University Press, 1970). It is possible that the North failed to approach its free labor ideal as much as it perceived itself to have done and that there were more similarities in economic movement in the antebellum United States in both sections than differences, striking as these variances might have been to the casual observer. See Edward Pessen, "How Different from Each Other Were the Antebellum North and South?" *American Historical Review* 85 (1980): 1119–49, and the discussion and defense in ibid., 1150–66.

6. R. Carlyle Buley, *The Old Northwest: Pioneer Period, 1815–1840*, 2 vols. (Bloomington: Indiana University Press, 1950), 1: 10–11, 14–15, 29, 47–48, 53; 2: 85, 96, 104, 105, 106, 107, 115, 156, 360–63, 378–82.

7. *Dred Scott v. Sanford*, 19 Howard at 393 (1857); Don E. Fehrenbacher, *The Dred Scott Case: Its Significance in American Law and Politics* (New York: Oxford University Press, 1978).

8. The problem of implied inferiority during Reconstruction is looked at in Wilbert H. Ahern, "Laissez Faire vs. Equal Rights: Liberal Republicans and Limits to Reconstruction," *Phylon* 40 (1979): 52–65. More modern echoes of the same are in Benjamin Schwarz, "The Diversity Myth: America's Leading Export," *Atlantic Monthly* 275 (May 1995): 57–67; Carolyn Lochhead, "The Yoke of Preferential Politics," *Insight on the News* 6 (25 June 1990): 22–24.

9. Philip S. Paludan, *A Covenant with Death: The Constitution, Law, and Equality in the Civil War Era* (Urbana: University of Illinois Press, 1975), xi, 61, 83, 129. See also Charles W. McCurdy, "Legal Institutions, Constitutional Theory, and the Tragedy of Reconstruction," *Reviews in American History* 4 (1976): 203–11. A similar dichotomy took place earlier in the 1840s during the Dorr War in Rhode Island, in which the Dorrites, hoping to force change in the state's restrictive constitution written during the original American Revolution, appealed to arms. The U.S. Supreme Court refused to engage in deciding the outcome, referring the matter to Congress under its constitutional power to guarantee "republican" governments in the various states, *Luther v. Borden* [1849]. The result was that the anti-Dorr forces were seated and declared the legal government. See George M. Dennison, *The Dorr War: Republicanism on Trial* (Lexington: University of Kentucky Press, 1976). Fuller implications of the court's position are explored in Peter J. Coleman, "The Dorr War and the Emergence of the Leviathan State," *Reviews in American History* 4 (1976): 533–38.

10. Harold M. Hyman, *The Era of the Oath: Northern Loyalty Tests during the Civil War and Reconstruction* (Philadelphia: University of Pennsylvania Press, 1954).

11. Eugene D. Genovese, *The World the Slaveholders Made: Two Essays in Interpretation* (New York: Random House, 1969), 99–102; and Genovese, *The Slaveholders' Dilemma: Freedom and Progress in Southern Conservative Thought* (Columbia: University of South Carolina Press, 1992).

12. C. Vann Woodward, "The Irony of Southern History," *Journal of Southern History* 19 (1953): 3–19, especially 5. See also Thomas L. Connelly and Barbara L. Bellows, *God and General Longstreet: The Lost Cause and the Southern Mind* (Baton Rouge: Louisiana State University Press, 1982); Emory Thomas, "Lost Cause Alive: Queries and Confederates," *Reviews in American History* 16 (1988): 403–9.

13. Prize Cases, 2 Black at 625 (1863); Harold M. Hyman, *A More Perfect Union: The Impact of the Civil War and Reconstruction on the Constitution* (New York: Alfred A.

Knopf, 1973), 141–42, 160, 162, 177, 194, 226; James G. Randall, *Constitutional Problems under Lincoln* (Urbana: University of Illinois Press, 1951), xi, 48–74, 114, 221, 308, 312, 515, 519.

14. Thomas J. Pressley, *Americans Interpret Their Civil War* (New York: Free Press, 1965), 25–78.

15. M. E. Bradford, *Founding Fathers: Brief Lives of the Framers of the United States Constitution*, 2d rev. ed. (Lawrence: University Press of Kansas, 1994), xvii.

16. Clarence L. Mohr, "Southern Blacks in the Civil War: A Century of Historiography," *Journal of Negro History* 59 (1974): 177–85; LaWanda Cox, "From Emancipation to Segregation: National Policy and Southern Blacks," in John Boles and Evelyn Thomas Nolan (eds.), *Interpreting Southern History: Essays in Honor of Sanford W. Higginbotham* (Baton Rouge: Louisiana State University Press, 1987), 199–253, especially 213–14.

17. Michael Les Benedict, "Equality and Expediency in the Reconstruction Era: A Review Essay," *Civil War History* 23 (1977): 322–35. Benedict examines the works of James C. Mohr, *Radical Republicans and Reform in New York during Reconstruction* (Ithaca, N.Y.: Cornell University Press, 1973); Herman Belz, *A New Birth of Freedom: The Republican Party and Freedmen's Rights, 1861–1866* (Westport, Conn.: Greenwood Press, 1976); and Glenn M. Linden, *Politics or Principle: Congressional Voting on the Civil War Amendments and Pro-Negro Measures, 1838–1869* (Seattle: University of Washington Press, 1976).

18. T. Harry Williams, *Lincoln and the Radicals* (Madison: University of Wisconsin Press, 1941); and Williams, "Lincoln and the Radicals," in Grady McWhiney (ed.), *Grant, Lee, Lincoln and the Radicals* (Evanston, Ill.: Northwestern University Press, 1964), 92–117.

19. Larry Gara, "Slavery and the Slave Power: A Crucial Distinction," *Civil War History* 15 (1969): 5–18; David Brion Davis, *The Slave Power Conspiracy and the Paranoid Style* (Baton Rouge: Louisiana State University Press, 1969).

Acknowledgments

A lot of people over the years contributed to this volume, many of whom were not aware of it at the time, some of whom were. Thirty years ago at Louisiana State University, Charles B. Dew took a Civil War buff and made him into a fan of the peace that followed. More than anyone else, he tried to make a historian of me, a process a lot of my critics would claim he failed at, but one that I am thankful he in large part accomplished. This volume is dedicated to him with gratitude and the deepest respect. The magnificent interpretations of T. Harry Williams did much to give a factual basis to my innate love of the South and its historical ironies. John L. Loos (the only mentor I ever had who pronounced my last name like a true *landsman*) more than anyone else understood the mind of a half-baked Arizona cowboy who missed the West's big sky, deserts, and canyons amid the bayous and Spanish moss of Dixie. James L. Bolner, John W. Clark, and Otis E. Young opened up the constitutional and economic sides of America's past, although my interpretation, having been influenced by the writings of the late M. E. Bradford, differs from theirs. Several mentors, James E. Sefton, Burl Noggle, Robert Holtman, James G. Zeidman, and Ron Smith, took an interest in my career early on and have unselfishly helped me countless times. And I am especially grateful to Paul Hubbard, who inspired me to "go for it" a long time ago, and for the reassuring enthusiasm of Jack Jackson and three Yellow Roses of Texas, Bertha L. Gable, Thelma Duty McKinney, and Jane Tuck. Todd Hallman at ABC-CLIO suggested the topic, got me started, and kept me on the straight and narrow. As usual, Robert Hershoff and the rest of the staff at the main library of the University of Arizona and Gloria Marx at the university law library provided critical help in finding needed resources. To these people belongs whatever merit this work possesses.

Introduction:

The Historians and Reconstruction

That more misconceptions exist about Reconstruction than about any other era of U.S. history can be traced to the historical writers. The violent controversy of the pen has led to the creation of a whole legion of overly dramatic and false stereotypes of Reconstruction's participants. The good and bad depend on who is writing and when. Some of the myths are easily deflated, for example, statements like these: the newly freed blacks instituted corrupt governments that stole from destitute Southern white taxpayers and threatened pure white ethnicity with racial amalgamation through unwanted interracial social contact; Carpetbaggers were evil and corrupt Yankees who invaded the prostrate South after the war to exploit the Union victory and who assisted in creating that horror of horrors, "Negro Rule"; Scalawags, the native white Southerners who supported Reconstruction, were low-born traitors to their race; Reconstruction was assisted by rude, occupying armies of bluecoats who forced the defenseless white South into submission through "Bayonet Rule."

But there are subtler stereotypes. Take the simple assertion that Radical Republicans in Congress defeated President Lincoln's mild Reconstruction program and inaugurated an era of drastic readjustment. This statement incorporates three misconceptions. First, it ascribes to an unstated number of individuals a common unity and assigns to them a crucial role in defeating one policy and implementing another. Yet historians still do not know for sure who the Radicals really were and what they believed. Nor do they know what Lincoln's postwar program for the South was. Second, it assumes a content and a chronological generalization, that Reconstruction began and ended on certain dates and involved setting up new regimes in the South and restoring them to the Union, rather than noting that many of Reconstruction's effects, like those concerning industrialization and race, continue on into modern times. Third, it generalizes about the severity of Reconstruction and the handling of a defeated enemy, when many of Reconstruction's programs, like public education and guaranteeing the right of women to hold property independent of their husbands, were clearly beneficial and others, like the general amnesty of 1872, were not severe at all.[1]

According to an old saying, history is written by the victors. Not so with Reconstruction. Indeed, it took the North nearly a hundred years to forge ahead of the South in interpreting Reconstruction history. And a Union victory took even longer in fiction, film, secondary school texts, and other indicators of popular understanding. Until the modern civil rights movement galvanized the Lyndon B. Johnson administration into proposing the Civil Rights Act of 1964 and the Voting Rights Act of 1965, popular culture was ruled by a consensus that the North was correct about the justness of the war and the South was correct about the injustice of Reconstruction.[2] This agreement held true in textbooks from first grade through college.

The North-South compromise was especially pervasive in historical fiction put on celluloid in Hollywood, beginning in 1915 with the first real U.S. feature-length film, D. W. Griffith's *The Birth of a Nation*, which brought to life Thomas Dixon's race-baiting, cliché-filled "Trilogy of Reconstruction" (*The Leopard's Spots* [1902], *The Clansman* [1905], and *The Traitor* [1907]). The film, which honored the Ku Klux Klan, was shown amid "oohs" and "aahs" at the White House (with an obviously upset President Wilson allegedly turning to U.S. Supreme Court Justice Edward White of Louisiana and croaking *sotto voce*, "That's the way it was, White, that's the way it was"). The trend continued with David O. Seltznick's 1939 box-office smash of Margaret Mitchell's magnificent novel about a liberated Southern woman writ large, *Gone with the Wind*, and with television's presentation in the 1980s of John Jakes's even bigger two-volume epic *North and South*, about a pair of families, one Northern, one Southern, who remain friends through the vicissitudes of the sectional conflict. Videos and repeat television performances, run with much fanfare, ingrain in the popular mind this portrait of national and local Reconstruction governments gone mad.[3]

These are the "moonlight and magnolia" themes of valiant soldiers in gray led by ingenious, gentlemanly officers and backed by proud, well-bred, beautiful women, outnumbered and overpowered by an advancing cold-blooded technocracy that destroyed a genteel (and in many ways superior) civilization, as Gen. William T. Sherman cut his heartless swath of destruction through the core of Georgia or Gen. Philip H. Sheridan burned out the verdant Shenandoah Valley of Virginia. With minor exceptions (like Yvonne De Carlo's and Sidney Poitier's characters in the 1957 movie *Band of Angels*), blacks appear in menial roles and are often slow-witted, fawning reincarnations of old-time "colored" movie icons Stepin Fetchit or Butterfly McQueen's wailing character in *Gone with the Wind*—loyal to their masters and mistresses to a fault. All of this "twistory" (propagandistic drama reminiscent of George Orwell's surrealistic novel, *1984*)[4] dismayed historian Fawn Brodie, biographer of nineteenth-century U.S. figures as diverse as Thomas Jefferson, Joseph Smith, and Pennsylvania Radical Republican Thaddeus Stevens. It was as if by "some quixotic revival the Lost Cause is no longer lost," wrote Brodie in 1962. Reinforcements for the "ghostly ranks of secessia" and the Ku Klux Klan kept reappearing, over and over again, causing her to ask with astonishment, "Who won the Civil War, anyway?"[5]

THE DUNNING SCHOOL OF
HISTORIANS

Brodie's question possessed a great deal of poignancy by 1962. Before 1900 most who wrote on the Reconstruction period had been participants: Republican party members and reforming idealists who saw the Civil War as brought on by the Slave Power Conspiracy; or Southerners who saw Reconstruction as an unnecessary assault on white, Christian liberties guaranteed under the Constitution before the Thirteenth, Fourteenth, and Fifteenth Amendments. As these participants grew old, a new breed of writer appeared on the horizon, the professional historian trained in the German method of scholarship with its emphasis on original sources, possessing the Ph.D., and interested in something called "social science." These Ph.D.'s, men like John W. Burgess, James Ford Rhodes, James

Schouler, and future president Woodrow Wilson (the first Southern-born aspirant to the office since Lincoln), using so-called scientific methods (that is, digging deep into the original documents) and influenced by Charles Darwin's theory of natural selection as applied by Herbert Spencer to human society ("Social Darwinism"), saw African Americans as innately lesser beings on the scale of human evolution who were prematurely thrust into positions of responsibility, making the period of Reconstruction a predetermined travesty.[6]

This marked a great change from the previous century of the Enlightenment, when all men were considered to be created equal and said to possess a divinity from God. These nineteenth-century historians were aided in their interpretations by the North's decision to stop protecting supposedly inferior blacks from allegedly natural white domination and the beginnings of the U.S. imperial drive into Asia and the Caribbean, brought on by the U.S. victory in the Spanish-American War. As white Southerners were quick to point out, the North now had its own "little brown brothers" overseas to "civilize with a Krag" (the standard infantry rifle of the time), as the South had been trying to do at home with African Americans for 200 years through slavery and lynchings.[7] The era was also marked by a new white unity, as white Southerners donned Yankee blue and marched to Cuba with their Northern brothers, led by former Confederate cavalry general "Fightin' Joe" Wheeler (who, during an especially tense moment, allegedly pointed to the Spanish position and ordered, "Get them damned Yankees" to the black "buffalo soldiers" under his command). Aging Civil War veterans held commemorative get-togethers at old battle sites, where they convivially agreed that both sides had fought honorably. Of course, conspicuous by their absence were the numerous uninvited black Union veterans.[8]

All of these forces came together at one of the nation's finest institutions of higher learning, Columbia University, under historian William A. Dunning. Born in New Jersey, the son of a small manufacturer, Dunning graduated Columbia in 1881. He was variously employed the rest of his life at the university as a professor of history and political philosophy, editor of the *Political Science Quarterly*, and president of the American Historical Association. Central to the "Dunning thesis" was the supposedly scientific innate inferiority of blacks and their incapacity for citizenship. The fact that they participated in Southern public life at all was akin to condemning the South to inept, corrupt, barbarian government, claimed Dunning. He condescendingly saw African Americans as not necessarily vicious but more as deluded and lazy, easily influenced by evil whites, the familiar Carpetbagger invaders from the North and their shiftless Southern allies, the Scalawags. All of them were abetted in their exploitation of the prostrate South by a Republican-dominated Congress led by the vindictive Radicals, intent on punishing and humiliating the white South for the war by imposing an unwanted, unwise form of "Negro Government" through the bayonets of the U.S. Army. Dunning saw Lincoln as a natural opponent of Radical ideas during the war, a position inherited by Lincoln's successor, Johnson. Dunning also depicted the Ku Klux Klan as an understandable response to the perceived excesses of Reconstruction's advocates.

Although he wrote two influential volumes on the Reconstruction period,[9] Dunning's greatest impact on U.S. history came through his graduate students, many of whom were from the Deep South and most of whom became important historians in their own right.[10] They came North already full of Dunning's racial prejudices, which they learned from their Confederate progenitors and their own experiences in the postwar South. Even though Dunning and his students were careful researchers, they were predisposed to overlooking the fact that Reconstruction began a revolutionary national trend of spending money on social programs for the poor. The corruption in state governments was really minimal, and most of the money was spent on social services (roads, bridges, railroads, education) that had been ignored before the war. Dunning's students also failed to appreciate that the Reconstruction period was typical for a postwar event, full of the collapsed morale, looser morals, and exploitative growth typical of the entire late nineteenth-century United States (much like during the 1920s after World War I). And they did not appreciate the humanitarian concern for the freedmen that stimulated much of the Reconstruction program.[11]

Nonetheless, the Dunning view came to dominate the Reconstruction story, reaching its epitome in newspaperman Claude Bowers's 1929 melodramatic best-seller, *The Tragic Era*.[12] An accomplished writer, Bowers took the Dunning thesis a step further in his rebuilding of the reputation of President Andrew Johnson. Dunning's students had disagreed on the role of Johnson, some seeing him as an embattled hero, others preferring to see him as an inept politician who made poor choices in his struggle with the Republican Congress. Calling it a "black and bloody drama," Bowers likened Reconstruction to the days of the French Revolution, giving the various American factions names like "the Directory" (Republican leaders) and "Montagnards" or "Jacobins" (Radical Republican rank and file) and condemning members of all the various Republican factions as venial hypocrites.

Johnson, on the other hand, Bowers portrayed as an honest, tender, able, and forceful politician, although not a polished conversationalist and somewhat inflexible. But Johnson was the heir to Lincoln's moderate plan of Reconstruction and definitely had the ethical edge over his opponents as he fought the bravest battle in U.S. constitutional history to preserve the nation's essential liberties. Bowers condemned Johnson's impeachment as the "Great American Farce." *The Tragic Era* was a thrilling tale that became a best-seller. It was contemporaneous with several other biographies friendly to Johnson and was bolstered by the assertion of historian Ulrich B. Phillips that the "Central Theme of Southern History" was that the South had been, was, and always would be "a white man's

country." Hollywood presented Bowers's version of history to the nonreading public in the 1942 film *Tennessee Johnson*, which starred Van Heflin as the courageous, beleaguered president.[13]

Although Bowers was a mite on the lurid side, the Dunning view retained its potency because of volumes that bracketed World War II and brought the story back to more cogent historical argument. In 1937 Paul H. Buck traced the reunification of the nation during the last four decades of the nineteenth century and accused the North of being an arrogant victor; he characterized Reconstruction as birthing an abnormal political condition that ran counter to the natural tendency of Americans for unification. He attributed reconciliation to Memorial Day celebrations that lauded all the boys in uniform as honorable; the 1876 national centennial celebration and its emphasis on the fruits of the revolution against the British; Northern relief aid during several severe yellow fever epidemics in the South; Southern salutes to Radical Republican Charles Sumner as a man of principle upon his death; the glories of the centennial of the Battle of Bunker Hill; national mourning for the shocking assassination of President Garfield in 1881; the admission in James Ford Rhodes's multivolume history of the United States that the South had been right in its stand over the "Negro Problem"; and the overwhelming desire of Southern volunteers to don "Yankee Blue" to fight in the Spanish-American War.[14]

Buck's work was joined by E. Merton Coulter's 1947 volume, *The South during Reconstruction*, the last great study of Reconstruction until the last decade. Coulter summarized his view of Reconstruction with a warning: "As each generation feels constrained to rewrite the past, points of view and methods of approach necessarily change," he wrote. "If they remain within reasonable bounds of established facts, they may well make lasting contributions in fresher interpretations and in the presentation of new information"; if not, they would not hold for long. Coulter concluded firmly, "There can be no sensible departure from the well-known facts of the Reconstruction program as it was applied to the South. No amount of revision can write away the grievous mistakes made in this abnormal period of American history." William Dunning would have liked that.[15]

THE AFRICAN AMERICAN CHALLENGE TO DUNNING

As the persons most adversely affected by the Dunning interpretation, it was quite natural that African Americans would raise the first challenges to the prevailing view. As with whites, initially it was actual Reconstruction participants who voiced their interpretations. Charlotte Forten, a New England schoolteacher, found newly freed slaves anxious to obtain an education. Robert G. Fitzgerald detailed racial animosities he witnessed in Reconstruction-era Virginia and North Carolina. Frederick Douglass admitted that Reconstruction (although he never used the word once) failed because of the violent opposition of Southern whites, compounded by the failure of Northern whites in Congress to guarantee blacks full civil rights. T. Thomas Fortune praised African Americans for their restraint when "freedom" merely exchanged slavery for a society in which they were denied a living. He too placed blame on the white South.[16]

Most creditable was the effort of John R. Lynch of Mississippi. A self-educated slave who rose to the speakership of the state house of representatives and eventually a seat in Congress, Lynch attacked the Dunning thesis outright through the person of James Ford Rhodes, a historian of some note who preceded Dunning with a similar interpretation. Contrary to the derogatory picture of Reconstruction presented in Rhodes's history, Lynch pointed out that blacks were deeply concerned with the welfare of all Mississippians and acted in a sensible, moderate way. At no time did blacks dominate the legislative process in Mississippi or any other state, Lynch said. He blamed the failure of Reconstruction on Northern whites, led along by unwise Supreme Court decisions detrimental to black civil rights.[17]

After the Reconstruction participants came the professional historians, African Americans who went through the same training as Dunning and his students, both in the United States and abroad. W. E. Burghardt DuBois, the first American black to earn a Ph.D. (1899), did much of his work in history, although his Harvard training was in sociology. Capitalizing on an 1883 account of blacks in America by self-trained historian George Washington Williams, DuBois challenged the prevailing doctrine with two seminal articles, praising the work done by black churches and schools and the federal relief agency established to guard the freedmen's civil and economic rights, the Bureau of Refugees, Freedmen and Abandoned Lands, popularly called the Freedmen's Bureau. DuBois, however, was critical of the short life span of the bureau (which completed most of its work in three years, continuing its educational efforts for four more years), saying that the project should have lasted more like 40 years. He saw the ballot as the key to real freedom and lamented its negation through the Ku Klux Klan and other organizations with the eventual acquiescence of the North. He challenged the charges that African American officeholders were ignorant, thieving incompetents. Using South Carolina and Mississippi (two states the Dunning school credited with the worst "Negro Rule") as examples, DuBois credited ex-slaves with three innovations in Southern government: real democracy for all, including poor whites and blacks; free public schools for the first time; and a myriad of social and economic legislation (internal improvements, penal reform, property-holding reforms for women and blacks). He also pointed out that both states kept their Reconstruction constitutions for over a quarter of a century, with no adverse effects.[18]

Although few noted DuBois's accomplishments at the time, he inspired others to take up the work while he retired to write a comprehensive history of the era. The most important was Alrutheus A. Taylor, a Fisk

University professor who wrote lengthy studies of African Americans in South Carolina, Virginia, and Tennessee during Reconstruction; a full-fledged attack on the Dunning thesis; and a review of the contributions of black congressmen. He conclusively proved blacks to be responsible and trustworthy in their approach to government.[19] In a similar fashion, Horace Mann Bond examined the role of African Americans in the social and economic life of Alabama Reconstruction. He found that humanitarian motives spurred Reconstruction on, only to fall victim to the exploitative forces of big business and finance. Of particular importance were the railroads competing for access to the new coal and iron fields around what would become Birmingham, with the Republicans backing one conglomerate and the Democrats another. Race and Reconstruction were merely a cover under which both sides operated to steal public money. Like others before him, particularly Carter G. Woodson, founder of the *Journal of Negro History* and author of a history of blacks in America, Bond asserted that public education was the era's finest achievement.[20]

Then DuBois came forward with his magnum opus, *Black Reconstruction*, in 1935. In one of the finest written volumes on the period, DuBois showed that African Americans responded to Reconstruction as an opportunity for self-improvement and became the dominant factor in the whole process. Instead of focusing on politics, DuBois examined the local economic scene for the real story of the era. Dismissing Burgess (a native Tennessean) as an ex-slaveholder, Dunning as a Copperhead (a Northerner who supported the South during the Civil War), and Rhodes (a businessman turned historian) as an exploiter of labor, DuBois forced his tale into a stilted Hegelian and Marxist framework that overlooked many of the actual events of the time, thereby causing too many to overlook its value.[21] (A modern critic of the economic class analysis school, still popular among American historians minus the Marxian straitjacket, dismissed this format in favor of a racial division thesis with a provocative chapter title: "How Many Niggers Did Karl Marx Know?")[22] But it was a popular thesis in the 1930s with the rise of the Soviet Union abroad and the New Deal at home. DuBois talked of a white-black alliance of proletarians, ignoring that poor whites hated blacks and filled the ranks of the Ku Klux Klan. He called Reconstruction a "splendid failure" brought down in the end by white economic dominance, a view that echoed T. Thomas Fortune's earlier work.[23] DuBois's volume was expropriated by white historian James Allen, who wrote a shorter version that became the basis of Howard Fast's novel *Freedom Road*, later produced on television in a two-night miniseries (of the same title) in 1979 with charismatic boxer Muhammad Ali in a starring role.

In 1943, DuBois revisited Reconstruction on paper 75 years after the passage of the Fourteenth Amendment, which he called the "capstone" of Reconstruction, and compared the treatment of African Americans in the South with the Nazis' treatment of the Jews. He appealed to white and black students to revise the falsehoods of that era and for the United States to purify not only itself but the world of discrimination against colored peoples of all kinds. DuBois had finally managed to do what the others had only attempted—he nailed a potentially fatal spike into the Dunning thesis.[24]

THE REVISIONISTS: THE CHALLENGE TO DUNNING EXPANDS

By the time of World War II the black arguments against the Dunning studies were gaining ground, aided by the crusade against fascism. As the clouds of war spread across Europe and Asia, two influential white historians joined the debate. Building on a book he had coauthored with colleague Robert Woody, Francis B. Simkins asserted the central issue of Reconstruction was race. He decried the works of historians like Claude Bowers and novelists like Thomas Dixon and Margaret Mitchell that glorify the Old South and legitimize the separation of blacks and whites in modern U.S. society. During Reconstruction, said Simkins, the races generally lived together quietly and the political aggressiveness of African Americans did not extend into other societal realms. Simkins stated that the reconstructing forces hardly touched the average Southerner's life and that the worst "crime" of the Carpetbaggers and Scalawags was that they crossed the racial barrier in politics. He called on historians to be more critical of events and sources to rise above Southern white political and social propaganda.[25]

Simkins was joined shortly in his "new viewpoints" by Howard K. Beale. Noting that Dunning and his students had already made one revision of history at the turn of the twentieth century, Beale said that things had gone too far and needed to be brought back to a form of reality through a second revision. He blamed many of the extreme positions not on Dunning but on Claude Bowers's recent polemic about Andrew Johnson and on that president's quarrel with the Radical Republicans, whom Bowers skillfully likened to the Jacobins of the French Revolution minus the guillotine. Beale called for treating Reconstruction as a part of U.S. history as a whole. For example, the corruption in the South was mirrored in the North; postwar immigration of Northerners to the South was not evil and vicious; and Reconstruction marked the beginning of the transfer of political power from agriculture to industry, a process already under way before the Civil War and one that would take over 100 years to effect. Indeed, Beale favored focusing upon economic struggle between rich and poor as the main theme of the era, putting race aside as a bogus issue.[26]

The questions raised by blacks like Taylor and DuBois, seconded by whites such as Simkins and Beale and ignored by Buck and Coulter, continued to fester. John Hope Franklin, a young black scholar who would lead the revisionist quest for the next 40 years, began his assault in the waning years of World War II. Franklin, like DuBois, was concerned that history ought to be utilized in the postwar world as "a manifestation of the inexorable march of man toward a better and finer civilization." In the past, commented Franklin, history had been used for

"breaking the peaceful relations of nations and for waging war." He hoped that, in the future, history would be used as "an active weapon of peace," to promote democracy and freedom by "tolerat[ing] no compromise and half hearted measures and know[ing] no color lines." In this light, three years later, Franklin went on to excoriate Coulter for writing, and the history profession for accepting, *The South during Reconstruction*. He found that Coulter's book ignored several revisionist studies, selectively used sources, quoted others out of context, and created a series of half-truths about Reconstruction and the role of blacks, whom it stigmatized as gullible, unclean in person, overly excitable, injudicious in temperament, and habituated to drunkenness. When Coulter compared Radical Reconstruction to fascism, Franklin angrily wondered whether the real fascist society was in fact the slaveholding regime of the Old South. Once again, Franklin called for a critical reexamination of Reconstruction as a national problem.[27]

During the ensuing two decades, historians tackled Franklin's challenge, using several themes to accomplish the task.[28] The first of these was the political party struggle in the North during the war. Because reunion became a problem the minute the South seceded and the North decided to fight for union, the politics of the war and Reconstruction are hard to separate.[29] The real question was whether the theme of domestic politics was to be that of the Democrats, who called for restoration with the slogan "The Union as it was, and the Constitution as it is." The Democratic party was one of strict adherence to the Constitution, from the time of Andrew Jackson to that of Woodrow Wilson. The Democrats' attitude on race was also consistent; they did not care much for blacks in the United States.[30] But they supported the preservation of the Union and joined with the Lincoln administration as "War Democrats,"[31] despite the fallacious tendency of historians to paint them all with the tar brush as "Copperheads."[32]

Unlike the Democrats, however, many

Republicans wanted more out of the war. With the South gone, the Republican party had a majority in both houses of Congress. This was their golden opportunity to alter the United States once and for all with their ideological program, which at a minimum involved emancipation. But they had to be careful lest they alienate Northern voters or split their own party by moving too quickly. Indeed, the only real theme in common with all Republicans was opposition to the Slave Power Conspiracy. But the principled group, the Radicals, kept the issue of reconstructing an altered Union before the nation, often chiding Lincoln and other more conservative Republicans to take a stand with them for total equality before the law. It was only when Lincoln achieved his second term (the first by any "Northern" president in the nation's history) that he felt able to move in their direction, although his assassination prevented anyone then or now from fathoming his real stand on the racial issues of his day.[33]

The revisionists also changed the commonly held interpretation of the Radical Republicans as the sole instigators of Reconstruction, as well as the view that Reconstruction was "radical" in any sense of the word. Even the capstone of Reconstruction, the Fifteenth Amendment, did not really grant African Americans the right to vote. It merely outlawed discrimination on the basis of race, color, or former condition of servitude. It did not take much—an unfairly administered literacy test, for example—to circumvent the amendment. Whether the Radicals acted out of principle or out of expediency to guarantee a Republican presidency and Congress for years to come is still subject for debate.[34]

The next revisionist theme involved the presidents associated with Reconstruction: Lincoln, Johnson, and U. S. Grant. Until the 1960s Abraham Lincoln's wartime Reconstruction policies were generally viewed in the light of his second inaugural speech: "with malice toward none and charity for all."[35] This led to much criticism of Lincoln as the "embodiment, not the transcendence, of the American ... racist tradition," particu-

larly in light of the fact that the Emancipation Proclamation had effect only within the Confederacy, where he had no power to act.[36] Historians have disagreed as to whether Lincoln was politically shrewd in issuing the Emancipation Proclamation when he did. Was he a conservative who took this radical step out of desperation to save the Union cause, a moderate racist who evidenced great personal growth as president (not in favor of equality, yet not anti-Negro), or a dedicated antislavery advocate turned opportunistically abolitionist for political reasons ?[37]

Others have questioned whether Lincoln and Republicans of whatever stripe disagreed on emancipation or Reconstruction, as Dunning writers said they did.[38] Yet another viewpoint asserted that Lincoln and the Republican party, especially the Radical branch, clashed meaningfully as to methods and timing in both emancipation and reunion with the South.[39] But when all is said and done, the truth remains that historians have no idea what Lincoln's true notions on emancipation and Reconstruction were. True, he seemingly dragged his feet in both areas, but this has been seen as bowing to Northern political realities, including an inherent race hatred. Defenders of Lincoln, however, point out that he moved rapidly, dropping former ideas of colonizing African Americans abroad after the war, as soon as the Republican party survived the off-year election in 1862 and won the battles of Gettysburg and Vicksburg the following year. The real problem with interpreting Lincoln was his untimely death, which made all historical speculation what one author has called "if history."[40]

What happened to the historical perspective on Lincoln is nothing compared to what befell the reputation of his successor. If there was one single hero of the "Tragic Era," it was Andrew Johnson, whom some biographers depicted as bravely holding to principle and standing firm against the excesses of the Radicals.[41] This view, though, was a switch from the perspective of earlier historians, who found him to be a failed president.[42] More recent revisionists have returned to the earlier interpretation, attacking Johnson from several angles, some of them mutually contradictory. One view of Johnson is that he was an inept politician who tried to isolate the Radical Republicans by vetoing basically Moderate Republican measures like renewal for the Freedmen's Bureau, the Civil Rights Act of 1866, and the Fourteenth Amendment, thereby cutting himself out of the picture and inviting impeachment. Another view presents him as a president whose ideological rigidity rendered him incapable of compromise after his appointed governments in the South imposed disfranchisement, discrimination, and segregation as the South's answer to African American rights. A third interpretation depicts him as a shrewd politician whose appeal to state rights and Negrophobia could have won the day if he had been willing to agree with Moderate and Conservative Republicans on some federal protection of the freedmen short of suffrage. Finally, others portray him as simply a provincial politician who was out of touch with the political realities of Reconstruction and the elements of the Republican party and who listened too much to the bad advice of his secretary of state, William Seward.[43]

Johnson suffered greatly as the position of the Radical Republicans improved in the eyes of revisionist historians. If the Republican Reconstruction program was limited in scope, as the revisionists say, Johnson by definition became a racist extremist.[44] His allegedly unreasonable actions drove Congress to impeach him (he wound up only one vote short of being convicted), citing his unwillingness to enforce congressional laws—never mind that the laws were poorly written and thus gave Johnson much latitude. Although revisionist historians saw Johnson's impeachment as necessary and executed in a fair manner, more general writers have condemned it as an excessive display of congressional power and a bill of attainder.[45] Impeachment's advocates, however, make a good point by emphasizing that the process was created to ensure that an executive did not acquire too much power. It seemed to have done the job, not only by

defeating Johnson's presidency, but also by ensuring the Republican nomination of a popular outsider, Gen. Ulysses S. Grant, rather than a Radical senator, Benjamin Wade of Ohio. (Wade, as president pro tem of the Senate, would have succeeded Johnson had the latter been found guilty; Wade voted to convict despite an obvious conflict of interest.)[46]

U. S. Grant, the first Republican to be elected to two terms as president (technically Lincoln received his second term as the nominee of the Union party, an alliance of Republicans and War Democrats), suffered less than Lincoln and Johnson from the inquiries of revisionist historians—if only because he started lower in esteem and never truly overcame his lousy historical reputation. (Historians still habitually and probably unfairly place him among the worst of U.S. presidents.) He was seen as a butcher of men in war and a shelterer of corrupt cronies in peace, where "Grantism" came to embody the worst of Reconstruction excesses.[47] Not until the 1930s did J. F. C. Fuller destroy the myth of Grant's military record, pointing out that both George B. McClellan and Robert E. Lee regularly lost more men in battle than Grant; William Hesseltine challenged Grant's reputed political ineptitude, having the temerity to label Grant a "politician," in the best sense of the word. The themes of Grant's military prowess through brilliant maneuvers to avoid unnecessary casualties and his newfound political acumen continued as his personal papers were printed as a Civil War bicentennial project.[48]

But no matter how Grant's defenders tried (in 1945 there were 91 Grant biographies, which compared favorably to 110 on Lincoln), the old image still haunted the general-turned-president. In a 1981 monograph, William S. McFeely revived many of the former interpretations that the prior half-century discarded. Preferring to look at "the man himself," McFeely accused Grant of being a butcher in war and a racist in peace, a hard-hearted man, impervious to the results of his failures in both arenas. Historians Richard N. Current, John Y. Simon,

James M. McPherson, and Brooks Simpson, however, came to Grant's defense, admitting he made mistakes (he was not happy with casualties in war or the loss of African American rights in peace) but averring he had an admirable character as he played the often poor hand that fate dealt him. At least Grant had tried to make Reconstruction a reality, consistently backing black rights during the war and later on, they concluded. But nearly a dozen of the best names in the profession praised McFeely's work as "a moving and convincing portrait of the whole Grant" and "a perceptive interpretation of that enigmatic personality," setting Grant historiography back fifty-odd years.[49]

After exploring the executive branch during Reconstruction, the revisionists turned their attention to the role of the judiciary. Earlier studies of the Constitution and the U.S. Supreme Court came from the Dunning era. They told the usual tale of Republican wickedness in expanding the normally "weakened spring of government" unnecessarily; they described the cowardice of the courts in folding before the Radical onslaught and expressed a fear that the Supreme Court was under actual attack from the Republican leadership.[50] Led by Harold M. Hyman and Stanley I. Kutler, who expanded on moderating pioneering work of James G. Randall,[51] revisionists questioned whether the Constitution had proved inadequate to expand and meet the needs brought on by a problem unperceived by the Founding Fathers. They saw the Radicals, indeed all Republicans, as operating in a relatively conservative manner that restricted attempts to reconstruct the South and actually expanded civil liberties (rather than restraining them as the old school had maintained), laying the foundations for the modern court system.[52] Critics have questioned whether the revisionists' "fervent liberal nationalism" was necessarily good in light of the all-encompassing powers of the modern federal government, but the new constitutional history seemingly had liberated historians from the Dunning approach once and for all.[53]

The revisionists also impugned Dunning by reexamining the roles of the main protagonists of the era: the Scalawags, the Carpetbaggers, and the African Americans. The Scalawags were Southern whites who for one reason or another backed the Reconstruction regimes. Roundly condemned by the Dunning historians as wartime Unionists who still hated the Confederates and now longed for the spoils of office under the victorious Yankees, Scalawags had been portrayed essentially as collaborators with the North and traitors to their race who manipulated gullible freedmen to loot the South and place it under the degradation of "Negro Rule." It fell to E. Merton Coulter to sum it all up, dismissing Scalawags as the dregs of society, untrained and untried in politics, those who could not get along, and "bushwhackers or deserters" during the war, although he admitted that a few "respectable, intelligent, realistic Southerners supported the Radicals." But it all led to a "blackout of honest government" that gave Reconstruction its well-deserved bad image in history.[54]

As revisionists entered the fray over the origins of the Scalawags, the picture changed completely. In 1944, David Donald suggested that Mississippi Scalawags were not Dunning's "white trash" but rather the most respected elements of antebellum and Confederate society. They were former Whig politicians who had been reluctantly swept up by the Democrats during the secession crisis, a thesis that Thomas B. Alexander extended to the rest of the South except South Carolina and Texas, which is generally referred to by historians as "persistent Whiggery." That picture was reinforced when T. Harry Williams found that the upper classes in Louisiana actually had tried to combine with the black voters to govern that state through the Louisiana Unification movement. Although Williams's unifiers, unlike Donald's and Alexander's Whigs, were against Republican rule, something was amiss here. These revisionists were putting forth the exact opposite of what Marxist historians like DuBois had posited in the 1930s; that is, they were maintaining that white upper classes—former planters who had worked with blacks all of their lives, not poorer "proletarian" whites—were African Americans' allies during Reconstruction. These Scalawags offered the blacks civil rights while they themselves received lower taxes and internal improvements (levees and railroads). The black/Scalawag union faltered when upper-class whites refused to permit social equality as well. Hence the ultimate Redemption of the South (the restoration of conservative white rule) rested with white unity on race more than with terrorizing blacks not to vote.[55]

But this historical debate is far from over. In 1963 Allen Trelease questioned whether the Donald thesis had any validity outside of Tennessee, North Carolina, and parts of Virginia. In an extensive study of the Southern states' voting records county by county, Trelease went back to the notion that Jacksonian Democrats, poorer whites, mostly wartime Unionists opposed to secession, supported the Reconstruction governments as Scalawags. The key was that Scalawags came from counties with few blacks and combined at the state level with African Americans to run the legislatures. Then John V. Mering questioned the validity of the theory of persistent Whiggery, asserting that few Whigs remembered the party battles of the 1830s and 1840s. They had taken such a convoluted path to the postwar Democratic party as to have forgotten their old ties. Other historians found once again that Donald's original Whig thesis was valid in Mississippi and Alabama, confusing the picture more. But by now even Donald was no longer convinced of his own original assertions.[56]

Until recently, the only solution for the revisionists was to declare that Scalawags had multiple motives (personal reasons, class hatred, greed, reformist tendencies, and Unionism) in their support of Reconstruction.[57] But an article by Armistead Robinson offered a way around the confusion. He found that at one time or another, all Southern whites of all classes had flirted with being Scalawags, hence the diverse answers as to who was a Scalawag that dominate Recon-

struction historiography. It all depended on when during the era one looks for the evidence, Robinson said; lower classes came over early on and then left before the wealthy came in, as Southern party goals fluctuated and changed. He also applied the same analysis to blacks, showing them not to be fixed in their political ideas, either.[58]

The historiography of the Carpetbaggers has been decidedly less complicated than that of the Scalawags. Suffering from the same stigma as the Scalawags, the Northern Carpetbaggers, according to Dunning's followers, came to exploit the prostrate South through manipulating the black vote. They received their name because allegedly all of their possessions could be stuffed into a carpetbag—they were that shiftless. These Yankees were viewed as the central cause of the grief of Reconstruction.[59] No one has spent more time debunking the Carpetbagger myth than Richard N. Current. In three publications spanning a quarter of a century,[60] Current claimed that the Carpetbaggers did not come to exploit the South during Reconstruction. He saw them more as typical Americans, much like those who went West, who wished to improve themselves economically through hard work. Most arrived before there was any hint of Reconstruction in a political sense; most entered business, a field Southerners tended to avoid in favor of planting; most entered politics after their businesses had failed, a common occurrence in the economic disasters that followed the Civil War; and most acted with a sense of responsibility, patriotism, and some personal ambition, rather than a desire to exploit their offices criminally. They stood on all sides of the Reconstruction issues. But if there was one issue over which Carpetbaggers agreed, it was their desire to have government influence the economic expansion of their state, section, and nation. They were essentially reformers who desired to change the government of their adopted states for what they saw as the better by eradicating the vestiges of slavery and rebellion. Unfortunately they could not agree on their local programs, and national leaders refused to assist them in their plight.[61] Their real fault in the eyes of Southern whites was that the Carpetbaggers were willing to associate with blacks more than "decent" whites ought to. [62]

Having debunked the human stereotypes of Reconstruction, the revisionists turned to economics. The economic conditions during Reconstruction had lost out for years to the political and social issues, especially among the Dunning scholars. But in the 1930s studies by Howard K. Beale and William B. Hesseltine maintained that Reconstruction was undergirded by a strong economic drive to make the agrarian South safe for Northern industrial investment. These ideas were further established by Charles and Mary Beard's thesis that the Civil War and Reconstruction made for a "Second American Revolution," this one economic, from agriculture to industrialism. As in most Reconstruction studies of that time, the Radicals became the villains of the story, striving to jack up the tariff rates to appeal to eastern voters, holding off the hike until after the election of 1866, and unjustly accusing the South of violence against Yankee immigrants and businessmen after the war (called "waving the bloody shirt," after Benjamin Butler literally waved on the floor of Congress the shirt of a Yankee scourged in Mississippi to make his point that the South needed thorough Reconstruction) to hold the vote of the western states.[63] This view of a Second American Revolution held for three decades until a series of studies questioned whether Republicans had any unified economic outlook at all. These studies asserted that there was no common ground among Radicals or any identifiable group of Republicans that would justify the idea that they had a unified economic approach. The party's factions were simply too diverse.[64]

Another economic tack was to examine the Civil War and Reconstruction as vehicles of economic change. The Beards said these events *were* such vehicles, both in the transfer of power from South to North and in bringing forward men concerned with industrial growth and the structure to make that growth. Other authors agreed.[65] Again

the Beard thesis held for three decades until it came under fire from Thomas Cochran, who posited that the era actually slowed the economy down relative to the decade that preceded it. He concluded that the era brought forth little constructive economic influence.[66] Cochran's notions were seconded by Walt W. Rostow and Douglass C. North[67] and became the vogue until the mid-1960s, when the Hagley Foundation Conference on Economic Change in the Civil War Era produced some new studies. The general import of these studies was that the real change came in the Republicans' willingness to finance the war through new taxes, including the first income tax in U.S. history. The government obtained greater revenues from sources other than the tariff, like stamp and excise taxes.[68] This brought the discussion back to the Beards, who had seen the high tariffs as an exploitation of the nation by big business, rather than as a necessary source of government income as before the war. Newer studies emphasized that Republicans North and South saw economic appeals as the best way to attract white Southerners to the party and that the party's failure to make good cost it its Southern branch after 1877.[69]

Finally, the revisionists took a look at the Compromise of 1877, the traditional end to Reconstruction with the restoration of white government to all of the Southern states. Paul A. Haworth made the original study of the compromise at the turn of the twentieth century. He emphasized the congressional passage of the electoral commission act that set up the process by which "Rutherfraud" B. Hayes became "ol' eight to seven" (in reference to the vote in the commission by which Hayes won the presidency). Haworth played down the secret Wormley Hotel conference that, according to revisionist historian C. Vann Woodward, was the key meeting. In that conference Ohio Republicans and Southern Democrats (really, old-time Whigs) allegedly made a deal to back Hayes; in return, the Republicans would get to organize the House of Representatives despite its Democratic majority and Hayes would withdraw the federal troops that had blocked the Redemption in the last three "rotten boroughs" of Reconstruction (Louisiana, Florida, and South Carolina). For its part, the white South agreed to protect black political and civil rights and vote with the Republicans on certain economic issues that would yield railroad development crucial to the South.[70] Recent historians have taken Woodward to task, pointing out that the Compromise of 1877 was never put into effect (a fact that Woodward had conceded all along) and that the real deal was the seating of a Republican on the U.S. Supreme Court;[71] or that the real compromise was the electoral commission, as Haworth had argued, and that the two political parties were so similar as to create an inertia in federal governance that existed until the Spanish-American War, which made the choice in 1876 one between Hayes or chaos;[72] or that Woodward's sources were skewed to produce a false picture of the Wormley conference's results.[73]

Yet in spite of the various monographs and articles that examined the forces and participants of Reconstruction from a revisionist viewpoint by 1959, historian Bernard A. Weisberger suggested something was lacking. There was still no new synthesis of Reconstruction; school textbooks still mouthed the outworn platitudes of the Dunning thesis. He called for historians to "come to terms with some larger problems of United States history." They had to grapple with the race problem, suggested Weisberger, recognizing the conflict inherent between the aspirations of blacks and the innate conservatism of the dominant white race. The whole notion of Reconstruction corruption, he continued, was but a part of a continuous trend common to the development of the United States. So was the change from an agrarian economy to an industrial one. Weisberger also opined that Reconstruction was not a constitutional aberration but a small part of the rise and decline of state power that was writ large in the twentieth century. Hence, Weisberger went on, the fact that the South was a colonial outpost of the industrial North after the war implies change that might not necessar-

ily be bad in the development of the world or our nation. Weisberger particularly called upon American historians to confront forces most Americans prefer to ignore— race antagonism, the manipulation of brute power, and class conflict. American history was not necessarily a success story full of unity and patriotism, Weisberger concluded.[74]

Meanwhile, as historians argued the realities of Reconstruction, several surveys of the period appeared. Hodding Carter wrote a lucid treatment of the era, but his moderate work was still marked by a defense of the white South that revisionists found offensive. Some historians, as they are wont to do, also criticized Carter for not being a professional researcher and relying too much on secondary sources. One suspects that this hides a secret admiration and jealousy of the quality of his prose rather than containing real substance.[75] No such reservations accompanied John Hope Franklin's volume, which found Radical rule in the South to be short-lived and relatively mild. It brought about needed improvements, he maintained, especially in public education and welfare for poor people. Although this was the first time blacks served in high political office, nationally and locally, he continued, these men generally were honest and competent in their service. If corruption prevailed, concluded Franklin, it was a national phenomenon, not unique to black Reconstruction in the South. The great fault of the era was that the same men who led the Confederacy returned to lead during and after Reconstruction. That so little criticism was levied at Franklin's work showed how far the list of Reconstruction villains and heroes had changed, for historians at least, in the preceding 24 years.[76]

Like Franklin's work, Kenneth M. Stampp's *The Era of Reconstruction* was in the mainstream of revisionism. Noted for his earlier famous and controversial assumption that African Americans were merely white people in black skins,[77] Stampp used the same supposition in his volume on Reconstruction published during the height of the civil rights movement. Following a standard revisionist essay on past authors, he be defeated when the Northern industrialists sold out their wartime principles to the entrenched Southern former slaveholding oligarchy, which instinctively feared a burgeoning black revolution. Between Aptheker and Wiley in tone stood Harvey Wish's seminal article on slave disloyalty in the Confederacy, which showed blacks to be serious people possessing a "folk opinion" that sanctioned "acts in behalf of freedom."[99]

Thereafter, historians felt obliged to include sections on blacks in their Civil War and Reconstruction monographs that have been described as "ghetto history," that is, sort of segregated "Jim Crow" appendages to the main story.[100] But the basic conclusion brought forth was that throughout the war white Southerners obtained black support only at a price, which in the end turned out to be a plan to enlist the slaves as soldiers to fight the Yankees, an act to be rewarded by emancipation.[101] Throughout the conflict blacks had remained loyal to themselves and their culture.[102]

Recent historians have found the same to be true of Reconstruction. Looking at the period from a black perspective, historians have attacked the validity of the Sambo stereotype as never truly internalized by slaves or freedmen. They have shown that upon emancipation African Americans sought out their families, often broken up by slave sales; maintained remarkably stable and long-lived marriages; created powerful, independent churches and benevolent associations that became the source of black leaders then and now; made the most of scant educational opportunities; created their own intellectual life; and established their own social patterns.[103] Critics, however, have pointed out that the resulting picture merely consisted of "moonlight, magnolias, and collard greens." It was too idealized, they claimed. Many of the African American "heroes" of Reconstruction were ineffective, especially black congressmen; the severe setbacks of the Gilded Age that followed Reconstruction (segregation, peonage, loss of voting rights) have been ignored (except for the notable case of Rayford W. Logan's *Betrayal of the Negro*);[104]

and these faults have been compounded by "a misguided form of white philanthropy and paternalism" that permitted conclusions to be drawn that were not supported by the facts and were often contradictory.[105]

But history from an African American point of view, romanticized or not, opened a whole new perspective on the Reconstruction era.[106] The result was the first real synthesis of Reconstruction historiography since Dunning's monograph 80 years ago: Eric Foner's massive 1988 volume *Reconstruction: America's Unfinished Revolution*. Foner began by starting the Reconstruction story from a whole new perspective, that of the black experience, relying on the recent explorations of black history. He put the onset of Reconstruction at 1863, the date of the Emancipation Proclamation. He viewed African Americans as the central figures of the era, not passive victims, who forced the United States down the road to change.

Foner credited blacks with causing the nation to see democracy as an interracial experiment, so revolutionary that nothing in the history of the world during the nineteenth century could match it. He paid special attention to black political leadership and the political mobilization of the black political community, lauding both. Next Foner looked at the changes that African Americans spearheaded in Southern society. The interaction between blacks and whites caused government to be used in new ways, Foner posited, primarily to the benefit of poor people. The result was an evolution in racial attitudes and an Americanization of the freedmen (which Francis B. Simkins had called attention to 40 years earlier) rather than the Africanization of America that Southerners had feared and William A. Dunning had emphasized.[107] Attitudes evolved so much so, Foner noted, that a significant number of Southerners from all levels of white society were willing to link their futures with those of blacks and the nascent Republican party in the South.

He also sought to place Reconstruction on state and local levels in a national context. According to Foner, what emerged was a central government that possessed vast new powers and a new set of goals that began the reforming impulse that became so common by the twentieth century. It was what other historians saw as the altering of "American exceptionalism": the abundance of free land, absence of a feudal past, or pragmatic liberalism in politics that set the nation apart from the rest of humankind.[108] The results of the war saw the United States evolve away from an antebellum experience, which had been dominated by the South and resembled much of the rest of the world in its cultural conservatism. The North's different vision of reform became the rule in the United States and transferred the burden of exceptionalism from the predictable, indolent South to the vibrant, changing North.[109]

A new federal-state relationship developed that fundamentally changed the whole concept of U.S. citizenship, Foner went on. The threat to local autonomy implicit in black political participation led eventually to the violent purging of African Americans from the political scene, he surmised.

Finally, Foner looked at changes in the postbellum economy and class structure in the North during Reconstruction. His examination of various Northern states was less involved than his discussion of the South for two reasons, he said: the lack of existing research into the North's response to Reconstruction, and a recognition that the South will always be the center of the story, for that was where blacks could have the greatest impact at that time.[110]

There are problems with this view. Foner had written extensively on the "free labor" ideology of the Republican party. He wondered what happened to this notion, which differentiated slave and free society, after the war. What he found was that it disappeared by the mid-1870s, to be replaced with the antilabor organization theme that dominated U.S. business philosophy until the New Deal in the 1930s. Foner said that this change had to be a contributing factor to the abandonment of Reconstruction's idealism, especially once the massive depression of 1873 is taken into account. But critic Michael Perman thought the "free labor" slogan to be mere window dressing. Once

slavery had disappeared, it no longer had relevance. Or better yet, once the slave power—the dominance of the South in U.S. politics—had passed, original Republican ideology was free to turn to its economic side, the building of the United States in the last half of the nineteenth century and the first third of the twentieth, much of it by government subsidy and friendly regulation. The result, as Foner and others have stated, was to leave African Americans not as slaves, but not yet fully free.[111] Perman also wondered if historians, Foner included, have asked the wrong question, why did Reconstruction fail? The real query, Perman countered, ought to be, why did Reconstruction occur in the first place? Why did it last as long as it did? Foner had mentioned this as a field for future inquiry, but only in passing, Perman said.[112]

Modern historians eschew present-mindedness, that is, reading current events into their works—and the "new synthesizers" are no exception. Yet when one collector of compositions feels compelled to assert that "there is no party line in the essays that make up this volume," the reader begins eagerly to look for one and rarely fails to find it.[113] When they assert that no historian should allow Reconstruction to be used "as a mirror of ourselves,"[114] what they really mean is do not disagree with our viewpoint, or be condemned as a Dunningite—a subtle form of reverse racism. This leaves us with those who are unabashedly willing to reveal their present-minded political agenda and go on from there with their biases flying. One of the best of these comes from an admitted nonhistorian (one is already refreshed to know he will not hide his partisanship behind the label of "scholarly"), Stetson Kennedy.

In his *After Appomattox*, Kennedy went over some of the same ground as Foner, but in a more popular, accessible approach. He admitted that he was writing not "*the* history of Reconstruction," but rather one version. He stated that the "very idea of a complete history of any decade, particularly that one, is beyond the realm of human capability." He then went on to relate Reconstruction to the present struggle for civil rights, a connection that new synthesizers deny was implicit in their work. One need not agree with Kennedy's precepts to admire and enjoy his study and its implications.[115] As Pitchfork Ben Tillman said 100 years ago, "Come out and say why you say this thing."[116]

To his credit, Foner admitted that modern Reconstruction history owed much to the civil rights movement—probably as much as Dunning owed to Social Darwinism.[117] And as Perman realized, that is the real weakness of Foner's work. Foner had done valuable service in synthesizing the work of those who preceded him on the importance of blacks in asserting their own values and needs in Reconstruction, but in the process he lost track of the white South, except as villain. In other words, Foner filled in the gaps left by earlier historians in assessing the role of African Americans, but he left significant gaps of his own in turn. Nonetheless, Perman concluded that "because this synthesis is so successful and thorough, it does raise one unsettling question and leave it unanswered—what is left to be done?"[118] That borders on the same attitude that rightly got Coulter in trouble 50 years ago.

HERE WE GO AGAIN

In reply to Perman's question, a great deal remains to be done. So long as there are historians, or those laypersons interested in history, there will be revision. Historians are as entrenched as government bureaucracy. One thing, for example, that revisionists, post-revisionists, and new synthesizers alike essentially ignored was the fact that Reconstruction was administered by the army. It (Reconstruction) was carved out in violation of George Washington's Newburgh address—a refusal to allow the army to get involved in politics, no matter how disgusting the outcome, impotent the politicians, or noble the cause. Revisionists pointed out that the war made the era special. It had no precedent; the peace had to be guaranteed, and ultimately force had to be used to counter violent Southern white obstruction of the "will of the nation"[119]—or was it merely the will of the Republican party?[120]

Yet few historians dealt with the military occupation of the South unless peripherally. At the time of Reconstruction the concepts of military government (in which the army replaces civil government) and martial law (in which the army assists the civil government in facing a crisis) were not developed. During the Civil War, Northern legal theorist Francis Lieber drew up certain rules for war and military occupation that the Lincoln administration issued in the form of general orders, based on prior experiences in the Mexican War. But there was no evidence that any Reconstruction commander in the South ever referred to them or had even heard of them. Scholars have argued since as to whether the occupation of the South was an instance of military government or one of martial law, leading to the suggestion that it be labeled "congressionally declared martial law." Others rejected this as confusing, leaving the whole matter in limbo.[121]

Oddly enough, many early studies and revisionist works agreed on one thing—that the army conducted itself well during the period. The difference was that Dunning saw military government as an aberration in U.S. history, while revisionists did not. Indeed they saw army numbers in the South so small as to be irrelevant to the overall process.[122] Harold Hyman theorized that the army went from executive control in 1865 to a legislatively directed form of control by 1868. He saw congressional desire to remove President Johnson as commander-in-chief as the main reason for the latter's impeachment, even though Johnson's position had been compromised already by (1) the Tenure of Office Act, which prevented him from removing officials appointed with Senate consent without concurrence of the same body (to protect the position of the Radical Republican cabinet spy, Secretary of War Stanton), and (2) the Command of the Army Act, which prevented soldiers from obeying any presidential order unless it was reissued through the commanding general (U. S. Grant, who by now was firmly in the congressional camp on Reconstruction matters).[123]

These viewpoints were challenged in James E. Sefton's full-length 1967 monograph on the army's role in Reconstruction. Calling the employment of the army to administer Reconstruction unique, Sefton went on to illustrate that the army automatically became a legislative agency whenever it administered measures legally passed by Congress. He also held that the numbers of soldiers in the South were irrelevant to their influence, particularly with respect to the role of the general officers and commandants of local garrisons. Although military men made mistakes and some officers were more inclined than others in favor of Reconstruction, Sefton saw the failures of the army in the South as the miscarriage of the congressional policy itself. He also methodically revealed the efforts of the army to enforce Reconstruction as a police force, and he questioned the wisdom of its domestic use (enshrined in the Posse Commitatus Act of 1878), aspects overlooked by the new synthesizers.[124]

Perhaps in no other area is the quarrel between the post-revisionists and the new synthesizers more clearly revealed than in the studies of the army's adjunct in Reconstruction, the Bureau of Refugees, Freedmen, and Abandoned Lands, the welfare agency established to supervise the three subjects in its title. Almost immediately, the agency concentrated on the freedmen, under the direction of its administrator, Gen. Oliver O. Howard, a one-armed veteran of the war. Known as the "Christian General" because of the religious principles that governed his life, Howard was generally treated as such by historians until William S. McFeely questioned whether Howard's paternalism actually concealed a latent racism.[125] His bureau faced the same charges, with post-revisionist historians questioning its policies as inadequate (intentionally or not) to combat the existing mores of Southern white society and presaging the Black Codes that threatened to return blacks to a form of pseudoslavery enshrined in the sharecrop and lien system.[126] Other historians, part of the new synthesis, found that blacks went forward to achieve their own freedom with the

assistance of those local bureau agents who cared, expanding on the thesis DuBois put forth eight decades earlier.[127]

There is a great deal of merit in these arguments because they go hand in hand with another facet of Reconstruction, white violence. The failure of Reconstruction has often been blamed on Southern violence epitomized by the Ku Klux Klan, the White Leagues, and the Red Shirts. Early historians found merit in the Ku Klux Klan, comparing it to the Republican-organized Union Loyal Leagues as political fronts for the philosophy of white supremacy. These historians attributed the violence of the Ku Klux Klan and its imitators in particular to outlaw elements that took over these once "noble" organizations, which had been designed to save the white South from the trials and tribulations of "Negro Rule" imposed by Yankee bayonets and aided by greedy Carpetbaggers and traitorous Scalawags. This led to the Klan's disbandment by more responsible leaders themselves.[128]

Some post-revisionists, like Michael Perman, also found that violence was more an undercurrent than a major theme of Reconstruction politics. Indeed, Perman asserted that the politics of Reconstruction were merely a continuation of themes from the eras that preceded and followed Reconstruction, rather than something unique. Perman saw in both political parties a competitive and an extremist group, the former often referred to as New Departure wings of the parties. These New Departure people were quite willing to accept the constitutional changes of Reconstruction (the Thirteenth, Fourteenth, and Fifteenth Amendments) and to go on from there, trying to build centrist coalitions that could govern. These centrists were generally Moderate Republicans in the North and Scalawags in the South, while their Democratic counterparts were Liberal Republican/Democratic fusionists in the North and South. Their main political focus centered around the defeat of the Radical Republicans in 1867 and the election of Ulysses S. Grant in 1868, as well as the railroad building that swept the whole nation after the war. It was these men who dominated the Redemption of the South before 1874, a fairly peaceful process marked by normal political competition among the Republican and Democratic parties.

By 1872, however, this New Departure idea began to fall apart under pressure to "redeem" the rest of the South, driven by the extremist factions in both parties in the South. The so-called Black and Tan Republicans (composed of blacks and Carpetbaggers) and Straight-out Bourbon Democrats (the Jacksonian Democrats and old-line secessionists in the South) claimed that the best way to win a political contest was to fully mobilize one's own constituency, rather than appealing to the "thinking element" of your opponent's. The goal of the Straight-out Bourbons became to capture the 20 percent of whites who voted Republican by appealing to racial solidarity and using violence to gut their opponents' ability to respond. These Democratic extremists ran on pre–Civil War issues, like opposition to state aid and lower taxes on land. Using the White Leagues, the White Liners, and the Red Shirts, they outfought their opposition to carry the day and "redeem" the rest of the South. The effectiveness of the Straight-out Bourbons' policy was demonstrated in the inability of the Scalawags to overcome the appeal to white solidarity and protect themselves and their Carpetbag and African American allies from violence without perennial appeals to Washington for help; in the end this help never came, and the continual appeals wore out Northern desires to help sustain a failing Reconstruction policy.[129]

Some critics, however, claimed that downplaying the impact of violence during Reconstruction defied reality. George Rabel placed Southern white violence in two categories: (1) random crimes of robbery, riot, assault, and murder, which predominated in the early years of Reconstruction and were typified by the Norfolk and Memphis Riots of 1866; and (2) the systematic political terrorism that began with the New Orleans Riot of 1866, passed on to the Ku Klux Klan movements of violence by men in disguise, and culminated in the White Leagues and other paramilitary groups that fought openly. Rabel was assisted in his view by studies that examined specific aspects of the violence issue, such as Allen Trelease's study on the Ku Klux Klan movement and Melinda Meek Hennessey's examination of the numerous race riots during Reconstruction.[130]

Of course, each side had ignored the possibility that both movements could have occurred simultaneously, something more like what William Gillette discussed in his reexamination of national policy and why it failed. Gillette considered that the failure of Reconstruction was made possible by the North's merely tenuous interest in black rights. On both the federal and state levels the Republicans did little to defend themselves or their partisans against guerrilla war, especially after suppression of the Ku Klux Klan movement under the Enforcement Acts wore out Northern resoluteness. So long as the fruits of victory, Union, and the Industrial Revolution (i.e., the prewar Republican free labor ideal) could be maintained in any other manner (historian C. Vann Woodward's "right fork" choice, epitomized by Atlanta newspaper editor Henry Grady's proindustrial "New South," as opposed to the "left fork" of agrarian protest symbolized by the later Populist Revolt), the blacks were hung out to dry by Northern inaction. The white South had always been violent, especially where race was concerned. That it should oppose black rights during Reconstruction should have come as no surprise in the North, which did not care much for black rights either. After all, white Northern soldiers who intimidated blacks during and after the war and discriminated against them in social and public accommodations, denied blacks the franchise whenever the issue came up for a popular vote.[131]

It is possible, however, that the real purpose of Reconstruction may not have been so noble as new synthesis history would have us believe—that in actuality Reconstruction was designed simply to keep African Americans in the South. There was a great fear, as during the days of slavery and the Underground Railroad, that blacks would flee their "natural" home for Northern paradise. So the South had to guarantee civil rights to keep African Americans happy there. This was the source of Northern concern about the Memphis, Norfolk, and New Orleans race riots; the passage of the Black Codes that limited blacks' rights as free citizens; and the turning down of the Fourteenth Amendment in 1866. The North disliked Southern violence toward blacks only insofar as it tempted blacks to move north. And the South resented outsiders interfering with their state sovereignty, war or not. As for conservative Southerners, even those who served in the 1865 Johnson-appointed provisional governments and were opposed to secession and against the Civil War were proud of their contribution to the cause of Confederate independence and still favored state rights.[132]

This means that the U.S. Constitution that revisionist historians praised for its adequacy in defeating the South proved inadequate in Reconstruction, even with changes. The South essentially had to approve the Fourteenth Amendment to gain readmission to the Union in 1868, but the amendment permitted the black vote only in the South and it disfranchised those who had led the move for Southern independence. So the South turned down the amendment. The Fifteenth Amendment did not grant anyone the right to vote. It merely prevented certain discriminations based on race. Literacy tests, property qualifications, and poll taxes were within the amendment's provisions until after the middle of the twentieth century; by 1870, however, both the North and South could live with these restrictions. Later in the nineteenth century, the South merely copied the limits on the black vote already practiced in the North in such "equal rights" states as Massachusetts. Historians like W. E. Burghardt DuBois and Kenneth Stampp recognized that the Civil War amendments, especially the Fourteenth, did have potential as the only real valuable outcomes of Reconstruction, but it took 100 years for that potential to be realized through the modern civil rights movement.[133]

The new interpretations of Reconstruction history were most welcome for the broader outlook they brought to the period. Modern historians seem to have ignored the injunction of C. Vann Woodward, however, who long ago warned revisionists to be wary of merely placing Southern whites in the villain's corner and elevating Dunning's evildoers to hero status; the whole picture was more complicated than that.[134] We thus return to Fawn Brodie's question, who won the Civil War anyway? The South may have been seen as winning Reconstruction's historical argument at the time Brodie wrote, but the ensuing three decades have changed all that. The new synthesis would stand by the century-old statement of James Ford Rhodes, that the South suffered the mildest punishment ever inflicted after an unsuccessful civil war for the crimes of treason and rebellion.[135] But then, after a twentieth century filled with world wars, genocidal dictatorships from the right and left abroad, imperial presidents, spendthrift Congresses, and power-grasping court systems at home, any nineteenth-century program—no matter how harsh or expensive it was then—can easily be perceived as conservative and inexpensive today. This is a problem inherent to modern historians trying to criticize a 130-year-old policy in light of present-day standards. The nineteenth century needs to be judged in terms of it own time, not ours, and Reconstruction rarely is.

There was a price paid by Southern whites for the rebellion. The white South lost an estimated $1.6 billion in slave property (3.5 million blacks at $500 each)[136] and another $1.25 billion for most of its industrial and agricultural infrastructure (some states lost more than others; some, like Texas, untouched by the passage of war, lost relatively little), its entire war debt, and its share of the Yankee war debt and pensions for U.S. soldiers (a tax that functioned for all effect as a war indemnity). By 1865, then, the South had lost 40 percent of its 1860 wealth, while the North had increased its wealth by 50 percent. At the turn of the twentieth century the South as a section had just begun to approach the level of wealth it possessed in 1860, a malevolent legacy of Reconstruction, according to some, that extended at least until World War II.[137]

In effect, the Southern landowners became bourgeois employers, and the once independent white farmers—their livestock and farms destroyed by the war and Southern Republican Reconstruction tax policies[138]—became agricultural wage earners, forced to produce only commercial crops, crushed with debt for foodstuffs, seed, and manufactured goods they never could pay off. The former slaves, of course, never even had such a meager chance for self-sufficiency.[139] It was this fact of agricultural peonage—brought on by racism, the lack of credit available after the war, and the withdrawal of black labor from the fields (caused by the desire of former slaves to work in other occupations, the wish of black women to tend to domestic chores denied them in slavery, and the lack of compulsion and need to work extra-long slave hours)—that caused the South to languish in defeat so long. True, historically speaking, other nations have suffered from worse economic consequences in defeat and recovered far more quickly,[140] but then they also had the benefit of more outside help to overcome the tendency of a ruined economy to become a "zero-sum game" of fixed resources in which a player can get ahead only at the expense of another. And in the postbellum South it was the former slaves who were relegated to the losing position, by force if necessary.[141]

The North erred in thinking that Appomattox was a peace treaty, rather than a temporary cease-fire, and thus it lost the peace. No wonder there was no Reconstruction Centennial; no celebration of the writing of the Fourteenth Amendment; no Reconstruction re-enactment units dressed in period costumes play acting the roles of freedmen, Scalawags, or Carpetbaggers; no celebration of the South having been converted into a massive "rotten borough," first by interventionist Radical Republicans and then by home-grown conservative Democrats. Indeed no one, black or white, North or South, really wanted to repeat Reconstruction's lessons all over again.[142] But repeat it they would by way of the modern civil rights movement, a whole new Second Reconstruction, and the emergence of a multicultural nation that has in turn spawned the "angry white male," the Contract with America, and the profoundest irony of all: a viable Republican party in the South dominated by those very whites whose ancestors rode with the ghostly apparitions of the Ku Klux Klan, leaving black Americans a dominant force in the Democratic party that had once crushed the hopes of their great-grandparents. Were it the plot of a novel, no doubt an editor would reject it as too improbable to be believed.

Notes

1. David Potter, "Explicit Data and Implicit Assumptions in Historical Study," in Louis Gottschalk (ed.), *Generalizations in Writing History: A Report of the Committee on Historical Analysis of the Social Science Research Council* (Chicago: University of Chicago Press, 1963): 184–85.

2. For the "Compromise of 1898" that portrayed the North as right about the war and the South as right about Reconstruction, see Paul H. Buck, *The Road to Reunion, 1865–1890* (Boston: J. B. Lippincott, 1937). For the shortcomings of textbooks, see Mark M. Krug, "On Rewriting the Story of Reconstruction in the U.S. History Textbooks," *Journal of Negro History* 46 (1961): 133–53. For an earlier article in the same manner, see Lawrence J. Reddick, "Racial Attitudes in American History Textbooks of the South," *Journal of Negro History* 19 (1934): 225–65. Also of related interest are Patrick J. Goff, "The Abolitionist Movement in High School Texts," *Journal of Negro Education* 32 (1963): 43–51; and Carl N. Degler, "The South in Southern History Textbooks," *Journal of Southern History* 30 (1964): 48–57.

3. Theodore L. Gross, "The Negro in the

Literature of Reconstruction," *Phylon* 22 (1961): 5–14; Jack Temple Kirby, "D. W. Griffith's Racial Portraiture," *Phylon* 39 (1978): 118–127; John Hope Franklin, *Race and History: Selected Essays, 1938–1988* (Baton Rouge: Louisiana State University, 1989), 10–24.

4. See Harold M. Hyman, "Introduction," in his edited volume, *The Radical Republicans and Reconstruction* (Indianapolis: Bobbs-Merrill, 1967), xviii.

5. Fawn Brodie, "Who Won the Civil War, Anyway?" *New York Times Book Review*, 5 August 1962, VII, 1. For the Lost Cause and its post–Civil War implications, see Rollin G. Osterweis, *The Myth of the Lost Cause, 1865–1900* (Hamden, CT: Archon Books, 1973), and Gaines M. Foster, *Ghosts of the Confederacy: Defeat, the Lost Cause, and the Emergence of the New South, 1865 to 1913* (New York: Oxford University Press, 1987).

6. For a modern rehash of similar arguments, see Richard J. Herrnstein and Charles Murray, *The Bell Curve: Intelligence and Class Structure in American Life* (New York: Free Press, 1994).

7. Francis B. Simkins, *Pitchfork Ben Tillman: South Carolinian* (Baton Rouge: Louisiana State University Press, 1944), 353–57.

8. Thomas J. Pressley, *Americans Interpret Their Civil War* (New York: Free Press, 1965), 152, 168.

9. William A. Dunning, *Essays on the Civil War and Reconstruction* (New York: Macmillan, 1897); Dunning, *Reconstruction: Political and Economic* (New York: Harper & Brothers, 1907).

10. For examples of Dunning students and their works or of others who wrote in the same vein, see John W. Burgess, *Reconstruction and the Constitution, 1866–1876* (New York: Charles Scribner's Sons, 1902); James Ford Rhodes, *History of the United States from the Compromise of 1850 to the Final Restoration of Home Rule at the South in 1877*, 7 vols. (New York: Macmillan, 1896–1906); James Shouler, *History of the United States of America under the Constitution*, 7 vols. (New York: Dodd, Mead & Co., 1880–1913); Woodrow Wilson, *A History of the American People*, 10 vols. (Harper & Brothers, 1902);

Walter Lynwood Fleming, *Civil War and Reconstruction in Alabama* (New York: Columbia University Press, 1905); Fleming, *The Sequel to Appomattox* (New Haven, CT: Yale University Press, 1921); Fleming (ed.), *Documentary History of Reconstruction: Political, Military, Social, Religious, Educational & Industrial 1865 to the Present Time*, 2 vols. (Cleveland: Arthur H. Clark, 1906–1907); James W. Garner, *Reconstruction in Mississippi* (New York: Macmillan, 1901); Hamilton J. Eckenrode, *Political History of Virginia during the Reconstruction* (Baltimore: Johns Hopkins University Press, 1904); William M. Caskey, *Secession and Restoration of Louisiana* (Baton Rouge: Louisiana State University Press, 1938); John Ficklen, *History of Reconstruction in Louisiana (through 1868)* (Baltimore: Johns Hopkins University Press, 1910); Ella Lonn, *Reconstruction in Louisiana after 1868* (New York: Russell & Russell, 1918); Garnie W. McGinty, *Louisiana Redeemed: The Overthrow of Carpet-bag Rule, 1876–1880* (New Orleans: Tulane University Press, 1941); Joseph G. de Roulhac Hamilton, *Reconstruction in North Carolina* (New York: Columbia University Press, 1914); C. Mildred Thompson, *Reconstruction in Georgia, Economic, Social, Political, 1865–1872* (New York: Columbia University Press, 1915); Charles W. Ramsdell, *Reconstruction in Texas* (New York: Columbia University Press, 1910); William C. Nunn, *Texas under the Carpetbaggers* (Austin: University of Texas Press, 1962); David Y. Thomas, *Arkansas in Civil War and Reconstruction, 1861–1874* (Little Rock: United Daughters of the Confederacy, 1923); Thomas S. Staples, *Reconstruction in Arkansas, 1862–1874* (New York: Columbia University Press, 1923); William W. Davis, *Civil War and Reconstruction in Florida* (New York: Columbia University, 1913); John Wallace, *Carpetbag Rule in Florida* (Gainesville: University of Florida Press, 1964), a volume written by an African American under the tutelage of Redeemer (white Democrat) Lieutenant Governor William D. Bloxham; E. Merton Coulter, *The Civil War and Readjustment in Kentucky* (Chapel Hill: University of North Carolina Press, 1926); John S. Reynolds, *Reconstruction in South Carolina* (Columbia: University of South Carolina Press, 1905.

11. Alan D. Harper, "William A. Dunning: The Historian as Nemesis," *Civil War History* 10 (1964): 54–66. For more on Dunning, see also Philip D. Muller, "Look Back without Anger: A Reappraisal of William A. Dunning," *Journal of American History* 61 (1974): 325–38.

12. Claude G. Bowers, *The Tragic Era: The Revolution after Lincoln* (Cambridge, MA: Riverside Press, 1929).

13. Hobert W. Winston, *Andrew Johnson: Plebeian and Patriot* (New York: Henry Holt, 1928); Lloyd P. Stryker, *Andrew Johnson: A Study in Courage* (New York: Macmillan, 1929); George F. Milton, *The Age of Hate: Andrew Johnson and the Radicals* (New York: Howard-McCann, 1930); and a later work on the same theme, Milton Lomask, *Andrew Johnson: President on Trial* (New York: Farrar, Straus & Cudahy, 1960). See also Ulrich B. Phillips, "The Central Theme of Southern History," *American Historical Review* 34 (1928–29): 30–43, quotes from 31 and 43.

14. Buck, *The Road to Reunion.*

15. E. Merton Coulter, *The South during Reconstruction, 1865–1877* (Baton Rouge: Louisiana State University Press, 1947), xi.

16. Charlotte L. Forten, "Life on the Sea Islands," *Atlantic Monthly* 13 (1864): 587–96; Ray Allen Billington (ed.), *The Journal of Charlotte L. Forten* (New York: Norton, 1981 [repr.]), 141–66; Pauline Murray, *Proud Shoes; The Story of an American Family* (New York: Harper & Row, 1956); Frederick Douglass, *The Life and Times of Frederick Douglass Written by Himself* (New York: Collier Books, 1962); T. Thomas Fortune, *Black and White: Land, Labor, and Politics in the South* (New York: Fords, Howard, Hulbert, 1884).

17. John R. Lynch, *The Facts of Reconstruction* (New York: Neale Publishing, 1913), 20–21, 48–49, and "Some Historical Errors of James Ford Rhodes," *Journal of Negro History* 2 (1917): 345–67. For a complete look at Rhodes, see Robert Cruden, *James Ford Rhodes: The Man, the Historian, and His Work, with a Complete Bibliography of the Writings of James Ford Rhodes* (Cleveland: Press of the Case Western Reserve University, 1961).

18. George Washington Williams, *History of the Negro Race in America from 1619 to 1880* (New York: G. P. Putnam's Sons, 1883); W. E. Burghardt DuBois, "The Freedmen's Bureau," *Atlantic Monthly* 87 (1901): 354–65; DuBois, "Reconstruction and Its Benefits," *American Historical Review* 15 (1909–10): 781–99.

19. Alrutheus A. Taylor, *The Negro in South Carolina during Reconstruction* (Washington, DC: Association for the Study of Negro Life and History, 1924); Taylor, *The Negro in the Reconstruction of Virginia* (Washington, DC: Association for the Study of Negro Life and History, 1926); Taylor, *The Negro in Tennessee, 1865–1880* (Washington, DC: Association for the Study of Negro Life and History, 1934); Taylor, "Historians of Reconstruction," *Journal of Negro History* 23 (1938): 16–34; Taylor, "Negro Congressmen a Generation After," *Journal of Negro History* 7 (1922): 127–71. See also Taylor, "Making West Virginia a Free State," *Journal of Negro History* 6 (1921): 131–73.

20. Carter G. Woodson and Charles H. Wesley, *The Negro in Our History*, 10th ed. (Washington, DC: Association for the Study of Negro Life and History, 1962); Horace Mann Bond, "Social and Economic Forces in Alabama Reconstruction," *Journal of Negro History* 23 (1938): 290–348; Bond, *Negro Education in Alabama: A Study in Cotton and Steel* (Washington, DC: Associated Publishers, 1939).

21. See Joseph Logsdon, "Black Reconstruction Revisited," *Reviews in American History* 1 (1973): 553–54. Logsdon thinks DuBois ought to be the primer for anyone engaging in a study of black history but points out that "provincial" American scholars are usually unable to cope with DuBois's depth of European training.

22 . See Clarence E. Walker, *Deromanticizing Black History: Critical Essays and Reappraisals* (Knoxville: University of Tennessee Press, 1991), and the discussion of this volume by Peter Kolchin, "Class Conscious-

ness," *Reviews in American History* 20 (1992): 85–90.

23. W. E. Burghardt DuBois, *Black Reconstruction: An Essay toward a History of the Part which Black Folk Played in the Attempt to Reconstruct Democracy, 1860–1888* (New York: Harcourt, Brace, 1935).

24. James Allen, *Reconstruction: The Battle for Democracy* (New York: International Publishers, 1937); Howard Fast, *Freedom Road* (New York: Duell, Sloan & Pearce, 1944); W. E. Burghardt DuBois, "Reconstruction, Seventy Five Years After," *Phylon* 4 (1943): 205–212. Daniel Savage Gray, "Bibliographic Essay: Black Views on Reconstruction," *Journal of Negro History* 58 (1973): 73–85, is the pivotal work on this topic and forms the basis for much of this discussion.

25. Francis B. Simkins and Robert Woody, *Reconstruction in South Carolina* (Chapel Hill: University of North Carolina Press, 1932), a volume that retreads the ground covered already by Alrutheus A. Taylor earlier. See Simkins, "New Viewpoints of Southern Reconstruction," *Journal of Southern History* 5 (1939): 49–61.

26. Howard K. Beale, "On Rewriting Reconstruction History," *American Historical Review* 45 (1939–1940): 807–27.

27. John Hope Franklin, "History—Weapon of War and Peace," *Phylon* 5 (1944): 249–59, quotes from 249, 250, 257; Franklin, "Whither Reconstruction Historiography," *Journal of Negro Education* 17 (1947): 446–61.

28. The rest of the material on revisionist changes and challenges, with some alterations, will follow the general presentation of Richard O. Curry, "The Civil War and Reconstruction: A Critical Overlook of Recent Trends and Interpretations," *Civil War History* 20 (1974): 215–38. On politics in the North, see also LaWanda Cox, "From Emancipation to Segregation," in John Boles and Evelyn Thomas Nolan (eds.), *Interpreting Southern History* (Baton Rouge: Louisiana State University Press, 1987), 204–209.

29. Examples of those historians who combine the two eras politically are Hyman (ed.), *The Radical Republicans and Reconstruction, 1861–1870*; Herman Belz, *Reconstructing the Union: Theory and Practice during the Civil War* (Ithaca, NY: Cornell University Press, 1969); Belz, *A New Birth of Freedom: The Republican Party and Freedmen's Rights, 1861–1866*; Hans Trefousse, *The Radical Republicans: Lincoln's Vanguard for Racial Justice* (New York: Alfred A. Knopf, 1969).

30. Forrest G. Wood, *Black Scare: The Racist Response to Emancipation and Reconstruction* (Berkeley: University of California Press, 1968); George M. Frederickson, *The Black Image in the White Mind: The Debate on Afro-American Character and Destiny, 1817–1914* (New York: Harper & Row, 1971).

31. Leonard P. Curry, "Congressional Democrats, 1861–1863," *Civil War History* 12 (1966): 213–29.

32. Richard O. Curry, "The Union as It Was: A Critique of Recent Interpretations of the 'Copperheads,'" *Civil War History* 13 (1967): 25–39; Curry, "Copperheadism and Ideological Continuity: Anatomy of a Stereotype," *Journal of Negro History* 57 (1972): 29–36.

33. Hyman (ed.), *The Radical Republicans and Reconstruction*; Trefousse, *The Radical Republicans*; T. Harry Williams, *Lincoln and the Radicals* (Madison: University of Wisconsin Press, 1939); Larry Gara, "Slavery and the Slave Power: A Crucial Distinction," *Civil War History* 15 (1969): 5–18.

34. John H. Cox and LaWanda Cox, "Negro Suffrage and Republican Politics," *Journal of Southern History* 33 (1967): 303–30; William Gillette, *The Right to Vote: Politics and the Passage of the Fifteenth Amendment* (Baltimore: Johns Hopkins University Press, 1966, 1969). The second edition of Gillette's book answers the Coxes' attack on him and his expediency view. See also Larry G. Kincaid, "Victims of Circumstance: An Interpretation of Changing Attitudes toward Republican Policy Makers and Reconstruction," *Journal of American History* 57 (1970): 48–66.

35. Arthur Zilversmit (ed.), *Lincoln on Black and White: A Documentary History* (Belmont, CA: Wadsworth Publishing Company, 1971), introduction. See also Cox, "From

Emancipation to Segregation," 219–23.

36. Lerone Bennett, Jr., "Was Abe Lincoln a White Supremacist?" *Ebony* 23 (1968): 35–38, 40, 42; Richard Hofstadter, *The American Political Tradition and the Men Who Made It* (New York: Alfred A. Knopf, 1948), 93–136.

37. Herbert Mitgang, "Was Lincoln Just a Honkie?" *New York Times Magazine*, February 11, 1968, 34–35, 100–107; Rhodes, *History of the United States from the Compromise of 1850*, 3: 633–35; James G. Randall, *Lincoln the President*, 4 vols. (New York: Dodd, Mead, 1945–55), 1: 123, 181–82, 2: 126–203, 4: 1–33; Allan Nevins, *The War for the Union*, 2 vols. (New York: Charles Scribner's Sons, 1959–1960), 2: 236–37; Benjamin Thomas, *Abraham Lincoln* (New York: Alfred A. Knopf, 1953), 188, 192; Benjamin Quarles, *Lincoln and the Negro* (New York: Oxford University Press, 1962), 36, 139; Harold M. Hyman, "Lincoln and Equal Rights for Negroes," *Civil War History* 12 (1966): 258–66; Ludwell H. Johnson, "Lincoln and Equal Rights," *Journal of Southern History* 32 (1966): 83–87; Cox, "From Emancipation to Segregation," 219–23. For an excellent piece of footnoted historical fiction on these matters, see William Safire, *Freedom: A Novel of Abraham Lincoln and the Civil War* (Garden City, NY: Doubleday, 1987).

38. Belz, *Reconstructing the Union*; Trefousse, *The Radical Republicans*; David Donald, "Devils Facing Zionwards," in Grady McWhiney (ed.), *Grant, Lee, Lincoln and the Radicals* (Evanston, IL: Northwestern University Press, 1964), 72–91.

39. Williams, "Lincoln and the Radicals," in McWhiney (ed.), *Grant, Lee, Lincoln and the Radicals*, 92–117; W. R. Brock, *An American Crisis: Congress and Reconstruction, 1865–1867* (New York: St. Martins Press, 1969).

40. V. Jacque Vogeli, *Free but Not Equal: The Midwest and the Negro during the Civil War* (Chicago: University of Chicago Press, 1967); LaWanda Cox, *Lincoln and Black Freedom: A Study in Presidential Leadership* (Columbia: University of South Carolina Press, 1981); Peyton McCrary, *Abraham Lincoln and Reconstruction: The Louisiana Experiment* (Princeton, NJ: Princeton University Press, 1978); Louis S. Gerteis, *From Contraband to Freedman: Federal Policy Toward Southern Blacks, 1861–1865* (Westport, CT: Greenwood Press, 1973); Walter A. Payne, "Lincoln's Caribbean Colonization Plan," *Pacific Historian* 7 (1963): 65–72; Paul J. Scheips, "Lincoln and the Chiriqui Colonization Project," *Journal of Negro History* 37 (1952): 418–53; Richard O. Curry, "The Civil War and Reconstruction," 220–24.

41. Dunning, *Reconstruction: Political and Economic*; Dunning, *Essays on the Civil War and Reconstruction*; Winston, *Andrew Johnson*; Stryker, *Andrew Johnson*; Milton, *The Age of Hate*; Bowers, *The Tragic Era*; Howard K. Beale, *The Critical Year [1866]: A Study of Andrew Johnson and Reconstruction* (New York: Harcourt, Brace, 1930).

42. Rhodes, *History of the United States from the Compromise of 1850*; Burgess, *Reconstruction and the Constitution*.

43. Eric McKitrick, *Andrew Johnson and Reconstruction* (Chicago: University of Chicago Press, 1960); Kenneth M. Stampp, *The Era of Reconstruction, 1865–1877* (New York: Alfred A. Knopf, 1965); John H and LaWanda Cox, *Politics, Principles and Prejudice, 1865–1866: Dilemma of Reconstruction America* (New York: Atheneum, 1963); Richard O. Curry, "The Civil War and Reconstruction," 225; Albert Castel, *The Presidency of Andrew Johnson* (Lawrence: University of Kansas Press, 1979); Hans L. Trefousse, *Andrew Johnson: A Biography* (New York: W. W. Norton, 1989). See also Carmen Anthony Notaro, "History of the Biographic Treatment of Andrew Johnson in the Twentieth Century," *Tennessee Historical Quarterly* 24 (1965): 143–55.

44. Michael Les Benedict, *A Compromise of Principle* (New York: W. W. Norton, 1974); Trefousse, *Radical Republicans*; Brock, *An American Crisis*; David Donald, *The Politics of Reconstruction, 1863–1867* (Baton Rouge: Louisiana State University Press, 1965). See also James E. Sefton, "The Impeachment of Andrew Johnson: A Century of Writing," *Civil War History* 14 (1968): 120–47.

45. Raul Berger, *Impeachment: The Constitutional Problems* (Cambridge, MA: Harvard

University Press, 1973); Irving Brandt, *Impeachment: Trials and Errors* (New York: Alfred A. Knopf, 1973).

46. Michael Les Benedict, *The Impeachment Trial of Andrew Johnson* (New York: W. W. Norton, 1973); Benedict, "The Rout of Radicalism: Republicans and the Elections of 1867," *Civil War History* 18 (1972): 334–44; McKitrick, *Andrew Johnson and Reconstruction*; Stanley I. Kutler, "Impeachment Reconsidered," *Reviews in American History* 1 (1973): 480–87.

47. Dunning, *Reconstruction: Political and Economic*; Buck, *The Road to Reunion*; George H. Mayer, *The Republican Party, 1854–1866*, 2d ed. (New York: Oxford University Press, 1967), 171–89.

48. J. F. C. Fuller, *The Generalship of U. S. Grant*, 2d ed. (Bloomington: Indiana University Press, 1958); William B. Hesseltine, *U. S. Grant: Politician* (New York: Dodd, Mead & Co., 1935). See also John Y. Simon et al. (eds.), *The Papers of Ulysses S. Grant*, 20 vols. to date (Carbondale: Southern Illinois University Press, 1963–), particularly the introductory materials to vol. 1. See also Ulysses S. Grant III, *Ulysses S. Grant: Warrior and Statesman* (New York: William Morrow, 1969); Bruce Catton, *Grant Takes Command* (Boston: Little, Brown, 1969); Catton, "The Generalship of U. S. Grant," in McWhiney (ed.), *Grant, Lee, Lincoln and the Radicals*, 3–31; John A. Carpenter, *Ulysses S. Grant* (New York: Twayne Publishers, 1970); David L. Wilson and John Y. Simon (eds.), *Ulysses S. Grant: Essays and Documents* (Carbondale: Southern Illinois University Press, 1981); Brooks D. Simpson, *Let Us Have Peace: Ulysses S. Grant and the Politics of War and Reconstruction* (Chapel Hill: University of North Carolina Press, 1991); Herman Hattaway and Archer Jones, *How the North Won: A Military History of the Civil War* (Urbana: University of Illinois Press, 1983); and William L. Richter, "The Papers of U. S. Grant: A Review Essay," *Civil War History* 36 (1990): 149–66.

49. William S. McFeely, *Grant: A Biography* (New York: W. W. Norton, 1981); Richard N. Current, "Grant without Greatness," *Reviews in American History* 9 (1981): 507–509; John Y. Simon, review in *Wisconsin Magazine of History* 65 (1982): 220–21; James M. McPherson, review in *Civil War History* 29 (1981): 362–66; Brooks D. Simpson, "Butcher? Racist? An Examination of William S. McFeely's *Grant: A Biography*," *Civil War History* 33 (1987): 62–83 (for reviewers and quotes). See also Arthur Zilversmit, "Grant and the Freedmen," in Robert H. Abzug and Stephen E. Maizlish (eds.), *New Perspectives on Race and Slavery in America: Essays in Honor of Kenneth M. Stampp* (Lexington: University of Kentucky Press, 1986), 128–45; and William L. Richter, "The Papers of U. S. Grant: A Review Essay," *Civil War History* 38 (1992): 342–48.

50. Wallace D. Farnham, "'The Weakened Spring of Government': A Study in Nineteenth Century American History," *American Historical Review* 68 (1963): 662–80; Dunning, *Reconstruction: Political and Economic*; Dunning, *Essays on the Civil War and Reconstruction*; Burgess, *Reconstruction and the Constitution*; Rhodes, *History of the United States from the Compromise of 1850*; and Alfred H. Kelly and Wilfred A. Harbison, *The American Constitution: Its Origins and Development*, 4th ed. (New York: W. W. Norton, 1970).

51. James G. Randall, *Constitutional Problems under Lincoln*, rev. ed. (Urbana: University of Illinois Press, 1951); Randall, *The Civil War and Reconstruction* (Boston: D. C. Heath, 1937). The Randall view is not yet passé; see Charles Fairman's magisterial study of the courts and Constitution, *Reconstruction and Reunion, 1864–1888*, 2 pts. (New York: Macmillan, 1971–1987).

52. Harold M. Hyman, "Reconstruction and Political-Constitutional Institutions: The Popular Expression," in Hyman (ed.), *New Frontiers of the American Reconstruction* (Urbana: University of Illinois Press, 1959), 1–39; Hyman, "Law and the Impact of the Civil War: A Review Essay," *Civil War History* 14 (1968): 51–59; Hyman, *A More Perfect Union: The Impact of the Civil War and Reconstruction on the Constitution* (New York: Alfred A. Knopf, 1973); Benedict, *A Compromise of Principle*. See also Stanley I. Kutler, *Judicial Power and Reconstruction Politics*

(Chicago: University of Chicago Press, 1968); Richard O. Curry, "The Civil War and Reconstruction," 228; William M. Wiecek, "The Reconstruction of the Federal Judicial Power, 1863–1875," *American Journal of Legal History* 13 (1969): 333–59.

53. William M. Wiecek, "The Reconstruction of the Constitution," *Reviews in American History* 1 (1973): 548–53; Cox, "From Emancipation to Segregation," 215–18.

54. Dunning, *Reconstruction, Political and Economic*, 116. The discussion here relies heavily on Frank Francis Wetta, "The Louisiana Scalawags" (Ph.D. dissertation, Louisiana State University, 1977), 1–48; Coulter, *The South during Reconstruction*, 124, 139, 142.

55. David Donald, "The Scalawag in Mississippi Reconstruction," *Journal of Southern History* 10 (1944): 447–60; Thomas B. Alexander, "Whiggery and Reconstruction in Tennessee," *Journal of Southern History* 16 (1950): 291–305; Alexander, "Persistent Whiggery in Alabama and the Lower South, 1860–1867," *Alabama Review* 12 (1959): 35–52; Alexander, "Persistent Whiggery in the Confederate South, 1860–1877," *Journal of Southern History* 27 (1961): 305–29; T. Harry Williams, "An Analysis of Some Reconstruction Attitudes," *Journal of Southern History* 12 (1946): 349–69. Donald later extended his view to include most of the South in his revision of the standard college text of its time, James G. Randall and David Donald, *The Civil War and Reconstruction*, 2d ed. (Boston: D. C. Heath, 1961), 626–629.

56. Allen Trelease, "Who were the Scalawags?" *Journal of Southern History* 29 (1963): 445–68. Otto Olsen confirmed Trelease's conclusions in North Carolina, "Reconsidering the Scalawags," *Civil War History* 12 (1966): 304–25; John Vollmer Mering, "Persistent Whiggery in the Confederate South: A Reconsideration," *South Atlantic Quarterly* 69 (1970–1971): 124–34; Warren Ellem, "Who Were the Mississippi Scalawags?" *Journal of Southern History* 38 (1972): 217–40; William M. Cash, "Alabama Republicans during Reconstruction: Personal Characteristics, Motivations, and Political Activity of Party Activists, 1867–1880"

(Ph.D. dissertation, University of Alabama, 1973); David Donald, review of Lillian Pereyra's *James Lusk Alcorn: Persistent Whig* (Baton Rouge: Louisiana State University Press, 1966), in *American Historical Review* 72 (1967): 707–708.

57. Hodding Carter, *The Angry Scar: The Story of Reconstruction* (Garden City, NY: Doubleday, 1959), 268; Stampp, *The Era of Reconstruction*, 162–64; Carl N. Degler, *The Other South: Southern Dissenters in the Nineteenth Century* (New York: Harper & Row Publishers, 1974), 192–228; Wetta, "The Louisiana Scalawags," 367–77. See also Sarah Van Voorhis Woolfolk, "Five Men Called Scalawags," *Alabama Review* 17 (1964): 45–55; Woolfolk, *The Scalawag in Alabama Politics, 1865–1881* (University: University of Alabama Press, 1967); and David G. Sansing, "The Role of the Scalawag in Mississippi Reconstruction (Ph.D. dissertation, University of Southern Mississippi, 1969).

58. Armistead L. Robinson, "Beyond the Realm of Consensus: New Meanings of Reconstruction for American History," *Journal of American History* 68 (1981): 276–97. For Southern Republican fiscal policies (primarily taxes on land to replace the antebellum taxes on slaves) that helped drive the small white farmer from its ranks, see J. Mills Thornton III, "Fiscal Policy and the Failure of Radical Reconstruction in the Lower South," in J. Morgan Kousser and James M. McPherson (eds.), *Religion, Race, and Reconstruction: Essays in Honor of C. Vann Woodward* (New York: Oxford University Press, 1982): 349–94.

59. Dunning, *Reconstruction: Political and Economic*, 116, 121, 210; Coulter, *The South during Reconstruction*, 126–27, 134, 140–41, 142.

60. Richard N. Current, "Carpetbaggers Reconsidered," in David H. Pinckney and Theodore Ropp (eds.), *A Festschrift for Frederick B. Artz* (Durham, NC: Duke University Press, 1964), 139–57; Current, *Three Carpetbag Governors* (Baton Rouge: Louisiana State University Press, 1967); and Current, *Those Terrible Carpetbaggers: A Reinterpretation* (New York: Oxford Univer-

sity Press, 1988). For a nice reprise of Current's study (with a catchy title to boot), see Stephen E. Maizlish, "A Look inside the Carpetbag," *Reviews in American History* 17 (1989): 79–84.

61. William C. Harris, "The Creed of the Carpetbaggers: The Case of Mississippi," *Journal of Southern History* 40 (1974): 199–224; Jack B. Scroggs, "Southern Reconstruction: A Radical View," *Journal of Southern History* 24 (1958): 407–29; Scroggs, "Carpetbagger Constitutional Reform in the South Atlantic States, 1867–1868," *Journal of Southern History* 27 (1961): 475–93; J. Mills Thornton, III, "Fiscal Policy and the Failure of Radical Reconstruction in the Lower South," in J. Morgan Kousser and James M. McPherson (eds.), *Region, Race, and Reconstruction: Essays in Honor of C. Vann Woodward* (New York: Oxford University Press, 1982), 349–94.

62. Thomas J. Pressley, "Racial Attitudes, Scholarship, and Reconstruction," *Journal of Southern History* 32 (1966): 88–93. See also John Hope Franklin, "Mirror for Americans: A Century of Reconstruction History," *American Historical Review* 86 (1980–1981): 1–14.

63. Howard K. Beale, "The Tariff and Reconstruction," *American Historical Review* 35 (1929–1930): 276–94; Beale, *The Critical Year [1866]*; William B. Hesseltine, "Economic Factors in the Abandonment of Reconstruction," *Mississippi Valley Historical Review* 22 (1935–1936): 191–210; Charles A. Beard and Mary Beard, *The Rise of American Civilization*, 2 vols. (New York: Macmillan, 1927). For an in-depth discussion, see Harry N. Scheiber, "Economic Change in the Civil War: An Analysis of Recent Studies," *Civil War History* 11 (1965): 396–411.

64. Stanley Coben, "Northeastern Business and Radical Reconstruction," *Mississippi Valley Historical Review* 46 (1959–1960): 69–90; Irwin Unger, *The Greenback Era: A Social and Political History of American Finance* (Princeton, NJ: Princeton University Press, 1964); Robert P. Sharkey, *Money, Class, and Party: An Economic Study of the Civil War and Reconstruction* (Baltimore: Johns Hopkins University Press, 1959); Walter T. K.

Nugent, *The Money Question during Reconstruction* (New York: W. W. Norton, 1967). For the epitome of the money issue as a straight economic problem divorced from Reconstruction issues, see Milton Friedman and Anna Jacobson Schwartz, *A Monetary History of the United States, 1867–1960* (Princeton, NJ: Princeton University Press, 1963), 15–134.

65. Beard and Beard, *The Rise of American Civilization*; Louis Hacker, *Triumph of American Capitalism* (New York: Simon & Schuster, 1940); Thomas Cochran and William Miller, *The Age of Enterprise* (New York: Macmillan, 1942).

66. Thomas Cochran, "Did the Civil War Retard Industrialization?" *Mississippi Valley Historical Review* 43 (1961): 197–210.

67. Walt W. Rostow, *Stages of Economic Growth*, 3rd ed. (Cambridge: Cambridge University Press, 1990); Douglass C. North, *Economic Growth of the United States, 1790–1860* (Englewood Cliffs, NJ: Prentice-Hall, 1960).

68. See various essays in David T. Gilchrest and W. David Lewis (eds.), *Economic Change in the Civil War Era* (Greenville, DE: Eleutherian Mills–Hagley Foundation, 1965).

69. Terry L. Seip, *The South Returns to Congress: Men, Economic Measures, and International Relationships* (Baton Rouge: Louisiana State University Press, 1983); Mark W. Summers, *Railroads, Reconstruction, and the Gospel of Prosperity: Aid under the Radical Republicans* (Princeton, NJ: Princeton University Press, 1984). See also the analysis by Michael Les Benedict, "The Politics of Prosperity in the Reconstruction South," *Reviews in American History* 12 (1984): 507–14.

70. Paul L. Haworth, *The Hayes-Tilden Disputed Presidential Election of 1876* (Cleveland: Arthur H. Clark, 1906); C. Vann Woodward, *Reunion and Reaction: The Compromise of 1877 and the End of Reconstruction* (Boston: Little, Brown, 1951); Woodward, *Origins of the New South, 1877–1913* (Baton Rouge: Louisiana State University Press, 1951), 1–75. This summary is taken from Gerald W. McFarland, "Another Perspective on the Compromise of 1877," *Reviews in American History* 2 (1974): 257–61; and

Michael Les Benedict, "Southern Democrats and the Crisis of 1876–1877: A Reconsideration of Reunion and Reaction," *Journal of Southern History* 46 (1980): 489–524.

71. Allan Peskin, "Was There Compromise in 1877?" *Journal of American History* 60 (1973): 63–75; C. Vann Woodward, "Yes, There Was Compromise," *Journal of American History*, 215–19. See also Carl V. Harris, "Right Fork or Left Fork? The Section-Party Alignments of Southern Democrats in Congress, 1873–1897," *Journal of Southern History* 42 (1976): 471–506, who doubted the deal ever went through.

72. Keith Ian Polakoff, *The Politics of Inertia: The Election of 1876 and the End of Reconstruction* (Baton Rouge: Louisiana State University Press, 1973). See also the discussion in Vincent P. DeSantis, "Rutherford B. Hayes and the Removal of the Troops and the End of Reconstruction," in J. Morgan Kousser and James M. McPherson (eds.), *Region, Race, and Reconstruction: Essays in Honor of C. Vann Woodward* (New York: Oxford University Press, 1982), 417–50.

73. Benedict, "Southern Democrats and the Crisis of 1876–1877," 489–524. See also David Donald, "Reconstruction," in John A. Garraty (ed.), *Interpreting American History: Conversations with Historians* (New York: Oxford University Press, 1970), 363–64; Thomas B. Alexander, "Persistent Whiggery in the Confederate South," 324–25; and Joseph F. Wall, *Henry Watterson: Reconstructed Rebel* (New York: Oxford University Press, 1957), had all expressed earlier doubts about Woodward's thesis but never went into detail about them.

74. Bernard A. Weisberger, "The Dark and Bloody Ground of Reconstruction Historiography," *Journal of Southern History* 25 (1959): 427–447.

75. Carter, *The Angry Scar;* Weisberger, "The Dark and Bloody Ground," 434.

76. John Hope Franklin, *Reconstruction: After the Civil War* (Chicago: University of Chicago Press, 1961); Gray, "Bibliographic Essay," 84–85; Staughton Lynd, "Rethinking Slavery and Reconstruction," *Journal of Negro History* 50 (1965): 206.

77. Kenneth M. Stampp, *The Peculiar Institution* (New York: Alfred A. Knopf, 1956), vii–viii.

78. Stampp, *The Era of Reconstruction*, 215.

79. Rembert W. Patrick, *The Reconstruction of the Nation* (New York: Oxford University Press, 1967); Avery O. Craven, *Reconstruction: The Ending of the Civil War* (New York: Holt, Rinehart, and Winston, 1969); Allen W. Trelease, *Reconstruction: The Great Experiment* (New York: Harper & Row, 1971). See also Forrest G. Wood, *The Era of Reconstruction, 1863–1877* (New York: Thomas Y. Crowell Co., 1975); David Lindsey, *Americans in Conflict: The Civil War and Reconstruction* (Boston: Houghton Mifflin, 1974).

80. Thomas J. Pressley, "Racial Attitudes, Scholarship, and Reconstruction: A Review History," *Journal of Southern History* 32 (1966): 88–93.

81. For a summary of the benefits of Reconstruction from a revisionist point of view, see Hyman, "Introduction," in his edited volume, *The Radical Republicans and Reconstruction*, lv–lxi. Cf. DuBois, "Reconstruction and Its Benefits," 781–99. A good summary of the revisionist point of view is the collection of articles in Kenneth Stampp, *Reconstruction: An Anthology of Revisionist Writings* (Baton Rouge: Louisiana State University Press, 1969).

82. Vernon L. Wharton, "Reconstruction," in Arthur S. Link and Rembert W. Patrick (eds.), *Writing Southern History: Essays in Historiography in Honor of Fletcher M. Green* (Baton Rouge: Louisiana State University Press, 1965), 295–315. A critique of Wharton as too glum is in Eugene D. Genovese, "On Southern History and Its Historians: A Review Article," *Civil War History* 13 (1967): 170–82, especially 178–79.

83. Herman Belz, "The New Orthodoxy in Reconstruction Historiography," *Reviews in American History* 1 (1973): 106–13; August Meier, "Negroes in the First and Second Reconstructions of the South," *Civil War History* 13 (1967): 114–30.

84. Eric Foner, "Reconstruction Revisited," *Reviews in American History* 10 (1982): 86. The following discussion is based on Foner's complete article, 82–100, and Eric

Foner, *Reconstruction: America's Unfinished Revolution, 1863–1877* (New York: Harper & Row, 1988), xix–xxiv.

85. C. Vann Woodward, "Seeds of Failure in Radical Race Policy," in Harold M. Hyman (ed.), *New Frontiers of the American Reconstruction*, 125–47.

86. Michael Les Benedict, "Preserving the Constitution: The Conservative Basis of Radical Reconstruction," *Journal of American History* 61 (1974): 65–90; Benedict, "Preserving Federalism: Reconstruction and the [Chief Justice Morrison R.] Waite Court," *Supreme Court Review* (1978): 39–79; Benedict, *A Compromise of Principle*.

87. Michael Perman, *Reunion without Compromise: The South and Reconstruction, 1865–1868* (New York: Cambridge University Press, 1973).

88. William Gillette, *Retreat from Reconstruction, 1869–1879* (Baton Rouge: Louisiana State University Press, 1979).

89. James C. Mohr, *The Radical Republicans and Reform in New York during Reconstruction* (Ithaca, NY: Cornell University Press, 1973); Mohr (ed.), *Radical Republicans in the North: State Politics during Reconstruction* (Baltimore: Johns Hopkins University Press, 1976); Eugene H. Berwanger, *The West and Reconstruction* (Urbana: University of Illinois Press, 1981); Felice A. Bonadio, *North of Reconstruction* (New York: New York University Press, 1970).

90. Claude F. Oubre, *Forty Acres and A Mule* (Baton Rouge: Louisiana State University Press, 1978); Eric Foner, *Politics and Ideology in the Age of the Civil War* (New York: Oxford University Press, 1980), 128–49. The land question had been brought up much earlier. See Staughton Lynd, "Rethinking Slavery and Reconstruction," *Journal of Negro History* 50 (1965): 207–209. Many question whether African Americans would have been able to hold on to their farms, given the poor economic conditions for agriculture in the late nineteenth century and the catastrophe that followed Native Americans after the Dawes Severalty Act (1887) granted the latter individuals farms, instead of reservations, that they were cheated out of in short order. See C. Vann

Woodward, "Emancipations and Reconstructions: A Comparative Study," in his *Future of the Past* (New York: Oxford University Press, 1989), 145–66; Belz, "The New Orthodoxy in Reconstruction Historiography," 109–11. Willie Lee Rose, *Rehearsal for Reconstruction: The Port Royal Experiment* (Indianapolis: Bobbs-Merrill Company, 1964), saw the land question as more important, as did Foner, who regretted its dominance to the exclusion of other factors, such as political and social rights, "Reconstruction Revisited," 86–87.

91. Lee W. Formwalt, "Antebellum Planter Persistence in Southwest Georgia— A Case Study," *Plantation Society in the Americas* 1 (1981): 410–29; A. Jane Townes, "The Effect of Emancipation in Large Landholdings: Nelson and Goochland Counties, Virginia," *Journal of Southern History* 45 (1979): 403–12; Joe Gray Taylor, *Louisiana Reconstructed, 1863–1877* (Baton Rouge: Louisiana State University, 1974); Jerrell H. Shofner, *Nor Is the Day Over Yet* (Gainesville: University Presses of Florida, 1974); William C. Harris, *The Day of the Carpetbagger* (Baton Rouge: Louisiana State University Press, 1979).

92. William S. McFeely, *Yankee Stepfather: General O. O. Howard and the Freedmen* (New Haven, CT: Yale University Press, 1968); Louis Gerteis, *From Contraband to Freedman*; Donald G. Nieman, *To Set the Law in Motion* (Millwood, NY: Kraus International, 1979); Leon F. Litwack, *Been in the Storm So Long: The Aftermath of Slavery* (New York: Alfred A. Knopf, 1979).

93. Robert C. Morris, *Reading, 'Riting, and Reconstruction* (Chicago: University of Chicago Press, 1981); Ronald E. Butchart, *Northern Schools, Southern Blacks, and Reconstruction* (Westport, CT: Greenwood Press, 1980); Kenneth B. White, "The Alabama Freedmen's Bureau and Black Education: The Myth of Opportunity," *Alabama Review* 34 (1981): 107–24.

94. Michael Les Benedict, *A Compromise of Principle*. For a discussion of the implications of this monograph, see Peter Kolchin, "The Myth of Radical Reconstruction," *Reviews in American History* 3 (1975): 228–36.

95. Foner, "Reconstruction Revisited," 87; Foner, *Reconstruction*, xxiii. For a different perspective of Reconstruction historiography from outside the United States, see John V. Bratcher (ed. and trans.), "A Soviet Historian [A. V. Efimov] Looks at Reconstruction," *Civil War History* 15 (1969): 257–64.

96. Robert L. Harris, "Coming of Age: The Transformation of Afro-American Historiography," *Journal of Negro History* 67 (1982): 107–21; Cox, "From Emancipation to Segregation," 199-202, 234–53.

97. Frank Tannenbaum, *Slave and Citizen: Slavery in the Americas* (New York: Alfred A. Knopf, 1947); Stanley M. Elkins, *Slavery: A Problem in American Institutional and Intellectual Life* (Chicago: University of Chicago Press, 1959); Ann J. Lane (ed.), *The Debate over Slavery: Stanley Elkins and His Critics* (Urbana: University of Illinois Press, 1971); Ulrich B. Phillips, *American Negro Slavery* (New York: D. Appleton and Company, 1918; Phillips, *Life and Labor in the Old South* (Boston: Little, Brown, 1930); Clarence L. Mohr, "Southern Blacks in the Civil War: A Century of Historiography," *Journal of Negro History* 59 (1974): 177–85.

98. Bell I. Wiley, *Southern Negroes, 1861–1865* (New Haven, CT: Yale University Press, 1938). The reissued 1953 hardback and 1965 paperback volumes had these terms edited out, producing a far different tone.

99. Herbert Aptheker, *The Negro in the Civil War* (New York: International Publishers, 1938); Harvey Wish, "Slave Disloyalty under the Confederacy," *Journal of Negro History* 23 (1938): 435–50.

100. I. A. Newby, "Historians and Negroes," *Journal of Negro History* 54 (1969): 34–47; Dudley T. Cornish, *The Sable Arm: Negro Troops in the Union Army* (New York: W. W. Norton, 1966), foreword to the Norton Library Edition. Cornish's book has since been replaced by Joseph T. Glatthaar, *Forged in Battle: The Civil War Alliance of Black Soldiers and White Officers* (New York: Free Press, 1989).

101. Emory M. Thomas, *The Confederacy as a Revolutionary Experience* (Englewood Cliffs, NJ: Prentice-Hall, 1971); Robert F. Durden, *The Gray and the Black: The Confederate Debate on Emancipation* (Baton Rouge: Louisiana State University Press, 1972).

102. This conclusion and the discussion above are from Clarence L. Mohr, "Southern Blacks in the Civil War: A Century of Historiography," *Journal of Negro History* 59 (1974): 177–95.

103. Led by Vernon L. Wharton, *The Negro in Mississippi, 1865–1890* (Chapel Hill: University of North Carolina Press, 1947), some of the more modern treatments included John Blassingame, *Black New Orleans, 1860–1880* (Chicago: University of Chicago Press, 1973); W. McKee Evans, *Ballots and Fence Rails: Reconstruction on the Lower Cape Fear* (Chapel Hill: University of North Carolina Press, 1967); Robert Cruden, *The Negro in Reconstruction* (Englewood Cliffs, NJ: Prentice-Hall, 1969); Joe M. Richardson, *The Negro in the Reconstruction of Florida, 1865–1877* (Tallahassee: Florida State University, 1965); Willie Lee Rose, *Rehearsal for Reconstruction*; Joel Williamson, *After Slavery: The Negro in South Carolina during Reconstruction* (Chapel Hill: University of North Carolina Press, 1965); Peter Kolchin, *First Freedom: The Responses of Alabama's Blacks to Emancipation and Reconstruction* (Westport, CT: Greenwood Press, 1972); Howard N. Rabinowitz (ed.), *Southern Black Leaders of the Reconstruction Era* (Urbana: University of Illinois Press, 1982); Edmund Drago, *Black Politicians in Reconstruction Georgia* (Baton Rouge: Louisiana State University Press, 1982); James Smallwood, *Time of Hope, Time of Despair: Black Texans during Reconstruction* (Port Washington, NY: National University Publications, 1981); Merline Pitre, *Through Many Dangers, Toils, and Snares: The Black Leadership of Texas, 1868–1900* (Austin, TX: Eakin Press, 1985); all of which reached its apex in the monumental volumes of Herbert G. Gutman, *The Black Family in Slavery and Freedom* (New York: Pantheon Books, 1976) and Litwack, *Been in the Storm So Long*.

104. Rayford W. Logan, *The Betrayal of the Negro: From Rutherford B. Hayes to Woodrow Wilson* (New York: Collier Books, 1965). Logan's volume was first put out in

1954 with the less inspired title *The Negro in American Life and Thought: The Nadir, 1877–1901.*

105. Dan T. Carter, "Moonlight, Magnolias, and Collard Greens: Black History and the New Romanticism," *Reviews in American History* 5 (1977): 167–73; John Hosmer and Joseph Fineman, "Black Congressmen in Reconstruction Historiography," *Phylon* 39 (1978): 97–107; Logsdon, "Black Reconstruction Revisited," 558; Richard O. Curry, "The Civil War and Reconstruction," 229–30; C. Vann Woodward, "Clio with Soul," *Journal of American History* 56 (1969): 18 (quote).

106. Peyton McCrary, "The Political Dynamics of Black Reconstruction," *Reviews in American History* 12 (1984): 51–58, especially 57–58.

107. Simkins, "New Viewpoints of Southern Reconstruction," 58–61; Dunning, *Reconstruction, Political and Economic,* 216, 278. Perhaps the best of this scholarship came from Edward Magdol, "Local Black Leaders in the South, 1867–1875: An Essay toward the Reconstruction of Reconstruction History," *Societas* 4 (1974): 81–110, an account of the influence of African American artisans in both white and black communities in the South, a theme expanded upon in his book, *A Right to the Land: Essays on the Freedmen's Community* (Westport, CT: Greenwood Press, 1977).

108. Lawrence Veysey, "The Autonomy of American History Reconsidered," *American Quarterly* 31 (1979): 455–77.

109. James McPherson, "Antebellum Southern Exceptionalism: A New Look at an Old Question," *Civil War History* 29 (1983): 230–44.

110. Foner, *Reconstruction,* xxiv–xxvii; Foner, "Reconstruction Revisited," 87–95; Michael Perman, "Eric Foner's Reconstruction: A Finished Revolution," *Reviews in American History* 17 (1989): 73–78.

111. Eric Foner, "The Meaning of Freedom in the Age of Emancipation," *Journal of American History* 81 (1994): 435–60. See also Belz, "The New Orthodoxy in Reconstruction Historiography," 109; Jane H. Pease and William H. Pease, *They Who Would Be Free: Blacks' Search for Freedom* (New York: Atheneum, 1974); Ira Berlin, *Slaves without Masters: The Free Negro in the Antebellum South* (New York: Pantheon, 1974); Vincent Harding, *There Is a River: The Black Struggle for Freedom in America* (New York: Harcourt Brace Jovanovich, 1981).

112. Michael Perman, "Eric Foner's Reconstruction: A Finished Revolution," 73–78.

113. Eric Anderson, "Afterward: Whither Reconstruction Historiography," in Eric Anderson and Alfred A. Moss, Jr. (eds.), *The Facts of Reconstruction: Essays in Honor of John Hope Franklin* (Baton Rouge: Louisiana State University Press, 1981), 219–28, especially 28.

114. Franklin, "Mirror for Americans," 1–14.

115. Stetson Kennedy, *After Appomattox: How the South Won the War* (Gainesville: University Press of Florida, 1995), vii–x, 287–91.

116. Quoted in Francis B. Simkins, *Pitchfork Ben Tillman: South Carolinian* (Baton Rouge: Louisiana State University Press, 1944), 355–56.

117. Foner, *Reconstruction,* xxi–xxii.

118. Michael Perman, "Eric Foner's Reconstruction: A Finished Revolution," 73–78, quote from 78. Other new synthesizers are very careful not to make this assertion, which is the full import of Eric Anderson, "Afterward: Whither Reconstruction Historiography," in Eric Anderson and Alfred A. Moss, Jr. (eds.), *The Facts of Reconstruction,* 219–28.

119. Hyman, *A More Perfect Union,* 543–53 and *passim.*

120. Dunning, *Essays on the Civil War and Reconstruction,* 174–75; Coulter, *The South during Reconstruction,* 159–61. Coulter emphasized that many generals were against Military Reconstruction (160) and soldiers often fraternized with their Southern charges (131) rather than be a part of this alleged violation of judicial, executive, and congressional legalities (130–32).

121. Hyman, *A More Perfect Union,* 156–70; Randall, *Constitutional Problems under Lincoln,* 238; William L. Richter, "'Devil

Take Them All': Military Rule in Texas, 1862–1865," *Southern Studies* 25 (1986): 5–30. See also David Y. Thomas, *A History of Military Government in Newly Acquired Territories of the United States* (New York: Columbia University Press, 1904); George W. Dennison, "Martial Law: The Development of a Theory of Emergency Power, 1776–1861," *American Journal of Legal History* 18 (1974): 52–95; George T. Baker, "Mexico City and the War with the United States: A Study of the Politics of Military Occupation," (unpublished Ph.D. dissertation, Duke University, 1970); Henry W. Ballantine, "Martial Law," *Columbia Law Review* 12 (1912): 529–38; W. S. Holdsworth, "Martial Law Historically Considered," *Law Quarterly Review* 18 (1902): 117–32; Ralph Gabriel, "The American Experience with Military Government," *American Historical Review* 49 (1944): 632–37; A. H. Carpenter, "Military Government of Southern Territory, 1861–1865," *American Historical Association Annual Report* (1900): 1: 465–98; Robert F. Futrell, "Federal Military Government in the South, 1861–1865," *Military Affairs* 15 (1951): 181–91; Frank Freidel, "General Orders No. 100 and Military Government," *Mississippi Valley Historical Review* 32 (1945–46): 541–56; James W. Garner, "General Orders 100 Revisited," *Military Law Review* 27 (1965): 1–48; David E. Engdahl, "Soldiers, Riots, and Revolutions: The Law of Military Troops in Civil Disorders," *Iowa Law Review* 57 (1971): 1–70.

122. Dunning, *Essays on the Civil War and Reconstruction*, 136–75; Franklin, *Reconstruction*, 119–21, 196. See also Cox, "From Emancipation to Segregation," 225–28.

123. Harold M. Hyman, "Johnson, Stanton and Grant: A Reconsideration of the Army's Role in the Events Leading to Impeachment," *American Historical Review* 66 (1960): 85–100; Benjamin P. Thomas and Harold M. Hyman, *Stanton: The Life and Times of Lincoln's Secretary of War* (New York: Alfred A. Knopf, 1962): 547–614.

124. James E. Sefton, *The United States Army and Reconstruction, 1865–1877* (Baton Rouge: Louisiana State University Press,

1967). Other studies, particularly in the Fifth Military District (Louisiana and Texas), have confirmed Sefton's major contentions, whether they favor military government as in Joseph Green Dawson III, *Army Generals and Reconstruction: Louisiana, 1862–1977* (Baton Rouge: Louisiana State University Press, 1982) and Robert W. Shook, "Federal Occupation and Administration of Texas 1865–1870" (Ph.D. dissertation, North Texas State University, 1970), or questioned its effect as in William L. Richter, *The Army in Texas during Reconstruction* (College Station: Texas A&M University Press, 1987). See also A. H. Carpenter, "Military Government of Southern Territory, 1861–1865," *American Historical Association Annual Report* (1900): 1: 465–98; William T. Alderson, "The Influence of Military Rule and the Freedmen's Bureau on Reconstruction in Virginia, 1865–1870" (Ph.D. dissertation, Vanderbilt University, 1952); James L. McDonough, "John Schofield as Military Director of Reconstruction in Virginia," *Civil War History* 15 (1969): 237–56; Sefton, "Aristotle in Blue and Braid: General John Schofield's Essays on Reconstruction," *Civil War History* 17 (1971): 45–57. Foner, *Reconstruction*, relegated the army's key role in the era to less than 10 pages out of 612, less than 2 percent of the total. On the limits of military use domestically, see H. W. C. Furman, "Restrictions upon the Use of the Army Imposed by the Posse Comitatus Act," *Military Law Review* 79 (1959): 85–129.

125. William S. McFeely, *Yankee Stepfather: General O. O. Howard and the Freedmen* (New Haven, CT: Yale University Press, 1968). Others more favorable to Howard were John Cox and LaWanda Cox, "General Howard and the 'Misrepresented Bureau,'" *Journal of Southern History* 19 (1953): 427–56; John Carpenter, *Sword and Olive Branch: Oliver Otis Howard* (Pittsburgh: University of Pittsburgh Press, 1964).

126. Cox, "From Emancipation to Segregation," 223–25. In defense of the bureau, see Martin Abbott, "Free Land, Free Labor, and the Freedmen's Bureau," *Agricultural History* 30 (1956): 150–56; Alderson, "The

Influence of Military Rule and the Freedmen's Bureau on Reconstruction in Virginia"; Victoria Marcus Olds, "The Freedmen's Bureau as a Social Agency" (Ph.D. dissertation, Columbia University, 1966); Richard Paul Fuke, "A Reform Mentality: Federal Policy toward Black Marylanders," *Civil War History* 22 (1976): 214–35. Those who question the bureau include Theodore B. Wilson, *The Black Codes of the South* (University: University of Alabama Press, 1965); Joe M. Richardson, "The Freedmen's Bureau and Negro Labor in Florida," *Florida Historical Quarterly* 39 (1960): 176–84; George D. Humphrey, "Failure of the Mississippi Freedmen's Bureau in Black Labor Relations, 1865–1867," *Journal of Mississippi History* 45 (1983): 23–37; J. Thomas May, "Continuity and Change in the Labor Program of the Union Army and the Freedmen's Bureau," *Civil War History* 17 (1971): 245–54; James Smallwood, "Perpetuation of Caste: Black Agricultural Workers in Reconstruction Texas," *Mid-America* 61 (1979): 5–23; N. Gordon Carper, "Slavery Revisited: Peonage in the South," *Phylon* 37 (1976): 85–99; Ira C. Colby, "The Freedmen's Bureau: From Social Welfare to Segregation," *Phylon* 46 (1985): 219–30. Ronald L. F. Davis, "The U.S. Army and the Origins of Sharecropping in the Natchez District: A Case Study," *Journal of Negro History* 62 (1977): 60–80, saw no bureau policy but the interplay of vast socioeconomic forces as defeating the bureau, while Paul A. Cimbala, "The 'Talisman of Power': Davis Tillson, The Freedmen's Bureau, and Free Labor in Reconstruction Georgia," *Civil War History* 28 (1982): 153–71, saw white expectations as critical to the stymied bureau programs.

127. These two historical viewpoints were graphically portrayed in Texas. See William L. Richter, *Overreached on All Sides: The Freedmen's Bureau Administrators in Texas, 1865–1868* (College Station: Texas A&M University Press, 1991), who put forth a post-revisionist view; Barry A. Crouch, *The Freedmen's Bureau and Black Texans* (Austin: University of Texas, 1992); and Nancy Cohen Lack, "A Struggle for Sovereignty: National Consolidation, Emancipation, and Free Labor in Texas," *Journal of Southern History* 58 (1992): 57–88, who posited the new synthesis.

128. Dunning, *Reconstruction, Political and Economic*, 121–23, 134–35, 181–88; Dunning, *Essays on the Civil War and Reconstruction*, 354–57; Coulter, *The South during Reconstruction*, 162–83.

129. Michael Perman, *The Road to Redemption: Southern Politics, 1869–1879* (Chapel Hill: University of North Carolina Press, 1984). For the economic picture before, during, and after the war, see Mark W. Summers, *The Era of Good Stealings* (New York: Oxford University Press, 1993); Summers, *Railroads, Reconstruction, and the Gospel of Prosperity: Aid under the Radical Republicans* (Princeton, NJ: Princeton University Press, 1984); and Summers, *The Plundering Generation: Corruption and the Crisis of the Union* (New York: Oxford University Press, 1987). On the inability of Southern Republicans to overcome the divisive racial issue, see Otto H. Olsen, "Southern Reconstruction and the Question of Self Determination," in George M. Frederickson (ed.), *A Nation Divided: Problems and Issues of the Civil War and Reconstruction* (Evanston, IL: Northwestern University, 1975), 113–41. See also the various state-by-state essays in Otto H. Olsen (ed.), *Reconstruction and Redemption in the South* (Baton Rouge: Louisiana State University Press, 1980).

130. George C. Rabel, *But There Was No Peace: The Role of Violence in the Politics of Reconstruction* (Athens: University of Georgia Press, 1984); Allan W. Trelease, *White Terror: The Ku Klux Klan Conspiracy and Southern Reconstruction* (New York: Harper and Row, 1971); Melinda Meek Hennessey, "Political Terrorism in the Black Belt: The Eutaw Riot," *Alabama Review* 33 (1980): 35–48; Hennessey, "Racial Violence during Reconstruction: The 1876 Riots in Charleston and Cainhoy," *South Carolina Historical Magazine* 86 (1985): 100–12; Hennessey, "Race and Violence in New Orleans: The 1868 Riot," *Louisiana History* 20 (1979): 77–91; Hennessey, "Reconstruction Politics and the Military: The Eufala Riot of 1874,"

Alabama Historical Quarterly 38 (1976): 112–25; and Hennessey, "To Live and Die in Dixie: Reconstruction Race Riots in the South" (Ph.D. dissertation, Kent State University, 1978); William Gillette, *Retreat from Reconstruction, 1869–1879* (Baton Rouge: Louisiana State University Press, 1979). The best short discussion of the whole problem is James M. McPherson, "Redemption or Counterrevolution? The South in the 1880s," *Reviews in American History* 13 (1985): 545–50. See also the introductory essay and the selections in Donald G. Nieman (ed.), *Black Freedom/White Violence, 1865–1900* (New York: Garland Publishing, 1994).

131. Gillette, *Retreat from Reconstruction*, 335–80; Olsen (ed.), *Reconstruction and Redemption in the South*, 1–12. For a critique of Gillette's and Olsen's approaches as an undermining of the economic determinism of earlier studies without offering anything of substance in exchange, see August Meier, "An Epitaph for the Writing of Reconstruction History?" *Reviews in American History* 8 (1981): 82–87. See also Woodward, *Reunion and Reaction*, 237–46; his critic, Harris, "Right Fork or Left Fork?" 471–506; and Patrick Riddleberger, "The Radicals' Abandonment of the Negro during Reconstruction," *Journal of Negro History* 45 (1966): 88–102. Also of interest is Logan, *The Betrayal of the Negro*.

132. Woodward, "Seeds of Failure in Radical Race Policy," 124–47.

133. Hyman, *A More Perfect Union*; Robert J. Kaczorowski, "To Begin the Nation Anew: Congress, Citizenship and Civil Rights after the Civil War," *American Historical Review* 90 (1987): 45–68; Kaczorowski, *The Nationalization of Civil Rights: Constitutional Theory and Practice in a Racist Society, 1866–1883* (New York: Garland Publishing, 1987); Kaczorowski, "Searching for the Intent of the Framers of the Fourteenth Amendment," *Connecticut Law Review* 5 (1972–73): 369–98; Kutler, *Judicial Power and Reconstruction Politics*; Wiecek, "The Reconstruction of the Constitution," 548–53; Wiecek, "The Reconstruction of the Federal Judicial Power, 1863–1875," 333–59;

DuBois, "Reconstruction, Seventy Five Years After," *Phylon* 4 (1943): 205–212; Stampp, *The Era of Reconstruction*, 215.

134. C. Vann Woodward, "Our Past Isn't What It Used To Be," *New York Times Book Review*, 28 July 1963, 1ff.

135. Rhodes, *History of the United States from the Compromise of 1850*, 5: 609; 6: 49–50.

136. Recent historians point out that the loss in slaves was really a transfer of ownership of capitalized labor from management to labor itself. See Roger L. Ransom and Richard Sutch, *One Kind of Freedom: The Economic Consequences of Emancipation* (Cambridge: Cambridge University Press, 1977), 52. This is true, economically speaking, but quite otherwise emotionally; see A. B. Moore, "One Hundred Years of Reconstruction of the South," *Journal of Southern History* 9 (1943): 153–80.

137. Moore, "One Hundred Years of Reconstruction of the South," 153–80; James L. Sellers, "An Interpretation of Civil War Finance," *American Historical Review* 30 (1925): 282–97; Sellers, "The Economic Incidence of the Civil War in the South," *Mississippi Valley Historical Review* 14 (1927): 179–90; Eugene M. Lerner, "Money, Prices, and Wages in the Confederacy, 1861–1865," in Ralph Andreano (ed.), *The Economic Impact of the American Civil War* (Cambridge, MA: Schenkman, 1967), 31–60; Lerner, "Southern Output and Agricultural Income, 1860–1880," *Agricultural History* 33 (1959): 117–25. See also William E. Parrish (ed.), *The Civil War: A Second American Revolution?* (New York: Holt, Rinehart & Winston, 1970); and William L. Barney, *Flawed Victory: A New Perspective on the Civil War* (New York: Praeger Publishers, 1975), 171–84.

138. Before the war, taxes had been paid primarily by slaveholders, exempting small white farmers—afterward taxes hit all landowners. See J. Mills Thornton, III, "Fiscal Policy and the Failure of Radical Reconstruction in the Lower South," in J. Morgan Kousser and James M. McPherson (eds.), *Religion, Race, and Reconstruction: Essays in Honor of C. Vann Woodward*, 349–94.

139. Harold D. Woodman, "Sequel to Slavery: The New History Views the Post Bellum South," *Journal of Southern History* 43 (1977): 547–56; Forrest McDonald and Grady McWhiney, "The South from Self-sufficiency to Peonage: An Interpretation," *American Historical Review* 85 (1980): 1095–1118, and discussion in 1150–66 of same journal issue. Although admitting the South was not booming as Republicans had hoped, Foner saw subtle changes in the economic system, particularly the nipping in the bud of a disciplined pseudoslavery, not measurable by statistics, that boded well for the future, *Reconstruction*, 397–410. For the economic and social plight of African Americans after the war, see Herbert G. Gutman, *The Black Family in Slavery and Freedom, 1750–1925* (New York: Pantheon Books, 1976); Pete Daniel, *The Shadow of Slavery: Peonage in the South* (New York: Oxford University Press, 1973); Litwack, *Been in the Storm So Long;* Roger L. Ransom and Richard Sutch, *One Kind of Freedom;* William Cohen, *At Freedom's Edge: Black Mobility and the Southern White Quest for Racial Control, 1861–1915* (Baton Rouge: Louisiana State University Press, 1991); Cohen, "Negro Involuntary Servitude in the South, 1865–1940: A Preliminary Analysis," *Journal of Southern History* 42 (1976): 31–60.

140. Ransom and Sutch, *One Kind of Freedom*, 40–55.

141. Jonathan M. Wiener, "Class Structure and Economic Development in the American South, 1865–1955," *American Historical Review* 84 (1979): 970–92.

142. C. Vann Woodward, *The Strange Career of Jim Crow*, 2d rev. ed. (New York: Oxford University Press, 1966), 8–10, 122–47, 150–91.

THE
ABC-CLIO
COMPANION TO

American Reconstruction, 1862–1877

Abolitionists and Reconstruction

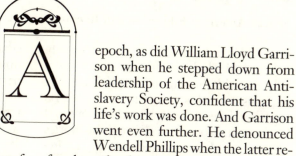

It is common to view American history from the perspective of eras or epochs. Although this concept of history helps in understanding certain themes, it can also be very limiting. Typical in this respect is the notion of seeing the abolitionists as a part of the antebellum period without realizing that their interest in black America stretched into the war and certainly into Reconstruction and even beyond. Yet somehow there is a feeling among historians that much of Reconstruction got lost somewhere along the line, especially the concept of "all men are created equal." This has been described by historian C. Vann Woodward as the war's "deferred commitment." The war saved the Union and freed African Americans from legal bondage, but the equality of people was forgotten. It was not an inadequacy limited to the South—indeed, the war's greatest fault was that equality never won over the average citizen of the North.

So what happened to the abolitionists during Reconstruction? Why did Radical Republicans abandon African Americans to the simplicities of alleged racial inferiority? Why did everyone seem to give up on the final step, the true Reconstruction of U.S. society? Part of the answer is that abolitionists did not end their activity with the war or Reconstruction. They continued to work actively for the extension of black civil rights from the political to the economic to the social spheres. They spoke out and campaigned against the bans on interracial marriage and supported the integration of public schools and public accommodations. But the concept of nationalism that emerged from the Civil War was a limited one. It did not include what we today view as more or less normal, the idea of state-planned reform. Indeed, most Americans and most abolitionists believed in self-help. It was not the government's responsibility to ensure social or economic equality; one had to achieve that by oneself.

Thus it was not uncommon for Americans to view Reconstruction as the end of an epoch, as did William Lloyd Garrison when he stepped down from leadership of the American Antislavery Society, confident that his life's work was done. And Garrison went even further. He denounced Wendell Phillips when the latter refused to do the same and took over the society for more work on black equality. The sad part was that there were places where state-directed economic improvement had proved useful. One of these was in the Sea Islands of South Carolina, where Northern missionaries and benevolent association members came south to help blacks make a successful transition from slavery to freedom. But in the nation at large these efforts were looked upon as the eccentricities of "do-gooders." Essentially the United States did the same thing it had done in the aftermath of its own Revolution—it created a conservative republic, this time without slavery, rather than an egalitarian, multiracial democracy. It was ready to free blacks to achieve the goal of Union, but it was unwilling to go farther and follow the slow and painful example of the Sea Islands toward racial progress. The failure rested not so much with the abolitionists as it did with the American people.

See also Freedmen's Aid Societies; Port Royal Experiment.

References Curry, Richard O., "The Abolitionists and Reconstruction" (1968); Davis, David Brion, "Abolitionists and the Freedmen" (1965); Dillon, Merton L., "The Failure of American Abolitionists" (1959); Donald, David H., "Towards a Reconsideration of the Abolitionists" (1956); Duberman, Martin, ed., *The Antislavery Vanguard* (1965); Frederickson, George M., *The Inner Civil War* (1965); McPherson, James M., "Abolitionists and the Civil Rights Act of 1875" (1965) and *The Struggle for Equality* (1964); Riddleberger, Patrick W., "The Radicals' Abandonment of the Negro during Reconstruction" (1960); Sproat, John G., "Blueprint for Radical Reconstruction" (1957); C. Vann Woodward, "Equality" (1958) and "Seeds of Failure in Radical Race Policy" (1966).

African American Education and Reconstruction

Reconstruction was begun haltingly and with contradictory methods during the

Civil War, not in 1865 as is commonly believed. Similarly, it ended just as disjointedly, not with the usual date of 1877. Nothing illustrates this better than the efforts made by dozens of Northern religious and benevolent associations to bring the glories of freedom through education to the ex-slaves. But what blacks wound up with was not the Northern free soil, free labor society the missionaries and teachers desired for them, nor the liberated autonomous world hoped for by African Americans themselves. It was somewhere in between, different from what preceded it, but probably too dependent on the white South. It was a capitalist society with remnants of the feudal slave-based society of the antebellum days intermixed. To the degree that it was new, postwar education of blacks must have had some positive influence. But the terms on which the former slaves received the gift of education were not determined by Northern teachers or skeptical Southern whites alone. This education was molded by the uses and needs of the black community, which in the end determined just how things would be.

In the early years of Reconstruction, missionaries and aid workers came South, seeking to relieve the misery of slaves who had fled their homes for freedom. The need for aid was so great that education took second place to survival. But education was never forgotten. It was seen by the Yankees as the only true route to freedom and self-sufficiency. There were 51 different freedmen's aid societies—20 secular, 31 sectarian—in the South during and after the war. When they took up the burden of education among the contrabands (the name given to slaves liberated during the war), they often found that blacks had already established schools of their own, run by literate former slaves who could pass on the basics of literacy. Many times, the incoming Yankees approached these early efforts with a condescending scorn, often reluctantly paying the teacher to continue, other times refusing to associate with the contraband teachers. The societies had problems with their own people, too, centering around the proper way to

educate blacks, which in the spirit of the times included religious training as a key part of all education. A person without moral education was deemed at best half ignorant. But the various church groups were not about to compromise on what they saw as they only true way to godliness and eventual salvation of the human soul.

Typical of the philosophical problems that existed was the claim of the American Missionary Association (AMA) to be inter-denominational. This claim was a fraud, of course, to anyone who was not a Congregationalist, the sponsoring body of the association. And the work of the association belied the claim, as its missionaries openly created Congregational churches everywhere its teachers went. But they were not alone. Baptists, Methodists, Presbyterians, and Quakers all competed for African Americans' souls as well as their minds. There was also competition from the secular associations, which claimed to be doing their work without denominational prejudices. That claim was true to some degree, but it was a poor church member indeed who would not stick a bit of the "true salvation" into his or her work, regardless of the parent association's denial of the same. The secular associations were eventually united under the guise of the American Freedmen's Union Commission (AFUC). And as a result of their demand for government assistance for a work that was too great in size and intent for uncoordinated, private action, Congress eventually established the Bureau of Refugees, Freedmen, and Abandoned Lands (commonly referred to as the Freedmen's Bureau). The bureau had its own department of education that was supposed to synchronize the education efforts among the freed people.

But why was there such an emphasis on education? African Americans needed a lot more than that to become full partners in U.S. society as free people. They needed political and economic power. In the end the schools fell under the control of whites who cared less for the problems of blacks as free persons, which meant that the schools proved totally inadequate for the monumental task they had undertaken. Education was important to the nineteenth-century American because it imparted the privileges and immunities of citizenship as well as its limitations, duties, and responsibilities. There was much doubt among white Americans of both sections (North and South)—even the strongest abolitionists—as to whether blacks would survive freedom. Indeed, intellectuals feared and ascribed much importance to racial differences. The hope was that the former slaves would be able to learn. The fear was that slavery had been such a deadening institution that it would be impossible to overcome the sense of inferiority it had implanted in the black psyche. But the gross immorality of slavery demanded that blacks be given the chance to be free Americans.

Education, then, was to Americanize blacks like any other immigrant group. This was important because the freed slave was not merely a citizen, but the black man was also a voter. Political rights were a privilege that had to be exercised responsibly. For those who doubted the wisdom of the black vote (it was not looked upon favorably by many Northerners, especially in the Old Northwest), education also instilled a sense of responsibility. There was also the hope that through education African Americans would overcome the hostility and prejudice directed toward them. It was hoped that as blacks demonstrated their ability to learn and absorb U.S. political and free market economic ideals, there would be no reason for whites to ostracize them. Education would bring economic mobility, allowing blacks to live like other ethnic groups in the United States. Black women would be taught homemaking skills to make their homes a refuge from the men's forays into the hostile world. The entire South would be transformed into an idealistic picture of a New England with a Southern drawl. Reconstruction was, after all, an institutional transformation. Every institution in the Old South would have to give way to the ideals presented by the Yankee victors, including public schools, democratized politics, proper economic activity (without slavery),

and a refined morality. Of course, this point of view smugly assumed that the South, white or black, did not possess any such concepts already.

For every secular or religious association that went South, education was the key to reforming the ex-slaves, restructuring the white South, and protecting the republic from the ills of slavery, secession, and treason. The core of this change would come from a religious point of view. The nineteenth century was a religious one; churches were influential, and truth was denominational, not general. Of course, in the eyes of Northern missionaries, the former slaves lacked the religious basis needed for becoming good citizens. No one of the "true faith" was going to give credence to African Americans' religious institutions and beliefs. The ex-slaves had to be Reconstructed along with the white South. These missionaries had little faith in the secular interplay of self-interest displayed by the Founding Fathers in the Constitution. The world was made up of the unbaptized, who had to be enlightened for their own and society's good. Unless African Americans received this great education they would be dangerous, unstable, and threatening. They would be susceptible to the evils of drink, vice, and even Roman Catholicism (the Protestant missionaries were a little late when it came to Louisiana, which had all three in abundance). With the proper schooling, though, they would become docile, tractable, and safe. This attitude gave the Congregationalists an advantage over all other Protestants—they had no white co-religionists in the South to worry about. They had not been rent asunder by the war and slavery.

All of this raised the question of what the real purpose of education was. Was it to make blacks a docile, obedient part of white society? Or was it truly to liberate them, to help them find their own unique way in the United States? One thing is clear: black education during Reconstruction did not promote African American liberation, in a modern sense. Rather, it was intended to make blacks a sober, clean, industrious,

African American schools were regulated and supported by the federal government through the Freedmen's Bureau. The schools emphasized discipline, domesticity, and piety, and spoke very little of liberty, democracy, and the rights of U.S. citizens.

thrifty people who would keep legal contracts especially as regarded labor. In short, the Yankee teachers hoped to replace the care and control exercised over African Americans by their former masters. No wonder the white South attacked school rooms, burned school buildings to the ground, and harassed and murdered teachers and students; furthermore, blacks were often disappointed about what they were taught.

There was an economic side to education, too. The creation of a hard-working, stable work force was part and parcel of education. This aspect of education was acceptable to the white South, and many planters sought to have schools placed on their property to have a say in the content of education. Implicit in this effort was the desire of Northern whites to educate blacks to accept their lot in the South and not to follow the thousands who took the Underground Railroad in search of a new life in the North. One of the key objectives of the Freedmen's Bureau was to achieve economic fairness for the ex-slaves in the South so that they would not want to leave their old homes. But this meant that African Americans would for the most part work on someone else's land, not their own.

The schools set up for African Americans by the secular and religious aid societies were coordinated and supported by the federal government through the Freedmen's Bureau. The first bureau law in 1865 was extremely vague in all aspects, leaving it to the commissioner, Bvt. Maj. Gen. Oliver O. Howard, to work out the details. The renewal of the bureau in July 1866 mentioned education for the first time when it appropriated money to repair and rent school buildings. What this all meant was that Howard and his assistant for education, John Alvord, could exercise much influence for good or ill over the activities of the already-existing aid agencies in the South. Howard was very liberal as to what "repair" and "rent" involved. He stretched the law to its limit, doing all he could to get schools built under these provisions. He also allowed "rent" to go toward subsidizing teacher salaries.

Howard and Alvord had the authority to determine which agency received federal aid, and in this respect the two men favored church-affiliated associations over secular ones to such a degree that the latter had pretty much disappeared by 1869. Since both Howard and Alvord were Congregationalists—as was Howard's brother, Charles, who served as bureau subassistant commissioner in Washington, D.C., secretary of the AMA's headquarters at Chicago, and school inspector for the AMA's operations in the Southwest (Mississippi, Louisiana, Arkansas, and Texas)—the primary beneficiary of this governmental support was the "nondenominational" AMA, much to the disgust of other supplicants. The government picked up Charles Howard's traveling expenses, even though he was technically on the AMA payroll. The superintendents of the bureau's educational efforts in the Southwest were all AMA men, too, except in Texas. There, a Unitarian and dedicated abolitionist who favored public education, Edwin Wheelock, blocked AMA attempts to control the state until he ran afoul of Bvt. Maj. Gen. Charles Griffin, who had Wheelock removed from office in 1867.

Although the bureau began with the intent of educating blacks to facilitate their liberation, it soon compromised its plan by emphasizing the more conservative concept of the school in place of liberation. Howard refused to fight President Andrew Johnson, who abolished the bureau's congressional mandate to distribute "abandoned lands" to the freedmen in 40-acre plots when he returned plantations to their pardoned owners. Eventually Howard compromised the bureau into extinction so that by 1869 only a weakened education division remained. Howard had agents lecture freedmen on how to behave; he curtailed independent economic activity, placing blacks at the mercy of planters; he stopped much of the bureau's judicial regulation of white-black relations; he increased education activities until the promise of black independence and political and economic power shifted to that of the offer of a schoolhouse. These changes reconciled the bureau more and more with the Southern white power structure. This shift was marked by more and more schools being located on plantations. This permitted planters to control curricula, tie blacks to the land, and isolate them from each other. The bureau also saddled the impoverished African Americans with more of the costs of education. Blacks had to buy the land, erect the building, and pay the teacher's board. Only then would the bureau step in to help. In the end, education became another force that limited black aspirations during Reconstruction and the period that followed.

Despite the limitations of black education in the South, hundreds of Northerners, mostly white women, flocked into the service. When they arrived in the South they met a host of problems. The school facilities were primitive (without proper floors, ill-lighted, drafty, cold, often without chalk, slates, maps, and books), as were the teachers' living quarters (if any were available at all). There was little chance for social life. The Yankee schoolmarms were isolated from the rest of white society; verbal assaults were common, as were the anonymous vulgar, threatening letters. The black community was often too poor to help out. Teachers quickly found out that corporal punishment was out of the question—it too strongly suggested slavery. But the lack of initial discipline was soon replaced by an eagerness to learn. Few teachers went South for monetary reasons; if they did they were soon cured of that idea. Wages were minimal, running around $40 a month. The better jobs, like that of superintendent, were reserved for males, who rarely numbered more than 17 percent of the teachers. (Texas military commanders preferred male teachers because they were easier to house, not needing the niceties that nineteenth-century Americans thought were essential for ladies.) Some of the teachers were black, but the agencies and the bureau tended to send them to remote places in the countryside, reserving the prestigious city jobs for whites. Although Southern whites were acceptable if they would take the oath that they had never aided the Confederacy, few volunteered, not desiring the ostracism that went with being a "nigger teacher."

The subjects taught in African American schools did not differ much from those taught in white schools at the time. They included reading, writing, grammar, diction, history, geography, arithmetic, and singing. The normal (teacher-training) colleges added orthography, map drawing, physiology, algebra, geometry, Latin, and Greek, as well as tips on how to teach. While the subjects might have been standard, their delivery was not. The largest publisher of texts was the American Tract Society (ATS), dominated by Congregationalists. Their "Freedmen's Library" had books that were patterned for the black scholar—or, better yet, what these whites thought black students ought to learn. The emphasis was on piety, domesticity, temperance, thrift, industry, discipline, order, and regularity in habits. The goal was to create the Anglo-Saxon image as the ideal for the ex-slaves.

These books gave a few ideas on how the U.S. government worked and a mild history of the American Revolution, but they had little to say about democracy, rights of the people, or liberty. They emphasized the Yankee missionaries' notion of African Americans as docile and tractable children. In their day the ATS tracts were perceived as outrageously racist, both by Northern blacks and by more secular aid societies. Many preferred the *Freedmen's Book*, by Lydia Maria Child, or the African Civilization Society's *Freedmen's Torchlight*, a monthly newspaper. These put a premium on black pride and independence of thought; they approached the student as an intellectual being. In no curriculum was the idea of Republican party politics expressed—nor was the concept of social equality. But both cropped up in individual schools, depend-

ing on the philosophy of the teacher. In truth, black education tended to be a form of white cultural imperialism that resulted in colonization, not liberation.

Regardless of the content of the education that they received, black students (who ranged in age from 6 to 60 and beyond) were enthusiastic to learn. Because many of the students were adults, schools were often held at night, to accommodate work schedules. They were held on Sunday, too, before church, although these were particularly religious in nature, embodying the theory that one could not fully comprehend the Bible if one could not read. Advancement tended to be rapid. Students applied themselves with zeal, as if trying to make up for the years when book learning by slaves was illegal. The community at large made many sacrifices to build a church and school (usually the same building). These buildings required labor, building supplies, and money that the black students could ill afford, given the grinding poverty of the postwar South.

But African Americans did not limit themselves to schools supported by the Freedmen's Bureau or various aid societies. They often independently found a teacher and set up a school on their own. Often a member of the local black community, probably a former Union soldier, would teach basic skills of reading and writing. In most cases the community would have to provide room and board for the teacher—away from the local white community. The sponsoring agencies often muted the efforts of black students and parents to gain control of their education or snidely remarked that the freedmen preferred to send their children to their own private schools of inferior quality. But the real lack of quality came with Redemption (the return of conservative white rule in the South), when the Southern states' school boards sent whites who could not find employment in a white school to teach blacks. Meanwhile the missionary societies shifted their support to the several black normal colleges, hoping to turn out African Americans who could go back and teach their own people.

The appearance of less qualified native whites as teachers in black schools marked a change in the funding of schools as envisioned by the Republicans with their "separate but equal" strategy. Now the philosophy became "separate but unequal" as African Americans turned up short in every monetary category. White schools expanded through construction of new buildings; black expansion often came through the use of structures abandoned for any other use. Black normal colleges were often equivalent to white high schools, and black elementary schools were frequently ungraded, throwing all students into a mishmash of haphazard learning. But the change was slow and halting. The Redeemers wanted to keep the missionary societies' buildings without having to fund the societies' teachers, yet at the same time they wished to manage the content of black education to keep "pernicious" Yankee ideas (like freedom and equality) to a minimum.

Blacks soon realized that in the absence of a missionary effort, the only way they would be able to counter the Redeemers was through schools taught by the recent graduates of their own normal colleges. Thus the shift away from white teachers was an African American–inspired move toward self-determination. According to this line of reasoning, no one knew more about the African American condition and what to do to change it for the better than blacks themselves. This was especially true when it became obvious that the integrated school concept in the original draft of the Civil Rights Act of 1875 had fallen by the wayside. But blacks were stymied in their drive for complete control by the states' desire to keep blacks off local school boards and to put white principals in control of local school districts. Because they could pay African American teachers less than whites, however, local school boards eventually responded well to black petitions for teachers from their own race.

Reconstruction and the ensuing Gilded Age were marked by the development of public education as a viable philosophy for the first time in Southern history. Blacks were included but were kept separate from the whole. As a result of one of the first successful protest movements after emancipation, blacks were to be educated by teachers of their own race. African Americans wanted education, but they wanted equality, liberty, and justice most of all. It was the Northern whites who said that education was the cure-all; and when this notion did not pan out, they blamed the failure on the patient, not the diagnosis. This was made evident in the failure of the federal education subsidy bill of New Hampshire Representative Henry W. Blair. Promising to help fund public schools in the South with the money allotted by racial quotas, the Blair bill failed for the last time in 1890, along with the Lodge Federal Elections Bill, designed to renew the old Force Acts and protect black voters. With the failure of these two measures, Reconstruction's time truly had passed.

In 1899 the informal system of separate education in the South and elsewhere received the blessing of the highest court in the land. In the case of *Cumming et al. v. Board of Education of Richmond County, Georgia* (not *Plessy v. Ferguson* as commonly supposed, which handled segregation in public accommodations) public education was determined to be a state and local function as determined by the taxes raised; it was beyond the scope of the Fourteenth Amendment's "equal protection of the laws" clause, and therefore segregation of education was not on its face discriminatory. The court was unanimous in its opinion, unlike in the *Plessy* case, which Justice John Marshall Harlan of Kentucky dissented. Harlan's willingness to write the court's opinion in *Cumming* is debated by historians and biographers to this day, but the decision gave the green light to the South's unequal approach to segregated education. Overcrowded black schools in the South went on double sessions and still could not keep up with the demand for increased classes and more school rooms. But white officeholders, guaranteed sole power by the white-only primary election system, seemed not to care.

Education could have been one element of many in a broad-based attack against discrimination and racism, designed to place the freed slaves in the mainstream of U.S. economic, political, and social life. Instead it became the sole means to that end. Schooling proved inadequate to the task, subverted to the purposes of stigmatizing and crippling African Americans for generations. The institutions that came South to help integrate blacks into the American dream had merely reinforced a separatist nightmare that was based on inequality and was confirmed by the U.S. Supreme Court.

See also Bureau of Refugees, Freedmen, and Abandoned Lands; Freedmen's Aid Societies; Washington, Booker T.

References Abbott, Martin, "The Freedmen's Bureau and Negro Schooling in South Carolina" (1956); Alexander, Roberta Sue, "Hostility and Hope" (1976); Armstrong, Warren B., "Union Chaplains and the Education of Freedmen" (1967); Beatty, Bess, *A Revolution Gone Backwards* (1987); Blassingame, John W., "The Union Army as an Educational Institution for Negroes" (1965); Butchart, Ronald E., *Northern Schools, Southern Blacks, and Reconstruction* (1980); Cornish, Dudley Taylor, "The Union Army as a School for Negroes" (1952); Franklin, John Hope, "Jim Crow Goes to School" (1959); Halstead, Jacqueline J., "The Delaware Association for the Moral Improvement and Education of the Colored People" (1972); Hornsby, Alton, Jr., "The Freedmen's Bureau Schools in Texas" (1972–73); Jackson, Luther P., "The Educational Efforts of the Freedmen's Bureau and Freedmen's Aid Societies in South Carolina" (1923); Jones, Jacqueline, *Soldiers of Light and Love* (1980); Kimball, Philip Clyde, "Freedom's Harvest" (1980); Kousser, J. Morgan, *Dead End* (1985); Kousser, "Separate But Not Equal" (1980); Low, W. Augustus, "The Freedmen's Bureau and Civil Rights in Maryland" (1952); Morris, Robert C., *Reading, 'Riting, and Reconstruction* (1981); Newby, Robert G., and David B. Tyack, "Victims without Crimes" (1971); Pearce, Larry W., "The American Missionary Association and the Freedmen's Bureau in Arkansas" (1971, 1972); Proctor, Samuel, "'Yankee School Marms' in Post-War Florida" (1959); Rabinowitz, Howard N., "Half a Loaf" (1974); Richardson, Joe M., "The Freedmen's Bureau and Negro Education in Florida" (1962); Schweninger, Loren, "The American Missionary Association and Northern Philanthropy in Reconstruction Alabama" (1970); Sherer, Robert G., *Subordination or Liberation?* (1977); Small, Sandra E., "The Yankee Schoolmarm in Freedmen's Schools" (1979); Smith, Thomas H., "Ohio Quakers and Mississippi Freedmen" (1969); Spivey, Donald, *Schooling for the New Slavery* (1978); Swint, Henry Lee, *The Northern Teacher in the South* (1941); Wesley, Edgar B., "Forty Acres and a Mule and a Speller" (1957); White, Kenneth B., "The Alabama Freedmen's Bureau and Black Education" (1981).

African American Leadership and Reconstruction

As professional historians began to write about Reconstruction at the beginning of the twentieth century, they had little good to say about African American leadership during the era. This unflattering view came despite the fact that between 1870 and 1901 two blacks were elected to the U.S. Senate, 20 were sent to the House of Representatives, and countless others served in state conventions, state legislatures, and local offices on the county and town levels. To give one an idea of the magnitude and importance of black leadership, there were 240 identifiable black political leaders in New Orleans and another 234 in Charleston alone during Reconstruction. Yet the ability of blacks to do a credible job in leading their people and their states during this era is an important part of Reconstruction that until recently was for the most part lost. Instead, books were filled with stories of "Negro Rule," the corruption of blacks in government, and the blunder and insult of putting the Southern whites under the government of black leaders, considered somehow innately unfit to do more than cultivate cotton.

The responsibility for this misrepresentation rests largely with a group of historians who studied under William A. Dunning at Columbia University. Most of Dunning's students were of Southern origins and had already heard of the evils of Reconstruction from their parents. By writing Ph.D. dissertations that became important books, these scholars retold the story of Reconstruction through the sociological "truths" of their day, which made much of the alleged racial inferiority of blacks from birth. But even with their racial bias, these studies varied in content as much as the students did in their own backgrounds and intellectual abilities. Some ignored the role of African Americans pretty much completely, focusing on the rousing tale of Radical Republicans in Congress, as well as Carpetbaggers and Scalawags in the South, who allowed blacks a role in government in the first place. Others, although critical of blacks' participation in Reconstruction, offered fairly balanced accounts, analyzing capable black leaders as "distinctly Caucasian" in their capabilities and conservatism.

One popular textbook of the times was entitled *Division and Reunion* (originally published in 1883 and reprinted several times through 1908); it was written by a noted political scientist from Princeton University who later became president of the United States, Woodrow Wilson. It portrayed unscrupulous Yankee adventurers and traitorous Southern whites, aided by a few shrewd and unprincipled blacks, who organized and plundered the South through governments that relied on the votes of their more ignorant cousins. Like others, Wilson saw the African American leaders and followers as the dregs of the population, easily manipulated by Scalawags and Carpetbaggers to loot the South under the cover of law.

But the height of this interpretation was not reached until 1929, when Claude Bowers, a Northern newspaperman with a distinct flair for the dramatic, wrote *The Tragic Era*, a onetime Book of the Month Club selection that has gone through numerous editions and is still in print. He portrayed African Americans as innocent, lazy, and childlike, with their capabilities and taste for corruption determined by the degree of blackness of their skin. In his view, malevolent was the control exercised over them by evil and cunning white renegades, the Carpetbaggers and Scalawags, under a Reconstruction program ramrodded through Congress by vile Radical Republicans intent on destroying U.S. democracy.

The standard approach to Reconstruction history did not go unchallenged. Blacks who either experienced Reconstruction or had relatives who did wrote their own histories, but circulation of these publications was not like that of Bowers and the other white accounts. The *Journal of Negro History*, a professional magazine founded in 1915, published many correcting and pioneering monographs that disagreed with the then-accepted interpretations. Lists of black leaders were compiled to stimulate further research; individual careers were examined to revise uncomplimentary and untrue portrayals of black leaders; and entire state studies were rewritten to revise the tale of corrupt, incapable black control and to point out that no state or local government was controlled entirely by blacks. Indeed, no black was elected governor of a state (although one served as governor of Louisiana for a month after the elected white governor was impeached), no black was elected mayor of an important Southern city, nor was any state constitutional convention or legislature controlled by blacks, with the exception of South Carolina. In addition, when blacks had power they often moved to bring Southern whites back into government rather than vindictively excluding them. The conclusion reached in these studies was that African American leaders, with rare exception, were men of ability, common sense, and fairness, worthy of the jobs they held.

The *Journal of Negro History* was joined in the coming decades by *Phylon* and the *Negro History Bulletin* in the reexamination of black history, especially Reconstruction history, in the United States. At the same time the tide slowly began to turn among professional historians, led by the most notable black scholar of his time, W. E. Burghardt DuBois. His *Black Reconstruction* attacked every premise of the works that preceded him. Although marred by a Marxist perspective that led him to criticize black leaders as "petty bourgeoisie" in their economic outlook, DuBois painted a different picture of African American leaders during the period. He emphasized their positive contributions to reforming Southern white governments. Most interesting, although he did massive research in primary documents, DuBois mostly used the secondary works already available from historians critical of Reconstruction. All he had to do was place a positive spin on those accounts to put the African American role in Reconstruction in a different, more complimentary light.

Other historians, black and white, followed in DuBois's wake. Studies of South Carolina and Mississippi, where black leadership had been criticized the most in traditional studies, found that historians had actually understated the ability of black leaders during reconstruction. Especially important has been the reexamination of black leaders and followers on a local level, which proves their roles to be more active than heretofore expected. New monographs of the period like John Hope Franklin's *Reconstruction: After the Civil War* (1961), Kenneth Stampp's *The Era of Reconstruction* (1965), and Eric Foner's *Reconstruction* (1988), have synthesized the picture of blacks during Reconstruction to show that they were not corrupt or vindictive, did not control state government, and generally served well when elected to public office. Indeed, Foner's book views the entire Reconstruction experience with African Americans' roles as his main emphasis. Numerous profiles of individual black leaders have now gone beyond mere rehabilitation to emphasize basic biographic information; the actual stands these leaders took on issues of the day; and how they attained, maintained, and finally lost power.

Black leadership was not unknown before Reconstruction. Even under the slave regime, preachers, sorcerers, gang leaders, drivers and foremen, skilled artisans, house servants, and free people of color all provided leadership among the black community, slave and free, North and South. During the Civil War black leadership displayed itself in many forms. In areas where Union troops were available to protect them, slaves followed their leaders into the Union lines to freedom. But where the Confederates ruled and could effect bloody reprisals, black leaders counseled caution lest a misstep lead to a massive retaliation by Confederate soldiers. But nothing so eroded the institution of slavery as the appearance of black men in uniform. This was discussed in the North in 1862 and adopted as policy by

Abraham Lincoln's administration in 1863 (and even accepted as a last-ditch proposal by the Confederate Congress in 1865). Blacks, from Frederick Douglass to the most downtrodden escaped slaves, sought the right to enlist and demonstrate their capacity to fight for their own freedom. By 1863, the Union army had adopted a near conscription policy, going into the camps of "liberated" slaves to compel service. Such activity, as well as the mass exodus of African Americans to free areas, practically extinguished slavery in the border states by 1864, making the Thirteenth Amendment abolishing slavery merely a legal recognition of real-world conditions.

As blacks had experienced slavery as a common bond, so too they approached freedom as a collective community. Under the slave regime they had learned to cope with the so-called peculiar institution and to hope for freedom. The village had been the center of West African society, only to be replaced by the slave quarters during bondage. African Americans bonded together to help each other face the problems of daily life. Slave weddings, no matter how informal, were important and even encouraged by smart masters as a way to give everyone a stake in remaining at home. Kinship was maintained despite slave sales. Indeed, much of what appeared to whites as useless wandering after slavery ended was actually an effort to reestablish contact with lost family members or a home once loved.

Religion was another unifying factor of the slave community, and exhorters (unlicensed preachers) were respected leaders of the local slave community. Drivers in the field, slave foremen who set the pace of work and often had to mete out punishment, were also important leaders. They could make or break the work effort and were listened to by worker and master alike. Artisans, carpenters, blacksmiths, wheelwrights, masons, coopers, shoemakers, and tailors, among others who had special talents that built the plantation and kept it functioning, were instrumental in the education of others and provided role models for the young. Even the house servants, often condemned by some as being allies of the white family, used their position to obtain a book education and pass it on to others. They were also excellent spies and kept the slave community informed as to what was going on in the "big house" and the world at large.

There were the rebels who never could put on the subservient act that survival as a slave required. Yet they too provided a leadership role. They kept the system honest in a sense—slaveowners had to be careful lest the individual rebels grew in number to become the whole slave community. In the United States slave rebellions and maroon communities (rebel towns organized in the swamps and woods—sort of slave versions of Robin Hood) were known, but they were less frequent than in Latin America (especially Brazil). Armed slave rebellions in the South were crushed without mercy. After one such uprising in 1811 in Louisiana was put down, the skulls of the participants were erected on poles along the Mississippi River to warn others. The Seminole wars in Florida were in large part due to the fact that enterprising slaves could escape to the security of the Indian towns and live there in freedom, even rising to become chieftains in the tribe. It was when whites tried to recapture their human "property" that the Indians fought back, frequently under the charge of black war leaders.

There were other, subtler ways in which rebels might exercise leadership. Feigning sickness or disability was one. Indeed, there is a story about a Mississippi slave who convinced his master he was blind and could not work. After emancipation he led the county in raising cotton, willing to work for himself but not someone else. Stealing prohibited food was another way one might show leadership for the community. As the old slave saw went, nothing tasted as good as stolen pork. Rather than initiating armed rebellion, American slaves specialized in work slowdowns or in fleeing to the woods in a general protest against conditions (sometimes the whole plantation would take off) and then renegotiating their return, much like a modern labor strike. The organizers

and negotiators, of course, were examples of early black politicians.

After the rush into freedom, the contraband camp became the new community. There they took up activities that had been prominent among the freed community in the North for years. They organized self-help organizations to acquaint newcomers with primitive social services, eschewing commonly available public charity from benevolent agencies. They protested working conditions on the plantations along the Mississippi where they were sent by Union military commanders and employed by Yankee contractors. But many preferred to work as stevedores (ship loaders and unloaders) or lease their own 5-acre farms (the ultimate recognition of freedom was to obtain a wage-paying job or one's own land). They opened up schools and churches to provide places to train their own future leaders—black soldiers were one source of educators, schooling having been one of the main off-duty goals in black regiments. They asked for the right to vote, but that would come only years later as a part of Military Reconstruction. They also asked for land—a request that would never come to pass except in select parts of the South, particularly along the southeast Atlantic coast. Often the quests led them off plantations and into towns, especially, in the jargon of the day, "freedmen's villages," where blacks lived in self-imposed segregation, as far as possible from constant white supervision. Some towns were substantial undertakings by both white and black laborers, but most were constructed by blacks themselves out of materials at hand.

All of these activities were led by men and women who for the most part remain unknown. But of those who are identifiable, at least some were skilled artisans from the slave era, and a large portion of the rest came from the ministry of the black church. Very often these activities were combined with farming. What set these individuals apart was their willingness to speak out on behalf of African Americans; to lead various social and political activities including protests of political and working conditions; to

A portrait of the first African American senator (seated, left) and representatives of the 41st and 42d Congress in 1872.

run for political office; to establish religious and educational facilities; to organize self-help organizations; to join the state militia and fight back against the Ku Klux Klan, the Red Shirts, the White Liners, and the White Leagues; and generally to make up their own minds independent of white desires. Reconstruction was, in the words of historian DuBois, a "mighty revolution of rising humanity." Even if most blacks might wind up in peonage and be denied the full fruits of their freedom, they were always aware of who within their own community might lead them with dignity.

Blacks throughout the South met in conventions to articulate their hopes and beliefs. Petitions were drawn up and sent to local governments, the state legislatures, and Congress. They usually opened up with a brief "thank you" to those who had helped out African Americans in the past and then went on to state the groups' wants and needs for the future. These included equality before the law; security of life and property; the unmolested right to establish schools,

churches, and newspapers; the right to vote; the right to serve on juries and give evidence before the courts; the right for labor to take the first lien on any crop; and the right to bear arms. In return the groups pledged to police the black community and curtail lawbreakers, to give a full day's work (usually eight or nine hours) for a fair wage, and to work closely with Southern whites to govern their states fairly. These petitions went unanswered until Congress passed the Military Reconstruction Acts in 1867, which began the long road toward political participation by black Americans in local elected government.

The first place black politicians came into public view was at the state constitutional conventions called at the behest of Congress as a part of Military Reconstruction. These conventions began in Montgomery, Alabama, the cradle of the Confederacy, on 5 November 1867 and concluded in Austin, Texas, on 8 February 1869. There the ten seceded states (excluding Tennessee) that had previously rejected the Fourteenth

Amendment met in conventions to alter their constitutions to accept the role of black Americans as free citizens, imbued with all the associated rights, and to recognize the loss of the Civil War by passing the Fourteenth Amendment (and in the case of Mississippi, Texas, and Virginia, as punishment for lagging behind or backsliding, the Fifteenth Amendment). Three states had African American majorities in their populations (South Carolina, Mississippi, and Louisiana), and two others had a black voting majority because of the disfranchisement of former Confederate officials (Alabama and Florida). But only in South Carolina (with 71 of 121 delegates), Florida (19 of 50), and Louisiana (47 of 97) did African Americans hold significant influence among the delegations. In Alabama, Virginia, Mississippi, and Georgia, black delegates had sizable blocs of influence but were well below a majority in numbers. The rest of the delegations were dominated by native whites, Scalawags, or Carpetbaggers. Only in Alabama, Florida, Mississippi, and Arkansas did Carpetbaggers control at least 20 percent of the delegates. The rest of the states were run by local whites of varying political loyalty during the war.

The black delegates to the state constitutional conventions were from rural districts with predominantly African American voting majorities and a higher value in crop lands or from similarly populated urban areas. Those districts with such a large black voting population that did not send African American delegates to the conventions generally sent Carpetbaggers, showing some hesitation to trust local whites. But the willingness of blacks to elect either their own race or Northern whites also demonstrated a political awareness. It proved that they would not be unwitting pawns in deciding questions of their own future. They would develop their own leaders who were sympathetic to the demands of the black community. These delegates came from former plantation areas, as indicated by the value of the lands on the tax rolls; this choice of representatives draws some doubt as to the alleged ignorance of the average fieldhand.

The urban areas produced another interesting Reconstruction political type: black Carpetbaggers, African Americans from Northern states who came South to take part in the biggest event of their time.

It is interesting that 100 of 192 delegates throughout the South were recognized as mulattos or of mixed race (if this could be determined at all), at a time when the census listed such individuals as only 13 percent of the population (admittedly census takers were horribly inaccurate in such determinations). Of all African American delegations, those in Texas, Mississippi, and Georgia were largely not of mixed race. Those in Virginia, Florida, North Carolina, and Alabama were evenly divided. Of the remaining delegations Louisiana had mostly mulatto delegates among the African American contingency, while South Carolina and Arkansas had slight mulatto majorities among their black members. This color distinction is important for two reasons: mulattos frequently were among the best educated, and thus most articulate, of the African American population nationally; and their color might suggest a higher antebellum status. Most mulatto delegates had been born free or had bought their freedom prior to the war.

But regardless of their actual color the African American delegates were highly educated men—a far cry from the average for blacks of their day. DuBois estimated that about 5 percent of all blacks were literate at this time, but 85 percent of the delegates could read and write, some of them, particularly in Louisiana, at a university level. Admittedly these statistics are based on likely faulty information, but the general drift of them still holds. This challenges that notion that black politicians were illiterate, as critics of Reconstruction had long maintained.

Of 226 black delegates (whose occupation could be determined) 50 were farmers but only 12 of these were listed as propertyless, though the latter make up the traditional picture of the black politician. Another group comprised 47 ministers of the gospel, many of whom came south with Northern benevolent or religious societies.

Others of this group were antebellum free men of color. As a group they were not wealthy, but they were among the most articulate in presenting black demands. A third occupational group consisted of 54 skilled laborers. Most of them were carpenters, blacksmiths, barbers, shoemakers, and tailors, occupations open to blacks (slave or free) before the war, and many of these individuals had been born free. These were prosperous men, indicating that they were successful in the communities from which they came. Finally, there were 41 blacks who worked in the professions or business. The largest bloc of this group were teachers. They often had connections with the Freedmen's Bureau or other Northern societies. This group included the most prosperous of all black delegates, particularly merchants from the bigger cities.

In the constitutional conventions blacks gained their power from bloc voting on issues. Not infrequently they were the most unified of all the factions and formed a critical part of the Republican party. The most important issues from their perspective were debtor relief, land reform, racial segregation in public facilities, and political rights. These delegates favored the usual Republican economic programs and public education. But there were conservatives among them, and mutual support on all economic issues was not guaranteed. Black delegates failed to gain racial equality because Republican whites, especially Scalawags, refused to unite with them on this count. As a group, the African American delegates refused to disfranchise permanently any white Southerner. But they did gain the franchise themselves and become a critical voice in Reconstruction governments throughout the former Confederacy.

The black legislators who served in the Reconstruction state governments—as well as those who followed until the turn of the century, when African American voters were disfranchised in the South—acted in different environments that determined their effectiveness. In South Carolina blacks accounted for 60 percent of legislators during Reconstruction; in Louisiana the figure

was 30 percent. Furthermore, these two states had a large proportion of free blacks in their antebellum population, concentrated in Charleston and New Orleans, who were landowners, artisans, or educated business and professional men. This gave these two states a pool of highly skilled African Americans to draw from for legislative service. In another group of Southern states—Florida, Georgia, Alabama, and Mississippi—blacks represented from 46 percent to 54 percent of the total population. But this number included fewer persons who had been free before the war and fewer from skilled trades from which to draw its leadership. Few owned land or ran businesses. In the Upper South (Maryland, Virginia, North Carolina, Tennessee, Kentucky, and Missouri), the pool of free and educated blacks for leadership roles was present, but the overall black population was too small to provide more than a few isolated opportunities to serve. Finally, in the frontier Southwest, Texas and Arkansas, not only did African Americans form a small percentage of the total population, they also were handicapped by the lack of a free, educated class (or an urban setting in which to develop one); thus they suffered on both counts during the post–Civil War period.

In almost all cases except South Carolina and Louisiana, black legislators had little time in which to serve during Radical Republican Reconstruction before their states were "redeemed" by the conservative whites. Nonetheless they acted in league with white Republicans to advance the party's economic program of public education, internal improvements, and civil rights. Blacks worked together as a bloc on public schools and civil rights but tended to be divided on individual, regional, and socioeconomic preferences on other problems. Indeed, blacks tended to differ among themselves along a conservative-radical scale much as did whites. This meant that differences among black leaders and the rank and file appeared immediately after emancipation and that African Americans were far from being passive objects upon whom white society could work its will.

Blacks refused to follow the rich white planters in 1867 because they mistrusted the latter's motives as Scalawags.

But as the Republican program changed from revolution to conservatism, the white yeomanry abandoned it in favor of the Democrats, racial solidarity, and Redemption of white home rule. In a pattern that would become common for the rest of the century, the white yeomanry proved too radical in their demands for debt reduction and a shift of taxes upon the rich. African Americans were then left to work out a conservative economic approach with the remaining Scalawags, the old-time Whigs, the former slaveholders. Hence, during the Gilded Age following Reconstruction, the South was ruled by a coalition of white and black conservatives who worked to nullify white farmer radicalism, forcing those farmers into third-party movements. Then, by the end of the nineteenth century, the conservative whites, stampeded by black defections to the Populist party of farmer radicals, joined with their former white enemies to disfranchise African Americans. However, the Fifteenth Amendment prevented disfranchisement based solely on race, so measures such as the poll tax and literacy tests, designed to exclude blacks, also affected the poorer whites, despite stratagems such as grandfather clauses that it was hoped would enable these whites to slip through the net.

As with the states, on the national level the influence of black congressmen was mixed. During Reconstruction, 16 African Americans represented their districts in the nation's capitol, 6 from South Carolina, 3 each from Alabama and Mississippi, and 1 each from Florida, Louisiana, Georgia, and North Carolina. All were Republicans. Like black leaders elsewhere these men received little attention from white historians, usually in passing. On the other hand, modern historians of the black experience in America have written many pieces designed to refute white racist accounts and attempt to recreate a glorified past of which black Americans might be proud. Unfortunately, the result has been a condescending treatment that led critics to label this kind of

history "moonlight, magnolias, and collard greens" (in reference to the similarly unrealistic treatment of the white South that came to be labeled "moonlight and magnolias"). These accounts describe black congressmen as witty, shrewd, eloquent, charismatic, brilliant, and militant. Yet few actually point out legislation or speeches in which this picture is advanced.

Critics say that as a group the black congressmen tended to support the Republican economic program and spoke out on only one issue that affected them most, political and racial equality. Overall these representatives seemed reluctant to cause trouble and for the most part just served. Indeed their ineffectiveness might be one important reason why the Redeemers won out in the end. Proponents of a more positive image of blacks in Congress reply that the latter did a credible job, especially in light of having been kept out of the political process so long and having to buck a powerful prejudice just to take in their seats. It is telling that so many black representatives went back to the South at the end of their terms and engaged in business and law, rather than accepting the inevitable "Negro patronage" jobs that abounded in Washington. They were protective of their race, Southern-loving, articulate, trained, nonvindictive, and as productive as the average congressional representative could be.

Black leaders were present in every aspect of Reconstruction, helping to formulate issues and responses that would meet the needs of the African American community. That they did not always succeed did not lessen their impact on the overall process. They constantly strove to direct Reconstruction to their advantage on national, state, and especially local levels. Indeed, the closer they operated on the grass-roots level, the more likely their success. As they operated on the state and national levels, black politicians tended to get lost in the one big fact that would eventually bring Reconstruction to an end—the United States was a white man's country bent on imperialism in North America and ultimately abroad; in the nineteenth century that fact determined, for good or ill, the direction the nation would take.

See also African American Education and Reconstruction; Bruce, Blanche K.; Cardozo, Francis L.; Cardozo, Thomas W.; Disfranchisement; Douglass, Frederick; Dubuclet, Antoine; Dunn, Oscar J.; Economic Disfranchisement; Lynch, James; Lynch, John R.; Pinchback, Pinckney Benton Stewart; Rainey, Joseph H.; Revels, Hiram R.; Ruby, George; Segregation (Jim Crow); Smalls, Robert; Washington, Booker T.

References Abbott, Martin, "Freedom's Cry" (1959); Barr, Alwyn, "Black Legislators of Reconstruction Texas" (1986); Berry, Mary Frances, and John W. Blassingame, Long Memory (1982); Blassingame, John W., Black New Orleans (1973); Carter, Dan T., "Moonlight, Magnolias, and Collard Greens" (1977); Cimprich, John, "The Beginning of the Black Suffrage Movement in Tennessee" (1980) and Slavery's End in Tennessee (1985); Drago, Edmund, Black Politicians and Reconstruction Georgia (1982); Cook, Samuel Dubois, "A Tragic Conception of Negro History" (1960); Cruden, Robert, The Negro in Reconstruction (1969); Genovese, Eugene D., Roll Jordan Roll (1974); Hermann, Janet S., "Reconstruction in Microcosm" (1980); Holt, Thomas, Black over White (1977); Hosmer, John, and Joseph Fineman, "Black Congressmen in Reconstruction Historiography" (1978); Jones, Howard James, "Images of State Legislative Reconstruction Participants in Fiction" (1982); Kolchin, Peter, First Freedom (1972); Logsdon, Joseph, "Black Reconstruction Revisited" (1973); Magdol, Edward, A Right to the Land (1977); Magdol, "Local Black Leaders in the South" (1974); McFarlin, Annjeannette Sophia, Black Congressional Reconstruction Orators and Their Orations (1976); Mohr, Clarence L., "Southern Blacks in the Civil War" (1974); O'Brien, John T., "Reconstruction in Richmond" (1981); Pitre, Merline, Through Many Dangers, Toils, and Snares (1985); Rabinowitz, Howard N., ed., Southern Black Leaders of the Reconstruction Era (1982); Richardson, Joe M., The Negro in the Reconstruction of Florida (1965); Reid, George W., "Four in Black" (1979); Robinson, Armistead L., "Beyond the Realm of Consensus" (1981) and "Explaining the Failure of Democratic Reform in Reconstruction South Carolina" (1980); Smith, Samuel Denny, Negroes in Congress (1940); Thornbrough, Emma Lou, ed., Black Reconstructionists (1972); Thorpe, Earl E., Black Historians (1971); Vincent, Charles, Black Legislators in Louisiana during Reconstruction (1976) and "Louisiana's Black Legislators and Their Efforts To Pass a Blue Law during Reconstruction" (1976–1977); Wagandt, Charles L., "The Army Versus Maryland Slavery" (1964) and The Mighty Revolution (1964); Williamson, Joel, After Slavery: The Negro in South Carolina during Reconstruction (1965); Woodward, C. Vann, "Clio with Soul" (1969) and "Flight from History" (1965).

African Americans and Reconstruction
According to historian William M. McPherson, the black experience in the United States has come close to success only three times since the Civil War. One such time was the civil rights crusade of the 1960s; another was the Populist revolt of the 1890s (although McPherson thinks that whites wanted fundamental economic restructuring of society, whereas blacks merely sought physical protection within the law and political recognition); and the third was during Reconstruction. Reconstruction was so important because it was the time when African Americans became free and began to operate farms independently or enter into businesses. It was when blacks participated in state constitutional conventions that developed liberal reform constitutions, many of which endured until the twentieth century. It was when they gained the right to vote and had an important hand in the running of state and local governments. But in the United States during Reconstruction, says McPherson, the perceived role of black people is distorted by five myths: the myth of the day of jubilee, the myth of the exodus, the myth of the prodigal son, the myth of 40 acres and a mule, and the myth of the menacing black man.

The first myth, the day of jubilee, concerns the way blacks approached the advent of freedom itself. Tradition has the slaves called in by their masters and told of emancipation and what it meant. The happy blacks then rolled their eyes, cried hosannas to Heaven, and began to cry and dance for joy. The suggestion was that they were childlike beings who would never make it on their own. Of course, the problem is that the reaction to emancipation was described not by blacks but by whites. Most of the slaves were illiterate (a condition enforced by law), and they generally did not widely describe what they felt until years later—and then often to white men of the Works Progress Administration interviewing them during the New Deal of the 1930s. African Americans knew that now they had a chance to work for themselves. It had become worthwhile to labor. But soon a new reality hit them hard. With the assistance of the federal Freedmen's Bureau, they soon had to sign annual contracts that gave them a portion of the crop but required them to labor in the fields as before. About the only change the average male field hand managed to negotiate was the right to work his own piece of rented land like an independent farmer—so long as he raised the cotton necessary to pay the owner off for the loans used for food, seeds, equipment, clothing, and shelter at the end of the year. This was no reason for the freed men and women to cheer, and indeed few said that they did.

The second myth was that of the exodus—that blacks wandered about aimlessly, uncertain of what to do. It is true that many blacks tested their freedom by going into a nearby town or walking miles down a road. No doubt that offered an exhilarating feeling. The former slaves could now move about without a pass—although the Union army reinstalled that humiliation in short order. Those who did truly move around for a long period of time often were looking for family and friends who had disappeared during slavery, sold elsewhere. This was especially true in Texas, where the lines of traveling emancipated slaves extended for days' worth of travel. But these people had been forcibly removed west of the Sabine River during the war to protect them from Yankee invasions and now were going "home" to seek spouses and children left behind.

Although African Americans might wander back to their old places, there was no real need for the old master's guiding hand, an element in the third myth, that of the prodigal son. This was the notion that blacks left the plantation for some time to go on their drunken sprees of joy without a care in the world and then returned to seek their former owners' forgiveness and protection. In reality, though, there was less movement than supposed, and most of it had a purpose. Many who went into town were looking for work—a scarce commodity in the war-torn South of 1865. When

they did not find want they wanted, they might return to sign a labor contract on the old plantation. But more often than not a freed man signed for his wife and family, demonstrating that there was a viable family structure that lingered over from slavery and continued during freedom. The old slave cabin might not have been much, but it was home and provided important psychological relief after a hard day's work. The large numbers of vagrants whom the army and planters saw after the war were really people declared as such under the law to maintain labor discipline and a guaranteed work force. It was not unusual to force blacks employed in town to sign a labor contract somewhere in the countryside, lest such persons be declared vagrants even though they were simply traveling on a day off work.

The myth of each head of a family receiving 40 acres of farm land and a mule with which to work it is one of the most enduring myths of Reconstruction. It is true that Congress in the first Freedmen's Bureau law instructed the bureau to administer all property abandoned by owners during the war and now under federal control. It is true that Congress saw the land being divided up and doled out among the freed slaves. But there was not enough abandoned land to accomplish this prodigious task. And President Johnson soon pardoned the original owners and returned the property to them. The Civil War was a revolution of sorts, but there would be no violation of property rights guaranteed under the Constitution. Few freedmen beyond the Sea Islands along the South Atlantic coast received any land unless they bought it.

However, blacks refused to abandon their hope until well after Christmas 1865 (when the land give-away was rumored to take place). This brings up the final myth of Reconstruction, the menacing black man. Although the first four myths suggested a childlike freedman who could not manage on his own, the fifth denied all that and created an ogre who would crush the white man's United States. African Americans were not willing pawns in the fight between

Northern and Southern white men. They had already demonstrated this during the war when they left their homes for freedom behind the Union lines and refused to work on plantations managed by Yankees unless there were major concessions in discipline and hours (demands that whites attributed to black "laziness"). Blacks in New Orleans ran a mock election for governor of the state in 1865, and their man received more votes than the incumbent governor had in the legitimate white-only election held a year earlier. When they continued their protest against not being able to vote a year later in a parade on the reconvened state convention, the result was a massive race riot. Southern whites were not about to allow the menacing black man to exist. Congress changed the situation by passing the Military Reconstruction Acts, which outlawed the state governments and set up new, provisional ones until a new state convention—elected with the participation of African American voters—could draw up a new state constitution that recognized the results of the war as embodied in the Fourteenth Amendment and allowed black men to vote permanently.

Even Yankee visitors to the South scornfully dismissed much of their own Reconstruction program as the creation of "Congo" governments. Indeed, one historian has suggested that the real goal of Reconstruction, besides ensuring the election of safe, loyal Republican governments in the South through black votes, was to keep African Americans in the South, happy in their jobs and protected in their social and civil rights; that way they would not emulate their cousins who had taken the Underground Railroad decades earlier to seek a better world in the North. After all, this reasoning went, African Americans had already shown their mobility since being freed by wandering the South. Better to keep them there and make them an exclusively Southern problem.

In reality the freed slaves posed little threat by their entry into the mainstream of U.S. political and economic life. They did not demand social integration. They actually preferred to return the disfranchised Confederates to full political rights. They did not even run the politics of any single state. No black state governor was ever elected during Reconstruction, and only a handful of lieutenant governors were, by prior agreement with the ruling whites of the Republican party. Black legislators might have acted a little pompously in their conduct of state business, but a country that survived Andrew Jackson's unruly inaugural could (and did) make it through Black Reconstruction with no real harm. And the corruption attributed to the Reconstruction governments, as well as the alleged black ignorance, were piddling affairs in light of the national scandals of the Ulysses S. Grant regime or those of the Democratic political machines that looted larger Northern cities at the same time. But reality was hidden behind the myths of black inferiority, which permitted the division of a nation by a means as diabolical as secession had been.

What, then, were African Americans' major concerns during Reconstruction? Family was one. Black families were often dismissed as matriarchal, without recognizing that all families in the United States tended to have a bigger role for women than did the idealized European family of the seventeenth century. This circumstance can partly be explained by the semi-frontier environment that existed nearly everywhere in the country. Women had to take charge whenever the men were out hunting or working. The industrialization of the nineteenth century increased this role. In this sense black families in Reconstruction and later were not that unusual. But there were important changes from the time of slavery: the male head of the family did not have to submit to every indignity dreamed up by his white master, and the family could not be legally split by sale at the whim of the white plantation owner.

Reconstruction did bring uncertainties of another nature, however, mostly economic. It was not unusual for a black family to move yearly, desperately seeking a landowner who would cut them a good deal at contract time and honor it at harvest, nine months later, without overcharging on all forms of credit. Blacks also saw the term *middle class* from a different perspective than whites. Because of the economic difficulties that came with second-class citizenship, a middle-class black family was one in which the head of household supported his wife and children, the local church, and his children's education. The wife's willingness to work and keep the others cognizant of the need for more effort was one of the factors that led to a family's success.

As important as families (and often more important) was the independent African American church. Much of the strength of black men and women came from their churches, which were different from the white churches at the time in that they adhered to a nationalistic theology of liberation, reform, and uplift. The church was at the center of the fight against slavery before the war and against discrimination afterward. Before the war in the South, whites in theory kept a close watch over the content of church sermons. But as soon as emancipation came, African Americans moved quickly to separate themselves from any white control, making churches the one arena in which black men and women could speak and act freely. For this reason ministers became leaders in the black community. They knew what the congregations wanted and could articulate it before the secular body politic, both black and white. They also led the way in expressing pride in their color and refusing to be "Jim Crowed," that is, segregated and put down.

Black ministers cleverly appealed to the American sense of fair play by stressing the patriotism of African Americans and asking that the rest of the country live up to the noble precepts enunciated in the Declaration of Independence. They told their people to stay in the South, save their money, educate themselves, promote racial cooperation, and denounce discrimination through word and deed. They also promoted a religion that buttressed the spirit through emotional appeals to a better world beyond the grave, emphasized through the medium of the "shout," an African tradition

brought to the New World by their ancestors. Through the African emphasis on community togetherness, the church became more than a religious center. It also performed many secular tasks like organizing beneficial societies, secret lodges, cooperative and building associations; acting as a job agency; performing considerable charitable and relief work; and providing a forum to discuss racial issues.

Many of the issues surrounding the forum of discussion concerned politics. Blacks strove continually to achieve the right to hold office, use public accommodations, and vote. Before the Civil War African Americans could not vote in the North or the South. Jacksonian democracy's quest for universal male suffrage was for whites only. Blacks were excluded from the electoral process except in New York and central New England, where their numbers were too insignificant to accomplish much. In the South they had no rights at all. African Americans, slave or free, saw the Civil War as the beginning of the realization of their dream to participate in politics. They were dismayed when President Abraham Lincoln kept political rights out of his Reconstruction plan, even as they cheered his hesitant steps toward emancipation. But with the accession of Andrew Johnson to power in the White House, blacks decried what they saw as a step backward in his recognition of the restored South, without any African American rights beyond the Black Codes, a recodification of the old slave laws.

Even before they gained the vote, black Americans took to the streets to protest second-class treatment, particularly in public accommodations. In Philadelphia, New Orleans, Charleston, Savannah, and Richmond they challenged special streetcars designated by race. But with the advent of Military Reconstruction, blacks entered the world of U.S. politics at last. They served in the state constitutional conventions and in local, state, and national government. They eschewed vindictiveness toward the unpardoned Rebels, asking that the latter's political rights be restored. They also helped write constitutions that abolished property qualifications to vote and hold office and that provided debtor's relief. In Louisiana and South Carolina, where they had the most political power, African Americans sought and obtained open access to public accommodations and civil rights. They backed the federal 1875 Civil Rights Act, which guaranteed such rights along with the right of impartial jury service.

Between 1869 and 1901 two blacks served in the U.S. Senate and 20 went to the House of Representatives. In South Carolina African Americans had a majority in the lower house of the legislature, and in Louisiana they were a strong enough minority to actually control policy. Outside of these two states their influence varied widely at the state level from little to none. But on the local levels they often controlled the government, sometimes virtually unchallenged. They soon learned the limits of coalition politics and found out that Scalawags would not support open public accommodations; in addition, Carpetbaggers would not go along with black control of the Republican party, preferring to split rule by prearrangement, giving the blacks the lesser of the available offices. Generally blacks did not wish to engage in a full-scale race war, which left them vulnerable to the rifle militias of white Redeemers, especially after the federal government refused to enforce its own laws guaranteeing black political involvement. After the North indicated in 1890 that it would not pass anymore enforcement laws, it was but a short road from Redemption (the return of home rule to the South) to complete black disfranchisement.

The political disfranchisement was reinforced by economic discrimination that was at best a repressive sharecrop system and at worst a form of peonage. Ironically, blacks themselves, with the active participation of the army and the Freedmen's Bureau, came up with the sharecrop system. It seemed to avoid the slave-like features of the gang and task system, under which the former slaves worked in the employer's fields in gangs and each worker had to complete a specified amount of work per day, and to deal with the shortage of credit. Sharecropping guar-

anteed that the laborer would get something tangible from a year's work and would be able to farm a specific piece of land. But the system's fault lay in the freedmen's lack of capital to begin each year. Black farmers had to buy everything on credit, from food (poor-quality "Negro food" that whites did not want) to tools, seeds, and farming implements. The creditor was the planter and the local store, often the same white man.

All it took was one bad year and the black laborer would be caught up in a never-ending cycle of debt. This was worsened by the store's doubling and tripling of prices and fancy accounting procedures that had all sorts of hidden interest fees. The whole process was made more prison-like by the arbitrary arrest of any African American without a labor contract for vagrancy and the leasing of such convicts to the highest bidder. The convict lease made money for the state and allowed authorities to forego expenses like jails. Often the lessee of convicts was the original contract holder, who now had a laborer at half the cost. Of course, the cost of the convict's "bail" was added to his or her original debt and the whole thing passed on to their children. Jail food was even worse than "Negro food," which increased health problems like trichinosis, jaundice, and pellagra.

The route through which most Americans learned to fight their way to a better economic status was the schoolhouse. And here, blacks lost out again. Prevented from obtaining an education before the war by law, blacks had to start from scratch after the Civil War. Fortunately, one of the better-managed programs of the Freedmen's Bureau was the coordination of the various benevolent and religious societies that sent teachers south to work among the freedmen. But blacks found that the best of intentions of the bureau and the benevolent societies was not enough. They constructed many of their own schools and found their own African American teachers, many of whom were veteran Union soldiers. No one knew the advantage of getting a good education better than African Americans of the Reconstruction era, probably because they had been denied one for so long. Old and young thronged to the schools, coming in for day, night, and Sunday classes. Planters soon discovered that they could attract a better laborer if they offered a school on the plantation. They also could control the content of the classroom work more easily that way, too. But in general whites believed that blacks lacked the wherewithal to learn, an attitude that was not necessarily limited to the South. Their best solution was to educate African Americans as a permanent underclass, submissive to their so-called white betters.

Between 1877 and the turn of the century, blacks fought to retain the gains they made during Reconstruction, but they were outnumbered in a fight against not only Southern whites but most white Northerners as well. Worse yet, the U.S. Supreme Court ruled on racial matters on the basis of Social Darwinism, the latest intellectual craze that "proved" that certain races were better than others. As described by a white man, Herbert Spencer, it was only a matter of time before blacks found themselves entrenched at the bottom of society again. This second-class treatment was topped by an entertainment industry that lampooned racial minorities mercilessly. Blacks suffered the worst, with the possible exception of the Chinese. The industry promoters, who merely served up popular superstition, characterized African Americans as lazy, licentious, ignorant, and dishonest. Minstrel shows featured whites made up in black face, with big lips and foolish costumes, singing outrageous "coon songs." Typical black Americans were depicted as playing the numbers (a form of gambling), acting servile and stupid in front of whites, being of cowardly character, lying, stealing, and eating watermelon. This image was clearly evident in the United States' first major movie hit, *Birth of a Nation*, which portrayed African American men with a sinister veneer as the source of incompetent "Negro Rule," Radical Reconstruction corruption, and a insatiable desire for white women that was checked only by the heroic riders of the Ku Klux Klan.

See also African American Education and Reconstruction; African American Leadership and Reconstruction; Disfranchisement; Segregation (Jim Crow).

References Bennett, Lerone, Jr., *Black Power, U.S.A.*(1967); Berry, Mary Frances, and John W. Blassingame, *Long Memory* (1982); Carter, Dan T., "Moonlight, Magnolias, and Collard Greens" (1977); Cruden, Robert, *The Negro in Reconstruction* (1969); Donald, Henderson H., *The Negro Freedman* (1952); Franklin, John Hope, and Alfred A. Moss, Jr., *From Slavery to Freedom* (1994); Gutman, Herbert G., *The Black Family in Slavery and Freedom* (1976); Harris, Robert L., Jr., "Coming of Age" (1982); Litwack, Leon F., *Been in the Storm So Long* (1979); McPherson, James M., "The Hidden Freedmen" (1970); Woodward, C. Vann, "Seeds of Failure in Radical Race Policy" (1966).

Alcorn, James Lusk (1816–1894)

A Mississippi Scalawag of importance, James L. Alcorn was born in 1816 in Illinois Territory, where his father ran a freighting service on the Mississippi River. The family moved to Kentucky, where Alcorn was educated in local schools and at Cumberland College. He married twice—first to Mary C. Stewart, with whom he had three children (she died in childbirth with the third), and then to Amelia Walton Greer, with whom he had five more. After teaching schools and acting as deputy sheriff in Arkansas and Kentucky, Alcorn moved to Mississippi in 1843. There he ran a plantation near Yazoo Pass, founded the Mississippi River levee system, and was a member of the state legislature as a Whig for 15 years. He ran for the U.S. House in 1856 but lost the election. He was also a delegate to the state constitutional conventions of 1851 and 1861, which considered secession. Although Alcorn was against secession personally, he was one of those Whigs who backed the proposal in 1861.

During the Civil War, Alcorn served as brigadier general of Mississippi state troops. Disappointed with the war and never much of a Rebel, he resigned his commission. Back home he was arrested as a disloyal civilian by the federal army and released on what he described as a "parole." He sold his cotton to smugglers in violation of U.S. regulations to get a cash advance upon which he lived during the war. He also watched much of the Vicksburg campaign from his front porch. He opposed the centralizing tendencies of a fellow Mississippian, Confederate president Jefferson Davis, but constantly gave of himself and his wealth to the Southern cause. Well known among Union provost marshals as "old Chief Secesh," he advocated what seemed to them to be Confederate sympathies to the end, refusing to take an oath of future loyalty to the Union. Late in the war Alcorn was among those Rebels who supported the notion of arming blacks as Confederate soldiers and rendering them free in return. He supported the Thirteenth Amendment at the end of the war. After he applied in person for a pardon, Alcorn was elected U.S. senator, but his application for a seat in that body was rejected along with others elected under President Andrew Johnson's Reconstruction proclamations.

Under the Military Reconstruction Acts, the Mississippi constitutional convention delayed the disfranchising of former Confederates. The inclusion of the disfranchising clause caused the constitution to be rejected by the voters. When Ulysses S. Grant was elected president, he favored separating the clause from the constitution and taking a vote on each. With the Congress now willing to accept the resubmission of the state constitution and the disfranchising provision separately, it was easy for Mississippians to accept the fundamental document and defeat the voting prohibitions. The Moderate Republicans then put up Grant's brother-in-law, Lewis Dent, for governor. The Radical Republicans nominated Alcorn as their candidate. Alcorn had been rejected by the Moderates, and he accepted the Radical nomination out of a desire for revenge as much as anything else. He called on the old Whigs to reject Dent as a dupe of the old Jackson Democratic clique, those who would run Mississippi from the capitol in the same style as before the war. The old Whigs, however, backed and campaigned for Dent. The decisive factor in the election was Grant's repudiation of his own relative as too much in

James Lusk Alcorn

league with Democrats under the catch-all label "conservative." Alcorn won with the support of African Americans and white (usually Carpetbagger) Radicals. The canvass was helped immeasurably by Gen. Adelbert Ames, military commander of the state, who removed from office as impediments to Reconstruction anyone who could be identified as moderate or conservative.

Alcorn's platform seemed quite radical to white Mississippians of that day, although in present-day terms it is rather innocuous. He worked for legal equality of all races and comprehensive civil rights laws (but he opposed social equality and public accommodations laws). He backed segregated public education (the all-black Alcorn College was named after him), expanding the judiciary (to protect loyal whites and blacks and give the party much patronage to grease the wheels of government), reduced taxes on land (to save the old planter class), leasing of convicts (to gain a steady source of labor for a massive public works system), and state aid to the construction of railroads (many of which had been wrecked by the passing armies of blue and gray). Democrats objected to the program as too pro-black and discriminatory against the white hill regions. For recognizing black rights Alcorn was condemned as "an open and avowed enemy of his race." Democrats claimed that Benedict Arnold's name carried less stigma than did Alcorn's. The program passed, however, and afterward Alcorn resigned his governor's position to assume a U.S. Senate seat. There he made quite a splash by arguing and debating with Ames, who had resigned from the army and was now the other U.S. senator from Mississippi, over the need for the Enforcement Acts, which Alcorn opposed. Yet he had failed to squelch violence against loyal whites and blacks while governor. Indeed, older histories saw his resignation and change of venue to Washington as a tacit admission of his failure as governor.

But the Democrats were not Alcorn's only opposition. Radical Republicans in the form of Carpetbaggers, who favored a looser system that would enable them to grease the wheels of government with money, objected to his squeaky clean government style. Although it can be said that Alcorn's program did discriminate by class, it never was dishonest. The Carpetbaggers soon latched onto Alcorn's real weak point with the masses of black voters. Alcorn might grant a certain legal equality (which no one could enforce in Reconstruction Mississippi), but he was a planter at heart. He was still an old slave master in his social attitudes. He would not get his hands "dirty" by giving in to black demands for social equality. He would not give a half share of offices to those whose votes put him in power, the freed slaves. Nor would he allow a public accommodations law. So when Alcorn came home to run for governor again in 1874, the Democrats, African Americans, and Carpetbaggers all opposed him and elected Adelbert Ames, the Carpetbagger who as military commander had helped put Alcorn in office in the first place.

Alcorn went back to Washington to serve out the remainder of his U.S. Senate term.

He voted continuously with the Republicans on Whiggish matters (economic development of the nation, particularly through internal improvements) and for the Compromise of 1877. After his retirement, Alcorn continued to practice law and develop his plantation lands. He served on the state levee commission and, although he was ignored by the Mississippi Republican party, he ran for governor again in the 1880s to no avail. He was also a member of the state constitutional convention in 1890, which disfranchised blacks within the terms of the Fifteenth Amendment, a step that Alcorn supported—again demonstrating his limits on behalf of racial equality. Alcorn hoped that disfranchisement would turn Mississippi back to a time when the "better" classes ran the state. Instead what happened was exactly the opposite, as the "rednecks" took over and the state stagnated in a way he never envisioned or would have approved of. To the end, Alcorn remained a Whig among Whigs rather than a real Republican. It was his example that led twentieth-century historians to theorize that many more upper-class men like him were the Scalawags of Reconstruction, not the poor "white trash" that the stereotypical legends indicate. But in reality Alcorn may have been the exception rather than the rule.

See also Ames, Adelbert; Morgan, Albert T.; Redemption of the South before 1874; Redemption of the South from 1874; Scalawags.

References Alexander, Thomas B., "Persistent Whiggery in Mississippi" (1961); Donald, David H., "The Scalawag in Mississippi Reconstruction" (1944); Harris, William C., "Mississippi" (1980) and "A Reconsideration of the Mississippi Scalawag" (1970); Pereyra, Lillian A., *James Lusk Alcorn* (1966); Wakelyn, Jon L., *Biographical Dictionary of the Confederacy* (1977).

Ames, Adelbert (1835–1933)

A Carpetbagger, U.S. senator, and governor of Mississippi, Adelbert Ames was born in Rockland, Maine. The son of a sea captain, he had accompanied his father on several sea voyages. He had a talent for art and mathematics and a New England horror with respect to the institution of slavery. He was a good son of his Puritan ancestors, a man with a conscience and a stern sense of duty. He was fastidious in personal conduct, dressing impeccably, rarely smoking or drinking, seldom swearing, and always behaving as a gallant gentleman with the ladies. It was no wonder that Ames made a good soldier. He graduated near the top of his class at West Point and at First Bull Run won the Congressional Medal of Honor for valor on the battlefield, serving with a gun battery until he dropped from the loss of blood caused by a leg wound. He rose in rank to brevet brigadier general, having fought with distinction on the Virginia Peninsula and at Antietam, Fredericksburg, Gettysburg, the siege of Charleston and Petersburg, and the final attack on Fort Fisher. At the end of the war he received the permanent rank of lieutenant colonel in the regular army. He thought of resigning his commission to enter private business, but he stayed on with the army as part of the occupation forces in South Carolina, then taking a leave of absence to tour Europe. He returned to Washington and met Blanche Butler, the only child of the infamous Benjamin F. Butler, Ames's one-time commanding officer during the war. Blanche was considered the belle of the capital, and Ames would eventually marry her.

Ames's station after his leave was with the occupation forces in Mississippi. He approached his duties with the same resolve he had shown in the war. His first duty was to assume the task of governing the state, the elected governor having been thrown out of office by the army command. However, Governor Benjamin Humphreys wanted to await the results of the upcoming election, and Ames decided to accommodate him. The Democrats won, partly because Ames's superior, Brev. Maj. Gen. Alvin C. Gillem, a Tennesseean who disliked Reconstruction, had stacked the deck in favor of whites. Humphreys was reelected and told Ames that he would not relinquish power unless forced to do so. Ames obliged him and marched him out of the governor's mansion between two files of soldiers. Ames thus became provisional governor of the state.

Immediately after he took over as president, Ulysses S. Grant appointed Ames to be military commander of Mississippi as well as provisional governor of the state. A Republican, Ames began to undo Gillem's pro-Democratic policies. He removed 2,000 men from offices to which they had been elected. He gave the positions to blacks, who made up a majority of Mississippi's population, and to loyal white Carpetbaggers. He cut the poll tax to allow poorer Mississippians to vote. He applied the tax to disabled Confederate veterans, who until that point had been exempt from paying it. He put African Americans on juries for the first time. He gave his support to the Radical Republicans when Carpetbagger Lewis Dent, brother-in-law of President Grant, threw his lot in with the Democrats. He also removed from office all Moderate Republicans who sided with Dent, and he appointed poll watchers from each party, one of whom had to be black. When the Radicals won with a ticket headed by Scalawag James L. Alcorn, Ames appointed the elected officials to office without waiting for the inauguration date. Alcorn, however, refused to take office before the inaugural, not wanting to be so obviously reliant on the army. Conservative whites accused Ames of being a Caesar—using his military power for selfish political ends, which, in Ames's case, was a seat in the U.S. Senate. The prophecy proved true, and Ames received the Republican party's nod for the Senate and was elected for the term ending in 1875. He resigned from the army to accept this new opportunity.

Along with the first African American to serve in the Senate, Hiram Revels, Ames presented his credentials, to which some in the Senate objected because their credentials had been signed by Ames himself as military commander. They also objected to Ames because he was hardly a true resident of Mississippi. Revels was seated immediately, Ames after a long hearing on a straight party vote. He did little to endear himself to white Mississippi when he married Blanche Butler, a headstrong woman who was smarter than he in politics and who did not like Mississippi from the first day she set foot on its soil. In the Senate, Ames supported the Enforcement Acts against the Ku Klux Klan, even though Governor Alcorn said the measures were not needed. When Alcorn removed certain black Republicans from office and appointed Democrats, Ames took advantage of the Senate recess to go South and campaign for Radicals in the 1871 by-elections. Ames managed to turn out the heaviest African American vote yet, and more blacks were elected than ever before. But the cost was splitting the Republican party among Moderates, Scalawags like Alcorn who had the support of Senator Revels and who wanted to cooperate with the Democrats, and rock-ribbed Radicals like Ames who relied on black and Carpetbag votes.

After the election, Alcorn replaced Revels in the U.S. Senate, where he and Ames debated each other over the Third Enforcement Bill. Alcorn claimed this bill, aimed at the Ku Klux Klan, was unnecessary, whereas Ames demanded its passage. Alcorn scorned Ames, who claimed to be a resident of Mississippi and a planter though he had no plantation. Ames dismissed Alcorn as a Democrat in Republican clothing. Ames also introduced a bill to desegregate the army, an idea 70 years ahead of its time. Ames believed that he would probably win reelection to the Senate from the Radical-controlled Mississippi state legislature, but he decided that a popular election triumph might solidify his chances for future office-holding. It would also remove the stigma of taking office by his own signature and of not being a bona fide resident. Thus he decided to run for governor. He took Blanche and the youngest of his two children back to Mississippi with him, but she did not like the heat and humidity and soon returned North. Ames stayed on to campaign. His willingness to cultivate black voters and not appear stuffy in their presence socially won him the Republican nomination. Senator Alcorn returned immediately to Mississippi and announced he would run against Ames as an Independent. Ames took the contest by 20,000 votes.

Ames resigned his Senate seat and brought his wife and children to Jackson, where he was inaugurated in January 1874. Blanche took to being first lady with a flair. She enjoyed the Mississippi winter, mild by comparison to New England's, and entertained mostly with her Carpetbag friends. She did her best to cut lard out of the cooking, going against Southern culinary traditions, and kept a good home. And she threw a gala bash at the end of the legislative term that lacked only liquor to make it the best in years. Blanche Ames did not approve of having drunks in the governor's mansion as others had done before.

The governor was not as pleased with the legislative term. His enemies looked at his balding pate and gave him the monikers "Addle-pate" (playing on his first name) and "old onion head." He spoke out for black education, the importation of manufacturers, the need of land distribution to the former slaves, and a frugal government. He made some progress in tax equalization and forced the railroads to pay taxes for the first time. He wanted Mississippi to outlaw drinking but had to settle for a county option. He vetoed measures that would have given debt and tax relief to farmers in the midst of economic depression, but he got them $100,000 in flood relief from Congress.

What worried Ames most was the storm coming in from white Democrats known as White Liners. These men intended to take over the state, and Ames was their chief target. They charged him with freeing an accused murderer, Carpetbagger Albert T. Morgan, who had had to shoot it out with his opponent to take over as sheriff at Yazoo City, a post to which he had been elected. They also began to "bulldoze" his black voters in acts of violence that spread throughout the state. Ames had no federal troops under his command, and the few in Mississippi preferred to sit on the sidelines. When the White Liners rioted at Vicksburg, Ames called the legislature into special session. But all they did was appeal to President Grant to send a company of troops to quell the violence. The president accommodated them, but this showed that the Ames administration could do little to preserve order itself. Even the so-called Gatling Gun Bill, allowing the governor to reorganize the militia and purchase fast-firing weapons for defense of the state government and blacks in the backcountry, did not help. The White Liners knew that if they killed enough African Americans to intimidate the rest but kept the number as low as necessary, they could keep the Grant administration from assisting Ames further.

That was exactly what happened. Republican refugees from the countryside flocked to Jackson to camp under the guns of the federal troops for protection. But they could not vote there. Ames telegraphed Grant for more soldiers to take the battle out into the hinterlands, but Grant's attorney general informed Ames that the nation was tired of the annual autumnal outbreaks of violence and that Ames would have to settle the problem on his own. Ames was faced with a grim reality. He had to put his mostly black militia in the field and risk an all-out race war or yield to the White Liners at the polls. Democrats sent telegrams to Grant assuring him that peace reigned in the state and questioning Ames's sanity and motives. They also offered Ames a military truce which he accepted. On election day 1875 the Democrats won a majority of 50,000 votes, demonstrating the efficacy of the First Mississippi Plan (also known as the Shotgun Plan) in regaining white control through controlled violence. The state was "redeemed" at last. The legislature was theirs. All that remained was to get rid of the Radical Republican executive branch, most of whom had not been up for reelection that year. Impeachment was the cure. Ames was accused of everything (absenting himself from the state, freeing accused criminals, degrading the judiciary, and so on) but corruption (even the Democrats knew the latter would not sell). Blanche Ames came up with the solution. The legislature agreed to drop all of the charges and Ames would resign the governorship and leave the state. But credit for the deal went to Robert Pryor, the legislative liaison to Ames.

Ames returned North to become a business success in his father's flour mill in Minnesota and then in textiles and real estate in Massachusetts. His family lived in luxury that merely increased when Blanche's father died in the 1890s. Ames became an avid golfer. He and his family vacationed in California, Florida, and Europe, especially Italy, where they owned a home at Lake Cuomo. When the Spanish-American War broke out he joined the volunteers as a general and served in Cuba at the siege of Santiago. Meanwhile historians began to fabricate tales of how corrupt he and his administration were during Reconstruction. One accused him of raising the state debt from almost nothing to $20 million. Ames wrote back and stated that records showed the state debt to be only $500,000 when he left office. This latter version was presented in another historian's book, James W. Garner's *Reconstruction in Mississippi*. Using papers that Ames graciously lent him, Garner also declared Ames to be corruption-free and credited his fall more to the spirit of the times than anything he did or left undone as governor.

But when his *Profiles in Courage* appeared in 1956, John F. Kennedy lauded Ames's Democratic opponents and declared that no state ever suffered more from Reconstruction mismanagement than had Mississippi. Despite protests from Ames's family to President Kennedy, the error remained uncorrected in all editions of the book. It remained for Ames's granddaughter to write the story from her grandfather's side, a task completed in a massive volume that came out in 1964. This book reiterated what Ames had told James W. Garner a half century earlier—Ames had resigned from the army to enter state politics because he "had a Mission with a large M."

See also Alcorn, James Lusk; Carpetbaggers; Redemption of the South from 1874.

References Ames, Blanch, *Adelbert Ames* (1964); Boatner, Mark M., III, *The Civil War Dictionary* (1959); Current, Richard N., *Those Terrible Carpetbaggers* (1988) and *Three Carpetbag Governors* (1967); Currie-McDaniel, Ruth, "The Wives of the Carpetbaggers" (1989); Garner, James W., *Reconstruction in Mississippi* (1901); Harris, William C.,

"Mississippi" (1980); Kennedy, John F., *Profiles in Courage* (1956); Sefton, James E., *The United States Army and Reconstruction* (1967).

Arm-in-Arm Convention

The month before President Andrew Johnson undertook his "Swing around the Circle" political tour designed to elect his supporters to Congress in 1866, a National Union political coalition met in Philadelphia to hold a convention of Conservative Republicans, Northern Democrats, and restored Southern Democrats with the intent of supporting the president's reelection in 1868. Participants were led onto the floor by James L. Orr of the South Carolina delegation and Darius N. Couch of the Massachusetts delegation, giving the event its popular nomenclature, the Arm-in-Arm Convention. Orr had been a brigadier general in the late Rebel army, a Confederate congressman, and a former governor of his state, while Couch was a former Union general and constant critic of the politics in the Union's old Army of the Potomac. Their two states represented the extreme poles of secession and the emancipation. Together the two men were a symbol of the reunified nation, of letting bygones be bygones; in the words of Louisiana delegate Richard Taylor (son of the late president and a Confederate general of note), who stood on a chair and yelled above the pandemonium, "Three cheers for the thirty-six states of the Union!"

The National Union party was the conservative outgrowth of Abraham Lincoln's wartime coalition of Republicans and Northern War Democrats, which had garnered big majorities for Lincoln and his running mate, Andrew Johnson, in 1864. Now president in his own right, Johnson hoped to move the coalition to the right and maintain its political clout in upcoming congressional contests in 1866 and the presidential election of 1868. The men behind the scenes were cabinet secretaries William H. Seward, Gideon Welles, and Hugh McCulloch, and a Conservative Republican senator from Wisconsin, James R. Doolittle. Supporting these men were

Thurlow Weed, Seward's perennial backer, and Henry Raymond of the *New York Times*. The basis of their organization would be Johnson's program of Reconstruction, recently challenged by Moderate and Radical Republicans in Congress who backed the Freedmen's Bureau Acts, the Civil Rights Act of 1866, and the proposed Fourteenth Amendment.

The Johnson coalition cut across party lines and relied too much on what many saw as unrepentant Southern Democrats. Therein lay its weakness. In a warning to Johnson, Secretary of War Edwin Stanton said that he would not be a part of destroying the Republican party. Nor would many Northern voters. Johnson's move smacked too much of the Democratic party and of giving in to rebellion, in the view of voters North of the Mason-Dixon line. Pennsylvania's Radical Republican candidate for governor had recently just avoided being assassinated. Race riots ravaged the Southern cities of Norfolk (April 1866), Memphis (May), and New Orleans (July). For the conference, Johnson had tried to remove the presence and support of Northern Peace Democrats (like Clement L. Vallandigham and Fernando Wood) accused of Copperhead (pro-Confederate) leanings during the war, but to no avail. Fortunately, a determined bid by floor leaders kept these Democrats from speaking and contaminating the convention further. But the enthusiasm of the August 1866 convention seemed to belie such restrained sentiments. The band struck up "Hail Columbia," "We'll Rally Round the Flag, Boys," and "Dixie," which it skillfully blended into a grand finale of the "Star-Spangled Banner."

The speakers were artfully chosen by Johnson's managers (called "the Ring" by Radical Republicans, as if to denote some sort of fraud). John Dix, running for the Democratic party as governor of New York, was the keynote speaker. He criticized Republican domestic economic policies (a national bank, tariffs, internal improvements). The Ring strictly controlled floor resolutions, recognizing predetermined nominators and seconds, allowing no discussion of the terms to maintain an outward show of unity, as the platform was hammered out behind closed doors. At dinner that night, Benjamin F. Perry of South Carolina described President Johnson as being "raised up by God to save the Republic," a sentiment that had already become a key part of Johnson's own psyche and speeches. The next day a 10-plank platform passed. It disavowed federal government interference with voting rules in the states, decried slavery, discredited the Confederate debt and made the Union debt sacred, thanked federal soldiers and sailors for their service, praised President Johnson's Reconstruction program, and thanked God for ending the war and saving the Union and the Constitution.

In Washington President Johnson hailed the convention's work as a "Second Declaration of Independence from the tyranny of an oligarchy, the worst and most odious of all forms of despotic tyranny." Senator Doolittle learned of Johnson's words with dismay and sent Johnson a cautionary note advising against "extemporaneous speeches." But the president was on a roll against the governmental body "called or which assumes to be, the Congress of the United States." He ignored Doolittle's advice and stepped on board the train, taking him on the first presidential off-year election campaign tour ever conducted. The Swing around the Circle would prove to be such a disaster that it would take generations before a president ventured into the congressional by-elections again.

See also Johnson and Reconstruction; Moderate Republicans and Reconstruction; Swing around the Circle; Washington Birthday Speech.

Reference Wagstaff, Thomas, "The Arm-in-Arm Convention" (1968).

Army and Reconstruction

It is one of the ironies of Reconstruction history that an entire century passed after the enactment of the Military Reconstruction Acts before a scholar turned full attention to the army's critical role in the era. Although minor investigations had been made, along with a few legal studies, James E. Sefton's full-length book *The United States Army and Reconstruction* (1967) was the first to focus on both the national and local aspects of military rule in the South between 1865 and 1877. It challenged the perspective of earlier scholars, particularly John Hope Franklin and Harold M. Hyman. Franklin had argued that the power and influence of the army during Reconstruction was minimal, limited by small numbers of soldiers at the government's disposal; Sefton countered that power and influence were functions of more than mere numbers. A few troops placed in key locations in a rural region could be dominant. In addition, Sefton believed that the blue uniform had a strong psychological effect on Southern whites. Few men dared attack an army unit because it could trigger a tremendous response from the army, the president, and Congress, as the Enforcement Acts demonstrated.

On a different level, Hyman had argued that the end of the Civil War saw Congress create two peacetime armies: a congressional force that dealt with Reconstruction, and the traditional force, controlled by the president as commander in chief, that handled all other duties (like guarding the coasts and fighting Native Americans). Hyman maintained that President Andrew Johnson, through his allegedly shortsighted Reconstruction policies, alienated the army's high command, forcing it to assist in the establishment of an independent force outside the president's usual influence. Sefton challenged this view, claiming the president was not as antimilitary as previously supposed. He viewed congressional indecisiveness in making up its own Reconstruction policies as the prime reason for the army's problems in the South. Besides, he concluded, Johnson never lost control of either army. Even under the Military Reconstruction Acts the president had certain powers, like appointing military district commanders, that he exercised to the limit.

According to Sefton, the army's role in Reconstruction passed through three stages. The first period ran from the end of the war to the passage of the Military

Reconstruction Acts, which corresponds to what is generally known as Presidential Reconstruction. At this time, the army had to administer the South without any real help from Washington, D.C., while Congress and President Johnson maneuvered for a position of dominance. The result was a great deal of confusion and frequent contradictions in policy between military departments (and even within departments), as totally inexperienced and sometimes incompetent officers sought to cope with the problem of civil affairs.

Next Sefton saw a period known as Military Reconstruction, lasting from 1867 to 1870. During this period, Sefton said, Congress emerged as the dominant branch of the federal government. In a vague set of laws, the Military Reconstruction Acts, Congress established a new Reconstruction program that finally placed the army in firm control of the Southern state governments. The new program set up five military districts embracing all of the former Confederacy except Tennessee, which had passed the Fourteenth Amendment and had been readmitted into the Union. Military Reconstruction lasted until 1870, when all of remaining Southern states achieved readmission to the Union by creating new constitutions that junked slavery and by electing loyal governments that approved the Fourteenth Amendment (the Carolinas, Florida, Alabama, Arkansas, and Louisiana) and, in some cases (Texas, Virginia, Mississippi, and Georgia), the Fifteenth Amendment.

The final era of military influence described by Sefton extended from 1870 to 1877, during which the army was charged with the unenviable task of preserving the new Republican regimes in each Southern state. The main thrust of this policy was the protection of loyal whites and blacks upon whose votes these governments depended for their existence. This was done by carrying out the provisions of the Enforcement Acts, patrolling polling places, and even installing one side or the other in power. Sefton found it difficult to call the army's role in any of these periods a success or a failure. He would rather blame the policy and those who created it for whatever shortcomings the era had. In keeping abreast of the twists and turns of events in the national capital, Sefton concluded that the army proved to be adaptable and flexible to civilian government's demands and that as an institution it rendered an overall credible, honorable performance.

Prior to Sefton's study, historians had satisfied themselves with casual references to "bayonet rule" and went on to the seemingly more exciting tales of the interaction of Southern Rebels, Carpetbaggers, Scalawags, and African Americans, as well as the resulting ills of statehouse corruption. Nowadays, historians do the same, but the heroes and villains have been reversed. Whether they reviled or found merit in the events they described, few historians examined and even fewer understood the role of the army in the process of Reconstruction. Commentators generally realize that one of Reconstruction's great weaknesses was the army's administration of civilian government, a unique aspect of the period. The idea of military supervision of civil government, regardless of how noble the objectives were, has always been reprehensible to Americans.

The tradition that the military forces were not independent from or superior to the civil power became ingrained in our own consciousness during the colonial period. Americans so objected to the use of British troops to enforce parliamentary legislation in the 1760s that they instituted mass protests that culminated in the so-called Boston Massacre. The event so shocked the British and colonial public that Parliament had to withdraw the soldiers from North America. When the army returned under the Intolerable Acts to administer Massachusetts colonial government, the Founding Fathers felt compelled to list this military supervision of civil government, with its attendant suspension of the local legislature, in the Declaration of Independence as a prime reason for the American Revolution. This suspicion of armed force was enshrined in the Articles of Confederation of 1781, which provided for no national defense force beyond the citizen soldier militia; Governor George Washington's Newburgh Address, in which he refused to countenance a military takeover of the national civil government in 1782; and in the later Constitution of 1789, which provided for a permanent national military establishment but always subordinated it to civilian leaders elected by the people.

Hence, any period of time in which the traditional constitutional guarantees of civil laws and courts are superseded by army supervision tends to be distasteful to the American palate. Reconstruction was such an era, in which military interference with civil government—above and beyond the merit of its programs designed to purify the former Confederate South— became an issue in itself. In the end, it was a crucial point that undermined the North's plans for Southern rehabilitation and caused Reconstruction to be discredited.

Lacking a solid tradition in martial rule, the army was plagued throughout Reconstruction by a lack of experience and legal precedent in military occupation and government. What little background the army possessed evolved out of the brief, dated supervision of government in Louisiana and western Florida before the War of 1812, as well as in eastern Florida after that conflict ended. A temporary stint of a similar scope occurred during the Mexican War in the occupied territories of New Mexico and California. Unfortunately, the army's experience with military government in these regions was not catalogued for later reference, and the personnel involved were either dead, retired, or stationed in areas not connected actively with the Reconstruction era after the Civil War.

Typical of the latter group was Bvt. Maj. Gen. Henry Wager Halleck, chief of staff to Lt. Gen. Ulysses S. Grant in 1865. Halleck had had more experience in military government than most officers. He had been secretary of state to the army regime in California, had helped draft the state constitution in 1849, and had written of his experiences in a treatise on international law in the 1850s. Yet Halleck became a nonentity

in Reconstruction. This was due partially to his penchant for alienating everyone he came in contact with and, more important, to his philosophy of military government. During and after the war, the general had demonstrated a fairly conservative approach to Reconstruction, much along the lines advocated by his close friend and rare defender, Maj. Gen. William T. Sherman. Both men tended to adhere to the notion that Reconstruction was solely a military problem, not a political one. This attitude irritated Secretary of War Edwin Stanton, who, in the aftermath of President Abraham Lincoln's assassination, removed Halleck as chief of staff and ordered him to Richmond to assume command there. In a vain effort to gain the secretary's favor, Halleck engaged in a brief tenure of absolute power. He went so far as to prohibit church services where the minister would not read a proscribed prayer for the president, and he refused marriage licenses to anyone who had not taken the oath of future loyalty, "to prevent so far as possible the propagation of legitimate Rebels."

But Halleck soon reestablished his conservative credentials by refusing to seize the Tredegar Ironworks as punishment for its support of the Confederacy, by recommending that freedmen stay at their old places of work, and by holding quick civil elections for a new Richmond city government. Believing Halleck's position to be too pro-Confederate, Stanton quietly transferred him to San Francisco, where the general remained harmlessly until 1869 in charge of the Department of the Columbia and Pacific. Then Halleck came east once again to head the Military Division of the South at Louisville. By that time Reconstruction was all but over in his new command area. He died three years later without having made a real contribution to the Reconstruction process.

Another officer who had made a noteworthy addition to the concept of military government before the war was Bvt. Lt. Gen. Winfield Scott, the conqueror of Mexico in 1847. At the city of Tampico, Scott had written a set of general orders intended to govern the conduct of soldiers and civilians during his famous campaign on Mexico City. Issued over the opposition of Congress, the James K. Polk administration, and fellow commander Maj. Gen. Zachary Taylor, these general orders authorized the use of military commissions to try all wrongdoers, civilian or military, for crimes ranging from simple theft and desecration of the church to rape and murder. In conducting these military commissions, Scott operated under the general rules established for the conduct of courts-martial in the Articles of War of 1806. But at the close of the Civil War Scott was dead; of 35 general officers significantly involved with the Reconstruction process, only 18 had had any experience in civil affairs under Scott. Those Reconstruction officers who did serve in the Mexican campaign were commonly junior combat leaders who had little contact with military government. And, as all of these men were to discern, it was one thing to manage civil affairs in a wartime situation, but quite another to continue in such a role after the fighting had subsided.

Hence wartime experiences in military government proved tentatively useful at best and inadequate at worst. Without an organized, accepted doctrine of military government, the generals had had to improvise from the beginning of the Southern occupation. The problem ultimately became the concern of various provost marshals in each advancing army. Originally conceived to handle troop discipline and to prevent disorder in the ranks, the provost marshal system had fallen into ruin by the time of the Civil War. The scattered deployment of prewar regiments in frontier duty stations and their isolation from the general public had made provost marshals unnecessary in the economy-minded army. All of this changed with the raising of massive civilian forces that campaigned the settled areas of the Eastern states. As the conquering federal soldiers advanced south, someone had to deal with the potentially disloyal Confederate civilians. Commanders casually delegated this responsibility to the provosts, a process that became more formal about the time of Bvt. Maj. Gen. John Pope's campaign into Virginia in 1862.

By the following year it had become obvious to high-ranking army officials that a more standardized conduct of war and occupation was needed. The Union record thus far was irregular. Officers like Halleck, Irwin McDowell, and George B. McClellan had followed a policy of respecting private property (including slaves, to the disgust of Radical Republicans) and Southern civil rights. Other generals, like Pope, Robert Milroy, and the infamous Benjamin F. Butler, had been harsher. The latter's conduct was so controversial that he was replaced by Bvt. Maj. Gen. Nathaniel Banks, who asked the War Department for a formal code of behavior to govern occupation of the South. The result was General Orders No. 100, entitled "Instructions for the Government of Armies of the United States in the Field," the first attempt to codify the rules of war by a Western nation.

Written by Prussian immigrant and renowned legal expert Francis Lieber, reviewed by a board of officers supervised by Bvt. Maj. Gen. Ethan Allen Hitchcock, and edited for distribution by General Halleck, General Orders No. 100 was based on Scott's occupation orders in Mexico, a bit of Grotius (the seventeenth-century Dutch international legal theorist), and the wartime experience of various Union generals, with a strong dose of Radical Republican abolitionism for good measure. It was designed to prove that Yankee war conduct and objectives were well within the realm of Western morality and international law. Often referred to as the "Lieber Code," General Orders No. 100 defined "civil war" as a conflict between two or more portions of a nation, "each contending for the mastery of the whole, each claiming to be the legitimate government." The South's secession was declared a "rebellion," or "insurrection of a long extant," a rising of a portion of the people against their legitimate government with the desire to "throw off their allegiance to it, and set up a government of their own." Under these orders, neither the treatment of captured Rebels as prisoners of war, the proclamation of martial law in Rebel territory, the honoring of Rebel flags of truce, nor a willingness on the part of the Union to negotiate with Rebel leaders, could be construed as legitimizing the Rebels' struggle or be taken as a promise of pardon or amnesty to any or all, a statement that echoed the U.S. Supreme Court's prior holding in the *Prize* cases (1863).

General Orders No. 100 further stated that martial law "was the direct outcome of enemy occupation or conquest." It did not have to be formally declared, and it would continue until canceled by special mention in a treaty of peace or by presidential proclamation. Martial law permitted local military officers to suspend the normal civil and criminal laws and substitute "military rule and force" and to dictate all laws on the basis of "military necessity." The latter term was defined as "those measures which are indispensable for securing the ends of the war, and which are lawful according to the natural law and useages of war." This allowed the annihilation of armed enemies but prohibited cruelty toward unarmed civilians or the undue destruction of their private property. In return the conquered population was expected to admit to outward loyalty toward the occupation forces. At all times the Lieber Code recognized the army's right to treat those truly loyal persons by a different standard than suspect civil inhabitants. Military commissions were to be established to enforce martial law, but if he deemed it reasonable, the commander could merely order the continuance of local laws and customs under his supervision, rather than replace them with his own ordinances. Technically, however, legislative, executive, and judicial functions of the occupied area's government ceased under martial law. These functions, like the right to tax, for example, were to be administered by the occupation forces.

The effect of General Orders No. 100 is still open to much controversy. The Supreme Court took favorable notice of it a year after it was issued in *ex parte Vallandigham* (1864). The set of orders was translated into German (Lieber's native tongue) at the end of the war; it was copied by numerous European nations during the last half of the nineteenth century and made the basis of the Hague Agreements on the civilized rules of warfare (a sort of contradiction in terms) at the turn of the century; it became a standard for the occupation of the Spanish empire during the Spanish-American War at the end of the century and a guide for army officers suppressing the Philippine Insurrection; and it guided the Rhine Occupation after World War I and the German and Japanese occupations after World War II. Yet in spite of the favorable worldwide influence of the Lieber Code, as well as army efforts to publicize it at the end of the Civil War, there is good reason to doubt that Reconstruction army officers were fully cognizant (if at all) of its implications. Although the conduct of Union soldiers during the war was by and large in agreement with the code, this may have been accidental rather than intentional. Yankee troop conduct might better be traced to the length of service of the soldiers, the weeding out of irresponsible officers, and the zealous efforts of General Halleck to ensure a decent standard of conduct.

There is no record of the high command referring its Reconstruction commanders to General Orders No. 100. Commanders in the field did not refer to it or suggest its contents as a guide for subordinates. It was not included in any of the orders traditionally passed from one command to another. And the code itself was nothing more than a set of guidelines that left much discretion in behavior by each commander and his subordinates. The main reason for the code's absence may be that military government developed independent of and prior to the Lieber Code.

The first step toward establishing military governments took place in the disputed border states, areas that the North could not bear to lose after secession of the Lower South. President Abraham Lincoln issued an executive proclamation on 29 April 1861, placing all territory between Washington and Philadelphia (a devious way to say the state of Maryland, especially the hostile pro-Confederate city of Baltimore) under martial law. In 1862, the army arrested William Offutt for legally recovering a slave under the Fugitive Slave Law of 1850, on the grounds that the slave was under military protection as an employee. In 1863, the whole state was put under military law, and in 1864, the freeing of Maryland's slaves by state action was enforced in military courts.

Missouri received its introduction to military government in July 1861, when local commanders visited nearby towns and organized pro-Union committees of public safety. In August Bvt. Maj. Gen. John Charles Frémont declared martial law throughout the state, took over the government (it had fled to the Confederacy anyhow), and freed all of the slaves. Lincoln endorsed all of this declaration except the freeing of the slaves—endorsing that portion would have sent every border state into immediate secession, and practicality was more important than morality at this juncture. On 2 December 1861, Bvt. Maj. Gen. Henry W. Halleck, with the president's approval, extended the military control for the duration of the war. Similar actions took place in Kentucky. (Because of their states' critical geographic locations, Kentuckians and Marylanders accounted for most of the political prisoners held without trial during the war.) In 1863, Bvt. Maj. Gen. Ambrose E. Burnside issued a further expansion of martial law in Kentucky that included a denial of the First Amendment right to disagree with any governmental policy vocally or in print. The military commanders regularly censored church sermons and prayers or insisted that such be delivered up for the Union war effort.

Military rule was expanded in 1862 to apply to all Rebels; insurgents; their aiders or abettors; those opposing the draft or enlistment and urging others to do the same; anyone who gave aid or comfort to the enemy; and anyone guilty of disloyal practices (a vague term never defined) anywhere in the United States. The War Department ordered all federal, state, and local law enforcement officials to arrest anyone who encouraged disloyal practices. Chief Justice Roger B. Taney (a Marylander) issued an opinion (*ex parte Merryman*) while on circuit in 1861 that military arrest could not take place and military commissions could not convene while civil courts were in session and operating freely, but the army ignored him and Lincoln refused to enforce the decision. The *Merryman* opinion would be restated by the whole court in an 1866 decision, two years after Taney died, but the war was over and the damage done by then. Martial law and military arrest were so effective that military prisons (labeled the "American Bastille" by dissenters, in reference to the infamous jail that symbolized the tyranny of French kings) overflowed with political prisoners; a special board consisting of Bvt. Maj. Gen. John A. Dix and retired New York judge Edwards Pierrepont had to be convened to investigate the cases and free those not openly pro-Confederate.

Generally military commanders had free reign to impose whatever laws they thought proper so long as they did not create national policy (which had been Frémont's sin). Most of their edicts were still local and municipal. Then in 1862, President Lincoln began a process that would mark the norm for military government in Reconstruction when he appointed Andrew Johnson to be the military governor of Tennessee. There never had been a military governor of a whole state before. Johnson was given the honorary rank of brigadier general and the job of rooting out disloyalty and forming a loyal government. Lincoln appointed military governors for other states as federal troops advanced into their areas. Other federal agencies accompanied the military governors and the armies into the South. Principal among them were (1) Treasury Department agents, who collected back taxes due and confiscated contraband property and goods (primarily cotton), and (2) after March 1865, agents of the Freedmen's Bureau, charged with enforcing the Thirteenth Amendment and helping refugees with transport and rations.

Military government could be quite all-encompassing. Commanders quickly assumed the executive powers of appointing and removing public and even quasi-private officeholders. The usual method was to administer the ironclad oath (one of never having willingly aided the Confederacy). It was given to all officeholders, and those who failed to take it lost their authority and position. Such interference extended to public universities, chambers of commerce, private library associations, and sextons of cemeteries. Local military commanders filled all sorts of political offices and held elections under orders from Washington for others. They supervised the convening of bodies to write state constitutions.

In addition to executive power, the commanders carried out judicial functions through courts-martial (usually reserved for soldiers) and military commissions (for the trial of civilians in place of criminal and civil courts). The tribunals usually had three to five members, and their jurisdictions extended from the ordinary crimes like fraud, embezzlement, bribery, breach of the peace, horse theft, rape, arson, receiving stolen goods, riot, assault, or election fraud to more war-related actions like correspondence with the enemy, blockade running, carrying mail to the Confederacy, running arms to the South, burning bridges and other acts of sabotage, hindering the draft or enlistments, or engaging in guerrilla warfare. President Lincoln even set up his own loyal court in Washington and sent it to Louisiana during the war to administer "loyal" justice.

Besides executive and judicial functions, military officers also got involved with economic matters, like trade, labor, and finance. Often they operated in conjunction with the treasury agents or were in direct competition with them. The army granted special licenses to trade in war zones and even with the enemy, particularly in cotton. To obtain a license one had to take the proper oaths, get letters of reference, and file the proper money guarantees with the government. The army also administered the government farms in the Mississippi Valley and elsewhere, provided black labor in the form of contraband blacks (i.e., slaves taken from Southern landowners) to private contractors, administered the wage arrangements, and provided protection for the operation of loyal plantations. If any African American behind the Union lines was not employed in some gainful job, he or she was sent to the contraband camps to become part of the general labor pool. This is one reason so many blacks latched onto a Union army regiment as a cook, preferring this form of quasi-freedom to enforced labor on army-administered plantations. Military governors also saw to it that no Confederate money exchanged hands in their districts and that all banks operated on specie (gold or silver coin) or greenbacks. The army also levied and collected local taxes.

The absolute nature of military government during the war, afterward during the more informal Presidential Reconstruction, and under the more rigorous Military Reconstruction Acts was evident to all who came in contact with it. Most commanders operated in a just and wise manner. Military courts were fair and above all speedy in their administration of justice. Some Southerners even voiced their desire to continue under military government indefinitely to avoid rule by the Scalawags, Carpetbaggers, and African Americans who made up the loyal governments installed after readmission and the end of army supervision. But the fairness and efficiency of military government begs the real question: was it the right thing to do?

Although Civil War and Reconstruction commentators made no distinction, there is now a recognized difference between martial law, in which the army helps an existing government weather a crisis, and military government, in which the army takes over the functions of civil government until the latter can be restored at a future date. Some have suggested that Reconstruction was merely a congressionally declared martial law. But if the distinction has merit, it would seem that the commanders who got along best in the South acted in the spirit of martial law. Those who had problems operated in the spirit of military government. Under the Military Reconstruction Acts either approach was permissible even after the state governments were declared illegal—it all depended on the desires, political skills, and prejudices of the individual army commanders.

The election of 1876, the so-called Crime of '76, was the last straw for those opposed to the military intervention in U.S. government that became so common during the Civil War and Reconstruction. The result was a rider to the Army Appropriations Bill for 1878 called the Posse Comitatus Act. Posse comitatus was an ancient English common-law concept in which the adult male populace of a county was to stand armed and ready to aid the sheriff or marshal in enforcing the law. The use of the United States Army to support the civilian governments in the South fell under this doctrine, the army acting in place of or as a supplement to the posse comitatus. But under the Posse Comitatus Act, no army officer of any rank could intervene to assist local, federal, or state law enforcement officials unless specifically ordered to do so by Congress or under the Constitution (by executive order of the president). The penalty was two years in jail or a $10,000 fine or both. The act's passage can be seen as a part of the Compromise of 1877, despite the year of the law (1878). The act has been amended twice since its initial passage. In 1900, because of the Klondike gold strike, Alaska was exempted from its protection, because law enforcement there was so haphazard. In 1947 the act was extended to include the air force when it separated from the army. As yet no one has been arrested and convicted of violating the act's provisions.

This is not to say that the army cannot be used at the prerogative of the president, just that everyone in all departments of government below the president cannot act without direction of executive proclamation or law of Congress. Strong federal executives used the posse comitatus 70 times from the beginning of the nation's history under the

Constitution of 1789 to the end of Reconstruction in 1877. George Washington used the army as a posse comitatus to suppress the Whiskey Rebellion in 1794; Thomas Jefferson used it to enforce the Embargo Acts in 1807; Andrew Jackson employed it during the Nullification Crisis in 1832; Franklin Pierce found it indispensable during the Kansas-Missouri Border Wars in 1854; and Abraham Lincoln used it to call up the militia in 1861 to suppress the Civil War.

Presidents continued to use the posse comitatus during Reconstruction and even after the passage of the 1878 act. President Rutherford B. Hayes used the army as a posse comitatus during the Lincoln County War in New Mexico Territory in 1878; Grover Cleveland called on it for putting down the rail strikes of 1894 (and his Democratic party lost an election partly because of it); Theodore Roosevelt employed it during the San Francisco earthquake; Woodrow Wilson made the army available to the states that sent their national guard troops overseas in World War I; Franklin Roosevelt used it to guard the banks during the Bank Holiday in 1933; and Dwight D. Eisenhower used it to enforce the integration of public schools in the South in 1958. Some authorities are now questioning whether the act was violated by the use of military-provided equipment in the 1993 attack on the Branch Davidian compound at Waco, Texas. But in the early 1990s congress had amended the Posse Comitatus Act to permit military assistance to civil law enforcement in the war on drugs, which confused the issue somewhat.

Essentially the law was, in the words of Congressman Knott of Kentucky (whose state had seen federal troops employed 441 times between 1871 and 1876 to stop Ku Klux Klan raids), "designed to put a stop to the practice, which has become fearfully common, of military officers of every grade answering the call of every marshal and deputy marshal to aid in the enforcement of the laws." Knott and others found one of the paramount principles of the American Revolution to be that soldiers were never to be used against their civilian compatriots, no matter how expedient it might seem at the moment. Historians, however, have tended to trace the collapse of Reconstruction to the race problem. And yet, had there been no race problem Reconstruction would still have had to overcome the onus of relying upon the army to enforce "proper" behavior in the South. Americans traditionally have perceived a distinction between the police officer's executive right to enforce the law through arrest and the power to legislate law and determine guilt. Military Reconstruction demonstrated that, even though the army theoretically possessed absolute power in the South, there were limits to its ability to effect through force a permanent change in the region's culture. And that is part of why Reconstruction failed.

See also Ames, Adelbert; Canby, Edward R. S.; Enforcement Acts; Griffin, Charles; Hancock, Winfield S.; Military Reconstruction Acts; Reynolds, Joseph J.; Schofield, John M.; Sheridan, Philip H.

References Alderson, William T., "The Influence of Military Rule and the Freedmen's Bureau on Reconstruction in Virginia" (1952); Ambrose, Stephen E., *Halleck: Lincoln's Chief of Staff* (1962); Ashcraft, Alan C., "Role of the Confederate Provost Marshals in Texas" (1968); Bailyn, Bernard, *Ideological Origins of the American Revolution* (1967); Baker, George T., "Mexico City and the War with the United States" (1970); Ballantine, Henry W., "Martial Law" (1912) and "Unconstitutional Claims of Military Authority" (1914–1915); Barr, Alwyn, ed., "Records of the Confederate Military Commission in San Antonio" (1966–1967, 1967–1968); Benet, Stephen Vincent, *Treatise on Military Law and the Practice of Courts Martial* (1868); Birkhimer, William E., *Military Government and Martial Law* (1904); Bluntschli, Johann Kaspar, *Das Moderne Kriegsrecht der Civilisierten Staaten als Rechtsbuch Dargestellt* (1866); Byrne, Frank L., "'A Terrible Machine'" (1966); Carpenter, A. H., "Military Government of Southern Territory" (1900); Davis, Ronald L. F., "The U.S. Army and the Origins of Sharecropping in the Natchez District" (1977); Dawson, Joseph G., III, *Army Generals and Reconstruction* (1982); Dennison, George W., "Martial Law" (1974); Dunning, William A., *Essays on Civil War and Reconstruction* (1897); Foner, Eric, *Reconstruction* (1988); Franklin, John Hope, *Reconstruction* (1961); Freidel, Frank, "General Orders No. 100 and Military Government" (1945–1946); Furman, H. W. C., "Restrictions upon the Use of the Army Imposed by the Posse Comitatus Act" (1959); Futrell, Robert F., "Federal Military Government in the South" (1951); Garner, James W., "General Orders 100 Revisited" (1965); Gerteis, Louis S., *From Contraband to Freedman* (1973); Holdsworth, W. S., "Martial Law Historically Considered" (1902); Holladay, Florence Elizabeth, "The Extraordinary Powers and Functions of the General Commanding the Trans-Mississippi Department of the Southern Confederacy" (1914); Hyman, Harold M., "Johnson, Stanton, and Grant" (1960) and *A More Perfect Union* (1973); Main, Jackson Turner, *The Anti-Federalists* (1964); Majeske, Penelope K., "Virginia after Appomattox" (1982); Maslowski, Peter, "'Treason Must Be Made Odious'" (1972); Matthews, Clifford, "Special Military Tribunals" (1951); McDonough, James L., "John Schofield as Military Director of Reconstruction in Virginia" (1969); Meek, Clarence I., III, "Illegal Law Enforcement" (1975); Moore, Wilton P., "The Provost Marshal Goes to War" (1959) and "Union Provost Marshals in the Eastern Theater" (1962); Rice, Paul Jackson, "New Laws and Insights Encircle the Posse Comitatus Act" (1984); Richter, William L., *The Army in Texas during Reconstruction* (1987) and "'Devil Take Them All'" (1986); Sefton, James E., *The United States Army and Reconstruction* (1967); Shy, John, *Toward Lexington* (1965); St. Clair, Kenneth E., "Judicial Machinery in North Carolina in 1865" (1953) and "Military Justice in North Carolina" (1965); Thomas, Benjamin, and Harold M. Hyman, *Stanton* (1962); Thomas, David Y., *A History of Military Government in Newly Acquired Territories of the United States* (1904); Ulrich, John William, "The Northern Military Mind in Regard to Reconstruction" (1959); Weigley, Russell F., *History of the United States Army* (1967).

Ashley, James M. (1824–1896)

James M. Ashley's branch of an old Virginia family migrated to Pennsylvania, where he was born in Allegheny County near Pittsburgh. Ashley's father took the family to Ohio and brought his son on frequent missions in the Ohio Valley, proselytizing for the Campbellites, an austere offshoot of Presbyterianism. Here James Ashley received an education by learning to read the Bible. He never went to school. On his father's missions, the boy encountered slavery in Kentucky and what would become West Virginia. He later fled his father's strict discipline and worked as a cabin boy on a river steamer on southern rivers. Ashley found slavery abhorrent, especially the reenslaving of blacks who had free papers, the general cruelty of bondage, and the blatant disregard for the feelings of human beings. He toured the rest of the South and found the story much the same. His outspokenness forced local officials in Virginia to ask him to leave the state for his own safety.

Ashley returned to Ohio and worked as a printer and newspaper editor and later as a boat builder. During his spare time he read law and was admitted to the bar in 1849. Shortly thereafter he married Emma J. Smith, a Kentucky woman, and set up a wholesale drug company in Toledo. At this time, with the annexation of the western territories that were a part of the Mexican Cession, Ashley became interested in politics. A lifelong Democrat up to that point, he broke with his party and backed the Free Soilers in 1848 and the new Republican party in 1854. He attended the Republican convention of 1856 that nominated John C. Frémont as the party's first presidential candidate and stood for Congress as a Republican in 1858. He was reelected four more times during the war and Reconstruction.

In Congress Ashley developed and led in the passage of much of the Radical Reconstruction program. He introduced the first wartime Reconstruction measure in 1861. Although it failed passage, it would be the core of Congressional Reconstruction after the war. He led the way in abolishing slavery in the District of Columbia in 1862. He introduced the Thirteenth Amendment in 1863 and, upon its failure, lobbied enough border state Democrats to change their votes that it passed two years later. Ashley considered this achievement the greatest triumph of his life. His final contribution was the introduction of the impeachment proceedings against President Andrew Johnson. Upon the Senate's failure to convict, Ashley suffered the rebuff of so many other Radicals that he lost the election of 1868.

After his defeat, Ashley accepted President Ulysses S. Grant's appointment as governor of Montana Territory. But his outspoken criticism of Grant's Reconstruction policy as weak and corrupt cost him the

James M. Ashley

job. Ashley then shifted his support to Horace Greeley's Liberal Republican campaign in 1872, his last political act. Ashley's political philosophy was one of emotional gut reaction to perceived wrongs rather than a consistent, organized ideology. He was Puritan in habit, thorough in his hatreds of opponents, suspicious of all motives, and somewhat vain as to his own importance. He was very courageous and willing to buck the system whenever he thought it was wrong; or as his opponents would have preferred to say, he was unbelievably obstinate in his views. These traits were not uncommon among other Radical Republicans. After his political career failed he entered railroading and built and managed the Ann Arbor line until his death.

See also Radical Republicans.

References Carter, Clarence E., "James Mitchell Ashley" (1964–1981); Horowitz, Robert F., "James M. Ashley and the Presidential Election of 1856" (1974) and "Land to the Freedmen" (1977).

Beecher, Henry Ward (1813–1887)

One of the premier churchmen of his day and a popular figure nationally, Henry Ward Beecher was born in Litchfield, Connecticut. He was the brother of Harriet Beecher Stowe (the author of *Uncle Tom's Cabin*) and son of Lyman Beecher, a renowned religious figure in his own right and backer of a revolt at Lane Seminary (where the directors did not want the slavery issue discussed on campus) that led many of the antislavery faculty and students to leave for Oberlin College. Henry Ward Beecher grew up in the Connecticut woods. He was a difficult student, bright enough but lazy in his studies—so much so that many thought him actually stupid. He bumped around from school to school until he came home one day and announced that he wished to go to sea. His father cleverly told him that he would have to learn navigation to be a credible sailor and sent him off to a Massachusetts academy for boys, where the young Beecher finally found himself. He learned how to study and became a leader in sports and oratory.

Beecher never went to sea; indeed, he never studied navigation. He was more interested in other things. He had been raised in the strict religious atmosphere of his father's home, one that encouraged seeking after one's salvation, strict discipline, and resourcefulness in all matters. But with ten brothers and sisters, there was very little affection from his overworked parents, which had led Beecher to become somewhat self-centered, shy, and lonely. At the time of his academy graduation, Beecher had yet to have the "religious experience" deemed so important for youth of his upbringing. He attended Amherst College but did poorly; he was more interested in phrenology, English classics, and oratory than in a particular course of study. He seemed to have come out of his shell, and he developed a reputation for hilarity, repartee, and practical jokes. His religion was marked with much uncertainty and doubt, exacerbated by the fact that his mother, on her deathbed,

made him promise to enter the ministry—something his father had expected him to do so all along. He followed his father out to Ohio's Lane Seminary and tried to study for assuming the cloth, but he found extracurricular activities more to his liking.

Beecher was a free spirit who liked to roam in the woods, knit, and even shoe his own horse. Although he spent time reading, lecturing, preaching, and teaching, he had little appreciation for systematic theology. In this he had a lot in common with his neighbors, and one May morning in the woods Beecher received his heavenly revelation at last. He discovered that God loved "a man in his sins, for the sake of helping him out of them" not "out of compliment to Christ, or to a law, or to a plan of Salvation, but from the fullness of His great heart." Beecher saw Christ as a constant companion, a friend who would uphold and sustain him always.

Beecher entered the ministry as a Presbyterian and experienced his first disappointment, the control of the church's General Assembly. Beecher tended to be a law unto himself, not only in religion but in all things. He had little use for conventionalities. He was of high spirits, genial in disposition, interested in all aspects of human existence, and free from the dour piety so common among churchmen of his time. And therein lay his public popularity. So Beecher received his license to preach from the New School Presbytery of Cincinnati, a body that allowed much diversity in belief.

Beecher as a preacher modeled himself and his message after the tremendously moving sermons of the eighteenth-century Congregational preacher Jonathan Edwards and the methods of the early Apostles as revealed in the biblical Book of Acts. He had but one aim as a preacher—to effect a moral change in his listeners. A sermon was only as good as its effect on one's heart. Combined with a great delivery, his popularity grew year by year. Beecher railed against the perceived evils of his day: gambling, drinking, womanizing,

Henry Ward Beecher

idleness, dishonesty, and popular amusements. He had a skill for shrewd analysis of the human motive, used graphic descriptions, employed a picturesque language, and displayed a trenchant style. As he put it to one of his brothers: "Preach little doctrine, except what is moldy orthodoxy." As Beecher's fame spread he received several invitations to preach at other, more prestigious congregations. But he refused them all until 1847, when he accepted the call to a small congregation of ten members called Plymouth Church in New York City (Brooklyn). Here, like his parishioners, he would become a Congregationalist, the most liberal denomination of his day, in which the individual churches were entities unto themselves, unlike the Presbyterians with their denomination-wide synods.

Beecher would parlay this modest beginning into a position of conspicuous influence unmatched by any other clergyman of his day. After the original sanctuary burned, Beecher built a new one that could hold better the estimated 2,500 parishioners a

week who came to see him from all parts of the country. He based his popularity on his unconventionality, audacity, wit, humor, theological latitude, dramatic presentation, and friendly intimacy with the congregation. He refused to use a pulpit, preferring to speak from a slightly raised platform to maintain intimacy with the crowd. He spoke out in favor of many burning political issues of the day—antislavery; opposition to the Compromise of 1850, which extended slavery into the Mexican Cession; disobedience of the Fugitive Slave Law; the use of force to make Kansas free soil; his support of Republican presidential candidates John Charles Frémont (1856) and Abraham Lincoln (1860); vigorous prosecution of the war and early emancipation; and quick readmission of the South to the Union after the war with civil rights guaranteed to blacks. But it was his sympathetic understanding of the human heart and his appreciation and varied application of fundamental spiritual truths that appealed to his listeners—and his readers. Beecher printed his sermons in pamphlet form, wrote magazine articles, and edited several Christian magazines and newspapers.

In neither his religious nor his political pronouncements was Beecher original. He followed rather than led and was moderate rather than innovative. He rarely looked at the subtleties of any idea. Instead he grasped the obvious, looked at the fundamentals, displayed the facts, and set everything forth with great clarity, persuasiveness, and unmatched wit. He was essentially a man of moods and impulses. He never really disciplined himself. He had no sense of self-sacrifice, no stern virtues. He did as he pleased. He acted just like the people who flocked to see him every Sunday. Like them, he had weaknesses and foibles that he could not or would not control, but he made it all understandable and within God's ability to forgive. His efforts on behalf of reform reflected his impulses rather than a well-thought-out rationale. He sympathized with the plight of African Americans as slaves and as free persons with less than equal rights; supported woman's suffrage;

and stood in favor of free trade—these seemed like natural things to do. They promised freedom from restriction. He embraced the theory of evolution with his own interpretation—it showed the constant improvement of human nature over the ages and denied the idea of original sin. It showed humankind always rising, something Beecher believed in implicitly.

With his flexible notions of religious truths it is somehow not surprising that Beecher became involved in the greatest public scandal of his time, the Beecher-Tilton affair. To this day defenders claim that he was falsely accused of carrying on a clandestine romance with the beautiful wife of his young protégé, Theodore Tilton. After all, Tilton had unconventional ideas about love and marriage that included non-monogamy, something that went against the accepted precepts of society. In any case, scandalous stories had circulated for years about Beecher's love life. Until 1870, however, they did little more than titillate members of his congregation and actually improve his image in the minds of his advocates. Then Tilton publicly accused Beecher of having an affair with his wife, Elizabeth, according to her own written admission. But Elizabeth retracted the admission, claiming it had been obtained under duress. Everyone kept it silent and denied everything for two years. Then a highly imaginative account of the relationship came out in one of the scandal sheets of the day, *Woodhull and Claflin's Weekly*, run by two allegedly reformed prostitutes, Victoria Claflin Woodhull and her sister, Tennessee Claflin.

For eight months the stories circulated in print and by word of mouth before Beecher felt it necessary to deny them. Twelve months later, Tilton accused Beecher again in print, and Beecher asked the church to investigate. They found him innocent—or at least there was no evidence to hang him with. Tilton then charged Beecher in court, asking damages of $100,000 for alienating the affections of his wife. The trial was a sensation, lasting six months and resulted in a hung jury (9-3 in favor of Beecher). A year

and a half later, another Congregational church council of 244 members cleared Beecher, unable to obtain any real proof that he did wrong. It is true that the evidence before any of the investigating bodies remains open to all sorts of interpretations to this day, but Beecher himself admitted to his attorneys one Sunday afternoon that although it was theologically "unlawful to pull an ass out of the pit on the Sabbath day …there never was a bigger ass or a deeper pit." As the *New York Times* concluded in 1875 after the whole thing subsided, "Mr. Beecher's management of his private friendships and affairs has been entirely unworthy of his name, position, and sacred calling." Or as another, blunter commentator put it, "Mankind has been falling since Adam, but it never struck bottom until Henry Ward Beecher came along."

The rest of Beecher's life was tarnished by the scandal. The trial had cost him $118,000 and, never a wealthy man, he remained relatively poor until his death. But his public popularity was probably enhanced rather than lessened. He went on the lecture circuit and people paid by the thousands to see and hear about repentance from a true reprobate. He lectured on the evils of labor unions (but later renounced his opposition), abolished Hell ("If ever a man had reason to wish Hell didn't exist it was Henry Ward Beecher," intoned one wag), talked about the God of love, and defended evolution as true religious doctrine in his book *Evolution and Religion*. He also attacked the corrupt judges of New York (a never-ending occupation), praised President Chester A. Arthur (one reformed sinner to another), and denounced noted Republican politician James G. Blaine as a corruptionist on behalf of Grover Cleveland (who, like Beecher, had had some problems of an amorous nature, having fathered an illegitimate child). Beecher also began a monumental work, *The Life of Christ*, but never finished it, leaving that to his sons. He died from a cerebral hemorrhage, active until the end. It was estimated that 40,000 persons viewed his body before it was buried at Greenwood Cemetery, a tribute to his influence on the popular culture of the Civil War, Reconstruction, and the Gilded Age and the shifting values of the Victorian America he epitomized.

See also Grant and the Scandals; Social Thought during and after Reconstruction; Woodhull, Victoria Claflin.

References Clark, Clifford E., *Henry Ward Beecher* (1978); Hibben, Paxton, *Henry Ward Beecher* (1942); McLoughlin, William G., *The Meaning of Henry Ward Beecher* (1970); Ryan, Halford R., *Henry Ward Beecher* (1990); Starr, Harris Elwood, "Henry Ward Beecher" (1964–1981).

Bingham, John A. (1815–1900)

Born in Mercer, Pennsylvania, John Bingham was educated in local schools and as a printer's apprentice. He went to Franklin College, a center of abolition early in the nineteenth century, and read law. He was admitted to the bar in Ohio and took up a lifelong residence at Cadiz. He became interested in Whig politics and stumped for William Henry Harrison's "Log Cabin" campaign in 1840. He was a Conscience Whig, against slavery, and by 1854 he had become a Republican and was elected to Congress under that banner the same year. He served every term but the 1862-1864 Democratic resurgence that followed the Emancipation Proclamation until 1873, when he lost once more and accepted an appointment as U.S. minister to Japan for 12 uneventful years.

Bingham was known as a resourceful speaker, full of the invective that marked the Civil War era. He never let fact get in the way of a telling story to make a point. His two biggest achievements known to the public were his parts in the trial of the assassins of President Abraham Lincoln and the impeachment of President Andrew Johnson. In both cases he was outspoken in his hostility toward the accused; although he had initially opposed the indictment of Johnson, he later bowed to party expediency. But his main achievement was his part in drafting the Fourteenth Amendment, particularly the controversial first section having to do with due process of the law, equal protection under the law, and the privileges and immunities of citizenship, all

of which were old abolitionist doctrines. In politics, Bingham is considered to be among the critical Moderate Republicans who were driven to the Radical policy of harsher Reconstruction by the intransigence of the South after the war (which President Johnson encouraged).

See also Fourteenth Amendment; Moderate Republicans and Reconstruction.

References Kendrick, Benjamin B., *The Journal of the Joint Committee of Fifteen on Reconstruction* (1914); Donald, David H., *The Politics of Reconstruction* (1965); McCormick, Thomas D., "John Armor Bingham" (1964–1981); Swift, Donald, "John Bingham and Reconstruction" (1968); Ten Broek, Jacobus, *Equal under Law* (1951, 1965).

Black Codes

From a modern perspective, one of the greatest follies the South committed during its self-administered form of Reconstruction under Andrew Johnson's plan of reunion was the passage of the Black Codes. These codes demonstrated that the white South would not handle the freed African Americans fairly. It was a poor strategy, coming so soon after the end of slavery. In reality some sorts of laws were necessary. Slavery had involved more than a system of labor. It actually governed all aspects of social contact between blacks and whites. The problem was whether the ordinances should have assumed the form that they did. The Black Codes primarily concerned themselves with African Americans as laborers. Social organization—segregation or integration of the races beyond work—was quite unstable during Reconstruction and would take nearly 30 years to work out.

The Black Codes began by defining who was legally a Negro. Generally this was accepted to be anyone of one-eighth "Negro blood"; this imprecise description gives modern sociologists chills, but white Southerners saw it as so precise as to give such a person a name—octoroon. African Americans received certain rights in the Black Codes. The laws legalized their marriages (blacks had lived together in family units during slavery, but they had no legality under law); tacitly recognized their right to a family name (many slaves had family names, some of them African in origin, but these names had not been legal); and permitted the emancipated to draw up contracts, sue or be sued, and attend schools for their race (all of which had been illegal activities under slave law). At the same time certain activities were prohibited to blacks. African Americans could not serve on juries, give testimony in court against a white, or carry firearms. Many of these prohibitions were also included in Northern states' Black Laws as part of a form of early segregation that evolved when slavery was abolished there after the American Revolution. Similar laws arose during the antebellum era in Southern cities, where the slave system often broke down under the anonymity of city life and the economic realities of hiring slaves out or of slaves hiring themselves out.

Next the Black Codes defined African Americans' status as laborers. (Few whites smugly assumed that blacks would become anything other than laborers.) Part of the problem was that whites were so propagandized by their own myths that an African American would not work once he or she became free. This notion had been reinforced by the former slaves who wandered as they sought true freedom and lost family members sold down the river years before. The compulsions varied from state to state and even by region or town within a state. But generally they took the form of a drastic imposition of the laws against vagrancy. All vagrants were to be arrested and placed to work on public roads or other projects. One was a vagrant if one had no labor contract with a white employer. Other jurisdictions could forcefully sign black vagrants over to private employers. Often blacks could own

In compliance with Black Codes, African Americans considered vagrants were forced into labor or jailed until they chose to work. In this undated illustration, a free man is auctioned off for such a purpose.

no property or only a small town lot. What these provisions did, and what Northerners and blacks themselves found so objectionable, was to place African Americans in a position somewhere between slavery and freedom. They could not be owned outright, but neither could they do what they pleased like truly free people.

In retrospect the Black Codes seem inexplicable until one takes a look their origins. Essentially the Black Codes were based on U.S. Army occupation regulations covering black laborers during and after the war. Some recent historians point out that the Southern governments had a different, more sinister intent, but since the laws are almost verbatim copies of army general orders, this seems untrue. Texas serves as a good example. The state's act to "Provide for the Punishment of Persons Tampering with, Persuading, or Enticing Away Laborers or Apprentices under Contract" allowed the imposition of fines and imprisonment on malefactors. The Freedmen's Bureau Circular Orders No. 14 also allowed the laborer to be fined, with the money withheld from wages due. The state law also forced employers to grant certificates to laborers who had completed their contracts, in order to speed rehiring of these laborers elsewhere. Another army edict also recommended that blacks work for a share of the crop instead of wages.

The Texas vagrancy law defined vagrants as anyone without visible means of support and making no effort to obtain work by honest employment (a description that included habitual drunks, idlers, prostitutes, and gamblers). Such persons could be put to labor on various public works until their fine was paid off, or in jail on bread and water until they desired to work. The army had enforced similar provisions around soldier camps for years and had further defined *vagrant* as anyone away from his or her place of employment for 24 hours.

But the military power structure enforced only part of the state's contract labor law. The army made contracts binding on the whole family if the head of family signed and made the contract a lien on a portion of the crop. It also established the provision that an employee could not leave the place of work without the employer's permission. All of these had a basis in army regulations, most coming from the Mississippi Valley and Louisiana experiments. But the parts enacted by the Texas state legislature that made fines double deductions on wages for feigned sickness or theft and forbade disobedience and any but "civil and polite" language to the employer or his family were disallowed, mainly because there was no appeal to an outside court.

So while the Black Codes had provisions in them that were unwise, they largely reflected the conqueror's handling of the problems of freed slaves. However, the codes fit right into the white South's expectations, too. Southerners were a bit surprised when Northern politicians disallowed them their congressional seats in December 1865 for agreeing with the army's own labor rules in the South. But Congress was also looking for excuses to reexamine Reconstruction from the ground up, and the Black Codes provided such an excuse, no matter who instituted them originally.

See also Johnson and Reconstruction; Lincoln and Reconstruction; Louisiana Experiment; Mississippi Valley Experiment.

References Carter, Dan T., *When the War Was Over* (1985); Crouch, Barry A., "'All the Vile Passions'" (1993); Davis, Ronald L. F., "The U.S. Army and the Origins of Sharecropping in the Natchez District" (1977); Dawson, Joseph Green, III, *Army Generals and Reconstruction* (1982); Humphrey, George D., "Failure of the Mississippi Freedmen's Bureau in Black Labor Relations" (1983); Litwack, Leon F., *North of Slavery* (1961); May, J. Thomas, "Continuity and Change in the Labor Program of the Union Army and the Freedmen's Bureau" (1971); Mecklin, John M., "The Black Codes" (1917); Nieman, Donald G., "The Freedmen's Bureau and the Mississippi Black Code" (1978); Perman, Michael, *Reunion without Compromise* (1973); Joe M. Richardson, "The Freedmen's Bureau and Negro Labor in Florida" (1960); Richter, William L., *Overreached on All Sides* (1991); Shofner, Jerrell H., "Custom, Law, and History" (1977); Wade, Richard C., *Slavery in the Cities* (1964); Wilson, Theodore B, *The Black Codes of the South* (1965); Wood, George A., "The Black Code of Alabama" (1914); Woodward, C. Vann, *The Strange Career of Jim Crow* (1966).

"Black Personality" in Slavery and Freedom

African Americans have the dubious honor of being one of the most psychoanalyzed groups in American history—particularly by whites. Much of this analysis concerns historical interpretations of slaves' psychological response to slavery and racism. Did the slaves and freedmen internalize their feigned laziness and inabilities until those traits became real, as plantation owners wanted to believe, or was every slave a Nat Turner, fighting the system with guile and dignity, as some African Americans forcefully state today?

Numerous black historians, from the eloquent W. E. Burghardt DuBois to Joseph Carroll to the popular Joel A. Rogers, have asserted African Americans' nobility as an enslaved people. But one of the better-known accounts comes from white Marxist historian Herbert Aptheker. In his *American Negro Slave Revolts*, Aptheker paints a picture of a continually resisting slave population that attacked the "peculiar institution" in a variety of ways, from sly day-to-day resistance to outright armed rebellion. Aptheker would prefer to use as his working definition of rebellion the one adopted by the antebellum Texas Supreme Court—an assembly of three or more slaves with arms intending to take their freedom by force. But he feels that a more widely acceptable definition of a revolt would be ten or more individuals intending to assert their freedom and being portrayed in contemporary literature as rebels; this definition also includes revolts in the transatlantic slave trade. Aptheker finds that there were at least 250 such slave revolts from 1526 to 1865 that affected African American slavery. In turn, he has been criticized for arguing beyond the evidence and failing to distinguish among rumor, discontent, and actual rebellion.

One of Aptheker's critics is another white Marxist historian, Eugene Genovese, author of the monumental study *Roll Jordan Roll: The World the Slaves Made*. Genovese thinks that black and leftist historians of the twentieth century have been too impressed by the notion that the masses are noble and, if not already ripe for revolt, can be educated to be so. He notes that it is sacrilege to suggest that slavery was a social system in which the vast majority lived in relative harmony, but he believes that the record shows that there was little organized, massive resistance to the slave regime. Genovese points out that there were bloody slave rebellions in the Caribbean and South America that lasted for decades, had thousands of participants, and cost hundreds of lives. Yet the record for the United States in the nineteenth century includes only the 1811 Louisiana Revolt, Nat Turner's 1831 attempt, and two others that were snuffed out before they got off the ground (one of which, Denmark Vesey's attempt in 1822 in Charleston, South Carolina, might not have occurred at all). There was no rebellion between 1831 and 1865, despite the occurrence of the Civil War. Genovese dismisses most of Aptheker's 250 revolts as panicked newspaper reports.

Genovese traces this alleged lack of a black revolutionary tradition to three factors. First was the heritage of the Africans involved in the slave system. Those in the United States came from Lower Guinea and represented more complex civilizations that had previously disciplined their people to servitude and class distinction, while the Latin countries used more Angolan and Congolese people, who lacked these cultural traits. Moreover, after the 1808 ending of the foreign slave trade, the United States had the only American-born African slave population in the world, which was even more acculturated to the New World. Genovese's second factor is the ratio of the white to black populations—in the United States this was decidedly in favor of the white master class (most Southern plantations had fewer than 20 slaves, few had over 50), which more actively patrolled and isolated blacks and put them at the mercy of white law. The third factor is the treatment of the slaves by their New World masters—which Genovese finds to be better in the United States than elsewhere, involving more food, leisure time, and family units; better housing; and less corporal punishment, epitomized by a feeling of duty and responsibility that saw many slaveowners characterize their slaves as "my people." Genovese finds that the American slave system was so repressive and yet so benign that revolt was impossible and impracticable.

Far more controversial than Genovese's view is the theory put forward by Stanley Elkins based on earlier work by his mentor, Frank Tannenbaum. Rather than seeing the U.S. slave system as the most benign, Elkins posits that it was the most repressive—so much so that it literally brainwashed the normal, varied psyche of an enslaved African into a new, warped personality, one of childlike meekness, humility, optimism, readiness to laugh and joke, happiness, and an emphasis on emotion rather than reason. Elkins refers to this character by an infamous name: "Sambo." This personality change was caused by the shock and detachment of free Africans as they were removed from their traditional milieu—the capture, march to the coast, sale and transport to the New World, resale and seasoning as a slave, and the need to internalize the standards of the new master as their own to survive. The isolation and closed nature of the new system, particularly in the United States, caused the crushing of Africanisms to the degree that the African American slave became a new cultural/racial type.

Elkins finds that the same sort of regression to childhood also occurred among European Jews incarcerated in Adolf Hitler's World War II concentration camps, which Elkins sees as comparable to the American slave system. He also poses three psychological theories to explain how this regression takes place: (1) a modified Freudian approach, in which the supposedly fixed patterns established in childhood are actually broken and reestablished by the shock of the enslavement; (2) Henry Stack Sullivan's *interpersonal theory*, which studied how immigrants became Americanized by adapting to the standards of those who held the keys to their personal security; and/or (3) an application of role psychology, in which one's role and one's self become confused through a system of reward and punishment. U.S. slavery was so pervasive as to kill all chance of rebellion, says Elkins. He points out that the rebel slave was a general type in Latin America, while in the United States the individual rebel was a noted exception. Hence U.S. slave revolts are known by those who led them—persons who developed personalities outside the norm—aberrations like Gabriel, Denmark Vesey, and Nat Turner.

But what if the "peculiar institution" was not as closed as the concentration camp, but more like a minimum-security prison? The constant terror of the camps was not present in slavery. Execution was not the goal. In such a system multiple personalities (even a false one to fool the white man and another, real one for life in the slave quarters away from white supervision) would develop. This is what many historians think actually happened under the slave regime of the American South. Kenneth Stampp joins other critics of Elkins to find at least four distinct slave personality types: Sambo, yielding, and accommodating—but who a wise master knew might become a rebel at any moment; another labeled Banzo, a type of slave common in ruthlessly exploitive and expanding slave systems, like that in Brazil or the American Old Southwest, who was overworked and fatigued to the point of not caring about life or punishment; a third called Jack, hard-working, efficient, and trustworthy, who took pride in the life of the slave quarters so long as he was treated with respect, honor, and trust; and Nat, the true rebel, a conspirator as well as an individual troublemaker, a class formed by those who never reconciled to the system, including runaways, thieves, arsonists, and saboteurs. (Naturally, the types could refer to either males or females, despite their implied gender.)

Argument as to the psychology of African American slaves continued into Reconstruction. Examinations into the Shelby Iron Works in Alabama and the Tredegar Iron Works in Virginia yielded different results. Black workers at Shelby seemed more reluctant to assert their freedom after the war. They were more interested in basic concerns such as food, shelter, and finding paying work for the next day. Freedom was not a time of joy or change—it was best met by old and tried methods that revolved around allowing the white managers to take the initiative. The black workers at Tredegar seemed less hesitant to go back to work and more willing to take the lead as freedmen. But they may have been assisted by the fact there was less damage of the industrial plant at Tredegar, by the desire of the plant's owner to get back into production using his old slave foremen and workers, and by the fact that the plant was located in the upper South, where slavery had a more benign reputation. Many of the hands had been living their own lives even as slaves and hired their own time, which carried on into freedom quite neatly.

Whether the former slaves would be independent-minded or "docile" was very important to the white South after the war. Southerners viewed the time following South Carolina's secession as the most troubling of their lives. Their whole world was upset by the Yankee victory, emancipation, and the uncertainties of Reconstruction. The white South seemed in a stir out of fear of the Sambo stereotype being replaced by free African Americans no longer compelled to do what whites deemed best. New modes of social control had to be developed. In this regard Southern whites evidenced little faith in the ability of blacks to act as free people. Whites envisioned two types of behavior from African Americans—the incorrigible rebel and the cooperative black who "knew his place" as a useful laborer. But regardless of their willingness or refusal to credit black adaptability to the new order, white Southerners believed that the place of former slaves was on the lower rungs of society, segregated from the whites until they could be taught the "responsibilities" of freedom (which revolved around the notion of servility) and free from the banal influence of Yankees, who did not "understand" blacks the way native Southern whites did. Those Southerners who believed that African Americans ought to have a modicum of civil rights or be in constant contact with whites saw this more as a way to ensure white control than as something all free peoples ought to enjoy. But above all, white Southerners wanted blacks to be industrious and happy, just like the stereotypical Sambo.

Modern sociologists have found that this imposed segregation had two different effects upon black people. Some came to hate themselves and their blackness. A lighter skin, straightened hair, and products that guaranteed them became the rage. But more often the separation led to increased black pride and a willingness on the part of African Americans to establish their own institutions for everyday survival. Black businesses grew in the late nineteenth century, as did black-owned streetcars, black churches, black libraries, black social and service clubs, black burial societies, and of course black colleges and universities. In these institutions, African Americans could live as adults, free people in every sense of the word, holding office, electing their own representatives, contributing to society in their own segregated way. In the metaphor of Booker T. Washington, blacks and whites were as separate as the five fingers and yet as unified as the whole hand.

But others wanted to go further and break what they saw as an unconscious dependency of blacks upon whites. Black thinkers like John S. Durham condemned the very African Americans whom whites admired most, the antebellum house servants, as pathetic imitators of the white man's luxurious social standards. Durham admitted that the field hands were full of ignorance and superstition, but he praised their ability to stand clear of dependence on the white man's civilization. Durham's highest praise, however, was reserved for the slave artisans and craftsmen who had developed the skills and independence of thought necessary to lead blacks into freedom. More important for African Americans' future was black writer Alexander Crummell. Although blacks were legally free, Crummell believed they would never achieve psychological independence unless they acquired a self-esteem that could only come by rediscovering both the black African past and a consciousness of social destiny. What Crummell hoped to form was an African American cultural and intellectual elite through his American Negro Academy, an organization full of college-educated blacks like W. E. Burghardt DuBois, the first black man to receive a Ph.D. from Harvard. By emphasizing what he called the "talented tenth" of blacks who were well beyond the world of the cotton patch in intellectual abilities and skills, DuBois hoped to develop an indigenous black middle class of white-collar workers and business owners—which came to be called in the twentieth-century North as the "New Negro."

See also African American Education in Reconstruction; African Americans and Reconstruction; Disfranchisement; Segregation (Jim Crow).

References Aptheker, Herbert, *American Negro Slave Revolts* (1943); Barr, Alwyn, "The Texas 'Black Uprising' Scare of 1883" (1980); Dew, Charles B., "Disciplining Slave Ironworkers in the Antebellum South" (1974) and *Ironmaker to the Confederacy* (1966); Elkins, Stanley M., *Slavery* (1959); Friedman, Lawrence J., "The Search for Docility" (1970); Genovese, Eugene D., *Roll Jordan Roll* (1974); Lane, Ann J., *The Debate over Slavery* (1971); Lynd, Staughton, "Rethinking Slavery and Reconstruction" (1965); McKenzie, Robert H., "The Shelby Iron Company" (1973); Meier, August, *Negro Thought in America* (1966); Stampp, Kenneth M., *The Era of Reconstruction* (1965); Tannenbaum, Frank, *Slave and Citizen* (1947); Toll, William, "Free Men, Freedmen, and Race" (1978); Wagstaff, Thomas, "Call Your Old Master—'Master'" (1969); Wood, Forrest G., *Black Scare* (1968).

Blaine, James G. (1830–1893)

James G. Blaine, perhaps the key politician of the Republican party after the end of Military Reconstruction in 1870 during the Gilded Age, was born in Pennsylvania. His parents moved the family to the Pittsburgh region, where Blaine received the best education available, including studies at Washington College, which allowed him to start his career of teaching. He taught at Georgetown Military School in Kentucky, found that he did not like the South, and returned to Pennsylvania to teach at the state school for the blind. At the same time he began to study law. He married Harriet Stanwood twice (there was some doubt as to the legality of the first ceremony), and through her family he managed to get into journalism in her home state of Maine, eventually buying the *Kennebec Journal.* From 1854 on he would be identified with his adopted state; he and his wife would raise seven children there, and his whole political career would take place out of there. He joined the Congregational Church and adopted the mores and social attitudes of upper New England. Blaine had a magnetic quality that naturally attracted people to him and his ideas; hence he was a perfect politician. He spoke magnificently and possessed a regal bearing that led to his political moniker, the "Plumed Knight." He never forgot a name or a face, an indispensable quality in dealing with the public.

Blaine got his political ideas from his family's old Whig associations. He was an admirer of Whig party organizer Henry Clay and, like Clay, was an advocate of nationalizing measures. But when Blaine went into his newspaper career, the Whig party was in dire straits, splitting up over the slavery issue. In writing on the Kansas-Nebraska Bill, Blaine took notice of the fledgling Republican party and was instrumental in organizing and publicizing its appearance in Maine. What he liked was not only its moralistic stand against slavery but its economic measures, which aped Henry Clay's old American System: the tariff, internal improvements, the national banking system, and free land in the West. Maine was rather isolated geographically on the American continent, but it possessed two real advantages for a political career—it had its elections first, making it the political trendsetter for the nation, and it possessed more than its fair share of brilliant politicians. The competition was good and intellectual. Moreover, after the contest, Maine politicos supported each other in Washington, and the voters kept them in office for long periods of time.

Blaine began his political life by becoming head of the state's Republican party in 1858, a post he held until 1881. In 1858 he was elected to the state legislature, the first of three terms, and served as speaker for four years. He was admired as a careful politician. Blaine had a reason for everything he did. His speeches were fine-tuned works of art that tended to give the listener more information about policy than most politician's efforts. He was not a windbag. In 1863, after winning a Union party (Republican and War Democrats allied together) victory for President Abraham Lincoln's war effort, Blaine entered Congress, serving in the House of Representatives until 1876 (he was speaker from 1869 to 1875) and in the Senate until 1881. During this time Blaine became a national figure. He was among the first to support African American suffrage. But he did not follow the lead of Radicals Charles Sumner or Thaddeus Stevens, the normal party bigwigs. Blaine joined with men like James Garfield and James Ashley of Ohio, which gave him a good position among the men who would carry the Republican standard after Military Reconstruction.

Indeed, Blaine regarded Stevens's death in 1868 as an "emancipation for the Republican party." When queried who would take Stevens's place, Blaine replied that he could see three men—the first two were Garfield and William B. Allison of Iowa; then, looking wistfully at the capitol dome, he smiled and said with feigned modesty that he did not know the other. During the Ulysses S. Grant administration, Blaine supported coming together with the South, opposing the Enforcement Acts. It is not that Blaine was a bigot so much as he had other plans in mind for the nation—issues like tariffs, taxes, currency, national expansion through railroads, and the United States' step onto the world stage—and Reconstruction was drawing away resources needed elsewhere. But Blaine also was not above "waving the bloody shirt" (i.e., telling graphic stories of conservative white political violence in the South) when it suited his purposes. He cleverly manipulated the issues of the Grant era to emerge as a Liberal Republican with Stalwart, or old Radical Republican, principles. He was very loyal and forward-looking but

James G. Blaine

not an extremist. But his personal enmity with Roscoe Conkling of New York would lead to many a party scrap that Blaine would have done well to avoid. The two were much the same, with conflicting ambitions for the White House. Gradually the party formed around them, the somewhat more idealistic Half-Breeds with Blaine, and the more crass Stalwarts with Conkling.

Oddly, as much as Blaine admired Clay, he would find that the presidency would elude him as much as it did "Harry of the West," and for the same reasons—corruption, or at least the appearance of it. Blaine's problem was the "Mulligan letters," which detailed Blaine's actions in an Arkansas railroad fraud. These letters came to light in the 1876 campaign, at a time when Blaine was rumored to be the Republican choice for president. He managed to secure the documents, refused to make them public as he had promised, and then read heavily censored selections to the House. These documents showed that Blaine had managed to save a federal land grant for the railroad in question and that, in exchange, the grateful executives worked out a secret scheme where Blaine could sell company bonds on commission. The scheme allegedly failed to gain Blaine any money and it lost money for the friends who invested. Blaine was mortified and made good on his friends' money losses, but he displayed regard only for his cronies and a disregard for any public interest (though such behavior was standard practice at the time). His problem was that this information looked bad at a time when certain Republicans hoped to put the Grant scandals behind them and appear more honest to the voters. The fact that Blaine became quite wealthy with no visible means of support beyond his congressional salary raised suspicions that his alleged losses in Arkansas were in truth vast profits achieved at public expense. The result was that the nomination went to squeaky-clean Rutherford B. Hayes, despite Blaine's penitent crying bout to reporters on the capitol steps.

Blaine never got over being bit by the presidential bug. He immediately began preparing for 1880. But at the convention Conkling and the Stalwarts were so against Blaine that the party turned to Garfield. As a consolation prize, Blaine was made secretary of state, a prospect that angered many Stalwarts and probably helped lead to Garfield's assassination by a disaffected office seeker. With Garfield's death, Blaine felt obliged to tender his resignation to the new president, Chester A. Arthur, Conkling's right-hand man in New York. But Arthur asked him to stay on. Blaine remained a few months, but his influence with Arthur was nil, and he left the administration to concentrate on the 1884 election. By this time, Blaine was the admitted choice of a majority of the party. His faction was gaining in power, helped by Arthur's conversion to civil service reform, and Blaine finally received the nomination. But the Democratic choice was a real reformer, Grover Cleveland, and the lingering suspicion about the Mulligan letters caused the reform-minded Liberal Republicans to bolt the party and vote for the Democrat. Then, at the end of the campaign, one of the dirtiest in American history (Cleveland had fathered a child out of wedlock, which made him a perfect target for a smear campaign), one of Blaine's supporters called Cleveland the representative of the party "whose antecedents are rum, Romanism [in reference to Roman Catholicism], and rebellion." The result was a change in enough Irish Catholic city votes to cost Blaine the contest narrowly.

Blaine retired to write his memoirs and a collection of his speeches. He declined to run in 1888 unless he received a unanimous nomination, an impossible condition. But under the victorious Republican standard bearer, Benjamin Harrison, Blaine was returned to the post of secretary of state. It was this term that made Blaine's reputation in American history. He was one of the few to foresee that the United States' future lay in the world at large, and he worked to start it off right. He readopted the pan-American notions that had been part of Henry Clay's program under the John Quincy Adams administration. Under the theme "America for the Americans," Blaine strengthened the United States' desire to build, without international support, a canal through the isthmus between North and South America, favoring a Nicaraguan route that would not be abandoned until Theodore Roosevelt decided on Panama. He stood between Latin America and Europe, refusing to allow the collection of debts owed by force but guaranteeing that the United States would enforce collection itself, which he did by negotiation rather than force. He mediated territorial disputes between Mexico and Guatemala and between Chile and Peru. He called a Pan-American Congress and drew up several trading treaties, favoring a policy of negotiated reciprocity over congressionally mandated tariffs. He began the series of events that led to the annexation of the Hawaiian Islands after he left office. He claimed that the Bering Sea was an enclosed body of water under the sole control of the United States.

Blaine retired ahead of the Harrison presidency in 1892, once again looking to gain the presidential nomination, but he was soon diagnosed as having Bright's disease, from which he died in early 1893. So passed the most important Republican of his time, and the only outstanding American in foreign policy between William H. Seward and John Hay. He was instrumental in moving the United States away from its concern with internal matters typified by the Civil War and Reconstruction and toward what Blaine and many others of his day thought were more important: building a unified nation and inserting the United States into its rightful place in the world. As such, the problems of Reconstruction and the place of African Americans as free persons were far from his mind and peripheral to his main concerns. He unwisely used the war to score political points—an act that cost Blaine his best chance at the presidency, a goal he ultimately found unattainable.

See also Conkling, Roscoe; Garfield, James A.; Hayes, Rutherford B.

References Fish, Carl Russell, "James Gillespie Blaine" (1964–1981); Muzzey, David S., *James G. Blaine* (1934); Russell, Charles Edward, *Blaine of Maine* (1931).

Brown, Joseph E. (1821–1894)

A Scalawag politician so flexible in his political principles and so adroit at changing sides that he was, according to historian C. Mildred Thompson, "first in secession, first in reconstruction, and very nearly first in redemption," Joseph E. Brown was born in South Carolina. His family moved to the Georgia backcountry, where his father farmed. Brown was educated at Anderson Academy in South Carolina; he taught school briefly and read law, being admitted to the bar in 1845. He also attended Yale Law School with the support of a benefactor. He married Elizabeth Gresham in 1847. Brown was a staunch prewar Democrat and a lifelong Baptist. Before the war Brown served one term in the state legislature and was appointed to the Georgia superior court in 1855. He resigned to become Georgia's governor in 1857 and was reelected every two years until his resignation in 1865.

Brown was considered the common man's candidate for governor and a radical state rights advocate. He was a red-hot se-

cessionist, so in favor of leaving the Union that he did not even await the secession of his state before calling for the seizure of Fort Pulaski near Savannah in December 1860. Though he led the way in seceding from the Union and joining the Confederacy, Brown remained opposed to central government. During the war he kept military supplies back from the armies in the field for the exclusive use of Georgia troops; he permitted legal draft dodging by enrolling a large number of able-bodied men in the home-guard Georgia Militia (about whom the derogatory folk song "Eatin' Goober Peas" was written); and although he encouraged the planting of food crops as opposed to staples when subsistence became critical after 1862, his pro–state rights population refused to heed his interference with their individual right to choose. He allied with fellow Georgian, Confederate vice president Alexander Stephens, in opposing Jefferson Davis's hearty prosecution of the war and no-surrender policy by trying to end the war through direct negotiation with the Yankees. Actions like these have caused many historians since to theorize that the South lost the war because of excessive adherence to state rights.

At the end of the war, Brown was arrested for calling a special session of the state legislature in violation of military orders and was taken to Carroll Prison in Washington, D.C., where several other arrested Confederate governors were lodged. He negotiated his own pardon from President Andrew Johnson by repenting of his secession as a mistake determined on the field of battle. Brown pledged to work for the restoration of Georgia to the Union and returned to Georgia to practice law at Atlanta. He accepted the terms of the Military Reconstruction Acts in 1867 and switched to the Republican party. This could be viewed as Brown keeping his promise to President Johnson, but more likely Brown wanted to control the party's initial Radical tendencies, prevalent among blacks and Scalawag yeoman farmers, to seize the state's plantations and divide up the land among themselves. Meanwhile he used his Republican political connections to dabble in railroad stocks and secure valuable real estate. For these properties to have any future value, Brown believed that Reconstruction had to be completed and Georgia returned to normal times.

Georgia Republican leaders could not have cared less about Brown's motives. They needed his name and organizing abilities behind the scenes at the state constitutional convention in 1868. But many Democrats did not feel so charitable. In the legislative election for U.S. senators, Brown lost to other candidates. Although Brown actively campaigned for Republican gubernatorial candidate Rufus Bullock (who won), he was very lukewarm in his support of Ulysses S. Grant for president. Grant lost in Georgia, largely because of Ku Klux Klan intimidation and race riots at Albany and Savannah, which reduced the large Republican majorities as of spring 1867 to negligible ones in the fall of 1868. In what critics saw as a blatant political payoff, Governor Bullock appointed Brown chief justice for the state supreme court. Brown served for a year and a half, ostensibly resigning to devote full time to his businesses.

In reality, however, Brown had been keeping a close eye on Republicanism in Georgia and found it lacking. The party was unable to prevent the expulsion of black legislators on a trumped-up technicality or to counter rising Ku Klux Klan raids in the countryside. The Republicans had had to call on the U.S. Army to reconstruct Georgia a second time by purging Democrats who could not take the ironclad oath (one of never having aided the Confederacy) in favor of their Republican runners-up. (The same thing happened in other states, like Texas and Mississippi, but in those cases the army was smart enough to take action before the legislature sat and Reconstruction ended.) At this point Governor Bullock's term was set to last until 1872, but the legislature would come up for reelection in 1871. The new body promised to be composed of anti-Bullock Republicans and Democrats, who had already threatened to impeach the governor. Only military intervention kept him in power, and Bullock saw no security in that.

At Brown's urging, backed by the approval of Democrats eager to be rid of Republican rule so easily, Bullock resigned from office and fled the state. Seeing that the future was not going to be determined by the feeble Republican administration of Reconstruction Acts, Brown took this opportunity to denounce Republicanism and switched back to the Democrats. Of course, he led the way in blaming all corruption on the departed governor, who in reality was as clean as could be, but it gave all Georgia Scalawags and home-born corruptionists a quick route to respectability. And it allowed Brown to complete a full circle in his political loyalties—Democrat before the war, secessionist in 1861, war opponent in 1863, Johnson and Union man in 1865, Radical Republican in 1867, Liberal Republican in 1872, and Democrat again in 1876.

Brown made his final conversion to the Democrats by doing them a favor in the neighboring state of Florida. The 1876 electoral vote there and in other states was in dispute. The Republicans needed all 20 votes in question to win the presidency. The Democrats needed but one. The Democratic National Committee asked Brown to go down and see that Florida stayed in the proper (Democratic) column. Brown labored mightily but could not get the Democratic victory counted. The Republicans still held the governing authority and counted their men in, locally and nationally. But Brown's willingness to go and document the Republican fraud, even when he was in poor health, put him in good stead with the Democrats back home. He also wrote several poignant editorials in Atlanta newspapers comparing the Republican win to the "Corrupt Bargain" of 1824, when Andrew Jackson had been cheated out of the presidency. When Georgia revised its Reconstruction constitution in 1877, Democrats began to bandy about his name for governor or U.S. senator.

Exactly what brought Brown together with his post-Reconstruction allies is unclear, but his desire to return to a modicum of respectability was an important part of it. Another part of it had to do with the desires of newspaper editor Henry B. Grady of the *Atlanta Constitution* to make Atlanta the rail center of the South. It all started when U.S. Senator John B. Gordon, a Confederate war hero and spokesman for sectional reconciliation on the basis of economic exploitation of the South and West, unexpectedly resigned his position. He had only a short time to serve, but the resignation allowed the governor, Alfred H. Colquitt, to appoint a successor. He picked Brown, even though Brown was still hated by many for being a Reconstruction Scalawag. Brown, Gordon, and Colquitt became known as "the triumvirate." From here on out, despite cries of collusion, the general pattern in Georgia was for one to be governor and the other two to be U.S. senators on an alternating basis, a process that ran Georgia through political patronage, peonage, the convict lease, and other graft and corruption until the Spanish-American War. But big business never had anything to fear from these men, who clearly represented what the "New South"—loyal, industrialized, and "Yankee-fied"—meant to the American public.

Politically secure, Brown also made a fortune in private business in Atlanta real estate, convict leases, and railroads after Georgia was "redeemed" (i.e., conservative white rule was reestablished). But try as he might, he could never buy back the respect that yeoman white farmers had given him before and during the war, when he was their best ally. In a last-ditch attempt Brown even flirted with the Populist Party just before his death in 1894. Hated by many, admired by the rest, Joe Brown had shown an uncanny ability over his controversial lifetime to come to the top with every turn of the wheel and make a fortune doing it.

See also Scalawags.

References Conway, Alan, *The Reconstruction of Georgia* (1966); Duncan, Russell, *Entrepreneur for Equality* (1994); Eckert, Ralph Lowell, *John Brown Gordon* (1989); Hesseltine, William B., and Larry Gara, "Georgia's Confederate Leaders after Appomattox" (1951); Nathans, Elizabeth Studley, *Losing the Peace* (1968); Parks, Joseph H., *Joseph E. Brown of Georgia* (1977); Roberts, Derrell C., *Joseph E. Brown and the Politics of Reconstruction* (1973); Thompson, C. Mildred, *Reconstruction in Georgia* (1915); Wakelyn, Jon L., *Biographical Dictionary of the Confederacy* (1977).

Brownlow, William G. (1805–1877)

Born in Wythe County, Virginia, William G. Brownlow became one of the most noted Scalawag politicians in the South. In his earliest years, his extended family kept moving south and west through the Appalachian highlands until most of them reached eastern Tennessee. By the time he was five years old both his father and mother had died. He and his brothers and sisters were sent to live with various relatives. Brownlow wound up with his uncle and grew hard and strong in the life of a mountain farmer. He had a rudimentary education, made better by an insatiable desire to read everything he could get his hands on. He apprenticed himself to a carpenter but found his true calling at a Methodist camp meeting, and he took up the duties of a circuit rider. Henceforth he would be known as "the Parson." He would have the strong convictions of an evangelical not only in religion but in his politics. He would speak in the words of religious argument, which made him an effective speaker and writer among people who thought the same, which included most of Tennessee. In 1836 he married Eliza O'Brien, with whom he had seven children.

Brownlow's first political utterances were in upland South Carolina in the 1830s, where he spoke out against the nullification theory of John C. Calhoun. He also pinned the blue cockade of the nullifiers to stray dogs as a sign of his disrespect. He took up writing, immodestly beginning with his autobiography and moving on to religious doctrine (he hated Presbyterians, believing them to be false thinkers and nullifiers) and politics. Although he was a Union man as strong as Andrew Jackson, Brownlow preferred the politics of Jackson's archrival, Henry Clay. So he named his newspaper *The Whig*, after Clay's Whig party—Whig because it opposed the policies of "King

William G. Brownlow

Andrew I of Veto Memory" as their revolutionary forebears had challenged those of George III. He was outspoken and was hated as much as admired, and like all Southern editors he was frequently shot at. It took real courage to put one's views before the public in those days. His views on slavery and plantation aristocrats were relatively mild. He believed that slaves were better off than free blacks, and he opposed those who wished to end the institution. He positively hated Jackson's political heir, Andrew Johnson, and lambasted the man continuously and very personally. He thought

himself quite a politician, but he was not an officeholder. Like many border-state Southerners, Brownlow backed the Constitutional Union party in 1860 and its candidate, former Whig John Bell from Tennessee.

Although Brownlow was a Bell supporter in 1860, he recognized the Lincoln victory and vowed to protect the government from the radical secessionists. When Tennessee joined the Rebel states in May 1861 (before its own secession), he condemned Governor Isham Harris's Confederate alliance as "the most outrageous, high-handed and infamous legislation ever known in the civilized world," virtually handing the populace a *fait accompli* on behalf of secession. This did not stop Brownlow. He called on every man to vote and give the Rebels the setback of their lives at the polls. Andrew Johnson came in from Washington, his train booed at every junction, to help rally antisecession sentiment. But the ordinance of secession carried by a voting ratio of 2 to 1. Brownlow announced that he would be available as a Union candidate, running on the platform of Lincoln's first inaugural speech, but he became ill and had to leave the contest to other men. The result was a pro-Confederate win and Harris's reelection.

With the fall of Fort Donelson in 1862 and the occupation of Nashville, Andrew Johnson became the provisional military governor. Johnson's prior support of the Breckinridge-Southern Democratic ticket in 1860 came back to haunt him in East Tennessee, as did his long-standing personal feud with Parson Brownlow. Brownlow knew that Johnson's legal standing was doubtful. It depended upon the guarantee clause of the Constitution in which Congress is charged with seeing that each state has a republican form of government (in reference to political theory, not a particular party). But Johnson held on through threats against his life and Confederate invasion. Meanwhile eastern Tennessee spent most of the war under Confederate military government. It was part of a critical railroad hookup between the eastern seaboard and the Deep South. Guerrilla warfare of the bloodiest kind was visited upon the population. Brownlow kept publishing his newspaper, the Knoxville *Whig*, until he was arrested and held for a short period of time as disloyal to the Confederate cause—an obvious understatement. When asked to be chaplain of a Confederate regiment, he snorted contemptuously, "When I shall have made up my mind to go to Hell, I will cut my throat and go direct, not travel around by way of the Southern Confederacy." Brownlow soon was run out of the state.

Not until the waning days of 1863 were the Yankees able to hold eastern Tennessee. Returning with the federal armies, Brownlow resumed publishing his paper, which he renamed the *Whig and Rebel Ventilator*, and once again he castigated the Confederacy and the plantation aristocracy, whom he blamed for the war. Although Tennessee voted in the election of 1864, with white voters who would not take the ironclad oath (of never having given aid to the Confederacy) prevented from voting, the overall vote was not counted. Shortly afterward, a convention met at Nashville under the Lincoln Plan of Reconstruction, and a new state constitution was drawn up that disallowed slavery and had a separate ordinance drafted to negate the Confederate military alliance. More than the required 10 percent of the voters approved of these measures, and on 5 April 1865, William G. Brownlow became the first elected loyal governor of Tennessee since the war had begun.

Brownlow had a typical Southern attitude when it came to people he hated. He condemned them in the vilest terms as a group but was quite forgiving to individuals. One of his first tasks as governor was to secure a pardon from President Andrew Johnson for former governor Isham Harris. In his inaugural address, Brownlow declared himself to be against slavery as an institution and vowed to promote the power of the federal government at the expense of the states. He praised the Union victory and promised no quarter for the Confederates. The Tennessee legislature was no Carpetbag body, but it was perhaps the largest

Scalawag institution in the whole nation. Much of its representation came from eastern Tennessee and from those in other parts of the state who had remained neutral during the war. As yet no blacks could vote—that would come only with the Fourteenth Amendment in 1868. Brownlow was in full agreement with the legislature on this point. The legislature did little to advance the cause of blacks as free persons beyond passing basic civil rights legislation. But Brownlow helped pass a law, much like the later federal Enforcement Acts, that prohibited one from using the state's roads or entering another's house for illegal activities and punishing any official who refused to prosecute such persons or any witness who refused to testify in such cases. Punishment included fines ranging from $500 to $20,000 and jail terms up to five years. His campaigns against the Ku Klux Klan were known locally as the "Brownlow Wars."

Brownlow's most important program was to keep Confederate whites from voting too soon and trying to upset the process of Reconstruction for the next five years. State courts declared voting in elections to be a privilege, not a right, that could be restricted, limited, or withheld at the pleasure of the sovereign people through their legislature. The test oath, usually ironclad (that is, an oath that the person had never given any support of any kind to the Confederacy as opposed to an oath of future loyalty to the Union), was required for practically everything under the law from voting, to running for office, to acting as plaintiff in a lawsuit. No marriage license was to be issued if the bride-to-be could not take the oath of loyalty. The Confederate uniform was banned from any public place. Business stocks held by secessionists were to be seized by the state.

An idea of how Brownlow's well-led forces worked can be obtained from Tennessee's passage of the Fourteenth Amendment; Tennessee was the only former Confederate state to do so. When Democrats boycotted the legislature, denying it a quorum, the speaker had four of them arrested. The detained men got a writ of habeas corpus. The legislature impeached and removed the judge from office for issuing the writ, and it hauled two of the detained Democrats into the legislature. A quorum was declared, the two refusing to speak or vote. When the speaker got a sudden, belated attack of fairness and refused to sign the vote, the president pro tem did it and the speaker was impeached and removed from office. Then Brownlow sent the ratification to Congress: "We have fought the battle and won it,... two of Andrew Johnson's tools not voting. Give my respects to the dead dog of the White House!" For its astuteness and Brownlow's leadership, Tennessee was declared to be readmitted to the Union in 1866, the only Southern state so honored at that point.

By 1868, however, it was becoming obvious that conservative (i.e., Democratic) forces would soon control state government. In 1869, as sort of a swan song, the Scalawag Republican legislature elected Governor Brownlow to the U.S. Senate, displacing Andrew Johnson's son-in-law at the same time that President-elect Ulysses S. Grant was replacing Johnson. Although Brownlow's mind was as sharp as ever, his body was worn out by his years of vigorous campaigning for the Union. He attended all of the Senate sessions of his six-year term but the last. He hated former Confederates and detested newly declared Scalawags like James Longstreet, who had tried to subdue eastern Tennessee for the South. To Brownlow a real Scalawag had to have been a wartime Union man. Nothing else was good enough.

Brownlow did little as senator beyond relish the passage of the Enforcement Acts and call for Tennessee's subjugation under them, which never happened. It seemed that God had willed that Brownlow live long enough to see his handiwork as the premier Unionist of the South undone. Not only did he live to see the Redemption of the entire region, he also suffered the humiliation of being succeeded by his old Democratic enemy, Andrew Johnson, in the Senate. Brownlow was too vindictive to be considered a statesman, and he lacked the training. But he was a natural for an era in which extremes often meant the difference between life or death, political success or failure. He was fearless, even reckless. He was the champion of the Union when it was an unpopular and dangerous cause. He remained a product of his times, a Scalawag Union man to the day he died.

See also Johnson and Reconstruction; Moderate Republicans and Reconstruction; Scalawags.

References Alexander, Thomas B., "Strange Bedfellows" (1952); Bergeron, Paul H., *Antebellum Politics in Tennessee* (1982); Coulter, E. Merton, *William G. Brownlow* (1937); Haskins, Ralph W., "Internecine Strife in Tennessee" (1965); Patton, James Welch, *Unionism and Reconstruction in Tennessee* (1934); Trefousse, Hans L., *Andrew Johnson* (1989).

Bruce, Blanche K. (1841–1898)

Born a slave in Farmville, Virginia, Blanche K. Bruce was taken by his owner to Missouri. His early life was much the same as that of his master's son, with whom Bruce played and learned, sharing a tutor (contrary to state laws against teaching blacks to read and write). At the outbreak of the Civil War, Bruce escaped to the Union lines in Kansas (he could have gone earlier during the Kansas-Missouri Border Wars, but he was always a cautious person) and returned as a free man to open a school for blacks at Hannibal and to learn the printing trade. He then studied for two years at Oberlin College in Ohio after the war and moved to Mississippi, where he had once lived briefly as a boy, and where, by saving and investing his meager salary, he eventually became a wealthy planter. He leased plantations, founded the town of Floreyville (wisely named after a local Carpetbagger of much political influence), and invested in abandoned lands.

After the passage of Military Reconstruction Acts in Congress, Bruce noted the dearth of African American politicians in the predominantly black Delta region and entered Republican politics, serving as sheriff, tax collector, county superintendent of schools, and member of the state levee board. He was also commissioner of elections and sergeant-at-arms in the state senate. Bruce had a dignified bearing, handsome look, and magnificent physique. He always kept vindictive statements and actions out of his policies, which appealed to many whites. He had much competition in Mississippi politics, including white Scalawags and Carpetbaggers, as well as many qualified blacks like John R. Lynch, Hiram Revels, and innumerable others. But Bruce had carefully stayed aloof from party factions and had the support of influential whites from the Delta. All sides competed for him, and finally the Radicals under Carpetbagger Adelbert Ames offered him the lieutenant governorship. Bruce declined; he wanted the U.S. Senate seat, a prized plum. By 1874 he was elected senator and became the first African American to serve a full term in that body (1875–1881), although Hiram Revels of Mississippi had been the first black Senator for the short two-year term starting in 1870 (this was done as a matter of course to stagger the election of senators throughout the South as their states rejoined the Union).

In the Senate, Bruce was escorted to the swearing-in by New York senator Roscoe Conkling (Mississippi's other senator, James L. Alcorn, was a political enemy back home), who remained Bruce's mentor despite having a reputation as a spoilsman (i.e., one who uses political office for personal gain). Bruce served on the committees on manufactures, education and labor, pensions, and the improvement of the Mississippi River and its tributaries. He opposed the removal of federal troops from the South, and he spoke out in favor of the admission of P. B. S. Pinchback as senator from Louisiana (Pinchback was not seated) and on the denial of black civil rights in North and South. But he failed to back up Governor Ames when the latter's government was run out of the state, believing (as did black Mississippi congressman John R. Lynch) that Ames's mismanagement had cost the party its control back home. He also attacked the Chinese Exclusion Bill and stood for a decent policy toward Native Americans, believing that the measures employed against them, like those against black

Blanche K. Bruce, the first African American to serve a full term in the Senate (1875–1881)

Americans, were contrary to American political principles. A temperance advocate who believed in frugal living habits, Bruce did much to clear up the defunct Freedmen's Savings and Trust Company and distribute its resources among the depositors.

Meanwhile, Bruce formed a triumvirate—composed of him (as national spokesman in Washington), Lynch (as head of the state party dispensing patronage), and James Hill (the black secretary of state under Ames who worked with local candidates and recommended appointments)—to wrest control of the Mississippi Republican party from whites. These three men managed to hold their influence until the 1890s, losing out only after the state disfranchised blacks under the limits of the Fifteenth Amendment by using literacy tests. Oddly, the triumvirate gave most of its political favors to whites, leaving few jobs for black supporters. This went along with Bruce's commitment to black acceptance in American society through assimilation. In the late 1870s he opposed the exodus of blacks (mostly from Mississippi) who traveled to Kansas to avoid discrimination, partly because he was a planter, like many whites, and partly because he believed that it represented running from the problem rather than trying to solve it where it existed. But while he spoke up in the Senate for aid to the participants of the exodus, he refused any such support for those who wanted to emigrate to Liberia on the African continent. He maintained that blacks in the United States were Americans and were no longer African any more than any other immigrants who had settled here.

Upon completion of his term Bruce continued his influence in Washington when he accepted an appointment from President James A. Garfield as registrar of the U.S. Treasury. He never went back to Mississippi. When he lost his government job to the incoming Grover Cleveland Democratic administration in the mid-1880s, he moved temporarily to Indiana, where he had relatives. Under the Benjamin Harrison administration (1889–1893), Bruce was recorder of deeds for the District of Columbia. By this time he was aware that the Northern Republicans would not protect Southern blacks when the Lodge Enforcement Bill failed in 1890. After a two-year hiatus occasioned by the return of Grover Cleveland's Democrats to Washington, both Bruce and Booker T. Washington were mentioned as possible cabinet appointees, but nothing came of it. Bruce managed, however, to regain his old treasury job and remained there until his death in 1898 from diabetic complications.

See also African Americans and Reconstruction; Alcorn, James Lusk; Ames, Adelbert; Exodusters; Revels, Hiram.

References Harris, William C., "Blanche K. Bruce of Mississippi" (1982); Houston, G. David, "A Negro Senator" (1922); Low, W. Augustus, and Virgil A. Clift, *Encyclopedia of Black America* (1981); Mann, Kenneth Eugene, "Blanche Kelso Bruce" (1976); McFarlin, Annjeannette Sophia, *Black Congressional Reconstruction Orators and Their Orations* (1976); Shapiro, Samuel, "A Black Senator from Mississippi: Blanche K. Bruce" (1982); Urofsky, Melvin I., "Blanche K. Bruce: United States Senator" (1967).

Bureau of Refugees, Freedmen, and Abandoned Lands (Freedmen's Bureau)

Created in the spring of 1865, the Bureau of Refugees, Freedmen, and Abandoned Lands, known as the Freedmen's Bureau, had as its goal, in simplest terms, to provide a shortcut from slavery to freedom for the South's 4 million African Americans. It would call for the greatest dedication, massive understanding, and unimaginable patience. It was a noble challenge, an opportunity to enrich the liberty of a whole people. But the failure of its charge could lead to disaster beyond comprehension. Established as a bureau in the U.S. Army under the secretary of war, the Freedmen's Bureau was a quasi-military organization governed by the articles of war. It consisted of a commissioner (Maj. Gen. Oliver Otis Howard) and his staff in Washington, as well as 10 (later 12) assistant commissioners in the field who would control the relationship between blacks and whites in 16 states and 2 territories below the Mason-Dixon line. Just who made up state and local bureau policies beyond the general guidelines from Washington is debatable. The responsibility lay with the assistant commissioners, but it is possible that they delegated most of the decision-making to unnamed staff officers. The core of bureau work, however, would be conducted by the numerous field agents under the assistant commissioners, another group that wound up making more policy. Their agencies would establish direct contact between the ex-slaves and the planters and between the newly freed African Americans and the average whites, who considered emancipation and equal rights to be a cruel joke played by Yankees for the Southern loss of the Civil War.

Being a bureau field agent would prove to be a difficult and dangerous job. In Texas, for example, 19 of the 234 field operatives (over 8 percent) died during their terms of service over a three-year period (1865–1868), 14 from disease, 1 in an accident, and 4 from bullets. Another 27 agents (roughly 12 percent) were the victims of assaults, all involving fisticuffs except for two that entailed firearms. Excluding the 15 disease and accident victims, 31 agents (over 13 percent) were the victims of some form of violence during their terms of office. Including disease and accident victims, about one in five faced an actual life-threatening or potentially life-threatening situation during his service. The morbidity among agents revealed that Northern whites were not as inured to the South's semitropical climate and its diseases as locals might be. The rates of assault and murder give stark testimony to the effect that bureau men had or potentially could have in a planting area, as well as the deep resentment it stirred among whites, unaccustomed as they were to the new social order.

The new order was puzzling to nineteenth-century Americans because the bureau entered the lives of Southern blacks and whites at many levels usually reserved for individual (as opposed to governmental) action. Initially, the bureau's main job was to help black and white refugees dispossessed by the war to return home. Indeed, many historians think that had the bureau not been charged with the function of assisting white loyal refugees, its enabling legislation might not have passed Congress. In the summer of 1865, all Southerners seemed to be moving. Much of this traveling was on the part of blacks. The whites saw this as typical of black "shiftlessness," indicating a people so irresponsible that they would not stay home and do their work. To some degree, the army agreed with this view and often helped planters capture and take black workers back to the plantations from where they came or required blacks to have passes to move about, lest they be declared vagrants and put to work on public projects like roads and bridges.

It is true that many former slaves tested their freedom by doing the one thing forbidden to them during slavery—they went down the road to see what was there. It was something a truly free person could do. Often, they soon returned home and reluctantly went back to the fields. But many African Americans had a more important purpose in their travels. They sought family and loved ones sold away years before. They wanted to find their wives, husbands, children, and old friends. So they wandered to those places where they had last seen or heard that their loved ones had been. Many Louisiana and Arkansas planters had taken their slaves into Texas for safe keeping during the war. These blacks now wanted to go back to their old homesteads and reunite with their families. Few of these black travelers had enough food to keep going. Many did not know where they were going. But the bureau helped them with sustenance, medicines, transport, direction, and care. The same was done for loyal, pro-Union whites, driven out of their homes through persecution during the war. But the bureau's refugee responsibilities, which included doling out rations, clothing, tents for temporary shelter, and transportation vouchers, were soon completed by early 1866.

The bureau's completion of its first task left the other functions spelled out in its full title: abandoned lands and freedmen. Throughout the war, a large group of reformers had been interested in giving the freed slaves an economic base of independence through the family farm, a concept evident in the phrase "40 acres and a mule." The former slaves were enthusiastic about the idea. In the South Carolina Sea Islands, land distribution had worked out well. The black farmers usually raised food crops rather than cash crops, but some even put in cotton. In the Mississippi Valley the government had put fugitive slaves to work on government-owned plantations leased out to loyal persons. The regulations concerning treatment of laborers on these government-operated farms became the basis for some of the first bureau directives. They did not really recognize the blacks as truly free, but they provided a minimum wage, set some standard as to treatment, and eschewed corporal punishment. But as the Mississippi Valley and other wartime experiments demonstrated, the government was in possession of thousands of acres of abandoned lands, especially in Southern states, where the armies had passed or the Confederate government had set up war industries.

Bureau operatives cautioned Commissioner Howard to make quick work of granting small farms to the freed people. They feared that President Andrew Johnson's liberal pardon policy would return white landowners to reclaim property in short order. Many of the plots had been seized under federal laws that provided for government title only temporarily. Small 20- to 40-acre plots were leased to black farmers and their families, with the bureau hoping to finance much of its work from this income. All over the Southern states blacks gathered at bureau headquarters hoping to receive their land grant at Christmas 1865, as rumor promised. Whites began to arm themselves, expecting a riot when the truth was learned. President Johnson, despite his initial statements about punishing Rebels, was patently against confiscation of property. He forced Howard to reverse the bureau's policy, with the result that the only freedmen who managed to

gain any kind of land were those in the Sea Islands along the South Atlantic coast. It was a disappointing and embittering experience for African Americans to see their little farms given back to the former slavemasters. But there would be more disappointments to come.

The biggest responsibility that the bureau faced after the war was protecting African Americans in their freedom. In essence this meant that the bureau took the place of the slavery system. Various labor systems had been tried during the war on the Sea Islands, on the occupied sections of the peninsula of Virginia, and in the states along the Mississippi Valley, especially Louisiana. By 1865, the bureau managers had some idea of the type of system needed to ensure labor for the South's staple crops to return the section to prosperity. They also had some idea of what had to be done to keep blacks at work and protect them from vicious and crooked contractors who might exploit them. This was not to be a kind system; anyone without a contract and visible means of support was treated like a

Freedmen line up to receive rations from the Freedmen's Bureau in this undated engraving. The Freedmen's Bureau was created in 1865 to free African American slaves, as well as to protect freed slaves from exploiting employers.

vagrant and put to forced labor. The bureau, like the army before it, did not set down hard and fast rules of labor. Basically, as long as local agents negotiated labor agreements that were just, provided for real freedom, and presented impartial enforcement, anything went.

Of course, in any contract system there are bound to be disagreements between the parties. Each field agent was to create a board consisting of himself and two local citizens to mediate such disputes. But the white citizens were constantly against the interests of black labor, and these boards soon fell into disuse; mediation fell to the bureau agent alone. This put great responsibility on the agents, of whom there were too few even when the army delegated commissioned officers to help out. Furthermore, bureau funds fell precipitously after President Johnson returned leased lands to their prewar owners through the pardon procedures, threatening the government's ability to fund agents' salaries. The main problem faced by agents was the contracting process. The fact that contracting could not be left to local law enforcement and courts had been proven by the Black Codes. Even though these codes were established on the basis of federal military regulations with the desire to restore order to chaos, the Yankees saw their application by Southerners as too discriminatory.

The labor contracts varied from plantation to plantation, agency to agency, and state to state. Depending on what a freedman and his family received in advances of goods (food and clothing), implements, and seed, he might get a share of the crop, a monthly wage, or compensation by task. Essentially the freedmen liked crop shares better than cash because they saw the former as a more tangible form of payment. The worst thing about the whole system was that blacks were less than really free; they were bound to the plantation by the contract, which often spelled out behavior, sick days, and absences as thoroughly as any planter or army officer had done before emancipation. Often there was a clause that any freedman who was absent before the end of the contract lost all shares. This allowed crooked planters to hire gunmen to run their laborers off at the end of harvest so the planters could claim the full crop.

Moreover, the years right after the war were renowned for their horrible weather, which caused bad harvests and put blacks in a crushing debt that was passed on from generation to generation. This has led many historians to blame the bureau for the peonage that set in after Reconstruction and was a hallmark of the South until World War II. Others point out that the bureau gave blacks a chance to prove that they could work as free laborers without the compulsion of slavery and safeguarded against the worst evils of an unfair legal system. And in many places in the South, the old plantation gang system of labor soon gave way to the croppers and landowning farmers, who worked small acreages as their own without supervision, could change jobs at will, and played landowners against each other for better conditions and wages.

Besides labor, the bureau provided African Americans with all sorts of legal protections and basic civil rights not available in local law. Here again, one can see differing viewpoints on the bureau's effectiveness among historians. That the bureau did much cannot be denied. The problem was that bureau personnel had a limited ideological framework from which to operate. Too often they saw compulsion as necessary to make African Americans fit into their vision of what freed people ought to be (as opposed to what blacks envisioned their freedom to be), as the army and white Southerners had done previously. Commissioner Howard made it clear from the onset of the bureau that he would enforce the law's edict that no Southern state could have its courts considered open to cases involving blacks unless the latter's testimony was accepted in all matters. The states complied readily enough in theory, but in actuality testimony given by African Americans was disregarded by white judges and juries.

The original bureau courts (when they had the time and money to operate) consisted of an agent, a representative for the white litigant, and one for the freedman. But a shortage of agents soon led to cases being given to the indigenous state court systems. The result was that the bureau was pitted against social, legal, political, and institutional forces that brought into question whether anything could have been done to guarantee justice for blacks. Legal harassment was common. Sheriffs, prosecutors, defense lawyers, and juries all conspired to delay justice and run up costs that few freedmen could afford to pay. The bureau usually acted only on individual cases of note, leaving most cases to the mercy (or lack of it) of the states. Blacks did their best to find a bureau agent who would take an interest in their cases, but often they languished in jail from a lack of bail. It helped to have a state legislator who was elected by a large black vote, and until the 1890s this happened all over the South in select counties, which ensured a more even application of justice. Still, as one Texas bureau agent aptly put it, generally blacks got a lot of law but very little justice.

One area in which the bureau's work was more uneven than its work in justice was the creation of health services in the South. Generally, the further away from Washington, D.C., a state was, the fewer health services it received. Yet these services were more important than administrators at the time believed. Good health affects not only life span, but also the ability of a population to work productively. The provision of health services also offered the white population one more way to control black laborers.

The level of health services provided was limited by the distrust of medicine that permeated the nineteenth century (one seldom went to a doctor unless near death), as well as the inability of the federal government to administer or provide health services for any part of the population, even through the Army Medical Corps. Thus, although the bureau's regulations provided for hospitals, dispensaries, and home health care, there was little to none provided in Texas and Florida, a little more in Kentucky and Tennessee, and less in the Carolinas aside from the Sea Islands. The rest of the South did

better, but the bureau medical system left little behind in the way of preparing blacks to assume health care activities on their own. As for the Southern states, whites were not about to "waste" tax dollars on caring for African Americans when even whites received no state aid. Black health during Reconstruction, when compared to that of whites, was much worse than it had been before the war.

Unlike its record for medicine, the bureau has received fairly universal praise in its development of educational systems for Southern blacks. This was the bureau's longest-running program, lasting until 1872. All other programs had been phased out in 1868. From the beginning, black education was affected by stereotypes. Most white Americans, North and South, could not envision an African American as much more than a day laborer, cook, or house servant. One did not need much schooling to swing a hoe. But blacks refused to be limited in their hopes for the future through education. Education was the original creator of black power in American history. From the beginning, blacks sought to move up the ladder in their own schools. Because the education system was segregated until 1954, African Americans were not prevented from becoming teachers, administrators, principles, superintendents, and trustees in their own schools. The bureau did encourage all of this; however, the numbers of students educated was very small in relation to the need.

Very important to early African American education were the Protestant church societies of the North. Hundreds of schools, some founded by blacks, were adopted by groups like the American Missionary Association (AMA), individual denominations of Northern churches (who often feuded with each other and the bureau over jurisdiction and the route to proper salvation), and secular freedmen's aid societies. The schools they founded and operated—providing teachers, books, buildings, and administrators—ranged from elementary to secondary to colleges. Soon black denominations like the African Methodist Episcopal and AME

Zion stepped into the picture. Black agricultural and mechanical universities founded under the Morrill 1862 Land Grant College Act sprang up in most Southern states. The problem for black college graduates was where were they going to find work. The answer was found in educating other blacks in schools and churches throughout the South. It is no accident that influential black leaders of the late nineteenth century were educators, ministers, or both. It is also no accident that one of the places African Americans demanded more than the traditional input in American society was through their schools, especially the many black universities.

Arguably the most influential black university was Howard University, founded by the AMA and administered by General Howard after the demise of the bureau. When Howard stepped down in 1875, the black students and faculty supported John Mercer Langston of the university's college of law as dean. But the AMA, despite its constant aid to black education, deemed an African American, even one as eminently qualified as Langston, to be the wrong person to lead what many saw as the national black university. Intrigue among the faculty and the need to cater to white philanthropic supporters kept the president of Howard white until after World War I.

Even worse was the competition between Methodists and Baptists on the local level. More than 90 percent of African Americans were of these two denominations; hence the black power struggles were immense, especially after the growth of Jim Crow segregation produced compensatory feelings of black pride and glory in separatism. "Home rule for our colored schools" had become a powerful slogan by the 1890s. The problem was solved by allowing a decentralization of power from the national finances provided by whites, permitting blacks to take over locally and allowing white contributors to still consider themselves to be running the schools on paper.

Yet although the universities and other schools founded by whites and later funded by whites and run by blacks (Howard, Fisk, Atlanta, Lincoln, Morehouse, and Wiley) produced the leadership class of the twentieth century (W. E. B. DuBois, James Weldon Johnson, James Farmer, Martin Luther King, Jr., Thurgood Marshall), many local black schools never rose much above the problems of Reconstruction. Whites sought to subvert the independent black school system and bring it under state control. This was done politically and through clandestine violence against schools, teachers, and individual students. The goal was to control the curriculum and operating funds, keeping blacks a "happy peasantry," always in a subordinate place. As it was, not more than one-sixth of the eligible black population was reached by educators during Reconstruction. But the education movement did accomplish three things: it awakened African Americans to the need of education; it led to the establishment of public education in the South; and it created the black colleges and universities that provided the graduates to expand that system in the future.

Along with school separation, which was not necessarily wanted by blacks, came certain institutions that African Americans wished to be kept separate. These revolved around the family and churches, areas in which blacks did not want white supervision but instead preferred their own institutions and customs. It gave them a needed break from white domination and prejudice. The religious views of African Americans tended toward the evangelical, often Methodist or Baptist, with local traditions thrown in. The church became the center of African American family life, the one place they could be themselves and develop their educational, social, and economic needs as well as the spiritual and moral. Black ministers were community leaders, along with artisans, a process that continued well beyond Reconstruction. It gave them a voice in the development and ordering of their own affairs. Most important were the aid societies that assisted the not so well-off after the bureau stopped relief activities in its first year of operation. The church also acted as an employment office and a place for bureau agents and Northern missionaries to make contact with the black community.

By its very nature, with the exception of ministrations to white refugees in its first year, the bureau tended to support segregation. Its services were for blacks only. The concept that any one group ought to receive largesse from the government had been anathema to the American experience in the nineteenth century. The bureau's labor policies created sharecropping and the lien, a form of peonage that doomed blacks (and then poor whites) for three generations. It short-term goals (ending destitution and providing clothing, rations, and shelter) were successful. Its intermediate goals (labor contracts, medical care) were less so. Its long-term goals (stability for African Americans, public education, employment opportunity, legal rights for blacks, African American voting rights, and the altering of state laws to treat blacks fairly) remained unmet for a century. What the bureau achieved during Reconstruction was the freeing of African Americans from slavery, but at the cost of making them second-class citizens. Yet, in the words of black historian W. E. Burghardt DuBois, the bureau represented "one of the most singular attempts to grapple with the vast problems of race and social condition." He and recent historians would say that the effort itself was ennobling, well worth it even though the ultimate ideals were never achieved then and are lacking today.

See also African American Education and Reconstruction; Black Codes; Captured and Abandoned Property Act; Confiscation Acts; Freedmen's Bureau Acts; Howard, Oliver Otis; Johnson and Reconstruction; Louisiana Experiment; Mississippi Valley Experiment; Port Royal Experiment; Southern Homestead Act; Virginia Experiment.

References Abbott, Martin, "Free Land, Free Men, and the Freedmen's Bureau" (1956) and *The Freedmen's Bureau in South Carolina* (1867); Belz, Herman, *Emancipation and Equal Rights* (1978), "The Freedmen's Bureau Act of 1865 and the Principle of No Discrimination According to Color" (1975), and *A New Birth of Freedom* (1976); Bentley George R., *A History of the Freedmen's Bureau* (1955); Bethel, Elizabeth, "The Freedmen's Bureau in Alabama" (1948); Bronson, Louis Henry, "The Freedmen's Bureau" (1970); Carper, N. Gordon, "Slavery Revisited" (1976); Cimbala, Paul A., "The 'Talisman of Power'" (1982); Cohen, William, "Negro Involuntary Servitude in the South" (1976); Cohen-Lack, Nancy, "A Struggle for Sovereignty" (1992); Colby, Ira C., "The Freedmen's Bureau" (1985); Cox, LaWanda, *Lincoln and Black Freedom* (1981) and "The Promise of Land for the Freedmen" (1958); Crouch, Barry A., *The Freedmen's Bureau and Black Texans* (1992); Currie, James T., "From Slavery to Freedom in Mississippi's Legal System" (1980); Davis, Ronald L. F., "The U.S. Army and the Origins of Sharecropping in the Natchez District" (1977); DuBois, W. E. Burghardt, "The Freedmen's Bureau" (1901); Foster, Gaines M., "The Limitations of Federal Health Care for Freedmen" (1982); Friedman, Lawrence J., "The Search for Docility" (1970); Guttman, Herbert G., *The Black Family in Slavery and Freedom* (1976); Harlan, Louis R., "Desegregation in New Orleans Public Schools during Reconstruction" (1961); Hasson, Gail S., "Health and Welfare of Freedmen in Reconstruction Alabama" (1982); Howard, Victor B., "The Black Testimony Controversy in Kentucky" (1973); Humphrey, George D., "The Failure of the Mississippi Freedmen's Bureau in Black Labor Relations" (1983); Jackson, Luther P., "The Educational Efforts of the Freedmen's Bureau and Freedmen's Aid Societies in South Carolina" (1923); Kolchin, Peter, *First Freedom* (1972); Lee, Anne S., and Everett S. Lee, "The Health of Slaves and Freedmen" (1977); Low, W. Augustus, "The Freedmen's Bureau and Civil Rights in Maryland" (1952) and "The Freedmen's Bureau in the Border States" (1969); May, J. Thomas, "Continuity and Change in the Labor Program of the Union Army and the Freedmen's Bureau" (1971) and "A Nineteenth Century Medical Care Program" (1973); McPherson, James M., "White Liberals and Black Power in Negro Education" (1970); Messner, William F., "Black Education in Louisiana" (1976); Morris, Thomas D., "Equality, 'Extraordinary Law,' and the South Carolina Experience" (1982); Nieman, Donald G., "Black Political Power and Criminal Justice" (1983) and *To Set the Law in Motion* (1979); Oakes, James, "A Failure of Vision" (1979); Olds, Victoria M., "The Freedmen's Bureau as a Social Agency" (1966); Oubre Claude F., *Forty Acres and a Mule* (1978); Pierce, Paul Skeels, *The Freedmen's Bureau* (1904); Raphael, Alan, "Health and Social Welfare of Kentucky Black People" (1972); Richter, William L., *Overreached on All Sides* (1991) and "Who Was the Real Head of the Texas Freedmen's Bureau?" (1990); Ripley, C. Peter, "The Black Family in Transition" (1975); Savitt, Todd L., "Politics and Medicine" (1982); Shlomowitz, Ralph, "'Bound' or 'Free'?" (1984); Shofner, Jerrell H., "Militant Negro Laborers in Reconstruction Florida" (1973); Small, Sandra E., "The Yankee Schoolmarm in Freedmen's Schools" (1979); Smallwood, James, *Time of Hope, Time of Despair* (1981); Stealy, John

Edmond, III, "The Freedmen's Bureau in West Virginia" (1978); White, Howard A., *The Freedmen's Bureau in Louisiana* (1970); White Kenneth B., "The Alabama Freedmen's Bureau and Black Education" (1981); Woody, Robert H., "The Labor and Immigration Problem of South Carolina during Reconstruction" (1931); Wynne, Lewis N., "The Role of Freedmen in the Post Bellum Cotton Economy in Georgia" (1981).

Butler, Benjamin F. (1818–1893)

New Hampshire–born cockeyed Ben Butler studied hard and was admitted to the bar after a brief stint at Waterville College (present-day Colby University). He became an excellent criminal lawyer and a Democratic politician. Moving to Massachusetts, Butler represented the poor Catholic mill hands at Lowell. He also fancied himself a military man and wrangled a major generalship of the state militia and commanded several summer encampments, which gave him the distinction of having as large a body of men as Lt. Gen. Winfield Scott, the general in chief of the whole federal army. In 1860 he attended the Democratic convention and voted for John C. Breckinridge. His support of the extreme Southern candidate cost Butler election to the governorship of his adopted state.

Declaring himself a Jacksonian Democrat (that is, opposed to secession), Butler led some of the initial Union troops to Washington during the critical first days of the war. He was the first to classify the slaves who fled to the Northern lines as "contraband of war," which in effect freed them and gave them their wartime nickname, "contrabands." Eventually sent to the Department of the Gulf, he commanded the federal occupation forces at the capture of New Orleans. His occupation of the Gulf ports and southern Louisiana was highly controversial (he hanged one man for insulting the U.S. flag), even criminal (he allegedly ransacked plantations that he declared, often without regard for the facts, to be Rebel-owned). The theft of silverware was so common under his command that Butler received the nickname "Spoons." He never quite outlived his declaration that women of New Orleans who insulted federal soldiers would be treated as "prostitutes plying their trade," which led to widespread condemnation, as well as a death sentence in absentia being placed on his head by the Richmond government. Hence Butler acquired another sobriquet, "Beast." Needing to have a less controversial man in charge to initiate Reconstruction in Louisiana, President Abraham Lincoln put Butler in command of an army group that was supposed to cooperate with Lt. Gen. U. S. Grant's 1864 campaign on Richmond, but incompetence on Butler's part led to his force being trapped on the Bermuda Hundred peninsula and to yet another nickname, "the Bottle Imp." Grant fired Butler after Lincoln won the elections of 1864 and Butler led a botched campaign against Fort Fisher at Wilmington, North Carolina.

After the war, Butler acted with the Radical Republicans to develop Military Reconstruction and impeach President Andrew Johnson. He led the way in Johnson's impeachment trial as part of the House prosecution team, where he managed to alienate many and actually made the president a sympathetic figure once again. He was the first to "wave the bloody shirt," literally waving the torn, stained garment of a whipped Carpetbagger above his head and calling for a stricter Reconstruction of the South. He served his state in Congress from 1866 to 1875. In 1876 he spent election night in a jail, visiting with the incarcerated candidate of prohibition and reform, Victoria Claflin Woodhull, a reformed prostitute and the first American female candidate for the presidency. He returned home to run for governor, losing in 1877 and 1879 but winning in 1882. Never one to let principle get in the way of practicality, Butler won elections not only as a Democrat and a Republican but also as a Greenbacker; and he unsuccessfully sought the presidency in 1884 under the label of the Anti-Monopoly party. He died in Washington in 1893, leaving behind a $7 million fortune and a reputation for audacity matched by few others.

Butler, Benjamin F.

See also Ames, Adelbert; Contrabands; Impeachment; Louisiana Experiment; Virginia Experiment.

References Boatner, Mark M., III, *The Civil War Dictionary* (1959); Butler, Benjamin F., *Autobiography and Personal Reminiscences of Major-General Benjamin F. Butler* (1892); Holzman, Robert S., *Stormy Ben Butler* (1954); Trefousse, Hans L., *Ben Butler* (1957).

Canby, Edward R. S. (1817–1873)

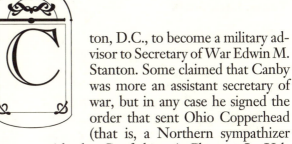

Born in Kentucky on the Ohio River, Edward "Sprigg" Canby was raised in Madison, Indiana, at that time a bustling, growing river town. He accepted an appointment to the U.S. Military Academy and graduated next to last in his class of 1839. He served in the Second Seminole War and was a staff officer in the Mexican War under Maj. Gen. Winfield Scott. But more than anything else, Canby was a paper shuffler, an officer in the adjutant general's office, a man who knew regulations and enforced them. He also served in California and for a time was a recruiting officer. He was with the ill-fated Utah Expedition, sent out to subdue the Latter Day Saints in the so-called Mormon War of the late 1850s, that nearly starved and occupied Utah only as part of a compromise between the federal government and church authorities. In 1860, Canby was sent to New Mexico to put down trouble between the Navajos and local settlers that had been brewing since the Mexican War. He had just completed a failed campaign against the tribe when the Civil War broke out in the East.

At the beginning of the Civil War, Canby became colonel of the newly raised Nineteenth Infantry. As such he was the senior officer left in New Mexico, so when the Confederates invaded in the winter of 1861, he received the duty of checking their advance. Canby wisely fell back past Santa Fe into southern Colorado, seeking to consolidate the few troops he had left after several disastrous defeats in southern New Mexico and covering his supply line to Denver. As Canby retreated his supply line got shorter and the Colorado volunteers came closer, until his forces managed to wreck the Confederate supply train after another Union loss at Glorieta Pass outside Santa Fe. The Rebels then found themselves overextended and had to do the same as Canby, fall back, all the way to Fort Davis in Texas. The result was that Canby became a war hero in a forgotten theater of the conflict. In the beginning of 1863, he arrived in Washing-ton, D.C., to become a military advisor to Secretary of War Edwin M. Stanton. Some claimed that Canby was more an assistant secretary of war, but in any case he signed the order that sent Ohio Copperhead (that is, a Northern sympathizer with the Confederacy) Clement L. Vallandigham into Confederate exile and was on the board that revised the Articles of War, the rules by which the U.S. Army is governed.

By summer, Canby was in New York City, where he and a brigade of combat infantry from the Army of the Potomac were charged with administering the draft laws. Although Canby had had nothing to do with the earlier riot there, he was the one who saw to it that the riot was never repeated and that the rioters were enrolled in the draft. In 1864, Canby took over the Division of West Mississippi and led the final successful assault on the forts at Mobile Harbor in Alabama. He then took over the Department of Louisiana and the Department of the Gulf, a bigger command area including Louisiana, with headquarters at New Orleans. In this capacity he received the surrender of Confederate armies operating east and west of the Mississippi River. He also had to administer Reconstruction for the first time.

Canby became involved with the Mississippi Valley Experiment and the creation of armed home colonies of freed slaves who worked for wages to produce cotton and were defended by their own militias. A Southerner by birth, Canby had a nebulous position on race. He firmly thought that it was a problem of correct concern to the federal government, but he was very conservative in that he believed that government help ought to be limited and curtailed at the first opportunity. But he would brook no racial incidents in his command area, whether by Southern whites or Northern soldiers. He tended to wind up in the middle between the Freedmen's Bureau and state officials on most matters. Although Canby did not believe that blacks ought to be forced to take jobs they did not want, once a contract was signed, the general saw to it that all sides abided by the terms exactly. He had a tendency to require that all problems involving African Americans be handled by the Freedmen's Bureau and that crime be handled by local authorities. But he stepped into both jurisdictions if they failed to act judiciously for all concerned. He knew the rules and demanded that others follow them. As a general Canby was a good adjutant. But he remained monotonously consistent all the time.

At first Canby expected Reconstruction to go along quickly. Like most Union soldiers, he was not against forgiving the enemy. He did his best to help surrendering Confederate soldiers to get home (and get out of his command zone). And initially the South seemed ready to submit to any program they considered fair. But Canby was in Louisiana, where politics had a way of being unfathomable to outsiders. Taking over from Bvt. Maj. Gen. Nathaniel Banks, Canby found that he was the heir to a program that was to reconstruct the state through a group of old planters who formerly were pro-Confederate but now were allegedly loyal. This seemed to contradict President Abraham Lincoln's desires to open Reconstruction up to a broader black-white coalition. Lincoln wanted Canby to loosen up the Reconstruction process; Canby sought to follow rules already established, many of which may have been unwise to follow and were idealistic but eminently practical. Like Lt. Gen. George S. Patton's use of Nazis in the occupation government of Germany after World War II, Canby was not opposed to letting Rebels run things, because they knew how to do it. They would simply have to be watched closely.

However, Lincoln's death brought a new hand to the helm in Washington. President Andrew Johnson's Reconstruction, although it was not necessarily planned that way, returned power to the prewar elites. Again, Canby saw his role as not to interfere with the political process, unless blacks and loyal whites were adversely affected. Canby preferred to cajole the elected officials into doing their duties. The city government of

New Orleans decided to press Canby and find out where the limits were. They attempted to sell certain city properties. Canby issued a direct order to the contrary. Then he ordered a city charter election that would put an elected government in power, the present one being a creature of Canby's military appointment under the order of President Lincoln, which Canby had opposed. He did not like the elected government any better than Lincoln's, but he abided by the election. Now it could alienate any property it wanted because it was no longer under military control. About this same time, a jealous Maj. Gen. Philip H. Sheridan, whose command area in western Louisiana overlapped with Canby's Department of the Gulf, got Canby transferred to Washington and took over the unified Gulf region. Officially, Sheridan charged Canby with certain financial irregularities (an investigatory board cleared him later), but Sheridan's real problem was that he hated asking a lower-ranking officer for supplies and logistical support.

Back in Washington, Canby headed the "Canby Claims Commission," which looked into property seized by the federal government during the war under the Confiscation Acts. After passage of the Reconstruction Acts, Canby was sent to the Second Military District (North and South Carolina) to replace Bvt. Maj. Gen. Daniel Sickles, who had interfered with operation of the circuit courts administered by Chief Justice Salmon P. Chase. Canby arrived in Charleston in the summer of 1867 to begin a portion of his career that would result in the readmission of four former Confederate states back into the Union (almost half of those ten that fell under the Military Reconstruction Acts) and earn him the title of "the Great Reconstructor." He considered his job to be a ministerial one of carrying out policy without favor to anyone. As always, he followed the rules already set down. Of course, that exasperated the various state politicos who hoped to find a way around various policies and actions, as they had with General Sickles, a known wheeler-dealer. The first thing Canby did was reorganize his states into military zones, with a troop contingent in each made up of infantry and cavalry. He refused to put soldiers in all county seats because that would spread his forces too thin. Instead he concentrated his men in isolated areas that were most likely to have trouble.

Next Canby made it a habit to investigate all reports and complaints so as to head off trouble before it started. He prohibited armed civilian groups from drilling, but he did not take their arms. He expected local authorities to enforce all laws fairly for both blacks and whites. He found that many of Sickles's appointees were not of a quality that he would have liked, so he augmented them with military commissions. His conviction rate was 80 percent. Canby apologized for it, considering it low, but it rated as one of the highest in Reconstruction. He concentrated on unlawful actions taken during the war against white Union men, unfair actions taken by state courts, and the transfer of cases to federal jurisdiction for which such transfer had been improperly denied. He changed jury rules in North Carolina that were based on property holding, as well as those in South Carolina that were based on race. Canby's rules made jury duty a responsibility for all registered voters who paid taxes. Color alone was an insufficient basis on which to include or exclude. He did not require every man to serve, as President Grant preferred, but again sought a middle road.

Canby was also hesitant about removing officials from office. The number of appointed officials he removed in the Carolinas is still unclear, but extant records point to fewer than 50. He preferred to cajole officials into doing their duty, and he seemed to have the ability to talk to both North and South in a diplomatic manner. He never tried to force his actions down the throats of Southern whites by direct military confrontation. He kept all of Sickles's registrars, merely modifying their rules of registration to make them as inclusive for both blacks and whites as possible. Canby did not try to interfere with the conduct of the state constitutional conventions.

Rather, he interested himself in the concerns of voters: safety, preventing economic discrimination against blacks by their employers (he taxed a county where African Americans had been unfairly fired to provide for their maintenance on a public dole), and closing down all other governmental functions to ensure that everyone could go vote. After the constitutions were approved by state voters, Canby appointed all elected officials to office so that the legislatures might get on with approving the Fourteenth Amendment and electing U.S. senators. This required him to force all elected officials to take the ironclad oath (of never having aided the Confederacy), which was an unpleasant experience for Democrats. But Canby pointed out that it was required under the Military Reconstruction Acts. He also immediately recognized both states' new constitutions as valid. By these methods, Canby kept the Reconstruction process going forward, with both North Carolina and South Carolina being readmitted into the Union on 24 July 1868.

Canby had been so successful in the Carolinas that the army decided to send him into two other states, Texas and Virginia, where the Reconstruction process had faltered under other generals. The state of Texas was a mess under Bvt. Maj. Gen. Joseph J. Reynolds. The Texas commander had been playing at politics, removing and appointing officials, setting Radical and Moderate Republicans at each other's throats, and ignoring the disruption of law and order in the countryside. Canby arrived in Austin just before Christmas 1868. Once again he divided the state up into military zones garrisoned by infantry and cavalry. Since distances were vast, he relied on telegraphic communication to call ahead for an arresting party to catch fleeing felons. He also expected the authorities to act—something no one else had done—and he got some results.

Then Canby recalled the state convention and tried to get it to write a constitution. Radicals and Moderates argued over esoteric issues like splitting the state into loyal and Rebel areas, the validity of all laws and contracts since 1861, and disfranchisement of white ex-Confederates so as to produce a Republican majority in any election. Canby tried to stay out of the picture, but when the convention adjourned without producing a constitution, he ordered a board consisting of one Radical, one Moderate, and his military aide to hammer together a constitution from the records left behind. But before Canby could supervise the election to approve the fundamental document (it ultimately would pass and is still the state's constitution), President Grant sent General Reynolds back to Texas and reassigned Canby to Virginia.

Canby faced a real problem in Virginia. Congress had just passed a law requiring that all officials in the unreconstructed states take the ironclad oath or resign. In the Old Dominion this involved 6,061 officials, of whom only 885 would take the proper oath. Even those who would take the ironclad oath were pressured socially and politically not to do so. Canby managed to fill 3,070 offices in less than six months, but this left 2,814 vacant offices—the very thing that cheap politics had produced in Texas and had led to such anarchy there before Canby's arrival. Virginia managed to pass a new constitution, the one that had been written 24 months before, by separating the fundamental law from the clause that disfranchised whites. The constitution passed and disfranchisement failed. Then Canby required that all elected officials take the ironclad oath as he appointed them to office. This was exactly what the voters had turned down. They accused him of trying to impose Radical Republican government over the expressed will of the people. But Canby pointed out that he had no choice under the laws. The thing that amazes one today is that Canby could make this explanation and get the white Virginians to accept it. Somehow they were convinced of his integrity and impartiality.

Canby also proposed a compromise that would allow the state legislature to ratify the Fourteenth and Fifteenth amendments before taking the oath. Then the state legislature would await congressional approval before passing more new legislation and would ignore the oath requirement thereafter. Under this charade, Virginia rejoined the Union in January 1870. Throughout it all Canby had the magic touch—he could get a convention, constitution, and voter acceptance seemingly anywhere. The whites might grumble, but they accepted it.

After Reconstruction was completed in 1870, Canby was sent out to the Pacific Coast to command the Department of the Columbia out of Portland, Oregon. In 1871, the Modoc Tribe in southern Oregon complained that the government had treated them unfairly, taking lands in violation of an 1864 treaty. The whites who had settled there treated the members of the tribe poorly. Led by a chief, Keintpoos, who also had the English name Captain Jack, a portion of the tribe left the reservation and refused to return. Not all of the tribe wanted to confront the whites, and Captain Jack had killed one of the compromisers. Attempts to arrest Captain Jack had turned the situation ugly. Attacks by both sides caused the Modocs to retreat to the lava beds in northern California, where they proved unbeatable. The secretary of the interior created a three-man commission to talk things out with Captain Jack. Canby was assigned to go along to protect the commissioners.

Initial offers made to Captain Jack included surrender and removal to Angel Island in San Francisco Bay, with final resettlement in Arizona Territory. Captain Jack was not impressed. A week of negotiations produced nothing worthwhile. Canby moved his soldiers into position to seal off the lava beds. In a meeting on 11 April 1873, Canby and the commissioners were attacked after the general refused to withdraw the soldiers. Canby fell at the first shot from Captain Jack's revolver. He was the first U.S. general officer to fall in a battle with Native Americans. Eventually Captain Jack and three others were hanged and the rest of the tribe transported to Indian Territory (present-day eastern Oklahoma). Canby was buried at Indianapolis, Indiana. The Great Reconstructor had finally found a situation that resisted rebuilding.

See also Army and Reconstruction; Davis, Edmund J.; Military Reconstruction Acts; Mississippi Valley Experiment; Reynolds, Joseph J.; Schofield, John M.

References Alderson, William T., "The Influence of Military Rule and the Freedmen's Bureau on Reconstruction in Virginia" (1952); Boatner, Mark M., III, *The Civil War Dictionary* (1959); Carrier, John P., "A Political History of Texas during the Reconstruction" (1971); Hamilton, Joseph G. de Roulhac, *Reconstruction in North Carolina* (1914); Heyman, Max L., Jr., "'The Great Reconstructor'" (1955) and *Prudent Soldier* (1959); Lowe, Richard G., "Republicans, Rebellion, and Reconstruction" (1968); Maddex, Jack P., Jr., *The Virginia Conservatives* (1970); Ramsdell, Charles W., *Reconstruction in Texas* (1910); Richter, William L., *The Army in Texas during Reconstruction* (1987) and "'We Must Rubb Out and Begin Anew'" *Civil War History*; Sefton, James E., *The United States Army and Reconstruction* (1967); Shook, Robert W., "Federal Occupation and Administration of Texas" (1970); Simkins, Francis B., and Robert W. Woody, *South Carolina during Reconstruction* (1932).

Captured and Abandoned Property Act of 1863

As federal armies advanced into the South, they captured large amounts of private property, much of it abandoned by fleeing owners. The armies really could not do much with this property because it had little direct military use. But since a lot of it was cotton that had already been sold or seized by the Confederate government and that had value on the open market, something had to be done. So Congress passed the Captured and Abandoned Property Act on 3 March 1863. It declared that under the "belligerent rights of confiscation" all moveable property of disloyal persons could be picked up by treasury agents, who would remove it for sale to the loyal states. The Department of the Treasury immediately sent out customs officials, agency aids, local agents, and supervisory agents to follow the armies into the Rebel states and seize this property. A general agent in Washington coordinated all of this work.

The field agents found that their work was dangerous. Rebel agents were about doing the same thing. Owners could show up and dispute the seizures violently. Seizable property was disguised with fake marks

of ownership (in the case of cotton) or hidden in woods and swamps to be claimed later. Transportation was lacking to move the seized goods to loyal areas, and the army was loathe to provide it. Fraud abounded, and agents took property exempted from seizure or owned by loyal persons and sold it for their own profit. About $30 million worth of property was seized during the war, of which 95 percent was cotton. About $25 million in net proceeds was realized by all parties.

Another aspect of the Captured and Abandoned Property Act was the taking of abandoned plantations. If the owner was absent aiding the Confederacy, treasury agents declared the property abandoned and held it with an eye toward possible return to its owner in the future. Loyal owners could file a claim for property return in federal courts within two years of the close of the war. Suspected or actual Rebels could do the same if they had either presidential amnesty or a pardon. But though land titles remained undisturbed, the intent was really wartime confiscation. Early on, the federal government decided to manage this property through a bureau of plantations to give employment to the large numbers of fugitive slaves who had fled to Union lines for freedom and security. Usually these properties were leased out to bidders on an annual basis, all rents and proceeds going to the war effort.

By 1865, administration of this captured or abandoned property passed into the hands of the new Bureau of Refugees, Freedmen, and Abandoned Lands. There it was held until claimed (for which one needed to provide a title and demonstrate loyalty, be it original or through amnesty or pardon) or eventually sold at auction. The owners who had the hardest time proving their loyalty, oddly enough, were the people who actually refused to aid the Confederacy. They often had few witnesses or documents to show, unlike pardoned Rebels. But in 1871, a bit late for the two-year limit after the war, the U.S. Supreme Court ruled in *Smith v. Kline* that all claimants were to be assumed loyal unless evidence to the contrary could be produced. But the uncertainty of U.S. title in any of the seized or abandoned lands defeated those who wished to grant homesteads to African Americans during Reconstruction, and it led to the passage of the Southern Homestead Act in 1866.

See also Bureau of Refugees, Freedmen, and Abandoned Lands; Confiscation Acts; Pardon, Amnesty, and Parole; Southern Homestead Act.

References Abbott, Martin, "Free Land, Free Labor, and the Freedmen's Bureau" (1956); Cox, LaWanda, "The Promise of Land for the Freedmen" (1958); Gates, Paul W., "Federal Land Policy in the South" (1940); Hoffman, Edwin D., "From Slavery to Self Reliance" (1956); Johnson, Ludwell H., "Contraband Trade during the Last Year of the Civil War" (1963) and "Northern Profit and Profiteers" (1966); Oubre, Claude F., *Forty Acres and a Mule* (1978); Randall, James G., *The Confiscation of Property during the Civil War* (1913) and *Constitutional Problems under Lincoln* (1964).

Cardozo, Francis L. (1837–1903)

A black officeholder who maintained his integrity amid the excesses usually associated with Reconstruction in South Carolina, Francis L. Cardozo (sometimes given erroneously as Cardoza) was born in 1834 in Charleston as a free man of color. His parents were Lydia Williams, a free woman of color, and Isaac N. Cardozo, a customs house clerk from a well-known Jewish family in the city. Francis Cardozo was educated in a school for free blacks in Charleston, went abroad, and completed his education at the University of Glasgow and seminaries at London and Edinburgh. He returned to the United States during the Civil War and took over a parsonage in New Haven, Connecticut. At the end of the war, Cardozo returned to South Carolina, where he organized schools for blacks. Upon the passage of the Military Reconstruction Acts, Cardozo entered politics and was elected to the state constitutional convention.

Throughout the convention Cardozo exhibited a moderate attitude and insisted that the floor be opened to all newspapermen so that the proceedings would be fairly reported. He was very solicitous of the public purse, opposing all steps that were unnecessary expenses, like appointing pages to the convention, defraying unlimited expenditures, and permitting lucrative travel monies for members. But he supported a petition to Congress asking for a million dollars to assist freedmen in buying abandoned plantations. Cardozo was also for universal male suffrage, opposing penalties against ex-Confederates. He also served on the committee on public education and worked out the details of the first tax-supported system of universal education in the state. In 1868 Cardozo was elected as secretary of state on the Republican ticket. His most notable act was to clean up the fraud associated with the state land commission and to reserve much land for the freedmen as intended in the original act creating the commission. An active politico, Cardozo became the head of the Union Loyal League in the state in 1872. He campaigned for the party, despite the monetary extravagances that alienated it from most native whites, asking that the regime be assessed on its merits rather than by the avaricious acts of a few. The result was a resounding approval by the voters at the polls.

In 1873, Cardozo became the state treasurer under the corrupt Franklin J. Moses, Jr., administration. Cardozo's policy was to restore the state's credit by adjusting and settling in an equitable manner the state's outstanding debts, resuming payment of the state's bonded debt, and reducing property assessment and rate of taxation by emphasizing a fair collection and disbursement of the state's monies. Much of Cardozo's policy was an able reaction to the legitimate complaints of several statewide taxpayers' conventions. Cardozo also pointed out that while the state debt was almost $16 million, over $7 million had been contracted by Democratic governments in power before the passage of the Military Reconstruction Acts. He was attacked viciously by the Charleston *News and Courier* after he canceled the newspaper's state printing contract, but the tone of these comments soon changed as it became evident that Cardozo was the lone honest man in an administration dominated by a greedy, corrupt governor. Numerous investigations by a hostile

Democratic state legislature proved that Cardozo's books were in order and that his policies were honest and good for the state. Nonetheless, the 1876 legislature indicted and convicted him for so-called irregularities when Wade Hampton's Red Shirt Democrats took over the state; Governor Hampton was forced to pardon Cardozo of all charges.

Unwilling to trust to himself to Hampton's protection forever, Cardozo left South Carolina and moved to the nation's capital. There he was employed by the post office for a while before becoming superintendent of public schools in the District of Columbia, a position he held until his death in 1903. Cardozo was a man with a passion for economy and honest administration in government. He did not give in to corruption at a time when thieving from the government was a common national disgrace. The constitution that he worked on lasted until 1895 and the Populist Revolt. And the parts with which Cardozo was most associated—free schools, the system of taxation, terms and elections of public officials, and the system of county government—were retained beyond that date in the new document, a fitting tribute to his able administration and contribution to South Carolina during Reconstruction.

See also African Americans and Reconstruction; Cardozo, Thomas W.; Chamberlain, Daniel H.; Moses, Franklin J., Jr.; Redemption of the South since 1874; Scott, Robert K.

References Richardson, Joe M., "Francis L. Cardozo" (1979); Simkins, Francis B., and Robert H. Woody, *South Carolina during Reconstruction* (1932); Sweat, Edward F., "Francis L. Cardoza" (1961) and "Some Notes on the Role of Negroes in the Establishment of Public Schools in South Carolina" (1961).

Cardozo, Thomas W. (1838–1881)

The brother of Francis L. Cardozo, who was a black politician in South Carolina during Reconstruction known for his integrity and honesty, Thomas W. Cardozo represents the other side of the coin, corruption and avarice. Born in Charleston the son of a free woman of color, Lydia Williams, and a Jewish customs house clerk, Isaac N. Cardozo, Thomas Cardozo lived in the much-privileged, much-oppressed world of Charleston's free black population. This gave him an ambivalent attitude toward other blacks—he felt an obligation to assist them, but at the same time wished to stay a step or two above them on the ladder of society, as his almost white color seemed to demand. He never wanted to "dirty" his hands too much with the affairs his own race. He attended private school in Charleston, but the death of his father sent him and his mother to New York City. There he continued his education and opened up a school for local blacks. At the end of the Civil War, Cardozo became associated with the American Missionary Association and supervised their schools in Charleston. It was here that his disturbing penchant for quarreling with others became evident. He also turned out to be quite a womanizer, and an affair with one of his students caused the AMA to give his job to his brother, Francis, forcing Thomas into the grocery business to survive.

Thomas Cardozo made many attempts to atone for his past and regain his stature with the AMA, to no avail. He then went to New York state and became associated with the Freedmen's Union Commission, which sent him and his wife to teach in schools in North Carolina. The failure of the commission to finance its operations adequately sent Cardozo over to the rival federal Bureau of Refugees, Freedmen, and Abandoned Lands, again as a teacher. After the passage of the Military Reconstruction Acts in 1867, Cardozo entered Republican politics. His presence on the ticket was blamed for the loss of his county to the Democrats. Cardozo belatedly recognized that local white Republicans were not about to allow a black to serve in any official capacity in local government. This realization sent him in 1871 to Mississippi, where his wife had relatives and the Republican party was more open. In Vicksburg, Cardozo joined the local Republican party and taught school until he had gained the proper residency requirements (six months) to run for office. Cardozo soon discovered that the large Republican majority in the area actually harmed local party efforts because it allowed much internal dissension to go unpunished. Nonetheless, Cardozo managed to get himself elected as clerk of the county court in 1872.

Cardozo immediately began to ingratiate himself with state party councils. He attended the Republican state convention in 1872, supported and campaigned for Ulysses S. Grant's reelection, worked for the election of John R. Lynch to Congress, and became a friend of future U.S. senator Blanche K. Bruce. He also wrote about Mississippi politics (in an inaccurate, propagandistic way) for the Washington *National New Era* newspaper. Still, Cardozo was a strong advocate for black civil rights, especially equal access to public accommodations, a problem that haunted many light-skinned African Americans of the upper classes like Cardozo. He was an advocate of Senator Charles Sumner's Civil Rights Bill (later the Civil Rights Act of 1875) that would cause the federal government to enforce these desires. He attended the National Equal Rights Convention in Washington, D.C., and got the Mississippi legislature to pass a stronger public accommodations law.

Meanwhile Cardozo did not lose sight of his own political advancement. By active campaigning he managed to get the nomination for the post of state superintendent of education on the Adelbert Ames ticket in 1874. He took a real interest in Mississippi's education system, white and black, and made regular field inspections. He backed local control of schools and a statewide adoption of uniform texts. But he did nothing to interfere with the segregated nature of the school system. Unfortunately, the vicious campaign that brought Cardozo to office led vengeful conservative whites, who had taken over in Vicksburg, to charge his successor as clerk of the county court with issuing fraudulent witness certificates. The conservatives decided to charge Cardozo with the same offense, although they had no real proof. The claim was that Cardozo had issued false certificates to the state and pocketed the money witnesses normally received. The indicted Cardozo posted a $22,500 bond that was backed by every prominent Republican in the state. The resulting trial ended in a hung jury; the jury of nine blacks and three whites divided largely along racial lines.

Prosecutors tried to bring the charges up again after a change of venue to Jackson. The Redemption of Mississippi by the White Liners (i.e., the return of white conservative home rule) meant that the prosecution would go on, and further investigation resulted in Cardozo's impeachment. The charges echoed the earlier court case (that he had issued false witness certificates and took the cash), but other new charges appeared, too. Cardozo was accused of embezzling funds from Tugaloo University as its treasurer; accepting bribes and kickbacks in choosing Mississippi's school texts; and cheating on the average daily attendance

Thomas W. Cardozo

records, splitting the difference in money with local principals. Although Cardozo did not intend to embezzle the money entrusted to him (he was just going to "borrow" it a while and return it, keeping the interest), the evidence against him made it clear that he had handed his opponents an issue over which he could be removed from office. Cardozo did not wait for the results; he resigned all offices and left the state, reportedly with $2,000 in state funds, forfeiting the amount bondholders had previously put up for him. In exchange for his departure, the state legislature dropped all charges. Cardozo went to Newton, Massachusetts, where he lived out his life as a local postal service worker.

Cardozo ought to have been the ideal candidate for Mississippi Republicans. He was well educated, urbane, articulate, and an obvious leader. But he also had a classic fault—he always hungered for more and better things, especially power. He tended to antagonize black and white supporters with his arrogant sense of superiority, a stuffiness that stemmed from his birth in Charleston and a lifelong social position outside both the white and black races. He personified an attitude too often associated with black leaders during Reconstruction, an inability to get in and mix with the African American masses. The tragedy was that slavery often prevented indigenous blacks from developing adequate leadership, which made them vulnerable to men like Cardozo—a corruptionist who betrayed his race and the whole Reconstruction process.

See also African Americans and Reconstruction; Ames, Adelbert; Cardozo, Francis L.

Reference Brock, Eugene W., "Thomas W. Cardozo" (1981).

Carpetbaggers

More so than for any other period of American history, the story of Reconstruction has been depicted as an encounter of good and evil. This clash was clearly (and heavy-handedly) portrayed in D. W. Griffith's movie *The Birth of a Nation*. The exaggerated facial contortions, portraying a twisted lust for money and innocent white women on the part of the cruel supporters of Reconstruction and an aura of simplicity for their Southern white opponents, would seem almost comical today—if the movie's topic were not so serious. The prime villains of any Reconstruction melodrama have to be the Carpetbaggers, who, in the words of Griffith, created an era of "cruel chicanery and political upheaval" in their "studied degradation of the conquered South."

According to the stereotype, the Carpetbagger was a low-life Yankee male, newly arrived from the North with every one of his belongings stowed in a carpetbag, a popular valise of the time made from carpet materials for sturdiness. He had a keen, corrupt manner, exceeded in its contemptability only by his lack of decency and honor. His manner was swaggering, his knowledge of what needed to be done to "save" the South from itself was repulsive in its pushiness, and his greed was insurmountable. A seeker of power and plunder, he took advantage of the Military Reconstruction Acts to sway the easily exploitable black voters and low-born Southern white traitors to their section of the country, the Scalawags. When the Carpetbagger was driven out of the South, by the noble ex-Confederate Redeemers, concluded the myth, he left behind a trail of corruption, misgovernment, and disturbed race relations.

Although the evil Carpetbagger is a caricature, it still holds in the popular imagination, North and South. Indeed, historians now like to use the term *outside whites* to get around the evils the stereotype suggests. But among historians of Reconstruction the Carpetbagger portrait has been changing for the last quarter century such that the stereotype is now hardly recognizable. Instead of poor, low-born adventurers out to exploit the South, these men are now seen as Northerners with money who came South to invest in the land and its potential for the good of their communities; men who arrived right after the war and had no notion of entering government; men who were interested in everyday business, not Reconstruction politics. Indeed, the Yankees who came South after Appomattox to invest in plantations and planting had little trouble with their Southern white neighbors beyond a little social ostracism, which was common in the nineteenth-century United States for any outsiders or newcomers to an established area.

The change came two years after these men arrived, when they wound up getting elected to office under the Military Reconstruction Acts with the support of the newly enfranchised African Americans. And that seems to be the key. A Northerner was not a true Carpetbagger unless he deigned to enter politics and encouraged political activity on the part of blacks. Republican politics was the central distinguishing feature of Carpetbaggers. And although there were Northern blacks who came South to do the same, at that time they were not defined as Carpetbaggers. The white South merely condemned them as "niggers," along with the former slaves. Indeed, whites found these blacks all the more despicable because they were educated and tended to school their brethren in the ways of freedom. They were dangerous to a status quo that depended upon white power through black ignorance.

Thus, to be a Carpetbagger in the Reconstruction sense of the word, one had to be a white Northerner who came south after the Civil War and at some time entered Republican politics. Most were former Union soldiers who had been away from the North so long as to see the South as their adopted homeland. Many had married Southern women. Most seemed to like the milder Southern climate. Others saw business opportunities in the great unexploited natural resources of the South. A lot of them wanted to grow staple crops—to become the owner or manager of a great plantation, like the ones they had passed by so often, or looted and burned, in military campaigns. They saw an appealing life and wanted to share in it.

The Yankees who came South and stayed saw the place as a new frontier. Actually, so did many Southerners who moved from east to west in the South at this time, search-

ing out opportunity without being condemned for doing so. The South was a land of opportunity, and the Northern emigrants expected to achieve much in business because they condescendingly saw the white and black Southerners as indolent. When the end of the war released them from military service, thousands of soldiers stayed in the South or returned to some spot they had seen as especially appealing during the war. Land was abundant and cheap. Cotton prices were sky-high, and labor was plentiful. These men obtained plantations or businesses, employed the freed slaves as wage laborers, and waited to get rich. But few made it in these farming endeavors. The Yankees were novices in the cotton culture. Southerners laughed as the Northerners tried to treat the black laborers as human beings. The Northerners also suffered from economic and social isolation as Southern whites ostracized them and their products.

But the main problem with planting in the South was the weather immediately after the war. Much of the South was under drought conditions. Every planter, neophyte Northerner or experienced Southerner, was at the drought's mercy. In addition, many planters fared poorly in their relations with black laborers in the field. The freed African Americans were also looking for opportunity, and working cotton was not necessarily high on their list. Those who did continue to work crops began to assert their own feelings as to how things ought to be done. Blacks worked less and less at gang labor for white-selected staples. More and more they took up individual plots of land upon which they raised whatever they pleased. A lot of planters were going broke by 1867, and the recently arrived Yankees led the pack. Many returned North to recover their fortunes; others stayed on, enduring the heat, eating food full of pork and lard (which Yankees found abominable to their palates), and banding together, seeking solace with others from the North.

Just as everyone seemed to be going broke (and the Northern newcomers had often invested thousands in their businesses), along came the Military Reconstruction Acts. A new field beckoned. Northerners in the South were among those who could vote without question. They could take any oath required, they were indisputably loyal to the Union, and they could hold office at a time when Southern whites were still suspect. They also believed that they had a responsibility to serve. It was like enlisting in the war all over again. They sympathized with Congress and the goals of Reconstruction. They had to complete the victory won on the battlefield in the halls of the state legislatures. It was their South, their home, too. Besides, the newly enfranchised blacks needed leaders who understood how the system worked. And when African American voters had to choose between ex-Confederates and ex-Federals, the Yankees got the benefit of the doubt every time. Hence the Carpetbaggers, willing to treat the blacks more fully as equal men, had great political power beyond their numbers. It should not be surprising that they won office frequently.

In spite of their numbers, it is often difficult to find adequate information about Carpetbaggers in the South. There were nine Carpetbag governors, for example—eight of whom came South well before the Military Acts were passed and one, Aldelbert Ames of Mississippi, who came as a military officer and military governor, not an adventurer in search of a political job. Two others had been Freedmen's Bureau officers (enough to ruin them for all "right-thinking" Southern whites), two more had been civilian governmental employees, two more planters, one a lawyer, and the last a minister of the gospel. All were respectable people. Like the Carpetbag governors, those 62 Carpetbaggers who served in Congress from the Southern states during Reconstruction (17 in the Senate and 45 in the House) do not necessarily fit the stereotype, either. Almost all were Union veterans. But two-thirds of the group were surprisingly well educated for their day. They had studied law, medicine, or engineering or were qualified college-educated teachers. They

stood well among other men in Congress regardless of where they were from. And 50 of the 62 had arrived in the South before the passage of the Military Acts, before African Americans could vote. Only 15 of the 50 served as Treasury agents, Freedmen's Bureau officials, or occupation soldiers. Seventy percent had entered farming or business professions before running for office. Even the 12 late arrivals who came after the Military Reconstruction Acts tried business endeavors before entering politics. Similar statistics hold true for the nearly 200 Carpetbaggers who served in Southern state constitutional conventions during the era.

But what kind of regimes did these Carpetbaggers establish? Were they corrupt and mismanaged? Although it is hard to generalize about a group of men of such wide experiences and personalities, a few things need to be noted about Carpetbag rule. First of all, 6 of the 11 former Confederate states (Texas, Tennessee, Alabama, Georgia, Virginia, and North Carolina) never had a Carpetbag governor. No Southern state had Carpetbaggers as a majority of its white Republican voters. Carpetbaggers had to have the support of Scalawags (white Republicans) and African Americans to hold office. The five Southern states that had Carpetbag governors (Louisiana, Mississippi, Arkansas, Florida, and South Carolina) had them only for a short period of time (usually one term of two years). Next, the extent of illegal and illegitimate spending under Carpetbag governors has been exaggerated on the basis of the worst cases possible, like Louisiana and South Carolina. Most of the money went to items that the South had been notably deficient in financing before the war: schools, roads, and various social and economic services. It was the change in spending mores brought south by former Northerners that accounted for most of the money and taxes raised.

Finally, the Carpetbaggers were no more corrupt than anyone else at the time, black or white, North or South. Though the Carpetbag governors are described as dishonest to a man in older historical accounts, the reality is more varied. Joseph Brooks of Arkansas never exercised uncontested power for good or evil and was thrown out by rival Republicans. Robert K. Scott of South Carolina and William Pitt Kellogg of Louisiana lived up to the stereotype of corrupt regimes. And Powell Clayton of Arkansas, Harrison Reed and M. L. Stearns of Florida, and Henry Clay Warmoth of Louisiana were accused of corruption but never proven guilty. Unlike the other accused governers, Warmoth admitted that he and everyone else, Democrat or Republican, black or white, made money off of Reconstruction. One historian asserts that if Warmoth were corrupt, Louisiana corrupted him; Warmoth did not corrupt Louisiana (though Warmoth did say that "corruption is the style" in Louisiana and maintained that he was honest because he could have taken more). In contrast to Warmoth and his suspected malefactors, however, stood Adelbert Ames of Mississippi and Daniel H. Chamberlain of South Carolina, who were scrupulously honest, upright men.

Southerners and historians later accused the Carpetbaggers of disturbing racial relations in the South, an accurate attribution. And in the end, this becomes the Carpetbaggers' real "crime." It is the reason that even the openly honest Carpetbaggers like Ames and Chamberlain were hated. Carpetbag regimes rested their power on a widened democracy (in that all men could vote and hold office); guaranteed political rights as represented by the Thirteenth, Fourteenth, and Fifteenth amendments and the Military Reconstruction Acts; reapportioned representation; election rather than appointment to office (with the notable exception of Louisiana); public schools, although these institutions did their best to avoid the question of integration; public accommodations (though Scalawags were not in favor of them); Northern emigration to purify the South and help Republicanism politically; and internal improvements like highways and railroads. It was the Carpetbaggers who led the war against the Ku Klux Klan and organized the Union Loyal Leagues and the so-called Negro Militias.

The Carpetbaggers believed in the justness of the war for the Union. In the end the Carpetbaggers lost everything they had. Up North their comrades in arms got tired of the fight. Down South their white Republican Scalawag allies abandoned them for the Democrat-Conservatives and the white racial unity necessary to counter the stance on racial issues that put the Carpetbaggers in power in the first place.

Why is the myth of the Carpetbaggers so enduring? A partial explanation is that the story has an element of truth in it. Some Carpetbaggers, though far from the majority, were criminal adventurers. Another reason is that academic historians have failed to communicate their more recent findings to the public. Historians tend to talk among themselves rather than appealing to the popular reader. And the myth also served a useful purpose to some. It allowed Southern whites of all political labels, even reformed Scalawags, to blame someone else for the troubles of Reconstruction—and it is convenient to blame outsiders who cannot defend themselves adequately. The myth of the Carpetbaggers also let the white South feel that scales of morality had been balanced. According to this reasoning, the South left the Union over the noxious slavery issue, but the Yankees perverted Reconstruction through the excesses and corruptions of the Carpetbaggers. The alleged harm caused by Carpetbaggers made the struggle of the Confederate soldiers for Southern independence noble by comparison.

Although the Carpetbagger stereotype needs to be viewed with a great deal of skepticism, it cannot be totally ignored, as some more recent commentators would have it. The Carpetbaggers' role in Reconstruction was way too important for that. It was the Carpetbaggers' need to earn a living through political patronage that gave the era much of its flavor of political factionalism based on personalities rather than ideology; and it was their inability to build unity in the fledgling Southern Republican party that was central to Reconstruction's failure. Even though they were a distinct minority within the Republican party in the

South, they were a driving force for a South that was far different from the one that preceded them and the one that followed.

See also African Americans and Reconstruction; Ames, Adelbert; Army and Reconstruction; Chamberlain, Daniel H.; Clayton, Powell; Grant and Reconstruction; Ku Klux Klan; Morgan, Albert T.; Redemption of the South before 1874; Redemption of the South from 1874; Reed, Harrison; Scalawags; Scott, Robert K.; Southern Carpetbaggers in the North; Tourgée, Albion W.; Warmoth, Henry Clay.

References Campbell, Randolph B., "Carpetbagger Rule in Reconstruction Texas" (1993–1994); Current, Richard N., "Carpetbaggers Reconsidered" (1964), Those Terrible Carpetbaggers (1988), and Three Carpetbag Governors (1967); Currie-McDaniel, Ruth, "The Wives of the Carpetbaggers" (1989); Foner, Eric, Reconstruction (1988); Harris, William C., "The Creed of the Carpetbaggers" (1974); Hume, Richard L., "Carpetbaggers in the Reconstruction South" (1977–1978); Kolchin, Peter, "Scalawags, Carpetbaggers, and Reconstruction" (1979); Maizlish, Stephen E., "A Look inside the Carpetbag" (1989); Mechelke, Eugene R., "Some Observations on Mississippi's Reconstruction Historiography" (1971); Powell, Lawrence N., "The Politics of Livelihood" (1982); Scroggs, Jack B., "Carpetbagger Constitutional Reform in the South Atlantic States" (1961) and "Southern Reconstruction" (1958); Stampp, Kenneth M., The Era of Reconstruction (1965), Thornton, J. Mills, III, "Fiscal Policy and the Failure of Radical Reconstruction in the Lower South" (1982).

Chamberlain, Daniel H. (1835–1907)

A South Carolina Carpetbagger, Daniel H. Chamberlain was the next to youngest of ten children born to a Massachusetts farmer. He grew up working on the farm, receiving a common school education. He also taught school to earn the money to go to a college prep school and eventually wound up at Yale College, where he worked at speech and debate, English composition, and classical languages (Greek and Latin). He graduated at the top of his class and went on to Harvard Law School. He was a confirmed antislavery Republican by now, but he was kept out of the war initially by the need to complete his education and repay some of the debts it cost him. Finally, the moral obligation of the war against slavery could no longer be denied. He enlisted in the Fifth Massachusetts (Colored) Cavalry,

as a lieutenant. Soon he was adjutant in a regiment whose colonel was Charles Francis Adams, Jr., of the famous Massachusetts family that produced two presidents. Chamberlain saw little action during the war, but his regiment did manage to occupy Richmond in April 1865 before being sent out to the Rio Grande to bluff the French out of Mexico.

Chamberlain came South in response to the accidental drowning of a friend who was serving as a teacher of freedmen. The boy's father asked Chamberlain to retrieve the body and bring it home. When Chamberlain got to Charleston, however, he learned that the friend had been swept out to sea when his boat capsized. Chamberlain notified his friend's father and stayed on to look things over. He saw the South as a place to make the money he needed to pay off his debts. He decided to enter planting. It would cost him more debt, but it promised to bring in riches beyond comprehension. Like most planters, however, Chamberlain was lucky to break even. After two years, the Military Reconstruction Acts opened up another possibility: he could serve in the state convention—called the "Congo Convention" by newspapers that denigrated its black majority—as a loyal white delegate. This option gave him a job that made good use of his legal education. He voted as a reformer for debt relief (he knew a lot about that first hand), redistribution of land among the freedmen, elective state offices rather than appointive ones, reorganization of the court system, and equal rights.

Chamberlain made a good impression on the Republican delegates. Governor Robert K. Scott appointed him attorney general for the new government. Chamberlain exuded the air of a college professor, with his slight build, premature balding, and neat style of dress. He had married a Massachusetts woman a year earlier and tended toward her Unitarian religion. He was noted for his honesty and fairness. He was also ambitious, already envisioning himself as Scott's replacement. He served on the state railroad and the land commissions, but like Scott was not involved in the corruption aside from backing erstwhile projects that ultimately backfired. He also appealed to the taxpayers in revolt, setting himself up as a alternative to Scott in the election of 1872. He proposed that corruption be controlled and that whites be given a better chance of electing representatives by a system of proportional voting. For example, if Charleston County had 18 representatives in the state legislature, give each voter 18 votes; this voter could cast them in any way he chose, up to all 18 for one candidate or in any other proportion he wished. Chamberlain also appealed to certain Democrats like James L. Orr who wished to create a single party of whites and blacks dedicated to honesty.

Chamberlain ran for governor against Radical Republican Franklin J. Moses in 1872 but lost out; Moses canvassed among black Republicans, who disliked Chamberlain's appeal to the ex-Confederates. But after two years of Moses and his cronies robbing the state blind, Chamberlain looked good in 1874. He also strengthened his support among black voters when he refused to keep black students out of the state university. Chamberlain held his ground even though all white students withdrew under protest. He received a majority of nearly 12,000 votes, many fewer votes than either Scott or Moses had received, but enough to win a convincing victory. As governor, Chamberlain tried to walk a narrow line between Republicans and Democrats, probably too difficult a job at that point in time for anyone. But he managed to put together a coalition of reform-minded blacks and whites in the legislature to work for an honest, economically run state government. Even hostile editors were impressed. He defeated many appropriation bills and kept tax rates down. Hence he was not ready when the Radicals revolted in the state legislature. The issue was the selection of judges for the state courts, a legislative function. The hostile legislators scheduled the event on two days when Chamberlain was scheduled to be out of town. The governor thought he had an agreement to postpone the selection, but when he returned from his trip a few days later, the judges had

all been chosen. They included some of the most radical and corrupt whites and blacks in the state.

Immediately the newspapers, friendly up to that point, sided with the red-hot Democrats and accused Chamberlain of trying to "Africanize the State." Chamberlain had one course open to him. He could refuse to sign the new judges' commissions. But Chamberlain rejected only two of the appointments; his stated reason was that these two men's terms would not expire until after the next legislature met, and that body ought to select its own judges. Chamberlain seemed once again to have taken the credible middle road. But in the upcountry, local white Democrats refused to go along with low-country compromisers. The upland Democrats wanted an independent, white-controlled party with its own Southern white candidate. They wanted Maj. Gen. Wade Hampton, a Confederate war hero. Hampton promised an end to both Reconstruction and Yankee-Negro government. White militia groups, the Red Shirts, began to organize and drill for action. Regular Republicans, especially in the legislature, responded in kind. They also accused Chamberlain of being too pro-Confederate in his appointments.

It soon became evident that the Democrats were not about to lose the election of 1876 in South Carolina to an honest vote. Smears of Republican candidates, including Chamberlain, became more and more exaggerated. Republican rallies faced the guns of the Red Shirts. South Carolina was about to use the First Mississippi Plan to "redeem" the state (i.e., return it to conservative white rule). The core of that plan was to make it too dangerous for Republican candidates to campaign and for black voters to ballot. Race riots spread all over the area west of Columbia, those at Hamburg and Ellenton being the worst. Blacks were shot down at random, in their homes, on the roads, and in marketplaces. It mattered little that they were not engaged in political activities. Rifle clubs heard speakers who warned that "the tall poppies will fall first." One speaker outlined his plan for South Carolina's "salvation": "I for one would shoot first Chamberlain…and such carpet-baggers; second, the miserable white native scalawags; and, lastly, the black leaders generally."

When Chamberlain appealed for federal military assistance, he was refused. South Carolina Democrats declared that his request proved he was out of touch with the state and that he ought to ask for the help of the white Democrats. Instead Chamberlain issued a proclamation for the rifle clubs to disband. Knowing that the illusion of nonviolence was more important than reality, Hampton and his men complied. But the Red Shirts kept on, calling their military companies such things as the Allendale Mounted Base Ball Club, Mother's Little Helpers, or the First Baptist Sewing Club. By now President Ulysses S. Grant had ordered every available soldier to the state to police the 1876 state and federal elections. But it was already too late. Blacks stayed home and did not vote, knowing that the troops would soon be gone, and with them the protection they offered. The result was a quiet election and a Democratic landslide. Although the electoral vote went for Republican Rutherford B. Hayes for president, everyone in South Carolina knew that made little difference. It was the Democratic victory in the state elections that counted, nothing else.

At first Chamberlain naively expected that the Hayes administration would not allow Hampton to take over. But when troops were withdrawn from Louisiana, he realized that a drastic change in the political scene was inevitable. Chamberlain left the state and took the New York bar exam. He kept track of the situation in South Carolina through newspapers. He saw that he was charged with the corruption of his minions and those of other administrations. His former political allies lied about the course of events in an effort to save their own skins. His indictment followed. Eventually it would be dropped for lack of evidence. As time passed Chamberlain did well for himself as a Wall Street lawyer. He wrote articles for leading law journals and took an interest in legal education. He defended himself in print for his actions as governor in South Carolina. He continued to speak out for civil rights for African Americans.

During the 1880s Chamberlain began to change. Soon he was speaking out on the futility of basing government on the vote of the "ignorant" black voters. He switched to the Democratic party and then became an Independent. As he spoke out against "Negro Rule" he lost many friends from his New England days, but he heard again from old adversaries in South Carolina, who were impressed with Chamberlain's newly acquired "wisdom" on race. He was invited back to South Carolina and represented it as it received its railroad. He was lauded in speeches given by the most vitriolic of his enemies from a quarter of a century earlier. He toured Europe and the Mediterranean. He outlived his wife and children, finally settling in Charlottesville, Virginia, where he passed out his years bedridden except for a few trips to the Johns Hopkins Medical Center for his health. He died in 1907, rejecting Christianity and all other religions as irrational. "Death ends all" were his final words.

See also Carpetbaggers; Moses, Franklin J., Jr.; Scott, Robert K.; Redemption of the South from 1874.

References Current, Richard N., *Those Terrible Carpetbaggers* (1988); Holt, Thomas, *Black over White* (1977); Sheppard, William A., *Red Shirts Remembered* (1940); Thompson, Henry T., *Ousting the Carpetbagger from South Carolina* (1926); Wellman, Manley Wade, *Giant in Gray* (1949); Williams, Alfred B., *Hampton and His Red Shirts* (1935); Woody, Robert H., "The South Carolina Election of 1870" (1931).

Chandler, Zachariah (1813–1879)

Born and educated in New Hampshire, Zach Chandler moved to Detroit in 1833, opened a general store, and graduated into trade, banking, and land speculation, becoming one of the richest men in Michigan. A Whig in politics, he served in the Zachary Taylor campaign and was elected mayor of Detroit in 1851. He tried for governor the following year but was defeated. Angered by the slavery issue, he was one of the original organizers of the Republican party in 1854 and a supplier of arms to the free soil (anti-slavery) settlers in Kansas. In 1856 he attended the Republican convention that nominated John Charles Frémont for the presidency and became a member of the national committee. In 1857 he succeeded Lewis Cass as U.S. senator, a position he held until 1875. In the Senate, Chandler was considered a Radical Republican, although he was not on speaking terms with prominent senator Charles Sumner of Massachusetts, among others. He was chairman of the committee on rivers and harbors, from which he dispensed much party aid in the form of "pork barrel" legislation and appointments.

At the outbreak of the Civil War, Chandler stood against secession and raised and equipped the First Michigan Volunteer Infantry Regiment. The war gave him a golden opportunity to make himself heard because he was on the critical joint committee on the conduct of the war, an investigatory body that prodded "politically incorrect" generals to accept the abolition and confiscation programs of the Radical Republicans. His prime enemy in uniform was Maj. Gen. George B. McClellan, whom Chandler accused of rank incompetence. Chandler also supported the Republican domestic program, especially the national banking system and the printing of greenbacks to finance the war.

Chandler was bitterly anti-British and proposed breaking relations with them because they had dragged their feet on paying the United States for damages incurred by the Confederate warship *Alabama*, which had been outfitted illegally in British ports. He suggested that the United States grant the same rights to any British enemy or colony that rebelled as England had given the defunct Confederacy. He was a die-hard Republican who chaired the party's national congressional campaign committee from 1868 to 1875. He was merciless in using political patronage to strengthen his own and the party's political base, and he ran Michigan as his own personal fiefdom. But the Democratic landslide of 1874 broke his power in the state, and he lost the upcoming Senate race. He accepted a position as secretary of the interior and partially cleaned up the corrupt and incompetent Indian agent system, until the Ulysses S. Grant administration fell from power in 1877. He returned to the U.S. Senate in 1879 but died before he could make his influence felt again.

See also Grant and Domestic Policy; Lincoln and Reconstruction; Radical Republicans.

References MacDonald, William, "Zachariah Chandler" (1964–1981); Williams, T. Harry, *Lincoln and the Radicals* (1941).

Chase, Salmon P. (1808–1873)

Born in New Hampshire, where he received an excellent education in public schools and from a private tutor, Salmon P. Chase went to Ohio under the care of his uncle, the first bishop of the Episcopal Church there. Completing his boyhood education under his uncle's guidance, Chase returned to New Hampshire to attend Dartmouth College. Graduating in 1826, he taught school in Washington, D.C., until he read for and passed the bar in 1829. He went back to Ohio to practice and became one of Cincinnati's best-known lawyers in short order. He lectured in the Lyceum (an adult education association) and wrote a collection of the laws of Ohio, which greatly enhanced his reputation and became a standard course of study. He gained many lucrative fees representing various banks, but his fees grew so pricey that his business fell off. Meanwhile, he married three women in succession, all of whom died early, and he fathered six children, only two of whom lived to adulthood.

Around 1840, Chase became interested in the antislavery movement. His main interest was free speech of abolitionists rather than the travails of African Americans or the need of the North to secede from the Union (an early abolitionist doctrine) to end the institution. Chase was a poor orator but a sound thinker and good writer. He worked behind the scenes for the Liberty party and later the Free Soil party in preparing speeches and platforms. Chase also devoted much work to defending fugitive slaves from being returned South, so much so that he was known as the "attorney general of fugitive slaves." He maintained that the Fugitive Slave Act of 1793 allowed recovery of runaways from the original 13 states but that states west of the mountains were protected from such measures by the Land Ordinance that preceded the Constitution itself. He maintained that evil laws could not properly be passed because they went against the superior laws of nature.

Although Chase had been a delegate to the 1832 presidential nominating convention for the coalition that eventually became the Whig party, he stayed out of politics until he joined with the Liberty party and the Free Soil party to oppose slavery in the 1840s. He was instrumental in dissolving the Liberty party and reconstituting it as the Free Soil party in 1848 and in nominating former president Martin Van Buren for president at a convention over which Chase presided. Working to manipulate the fragmented parties represented in the Ohio legislature, Chase managed to get himself elected to the U.S. Senate in 1849. He fought against the Compromise of 1850, which among other provisions permitted slavery in the New Mexico Territory, and tended to side with the Democrats in organizing the Senate for business. But in reality he was not happy with either the Democrats or the Whigs. He became the leader of the opposition to the Kansas-Nebraska Act in 1854, because it permitted slavery in territory in which it had been previously outlawed, and in 1855 the "Anti-Nebraska" convention in Ohio nominated him as a candidate for governor under the new Republican label, after the Democratic-dominated state legislature refused to reelect Chase to the U.S. Senate. He was reelected governor in 1857, and his administrative abilities and stance in favor of black rights made him a power to be reckoned with in the Republican party nationally. In 1860, as the nation threatened to break up over the slavery issue, Chase was returned to the Senate as a Republican.

Chase, however, had bigger things in mind. He was bitten by the presidential bug in a big way. The rest of his life would see him jockeying for the presidency, always unsuccessfully and often embarrassingly. His greatest asset was the able assistance of his knowledgeable daughter, Kate, whose tremendous personality often made up for her father's shortcomings. He came up short for the nomination in 1860, but the winner, Abraham Lincoln, included him in his cabinet (along with everyone else who had sought the Republican nomination that year, like William H. Seward, Simon Cameron, and Edward Bates) as secretary of the treasury. As the head of the Department of the Treasury, Chase was brilliant. He reorganized the almost bankrupt treasury, recommended new taxes, supported confiscation of Rebel property, borrowed money and maintained the national credit, created greenback currency (putting his face on the dollar bill so that every voter might have in his pocket a miniature campaign poster for the 1864 presidential race), established the national banking system that had been the keystone to the Republican platform, and administered the department so well on a day-to-day basis as to still be considered one of the best secretaries the treasury has ever had.

On the other hand, Chase could not stop seeking the presidency, a process he hoped to abet by advancing a Radical Republican program. He backed Maj. Gen. Benjamin F. Butler's idea of declaring runaway slaves "contraband," opposed colonization of ex-slaves abroad, supported the Emancipation Proclamation, advocated arming blacks as soldiers, criticized the army's employment of freed blacks in government plantations as reenslavement, and advocated land redistribution among the freed slaves. He was especially miffed when President Lincoln tended to ignore his freely offered advice; the president preferred to rely on the more moderate tenets of Secretary of State Seward. Chase described details of secret cabinet discussions to the Radical Republicans, who considered Lincoln to be dragging his feet on the slavery issue, and he claimed that the president's advisors were hopelessly under the hand of the allegedly scheming Seward.

When Lincoln called Chase's bluff in front of a congressional delegation (Chase either had to deny that the cabinet was bickering or reveal that he was a congressional mole), Chase resigned his office. Seward had already tendered his resignation to give Lincoln a free hand with Congress, but Lincoln returned both documents and asked the two men to stay on for the good of the country. Thus began a charade of Chase regularly handing in his resignation during the next year, only to see Lincoln refuse it.

Finally, in 1864, Chase unwisely supported the "Pomeroy Circular," which claimed that Lincoln needed to be replaced with a better man (like Chase) in order for Republicans to win the election later that year. Once again Chase felt obliged to resign, but Lincoln kept the letter to see the secretary squirm. In July, over a minor patronage problem, Chase resigned once more; this time, considering Chase no longer to be a possible presidential rival, Lincoln accepted it. Chase was mortified. Lincoln then dangled the possibility of a Supreme Court seat before Chase; after an appropriate period of cat and mouse during which Chase begged for the job, Lincoln put him up for chief justice. Many in Congress knew of Chase's duplicitous character and were not pleased with the nomination, but Lincoln insisted.

As chief justice Chase had his good and bad moments. He continued to be active in his support of the Freedmen's Bureau, the granting of the franchise to blacks, and numerous freedmen's benevolent societies. He stayed out of Congress' dispute with President Andrew Johnson over the nature of Reconstruction, although he drew up a preliminary draft for what would become the Fourteenth Amendment. After the passage of the Military Reconstruction Acts, Chase refused to ride circuit in Virginia and North Carolina until those states had been readmitted to the Union, fearing that to sit in militarily occupied areas would make the court lose prestige and recognize the legitimacy of the Johnson governments. He refused to preside over the case of Jefferson Davis until after Johnson's pardon of the

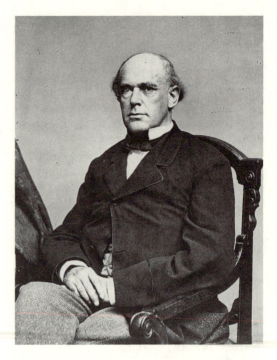

Salmon P. Chase, the "attorney general of fugitive slaves"

former Confederate president made the point moot. Chase declared his own greenbacks as not good enough for legal tender and then saw a reconstituted court reverse him. He dissented from the court majority in key cases concerning Reconstruction, but he wrote the majority opinion in *Texas v. White*, which decided that the nation was an indestructible, perpetual Union of the states. He supervised the impeachment of Johnson and kept the hearing fair. And, of course, he had friends put his name up before the Republican convention in 1868, only to lose out to Ulysses S. Grant. He also toyed with the possibility of running as a Democrat, but this idea was not well received.

Historians consider Chase's Supreme Court to be one of great unity, an amazing feat when one looks at the numerous prickly personalities who served, including Chase himself. Of 170 cases, there was dissent for various reasons in only 20. Once again Chase proved to be an able administrator. He also managed to walk the court down a fine line between its own independence as a branch of government and possible domination by a Congress interested in its own supremacy in government. In 1870, Chase suffered a stroke that left him partially paralyzed on his right side and unable to speak. He refused to resign the bench and, although he missed one term, recovered enough to sit on the bench for two more terms and consider another presidential bid in 1872, as a Liberal Republican. Once again his daughter Kate ran the campaign, trying to convince the skeptical delegates that the chief justice was up to the job. But a second stroke felled him on a campaign trip to New York City, where he died on 6 May 1873.

See also Supreme Court and Reconstruction; Theories of Reconstruction; Waite, Morrison R.

References Donald, David, ed., *Inside Lincoln's Cabinet* (1954); Fairman, Charles, *Reconstruction and Reunion* (1971–1987); Gerteis, Louis S., "Salmon P. Chase, Radicalism, and the Politics of Emancipation" (1973–1974); Kutler, Stanley I., *Judicial Power and Reconstruction Politics* (1968); Sefton, James E., "Chief Justice Chase as an Advisor on Presidential Reconstruction" (1967); Silver, David M., *Lincoln's Supreme Court* (1956).

Civil Rights Acts

During the Reconstruction era Congress passed several acts designed to secure social and political rights to the recently freed slaves: the Civil Rights Acts of 1866 and 1875 and the Enforcement Acts of 1870 and 1871. These measures were to be the only civil rights legislation on the federal level until 1957; even though many of their features were limited by the Supreme Court by 1898, they would set an example for the legislation and executive orders of the so-called Second Reconstruction of the 1960s.

Drawn up by the Joint Committee of Fifteen on Reconstruction, the Civil Rights Act of 1866 nationalized citizenship for the first time in American history (it had been a prerogative of the individual states before the Civil War) by defining a citizen as anyone born or naturalized in the United States. All citizens received certain rights, among them the right to jury trial, the right to sue and be sued, the right to give evi-

dence, the right to be on juries, and the right to receive full protection of the laws. No one could be denied these rights without due process of the law (a court proceeding), and the federal courts were to have sole jurisdiction in these cases. This measure was a part of Moderate Republican Reconstruction and had to be passed over President Andrew Johnson's veto. The president's refusal to include this measure voluntarily as a part of Reconstruction caused Congress to put part of this measure in the first section of the Fourteenth Amendment. Doing this allowed Congress to guarantee the measure's availability to future generations, protected from ordinary repeal, and to overcome the possibility that the U.S. Supreme Court might find the measure contrary to the ruling in an 1857 case, *Dred Scott v. Sanford*, which declared blacks, free or slave, not to be U.S. citizens. This was the first major piece of legislation enacted by Congress over a presidential veto in American history.

The Civil Rights Act of 1875, a lifelong project of Massachusetts senator Charles Sumner, was the congressional answer to the Supreme Court's curtailing of the wider implications of the Fourteenth Amendment. It was essentially the United States' first public accommodations law; it guaranteed citizens of every race the "full and equal" enjoyment and use of inns, public conveyances, and theaters and other places of public amusement. It also had a section stating that race was not to be a factor in excluding persons from service on grand (indictment) and petit (trial) juries. However, to the disappointment of many, it left out any mention of equal schools, cemeteries, and church attendance. The latter measures were politically inexpedient as far as Congress was concerned, because the North and South were filled with voters prejudiced against African Americans in the more personal areas of American life. Indeed, if the Civil Rights Act of 1875 had not been presented as a memorial to Senator Sumner, who had just died, it might not have been enacted at all. In both the North and South, people thought the demands of the bill to be an invasion of individual personal prerogatives. But the act went a long way in correcting what blacks and their white allies saw as the shortcomings presented in the restrictions on the Fourteenth Amendment in what were known as the *Slaughter House* cases (1873). The Supreme Court gutted the public accommodations sections of the act in the 1883 *Civil Rights* cases, although it upheld the jury section in *Strauder v. West Virginia* (1879).

See also Enforcement Acts; Johnson and Reconstruction; Supreme Court and Redemption.

References Beale, Howard K., *The Critical Year [1866]* (1930); Clark, John G., "Historians and the Joint Committee of Reconstruction" (1961) and "Radicals and Moderates in the Joint Committee on Reconstruction" (1963); Donald, David H., *Charles Sumner and the Rights of Man* (1970); Foner, Eric, *Reconstruction* (1988); Franklin, John Hope, "The Enforcement of the Civil Rights Act of 1875" (1989); Hyman, Harold M., "Reconstruction and Political-Constitutional Institution" (1959); Kelly, Alfred H., "The Congressional Controversy over School Segregation" (1958–1959); Kendrick, Benjamin B., *The Journal of the Joint Committee of Fifteen on Reconstruction* (1914); McKitrick, Eric, *Andrew Johnson and Reconstruction* (1960); McPherson, James M., "Abolitionists and the Civil Rights Act of 1875" (1965); Murphy, L. E., "The Civil Rights Law of 1875" (1927); Riddleberger, Patrick W., *1866* (1979); U.S. Congress, "Report of the Joint Committee on Reconstruction" (1866); Vaughn, William P., "Separate and Unequal" (1967); Weaver, Valerie W., "The Failure of Civil Rights 1875–1883 and Its Repercussions" (1969).

Clayton, Powell (1833–1914)

Powell Clayton, a Carpetbag governor of Arkansas, was from a Pennsylvania family that had come over with William Penn (the state's founder). Since that time, the family had great influence in Pennsylvania and Delaware, one ancestor serving in the U.S. Senate and another as secretary of state. Clayton himself was from the area near the Delaware line, and he studied engineering in schools in both Delaware and Pennsylvania. After graduation Clayton went to Kansas in 1855. He was not a fighter in the slavery wars that plagued that territory. He went to Leavenworth because he disliked the free soilers (antislavery advocates) at Lawrence. He was elected to the post of city engineer as a Democrat (his family had been noted Whigs). But although Clayton was not an abolitionist, he was an unequivocal Unionist. When the Civil War came, he raised a company and went off to fight as a captain of infantry. After a short three months of enlistment, he raised a cavalry regiment (better to ride than walk in this war) and rode off to free Arkansas from the Rebels. He rose in rank to brevet brigadier general when he made a name for himself defending Pine Bluff from a Confederate attack in 1863. He credited his able defense to the black laborers who rolled the cotton bale forts into place. As a commander in guerrilla-plagued Arkansas, Clayton's two main jobs during the war were aiding loyal white and black refugees and suppressing bushwhackers. Experience in both fields would serve him well later.

After the war Clayton settled down in Pine Bluff to plant cotton. He married an Arkansas woman, apparently with the blessing of her Rebel parents. As President Andrew Johnson squared off against Congress, Clayton found himself growing disillusioned with the Democratic party. He saw more and more hostility among his neighbors, Rebels who had not been sufficiently cowed by the results of the war. Clayton declined an opportunity to run for Congress on the Democratic ticket. But he was worried by the growing number of raids by night riders and the threats against all Yankees. After the passage of the Military Reconstruction Acts, Clayton decided that he had to stand for Union once again and joined with local black and white Republicans. He quickly rose to the top of the state's party infrastructure and would dominate it until his death.

Elected governor in 1868, Clayton addressed a Republican-dominated legislature, most of whom were native whites (Scalawags, in the parlance of that time). He spoke in favor of transportation projects, especially railroads; public schools; creation of a loyal militia; and encouraging emigration from outside the state. But trouble was not long in coming. At a gathering of local black Republicans in Little Rock, the meeting was

Powell Clayton

emerged from four years of war unscratched.

All was not roses in Arkansas despite the destruction of the Klan. Many residents believed that Clayton's militia had the sinister motive of sweeping the state for Republican political victories, a sort of Klan in reverse without the secrecy. Many Scalawags believed that Clayton supported black rights too fully. But business boomed and peace generally reigned, so that even Clayton's most outspoken enemies had to admit that his regime was doing well. He revived the state's credit rating, made the atmosphere congenial for railroad and logging investors, and kept public schools active. Clayton put his plantation at Pine Bluff under the management of his younger brother and moved with his wife to a row of new homes built on a bluff above the river in Little Rock, dubbed the "Robbers' Roost" by local Democrats since so many of the houses were occupied by Carpetbaggers.

Clayton's real opposition came from fellow Republicans, not Democrats. The anti-Clayton Republicans were led by Lieutenant Governor James M. Johnson, and like him most were Scalawags. They claimed that Clayton's administration was filled with bad management, and they began talks with the Democrats on possibly joining forces. When Clayton left the state on a trip to New York to fund the state debt, Johnson started a rumor that Clayton had absconded with the state treasury. Johnson also decided to come into Little Rock from his Ozark home and take over the government. Only a warning from friends and a fast steamboat got Clayton back in time to avert disaster.

Clayton then went on a political offensive of his own. Claiming that a technicality disqualified Johnson, Clayton challenged the lieutenant governor to prove that he was entitled to his position. Clayton also offered an olive branch of his own to the Democrats. Since Clayton actually had control of the government, the Democrats sat back and awaited developments, which was exactly what Clayton wanted. But the more extreme Radicals were dismayed at Clayton's willingness to play politics so

attacked by Klansmen under the cover of a fire department wagon. Clayton could not fathom the fear of black-dominated government in Arkansas because only a quarter of the state's population was black. But attacks on Republicans continued, many of them racially inspired. Unlike other Reconstruction governors, Clayton did not hesitate a moment. He proclaimed martial law, called out the "black and tan" militia (most of whom were Unionists from the Ozarks and former slaves from the Arkansas and Mississippi river bottoms), and pacified the whole state in a series of military campaigns reminiscent of those he fought successfully during the war. He used agents and spies to join the local klaverns and tip the militia off as to the Ku Klux Klan's next moves. Clayton marked his men with red scarves and hatbands, and the arrests these men made paid off in numerous convictions and hangings that gave the governor a national reputation. Meanwhile a hunting accident caused him to lose his left hand—after he had dangerously. The legislature tried to impeach Clayton but could find no reason to file charges. In a complicated set of negotiations, Clayton agreed to drop his charges against Johnson, who would resign the lieutenant governorship if Clayton would make him secretary of state. The legislature would then elect Clayton to the U.S. Senate, and the governorship would go to the state senate president, one of Clayton's Carpetbag friends. In Washington, Clayton found himself at home with Maine senator James G. Blaine, who had an interest in Arkansas railroads that would eventually cost Blaine the presidency in 1884.

With Clayton in Washington, the state Republican party divided up between (1) the Radical Republicans, or "Brindletails," led by Joseph Brooks, a Carpetbagger from Iowa and a man of the cloth, and (2) the Moderate Republicans, or "Minstrels," under Clayton's heir apparent, Elisha Baxter, an Arkansas Scalawag. When the legislature sent Clayton ally Stephen W. Dorsey to the other U.S. Senate seat and put Clayton's two brothers in important local positions, it seemed that the state was to be in Clayton's hands forever. The legislature decided to recognize Baxter as the elected governor, a stunt challenged by rival Brooks in a political free-for-all known as the Brooks-Baxter War. But Baxter soon proved to be too independent to suit Clayton. He was appointing too many Democrats to office; he refused to authorize the railroad bonds that Clayton and Blaine found so appealing. Evidently Baxter feared that Clayton would try to have him impeached and replaced with Clayton's brother John, the new president of the state senate. So Clayton threw his support to Brooks and had President Grant recognize him as the legal governor. Both sides assembled armed men to back their point of view, but Baxter still held the statehouse and the legislature recognized his claim. Grant, thoroughly sick of these petty squabbles from the South, decided to accept Baxter instead, and Clayton's side lost out. By now the Republican party was so divided that it lost the general election to the Democratic candidate, Augustus H. Garland.

With the Republicans split and the Democrats in power, Garland's supporters decided to cut a deal with Clayton to divide up offices among them, in order to keep blacks from gaining control in the counties they dominated along the Arkansas and Mississippi rivers. Clayton agreed. This made him the Republican boss to be reckoned with for years to come. When he finished his term in the Senate, Clayton returned to Arkansas, where he dabbled in railroads and real estate, making a small fortune. In 1897 he went to Mexico as President William McKinley's ambassador. His greatest diplomatic coup was to settle claims between the Catholic Church of California (as representative of the Vatican) and the Mexican government for confiscated church lands inside Mexico. Clayton retired to Washington, D.C., in 1905 and wrote his own account of the turbulent times of Arkansas' Reconstruction. In 1914 he died a few days after he finished the manuscript, which was published the following year.

See also Carpetbaggers.

References Boatner, Mark M., III, *The Civil War Dictionary* (1959); Clayton, Powell, *The Aftermath of the Civil War in Arkansas* (1915); Current, Richard N., *Those Terrible Carpetbaggers* (1988); Driggs, Orval T., "The Issues of the Powell Clayton Regime" (1949); Harrell, John M., *The Brooks and Baxter War* (1893); Swinney, Everette, "United States vs. Powell Clayton" (1967); Thompson, George H., *Arkansas and Reconstruction* (1976).

Colfax, Schuyler (1823–1885)

Schuyler Colfax, vice president of the United States during the first U. S. Grant administration, was born in New York City. His father died when Schuyler was a boy, and his mother's new husband took the family to Indiana in 1836. His stepfather was a local politician who eventually appointed Colfax to the position of deputy auditor at South Bend, a position he held for eight years. He was also a newspaper correspondent and publisher, and he read law on the side. Like his stepfather, Colfax was a Whig. He took an early interest in politics, campaigned for Henry Clay's presidential bid in 1844, and attended the national Whig conventions in 1848 and 1852. He was also a delegate to the Indiana constitutional convention in 1850 and unsuccessfully ran for Congress in 1851. He joined the new Republican party in 1854 and helped organize it in Indiana, winning a seat in the U.S. House in 1855. He served continuously until 1869, being elected speaker in 1863. He was a proponent of free soil (i.e., no slavery) in Kansas and organized the first transcontinental mail service as chairman of the committee on post offices and roads. He was strongly considered for becoming postmaster general under Abraham Lincoln, but the president turned him down in favor of Edward Bates of Missouri. Upon the death of his first wife in 1863, Colfax married a niece of powerful Republican leader Senator Benjamin Wade, a wise political move.

As Speaker of the House, Colfax was an advocate of reformist positions concerning African Americans, like emancipation, military service, and the vote, which made him the perfect Radical Republican counterbalance to the moderation of Ulysses S. Grant in 1868. Grant offered him the position of secretary of state in 1871, but Colfax declined. Grant then dumped him from the administration in the election of 1872, when Colfax flirted too long with the Liberal Republicans. But Colfax would not have lasted anyhow because he became involved in the Crédit Mobilier railroad scandal. It turned out that Colfax, while he was speaker, had accepted 20 shares of stock, uncounted "dividends," and a campaign contribution of $4,000 from a contractor who supplied envelopes to government offices. Colfax maintained his innocence until the end, but his story was not convincing, even to friends. After his forced retirement he spent much of his time as a paid lecturer and as a member of the Odd Fellows lodge. He died suddenly while on a trip to Minnesota on 1885. His body was returned to South Bend for burial.

See also Grant and Domestic Politics.

References MacDonald, William, "Schuyler Colfax" (1964–1981); Smith, Willard H., *Schuyler Colfax* (1952).

Colonization of African Americans Overseas

The idea of relocating enslaved black Americans to Africa became very compelling to many after the War of 1812. Because slavery looked pretty much unprofitable at the time, and because the soils in the Southeastern Atlantic states were becoming exhausted by intensive agriculture and the accompanying erosion, it was hoped that many slaveowners would avail themselves of this chance to get rid of the "peculiar institution." In 1816, led by notable politicians like President James Monroe, former president James Madison, and Speaker of the House Henry Clay, the American Colonization Society was formed. It was to free blacks from slavery and send them to a spot on the African coast that eventually became the nation of Liberia. Money to compensate the slaveowners for emancipation would be provided from the tariff on imports, which was also mentioned as a source of funding for various internal improvements and would serve the purpose of protecting the fledgling U.S. industries from the import of cheap foreign goods.

Then came the boom of upland cotton in the Old Southwest, particularly in the Mississippi Delta region. All of a sudden, slaves had real worth. They could be sold to the Deep South from slaveholding states further north, or a plantation owner could move his whole operation to the new rich soils to profit immensely. Many historians think that investment in cotton, slaves, and land was the single most profitable economic endeavor of the first half of the nineteenth century, even outdoing railroads. As the Deep South expanded economically, the strife between North and South grew accordingly. Now it looked like slavery was here to stay. It even had application in industries and mining, which threatened to extend it into the arid Southwest, once thought unfit for white Americans. Still, many adhered to the old colonization idea, and one of these individuals was Abraham Lincoln, destined to become sixteenth president of the United States in 1861.

Lincoln was an advocate of Henry Clay's

political and economic policies all of his life. On colonization he advanced Clay's notion that there was "moral fitness in the idea of returning to Africa her children, whose ancestors have been torn from her by the ruthless hand of fraud and violence." After his inauguration, Lincoln looked into colonization as a way to handle the large numbers of blacks who had fled to Union lines for protection from their masters. Congress endorsed the president's suggestions on 16 April 1862, when it passed a law to end slavery in the District of Columbia. Part of the measure called for $100,000 to be appropriated to remove such freed slaves to Liberia, Haiti, or anywhere they wished to go and would be well received. Each immigrant was to receive not more than $100. Later, on 16 July an additional $500,000 was appropriated to extend the project further. Both equal rights advocates, like Senator Charles Sumner of Massachusetts, and most blacks themselves protested the plan as unfair. But the president mentioned the plan to border-state white political leaders as a possible approach to the compensated end of slavery he was recommending to them. Lincoln also tried to interest a delegation of freed blacks in the concept, to no avail.

Nonetheless, Lincoln instructed Secretary of State William H. Seward to look into which nations in the Caribbean or Latin America (either independent republics or colonies of European powers) might be used. Most of Central America and South America except for New Grenada (present-day Colombia) and Ecuador rejected the idea. But several Caribbean islands (Danish, Dutch, and British), Haiti, and Liberia expressed interest. By this time, however, even Lincoln realized that there could be no forced deportation of African Americans. So he tried to get volunteers to show how it would work and thereby interest others. Two colonies were examined, one at Chiriqui on the Isthmus of Panama and another at L'Isle à Vache off the coast of Haiti. The Panamanian effort fell through because of disputes over the land titles between New Grenada and Costa Rica. Besides, no one wanted to

go to Chiriqui because a prior examination proved that alleged coal fields were of doubtful value. And there was also some private consideration of the United States claiming the isthmus for a future canal.

The L'Isle à Vache project, on the other hand, went a lot farther. An entrepreneur, Bernard Kock, described the island as 100 square miles of tropical paradise. Sugar, cotton, coffee, and indigo were possible crops. Timber was plentiful. At $50 per person Kock agreed to take 5,000 African Americans to the place and set them up in their own independent homeland. Kock promised to establish comfortable homes, garden lots, churches, and schools, and to guarantee employment for four years. Then Lincoln heard that Kock was in receipt of fugitive blacks from the American South and had contracted with other entrepreneurs to transport them to L'Isle à Vache at a hoped-for profit of 600 percent after nine months' work. Lincoln canceled all government contracts with Kock immediately. But another group of capitalists secured a governmental contract to transport up to 500 volunteers from among freed slaves staying at Fortress Monroe. The project was plagued by disease from the day the ships sailed. The colonists found that the island was a virtual wilderness, and the Haitian government was hostile to their arrival. More disease put an end to the expedition. In 1864 Lincoln sent another vessel to remove all of the colonists who wished to return to the United States. On 2 July 1864, Congress repealed its appropriations for all colonization efforts.

But that did not end the project, at least according to Benjamin Butler, although historians generally dismiss these undocumented assertions as suspect. Butler reported years later that Lincoln had still wanted to advance a colony in 1865, shortly before his assassination. This time the place of interest was Santo Domingo. But Butler looked into the project at the president's behest and found that all of the available U.S. shipping that could safely be used could not transport African Americans fast enough to beat their own birth rate. James

H. Lane suggested that blacks be colonized on land west of the Colorado River in Texas, but this idea was received with a lot of hostility in Texas, as well as in Congress. It really did not matter. After blacks had fought in the Civil War for their own freedom, it became morally and politically impossible to propose that they leave the country of their birth. And forceful repatriation was out of the question. So the colonization of American slaves to a colony overseas was taken out of consideration for a while, only to be resurrected later when the Ulysses S. Grant administration tried to buy Santo Domingo from its own corrupt dictator. Senator Charles Sumner made stopping this scheme a priority during his last years in the Senate.

See also Emancipation; Exodusters; Lincoln and Reconstruction.

References Boritt, Gabor S., "The Voyage to the Colony of Lincolniana" (1975); Gold, Robert L., "Negro Colonization Schemes in Equador," (1969); Lockett, James D., "Abraham Lincoln and Colonization" (1991); Neely, Mark E., Jr., "Abraham Lincoln and Black Colonization" (1979); Stadenraus, P. J., *The African Colonization Movement* (1961); Wesley, Charles H., "Lincoln's Plan for Colonizing the Emancipated Negroes" (1919).

Come Retribution

The assassination of President Abraham Lincoln is too often seen as an event in isolation committed by a man on the brink of insanity, John Wilkes Booth, as a sort of last explosion of frustration to avenge the defeated South. This theory does not take into account Come Retribution, a Confederate secret service plan to kidnap Lincoln and hold him ransom for the South's independence. Detailed in a recent study by researcher William A. Tidwell, Come Retribution challenges all of the ordinary assumptions and portrays Lincoln's death as a logical outcome of a well-thought out plan gone awry. Tidwell, a former Central Intelligence Agency operative, takes a new look at existing Civil War records and finds much that historians had overlooked or dismissed as gibberish but that immediately draws the eye of an experienced intelligence officer like himself. In his study he proposes a theory that seeks to answer, among other things, the question of why Booth killed Lincoln.

The South in 1865 had everything to gain from the traditional theory that Booth was a half-crazy man who went berserk. That theory put an end to a lot of searching into motives that might have embarrassed Southern leaders resting uncomfortably in Yankee jails. The story is further confused by the notion that Lincoln was the South's best friend in Washington, as illustrated by his lenient wartime Reconstruction policy, the famed Ten Percent Plan. Scores of stories—some professionally researched, some not—have appeared since Otto Eisenschiml's 1938 book *Why Was Lincoln Shot?*, variously linking Booth to Radical Republicans, claiming that he disappeared only to resurface again 40 years later to confess his crime before dying, and positing Booth's connection to an ill-conceived plan to kidnap the president and take him south to save the Confederacy. Only the last notion is indisputably true. The kidnapping plan formed the basis for the president's assassination and is the focus of Tidwell's inquiry.

Tidwell is the first to admit that his story is conjecture. But it has escaped much of the criticism raised against others working in the field. Tidwell believes that the origins of the assassination of the president lay in a botched Union raid against Richmond, Virginia, led by Brig. Gen. Judson Kilpatrick and Col. Ulrich Dahlgren, in the spring of 1864, a few months before Lt. Gen. Ulysses S. Grant's campaign against the Confederate capital that would end the war a year later. A Confederate search of the battle sites after the fighting was over revealed numerous papers about the failed expedition, including the known objectives of freeing federal soldiers, burning Richmond and, more important, a secret plan to assassinate Confederate president Jefferson Davis and his cabinet.

In that age of romantic chivalry, the South was outraged by these plans. Lincoln had lived in a Southern city (Washington) for four years without an assassination even being contemplated. Many in the South urged retaliation. Ostensibly Southern leaders refused to countenance such a move. But Tidwell maintains that secretly they did. The plan was one not of assassination but of kidnap. It was conceived as Grant tightened his hold upon Richmond and Petersburg in the fall of 1864, with Confederate chances on the battlefield seeming to be waning with the losses of the Shenandoah Valley in Virginia and Atlanta in Georgia. Southern agents would take the president into Richmond, the idea went, using the Confederate secret mail line that ran from Washington to just north of Richmond. The Confederate agent who led the kidnap team was actor John Wilkes Booth.

Lincoln had the habit of traveling through the District of Columbia relatively unprotected. Relying on the president's lack of protection, Booth and his conspirators picked a time and spot to make their move. But Lincoln, on a whim, changed his route and time of travel, causing the plan to fall flat. It was too late to try again because doing so would not correspond with the spring 1865 campaign developed by General Lee and Jefferson Davis. This plan called for abandoning Richmond after an attack by Lee's army to throw Grant back on his heels for a few days. With a day or two's head start, Lee hoped to get his army to the railroad behind Richmond, where he had stored supplies. Then he would head south and join with another Confederate force led by Gen. Joseph Johnston and crush the Yankee army under Maj. Gen. William T. Sherman in North Carolina. This accomplished, Lee hoped to utilize his central position to swing back on Grant and defeat him as he struggled to move forward on a lengthy supply line. The war was still winnable, Lee reasoned, if the Confederates could move with the rapidity for which they were famous.

To keep Sherman and Grant from communicating among themselves and with the coordinating general staff and Lincoln in Washington, the Rebels came up with a new wrinkle in Come Retribution. They would blow up the White House, hopefully with Lincoln and some of his cabinet and military men in it. This would so confuse the situation that the North would be in chaos for days, allowing the Confederate campaign to get under way. Lt. Col. John Singleton Mosby would take Confederate explosives expert Thomas F. Harney to Washington to connect with Booth's agents, who would help Harney do the job.

But bad luck dogged the Confederates in 1865. Outside Washington, Mosby's escort ran into a Yankee cavalry patrol; in the ensuing gunfight, explosives expert Harney was captured and jailed in the Old Capitol Prison. Meanwhile, Lee began his breakaway from Grant only to find that Grant was faster than he. In a week of hard marching and numerous fire fights, Grant cut Lee off from his stored supplies and ran his army down, forcing Lee to surrender at Appomattox Court House. This left Booth in a quandary. What was he to do without further orders? He decided on his own to improvise on Come Retribution with his own people. With no explosives expert, he would rely on assassination to accomplish the same thing. He did not know that Lee's surrender had made the whole plan irrelevant. He picked out President Lincoln, Vice President Andrew Johnson, Secretary of State William H. Seward, and Secretary of War Edwin M. Stanton as his targets. He would use many men he had known since childhood (most of whom proved untrustworthy) and escape by way of the same route that the kidnapped Lincoln was to have been hustled to Richmond.

That Booth failed was the fault of poor personnel. Johnson and Stanton were never attacked. Another compatriot almost killed Seward and his son, and Booth killed Lincoln. Along with Confederate courier Davy Herold, Booth fled out to Surratt's Tavern, down to the house of Dr. Samuel Mudd (a Confederate sympathizer who may have known Booth from before the war), where Booth's injured leg was set, and on to Virginia's Northern Neck just south of Port Royal. At Garrett's Farm, a pursuing Yankee Cavalry squadron killed Booth and arrested Herold. The young Herold was brought to Washington, where he joined the other conspirators, four of whom were hanged (Herold; Mary Surratt, who probably knew nothing of the plot, although her son John did; Lewis Paine, who nearly killed Seward; and George Azerodt, who was to have killed Johnson but panicked) and three more of whom (the hapless Dr. Mudd and a couple of innocent theater workers) were sent to a military prison off the Florida Keys in the Dry Tortugas.

Many historians of the Civil War question whether Tidwell is mistaken in including honorable men like Davis, Lee, and Mosby in the plot. They prefer to see a "rogue" member of government as initiating the process without the others knowing. The preferred villain is Judah P. Benjamin, variously secretary of state, secretary of war, and attorney general of the Confederacy. But Benjamin could not have acted without the cooperation of Davis, who had cosigned money vouchers, in accordance with Confederate law, to finance a secret unnamed project. Davis's main military advisor was Lee. And Lee, Mosby (Lee's prime informant on affairs in northern Virginia), and others like Secretary of War John C. Breckinridge (former U.S. vice president under Buchanan) had all been at Richmond at the time the meetings to plan such activities took place. Moreover, Tidwell points out that nearly 1,000 men from selected Virginia regiments in Lee's army (all from locations along Booth's route to safety with Lincoln as prisoner) got furloughed home just as the kidnapping was to take place—a unit Tidwell sees as a blocking force to hold off expected Union pursuit. These men never surrendered at Appomattox with their parent units. They instead surrendered at Ashland Station, now a federal provost marshal's headquarters, in the weeks following the fall of the Confederacy.

If Tidwell and others who agree with him are right, the Civil War brought out heretofore unthinkable measures on both sides as they fought desperately for their vision of America's future. Perhaps it was just as well that it took 130 years to unravel the whole story. Tidwell sees Lincoln's assassination

as part of the clandestine activities of a Confederate secret service that included the Rose Greenhow spy ring in Washington, D.C., and activities in Canada that led to several attempts to free Confederate soldiers held prisoner in Northern states. He speaks of a reorganized Confederate secret service act passed in 1865 that rivaled anything done in North America until the advent of the Central Intelligence Agency in 1947. A lot of hanging might have resulted had the whole truth according to Tidwell been known during Reconstruction.

See also Davis, Jefferson F.; Lincoln, Abraham.

References George, Joseph, Jr., "Black Flag Warfare" (1991); Hanchett, William, *The Lincoln Murder Conspiracies* (1983) and "Lincoln's Murder"; Tidwell, William A., *April '65* (1995); Tidwell, William A., with James O. Hall and David Winfred Gaddy, *Come Retribution* (1988); Turner, Thomas R., *Beware the People Weeping* (1982).

Command of the Army Act

Section 2 of the Army Appropriations Act of 1867, known as the Command of the Army Act, provided that the headquarters of the general-in-chief be fixed at Washington, D.C., and that the general (Lt. Gen. Ulysses S. Grant) could not be suspended, removed, or reassigned to duty elsewhere, unless he requested it, without the express concurrence of the U.S. Senate. All orders to the army in the field from the president or the secretary of war had to go through the general-in-chief to be valid. To obey any order not so routed could lead to imprisonment from 2 to 20 years. The notion was to fix Grant in the office; he was leaning toward the Radical Republican view at that time and believed Congress to be the supreme branch of the government and voice of the people. Another goal was to prevent President Andrew Johnson from interfering with Radical or Military Reconstruction (he had tried to send Grant away to Mexico on a diplomatic mission months earlier). The law was never tested because Grant and Johnson never came to open disagreement over any of the president's requests. Another section of the same measure disbanded all existing militia organizations in the Southern states to prevent armed interference with Reconstruction.

See also Radical Republicans and Reconstruction.

Reference Sefton, James E., *The United States Army and Reconstruction* (1967).

Compensated Emancipation

Throughout the eighteenth and nineteenth centuries, many Americans, North and South, advocated getting rid of the institution of slavery by paying off the slave owners to allow emancipation. But the movement's chance of success was already negligible even before the radical abolitionists appeared on the American political scene, even though new compensation schemes appeared right up to the end of the Civil War. Very often, but not always, these compensation schemes included colonization of African Americans in Africa or in some tropical clime in the Western Hemisphere.

The first public suggestions for compensated emancipation occurred shortly after the American Revolution. Thomas Pownall, once a royal governor of Massachusetts during the French and Indian War, advocated establishing a black state in the western territories between the Appalachians and the Mississippi obtained at the Peace of Paris (1783). Quaker abolitionist Anthony Benezet seconded the notion. Both men were interested in the new nation living up to the noble precepts stated in the Declaration of Independence. In 1790, Elbridge Gerry of Massachusetts proposed that petitions from several state abolition societies be answered by emancipating slaves gradually as monies became available from the sales of western lands. Ten years later another Massachusetts representative, George Thatcher, in response to a petition made by free blacks from Philadelphia to end the fugitive slave law and the Atlantic slave trade, asked that Congress investigate methods to finance the end of all slavery in the United States. In all cases lack of support in the North and vociferous criticism from Southerners, especially South Carolinians, ended the debate. The suggestions, however, seemed thereafter to connect the idea of compensated emancipation with settlement of African Americans in, or the sale of, the western lands.

By the end of the War of 1812, the idea of compensated emancipation had become linked with the notion of sending liberated slaves to Africa. This period was the heyday of the American Colonization Society, backed by men like Henry Clay and former presidents Thomas Jefferson, James Madison, and James Monroe. All feared the difficulties of assimilating freed blacks into white society and government and saw transportation overseas as a logical (albeit racist) solution. When the controversy over the admission of Missouri as a slave state came to a head in 1820, Henry Meigs of New York submitted a proposal arguing that it was a good time to get rid of slavery altogether by using monies from the sale of public lands. After the admission of Missouri as a slave state, Meigs reintroduced his project, adding to it a clause to set aside 500 million acres especially earmarked for the ending of slavery. When a master decided to free his bondservants, he would receive a government scrip that entitled him or his heirs to a land grant from the selected territory. Not only would slavery end, but the settlement of the West would thereby be stimulated. However, neither of Meigs's proposals received any real consideration.

Other ideas followed those of Meigs. One of them tied compensated emancipation to the ending of the national debt (something President Andrew Jackson accomplished in 1835), whereupon all federal monies would be turned to the emancipation project. Henry Clay introduced compensated emancipation as a part of his American system of financing economic growth. To overcome Southern opposition, Clay emphasized that his program was not one of abolition but rather a government effort to allow individual slave owners a choice of emancipation if they so desired. Clay would finance his program through the proceeds from public land sales, once again. Clay made numerous efforts to gain some form of compensated emancipation but failed each time. Daniel Webster of Massachusetts joined Clay in the last of these schemes in 1850.

No matter how reasonable these compensation plans seem today, at the time they were envisioned to be just as revolutionary as uncompensated abolition. It was not until the bloodbath of the Civil War and Lincoln's backing of the Emancipation Proclamation and the Thirteenth Amendment that these plans were seen as the conservative approach they truly were. Lincoln, with the backing of many abolitionists, offered to pay for the slaves of the loyal border states during the war several times, only to be rebuffed. It was not until 1865 and the passage of the Thirteenth Amendment that Southerners were willing to consider compensation for their slave property. Many slaveowners held their chattel until 1866, hoping in vain that Congress might vote some form of compensation, but by then it was too late. Furthermore, it cannot be said that nonslaveholding states would have permitted the creation of a black commonwealth in the West paid for by land sales, either. All of which suggests that there was more to slavery than forced labor—it had a lot to do with whites' notions of refusing to accept blacks as a part of the American experiment. Slavery was as much a social system as the segregation that followed it, both before the war in the North and after the war in the South.

See also Colonization of African Americans Overseas; Cox Plan of Reconstruction; Emancipation; Lincoln and Reconstruction.

References Fishel, Leslie H., "Repercussions of Reconstruction" (1968); Fladeland, Betty L., "Compensated Emancipation" (1976); Litwack, Leon F., *Been in the Storm So Long* (1979); Myrdal, Gunnar, *An American Dilemma* (1964); Schultz, John H., "Thomas Pownall and His Negro Commonwealth" (1945); Staudenraus, P. J., *The African Colonization Movement* (1961); Zilversmit, Arthur, *The First Emancipation* (1967).

Compromise of 1877

See Election of 1876 and Compromise of 1877.

Confederate Brigadiers

With the exception of Texas, which was late in implementing Andrew Johnson's Reconstruction plans, the Southern states established new "reconstructed" governments in the fall of 1865. Part of this process was to elect representatives and senators. If these individuals were seated in the upcoming session of Congress, it would signify that the Reconstruction process initiated by the executive branch was recognized as valid by the legislative branch of the federal government. When Northerners saw the names of the men elected to represent the South, they professed shock, and Congress refused to seat them on the floor. The men were pretty much the same ones who had led the South out of the Union four years before and had sustained the Confederacy through the war. Historian W. E. Burghardt DuBois counted up the toll for posterity: the vice president of the Confederacy (Alexander Stephens), four Confederate generals, five Confederate colonels, six Confederate cabinet officers, and 58 Confederate congressmen, none of whom was able to take the required oath of loyalty to the Union without a special pardon. These men received the disparaging nickname "the Confederate Brigadiers."

In reality, DuBois underestimated the military figures. There were 10 generals and 5 officers of lesser rank. But these individuals were not devout secessionists, as contemporary newspapers and later historians assumed. Of 80 senators and representatives, only 7 had been supporters of secession in 1860 and 1861. Seventy had opposed secession until the election of Abraham Lincoln as president, and 44 had remained opposed until their states voted to leave the Union. However, most had supported the Confederacy after its creation, either as military men or as civil functionaries. Five had been peace candidates during their elections, however, on platforms that came close to treason to the Confederacy. Fifteen others were openly and consistently Union men throughout the war. Another 16 were openly neutral to the war effort. Of the 11 state governors, only 3 had been secessionists and 4 more would ultimately become Republicans during Radical Military Reconstruction. These men were willing to admit to the loss of the war, the end of slavery, the supremacy of the federal government, and a temporarily diminished political role for the South nationally; but none of them, not even the most devout Unionists, were willing to concede equal civil rights, much less the vote, to African Americans. This fact made them poor choices for reconstructing the South, as their support for the oppressive Black Codes demonstrated.

See also Black Codes; Johnson and Reconstruction; Moderate Republicans and Reconstruction.

References Carter, Dan T., *When the War Was Over* (1985); DuBois, W. E. Burghardt, *Black Reconstruction* (1935).

Confiscation Acts

In response to Confederate measures that confiscated all debts due Northerners (passed on 21 May 1861) and alien property (30 August 1861), the U.S. Congress began its own confiscation program embodied in two pieces of legislation: the Confiscation Acts.

The Confiscation Act of 1861, passed on 6 August 1861, and known as the First Confiscation Act, condemned all property used to further the rebellion against the United States. It was limited in scope and stated that confiscation had to take place through a court proceeding. The U.S. attorney could initiate proceedings, or a private citizen could file information that, if found to be true, would entitle the informer to half of the proceeds from the condemned property. Maj. Gen. Benjamin Butler said that he used the ideas expressed in this act even before its promulgation to confiscate fugitive slaves coming into his lines at Fortress Monroe, Virginia, in 1861; he declared such slaves to be contraband of war, which led to these individuals being called "contrabands" during the rest of the war.

As the war lengthened and Northern battlefield losses grew, clamor for a harsher policy of confiscation of Rebel property arose. The 1861 law was cumbersome in its insistence on court proceedings and gave the benefit of the doubt to the alleged Rebels. The Second Confiscation Act of 17 July 1862 was designed to be truly punitive in nature; it involved the outright seizure of all property of those who aided the rebellion. The law inspired much debate concerning its harshness and whether it recognized the Southerners as belligerents (as opposed to rebels), especially with respect to Democrats from border slave states. Indeed, President Abraham Lincoln once considered vetoing the measure, but in the end he signed it. As passed, the Second Confiscation Act permitted the immediate seizure for the offender's lifetime of all property of anyone who was an officer of the Confederacy (civil, military, or naval). All others in any part of the United States or occupied territory would be given 60 days to change their allegiance by taking an oath of loyalty to the Union government. After that time their property could be taken if they could be declared as Rebels in a court proceeding.

The Confiscation Acts were enforced during the war, but few felt their effect unless they had their own property seized. Financially the acts failed to take enough Rebel-owned property to cause any discomfort to the Confederate cause. After the war, confiscation proceedings actually increased, but because the courts had to be used and the backlog was tremendous, little was actually taken. Amnesty and pardon of most Rebels led to a return of property to its original owner in most cases. Even in the case of Arlington, the ancestral home of the wife of Confederate general Robert E. Lee, the family received a settlement for the estate, which had in the meantime been converted into the National Cemetery.

See also Contrabands; Virginia Experiment.

References Lucie, Patricia M. L., "Confiscation" (1977); Randall, James G., *The Confiscation of Property during the Civil War* (1913) and *Constitutional Problems under Lincoln* (1964).

Congressional Reconstruction

During the Civil War and Reconstruction eras, Congress put forth three proposals to reunite the nation. The first was the Wade-Davis Bill of 1864, in response to President Abraham Lincoln's Ten Percent Plan. The bill proposed that Congress have a voice in Reconstruction and questioned whether Lincoln's plan really represented a democratic proposal because it relied on only a small group of the registered voters in 1860 to get it started. Congress preferred involving a majority of registered voters and wanted to restrict initial voting to those who had never rendered support to secession or the Confederacy. Lincoln pocket-vetoed the measure, indicating that he preferred to have a freer hand in setting Reconstruction terms for the defeated South. But by refusing to seat the representatives and senators from the Southern governments established under Lincoln's plan, Congress parried the president's attempt to reconstruct the South by exercising his alleged war powers. Lincoln's death left Reconstruction in limbo by 1865, necessitating a reexamination by the executive and legislative branches.

Congress' response was the second legislative Reconstruction program, which included the Fourteenth Amendment and the measures that led up to it (the renewal of the Freedmen's Bureau and the Civil Rights Bill of 1866). When President Andrew Johnson continued the Lincoln wartime policy of ruling during congressional recess through presidential proclamation, Congress refused to seat the representatives from his Reconstruction program in December 1865. Instead it proposed that the federal government protect the newly freed blacks through continuing an existing agency, the Bureau of Refugees, Freedmen, and Abandoned Lands, or the Freedmen's Bureau. It also proposed that citizenship and certain civil rights be granted by law to African Americans to counter the effect of discriminatory Southern state laws known as Black Codes and a prewar U.S. Supreme Court decision (*Dred Scott v. Sanford*, 1857) that said that blacks were not citizens. When President Johnson vetoed these acts and ridiculed Congress, the legislators repassed both proposals over his veto and sought to enshrine citizenship and equal rights in a constitutional amendment (the Fourteenth). When all of the Confederate South (except Tennessee) and two border slave states that had remained loyal during the war (Delaware and Kentucky) refused to endorse this program, it failed, causing Congress to reassess its position once again.

The impasse over the Fourteenth Amendment led to the third congressional Reconstruction plan, known as Radical Reconstruction or Military Reconstruction. This was a demanding program that nullified presidential interference and compelled the South to act as Congress desired under the supervision of the U.S. Army. The 39th Congress, immediately upon its adjournment, called its successor into session to prevent a gap in legislative supervision, which presidents had previously taken advantage of to circumvent Congress. Further, the president was prohibited from giving direct commands to the army in the field and was not allowed to remove executive officials who had been appointed with the advice and consent of the Senate without Senate concurrence. Congress also passed four Military Reconstruction Acts that required the Southern states to write new state constitutions, grant the right to vote to black males, and approve the Fourteenth Amendment (a process completed by all but Texas, Mississippi, and Virginia by 1868) and, in some cases, the Fifteenth Amendment (a process completed by the three laggards and by Georgia, which had to be reconstructed twice under the Military Reconstruction Acts, by 1870). Except for the enforcement of the Reconstruction provisions on behalf of black citizens, Congressional Reconstruction was over.

See also Bureau of Refugees, Freedmen, and Abandoned Lands; Civil Rights Acts; Command of the Army Act; Enforcement Acts; Fortieth Congress Extra Session Act; Fourteenth Amendment; Johnson and Reconstruction; Joint Committee of Fifteen on Reconstruction; Lincoln and Reconstruction; Military Reconstruction Acts; Moderate Republicans and Reconstruction; Radical Republicans and Reconstruction; Tenure of Office Act; Wade-Davis Bill; Wade-Davis Manifesto and the Elections of 1864.

References Coulter, E. Merton, *The South during Reconstruction*, (1947); Craven, Avery O., *Reconstruction* (1969); Foner, Eric, *Reconstruction* (1988);

Franklin, John Hope, *Reconstruction* (1961); Patrick, Rembert W., *The Reconstruction of the Nation* (1967); Sefton, James E., *The United States Army and Reconstruction* (1967); Trelease, Allen W., *Reconstruction* (1971).

Congressional Supremacy

When the Republicans took control of the federal government in 1861, the power of the presidency was at a low ebb. Ever since the American Revolution there had been a strong commitment to legislative supremacy vis-à-vis the executive branch of government. Various state constitutions of the time put political power in the hands of the elected representatives of the people. King George III had shown Americans enough of executive tyranny. This led to the Articles of Confederation (1781), in which Congress was specified as the supreme branch of government. However, criticism arose that the government was too weak to do much of anything, especially in defense or the promotion of economic harmony. The result was the ratification in 1787 of the U.S. Constitution, a document seen as almost holy today, but one that was seen as an usurpation of power from the states by the central government at the time it was written.

The executive-legislative argument became central to early party battles in American history. Usually the party out of power favors a more powerful Congress—a place where they at least have some say on what is going on. This struggle reached a fever pitch in the 1830s when the opposition to Andrew Jackson, the first really strong executive under the Constitution, became angry with his leadership. He was compared to King George III and given the title of King Andrew I of Veto Memory, because he made great use of that prerogative to defeat the measures of his adversaries. Jackson believed that because he was the only member of the federal government elected by all the people, he had a clearer right to power than Congress, which represented small districts of special local interests. His opponents took on the name Whigs, a reference to those, both in America and in the English

Parliament, who had supported the American Revolution. And because the Whig candidates rarely seemed to win the presidency, the Whigs put forward the idea that Congress, elected by the people every two years, was actually the body of government most answerable to the people. Some state legislatures, particularly in the South, even sent instructions to their representatives and senators, telling them how to vote on certain issues.

By the era before the Civil War, the United States had gone through a series of political administrations that appeared particularly gutless, especially when compared to those of Jackson and his student, James K. Polk, who preceded these weak executive leaders, and Abraham Lincoln, who followed. Taking their cue from the defunct Whigs, which had been destroyed in part over the North-South split over the slavery issue, the new Republican party put forth the doctrine of the Whigs—that the branch of government closest to the wishes of the people was Congress. The president was charged with enforcing Congress' laws and the courts with interpreting them, leaving all duty of correction and initiation of law to the legislative branch. Lincoln, of course, ruled as much as possible by presidential decree, using the adjournment periods of Congress to make his biggest statements in policy. This so angered the Radical Republicans (and they were not alone in the party) that in 1864 they passed the Wade-Davis Bill, followed by the Wade-Davis Manifesto in answer to Lincoln's veto, stating that the problem of Reconstruction was a congressional responsibility. Congress would establish policy through law, the president would enforce those laws, and the Supreme Court would find those measures constitutional.

When Andrew Johnson, "His Accidency," having achieved the presidency through Lincoln's death (though Johnson was really a Democrat), tried to continue with Lincoln's independent policy of Reconstruction, Congress impeached him and cut him down. They warned the Supreme Court not to interfere; they removed cases from the court's appellate jurisdiction (a perfectly legal move) and threatened to allow their man in the White House, President Ulysses S. Grant, to pack the court with members approved by the Senate. The appointment process was watched through the Tenure of Office Act, which allowed the Senate to confirm any presidential patronage changes. Any president who failed to follow the recommendations of powerful representatives and senators in appointing people to local positions, like the New York City customs house, wound up in trouble when it came to executive monetary bills (which would be loaded with riders to force the president to admit to congressional control or shut down the whole government) and party renomination time. The veto power was also to be used sparingly, not in a "wholesale manner" as Jackson, Lincoln, and especially Johnson had done. The result was a parade of presidents whom most students of American history cannot name and whose policies remain basically unknown. It would take a man of the character of Theodore Roosevelt (another accidental president, having come to power as a result of William McKinley's assassination) to put the concept of legislative control aside until Representative Newt Gingrich and his Contract with America revived it 94 years later.

See also Johnson and Reconstruction; Lincoln and Reconstruction; Moderate Republicans and Reconstruction; Radical Republicans and Reconstruction; Supreme Court and Reconstruction; Wade-Davis Bill; Wade-Davis Manifesto and the Elections of 1864.

References Main, Jackson Turner, *The Sovereign States* (1973); McCormick, Richard P., *The Second American Party System* (1966); White, Leonard D., *The Jacksonians* (1954) and *The Republican Era* (1958).

Conkling, Roscoe (1829–1888)

Born in Albany, New York, Roscoe Conkling was educated in local academies and entered the Mount Washington Collegiate Institute in New York City in 1842. He went to Utica, New York, where he spent the rest of his life, and studied law. Upon passing the bar in 1850, Conkling was immediately appointed district attorney. He served two years and opened his own law firm in partnership with Thomas H. Walker of Utica. He also entered Whig politics and was soon considered one of the great speakers of his day, although he had not yet reached 30 years of age. He was elected mayor of Utica in 1858 and went to Congress that same year. He also married Julia Seymour, sister of Horatio Seymour, a prominent Peace Democrat, later governor of the state during the Civil War and Reconstruction presidential candidate in 1868. Conkling eschewed tobacco and alcohol and exercised and boxed to keep in shape. He once acted as bodyguard to the frail senator Thaddeus Stevens after a particularly biting speech caused some Southerners to charge the podium. Conkling advocated a vigorous prosecution of the war and supported the tougher measures of Reconstruction.

Conkling and his ambitions ran head on into those of his chief competitor for party leadership, James G. Blaine. Neither man liked the other. Both were vain, great speakers, and from the same general part of the country (Blaine was from Maine). Matters were helped little when Blaine jeered publicly at Conkling's "haughty distain, his grandiloquent swell, his majestic, supereminent overpowering turkey-gobbler strut." One suspects that Blaine might as well have been describing himself. But in Conkling's case it was apt. Conkling was not called the "Adonis of the Senate" after his 1867 election to that assembly for nothing. For the next ten years Conkling came to dominate New York Republican politics in cooperation with the "Customs House Ring" in New York City, headed by Chester A. Arthur and Alonzo B. Cornell. Their power came from control of the appointments to the various patronage spots available in that largest of U.S. port cities. Not able to wrangle the Republican presidential nomination for himself, Conkling had to be satisfied with denying it to Blaine and trying to get Grant to run for a third term. He was offered two spots on the U.S. Supreme Court but declined both (one was for chief justice) to concentrate on partisan politics, his forte.

Conkling selfishly regarded all appointments concerning New York men and New York jobs as his own private preserve. Woe to any president who ignored Conkling's wishes. He battled both Rutherford B. Hayes and James A. Garfield for not listening to his preferences or for trying to clean up the appointment process with respect to the New York customs house. Eventually Conkling got Cornell the post of governor, Arthur the position of vice president (then chief executive upon Garfield's assassina-

A political cartoon from the late 1870s depicts Roscoe Conkling in his ill-fated pursuit of the Republican presidential nomination in 1880. The caption reads "Eagle: 'Perhaps you would like to pluck me.'"

tion), and another lieutenant, Thomas C. Platt, the other Senate seat. Those Republicans who backed Conkling, from many states besides New York, were called Stalwarts. They differed from their party opponents, the Half-Breeds, only in their open desire for the spoils of office. When Garfield and Arthur ignored Conkling's desires on appointments, Conkling and Platt both resigned their Senate seats in 1881. Platt would return later, but Conkling had overplayed his hand. Things were changing; Blaine would take over the party outside the state, and Conkling had lost much of his power inside New York to newer and younger men. He never served his state or nation again. Conkling moved to New York City and practiced law for the remainder of his life, dying there seven years later, supposedly of overexertion during a snow storm—an ironic fate for a man who had made physical fitness the hallmark of his life.

See also Blaine, James G.

References Chidsey, Donald B., *The Gentleman from New York* (1935); Jordan, David M., *Roscoe Conkling of New York* (1971), Paxon, Frederic L., "Roscoe Conkling" (1964–1981).

Contrabands

In May of 1861, several fugitive slaves fled to Union lines on the Virginia Peninsula at Fortress Monroe. Their owner soon appeared and demanded that the bondsmen be returned under the Fugitive Slave Law of 1850. The post commandant, Maj. Gen. Benjamin Butler, a Massachusetts Democrat turned Republican, refused. He claimed that the Southerner was from a seceded state, which had lost all right to the benefits of U.S. law. He also asserted that the fugitives in question had been working on constructing Confederate fortifications and could not be returned. Rather, they were "contraband of war" and therefore seizable. His report to headquarters became public, and the term *contraband* came to refer to any fugitive slave who fled to Union lines for freedom and protection during the war. After the war, *contraband* was replaced by the term *freedman*.

See also Virginia Experiment.

References Gerteis, Louis, *From Contraband to Freedman* (1973); Randall, James G., *Constitutional Problems under Lincoln* (1964).

Corruption as a Problem in Reconstruction

One of the more enduring themes of the Reconstruction era has been its corruption. No matter how good the intentions of Republican governments in the South, in the end these systems of rule were viewed as the epitome of the ills that accompanied the "Blackout of Honest Government" or "Great Barbecue," as the capitalism gone rampant in the nineteenth century was called. But such an explanation, although it has merit, does not adequately explain that the Reconstruction governments (on national, state, and local levels) simply continued an emphasis that had been a part of the nation from its beginning. The "reforms" of Reconstruction initiated by the "good government" people (be they Liberal Republicans in the North or Redeemers in the South) tended to be driven by the actual or perceived presence of corruption. Often the reformers, especially big-city Democrats and the Southern Redeemers, merely funneled the graft to their own side rather than clean up the malaise. The corruption was not simply a result of entrusting the vote to uneducated and allegedly unqualified black voters in the South.

The American fascination and horror at corruption in government is older than the nation itself. The Founding Fathers talked of how the British system was corrupting the pure republican institutions of the New World, and such a feeling helped lead the way to the American Revolution. It was a reccurring theme of the "Revolution of 1800" that put the Jeffersonians in power, and it was an integral part of the Jacksonian era before the Mexican War. Both Thomas Jefferson and Andrew Jackson, especially the latter, believed that they were taking the nation back to an earlier time of political purity. Neither really accomplished his goal, but their efforts led to a critical change in the American party system each time.

What most historians forget was that the 1850s marked another era in which complaints over the ills of corruption were present everywhere across the American political landscape. The depth of the corruption and the fears of those who opposed it ran deep and were an important undercurrent among the causes of the Civil War. Both the Republicans in the North and the Fire-Eaters (Secessionists) of the South sought to cleanse the nation, the former by getting rid of the ills of slavery or the Slave Power, the latter by eliminating the damned Yankee moralists who reputedly sold wooden nutmegs and unnecessarily interfered with a booming cotton economy that drove the nation's progress.

Political corruption, the illegal obtaining of private profit or advantage through the political system and the subversion of the political process for personal ends beyond those of ambition, helped discredit the Democrats and destroy the Whigs in the decade before the Civil War. That is, the war came as much because of the activities of a "plundering generation" as because of the "blundering generation" previously seen by historians. The plundering became a sectional competition, particularly in the creation of potential railroad routes to the West. Because there were insufficient private resources to construct so long a line and the government could afford to assist only one transcontinental route, where the route began was essential. And to the disgust of Northerners, the South had the best possible passage. It was suited to all seasons, ran around the Rocky Mountains and across the Continental Divide at the lowest spot in New Mexico Territory, and had the most potential customers already available (in Texas). Extension of the southern limits of the United States to its present border in Arizona and New Mexico through the Gadsden Purchase in 1854 guaranteed that the southern route would be available.

To counter this advantage, the North flexed its own political power to prove that the Central Overland route would be the best. This route came out of the center of the nation and could cross the Rockies at South Pass, the traditional crossing for the Oregon and California Trails. The North sponsored several programs to prove that its choice was a viable competitor to the South's. One was the spectacular Pony Express, delivering the mail even throughout the notorious winters on the Great Plains, but the most important was a measure intended to create a territory west of Missouri to entice settlement and negate the South's Texas advantage. However, the men who wanted the Northern route did not have the votes needed without Southern support. The result was the Kansas-Nebraska Act, which repealed the Missouri Compromise and opened the whole West above the 36°30′ line to slavery. Northern settlers rushed to Kansas to stop the extension of slavery, but the railroad men tried to buy Congress' approval of a proslavery state constitution for Kansas. On top of that, the U.S. Supreme Court endorsed the whole Southern position in the *Dred Scott* case (1857). The whole situation looked corrupt, and to a large extent it was. But it spurred the organization of a Northern party, the Republicans, dedicated to cleaning out the Slave Power in Washington, and it brought the Civil War that much closer. The election of Abraham Lincoln with a purely Northern vote triggered the South to leave this den of thieves, as Southerners saw it, who would not allow the South's political acumen, endorsed as constitutional by the highest court in the land, to carry the day.

Of course, most politicians were not corrupt in the 1850s, Congress acted for other reasons than bribery and railroad interests, and the Civil War was not caused by political corruption alone. Nor is this entry a full account of why the war came. But there were large groups of persons who tacked the corruption issue onto the sectional controversy. Many saw the development of American economic potential with government assistance—the essence of Alexander Hamilton's economic program and Henry Clay's American System—as corruption in itself. They proposed, along with Jefferson and Jackson, that government be curbed in its powers and that special privilege (usually defined as anything that goes to the other guy to your detriment) be obliterated. Of course, each reform element, as it took charge, streamlined the corruption process for its own ends.

Generally Americans could agree that paying off a judge or jury, voting for or against a proposed law in exchange for money, rigging an election, allowing ineligible persons to vote, and using public office for personal gain were pretty much illegal. But at the same time, just as they condemned these practices, Americans also admired the people who could do these things and get away with them. Such political depravity brought a whole new set of words into the American language: "pipe laying," "suckers" and "strikers," "wire-pullers," "shoulder hitters," "plug-uglies," "grinding" and "smelling" committees, and "Plaquemining" (referring to the Louisiana parish that made political skullduggery into a fine art). But nothing topped the Rhode Island temperance election that was decided when the "drys" bought the deciding four votes with a gallon of Holland gin. But it was for such a good cause, whined the perpetrators when their actions were discovered. Indeed, there were many feeble excuses that accompanied such acts.

Why were the 1850s so corrupt? Some blame the gold strike in California, others the decline of the Jacksonian party system, and still others the draw of financial gain associated with internal improvements (railroads, canals, roads). Part of the apparent prevalence of corruption stems from the fact that newspapers were developing a national reporting network (sending their own reporters to Washington, for example), which made the public aware for the first time of how the wheels of government were greased. This caused many to fear for the safety of the nation itself. Greed threatened republican simplicity. But the Civil War and its many contradictions—the need to treat the Confederate soldiers as prisoners of war rather than Rebels to be hanged; the need to trade food and medicines to the South for its cotton to bolster Yankee monetary exchange abroad; the commission system of paying off treasury and tax agents who went South to find sources of traditional income now cut off by war; the commission agents who could expedite anything for a fee; and the shoddy contractors who sold the government dead cavalry horses, sand in place of gunpowder, cardboard shoes instead of leather, and felt uniforms that fell apart when used—did a lot to expedite the continued use of political "influence."

After the war, Reconstruction offered the Republicans an opportunity to extend their political influence into the South. But their identification with African American freedom, equal rights, and the franchise made them anathema to the white South. The free blacks were a continuing visual reminder that the Confederacy had failed. Yet no matter how the Republicans might want to look at it, they could not win the South without some of the Rebel white vote. Too few states had a black voting majority, and too few had sufficient white Unionists to help flesh out the count (besides, the white Unionists looked down on the freed blacks as much as the Rebels did). So to counter the racial distaste the party had among whites, the Republicans tried to emphasize economic assistance. The South had been wrecked by the war. Especially affected was the South's transportation system, and without it no crop, no manufacture, could get to market. At first many doubted that the South had the gumption to recover from the war. But it did recover because the damage was not universal; because the North and the world still needed cotton and the South had the black labor to produce it (although the system changed from gang work to that of the individual sharecropper); because the North was willing to help in the recovery after certain loyalty conditions were met (the Reconstruction process itself); and because enough Southerners (Scalawags) were willing to go along to achieve ultimate sectional, economic, political, and social independence—something usually categorized in the eras after Reconstruction as the New South movement.

The method of Northern assistance was to be the construction of railroads. The problem was, how much would the South pay for that help? But the conservatives who took over the Southern governments in 1865, in their attempt to revitalize the South, failed economically as much as they did politically. There was too much baggage left over from before the war: state debt, inadequate finances, an inability to cope with African Americans as a free persons, and a proud unwillingness to bow to the conqueror. The result was Military Reconstruction in 1867 and the disfranchisement of the old ruling class, whom the Republicans tended to blame for every malaise (political, economic, or social) they encountered. The new Republican governments went to work to institute the "Gospel of Prosperity." This was an appeal to the voters to adopt the Yankee vision of progress through industrial growth. In the state constitutional conventions the delegates voted for debt relief, homestead exemption (that is, exemption of one's home from taxes), and aid to the poor and destitute. But under the radical veneer was a conservative bedrock that refused to allow a type of Reconstruction that would root out every vestige of antebellum, Confederate wartime, and conservative postwar government. Such a Reconstruction would have meant starting all over again; every contract (even marriages) would have had to be nullified and renegotiated. It was too big a task.

Nonetheless, the conventions, as well as the governments elected under the constitutions the conventions wrote, did permit state aid for internal improvements and encouraged all sorts of business activity. They did allow African Americans equal rights under the law, universal adult male suffrage, and in a few cases open access to public accommodations. They did create public education systems, albeit usually segregated ones. They did provide for taxes to finance these items. And they elected fairly conservative governments to carry these policies into effect. It was hard for the Southern conservatives to argue with the Republican program because it was the kind of program they would have put in place themselves, at least with respect to the economic parts.

Many of them joined the Republican party as Scalawags. The party opened its arms to them, driving out the more radical white yeoman farmers who had helped start the party up and at the same time expected blacks to vote Republican without question.

However, the Southern conservatives who took over the Republican party and made its economic philosophy their own needed white yeoman farmer support to control their states after the inevitable withdrawal of federal troops. To obtain this support they had to get rid of the Carpetbag Republicans and their notions of racial equality. The conservatives accomplished this by returning to the Democratic label, advocating racial unity, and employing violence through the Ku Klux Klan and the rifle clubs. Once the conservative native whites had control of the government and the Democratic party well in hand, they intimidated black voters, promoted the myth of a corrupt Republican Reconstruction, and spoke of the dream of the Lost Cause of Southern independence to keep the white farmers in line for a generation.

Abandoning blacks to their white antagonists was not the intent of the Republican program—but that was exactly what happened. In effect, the corruption that greased the wheels of progress, through a government that was still very limited in scope and needed more expansive powers, subtly changed the emphasis of Reconstruction just enough to compromise its original idealistic objectives. This shift was evident in the North as well as (or perhaps even better than) in the South. An economic expansion that was marked by scandals in Washington in nearly every department of government, in both houses of Congress, and in most major cities led to a demand for reform. By 1872 reform had become the new crusade, and Reconstruction had been branded as a part of the sickness of corruption. In reality, the corruption was no worse than in the 1850s. Most scandals were due to incompetence, negligence, or extravagance. There was no real crime intended. And the corruption was scattered rather than systemic in its effect—isolated pilfering. The reformers were not attacking the system so much as the idea of corruption. The corruption issue gave them an edge over the opposition, but the intent was never to change how government worked, just who worked it.

Nothing revealed the limits of reform more than the Election of 1876 and the Compromise of 1877. To obtain a reform-minded president from their own party, both Republicans and Democrats resorted to shameless political corruption. The Republicans did a better job and took the prize, installing Rutherford (or was it "Rutherfraud," as his enemies insisted?) B. Hayes in the White House. But Hayes did not change much with respect to how the system worked. He expected political appointees to contribute a large percentage of their salaries to the party; there were spoils for everyone, even the relatives of Benjamin F. Butler of Massachusetts, whose name was synonymous with payoffs; the members of the Louisiana Returning Board, which had voted for Hayes, all got federal jobs; and President Ulysses S. Grant's personal secretary, Orville Babcock, who fairly reeked with the stench of corruption, found a political sinecure courtesy of the "scrupulous" President Hayes. In the South the "honest" Redeemers (white conservatives) cut "extravagant" Republican expenditures to the bone, and along with them spending on public education, social services, and aid to business. For the Redeemers, "good government" was cheap, too.

Nonetheless, the postwar corruption had a different flavor to it than that which dominated the 1850s. It was not connected to the fragility of the nation. The country had survived a civil war that threatened its very being and had been saved. Nothing could compare with that. Of course, Northerners saw Union as the result and Southerners looked to Redemption, but the sense of salvation was universal. The postwar era had nothing like the prewar Slave Power to which corruption could be connected. The political boss or the "robber baron" was simply too weak to provide the same kind of danger. But there was a new phenomenon.

For the first time in American history, political parties became fixed in the nation's eye. The Republicans and Democrats entered a new age in which they were seen as part and parcel of the republic's very existence. Before the war, anyone could form a new party to clean up the system. Now the two major parties acted together to keep all competition within their control, as the national Populists found out in the 1890s, and the local Independents, Greenbackers, and Readjusters found out in the South in the 1880s. There was also a realization that corruption tended to make government work, so long as the ruler and ruled alike both accepted the terms of the process; if not, then corruption led to deadlocked government.

In the end, the corruption of the reformers caused a loss of Americans' trust in government itself. There was a belief that rogues ran rampant in the halls of power, locally and nationally. This in turn encouraged the increased use of corrupt methods, desensitized voters and politicians to the abuse of the public purse and trust, and put the legitimacy of democratic government into question. This shift led to the rise of a new set of reformers in the long run, individuals interested not so much in the right of blacks and propertyless whites to vote but rather in preventing predatory elements from gaining control of the government and manipulating it for their own ends. These reformers were called Progressives, and they made clean government a cause for whites only.

Thus, corruption has long had an influence in American government. For the Jeffersonians, corruption created a concern for the fragility of republican government itself. For the Jacksonians it created a demand for the popular vote and "rotation in office" to continually clean the old rascals out. For the ideologues of North and South in the 1850s, it showed how meaningless the Jacksonian system was and how the Slave Power or the advocates of centralized power managed to obtain an unfair advantage. For the Progressives corruption was an argument for government to protect the citizen against the evils of Big Business. For the modern Conservative corruption is an argument for Big Government to be downsized to rehabilitate individual initiative. But for the politicians of Reconstruction, corruption was nothing unusual; it was merely a propagandistic tool used to cover up the reformers' own licentiousness. It was not the reason Reconstruction failed, but it provided a convenient excuse for letting it go down.

See also Beecher, Henry Ward; Grant and the Scandals; Redeemers.

References Eaton, Clement, *The Waning of the Old South Civilization* (1968); Foster, Gaines M., *Ghosts of the Confederacy* (1987); Govan, Gilbert E., and James W. Livingood, "Chattanooga under Military Occupation" (1951); Johnson, Ludwell H., III, "Contraband Trade during the Last Year of the Civil War" (1963), "Northern Profit and Profiteers" (1966), and *Red River Campaign* (1958); Osterweis, Rollin G., *The Myth of the Lost Cause* (1973); Parks, Joseph H., "A Confederate Trade Center under Federal Occupation" (1941); Robinson, Armistead L., "Beyond the Realm of Consensus" (1981); Summers, Mark W., "'A Band of Brigands'" (1984), *The Era of Good Stealings* (1993), *The Plundering Generation* (1987), and *Railroads, Reconstruction, and the Gospel of Prosperity* (1984); Williams, T. Harry, "An Analysis of Some Reconstruction Attitudes" (1946) and "The Louisiana Unification Movement of 1873" (1945).

Cox Plan of Reconstruction

By 1865 it was evident that the fall of the Confederacy was just a matter of time. Ohio, like other Northern states, had to readjust its thinking from prosecuting the war to ensuring the peace. Republicans agreed that the Southern slaveholders were responsible for the rebellion, and they believed that the planters' political power had to be broken. Some of them also believed that the freedmen could provide a loyal wedge into Southern politics. They believed that blacks deserved some rights, especially the right to collect the proceeds of their labor and to vote in the South (though generally not in the North), and to preserve their freedom. But they and their Democratic opponents, who just could not take control of Ohio during this period so long as Reconstruction dominated political discussion, did agree on one thing—white supremacy, in the nation and in the individual states. However, the Democrats tried to appeal to the white voters' basest feelings on race. They were unwilling to grant blacks much of anything when it came to civil rights and nothing when it came to social position.

One of the Republican politicians who sought an answer to the problem of free blacks in white America was Jacob D. Cox. A war hero at Antietam, a major general in the Union army, and a man experienced in the occupation of the South Atlantic coast, Cox was acknowledged statewide as an expert in the "Negro problem." Republicans feared that Andrew Johnson's Reconstruction of the South, which made no reference to the rights of African Americans, would hurt them in state elections as Democrats would brand them "Black Republicans." They wished to keep the Union party alliance of Moderate Republicans and War Democrats that had won the rebellion and had elected Abraham Lincoln in 1864. Could Cox find a way?

Cox believed that he could find a middle ground between the Radical Republican stance favoring equal rights for African Americans and the no-rights position of Democrats. Cox was an antislavery man from way back and had attended Oberlin College, a hotbed for abolition before the war. It was in answer to a letter from the college faculty that he framed his concept of a Reconstruction that would guarantee a significant degree of political and civil rights and still maintain white supremacy as the guiding principle of American government. In his Oberlin letter, Cox stated that he was in favor of black voting rights as a condition of readmitting the South to the Union. But he went on to define his concept of how this could work. Cox proposed that an area along the Southeastern Atlantic coast from Charleston south to and including all of the Florida peninsula should be cleared of all whites and set aside as an all-black territory. Within its boundaries, blacks would be able to rule themselves politically and economically in peace.

A similar program on a small scale had already been tried under Maj. Gen. William T. Sherman's Special Field Orders No. 15. Cox's proposal would widen the effect of Sherman's approach. (President Johnson had not yet returned this land to its white prewar owners.) Cox ridiculed the notion accepted by Radicals that the vote would protect blacks in the South or elsewhere. Instead he believed that granting African Americans the right to vote in the South would only lead to a race war. This he hoped to avoid, while still guaranteeing blacks full citizenship. So long as blacks stayed in their reserve, they would be equal citizens. Outside this area, they would be second-class citizens at the mercy of local law.

Although Cox put forth this grandiose scheme in theory, he did not present any practical ideas of how to fund it or carry it out. The relocation would have to be forcefully enacted, something on a larger scale than had been done to the Cherokee, Choctaw, Chickasaw, Creek, and Seminole tribes when Andrew Jackson deported them to Indian Territory in the 1830s. The Native American example was not too pleasing, either. There had been massive starvation and death from exposure to the elements. Tribal elements had resisted the government's action by force, and not all of them had been removed yet. But Cox did offer a way to take race out of the picture in Reconstruction America, no matter how impractical his proposal was. Cox and his Union party took 53 percent of the Ohio vote and captured both houses of the state legislature, giving Republicans their largest peacetime victory so far in the state. He had managed to stand simultaneously for reunion, a secure future, the guarantee of basic rights for African Americans in the South, and the denial of black social, political, and economic equality in Ohio.

See also Ethridge Conspiracy of 1863; Johnson and Reconstruction; Special Field Orders No. 15.

References Ahern, Wilbert H., "The Cox Plan of Reconstruction" (1970); Bonadio, Felice A., *North of Reconstruction* (1970); Sawrey, Robert D., *The Dubious Victory* (1992).

Davis, Edmund J. (1827–1883)

E. J. Davis, the Scalawag governor of Texas during Reconstruction, was born in St. Augustine, Florida. He moved to Texas with his widowed mother when he was ten years old. Settling in Galveston, he read law, was admitted to the bar, and practiced his profession at Corpus Christi, Laredo, and Brownsville. He was deputy collector of customs at Laredo in the early 1850s and then elected district attorney at Brownsville. His service impressed the right people, and he was made district judge for the Lower Rio Grande Valley, a position he held until he refused to take an oath to the Confederacy. Davis was defeated in the election to the secession convention, a fact that some attributed to his Union support. But it is more likely that he represented Union feelings prevalent throughout most of the border region, dependent as it was on the federal government for its economic activity and protection.

During the war, Davis organized a Union cavalry regiment. He was captured soon after and barely escaped being hanged for treason against Texas and the South. He returned to the First Texas (Union) Cavalry, composed of local Hispanics, Union men, and a few Confederate deserters, and led it on a raid to Laredo, but he was defeated by Rebel troops led by Santos Benavides. He was then transferred to the Louisiana theater, where he and his regiment served the rest of the war, with Davis being promoted to brigadier general. After the war, he declined an appointment to the Texas supreme court offered by Maj. Gen. Philip H. Sheridan.

But Davis did take a consistent, loyal position in Texas politics, lamenting the lack of a true Republican party in 1866, when the state went back to proto-Confederate rule. He recommended that a loyal state militia be organized to protect Texas' Union population, which included a fourth of all whites as well as all of the former slaves. He also took the lead in suggesting that Union men organize their own convention of all males, black and white, pledged to universal adult male suffrage and declaring themselves Republicans. Davis was a man ahead of his time, but his idea was taken up by others at Houston a year later, after passage of the Military Reconstruction Acts. Delegates of both races from 27 counties attended and agreed to promote the Republican party through the use of Union Loyal Leagues. Along with other Republicans he recommended a full slate of officers for the army commandant, Bvt. Maj. Gen. Charles Griffin, to appoint for his home district.

In 1868, Davis was elected delegate to the state constitutional convention, where he became the convention chairman. The Texas convention process was held up by a philosophical division between Republicans that was exploited by conservative Democratic delegates. Essentially, the Republicans were divided over whether they should disfranchise former Confederate whites in the new constitution; split Texas into former Rebel, African American, and Union white–dominated states (Texas had a special provision in the Compromise of 1850 that permitted it to be divided into as many as five states); and adopt a provision of ab initio (declaring all legal acts committed since the 1861 secession as null and void). Davis led the Radical Republicans, who favored all three positions. However, Texas Loyalists could not win an honest election even with all the black vote because the ex-Rebels held a majority of registered voters. Thus, the Moderate Republicans, who opposed each of these proposals, favored combining with "right thinking" men of the Democratic party; they were led by Andrew J. Hamilton, once President Andrew Johnson's provisional governor and, like Davis, once a Union brigadier general. The debate on these positions was long and involved, but the outcome was to extend the convention into two sessions and delay the state's readmission to the Union until 1870.

Most Texas Radicals were angered at Hamilton's willingness to compromise with the old secessionists. With Davis using the power of the chair to their advantage, they finally moved the convention to authorize the division of the state, though they used several dubious parliamentary procedures, including voting without a quorum. As part of this measure, Davis proposed that all voters take an oath that was similar to the Union's wartime ironclad oath—that the voter had never directly or indirectly willingly aided or abetted the Confederate cause. This measure was defeated when four African American Republicans crossed over and voted with the Hamilton Moderates. The result was a document that recognized universal adult male suffrage (the delegates had considered offering the franchise to women but eventually dropped the issue), the supremacy of the U.S. Constitution as amended and all federal treaties and laws, the full freedom of blacks, easier access to corporate charter, state financing of internal improvements, and a dual (segregated) public education system. Historians credit it with being a truly progressive fundamental law for its day—it is still the state constitution 125 years later.

Radicals, however, including Davis, did not like the absence of the issues of principle, especially the lack of both disfranchisement for ex-Rebels and the ab initio clause. On the other hand, many conservatives considered the document way too innovative in other areas. When the convention adjourned without having made any provision to preserve its records, Hamilton seized those records from the secretary and turned them over to Bvt. Maj. Gen. E. R. S. Canby, the federal army commandant for the state. Canby appointed a committee of three (a Moderate Republican, a Radical Republican, and his staff adjutant) to organize the documents and print the constitution, which was offered to the people that winter. The Moderates put forward Hamilton as their choice of governor by acclamation. It quickly became evident that the Radicals were in deep trouble. By this time, President Ulysses S. Grant had replaced Canby with Bvt. Maj. Gen. Joseph J. Reynolds, who had been a Moderate supporter in an earlier tenure in Texas. Reynolds once again took up the Moderate cause, removing officials and appointing Hamilton's men at every chance.

Meanwhile the Radicals met in a party convention (boycotted by the Moderates) at Houston and nominated Davis. It was then that E. J. Davis pulled off the most brilliant political maneuver of the election. The Houston platform was almost an exact duplicate of that of the Moderates: an acceptance of the constitution and everything it stood for. The whole state was aghast. What had the past two years' political infighting been about anyhow? Where were disfranchisement, division of the state, and ab initio? Ultra-Radicals were enraged, but they really had no place to go. They would in the end have to accept Davis's new platform. Hamilton cried foul. The Radicals had stolen his platform. Moreover, the state was rife with rumors that General Reynolds would support the Davis ticket in exchange for a U.S. Senate seat under the new government, a proposal Hamilton had already refused to make on his own, over the objections of his political managers. Both sides went to Washington to obtain the support of the Grant administration. Grant chose to support the Radicals. They were consistently loyal, they had not made any overt appeals to the former Confederates, they worked well with black voters, and they had the support of General Reynolds, with whom Davis had made the deal to change the platform in the first place. And Reynolds and Grant were old West Point classmates. Federal patronage went to the Radicals. So did the state patronage. General Reynolds made the final recommendations in both cases.

When duplicate returns from two counties threatened to keep Davis from the governorship, Reynolds counted the totals on behalf of the Radicals (there was an 800-vote difference in the end, with half of the registered voters staying home). The result was a Radical electoral win in December 1869, with the erstwhile support of General Reynolds. (Bvt. Maj. Gen. Adelbert Ames would pull off a similar ploy in Mississippi.) Davis took office immediately, because the provisional governor (a Moderate) had resigned rather than be tainted with this mess. After the election Reynolds, with the approval of Grant, appointed all elected officials to office. This made them federal appointees and subject to taking the iron-clad oath. Reynolds removed from office those who could not take it, Hamilton's Moderate-Democratic fusionists, and appointed their runners-up (mostly Radicals) in their place. The first order of business for the legislators was to endorse the Fourteenth and Fifteenth amendments to the U.S. Constitution. Then they proceeded to elect U.S. senators. Reynolds lost out to two Radical Republicans, one of whom was Lieutenant Governor J. W. Flannigan.

The Davis administration, the only Republican administration elected in Texas during Reconstruction, remains highly controversial to this day. Early historians reserved for it much acrimony, but modern historians find in it much nobility. An amazing thing is that one major published history of the era is entitled *Texas under the Carpetbaggers*—even though Davis and most Texas Republicans were home-grown Scalawags. It would probably be fair to say that Davis ruled from an impossible position, because he lacked a true majority vote, and that he made some unfortunate decisions, often with the best intentions in mind, that backfired. A continuation of white violence led Davis to call for a state militia to replace the army, which then moved to the frontier, and a state police to replace the rebellion-tainted Texas Rangers. Recent studies credit the militia and police with more being more effective than once supposed, although the state adjutant general absconded to Europe with nearly $40,000 in state funds. The main complaint white Texans had about the police and militia was the groups' high proportion of black officers and rank and file, as well as Davis's declaration of martial law to protect African Americans and loyal white citizens. But the police and militia kept the law, especially around polling time, and led to the myth that the army had stationed black soldiers in eastern Texas during Reconstruction.

Another Davis program later condemned for its expense was the creation of the segregated public school system. Like most Reconstruction state institutions in most Southern states, this system was highly centralized, with appointments made in Austin. The Democrats would keep the system after Redemption, but they returned it to local control, which effectively gutted it as far as blacks were concerned. Commerce and industry received a boost from the Republican legislature, and the state debt went up as much because of needed expenses for increased public services as because of fraud. Interestingly, after Redemption, the Democrats continued to assist transportation projects as much as the Republicans had done. Perhaps the stupidest thing Davis did from a public relations point of view was to pardon the Kiowa-Comanche chiefs Satanta and Big Tree after their companion Satank had been "shot while trying to escape" from Fort Sill in Indian Territory. Actually Davis had been undermined here by the federal government, which let the two men go without adhering to Davis's conditions the their bands turn in their weapons and horses first, but he took the brunt of public criticism for approving their release at all.

By 1873, it was obvious that the Republicans were done for in Texas. All four congressional seats had gone to Democrats in 1872, as had the state legislature. Davis had been indicted for vote tampering but was acquitted in two sensational trials. The feuding in Republican party ranks was still going on. This time whites would turn out en masse to vote for Davis's Democratic opponent, Richard Coke. General Reynolds, who had tried one more time for the Senate seat in 1871, had been transferred to a post in the West and was no longer around to help with the count. As expected, the totals showed Coke with a large majority, but Davis seized upon a technicality to sue for retention of his office. His contention maintained that a new election law had repealed only the first part of the old ordinance, but not the second part, which required that the election last for four days (it had not). Since the two sections were separated by a semicolon—punctuation being very important in many types of legal documents—the suit became known as the *Semicolon* case. Both sides sent armed men to Austin to defend their candidate. The Radicals appealed to Grant for military assistance to save Texas from "Ku Klux Democracy." Grant said that the dispute involved state law and the federal government had no interest in it. He lectured Davis on the need of yielding to the voice of the people.

Faced with no help from Washington, outnumbered in the military realm, and with the people and politicians ignoring the *Semicolon* case, which Davis had won in a Republican-dominated court, the governor stepped down. The Democrats wisely refrained from any overt violence so that Grant would have no reason to change his mind about federal intervention. Davis stayed on in Austin and practiced law. He headed the Texas Republican party until his death, standing for governor once again in 1880 (he lost by 100,000 votes). He was considered for a position in the Chester A. Arthur cabinet but failed to win a previous congressional election, which caused Arthur to recognize him as a potential political liability. He was never accused of personal dishonesty at any time. His personal and social conduct remained above reproach in every way. His beliefs in the Union cause never slackened either. He never thought that his fellow Texans were anything but unreconstructed Rebels. E. J. Davis died in 1883, a Scalawag to the end and proud of it.

See also Scalawags.

References Baenziger, Ann Patton, "The Texas State Police during Reconstruction" (1968–1969); Baggett, James Alex, "Birth of the Texas Republican Party" (1974–1975) and "The Rise and Fall of the Texas Radicals" (1972); Campbell, Randolph B., "Carpetbagger Rule in Reconstruction Texas" (1993–1994); Carrrier, John P., "A Political History of Texas during the Reconstruction" (1971); Crouch, Barry A., "'Unmanacling' Texas Reconstruction" (1989–1990); Field, William T., Jr., "The Texas State Police" (1965); Gillette, William, *Retreat from Reconstruction* (1979); Gray, Ronald N., "Edmund J. Davis" (1976); Moneyhon, Carl, *Republicanism in Reconstruction Texas* (1980); Nunn, W. C., *Texas under the Carpetbaggers* (1962); Perman, Michael, *The Road to Redemption* (1984); Rabel, George C., *But There Was No Peace* (1984); Ramsdell, Charles W., *Reconstruction in Texas* (1910); Richter, William L., *The Army in Texas during Reconstruction* (1987); Russ, William A., Jr., "Radical Disfranchisement in Texas" (1934–1935); Sandlin, Betty Jeffus, "The Texas Reconstruction Constitutional Convention of 1868–1869" (1970); Singletary, Otis A., *Negro Militia and Reconstruction* (1957); Sneed, Edgar P., "A Historiography of Reconstruction in Texas" (1968–1969); Thompson, Jerry Don, *Vaqueros in Blue and Gray* (1976); Wallace, Ernest, *The Howling of the Coyotes* (1979); Waller, John L., *Colossal Hamilton of Texas* (1968); Webb, Walter Prescott, *The Texas Rangers* (1965).

Davis, Henry Winter (1817–1865)

Born in 1817 in Annapolis, Henry Winter Davis was the son of an Episcopal rector who was the president of St. Johns College. Davis was raised in an upper-class setting and graduated from Kenyon College in 1837 with an education in the classics and an interest and skill in forensics. He went on to study law at the University of Virginia and practiced his profession at Alexandria and then Baltimore, where he lived the rest of his life. A polished orator, Davis was a Baltimore politician of the old Whig party. A man of medium height, clean-shaven except for a mustache (the full kind often called a "soup-strainer") at a time when the beard was coming into style, he was known for being a natty dresser. He delivered his oratory with a high, clear voice, essential at a time when loudspeakers were unknown. He was elected to Congress in 1855 and served three terms before being retired for two years; he then returned for one more term that ended just before his premature death. Much of his political power stemmed from a gang of dock workers known as the "plug uglies" who often rioted in select places on election day, scaring off opposition voters to Davis's advantage. To this day biographers are unable to explain how a Davis, a man from such an upper-class environment, could control and work with such lower-class thugs. But it speaks volumes about his oratory and cold political realism.

Part of his appeal was undoubtedly his affiliation with the anti-immigrant American party (the Know Nothings), a common move for old Southern Whigs like Davis in the 1850s. In Congress he was known for his outspokenness and hatred of the Democrats. Davis was against any talk of secession and denounced such threats during the 1856 presidential election, which featured the antislavery Republican party for the first time. Davis was openly for the Union; he favored anyone with the same view who could win the presidency or a seat in Congress. He spoke out against the crooked, proslavery Lecompton constitution in Kansas and criticized the James Buchanan administration in every aspect. But Davis overdid himself in the vicious and prolonged fight for the speakership of the House of Representatives in 1859. It was possible for the Democrats to keep the speakership if the American party stood with them. With the exception of Davis, the entire party, composed primarily of Southern slaveholders (like Davis himself), went for the Democratic candidate. The acid-tongued Baltimore man, however, cast his lone vote for the Republicans, giving them control of the House for the first time in their existence. Davis's vote earned him the disparaging label "Black Republican" and the censure of the Maryland state assembly, costing him his reelection in 1861. He was verbally pilloried and often hung in effigy throughout the South.

By his 1863 reelection, Davis had long abandoned the conservative principles that held the Whigs together and had joined the Union party, a combination of ex-Whigs, Republicans, and loyal Democrats. But the party was stifled in Maryland by its refusal to consider the issue of its time—the abolition of slavery in the state. Davis knew that the institution was doomed. There were too many assaults on its fragile fabric. The state was too close to Pennsylvania and freedom, the majority of the white population was against the institution as an aristocratic holdover, and the Emancipation Proclamation pointed the way of the future. Davis appealed to white middle-class town dwellers, small farmers, and artisans to rid the state of the anachronism of slavery. He shrewdly pointed out that black soldiers allowed the poorer whites to stay home from the war and that the richer slaveholders could buy an exemption. With respect to interracial marriages, Davis declared that any whites feeling so inclined should petition the state legislature for special punishment for their weaknesses. Using the aid of federal soldiers to shield his crooked election-day antics, Davis and his Radicals elected an emancipationist majority to the state legislature. On 1 November 1864, the drive to free the slaves met with success. Davis went on to champion black suffrage, seeing in the black vote a way for his political machine to move out of Baltimore and into political bastions previously held by Democrats.

Davis also had a national reputation as a strong opponent of Abraham Lincoln, and some credited him with more influence on the Radical wing of the party at this time than Representative Thaddeus Stevens of Pennsylvania. Davis's quarrel with Lincoln was personal as well as philosophical. Allegedly Davis had been considered and rejected by Lincoln for first the vice presidency and then a cabinet position in 1861. But Davis particularly disliked the slow steps Lincoln took toward emancipation and what Davis saw as his flawed plan of Reconstruction. Along with his U.S. Senate ally, Benjamin Wade of Ohio, Davis introduced the Wade-Davis Bill into Congress. Originally written by Republican Senator Ira Harris of New York, his measure would counter Lincoln's Ten Percent Plan by requiring that a majority of a state's voters in 1860 take an oath of future loyalty to begin the process and that actual participants in voting and officeholding be limited to those who could take an additional ironclad oath (of never having aided the Confederacy). When Lincoln pocket vetoed the bill, Wade and Davis issued their so-called manifesto, which condemned Lincoln's approach as undemocratic and dangerous to the "proper" cleansing of the soon-to-be-reunified Union of rebellion.

Davis, a civil libertarian, believed that President Lincoln had overstepped his powers as president when he denied the writ of habeas corpus and relied on military courts to try wartime dissenters. He also stood forthright against the notions then prevalent of transporting the freed slaves to the Caribbean or to Africa, maintaining that they had earned the right to be Americans through their labor and service in the Union armies. Davis traveled widely during the war, in Maryland and the North in general, speaking on behalf of the Union. When Lincoln took the support of most Marylanders in the Union party and received the Union party nomination, Davis refused to run for Congress another time. Instead he concentrated on building up his political machine by securing the post of Baltimore port collector for one of his cronies. At the height of his state power, Davis died of pneumonia in December 1865. Thus was stilled one of the most outspoken Radical Republicans and an ever-controversial voice against the exclusive Presidential Reconstruction of the nation.

See also Wade-Davis Bill.

References Belz, Herman, "Henry Winter Davis and the Origins of Congressional Reconstruction" (1972); Curry, Richard O., *Radicalism, Racism, and Party Realignment* (1969); Hentig, Gerald S., "Henry Winter Davis and the Speakership Contest of 1859–1860" (1973) and *Henry Winter Davis* (1973); Steiner, Bernard C., *Life of Henry Winter Davis* (1916); Tyson, Raymond W., "Henry Winter Davis" (1963).

Davis, Jefferson F. (1808–1889)

Jefferson Finus (signifying he was to be the last child of his parents) Davis, president of the Confederacy, was born in Kentucky, but his family soon moved to Mississippi. There he was educated in private schools before returning to Kentucky to attend Transylvania College. Receiving an appointment to the United States Military Academy, where he was a contemporary of Robert E. Lee, Joseph E. Johnston, and Albert Sidney Johnston, Davis graduated in 1828. He served as an officer for seven years along the western frontier. In 1835 he married the daughter of his regimental colonel, Zachary Taylor. He resigned his commission and took his new wife to a plantation in the Felicianas north of Baton Rouge, Louisiana, where she died of a fever. Heartbroken, Davis lived the life of a recluse for several years at his brother Joseph's landholdings back in Mississippi.

Through the influence of his brother, Davis read widely and reentered public life in 1843 as a candidate for Congress. He lost the election but did serve as a presidential elector in 1844 for James K. Polk. He stood for Congress again in 1845 and won the election, but he resigned his seat when the Mexican War broke out. Davis had the necessary influence and education to become the colonel of the First Mississippi Rifle Regiment, the Red Shirts. When he reached Texas he found his former father-in-law in command, and under his tutelage, Davis took a conspicuous part in several battles. The most important of these battles was at Buena Vista, where Davis managed to defeat a Mexican turning maneuver by deploying his regiment and the Third Indiana Infantry in an inverted vee. This unorthodox lineup made him a national hero and gave him the reputation of being something of a military genius. Later, disgruntled Confederate military and political men would assert unfairly that Davis's meddling in Civil War field campaigns on the basis of his reputation in Mexico cost the Confederacy its independence; they suggested that the Confederacy's tombstone ought to read "Died of an Inverted Vee."

Davis parlayed his military reputation into a national political career in the 1850s. He was elected to the U.S. Senate, where he served as chairman of the military affairs committee and spoke out for retaining all of Mexico conquered by the United States during the Mexican War—a position that was defeated by South Carolina Senator John C. Calhoun, who was fearful that such a move would revive the slavery question (it did). Davis also spoke out on behalf of Southern rights in the debates over the Compromise of 1850. He even suggested that the South secede rather than submit to what he saw as Yankee perfidy: stealing the fruits of war by preventing the westward movement of slavery. He resigned his seat and went home to run for governor on the Secessionist ticket, but he lost the race to a Union man by fewer than 1,000 votes.

The loss discredited Davis much, but he recovered when his old friend, Franklin Pierce, was elected president in 1854. Pierce invited Davis to come to Washington and serve as secretary of war. Though he was not sure he wished to compromise his principles, Davis yielded under the constant demands of the president-elect and became one of the more innovative secretaries the Department of War ever had. He experimented with camels as beasts of burden, established numerous forts to protect western travelers, and reorganized the numerous types of mounted regiments (dragoons, mounted rifles, and cavalry) in the army into five units of modern light cavalry. He also supported the building of a transcontinental railroad and was instrumental in getting the Gadsden Purchase to make the railroad possible by a Southern route out of New Orleans or Memphis.

At the end of Pierce's term, Mississippi returned Davis to the Senate. There he stood for the repeal of the Missouri Compromise and the extension of slavery to all of the western territories under a formula put forward by Illinois Senator Stephen A. Douglas called popular sovereignty—letting a territory's new state constitutional convention decide. When the process yielded a free-state solution in Kansas, Davis joined other Southerners in reading Douglas out of the party as a traitor to the South. (Douglas had promised a proslavery Kansas.) When Douglas managed to gain the party nomination in 1860, Davis and other Southerners bolted the party and set up Vice President John C. Breckinridge as their candidate. With a split Democratic party, the rival Republicans easily elected Abraham Lincoln as president. Davis was mortified, but he urged the nation to stay whole. Unfortunately, the crisis had passed beyond the control of the politicians, and the secession of the Lower South (South Carolina, Mississippi, Florida, Georgia, Alabama, Louisiana, and Texas) was the result.

Given that he had dragged his feet in the secessionist cause, Davis was stunned when he was elected president of the provisional government of the Confederate States of America at Montgomery, Alabama. Davis organized a cabinet made up of conservative Southerners like himself and set about to unify the South behind him. The refusal of the Lincoln government to give up forts Sumter (Charleston, South Carolina) and Pickens (Pensacola, Florida) forced the Confederates to fire the first shot or appear less than independent. The result was to unify the South (and the North) and cause a second secession, this time of the Upper South (Arkansas, Tennessee, Virginia, and North Carolina). Eventually Davis was popularly elected to head the Confederate government, now located at Richmond, Virginia. Much has been written about Davis's inability to work with people of all beliefs, his favoritism to old West Point cronies, his preference for field command over political leadership (he had a neuralgia of the eye that intensified while he was in Richmond and mysteriously disappeared when he went out into the countryside to campaign or inspect the troops), and his willingness to argue an issue to its fine points. But all in all he did manage to take a nation built from scratch and in four years nearly break up the whole United States. There was probably no one else who could have done better.

As president, Davis instituted the first national draft of soldiers and preserved the writ of habeas corpus and free speech despite the war and many outspoken opponents in the South (the groups against him were either more radical in their pursuit of independence or were openly pro-Union). He moderated those who wished to reopen the slave trade, kept the tariff low, instituted a secret service that probably surpassed the modern Central Intelligence Agency in its audacity, and obtained the enlistment of black Confederate fighting men in exchange for their independence. He put 1 million men in the field (out of a white population of 7 million) and required the North to raise twice that number to defeat him. Even as the final campaign began in 1865, Davis and Robert E. Lee were planning to unite with the remaining Rebel forces in North Carolina to defeat the Union armies. Davis fled south, hoping to get out to the western part of the Confederacy, but he was taken by Union cavalry in Georgia, allegedly dressed in a woman's shawl (which soon became a full outfit of women's clothes, as the story grew in the Northern yellow journalistic sheets of the day). Some historians believe that Davis tried to escape because of Lincoln's assassination. But more recent research reveals that his departure was a part of an involved plan that went awry because of Lt. Gen. Ulysses S. Grant's unexpectedly quick pursuit of Lee's army.

Davis spent the next two years under arrest in Fortress Monroe, Virginia. His case presented the Union with some complex legal issues. Secretary of War Edwin M. Stanton and Judge Advocate General Joseph Holt believed him complicit in Lincoln's death, but they could not prove anything. Had they the time and skill of recent historians, who have linked the Confederate government with John Wilkes Booth, it is doubtful Davis or Lee would have escaped the hangman's rope. President Andrew Johnson refused to set Davis free, but he and his government did not charge Davis either. After much thought they decided to try Davis for treason. Johnson set up a special board made up of the attorney general and several prominent attorneys to bring forth the charges. It was decided to try Davis in Virginia, the site of his most heinous "crimes," although many wanted to try him in Pennsylvania, seeing him as "constructively" present during the 1863 invasion.

The federal court in Virginia was in the circuit of Chief Justice Salmon P. Chase. He refused to appear in court so long as Virginia was occupied and under the jurisdiction of the federal armies. The other member of the circuit court was Judge John Underwood. Chase was willing to let Underwood try Davis alone, but Johnson's cabinet thought Underwood too lenient and of suspicous loyalty. Worse yet, how could the government get a jury that would convict Davis? It would look bad to bring him to trial only to have Southerners set him free. Indeed, how could a fair panel be

picked anywhere in the country? But Judge Underwood did manage to convene a grand jury that indicted Davis on a charge of treason. An asked-for murder indictment was let go at this time. There was much confusion as to the proper proceedings anyway. The prisoner was still in military custody, and the government was still unready in its case. But Johnson said that Underwood could grant bail if he desired. Underwood believed that Davis deserved bail, but it would have been political suicide to allow it then. So Davis sat in jail longer.

Meanwhile Davis's attorney, a prominent Democrat, Charles O'Connor of New York, moved for a writ of habeas corpus. This would force the government to bring charges against Davis or grant him bail. But would the War Department respond to the writ? Secretary Stanton said it would. The local federal prosecutor asked for assistance during the hearing but was refused. He therefore had a weak case that he had been forced to draw up hurriedly. Finally, special prosecutor William M. Evarts appeared and told the court that the government's case was not ready and that Davis could be put out on bail.

Jefferson Davis was released on 13 May 1867, upon a bail bond signed by Yankee publicist Horace Greeley ("Forward to Richmond" had been the pro-Union banner headline of his *New York Tribune* during the war) and other long-time Davis opponents who were weary of the concept of a harsh peace and hoped his release might bind up the wounds of war and promote black civil rights and the vote. O'Connor believed that Davis would never be tried now. But the government was not yet ready to give up. Radicals in Congress still wanted Davis tried for murder and, in a rare case of agreement, President Johnson concurred. The government reorganized its prosecutorial team to make a better effort. Trial date was set for the fourth Wednesday in March 1868.

The government team then sought to gain an indictment. The statute of limitations for all crimes then was three years, which was fast approaching. But try as they might, the legal team could not agree on a way to proceed, and the investigators in Virginia did little to help out. Meanwhile, the U.S. Senate impeached President Johnson, and he employed several of the legal team, including Evarts and Attorney General Henry Stanbery, in his own defense. If Johnson were convicted, the new president would be Benjamin Wade of Ohio, a red hot Radical. O'Connor feared that Davis would be tried and convicted in short order if Wade took the helm; he advised Davis to jump bail and flee the country if Johnson were convicted. The president was not convicted, but Davis's trial was delayed again.

By now it appeared that the government would have to risk all on one throw of the dice. It was likely that at least one man on a jury of 12 in Virginia would vote on Davis's behalf and find him innocent. A great revival of Davis's reputation had taken place because of his stoic demeanor and apparent willingness to accept his fate, which had been publicized by a compassionate but largely apocryphal account of his postwar political ideas and travails in jail, taken from notes recorded by his physician, John J. Craven, and ghost-written and enhanced by Charles G. Halpine, a Northern Democratic propagandist. Besides, Davis and other high Confederates had already been punished through the no-officeholding clause of the Fourteenth Amendment. Indeed, O'Connor moved for dismissal on the basis of double jeopardy. But Chase, who was willing to come to Virginia now that it was readmitted to the Union, and Underwood split on their ruling, which meant that the final say would have to await the spring 1869 meeting of the whole Supreme Court. President Johnson did not wait that long. On 25 December 1868, he issued a blanket amnesty for all those who took part in the rebellion, including Davis. The Virginia circuit court moved for a *nolle prosequi* (no further prosecution) motion to be entered in the Davis case and the appeal to the Supreme Court dismissed. On 16 February 1869, Davis was a free man, not liable to prosecution in any jurisdiction of the United States.

Davis traveled for a while, finally settling down in Memphis to head an insurance company. His business failed during the economic panic of 1873, and several opportunities in New Orleans never materialized. He retired to Beauvoir, a home near Biloxi, Mississippi, given to him by a friend. There he lived out his days, writing a defense of his actions as Confederate president (*The Rise and Fall of the Confederate Government*, in two long volumes) and relishing the role of an elder statesman who had never surrendered, stripped of his rights as a citizen, unreconstructed to the end. He died in New Orleans on a business trip. His body was later disinterred and shipped to Richmond in a procession across a half dozen Southern railroads that rivaled that of Abraham Lincoln's journey to Springfield 23 years earlier.

See also Come Retribution; Greeley, Horace; Johnson and Reconstruction; Lincoln, Abraham.

References Cooper, William J., Jr., "A Reassessment of Jefferson Davis as War Leader" (1970); Davis, Varina Howell, *Jefferson Davis* (1890); Dodd, William E., *Jefferson Davis* (1907); Eaton, Clement, *Jefferson Davis* (1977); Eckenrode, Hamilton J., *Jefferson Davis* (1923); Hanchett, William, "Reconstruction and the Rehabilitation of Jefferson Davis" (1969–1970); Nichols, Roy Franklin, "United States vs. Jefferson Davis" (1925–1926); Potter, David, "Jefferson Davis and the Political Factors of Confederate Defeat" (1960); Strode, Hudson, *Jefferson Davis* (1955–1964); Vandiver, Frank E., "Jefferson Davis" (1977).

Davis Bend Experiment

As the Union army moved southward, it came across many abandoned lands and slaves, a circumstance that offered the possibility of improvising a truly radical change in Southern society, with free black laborers farming their own land. Unlike the Port Royal experiment, which was located in the South Atlantic Sea Islands and run by abolitionist idealists from New England, wartime western experiments in the Mississippi Valley were geared more toward the mainstream views of the Republican party, a hard-hearted practical application of the prewar free labor ideology. None achieved its goals more so than the free labor experiment at Davis Bend, Mississippi, located on the Father of Waters about 25 miles south of the Confederate fortress at Vicksburg.

The man in charge of the Davis Bend experiment during the Civil War was John Eaton, an antislavery man but not an abolitionist, whom Maj. Gen. Ulysses S. Grant had placed in charge of the thousands of slaves who fled slavery for security behind the Union army's lines. Eaton gave careful thought to the notion that these blacks could be settled on abandoned lands and allowed to farm; thus, the slaves could change from what Eaton condescendingly saw as "children" into a truly adult free persons, demonstrating their ability to become full citizens after the war. Basically Eaton envisioned a postwar South full of wage-earning freed people, each family on its own plot of land "under the kindly but faithful care of some worthy friend." He would attempt two forms of free labor: one in which the former slaves would work cash crops like cotton as before the war, but now earning a fair wage; and the other an independent small farm raising such crops as the black family desired. In both cases Eaton envisioned the African Americans leasing the land rather than owning it.

Eaton used the old plantation approach throughout Mississippi, Tennessee, and Arkansas, but he reserved his latter experiment—the independent black farmer concept—for his showpiece at Davis Bend. Eaton feared that Northern land and labor speculators under the guise of the Department of the Treasury would ruin his chance for conducting the free labor experiment, so in 1864, with General Grant's assistance, he shut off the peninsula at Davis Bend (actually an enclosed loop formed by the Mississippi River on three sides) from everyone but the former slaves. The experiment at Davis Bend would be managed by Lt. Col. Samuel Thomas, a brash, young Ohioan "of the right Christian spirit," according to Eaton. Thomas set to work, marked off plots ranging in size from 10 to 150 acres, and doled them out to the freedmen. The project was an instant success. Early on

Thomas noted that his black charges worked much harder than those left on a plantation system. Unfortunately, their magnificent cotton crop was almost destroyed by army worms. Nonetheless, individual black farmers managed to obtain profits ranging from $500 to $2,500 each.

News of Eaton's experiment soon reached Washington, and an impressed President Abraham Lincoln ordered the project to continue in 1865. Eaton changed the formula somewhat and now established 181 cooperatives of 3 to 25 African American farmers, who were given land in proportion to the size of their companies. The army worm stayed away in 1865, but early rains threatened to ruin the cotton crop once again. Hard work allowed the former slaves to foil the rains and resulted in a total shared profit on 5,000 acres of nearly $400,000. Taking a leaf from the management book of the Joseph R. Davis family (Joseph's brother Jefferson was president of the Confederacy), the former slaves were allowed to police the farms themselves and punish lawbreakers through their own courts, run solely by their elected leaders. Eaton also brought in teachers and established a half dozen schools at the Bend.

After the war, the Freedmen's Bureau took over the administration of Davis Bend under the bureau's state assistant commissioner, Samuel Thomas, the same man who had begun the wartime project at Eaton's behest. The land was eventually returned to Joseph R. Davis, its original owner, and he leased it to his former slave foreman, Benjamin Montgomery, an extremely capable man who had managed the Davis plantations while a slave. (Davis had run his plantations according to the ideas of Robert D. Owen, a utopian philosopher; as a result, the slaves were allowed much autonomy.) However, Montgomery seemed to grate on Thomas's soul. Perhaps Montgomery was too clever to suit the Yankee bureau man, who shared the prevailing prejudices of his time. Thomas was glad to see blacks succeed, so long as they did it in their proper subordinate place. He was especially angry when Davis, a former Rebel, sided with

Montgomery on various contentious issues. For instance, Davis supported the firing of a crooked white Carpetbagger and cotton gin operator whom Thomas backed, and he disbelieved Thomas's accusation that Montgomery then tried to fleece his black neighbors by overcharging for ginning their cotton. In the end, Davis and Montgomery joined forces to get rid of Thomas as head of the bureau in Mississippi; Davis sold his land to Montgomery, his former slave, for $300,000 in November 1866. Davis Bend was one of the few labor experiments in the South that showed what blacks could do on their own. It became the inspiration for the all-black town of Mound Bayou when Montgomery's high rental fees drove many blacks away. But it was doomed to failure by forces beyond the control of the successful black farmers, including the pardon policy of President Andrew Johnson, which returned land to secessionist slaveholders, and the conservatism of the Constitution and the Republican party.

See also Mississippi Valley Experiment.

References Benedict, Michael Les, "The Rout of Radicalism" (1972); Hermann, Janet S., *The Pursuit of a Dream* (1981) and "Reconstruction in Microcosm" (1980); Hesseltine, William B., "Economic Factors in the Abandonment of Reconstruction" (1935–1936); Ross, Stephen Joseph, "Freed Soil, Freed Labor, Freed Men" (1978).

Disfranchisement

American historians and political scientists who investigate and theorize on the impact of voting statutes usually concentrate on the expansion of the franchise while virtually ignoring the contraction in the franchise that might have occurred. This makes American history a success story, inasmuch as more people are qualified to vote today than could, say, in 1789, when all sorts of property and religious restrictions limited the electorate to very rich men of the "proper" beliefs. The biggest expansions of the vote are usually seen as the one preceding the era of Jackson in the 1820s, the one during the first Reconstruction in the 1860s, and that of the second Reconstruction, the

civil rights movement 100 years later.

But there are regressive periods in American history when the vote was reduced rather than expanded. Two of those are germane to Reconstruction. The first occurred during the expansion of the vote to blacks, when the Republicans sought—through the Fourteenth Amendment and various state laws that imitated it—to limit both the right of former Confederates to exercise the franchise and their traditional leadership role in the South, permitting Reconstruction to advance unimpeded in its early stages. The second occurred after Redemption, when the traditional white leadership of the South limited the vote through legal and constitutional means within the scope of the Fifteenth Amendment to deny the franchise to blacks and certain lower-class whites.

WHITE DISFRANCHISEMENT DURING RECONSTRUCTION

The aims of the Radical Republicans in the Military Reconstruction Acts were predicated on two policies, the enfranchisement of the African Americans and the disfranchisement of the leaders of the Confederacy, defined as those who had once taken an oath to the United States and then made a subsequent pledge of loyalty to the Confederate States. It was hoped that loyal voters might thus be given a chance to reconstruct state constitutions and governments without the obstructionism of Rebels. Many commentators at the time wondered if this was not throwing the government into the hands of allegedly ignorant blacks. But there was a long tradition of American political thinking, beginning with Thomas Jefferson and reaching its culmination with Andrew Jackson, that held that any citizen was smart enough to handle the responsibilities of voting and holding office. Nothing that blacks did in Reconstruction matched the riot that took place during Jackson's first inaugural. Besides, the new approach to voting rights offered a quick way in which to introduce the Republican party into the South—perhaps the only viable way, because there were as many Union Democrats as Republicans and too few Republicans to affect the Deep South states.

The problem was, who should be disfranchised? Particularly important was what was to be considered "aid and comfort" to the enemy. The Military Reconstruction Acts were not explicit about this. Obviously those who had taken an oath before the war to the United States and then taken a subsequent one to the Confederate States were affected. This notion also exempted anyone who was under 21 when the war began. So it was left up to the five military commanders to work things out, which meant that there would be five different notions of who ought to be excluded from the process of Reconstruction. The actual disfranchising came about when one registered to vote. The individual commanders of the five military districts would have numerous interpretations of their instructions to iron out. It came to be quite an involved process that had many political overtones.

First, the military commander had to find enough loyal men who could take the ironclad oath of 1862 (one of never having given aid or comfort to the enemy). Then these men would make the decision concerning who was loyal enough to vote. Commanders usually ordered the elected governors (declared provisional by the Military Reconstruction Acts) to submit a list of those who could take the oath in any one electoral district. Then appointments were made from the list. If the appointee accepted, the job was done. But of course there were numerous objections to anyone picked, some valid, most superfluous. The commanders would then promulgate an order that would give probable descriptions of those who would be disfranchised. These included individuals who had taken the double oath, most executive and judicial officers of the state during the war, anyone who voluntarily engaged in the rebellion, and all those who lent aid or comfort to the Confederate war effort. Bvt. Maj. Gen. John M. Schofield, commander of the First Military District (Virginia), defined the latter not to include parents who gave their son in the Confederate army food or clothing for his own use, but it did apply to parents who gave their son a weapon, horse, or something that might be used for a "hostile purpose." This rule probably raised as many questions as it settled, but it gives an idea of what the registrar faced in doing his job. No wonder one disgruntled historian described registrars' actions as the "arbitrariness of petty officials" and dismissed the officials as "little despots."

Any registration board's decision could be appealed up the military chain of command. This mitigated the board's effect, unless the commander was Maj. Gen. Philip H. Sheridan of the Fifth Military District (Louisiana and Texas). When Sheridan inquired as to the restrictions of the law, Lt. Gen. Ulysses S. Grant informed him that the matter was under the domain of Andrew Johnson's attorney general, Henry Stanbery, who was mulling it over before rendering an opinion. Meanwhile Grant told Sheridan to go ahead and give any interpretation that he wanted. Sheridan decided to disfranchise anyone who held any public office, right down to sextons of cemeteries. When Stanbery's decision called for a milder approach, Congress stepped in and put much of Sheridan's policy into law in the form of the Third Reconstruction Act.

According to the eighth census (1860), on the basis of male population only one Southern state, South Carolina, was guaranteed a majority of black voters after the Civil War. Louisiana and Mississippi were so close that they could go either way. But once the chosen whites had been disfranchised, Florida and Alabama had a black majority, while Georgia, Arkansas, Texas, and Virginia had their white majorities severely reduced. This was a far cry from having state conventions dominated by black delegates, but black voters did return a large number of Carpetbag and Scalawag delegates, guaranteeing a Republican majority in most conventions. This allowed Radical Republicans to achieve such goals as punishing the traitorous Southern whites for the war and preventing them from disrupting the councils of the victors. But a large part of the Radicals' triumph came from the fact that many eligible whites refused to register and even more refused to vote after registering, giving the reconstructing forces a de facto victory.

Despite two and a half centuries of slavery and exploitation, African Americans did not demand further disfranchisement of their former masters by the state constitutional conventions. Indeed, considering the wrongs that they had faced, American blacks tended to be quite forgiving of the past. It was the Carpetbaggers and Scalawags who looked upon disfranchisement with interest. The severest disfranchisement laws, with the possible exception of Louisiana's, existed in West Virginia, Missouri, and Tennessee. These were states in which white loyalists were plentiful, blacks were relatively few, and disfranchisement laws were written and put into effect during the war, long before the Military Reconstruction Acts were even thought of.

Of the Southern states under the jurisdiction of the Military Reconstruction Acts, Florida, Georgia, South Carolina, North Carolina, and Texas disfranchised very lightly if at all, sticking with the Fourteenth Amendment's provisions of excluding those who took the double oath. South Carolina had the only state convention with a black majority among its delegates, indicating that African American politicians were quite astute in recognizing that the long-term effects of vindictiveness were counterproductive. Alabama, Virginia, Mississippi, and Louisiana went far beyond the Fourteenth Amendment, with the worst-case scenario being Louisiana. Under section 99 of its 1868 state constitution, Louisiana excluded from the polls anyone who had held a civil or military office under the Confederacy for one year or more, anyone who attended the state secession convention, anyone who had voted for the secession ordinance among the general public, and anyone who had advocated treason by writing or publishing newspaper articles or preaching a sermon against the United States (not an uncommon "crime" in the Civil War Bayou State). The Louisiana requirements could be lifted if one were willing to swear in writing and file with the secretary of state an oath that he believed the rebellion and his part in it were morally and politically wrong and that he regretted any aid or comfort he had given the enemy.

Despite such devices as Louisiana's disfranchisement law, African Americans did not control any government. They could vote only for whites, or at best for whites and blacks, through a previously agreed upon division of offices. No black was elected governor of a Southern state, and some even doubt the legality of P. B. S. Pinchback's five-week term in Louisiana. As it was, Republicans could no more count on black voters to blindly elect them than Democrats could for blacks to vote against them. The split of Southern Republicans into Radical and Moderate blocs (usually but not always represented by Carpetbaggers and Scalawags, respectively, with blacks caught in between) neutralized much of the force of Republican power and led to Redemption everywhere by 1877. But the initial effect of disfranchisement would be remembered 20 years later and brought out again, this time by establishment Democrats under the guise of "cleansing" Southern elections of opposition elements, both white and black.

BLACK DISFRANCHISEMENT AFTER REDEMPTION

The period that followed the Redemption of the South—the restoration of whites (usually referred to as Bourbons, because like the French royal family, they neither learned from nor forgot the past) to political control—did not seal the fate of the Reconstruction reforms in politics, economics, or social contacts among whites and blacks. Indeed, the next 20 years, from Reconstruction to the Populist revolt, could best be described as a period of transition—a time of uncertainty and fluctuation.

The fear among Southern whites was that the Yankees would pass another civil rights or enforcement measure to continue the spirit of Reconstruction. Such a measure might emanate from humanitarian motives or from political realities. Not all white politicians in the South were convinced that the Democratic party was the forum in which all problems should be raised. The constant flow of Fusionists (who were willing to combine tickets, usually with Republicans), Independents (who were unwilling to combine with others lest principle be diluted), Republicans (the regular party, often called the "Black and Tans" because of their biracial membership), and so-called Readjusters (who were interested in re-funding the horrendous state debts) merely presaged the ultimate third party, the powerful Populists (agrarian radicals who wished to reform the corrupt establishment) in the 1890s. All of this turmoil gave Southern blacks greater political leverage throughout this period than historians (or contemporaries) have been willing to admit.

Throughout the 1870s, the two sections had an equal voter turnout in national elections. But in the 1880s, the North began to forge ahead in voter participation by 10 to 12 percent as the South began to turn to disfranchising laws, extensive fraud, and weaker party competition. By 1896, the North was achieving record voter turnouts, while the South was experiencing record nonparticipation as the Populist movement collapsed there first. The lull in Southern voter interest became permanent as new restrictive laws and state constitutions took over. By the turn of the century, Southern voter participation was half that of the North and most of it was in the Democratic column. The one-party South had been achieved, making the party a sort of private club for whites, especially the rich and better educated. This "Solid South" would endure until the civil rights and conservative Republican movements of the second half of the twentieth century.

Throughout this period until the 1890s, African American votes were important to Southern political strategies. In nearly every state a majority of black males voted and a majority of them tallied in the Republican column. The Democrats based their appeal to whites on the basis of this active black vote. In counties with less than 30 percent black residents, 54 percent of whites voted Democratic. But in counties with a black population over 30 percent, white support of the Democratic party topped out at just over 92 percent. These black belt counties (actually named after the color of their fertile soils, not the skin color of the population) were the parts of the South where the contrast between the races was most pronounced politically, economically, and educationally. It was here that the revolution represented by Radical Reconstruction had been the most successful, where the black politicians and their white Carpetbag and Scalawag allies had ruled the longest.

After Reconstruction, whites took several approaches to power in the South. Some counties chose the First Mississippi Plan and drove blacks from the polls by force. Others had local governments appointed by the state government, obviating the need for local elections. The rest either took the road of counting blacks out—through corrupt officials and fraudulent election returns or by cutting deals whereby whites and blacks arbitrarily divided up the offices by race, which permitted the whites always to achieve a partial victory—or continued the Reconstruction party battles. Sometimes the Republicans and blacks won, other times the Democrats and whites did. But intimidation and chicanery were the order of the day and became more evident as the decades advanced. It was these black belt counties that had the most to lose if a Fusion party came to power based on the votes of poorer whites and blacks. In such cases the whites in the black belt would have to pay taxes to African American tax collectors, argue cases before black judges and juries, and apply to a black legislator for favors. They would even have to pay money to black school districts—as the Southern saw went, to educate a black was to ruin a good field hand.

But despite the fear that Reconstruction might return, opposition parties abounded in the South. Upper-class Bourbons constantly cut back on public services, which harmed and irritated poorer whites and

An 1867 Harper's Weekly *cartoon depicts both the frustration of the disfranchised Confederate and the elation of the newly enfranchised African American.*

blacks alike. They also backed policies that aided big business, much of it Yankee owned and managed, at the expense of the less wealthy. These things became more and more regressive as the decades wore on, aggravated by the deflation of the late nineteenth century; the sharecrop and the lien, which prevented crop diversification in grasses and food crops in favor of cash staples like cotton; and a regressive, malapportioned tax system that was often accompanied by corrupt collection and spending. As much as the former Confederate fighting men loved the "Lost Cause" expounded by Bourbon Democrats, the latter's misdeeds were too much. As opponents of the Bourbons looked for allies to combat this system,

they—like all "outs" in the postwar South—began to look to African Americans at home and to the national Republican party in Washington, D.C., for federal patronage.

Even though Republican support of the Southern branch of the party and Reconstruction had wavered, many national party leaders were holdovers from Reconstruction days. Some still had the idealism that led to egalitarianism and a hatred of racial oppression. Others might not be so noble philosophically, but they did want to see a free ballot and fair count down South. Both groups "waved the bloody shirt" (i.e., told graphic stories of conservative white political violence in the South) for political advantage; they believed the atrocious stories emanating from the South. This meant that a lot of Republicans—perhaps not the party bigwigs, but the second echelon—believed that the federal government owed some form of protection to Southern dissenters regardless of race. National Democrats viewed this Republican proclivity to resurrect Reconstruction as a violation of the Compromise of 1877. They condemned it as an unconstitutional interference with the states, a faulty desire to bring back to life a policy that led to unparalleled corruption and the imposition of "Negro Rule" on the white South. Republicans complained that post-Reconstruction Southern state governments had instituted "new forms of servitude" upon blacks (violations of political rights, tennantry and the lien, segregation, and the denial of public services), to whom the North owed a great debt for their loyal service during the Civil War.

The Republican policy toward the South had two contradictory aspects. Some wanted to go the route of the Compromise of 1877 and industrialize the South, bringing the "better classes" (the Bourbons, the old-time Whigs) to the party's favor by wedding them to economic policies of high tariffs and government aids to business, especially internal improvements like railroads, and by permitting them to paternally "protect" African Americans. This line of thought was what had produced the upper-class Scalawags of Reconstruction in the early 1870s. The other route was to appeal to Southern white dissidents and traditional black Republican voters by stressing honest elections, fair taxes, support for public education, and racial democracy. This reasoning had been prevalent early in Reconstruction (the late 1860s) and had resulted in common whites acting as Scalawags in support of the Republicans. It had crumbled when the traditional upper-class former slaveholders absorbed the party leadership and neutralized the revolutionary aspects of Reconstruction.

The first course had been supported by the Rutherford B. Hayes administration. But disillusionment set in when the Re-

deemers failed to deliver the needed votes of support because economic depression had diluted the willingness of the lower classes of either race to follow. In addition, the Redeemers were disappointed when Hayes failed to honor his promise of economic development. Thereafter Republican administrations fluctuated among who they thought were the proper party representatives in the South: the upper-class whites or the lower-class dissidents of both races. Sometimes Republicans worked with both, depending on local circumstances (issues varied greatly among states). The willingness of the national Republicans and lower-class whites to work with black voters in Fusion, Readjuster, Greenback, and Independent parties nearly caused the Bourbons to lose power everywhere in the South (indeed, they did lose power briefly in Virginia and Tennessee). Only South Carolina Democrats managed to weather the storm by limiting voter (especially black voter) participation through the "eight box law," which forced the voter to place his ballot in the correct box or have it nullified—of course, the order of the boxes was switched often and the labels were difficult to read.

By the 1890s the Bourbon Democrats had to do something to hold back the dissident tide. The whole nation was facing the greatest political turmoil since the Civil War. Depression had led to the formation of the People's party, the Populists, made up of farmer and labor elements tired of Conservative Republicanism and Grover Cleveland Democracy (both of which amounted to the same thing). Southern Democrats wanted to make the final move to contain the dissident vote within the boundaries of the Fifteenth Amendment, before the Populists could sweep them from power.

But the Republicans took over both houses of Congress and the presidency in 1888. For the first time in decades the party had the power to block Southern Democratic interference (intimidation of voters, violence, miscounted ballots, unfair procedures at the polling places) with the electoral process and ensure a free vote and a fair count through federal regulation. The Republicans quickly passed a higher tariff (the McKinley Tariff Act), an antitrust bill (the Sherman Antitrust Act), increased pensions ("God help the surplus!" cried its triumphant administrator) for Union veterans of 90 days' service or more (the Dependent Pension Act), and a currency expansion measure (the Sherman Silver Purchase Act). Then the party introduced the Lodge Force Bill, or Federal Elections Bill, which would extend the Second Enforcement Act of 1871, providing for federal election supervisors in 34 Southern and 129 Northern cities; this allowed federal officials to supervise elections and voter registrations in any congressional district where 100 voters asked for it. Introduced by U.S. Senator Henry Cabot Lodge of Massachusetts, the measure quickly passed the House but was defeated on a procedural motion by one vote in the Senate. The bill was really pretty mild, but it would have guaranteed the election of Republicans or Populists in every Southern state by focusing on cleaning up the electoral process. It would all be followed by the second Cleveland administration's repeal of all remaining federal election statutes in 1984. The way was open for the Bourbons to permanently "fix" Southern electoral processes their way and create a multitude of one-party states ruled by the "correct" whites alone. The extralegal fraud was to be made legal.

Mississippi did not even wait for the federal process to be played out. In 1890, it convened the first state constitutional convention since Reconstruction and wrote disfranchisement of blacks and poor whites into the state's fundamental law, the so-called Second Mississippi Plan. The rest of the South followed suit, although only South Carolina, Louisiana, Alabama, and Virginia followed Mississippi's example and called constitutional conventions to accomplish the job. The rest, even the states with new constitutions, passed normal laws that did the trick. Numerous devices were tried, each state in effect becoming a laboratory for the others to copy. Florida copied South Carolina's eight-box scheme; Alabama and Florida instituted Tennessee's secret (Aus-

tralian) ballot law; and Tennessee, Arkansas, Florida, and Mississippi used the poll tax after Georgia proved it effective. But all such maneuvering had to be subtle because the Fifteenth Amendment prohibited it from being overtly based on race and the Fourteenth Amendment threatened to reduce the representation of any state should it discriminate against any group of voters.

But there were legal ways to achieve a reduction in select groups of voters, some of which were also actively used in the North. Frequent registration was one of these. By making voters register every so many years, or during a specific month, many were discouraged. More important was granting great discretionary powers to the registrars. They were the ones who determined the literacy of the applicant and his qualifications for exemption from literacy tests. They oversaw such regulation as Louisiana's grandfather clause (if one's grandfather had voted before 1867, one could not be turned down—of course, only white grandfathers voted before that date) or the understanding clause (the registrar read part of the constitution to the applicant and the latter had to explain what it meant—and some parts of the constitution are more easily understood than others). Failure to know extraneous information, like your neighbor's full name, the exact date of your birth (many blacks were not sure), or your street address (black communities often did not have these) could disqualify a potential voter. The law always called on registrars to verify these things "as near as may be," which gave the registrar the ability to be tough on one voter and easier on another. Confederate veterans and their heirs were always given the benefit of the doubt, appealing to Southern whites' vulnerability to images of the Lost Cause.

Other disqualifying features included minimum property ownership requirements (blacks and lower-class whites were renters) and the payment of fees to vote, like a poll tax. The real crux was to require that the voter show his registration certificate and current poll tax receipt. Some states required that several years' worth of receipts be shown, something difficult for sloppy record keepers to do. Residency requirements limited the vote to those who had stable jobs and families and stayed in one place, usually a year in the county and several years in the state (sharecroppers moved about a lot to gain a better contract deal).

The biggest help to Democrats was the secret ballot. Before the "reforms" of the 1890s, parties handed out their own ballots, encouraging voters to select a straight ticket and not requiring any literacy at all. When a ballot box needed to be stuffed, the Democrats would insert enough undersized, fraudulent ballots—"little jokers," in the parlance of the trade—to win the precinct. When the ballots were tallied, too many for the number of voters would be found. Then a reliable party man would be blindfolded (to keep things "honest") and would withdraw enough excessive ballots to make the count right. Of course, he pulled out only the full-sized ballots, guaranteeing a Democratic victory. But the secret ballot, part of what was called the Dortch Law in Tennessee (which had originated this bit of electoral chicanery), was seemingly better and more honest. Both parties appeared on the ballot, allowing a split vote. But the ballot's format could be made unbelievably long and complicated. More important, one had to read to fill it out, and no help was allowed (unless one had voted before the Civil War). Also, voters were limited in the time they could take to mark the secret ballot, and any mistake voided one's vote for that election.

Finally, there was the all-white primary. The Bourbons claimed that if blacks were excluded as an independent voting block that shifted from side to side and thus controlled elections (a false charge), whites could then disagree on all issues without the fear of "Negro Rule." Elections could be honestly run. In the general election, all participants in the white primary would pledge to vote for the candidates picked in the primary. Often the Democratic party would be made a private club restricted to members only, like the Jay Bird Association of Ft. Bend County, Texas, in which case the primary became an exclusive club elec-

tion. The result was that elections became personality contests, going to the candidate who had the funniest stories, the best singing voice, the firmest handshake, or the broadest smile. With no issue but race being considered, political campaigns soon degenerated into demagoguery, "a sort of legalized knife fight and perpetual stomping contest," in the words of one observer, as each white candidate tried to hang the label of "nigger lover" on his opponent.

With the U.S. Supreme Court's endorsement of disfranchisement on some other basis than race alone, *Williams v. Mississippi* (1898) gave the South the go-ahead to make disfranchisement of blacks an established fact. The various disfranchising methods worked like a charm. By the end of the century, the vote for the Democrats had declined by half, but the vote for opposition parties dropped by two-thirds. Seventy percent of adult male Southerners did not vote. Some blacks still voted, but their numbers were so small as to be unimportant. Except for Tennessee and North Carolina, where mountain Republicanism still existed, the Republican party was a mere cipher. As the joke went in Louisiana, the Republican party was so insignificant that its members could hold their state convention in any telephone booth. Blacks were totally dependent on national Republican patronage, and this patronage ended in 1913, when Woodrow Wilson, the first Southerner in the White House since Lincoln, became president.

The loss of political power hit the black community hard. The state governments no longer had to recognize African Americans. The biggest loss was in education. The governments dispensed school funds to the counties for disbursement to local schools. All too often, little or nothing went to the separate, supposedly equal, black system. By matching the funds of localities that were willing to tax themselves, the states fostered an education system that was underfunded in rural areas dominated by poor whites and blacks and well funded in urban areas of upscale whites. The loss of political power directly affected access to governmental services. What had started out as an extralegal system of voter fraud was now entrenched as constitutional prerogative on the state level and was allowed to pass for electoral reform in the eyes of the nation. It would take 60 years before the nation saw disfranchisement for what it really was, a contraction of democracy, so humiliating in its effect as to be a contradiction of everything the country prided itself on.

See also Economic Disfranchisement; Redemption of the South since 1874; Segregation (Jim Crow); Washington, Booker T.

References Argersinger, Peter H., "The Southern Search for Order" (1975); Eaton, Clement, *The Waning of the Old South Civilization* (1968); Foster, Gaines M., *Ghosts of the Confederacy* (1987); Fredman, L. E., *The Australian Ballot* (1969); Hair, William Ivy, *Bourbonism and Agrarian Protest* (1969); Holmes, William F., "The Leflore County Massacre and the Demise of the Colored Farmer's Alliance" (1973); Jones, Robert R., "James L. Kemper and the Virginia Redeemers Face the Race Question" (1972); Key, V. O., Jr., *Southern Politics in State and Nation* (1949); Kirby, Jack Temple, *Darkness at the Dawning* (1972); Kousser, J. Morgan, "Ecological Regression and the Analysis of Past Politics" (1973) and *The Shaping of Southern Politics* (1974); Lewinson, Paul, *Race, Class, and Party* (1965); Mabry, William Alexander, "Disfranchisement of the Negro in Mississippi" (1938); Moore, James T., "Black Militancy in Readjuster Virginia" (1975); Osterweis, Rollin G., *The Myth of the Lost Cause* (1973); Potter, David M., *The South and the Concurrent Majority* (1972); Russ, William A., Jr., "Disfranchisement in Louisiana" (1935), "The Negro and White Disfranchisement during Radical Reconstruction" (1934), "Radical Disfranchisement in Texas" (1934–1935), and "Registration and Disfranchisement under Radical Reconstruction" (1935); Simkins, Francis B., *Pitchfork Ben Tillman* (1944); Tindall, George B., *The Disruption of the Solid South* (1972); Welch, Richard E., Jr., "The Federal Elections Bill of 1890" (1965); Williams, Frank B., "The Poll Tax as a Suffrage Requirement in the South" (1952); Wood, Forrest G., "On Revising Reconstruction History" (1966); Woodward, C. Vann, *Origins of the New South* (1951), *The Strange Career of Jim Crow* (1966), and *Tom Watson* (1938).

Doolittle, James R. (1815–1897)

Born and raised in western New York state, James R. Doolittle was educated locally and graduated from Hobart College in 1834.

He married and began his career in law in 1837. He also took part in politics as a Democrat, supporting James K. Polk in 1844 and writing the "cornerstone resolution" passed at the party's New York convention in 1847, declaring support for a free soil (i.e., antislavery) position. Rejected by the party leadership, Doolittle supported former president Martin Van Buren and the Barnburner (or free soil) faction of the Democratic party in 1848. The cornerstone resolution became a part of the Free Soil party platform in 1848 and the Republican party platform in 1856, but it was rejected by the national Democratic party throughout the 1850s. By 1851, Doolittle had moved to Racine, Wisconsin, where he was elected judge on the Democratic ticket. In 1856 he switched to the Republican party. He was elected to the U.S. Senate, serving two terms until 1869. Doolittle was a commanding presence when he gave a speech. His voice was so clear that he could address thousands without amplification. He was a fundamentalist Protestant and an expert on the Bible and prophecy. In politics he was a Jeffersonian, reading the Constitution quite literally without creative interpretations.

Nationally Doolittle's career divides itself neatly into two periods, separated by the death of Abraham Lincoln. Before and during the Civil War Doolittle supported the nullification of the fugitive slave laws by state conventions and opposed secession. After secession he advocated no compromise with the slave states on principle. But he always favored legislative action and a constitutional amendment to end slavery. He was considered one of Lincoln's important wartime advisors and close personal friends. "I believe in God Almighty!" Doolittle told doubters who felt Lincoln ought to be dumped in 1864. "Under Him I believe in Abraham Lincoln!" he concluded, to the cheers of the party faithful. Lincoln's assassination ended all that.

With the accession of Andrew Johnson to power, Doolittle returned to his old Democratic philosophy. He abhorred the Radical Republican notion of thorough Reconstruction because he believed it was unconstitutional to keep the Southern states out of the Union. He saw the various theories of Reconstruction as so much political double-talk. He rationalized Johnson's policies as the continuation of Lincoln's just wartime plans. And, of course, he voted to acquit Johnson during the impeachment trial. By 1868 he was supporting Horatio Seymour, the regular Democratic nominee, over Ulysses S. Grant. The Wisconsin legislature asked Doolittle to resign, but he refused. In 1869 he ended his second term in the Senate; after an abortive attempt to run for governor of Wisconsin on the Democratic ticket, he retired to Chicago, where he practiced law until his death, permanently exiled from his adopted home state.

See also Impeachment; Johnson and Reconstruction; Moderate Republicans.

References Cox, John H., and LaWanda Cox, *Politics, Principles and Prejudice* (1963); Donald, David H., *The Politics of Reconstruction* (1965); Schafer, Joseph, "James Rood Doolittle" (1964–1981).

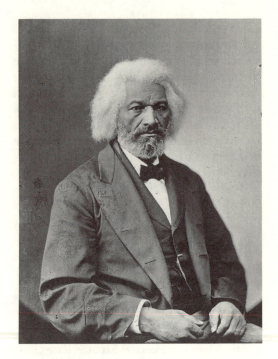

Frederick Douglass

Douglass, Frederick (ca. 1817–1895)

Frederick Douglass was born a slave in Talbot County, Maryland, of a black mother, Harriet Bailey, and an unknown white father, and was originally named Frederick Augustus Washington Bailey. He experienced the usual travails of slavery—neglect, cruelty, and hard work—but he chaffed most under the restraint of his ambition as a very talented person. He struck back at his cruelest master and learned the value of well-placed resistance. He was sent to Baltimore to become a house servant and learned to read and write with the connivance of his mistress. "A city slave is almost a freeman," he said, "when compared with a slave on a plantation." But the settlement of his dead master's estate sent him back into the fields he hated. Frederick soon developed a plan to escape with several of his fellows, but the plan was betrayed and he was jailed. Eventually his new master decided to return him to Baltimore, where he became a ship's caulker and hired his own time, that is, he sold his services himself but had to pay his master a percentage of his earnings. In 1838, he escaped to New York City and assumed the name under which he became famous, Frederick Douglass.

In New York Douglass married a free woman of color whom he had met in Baltimore, and they went to Massachusetts, where he worked as a common laborer. There, for the first time, he came into intimate contact with abolitionists. Upon hearing Douglass speak to a group of blacks at a local meeting, the organizers asked him to address a whole convention. Although Douglass stammered with nervousness, his well-chosen words and charismatic personality were immediately evident. The Massachusetts Anti-slavery Society hired him as an agent on the spot. He then began what would be a lifelong commitment to free blacks from slavery and the pernicious effects of the second-class citizenship that followed. In the process he was mobbed, beaten, mocked, and humiliated by being refused access to public accommodations, but he never faltered in his task.

Douglass was over six feet in height, built

like the former laborer he had been, with a proud head crowned with frizzy hair. His voice was sonorous and his manner of speaking and writing so educated that many doubted his story of having been born in slavery. Douglass did not lower his eyes, mumble apologies, smile, and shyly step back, as so many blacks of his time did, slave or free. He was simply too much of a commanding presence for whites to imagine him as ever having been in bondage. To prove his story, Douglass wrote his memoirs of slavery in 1845, a volume that white friends urged him to burn because it was too daring in content and so self-implicating that they feared he might be reclaimed as a fugitive and resold into slavery. But Douglass published his *Narrative of the Life of Frederick Douglass* and then took a vacation to Europe to let the controversy die down. In England he noticed immediately how differently he was treated; for the first time in his life he was truly a free man. Here he began to change from a man concerned with emancipation of his people to one who would become the premier spokesman for African American social equality and economic and spiritual freedom.

Douglass returned to the United States with enough money to buy his freedom and set up a newspaper, *The North Star* (the "drinking gourd," or Big Dipper, which was the traditional beacon to freedom among slaves), to publicize his ideas. This caused much jealousy among the white abolitionist community, which accused him of splintering the antislavery effort. His critics said that by buying his freedom he had sanctioned slavery (a notion that, of course, ignored the fact that he was no longer liable to be sent back South). Douglass also angered many in the North by marrying a second time, to a white woman, criticism he tossed off by saying his first wife "was the color of my mother, and the second, the color of my father." Unflattering biographers have also accused him of many extramarital affairs with women of all colors. Besides abolition, Douglas supported advancing the rights of women ("right is of no sex," he maintained, a revolutionary idea in

his time) and counseled radical abolitionist John Brown in his raid on the U.S. arsenal at Harpers Ferry. The latter incident led to a call in Virginia for Douglass's arrest, so he went to Canada and England and lectured for the next six months until the chance of being apprehended faded.

The Civil War brought Douglass to the forefront of black liberation activities. He spoke against slavery as the true cause of the war and called for immediate freedom for all slaves. He worked hard for the right of blacks to enlist and help emancipate themselves. He was instrumental in the organization of the Fifty-fourth and Fifty-fifth Massachusetts (Colored) Volunteer Infantry Regiments, to whose service he contributed two sons. He hinted that the war could not have been won but for the help of the black volunteers. He conferred with President Abraham Lincoln, which raised his stature to being the most important African American in the country. During Reconstruction Douglass urged Congress to grant the right to vote and secure civil and social rights for the former slaves. For a while he was marshal and recorder of deeds for the District of Columbia. He also served on the Santo Domingo Commission and as U.S. minister to Haiti.

Throughout all of the Civil War, Reconstruction, and the rest of the nineteenth century, Douglass sought to keep intact the unity of blacks and whites on behalf of the cause of freedom and equality. He believed that the war was more than a battle for Union. It was a fight for the proper moral ideology that had to be guarded against what he saw as the historical amnesia implicit in the myth of the "Lost Cause" of the Confederacy and the resurgent racism that accompanied it. His whole being demanded that future generations see the conflict from an African American and abolitionist perspective, rather than as a war in which all were brave soldiers for their own beliefs.

He continued to advance his own thirst for knowledge and the cause of black and women's rights to the day of his death after attending a women's rights conference. "Now as always," he once wrote, "I am for any movement whenever there is a good cause to promote, a right to assert, a chain to be broken, a burden to be removed, or a wrong to be redressed." On the other hand, Douglass never believed that prejudice absolved its victims from the exercise of personal responsibility. "By the power that is within you, do what you hope to do," was his constant advice. Douglass never was against cooperation with whites. He believed that African Americans were of the New World first and that to condone establishing a black nation within a nation was an anomaly, "and we have no more right to foster it than men of any other race." But he was never ashamed of his color, either. "I utterly abhor and spurn with all contempt possible that cowardly meanness which leads any colored man to repudiate his connection with the race," he stated, in a phrase typical of Douglass's powerful tone. At the same time, Douglass was enough of a realist to warn his brethren that while whites would do much for African Americans, "whenever the American people shall become convinced that they have gone too far in recognizing the rights of the Negro, they will find some way to abridge these rights."

When he died in 1895, five states adopted resolutions of regret, and two U.S. senators and a Supreme Court justice were among the honorary pallbearers. By the time of his death, however, Douglass recognized that the cause of freedom had suffered a setback in the latter part of the nineteenth century. But he was not without hope. He preferred to see the cause as being like Lazarus, not dead but asleep. In this manner he accurately perceived the coming of the Second Reconstruction that arrived with the advent of the freedom riders and the marches of Martin Luther King, Jr., and was secured by the Civil Rights Law of 1964 and the Voting Rights Act of 1965. "Fellow citizens," he intoned at a Memorial Day convocation the year before he died, "I am not indifferent to the claims of a generous forgetfulness, but whatever else I may forget, I shall never forget the difference between those who fought for liberty and those who fought for slavery; between those

who fought to save the Republic and those who fought to destroy it." He never ceased to see African Americans as the mirror of American democracy by which all other things must be measured.

See also African Americans and Reconstruction; Emancipation.

References Blight, David W., "'For Something Beyond the Battlefield'" (1989); Chesnut, Charles Haddell, *Frederick Douglass* (1899); Douglass, Frederick, *The Life and Times of Frederick Douglass Written by Himself* (1881) and *Narrative of the Life of Frederick Douglass* (1845); DuBois, W. E. Burghardt, "Frederick Douglass" (1964–1981); McFeely, William S., *Frederick Douglass* (1991); Quarles, Benjamin, *Frederick Douglass* (1948), "Frederick Douglass" (1981), *Lincoln and the Negro* (1962), and *The Negro in the Civil War* (1953); Washington, Booker T., *Frederick Douglass* (1906).

Dubuclet, Antoine (1810–1887)

The black treasurer of the state of Louisiana from 1868 to 1878, Antoine Dubuclet was born a free man of color in Iberville Parish. His black father was a landholder and slaveholder of some wealth (not a rare occurrence in pre–Civil War Louisiana) whose early death sent the remaining Dubuclets to New Orleans, where his mother hoped to educate the family better. Antoine, however, remained behind on the plantation. As the eldest son, already educated at home, he managed the sugar production until 1834, when the land was divided up among him and his ten brothers and sisters. During this same time, Dubuclet met and married Claire Pollard, a wealthy free woman of color whose own sugar plantation was located near New Orleans. When she died in 1852, Dubuclet married again. He fathered 12 children between both women, and by 1864 his property holdings were worth almost $100,000, including more than 100 slaves. This made him the wealthiest free black in Louisiana and the South, and one of the richest men in all Louisiana, regardless of color, to boot. In the fashion of the time, Dubuclet sent his children to France to be educated free from the baneful influences of slavery and racial discrimination.

The coming of the Civil War caused great changes in the plantation system of the South, particularly in Louisiana, which became one of the first areas occupied by federal troops in early 1862. Dubuclet was reputedly a kind master, but he was a slave driver nonetheless, and his people fled to freedom along with those of his white neighbors. Dubuclet would now have to hire his labor. Although there is no record of his Civil War experiences, civilian or military, Dubuclet emerged during Reconstruction as a loyal supporter of the Military Reconstruction Acts and the Republican regime in the state. Though not a member of the conventions in 1864 or 1867, Dubuclet was an important enough in party circles to be placed on the Republican ticket as nominee for state treasurer and was elected in 1868 along with the rest of the Henry Clay Warmoth regime.

When Dubuclet assumed office, the Louisiana state treasury was bankrupt. Dubuclet worked to halt all unnecessary expenditures and end extravagant appropriation bills. He asked the state assembly to reconsider the whole tax and revenue collection system, and he recommended that an act be passed making greenbacks the only acceptable currency with which to pay state debts. But he faced a political system riddled with patronage and fraud, and his wise recommendations were ignored. In spite of the prevalance of the unethical monetary practices of black and white politicians, Dubuclet attempted to halt the payment of dubious claims and, when necessary, was even willing to take malefactors to court to protect the integrity of the state treasury. According to the constitution, the state treasurer was to be elected for two years at first and every four years thereafter. Dubuclet's reelection in 1870 demonstrated he had much support among blacks and whites of all political persuasions, and he received much campaign support from conservative newspapers. This success was repeated in 1874 when he gained a third term. He guaranteed honesty among the treasury officials through nepotism, employing his sons as assistant clerks.

Dubuclet had now served as state treasurer under three governors: Warmoth; his successor upon impeachment, P. B. S. Pinchback; and William P. Kellogg. Only the latter could really be seen as interested in assisting Dubuclet in reducing the state's indebtedness, which was accomplished by a funding bill that converted the whole amount owed into bonds redeemable in 40 years. Because Dubuclet's term would be up in 1878, he was retained in office by the Democratic Redeemers who took over in the election of 1876. But the legislature subjected him and his department to an intensive investigation, led by Edward D. White, a future U.S. Supreme Court justice appointed during Grover Cleveland's second administration. The White committee found some alleged minor irregularities, but a minority report cleared Dubuclet completely, leading one to suspect that White and the Democratic majority did not wish to find Dubuclet totally clean lest the Redeemer myth of Reconstruction corruption be mitigated. In any case Dubuclet still must rank as one of the cleanest politicians of his era. Dubuclet decided not to run in 1878; the divided Republican party was having little success in fielding a winning ticket anyhow. Dubuclet returned to his Iberville Parish estate, which he eventually sold to his son, and lived there with his mistress, his second wife having died. He passed away in 1887, never entering politics again.

Dubuclet's clean career as state treasurer stands in contrast to the corruption that infected Louisiana during Reconstruction. It earned him bipartisan praise. His record looks even better when one examines the term of the Democratic treasurer, E. A. Burke, who followed him. Burke bilked the state out of an estimated $1.2 million before he fled to Honduras a jump ahead of the law, where he remained a fugitive from justice until his death in 1928.

See also African Americans and Reconstruction; Pinchback, Pinckney Benton Stewart; Warmoth, Henry Clay.

Reference Vincent, Charles, "Aspects of the Family and Public Life of Antoine Dubuclet" (1981).

Dunn, Oscar J. (ca. 1820–1871)

Born of an unknown father and a free woman of color who ran a rooming house for white actors, Oscar J. Dunn was apprenticed to a painter and plasterer in New Orleans. He had no formal education, but somewhere along the line, probably from his mother's boarders, he picked up a good command of language, written and oral, and he was noted as an excellent fiddle player. He was not enamored with his life as an apprentice, which is evident by his running away numerous times. He later took up the trade of barber, buying his own shop, and he also taught music. Following the occupation of New Orleans in the spring of 1862, it is said that Dunn enlisted in the Corps d'Afrique, some of the first blacks to be accepted into the Union army. He had leadership talent and rose to the rank of captain, but he resigned his commission when an inferior white candidate was promoted over him. In any case he did establish an employment office for the newly freed slaves in 1865, and he later worked as an inspector for the federal Bureau of Refugees, Freedmen, and Abandoned Lands. He also registered many blacks to vote and helped sponsor a mock election of all races that sent Carpetbagger Henry Clay Warmoth to Congress to be seated as Louisiana's nonvoting "territorial representative."

Meanwhile, Dunn became secretary to the Freedmen's Saving and Trust Company and organized a people's bakery, owned by its employees. He was in favor of reconvening the state constitutional convention and thus was unfairly blamed for the ensuing New Orleans Riot of 1866. Evidently Dunn's reputation preceded him because Maj. Gen. Philip H. Sheridan appointed him to the commission council of New Orleans in 1867 under powers granted by the Third Military Reconstruction Act. Dunn proposed that the city establish a public education system open to all children irrespective of race and to be fully integrated. Although his proposal became the basis of the state constitution sections on education in 1868, it was reality only for about a decade in New Orleans. He also spoke out in favor of a more efficient fire-fighting system, the appointment of only qualified electors to city patronage posts, and a tighter management of city government under the mayor. When the state Republican convention nominated Henry Clay Warmoth as governor in 1868, it tendered the lieutenant governorship to another politician. But the man refused the post, leaving the position open for Oscar J. Dunn, by now the acknowledged leader of the city's powerful contingent of black voters. The election of the Moderate Republican ticket of Warmoth and Dunn placed the black plasterer in power as the first African American to hold an executive post in Reconstruction.

Aside from his duties as lieutenant governor of presiding over the state senate, Dunn was president of the board of New Orleans metropolitan police, a member of the senate printing committee, and president of the board of military pensions. He insisted that all members of the state senate take the ironclad oath (one of never having aided the Confederacy) before being seated, a step that sent several prominent Democrats home. It was soon evident that Louisiana had three aspirants to the open U.S. Senate in 1871: Warmoth, senate president pro tem P. B. S. Pinchback (an African American from Ohio), and Dunn. The latter had the advantage over the other two, both of whom were Carpetbaggers and hence outsiders to many in Louisiana. Dunn got the chance to demonstrate his abilities further when Warmoth retired to the Mississippi Gulf Coast with an injured foot. As Warmoth was out of the state, the governorship devolved upon Dunn. Angry that Warmoth seemed in league with prominent Democrats and ex-secessionists, Dunn and other African Americans hoped to gain a better patronage position with Warmoth temporarily gone. Warmoth was warned as to the situation and returned to oust Dunn before he could fairly act, but many expressed their desire to see an honest man like Dunn advance somewhere in state or national government. Dunn represented a growing reform movement among blacks and whites alike.

Both Warmoth and Pinchback had the reputation of being political hacks who would sell any position for a price. Dunn, in contrast, was viewed as an honest man, a fact that endeared him to the Ulysses S. Grant administration nationally and to many voters of both races locally. He also managed to take over the Louisiana state central committee of the Republican party, which held the nomination procedure in its hands. With these assets, Dunn could mount a creditable reform campaign for the open U.S. Senate seat in 1871. Warmoth and Pinchback also claimed to have control of their own well-bought versions of the state central committee, and each man claimed to be the regular, legal candidate. However, the whole picture abruptly changed as Dunn took sick. Rumors spread that he had been poisoned at a $1,000-a-plate dinner the night before. But Dunn had been experiencing what he described as a chest cold for weeks, and it is possible that he had an allergic reaction to the patent medicines he took. He began to vomit violently and cough up phlegm and a bloody mucus. Doctors diagnosed a congestion of the brain and lungs. By morning Dunn gave out a death rattle in his throat, sobbed, and died.

A local coroner responded to the rumors of poisoning by asking Dunn's family to permit an autopsy. But the family refused, satisfied that he had died a natural, although unexplained and unexpected, death. Although Dunn had been attended by several physicians during his sickness, none agreed as to the reason for the lieutenant governor's death. The coroner suspected arsenic poisoning (as do modern analyzers), having autopsied a similar case the week before. Arsenic was also known to be a common voodoo concoction popular in the city. But three doctors (all white, implying to some that they were Warmoth hacks) signed the death certificate, making it official and negating an investigation. Dunn's skilled black doctor, L. C. Roudanez, however, was not among the signers, a fact that caused much suspicion then and now. Meanwhile, Warmoth and Pinchback (who had advanced to lieutenant governor in Dunn's absence, in accordance with the state constitution), both of whom stood to gain from Dunn's death, continued to fight it out over the U.S. Senate seat, able to devote full attention to each other now that Oscar J. Dunn was gone.

See also Pinchback, Pinckney Benton Stewart; Redemption of the South since 1874; Warmoth, Henry Clay.

References Christian, Marcus B., "The Theory of the Poisoning of Oscar J. Dunn" (1945); Perkins, Archie E., "Oscar James Dunn" (1943); Vincent, Charles, *Black Legislators in Louisiana during Reconstruction* (1976).

Eaton, John (1829–1906)

Originally from New Hampshire, where he attended Dartmouth College to study theology, John Eaton enlisted as the chaplain of the Twenty-seventh Ohio Volunteer Infantry. In this capacity he was appointed by Maj. Gen. Ulysses S. Grant as superintendent of freedmen for Mississippi, northern Louisiana, Arkansas, and western Tennessee, a position he held until the end of the war, winding up as a brevet brigadier general. Eaton worked the contrabands (the name given to liberated slaves during the Civil War) in abandoned fields at Corinth, Mississippi, and Grand Junction, Tennessee, where the largest camps of blacks were. He got into several squabbles with the army's adjutant general, Lorenzo Thomas, over recruitment of blacks as soldiers and how they should be employed by private contractors on abandoned plantations. At the end of the war Eaton remained in Tennessee, editing a Memphis newspaper and serving as state superintendent of education. He was also a commissioner for the U.S. Bureau of Education, president of two colleges, and the individual in charge of restoring the education system of Puerto Rico after the Spanish-American War. He wrote several accounts on Mormonism (he had been in Salt Lake City for a period of time) and about his wartime experience with black labor. He died in Washington, D.C., in 1906.

See also Mississippi Valley Experiment.

References Bigelow, Martha M., "Freedmen of the Mississippi Valley" (1962); Eaton, John, *Grant, Lincoln, and the Freedmen* (1969 [1907]); Gerteis, Louis S., *From Contraband to Freedman* (1973); Ross, Steven Joseph, "Freed Soil, Freed Labor, Freed Men" (1978); Wiley, Bell I., "Vicissitudes of Early Reconstruction Farming in the Lower Mississippi Valley" (1937).

Economic Disfranchisement

With respect to observers of the South around the time of the Civil War, two statements seemed almost universal. During the antebellum years it was said that all Southerners, especially the white nonslaveholders and the enslaved blacks, were lazy. After the Civil War the comments took the line that most Southerners, white or black, lived in wretched misery.

That the slaves sought to do as little work as possible, given the compulsory and personally unprofitable nature of their labor, is not surprising. But what of the Southern white who seemed to do little but lie in the shade and commune with his hounds? Recent investigators have theorized that the Southern nonslaveholders had little to do because they lived a lifestyle based on the herding of wild hogs, as derived from the Celtic societies of Britain and Ireland from which most of their ancestors came. The only work required was to mark the yearlings in spring and collect the herd for market in the fall. The diet of pork was augmented by home-grown vegetables, all of which grew wild in the Southern heat and humidity and went to seed each year, keeping the agricultural tilling common to the rest of the country to a minimum. In truth, the South had the best of all worlds: economic abundance with little effort. As for being lazy, a term that Yankees condescendingly utilized, Southerners would substitute the descriptive adjective *leisurely*.

But when African Americans achieved emancipation at the close of the Civil War, they did not inherit the independent lifestyle of the nonslaveholding whites. Instead the planters tried to substitute a form of pseudoslavery by implementing the Black Codes. The idea was to create an agricultural system that resembled slavery as much as possible within the demands of freedom. For the first several years after the war, planters tried to get blacks to live on the plantation in select "towns" and work the staple crops with supervised gang labor, just like before the war; the difference was that blacks would now receive a share of the proceeds at harvest. The planters were assisted in this effort by the activities and edicts of the army and the Freedmen's Bureau, which had taken over the management of black labor on abandoned plantations during the war. But African Americans refused to work in this fashion. It reminded them too much of slavery. They boycotted the extension of slavery under this guise, and whites condemned them as lazy. Finally blacks and whites came to an agreement—blacks would work the land in family units as tenants, each unit being a small "farm" within the planter's whole plantation, and they would pay rent for their house and land out of their share of the crop.

But the black tenant farmer had a problem—there was no payday until the crop had been harvested and sold. So he needed credit, supplies, draft animals, and implements until the harvest was accomplished. The planter had the means to provide the credit, so he loaned the necessary items to the tenant at a usurious interest rate (at least 50 percent was common). To make the whole process convenient for the tenant, the planter either went in with a local store owner to provide these services or, ideally, ran the store himself. Prices were double or triple what the goods ordinarily sold for elsewhere (on top of the loan interest). Books were kept and the "deducts" taken from the share of the crop that was owed the tenant at the end of the season, after the landowner's share of the crop was secured. When the whole process was totaled up at the end of the year, the tenant usually found that his family was short of full payment. So the landowner would offer a loan on the next year's potential crop (called the lien). All credit was to be paid off in the form of cash crops like cotton. Food was sold at the store—on credit of course. So the vicious cycle continued until the mountainous debt became unmanageable and was permanently passed on from generation to generation. This system was a lot more profitable than slavery for the landowner, and the tenant took all the risk. Some lucky farmers were able to beat the odds and emerge with their own land or a business, but they were few and far between. It took only one bad year of no rain to put oneself in debt for life.

But blacks were not alone in being mistreated by the sharecropping system. For instance, a white hog farmer who went off to war against the North may have come home to find that his livestock had been rustled by the passing Union and Confederate armies or by brigands of both races who roamed the South during the conflict. Such a white farmer found himself in a trap after the war. As blacks gained their political rights, they combined with the planters to fence off the land, something the big landowners had wanted for years but had lacked the political power to achieve before the war. However, the open range had been essential to healthy hog raising. Now the hogs had to be raised in pens, wallowing in their own feces and urine, rather than in the cool forests where they had run wild (a hog cannot survive temperatures above 98°F without shade and a mud skin covering). This led the hogs to become unhealthy and to pass on that ill health, in the form of trichinosis, to the humans who ate the pork. In addition, fewer hogs could be kept because feeding them in a confined space cost more money than letting them run wild in the acorn forests. At the same time, the time-honored trail drive method of taking hogs to market was curtailed in the interest of the developing railroads. The small white farmers could not afford to send hogs to market by rail—that was too expensive. The result was that white farmers had to turn to the plow for income. But like black sharecroppers, they needed loans to get started. The local store was happy to help out a Confederate veteran—for the usual price already being charged to blacks. Loans were made with the farmers' land as collateral, and loans could be obtained only to grow cotton, not food for the farmers and their families. They were forced to buy food from the company store, only deepening their debt to the company. By 1890 both white and black farmers were in a real credit crunch. The lucky ones, mostly whites (because wage jobs were traditionally reserved for them to keep them socially above the poor blacks), got jobs at the textile mills, coal mines, or lumber mills. But they, too, faced creditors who trapped them in a cycle of debt.

With this kind of a bloodsucking credit system—in the end, as the song has it, you really did owe your soul to the company store—one might wonder what kept people from packing up and leaving the country for somewhere else. Presumably one could at least shop around for a better employer? The answer was that the credit system got its teeth from contract labor laws and the convict lease. Each laborer signed himself and his family up for a one-year stint on a piece of land. This was a legal contract, enforceable in court. Should any other planter (or employer) interfere with the original contract, that person could be taken to court for "enticement" of a laborer and jailed or fined. Emigrant labor laws kept anyone from taking labor away from the state. And vagrancy laws were strictly enforced—no contract and no income meant that one went off to jail.

Jail was where a person's real troubles began. Southern penal laws were run on a surety basis. Convicts were put to work within the jail system or contracted out to private companies as a cheap labor pool. Common sentences for vagrancy were 6 to 12 months on the chain gang. Any interested citizen could pay a convict's fine and put him or her to labor until the fine was worked off. It was also possible for a planter or employer to charge a hired contract laborer with a false crime (e.g., saying that he or she had obtained credit under the "false pretense" of agreeing to work it off and then had failed to work "adequately" to the creditor's satisfaction) and then to buy out the fine and put him or her back to work more cheaply than before. Of course, judges and sheriffs received kickbacks to keep the system well oiled with an automatic presumption of guilt.

The ironic thing was that the Southern penal system had its inception during Radical Reconstruction, when the state governments composed of Scalawags, Carpetbaggers, and African Americans had to improvise to create a prison system with minimum financial outlays. Alabama and Texas tried to maintain minimal supervision of prisoners, who were leased out. Virginia and the Carolinas tried to establish actual prisons that had their own indigenous industries. However, the rest of the Confederate states, plus Missouri and Kansas, had a convict lease system that could be described at best as brutal and corrupt. Living conditions in these convict lease camps were miserable. The prisoners ate and lived in an environment that made slavery look truly benign. At night they were shackled to their bunks in long communal dormitories. Women prisoners were given over to the most obedient male prisoners and raped. The prettiest ones went to the guards. Railroads, local public works, mines, pitch and resin factories, and hemp plants used jail inmates to carry out their tasks, often at great profit to the contractors, who skimped on everything but discipline.

Many historians wonder whether more decisive federal action on behalf of the freedmen would have produced better economic results during the period after the Civil War. But historian C. Vann Woodward demurs from this viewpoint. Woodward fears that confiscating Southern plantations and doling out the land to the ex-slaves would have merely consigned the land to eventual expropriation by Northern speculators and railroad interests, as happened to the land obtained by blacks under the Southern Homestead Act. He also believes that to have placed African Americans under a lengthy national benevolent guardianship would have been counterproductive, too, if federal policy toward Native Americans is a fair indication. If Woodward is correct, then Reconstruction's shortcomings were probably inevitable, given the U.S. commitment in the nineteenth century to white supremacy and untamed exploitation of natural resources. The credit crunch that destroyed the better-off white farmers by the 1890s would have done the same to blacks regardless of their landholdings.

The result was that, by the turn of the century, the South wound up with a system of peonage—involuntary servitude based on debt—that was contrary to an 1867 federal law. But this system had gone unchallenged since its inception during Reconstruction (except for during the Populist revolt of the 1890s, which merely inspired the powers that be to disfranchise indebted black and white farmers to prevent their interference). Economists have labeled this American gulag as the "Prussian Road" to modernity, one based on compulsion rather than the natural economic laws of supply and demand and mobility of labor. It took the throes of a half dozen court cases, two world wars, and the Great Depression before the system was crushed and a freer society emerged in the last half of the twentieth century.

See also African American Education and Reconstruction; Black Codes; Bureau of Refugees, Freedmen, and Abandoned Lands; Disfranchisement; Exodusters; Mississippi Valley Experiment; Segregation (Jim Crow); Washington, Booker T.

References Bacote, Clarence A., "Negro Proscriptions, Protests, and Proposed Solutions in Georgia" (1959); Cable, George W., "The Convict Lease System in the Southern States" (1884); Carleton, Mark T., *Politics and Punishment* (1971); Carper, N. Gordon, "Slavery Revisited" (1976); Cohen, William, "Negro Involuntary Servitude in the South" (1976); Daniel, Pete, "The Metamorphosis of Slavery" (1979) and *The Shadow of Slavery* (1973); Eckert, Edward K., "Contract Labor in Florida during Reconstruction" (1968); Kolchin, Peter, "Race, Class, and Poverty in the Post–Civil War South" (1979); Krebs, Sylvia, "Will the Freedmen Work?" (1974); Logan, Rayford W., *The Betrayal of the Negro* (1965); Magdol, Edward, *A Right to the Land* (1977); Mandle, Jay R., *The Roots of Black Poverty* (1978); McDonald, Forrest, and Grady McWhiney, "The South from Self-Sufficiency to Peonage" (1980); McKelvey, Blake, "Penal Slavery and Southern Reconstruction" (1963); Novak, Daniel A., *The Wheel of Servitude* (1978); Ransom, Roger L., and Richard Sutch, *One Kind of Freedom* (1977); Reid, Joseph D., Jr., "Sharecropping as an Understandable Market Response" (1973) and "White Land, Black Labor, and Agricultural Stagnation" (1979); Roark, James L., *Masters without Slaves* (1977); Schweninger, Loren, "Prosperous Blacks in the South" (1990); Shlomowitz, Ralph, "The Origins of Southern Sharecropping" (1979); Shofner, Jerrell H., "Custom, Law, and History" (1977); Weaver, Herbert, *Mississippi Farmers* (1945); Wiener, Jonathan M., "Class Structure and Economic Development in the American South" (1979); Wilson, Theodore B., *The Black Codes of the South* (1965); Woodman, Harold D., *King Cotton and His Retainers* (1968) and "Post Civil War Agriculture and the Law" (1979); Woodward, C. Vann, "Reconstruction" (1989).

Election of 1868

The Republican party is all too often characterized as the party of Big Business. But Big Business does not vote in sufficient quantities to elect anyone. In truth, the late nineteenth-century Republican party's strength was dependent on the suffrage of small businessmen and farmers. It also appealed to loyal Union men, blacks and white, through the slogan "Vote as you shot" and through its main lobby of veterans, the Grand Army of the Republic. There was no unity on economic questions. The party was split over questions of tariffs, internal improvements, and the national banking system. But it managed to vote in enough varied economic measures to please a wide audience.

In 1868, the Republican party was going to stand on its record and past legislation. It had no new program to offer. Doubters were to be won over by appealing to the patriotism of the supporters of the Union. The Republican platform had a wide appeal in its various parts but not, perhaps, as wide an appeal as a whole. It appealed to businessmen and labor through the Morrill Tariff of 1862, which had raised rates on imported goods to 50 percent of their value. It also offered an emphasis on internal improvements, typified by the Pacific Railroad Act of 1862 and its amendment in 1864, which linked markets and factories nationwide. The financial community was pleased with the national banking system, which gave a unified control of banking standards and a single, reliable currency. Agricultural interests liked the Homestead Act of 1862, which opened up 160 acres of public land to anyone who would improve it and could last on it for five years. Then there was the Morrill Land Grant College Act, which created agricultural and mechanical colleges through federal land grants given to the states; the sale of these lands financed colleges that taught subjects for the average American and also offered military science to keep the nation's youth prepared to meet further rebellion.

And, of course, there were civil rights for the nation's blacks. Some have argued quite forcefully that the popular vote throughout the balance of the nineteenth century was close enough that black voters provided the small majorities that allowed Republicans to carry states with large urban areas. Whenever Republicans got a bit smug about expecting the African American vote, blacks withheld their votes or went Democratic, as in 1884 or 1892, and the presidency changed hands (although Grover Cleveland's Democrats were not much of a change, being closet Republicans in economic policy). But others are not so sure that blacks alone determined control of the presidency.

Standing on their record and repudiating the Radicalism typified by the persecution of Andrew Johnson through his impeachment, the Republicans came to Chicago in 1868 for their national nominating convention. Here they played their trump card, the nomination of the popular war hero Ulysses S. Grant. The scene was set by a soldiers and sailors convention held just down the street. There, veterans denounced the seven Republican "traitors" who had voted to acquit President Johnson. They marched past pro-Democratic newspapers singing ribald songs. The convention band played the "Rogue's March" in "honor" of Johnson and his cabinet. And, of course, the veterans petitioned the Republican conventioneers to do the honorable thing for the nation's future by nominating General Grant for president. In much the same way he won the war he could also secure the peace, went the reasoning. The highlight of the veteran's show was the speech of Jesse Grant, the general's father. Playing the humble farmer to the hilt (he would not have missed this opportunity to shine for anything), Jesse Grant claimed to be astonished that he "who had done nothing in particular in the great war should be called upon by the braves of the nation to speak." Voices in the crowd, probably on cue, shouted back, "You had a boy—that is enough!"

Of course, the Republicans had more to offer the nation than a war hero for their presidential candidate. Salmon P. Chase (Lincoln's one-time secretary of the treasury, now chief justice of the Supreme Court and a perennial presidential candidate, whom detractors likened to a fourth member of the Trinity) had much support from white Radical Republicans in the South as well as New England bankers (the National Banking Act was his doing). Chase probably would have made it in normal times, but Grant's stand against Johnson over the Tenure of Office Act plus his military reputation were too much to top.

However, Grant's prestige was not enough to stop Benjamin F. Butler of Massachusetts. Spurred on by friends' remarks that he was Grant's equal in every way, all Butler really wanted was an apology from Grant for sarcastic remarks he had made about Butler's poor generalship during the war. So a weird deal was worked out in which Grant apologized to Butler by inviting him to a reception, where an incident was staged in which the Beast of New Orleans (as Butler was known) "saved" Grant from some blackmailing woman from California, who insisted that Grant owed her money from before the war. It was all nonsense (there was never any blackmailing "other woman" for the straitlaced Grant), but it allowed Butler to save face, and it showed that Grant was a man who favored party unity at all costs, something politicians like to know about outsiders such as hero generals. So with the endorsement from the soldiers and sailors, John A. Logan of Illinois, a political general and Democrat-turned-Republican, made the nominating speech. Lo and behold, no one else was put forward. And Grant received the nomination unanimously by acclamation. The vice president's slot went to "Smilin'" Schuyler Colfax, speaker of the House, who had let Representative Thaddeus Stevens run everything. It was said that Colfax was so amiable that he never lost a friend or made an enemy, which did not hurt him among party stalwarts.

Grant accepted the nomination through the traditional letter. Brilliantly, Grant declared that he would have no policy to enforce against the will of the people, which meant that he would do Congress' bidding as opposed to following Johnson's independent streak. This pleased Republican theorists, who believed that that was the president's constitutional role. Grant closed with a heart-rending plea to a war-weary, Reconstruction-weary nation: "Let us have peace." Then he went on a tour of the West, with generals William T. Sherman (who thought Grant was nuts to accept a political role and said so) and Philip Sheridan, letting others carry the campaign for him as tradition would have it. The platform endorsed the outcome of the war, approved of the Reconstruction Acts, pledged payment of the national debt in gold or its equivalent, permitted suffrage to be settled by the states (allowing blacks to vote in the South through the Reconstruction Acts but letting Northern states deny them the right), and ignored the tariff question (hoping to attract the votes of War Democrats who had supported Lincoln in 1864). Triumphantly the party declared to its Democratic opponents: "Match him!"

Matching Grant was out of the question for the Democrats, who were still ailing from the political throes of Civil War and Reconstruction. As they met in New York City (they had their own soldiers' and sailors' convention down the street, too), the party did have several possible courses of action. They could openly challenge the Republicans and Reconstruction by nominating President Johnson. But the losses to Johnson's supporters in 1866 did not bode well for this course. Or they could challenge Reconstruction policy by nominating their own war hero, Maj. Gen. Winfield Scott Hancock, who had ruled Louisiana and Texas in a manner to appeal to moderates all over the nation and had none of Johnson's liabilities. Or they could accept Reconstruction and the African American vote as established facts and nominate a man like Senator Thomas A. Hendricks of Indiana, committed to constitutional government and state rights. This same course of action could be taken with another declared nominee, Salmon P. Chase of Ohio. Having been denied the Republican nomination, Chase declared that he had been a Demo-

crat all along—he had parted with the Democratic party only over the slavery issue. There was a lot of Wall Street support for Chase within the party, and many admired the national banking system he had set up during the war.

Finally, the Democrats could ignore Reconstruction and focus on the prewar economic issues that had been enacted by the Republicans under Lincoln when the South was out of the Congress. The big issue here was to pay off the war debt in greenbacks (paper dollars) unless the terms of those debts specifically stated that payment must be made in gold. "The dollar that paid the soldier can pay the bondholder," went the call, issued by George Pendleton of Ohio. There was a lot of appeal to this concept, and Pendleton's "Ohio Idea" became the main plank of the Democratic platform. The Democrats also asked the nation to forget the war, pledged to declare the Reconstruction Acts null and void and to let all of the states settle their desires on suffrage, and promised to withdraw the U.S. Army's occupation force from the South. But the delegates deadlocked on nominating Pendleton. After numerous votes, the convention finally nominated its speaker, Horatio Seymour of New York. His vice presidential nominee was Frank Blair of Missouri, a political general of some ability from an old family that had put Andrew Jackson in the presidency 40 years earlier.

The Democratic ticket was bottom heavy. Blair was a good man, but he was not the candidate. Seymour, on the other hand, had numerous liabilities. He was little known outside New York, and then only as its governor who had been tarred with the brush of disloyalty during the war, which he had vocally opposed. Many suspected him of being a Copperhead, a secret Rebel sympathizer, and he had been accused of suspicious activities during the massive New York City antidraft riots in 1863 (it had taken a brigade of infantry and a battery of artillery right off the field of Gettysburg to put rioters down bloodily). Worse yet, he was a hard money man who wanted to repay the war bonds in gold, just like the Republicans.

Horace Greeley of the *New York Tribune* wrote that the Republicans themselves could not have picked a better pair than Seymour and Blair to run against. With Seymour, a suspected Copperhead who had disowned the platform, and Blair, who had left the Republican party at the end of war over the race issue, the debate raged over the Reconstruction issue, the Republican's strongest point. The Republicans "waved the bloody shirt" with zeal (i.e., told graphic stories of conservative white political violence in the South). "Scratch a Democrat and find a Rebel," went one slogan. "Grant acts, Seymour talks, and Blair blows," went another. The song of the day was: "Oh! God was kind and Heaven true when it gave us a man like U—Lysses Grant, when it gave us a man like you." The result was a smashing electoral victory for Grant and the Republicans (214-80) and a narrower popular victory of 300,000 votes out of nearly 6 million cast. Outgoing President Johnson never bothered to show up for the inauguration, as he and Grant were still bitter enemies over the Tenure of Office Act.

See also Butler, Benjamin Franklin; Grant, [Hiram] Ulysses Simpson; Grant and Domestic Policies; Grant and Reconstruction; Grant and the Scandals; Impeachment; Tenure of Office Act; Waving the Bloody Shirt.

References Carpenter, John A., *Ulysses S. Grant* (1970); Coleman, Charles H., *The Election of 1868* (1933); Hesseltine, William B., *Ulysses S. Grant* (1935); Logan, Rayford W., *The Betrayal of the Negro* (1965); McFeeley, William S., *Grant* (1991); Richter, William L., "The Papers of U. S. Grant" (1990 and 1992); Simpson, Brooks D., *Let Us Have Peace* (1991).

Election of 1872

By the time of the 1872 election, the Ulysses S. Grant administration had caused quite a bit of disillusionment among the party and the public at large. Some of it was embarrassing, such as Senator Charles Sumner introducing a constitutional amendment limiting a president to one term. True, it would exempt Grant, but on the other hand, everyone knew at whom it was aimed. Other criticism was of the "damned if you do, damned if you don't" variety. Grant was lambasted as soft on civil service reform; for being associated with the most corrupt elements of the party; as too harsh on Reconstruction enforcement; as not harsh enough on Reconstruction enforcement; and as soft on the protective tariff. Those who opposed Grantism within the party were called Liberal Republicans. Most were journalists, professional reformers, and intellectuals. They lacked political skills but made up for it with a lot of enthusiasm. They were liberal not in the twentieth-century sense of wanting government services, but in the traditional sense of desiring honest, constitutional government. They decided not to challenge the political professionals of the Republican party but to step aside and form a new party to challenge all of the status quo.

Led by German immigrant and former Union political general Carl Schurz, the Liberal Republicans met in Cincinnati, Ohio. Their platform was full of the reforms of the hour. While they agreed with Reconstruction in principle, they found it lacking in practice. Their solution to the corrupt boroughs of the South was to call for universal amnesty and a withdrawal of federal troops from the civilian political arena. The Liberals believed that something basic was amiss with governments that could not appeal on the basis of calm, political argument and the vote of the whole public. Of course, this ignored the reality of the South, where blacks would not be allowed to vote at all if the troops were gone. Another platform plank was the call for civil service reform and a general cleaning up of government. Liberals endorsed the paying of the national debt in gold (in their opinion, *real* hard money, not inflated greenbacks, was the only honest way). But they disagreed on the tariff issue. Some wanted it higher, some wanted it lower. So in the end the party said they would refer it to the people. This made them look weak and willing to drop principle for expediency.

Up to this point the Liberals stood a good chance to win. But then they got down to the process of nominating a candidate—the place where third parties often fail. There were several possibilities. One was Judge David Davis of Illinois, who had been Abraham Lincoln's campaign manager. But he had the support of a labor convention and the Liberals were probusiness. Another was Lyman Trumbull of Illinois, the senator who had attempted to compromise with Andrew Johnson over the Freedmen's Bureau Act and the Civil Rights Act of 1866. He had shown much resolve in not voting for Johnson's conviction—he was one of the notorious seven Republicans of principle. But he was viewed with only lukewarm enthusiasm because Davis had already sewed up the votes of the Illinois delegation. A third possibility was Charles Francis Adams of Massachusetts. From a distinguished, principled family that had already produced two presidents (never mind that they rated high among the most hated during their terms), Adams had done an outstanding job as Lincoln's minister to Great Britain during the Civil War. Adams posed a real threat to the ability of the regular Republicans to get their candidate elected. So, to remove Adams as a potential candidate for another party, the regular Republicans asked him to represent the United States in the *Alabama* claims, which concerned the United States' desire for reparation from Britain for several ships outfitted there for the Confederacy during the war. Adams could not turn down the chance to clear the slate with the British, and he accepted the appointment, which effectively removed him from consideration as the Liberal candidate.

In the end it was a man behind the scenes who garnered the nomination. He was picked by other men behind the scenes, four newspaper editors known as the "Quadrilateral." These men, who trumpeted reform in their papers, were Murat Halstead of the Cincinnati *Commercial*, Samuel Bowles of the Springfield (Massachussetts) *Republican*, Henry Watterson of the Louisville *Courier-Journal*, and Horace White of the Chicago *Tribune*. These men and Carl Schurz had favored Adams, but now that was irrelevant. As they pondered what to do, another editor asked for admittance to their group. He was

Whitelaw Reid of the powerful New York *Tribune*. His paper was critical to the reform movement because its influence was nationwide. Soon the persuasive Reid was bending the other four to his way of thinking. The man he believed could lead the Liberals to power was none other than his boss, Horace Greeley. And on the sixth ballot, Greeley became the standard bearer. His running mate was B. Gratz Brown, a Missouri Radical Republican and a crony of Schurz.

Greeley's nomination has been dismissed as the work of political amateurs, but this is not wholly true. If there were any real politicians or men who understood American politics, it was the members of the Quadrilateral. Greeley was stronger than he seemed on the surface, but his nomination was kind of a fluke. The first response to his candidacy was amusement. "No two men could look each other in the face and say Greeley without laughing," was one comment. Other analysts called Greeley "a tremendous political mouse" or "an eccentric philosopher." Another commentator put it in one word: "absurd." Others saw him as "chimerical and vacillating, visionary and discrete, malignant and crotchety" or as "a grandmother and a trickster." One critic labeled him "totally destitute of sound judgment." Greeley was truly representative of the crackpot reformer. He was lovable but idiotic, wise but full of buncombe. He was an American institution. He is best remembered for his advice "Go west, young man," but he was also instrumental in forcing the First Battle of Bull Run with his daily banner headline, "Forward to Richmond." Then he became disillusioned with the war and advocated peace. He advanced the "Prayer of 20 Millions" by advising Lincoln to emancipate the slaves. He was a man of insatiable curiosity, and he looked like someone who had just stuck a bobby pin in a light socket, with his sort of wide-eyed amazement.

Greeley was many things to the American people, but presidential candidate was not high on the list. A whole generation of Democrats had been raised to hate him and his loony ideas. If he were to win against

Grant, he had to shed this liability. It was a tall order. When the Democrats met at Baltimore, the outcome of the election rested in large part with their convention delegates. The Democrats reluctantly admitted that they could not come up with a man who could take on Grant and Greeley at the same time. So they fell into step behind Greeley and the Liberals. But large numbers of Democrats had the same attitude as former Confederate lieutenant general (and soon to be Imperial Grand Wizard of the Ku Klux Klan) Nathan Bedford Forrest. He said he would support Grant, because at least Grant had not advocated emancipation and hatred of the white South for 20 years before the Civil War (something Greeley had done). Forrest was not alone, North or South. At the same time, Grant represented a strong Reconstruction and support of black rights, which appealed to many old abolitionists in the North. Politics truly makes for strange bedfellows.

As the Democrats fumed about siding with the Liberal Republicans, Greeley and all, the regular Republicans met at Philadelphia. Party regulars controlled the convention machinery and saw to it that anti-Grant delegates were scattered in their placement on the floor so that they could not communicate and coordinate their opposition. Grant won on the first ballot and, as a sop to honest government, Vice President "Smilin'" Schuyler Colfax, implicated in the Crédit Mobilier railroad scandal, was dropped for Henry Wilson, a U.S. senator from Massachusetts. (Wilson had once dallied with Confederate spy Rose O'Neal Greenhow and prematurely revealed the Yankee advance on First Bull.) They ran on the same platform as for the last election: vote the way you shot.

The Republican campaign was not harmed any by Greeley's decision to break with precedent and stump for himself. Grant sat back and let his cronies do it for him, preserving the nineteenth-century myth that the office sought the man, not the other way around. Greeley screeched in a high squeaky voice at every stop, emphasizing sectional reconciliation, "peace not vengeance." His favorite line was to extend "the hand of reconciliation" to the South. Grant's supporters had a field day with that. Especially effective was Thomas Nast's series of cartoons in *Harper's Weekly*, a nationally circulated news magazine. The theme was Greeley's "Hand of Reconciliation"— extended to John Wilkes Booth over Lincoln's grave; extended to a Confederate soldier guarding the rotting hell-hole of the prisoners-of-war camp at Andersonville; extended to a Ku Klux Klansman over the body of a mutilated black voter. Greeley commented that he hardly knew if he were running for the presidency or the penitentiary. But Nast's attack pretty well blew to pieces Greeley's farmer-philosopher image and revealed what allowing the white South to take control of Reconstruction would mean.

When the results came in Greeley had lost to Grant even more decisively than Seymour had in 1868. The electoral vote was 286 to 62; the popular vote 3.6 million to 2.8 million. Greeley had exhausted himself during the campaign and died heartbroken three weeks later. When the electoral college met to cast their votes, all but ten of the electors who were pledged to Greeley cast their votes for other living Democrats (completely permissible under the Constitution, because political parties are not recognized under it). Grant had won his second term under conditions that meant the anomalies of his first term would be multiplied and made much worse. The corruption of the Great Barbecue was on and the Era of Good Stealings had just begun.

See also Election of 1868; Election of 1876 and Compromise of 1877; Grant and Domestic Policies; Grant and Reconstruction; Grant and the Scandals; Woodhull, Victoria Claflin.

References Carpenter, John A., *Ulysses S. Grant* (1970); Downey, Matthew T., "Horace Greeley and the Politicians" (1966–1967); Hesseltine, William B., *Ulysses S. Grant* (1935); Josephson, Matthew, *The Politicos* (1938) and *The Robber Barons* (1934); McFeeley, William S., *Grant* (1991); McPherson, James M., "Grant or Greeley?" (1965–1966); Riddleberger, Patrick W., "The Break in the Radical Ranks" (1959); Simpson, Brooks D., *Let Us Have Peace* (1991); Summers, Mark Wahlgren, *The Era of Good Stealings* (1993).

Election of 1876 and Compromise of 1877

In 1876, the Republican party met in Cincinnati determined to take the presidency once again. Initially backers of President Ulysses S. Grant hoped to run the popular general for an unprecedented third term. But the tradition of the two-term limit established by George Washington and the corruption of Grant's cronies during his two terms soon put an end to the effort. Obviously the party would face a clean Democratic candidate, and it would have to preempt the honesty issue if it were to win. Benjamin Bristow, one of those who had worked to clean up Grant's cabinet and destroy the corrupt Whiskey Ring, was an obvious choice. But Bristow had angered the old pols during his purge, and Grant, after being blocked at the convention, responded to their feelings by firing Bristow.

The main contenders for the nomination after Bristow and Grant were party regulars: U.S. senators James G. Blaine of Maine and Roscoe Conkling of New York. Blaine was an expert at waving the bloody shirt (i.e., telling graphic stories of white political violence in the South). He once said that he could forgive Jefferson Davis for treason but not for the brutal Andersonville prisoner-of-war camp. Known as the "Plumed Knight," Blaine entered the race too early and peaked too soon. His demise came when a man named James Mulligan surfaced with letters allegedly written by Blaine concerning the senator's involvement in an Arkansas railroad scandal. Blaine, who had indignantly demanded a congressional investigation, suddenly retreated and made an effort to buy the letters or shut Mulligan up. In a meeting with his accuser, Blaine snatched the letters and fled, refusing to return them or make them public. The clamor rose to great heights, and Blaine promised to release an edited version, cleansed of personalities to protect the in-

A crowd gathers around a lamplight in New York to read an election bulletin (left) while South Carolina plantation hands travel to the polls (right), two characteristic election scenes from an 1876 issue of Frank Leslie's Illustrated Newspaper.

nocent (as if there were any). He read the doctored versions on the floor of the Senate. Then he closed with a flourish that condemned his Arkansas accusers as nothing more than ex-Confederates trying to assault a lover of the Union. He claimed to have a telegram that would clear him but dared not release it lest others' reputations be unintentionally smeared. It was a great ploy but it did not wash, and he lost his chance for the nomination.

Blaine's colleague, Roscoe Conkling, a tall, bearded, well-muscled, good-looking man, was known as the "Apollo of the Senate." An excellent speaker and very gregarious, he had a reputation as a spoilsman, taking his cut of all activities in his state and elsewhere. Of course, Conkling had never been trapped publicly in his wheeling and dealing, and no one had caught him in bed with the wrong woman, but rumors abounded. Conkling never admitted or denied anything; he just smiled like the Cheshire cat and made clever jokes as an aside. But in a year like 1876, the mere hint of scandal was enough to give delegates a second thought, so Conkling went the way of Blaine, just more quietly.

Unlike Blaine or Conkling, the Republicans needed a man who was well known enough to attract the public and clean enough to keep them interested. But he also had to be a party regular who had not bolted with the Liberals in 1872. It took seven ballots to get rid of the chaff, but then the party nominated the perfect candidate, Governor Rutherford B. Hayes of Ohio. A former Union officer, Hayes was an Ohio native whose father had died young. He grew up surrounded by his sister and mother. As a youth he attended Harvard and became a lawyer. He married Lucy Webb, a strict, upright, religious woman who detested the use of liquor. She served lemonade, even at state functions, and won the moniker "Lemonade Lucy" from the not-so-dry reporters and politicians..

Hayes was a strong Republican supporter who had been elected to the House of Representatives while serving with the army. He supported Reconstruction (but believed that African Americans needed education before receiving the vote), and he became governor on a platform that advocated civil service reform and efficient, honest government. He had remained loyal to Grant in 1872, even though his support of the national ticket had cost him reelection. But he regained the governorship in 1875, even though the Democrats had taken the rest of the state. He was a proven vote-getter, and, upon accepting the presidential nomination, he pledged to clean up Washington and withdraw federal troops from the South (that is, he would not allow them to prop up allegedly unpopular, corrupt, nonwhite state governments).

Just as Hayes had struck the proper stance for the Republicans, the nomination of Samuel J. Tilden did the same for the Democrats. The Democrats backed him with a platform pledged to the end of Reconstruction and the end of governmental corruption at all levels. Tilden, a New York native, grew up with little formal education, read law with a local attorney, and became one of the first successful corporate lawyers in American history. Actually, his career sounded a lot like young Abe Lincoln's. But the comparison paled during the crisis of the Union. Tilden was a state rights Democrat, a critic of the draft, and a supporter of Andrew Johnson during Reconstruction. But he was smart enough to clean up New York's corrupt Tweed Ring, which gave him a clean enough look to go on to the governorship of that state in 1874. There he became the quintessential reformer, promoting honest, efficient, economical government. That Tilden—rumored to have accepted handouts from the Union Pacific railroad's construction company, the Crédit Mobilier—could run as a clean candidate says something about his ability to change with the demands of the hour. But he had some peculiarities that could not be covered up. He was an old bachelor and a health nut who swallowed pills by the dozens and tried to eat right—a bit strange to "normal" people committed to sweets, booze, and gluttony.

There was very little to differentiate

Hayes and Tilden. They had the same outward image, a bit eccentric but clean in a political sense. Both pledged to clean up Washington and end Reconstruction. Both had reformist backgrounds. Both were reliable party regulars through thick and thin. As custom demanded, neither candidate spoke but let party pros do it for him. The only substantial discrepancy between the two was that Hayes was married and Tilden was a bachelor; Republicans tried to play up this point by accusing Tilden of not having enough faith in American women or the future of the nation to wed and father a family. But that was not enough for the Republicans to discredit Tilden's whole campaign. This left the usual approach of "waving the bloody shirt," a natural against any antiwar Democrat. But 1876 was not a normal year. When the votes had been counted, Tilden was the popular choice by a quarter million out of eight and a quarter million votes cast. But the electoral vote was Tilden 184 and Hayes 165, with 20 electoral votes undecided. A candidate needed 185 to become president. The orders went out to local party ramrods to sit tight and await further orders. The contest was not over yet.

The key to the election was to clean up the 20 contested votes so the electoral college could function. Hayes had to have all; Tilden needed only one. The votes were scattered among four states: Oregon had one; South Carolina had seven; Florida had four; and Louisiana had eight. Oregon turned out to be clearly for Hayes because of Democratic irregularities in the original count. This left the 19 votes from the occupied South up for grabs. The problem in the Southern states was that their electoral votes were authenticated by state institutions known as returning boards. State governors appointed these boards, a fact that made their membership essentially Republican. But the Democrats claimed fraud and established their own returning boards that sent in duplicate electoral votes for Tilden. In Louisiana, for example, to cite an extreme case, Democrats claimed to have elected their man as governor in the last election but that this man had been pre-vented from taking office by the interference of federal troops on behalf of the Republicans. So he just set up his own shadow regime, appointed his own returning board, and sent in the "real" vote. Louisiana being Louisiana, there were also three other Louisiana returning boards claiming legality. Similar quirks accounted for duplicate returns elsewhere.

Both parties sent "visiting statesmen" to the South to look into purchasing the votes necessary to elect their brand of reforming president—rather ironic given the emphasis on honesty promoted during the campaign. The returning boards were very receptive. In fact, a couple of Republican boards indicated that they would be happy to go for Tilden, the Democrat, for a price. But they would go only as a bloc, and Tilden needed only one vote. Louisiana and Florida would sell out to the Democrats for $200,000 per entire board. At this juncture the visiting Democratic statesmen refused to bribe more than the one elector they needed. In the end, the boards (one Republican board and one Democratic board in each state) held firm and the stalemate continued. The electoral college turned the problem over to Congress. The problem there was, who counts the votes? The Constitution did not specifically say. It just said that the votes would be opened and counted in front of both houses. If the House did the counting, the winner would be Tilden because the speaker of the house was a Democrat. The opposite was true of the Senate; dominated by Republicans, it would count Hayes in. Again stalemate threatened.

As the process stagnated, there was much fear that organized party militia units would storm Washington to force the count to go their way. Something had to be done to stop the "Mexicanization of American politics," as the commentators of the day referred to the problem. Indeed, the whole Reconstruction era seemed to place political problems in the hands of armed units in the form of the army (under the Enforcement Acts) or irregular organizations like the rifle clubs, especially in the South. In desperation, the leaders in Congress decided to appoint an electoral commission of 15 members to examine the returns and determine which were valid. The commission was to have five senators (divided three to two in favor of the controlling Republicans; each body elected its own committee members), five from the House (three to two in favor of the Democrats), and five from the Supreme Court (divided two to two, with one "independent" or "neutral" judge who would obviously make all the decisions no one else could face up to).

The important thing was who would be the neutral judge (if there were such a man). Judge David Davis, once the campaign director for Lincoln in 1860, was an independent-minded Republican. The creators of the commission expected him to be the odd vote. But then the Tilden managers made an unwise move: They asked the Democratic-controlled state legislature of Illinois to elect Davis to the Senate, hoping to commit him ahead of time to their cause. But Davis had more integrity than that and probably was a mite thankful for the chance to opt out of the whole process. He resigned his judgeship and accepted the Senate seat, leaving the choice of the fifth man to a court dominated by staunch Republicans. Nominating Judge Joseph Bradley to fill Davis's seat, the electoral commission ultimately voted eight to seven to accept the Republican returning boards' contentions at face value and to count all of the 19 disputed votes for Hayes, making him the next president of the United States by one vote (185-184).

The electoral commission's decision needed to be accepted, however, by both houses of Congress. The Republican-controlled Senate voted quickly to accredit the commission's decision. But the Democratic-dominated House began a lengthy filibuster (allowed under the rules then but not now) that lasted the whole month of February 1877. As the House talked the problem to death, the March 1877 inauguration date was fast approaching. Something had to be done by then to satisfy all sides. Hayes was already known as "ol' 8 to 7" and as "Rutherfraud" B. Hayes. The armed mobs were back in the streets. Suddenly, as things

looked bleakest, Southern Democrats broke with their Northern brethren and voted to end debate and accept the electoral commission's decision on behalf of Republican Hayes. The nation had a president.

But why did the Southern Democrats take this course? The traditional reason given is that Hayes's managers met with the Southern Democratic leaders at the Wormley House (a hotel) and negotiated an agreement to accept Hayes as president if he would end Reconstruction and the occupation of the South by federal troops. But both Hayes and Tilden were already committed to that course. Something more had to be involved. The real reason was that the Civil War and Reconstruction had warped the political process in the South. There were many Southern Democrats who were really Republicans when it came to economic issues—old Whigs, in effect. But the throes of Reconstruction had driven all whites into the Democratic party to show a solid front against the reconstructing Republicans, who based their strength on the votes of the former slaves. These Whig-like Southern Democrats met with the Republican managers at the Wormley House and cut a deal. Hayes and the Republican party would confirm their commitment to withdraw the federal occupation forces; give Southern Democrats control of patronage in the Southern states by supporting former Confederate general David Key as postmaster general (cutting out the Southern Republican loyalists, black and white); and promise the Southern Democrats federal aid for internal improvements, letting the Southern whites in on the corruption known as the Great Barbecue (the key was to build the Texas & Pacific Railroad to connect with the Southern Pacific coming out of California). In exchange the Southern Democrats would make Hayes president by ending the House filibuster and by voting for the electoral commission's decisions; they would also elect a Republican speaker (James Garfield) to organize the Democratic-dominated house.

More recent historians question whether the Wormley conference really did anything that had not already been accomplished, but what the conference did achieve was to allow each side to reassure the other that it would live up to the deal. And it permitted Southern politicians to keep their white electorate happy by creating the myth of the Wormley House agreement for the press and popular consumption—the withdrawal of the troops and an end to Reconstruction on behalf of the white South. Ending Reconstruction had come to be viewed as a reform of government for the public good. This viewpoint covered up the betrayal of African Americans and made the policy palatable North and South.

In the end the deal was only partly consummated. Hayes became president but refused to let the internal improvements, the center of prior corruption, continue. The Southern Democrats retaliated by organizing the House for their own party. But the true significance was that the Wormley House agreement, the real Compromise of 1877, returned American politics to the give-and-take that had been normal until the issues of slavery, Civil War, and Reconstruction prevented splitting the difference in national politics.

See also Election of 1872; Grant and Domestic Policies; Grant and Reconstruction; Grant and the Scandals.

References Benedict, Michael Les, "Southern Democrats in the Crisis of 1876–1877" (1980); DeSantis, Vincent P., "Rutherford B. Hayes and the Removal of the Troops and the End of Reconstruction" (1982); Fairman, Charles, *Five Justices and the Electoral Commission of 1877* (1988); Harris, Carl V., "Right Fork or Left Fork?" (1976); Haworth, Paul L., *The Hayes-Tilden Disputed Presidential Election of 1876* (1906); House, Albert V., "The Speakership Contest of 1875" (1965); Peskin, Allan, "Was There a Compromise of 1877?" (1973); Polakoff, Keith Ian, *The Politics of Inertia* (1973); Pomerantz, Sidney I., "Election of 1876" (1971); Rabel, George C., "Southern Interests and the Election of 1876" (1980); Williams, T. Harry, *Hayes of the Twenty-Third* (1965); Woodward, C. Vann, *Origins of the New South* (1951), *Reunion and Reaction* (1951), and "Yes, There Was a Compromise of 1877" (1973).

Emancipation

During and after the Revolutionary War, many Americans began to feel very uneasy with the contradictions between the principles of the Declaration of Independence and slavery, which had been legal in all of the 13 colonies. Gradually, states above the Mason-Dixon Line (the southern border of Pennsylvania) began to abandon the so-called peculiar institution, a process that took until 1832. Usually the slaves were freed either outright or by adulthood, between the ages of 18 and 21. At the same time, Congress organized the western territories such that those northwest of the Ohio River had slavery excluded from their boundaries upon statehood (via the Northwest Ordinance of 1787). There were several exemptions to the territorial exclusion, most involving slaves held by English (as of 1795) and French (as of 1763) colonists before the United States assumed control, but these were relatively minor. The only marring of this emancipation record was in Illinois, where, upon the state's separation from Indiana, the territorial legislature legalized a form of slavery through a lifetime indenture and provided for the "hiring" of blacks originally enslaved in other states. At the same time, free African Americans were practically prevented from entering the area. The culmination of this process was reached in 1823, when by a close vote slavery was prohibited in Illinois according to the provisions of the Northwest Ordinance.

This process of eliminating slavery in the Old Northwest was well known to people from the South like the Lincolns, poor non-slaveholding families who fled across the river to get away from the slave-dominated economy of the South. Abraham Lincoln first encountered slavery as an institution in 1831 when he accompanied a flatboat to New Orleans. He saw the evils of slavery once again on a trip to St. Louis ten years later and resolved to hit the institution hard if ever given the chance. The opportunity soon followed in his service in the Illinois legislature at the time of the murder of noted abolitionist Elijah P. Lovejoy, whose family Lincoln knew. Although the state legislature confirmed its support of slavery as guaranteed under the U.S. Constitution, Lincoln and four others condemned it as an immoral institution. At the time of the

Mexican War, Lincoln was serving in Congress, and he sided with those who believed that the ability of Congress to govern the territories could include regulating, or even eliminating, slavery there. He attempted to test this concept by introducing a bill to eliminate slavery in the District of Columbia (a perpetual territory run by Congress), but the measure was amended to death. Lincoln retired at the end of his term because of a prior deal guaranteeing rotation of office among several men and because of his unpopular stance against the Mexican War.

Lincoln soon returned to the political fray in 1854 when the Congress voted to destroy the Missouri Compromise of 1820 and to allow slavery to be extended into all territories; each territory, through a popular vote in the state convention, was then to decide on the issue of slavery upon application for statehood. This concept of popular sovereignty, developed by an Illinois senator and Democratic aspirant for the presidency, Stephen A. Douglas, would guarantee slavery in any territory until statehood was petitioned for. It was contrary to Lincoln's avowed stance that Congress could regulate or destroy slavery in any territory under the Constitution. But Lincoln's view was challenged by the 1857 U.S. Supreme Court in the case *Dred Scott v. Sanford*, which declared that popular sovereignty was constitutional, and further that no black could be a citizen of the United States. Because Douglas was running for reelection to the Senate the following year, Lincoln agreed to take him on for the Republican party. During the ensuing Lincoln-Douglas debates, Lincoln defended Congress' right to regulate or eliminate slavery in the territories and managed to force Douglas to admit that Congress could deal slavery in the territories a death blow by not actively legislating its protection. This admission would cost Douglas the presidency two years later and gain the then-unknown Lincoln a national reputation and the presidency in his own right as a Republican in the election of 1860.

Although the Republicans were willing to guarantee slavery where it existed in the states, the election of Lincoln by a majority vote in the North touched off secession of the South. In the attempted compromises that followed, Lincoln promised to defend every state's right to its own institutions, but he refused to denounce the Republican platform's stand against slavery in the territories, and he pledged to defend the Union of all the states. The war then became inevitable. Although the war's announced purpose was to save the Union, what to do about slavery became an integral part of it immediately. When slaves fled to Yankee lines for freedom and safety, Union commanders were supposed to return them under the Fugitive Slave Law of 1850. At first many of them did so. But as the war went on, more and more commanders adopted the expedience of Maj. Gen. Benjamin Butler at Fortress Monroe on 30 May 1861. Butler declared that the slaves were contraband of war because they had been employed actively in support of the rebellion through raising foodstuff and building fortifications. Lincoln did not like this approach, because he feared that it might compromise his efforts to keep the border South in the Union. But Butler's policy was relatively mild when compared to that of Maj. Gen. John Charles Frémont, federal commander in Missouri. Prompted by Union victories in the West, Frémont, the first Republican candidate for president in 1854, issued a proclamation freeing all slaves in his command area on 30 August 1861. Lincoln let Butler's policy stand, but Frémont's threatened to drive four more states from the Union. Lincoln asked Frémont to substitute a congressional act for Frémont's own policy. Frémont refused and Lincoln removed him from command.

The congressional measure Lincoln had wanted Frémont to recognize was the First Confiscation Act of 6 August 1861. It allowed the confiscation of property, including slaves, of anyone found in sympathy and support of the rebellion. But the procedure was not arbitrary—it had to be effected through a court process. Meanwhile, the president attempted to convince loyal slaveholders to emancipate the slaves voluntarily through a compensation process. He hoped that Congress might accept such emancipations in lieu of direct taxes in support of the war. Lincoln looked for a "laboratory" in which to try out his idea; he came up with the smallest slave state, in terms of both size and number of slaves, Delaware (which had 1,798 slaves in 1861). But the hostility of local slaveholders, who saw in this scheme as an attempt to introduce total emancipation throughout the South as a war aim, caused its failure. Lincoln then turned to Congress directly. In March 1862, he asked for passage of a joint resolution that the federal government would cooperate with any state that voluntarily emancipated its bondservants through compensation at $400 per adult slave. Lincoln believed that the cost of the war for half a day would pay for Delaware's slaves; the rest of the border states, Maryland, Kentucky, and Missouri, plus the District of Columbia, could be financed at the same rate for what it cost to run the war for just under three months.

None of the border states appeared interested. Congress moved to eliminate slavery in the District of Columbia at $300 dollars per slave. It sought to appropriate a further $100,000 for transporting the freed blacks beyond the borders of the United States to Liberia or Haiti. Meanwhile, on 9 May 1862, another field commander, Maj. Gen. David Hunter, freed by military order all the slaves along the Atlantic coastal islands in South Carolina and Georgia. Worse yet, from the perspective of quelling the fears of the border South, he also enrolled males in the first black infantry regiments of the war. Hunter claimed that the enrollment was a matter of military necessity, because he had insufficient numbers of white troops to defend his military district. Lincoln denied knowledge or responsibility for the order as soon as the news reached Washington. But he used the occasion to admonish the border states to rethink the emancipation problem and to act and receive compensation before the war made such a policy unavailable.

Congress had already given new meaning to Lincoln's warning. On March 13, 1862, it had amended the Fugitive Slave Law of 1850 to make it a violation of law for any military or naval officer or enlisted personnel to return any fugitive slave to its owner. On 5 June 1862, it recognized the nations of Haiti (which, after the United States, was the second nation in the Western hemisphere to declare its independence from European domination) and Liberia (the African home in exile of freed American slaves since the 1820s). The Senate then passed another measure that endorsed a treaty between the United States and Great Britain for suppression of the African slave trade. Finally, Congress enacted a bill that freed all slaves in the territories, a key point in the Republican 1860 platform and Lincoln's lifelong ideal of no slavery in the West.

On 17 July 1862, Congress passed its most severe measure yet, the Second Confiscation Act. It seized all property (including slaves) of anyone found guilty of treason or rebellion. It also freed any slaves who managed to reach the safety of Union military lines or were captured by the federal armies or abandoned by their owners. The process was roundabout—the fugitive was declared a prisoner of war under federal control and then freed by act of Congress, giving substance to the myth that Lincoln and his government were acting within the states to interfere with slave property that was still protected by the Constitution. And it authorized the president to employ freed African Americans in any manner he saw fit to prosecute successfully the end of the war. In effect, it permitted the enrollment of blacks as soldiers for the first time. Once again Lincoln warned the loyal slave states to reconsider emancipation on their own with federal compensation. He cautioned them that if the war continued, he would act to destroy all slavery with no monetary indemnification.

Meanwhile, Lincoln had already been mulling over total uncompensated emancipation. He told Secretary of State William H. Seward and Secretary of the Navy Gideon Welles that he believed that emancipation could be instituted as a war measure against the Confederates. On 21 July he approached the whole cabinet on the measure. He maintained that it would bring a moral outlook to the Union cause that it sadly lacked, especially in the monarchies of Europe, which were flirting with recognizing the Confederacy. He believed that field commanders should actively feed their troops with Southern crops, that African Americans should be paid for their labor to the Union cause, and that in the end all blacks ought to be colonized overseas. He once again wished to caution all slaveholders, loyal or rebel, that the Confiscation Acts provided for the summary seizure of slaves, stating that he would free all slaves in rebellious areas through an executive proclamation on 1 January 1863. Only Seward and Secretary of the Treasury Salmon P. Chase agreed with his proposals. But Seward suggested that Lincoln await a Union field victory, because the war had been going badly, especially in the East, and emancipation might be seen as a last gasp for Union survival rather than a stand on the higher ground of morality. Lincoln agreed.

Lincoln's more radical and conservative political enemies of both parties leaped on him for indecision in the mater of confiscation. Lincoln intentionally kept them in the dark about his resolve to emancipate all slaves in disloyal areas at the beginning of the next year. But when popular newspaper editor Horace Greeley of the *New York Tribune* asked him to free all the slaves outright, calling it the "Prayer of 20 Millions," Lincoln replied publicly and quickly. The president said that his main purpose in fighting the war was restoration of the Union in the shortest possible way under the Constitution. If he could do it by freeing some of the slaves, all of them, or none of them, he would. Meanwhile, he told another group of petitioners that any emancipation at that time would be as ineffective as "the Pope's bull against the comet."

Lincoln received his victory in September when the Army of the Potomac drove Robert E. Lee's Confederate forces out of Maryland at the Battle of Antietam. It was not much of a victory—Lee had withdrawn more or less voluntarily when he should

have been destroyed—but it was all Lincoln had. He seized the moment at once. On 22 September 1862, he issued the preliminary Emancipation Proclamation. It contained all of his previous ideas, including renewal of compensated emancipation for loyal states, voluntary colonization of freed blacks overseas, and military emancipation of all slaves in states in rebellion against federal forces on 1 January 1863. In the fall elections, the Republican party took a shellacking, but it still managed to retain a majority in both houses of Congress. In December Congress rejected a resolution from Representative George H. Yeaman of Kentucky condemning the Emancipation Proclamation as an unwarranted, unconstitutional interference with the domestic institutions of the states and a dangerous war message. Then it passed a resolution of the exact opposite intent. It was the only vote Congress took on the measure. Lincoln gave copies of the Emancipation Proclamation to his cabinet for final discussion on 31 December. With minor revisions, it was issued 1 January 1863.

Lincoln has traditionally been praised as a forward-looking hero in the egalitarian tradition. But with the advent of the modern civil rights movement in the 1960s, he was seen as morally deficient—a traditional white racist. A more realistic view might be that he was a disciple of Henry Clay, the premier politician his day, known as the Great Compromiser or the Great Pacificator. Clay was a leader of the old Whig party and a man much admired by a young Abe Lincoln. Even though the Democratic party was the main political organization in Illinois, Lincoln had chosen to join Clay's Whigs in the 1830s. He internalized much of Clay's middle-of-the-road philosophy on race. This involved seeing blacks as human beings not to be enslaved but still not the equals of whites.

Unlike the more open racists of his time, Lincoln believed that African Americans had the ability to govern themselves in their own nation. But Lincoln, like Clay, believed that this quality would not evidence itself in the United States because of the limiting aspects of white racism. Indeed, both men feared a race war. So Lincoln openly advocated Henry Clay's solution to race—a gradual compensated emancipation of the slaves and their colonization overseas. This involved sending blacks to Africa (hence the American backing of the nation of Liberia, founded by freed American slaves) or removing them to some allegedly idyllic spot in the Caribbean or Latin America. In the words of one historian, Lincoln saw the African American as "A Man but Not a Brother," a quality recognized by no less than the great black abolitionist and orator of the nineteenth century, Frederick Douglass.

Nonetheless, it would be incorrect not to recognize Lincoln for the revolutionary that he was. Outwardly he was moderate, reasonable, kind, liberal (in the classical sense), conservative, pragmatic, flexible, pious, and law abiding. But underneath that placid, somewhat morose exterior, this most skillful politician of his age was a man of steel. Lincoln's conviction that slavery was wrong never faltered. He stood four-square behind the Republican ideology of free men and free labor, and he achieved the biggest revolution in American history by patiently adhering to the unconditional surrender of the Confederacy and its principles. Emancipation was the cornerstone of that revolution.

See also Colonization of African Americans Overseas; Confiscation Acts; Lincoln and Reconstruction; Seward and Reconstruction.

References Belz, Herman, *Emancipation and Equal Rights* (1978), *A New Birth of Freedom* (1976), and *Reconstructing the Union* (1969); Bennett, Lerone, Jr., "Was Abe Lincoln a White Supremacist?" (1968); Blackiston, Harry S., "Lincoln's Emancipation Plan" (1922); Current, Richard N., *The Lincoln Nobody Knows* (1958); Eberstadt, Charles, "Lincoln's Emancipation Proclamation" (1950); Foner, Eric, *Reconstruction* (1988); Franklin, John Hope, *The Emancipation Proclamation* (1963); Frederickson, George M., "A Man But Not a Brother" (1975); Hesseltine, William B., "Lincoln and the Politicians" (1960) and *Lincoln's Plan of Reconstruction* (1960); Klement, Frank L., "Midwestern Opposition to Lincoln's Emancipation Policy" (1964); Lucie, Patricia M. L., "Confiscation" (1977); McPherson, James M., *Abraham Lincoln and the Second American Revolution* (1990); Mitgang, Herbert, "Was Lincoln Just a Honkie?" (1968); Oates, Stephen B., *With Malice toward None* (1977); Olsen, Otto, "Abraham Lincoln as Revolutionary" (1978); Quarles, Benjamin, *Lincoln and the Negro* (1962); Randall, James G., *Lincoln the President* (1945–1955); Safire, William, *Freedom* (1987); Strickland, Avrah E., "The Illinois Background of Lincoln's Attitude Toward Slavery and the Negro" (1963); Stutler, Boyd B., "Abraham Lincoln and John Brown" (1962); Trefousse, Hans L., *Lincoln's Decision for Emancipation* (1975); Zilversmit, Arthur, ed., *Lincoln on Black and White* (1971).

Enforcement Acts

After the passage of the Fourteenth and Fifteenth amendments, Congress passed several measures designed to enforce them, sometimes referred to as the Civil Rights Acts of 1870 and 1871. The punitive nature of these laws led them to be popularly called the Force Acts. Congress considered a total of five Enforcement Acts, their formal name, of which three became law. Their implementation became one of the controversial issues of Reconstruction, involving the federal court system from bottom to top.

The First Enforcement Act, passed on 31 May 1870, was designed to enforce the right to vote (the Fifteenth Amendment). It declared that citizens otherwise qualified should be entitled to vote without distinction of race. It also declared that any prerequisite to voting must be equal for all voters regardless of race. Any official who failed to obey this measure was liable to fine (up to $500) or imprisonment (up to one year) or both (most of these terms were served locally in county jail). It also outlawed any combination or conspiracy to deny, intimidate, or threaten voters. It repeated much of the content of the Civil Rights Act of 1866 with respect to the right to sue or be sued, give evidence, and hold and convey property as any white citizen. Any official who acted to deny these rights could be removed from office, in addition to other fines and jail sentences. Finally, it prohibited conspiracies by disguised persons or groups using the public highways to deny anyone a right guaranteed under the constitution. This part was punishable by a healthy fine

($5,000) and jail term (up to ten years) in a federal penitentiary (the Albany, New York, facility was the one generally used in these convictions). Any state crime (murder, rape, assault, and the like) committed by a Klansman was to be tried in federal court, and sentences applicable in the state of occurrence could be applied by the federal judge.

Republicans realized that the election of 1870 had decreased their majority by some 60 votes. They feared that if they did not act immediately to increase the effect of the First Enforcement Act it might not be done later. Sections of the first act were mutually contradictory and vague, and the Second Enforcement Act, passed on 28 February 1871, united them in wording and intent. The second measure permitted no one to deny the right to vote through bribery or intimidation. It standardized penalties at $500 or up to three years' imprisonment, and in any town of 20,000 inhabitants or more it established a system of poll watchers from each political party appointed by local federal judges and assisted by special U.S. marshals to establish order at polls and prevent any irregularity. A state returning board was to check all votes to ascertain their validity. All ballots in any federal election were to be printed to prevent ballot box stuffing or other fraud. It was this law that many historians think was designed to regulate voting in Northern cities where Democratic machines ruled, rather than to assist blacks in the South as the law claimed on its surface.

The Third Enforcement Act, also known as the Ku Klux Act, was passed on 20 April 1871. It was designed to prevent individuals, state officials, or organized conspiracies from depriving persons of their civil rights, particularly in the South where the Klan rode. Whereas the Civil Right Act of 1866 had permitted a criminal remedy, this measure allowed the offended party to take action in civil court, too. It also defined conspiracy as two or more persons using the public roads, wearing a disguise, or violating the property of another to deny someone his civil rights. It permitted the president to use the army and navy to assist U.S. mar-

shals or enforce court orders independently and to suspend temporarily the writ of habeas corpus. Any official who failed to use his office to prevent a violation of this measure was declared liable, with fines of $1,000 or more and jail terms of one year to life if the violation resulted in a death.

Over 7,000 cases were tried under these acts from 1870 to 1896, when they expired. Hundreds of fines and jail sentences resulted, yet disfranchisement and intimidation of black voters continued, in spite of the destruction of the Ku Klux Klan. The conviction rate was 74 percent in 1870, 41 percent the following year, back up to 49 percent in 1872, and 36 percent in 1873. After 1874, conviction rate was around 10 percent, which remained true for the next 20 years. What happened to these measures, the supposed heart of the Grant administration's Reconstruction program? The year 1874 was important. It was an off-year election of Congress, and the Democrats were pressing the Republicans hard about the cost—monetary, moral, and constitutional—of enforcing an unpopular policy on the South. How much longer did this have to go on? Had not the worst of the Ku Klux Klan activity been stopped? Could not blacks protect themselves like any other citizen? Did they need special treatment forever? These issues struck hard throughout a North that was tiring of seemingly perpetual Reconstruction.

But there were other problems with the Enforcement Acts. In 1874, cases from South Carolina and Louisiana began to wend their way through the federal court system, challenging the notion that the federal government could pass laws that affected individuals rather than the states. Eventually, these cases (*United States v. Reese, et al.* and *United States v. Cruickshank, et al.*) would gut the acts of their strongest punitive provisions. Prosecutors awaiting the U.S. Supreme Court decisions that would come two years later put many cases on hold. Even so, there were problems in the states themselves. State and local authorities often refused to assist federal officers in the solution and prosecution of

Ku Klux Klan cases. After that, finding a grand jury that would indict and a petit jury that would convict was a real problem. Any conservative white on the panel could mean a hung jury, and black jurymen alone gave these cases a bad taste, North and South.

Worse yet, Congress had passed a good law but had not provided for its adequate funding. The hundreds of court cases cost money to prosecute and flooded an antiquated federal court system that was undermanned and ill prepared to process so many trials. Also, federal officials in the field were of a diverse lot. Some of them were as against prosecuting the cases as white Southerners were. Others were susceptible to bribery, intimidation, and political partisanship. And the Grant administration warned local federal officers not to be overly zealous, as the process was so controversial that it could be envisioned as a disguised political action and might cost the administration votes nationally and locally.

The unevenness in the enforcement of the Force Acts can be seen in two states where the trials were numerous, Mississippi and South Carolina. In the northern half of Mississippi, the federal courts racked up the highest conviction rate (55 percent, five times the South Carolina rate and twice the national average) of Klansmen in the South. The cases were brought mostly by Southern white natives, many of whom had served in the Confederate army, in the face of unbelievable opposition that included ambushes of arresting authorities, ostracism by one's neighbors, common assaults, threats, arrest by state officials on trumped-up charges, and minimal military assistance. Yet this great statistical success was marred by that fact that it did nothing to stop the intimidation and disfranchisement of black voters. The reason for the high conviction rate was found in the person of the local federal judge, Robert Andrews Hill. It was his announced policy to convict but assess light punishment. He believed that certitude of conviction, not punishment itself, was the key to law enforcement. The result was that even white juries had little trepidation in convicting their neighbors when a $25 fine and posting of a $1,000 bond to keep the peace were the penalties. Only in 5 percent of the cases tried did Judge Hill send men to the state penitentiary or to the federal institution at Albany, New York.

South Carolina was a bit different from Mississippi. Here the federal prosecutors did their best to put real teeth in the Enforcement Acts. But the result was the same in Mississippi—it just used up a little more effort. The key figure here was federal prosecutor David T. Corbin, a Vermont Carpetbagger who had served in the Union army and the Freedmen's Bureau before becoming the U.S. government's lawyer in South Carolina. He was assisted by a battalion of the Seventh Cavalry under Maj. Lewis Merrill, an active, energetic officer with an outstanding war record. Merrill arrested hundreds of Ku Klux Klan suspects, of whom 85 percent were not prosecuted or not convicted. Corbin tried to do something quite radical for his day but accepted in ours—he argued that the Fourteenth Amendment allowed the Bill of Rights to be applied to the actions of the states as well as to those of the federal government. He was particularly interested in getting the states to guarantee the Second Amendment (the right to bear arms) and the Fourth Amendment (which prevents government intrusion into private homes without a warrant), reasoning that these were some of the privileges and immunities of citizenship mentioned in the Fourteenth Amendment. He took this tack because many of the offenses against blacks were not voter related but instead involved assaults on children and women, who could not vote and thus could not be considered protected by the Force Acts in any other way.

South Carolinians rebelled against Corbin's tactic and, led by Wade Hampton, established a defense fund for the accused. They hired Reverdy Johnson and Henry Stanbery, well-known conservatives who had defended President Andrew Johnson during his impeachment. These two legal giants moved to quash the 11-charge indictment against the first of the accused. To

Corbin's disappointment, a Republican judge threw out 9 of the 11 charges, including Corbin's notion of applying the Bill of Rights against the state, even though the accused admitted to having taken an oath to the Klan and its precepts. It was an ominous ruling that indicated how Reconstruction was going, not only in South Carolina, but in the nation. Corbin tried again in other cases. This time he tried prominent local people of influence. The victims identified the accused as the perpetrators, and Corbin took the time to lay out the whole method of operation of the Klan—including the gristly details of murder, torture, rape, and beatings—for the national press. Forty-nine defendants pled guilty to lesser counts in exchange for dropping more serious charges.

But when the case concerning the Fourteenth Amendment applying against state or individual action came up (*United States v. Avery*), the U.S. Supreme Court chose to ignore these issues and rule on procedural matters, which left the federal officials in South Carolina little ground upon which to continue prosecution. Then U.S. Attorney General George Williams ordered Corbin to enter *nolle prosequi* (no further prosecution) in all remaining cases "for the sake of the public good." The result was that no substantial constitutional gains resulted from the South Carolina Ku Klux Klan trials. Unlike the Military Reconstruction Acts, the Fourteenth and Fifteenth amendments did not offer a positive grant of franchise to African American males. They just said that race could not be the factor upon which the vote was denied. This decision showed a deep reluctance on the part of even Radical Republicans to interfere in traditional state prerogatives. If the threat of the Force Acts should expire, the white South could easily find other legal methods to deny the vote to blacks or anyone else though the application of comprehension, reading and writing, and poll tax requirements.

After the initial three Enforcement Acts, Congress considered two other Force Bills in 1875 and 1894. The Fourth Enforcement Bill, one that would have given the president the right to suspend the writ of habeas corpus in Alabama, Arkansas, Mississippi, and Louisiana for two years, passed in the House. It failed in the Senate, which had its own approach that was realized in the Civil Rights Act of 1875, a tribute to Senator Charles Sumner of Massachusetts, who had just died. In the 1890s, Senator Henry Cabot Lodge of Massachusetts introduced another measure (the Lodge Force Bill) in an attempt to circumvent Southern attempts to deny blacks the vote within the terms of the Fifteenth Amendment through such devices as literacy tests. The bill proposed supervision of the polls, but it failed, giving the South the green light to proscribe African Americans from voting until 1965, when the problem was successfully attacked through the Voting Rights Act of that year. Unfortunately, the North did not object to Southerners disallowing blacks to vote in 1890; they merely objected to the fact that Southerners who got seats in Congress were representing a population that largely did not get to vote. The Lodge Bill fell to interest in tariffs and silver coinage, key issues in the depressed economy of the time.

See also Civil Rights Acts; Fifteenth Amendment; Fourteenth Amendment; Grant and Reconstruction; Ku Klux Klan; Redemption of the South before 1874; Redemption of the South from 1874; Supreme Court and Reconstruction.

References Avins, Alfred, "The Ku Klux Klan Act of 1871" (1967); Cresswell, Stephen B., "Enforcing the Enforcement Acts" (1987); Fairman, Charles, *Reconstruction and Reunion* (1971–1987); Faulkner, Harold U., *Politics, Reform, and Expansion* (1959); Frantz, Laurent B., "Fourteenth Amendment against Private Acts" (1964); Gara, Larry, "Slavery and the Slave Power" (1969); Gillette, William, *Retreat from Reconstruction* (1979); Hall, Kermit L., "Political Power and Constitutional Legitimacy" (1984); Hall, Kermit L., and Lou Falkner Williams, "Constitutional Tradition Amid Social Change" (1985); Hesseltine, William B., *Ulysses S. Grant* (1935); Kaczorowski, Robert J., "To Begin the Nation Anew" (1987) and *The Nationalization of Civil Rights* (1987); Swinney, Everette, "Enforcing the Fifteenth Amendment" (1962); Williams, Lou Falkner, "The South Carolina Ku Klux Klan Trials and Enforcement of Federal Rights" (1993); Woodward, C. Vann, "Seeds of Failure in Radical Race Policy" (1966).

Ethridge Conspiracy of 1863

In December 1863, at about the same time that President Abraham Lincoln was to announce his Ten Percent Plan of Reconstruction, Emerson Ethridge, acting clerk of the U.S. House of Representatives, put into play a plan to turn control of the legislative body over to a moderate coalition of Democrats and Republicans by refusing to seat certain Radical Republicans. At the time the clerk had great power in both houses to determine who had been legally elected through the expedient of reading the roll on the first day. If one's name were omitted, that person was not seated until there was a full investigation into the legality of his election. This cannot be done today because the powers used 100 years ago have been institutionalized and made nonpolitical. The whole concept was made possible by a measure passed the year before, when Congressman James M. Ashley wanted the clerk to exclude any representative from an occupied state by refusing to seat Lincoln's "reconstructed" governments in the Mississippi Valley.

Ethridge was a Union man from East Tennessee who had not seceded with his state and resented being treated as less than loyal by Ashley's bill. He was dismayed with the course of the war, too. Militarily, the Union seemed to be in a stalemate at best, losing at worst. Despite great Union victories at Gettysburg, Vicksburg, and Chattanooga, strong Rebel armies were still in the field. Politically, Lincoln seemed to be in the clutches of the Radical Republicans; he was freeing the slaves through executive proclamation (in the manner by which he ran most of the war), sending Carpetbaggers down to run the loyal Southern border states, and passing economic measures oriented to Northeastern business interests (a high tariff, internal improvements, a national banking system). What Ethridge thought the nation needed was a moderate constitutional party of War Democrats and middle-of-the-road Republicans to put a brake on things domestically while the war was won. He promised the Democrats the speaker's chair, under the Union party label, which stood for a pro-war policy, if they cooperated.

Unfortunately for Ethridge and his plan, the Democrats failed to deliver enough votes to confirm his action. The fact that the Radicals could gain the backing of moderates from their own party and several border-state Union men, like Henry Winter Davis, indicated that the conservative resurgence against the Lincoln domestic and war policies, evident in the Democratic victories in the North in the 1862 congressional elections, was over. The Radicals were to surge forward and send up the harsher Wade-Davis Bill to counter Lincoln's plan of Reconstruction; they used Ethridge's idea in reverse to unseat the Andrew Johnson Reconstruction governments in 1865. The Ethridge conspiracy probably marked the beginning of the end for conservative hopes of a Reconstruction based on the prewar Constitution, even though the Union party would be the device used to reelect Lincoln in 1864 and to pass the Thirteenth Amendment in 1865.

See also Cox Plan of Reconstruction; Johnson and Reconstruction; Lincoln and Reconstruction.

Reference Belz, Herman, "The Ethridge Conspiracy of 1863" (1970).

Exodusters

In addition to government colonization projects during the Civil War and Reconstruction designed to solve the racial problem by sending blacks out of the country to Africa or the Caribbean, there were several African American–inspired "exodus" projects to accomplish the same feat. These projects came into being after it had been amply demonstrated that Reconstruction was not to be the panacea many had hoped for in providing equal treatment for the former slaves. The goal of these various projects was for blacks to remove themselves to Africa or to someplace within the United States where the "exodusters" might live in safety and comfort. The idea of colonization in Africa had been broached several times before the war. The American Colonization Society had been formed after the War of 1812 with that goal in mind, remov-

Exodusters Benjamin Singleton (left) and A. McClure (right) prepare to leave Nashville in search of a safe place to stake a claim.

ing freed slaves to their ancestral homeland. In 1816, a black sea captain, Paul Cuffee, took 38 American blacks to Sierra Leone, a British colony set up for Britain's own freed slaves. The founding of Liberia by American expatriates soon followed. But generally most American blacks—freed, about to be freed, or enslaved—were not too keen on moving to Africa. They had been in the New World so long and had worked hard in the fields and homes of whites. They had earned a permanent place in America and sought to realize this.

When the Civil War broke out this claim became more certain as African Americans joined the Union armies to free their brothers and sisters still in bondage. But the variations in living conditions of blacks as free persons both in the North and especially in the South maintained interest in colonization projects as a constant undercurrent in American life. The creation of the Reconstruction governments, with their advance in black civil and political rights, made any plans to leave pretty speculative, but the advent of Redemption in the 1870s renewed interest. This realization helped William Coppinger, the white corresponding secretary for what remained of the American Colonization Society, to establish contact with a black Baptist preacher out of Charleston, South Carolina, Cornelius

Reeves. The latter said that he knew of thousands of South Carolina blacks who were interested in relocating to Africa.

Upon being prodded by Coppinger, Reeves produced a list of 286 names, and the society arranged for a ship to carry them abroad. But the ship would not arrive at Charleston until spring, and the hopeful immigrants, upon discovering that no employer would sign a six-month labor contract, were left destitute. Furthermore, local whites evidently were worried at losing any number of black laborers; they contacted the intended travelers and concocted a story that the immigration plan was a scheme devised by Reeves and other to reenslave them in Brazil or Cuba. Nonetheless, Coppinger came down to Charleston to coordinate activities and in the end the ship departed for Africa with 321 souls, many of whom replaced some of the originals who had since dropped out. Another cargo of almost the same number followed six months later. Over 450 left the following year (1867), none in 1868, and only 160 in 1869. The problem was not so much the lack of desire on the part of African Americans to leave, although the initial successes of Radical Reconstruction did discourage such immigration, as it was a decline in philanthropic money being devoted to transportation abroad. The donors were more interested in education and relief within America.

In all of these colonization schemes it seems that the people most interested were those with the least to lose economically in the South. Hence they were usually very poor and unable to pay for the necessary transportation. In northwestern Louisiana, Henry Adams, a black laborer and Republican organizer, developed a plan for relocation to Africa that would have the federal government provide the transportation, much as the Freedmen's Bureau had done for wartime refugees. Like Coppinger and Reeves, Adams had lists of blacks who wanted to start anew in some place without the racial disadvantages that Redemption forbode. Adams sought to convince the federal government that it ought to enforce the

political and civil rights it had promised during Reconstruction or pay for African Americans' transport to another place. Mass meetings of thousands around Shreveport gave impact to his assertions, as did the bloody violence of the White League as it recaptured the Louisiana state government. Again, the lack of funds meant that the program never could get off the ground.

But the collapse of Reconstruction soon brought new interest to colonization as a concept. Black Americans were not as interested in going to Africa or any other specific spot as they were in improving their prospects for the future anywhere they could do so. So if Liberia looked like a less-than-perfect prospect (and it was), then the proponents of relocation merely looked for a new place to go to. Liberia appealed to blacks in the South Atlantic regions, but those from Kentucky or the Old Southwest, for example, were just as likely to look fondly on the American West, particularly Kansas. And it was here that the name "exoduster" became famous. The number of African Americans who went to Kansas in 1879 was never very big; say, around 25,000. But this still was the largest single group that was successful in leaving the South until World War I and the migration to Northern cities.

Kansas in 1879 still recalled the "Bleeding Kansas" of before the Civil War, and that meant radical abolitionist John Brown to America's blacks. African Americans' interest in settlement on the Great Plains came from many sources, not the least of which was the free land provisions of the Homestead Act of 1862 and the fact that many white Kansans welcomed them. Instrumental in the Kansas exodus was Benjamin "Pap" Singleton, by his own account an ex-slave from Tennessee. He had run away to freedom when young and returned with the conquering Union armies. He distrusted current black leaders and politicians and felt that black prosperity was dependent upon obtaining adequate farmland. In the mid-1870s he traveled to Kansas and began to promote land like any other entrepreneur, but this time for blacks only. He was directly responsible for bringing 1,100 Tennessee blacks to Kansas before the actual 1879 exodus; indirectly, through speeches, broadsides, and handbills, he may have inspired many more from all over the South to go west.

In 1879, however, the magnitude and character of the Kansas exodus changed markedly. Not only did more go than before, they were the poorest and most downtrodden the black South had to offer. The draw was free land, and the U.S. Senate helped indirectly by holding hearings to consider a transportation subsidy bill. Although the measure was never passed, blacks congregated at railroad and steamship terminals in large numbers, inspired by what came to be called "Kansas fever." Local white planters, fearful at losing their hands, urged the operators to deny them passage. As the trains and boats passed them up, the exodusters reluctantly came to realize that without money for passage they were doomed to remain where they were. By June the fever had run its course, and most returned home to the peonage that awaited them there. Those who did not go on their own were sent on their way by force or drafted into local prison chain gangs.

The exodusters got a second burst of excitement when a plan was devised to send them to Indiana to fill the state with potential Republicans and deny it to the Democrats. This plan actually had backing in the U.S. Department of the Treasury, and it attracted the attention of Thomas Conway, former Freedmen's Bureau head in Louisiana and still a force among blacks there. In the end, more blacks went to Indiana from North Carolina, and their reception was not that they had hoped for. A Senate inquiry broke down on party lines, with Republicans defending the emigrants and Democrats decrying the dumping of unwanted citizens on Indiana soil.

Regardless of what inspired the blacks to want to leave the South, it was indicative that racial relations during Reconstruction and Redemption were not what they should have been and that Southern blacks despaired of getting equality or justice at home. The exodus was a theme that would reappear again and again in the twentieth century and still remains an integral part of black thought today.

See also Colonization of African Americans Overseas; Economic Disfranchisement.

References Cohen, William, *At Freedom's Edge* (1991); Little, Monroe H., "Making a Way out of No Way" (1977); Painter, Nell Irvin, *Exodusters* (1976); Woodward, C. Vann, "Seeds of Failure in Radical Race Policy" (1966).

Fessenden, William P. (1806–1869)

Born out of wedlock in Boscawen, New Hampshire, William P. Fessenden spent his early years in the care of his grandparents in Maine. When his father finally married, William was brought into his new family. He was a sharp child, and his entrance into Bowdoin College was delayed merely because of his youth. His diploma was withheld for a year, however, because of bad conduct and swearing while he was a student. Years later he would receive an honorary doctorate from the same institution and serve on its governing board. He studied law after his graduation and moved to Portland, where he practiced his profession and stayed the rest of his life. He was engaged to the sister of poet Henry Wadsworth Longfellow, and her death shortly before their planned marriage was a real blow. Some time later, however, he married Ellen Deering. He entered politics about the same time, running as an anti-Jackson candidate for the state legislature and accompanying Daniel Webster during campaigns. Eventually, though, Fessenden refused to support the swarthy Webster for president in 1852, considering the man to be too likely to abuse alcohol.

Meanwhile Fessenden proceeded to build up one of the finest law practices in New England in partnership with William Willis. He served a second term in the state legislature and one term in Congress as a Whig. In Washington he learned to dislike slavery, and his opposition to the institution grew until he became one of the original organizers of the Republican party. Before that, however, he served two more terms in the state legislature and tried several times unsuccessfully for the U.S. House and Senate. As Maine came more and more to embrace Fessenden's attitude on slavery, he gained stature and was elected to the U.S. Senate as a Republican in 1854. He would hold that seat until his death in 1869, with a brief time out when he served as the secretary of the treasury in 1864 and 1865. In the Senate Fessenden spoke out against the extension of slavery into the territories and earned the reputation of being one of the great debaters against the Southern institution. But Fessenden's real power was in the finance committee, which he came to chair. As such he helped fund the Union war cause through the backing of higher wartime taxes, the national banking system, and the printing of paper money, which he opposed but admitted had to be resorted to because of the unprecedented emergency of the rebellion. Once the war ended he led the call for fiscal conservatism and a recall of greenbacks.

During Reconstruction Fessenden was considered a Radical Republican without the petulance and viciousness attributed to most of them. He was against outright confiscation of Rebels' property and was not as enthused as others about punishment. But his view of Reconstruction was not far from that of Representative Thaddeus Stevens of Pennsylvania. Fessenden saw Reconstruction as a congressional function, with the South reverting to conquered provinces. He had little respect for President Andrew Johnson (who was just too Southern to suit a die-hard Yankee like Fessenden), and he thoroughly disapproved of Johnson's policies and conduct as too sympathetic to Rebels. As chairman of the joint committee on Reconstruction, Fessenden conducted the investigation that led to the Fourteenth Amendment and the justification of the Military Reconstruction Acts. But he disapproved of the Tenure of Office Act (which restricted the president's ability to remove appointees without Senate approval) and the impeachment of the president, and he refused to vote to convict, despite his position as majority leader. Fessenden faced a storm of criticism, and many doubted whether he could win another senatorial term, but he died before the question was raised formally in the Maine state legislature. After his death many former critics came over to his viewpoint on presidential power and hailed him as a principled man who had voted his conscience on a very difficult issue.

Fifteenth Amendment

See also Chase, Salmon P.; Joint Committee of Fifteen on Reconstruction; Moderate Republicans and Reconstruction; Radical Republicans and Reconstruction.

References Jellison, Charles A., *Fessenden of Maine* (1962); Robinson, William A., "William Pitt Fessenden" (1964–1981).

Fifteenth Amendment

The Republicans saw the African American vote as central to a true Reconstruction of the nation after the Civil War. This point of view was due in part to the fact that the South would reenter the Union with the freed slaves counting as whole persons for purposes of representation and taxation. In other words, even though Southerners had lost the war and had been forced to free the slaves by the Emancipation Proclamation and the Thirteenth Amendment, they would actually gain seats in the House of Representatives. This threatened Republican control of the nation, given that Northern Democratic votes were already challenging Reconstruction and other domestic policies (transcontinental railroad, national banking system, land grant colleges, higher taxes and tariffs). Another reason Republicans wanted African Americans to vote was that the number of black voters would help the party gain a political toehold in the Southern states—something that could be obtained no other way. There were too few whites willing to go against the "Lost Cause" of the Confederacy consistently. (Fortunately for the Republicans, blacks had no qualms about voting Republican all the time.) Finally, there was the notion that through the ballot and their voting strength blacks would command a respect for their rights that they could obtain by no other method. The North knew that it could not police the South with soldiers forever. Sooner or later African Americans would have to guarantee their own rights and economic independence, and the ballot offered a way to work toward this goal.

But there was a bit of a problem with granting African Americans the vote. As past elections had shown, Northern voters were unalterably opposed to blacks voting in their precincts. Even Radical Republicans like Thaddeus Stevens of Pennsylvania knew that to grant all blacks the vote nationwide would kill the party's chances in the congressional elections of 1866 and the presidential contest in 1868. State after state had rejected post–Civil War referenda designed to allow blacks to vote in the North. To insist on blacks voting up North would hand control over to President Andrew Johnson. So something hypocritical, yet eminently politically wise, was needed to allow the black vote in the South but to preserve the North for whites only. The result was seen in (1) the Fourteenth Amendment, which allowed Congress to reduce a state's representation by the same proportion that it systematically denied the vote to any part of its male population, and (2) the Military Reconstruction Acts, which required the South to register and count black voters in all elections and to approve the Fourteenth Amendment. In the presidential election of 1868 the nation voted with a not-too-subtle double standard that had blacks voting in the Reconstructed South by federal law but not in the North.

But the elections in 1867, in which Radical Republicans were hit hard, and the presidential election of 1868, in which Grant was rumored to have won only because of the black vote from the South, showed the precarious nature of Republican power in Washington, D.C. Radicals argued that the party was losing many white votes in the North anyhow, so now was the time to extend black voting everywhere. There were compelling reasons beyond mere politics to do so. Blacks had fought willingly for the Union, and social justice dictated that all should be treated the same. But others were not so sure. Whites feared political equality would lead to social equality (or as numerous shallow-minded candidates would put it, then and now, "Do you want a black man marrying your daughter?"). The matter would have to be rehashed many times before a proper formula could be found to appeal to all factions of the party. The end result was an amendment to the Constitution that was worded in such a manner as not actually to grant the franchise to African Americans but also not to permit them to be refused the vote solely on the basis of race. The Fifteenth Amendment established impartial but not universal suffrage. The states could still reject voters on any factor but color or former condition of servitude.

Having produced essentially a weak amendment, the Republicans faced the problem of ratification. At first the process looked good. The New England states, except for Rhode Island, which feared the effect of the measure on stimulating the Irish to vote, voted in accordance with their strong abolitionist leanings. The South joined in voting for the amendment. Most of the legislatures were Republican; there was a large black vote already; and Southern whites figured that if the South had to let blacks vote, why not the North? The border states disliked the idea immensely. However, the border states with legislatures dominated by Republicans—West Virginia, Maryland (which had already established the black right to vote through prior state action), and Missouri—passed the amendment. The rest voted it down (Delaware and Kentucky) or refused to vote at all (Tennessee). Much of the Far West (California and Oregon) rejected the measure, fearing its effect on allowing the Chinese to vote. Only Nevada, removed from the implications of that question, approved of it. The Middle Atlantic states and the Old Northwest (today's Middle West) split almost equally between Republicans and Democrats and, given the strong Southern heritage in the area along the Ohio River, passed the amendment only as a party measure.

In the end, the proportion of states required to pass an amendment (three-fourths) was lacking. But there was a solution. Three Southern states (Texas, Mississippi, and Virginia) had yet to complete Reconstruction. A fourth, Georgia, had been thrown out a second time when it refused to seat elected black legislators. These states were now required to ratify the Fifteenth Amendment (in addition to the

Fourteenth Amendment) to regain their places in the new Union. The new amendment became a part of the Constitution on 30 March 1870. But almost immediately it began to be ignored in the South. Congress tried to enforce both the Fourteenth and Fifteenth amendments through the Enforcement Acts, only to see both measures restricted by adverse Supreme Court decisions. By 1898, the Fifteenth Amendment had been totally circumvented in the South by limits on voting that were not overtly based on race, like literacy tests, grandfather clauses, and the poll tax and by the white primary. After that point, until the Voting Rights Act of 1965, only in the North did blacks have a legitimate chance to vote, courtesy of the Fifteenth Amendment.

See also Election of 1868; Enforcement Acts; Grant and Reconstruction; Redemption of the South before 1874; Redemption of the South from 1874; Supreme Court and Redemption.

References Benedict, Michael Les, "The Rout of Radicalism" (1972); Braxton, Allen Caperton, *The Fifteenth Amendment* (ca. 1903); Brock, W. R., *An American Crisis* (1963); Coleman, Charles H., *The Election of 1868* (1933); Cox, LaWanda, and John H. Cox, "Negro Suffrage and Republican Politics" (1967); Gillette, William, *The Right to Vote* (1969); Hesseltine, William B., *Ulysses S. Grant, Politician* (1935); Logan, Rayford W., *The Betrayal of the Negro* (1965); Mathews, John M., *Legislative and Judicial History of the Fifteenth Amendment* (1909); McFeeley, William S., *Grant* (1991); Woodward, C. Vann, "Seeds of Failure in Radical Race Policy" (1966).

Fish, Hamilton (1808–1893)

The son of upper-class New York parents, Hamilton Fish grew up to become one of the most important secretaries of state in the nation's history and one of the only decent cabinet picks that Ulysses S. Grant made. Fish had a private education and graduated from Columbia University with the highest honors. He read law and entered practice, moving into Whig politics from a Federalist party tradition. He ran for state assembly in a Democratic district and lost, but he managed to win a congressional seat for one term in 1842. When he was not returned to Congress, Fish turned to the lieutenant governorship of New York, only to lose the

Hamilton Fish

scape, but he never embraced the slavery issue as the main concern of American politics. After his Senate term expired, Fish took his family to Europe for a two-year vacation. When he returned he decided to work actively for the election of Abraham Lincoln, and he advised the outgoing James Buchanan administration to get tough with the South. During the war he worked on the New York state defense committee and negotiated the exchange of prisoners of war.

After the war Fish had no special claim to a position in the Grant administration beyond the fact that he had entertained the president-elect and knew him personally. In truth, Fish really did not want to serve, having retired from politics. But Grant insisted and sent his personal aide, Orville Babcock, to ask Fish to come aboard. Fish agreed only to help the administration get started but stayed on for Grant's two terms, during which time he became a pillar of honesty and moderation. As secretary of state, Fish reluctantly supported Grant's desire to annex the ill-governed republic of Santo Domingo, a stand that cost him an old friendship with opposing Senator Charles Sumner. Fish also had much difficulty charting a middle course between Cuban insurrectionists and the government of Spain, which he pressured to recognize legitimate claims for damages filed by American citizens. He attempted to negotiate a Central American canal with Colombia and Nicaragua in succession but failed in both efforts. He also failed to obtain a convention with Korea for American trading interests.

But in other areas Fish was more successful. He acted as a protector of German citizens in France during the Franco-Prussian War and kept the conflict from spreading to their Asia colonies. He reduced incursions along the Mexican border with much tact. He had the Russian minister to the United States recalled for interfering with negotiations with Great Britain, which had turned a blind eye to Confederate shipbuilding efforts in Britain during the Civil War. These *Alabama* claims, as they were known, in the end became Fish's greatest claim to fame. He skillfully presented the

race. A special election for the same office a year later proved successful, and in 1848 Fish moved on to the governor's chair, where he opened a statewide free school system and modernized the Erie Canal. He was opposed to the extension of slavery into the territories obtained from Mexico. He was slated to be placed in President Zachary Taylor's reorganized cabinet, but the president's death ended that plan.

Although Fish was not renominated as governor, the Whigs put him forward as their candidate for the U.S. Senate. In a hotly contested race in the state legislature, Fish emerged triumphant despite his refusal to denounce the Compromise of 1850, which permitted slavery to advance into the Mexican Cession, in contradiction of his own earlier announced position. In Washington he generally followed the lead of the senior New York senator, William H. Seward, and his home-state backer, Thurlow Weed, without much imagination. He became a Republican only because the Whigs were disappearing from the political land-

American viewpoint and carried the negotiations through to a successful conclusion. He also got England to agree to the notion that extradition of a wanted person need not be accomplished only through charges identical to those in the asking nation's courts; instead, persons could be extradited for any other viable reason.

After the end of his tenure as secretary of state, Fish retired to New York to live the life of a man of means, culture, and good taste. He enjoyed his family and had eight children with his wife, Julia Kean, who was considered a most gracious hostess. He was assisted in many of his public jobs by his son Hamilton, who became an important man in his own right and achieved special notoriety years later by receiving a personal rebuke from President Franklin D. Roosevelt for his opposition to the New Deal. The senior Fish lived out most of the rest of the nineteenth century, serving as a trustee of Columbia University, president-general of the Society of Cincinnati, president of the Union League, and president of the New York Historical Society.

See also Grant and Domestic Policies; Foreign Policy during Reconstruction; Grant and the Presidency.

References Fuller, Joseph V., "Hamilton Fish" (1964–1981); Nevins, Allan, *Hamilton Fish* (1936).

Force Acts
See Enforcement Acts.

Foreign Policy during Reconstruction

The foreign policy of the United States was admittedly not the crucial issue facing the nation during Reconstruction; it rated far behind the Southern question and the conquest of the American West. Nonetheless, it had important implications for the future. It was during Reconstruction that the country took its first steps toward world power. One of the men most responsible was Secretary of State William Seward, the Abraham Lincoln cabinet holdover who had much domestic influence with President Andrew Johnson and an almost uncontested

mastery of foreign affairs. The rationale of much of Seward's policy was the Monroe Doctrine, that cardinal principle of American foreign policy stating that no European encroachment in the New World would be countenanced. But the Civil War had turned American interest inward so much as to permit the invasion of Mexico by France, on the pretense that French claims against Mexico, which was experiencing constant, violent changes of government, would not be paid unless the country were stabilized from the outside. This notion was given much creditability because Mexico had experienced 36 changes of government and 73 presidents in a mere 40 years of independence from Spain. In 1863 France (at first helped by Britain and Spain, who soon withdrew) invaded Mexico and installed an Austrian prince, Ferdinand Maximilian, as emperor of Mexico.

Most Mexicans, especially those interested in a republican form of government, were unwilling to submit to this incursion from the outside. But until the end of the American Civil War, the French pretty much had driven President Benito Juárez and his supporters into the vastness of the Mexican north. There, Juárez's forces were cut off from much of the outside world, a process abetted by the Confederacy, which had hoped for French help on the diplomatic scene in exchange. After the war, mercenaries from both the Union and Confederacy drifted south to fight on both sides of the Mexican Civil War. Seward had at first proposed a declaration of war against this act contrary to the Monroe Doctrine, but President Lincoln pointed out that the war with the Confederacy was enough. The Mexican minister to the United States, Matías Romero, ably pushed the Lincoln administration to regard French invasion as a North American problem. Just as Lincoln hoped to preserve democracy in the United States by crushing the South, Matías Romero pointed out it would be but half a victory should Juárez go under at the same time south of the border. Unfortunately, Union efforts to capture and hold Texas seemed doomed to defeat; indeed, the last land battle of the war was a Yankee defeat near Brownsville at Palmetto Ranch in May 1865.

Meanwhile increasing losses in men and money and the maneuverings of Otto von Bismarck to unite the various German states into one kingdom under Prussia had caused France's Napoleon III to reconsider his Mexican venture. But he needed somehow to save face as he pulled out. The Lincoln administration (and later the Johnson one, too) immediately sent 25,000 troops to the Texas border in the spring of 1865, not only to force Texas into surrendering, but with an eye toward threatening the French across the Rio Grande. Dissatisfied with the slow pace of negotiations for the removal of the 28,000 French soldiers supporting Maximilian, Maj. Gen. Philip Sheridan took a federal cavalry contingent right through Texas to the border, creating a graphic realization of what could be done should France drag its feet. An actual raid across the Rio Grande below Brownsville by mercenaries with unofficial Union military support compounded the bleak picture awaiting France's Mexican venture.

In Washington, Matías Romero invited either Lt. Gen. Ulysses S. Grant or Maj. Gen. William T. Sherman to lead an expedition to relieve Juárez, and Grant spoke in favor of it. When Grant got Bvt. Maj. Gen. John Schofield to accept such a commission, Seward appointed Schofield to a diplomatic post to prevent a military response. Seward told Schofield to make a nuisance of himself in Paris and tell Napoleon to get out of Mexico. But when Schofield got to France, Seward's minister there, John Bigelow, kept him from the government, probably by prior arrangement with Seward. But the point had been made—the French expedition was as good as over. In January 1866, Napoleon III agreed to a staged withdrawal over an eighteen-month period. Juárez immediately attacked the withdrawing French, using American military equipment somehow "lost" on the border and "recovered" by the Mexicans for just that purpose. Maximilian unfortunately decided that he had a princely obligation to stay behind to

"save" Mexico from itself. The result was his capture and execution at Querétaro, north of Mexico City, in the spring of 1867.

After the expulsion of the French from Mexico, Seward began to expand his horizons and his view for the future of the United States in the world. In this he was perhaps the first to accurately foresee the entrance of the United States onto the world stage as an imperial power coequal to any European nation. Seward would not realize this in his lifetime, but he began to lay the essential preliminary foundation upon which his successors would build. And the Monroe Doctrine would be a perfect cover for his activities. Americans on the Pacific coast had long coveted Russian America, as Alaska was then called. But the Civil War had put off a decision on the purchase of this piece of European-controlled real estate on the shores of North America. The Russians, however, were interested in selling Alaska because it was not a viable economic endeavor and it was expensive to maintain and impossible to defend. So Czar Alexander II found himself in the same position as Napoleon I had been before his sale of Louisiana to Thomas Jefferson—in need of making the best of a lousy deal. Like the French at the beginning of the century, the Russians found the United States the right power to sell to—small, not too powerful, and not European-based. In short, the United States was not a competitor. The czar promised his minister to the United States, Baron Edouard de Stoeckl, a $17,000 bonus to make the deal, but he warned the minister not to get less than $5 million. Could Stoeckl convince the United States to buy?

The answer was an unreserved yes, as far as Secretary of State Seward was concerned. He had noticed the effect of the Confederate raider *Shenandoah* in the last months of the war as it destroyed the Yankee whaling fleet, ship by ship, aided by the lack of U.S. naval bases in the northern Pacific. With the end of the war, Seward was determined to gain U.S. naval bases in the Pacific as well as in the West Indies to reduce the threat to the U.S. merchant fleet. This made him interested in Alaska, Hawaii, Midway, the Danish West Indies, and Santo Domingo. (It also compelled Lincoln and Grant to look longingly at Santo Domingo more than they ought to have done—both as a naval base and as a place to send America's blacks for a new start, solving the problem of racial discrimination against freedmen at the same time.) So Seward went to work lining up Congress ahead of time, reminding it and the American people of their prewar desires to advance into the Orient and the Caribbean.

According to the tale, Stoeckl found Seward one night playing whist (a card game). He told the secretary of state that he could sell Russian America to the United States and offered to come by the next day and work out the details. "Why wait?" Seward wanted to know. He said that he would get his staff and Senator Charles Sumner, chairman of the foreign relations committee, together and Stoeckl could round up his own people, too. By the next morning, the treaty was ready and President Johnson sent it to the Senate. There Sumner gave it his unreserved approval (calling it Alaska for the first time) and it passed 37 to 2.

But it took a year to get the $7.2 million from the House, the proceedings extending right on through the impeachment process against Johnson. It was the lack of familiarity about Alaska and the hatred for anything Johnson did that made its purchase a joke. It took $165,000 in bribes to key congressmen to get the purchase accepted. (The bribe money came out of a $200,000 slush fund, which explains why the price was $7.2 million and not $7 million; Congress voted in effect to pay itself off.) Of course, Seward said he knew nothing about that. But as the public ridiculed "Seward's Ice Box," the secretary also appropriated Midway Island unnoticed by simply landing a force of sailors and marines on it. But the Danish West Indies would have to wait. The Danes tried to drive a hard bargain, and the problem dragged out past Seward's time in office. Grant did not choose to pursue it further, being more interested in Santo Domingo.

Hamilton Fish followed Seward into the secretary's job at the behest of President Grant. Fish was willing to look into the Santo Domingo annexation project, even though he had his doubts about the honesty of Grant's personal envoy, Orville Babcock, or the wisdom of any annexation beyond the acquisition of the naval base at Samana Bay. But when Babcock returned, Fish sent the resulting treaty to the Senate, where it ran afoul of Senator Charles Sumner, who blocked its ratification. Because of his willingness to work with Grant on this issue, Fish lost his lifelong friendship with Senator Sumner, which hurt him grievously.

The most notable achievement of Fish's tenure as secretary of state was the Treaty of Washington, which settled the contentious *Alabama* claims with Great Britain, held over from the days of the Civil War. Britain had declared itself neutral during the war, but in certain aspects its neutrality was decidedly pro-Confederate. Its building of ships (such as the *Alabama*) for thinly disguised Confederate agents was a case in point, as was its recognition of the South as a legitimate belligerent (rather than as a rebellious part of the Union). An earlier treaty had attempted to settle these problems but was marred by the desire of Radical Republicans to have Britain pay off claims of Northern citizens whose cargoes and ships were sunk by British-built raiders flying the Rebel flag. The result was an official standoff that lasted until 1873. When Fish let it be known secretly that he did not agree with the exorbitant sums and land claims against British territory in Canada that Congress put forward, the British opened up discussions again through the government of Canada. This time the negotiations included other matters like boundaries, fishing rights in the Atlantic, and trade.

The Treaty of Washington (1871), which grew out of these contacts, emphasized the need of a neutral country to be diligent in preventing the arming of belligerent vessels in its ports. When the British refused to admit their fault in advance of a monetary settlement, Fish began to pile on a series of minor claims at the Geneva arbitration hearings that threatened to raise the jackpot considerably. The British decided to admit its failure during the war, and settlement was established at the sum of $15.5 million. The debate over fishing rights and trade proved more enduring and dragged on for years. But the territorial settlement of the boundary through the San Juan Islands in Puget Sound was arbitrated by Kaiser Wilhelm I of Germany in 1872, mostly to the United States' advantage.

A final nasty foreign policy problem during the Grant administration was the armed insurrection in Cuba. This insurrection threatened American economic interests, which claimed damages against arbitrary actions of Spanish officials there. These problems occupied Fish throughout his eight-year term as secretary and often proved embarrassing. He had to try to get the Spanish to negotiate with the rebels to end the conflict and at the same time prevent Congress from recognizing the rebels as belligerents, which would extend and deepen the war and further damage American businesses. Fish also wanted to end slavery, which was still legal on the island; this provided the basis for some in Congress to call for American intervention. While Fish was engaged on other matters, President Grant moved to recognize Cuban belligerency. Although Fish was not opposed to this in principle, he preferred to keep it back to prompt Spain to negotiate. Grant agreed after a belated consultation with Fish and allowed the secretary to delay promulgation of the decree. There was little else Grant could do, because the president needed Fish's support on the Santo Domingo situation and he dared not alienate him over Cuba. Meanwhile Spain promised reforms on the island and a redress of the rebels' grievances. More important, Spain offered to negotiate on American claims for the first time.

Just as Fish thought he was getting somewhere, one of those unintended incidents that plague orderly diplomacy occurred. The steamer S.S. *Virginius*, which had an American crew and registry but was in the employ of the Cuban revolutionary committee in New York City, was captured by the Spanish in the midst of conveying mercenary soldiers and military goods. Local Spanish authorities executed the captain and 53 of the crew—after all, everyone knew the ship and its activities well. War fever swept through both nations. Fish demanded that Spain release the ship and the rest of its crew and passengers, punish the guilty officials, and fire a 21-gun salute to the American flag. He gave Spain 12 days to act or he would sever all diplomatic relations. The Spanish minister in the United States asked if his country might not dispense with the salute (an especially galling idea to the proud Spanish) if he could prove that the *Virginius* were illegally registered. This was easily done, and Fish acquiesced. But the questions of indemnity and punishment of the responsible officials dragged on for months with no settlement.

In the meantime, the Spanish government had a change in its monarchy, and Fish threatened to withhold recognition of King Alfonso XII unless an immediate settlement on outstanding problems, especially claims of American losses relating to the *Virginius*, were forthcoming. The new Spanish government agreed to indemnify the United States on the *Virginius*, which opened up the possibility of broader negotiation once again. Fish pointed out that the Cuban revolutionary mess had to be settled, as promised earlier, if U.S.-Spanish relations were to improve. Otherwise, he intimated that outside powers might feel obliged to intervene and force a settlement. Spain quickly agreed to Fish's proposals, which included reform of Spanish government on the island with a view toward eventual independence and the abolition of slavery. Spain dragged out the negotiations until it could place enough troops to stop the revolution in its tracks. Then it met an arbitration panel's determination of the amount owed the United States for prior claims, and the Cuban problem was solved until it sprang up anew in the 1890s.

In cooperation with other European powers and Japan, Fish also handled other, more minor problems, such as the protection of the interests of German subjects caught inside France during the Franco-Prussian War; a failed U.S. attempt to extort a convention on the surrender of shipwrecked American seamen from Korea; and the expansion of American rights in China. He tried to get a treaty with Colombia opening up the Panamanian isthmus to an American canal, but the document was so amended by the Colombian congress as to be nullified. A later negotiation for the same rights to cross Nicaragua failed when the country refused to grant Americans a neutral zone outside Nicaraguan law. Although the United States was still dominated by internal issues arising from the resolution of the Civil War and the settlement of the West, the diplomacy of Seward and Fish marked the hesitant beginnings of a policy that would take the nation onto the world stage in the 1890s, as evidenced by the settlement of the Spanish-American War and the absorption of Spain's Caribbean and Asian empires.

See also Fish, Hamilton; Grant and Domestic Policies; Grant and the Presidency.

References Beisner, Robert L., *From the Old Diplomacy to the New* (1975); Campbell, Charles S., *The Transformation of American Foreign Relations* (1976); Donald, David H., *Charles Sumner and the Rights of Man.* (1970); Ferrell, Robert H., *American Diplomacy* (1969); Fuller, Joseph V., "Hamilton Fish" (1964–1981); LaFeber, Walter, *The New Empire* (1963); Nevins, Allan, *Hamilton Fish* (1936); Plesur, Milton, *America's Outward Thrust* (1971); Spence, Clark C., "Robert Schenck and the Emma Mine Affair" (1959); Taylor, John M., *William Henry Seward* (1991); Van Deusen, Glyndon G., *William Henry Seward* (1967).

Fortieth Congress Extra Session Act

The Fortieth Congress Extra Session Act was a measure passed by the outgoing Second Session of the Thirty-ninth Congress. Its purpose was to call into session the Fortieth Congress immediately upon adjournment of the Thirty-ninth Congress. The idea was to create a Congress with three sessions (instead of the usual two) that would not adjourn until President Andrew Johnson had been thoroughly defeated in his attempts to reconstruct the South through presidential proclamation. Because both Johnson and his predecessor, Abraham Lincoln, frequently acted in the gaps between congressional sessions, this measure would curb executive interference.

See also Johnson and Reconstruction; Moderate Republicans and Reconstruction.

Reference Trefousse, Hans L., *Andrew Johnson* (1989).

Fourteenth Amendment

When Congress repassed the Freedmen's Bureau and Civil Rights bills of 1866 over President Andrew Johnson's vetoes, it indicated that it would not accept Johnson's view on Reconstruction. This meant that Congress now had to suggest a definitive alternative program, a responsibility that fell on the Committee of Fifteen on Reconstruction. Historians have traditionally examined the origins of the Fourteenth Amendment as a sort of plot to advance Reconstruction toward more and more vindictive ends that would make the process unpalatable to the white South. Modern authors have seen the amendment more as a sign of Congress searching for some solution that all could live with, given that the president had thrown down the gauntlet over the Freedmen's Bureau and Civil Rights bills of 1866.

The reason Congress put forward an amendment rather than another bill was to ensure that a succeeding Congress would not be able to alter it by mere majority vote—a real problem, it turns out, given the tenuous hold of the Republicans on the national and particularly Southern state governments. The Fourteenth Amendment, which all the seceded states were expected to ratify, was to represent some sort of Civil War peace treaty. (There never was an official peace treaty.) Ironically, however, Congress refused to admit that the seceded states were full-fledged states in the Union, and there was legitimate doubt as to whether they could ratify any amendment given their status. Even though many commentators today believe that the Fourteenth Amendment was something quite in the realm of continuing constitutional development, it was a revolutionary document. It was the first amendment that operated directly upon the states rather than the federal government.

Its first section was basically a repetition of the statement in the Civil Rights Act of 1866 that nationalized citizenship. Before the Civil War, citizenship was guaranteed by the states. Now it was nationalized, and the power was given to the states only in the absence of action by the federal government. And for the states to exercise this power, they had to stay within certain boundaries. They could not make or enforce any law that "abridged the privileges or immunities" of citizens, deny a citizen "equal protection of the laws," or deprive anyone of "life, liberty, or property, without due process of the law." This section overturned the 1857 *Dred Scott* decision, in which the U.S. Supreme Court had declared that blacks were not citizens; this decision had threatened the constitutionality of the Civil Rights Act of 1866.

The second part of the amendment handled the problem of Southern representation. Because of racist tendencies among Northern voters, Republicans in Congress did not wish to alienate their constituency by granting African Americans the vote outright. Every time some movement to free blacks or expand their rights had taken place during the war, the Republican vote had dropped precipitously in the North. But Republicans knew that to hold on to the nation with the increase in Southern representation that came from freeing the slaves, they would either have to grant blacks the right to vote (blacks would vote for the party that freed them from slavery, the Republicans smugly assumed) or somehow reduce this representation. So the second section apportioned representation in Congress among the whole numbers of persons in the several states, recognizing an African American as a complete citizen (not three-fifths of one person, as before the war). But if any male over the age of 21 and a citizen of the United States were denied the vote (except for participation in rebel-

lion or conviction of a crime), a state's representation could be reduced in direct proportion. In effect this forced the South to permit blacks to vote or accept a loss in representation in Congress. The weakness of this part of the amendment, of course, was that the white Southern establishment just might accept the deal, deny African Americans the right to vote, and take the loss. And it ignored gender, a matter that did not sit well with advocates of women's suffrage, many of whom had been ardent abolitionists before the war.

The third section concerned the whites who had taken an oath to the United States before the war in any capacity and then taken a similar oath to support the Confederacy. These men would be denied the vote until Congress decided by a two-thirds vote at some future date to give them a special amnesty (done at various times between 1872 and 1898). Another section of the amendment validated the Union war debt and nullified the Confederate war debt, implying that the Confederacy never existed as a legitimate entity. The final section allowed Congress to make such laws as it thought necessary to enforce the amendment. It was this section that would permit Congress to pass the Enforcement Acts in 1870 and 1871.

The proposals that made up the final draft of the Fourteenth Amendment were not set in stone. At any point President Johnson might have altered the process had he been willing to compromise with Congress on Reconstruction. But Johnson instead decided to oppose the amendment completely, asserting that it denied states equal representation in Congress as guaranteed in the Constitution. He also insisted that Southern congressmen be admitted immediately to debate and vote on any Reconstruction matters, including the amendment's final form before it went to the states. By now, however, the Republicans were not about to junk months of work to satisfy a man they thought to be mad, a traitor, or a damned fool—maybe all three. But Johnson's opposition led Southerners to vote the amendment down in every

Southern state except Tennessee, where the Republicans had by chance obtained a majority in the legislature, which they manipulated mercilessly. In most of the South the vote against the Fourteenth Amendment was unanimous or so lopsided as to be virtually so. The result was that Congress admitted Tennessee back into the Union and turned to considerations of more drastic policies to coerce the rest of the South to admit complete defeat in a war that had ended on the battlefield two years earlier. Part of that admission would be Southern ratification of the Fourteenth Amendment, now so necessary because too many Northern states had also rejected it. The amendment would achieve final approval on 28 July 1868, right after the readmission of North Carolina, South Carolina, Georgia, Florida, Alabama, Mississippi, and Louisiana into the Union.

It is fair to say that no other amendment has been as controversial as the Fourteenth. Its meaning has been challenged by every generation of American lawyers, historians, and legal critics. Although it seems, in the words of one researcher, that the amendment "was to be, *par excellence*, the Negroes' charter of liberty," others assert that no clear-cut picture of the framer's intended meaning can be had. Another legal scholar found that little beyond the definition of citizenship was germane. *Privileges* and *immunities* are nowhere defined; equal protection of the laws seems to preclude most legislation to aid people of different classes and needs; and due process appears to be a vague reference to a common-law procedural concept dating back to England's Magna Carta. The amendment's only apparent meaning was to attack the racism rampant in the Black Codes, in conjunction with the Thirteen and Fifteenth amendments and the Civil Rights laws of 1866 and 1875 and the Enforcement Acts of 1870 and 1871.

But there are even more dubious legal doctrines that have resulted from the Fourteenth Amendment. In 1882, while arguing a case before the U.S. Supreme Court, Senator Roscoe Conkling of New York maintained that the citizenship section was drawn up to make corporations legal persons exempt from state regulatory action. This so-called conspiracy theory led to a court that forced Congress to institute the Interstate Commerce Commission in 1887, as well as the tremendous federal regulatory action that followed in the twentieth century, culminating in the New Deal's (1937–1938) attack on the Court for its interpretation of "substantive due process," upon which the conspiracy theory was based. Following World War II the Court, led by Associate Justice Hugo Black, began to entertain a different concept: forcing the states to comply with the Bill of Rights (which previously had applied only to the federal government). This theory was first argued in the South Carolina Ku Klux Klan cases of the 1870s by federal prosecuting attorney David T. Corbin, who was primarily interested in placing the restrictions of the Second Amendment (the right to bear arms) and the Fourth Amendment (under which the government needs a warrant to intrude in an individual's home) against state authorities who acted in concert with the Klan. Although the court initially rejected Black's notion of incorporation, it has since accepted the idea on a case-by-case basis such that today Black's suggestion is good law.

What we are left with is a hodgepodge of often contradictory legal ideas. The terms *due process* and *equal protection* have rationalized a lot of things since 1868, but rarely did they protect blacks against racism during Reconstruction. In public schools the terms condoned the concept of "separate but equal" in public accommodations (as a result of *Plessy v. Ferguson* in 1896) and the assignment of children to schools by race (from *Cumming v. Georgia* three years later). Then, in 1954, according to a court majority in *Brown v. Board of Education*, these same words meant that American schoolchildren ought not be assigned to school on the basis of race. But in 1971 the court found, in *Swann v. Charlotte-Mecklenburg*, that assignment by race was permissible once again and ought to be encouraged by local government busing of children to select locations.

It was this same set of words that resulted in the constitutional right to abortion in 1973—something far from the minds of the framers, no matter how one reads the amendment. The same words have also been used to find that religion and public schools do not mix, resulting from a First Amendment that was designed to keep the federal government out of religious matters entirely, leaving them to the states. It is also the basis of those who are opposed to capital punishment, from an Eighth Amendment that also reserved such matters to the states in the 1790s.

In other words, court interpretation of the Fourteenth Amendment has reversed the Bill of Rights from the way the framers wrote it (restrictions on the central government) to what the United States has today—the exact opposite (restrictions on the states)—through a process called hermeneutics or the interpretations of legal scholars made into law through court decisions without legislative or popular action.

See also Black Codes; Civil Rights Acts; Enforcement Acts; Freedmen's Bureau Acts; Johnson and Reconstruction; Joint Committee of Fifteen on Reconstruction; Military Reconstruction Acts; Moderate Republicans and Reconstruction; Radical Republicans and Reconstruction; Supreme Court and Redemption.

References Avins, Alfred, "The Ku Klux Klan Act of 1871" (1967); Beale, Howard K., *The Critical Year [1866]* (1930); Clark, John G., "Historians and the Joint Committee of Reconstruction" (1961) and "Radicals and Moderates in the Joint Committee on Reconstruction" (1963); Collins, Charles Wallace, "The Fourteenth Amendment and the Negro Race Question" (1911) and *The Fourteenth Amendment and the States* (1912); Fairman, Charles, "Does the Fourteenth Amendment Incorporate the Bill of Rights?" (1952–1953); Flack, Horace E., *The Adoption of the Fourteenth Amendment* (1908); Frankfurter, Felix, "Memorandum on 'Incorporation' of the Bill of Rights into the Due Process Clause of the Fourteenth Amendment" (1964–1965); Graglia, Lino A., "Does Constitutional Law Exist?" (1995); Graham, Howard J., "The 'Conspiracy Theory' of the Fourteenth Amendment" (1938), and "Procedure to Substance" (1952–1953); James, Joseph B., *The Framing of the Fourteenth Amendment* (1956) and "Southern Reaction to the Proposal of the Fourteenth Amendment" (1956); Kaczorowski, Robert J., "To Begin the Nation Anew" (1987), *The Nationalization of Civil Rights* (1987), and "Searching for the Intent of the Framers of the Fourteenth Amendment" (1972–1973); Kendrick, Benjamin B., *The Journal of the Joint Committee of Fifteen on Reconstruction* (1914); Kousser, J. Morgan, *Dead End* (1985); Lacy, Alex B., Jr., "The Bill of Rights and the Fourteenth Amendment" (1966); Lien, Arnold J., *Concurring Opinion* (1957); McKitrick, Eric, *Andrew Johnson and Reconstruction* (1960); Mendelson, Wallace, "A Note on the Cause and Cure of the Fourteenth Amendment" (1981); Morrison, Stanley, "The Fourteenth Amendment Challenged" (1948); Richter, William L., "One Hundred Years of Controversy" (1968–1969); Riddleberger, Patrick W., *1866* (1979); Russell, James F. S., "Railroads in the 'Conspiracy Theory' of the Fourteenth Amendment" (1955); Suthron, W. J., "Dubious Origins of the Fourteenth Amendment" (1953–1954); Ten Broek, Jacobus, *Equal under Law* (1951, 1965).

Freedmen's Aid Societies

Before the Civil War had barely started, various abolition societies already began to look to Reconstruction of the Union and liberation of the slaves. It was to them a great opportunity to purge the nation for what they saw as a grievous sin. They would go South and redeem the freedmen, educate them, and make them black moral counterparts in a re-creation of New England society located in a rejuvenated South. The first of the freedmen's societies was the American Missionary Association (AMA), started in 1846 by such abolitionists as Arthur and Lewis Tappan, Edward Beecher, S. S. Jocelyn, Joshua Leavitt, John Greenleaf Whittier, and Gerrit Smith. Reorganized under George Whipple in 1861, the AMA moved down to Virginia and began ministering to the camps of contrabands (slaves escaping to the jurisdiction of the Northern armies) at Fortress Monroe. They were soon followed by Methodists and Baptists, with no sect wishing to yield the harvest of souls to another, less "enlightened" group.

As the sectarian societies moved south, various nonsectarian groups also organized with the notion to send relief to the destitute freedmen. The first such group began in New England, but soon others cropped up in many Northern cities, such as Cincinnati, Chicago, Cleveland, Detroit, New York, Philadelphia, and Baltimore. The result was a confusion of well-intended voices that was solved somewhat when the nonsectarian groups united under the banner of the American Freedmen's Union Commission (AFUC). Their leaders included such men as Levi Coffin, Salmon P. Chase, William Lloyd Garrison, Phillips Brooks, John Greenleaf Whittier, Henry Ward Beecher, Edward Everett Hale, Edward Atkinson, John A. Andrew, and Edward L. Pierce. By 1866, with the encouragement of the federal Bureau of Refugees, Freedmen, and Abandoned Lands, most independent groups had affiliated with either the AMA or AFUC. Perhaps one-half of the $12 million appropriated to the bureau by 1872 was turned over to the various benevolent societies.

The secretary of the AFUC was Lyman Abbott, a New Englander who believed in the Northern mission to civilize the South through a revolutionary transformation of people's minds. He liked to work through the reconstructed governments and their superintendents of public instruction. But he found his hardest fight to be among the contributing members, each interested in a different religious "truth" for the freedmen. He soon found that the only way to obtain the cooperation of Southern whites was to renounce the notion of integrated education and concentrate on each race alone. But in the end Northern aid societies probably did not educate more than 10 percent of the blacks who were available to learn between 1865 and 1869.

Abbott's counterpart in the prestigious Peabody Fund was Barnas Sears, a New England Yankee who took an even more racially divisive view of education in the South. Contributing about $2 million to the support of Southern public education, Sears discovered that he had to face up to separation by race if he hoped to accomplish the fund's goal of reestablishing Southern

A Pennsylvania Freedmen's Relief Association newsletter depicts one of the many schoolhouses sponsored by the Freedmen's Aid Societies.

schools after the war. The Peabody Fund had certain requirements that each school it helped had to meet: the school had to be public, it had to have a term of at least ten months, it had to have an attendance rate of 85 percent of those enrolled, and local citizens had to contribute at least twice as much to schools as the fund. From the beginning, through a series of Southern tours, Sears found that the only way to gain local white support was to separate the races in school. This he unabashedly did, granting less money for an African American school as for a white one in the same straits. The Peabody Fund also tended to stick to school systems in larger urban areas. This meant that the fund generally financed white schools and refused to help schools in Louisiana and South Carolina that were integrated by state law.

Sears claimed that the Peabody Fund was going to stay out of politics, a naive concept, if he ever believed it. He quarreled incessantly with the superintendents of education in Louisiana, Thomas Conway and William G. Brown, who believed that their states qualified for funds despite their integrated systems. He also lobbied to get the integrated education clauses pulled out of the Civil Rights Act of 1875, the public accommodations law. Ignoring Senator Charles Sumner and his allies, who favored a strict integration of all public facilities including education, Sears went to other senators and representatives and convinced them that to integrate schools would drive whites out of the public education system and into private schools. An interview with President Ulysses S. Grant found the chief executive in complete agreement with Sears. The result was a public accommodations law without the education clauses and a guarantee that Southern schools would be "separate but equal" 30 years before the U.S. Supreme Court would endorse such an approach.

Unlike Sears, the religious and benevolent societies had strong ties to the Radical Republicans in Congress and to Republican governments in the Southern states; these ties delayed the societies' acceptance of segregated schools. The missionaries and teachers often belonged to the Union Loyal Leagues and encouraged their black charges to make the most of the freedoms granted under the Military Reconstruction Acts. But their main concern was the education of the children. At first they were concerned with any and all children, but as the realities of Southern prejudices came to the fore, they tended to focus solely on African American children (except for Berea College in Kentucky, which was evenly split among the races). The North had set the blacks free, these groups reasoned, and now it had a duty to educate them to meet the obligations and opportunities of citizenship. By 1869, there were nearly 10,000 teachers from the societies in the South. By 1881, they spent $21 million in their endeavor.

As the several Southern states returned to the Union with loyal governments, the societies, led by the AFUC, tended to turn their efforts over to the states. The societies also tended to become more independent of each other and more interested in converting blacks to their denomination, rather than merely educating them in a secular fashion. The result was that, after the Freedmen's Bureau disbanded and ceased its coordination effort, the societies began to compete rather than cooperate, diluting their contribution's overall effect. Hit hard by the economic panic of 1873 (which reduced the contributions that kept the societies going) and faced with the white Redemption of each state (which threatened their very existence), the societies became conservative and cautious in dealing with the Southern powers that be. It was obvious that if their gains were to be consolidated, the aid groups would have to reach an agreement with the Redeemers.

The result was that the societies acquiesced to segregated education. Normal colleges like Atlanta, Fisk, Hampton, and Talledega were to provide teachers for the separate black education system. The AMA condoned this separation in 1882 when it allowed white Congregationalists in Atlanta to organize all-white churches in a synod separate from the mixed congregations that had existed earlier in Reconstruction. African Americans had finally been turned over by their alleged friends to the not-too-tender mercies of the white South in every aspect of life.

See also Abolitionists and Reconstruction; Bureau of Refugees, Freedmen, and Abandoned Lands; Louisiana Experiment; Mississippi Valley Experiment; Port Royal Experiment; Virginia Experiment.

References Brown, Ira V., "Lyman Abbott and Freedmen's Aid" (1949); Butchart, Ronald E., *Northern Schools, Southern Blacks, and Reconstruction* (1980); Drake, Richard B., "The American Missionary Association and the Southern Negro" (1957) and "Freedmen's Aid and Sectional Compromise" (1963); Harlan, Louis R., "Desegregation in New Orleans Public Schools during Reconstruction" (1961–1962); Kelly, Alfred H., "The Congressional Controversy over School Segregation" (1958–1959); Vaughn, William P., "Partners in Segregation" (1964) and "Separate and Unequal" (1967); West, Earle H., "The Peabody Fund and Negro Education" (1966).

Freedmen's Bureau

See Bureau of Refugees, Freedmen, and Abandoned Lands.

Freedmen's Bureau Acts

Congress passed the initial act for the Bureau of Refugees, Freedmen, and Abandoned Lands (better known as the Freedmen's Bureau) in the waning days of the Civil War. Its main purpose was to give assistance to loyal refugees, black or white, who had been dispossessed by the war. As time went on, however, the bureau became more of a social agency dedicated to helping freedmen make the transition between slavery and freedom. It was this concept that led to controversy over the act's renewal. In the nineteenth century no group of persons except merchant seamen had ever received government largess. Hence the bureau presented a revolutionary concept that would not become accepted until the throes of the Great Depression led politicians and citizens to rethink the role of government during the New Deal in the 1930s.

ACT OF 3 MARCH 1965

Instituted for the duration of the war and one year after, the Bureau of Refugees, Freedmen, and Abandoned Lands was to be a bureau of the War Department and would have jurisdiction in the Rebel states or any territory occupied by the United States Army. The bureau was to administer the three topics suggested by its title. It was to be headed by a commissioner appointed by the president with the advice and consent of the Senate at a salary of $3,000 a year; it was to have a staff of ten clerks. Both the commissioner and the chief clerk had to be bonded. The secretary of war was authorized to allow the bureau rations, clothing, fuel, and temporary shelter by proper requisition.

To help him in his duties, the commissioner was permitted to appoint up to ten assistant commissioners in the insurrectionary states. These men were to be paid $2,000 annually and had to post bond with the U.S. attorney general. Any military officer could be detailed to any bureau position without any increase in his normal salary—a cost-saving measure. Each assistant commissioner was to make written reports to the commissioner and the latter to Congress at the beginning of each session. Special reports had to be made on request of any superior officer or Congress. All officers of the bureau had to subscribe to the ironclad oath (one of never having aided the Confederacy).

The commissioner was authorized to set aside, under the president's direction, any lands that were abandoned or to which the U.S. government had acquired title. These lands could be offered to male heads of households, black or white, for the next three years, with rent not to exceed 6 percent of the value of the land per year as assessed in 1860. The amount of land for any one household was not to exceed 40 acres. These renters would be given the right to buy the land at any time during its rental.

ACT OF 16 JULY 1866

This measure, also known as the Freedmen's Bureau Renewal Act, was to continue in force and amend the act of 1865 for the next two years. The jurisdiction of the bureau was extended to all loyal refugees and freedmen in any part of the nation. The purpose of bureau aid was to get families back on an independent footing as soon as possible. Two additional assistant commissioners were authorized beyond the ten specified in the first act. The commissioner and his assistants were to cooperate with the religious and secular benevolent associations that sent members south for purposes of educational, religious, and moral instruction; in particular the bureau's workers were to help obtain the use of select buildings for the associations' classes.

The second bureau act confirmed the possession of lands granted to African Americans in the Sea Islands below Charleston, South Carolina, which had been condemned for nonpayment of federal taxes in September 1863. The plots were to be limited to 20 acres for each family. Those lands in the general area that had been granted to blacks under Gen. William T. Sherman's Special Orders No. 15 were also confirmed in title. Vacant lands in theses areas were to be sold exclusively to African Americans at $1.50 an acre. Such titles could not be alienated within the first six years of ownership. Other lots in and around the area that once belonged to the Confederate States of America were to be sold at public auction. None of these procedures would affect lands reserved for the exclusive use of the military and naval forces of the United States.

Finally, in all Rebel states the bureau was to guarantee the rights of every citizen regardless of race to sue or be sued, to make or enforce contracts, to sell or hold property, and to have equal protection under the law. No black person could be punished more for law violations than any white person. The president or the bureau had the authorization to ask for and receive military protection and assistance in enforcing these matters until such time as the former Confederate states were readmitted to the Union by their representation in Congress.

ACT OF 6 JULY 1868

This measure extended the first two bureau acts for the period of one more year, or until such time as specified otherwise by the secretary of war. All officers serving with the bureau who had been mustered out of the military service could be retained as civilians at the same rate of pay. The bureau would be phased out in any insurrectionary state when that state was readmitted into the Union, unless conditions warranted its continuance beyond that time. The educational operations of the bureau were exempt from any closure date and were to be continued until black children were guaranteed a free, public education. All unexpended monies held by the commissioner for any particular jurisdiction after the closure of the bureau field offices there were to be applied to the educational effort. All buildings owned by the bureau for education were to be sold to local school trustees and the proceeds returned to the treasury.

ACT OF 25 JULY 1868

This act guaranteed that Maj. Gen. Oliver Otis Howard would continue as head of the bureau until his death or resignation. Any successor, civilian or military, would be appointed by the president with the advice and consent of the Senate. All assistant commissioners, clerks, and field agents were to be appointed by the secretary of war on the advice of the commissioner. In case of a vacancy in the office of commissioner, the acting assistant adjutant general of the bureau would fill in temporarily until a successor could be found. Finally, the measure specified that all bureau operations would be closed down on 1 January 1869. (The educational functions continued until the economic panic of 1873 closed them down as well.)

See also Bureau of Refugees, Freedmen, and Abandoned Lands; Howard, Oliver Otis; Louisiana Experiment; Mississippi Valley Experiment; Port Royal Experiment; Virginia Experiment.

References Bentley, George R., *A History of the Freedmen's Bureau* (1955); Bremner, Robert H., *American Philanthropy* (1960); Bronson, Louis Henry, "The Freedmen's Bureau" (1970); Olds,

Victoria Marcus, "The Freedmen's Bureau as a Social Agency" (1966); Pierce, Paul Skeels, *The Freedmen's Bureau* (1904).

Freedmen's Savings Bank

In operation from March 1865 to July 1874, the Freedmen's Savings Bank was an attempt by Reconstruction-era America to instill middle-class mores in the newly freed slaves. Originally Anson M. Sperry, a paymaster of a white Illinois regiment who had a philanthropic interest in assisting blacks, tried to set up the bank; he tried to incorporate as its base of operations the military banks that had opened up among the soldiers of black Union army regiments at Norfolk, Virginia, and Beaufort, South Carolina, as well as the autonomous Free Labor Bank of New Orleans. But these institutions refused to give up their independent status. That left it up to John W. Alford, a Connecticut abolitionist who had worked to organize schools among free blacks in the North before the war and among the African Americans who followed in the wake of Maj. Gen. William T. Sherman's march across Georgia, to get the bank chartered.

Alford at the time was superintendent of schools and finances for the Freedmen's Bureau; he went to Congress and obtained a charter to establish the bank in New York City. There was little debate on the measure; it was deemed such a display of common sense that no one questioned its wisdom. It was to be an investment bank, not one that engaged in day-to-day general banking services. Congress reserved for itself the right to inspect the books at any time. Alford created the first and main office in New York City in April 1865. He then traveled throughout the South on behalf of the bureau and the Freedmen's Savings Bank, reporting on conditions among recently freed slaves and setting up bank branches. The result was the creation of 33 branches throughout the South, something Congress had not foreseen but did not discourage, either. Alford assigned Sperry, now a bureau official, the task of going among black soldiers of the Army of Observation (a force primarily made up of U.S. black infantry stationed along the Rio Grande to neutralize and intimidate the French effort in Mexico) to create savings branches in each regiment to invest money in stocks, bonds, treasury notes, and other securities. These soldier banks also helped the men transfer payments to their families back home.

The original backers of the institution were New York and Boston financiers and philanthropists who had connections with the abolitionist movement, the Freedmen's Bureau, and the American Missionary Association (a benevolent association for freedmen, firmly connected with the Congregational Church). These men saw the bank as a moral imperative, a way to imbue African Americans with middle-class values of self-sacrifice and frugality. They would encourage Southern blacks to set up societies among themselves to collect money and deposit it in one of the Freedmen's Savings Bank's branches. The problem was that the deposits slips were kept in a slipshod manner that in effect lost the money within the system. But the philanthropists did their best to keep an eye on the investments, assuring the freedmen who invested that they would be paid back handsomely.

Unfortunately for the bank's future, the safeguards and conservative actions of its founders were nullified when the institution transferred its headquarters to Washington, D.C. The New York office then became a collection point for all the branches in the South. The move effectively put the bank's operations beyond its founders, who began to drift off to other causes. The result was a new board of directors who were an integral part of the systemic corruption known as the Great Barbecue that plagued any money venture of this period. The new director wanted more interest. So the board secured a new charter from Congress that opened the bank's investment up to anything available. The motive presented to Congress looked good—more money for the black investors—but Congress was too busy with bigger frauds of its own to be concerned with possible wrongdoings at the Freedmen's Savings Bank. By the early 1870s the bank had attracted much money for the directors to play around with. There were about 72,000 black investors, of whom 3,000 had individual portfolios of over $50,000 each. Another 30,000 had accounts that averaged around $50 each, and 15,000 other investors had small accounts averaging less than $5 each. But the total amount saved was $57 million. This compared with ordinary commercial banks of the era, for which depositors possessed accounts averaging $215 each. The different amounts saved give some idea of how difficult it was for blacks to invest their meager incomes, but it also illustrates that they were trying as hard as they could to enter the American investment dream.

A sampling of the background of the African American investors as of 1870 reveals a different picture than what the bank started off with in 1865. Originally much of the bank's business was among black soldiers. But five years later the investors represent a cross section of the African American community during Reconstruction. Forty percent of the depositors were farmers. The next largest group (25 percent) included unskilled laborers and domestics. Next were the artisans, who accounted for about 15 percent of the total. Next came the local savings "societies," many of them church related and benevolent in nature, over 70 of which were from Charleston, South Carolina, alone. Only about 5 percent of the depositors were business and professional people, mostly politicians, journalists, teachers, and ministers. The by-laws of the bank prevented investing money in black businesses early on, and the directors refused to consider such investment later; thus, the money local blacks saved was largely lost in its effect on the development of the black community.

The new board of directors did not wait long to do as it pleased with this tidy sum. These men took advantage of the inexperience of blacks involved in the bank's operation (there were 21 black cashiers—seven from the North—all of whom had been free before the war) to invest in real estate of doubtful value and to waste deposits on the erection of fancy bank offices, rather than investing in government bonds and other more conservative securities. Funds were largely invested in high-risk loans and investments that would return more interest (unless, of course, the investments folded). Speculative stocks and mortgages became the norm for the bank's holdings. The new directors also entered an agreement with the powerful Jay Cooke and Company, whose boss who had won the title of financier of the Union war effort. Cooke's bankers began to raid the Freedmen's Savings bank of its quality investments; they dumped their own poorer investments into the freedmen's portfolios. The black bank also invested much deposit money in the District of Columbia, which wasted it in political patronage schemes involving dubious internal improvements.

Even though some congressmen had their doubts about the new charter (they ought to have known what was happening, given their own corrupt tendencies), Congress neglected to check up on the Freedmen's Savings Bank's operations until 1873. By then it was too late. The nation had slumped into the lengthy economic panic of 1873 (which would last five years or more), and one of the first victims was none other than Jay Cooke and Company, disastrously overextended in railroads that had gone broke. The comptroller of the U.S. Treasury, John J. Knox, found that the Freedmen's Savings Bank was rife with fraud and ill-conceived banking practices. Many records were a mess, others were nonexistent. By the time a second investigation was made, the bank had suffered three runs on its resources by creditors and depositors that consumed $1.8 million. Bank directors began to liquidate their own accounts while actively soliciting more from blacks throughout the South.

With a portfolio that consisted of outstanding loans from companies that had gone broke in the economic depression, drained assets that had gone to its directors rather than the depositors, and poorly kept records and outright errors in bookkeeping ($40,000 could not be found at all), the Freedmen's Savings Bank was in deep trouble. The directors elected Frederick Douglass to the board in 1874, and he sent a quieting telegram to the Southern depositors before he actually realized the extent of the trouble in Washington. After examining the various congressional investigations documents, Douglass changed his stand and warned blacks not to send any more money to the bank. Under Douglass's prodding, Congress passed a law designed to separate the past and future operations of the bank. Nine days later the Freedmen's Savings Bank folded, too far gone to take advantage of any new situation. Over 61,000 depositors lost nearly $3 million of savings.

It was a staggering blow to Southern blacks. Even though various comptrollers of the U.S. Treasury (one of whom, appointed by Grover Cleveland, was William L. Trenholm, former Confederate secretary of the treasury and the only one who sought to funnel money out of wasted administrative efforts to return something to the small depositors) tried to get Congress to buy out the African American depositors dollar for dollar, nothing came of their efforts. Black politicians like Representative Joseph H. Rainey of South Carolina and Senator Blanche K. Bruce of Mississippi failed to gain further consideration of saving the bank. Many depositors lost their life's savings, not to mention a loss of self-respect (Southern whites unfairly gloated that the situation proved African Americans were unready for freedom) and a loss of their trust in banks, regardless of their management. The divorce of philanthropy from the bank, its greedy directors, and the loss of the clients' savings had unnecessarily harmed a proud drive toward self-sufficiency and assimilation. The experience left a legacy of suspicion and failure that remained a hot issue in the black community well into the twentieth century.

See also Bruce, Blanche K.; Grant and Domestic Policy; Grant and the Scandals; Rainey, Joseph H.

References Fleming, Walter Lynwood, *The Freedmen's Savings Bank* (1927); Gilbert, Abby L., "The Comptroller of the Currency and the Freedmen's Savings Bank" (1972); Lindsay, Arnett G., "The Negro in Banking" (1929); Osthaus, Carl R., *Freedmen, Philanthropy and Fraud* (1976); Story, Ronald D., "'That Damned Pack of Sharpers'" (1977).

Garfield, James A. (1831–1881)

The last American president who could claim birth in a log cabin, James A. Garfield, whose father died when he was but two years old, grew up in an atmosphere of poverty and uncertainty. He worked hard as a youth, and by the time he reached 30 had managed to scrape together an education that included public school and college. He had married and even won a seat in the Ohio state legislature by the onset of the Civil War. A lifelong lay preacher among the Disciples of Christ, Garfield was an outstanding speaker. The state of Ohio sent him out to recruit soldiers. But Garfield wanted more, so he helped raise and then command the Forty-second Ohio Volunteer Infantry. Although he was not a military man by training, he had an ability to read and understand books on drill and tactics, making him a most credible civilian soldier. He won a battle as the head of a brigade and fought on the second day of the Battle of Shiloh. Promoted to brigadier, Garfield served on the court-martial of Fitz John Porter (a famous Union general accused and convicted of not obeying orders on the field of Second Manassas) before his health collapsed and he went home on furlough.

After a brief rest Garfield returned to the front with the Army of the Cumberland. Maj. Gen. William Rosecrans gave him a choice of assignments—Garfield could have his brigade back or be the general's chief of staff. Garfield chose the latter as more challenging and useful in advancing his career. As chief of staff, Garfield created a good intelligence operation that allowed the Army of the Cumberland to capture Chattanooga without firing a shot. But the system broke down as Rosecrans constantly changed position and moved into Georgia. The result was the disastrous Battle of Chickamauga that nearly cost Rosecrans his whole army. Driven back to Chattanooga and besieged, Rosecrans was replaced by the only Union hero the Army of the Cumberland had, George Thomas. Garfield skill-fully kept his own reputation separate from that of Rosecrans by accepting responsibility for nothing; he managed to emerge with a clean slate and a promotion to major general. He quickly resigned his military position before prying eyes found out the truth about his role at Chickamauga and accepted election to the U.S. House of Representatives from his home district. As President Abraham Lincoln put it, he could make dozens of major generals but loyal administration Republican politicians were in short supply.

Garfield now had a position that he would be returned to eight times in the succeeding years. He was very popular in his home district and an able supporter of coercion of the South during the rest of the war and Reconstruction. He ably jockeyed for position on the committees on appropriations and ways and means to be able to take over the House floor leadership after the death of party leader Thaddeus Stevens in 1868. Working hand in hand with the new Republican Senate leader, James G. Blaine of Maine, Garfield stood for resumption of specie (gold) payments on greenbacks (paper money) and a moderate tariff policy. But his leadership career was marred by two scandals. Garfield's name was on the bribery list of the Crédit Mobilier railroad scandal, and he was mentioned for receiving kickbacks in the DeGolyer paving contract for the District of Columbia. Garfield explained away the Crédit Mobilier link as untrue (there was no other proof), but the DeGolyer accusation stuck. Nonetheless, his reserve of popularity was such that he managed to win reelection in 1874. By the end of Reconstruction Garfield was ready to become House speaker as a part of the Compromise of 1877, and by 1880 he wanted the vacant U.S. Senate seat; the venerable Ohio senator John Sherman, then in the Rutherford B. Hayes cabinet, wanted the presidency.

But the tables were turned on both men in the ensuing Republican national convention. Deadlocked among several presidential choices including Sherman, the delegates decided to choose a "dark horse" candidate, Garfield himself. Sherman was outraged because Garfield had already won the Senate seat weeks before and still held his House seat, too. But Garfield mollified Sherman by resigning both seats and allowing the latter to return to the Senate as Garfield prepared to run for the presidency against Democrat Winfield Scott Hancock. In a close race, Garfield became chief executive, but only with the reluctant support of former president Ulysses S. Grant (who had wanted a third term and was angry with Garfield for preventing it) and Senator Roscoe G. Conkling of New York, a Grant supporter. As president, Garfield faced insurmountable problems in juggling appointments between the two Republican party factions, the Stalwarts (remnants of the old Radical Republicans but without the idealism; led by Conkling) and the Half-Breeds (remnants of the old Liberal Republicans; led by Senator Blaine), both of which sought appointments to the exclusion of the other.

By selecting Blaine as secretary of state, Garfield seemed to indicate that he favored the Half-Breeds, even though he had accepted Conkling's right-hand man, Chester A. Arthur, as vice president. Conkling then proceeded to block senatorial approval of the president's choices for federal positions in New York state through a process called "senatorial courtesy," which meant that the Senate would accept no one unless the U.S. senators from the state in question approved. This petty argument stagnated government business throughout the summer of 1881, which prompted Garfield to make a political tour of various Northern states to cement his support. Intending to visit Williams College in Massachusetts, from which he had graduated, Garfield went down to the Washington railroad station to board the presidential train. Out of the crowd came a disappointed office-seeker, Charles J. Giteau, who shot and mortally wounded Garfield, screaming, "I am a Stalwart and Arthur is president now!" Garfield lingered on for 11 weeks before passing away. His assassination (the second of a president in American history) silenced much criticism and led to laudatory biographies that have covered up any character flaws, securing for him a martyr's role in the eyes of future generations.

See also Election of 1876 and Compromise of 1877.

References Paxon, Frederic L., "James Abram Garfield" (1964–1981); Peskin, Allan, *Garfield* (1978); Smith, Theodore C., *The Life and Letters of James Abram Garfield* (1925); Taylor, John M., *Garfield of Ohio* (1970).

Grant, [Hiram] Ulysses Simpson (1822–1885)

Hiram Ulysses Grant was born at Point Pleasant, Ohio, on 27 April 1822. He came from a solid middle-class family; his father was a farmer and a tanner, a trade to which the young Grant never warmed. Biographers used to talk of Grant's miserable youth, his happiness allegedly hampered by his braggart father, who kept reminding him of his boyhood blunders. But nowadays historians think that Grant's childhood was never so unhappy. He was an excellent horseman by nature, and neighbors liked to have him tame horses for them. He was a fine rider and teamster at an early age. He attended local schools and academies and had a fairly good education for his day. His father was a local politician of sorts, a talent he would never let go of, and he managed to get his son an appointment at West Point—a free education and one of the best then available.

It is said that Grant took a look at his trunk around the time of the appointment and realized his initials spelled out "HUG." He was aware of the penchant of cadets to make up nicknames, so he asked Congressman Thomas L. Hamer to put him down on the appointment sheet as "Ulysses Hiram Grant." But Hamer could not remember the "Hiram" part—everybody called Grant "Ulyss" anyhow—so he registered the boy as "Ulysses Simpson," (Simpson being his mother's maiden name). Grant arrived at West Point, signed in as "Ulysses Hiram Grant," and was informed that no such name was on the roll. There was a "Ulysses

Simpson Grant," however. Grant, ever practical with nonsensical regulations, scratched out his signature and scrawled "U. S. Grant"—and so he stayed the rest of his life. His nickname was "Sam," as in "Uncle Sam"—he could live with that.

Grant did well at West Point. He excelled in horsemanship, was above average in mathematics and engineering, and survived the rest of the course to graduate twenty-first out of 39 in 1843. In those days one did not receive a commission as a second lieutenant automatically. A vacancy had to open up somewhere in the small U.S. Army first. So he became a brevet second lieutenant, a temporary appointment, in the Fourth Infantry, and he was sent off to Jefferson Barracks near St. Louis. There he met a local planter's daughter, Julia Dent, whom he married when he came home from Mexico. He finally received a full second lieutenancy in the Eighth Infantry and was shipped off to Texas to guard against Mexican intrusions over the Rio Grande into the disputed area south of the Nueces. In this capacity he fought under Maj. Gen. Zachary Taylor in the early battles of the Mexican War. He learned from the ragged-looking Taylor that calmness under fire and solid thinking meant more than spit and polish in a general.

When the main U.S. campaign against Mexico City was launched, Grant's regiment was transferred to Maj. Gen. Winfield Scott's command. Grant served as Scott's regimental supply officer and learned that an army supply line did not have to stretch to a base (which could be attacked) if the force could live off the country. Scott also showed that having a little imagination and not letting the enemy spook you could pay off big dividends in a campaign. Grant learned from both Taylor and Scott that one must not allow oneself to get involved with civilian policy decisions—a matter that cost both generals much worry in Mexico. Grant also showed himself to be a brave officer, hauling a small cannon into one of the custom house towers outside Mexico City to cover the infantry assault.

Returning home to marry Julia, Grant served with his regiment at Sackett's Harbor, New York, and then was transferred to the Pacific coast. He could not afford to take Julia with him, and in California the lonely captain (having been promoted for bravery in Mexico) took to drink. He became an embarrassment to his colonel, Robert C. Buchanan, a stickler for military discipline and a man who disliked the young officer from time they had both been in St. Louis. Buchanan offered Grant a choice of court-martial or resignation. The homesick captain turned in his commission and went back to Julia. In Missouri Grant worked hard as a farmer and businessman but was wiped out in the panic of 1857. So he went back to his parents's home, now in Galena, Illinois, and worked in his father's store, a humiliating experience.

When the Civil War came, Grant thought enough of his own abilities to ask for a regimental command; through his congressman, Elihu Washburn, he became colonel of the Twenty-first Illinois Volunteer Infantry. His ability to turn this raw company of men into a top-notch regiment impressed the right people (Congressman Washburne saw to that), and President Abraham Lincoln made him a brigadier general. Grant was on his way to fame. He was very lucky, one of the qualities of any good officer, because he got to work his way up from smaller to bigger unit command and from skirmishes to battles. Thus he gained his experience in nice little steps that allowed him to digest the lessons he gained from command. He also happened to be in the right place at the right time to make an impact on the course of the war. His opponents happened to be pretty poor early in the war, which helped him a great deal, as at Ft. Donelson, where he became the first Union general to capture a whole enemy army. His terms to the Confederates, "unconditional surrender," not only jibed with his initials but also made for good news copy.

Grant kept moving south into the Tennessee and Cumberland valleys, where he was surprised by the Rebel army at Shiloh Church near Pittsburgh Landing, Tennessee. Although Grant's men took a shellacking on

Ulysses S. Grant

the first day, he kept his cool and drove the Confederates back a day later, holding the field. Rumors that Grant was drunk (he was not) caused Lincoln to ask his administration what brand of whiskey it was so he could send a barrel to his other generals. Lincoln refused to sack Grant. "He fights," was the president's simple analysis. Instead Grant got a promotion to major general and the task of taking the Confederate fortress at Vicksburg. He kept at the project the better part of a year, finally cutting loose from his supply line and (like Scott in Mexico) moving around the Rebels's south flank to bottle them up in the city. The city fell after a short siege on Independence Day, the day after the Union victory at Gettysburg. Grant had captured his second Confederate field army. Later that same year, after Yankee defeats south of Chattanooga, Grant transferred there, broke the Rebel siege of the town, and routed their army.

By now, it had become obvious to the men at Washington that Grant had to be brought east to fight the Confederacy's first team, Robert E. Lee's Army of Northern Virginia. At the same time he became lieutenant general and commander of all Union armies. He decided to accompany the Army of the Potomac in the field, both to avoid Washington politics and to keep an eye on the fight against Lee. Although the Richmond campaign of 1864 was a frustrating experience for Grant, he never lost sight of his objective. Despite losing nearly 100,000 casualties (earning him the nickname "butcher," although he actually lost fewer men proportionally than Lee during the war), Grant kept moving southward and managed to bottle Lee up in Petersburg. It would take nine months to force Lee into the open and corner his force at Appomattox Courthouse through a brilliant campaign of rapid maneuvering. Lee's surrender marked the third time a Confederate field force had given up to the man whose pre–Civil War experiences one historian characterized as "40 years of failure." Now he was the hero of the Northern war effort.

The Civil War had made Grant. Although the nation was plunged into despair by Lincoln's assassination, Grant allowed it to revive itself by honoring him. He reviewed the massed armies in Washington in May 1865 and toured the North, receiving several college degrees and the plaudits of a grateful nation. During Reconstruction Grant at first favored President Andrew Johnson's go-easy plan. He toured the Southeast for the president and reported favorably on the willingness of the South's leaders to come back into the Union and recognize the results of the war. But as Johnson and Congress came to blows over the course of Reconstruction, Grant began to change his course. In the 1866 "Swing around the Circle," when Johnson took Grant and other dignitaries around the country with him to campaign for Democratic congressmen, Grant backed off halfway through the trip and abandoned the president to his fate. He also deeply resented the president's effort to involve him in the squabble over the Tenure of Office Act, which was enacted to prevent Johnson from removing political appointees favored by the Radical Republicans.

When the Republicans failed to convict Johnson during his impeachment, they began to look around for a candidate who could unite the North behind their Reconstruction efforts. Nominated by acclamation, Grant handily beat his Democratic opponent in the electoral vote, although the popular vote was quite close. As president, Grant made a good general. His inexperience in civil administration, his lack of political finesse, and his reticence made him defer to Congress in most matters. However, he tended to defer too much to his supposed friends, and the result was that his administration was tainted with corruption from the start. For cabinet positions he tended to pick businessmen who little understood government. He appointed them much as a general would his staff, rarely asking them if they could serve and often overlooking their lack of qualifications or conflicts of interest. His Reconstruction program brought the South back into the nation but led to the army's policing a series of "rotten boroughs" whose votes went to the highest bidder. Accused by many modern writers of being a racist, Grant had one distinction above most of his day—he honestly believed in equal rights under the law. He just was not a good enough politician to bring it all off. And that remains his tragedy. Sometimes decency is not enough. By the end of his eight years, Grant's reputation as president had been stained so badly that he has yet to recover, historically speaking.

Some of his cronies spoke of a third term, and Grant himself wanted one because he was flat broke. After a prolonged world tour, he retired to New York and went into private business. His success was no better than before the war. Heavily in debt, the heavy smoking-Grant learned that he was stricken with oral and throat cancer. He had received many boxes of cigars as gifts during the war from a grateful North, and the shy Grant took up smoking so as not to offend his public. The habit had finally caught up with him. He wrote his memoirs to clear up his debts and leave his family with something after his passing, even though Congress had restored him to his rank and voted him a pension. He wrote under tremendous pain, valiantly holding on until the task was finished. Edited by Mark Twain, who found Grant to be a natural writer, the memoirs became a best-seller. But Grant died in July 1885 before their publication and was interred in the great mausoleum at Riverside Park in New York City overlooking the Hudson.

See also Grant and Domestic Policies; Grant and the Presidency; Grant and Reconstruction; Grant and the Scandals; Johnson and Reconstruction; Moderate Republicans and Reconstruction; Radical Republicans and Reconstruction.

References Carpenter, John A., *Ulysses S. Grant* (1970); Catton, Bruce, "The Generalship of U. S. Grant" (1964), *Grant Moves South* (1960), *Grant Takes Command* (1969), and *U. S. Grant and the American Military Tradition* (1954); Current, Richard N., "Grant without Greatness" (1981) and "President Grant and the Continuing Civil War" (1981); Fuller, J.F.C., *The Generalship of U. S. Grant* (1958); Goldhurst, Richard, *Many Are the Hearts* (1975); Grant, Ulysses S., *Personal Memoirs of U. S. Grant* (1886); Grant, Ulysses S., III, *Ulysses S. Grant* (1969); Hagerman, Edward, *The American Civil War and the Origins of Modern Warfare* (1988); Hesseltine, William B., *Ulysses S. Grant: Politician* (1935); Lewis, Lloyd, *Captain Sam Grant* (1950); Mantell, Martin E., *Johnson, Grant, and the Politics of Reconstruction* (1973); McFeely, William S., *Grant* (1991); Richter, William L., "The Papers of U. S. Grant" (1990, 1992); Simpson, Brooks D., "Butcher? Racist?" (1987) and *Let Us Have Peace* (1991); Zilversmit, Arthur, "Grant and the Freedmen" (1986).

Grant, U.S., and Domestic Policies

The Civil War caused a tremendous business expansion in the North, the problems of which came to a head during the Ulysses S. Grant administration and would result in big business becoming a major voice in the Republican party once dominated by farmers and small businessmen. The two problems of concern to business at this time were taxes and the tariff on foreign imports. The war had caused all taxes to rise precipitously and new ones, like the income tax, to be imposed. At the same time the Republicans had elevated the tariff to new heights as part of their political platform. Now that the war was over, Americans expected relief on both accounts. Everyone wanted taxes reduced, but the tariff was another matter. Business and labor groups wanted to keep out goods from lower-wage-paying producers overseas in favor of better profits to American owners and higher wages to American workers.

Grant appointed a special tax commission under David A. Wells, a professional economist once considered as a possible secretary of the treasury. Grant had promised lower taxes in his inaugural message and pledged economy in government to help reduce costs (a common promise for an incoming administration). The Wells committee took a look at the taxes and suggested that nearly all be repealed or reduced dramatically. This was very good publicity for the Republicans and raised their esteem among the voters. But Wells also suggested that the protective tariff be cut to nothing. He said that the tariff did not so much protect American infant industries from unfair foreign competition as it permitted existing industries to raise prices to just under the tariff costs to foreign competitors for extra unearned profits. Wells correctly saw that the difference came out of the pockets of American consumers.

The Republican Congress thanked Wells for his concern and lowered taxes as he suggested. But it kept the high tariff intact. It was too big a pork barrel issue—too many people of influence in the party were making money off the tariff differential. They all banded together and voted for the tariff to protect themselves and their colleagues. The Republicans were not above playing the tariff card in a wholly arbitrary manner. For example, they cut all tariffs 10 percent in 1872 to help Republican congressmen win their seats and then raised it back up after the victory. The tariff would continue to be a political football until the New Deal of the 1930s, when Congress turned the tariff-making powers over to the president, who used it as a treaty-making device through the Department of State.

Along with the tariff, civil service reform was a hot issue during the Grant years and after. Ever since the days of Andrew Jackson (in the 1830s) the so-called spoils system

had been in operation with respect to government jobs on all levels. Jackson had theorized that anyone could work for the government—it took no special skills to push a pencil and file papers—and that for the sake of democracy the principle of "rotation in office" ought to be practiced. This meant that incoming administrations fired all prior appointees for their own people. It was a great device to give the general public a stake in the outcome of elections and guarantee party loyalty. If a congressman did not vote a party line, someone else would get the patronage to his district. If the voter did not vote right, he could kiss the local postmaster's job goodbye. (In those days there was no secret ballot; one voted by public declaration at the polling place—which was often dangerous because thugs from both sides supervised the process and administered punishment on the spot.)

There had been much criticism of this winner-take-all approach to government jobs. The problem got so bad that each election caused a hiatus in government services as the incoming new appointees took over and learned the job. Different succeeding presidents of the same party cleaned out their predecessor's job seekers, regardless of party loyalty. Critics suggested that government jobs were more technical than Jackson had reckoned and that skills needed to be known to function in them efficiently. Besides, jobs went to party contributors or were bought by competitive bidding that led to much corruption. Civil service reform became an imperative for honest government, although cynics would deem honest government an oxymoron.

The first improvement was to put forth merit examinations rather than party affiliation as the basis for acquiring government jobs. This system had been introduced in various European countries to great effect, and American intellectuals wanted a similar improvement here. After all, the role of government was increasing and becoming more important year by year. The number of government slots had nearly tripled from the beginning of Abraham Lincoln's administration in 1861 to the end of Grant's in 1877. Grant seemed to agree with this assessment. At first he appointed people only to offices that had become vacant through death or resignation. But Grant's appointees were usually old army buddies or relatives from his wife's family, the Dents, whose number appeared legion to neutral observers. And Congress did not like this approach. If they couldn't offer government jobs, how were they to pay off all the dedicated campaign workers and monetary contributors? Congress found especially offensive the fact that Grant's father, Jesse, came to Washington and sought to control patronage on behalf of his many friends. Indeed, if a civil service exam were instituted, commentators suggested, its only questions would be: "Were you a contributor to any of President Grant's three homes?" and "Are you a member of the Dent family or otherwise connected by blood or marriage to General Grant?"

Grant indicated that he would be open to a deal on civil service appointments—a fairly astute move for a man considered to be too apolitical as president. If Congress would modify the Tenure of Office Act, which limited presidential powers of appointment, he would consult with congressmen on local appointments. So Congress allowed him the right to remove executive officials more freely without resort to the act's advice-and-consent provision unless it found the change to be especially offensive. And Grant wound up approving as many as 150 appointments a day to local machine positions in consultation with the appropriate congressman, much to everyone's glee on Capitol Hill. But certain Republican reformers (who would later bolt the party as Liberal Republicans in 1872) wanted more. They introduced a civil service reform bill into the Senate, where it languished, bottled up in committee by the spoilsmen.

Grant ignored the old pols in the Senate and went ahead and established an independent Civil Service Commission under an executive order. It was headed by George W. Curtis of *Harper's Weekly*, an influential national illustrated news magazine, and Joseph Medill of the Chicago *Tribune*, the

Middle West's most important newspaper. Both men were active reformers who had trumpeted the civil service issue before the American public. Grant figured that if they wanted to see something done, they ought to do it themselves. The report of the Civil Service Commission arrived in the White House in December 1871. It recommended that federal jobs be classified and that each class be divided into two grades. All positions should be filled by competitive exam. Promotions would also be made based on a competency test. No political assessments would be levied against any appointee by any political group. Grant announced that the commission's report seemed fair to him. The problem was that most positions of importance still had political input and came under the advice and consent of the Senate. Although Grant offered to continue the commission's mandate, both Curtis and Medill realized that he would do little actively to encourage change. Neither Congress nor the public was sufficiently aroused, which postponed the matter until the assassination of James A. Garfield in 1881 by a disappointed office-seeker changed everyone's perceptions.

However, the first assault against public confidence in business and government came in 1873, well before the death of Garfield. The obvious corruption in government, the overextension of investors in railroad stocks of dubious quality, the overbuilding of transcontinental railroads, and the withdrawal of silver from circulation caused a major economic contraction and the failure of several New York banking firms, particularly Jay Cooke and Company. Cooke, known as the "financier of the Civil War," the exclusive seller of government war bonds, and a major contributor to Republican campaign funds, was overextended in Northern Pacific Railroad stock and could not meet his debts. In his wake there was a run on banks throughout the nation, and some 5,000 businesses worth a total of over $2.28 million failed. The panic of 1873, as the depression came to be known, saw Grant suggest a revolutionary concept for the first time in American history—that the government employ the poor to save them from ruination. But the idea was 60 years ahead of its time and was dismissed in Congress as the ranting of a naive general who did not understand reality.

The contraction of the economy meant that the Republican pledge to pay off the war bonds in gold was a heavier burden than usual. Following the rejection of Grant's suggestion of full employment, the public demanded that the government do something inflationary to relieve the stress. This naturally led to a reexamination of the money question. Next to Reconstruction, the money question was the hottest issue of the era. It had originated during the Civil War, when the Lincoln administration had taken the nation off the gold standard and began to pay its debts in paper currency called greenbacks (referring to the color of the back of the bill). Over $450 million in paper currency was issued in 1862 and 1863 alone, and this created a whole series of problems. First, great inflation reduced the value of the paper dollar by half. Then there was the problem of whether the government would make the greenbacks as good as gold after the war. Finally, the money question also concerned Civil War bonds. The bonds were issued in such a manner as to throw into question the manner in which they were to be paid off. They were 5-20 bonds, which meant that one could receive their face value in 5 years or hold them 20 years and get face value plus 6 percent interest. The law guaranteed that the interest would be paid in gold, but it was silent as to how the principle would be repaid. Many people favored the suggestion of Ohio congressman George Pendleton to pay off the principal in inflated paper dollars. This "Ohio Idea" had the slogan "The dollar that paid the soldier can pay the bondholder." But the Republican platform under which Grant was elected pledged to pay off both principal and interest in gold. Grant refused to back down from this promise because doing so would affect the reputation of the U.S. government as a borrower in the future. In 1869, Congress backed Grant up with the Public Credit Act, which said that the bonds would be paid in gold or its equivalent, nothing less.

But the bond question was an adjunct to the real debate, which was over the greenbacks themselves. As Grant well knew, there were two schools of thought on greenbacks. The first involved the soft money people. These advocates were against resumption (that is, making the greenbacks equal to gold and taking them out of circulation gradually as they were redeemed; this would contract the currency available in the economy). They preferred to keep the greenbacks in circulation to keep the money supply more flexible and slightly inflationary. This would help debtors, who could pay back their loans in paper worth less than when they borrowed it. Several groups supported greenbacks. Politicians, mostly Democrats, wanted to get away from the perennial Reconstruction issue and back into the economic questions that had been so good to the party before the Civil War. Oddly enough, some Republicans (especially small businessmen backed by the Radicals) stood with the Democrats on this issue because of the middle-class origins of their constituents.

Grant was aware that some businessmen also favored a flexible currency, especially those on the make who need to borrow to succeed. Moderate inflation would make those debts easier to pay back. Labor also favored greenbacks because their presence eased up on credit and made loans easier to pay back. They believed that this would give them an edge over the normally usurious bankers. Then there were the farmers, who traditionally had been against greenbacks, but the Civil War had changed that. To succeed farmers now had to invest large sums in the new machines of agriculture: steam tractors, threshers, and cutting devices. Because of the lousy weather and poor crop prices that followed the war, farmers had gone from being creditors to debtors. They believed that the low prices were being set by gold-minded bankers and sought to attack the bankers through easier credit and cheaper money. It was a fight that would see its nineteenth-century culmination in the 1890s with the agrarian radicals known as Populists.

The second school of thought on the money issue during Grant's presidency was the hard money interest. These people favored specie (actual coin minted from precious metals, usually gold alone because silver was somewhat inflationary). There were all sorts of way to get the United States back on the gold standard, including redeeming paper on a one-to-one basis with gold and then retiring the paper, but the gold bugs (as they were called) preferred that it be done quickly, cheaply, and as painlessly as possible. They too had several groups that supported their view. First came the Protestant churches. Hard money represented virtue and honesty. It was not right to borrow a dollar worth 100 cents and pay it back years later with dollars worth 50 cents (or whatever amount). Other individuals in favor of hard money were academics, especially economists. At that time economic theory was closely related to religion in that it had a strong moral strain and was classified as "moral philosophy." These men believed that capital (goods that made goods) was more important than money supply.

As Grant found out, the reformers of the era also stood behind hard money. These men were Liberal Republicans during Grant's terms and were later labeled "mugwumps." They saw easy money as the root of all evil when it came to tempting politicians to go bad. They, too, wished to restore a moral one to society and purge it of all corruptions, of which easy money was one. They tended to be based in New England and centered at Harvard University. Finally, certain businessmen were for hard money. These included bankers, merchants, and textile manufacturers—generally men who were owed money. These were established businessmen, not ones in search of success. They had their wealth and intended to keep it. Many were engaged in international trade, where gold was critical as a common unit of value among all currencies. This was the position of the National Board of Trade, for example.

In the middle of the soft money/hard money fight stood President Grant. He saw Republicans on both sides of an issue that threatened to split party and country, especially after the panic of 1873 sent the debate to a fever pitch. Secretary of the Treasury Hugh McCulloch, a Republican who had served under Lincoln and Johnson, had been retiring greenbacks gradually since 1867. But the soft money people wanted this stopped. Grant's proposed solution was to make greenbacks equal to gold. This would keep an inflationary amount of money in circulation but make it stable in value. It gave a little to both sides, again demonstrating that Grant was not an entirely inept politician.

But before he could get Congress to go along, the Supreme Court stepped into the question with the *Legal Tender* cases. The court's chief justice at this time was Salmon P. Chase, former secretary of the treasury under Lincoln and a man constantly with his eye on the presidency. Chase had written the law in 1862 that created the greenbacks. But he was always suspicious of them, acting in their favor only as an extreme war measure. He now decided to play for hard money support. In the case *Hepburn v. Griswold* (1871), he led the court in writing the majority decision that declared greenbacks to be legal tender only for debts contracted after 1862. The implication was that greenbacks might be of doubtful value even after that time, although the case stated otherwise.

The indecisiveness of the *Hepburn* case could not be allowed to continue. If greenbacks were later declared illegal for all debts, payments after 1862 would have to be renegotiated and repaid—just as those contracted before 1862 and paid off in greenbacks would now have to be reworked. However, it so happened that the Hepburn case had been decided by a court that was two members short. Grant had appointed William Strong and Joseph P. Bradley to the bench before the *Hepburn* case, but they had been unable to take their seats in time to participate. In 1871 another case, *Knox v. Lee*, arrived before the highest bench in the land. This time, with Strong and Bradley participating, the court reversed itself, the ever-flexible Chase again with the majority. In the Knox case, the court did the common-sense thing and ruled that greenbacks were legal tender for all debts. The court left it up to Congress as to what the greenbacks were worth compared to gold. Because the votes of Strong and Bradley were critical to the new ruling, Grant was accused of packing the court. This was not so. The president had appointed the two men with other considerations in mind before their views on money were known.

The court decisions threw the money issue back into the political area. In response to the panic of 1873, Congress passed the Inflation Bill in 1874. This would have increased the number of greenbacks in circulation to alleviate the worst effects of the depression. But Grant vetoed this measure, saying it was too late. He essentially used the Protestant moral argument. But by his actions he froze the money supply. Congress tried to override his veto but failed. Trying a different tack, Congress passed the Banking Act of 1874, which shifted some existing paper from East to West, where the short money supply had hit people hardest. Because it did not increase the existing supply, Grant signed the measure into law. But something had to be done to unite the Republican party over the money question in the election of 1876. The result was what Grant had originally proposed at the beginning of his administration. In the Resumption Act, Congress provided that all greenbacks already in circulation would be kept until 1 January 1879. Then they could be redeemed in gold. But for each $80 of greenbacks turned in, $100 in new federal bank notes could be issued. This gave the money a gold base and a moderate inflation and took the money issue out of the 1876 contest, much to the Republicans' relief.

After the election of 1876, the money question cropped up again and played a part in the not-too-cozy alliance of Republicans and Southern Democrats that got Hayes elected as part of the Compromise of 1877. In 1873 the Republicans had taken silver out of circulation in the Silver Demonitization

Act. This step, one of deflation in the midst of depression, received the onus of being remembered among soft money people as "the Crime of '73." A myth arose, initiated by Maine Republican George Weston, that a Jewish banker, Ernest Seyd, had bought off Congress with a half million dollars so that foreign bondholders would be paid off in gold instead of paper or silver. This led to a conspiracy theory about U.S. gold reserves being sold off to foreign Jews. In reality Congress demonitized silver in response to a money theory known as Gresham's law, which states that when two metals are in circulation, the cheaper will drive the dearer out. Interested in protecting gold, Congress dropped the cheaper silver coins.

But with the Compromise of 1877 and the return of home rule to the white South, Southern Democrats decided that they could come out in favor of economic inflation. This was contrary to the understanding of the compromise, but the Southerners did not think that the Republicans were keeping their end of the bargain, either. The result was a rejuvenated Democratic party and the passage of the Bland-Allison Act in 1878. This act reintroduced silver coins as legal tender for all debts but kept the ratio of silver to gold at 16:1 to undercut the fears of Gresham's law. Hayes vetoed the measure, but the Democrats repassed it over his protest. When the Democrats threatened to repeal the Resumption Act and keep all greenbacks in circulation without a gold backing, Hayes and the Republicans compromised with them in the Fort Act, which kept resumption but permitted an extra $46 million to be kept in circulation after 1 January 1879, and redeemable in gold. By this time the effects of the panic of 1873 had eased, and the money issue declined in importance until the Populists brought it up again in the panic of 1893.

See also Election of 1876 and Compromise of 1877; Grant and the Presidency; Grant and Reconstruction; Grant and the Scandals.

References Barrett, Don C., *The Greenbacks and the Resumption of Specie Payments* (1931); Beale, Howard K., "The Tariff and Reconstruction"

(1929–1930); Coben, Stanley, "Northeastern Business and Radical Reconstruction" (1959–1960); Fairman, Charles, *Reconstruction and Reunion* (1971–1987); Friedman, Milton, and Anna Jacobson Schwartz, *A Monetary History of the United States* (1963); Graham, Frank D., "International Trade under Depreciated Paper" (1922); Hammond, Bray, *Sovereignty and an Empty Purse* (1970); Hesseltine, William B., *Ulysses S. Grant, Politician* (1935); Hoogenboom, Ari A., *Outlawing the Spoils* (1961); Hurst, James Willard, *A Legal History of Money in the United States* (1973); McFeeley, William S., *Grant* (1981); Nugent, Walter T. K., *The Money Question during Reconstruction* (1967); Schell, Herbert S., "Hugh McCulloch and the Treasury Department" (1931); Sharkey, Robert P., *Money, Class, and Party* (1959); Unger, Irwin, "Businessmen and Specie Resumption" (1959) and *The Greenback Era* (1964).

Grant, U.S., and the Presidency

Along with Zachary Taylor and Dwight D. Eisenhower, Ulysses S. Grant was one of the United States' three professional military men who served as president. Many others had military experience but were not career soldiers. They were generally professional politicians or came through the political world. All of the military presidents were similar in one salient respect—they did not understand the role of the presidency in American politics. They thought as top dog all they had to do was issue an order and it would be carried out. In politics, however, the order becomes a proposal that may never see the light of day.

Of the military presidents, Grant was especially ignorant of what the political world was like. By the time he caught on, a lot of bad mistakes had already been made. He started off with the mistaken belief that Congress was the sovereign voice of the people and that the president was merely their deputy. So when Congress spoke out on an issue, Grant felt obliged to go along with it and not throw in his opinion. Of course, the American system is predicated on the president combating Congress to reach a consensus. Like other military presidents Grant did relatively little with the power he had. He acted as if he were still a general in the army—he carried out the orders of his superiors, the civilian branch of

government. He was little more than an administrative officer. This was Grant's greatest tragedy as president, because he served at a time when Americans needed an imaginative executive to reconstruct the nation. Without Grant actively taking a role, his administration became bogged down in the morals (or lack thereof), economics, corruption, and submission to the desires of big business. Grant was too willing to do the bidding of others. Worst of all, he took the advice of the wrong people.

What Grant wanted was noble. He hoped to help the nation make a transition from war to peace, restore the currency, balance the budget, promote economic expansion, and reunite the North and South without sacrificing the position of black Americans as freed people in the process. What he found out was that the ways of government are tricky. The few decisions he made got twisted around as they progressed down the ladder of control and came out as unrecognizable from the policy he desired. Actually, the very purity of Grant's motives worked against him. He had to make deals with shabby politicians, whom he disliked, to get anywhere; by the time he understood how things worked it was too late. He had become a victim of the system.

An example of how Grant worked as president came to the fore almost immediately as he picked his cabinet. In making his appointments Grant did not consult with the party bigwigs or even with the men he chose. Many like to point to this as a sign of Grant's independence from the politicians. But the system worked by the politicians being able to funnel patronage to the deserving, those who supported the party with money or deeds. Grant angered both Republicans and Democrats by ignoring them. He also revealed that he was a novice who could be duped. Grant had two considerations when it came to choosing cabinet members: he wanted to act independently of both parties, and he did not want to be overshadowed by big names as he felt Abraham Lincoln had been with William H. Seward, Salmon P. Chase, Edwin M. Stanton, and others. (It did not occur to Grant that Lincoln had relished the challenge and believed that these men were most effective in their valuable posts, where he could keep and eye on them, rather than off somewhere making trouble independently.)

Grant got off to a bad start by giving two important cabinet posts out as personal compliments, with the understanding that the recipients would resign shortly. This was great for his old congressman, Elihu Washburn (who became secretary of state) and Maj. Gen. John Schofield (who took the position of secretary of war), but it cheapened the positions in the eyes of many, especially after Schofield left the post in one week! Washburn was not so abrupt, but eventually the posts went to two important men—the State Department to Hamilton Fish, arguably the single best appointment Grant ever made, and the War Department to John Rawlins, the most important person from Grant's old wartime staff. It was Rawlins who made Grant's military staff function and kept Grant on the straight and narrow concerning a multitude of questions, from slavery to not drinking. Perhaps the worst event of Grant's early presidency was Rawlins's unexpected death in 1869, which left Grant without the political skills that Rawlins possessed (and Grant lacked). Rawlins's presence would have undoubtedly made Grant a better president.

Grant delighted in springing cabinet positions upon the unsuspecting and unqualified. A. E. Borie, a Pennsylvania businessman, came into Washington to introduce some friends to the president. Grant asked him if he knew who the man from Pennsylvania was. Borie did not and ignored the question because it made no sense. The man was Borie himself, as he found out when he read his hometown newspaper and realized he had been nominated for secretary of the navy. He was not *asked* to serve; Grant gave him a order like a junior officer. Borie declined but then accepted after Grant called it a personal favor. Grant's candidate for the U.S. Treasury was department store magnate and party contributor A. T. Stewart. Grant thought a successful businessman

would save the country money through good management. But Stewart was ineligible to serve under an old law defining conflict of interest. Grant asked that he be exempted, but the Senate, led by Charles Sumner of Massachusetts, refused, hoping to teach Grant how important the Senate's advice and consent was.

With such a cavalier attitude, it was no wonder that Grant appointed 25 men (excluding Schofield and Stewart) to serve him in seven cabinet positions over his two terms. (This is comparable with 29 for Theodore Roosevelt in eight years, 25 for Franklin D. Roosevelt in thirteen years, and 23 for John Tyler in four years.) The Grant White House was known for its army camp atmosphere; indeed, his official wartime staff all received comparable positions under Grant as president. He was well aware how a commanding general ought to act, but he never really quite caught on to being a politician—although one of his main biographers thinks that he did better as president than might be expected in the long run.

See also Grant, [Hiram] Ulysses Simpson; Grant and Domestic Policies; Grant and Reconstruction; Grant and the Scandals.

References Carpenter, John A., *Ulysses S. Grant* (1970); Catton, Bruce, *U. S. Grant and the American Military Tradition* (1954); Current, Richard N., "Grant without Greatness" (1981); Grant, Ulysses S., III, *Ulysses S. Grant* (1969); Hesseltine, William B., *Ulysses S. Grant, Politician* (1935); McFeeley, William S., *Grant* (1991); Richter, William L., "The Papers of U. S. Grant" (1990 and 1992); Simpson, Brooks D., "Butcher? Racist?" (1987) and *Let Us Have Peace* (1991); Zilversmit, Arthur, "Grant and the Freedmen" (1986).

Grant, U.S., and Reconstruction

The one thing Grant wanted to do as president was complete what he had begun at Appomattox—to end the Civil War and reunite the nation. So he proceeded to hasten the completion of Reconstruction in those four states that had not finished the process by the summer of 1868. He also came out squarely behind the proposed Fifteenth Amendment. The election of 1868 had been marked by a discrepancy in African American voting rights in the North and

South. In the South, black males had the right to vote in all elections because of the Military Reconstruction Acts. In the North, however, state governments could decide the circumstances under which black males were allowed to vote, and in many Northern states blacks could not vote at all. There were all sorts of idealistic and practical political reasons to allow blacks the vote nationwide. If African Americans were good enough to serve 180,000 strong in the Union armies, they were good enough to vote. There was also the belief that everyone ought to have an equal chance in life under the law—it would help African Americans protect their freedom and other civil rights. And it would ensure the Republican party a source of reliable votes for years to come.

Grant was one of many who believed that the right to vote flowed from the willingness of blacks to serve in the war to gain their freedom and that it would help guarantee that Reconstruction's benefits would be lasting. He understood the political angle, too. But there was a catch—many close Northern states might go Democratic over the issue. Wisconsin, Michigan, Ohio, New York, Connecticut, and Kansas had already defeated proposals for universal male suffrage. It never even came to a vote in Indiana, Illinois, Pennsylvania, and New Jersey. Radicals like Thaddeus Stevens of Pennsylvania had granted African American males the right to vote in the District of Columbia in 1866, but the backlash against this step in 1867 caused the general push for a constitutional amendment to lag. But now Republicans figured that, if it were done quickly, the fervor against it would subside by the next presidential election. Republican politicians decided to take the chance that since there were relatively few blacks in the North, most of the effect would be to neutralize the hostile white vote in the South. The result was the Fifteenth Amendment, a proposal that did not grant the black vote so much as it restricted how the vote could be limited. Its negative wording would cause problems later.

The Fifteenth Amendment passed with much hostility in the North but with enthu-siasm in the South, which was happy to force the Yankees to live by their own reforms. The only part of the North that accepted the Fifteenth Amendment readily was New England. The only state in that region that did not like the amendment was Rhode Island—not because it disliked the black vote (which it had had since 1840) but because it did not wish to let the Irish into the polls. In the Border states, Tennessee refused to consider the amendment, Delaware and Kentucky rejected it, and Missouri and West Virginia passed it. In the Far West only Nevada passed it; California and Oregon rejected it out of fear the Chinese would get the vote. In the Middle West the amendment passed mostly as a party measure, particularly in states with a small black population. In the others a little political chicanery helped—Illinois, for example, passed it by voting without a legal quorum.

The key areas were Ohio, Indiana, Connecticut, and the Middle Atlantic states, where the Republicans and Democrats were nearly equally divided. This was the section of the country for which the Republicans wanted the Fifteenth Amendment, politically speaking. A small number of votes in the Republican column for these states would guarantee the party a victory in the future. The Republicans' loss in the elections of 1876 (in Connecticut, Indiana, and New York), 1884 (in the same three states), and 1894 (those three states plus Illinois) led to the Compromise of 1877 and two Grover Cleveland presidencies for the Democrats. Indeed, except for the time of Cleveland's terms, the Republican political strategy embodied in the Fifteenth Amendment held until 1912, when Woodrow Wilson took two terms. The black vote stayed Republican steadily until 1936, the time of Franklin D. Roosevelt's election to a second term, after which it has been firmly in the Democratic column to the present time.

But the close vote on the Fifteenth Amendment meant that the Republicans had to get four more states to ensure ratification. These states were the laggards in Southern Reconstruction: Virginia, Georgia, Mississippi, and Texas, not yet readmitted into the

Union. Each state was unique in its problems. Virginia had refused to approve of its Reconstruction constitution because the document provided for disfranchisement of Confederate military and civilian officials who had taken one oath to the United States and then a later one to the Confederacy. The purpose of that measure was to trim the number of white voters, who outnumbered African Americans and their white Radical allies. Maj. Gen. John Schofield told Virginia's state constitutional convention that disfranchisement would destroy the constitution in the eyes of the voters, but to no avail. However, he did convince President Grant, who supported submitting the constitution and the disfranchising sections separately. The voters accepted the constitution and rejected the disfranchisement clause. Then the Republican factions split evenly over the ensuing state election and a stalemate followed. Grant once again intervened in the process but in an oblique fashion by meeting with his old foe, Robert E. Lee. Although Grant made no public statement, the meeting was seen as an indication that all ought to follow Lee's more moderate course. The Conservative Republicans were elected and ratified the Fifteenth Amendment, ending Virginia's government under the Military Reconstruction Acts.

Unlike Virginia or any other Southern state, Georgia had the dubious privilege of being reconstructed twice. It had been readmitted along with six other states (the Carolinas, Florida, Alabama, Arkansas, and Louisiana) in the summer of 1868 after ratifying the Fourteenth Amendment. Then the conservative legislature (like Virginia, Georgia had a white majority of voters) refused to expel white members who held office in violation of the Fourteenth Amendment (the double-oath clause); rejected Republican favorites for U.S. senators (senators were voted on by the state legislatures until 1914); and expelled all of its black members. It also had the unmitigated gall to vote Democratic in the presidential election of 1868 and had an especially active branch of the Ku Klux Klan roaming the countryside. This led Congress to question the admissibility of Georgia's representatives and to expel them and return Georgia to the jurisdiction of the army. A board of military officers supervised the cleaning out of the legislature of illegally serving whites, the return of the legally elected blacks to the legislature and local offices, and the reelection of new Republican national representatives. In addition, while they were at it, Congress saw to it that the Georgia legislators ratified the pending Fifteenth Amendment.

After the Georgia fiasco, Grant came to doubt the loyalty of Moderate Republicans in the South. Too many of them had joined with Democrats to proscribe black rights. So Grant decided that he would support the more Radical Republicans hereafter, which affected the results in Mississippi and Texas. In Mississippi, an attempt had been made to disfranchise whites who had taken the double oath. But black delegates to the state constitutional convention refused to allow this attempt and helped vote it down as unfair. Moderate leaders, realizing that Grant was not too prone to see things their way after what had happened in Georgia, nonetheless decided to call his bluff. They put Lewis Dent, the president's brother-in-law, at the head of their statewide ticket. Grant was a great practitioner of nepotism, and the Moderates felt that he would not go against his own family member. But this was too blatant—to the point of insulting Grant's intelligence. Besides, his cabinet, especially Attorney General E. R. Hoar and Secretary of the Treasury George Boutwell (who had the distinction of being honest men to boot, unlike many of Grant's appointees), ardently supported Grant's desire to back Radicals. Grant wrote his brother-in-law, explained the political facts of life to him, and backed the Radicals' James L. Alcorn. Mississippi then ratified the Fourteenth and Fifteenth amendments and rejoined the Union in 1870.

Unlike Mississippi, where the registered voters were predominantly black, Texas was like Virginia and Georgia, where white registrants dominated the polls. The Texas state constitutional convention split over several issues. One was the Radical suggestion that Texas be divided into at least three states (an option allowed by the 1845 Treaty of Annexation). Another idea was to disfranchise anyone who could not take the ironclad oath (of never having aided the Confederacy) or who had taken the double oath. A third was that Radicals wanted all acts committed under the Confederate government declared null and void from their inception. This threatened to open a whole can of worms (including negating all marriages) that few wished to face. But the Radicals were adamant through two convention sessions that did little but prolong the debate and military rule.

Finally the convention adjourned without a constitution. Maj. Gen. E. R. S. Canby formed a board consisting of his aide and one Moderate and one Radical Republican to put a constitution together. Grant, meanwhile, decided to return an old West Point classmate, Maj. Gen. Joseph J. Reynolds, to Texas to replace the politically unreliable Canby, who was too fair. Reynolds switched patronage to the Radical Republicans, became acting provisional governor when Moderate Republican E. M. Pease resigned in disgust, counted in the Radicals during a controversial election that was noted for its irregularities, and then appointed all those who had been elected to office before Reconstruction ended so that he could force them all to take the ironclad oath. Reynolds replaced those who refused with loyal Radical appointees. The new legislature ratified the Fourteenth and Fifteenth amendments, and Texas rejoined the Union. In this way, the South offset the lack of Northern support, and the Fifteenth Amendment passed and became a part of the Constitution on 30 March 1870.

With the readmission of Virginia, Georgia, Mississippi, and Texas and the ratification of the Fifteenth Amendment, Grant had completed the technical process of Reconstruction and the South was back into the Union. But the problems of Reconstruction would haunt Grant and Republicans in Washington in the form of increasing violence in the South, particularly around election time. At first this violence was clandestine, reflecting the fact that whites were not fully united against Reconstruction. Later this violence would become quite open and blatant, indicating that whites at last were unified in their desire to destroy as much of Reconstruction as possible and "redeem" the South. Through it all, Grant stood valiantly against violence and racism until, in the end, his whole administration fell as the nation registered its disgust and weariness with Reconstruction in the of election of 1876.

The violence of Reconstruction prevalent during Grant's presidency was epitomized by the the Ku Klux Klan. Organized by six bored Confederate veterans in Pulaski, Tennessee (at first as a lark, then as the perfect vehicle to terrorize Reconstruction advocates), Klansmen became folk heroes to the defeated white South. In fantastic disguises, these hooded ghosts claimed to be the Confederate dead, returned to earth to haunt the foes of the South. As Military Reconstruction became a reality, the disguised night riders offered a way to oppose soldiers, blacks, Carpetbaggers, and Scalawags without risking retaliation or arrest. The month after Congress passed Military Reconstruction, Ku Klux Klan representatives from various states met at the Maxwell House Hotel in Nashville to organize and coordinate efforts in every state. The group's goal was to uphold the supposedly weak, innocent, defenseless, and oppressed Southern whites by purpose, and against the political and social effects of Reconstruction.

The delegates at Nashville elected Lt. Gen. Nathan Bedford Forrest, the famous, indeed notorious, Confederate cavalryman who was the scourge to Yankees during four years of war in the Deep South, as imperial grand wizard. The "empire" was then divided into realms (headed by grand dragons), dominions (grand titans), provinces (grand giants), and dens (grand cyclopses). These men considered themselves to be not lawbreakers but law enforcers. They were to combat the "illegal" activities of Republican-dominated courts, state legislatures, and local officials and to compromise black political power in the South. They used threats, exile, flogging, mutilation, shooting, stabbing, and hanging to accomplish their goals. The Klan's victims were many and varied. They included members of the Union Loyal Leagues, Yankee schoolteachers, Republican politicians, black community leaders, or anyone who was important to the success of Reconstruction. The Klan became so notorious that the group was known the world over.

Initially the Klan was quite successful. Black voting declined by 1869. But there was a problem within the Ku Klux Klan movement—it could not be controlled. Those disguises could conceal the identities of men doing things that had little to do with Reconstruction, including personal vendettas, ordinary (as opposed to politically inspired) robbery, and murder. General Forrest ordered the Klan's disbandment, which was done in most of the Gulf South (though it is doubtful that the organization was ever fully organized in many states like Texas and Florida).

The real impetus to disband, however, was the effort of the Grant administration to compromise Ku Klux Klan activities, especially in the Atlantic coast South, Louisiana, and Kentucky, hotbeds of antiblack violence. In 1870, Congress passed the first Enforcement Act ("Force Act," in the vernacular of the day). This measure forbade state officials to discriminate against voters because of race, to bribe or intimidate a voter for any reason, or to use the threat of employment or occupational discrimination to affect votes. Since blacks were tenants on the land, the threat of the landowner to force a "correct" vote was very real, especially because there was no secret ballot at that time in the United States (the secret ballot was an Australian idea incorporated in the United States after 1900). The Force Act also prohibited disguised groups on the public highways or on anyone's property with the intent to do anyone harm.

The Force Act did not do the job. Congress had to amend it with new measures. The Second Force Act provided federal supervision of all voter registration. A Third Force Act soon followed. It prohibited any act or conspiracy to overthrow the federal government by force. It also forbade the intimidation of any public official or members of a jury. Finally, it allowed the president to suspend the writ of habeas corpus in disaffected areas and to use the army and navy to put down dangerous and illegal combinations or groups of people. President Grant immediately utilized the provisions of the Force Acts to stop Ku Klux Klan activities in Georgia and South Carolina. Grant put over 40 counties under martial law. The Seventh Cavalry was withdrawn from the Great Plains and sent into Kentucky, South Carolina, and Louisiana to give the laws impact (General Custer was not with his regiment; he was facing one of the numerous courts-martial that dotted his checkered short career). Hundreds of citizens were arrested, tried, and convicted (one Texas suspect was captured in Canada and extradited to face trial). But in reality, even though Grant saw to it that the Klan was destroyed, it had already accomplished many of its objectives and the Radical portion of Reconstruction had been blunted. The effort to restore white supremacy and establish "law and order" through traditional racial mores had begun.

As the Ku Klux Klan episode demonstrated, everything in secession, Civil War, and Reconstruction began and ended with the problem of race. The movement for Southern independence was dead. Slavery was over. But race remained behind; it was at the bottom of the antebellum quarrels and still very much alive during Reconstruction. The "American Dilemma," as Swedish sociologist Gunnar Myrdal once called it, was an enduring constant. It is possible that fallible human beings could not solve the race problem directly after the Civil War. But the greatest failing was not that the problem went unsolved, but that a deal was reached among whites North and South not to try to resolve it at all.

But, to his credit, Ulysses S. Grant did try. He approached the Reconstruction problem having several advantages, including an instinctive sense of fairness and humanity. He did not believe in punishing the South; he wanted the Union restored quickly; he believed that African Americans ought to be protected in their freedom. But the problem was staggering. The South had played its hand poorly. It had acted as if it would reenslave the blacks. This played into the hands of the most unscrupulous and least responsible men in the North. These people did not care about African Americans' place in society. They merely wished to manipulate blacks and the Southern situation for political power, graft, and corruption. Grant could not keep up with the intricacies of the problem, nor could most Americans. Blacks' civil rights could not be secured without the vote, so he backed the Fifteenth Amendment. Fraud and intimidation unfairly kept blacks from the polls, so he sent federal troops to curb these evil conditions. Step by step, repression took the place of reconciliation, and blacks' rights as free people were lost in the struggle to break the will of the white South. Grant lacked the political skill to keep from being maneuvered into a position where the most extreme measures became his policy and where the most violent Northern partisans claimed him as their leader.

Grant did not believe that African Americans should be thrown to the wolves. Most Republicans agreed. But most whites did not have any taste for keeping Republican politicians in control of Southern states at the point of a bayonet. In reality Grant belonged with the Liberal Republicans, who sought a reconciliation with the white South. But he could not cross the gulf between himself and the Liberals, which was widened by their opposition to his reelection in 1872. He saw them as narrow-minded and unrealistic reformers. They saw him as a crook involved in constant scandal. But though Grant could not work with the Liberals, he could get along with the Radicals and Stalwarts. They knew how to appeal to his hope that the Union victory was not in vain. When the Ku Klux Klan rode, the Radicals and Stalwarts portrayed them as ghostly Confederate armies, led by

Democrats, who would make the Civil War a useless sacrifice. There could be no retreat in the face of that image, and Grant felt it. He made Reconstruction harder and harder until the Northern populace broke under the strain. This made white America do what it had largely been inclined to do anyway—ignore race. Instead it focused its attention on conquering the great West.

Grant tried his best. He always maintained that the race problem had to be grappled with and defeated. If Reconstruction were subverted in the end by corrupt people with unworthy motives, Grant tried to keep them pointed toward noble ends. He knew that African Americans had to be protected in their freedom; this was the one issue that the most radical politicians used to preserve their power until everyone else grew tired of the perennial problem and blacks lost that which they had fought for the most. By 1874, the situation in the Southern states was becoming unmanageable for the Republican party. In Texas and Arkansas both Republicans and Democrats claimed to have won state elections, and both sides had private armies to fight for control. Grant's policy was to shore up Republicans as long as he could, but in these two cases, the cause was hopeless. The Democrats soon took control.

The reason behind Grant's inability to act in Texas and Arkansas was his greatest embarrassment. It concerned a situation in Louisiana that was a total mystery to anyone unfamiliar with its political mysteries and idiosyncrasies. Louisiana had become a sort of national scandal that colored all of Reconstruction. Louisiana had the most obvious scoundrels, the most unbelievable fraud, and the worst violence. Neither side was right; neither was worth supporting. The White League, a sort of Ku Klux Klan without the sheets, engaged in open massacres of white and black opponents. Grant sent Maj. Gen. Philip H. Sheridan down to survey the problem. Sheridan branded the whites "banditti" and called for the army to intervene. But the House of Representatives in Washington was controlled by the Democrats, who refused to fund such an intervention. Grant condemned the House and called upon it to force the South to make good on the promises that had allowed its readmittance in 1868. But the House would have none of that. It dwelled on corruption, horrors of Carpetbag rule, the un-American nature of military intervention, and alleged African American misdeeds and inferiority.

But Grant and his advocates managed to get a fourth Enforcement Bill passed in the House, one that would give the president the right to suspend the writ of habeas corpus in Alabama, Arkansas, Mississippi, and Louisiana for two years. However, the Senate rejected the bill in favor of its own approach: the Civil Rights Act of 1875, a tribute to Senator Charles Sumner of Massachusetts, who had just died. Sumner had wanted it passed in conjunction with the Amnesty Act of 1872—the one an act of justice, the other an act of forgiveness, Sumner had reasoned. The Civil Rights Act of 1875 included a public accommodations section preventing race-based discrimination in theaters, streetcars, railways, hotels, schools, cemeteries, churches, and courts of law. Grant threatened to veto the bill in 1872, claiming it interfered with individual choice. But in 1875, it passed and Grant signed it when the part on schools and cemeteries was left out. The U.S. Supreme Court would rule it unconstitutional in 1883, claiming that social rights were not matters of government.

In the South in 1875, the style was to organize "rifle clubs" to drive out unwanted Carpetbaggers and police the polls, seeing to it that only whites and a few select blacks got the vote. This intimidation was quite open, so that Reconstruction supporters would know whom to fear. It also marked the first time that whites opposed to Reconstruction were united in their approach. No one wanted to see if they could live with it any more. They were going to crush it with violence. Because this concept was developed first in Mississippi, it came to be known as the Mississippi Plan (or the Shotgun Plan, in reference to the weapon of choice in its enforcement). Louisiana had its White Leagues, who took on the Recon-

struction forces in a pitched street battle in New Orleans. South Carolina had Wade Hampton's Red Shirts. But these groups and plans were all part and parcel of the same thing. The Carpetbag governor of Mississippi, Adelbert Ames, faced a dilemma. He could call up the state militia, primarily composed of black units, and institute a race war, or he could appeal for federal troops to crush the rifle clubs. But the national Republican party was thinking ahead to the presidential election of 1876 and refused to back Grant if he acted. The state legislature impeached Ames on trumped-up charges and dropped them when he agreed to leave Mississippi. The state went to the Democrats. State after state followed Mississippi, and by 1876 all of the South had been "redeemed" except Louisiana, Florida, and South Carolina. They would have a lot to say about who would be Grant's successor.

See also Election of 1876 and Compromise of 1877; Grant, [Hiram] Ulysses Simpson; Grant and Domestic Policies; Grant and the Scandals; Ku Klux Klan; Rifle Clubs; Shotgun Plan.

References Carrier, John P., "A Political History of Texas during the Reconstruction" (1971); Carter, Hodding, *The Angry Scar* (1959); Cox, LaWanda, *Lincoln and Black Freedom* (1981); Dawson, Joseph Green, III, *Army Generals and Reconstruction* (1982); Gillette, William, *The Right To Vote* (1969) and *Retreat from Reconstruction* (1979); Hesseltine, William B., *Ulysses S. Grant: Politician* (1935); Olsen, Otto H., "The Ku Klux Klan" (1962) and "Southern Reconstruction and the Question of Self-Determination" (1975); Rabel, George C., *But There Was No Peace* (1984); Ramsdell, Charles W., *Reconstruction in Texas* (1910); Richter, William L., *The Army in Texas during Reconstruction* (1987); Sefton, James E., "Aristotle in Blue and Braid" (1971) and *The United States Army and Reconstruction* (1967); Simpson, Brooks D., *Let Us Have Peace* (1991); Taylor, Joe Gray, *Louisiana Reconstructed* (1974); Trelease, Allan W., *White Terror* (1971); Wallace, Ernest, *The Howling of the Coyotes* (1979); Williamson, Joel, *After Slavery* (1965); Woodward, C. Vann, "Seeds of Failure in Radical Race Policy" (1966); Zilversmit, Arthur, "Grant and the Freedmen" (1986).

Grant, U.S., and the Scandals

The problem with Ulysses S. Grant's presidency was not what was done but rather what was not done. Grant's record has been perpetually darkened with the shadow of a few tragic might-have-beens. Nothing illustrates this more than the scandals that compromised his regime. An emphasis on great wealth came into being during Grant's administrations. This was not old wealth, seasoned with a sense of public responsibility, but new, brash, vulgar wealth that reveled in its pursuit of more suckers to be plucked. The Civil War had destroyed more than the Confederacy; it crushed the restraints and decorum that had marked the antebellum era. An individual wise in the ways of the world might have been able to see that not only should the ambitious human predators be restrained, but they should never be given free rein to corrupt the government itself.

But by the time of Reconstruction, the North had spent most of a generation adulating the go-getter, the promoter, the entrepreneur who constructed a new railroad, factory, or business of any kind. The American dream has always been based on a desire to accumulate wealth coupled with the right to do almost anything. One had the right to do better in life than one's parents. Grant had exacting personal standards in his own world; he could size up an officer or soldier in mere seconds. But he was lost in the civilian world, as marked by his business failures. He could operate a small-town tannery or general store or even supply an army, but he had no concept of how to run a whole industry like the titans of business now emerging in American society. Outside the military world, Grant became a babe in the woods, overawed and gullible, a rube looking to be had. And it did not take long before the jackals moved to cash in on his innocence.

During Grant's first administration, the scandals that plagued him were more a matter of being too close to the malefactors rather than being in league with them. For instance, there was the gold scandal, which concerned Grant's involvement with the likes of Jim Fisk and Jay Gould, who had already made fortunes in their underhanded railroad dealings. Gould and Fisk began to

buy gold to force up its price. The plan was to buy and buy until the market became overheated and then suddenly sell, leaving the speculators to deal with the crash when reality struck. The whole plan depended on the U.S. government keeping its supply of gold off the market. If the government stepped in, the price would crash prematurely, leaving Fisk and Gould in the lurch, too. The two men thought they had Grant's agreement to hold the treasury in check. But Grant never understood what was going on and finally authorized the treasury to inject its gold into the market to stabilize it. Gould found out about the government move; Fisk did not. Gould saw no reason to tell his partner in crime as he shifted all of his options to sell. The next day Fisk went under with the rest of the speculators, and Gould alone made money.

Right on the heels of the gold scandal was the Santo Domingo scandal. Comprising the eastern two-thirds of the Caribbean island of Hispaniola, Santo Domingo (the present-day Dominican Republic) was the site of one of Christopher Columbus's original settlements in the New World. It had as its ruler in the late 1860s one Buenaventura Baez, a corrupt dictator who stopped at nothing where money was concerned. One day he got the bright idea that he could sell his impoverished country to the United States. The Americans had always shown a great interest in the Caribbean, especially before the Civil War, when the Greater Antilles were part of the "golden circle" that would extend Southern slavery and American democracy into the Gulf. Although the Americans seemed more interested in Cuba, Baez believed that with the proper prompting their interest could be shifted to his island. After all, Abraham Lincoln had tried to set up colonies of freed American slaves on Santo Domingo's north coast during the recent Civil War.

So Baez sent word to the U.S. government that the Dominicans were ready for annexation at the proper price. Grant was interested because Santo Domingo was strategically located with respect to some of the world's busiest shipping lanes and promised a direct link to the isthmus of Panama. Grant also wondered if Lincoln had not been right about the need to colonize African Americans abroad as the only way for them to truly achieve racial justice. Santo Domingo was big enough for three or four states for them. But then he blew it. Instead of sending a Department of State envoy to work out the details, Grant sent down Orville Babcock, his wartime aide-de-camp and now presidential assistant. Babcock was sort of a North American version of Baez when it came to monetary items—an expert at getting the fast buck. He also had a glib tongue, as far as Grant was concerned. The president instinctively trusted him. Babcock drew up a favorable treaty (from the standpoint of his and Baez's greed), brought in the U.S. Navy to advance Baez's interests against his more democratic opponents, and even sent American military supplies to Baez's forces in their domestic civil war.

If the treaty were to be approved in the U.S. Senate (it needed a two-thirds vote), it had to get a favorable review in the Foreign Relations Committee, whose chairman was none other than one of the great moralists and antislavery men of his day, Senator Charles Sumner of Massachusetts. Since much of the population of Santo Domingo was black, Sumner was going to safeguard their rights as fully as he did those of African Americans at home. Grant went to the committee in person to plug the treaty, and when Sumner asked questions that Grant could not answer, Grant volunteered to send Babcock over to sort it all out. Sumner was agreeable. "Mr. President," he intoned as only Charles Sumner could, "I am an administration man and whatever you do will always find in me a most careful and candid consideration." To Grant's simple ears, that was a "yes" on the proposed treaty if he ever heard one.

But Sumner's prying was nothing if not thorough. He soon saw through Babcock's machinations and was horrified at the clipping that the U.S. government was about to take. Baez was not even accepted as the ruler of Santo Domingo by all of its citizens; he

was corrupt, brutal, and a notorious wheeler-dealer to boot. Not only would the federal government have to guarantee the Santo Domingo national debt (which was quite large), but it would have to go against the wishes of Haiti, which shared the island, and most of Europe as well. The island was too expensive in a monetary sense, in a moral sense, and in a political sense. Sumner recommended that the Senate turn it down, which it promptly did. Grant was furious. What had happened to the "administration man" that Sumner had sworn he was? As Sumner and Grant carped about loyalty and morality (topics that Sumner had few peers in being able to debate), the public mistakenly got the notion that Grant had endorsed all of Babcock's crookedness and, indeed, had encouraged it from the start. The president had not, but he evidenced a great gullibility and a willingness to attach his reputation to lesser individuals who did not deserve his support.

Grant was beginning to see his star tarnished by men he foolishly considered his friends but who were in reality grifters without a shred of integrity. Nothing showed their true colors more than the Crédit Mobilier scandal. After passage of the Pacific Railroad Act in 1862 and its amendment in 1864, railroad investment became increasingly attractive to various entrepreneurs in the United States. As lucrative as the rail investments might be, the construction and management of the transcontinental railroad (the Union Pacific) offered more to those wise in the ways of maximizing profit at public expense. Their efforts went into establishing a construction company to build the railroad across the plains and mountains. This company was called the Crédit Mobilier of America to differentiate it from the corrupt French company of the same name that was involved in the construction of the Suez Canal—which should have been an omen of things to come for Grant.

The Crédit Mobilier was set up in Pennsylvania under charter from the state legislature at the behest of Thomas Durant, a manipulator of stocks in what later became

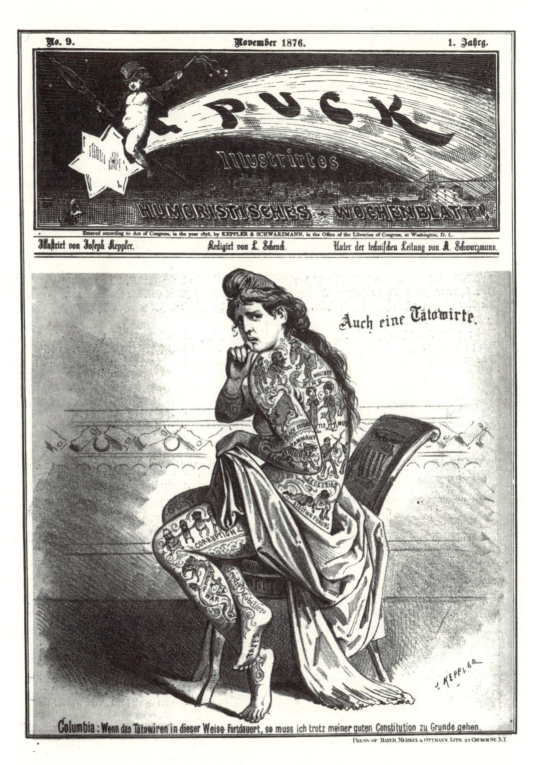

A tattooed Columbia appeared on the cover of a 1876 edition of Puck *magazine. Each tattoo represents a different Grant scandal, such as "Black Friday" and "Election Frauds."*

the Rock Island Lines. The Crédit Mobilier was a construction company, so far as the public knew, with which the railroad contracted to build the line to the west. What the public did not know was that the company was essentially run by the same men who directed the railroad. They bought items cheap and sold them to themselves at a high price, charging the federal government the higher price and pocketing the difference. If the profits were not in cash, they came in the form of securities that allowed the men to control the railroad and its land grants, particularly the timber and mineral rights that came with them.

It was nothing new—business was done that way then (quite openly, actually, by today's standards). At first the Crédit Mobilier contracted to lay the rails onto the plains for the first 200 miles at a profit to themselves of just over $5 million. That was a poor show. The Boston investors complained, so Representative Oakes Ames (who was on the House Committee on Pacific Railroads) was put in charge. He laid the next 600 miles of track and overcharged the government and first–mortgage common stockholders (the manipulators never used their own money) almost $30 million. The system was beginning to hum. But the problem was the five directors appointed by the federal government. What if one of them blew the whistle? What if the rumors of profit caused some crusading congressman to investigate? Ames had the solution. He went around among the directors and his political peers and distributed shares in the Crédit Mobilier ("where it would do the most good," he later said), free to some, at a small cost to others. Such a move was not unusual during that era, later remembered by Mark Twain as the "Gilded Age."

Among those blessed with Crédit Mobilier shares were the vice president of the United States, Schuyler Colfax; the speaker of the house, future president James A. Garfield; perennial presidential hopeful Senator James G. Blaine; and a slew of normally moralistic Radical Republicans. Everyone was in on the take, except Charles Sumner and his kind. To this day no one knows the names of all of those involved in this scandal. Suffice it to say that the estimated six dozen individuals did not lose face in financial wizardry. They came from Boston, Chicago, Philadelphia, and New York City. They included Samuel J. Tilden, a corporate lawyer and future Democratic candidate for the presidency in 1876 (who ran on an honest government platform, of course).

The problem lay in the fact that some of those paid off believed that they had been cheated out of their fair share of the greed. One of them took Oakes Ames to court—a very unwise move. Trials had a way of engaging the public's usually diverted attention. Then, in 1871, well after the Pacific Railroad had been finished and nearly everyone paid off, a combination of directors elected Thomas A. Scott as president of the Union Pacific. Scott was big in the Pennsylvania Railroad, and his election looked like a nationwide railroad power grab to many. So they backed the litigation against Ames and banded together to throw Scott out of his presidency. In revenge, the Scott group then leaked old letters in which Ames had named those whom he had bribed. The muckraking New York *Sun* got a hold of the letters and the story went public with a bang—right in the middle of the election of 1872. President U. S. Grant, all of Congress, and one-third of the Senate were up for reconsideration. And although the president was clean, the rest of his administration was not.

There was no way around it. Congress would have to investigate. Of course, everyone professed wide-eyed innocence. But the facts were out, and the government had to take the Crédit Mobilier to court. Naturally the suit was civil, not criminal (one did not send such upstanding citizens as congressmen to jail in the nineteenth-century United States), and eventually the Supreme Court ruled that the government could not collect even on the fraud until 1895, 30 years after the first bonds went out, as stipulated in the federal charter. The only ones who really suffered were Oakes Ames and Vice President Colfax. Ames lost his congressional seat—but he kept his cash. Grant won a second term by dumping Colfax from the ticket. But Grant might have been unseated, too, had the opposition not backed ending Reconstruction and abandoning the former slaves to Southern white rule, something Grant nobly refused to do. But with four more years of scandal in the offing, such compunctions would change mightily by 1876.

During Grant's second term the scandals grew worse and more frequent until they seemed universal, striking nearly every government department. George M. Robeson of New Jersey was the head of the Department of the Navy. Along with Hamilton Fish in the State Department, Robeson had the distinction of serving in Grant's cabinet the longest, nearly eight years. After the election of 1872, someone in Congress noticed that Robeson, a relatively poor man most of his life, was living pretty high on the hog. In fact, closer investigations proved the secretary had cleared $320,000 during his tenure. Unfortunately, he received this money as kickbacks from friends to whom he awarded government shipbuilding contracts. But by the time Congress got to the bottom of it, the election of 1876 was on and there were bigger fish to fry in the pan of governmental fraud. So Robeson left office relatively untouched. Nonetheless, it all happened on Grant's watch, as the newspapers were quick to point out.

Not to be outdone, the Department of War's secretary, William W. Belknap, collected his kickbacks from agents of the Bureau of Indian Affairs out west (the bureau being a function of the army in those days). The first bribes actually went to Mrs. Belknap, who had obtained the appointment of C. P. Marsh as agent at the Comanche-Kiowa Agency at Ft. Sill, Oklahoma. But Marsh was smarter than to go out on the Southern Plains to live. He merely wrote the incumbent and told him that for $1,000 a month Marsh would stay home and let him keep the job (it was an especially lucrative post). The agent agreed, and Marsh paid half of the take to Mrs. Belknap to support her lavish lifestyle in Washington society. When Mrs. Belknap died suddenly,

her widower told Marsh to keep the payments coming. He had married his first wife's sister, and she turned out to be even more expensive to maintain. When the fraud was revealed, Belknap offered to resign. Since he was an old war buddy and the president got the odd notion that it was all the dead Mrs. Belknap's fault, Grant let Belknap go to protect the family's reputation. Of course, this made the whole cover-up Grant's responsibility, and Belknap let him assume the blame for the whole deal. Belknap's resignation killed a pending impeachment proceeding. The expected criminal suit was dropped when the Department of Justice said there was insufficient evidence to prosecute.

Minor functionaries in the Department of State also wished to get in on this corruption, but Secretary Hamilton Fish was too honest to let that happen. There was one problem, however: Fish could not regulate the overseas appointments because they were a presidential perk. The U.S. minister to Britain was Robert Schenck. A mediocre Union general under the command of men fully as incapable as he, Schenck had run afoul of Confederate genius Stonewall Jackson in the 1862 Valley campaign. After that debacle, Schenck resigned and went to Congress, where his talents might better be utilized. His one real claim to fame was that he was reputed to have introduced draw poker to the British upper crust. He wrote a manual of play, which entitled him to the nickname "America's literary ambassador." He also introduced the British to the challenge of American corporate finance by circulating and selling stocks in the Emma Silver Mine. Since he was a secret member of the board of directors in addition to being a U.S. minister, he learned of the mine's demise weeks before the news became public in England. Quickly, Schenck unloaded all of his own stock at a profit to his British acquaintances. The whole thing eventually went public, and the British sent him home in disgrace. Under pressure, Schenck had to resign—a rich man.

Since the executive departments were getting rich off the corruption, Congress wanted in on the public largesse, too. The scheme was a measure that came to be called the Salary Grab Act of 1873. With the approaching centennial of the American Revolution, executive salaries became an issue. The president was still paid the same $25,000 that George Washington had received. The public sentiment was about evenly divided between those who thought that the office was worth twice as much as President Grant was paid and those who said that Grant ought to live more simply. The early Congress had refused to pick up George Washington's expenses as president, having learned from his Revolutionary War service that his spending rivaled that of King George. So the annual salary had been slapped on the office as a cost-saving measure. There had since been many efforts to raise the executive salary, but all had failed in the more parsimonious times preceding Reconstruction.

The usual attempt to raise executive salaries would have had a similar fate in 1873 if not for the imaginative intervention of Congressman Benjamin Butler of Massachusetts. Butler knew there was money to be made from the sentiment that the president needed a salary hike. So he amended the bill to give Grant a salary increase to $50,000 annually; the vice president, Supreme Court justices, and the speaker of the House of Representatives were moved up to $10,000 and members of Congress to $7,500. Then came the kicker—all salaries were to be retroactive back to 1871. Even the American public, which had grown numb to such scandals, was outraged. The 1874 elections returned a large number of Democrats to Congress, and they promptly lowered only the congressional salaries. But the instigators then sent a bill through that also cut Grant's salary. He vetoed the measure and ended up looking like he had been in cahoots with the salary grab scheme. In fact, Grant was not involved with it, but the raise was the only reason he did not leave office in great debt.

Although the public blamed Grant for much of the salary grab, the scheme paled in comparison with what happened in the Department of the Treasury. In fact the treasury scandals were so big that in the end they took the heat off everyone else. Prior to 1872, the government had awarded a percentage of delinquent taxes to those who reported them. This had led to false charges and blackmail by disgruntled employees, neighbors, and such and had been discontinued in 1872. Instead, a series of contract tax collectors were employed. Secretary of the Treasury W. A. Richardson appointed a crony of Ben Butler, John D. Sanborn, to one of the collector slots. Sanborn was to ferret out unknown delinquent taxes and take half of what was collected. His entry into district offices was assured by a letter from Richardson, asking that he Sanborn given full cooperation.

Sanborn was no idiot. If the government did not know who was not paying their taxes, he probably was not going to find them out either. So instead of seeking out the unknown, he took Richardson's letter to the Boston internal revenue office and got a list of already known delinquents. Then he collected their payments and took 50 percent off the top. Then, on a hunch, he made a list of 600 railroads and arbitrarily charged them with delinquent taxes. A large number confessed to the accusations and paid up to Sanborn, who took half. Complaints led to a congressional investigation, which revealed that Sanborn had made $213,000 off the government but that he had not directly discovered any new delinquent taxpayers. It was suspected that Ben Butler had received a healthy cut of Sanborn's income, but no such evidence could be produced. Congress decided to censure Richardson, who resigned (for President Grant's sake, he said). Grant was appreciative and made Richardson a federal judge after the whole affair cooled off.

Richardson's successor, reformer Benjamin Bristow, went on a crusade to clean up the treasury that made him a top contender for president on the honest government ticket in 1876. He found that his biggest obstacle in ridding the department of crooks was that they were all Grant's friends and supported the president for an unprecedented third term. Bristow decided that if he exposed them to the public, he could not only straighten out the mess at the treasury but become president as well. His target was something known as the Whiskey Ring. Composed of brewers and distillers of alcoholic beverages, who were supposed to pay federal excise taxes, the Whiskey Ring had been in existence for years. Basically, the ring paid off tax collectors to report lower production (leading to lower taxes). It was sort of an entrenched tradition that no one had touched before Bristow made his move in 1875. The secretary had tried for months to catch the Whiskey Ring, but tipoffs from inside the department had allowed the culprits to slip through his hands. The secretary then collected a secret police force loyal only to him and made many surprise raids in Chicago, Milwaukee, and St. Louis.

The most important catch was the collector of internal revenue at St. Louis, John McDonald. An illiterate political manipulator and astute judge of people, McDonald was an old friend to the president. McDonald had been protected by Missouri Republicans, many of them on the take, but there had been a recent shift in Republican personnel to the Carl Schurz group. And Schurz was the rare man of integrity, a Liberal Republican who opposed all graft and corruption. But because the Liberals had been against Grant's reelection in 1872, Grant took Schurz's complaints against McDonald as mere political hogwash. Grant should have known better. McDonald had asked the president for a letter of introduction to Jim Fisk and Jay Gould right after the gold scandal. Grant refused the letter, but when McDonald came back with a request to be appointed collector at St. Louis, the president readily assented. McDonald was a staunch Grant man, and the president had hoped that his political savvy would neutralize Schurz and his ally, B. Gratz Brown, in Missouri.

All of that was true, but so was the fact that McDonald was the head of the Whiskey Ring's St. Louis operations. McDonald would bring local distillers up on minor charges and then not prosecute them for a kickback. He had confided everything in Grant's most trusted aide, Orville Babcock, but Babcock was very understanding for a price. McDonald found this more than reasonable. He gave Babcock $25,000 right of the top and kept him regularly supplied with cigar boxes of $500 bills, large diamonds, vacations with paid expenses, and even a sylph's charms (a polite way at that time to refer to a practitioner of the world's oldest profession). Fortunately, as Babcock was well aware, Grant had heard "thief" so many times that he refused to believe such charges any longer. He saw everything as politically inspired drivel launched against trusted subordinates by Democrats and Liberal Republicans. Grant was personally so squeaky clean that he could not believe that his trusted aides, men who had stood shoulder to shoulder with him against the Rebels, and cabinet members, men of the business community whom Grant unabashedly admired, could be less trustworthy than he. And led by Babcock these men all played on Grant's soft heart for their own benefit.

Yet Grant made other mistakes. He accepted gifts from these men, especially several prized race horses. He never seemed to realize that the givers might expect something later or that it would look bad if the public ever found out. He was truly ripe for the plucking. In this state of mind, the president was horrified to find that his secretary of the treasury was in league with his critics. At least that is what Grant thought (guided by Babcock) when Bristow revealed all of his findings in the McDonald matter. But Bristow refused to back down. He presented facts that even Grant could not deny, including a bunch of telegrams informing McDonald of Bristow's failed raids, signed "Sylph." McDonald had to go; Grant accepted the man's resignation and gave Bristow a free hand to clean up the Whiskey Ring. Bristow informed him that "Sylph" was Babcock. "Let no guilty man escape," Grant said. "No personal consideration should stand in the way of performing a public duty.... If Babcock is guilty, there is no man who wants him so proven guilty as I do, for it is the greatest piece of traitorism to me that a man could possibly practice."

But in spite of his declaration to Bristow, Grant kept Babcock in his job, convinced deep down that Bristow was wrong about him. Babcock and Grant had several private and intense talks, the aide showing how Bristow was seeking the presidency over Grant's ruined reputation. He even convinced Grant that the "Sylph" telegrams were the work of Babcock and McDonald working to protect the president from a blackmailing woman (as if Grant ever did anything to be blackmailed about). Babcock asked his old general for a military trial, and the president appointed a board consisting of generals Alfred Terry, Winfield S. Hancock, and Philip H. Sheridan.

However, the St. Louis court would not quash Babcock's indictment there or give Grant's military board any evidence. Babcock condemned the court as led by "Rebels," said political plotters wanted to ruin him to get at Grant, and assisted a private investigation authorized by the president to seek out the "facts." The trial in St. Louis convicted all of the accused except Babcock (McDonald got 18 months), who produced an affidavit from Grant that he was as pure as the driven snow. The court did not wish to challenge the president's veracity through a mere deposition and felt obliged to let Babcock go. Babcock and Grant then had a heart-to-heart conference after which Babcock resigned to be director of public works for the District of Columbia, where he dropped from the public eye. Grant, meanwhile, turned his fury on Bristow, whom he allowed to continue in place until after the election of 1876, when the reformer was fired. Once again the president covered up for his friends' poor reputations by compromising his own. "Grantism" came to mean the worst in crooked government, a castigation that has endured up to the present day, and did much to compromise the continuance of the Reconstruction he supported.

See also Beecher, Henry Ward; Grant and Domestic Policies; Grant and the Presidency; Grant and Reconstruction; Tweed Ring.

References Boynton, H. V., "The Whiskey Ring" (1876); Donald, David H., *Charles Sumner and the Rights of Man* (1970); Hesseltine, William B., *Ulysses S. Grant: Politician* (1935); Mayer, George H., *The Republican Party* (1967); McDonald, John, *Secrets of the Great Whiskey Ring* (1880); McFeeley, William S., *Grant* (1981); Prickett, Robert C., "The Malfeasance of William Worth Belknap" (1950); Spence, Clark C., "Robert Schenck and the Emma Mine Affair" (1959); Sproat, John G., *The Best Men* (1968); Tansill, Charles C., *The United States and Santo Domingo* (1938); Webb, Ross A., *Benjamin Helm Bristow* (1969).

Greeley, Horace (1811–1872)

Horace Greeley, the most important newspaper editor and reformer of his time, was born in Amherst, New Hampshire. His father was a hardscrabble farmer who moved the family to various farms in Vermont and Pennsylvania. Greeley received a modicum of education and was apprenticed to a newspaper editor at age 14. The owner soon died, but Greeley kept at newspaper work the rest of his life. With about $25 and all of his belongings wrapped in a large handkerchief, he arrived in New York City in 1831. He was a tall, scrawny boy who lost one job because the editor would not have only good-looking men about him in his office, lest the public be turned away. The precocious Greeley was soon writing small pieces independently and then larger ones and editorial commentaries, too. He came to the notice of James Gordon Bennett, who offered him a partnership in the New York *Herald*, but Greeley had already started a literary magazine, the *New Yorker*. The sheet was a literary masterpiece and gained in reputation and circulation monthly, but Greeley still worried about debt. Nonetheless, he married Mary Cheney, a schoolteacher, and kept writing, earning a wide reputation for his articles.

Ultimately the *New Yorker* failed, which was probably a good thing because literary writing was not Greeley's main interest— politics was. He accepted the challenge from William H. Seward, later Abraham Lincoln's secretary of state, and Thurlow Weed, probably the most powerful political kingpin in upstate New York, to publish a Whig newspaper in the city. His papers ran often for a short time, and Greeley never made much money at it, but he was a natural commentator and made important friendships each time he started anew. In 1840 he opened up the *Log Cabin*, a sheet dedicated to the election of William Henry Harrison, and became an instant success. Greeley also made speeches and stumped the state for Harrison. After the election, Greeley took stock of the newspaper industry in New York City. There were 12 different papers a day published, but not one was dedicated to the Whig party cause. So Greeley took what was left of the *New Yorker* and the *Log Cabin*, borrowed a thousand dollars, and merged them into one publication, which he named the New York *Tribune* in 1841. The other editors attacked him immediately, and the result was a rising subscription rate and a newspaper that made Greeley not only famous but rich.

Greeley proceeded to set a new standard in American journalism. He emphasized good taste, high moral standards, and intellectual appeal. He also made good use of the editorial comment page, writing wholly partisan pieces but with an appeal to reason and accuracy. But most of all the newspaper was Greeley's personal sounding board, and he had a lot to sound off about. At one time or another he backed seemingly every crackpot idea that circulated in nineteenth-century America. He was an egalitarian who saw aristocratic plots behind everything. He spoke out on behalf of utopian socialism, advocated communal living, and invested in the utopian movement through its banks. He was for the free distribution of land in the West ("Go west, young man" was ever his advice to those seeking to make their fortune) and against economic advantage to the rich. He railed against railroad land grants, assailed corporate heartlessness, stood against the exploitation of workers, and wrote against wage slavery as fervently as he campaigned against chattel slavery. He opposed the death penalty, was for freedom of speech, favored women's rights (so long as they did not get the vote), wanted to restrict the sale of liquor, favored a protective tariff, formed one of the first labor

unions for printers in America, and was an avid fan of phrenology (he had an especially bumpy head, sort of a phrenologist's dream, as it were).

Greeley's thinking was never consistent; he was always changing his mind on this or that, but he was never idle. He was a moral leader, a popular teacher, the champion of new ideas. He walked about town, curious about everything. He dressed in a broad-brimmed hat with a wide cravat that was never tied straight, baggy pants, disheveled shirt, and a long linen duster with a multitude of pockets, each filled with little notes he was always making to himself. Pieces of paper dropped out of his pockets, making it fortunate that littering was not a crime in those days. His handwriting was abominable, and legend had it that only one copyboy at the *Tribune* could read it with any degree of consistency. This riled the more important junior editors because the lad lorded it over them each time one of Greeley's missives appeared. One day these editors went to a slaughterhouse and picked up a chicken's foot and brought it back to the office. Ever so quietly they dipped it into an ink well and stamped it about on a piece of paper. When the ink had dried, one of them held it up and yelled for the boy to translate Greeley's latest word. The impetuous kid sat down and worked feverishly for some time on the effort, never suspecting that the whole office was snickering behind his back. Finally one of the staff asked him if he had finished as they were about to go to press. Not yet, he replied, there was one word he could not fathom. Before the dumbfounded editors could stop him the youth went into Greeley's office and asked him what the word was—and Greeley told him.

By the time of the Civil War Greeley's paper was circulated all over the North (his antislavery ideas made it unacceptable for Southern readers). He opposed the war with Mexico as the advance of slavery into new western lands; opposed the extension of slavery into the Mexican Cession; and was livid about the creation of Kansas and Nebraska, with slavery allowed above the old Missouri Compromise line of 36°30′ (the northern border of Arkansas). He helped abolitionists arm the Yankees who went out to save Kansas from slaveholders, and he applauded resistance to the Fugitive Slave Act of 1850. He was one of the first editors

to join the Republican party, giving it instant access to homes all over the North. Of the *Dred Scott* decision that declared African Americans not to be citizens, he wrote that it was "entitled to as much moral weight as

PUBLISHED BY CURRIER & IVES.   Entered according to act of Congress in the year 1872 by Currier & Ives in the Office of Librarian of Congress at Washington.   125 NASSAU ST. NEW YORK

A PHILOSOPHER IN ECSTASY.

(By George! I've got it !!)

New York Tribune *founder Horace Greeley leaps for joy after receiving the Liberal Republican presidential nomination in this 1872 illustration.*

would be the judgment of a majority of those congregated in any Washington barroom." He fell out with Seward and Weed, declaring them too moderate on the slavery question, and backed Abraham Lincoln in 1860. Although he was a member of Congress briefly in the late 1840s, Greeley never served in any other political office. But he was the best-known politician in the nation because of his constant barrage of editorials on every issue.

The war brought him new opportunities to educate America on its moral duty to clean up the slavery problem. He believed that secession was a right if the great majority of the South wanted it, then professed to see a conspiracy of rich slaveowners as its guiding force. After the war began Greeley became an instant military genius, in his own eyes at least, and covered the masthead of page one with the slogan "Forward to Richmond!" (although in truth the headline was from one of his editors, Richard Henry Dana). He allied himself with the Radical Republicans and pushed emancipation, regardless of its cost. He called it the "question of the day" and begged Lincoln act in an editorial entitled "The Prayer of Twenty Millions." But the man who had wanted war in 1861 changed his mind as the conflict dragged on, and by 1864 he had become a peace-at-any-price advocate. Lincoln shrewdly let him go talk to Confederate peace commissioners, where Greeley found to his chagrin that the South's only uncompromisable condition for ending the war was an independent Confederacy. Greeley also supported Lincoln, whom he had berated for so long as ineffectual on most issues, in the 1864 election, which angered the Radicals. By the end of the war Greeley had been on so many contradictory sides of so many questions that most of the North thought he was going daft.

Reconstruction was not much different. Greeley endorsed Radical Military Reconstruction and the Fourteenth and Fifteenth amendments. He permitted the *Tribune* to support the impeachment of Lincoln's successor, Andrew Johnson, but the policy was one of a junior editor rather than Greeley himself. Once again the great editor was changing his mind. He went in on Jefferson Davis's bail bond, even though the action cost him fully one-half of his subscribers. Greeley was slowly coming to be disenchanted with the corruption that Reconstruction came to embody in the South. He saw Grant as a weak president of poor leadership qualities. Greeley was in favor of a single presidential term anyway, and he believed that Grant ought to step down in 1872. He also believed that time had come to let wartime animosities pass. By this time, however, the *Tribune* had become more than Greeley—it was now a great institution in itself. Even if Greeley did not care where his cockeyed ideas carried the paper, his editors did. But Greeley did not understand the change that was taking place. He knew that he was a good, humane man and represented the idealism that had made America great. And he knew that such a man was what the nation needed in 1872 to bring the country back to its senses as a healed, unified entity.

Led by Whitelaw Reid, one of Greeley's editors, the Liberal Republicans (the reform element of the party that bolted when Grant was renominated) nominated Horace Greeley for president during the summer of 1872. Greeley had not pushed the nomination, but he did not shrink from accepting it. Resigning from the *Tribune*, Greeley took to the stump. His acceptance was a real shock to the political professionals. It was said that no two men could look each other in the face and say "Greeley" without laughing. Others saw Greeley as a "ridiculous political mouse," "an eccentric philosopher," "a grandmother and a trickster," and "totally destitute of sound judgment." Historians have written him off as a nominee made by a combination of political idiots and political buccaneers, but the fact remains that he was put up by professionals and newsmen who had been writing about politics sensibly for decades.

Opponents assaulted Greeley the candidate without mercy. Greeley spoke of North and South clasping hands over the bloody chasm of war. He spoke of removing political disabilities from white Southerners and uniting the nation once again. Pundits and cartoonists had a field day with him. None was more effective than Thomas Nast, who took the theme of "hands across the chasm" and made it Greeley's political tombstone. He showed Greeley reaching across dead blacks to grasp hands with the Ku Klux Klan or reaching across the Union graves at the infamous Andersonville prison to grasp the hands of Confederate soldiers. Greeley himself said it was hard to tell if he were running for the presidency or the penitentiary. In the end he lost out to the better-organized Republican machine, a fear on the part of the financial markets that he was economically untrustworthy, and the impossibility of reconciling Democrats and Republican reformers under one banner.

The loss hit Greeley personally. It was compounded by the death of his wife at about the same time. He wandered back to his beloved *Tribune* only to find Reid and others in power and unwilling to let him back in (was this Reid's motive in nominating him all along?). His mind and body both broke. He died insane on 30 November 1872. In death the nation paid him a tribute that it never did while he was alive with a massive funeral procession in New York City. His failings were no longer important. He was praised for the very things that cost him a presidential victory, his editorials, his intellectual curiosity, his moral stand on issues most were willing to compromise out of a lack of personal courage, and his overall eccentricities. Reid reorganized the staff and the front page with the masthead "Founded by Horace Greeley" and erected a statue to him in the hallway. At the corner of Broadway and Sixth Avenue another bronze appeared, with the intersection being called "Greeley Square." And so passed not only a man but an American institution.

See also Election of 1872; Liberal Republicanism.

References Hale, William Harlan, *Horace Greeley* (1950); Linn, William Alexander, *Horace Greeley* (1926); Lunde, Erik S., *Horace Greeley* (1981); Nevins, Allan, "Horace Greeley" (1964–1981); VanDeusen, Glyndon G., *Horace Greeley* (1957).

Griffin, Charles (1825–1867)

Born in Granville, Ohio, Charles Griffin graduated from West Point in 1847. He arrived too late to fight in the Mexican War, but he served on the western frontier in New Mexico Territory before teaching artillery tactics at his alma mater. In 1861 he was a captain in the artillery and was placed in charge of the West Point battery of light artillery that gained fame at First Bull Run when it was overrun in the final Confederate attack. Griffin returned to Washington, D.C., where he spent the winter reorganizing his unit and courting Sallie Carroll, whom he would marry. An energetic officer, Griffin transferred to the volunteer service, where promotions came faster, and by 1862 he was in command of a brigade of infantry. He participated in every campaign of the Army of the Potomac and by the end of the war was a brevet major general in charge of a corps. Griffin's men took the formal surrender of the Confederates at Appomattox.

After the war, Griffin, like all regular officers, was reduced in actual rank. He became colonel of the Thirty-fifth Infantry, one of the occupation regiments assigned to Texas. Griffin was known as an unyielding officer of fiery temper, arrogant, egotistical, and very close to insubordinate in most of his public utterances. But he was tough and reliable, and those qualities endeared him to Maj. Gen. Philip Sheridan late in the war. And Griffin was a die-hard Union man, which reflected in his support for the Republican party, especially the Radicals. General Sheridan, after a year of frustration in commanding the occupation forces in Louisiana and Texas, became well aware that he needed a subordinate who could run Texas while he kept an eye on Louisiana. He called on Griffin.

When he arrived in Galveston to take charge, Griffin found the Reconstruction of Texas in a shambles. The elected governor, James W. Throckmorton, a former Whig who had donned the gray only to fight Indians in the Texas frontier, had outmaneuvered Sheridan and his Texas commanders time and time again. By pointing out the increased Native American raids on the northwest frontier, as well as misconduct by the Freedmen's Bureau and the army (including freeing black soldiers who murdered a white citizen; helping two horse thieves kill their accusers, who were alleged Rebels; and burning down the business section of Brenham during a drunken brawl), Throckmorton was forcing Sheridan to transfer Reconstruction garrisons to the western frontier. This helped curtail the Indian incursions but opened up the interior to numerous atrocities against African Americans. Moreover, the Andrew Johnson plan of Reconstruction was not going well. The Texas legislature had passed the notorious Black Codes, refused to consider the Thirteenth Amendment, rejected the Fourteenth Amendment outright, proposed to enroll state troops (former Confederates) ostensibly to fight Indians, and elected two uncompromising Rebels as U.S. senators. There was a lot for Griffin to do.

Griffin knew that he did not possess adequate authority to move against the Texas state government, but he was also aware that Congress was debating the expansion of his powers through the Military Reconstruction Acts. So Griffin bided his time, took the reins of the semi-independent Freedmen's Bureau, unfairly but effectively blamed the bureau's outgoing commander for all of the problems between civilians and soldiers, gave in on the surface to Throckmorton's demands by shifting some troops westward, and secretly planned his countermoves. Meanwhile, many members of the nascent Texas Republican party believed Griffin to be somewhat of an ineffectual humbug, as he wished the whole state to think. With the passage of the Military Reconstruction Acts, however, Griffin began his assault on what he saw as the backsliding of the civilian regime in Texas. Griffin told state Republicans that anyone impeding the Reconstruction process would be done away with. He especially targeted the wily Governor Throckmorton. But he had to go through the ponderous chain of command that included General Sheridan in New Orleans.

Leaving political removals until later (no one was yet sure that commanders had such powers under the initial Military Reconstruction Acts), Griffin turned to the problem of equal justice. One area in which Griffin took an interest was the number of blacks incarcerated in Texas jails, particularly at the state penitentiary at Huntsville. Under the guise of a Freedmen's Bureau inspection, Griffin recommended that many prisoners be released because they were serving time for crimes that would have merely called for a whipping in slavery days. He believed that they were unfairly convicted because courts excluded blacks from testifying and being impaneled on juries. Governor Throckmorton was outraged at these ideas, which he considered to be no more than fuzzy thinking on how to prevent and punish crime.

But Griffin knew that black testimony and the use of black jurors was nonexistent in state courts, so he moved against the problem in another way. The general issued an order that any post commander could take any case in which an African American was a party out of the civil and criminal courts and send it to Griffin for review. He then required that all jurymen take the iron-clad oath to serve (that is, an oath that one had not aided the Confederacy); this effectively limited jurors to blacks and pro-Union whites. The result was a protest that went all the way to Washington and brought in Lt. Gen. Ulysses S. Grant. The commanding general of the army finally ruled that Griffin was a mite too enthusiastic in his stance and that all persons, regardless of color or past loyalties, ought to be a part of the jury system. Griffin did not wait for this bit of inevitable criticism. He issued the only public accommodations law promulgated by any regime in Texas Reconstruction (and later ignored by everyone). He sent his soldiers out into the field to protect loyal citizens and assist Freedmen's Bureau officers in their duties (he was the only general in Texas to do this so consistently and methodically during the whole Reconstruction period).

Griffin also administered the registration of voters for the election of the new state constitutional convention required under the Military Reconstruction Acts. Registrars were federal employees and thus had to take the ironclad oath to serve. All voters had to take an oath of future loyalty and not be among the classes excluded from participation under the Fourteenth Amendment (people who had taken an oath to the United States and then to the Confederacy). But Griffin, with Sheridan's approval, allowed the registrars to go further and exclude anyone whom they suspected of latent disloyalty. It was a position that Congress would endorse in the Third Military Reconstruction Act, but it caused much dissatisfaction among Texas whites of the former Confederate variety.

Although things looked good on the surface, Griffin and the Republicans knew that patronage would be the only way to get rid of ex-Rebels in political positions and cleanse the state of treason. And here they ran into a big problem, General Sheridan. He would not allow the wholesale removals that were so important to building the Republican party. And no matter how hard he tried, Griffin could not change Sheridan's mind.

But Griffin was vindicated once again in the Third Reconstruction Act. Griffin immediately wrote Sheridan to explain how Governor Throckmorton had impeded Reconstruction (1) by helping the military government register voters but dragging his feet in the equal participation of blacks in the legal system (although he cleverly covered his tracks by pardoning black prisoners held for petty crimes at Huntsville); (2) by failing to insist on the protection of the political rights of African Americans (the governor kept up a constant barrage of complaints about Indian troubles and the army's inability to protect whites on the frontier); and (3) by quietly appointing conservative Democrats to fill vacant offices. Sheridan went into immediate action when notified of the Third Military Reconstruction Act. He removed Throckmorton from office and replaced him with Unionist Elisha M. Pease, the man who had overwhelmingly lost to Throckmorton in the gubernatorial election the year before.

In retaliation, President Andrew Johnson promptly removed Sheridan from office for exceeding the wisdom of his powers and replaced him with a known Democrat and opponent to Military Reconstruction, Maj. Gen. Winfield Scott Hancock. Pending Hancock's arrival (he had to consult with the president in Washington first), Sheridan turned his position over to Griffin, the next ranking officer, and gave him full power to act in any way he wished as Sheridan left for reassignment on the Great Plains. Griffin did not delay. He promptly began to clean out all Democrats in the state executive department, as well as in the state supreme and district court systems. Outgoing Governor Throckmorton condemned Griffin for posterity: "He is a dog—mangy—full of fleas…as mean as the meanest radical Republican in Texas, and that is saying as mean a thing of a man as can be said."

Suddenly, as the Texas Republicans seemed at the height of success, a virulent yellow fever epidemic swept up the Gulf Coast from Mexico. Everyone turned to combating the dreaded disease, and Griffin was in the forefront. Army authorities recommended that he move himself and his family away until the epidemic ceased with cooler weather. Griffin refused, likening his leaving to abandoning a post in battle. Griffin's family contracted the disease. His little boy died. Then Griffin himself fell ill. On 15 September 1867, Charles Griffin died from the complications of yellow fever. His parting was a disaster for Texas Republicans. He had left before his program of removing Democrats and replacing them with Republicans had fairly begun. No one knew if they would see his like again—an army officer who understood the political realities of the Military Reconstruction Acts and carried them out so as to cause a real change in the South to guarantee the results of the war.

See also Army and Reconstruction; Military Reconstruction Acts; Reynolds, Joseph J.; Sheridan, Philip H.

References Baggett, James Alex, "Birth of the Texas Republican Party" (1974–1975) and "Origins of Early Texas Republican Party Leadership"

(1974); Boatner, Mark M., III, *The Civil War Dictionary* (1959); Carrier, John P., "A Political History of Texas during the Reconstruction" (1971); Ramsdell, Charles W., *Reconstruction in Texas* (1910); Richter, William L., *The Army in Texas during Reconstruction* (1987), *Overreached on All Sides* (1991), and "Tyrant and Reformer" (1978); Sefton, James E., *The United States Army and Reconstruction* (1967); Shook, Robert W., "Federal Occupation and Administration of Texas" (1970).

Hancock, Winfield Scott (1824–1886)

A Pennsylvanian, Winfield S. Hancock graduated from West Point in 1840. He served in the Seminole War and in the Mexican War and received a brevet for bravery at Churubusco. After the Mexican War he served on the western frontier, where he was involved in the Kansas-Missouri border wars and wound up as chief quartermaster of the California command. With the outbreak of the Civil War, Hancock was brought east as a brevet brigadier general. He fought on the Virginia Peninsula, where he earned his nickname, "the Superb," in the sharp fight at Williamsburg. He continued with the Army of the Potomac in every campaign it fought, rising from brigade to corps command. His conduct at Gettysburg, where he selected the Union position and turned back several Rebel assaults, won him the thanks of Congress. His bravery had a price, however; he was severely wounded, suffering a hip injury that would plague him for years. In 1864, Hancock led his corps on the Richmond campaign, watching them disintegrate at Ream's Station, totally worn out from the incessant fighting around Petersburg. Hancock, too, was exhausted. His wound reopened, and he had to retire from front line duty. He was placed in charge of the Veteran Reserve Corps made up of wounded men like him, too valuable for the service to lose but unable to fight day in and day out.

Because of his war service Hancock became the junior major general of the army after the war. He served on several boards and commissions and was posted to the Great Plains, where he fought the Cheyenne in 1866. A well-known Democrat, Hancock was one of many Civil War generals who had doubts as to the wisdom of the army getting involved with the politics of the Military Reconstruction Acts. When President Andrew Johnson became particularly miffed at the pro-Republican stance of Maj. Gen. Philip H. Sheridan in the Fifth Military District (Louisiana and Texas), he pulled Sheridan out and sent him to the frontier to replace Hancock, who had not done well against the Cheyenne. Then Johnson used Hancock to blunt the Radical Republicans' plans for the South by putting him in charge of the Fifth Military District. Since the whole Gulf Coast was full of yellow fever, Johnson ordered Hancock to Washington for consultations before sending him to the Deep South. Hancock would delay his arrival until the frosts of November put an end to the fever epidemics in Louisiana and Texas.

Hancock was well aware what awaited him in Louisiana and Texas. Upon his arrival at his New Orleans headquarters, he began by issuing General Orders No. 40, in which he stated that it was time for the civil authorities to take power in the South. He saw the army's role as incidental to theirs, one of support, not of policy making. The army would not interfere with the right to trial by jury, the writ of habeas corpus, freedom of the press, freedom of speech, and the right to private property. The army would act only if the civil authorities refused. Conservative whites hailed Hancock's order as a fresh breath of American liberty. Although little had changed as far as announced policy was concerned, the attitude of Hancock and his staff was decidedly against interfering in local matters except as a positively last resort. But there was more to the whole situation than mere pronouncements. Prior to Hancock's arrival, both Texas and Louisiana had had a vigorous cleansing out of allegedly disloyal Democrats in favor of Republicans. Now in both states the ousted officials, all elected in 1866, petitioned to be restored to their rightful places. But Hancock could not do this without creating an insurmountable controversy, so he allowed all things to stay as they were when he arrived. Hancock was wise to let it go at that. Already Radical Republicans in Congress were moving to cut back the army by removing the position of junior major general (Hancock) from the list of active officers. But in reality they could do little. Hancock was acting well within his prerogatives as district commander under

Congress' own Military Reconstruction Acts.

Hancock next reopened all voter registration and liberalized the regulations excluding whites for past Confederate service. Several thousand voters were registered under Hancock's move, but this probably did not materially affect politics in either of the states under his command. Then Hancock got into an open tiff with Bvt. Maj. Gen. Joseph J. Reynolds, his subordinate in Texas, and Texas provisional Governor Elisha M. Pease. Reynolds had placed the Republicans in control of local politics in Texas just before Hancock's arrival in New Orleans. In answer to complaints from those replaced, Hancock ordered the suspension of all changes in officeholders. He also commanded that all military trials, whether by military commission or Freedmen's Bureau agents, be submitted to the civil courts. This would of course put loyal black and white defendants at the mercy of the local courts and their Democratic juries.

When Pease protested Hancock's vision of Texas under civil government, Hancock retorted that Texas was at peace and that the civil processes were more than adequate to preserve law and order. He condemned petitioners from all sides who seemed to think that he had the power to set aside election results or any adverse ruling from any source. He refused to assume and exercise any arbitrary powers. Pease retorted that the Military Reconstruction Acts imposed unusual conditions upon the state. There was no legal government in Texas, Pease said, and the concept that Texas was at peace was naive—there was an open race war on, and it was the army's duty to stop it. He blamed an outrageous increase in crime to Hancock's General Orders No. 40.

Hancock waited some time before replying to Pease's accusations. Then he icily opened his letter by saying he found Pease's assertions interesting but had not received his communications until after Pease had released them to the newspapers. Hancock admitted that he could essentially do as he pleased in Texas and Louisiana under the congressional laws, but he denied that possessing a power meant that it was always wise to use it. He said that a location's inability to rely on peace officers in all cases was not a mandate for the army to act. Such problems were found all the time in all parts of the country without army interference being necessary to counteract them. Further, Hancock went on, he resented Pease blaming General Orders No. 40 as the cause of difficulties in Texas. There was no way that the announcement of basic American principles of law and government could aid crime. He told Pease that his letter reeked of bad temper and illogical conclusions and that just because Pease and the Republicans did not like or agree with elected officials and their policies did not meant that they ought to expect the army to intervene. That was what elections were for. So stop complaining, Hancock concluded, and get on with the process of making a new constitution and electing new officials.

Hancock's biographers have lauded the general's refusal to make Reconstruction a process outside the general principles of American government. But, of course, that point of view ignores the fact that what he did also spelled death to the Republican party in any state like Texas that had a white majority. Louisiana Republicans might be able to survive Hancock's approach, but Texas Republicans could not. And that, of course, is exactly what President Johnson had in mind when he sent Hancock down South. Hancock next turned to General Reynolds and ordered him to shift the army from the Texas interior to the frontier. Reynolds was to stop enforcing law and order on behalf of black and white Union men and guard against Native American incursions on the settlements. But Reynolds dragged his feet, hoping that Republicans in Texas and Louisiana would gain a reprieve from Lt. Gen. Ulysses S. Grant. Meanwhile, Hancock replaced Bvt. Maj. Gen. Joseph Mower in Louisiana with Bvt. Maj. Gen. Robert C. Buchanan. Mower had paralleled Reynolds's actions in Texas by placing Republicans in power in Louisiana. Hancock no longer had confidence in Mower. Hancock also drove from power

Provisional Governor Benjamin F. Flanders, who refused to cooperate with Hancock's "Democratic" policies.

When the Republican New Orleans city council voted to fill a vacant city office, Hancock moved to clean out this Radical stronghold (once appointed by Sheridan). He telegraphed his action to Grant, the army's commanding general. Grant now saw his opening and moved against Hancock, whom he despised for not following Congress' biding or the will of the people (the Northern people), at least as Grant saw it. He refused to allow Hancock to make his removals and replacements. Grant said that Hancock was going against his own public pronouncements that civil government had been restored in the Fifth Military District and that as a federal official Hancock ought not interfere with a local government he did not like. Hancock sullenly obeyed the order. Shortly thereafter Hancock tried to replace the New Orleans street commissioner (a position noted for its access to political graft). Grant once again told him to stop interfering with the local government. Hancock resigned his position, compromised as he saw it by a lack of support from on high.

Hancock would continue in the army for some years, running the Military Division of the Atlantic and the Department of the Dakotas. He ran for president on the Democratic ticket in 1880 against James A. Garfield and lost narrowly, by 10,000 popular votes. His popularity among the voters and veterans never waned, despite his opposition to Reconstruction and the Republican party. Democrats saw him as a savior from Radical generals like Sheridan, Griffin, Mower, and Reynolds. But Southern Republicans envisioned him as the devil incarnate, a foolish man who would compromise party principle for some ethereal notion of what the Founding Fathers deemed was the spirit of American government. He could never seem to rise above principle to practicality, the way so many of that era did, and that made him special in a time marked by political and monetary greed. But he also did not understand that the period itself was

General Winfield Scott Hancock

so unique that it might have called for revolutionary approaches to guarantee the freedom of African Americans and quash a lingering and incipient rebellion.

See also Army and Reconstruction; Military Reconstruction Acts; Reynolds, Joseph J.; Sheridan, Philip H.

References Boatner, Mark M., III, *The Civil War Dictionary* (1959); Carrier, John P., "A Political History of Texas during the Reconstruction" (1971); Dawson, Joseph Green, III, *Army Generals and Reconstruction* (1982) and "Army Generals and Reconstruction" (1978); Hancock, Almira R., *Reminiscences of Winfield Scott Hancock* (1887); Richter, William L., *The Army in Texas during Reconstruction* (1987); Sefton, James E., *The United States Army and Reconstruction* (1967); Shook, Robert W., "Federal Occupation and Administration of Texas" (1970); Taylor, Joe Gray, *Louisiana Reconstructed* (1974); Tucker, Glenn, *Hancock, the Superb* (1960).

Hayes, Rutherford B. (1822–1893)

Born in Ohio after his father had died, Rutherford B. Hayes was raised by his mother and sister with assistance from his uncle, Sardis Birchard. He was educated in a local academy and by private tutors, and he hoped to attend Yale until financial realities sent him to local Kenyon College. The result was that he never lost his Midwestern point of view. He remained a conservative, cautious man all of his life. He also had a strange, overly dependent relation with his mother and his sister Fanny, who went insane and died after he married. After graduating college he read law and finally managed to attend Harvard Law School for a year and a half.

He returned to Ohio and opened a law office near his uncle's home at Lower Sandusky, where he practiced for five years at the time of the War with Mexico. He thought of volunteering for the war in the arid Southwest to clear up a bronchial condition, but doctors advised against it. After the war he traveled to Texas and visited Guy M. Bryan, a Harvard classmate and plantation owner, with whom he kept up a lifelong correspondence. In Texas Hayes came to see slavery as essentially a benign institution of racial control, which may have colored his attitude toward the South in years to come. He returned to Ohio, this time setting up a law practice in Cincinnati from which he grew rich. He married Lucy Webb, a temperance supporter who would ban alcohol from the White House and earn the somewhat derisive moniker "Lemonade Lucy" in later years. ("You are sister Fanny now," he told her when his sister passed away later.) He began to dabble in local politics as a Whig. The growth of the slavery issue, especially its spread into the West, made Hayes a Republican by 1856, although he was reserved in his condemnation of any viewpoint.

Although Hayes hoped to see the Civil War restrained, after its outbreak he became active and eventually accepted the post as major of the Twenty-third Ohio Volunteer Infantry, eventually advancing to regimental and brigade command. He served against Stonewall Jackson in the Shenandoah Valley in 1862 and was wounded in the arm at the Battle of South Mountain preceding the massive fight at Antietam. Hayes and his men then fought

guerrillas in the mountains of West Virginia and were important in checking flamboyant Confederate cavalryman John H. Morgan during his 1863 raid in southern Ohio. In 1864, Hayes and his troops were part of the Army of the Shenandoah under Maj. Gen. Philip H. Sheridan and were active in sweeping Confederate control from the Shenandoah Valley. He spent the rest of the war in garrison duty, achieving the rank of brevet major general.

In the fall of 1864, Hayes was elected to Congress from Cincinnati, even though he had refused to campaign for the seat. He resigned his military rank and took office in June 1865 only after the surrender of the last of the Rebel forces. He generally voted with the Republican party on Reconstruction questions, even though he was not a Radical and he disapproved of their hostile methods toward the South. He was reelected in 1866 but resigned the position in June 1867 to run for the party as governor of Ohio. Hayes narrowly won the governor's chair and, hampered by a Democratic legislature, got little done. But he did make some prison reforms and set up a better regulation of charities. His popularity with the voters remained high, and in 1869 Hayes won a second term. Now with a Republican majority in the legislature, Hayes came out against high taxes, reformed the care of the insane, supported creation of a state agricultural college, and attacked railroad management for disregarding the public good. He recognized the principle of merit in political appointments, even going so far as to appoint able Democrats to office. He combated election fraud, created a geologic survey department, and encouraged the preservation of historical records. By now he was viewed as a capable administrator of national importance, but Hayes instead chose to retire from the governorship and preserve its two-term tradition. He stood for Congress again but was defeated.

The next few years found Hayes devoting himself to the law, real estate, and local public service. But with the Democratic resurgence of 1874, state Republicans approached him with an offfer to back him not only for a third term as governor but for president of the country as well. Suddenly the man without real ambition felt the bite of the presidential bug in a big way. He won the governorship; he offered not only an ability to get votes, but a reform record as someone who had stayed loyal to the party despite his disagreements with it. With the backing of Senator John Sherman and Representative James A. Garfield, Hayes went to the Republican convention, which by able maneuvering was held in his hometown of Cincinnati. He won the nomination after opponents to the candidacy of James G. Blaine settled on Hayes as an appealing, unoffending alternative. The presidential election of 1876 hinged on whether Hayes could take all of the disputed votes in the Republicans' "rotten boroughs" of the South plus one in Oregon, a process that was accomplished by bribery without Hayes's direct participation. It seems that Hayes was not against the deals that his managers made with conservative white Southerners to allow the final Redemption of their states by the removal of federal troop support; this process was assisted by letters to him, some sycophantic, some sinister, from old friend and now Texas Redeemer, Guy M. Bryan.

Hayes ended federal support for the "black and tan" (biracial) governments in the South—this was something both he and Democratic opponent Samuel J. Tilden had promised, but Hayes's war record and party label allowed white America to feel more comfortable with the move. Hayes almost backed out on this plan until a "special" tour of the South and a private talk with South Carolina's Wade Hampton convinced him that any future bloodshed in a race war would be on his hands and that Southern whites would "take care" of their black population (after all, that was what Hayes had seen during his visit to Texas many years before).

In other matters, Hayes issued an executive order (he could not get a congressional law for civil service reform) forbidding monetary assessments (that is, donations to party funds) and political assignments from appointed officeholders. He cleaned up the New York customs house corruption (to the dismay of New York Senator Roscoe Conkling and Chester A. Arthur, the commissioner). He used federal troops to suppress the bloody rail strike of 1877 (to the dismay of union leaders nationwide) and vetoed a Chinese exclusion bill (threatening party support in the West). He came out on behalf of the resumption of specie payments and the end to greenbacks (alienating the gold lobby and debt holders in general but endearing him to Western silver producers as he would return the paper dollar greenbacks with gold and silver coins).

By the end of his term it was obvious that Hayes was going to be a one-term president, something that he did not oppose. He retired to his Ohio home and devoted himself to library work, filling his time with many speaking engagements and various humanitarian causes, like prison and education reform. His wife died in 1889, a severe blow to him, but he remained active until his own death four years later, which had been hastened by exposure to bad weather while attending a meeting of trustees of the state university. His funeral brought forth accolades for his patriotism and common-sense dedication to reform, overlooking the long-range implications of his failed Southern policy.

See also Election of 1876 and Compromise of 1877.

References Barnard, Harry, *Rutherford B. Hayes and His America* (1954); Eckenrode, Hamilton J., *Rutherford B. Hayes* (1930); Haworth, Paul L., *The Hayes-Tilden Disputed Presidential Election of 1876* (1906); Hoogenboom, Ari A., *The Presidency of Rutherford B. Hayes* (1988) and *Rutherford B. Hayes* (1995); Nevins, Allan, "Rutherford Birchard Hayes" (1964–1981); Williams, T. Harry, *Hayes of the Twenty-third* (1965) and *Hayes: The Diary of a President* (1964).

Holden, William W. (1818–1892)

North Carolina has a history of villains, ranging from Blackbeard the pirate to Tom Dully [Dula] of folk song fame, but few have exceeded that hatred inspired by William W. Holden, the state's Reconstruction governor. Holden was born in Orange County, and little is known about his early life. He was largely self-made; he attended a "field school" and became a printer's apprentice. Originally a Whig newspaper editor, Holden switched to advocating Jacksonian Democratic views, if for no other reason than to stimulate debate over political issues of the day. As a writer he was distinctly partisan and frequently abusive, in the style of the times. As a participant in the demise of the Whig party in the 1850s, Holden made many lifelong enemies. His involvement also enhanced his reputation as an opportunistic, bitter, unscrupulous, and arrogant demagogue.

In the late 1850s Holden entered state politics, running for governor and U.S. senator and failing to achieve either position. In 1860 he backed the presidential aspirations of Stephen A. Douglas and cautioned the eager secessionists to wait until President Abraham Lincoln did something overt before considering leaving the Union. When Fort Sumter was fired upon, Holden came out wholeheartedly for secession, although he tempered it somewhat by voting for the "right of revolution." But he soon saw that secession Democrats, in league with Confederate president Jefferson Davis, were squeezing him out of the party. This caused Holden to organize the Conservative party, a combination of Douglas Democrats and ex-Whigs. For their front man they chose Zebulon Vance, who became North Carolina's governor in 1864 on a program that criticized the war. Holden also dabbled with the more radical secret peace society known as Heroes of America. Once Holden's association with this group was revealed, many Whigs and Democrats of all hues charged him with treason to the Confederacy, but the outcome of the war saved him from any real embarrassment.

As Reconstruction began, President Andrew Johnson appointed Holden as his first loyal governor in the South. This was not hard to believe because Johnson and Holden thought much alike, if Holden's editorials were any indication. But it angered many in the state who thought that Holden had proved much too flexible in the past to be trusted now. In the words of one observer, the Yankees "have taken the lowest, most abject & degraded man they could find among us—one Holden—& exhalted him to the post of governor." The "Pope of Hargett Street" (a reference to his address in Raleigh) was condemned as "a base born bastard with neither the breeding [n]or the instincts of a gentleman." But Holden surprised many of his detractors when his administration proved to be one of moderation and feeling. Many feared that to reject him in the election of 1866 would cause the North to misinterpret the sincerity of North Carolina's submission to defeat. But at the last moment the Conservatives put forward Jonathan Worth, a relative political unknown of principled Union credentials, who had been serving as state treasurer. The result was that Holden was repudiated at the polls, his past reputation as an unprincipled and "malicious prince of demagogism" doing him in.

Worth was typical of the men elected in the South in 1866. He was a slaveholder who doubted the wisdom of emancipation. His attitude was that if the Yankees thought so much of African Americans as free people, why did they not invite them to come live up North and grant them the vote and civil rights in their own state constitutions? But the imposition of the Military Reconstruction Acts on North Carolina and the South would render Worth's doubts moot. It was no surprise that the leader of the new Republican party, in league with other Scalawags, blacks, and Carpetbaggers, was none other than the ever-flexible Holden. Guiding the party to a fairly moderate stance on such issues as disfranchement for ex-Confederates (there was none on the state level), Holden ran for and won the governor's chair in 1868; the Republicans also took over the state legislature.

Although many hated Holden for his support of black civil rights, blacks were really minor participants in North Carolina politics because they were only a small part of the overall population, except in selected eastern counties. The real struggle took place between Union (Carpetbag and Scalawag) and Rebel whites over state-backed economic growth subsidies, particularly to railroad companies. Realizing this, the Conservatives at first decided to ignore the governor and concentrate on his less–than–reputable Republican cronies. The issue that became the hottest of all was the state backing of numerous railroad bonds. In this, Holden inevitably became linked up with two con artists extraordinaire, Milton S. Littlefield and George W. Swepson. Holden was probably honest in terms of his financial dealings, but he became tainted when he issued a series of bonds for a railroad in the Piedmont and Appalachian sections of the state that turned out to be fraudulent. In this regard Holden was a lot like President Ulysses S. Grant—he never repudiated his friends and thus was guilty by association, if nothing else.

The problem that did Holden in was the suppression of the Ku Klux Klan in Alamance and Caswell counties. Authorized to raise a state militia to protect loyal white and black voters, Holden brought in from East Tennessee a man named George W. Kirk, whom he made colonel in charge. The result was the so–called Kirk-Holden War, as Kirk's men attempted, with mixed results, to put down Ku Klux Klan violence. Kirk did well in the two counties where he operated (both dominated by white Loyalists), but this left the rest of the state (especially the African American and Republican east) wide open to voter intimidation. Criticism of Holden reached a new peak because the attack on the Klans came just before the state election of 1870, one in which Conservatives hoped to retake the legislature. Calling him "one of the most unscrupulous despots and vindictive tyrants that ever disgraced the annals of modern history," Conservatives accused Holden of "playing the part of a reckless partisan" to tip the elections toward the Republicans by intimidating voters through a rampage of the Republican-organized state militia in one "last desperate act of his official insanity." One critic, newspaper editor Josiah Turner, Jr., went to the scene of the military operations and wrote of how "the devil incar-

nate," Holden, through Kirk's Republican militia, "robbed, despoiled, and plundered the people." Turner dared Holden to have him arrested and Holden foolishly had it done, making Turner the martyr of the hour and guaranteeing a Conservative victory in the legislative contests.

When the new legislators took their seats, many called for Holden to be removed. "Impeach the Traitor, the Apostate, and the Renegade, and drive him into the infamous oblivion which is so justly due," cried his critics, labeling him "the vilest man that ever polluted a public office." The legislature put on an impressive show trial that ignored the Ku Klux Klan attacks on white and black Republicans and portrayed Holden as a violator of civil liberties through his militia campaign and arbitrary arrests. The trial was so skillfully handled that even Republican newspapers in the North took up the hue and cry. Holden did not even await the verdict before he left Raleigh and headed to Washington, D.C., to ask for the assistance of the Grant administration. But while the president and his advisors had nothing but sympathy for Holden's impeachment and impending guilty verdict, they dared not intervene for political reasons of their own. Holden returned to North Carolina, abandoned by the federal government, deposed by the state legislature, and under legal assault through a lawsuit for damages filed by Turner (which was eventually dismissed from court).

Amazingly, Holden was readily accepted back home. He became active in the First Baptist Church, served in a state education convention, and was made postmaster by President Grant. But most of all, he hoped to expunge the disgrace of the impeachment from his public record. This took the form of Holden seeking to regain "his citizenship," as he called it, the right to hold state office again. He continued to work on a one-on-one basis, writing letters and speaking to persons on the street. But he refused to engage in public speaking. Holden took heart when the Republicans retained the governorship in 1872, but the legislature was still firmly in Conservative hands. They sidestepped the issue of exoneration, asserting that a state convention would have to do it. This opportunity appeared in 1875, as the state assembled delegates to get rid of the state's Reconstruction constitution. However, on a straight party vote (53–56) the delegates refused to remove Holden's political disabilities. This inspired the angered ex-governor to write a heated letter to U.S. Senator James G. Blaine, criticizing how Democrats were eager to receive amnesty and pardon for their own sins of secession and war but were unwilling to grant the same to those whose only crimes were standing for Union and civil rights for all.

Blaine publicized North Carolina's problems in a national forum, which enraged state politicos. They based their 1876 gubernatorial campaign on Holden's perfidy and captured the state house at last. But Holden went into print, too. In several long essays he refused to apologize for his Reconstruction administration and defended the Kirk-Holden War. He said that he had nothing to do with the numerous fraudulent railroad bond issues and defended his friend Swepson, despite much evidence that the man was a fraud. Holden even entered a banking partnership with Swepson that was terminated only at the latter's death. During the 1880s, however, Holden mellowed and began to engage in several projects that helped restore his reputation in the state. He gave an address on North Carolina journalism and ignored his own considerable contribution. He reconciled with Zeb Vance and began to write a massive history of North Carolina designed to "do justice to all of the public men of the state, living and dead." But the old man's health began to catch up with him. Holden suffered a stroke that limited his ability to write. He had to dictate all correspondence.

At the end of the decade he tried one more time to regain his political rights. He approached newspaperman Josephus Daniels and through legislator Charles M. Cooke had a resolution presented that would restore his political rights and leave the question of the impeachment un-

touched. But the resolution merely caused old hatreds to flare up and failed. Holden then had another stroke, which left him bedridden. Josiah Turner reinstituted the old false arrest suit and won a judgment that threatened to wreck his family's fortune. An appeal brought relief in 1894, when the court dismissed the case on the basis of the original dismissal from years earlier. But Holden would never live to see the victory. He died two years earlier. And in his funeral procession was the only vindication he would ever get—a public procession, the lowering of the flag to half–mast, and a public burial attended by blacks and whites from all political persuasions. Josephus Daniels had written his obituary some time earlier. Holden had "made stronger friends and bitterer enemies than any other man in our history," Daniels concluded, "[but w]hatever people in the future may think of him, one thing is certain—they will think of him."

See also Ku Klux Klan; Scalawags; Tourgée, Albion W.

References Boyd, William K., "William W. Holden" (1899); Ewing, Cortez A. M., "Two Reconstruction Impeachments" (1938); Folk, Edgar Estes, "W. W. Holden and the Election of 1858" (1944) and "W. W. Holden and the North Carolina Standard" (1942); Folk, Edgar Estes, and Bynum Shaw, *W. W. Holden* (1982); Hamilton, J. G. de Roulhac, *Reconstruction in North Carolina* (1914); Harris, William C., *William Woods Holden* (1987) and "William Woods Holden" (1982); Lancaster, James L., "The Scalawags of North Carolina" (1974); Olsen, Otto H., "The Ku Klux Klan in North Carolina" (1962); Raper, Horace W., *William W. Holden* (1985); Russ, William A., "Radical Disfranchisement in North Carolina" (1934); Trelease, Allen W., *White Terror* (1971); Tucker, Glenn, *Zeb Vance* (1965); Wakelyn, Jon L., *Biographical Dictionary of the Confederacy* (1977); Walker, Jacqueline Baldwin, "Blacks in North Carolina during Reconstruction" (1979); Yates, Richard E., *The Confederacy and Zeb Vance* (1958); Zuber, Richard L., *Jonathan Worth* (1965).

Howard, Jacob M. (1805–1871)

Born in Vermont, Jacob M. Howard was educated in public schools and private academies, receiving a degree from Williams College in 1830. He began to read law and was admitted to the bar in Michigan, where he had moved in 1833. Setting up a practice in Detroit, Howard did well as an attorney, but he much preferred politics. His first political move was to become a Whig candidate to the state assembly in 1838. Changing to the new Republican party in 1854, Howard served as state attorney general until 1861. He was then sent to the U.S. Senate, where he served until 1871 as a Radical Republican. Howard drafted the Thirteenth Amendment, opposed Presidential Reconstruction, and favored extreme punishment of the South through the Fourteenth Amendment and the Military Reconstruction Acts. He was a member of the Joint Committee of Fifteen on Reconstruction and was in charge of investigating conditions in Virginia and the Carolinas. Howard was an excellent speaker but somewhat ponderous in his presentation of a topic. He read widely in law, history, classics, and literature and even translated and published the memoirs of the Empress Josephine from the original French. Howard was interested in transportation and chaired the Senate committee on Pacific railroads. He drew up the final report on President Andrew Johnson's removal of Secretary of War Edwin M. Stanton, which led to the chief executive's impeachment (Howard voted to convict). He died of a stroke within a month of ending his term as senator in 1871.

See also Johnson and Reconstruction; Moderate Republicans and Reconstruction; Radical Republicans and Reconstruction.

Reference Knauss, James O., "Jacob Meritt Howard" (1964–1981).

Howard, Oliver Otis (1830–1909)

Born in Leeds, Maine, Oliver Otis Howard graduated from Bowdoin College in 1850 and West Point in 1854. He served as an ordnance officer, fought in the Third Seminole War, and taught mathematics at the military academy until the Civil War broke out. He helped organize and train the Third Maine Volunteer Infantry, and he served as its colonel and brigade commander at First Bull Run, the first of 20 major engagements

he fought in during the war. He was soon promoted to general officer. He lost his right arm on the Virginia Peninsula in 1862 at the Battle of Fair Oaks. Allegedly, fellow general Philip Kearney, who had lost his left arm at Mexico City 15 years earlier, came in to cheer Howard up; in his only recorded wisecrack, Howard proposed that the two men buy their gloves together in the future. Howard returned to the front within three and a half months and fought as brigade and division commander at all major battles in the East through Gettysburg. He advanced to corps command, taking over the XI Corps of the Army of the Potomac, a hard-luck unit largely composed of German immigrants whose flight both at Chancellorsville and the first day of Gettysburg caused Union defeats.

After the Pennsylvania campaign, Howard's XI Corps, together with the XII Corps, was sent to the West, where they fought well at Chattanooga and took Lookout Mountain, a fortified position so high that the fight was known as the "Battle above the Clouds." Taking over the combined XI and XII corps, Howard fought in the Atlanta campaign, advancing to army command under Maj. Gen. William T. Sherman. Howard commanded one of the wings in the March to the Sea from Atlanta to Savannah and continued in this role as the Union armies moved through the Carolinas; along the way he changed his record in the East from one of "diligent mediocrity" to one of occasional brilliance. In 1865, Secretary of War Edwin M. Stanton handed Howard a basket of memos and communications and thereby named him the first and only commissioner of the Bureau of Refugees, Freedmen, and Abandoned Lands.

Although recent historians have criticized Howard's condescending racism, summed up in the title "Yankee Stepfather," he was probably as good a man as was available at the time to do the job. He was honest, had the interests of African Americans at heart, and approached the problems in the spirit of a devout Christian, which led to another of his nicknames, the "Bible general." He came across as a bit much to "drunken, licentious, or profane" soldiers, agents, and freedmen who fell beneath his high standards once in a while, but he was a decent, moral man in a job that called for one. He believed that the key to bureau work was "virtuous intelligence and industry." Bureau agents ought to act "above corruption and prejudice," do "simple justice" to all regardless of "color or rank," and act "wisely, faithfully, consciously, fearlessly" while taking care "not to overdo, nor come short of duty." Unfortunately, not everyone measured up to Howard's expectations.

Howard fully realized that the change from slave to free society would be a long and arduous one, and he worked ever patiently to achieve it. Like many nineteenth-century intellectuals and reformers, he put his faith in God and education. He founded several black institutions of higher learning, of which Howard University in the District of Columbia is the best known, and worked tirelessly to keep the bureau as nonpolitical as possible. It is possible that the bureau might have continued longer had he made it an adjunct of the Republican party, but he refused. For all of his hard work he was accused of mismanagement of funds and investigated by Congress, but he was soon found innocent of any charges.

Howard went on to the Great Southwest, where he negotiated the end of the Apache Wars by bravely confronting the Chiricahua chieftan, Cochise, alone in his stronghold, and by impressing the Apaches with his Christian decency. Unfortunately, the rest of the government was not so just; Howard's treaty was unilaterally altered, and the reservation he promised was given over to the cattle and mining barons. Then the Apaches were sent to the bleak sand barrens of San Carlos. Meanwhile Howard took over the Department of the Columbia and was there during the Nez Percé War against Chief Joseph, whom he helped hound into submission. In 1886 he returned to the Department of the East, where he served until his retirement in 1894. He remained interested in the field of black education the rest of his life and wrote several historical books, including his memoirs, which he finished two years before his death.

See also Bureau of Refugees, Freedmen, and Abandoned Lands.

References Carpenter, John A., *Sword and Olive Branch* (1964); Catton, Bruce, *The Army of the Potomac* (1951–1953); Cox, John, and LaWanda Cox, "General O. O. Howard and the Misrepresented Bureau" (1953); Howard, Oliver Otis, *Autobiography of Oliver Otis Howard* (1908); McFeeley, William S., *Yankee Stepfather* (1968).

Impeachment

As of March 1867, the Republican Congress had tried to subordinate President Andrew Johnson to its will through measures like the Command of the Army Act, the Tenure of Office Act, and the Military Reconstruction Acts; they had also called one congressional session immediately after the previous one ended so as not to allow Johnson to act alone during the traditional recess. Johnson, however, managed to do much within the limits of the laws to frustrate the Radical program. He relied on appointment and pardoning powers that Congress really could not touch. Most of all, he was able to guide Reconstruction through his assignments of officers to Reconstruction districts in the South. In the late summer of 1867, he transferred Radical hero Maj. Gen. Philip H. Sheridan from the Fifth Military District (Louisiana and Texas) to the Plains and placed Democratic hero Maj. Gen. Winfield Scott Hancock in control at New Orleans. Hancock immediately issued General Orders No. 40, which essentially returned government to civilian hands. Johnson followed the same policy in the Second Military District (the Carolinas) and the Third Military District (Georgia, Florida, and Alabama) by replacing Republican-leaning generals Daniel Sickles and John Pope with more moderate generals like George G. Meade and E. R. S. Canby. Other officers, like Bvt. Maj. Gen. E. O. C. Ord in the Fourth Military District (Arkansas and Mississippi), were already against a vigorous Military Reconstruction from the start or, as with Bvt. Maj. Gen. John Schofield in the First Military District (Virginia), were very circumspect in stretching the limits of their authority.

Many Republican party members, especially Radicals, regarded Johnson with pure hatred. This man was thwarting the acts of Congress, a body that, in the eyes of Republicans, was the will of the Northern people. They deeply resented Johnson, who admired the concept of a strong, active president. In their view, he had to be curbed. The

only real way to stop Johnson and completely humiliate him was to impeach him. Impeachment is the bringing of charges against an elected or appointed public official. It is an indictment. In the case of the president, the House of Representatives impeaches and acts as prosecutor. The Senate acts as jury, and the trial is overseen by the chief justice of the U.S. Supreme Court (in this case, Salmon P. Chase, a former member of Abraham Lincoln's cabinet and a Radical Republican). If found guilty, the accused is removed from office. Then separate civil or criminal charges can be filed in ordinary courts. Until Johnson could be removed from office, he would be immune to ordinary prosecution. According to the Constitution, the president could be impeached only for treason, bribery, high crimes, or misdemeanors. What the latter two categories could include was a vague area, and the Radical Republicans zoomed in on this uncertainty immediately.

By 1866, many devout Radicals already wanted to ruin the president. Johnson had spoken of hanging traitors and had pardoned them instead. He was against the Freedmen's Bureau renewal and the Civil Rights Bill and had insulted congressmen publicly in a personal manner. Congress James M. Ashley of Ohio introduced the Ashley Resolution, which asked the House judiciary committee to look into the president's conduct and recommend impeachment to the whole House. The possible charges were that Johnson had aided in Lincoln's assassination (Ashley went so far as to try to bribe a jailer to so testify), that he was in league secretly with the Confederacy during the Civil War (either this charge or the previous one could brand him a traitor), that he had been bribed to issue so many pardons to former Confederates (a high crime), and that he had committed adultery while in office (wags wondered aloud whether this ridiculous charge was a high crime or a misdemeanor). To the disappointment of many, the judiciary committee failed to return a bill of impeachment.

"I'll take [Johnson's] record, his speeches, and his acts before any impartial jury," stormed a disappointed Thaddeus Stevens, "and I'll make them pronounce him either a knave or a fool, without the least bit of trouble." That may have been so, but those were not impeachable crimes under the Constitution. Nonetheless, Stevens raged on: "My own impression is that we had better put it on the grounds of insanity or whiskey or something of that kind. I don't want to hurt the man's feelings by telling him he is a rascal. I'd rather put it mildly and say he hasn't got off that inauguration drunk yet, and just let him retire to get sobered." When a fellow congressman protested Steven's invective and pointed out that the president was a self-made man, Stevens retorted, "Glad to hear it; for it relieves God Almighty of a heavy responsibility!" Congress also thought of impeaching Johnson for vetoing too many bills (he used it 20 times in 3 years; the previous record was Jackson's 11 times in 8 years), but in reality Congress lacked a real charge at this time.

By the following year, Congress had a new weapon to use against the president, the Tenure of Office Act. Essentially this act stated that anyone appointed by the president with the advice and consent of the Senate had to be removed in the same fashion. The tenure of office was designated to be the term of the appointing president plus one month. The act was designed to protect Radical sympathizers in the executive department who spied on Johnson and tipped off Congress as to his possible next moves. But it was especially there to shield Secretary of War Edwin M. Stanton. He was the civilian head of the War Department and thus one of the men through whom orders to the army had to proceed, according to the Command of the Army Act.

Thus Stanton, along with Lt. Gen. Ulysses S. Grant, kept the field officers from taking orders directly from Johnson that might compromise Reconstruction (although neither had been able to halt Johnson's annoying habit of appointing military district commanders who disliked congressional policy). Stanton was a patho-

President Andrew Johnson (right) receives an impeachment summons from his White House office in this undated illustration.

logical liar—driven to fabricate anything for the good of the country, the party, or himself (he has even been accused of doctoring John Wilkes Booth's diary and hanging the conspirators to shut them up); he spoke with the authority of a saint, and he often seemed to confuse himself with God. He was, however, financially honest and an effective wartime administrator who had done much to win the war. He was flexible enough to both inform upon Johnson to his Radical cronies and also help the president write his veto messages.

Johnson soon figured Stanton out and decided to test the Tenure of Office Act by firing him. Stanton would not resign if confronted, and Johnson knew this, because Stanton considered his two-faced policy necessary to save the nation from Rebel rule. So the president bided his time and waited. No congressman worth his salt could abide a prolonged stay in Washington. Sooner or later Johnson's protectors would have to go home and politick. Johnson's chance came in the summer of 1867 when the Fortieth Congress figured the president was in check and declared a recess from July to November. This was the opportunity for Johnson to remove the various Republican military commanders in the South. For good measure he removed Stanton, too. Then he informed Congress of his deeds, as the Tenure of Office Act provided, when they reconvened in December. Congress would then advise and consent.

Johnson was rather clever—too clever as it turned out—in his choice for Stanton's interim replacement: none other than Commanding General of the Army Ulysses S. Grant, a war hero with whom even the Radicals would not dare to trifle. Johnson explained to Grant what he was up to. He wished to test the Tenure of Office Act in court. Stanton stepped down with real alacrity—he was afraid of standing up to a man of Grant's reputation. But as much as Johnson had figured out what made Stanton tick, he had not done so for Grant. The general was a great unknown politically, and he was not happy with Johnson for dragging him out on the embarrassing political tour known as the "Swing around the Circle" in 1866. Grant did not understand the give and take of politics—he believed that Congress, as the true representatives of the people, was right in any political quarrel with the president. He also found out that if he cooperated with Johnson and they lost their case, he could be fined $10,000 and get five years in jail if he refused to give the office back to Stanton. But hanging tough was essential if Johnson were to get a test case in the federal courts. Finally, unknown to Johnson, Grant was getting the presidential bug—the Republican presidential bug.

So when the second session of the Fortieth Congress met, voted not to concur in Stanton's removal, and ordered him back into office, Grant returned the keys before Johnson could stop him. Stanton had planed to resign after Congress vindicated him, but the Radicals convinced him to stay on. Thus Johnson, in order to get what he thought was a good test case, had to remove Stanton outright while Congress was still in session. In Johnson's eyes, the secretary was not actually protected by the act because Lincoln had appointed him; Lincoln had

been dead for years, well beyond the one-month period after a president leaves office during which an appointed official can keep the position. But Johnson had to get someone to become secretary in Stanton's place.

Johnson looked for another war hero—he tried generals William T. Sherman and George Thomas—but all refused to get involved. Finally, Adj. Gen. Lorenzo Thomas agreed to confront Stanton and demand he get out. But Thomas was a poor choice. The public had never heard of him. He was 63 and one of numerous officers who spent their careers in the "housekeeping" (support) branches of the service rather than a combat arm. He was disliked in the service as a fussy paper shuffler. Thomas went into Stanton's office and asked him to surrender his keys and papers. Looking over his thick glasses at the scrawny figure before him, an incredulous Stanton begged time to remove his personal items. Thomas gave him 24 hours. Then Stanton said that he did not know if he would give up at that time or not.

Thomas ignored the secretary's remark and came back the next day, after an all-night drinking binge to celebrate his new appointment. He found Stanton barricaded behind his office door, standing on his desk and peering through the pane of glass above the door. The secretary had in his hand a one-word telegram from Radical Senator Charles Sumner. "Stick!" it said. Thomas told Stanton to get out. Stanton threatened to remove Thomas from his treasured adjutant general's position. Then the secretary noticed Thomas's red eyes and slurring voice. Wise in the ways of a hard-drinking army, Stanton invited Thomas in for a drink. As the whiskey flowed, Stanton pointed out just what a fool Thomas was to do the bidding of the traitor president. Thomas stumbled into Johnson's office to confront him. The exasperated president sobered the adjutant general up and sent him back to besiege Stanton, who ate, slept, and worked while cooped up in his office 24 hours a day. Thomas sat in the anteroom, waiting for Stanton to give up. Occasionally Thomas would leave to eat or answer the call of nature, and Stanton would step out on his own, with a band of spies left behind, watching for Thomas's return so the secretary might beat him back. It became a national joke. But Stanton knew that he was doing what the Radicals wanted and held on.

As Stanton held out valiantly, the House of Representatives passed the Covode Resolution, impeaching the president for "high crimes and misdemeanors." The Bill of Particulars had 11 accusations, 8 of which concerned violations of the Tenure of Office Act. Article 9 was the "Emory article." It accused the president of violating the Command of the Army Act by sending an order directly to Bvt. Maj. Gen. William H. Emory. The general had refused to obey and reported the attempt to Grant, who told Congress. Article 10 was the "Butler article," named after Radical congressman Benjamin F. Butler of Massachusetts. It accused Johnson of using foul language disrespectful of Congress—true, but more a matter of bad taste than a high crime or misdemeanor in anybody's book. Article 11 was the "Omnibus article." It was a catchall that accused Johnson of not faithfully executing the Military Reconstruction Acts. This was false. Johnson was meticulous in his obedience, although he worked the loopholes patiently and effectively. Everyone knew that the House had a poor case. Johnson was right, the Tenure of Office act did not really apply to Stanton. But in the Republicans' view, the Senate was not supposed to vote as an impartial jury—it was to act as a political body and vote the party line.

Johnson, aware of the farcical nature of the impeachment proceedings and wishing to keep intact as much of the executive's traditional independence of the legislature as possible, refused to patronize the process. He sent his attorneys, Henry Stanbery (who resigned as attorney general to defend the president) and William Evarts (one of the most respected attorneys of the day). They stuck to the legal facts: Stanton was not under the protection of the Tenure of Office Act because Lincoln, who had appointed him, had been dead (and thus out of office) more than one month; Stanton was still in office anyway, so no crime had been committed; and none of the so-called high crimes and misdemeanors were impeachable offenses, but rather political disagreements natural under the American system of government.

Facing Johnson's attorneys was the prosecution, a group of managers appointed by the House of Representatives. The leaders were Thaddeus Stevens and Benjamin Butler. Because Stevens was slowly dying, Butler carried on all of the real work. They had a lousy case, but it mattered little. All they wanted was 36 senators to vote "aye" to remove the president. "If we don't do it," warned Stevens, "we are damned to all eternity. There is a moral necessity for it, for which I care something; and there is a party necessity for it, for which I care more. In fact, the party necessity is the moral necessity; for I consider that when the Republican party dies, this country will be given over to the so-called Democracy, which is worse than the Devil." Stevens called Johnson worse than Judas Iscariot, a frightening charge to Bible-conscious nineteenth-century America. "Would to God that he had the repentance of that remorseful malefactor," Stevens said, "who had been guilty of no indictable offense, but had simply indicted by a kiss the Master who trusted him." Steven's hatred for Johnson was starkly revealed in his constant use of chilling metaphors like "the ax of the executioner is uplifted," "killing the Beast," and "tortured on the gibbet of everlasting obloquy."

Stevens had a certain flair about him that was not evident in Butler, who tended to offend the public and the Senate. Butler refused to stop the trial when Johnson's head lawyer, Stanbery, took ill. "While we are waiting for a few days for the Attorney General to get well," Butler protested, "numbers of our fellow citizens are being murdered day by day. There is not a man here who does not know that the minute justice is done on this great criminal, these murders will cease." When Evarts claimed the right of free speech for the president, Butler remarked, "The counsel for the president claims the freedom of speech and we claim the decency of speech." Butler, who was known for his light-fingered wartime Reconstruction of the Gulf Coast (during which time he acquired the nickname "Spoons," in reference to the silverware he allegedly stole), was hit hard for his insensitivity to Stanbery, Evarts, and the president. "Butler, fresh from the plate closets and bank vaults of New Orleans, representing the outraged virtue and integrity of the party of 'moral ideas,'" intoned the New York *World* in a telling Shakespearean analogy, "recalls more vividly than his language the spectacle of old Falstaff, preaching virtue in Mistress Quickly's tavern."

But the theatrics of the trial could not delay the Senate's vote on the real charges. Chief Justice Chase, as political as anyone and possibly seeking a presidential nomination with the Democrats (a party from which he had migrated to become a Radical Republican), kept the proceedings as close to law and the Constitution as he dared. The House managers sought to belay this influence by voting on Article 11 first. It was vague—most Republicans believed that Johnson had acted to obstruct Reconstruction, so one could vote "aye" with a clean conscience. But it also would amount to passage of a legislative bill of attainder (punishment of the president for no real impeachable offense, as defined in the Constitution), which was unconstitutional in itself. The most interesting side question was whether Ohio's Benjamin Wade, the senior member of the Senate (and its president pro tem), would vote at all. He would be the man who would assume Johnson's seat if the president were removed. He thus had a special, conflicting interest. But Wade was not about to miss his chance to be elevated to the highest office in the land. He voted guilty.

But only 32 others followed Wade, Butler, and Stevens. The Senate was one vote short of conviction (35-19). Seven Republicans had broken with their party and voted with the dozen Democrats to acquit, including long-term Moderate Republicans like Lyman Trumbull and William Pitt Fessenden, who were considered men of impecca-

ble honor and integrity. "We are sold out!" screamed Butler. "The country is going to the Devil!" raged Stevens. The Senate adjourned ten days while unbelievable pressure was brought to break one of the Republican dissenters. But when it reconvened, the Senate still produced the same vote on two other charges. The trial was over. Andrew Johnson was still president.

Some historians have pointed to Republican Senator E. A. Ross of Kansas as the one vote that saved Johnson. But in reality, there were others who would have voted to acquit had it been necessary. But only seven had to risk their political careers: young men who could start over, old men who could retire. What the acquittal did guarantee was that prominent Radicals like Chase and Wade would not receive the nomination of either party. The Republicans realized that they had overreached in passing Military Reconstruction and making the impeachment attempt. They had lost key local elections in 1867 (in those days some congressional seats were filled in odd years, according to state preference). The party now withdrew from ideology and went for practicality, or what politicians call availability. They turned to war hero Ulysses S. Grant, the man who had refused to stand by Johnson in challenging the Tenure of Office Act. He was a war hero, beloved by the voters, and a believer in congressional domination of government.

See also Johnson and Reconstruction; Radical Republicans and Reconstruction.

References Benedict, Michael Les, *The Impeachment Trial of Andrew Johnson* (1973) and "The Rout of Radicalism" (1972); Berger, Raul, *Impeachment* (1973); Brandt, Irving, *Impeachment* (1973); Brodie, Fawn, *Thaddeus Stevens* (1966); Current, Richard, *Old Thad Stevens* (1942); Korngold, Ralph, *Thaddeus Stevens* (1955); Kutler, Stanley I., "Impeachment Reconsidered" (1973); Lomask, Milton, *Andrew Johnson* (1960); Mantell, Martin E., *Johnson, Grant, and the Politics of Reconstruction* (1973); Sefton, James E., *Andrew Johnson and the Uses of Constitutional Power* (1980) and "The Impeachment of Andrew Johnson" (1968); Thomas, Benjamin P., and Harold M. Hyman, *Stanton* (1962); Trefousse, Hans L., "The Acquittal of Andrew Johnson and the Decline of the Radicals" (1969), *Impeachment of a President* (1975), *Benjamin Franklin Wade* (1963), and *Ben Butler* (1957).

Jim Crow
See Segregation.

Johnson, Andrew (1808–1875)
Andrew Johnson, born in Raleigh, North Carolina, lost his father at an early age and was apprenticed to a tailor. He became interested in his own education through the promptings of a customer and spent the rest of his youth and part of his early adulthood learning to read and write, encouraged by employers and later his wife. He violated the terms of his apprenticeship and relocated to Greenville, Tennessee, in 1827, traveling with his mother, for whom he always showed the greatest affection. He met and married Eliza McCardle the following year. He became interested in the problems of his fellow workers and non-slaveholding whites in general and ran for alderman, serving three terms. Johnson became mayor of Greenville in 1830. He served four terms and was also appointed by the county court to the board of supervisors of Rhea Academy.

Johnson was well liked for his political support of the middle class and poor whites in his area. He was sent to the state legislature in the late 1830s, where he worked on the new state constitution of 1839. He opposed internal improvements as wildly speculative endeavors, which cost him a second term, but the economic panic of 1837 proved him right. He made it back to the state legislature, eventually going on to the state senate in 1841. In the senate he introduced a much scaled-down measure for internal improvements that passed. He stood for Congress in 1843 and served the next ten years in the House of Representatives as a Jacksonian Democrat. He supported refunding a fine imposed earlier on Andrew Jackson for alleged military improprieties, called for the annexation of Texas, favored the war measures against Mexico asked for by James K. Polk, advanced all internal improvements that were national in scope, voted for the lower tariff of 1842, and introduced a homestead bill to provide settlers free land in the West that failed in passage.

He spoke out on behalf of Polk's use of the veto, calling it a conservative measure that allowed the president—as the only true representative elected by all the voters—to delay unwise, hasty, or unconstitutional legislation until it could be more fully considered by the people. It was a position he would adhere to all his life and was very Jacksonian in its origins.

In 1852, Johnson was elected governor of Tennessee, where he made many enemies in the slaveholding parts of the state by advocating the rights of nonslaveholding whites. He went on to the U.S. Senate five years later, a tremendous achievement for a man who came to the state penniless and fleeing an apprenticeship. Much of his success as a politician was due to his speaking style, provocative yet intelligent, and always very personal in his attacks on his opponents. While in the U.S. Senate, Johnson reintroduced a homestead measure (which failed again) and became an outspoken advocate for Union in the sectional conflict that was coming to a head. A slaveholder himself by now, Johnson was leery of the constant abolition petitions sent to Washington and the pamphlets that antislave societies wanted sent through the mails. He supported the Southern Democrats in 1860, but he refused to withdraw with his state in 1861 after the election of Abraham Lincoln—making him the only senator from a seceding state to stay on in Washington.

Johnson's uncompromising Unionism made him an instant man of importance. Since Tennessee was one of the first Southern states to be occupied by Union soldiers, Lincoln appointed Johnson as the state's military governor in 1862. His wife and family were still behind Confederate lines, and he was threatened with possible assassination, but Johnson went on with the work of running a loyal government without a second thought. His bravery and outspokenness earned him the vice presidential slot with the Union party (a wartime combination of Republicans and Northern war–supporting Democrats) in 1864 to draw the votes of border states and wavering Democratic districts in the North. Sick to his stomach at his inaugural, Johnson unwisely took some liquor for strength; however, he had not eaten since the previous day and the libation caused him to be woozy and unfairly accused of drunkenness. Within six weeks, Johnson would become president as Lincoln fell mortally wounded to John Wilkes Booth's pistol.

As the accusations of drunkenness showed, Johnson had (and still has) a controversial reputation. Although it was popular a half century ago to portray him as an embattled hero fighting against vindictive opponents for the good of American democracy, even among the first writers on Reconstruction, Johnson always had his critics. He was tactless, egotistical, overly self-confident, a gut-fighter on the stump, fond of making shocking off-the-cuff statements, a loner, and somewhat radical in the sense that he was always outside the mainstream of thought in his state and the nation. At first his uncompromising attitude impressed Republicans, who wanted a tougher peace with the South than the seemingly moderate Lincoln proposed. But no sooner did Johnson take office than he began to moderate. Historians blame this variously on the influence of Secretary of State Seward or the responsibilities of the office. But also important was the fact that the rich Southerners, the former slaveholders, Johnson's old political enemies in Tennessee, whom he had excluded from the political process unless they pled their cases individually, came forward and begged his forgiveness. And like them, Johnson had little sympathy for black Americans.

Merely being asked for forgiveness seemed to be what Johnson craved more than anything else. He forgave them right off. Then these men went back home and proceeded to wreck what chance the South had to Reconstruct itself. They passed the notorious Black Codes, which severely hindered the political participation of African Americans as free people; they elected former Confederate congressmen, generals, and even the Rebel vice president to office; and they permitted a series of race riots that were highly publicized in the North. But Johnson himself had a great void in his own thoughts on Reconstruction. He was essentially a Democrat, and he had little sympathy for Northern Republicans, who needed some guarantee that they would not be swamped by returning Southern Democrats in congressional votes and policymaking. Johnson should have known better. Already Congress had indicated to President Lincoln that they wanted a voice in Reconstruction with the passage of the Wade-Davis Bill in 1864. And upon Lincoln's pocket veto of this measure, the legislators had issued a Wade-Davis Manifesto, warning the executive branch that members of Congress would be key participants in the future of Reconstruction, or else.

But Johnson went on to issue his own Reconstruction program, part of which recognized the Lincoln-appointed governments in Louisiana, Arkansas, and Tennessee. Congress was not opposed to the president participating in the Reconstruction process—after all, Johnson had to act when they were out of session. The thing that did him in was his refusal to meet Congress halfway on key measures the Republicans saw as critical to Southern readmission, like the Freedmen's Bureau renewal, the Civil Rights Act of 1866, and the Fourteenth Amendment. People could disagree on the necessity of these measures, but Johnson did not merely argue, he shot off his mouth in public, accusing the Republican leaders by name of trying to destroy traditional American government, isolating himself from any reasonable compromise effort. Then he went on the campaign trail—a move known as the Swing around the Circle—and spoke out against his opponents in city after city. Aware of his tendency to respond to hecklers, Republican advance men went around and set up confrontations. Johnson made even more intemperate replies that so alienated the Northern voters they returned a veto-proof two-thirds Republican majority to Congress. This Congress was called into session immediately after its predecesor went out of session—a move intended to limit the presi-

A political cartoon satirizing Andrew Johnson as "King Andy" illustrates Americans' growing animosity toward the presidential candidate. Lady Liberty sits in shackles (lower right) as Secretary of State William H. Seward draws a curtain and points to the line of congressmen, each awaiting to be beheaded.

dent's ability to act in Congress' traditional absence. Reconstruction policy making had been transferred from the executive to the legislative branch.

Congress sought to restrain the president's power through acts that limited his removal of executive appointees and his control of the army in the South; along the way it established Military Reconstruction. Johnson acted to enforce these measures, but he also took care to obstruct them within the law (e.g., by appointing military commanders in the South who were against army control of civilian government). He also sought to test the validity of the Tenure of Office Act, which limited Johnson's ability to make appointments; this led directly to his impeachment. The trial was a sloppy proceeding. Congress figured that the Senate would vote on political questions rather than actual accusations. Johnson conducted an admirable defense through his lawyers and managed to diffuse a lot of animosity toward himself though moderate appointments and the fear that unpopular Republican Senator Benjamin Wade would become president if Johnson were convicted. He was sustained as president by one vote. Johnson then proceeded to offer himself as a presidential candidate for the Democratic party but was rejected as too much of a liability. He retired for a while to Greenville but returned to Washington as a U.S. senator when the Democrats took over Tennessee in 1875. Johnson saw his swearing in before a body that had tried to convict him eight years earlier as a personal vindication. On a trip home in July 1875, he collapsed and died of multiple strokes. He was buried at Signal Hill outside of Greenville, his body wrapped in the American flag and his head resting on a copy of the U.S. Constitution— treasured objects he had defended during the Civil War and Reconstruction.

See also Congressional Reconstruction; Impeachment; Johnson and Reconstruction; Lincoln and Reconstruction.

References Beale, Howard K., *The Critical Year [1866]* (1930); McKitrick, Eric, *Andrew Johnson and Reconstruction* (1960); Milton, George F., *The Age of Hate* (1930); Riddleberger, Patrick W., *1866* (1979), Sefton, James E., *Andrew Johnson and the Uses of Constitutional Power* (1980); Stryker, Lloyd P., *Andrew Johnson* (1929); Thomas, Lately, *The First President Johnson* (1968); Trefousse, Hans, *Andrew Johnson* (1989); Winston, Hobert W., *Andrew Johnson* (1928).

Johnson, Andrew, and Reconstruction

Andrew Johnson, picked as the vice presidential candidate to broaden the appeal of the Union party (a combination of Republicans and War Democrats) in 1864 and to get rid of then vice president Hannibal Hamlin, whom Lincoln saw as a disloyal spy for his radical opponents within the Republican party, became president upon Lincoln's death. No one had thought that in their hour of triumph that the Republicans would be saddled with a Democrat as party leader. "Why couldn't we have got an American for the job?" groused Pennsylvania congressman and Radical Republican Thaddeus Stevens, putting voice to many other's thoughts about the Tennessean's accession to power. It was bad enough that Johnson might not support the Republican hopes for the future of the United States. What was worse was that he was a strict constructionist—he believed in the very letter of the Constitution, hardly the man that innovative Republicans like Lincoln, accustomed to stretching the document to its limits, could work with. Yet initially Johnson fooled his doubters. He spoke of how "treason must be made infamous." He hated the plantation aristocracy. He hinted at hanging Rebel leaders. Radical Republicans began to wonder if the assassination of Lincoln had not been the judgment of the Lord for Lincoln's hesitancy in advancing the freedom and civil rights of the slaves. Johnson looked to be all right.

Johnson soon put an end to this rank speculation when he issued his Proclamation for Reconstruction on 29 May 1865. Unlike Lincoln's single Reconstruction proposal, Johnson issued one for each state, beginning with North Carolina. But all said essentially the same thing. And like Lincoln, Johnson assumed that secession was void from the outset and that the president should take the lead in Reconstruction without waiting for the reconvening of Congress in December 1865. The first thing Johnson did was to recognize the "Lincoln governments" in Louisiana, Arkansas, Tennessee, and Virginia. This may have not been a wise thing to do because Congress had already refused to seat them earlier. The rest of his plan, however, was more like the Radical Republicans' Wade-Davis Bill than Lincoln's wartime measure. Johnson expected a majority of the voters registered in 1860 to take an oath of future loyalty to the United States. Since the war was over it was logical that more had to be done than Lincoln had called for in 1863.

Like all other plans of Reconstruction, Johnson's excluded certain classes from initial participation in forming loyal governments. These included the usual higher officials, civilian and military, of the seceded states and the Confederacy, 14 separate classes in all. But Johnson added a new class. He excluded all persons worth $20,000 or more from the initial amnesty. These persons had to appeal directly to the president for individual pardons. This was at a time when people were still unsure if hanging or property seizure or permanent exclusion from political and civil rights might pertain to supporters of the defunct Confederate government. It was important to get a pardon to be exempted from future executive or legislative punitive actions. So 16,000 applied, often utilizing the services of a pardon broker, who for a fee would guide the application to the proper hands. And Johnson forgave 13,500 of them—about 85 percent. Virtually all of these applicants were former planters, the very men whom Johnson had fought during his political career as the defender of the average non-slaveholding Southern white. They came, they crawled, and Johnson loved it. And afterward he took their political advice.

Once Johnson had given the initial amnesty, he appointed a provisional governor for each state. In the case of several states, he accepted the Unionists whom Lincoln had put in power. In others he appointed his own man, always a Union supporter. The provisional governors, with the assistance of the occupying federal forces, were to supervise the amnesty process (taking the oaths) and then call the elections for a constitutional convention. The convention would write a new state constitution that had to repudiate secession, declare the Confederate war debt invalid, abolish slavery on the state level, and recognize the Thirteenth Amendment, which ended slavery nationally. No other action outside the amendment was required as to the status of African Americans in the reconstructed South. Then a new election would be called, and the voters would vote on the constitution and elect a new slate of state and local officials, as well as House members and U.S. senators.

The various states did some interesting things under Johnson's plan. Nearly all changed their constitutions to allow for the apportionment of representatives to state legislatures based on white population only. Before the war most Southern states had used the federal three-fifths formula, counting this proportion of slaves for the purposes of representation. This method had given the planters a disproportionate number of legislative seats and stacked all legislation their way. Under the new approach, however, it appeared that the small white farmers who disliked the planters as Johnson did would finally be heard. Conventions in Mississippi and South Carolina talked their way around the repudiation of secession; others refused to get rid of slavery on the state level, merely adopting the Thirteenth Amendment (but Mississippi refused to do even that), which negated state laws permitting slavery; most did not want to negate the Confederate war debt, pleading that it was so bound up with the prewar peace debt as to be indistinguishable (but Texas repudiated all state and national debts contracted since 1861); and Arkansas voted Confederate soldiers a pension, tacitly recognizing the validity of the Confederacy. But essentially all former Confederate states complied with Johnson's requests to one degree or another, and by December 1865 their representatives were waiting for

Congress to meet and give them their seats on the floor, with the president's approval.

Johnson was being a bit naive if he expected the governments he established to receive anything but the short shrift Lincoln's governments received earlier. In reality Johnson had done the South a great disservice. He had implied that if they did his bidding they would be back in the Union with full rights and no hard feelings. But the Northern public was not pleased with the Johnson governments. Unwisely, Southerners had assumed that the North would feel better able to deal with the same men who had represented the South before and during the war. As quickly as the excluded Confederate leaders got their presidential pardons, they stood for election and won. The Southern representatives waiting at the doors of Congress had been officers in the Rebel army and congressmen in the Richmond government; one of them had even been the vice president of the Confederacy. They were grouped under the derisive label "the Confederate Brigadiers."

This turn of events shocked even Johnson. He had expected that the poorer whites would stand together and repudiate the planters—a bit presumptuous, given that he had not done so himself through his liberal pardon policy. And the representatives came with more political baggage. There had been a series of race riots in the South that indicated that blacks would not be respected in their new status as freedmen, a fact that was reinforced by discriminatory laws known collectively as the Black Codes. In addition, the new white governments had excluded all blacks and some poor whites from voting by means of property qualifications, and they refused to finance public schools (half of Mississippi's state budget would go for artificial limbs for veterans). But Johnson was not about to admit that he had blundered. This would turn the whole process over to Congress. So he made the best of a lousy situation and accepted all that had passed. He was now controlled by the very men he had tried to exclude from the reconstructing process in the first place.

To understand Johnson's seeming political ineptness, one must remember that he was above all still a Jacksonian Democrat. He became president through an unfortunate assassination of the Republican party leader, President Lincoln. Johnson was a loyal Union man, but he hated Republicans otherwise. He and the Republicans had some things in common: a hatred of both secession and the planter aristocracy and a love of both the United States undivided and the end of slavery to break the Slave Power Conspiracy (the political influence of slaveowners). But Johnson was not about to help the Republicans expand their party to the South; he would not support a slow or difficult Reconstruction; he was against the Republicans' economic measures enacted during the war (high tariff, high taxes, national banking system, massive internal improvements), except for the Homestead Act; and he was against equal political and civil rights for African Americans. He wanted the South back in the Union fast so he could get all of those Democratic votes to back him in Congress. Unfortunately, Congress rules on its own members' suitability for being seated, and the Republicans drew back to look into the advisability of seating any of Johnson's representatives by creating a Joint Committee of Fifteen on Reconstruction to investigate the whole executive Reconstruction phenomenon.

See also Black Codes; Congressional Reconstruction; Ethridge Conspiracy of 1863; Impeachment; Johnson, Andrew; Joint Committee of Fifteen on Reconstruction; Lincoln and Reconstruction; Pardon, Amnesty, and Parole; Race Riots that Influenced the Reconstruction Acts; Seward and Reconstruction.

References Beale, Howard K., *The Critical Year [1866]* (1930); Brock, William R., "Reconstruction and the American Party System" (1975); Burgess, John W., *Reconstruction and the Constitution* (1902); Carter, Dan T., *When the War Was Over* (1985); Castel, Albert, *The Presidency of Andrew Johnson* (1979); Cox, John, and LaWanda Cox, "Andrew Johnson and His Ghost Writers" (1961–1962) and *Politics, Principles, and Prejudice* (1963); Dunning, William A., "More Light on Andrew Johnson" (1905–1906); Gipson, Lawrence H., "The Statesmanship of President Johnson" (1914–1915); Lomask, Milton, *Andrew Johnson* (1960); McKitrick, Eric, *Andrew Johnson and Reconstruction*

(1960); Milton, George F., *The Age of Hate* (1930); Perman, Michael, *Reunion without Compromise* (1973); Riddleberger, Patrick W., *1866* (1979), Sefton, James E., *Andrew Johnson and the Uses of Constitutional Power* (1980); Stryker, Lloyd P., *Andrew Johnson* (1929); Thomas, Lately, *The First President Johnson* (1968); Trefousse, Hans, *Andrew Johnson* (1989); Winston, Hobert W., *Andrew Johnson* (1928).

Joint Committee of Fifteen on Reconstruction

The Joint Commission of Fifteen on Reconstruction was formed in December 1865 to investigate conditions in the former Confederate states and recommend a program to ensure those states' loyalty and readmission to the Union. It was the body that brought about both Moderate Republican Reconstruction (renewal of the Freedmen's Bureau Act, creation of the Civil Rights Act of 1866, and the Fourteenth Amendment) and Radical Republican Reconstruction (the four Military Reconstruction Acts).

The first act of the committee was to investigate conditions in the South. The intent was to show that the South remained unrepentant in the face of President Andrew Johnson's Reconstruction program, which had already been completed and had sent representatives to Washington. These men, collectively referred to as the "Confederate Brigadiers," had already been refused seats on the floor of Congress pending the investigation. The report of the committee was presented in four parts in addition to a general report. The first part was an intensive look at Tennessee; the second concerned itself with Virginia and the Carolinas; the third covered Georgia, Mississippi, Alabama, and Arkansas; and the fourth examined Florida, Louisiana, and Texas. The committee's conclusions were that the Confederacy was a disorganized community lacking civil governments or constitutions or any proper relations with the United States beyond that of military conquest; that Congress could not recognize any group of representatives from that area; and that Congress would have to revamp conditions in the South to ensure the civil rights of all persons, equality of representation, the purging of all conditions of rebellion and the holding of office by the perpetrators of secession, and the right of suffrage to all loyal persons.

The committee then proceeded to recommend several measures to Congress that together represented Moderate Republican Reconstruction. The committee's go-between was Moderate Republican Senator Lyman Trumbull of Illinois, who somehow got the impression that Johnson would be reasonable and would work with Congress in developing a new program. Instead Johnson met Congress head on, asserting that he would act by executive proclamation and that Congress should merely endorse his plan. Besides, Johnson maintained, the measures proposed by Congress at the recommendation of the committee were blatantly unconstitutional because they would upset the federal system and interfere with prerogatives normally left to the states under the Constitution.

At first Congress wondered if the president might not have a good case. They upheld his veto of the renewal of the Freedmen's Bureau bill. But when Johnson got personal in his invective, Congress reconsidered its position. It then repassed the Freedmen's Bureau Act, added the Civil Rights Act of 1866, and wrapped its whole program up in the proposed Fourteenth Amendment to the Constitution, all products of the joint committee. When only Tennessee approved the amendment, Congress readmitted that state to the Union and, reinforced by overwhelming Republican victories in the 1866 congressional elections, brought forth Military Reconstruction to coerce the South into the "proper" course of action.

It was commonplace for historians to see the joint committee as dominated by Radical Republicans from the start, loaded, as it were, for the final humiliation of imposing Military Reconstruction on the South. More recent studies disagree with this notion, however, pointing out that the committee and all Republicans in general held to certain principles that they believed the

South ought to adopt as conditions of readmission to the Union. Indeed, Congress had already warned President Abraham Lincoln during the Civil War through the Wade-Davis Bill that it considered its role in Reconstruction to be essential and not to be compromised by executive action. Johnson ought to have taken note, historians conclude. After all, the incoming representatives—prominent Confederates every one—were from a part of the nation that had just engaged in a viable four-year rebellion, had massacred black soldiers at Fort Pillow when they tried to surrender, had abused Union soldiers at Andersonville and other prisons, and had rioted against the freedmen at Norfolk, Memphis, and New Orleans within the year while claiming to have been reconstructed through the president's program.

So Congress, regardless of the ideology of the Republicans that made up its majority, was in agreement that Reconstruction was its responsibility and that some provision had to be made in regard to the civil rights and personal protection of African Americans through citizenship and the vote. As such, the actions of the Joint Committee of Fifteen on Reconstruction correctly denoted the mood of Congress and, through the vote received by Republicans in the fall of 1866, the North. To plead security for the Union and civil rights and the vote for threatened blacks in 1866 was not merely "waving the bloody shirt" (i.e., a political tool of telling graphic stories of conservative white political violence in the South). It was reality. These issues would be callously propagandized and exploited for political advantage in the 1870s, but in the 1860s they were valid political considerations shared by the Republican party and the North as a whole; they were accurately accounted for in the measures recommended by the joint committee.

See also Moderate Republicans and Reconstruction; Radical Republicans and Reconstruction.

References Clark, John G., "Historians and the Joint Committee of Reconstruction" (1961) and "Radicals and Moderates in the Joint Committee on Reconstruction" (1963); Kendrick, Benjamin B., The Journal of the Joint Committee of Fifteen on Recon-

struction (1914); Lowe, Richard G., "The Joint Committee on Reconstruction" (1992); U.S. Congress, "Report of the Joint Committee on Reconstruction" (1866).

Julian, George W. (1817–1899)

Born in a log cabin in Wayne County, Indiana, George Julian came from a French/Huguenot background (his real family name being St. Julien). His father died when George was six, and his mother raised the family. Julian had a common school education and read law, practicing his profession in northeastern Indiana. In 1845 he was elected to the Indiana state legislature as a Whig, but he voted with the Democrats against repudiation of state canal bonds. He also began to speak out and write newspaper pieces attacking slavery. The Whigs refused him a renomination, this time to the state senate, so Julian went over to the Free Soil party in 1848 and supported Martin Van Buren. Julian himself ran for Congress as a Free Soiler and was elected in 1848. He voted against the Compromise of 1850, which extended slavery into the Mexican Cession below the 36°30′ Missouri Compromise line. In 1852 he ran as vice president on the unsuccessful Free Soil ticket. By 1854, Julian was one of the leading organizers of the Republican party, and he actively supported the John C. Frémont ticket in 1856. Four years later he was elected to Congress, where, upon the outbreak of war, he urged the abolition of all slavery as a war measure and was instrumental in the passage of the Homestead Act in 1862. Although he was disappointed in the hesitancy of President Abraham Lincoln to emancipate the slaves and impose harsher conditions on the wartime Reconstruction of the South, Julian never broke with the chief executive as so many other Radicals did in 1864.

Upon Lincoln's assassination, Julian felt no compulsion to go along with President Andrew Johnson's Reconstruction program. Julian now came forth publicly and called for harsh punishment of Southerners, particularly through land confiscation and the granting of land and suffrage to the freedmen (he also proposed a constitutional amendment granting the vote to women). He was one of the committee of seven that prepared the impeachment charges against Johnson. But the waning of radicalism upon the president's acquittal caught Julian full force, and he failed to achieve renomination in 1870. He became a Liberal Republican in 1872 and became a lifelong champion of various reforms. He supported the Democrats in 1876 and was made surveyor general for the Territory of New Mexico, during which time he uncovered many frauds. He supported the Gold Democrats, who favored basing the currency on gold, in 1896 and published his political philosophy and speeches, as well as a biography of Joshua R. Giddings, an early abolitionist. He died at his Indiana home at the end of the century, ever the principled idealist and an anathema to regular party politicians.

See also Southern Homestead Act.

References Clarke, Grace Julian, *George W. Julian* (1923); Haworth, Paul L., "George Washington Julian" (1964–1981); Julian, George W., *Political Recollections* (1884); Turnier, William J., "George W. Julian" (1967).

Ku Klux Klan

In late December 1865, six young former Confederate soldiers sat bored in the office of Judge Thomas M. Jones in Pulaski, Tennessee. They wanted something "fun" to do. One suggested that they organize a secret society. They thought it over all the next day and reconvened in the judge's office again the next night. They elected a chairman and a secretary and divided themselves into committees to consider at length such things as ritual, rules, and a name for their club. The third meeting took place at a home one of the young men was house-sitting. Here, they agreed to everything but a name. Hereafter the meeting house would be called a "den," the den leader would be the "grand cyclops," his aide was the "grand magi," the secretary was the "grand scribe," the greeter of initiates was the "grand turk," the den's two guards were "lictors," and the grand cyclops' two messengers became "night hawks," while the rank-and-file members would be "ghouls." Finally, one of the men, being a scholar of the classics, suggested a name for the new organization: "Kluklos," Greek for "circle." They spoke some more, and eventually John C. Lester, John B. Kennedy, James R. Crowe, Frank O. McCord, Richard R. Reed, and J. Calvin Jones (the judge's son), settled on the alliterative "Ku Klux Klan" for the name of the new club designed, as they saw it, to put some zip in dull old Pulaski.

The boys decided to put on Halloween-like disguises and celebrate the founding by galloping on horseback up and down Pulaski's streets. Not surprisingly, everyone was a bit uneasy about their antics and evil costumes, especially African Americans. From here on out, the club required that all members wear robes and cardboard masks, some of grotesque size, and pretend to be the Confederate dead risen up from their graves at Shiloh and thirsting for revenge against the Yankee soldiers, former slaves, Carpetbaggers, and Scalawags—the occupiers and alleged despoilers of the culture of the Old South. "That's the first drink I've had since I was killed," went what would become a traditional incantation, " and you get mighty thirsty down in Hell." As he spoke, the "ghost" would pour a whole bucket of water into his mouth (actually into a concealed funnel and tube leading to a gigantic, concealed oilcloth bag). From this beginning came the society of white regulators that would terrorize the supporters of Reconstruction. The Civil War that had been lost on the far-off battlefields of Virginia and Tennessee by the Confederate armies was about to be won on the back roads, swamps, and byways closer to home by a potent new guerrilla force.

After its more-or-less accidental initial organization, the Ku Klux Klan spread rapidly throughout the rest of the South, with the purpose of expediting white control of the ex-Confederate states and countering the Republican Union Loyal Leagues. Newspaper stories, pro and con, kept the Klan in the public eye. Fear of "Negro insurrection" fed its expansion. The Klansmen saw themselves like the Sons of Liberty of the American Revolution. Their activities mimicked tarring and feathering British tax collectors and throwing tea into Boston Harbor, but often with a more murderous twist. Perhaps a more appropriate analogy was the "patrol" instituted among whites in the days of slavery to watch the roads at night to make sure no blacks roamed freely without a pass or conspired against the powers that be.

The Klansmen were seen by many as modern Robin Hoods of white supremacy. They were glorified by Thomas Dixon's fictional Ku Klux Klan trilogy (*The Leopard's Spots* [1902], *The Clansman*, [1905], and *The Traitor* [1907]), which became the basis for the first hit movie of the twentieth century, D. W. Griffith's *The Birth of a Nation*. (Incidentally, this film introduced the notion of the fiery cross into Klan ceremonies; that symbol was never used in the Reconstruction Era, but it looked good on film.) Later, Rhett Butler rode with the hooded vigilantes in *Gone With the Wind* and was saved from arrest by Yankee troopers on the word of an Atlanta madam that he and his cronies spent the evening with her girls. Historian Hodding Carter spoke of the aura of the Reconstruction Klans in this way: "Your grandfather, God bless his memory, was one of them. And we hadn't been married more than a year when I sewed his robe together for him and out he would ride, night after night, night after night. Terrible times they were, but we won out in the end."

As the Ku Klux Klan grew, haphazardly and undisciplined, new levels of control were added, like the grand dragon and his staff of hydras for each state, culminating in 1867 with the election of former Confederate cavalry general Nathan Bedford Forrest as grand wizard, the head of all the Klans, and a staff of ten genii. Many names came to be used: the Knights of the White Camellia, the Knights of the Rising Sun, Pale Faces, the Invisible Circle, the Families of the South, and, of course, the Knights of the Ku Klux Klan. Some organizations were more secret than others, but all had the goal of restoring political and social control of the South to the whites who held it before the loss of the war, by violence if necessary—and it usually was necessary. And who better to lead this "invisible empire" than General Forrest, the instigator of the 1864 Fort Pillow massacre in which surrendering black and white Union soldiers, former slaves and white Loyalists, were shot down as traitors to the Confederacy and the Old South. "That's a good thing; that's a damned good thing," he is reputed to have said when told of the Klan. "We can use it to keep the niggers in their place."

Not all members wished to be as blunt as General Forrest. The Klan's motives were covered up by a grand-sounding "Prescript," the Klan's constitution, in which the name of the organization was never mentioned. In its place were three asterisks (* * *) for "Ku Klux Klan," two (* *) for "Ku Klux," and a single asterisk (*) for "Klan." Indeed, when questioned by a congressional investigating committee, Forrest claimed membership in an organization that had in place of its name "three stars." But by the time the committee had finished questioning him, he had contradicted himself and obfuscated his testimony so much that no one was quite sure what he claimed, setting a precedent for such testimony that still holds. The Prescript's statement of purpose defined the * as "an institution of Chivalry, Humanity, Mercy, and Patriotism" dedicated to protecting the weak, especially widows and orphans of Confederate soldiers, to protecting the Constitution as it stood before the Reconstruction amendments, and to preventing invasion from outside domestic (Scalawag) and foreign (Carpetbag) enemies—in other words, to keep the South for native-born whites only.

The * * oath was sort of a reverse of the ironclad oath the Union required of Southern whites who wished to hold public office—one had to swear that he had not given aid or comfort to the forces of Reconstruction, such as the Union Loyal Leagues or the Union army. Over a half million men filled * ranks in short order as their program went forth. The usual procedure was to issue a warning, administer a whipping if unheeded, and then resort to murder or exile of the major resisters. The * * * had its own "judiciary branch," and there were instances where victims of * * "justice" were released from further civil or criminal prosecution because of "double jeopardy." Of course, it was not unusual for the judge, sheriff, and arresting posse to be the grand cyclops, grand magi, and ghouls of the local * * * den.

Like the Prescript, every Ku Klux message and warning was written in code. There were two versions of this code—the original and a revised version (given here). In the latter, instead of the months, one would see for January, Dismal Moon; February, Mystic Moon; March, Stormy Moon; April, Peculiar Moon; May, Blooming Moon; June, Brilliant Moon; July, Painful Moon; August, Portentous Moon; September, Fading Moon; October, Melancholy Moon; November, Glorious Moon; December, Gloomy Moon. Days, from Sunday to Saturday, were White, Green, Yellow, Amber, Purple, Crimson, Emerald. The hours of the clock (starting at 1 o'clock) were Fearful Hour, Startling Hour, Wonderful Hour, Alarming Hour, Mournful Hour, Appalling Hour, Hideous Hour, Frightful Hour, Awful Hour, Horrible Hour, Dreadful Hour, Last Hour (midnight—the Klan rarely worked during daylight hours). The letters of the code word CUMBERLAND gave the numbers from 1 to 0 in the revised version (no number code was in the original Prescript). Hence if a grand cyclops wished to call a meeting of the den for Thursday, 25 July, at 9 o'clock p.m., the notice would read: Purple Night, Painful Moon, UE, Awful Hour. It was all a bit spooky.

On a raid, the Klansmen and their horses were disguised with flowing robes. No one was to speak. Instead, each raider carried a throaty-sounding whistle. When at rest, one blast meant move, three blasts meant danger, and a series of short toots was a request for aid. Many groups served with military discipline. One Mississippi Carpet-bagger who was whipped remembered that the leader reprimanded those who cursed him and that, except for the whipping, all was decorum. But other groups were not so "nice" in thought, talk, or action, the ideals of the Prescript be damned. It soon became apparent that something national had to be done to counteract Klan activities, which had expanded into a conspiracy that covered most of the South, lest the violence and intimidation overthrow the influences of local and state government.

But just as a Democratic state government did not necessarily support the Klan, a Republican government rarely acted with enough force to crush it. Most state officials feared that relying on martial law and a loyal militia that was composed of black and pro-Union whites would institute a race war. The only exception to this rule was in Arkansas, where Governor Powell Clayton used his militia units and an active anti-Klan law to destroy the Klan's influence by the

A Carpetbagger begs surrounding Ku Klux Klan members to spare his life in this 1871 engraving. African Americans, Carpetbaggers, and Scalawags were frequent targets of early Klan violence.

245

end of 1869. Considering that the Klan and related organizations could mount raiding parties of up to 150 men, Clayton's pursuit of them, using Union whites from the northeastern counties and black units from elsewhere in an integrated army that scoured the state from top to bottom, was spectacular.

Not everybody had the imagination or the resources to follow Clayton's success in Arkansas. Governor W. W. Holden of North Carolina, a state as fully plagued with Ku Klux Klan activity as Arkansas, sent a request to President Ulysses S. Grant for federal assistance. The result was Grant's annual message to Congress in December 1870 asking that it look into the Klan and pass necessary legislation. Congress, looking forward to the fall elections, had already passed the First Enforcement Act on 31 May of that year, geared toward protecting loyal whites and blacks in the exercise of the vote. The act prevented bribery and intimidation of voters by combinations of persons in disguise; authorized federal troops to act; and provided that if a person or persons deprived anyone of any right or privilege of citizenship and committed a state crime at the same time, that person could be tried in federal court and given the same punishment as would be provided by the state in which the incident occurred. But little was done to carry out the measure.

Congress moved to look into the problems faced in North Carolina as a result of the Ku Klux Klan. The result was the Second Enforcement Act to tighten up election procedures, given that Congress perceived the Klan to be mainly a political entity. But a stringent anti-Ku Klux Klan law failed when Moderate Republicans bolted and voted with the Democrats against its suspension of habeas corpus. President Grant then took what was for him a revolutionary step. He disliked interfering with Congress, but he had received so many complaints from the Carolinas that he conferred with congressional leaders. They told him that they would act if he wrote out a request. Grant did so on the spot. The result was the Third Enforcement Act (the Ku Klux Act)

on 20 April 1871. Seeking to enforce the Fourteenth Amendment, the Ku Klux Act made it a federal crime (1) to conspire or go in disguise on the public highways or upon the premises of another for the purposes of depriving anybody of equal protection of the laws or the privileges and immunities of citizenship, or (2) to hinder state authorities from protecting anybody in the same rights. One could be tried in both criminal and civil courts, fined up to $5,000 and imprisoned or both, and then sued by the victim. The president could authorize the use of the army and navy to assist in the enforcement of the laws and suspend the writ of habeas corpus to hold suspects.

Next Congress looked into Ku Klux Klan activity throughout the South, one of the largest, most involved investigations up to that time. Subcommittees went into each state and gathered evidence. Republicans wanted to look at violence and intimidation, whereas Democrats preferred to check into the malfeasance of Republican officeholders. But each side got to cross-examine the other's witnesses. In the end, the committee report asserted that the Klan was at the base of an effort to deprive African Americans of their civil rights and gut the Republican party in the South. That was pretty much right on the mark, despite Democratic and Southern white protests to the contrary. At the same time, Congress decided to remove Confederate political disabilities under the Fourteenth Amendment to lessen the feelings of injustice felt by whites.

Although federal prosecutors could not apply the Ku Klux Act retroactively, the First Enforcement Act allowed them to go ahead with their cases now buttressed by the fact that Congress meant business. Hundreds of indictments occurred in district after district, with federal grand juries willing to go ahead where local grand juries had proven hesitant or unwilling. Convictions and acquittals followed. Many accused had their legal fees paid for by local white citizens who viewed them as heroes. But Klan activity dropped off everywhere the law was enforced.

The center of the federal effort, however,

was in South Carolina (the only place where habeas corpus was suspended), Kentucky, and northern Louisiana. Since George Armstrong Custer, a Civil War hero now in command of the Seventh Cavalry, was off at one of his frequent appearances before a court-martial, his regiment was divided up into battalions (thirds) and sent to the disaffected places to put teeth into the prosecutions. Over 200 were arrested in South Carolina alone. Another 500 gave themselves up voluntarily. Northern newspapermen on hand for the trials remarked at how few of the accused displayed any remorse for their activities and that any public sense of right and wrong was entirely lacking. Only about 50 South Carolinians wound up in the federal penitentiary at Albany, New York. Those who confessed without a trial were usually given suspended sentences. Most were never brought to trial. Recent scholarship has shown that much of the policing of polls, though seemingly conducted to guard against antiblack terrorists in the South, was conducted in Northern cities to stifle the Northern Democratic opposition to Republican reelection. And there were almost equal numbers of indictments brought in the North as in the South until 1876.

As historian Hodding Carter has pointed out, many Southern whites still regard Reconstruction as an evil nightmare, just as many African Americans recall it for what it promised but never was, a glorious dream. It is in the light of these two viewpoints that the story of the Klan has to be seen. The federal government's effort against the Klan broke the group's campaign of terrorism, oddly enough, with the conviction of relatively few Klansmen (continued prosecutions would last until 1897 at the rate of 200 cases a year and relatively few convictions). But it was already too late. The Klan's program of terror had already revealed how to return Democratic majorities in most Southern states. The new violence would be quite open, practiced under the guise of the

rifle clubs, the White Leagues, and the Red Shirts. The Supreme Court would nullify the effectiveness of laws against the Ku Klux Klan by 1876, when it declared that the federal government could legislate against state actions, but not the actions of individuals, under the Fourteenth Amendment. And in the 1890s Congress itself would refuse to renew the Force Acts, giving official endorsement to the new society that emerged from the Ku Klux Klan–inspired chaos of Reconstruction.

See also Enforcement Acts; Grant and Reconstruction; Race Riots that Influenced the Reconstruction Acts; Rifle Clubs; Union Loyal Leagues.

References Ayers, Edward L., *Vegeance and Justice* (1984); Beck, E. M., and Stewart E. Tolnay, "The Killing Fields of the Deep South" (1990); Carpenter, John A., "Atrocities during the Reconstruction Period" (1962); Carter, Hodding, *The Angry Scar* (1959); Chalmers, David M., *Hooded Americanism* (1968); Cresswell, Stephen, "Enforcing the Enforcement Act" (1987); Escott, Paul D., "White Republicanism and Ku Klux Klan Terror" (1989); Grimshaw, Alan, "Lawlessness and Violence in America and Their Special Manifestations in Changing Negro-White Relationships" (1959); Hackney, Sheldon, "Southern Violence" (1969); Horn, Stanley, *Invisible Empire* (1939); Nieman, Donald G., ed., *Black Freedom/White Violence* (1994); Olsen, Otto H., "The Ku Klux Klan" (1962) and "Southern Reconstruction and the Question of Self-Determination" (1975); Peek, Ralph L., "Lawlessness in Florida" (1961–1962) and "Military Reconstruction and the Growth of Anti-Negro Sentiment in Florida" (1968–1969); Phillips, Paul D., "White Reaction to the Freedmen's Bureau in Tennessee" (1966); Sefton, James E., *Army and Reconstruction* (1967); Shapiro, Herbert, "Afro-American Responses to Race Violence during Reconstruction" (1972) and "The Ku Klux Klan during Reconstruction" (1964); Simkins, Francis B., "The Ku Klux Klan in South Carolina" (1927); Singletary, Otis A., *Negro Militia and Reconstruction* (1957); Stagg, J. C. A., "The Problem of Klan Violence" (1974); Swinney, Everette, "Enforcing the Fifteenth Amendment" (1962); Trelease, Allan W., *White Terror* (1971); U.S. Congress, *House Reports*, "Condition of Affairs in the Late Insurrectionary States" (1873); Williams, Lou Falkner, "The South Carolina Ku Klux Klan Trials and Enforcement of Federal Rights" (1993); Woodward, C. Vann, "Seeds of Failure in Radical Race Policy" (1966).

Liberal Republicanism

By the time of the 1872 election, the Ulysses S. Grant administration had cause quite a bit of disillusionment among the Republican party and the public at large. Those within the party who opposed Grantism were called Liberal Republicans. Most were journalists, professional reformers, and intellectuals. They often lacked political skills but made up for it with a lot of enthusiasm. They were liberal not in the twentieth-century sense of wanting government services, but in the traditional definition of desiring honest, constitutional government. Led by German immigrant and former Union political general Carl Schurz, they decided not to challenge the political professionals of the Republican party but to step aside and form a new party to challenge all of the status quo.

Their beliefs reflected the reforms of the time. While they agreed with Reconstruction in principle, they found it lacking in practice. Their solution to the corrupt boroughs of the South was to call for universal amnesty and a withdrawal of federal troops from the civilian political arena. The Liberals believed that something basic was amiss with governments that could not appeal on the basis of calm, political argument and the vote of the whole public. Another Liberal idea was civil service reform and a general cleaning up of government. They also believed in paying off the national debt in gold, not inflated greenbacks, as the only honest way. But on the tariff issue, some wanted it higher, some wanted it lower.

During the 1872 election the split between the Liberals and the regular (or Stalwart) Republicans—represented by their candidates for president, newspaper editor Horace Greeley and President Grant, respectively—threatened to swamp the Grand Old Party. But Greeley's eccentricities, the Liberals' willingness to leave African Americans to the mercy of the Southern whites, and their alliance with the Democrats proved too much for voters to swallow. Grant won a resounding victory. In 1876, the Republicans united behind reformist candidate Rutherford B. Hayes and eked out a narrow victory by manipulating the electoral college vote in a temporary deal with the Southern Democrats to end Reconstruction.

After Reconstruction officially ended with the symbolic withdrawal of the federal soldiers back to their garrisons as a part of the Compromise of 1877, Republicans once again divided into two factions, the Stalwarts and the Half-Breeds. The Stalwarts were headed as usual by Senator Roscoe Conkling of New York; they represented the decline of Republican Reconstruction idealism, a drive for spoils of office, and an amoral party loyalty on all issues. The Half-Breeds were led by Senator James G. Blaine of Maine, who picked up the old Liberal Republicans and their reformist attitudes. The party stagnated in the 1880 convention over the Stalwart desire to renominate U. S. Grant for a third term. Blaine outmaneuvered the others by shifting his support to a dark horse candidate, Brig. Gen. James A. Garfield, former chief of staff of the Army of the Cumberland and a Union hero of the 1863 Battle of Chickamauga.

The Democrats went with their own war hero, Maj. Gen. Winfield Scott Hancock of Gettysburg fame. In a close race, the Republicans managed to carry the day another time through the use of "soap," slang of the time for the buying of votes and the counting of grave stones (casting ballots in the name of dead men). Garfield came into office as an ardent advocate of civil service reform, but he had to compromise with the Stalwarts to gain the nomination and election by taking as his vice president Conkling's right-hand man, Chester A. Arthur, a noted spoilsman from the notorious New York Customs House Ring. The party's internal fight broke wide open when Garfield appointed Half-Breeds to the New York patronage spots. Just as Garfield and the Half-Breeds seemed certain to win everything, fate intervened—as the president accompanied Blaine to the Washington railroad station, two shots rang out, one of which hit Garfield in the back. Behind him the assassin, Charles Guiteau, disgruntled over not receiving a patronage spot, shouted out, "I am a Stalwart and Arthur is President now!" He was later declared insane but hanged anyway. Garfield's assassin put his finger on the exact quandary facing Garfield's party supporters. What would Arthur, the "gentleman boss," do to them?

The president hung on for 11 weeks before dying, and the suspense of Arthur's takeover grew hour by hour. To everyone's surprise, Arthur read of the public's disgust with the spoils system, as typified by the assassination, and he turned on his former cronies (the really corrupt ones anyway) and appointed good men of all factions to patronage positions. There was more grief in store for the old-time spoilsmen who once counted Arthur as one of their own. The new president supported and got through Congress the first major civil service reform of the century, the Pendleton Civil Service Act of 1883, which set up a commission to establish competitive examinations for hiring and a merit basis for promotion.

Although the Pendleton Act really did little beyond insulating 10 percent of the officeholders from patronage appointments, it set the United States on the road to the modern civil service system—a surprising achievement for one of the consummate spoilsmen of his time. The result so weakened the Stalwart faction that when Arthur sought to gain nomination and election to the presidency in his own right in 1884, the Half-Breeds dumped him for a real reformer, Blaine himself, though Blaine had moral problems of his own, being implicated in several monetary scandals of the time. Arthur got his revenge that fall when the Republicans, for the first time since the Civil War, fell to the Democrats, led by their own reform-minded man, Grover Cleveland. Much of Cleveland's support came from Liberal Republicans, now called "Mugwumps," who bolted the party for what they saw as the better man. The advent of the respectability of reform owed much to Arthur's own ability to rise above his past. But then, this overlooks the cynical, realist tradition in American politics that a re-

former is one who gives for free to the capitalists that for which the real politician charges dearly. This cynicism became the major criticism of Cleveland through his two disconnected administrations, and it haunted the Republicans until the advent of Theodore Roosevelt.

See also Blaine, James G.; Conkling, Roscoe; Election of 1872; Election of 1876 and Compromise of 1877; Greeley, Horace.

References Dobson, John M., *Politics in the Gilded Age* (1972); Hofstadter, Richard, *The Age of Reform* (1955); Hoogenboom, Ari A., *Outlawing the Spoils* (1961) and *The Presidency of Rutherford B. Hayes* (1988); Morgan, H. Wayne, *From Hayes to McKinley* (1968); Polakoff, Keith Ian, *The Politics of Inertia* (1973); Riddleberger, Patrick W., "The Break in the Radical Ranks," 1959; Smith, Ronald D., and William L. Richter, *Fascinating People and Astounding Events from American History* (1993).

Lincoln, Abraham (1809–1865)

Born near Hodgensville, Kentucky, Abraham Lincoln was the second child of carpenter/farmer Thomas Lincoln and his wife, Nancy Hanks Lincoln. Young Abe was named after a grandfather killed by Indians some years earlier. In 1817, the family moved to southern Indiana, near Gentryville, where Lincoln's mother died of undulant fever. Two years later his father married Sarah Bush Johnston, a widow with three children of her own. She was a strong, cheerful woman who modernized the Lincoln homestead and brought a love of education, which she imparted to Abe over the objections of his father. Largely self-educated, young Lincoln worked hard at physical labor (he grew to 6' 4" in height and was quite muscular and strong all of his life) and clerked at James Gentry's store. At age 19 he accompanied the Gentrys down river on a raft to New Orleans, where he encountered slavery for the first time and gained an uncompromising hatred for the institution. The Lincolns then moved to Illinois. Abe accompanied the family but soon set out on his own. He was about to accompany another flatboat down river, but a delay in the trip caused a storekeeper in New Salem to hire Lincoln on as a clerk. Lincoln stayed on at New Salem, where he held down a series of jobs. He was well liked, and during the Black Hawk War he enlisted as a private only to be elected captain of the local militia.

The war proved uneventful for Lincoln and his men, and they returned home, where he tried to go into storekeeping himself and failed. He paid off the debt incurred only after he became a congressman, ten years later. Meanwhile, he was elected to the state legislature as a Whig (those opposed to the policies of Andrew Jackson) and was instrumental in getting the state capitol moved from Vandalia to Springfield, in his own district, a town to which he promptly moved. He also read law and was admitted to the bar. Lincoln and many other young men of the town courted a visiting Kentucky belle, Mary Todd. The Todds were definitely upper-crust, rich, educated, and cultured—as Lincoln reputedly said: "God needed only one 'd' to spell His name; the Todds took two."

Legend has it that, by prior agreement, Lincoln's friend Billy Herndon won the first shot at vivacious Mary, only to ruin his chances when he complimented her on her dancing, likening it to the graceful moves of a serpent. She left him standing alone on the dance floor. Then Lincoln approached her, and they eventually were married, even after bashful Abe stood her up at the altar a time or two. The marriage turned out to be rather tumultuous, but they stayed together and raised four sons, two of whom died young. Most of the crazy stories about Mary Lincoln's behavior are traceable to Billy Herndon, Mary's rejected suitor and Abe's law partner. He noted that Abe seemed more and more melancholy as the years passed and blamed it on Mary's temper, dismissing her as the "she-wolf of this section" and the "female wild cat of the age." Herndon also spoke of Anne Rutledge, Abe's supposedly one and only true love, who went to a tragic early death, a tale that has been expanded on by romanticists ever since.

Feuding or not, the Lincolns lived most of their adult lives in Springfield, where he earned the reputation of being an outstanding courtroom lawyer and she one of being a sharp-tongued woman who dominated her husband at home. Lincoln ran for Congress in 1846 and served one term, being remembered for the "spot resolution." This was a Whig attempt to reveal President James K. Polk's message for war on Mexico as a sham by requesting he show the "spot" upon which "American blood had been shed on American soil." The spot was, of course, disputed territory at best and Mexican soil at worst. Lincoln retired after the one term, supposedly by prior agreement, but his antiwar attitude would probably have cost him the seat in prowar Illinois anyway.

Lincoln dabbled in politics and law for some years until the opening of Kansas to slavery above the old Missouri Compromise line brought him back into the fray fulltime. Lincoln helped organize the Republican party in the state, and it decided that he should take on the architect of slavery in the territories, his old friend and political opponent (and an active suitor of Mary Todd in the old days) Stephen A. Douglas. A powerful Democrat and U.S. senator from Illinois, Douglas hoped to make his 1858 reelection the springboard for the presidency in 1860. Lincoln accepted the assignment in his famous "House Divided Speech," in which he said that the United States could not remain half free and half slave and survive as a nation. One side or the other had to come out on top. Because of the expense of the campaign, the Lincolns and Douglases traveled together on a special campaign train and engaged in a series of debates (seven, one in each of Illinois' congressional districts) on the issues of the day.

They made a strange pair, Lincoln a foot taller than the "Little Giant" (Douglas's nickname) and speaking in a high-pitched voice that contrasted with Douglas's baritone. Both men used racial prejudice to discredit the other, each trying to avoid being seen as too friendly toward blacks; this task was easy for Douglas (whose wife's family owned slaves) but harder for Lincoln, a "Black Republican," in the parlance of the day. Lincoln lost the race, but he came much closer than expected as a result of the so-called "Freeport question." He asked

Douglas if slavery could be legally kept out of the territories in violation of the Little Giant's doctrine of "popular sovereignty," which allowed such slavery until the territory made a firm decision when it voted on statehood. Douglas had to answer yes to win the Senate seat, but he had to answer no to hold the South in the 1860 presidential race. Douglas habitually crossed his bridges as he came to them and answered yes. He pointed out that if the territorial legislature never passed any laws condoning slavery, then slavery would automatically cease to exist even before the final vote for statehood. No one could be enslaved without a positive law supporting the institution, Douglas admitted. He won the Senate seat with the support of the Illinois legislature, but he lost the support of the South forever, his duplicity revealed by Lincoln's question.

Lincoln's skill in compromising Douglas put him in demand as a speaker throughout the North. Soon it became obvious that he could carry three key states (Illinois, Indiana, and Pennsylvania) that the Republicans had failed to take four years earlier. If this were done, Lincoln and the Republicans could win the presidency without a single electoral vote below the Ohio River. Although several other men had more notoriety than Lincoln, none could perform the magic task of taking the three states. This fact, combined with masterly manipulation of the Republican convention and his rivals knocking each other off in a bitter contest, put Lincoln at the head of the Republican ticket in 1860. The Democrats split between Douglas and the Southern branch of the party, taking 1 million more popular votes combined than Lincoln. But even if everyone had united behind Douglas, Lincoln still would have taken the presidency because of the quirks of the electoral vote, which gave a simple majority to the Northern states that voted for Lincoln in close popular races.

Because of Lincoln's ability as president to make appointments to executive offices and the U.S. Supreme Court, the rabid secessionists in the South decided to leave the Union. Although Lincoln tried to allay their fears with a moderate inaugural speech, he refused to give in on the question of the advance of slavery into the territories or to yield federal properties still held in the seceded states. The result was war and further secessions as Lincoln assigned a quota of militia to every state to help suppress the rebellion. Lincoln demonstrated his political acuity and self-confidence right off in his appointments to his cabinet (he was "Humble Abe Lincoln" only as a public front). At least four members were political rivals within the Republican party (Simon Cameron, William H. Seward, Salmon P. Chase, and Edward Bates) and two of them (Seward and Chase) considered themselves superior to him in intellect (Seward would soon come around, but Chase never quite caught on).

The Lincoln presidency was a balancing act of wartime and domestic issues. He had to move on the military issue in such a manner as not to offend the still-loyal border slave states of Missouri, Kentucky, Maryland, and Delaware. Maryland determined Delaware's stand as a result of geography, if nothing else. Because Maryland was so critical to Northern control of the nation's capital, it was immediately occupied by federal troops and dissidents were arrested. Missouri was held by decisive advances of federal forces under Frank Blair and Bvt. Brig. Gen. Nathaniel Lyon. Kentucky was so critical to the Confederacy that they occupied it first, breaking its neutrality and permitting quick federal advances to key points. But Lincoln believed that he could not respond to the demands by many Northerners that he free the slaves immediately as a wartime measure. He feared repercussions that might extend even to the Old Northwest, states above the Ohio River like Illinois and Indiana where negrophobia was common. Meanwhile Lincoln carried out much of the domestic Republican program, including internal improvements like the Pacific Railroad, establishing land grant colleges, raising the tariff, creating a national banking system, and implementing a homestead act.

The president refused to call Congress

into session at the war's start, preferring to rule by executive proclamation, a practice that he continued throughout the duration of his term and that has drawn much criticism then and now from Democrats, Radical Republicans, and of course proto-Confederate historians. Lincoln's political success came from an excellent ability to appear anti-Southern without at the same time seeming pro-African American. His Emancipation Proclamation freed only the slaves outside the jurisdiction of the Union army. Further, he was willing to grant African Americans technical freedom without attacking any of the traditional racism of the North. Moreover, the litany goes on, the corruptions of the Republican era that mar the history of Reconstruction and the subsequent Gilded Age began with the Lincoln administration and were justified as necessary wartime measures, like the Pacific Railroad. Lincoln reinstituted the economic policies that Alexander Hamilton and Henry Clay had failed to sustain against Southern and Western opposition led by the Jacksonians; these policies were embodied in the Republicans' domestic programs and heavy taxes, including the first U.S. income tax. The result was that for the first time in U.S. history creditors had the upper hand over debtors and the developed East could exploit the developing West and defeated South.

Lincoln also expanded the powers of the presidency in such a manner as to alter the basis of the Federal Union. He was the country's first imperial president, as he summoned the militia, expanded the U.S. Army, decreed an illegal blockade, defied the Supreme Court, suspended the writ of habeas corpus and created a Yankee gulag (called the "American Bastille" by his critics), transferred millions of dollars from authorized accounts to his pet projects, and pledged the nation's honor and credit to others—all without the necessary participation of Congress under the Constitution. Some have accused Lincoln of leading the North in such a manner as to put the domestic priorities of his political machine ahead of the lives and well-being of his soldiers in the

field. He fought and fought until he could find a Republican hero in a field general. The result was the firing of Democrats like George B. McClellan, Don Carlos Buell, and Fitz John Porter and the elevation of mere political hacks to army command, men like Nathaniel P. Banks, Benjamin F. Butler, John C. Frémont, and John A. McClernand. The same held true of his cabinet, especially the original one, in which Simon Cameron robbed the Union blind, a process Lincoln covered up as necessary to save the Union. Even one of his hack generals, Henry W. Halleck, admitted such command decisions were "little better than murder."

Next, he compromised the integrity of his office to further prosecute the war. Each time peace was in the offing, Lincoln upped the ante or stalled so as to make compromise impossible. Peace could come only on his terms, reasonable compromise take the hindmost. Lincoln's search for an expedient peace cost the nation over 100,000 lives. And worse, the war had been his to start, a responsibility Lincoln sought to transfer to Jefferson Davis by arranging to have the South fire the first shot, after several reasonable attempts by politicians of both sections to compromise the crisis failed because of Lincoln's refusal to consider them. These compromise attempts included the South's offer to pay for Fort Sumter and other federal installations in the South (which Lincoln kept secret from the public) and an offer to keep the Mississippi River open to Midwestern commerce.

Finally, Lincoln altered the language of American political discourse so that it was next to impossible to reverse the ill effects of trends set in motion by his executive fiat. He put it all in the rhetoric of Scripture, making every "good cause" then and since a reason to increase the scope of government. All that counted was the goal; the means to achieve that goal became irrelevant. That Congress thought it was getting short shrift from Lincoln can be seen in its response to Lincoln's proposal to reconstruct the South. Lincoln proposed that whenever 10 percent of the population of any state occupied by the Union Army took an oath of future loyalty and drew up a new state constitution devoid of slavery, that state ought to be considered reconstructed and considered for readmission to the Union.

Congress responded with its own Wade-Davis Bill suggesting that 50 percent was a more operable number for the future loyalty oath and that the actual voters electing the constitutional convention should be restricted to those who could swear never to have given aid to the enemy. When Lincoln gave this measure a pocket veto (that is, let it lie on the table 14 days after Congress had adjourned), the two principal sponsors issued the Wade-Davis Manifesto accusing the president of interfering with Congress' prerogative to reconstruct the South and guarantee a republican form of government in the various states. (The term *republican*, which refers to a type of government, is distinct from the Republican party.) Lincoln responded that he had no real objection to the congressional measure but that he did not want to be limited in his approach. Any state that preferred to come in under the terms of the Wade-Davis Bill could do so. It was typically Lincoln—almost too clever and quite maddening to his critics.

Despite Lincoln's "with malice toward none; with charity for all" pledge in his second inaugural speech and the decent terms granted the surrendering Confederate armies, no one really knew what his postwar stance on Reconstruction would have been. An assassin's bullet silenced the only man who really knew where Lincoln stood—if indeed he had a position; as one writer put it, Lincoln was "the most shut-mouthed man" anyone in Washington had ever met. Regardless of how one feels about Lincoln, the proof of his policy was in winning the greatest war the United States has ever fought. He always believed that he had a divine purpose in life, although he would have been the first to admit that he did not know exactly what it was. But he saw himself as impelled by incidents outside his control, rather than as a molder of events. It was the very same measures he undertook, to the howl of his critics, that made that victory

possible and guaranteed his position as the greatest president next to George Washington that the nation ever had. If nothing else, Lincoln had an amazing ability to mold the public's thinking into accepting policies that most of them were opposed to at the start of the war. And it was the very hesitancy in executing them, which so aggravated his Radical Republican critics, that made him a true reflection of how the nation at large felt about what the war meant.

See also Congressional Reconstruction; Emancipation; Johnson and Reconstruction; Lincoln and Reconstruction; Wade-Davis Bill.

References Bradford, M. E., "Against Lincoln" (1990) and "The Lincoln Legacy" (1985); Charnwood, Godfrey Rathbone Benson, Lord, *Abraham Lincoln* (1916); Cox, LaWanda, *Lincoln and Black Freedom* (1981); Current, Richard N., *The Lincoln Nobody Knows* (1958); Donald, David H., *Lincoln* (1995) and *Lincoln Reconsidered* (1956); Fleming, Thomas, "Lincoln's Tragic Heroism" (1989); Graebner, Norman A., ed., *The Enduring Lincoln* (1959); Hesseltine, William B., *Lincoln's Plan of Reconstruction* (1960); Jaffa, Harry V., "Lincoln's Character Assassins" (1990); McPherson, James M., *Abraham Lincoln and the Second American Revolution* (1990); Nevins, Allan, *The War for the Union* (1959–1971); Oates, Stephen B., *Abraham Lincoln* (1984); Olsen, Otto H., "Abraham Lincoln as Revolutionary" (1978); Paludan, Phillip S., *The Presidency of Abraham Lincoln* (1994); Randall, James G., *Lincoln the President* (1945–1955); Randall, Ruth Painter, *Mary Lincoln* (1953); Sandburg, Carl, *Abraham Lincoln* (1926–1939); Thomas, Benjamin, *Abraham Lincoln* (1952); Williams, T. Harry, *Lincoln and His Generals* (1952) and *Lincoln and the Radicals* (1941); Zilversmit, Arthur, ed., *Lincoln on Black and White* (1971).

Lincoln, Abraham, and Reconstruction

Foremost among President Abraham Lincoln's announced war goals was the restoration of the Union. Emancipation was more of an opportunity presented by the war, and equality was even more remote as an ideal. (Historian C. Vann Woodward called equality the "deferred commitment," one that never came about.) So for all practical purposes the minute the South seceded there was the notion of Reconstruction—even during the secession crisis itself. Before his home state of Virginia seceded, Senator

Robert M. T. Hunter suggested an outward alliance between the North and South with separate economic and domestic institutions and a dual presidency, one executive from each section. Congress would be denied power to deal with slavery in the territories (the actual cause of the breakup). Indeed, slavery was to be guaranteed access to all territories, and each territory would decide on its status as slave or free by a popular vote upon its admission to the new Union. To clean up another aggravating problem, Hunter proposed that the federal government pay for all fugitive slaves who escaped into free states.

Not to be outdone, Illinois Senator Stephen A. Douglas, Lincoln's old debating opponent in 1858, came forward with a plan of his own. Douglas was solidly behind Lincoln's effort to prevent secession by force. But instinctively he tried to find a compromise for the whole secession crisis as he had done years earlier in the Compromise of 1850, which had solved the question of slavery in the Mexican Cession. Unfortunately, events moved too quickly toward war, and the plan lay dormant in Douglas's personal papers, found after his death in June 1861 (he had exhausted himself to death trying to heal the secession crisis and then rallying the North around Lincoln through personal intervention). Like Hunter he would have recognized the disunion as fact and substituted an economic union for the old United States. All of the old tariffs, trade regulations, patents, and copyright laws would still apply uniformly between the two republics. Each country would guarantee the other's territorial integrity, and neither would add territory or change its boundaries without the other's consent. Because the tariff was a thorny problem to begin with, its proceeds were to be divided between the two republics on the basis of population (including three-fifths of the slaves, the old federal formula).

Many of Hunter's and Douglas's ideas, in varied forms, were present at the Washington Peace Conference of 1861, a belated effort sponsored by the border South to head off secession and war (after all, these states knew very well that any North-South war would be fought on their lands). After much talk the "Old Gentleman's Convention" (many of the sponsors and delegates were elderly ex-Whigs) proposed a Thirteenth Amendment to the Constitution and a reunification of the nation under the old Constitution. This amendment would draw the 1820 Missouri Compromise line of 36°30′ across the western territories to the eastern border of California. Above the line slavery was not to be had. Below the line slavery was to be guaranteed. Territories would become states in the traditional manner. No new territories could be added to the United States without a majority of senators from both sections concurring.

The proposed amendment also guaranteed slavery in the states where it existed and in the District of Columbia so long as it existed in Maryland. Slavery could not be abolished in any state without concurrence of the slaveholders. All fugitive slaves were to be rendered back to their states of origin. If this could not be done because of mob action or the inaction of state or federal officials, the federal government would compensate the slaveholder, an action that would end all claims on the fugitive. The slave trade was to be prohibited in the District of Columbia (something already accomplished by law in the Compromise of 1850) and between the United States and foreign countries (accomplished by law in 1808). The amendment could not itself be amended without the agreement of all the states. But many in the North and South were fed up with compromise by this time, and Lincoln's tough inaugural speech put an end to the effort.

Lincoln was not against a Reconstruction effort. He dismissed the questions of many politicians as to what was the status of seceded states: Had they lost their rights as states? Were they still in the Union? Could they be punished for secession? Lincoln said these were really pernicious abstractions, semantic quarrels of no value. He held that the Southern states were still states but out of their proper relation to the rest of the nation. The object of Reconstruction was to make these relations normal again. And Lincoln believed that he had the right and obligation to begin the process through his executive powers of amnesty (to forgive a group of a wrong) and pardon (to forgive an individual) under the Constitution. So if the Southern people did certain things, Lincoln would grant them amnesty.

On 8 December 1863, Lincoln issued his Proclamation of Amnesty and Reconstruction. The demands of the war necessitated that he do something. But rather than view Lincoln's proclamation as an incontrovertible plan (as Congress and future historians would), it is better to see it as he did—as a proposal that did not exclude future changes. First, Lincoln said, residents of seceded state had to take an oath of future loyalty to the United States and recognize all Union wartime acts regarding slavery. Such acts included the Second Confiscation Act (which freed slaves used to further Confederate military aims), the Emancipation Proclamation (which had freed all slaves inside the Confederate lines), and Congress' ending of slavery in the territories and the District of Columbia. Lincoln did not require the applying state to end slavery; he doubted he had the power to do this. But by making their application and recognizing wartime acts, the states would indirectly end up doing so anyhow. It was typically Lincoln, working around a problem rather than confronting it head on and alienating people. But it tied Reconstruction to the ending of slavery, once and for all.

Next, Lincoln's proclamation continued, when 10 percent or more of the voters registered in 1860 swore such an oath of future loyalty, that number could establish a loyal state government. They would call a state constitutional convention, elect delegates to the convention, and draw up a new state constitution that recognized the wartime acts of the Union. Then they would elect local officials, a state legislature, and a governor and send their duly elected representatives and senators to the U.S. Congress to be seated. Certain high-ranking officials of the Confederate and state government and military could not participate in the

process. This was a practical matter and good politics. Someone had to pay for secession and the war. But Lincoln would receive their individual supplications for pardon later, after the readmission process had worked itself out. Finally, Lincoln offered his plan only to states that had been occupied by the Union army. This limited his plan to essentially three areas, the northern half of Arkansas, most of Tennessee, and the southeastern third of Louisiana.

All three areas went through Lincoln's program and presented their representatives and senators for seating in Congress. And here Lincoln's plan ran out of steam. Congress had already protested the mildness of Lincoln's program in the Wade-Davis Bill, which the president had pocket vetoed, provoking a hostile attack on his refusal to work with Congress on the Reconstruction matter. Both houses refused to seat the men from Lincoln's allegedly reconstructed states under its constitutional right to investigate and determine if the supplicating states had truly republican forms of government. (In this case, *republican* refers to a type of government, not a political party, though many critics claimed that Congress saw no difference.) And Congress, which considered 10 percent an unusually small number for the American way of majority-based government, asserted its right to have played a part in determining the Reconstruction process; it noted that the newly emancipated African Americans did not have a sufficient role in the program or an assured status in post–Civil War America. Such objections lead naturally to the question, what was Lincoln up to?

Historians speculate that Lincoln realized that, during a war as hotly contested as the American Civil War, 10 percent of the population was all that the president could reasonably expect to go along with an early Reconstruction. If these few would cooperate, Lincoln hoped that others would join in and the process would mushroom to include many more. There was also a possible political motive in Lincoln's mind. The president had been a Whig party member before becoming a Republican. The Whig party contained those who were opposed to the Jacksonian Democrats in the 1830s and 1840s. The party had been led by Henry Clay (Lincoln's political hero as a young man) and quite often contained the better elements of society, North and South, in its membership. These were conservative, business-oriented men who championed Clay's American System, which promoted economic development of the nation through governmental action. Indeed, the Republicans' domestic program of internal improvements (transportation projects like railroads, roads, bridges, and canals), land grant colleges, a national banking system, high protective tariffs on foreign goods, and the homestead grants in the West were Whiggish in their conception.

The Democrats saw this program as economic favoritism on behalf of the rich and as hostile to state supremacy under the federal system established by the Constitution. Lincoln needed to get around this hostility after the war, lest Southern Democrats come back to Congress and overwhelm the current Republican majority. As the 1861 Washington Peace Conference had demonstrated, there were a lot of old Southern Whigs who had been less than enthusiastic about secession (this was especially true in the southeastern third of Louisiana among the big sugar planters there). Lincoln was well aware of this and moved to capitalize on it to extend the Republican party into the South during and after the war through the votes of conservative slaveowners. That many of the Scalawags who cooperated with Reconstruction later turned out to be Lincoln's sought-after Whigs merely demonstrates Lincoln's political perspicacity.

Hence Lincoln had initially moved slowly on emancipation, considering such things as a gradual emancipation lasting until 1900, the colonization of freed blacks in the Caribbean to solve the race problem (an old Clay solution to racial animus represented best in the American Colonization Society), or turning African Americans over to the "better" elements of white society for protection as second-class citizens. The old Whigs were such a responsible class of per-sons to whom blacks could be trusted, Lincoln hoped. Thus the president wanted to expand and extend the Republican party to the South, based on old prewar loyalties, to gain a lasting majority position in the post-war United States. That he was willing to sacrifice black aspirations as free people and work with former slaveholders brings into question his racial idealism. It also caused the more radical elements of the Republican party to question Lincoln's loyalty to them and their principles of freedom and equality of all persons.

It is quite possible that Lincoln had continued throughout the war in the same misconception that had marked his actions during secession crisis—that the South was really full of all sorts of secret loyalists. That he was ready to alter his thinking on the South and Reconstruction is seen in his willingness to accept a more complete plan of military occupation and supervision of the defeated South, particularly in Virginia and North Carolina, that Secretary of War Edwin M. Stanton presented to him at a cabinet meeting the morning of the day he was assassinated. Lincoln asked that the plan be altered somewhat but drawn up formally so that it could be discussed with an eye to the fact that he needed to have a plan in operation before Congress reconvened in December 1865. Lincoln was not committed to any specific plan, but he did seem determined that he and not Congress would be the guiding light of Reconstruction.

See also Congressional Reconstruction; Emancipation; Ethridge Conspiracy of 1863; Johnson and Reconstruction; Seward and Reconstruction.

References Belz, Herman, *Emancipation and Equal Rights* (1978); Donald, David H., *Lincoln Reconsidered* (1956); Graebner, Norman A., ed., *The Enduring Lincoln* (1959); Gunderson, Robert Gray, *Old Gentlemen's Convention* (1961); Hesseltine, William B., *Lincoln's Plan of Reconstruction* (1960); Hofstadter, Richard, *The American Political Tradition and the Men Who Made It* (1948); Hyman, Harold, *Era of the Oath* (1954); Mallin, William D., "Lincoln and the Conservatives" (1962); McCrary, Peyton, *Abraham Lincoln and Reconstruction* (1978); Oates, Stephen B., *With Malice toward None* (1977); Paludan, Phillip S., "The American Civil War" (1974); Randall, James G., *Lincoln the President* (1945–1955); Rosenberg, John S., "Toward a New Civil War Revisionism" (1969); Stampp, Kenneth

M., *The Era of Reconstruction* (1965); Thomas, Benjamin P., and Harold M. Hyman, *Stanton* (1962).

Longstreet, James (1821–1904)

A Confederate Civil War hero, James Longstreet became one of the most noted and reviled of Southern Scalawags during Reconstruction. Born in South Carolina and raised in Georgia by his uncle, Augustus Baldwin Longstreet, the literary man and politician, James Longstreet graduated from the U.S. Military Academy in 1842. He served with the infantry in Mexico and was severely wounded at Chapultepec. After the war he stayed in the army and rose to the rank of major in the paymaster's department. Resigning his commission in 1861, Longstreet entered Confederate service a brigadier general. His brigade was lightly engaged on the flanks of the battlefield at First Manassas. He served under Joseph Johnston in the Peninsular campaign and fought indecisively at Fair Oaks before Richmond. Under Robert E. Lee, who had replaced the wounded Johnston, Longstreet commanded one of the assault divisions that drove the Union army from the environs of the Confederate capital.

Lee then divided up his army between Longstreet and Thomas J. "Stonewall" Jackson for the drive on Washington that resulted in the battles of Second Manassas and Antietam Creek. Retreating to Fredericksburg, Longstreet was still commanding half of Lee's army when his men defeated the Union forces at the stone wall before Marye's Heights. Always maneuvering for an independent command but never able to shine alone, Longstreet spent the spring of 1863 at Suffolk, Virginia, where he once again was mediocre in operations. Back with Lee as a corps commander, Longstreet made numerous controversial moves at Gettysburg that critics (spurred on by his becoming a Republican after the war) claimed cost Lee the battle. In the fall of 1863, most of Longstreet's corps went to the western theater of war, where they proved to be a decisive force at Chickamauga for the South. But Long-

James Longstreet

street joined the other corps commanders in quarreling with his inept superior, Gen. Braxton Bragg, and received an independent assignment to recapture Knoxville from the Yankees. Longstreet bungled the job once again. Back in Virginia with Lee in 1864, Longstreet's corps saved Lee's army at the Wilderness. But Longstreet was severely wounded in the neck by his own men in a friendly fire incident (these were quite common in the Civil War) and missed the rest of the 1864 battles. Rejoining Lee in 1865, Longstreet surrendered with him at Appomattox.

At the end of the Civil War Longstreet was a civilian for the first time in his adult life. He moved to New Orleans and became a cotton broker and sold insurance. He was doing reasonably well in business at the time the Military Reconstruction Acts. A local newspaper asked several prominent citizens, including Longstreet, to advise the state on how to proceed in the chaotic times that faced them. Longstreet answered immediately and recommended that New Orleans, Louisiana, and the South follow the congressional plan to the letter. After all, Longstreet reminded his readers, the South had lost the war. Had Longstreet stopped here, nothing more would have been said. But somehow, once started, he could not keep his opinions out of print. He began writing to the newspaper on his own, and each time he got further and further in trouble. He spoke with the "bluntness of a soldier" when the evasiveness of a diplomat might have served him better.

Longstreet now said that Appomattox marked three developments: the end of secession, the end of the blacks as slaves, and the end of the Confederacy. He also said that the South had lost the power to resist Yankee demands by its very surrender in 1865. It was one of the "hazards of revolution." But Longstreet still viewed the peace as a battlefield with obvious objectives and absolute values. His past as a lifetime soldier had not put him in contact with the vagaries and nuances of the civilian political world. Everything was up for grabs in 1867, but in his next letter he crossed over to the Reconstruction side. In so doing he became a Scalawag, quite inadvertently perhaps. The letter was actually written to a private party, but the New Orleans *Republican* got wind of it and then obtained the full text. The general said that he would work with any faction to bring peace to the new Union. He stated that the Military Reconstruction Acts ought to be viewed as peace offerings. He feared that the Democrats were living on political principles lost in the war. He came out in favor of giving African American men the right to vote and said that the same right ought to be extended to the North. The *Republican* hailed Longstreet as the Republican party's newest recruit and asked Congress to restore his full rights of citizenship.

The rest of the New Orleans press went after the general's hide. They declared he was surrendering before the battle had been joined. His sincerity was no excuse for stupidity, said one sheet. Others pointed out that Abraham Lincoln's wartime Reconstruction had been trashed by the harsher congressional proposal and they wanted nothing of a second Reconstruction. They had done it once already. Rumors had

Longstreet being mentioned as the new Republican senator from Louisiana, which made the whole letter look like a political payoff. Only an African American newspaper, the *Tribune*, questioned the tenor of Longstreet's suggestions. The paper's editors correctly saw that he envisioned the black vote as an experiment to be extended to the North, but one that could be rescinded at any point in the future. They believed that there were sufficient able Republicans in the Louisiana party that raising the Rebel flag to attract more was unnecessary.

Longstreet was appalled that citizens had misconstrued him to be a Southern traitor. He tried to explain himself in other letters, but no one was listening anymore. He wrote General Lee and asked his endorsement, but the man refused. Lee was willing to obey the laws, but he would not endorse the course of "the dominant party" as Longstreet had done, something that Lee viewed as "a great mistake." Longstreet's business and social connections fell away. Congress did relieve him of his political proscriptions (some protested because he did not ask that this be done). When a fellow army friend, Ulysses S. Grant, became president in 1869, he offered Longstreet the post of surveyor of customs for the Port of New Orleans. Out of money and lacking any job prospects, Longstreet accepted and became a Scalawag in fact as well as name. That the customs house was the center of the most radical and corrupt Carpetbaggers in Louisiana did not help the general's reputation any.

In support of the Republican administration of Louisiana, Longstreet was involved in the final battle against the White League as the forces of Redemption swept the state in 1874. In order to woo Longstreet from the customs house faction of the Republican party, outgoing Governor Henry Clay Warmoth had appointed him major general of the Louisiana state militia. Longstreet also got a postmasters job. But when the Warmoth faction went over to the Democrats, Longstreet went back to the Republicans. Led by their gubernatorial candidate, William Pitt Kellogg, the Republicans kept Longstreet as head of the state militia and added the New Orleans metropolitan police to his command. Longstreet actively used his men to put Kellogg in power and keep him there. In June 1874 the general led the militia and police in the Third Battle of New Orleans (or the Battle of Canal Street) when the Republicans contested with the pro-Democratic White League for control of the city. Valiantly Longstreet rode forward to order the White Leaguers to disperse. The front rank pulled him from his horse and opened fire on the Republican militia and police. Without their leader Longstreet's men broke and ran. The general was hit by a spent bullet, probably from his own men. The regular army soon saved Kellogg, but the Democrats had confined Republican rule to the federal buildings in New Orleans until the troops were withdrawn in 1876 and the state was redeemed.

Longstreet survived his wound, and the White Leaguers let him go. They were Confederate veterans, too, and were not about to execute "Lee's War Horse," as Longstreet was popularly known. Longstreet could read the handwriting on the wall. Republicanism in Louisiana was dead and his reputation ruined. He moved back to Georgia, where he lived out his long life. He still accepted federal appointments as his income. At various points over the next 25 years, he was U.S. minister to Turkey, U.S. marshal for Georgia, and U.S. railway commissioner. His political jobs became his livelihood. He remarried late in life, and his new wife became one of his principal defenders as die-hard Democrats attacked him for his wartime command actions. Led by Jubal Early, they accused him of dragging his feet at Gettysburg and costing the South the whole war. Longstreet answered his critics in his own volume, *From Manassas to Appomattox*, published eight years before he died; his book was reinforced by his wife's biography of him after his death. His story demonstrated how easy it was to be condemned by the extremes when one tried to walk the narrow line down the moderate center in a volatile period like Reconstruction.

See also Scalawags.

References Eckenrode, Hamilton J., and Bryan Conrad, *James Longstreet* (1936); Longstreet, Helen D., *Lee and Longstreet at High Tide* (1904); Longstreet, James, *From Manassas to Appomattox* (1896); Pearce, Haywood J., Jr., "Longstreet's Responsibility on the Second Day at Gettysburg" (1926); Piston, William G., *Lee's Tarnished Lieutenant* (1987); Richter, William L., "James Longstreet" (1970); Sanger, Donald B., and Thomas R. Hay, *James Longstreet* (1952); Tucker, Glenn, *Lee and Longstreet at Gettysburg* (1968); Wakelyn, Jon L., *Biographical Dictionary of the Confederacy* (1977); Wert, Jeffrey D., *General James Longstreet* (1993).

Louisiana Experiment

Nowhere in the South did Reconstruction last longer than in Louisiana. The fact that Reconstruction did not end there until 1877 was due to many factors: the Union forces' occupation of the southeastern third of the state early in 1862; the complexities of the state's population, which included cosmopolitan New Orleans, with its industrial and laboring classes and the largest group of immigrants outside of New York City; a countryside made up of large slaveholding plantations and small nonslaveholding farms; a large black contingent that included not only slaves of varying skills ranging from farm hands to artisans, but numerous free persons of color, some of whom owned slaves and plantations of their own; the largest and best-educated group of African Americans in the South, mostly located in New Orleans, many of whom had the blood of the state's most prominent white families in their veins; and the vicious nature of politics in Louisiana.

The first military ground commander in Louisiana was the infamous Maj. Gen. Benjamin F. Butler, fresh from Fortress Monroe, Virginia, where he had declared runaway slaves behind his lines to be contraband of war, thereby initiating one of the first freedom policies of the war. Butler's first goal in Louisiana was to stabilize the civilian population to prevent it from interfering with the movement of his troops and spreading the dreaded yellow fever so prevalent in the region. Because blacks accounted for more than half of the population of the area he occupied, he turned his attention to them right off. No blacks from elsewhere in the state were allowed to enter the city of New Orleans or army camps. Those who fled to the Union lines were immediately gathered up, shipped back to their home plantations, or consigned to augment the work force of nearby plantations. Butler used military power to enforce this policy, making him quite the reverse of the abolitionist general he was portrayed as by historians based on his Virginia record.

Under fire from subordinates and politicians back North for his reenslaving policies, Butler made a few modifications that summer. Goaded on by unruly abolitionist subordinates, the threat of Confederate attack on Baton Rouge, and the Union War Department, Butler enrolled the Louisiana Native Guards in three regiments in the summer of 1862. These were free blacks from New Orleans who had stood side by side with Andrew Jackson during the War of 1812 and whose organization had been maintained by the state. Contrary to existing custom in the rest of the nation, the Native Guards had their own black officers, once commissioned by the state of Louisiana.

Having duly astonished his critics on the black soldier issue, Butler rounded up all contrabands (the name given to slaves who crossed into Union lines) and sent them to loyal citizens' plantations south of New Orleans. Soldiers were stationed nearby to guard blacks from reenslavement by Southern raiders—and to keep order among the freedmen, who protested the quasi-slave system by fleeing to New Orleans or engaging in labor strikes for better conditions on individual plantations. As Butler's men collected black "vagrants" and forced striking laborers back to work, the general moved into parishes (Louisiana's version of counties) to the north and west and extended his contraband program there. Butler was quite liberal as to who was a loyal planter. All the owner had to do was sign a contract that regulated hours of labor and stipulated a small salary for the black laborers assigned to him. Past or present political affinities were not important.

By January 1863, President Lincoln had removed Butler from command and re-placed him with a less controversial man, Maj. Gen. Nathaniel P. Banks, who, like Butler, was a Massachusetts Democrat turned Republican. Banks provisionally retained Butler's labor system and organized a committee of planters to suggest changes. Meanwhile he had his staff, called the Sequestration Commission, take a look at Butler's old system. They essentially found it to be workable and incorporated most of it into their recommendations. They suggested that planters and African Americans enter into yearly contracts and that corporal punishment be abolished in favor of a system of fines. They required the employers to pay a salary and provide food, clothing, basic medical care, and a plot upon which the black families could raise vegetables. The former slaveholders praised the system's ability to regularize labor and restore agricultural production in the state.

Indeed, except for regularizing the rules, all Banks did differently in terms of the labor situation was ask for planter input. He got it. In February 1863, the planters' committee reported. They stressed the need for discipline of the black work force, a restoration of civilian government, the re-creation of patrols to search for stray freedmen, and the protection of federal military units. Banks promised to hold blacks to their contracts and to stifle labor complaints through a new military agency (variously called the Commission of Negro Affairs under the corrupt George Hanks or the Bureau of Free Labor under the capable Thomas Conway) to supervise the labor contract process. The agency was also to provide for black medical care and education, but the small sums allocated for these functions compromised their importance. Federal troops were provided to keep order in the planting areas.

When it came to the enrollment of black soldiers, however, Banks altered Butler's program significantly. Butler had enlisted the Louisiana Native Guard with its black officer corps intact. In Banks's view, making African Americans officers, and by implication gentlemen, would not do. No other regiment in the country had such a luxury.

The rule was black troops led by white officers. So Banks began to purge the black officers from the service. He then expanded the "Corps d'Afrique," as he now labeled the Native Guard, into 20 regiments. When necessary, black recruits were dragooned off plantations or the streets of New Orleans. Organized into a brigade under Brig. Gen. Daniel Ullmann (who had done most of the recruiting and training), the Corps d'Afrique played a key role in the capture of Port Hudson in 1863, a post north of Baton Rouge that, along with Vicksburg, had blocked the river for the Confederacy.

The arrival of officials from the Department of the Treasury in summer 1862 to engage in the cotton and sugar trade discomfited Banks somewhat more than it had Butler, who had ignored them so long as he received his portion of the accompanying graft. But Banks was different—he was basically honest in this respect. Seeking to compromise Banks, the treasury agents protested that he was in league with the planters and had virtually reenslaved the contrabands. Banks retorted that the treasury men were trading across enemy lines and aiding the armies opposed to him. The fact that the treasury program relied on army supplies and protection was the only thing that kept the men from Banks's throat. The general helped his case by telling Lincoln that a speedy, easy Reconstruction depended upon keeping the planters on his side.

Hence Banks did not report attempts by black leaders to obtain integrated public services, land, and the right to vote, though many of these efforts were cheered by white workers in New Orleans led by Thomas J. Durant, a utopian socialist newspaper editor and labor organizer. The upshot of this was that Lincoln's Reconstruction of Louisiana was perhaps more conservative than it might otherwise have been had the president known there was so much radical support. Banks ignored Durant and the working men of New Orleans in favor of a government based on planter support. The planters were led by Michael Hahn, a pliable man who did Banks's bidding and created a reconstructed government based on the old 1852 state constitution, cleansed of slavery, rather than a new document that would have liberalized the representation of working-class whites. Maybe the historical critics of the Lincoln/Banks policy are right when they say it did not live up to its full potential—but it is also possible that, during a fratricidal war, Lincoln and Banks were smart enough to understand the limits of what could realistically be done. And that is the definition of a good politician, which each man was.

Unfortunately, Banks had to produce a military victory to validate his Reconstruction program, and here he faltered. In the 1864 Red River campaign, Banks lived up to his moniker, "Nothing Positive," and allowed an inferior Confederate force to run his men off the field at Mansfield and Pleasant Hill. A disappointed Lincoln divided Banks's command area in half on the Mississippi River and replaced him with Maj. Gen. Stephen A. Hurlbut in the east and Maj. Gen. E. R. S. Canby in the west. Under the new administration in 1865, the treasury men proposed new regulations that greatly liberalized discipline and increased wages, but the planters appealed to the local provost marshals, who sided with them. Acting on the provosts' reports, General Hurlbut basically continued Banks's old contract labor program until the arrival later that same year of the Freedmen's Bureau, for which the first head in Louisiana would be Thomas Conway, the former head of Banks's Bureau of Free Labor. The wartime labor system in Louisiana, as elsewhere, was one of benevolence tempered with repression. It was not slavery, but it was not freedom, either. Nonetheless, it showed that blacks had emerged from slavery with a program for freedom. What they really needed was to articulate this desire to the powers that be and gain the latter's real commitment on a permanent basis. This, however, was not to be.

See also Mississippi Experiment; Port Royal Experiment; Ten Percent Plan; Virginia Experiment.
References Berlin, Ira, et al., *Slaves No More* (1992); Cornish, Dudley, *The Sable Arm* (1966); Cox, LaWanda, *Lincoln and Black Freedom* (1981); Dawson, Joseph Green, III, *Army Generals and Re-*

construction (1982); Gerteis, Louis S., *From Contraband to Freedman* (1973); Johnson, Ludwell H., "Contraband Trade during the Last Year of the Civil War" (1963) and "Northern Profit and Profiteers" (1966); May, J. Thomas, "Continuity and Change in the Labor Program of the Union Army and the Freedmen's Bureau" (1971); McCrary, Peyton, *Abraham Lincoln and Reconstruction* (1978); Messner, William F., "Black Violence and White Response" (1975); Ripley, C. Peter, *Slaves and Freedmen in Civil War Louisiana* (1976); Robinson, Armistead, "Reassessing the First Reconstruction: Lost Opportunity or Tragic Era?" (1978); Treagle, Joseph G., Jr., "Thomas J. Durant, Utopian Socialism, and the Failure of Presidential Reconstruction in Louisiana" (1979); Wetta, Francis Joseph, "The Louisiana Scalawags" (1977); Wiley, Bell I., "Vicissitudes of Early Reconstruction Farming in the Lower Mississippi Valley" (1937); Williams, T. Harry, "General Banks and Radical Republicans in the Civil War" (1939).

Lynch, James (1838–1872)

James Lynch was born in Baltimore in 1838 of a free mulatto father, a merchant who had just purchased the freedom of his wife. He was educated in Maryland and New Hampshire. Lynch entered the ministry at age 19 and served pulpits in Indiana and Illinois. In the latter state he met and married a woman and then moved with her to Philadelphia, where he edited *The Recorder*, a popular Methodist magazine. He stayed in Philadelphia until 1864, when he went to Georgia and set up a church and schools for freedmen at Savannah after its capture by Maj. Gen. William T. Sherman's army. Lynch was an accomplished speaker and organizer, and when he heard that local blacks expected to gain land and live separately from whites, he rebuked them and spoke of the need for an integrated society of all races after the war. Lynch soon returned to Philadelphia and stayed there for the next two years. When Congress passed the Military Reconstruction Acts in 1867, he went to Mississippi along with Hiram Revels to be "religious and moral educator of my race," as he put it. Lynch saw it as his duty to assist less fortunate blacks make the transition from slavery to freedom.

Early on Lynch realized that if he were to have a proper impact on Mississippi Reconstruction he would have to enter politics. Along with his religious and educational activities, Lynch served as a registrar of voters. He impressed upon Mississippi's blacks the necessity of voting the Republican ballot and trusting in the congressional solution for Reconstruction. But Lynch was against the Union Loyal Leagues as too provocative to whites. Nonetheless, his political organization of freedmen under the party banner brought him to the attention of Republican leaders and they made him vice president of their Mississippi party. Lynch went to work traveling the backcountry and speaking on behalf of the constitutional convention, a courageous act given that an African American had never done this before. As Lynch spoke on the necessity of blacks and whites cooperating in the new society, he was received well by both races. Lynch himself did not serve in the convention, but he had done much to give it its Republican majority and many of its 17 black members. Lynch was not happy with the proposed constitution's disfranchising and officeholding proscriptions against former Confederates. He believed them wrong in principle, and he recognized the practical problems of giving Conservative whites a free rallying point, but his church work kept him from influencing the proceedings.

As Lynch expected, whites used economic and physical intimidation to organize and prevent blacks from carrying the constitutional election. Rather than separating out the constitution's objectionable clauses as recommended by Lynch (who had been elected to the state legislature in elections that simultaneously rejected the proposed government, rendering his election null and void), the Republicans sent a delegation to Washington hoping to get assistance from Congress. The result was a split in the state Republican party over the disfranchising and officeholding exclusions. Eventually the Ulysses S. Grant administration adopted the view held by Lynch and Republican moderates in the state and separated the proscriptive clauses from the rest of the constitution. The proscriptions failed and the constitution passed. Lynch sided with James

L. Alcorn, Mississippi's Scalawag governor, in a moderate course and started up the *Colored Citizen*, a newspaper at Jackson for which he was editor. Lynch appreciated the work of Radical Republicans for blacks' civil rights but maintained that proscriptions against whites would upset the whole program in the long run. He seemed to recognize that the success of Republicanism and African Americans as free people depended upon whites and their attitudes.

But there was one point on which Lynch was not willing to compromise—the equal treatment of blacks under the law. He also believed that offices should be apportioned among the races so that all would get a chance to serve. In return for such treatment he was willing to accept segregated schools and individual social preferences. He believed that full access to public accommodations would come in due time as soon as blacks demonstrated their capabilities to rule. Unfortunately, his main problem turned out to be not native Mississippians but Yankee Carpetbaggers, who talked up a good program in league with blacks only not to let them participate. In the new order, however, Lynch was elected secretary of state for the incoming James L. Alcorn administration. Now recognized as a silver-tongued orator for the Reconstruction cause, Lynch was thought indispensable for Republican success. Lynch spoke on behalf of his usual principles: a kind approach to foes, removal of Fourteenth Amendment proscriptions, and education for the masses. As the first Reconstruction legislature met, their first job was to choose three U.S. senators, two of whom would be short-term appointments and one a full-term position. Blacks expected that one of these would be theirs, and James Lynch had much support for the job.

But Lynch knew that several prominent white Carpetbaggers were distinctly hostile to him and withdrew his name in favor of Hiram Revels, an obscure black minister who had rather reluctantly entered politics recently. Then Lynch went to work getting the Mississippi legislature to approve the Fourteenth and Fifteenth amendments,

conditions of readmission to the Union. Lynch believed that both amendments (less the Fourteenth's proscriptive clause) would cause racial conflict to wither away, a rather naive view from the perspective of 130 years later, but it gives some idea of the idealism with which he and others approached the problem of Reconstruction. He went to work as secretary of state, making sure to do an especially good job so as to demonstrate the ability of blacks to serve in the government. He was responsible for election administration, procurement of election data, state printing (a fine patronage opportunity), accounting for and disposing of state lands (he began to clear up the muddle from before the war and get much land assigned to educational purposes), and serving on the state board of education. Lynch found that it was normal to have to pay some of his expenses out of his own pocket. But his pride and joy was the new state education system, which he was mostly responsible for creating.

Lynch also began to look into the pernicious effects of the sharecrop and tenantry system that would plague generations of Southern farmers, black and white. Lynch hoped to impose upon white landowners to give up some of their property for blacks; unfortunately, this ran counter to the current of nineteenth-century farming, which was killing the small farmer with debt and resulted in the Populist revolt in the 1890s. Already white landowners were beginning to feel the pinch of credit and were looking to find white immigrants and lumber companies to purchase most of their lands. Lynch took to the stump in the state by-elections of 1871 to campaign for Republican candidates. He seemed to sense that his influence was waning, a conviction made solid when he failed to gain the party's congressional nomination from the Jackson-Vicksburg district in 1872. White Carpetbaggers were unwilling to have a black man of such demonstrated abilities as Lynch in the party, and enough black partisans went along in an effort to discredit him for their own gain. New heroes like the more radical Adelbert Ames and John R. Lynch (no relation to James) came to the fore.

James Lynch campaigned nationally for the Grant ticket in 1872, and upon his return from the North he was stricken with Bright's disease, complicated by a bronchial ailment. He died in December 1872 at age 34 and was buried in the white Greenwood Cemetery at Jackson. With him died a special kind of moderate solution for complicated problems such as Mississippi. The nation moved toward the end of Reconstruction with all of the hostilities that Lynch had fought against throughout his political career. His memorial still stands in a white cemetery; its inscription defines Lynch for all time—"True to the Public Trust."

See also African Americans and Reconstruction; Alcorn, James L.; Ames, Adelbert; Lynch, John R.; Revels, Hiram.

Reference Harris, William C., "James Lynch" (1971).

Lynch, John R. (1847–1939)

John R. Lynch was born on a Louisiana plantation to a slave mother and her white master. His father died before he could complete the formalities of emancipation. The executor of the will promptly sold boy and mother to someone in Mississippi, and the family was split up, with Lynch working on a plantation outside of Natchez. When federal occupation troops came into the area in 1863, Lynch and other slaves fled to their camps and became free. He had tried to pick up the elements of an education while still a slave, but his owners frowned on bondsmen who appeared to want to know too much. In 1866 he went to school at a Northern white missionary's establishment, but overall Lynch's education remained informal at best, prompted by a never-ending curiosity for books and newspapers. As he read he learned to convey his thoughts to others, developing an ability for public speaking and debate that would later prove invaluable. In 1867, when the Military Reconstruction Acts opened up the world of politics for the South's blacks, Lynch was just 20 years old. But he nonetheless became active in political organizations like the Union Loyal League and wrote and spoke on

behalf of the new state constitution. In 1869, the state's military governor, Bvt. Maj. Gen. Adelbert Ames, made Lynch a justice of the peace at age 21.

Lynch was soon elected by local blacks to the state legislature, where he served until 1873. He was an active and popular member among all factions and races. He spoke out often, offered bills and amendments, and made a good impression, even if his measures were not always successful. He served on committees on elections, education, and justice. He even began to act as an unofficial majority leader. In 1872 he sat on the committee on credentials, which judged whether members deserved to be seated from their districts, and advanced to speaker of the house. When the house could not agree to a congressional redistricting plan, it placed the project solely in Lynch's hands. He drew up the districts and the members agreed that his plan was well done, with five districts safely Republican and one Democratic. In 1872 he was sent to the Republican national convention; he returned home to defeat a white Carpetbagger for the honor of representing Mississippi in Congress. At age 26 he was the youngest member in the Forty-third Congress. Yet he had much legislative experience and knew how to handle the requests of his constituents. His major interest was Charles Sumner's Civil Rights Bill, which would guarantee entrance into public accommodations for all Americans regardless of race, something Lynch saw as "an act of simple justice." This made many whites back home determined to unseat him, but Lynch beat a popular white Democrat in a close vote.

Even as Lynch held on to his congressional seat, however, the Democrats took the state government and proceeded to redistrict the state's congressional delegation. This forced Lynch to run against Col. James R. Chalmers, a popular Confederate cavalry leader who was implicated in the massacre of black and white loyal troops at the Battle of Fort Pillow in 1864. Lynch was promptly counted out, and the new Democratic-controlled Congress refused to accept his challenge to the vote totals. In 1880 Lynch ran against Chalmers again. Once again

Lynch challenged the final vote count in which thousands of black votes were challenged and thrown out. This time Lynch's principled appeal was favorably received and he was seated. Chalmers was so disgusted with the failure of Mississippi Democrats to support him that he quit politics altogether. But Lynch had to run again almost at once because the appeal had taken so long. In 1882, he lost a fair race to white Democrat, Judge Henry S. Van Eaton, by 800 votes. Lynch continued to serve as the head of the state Republican machine, which he ran in league with Blanche K. Bruce and James Hill, two other African American politicians in Mississippi. During this time he served as preliminary chairman of the 1884 Republican national convention and in his keynote address publicly condemned Democrats for their continued vote fraud in Mississippi. It would take 74 years before a black man would give a keynote address to another national convention of either party.

Lynch's retirement from politics and the stirrings of disfranchisement of blacks all over the South as of 1890 caused him to be active in other ways. He declined a political appointment offered by President Grover Cleveland because he believed that it was contrary to his political loyalties. He did, however, serve as fourth auditor of the Treasury Department under Benjamin Harrison, a Republican. He bought and sold real estate in Mississippi and actually became quite wealthy. He also began to study law formally and passed the bar exam in 1896 on the second try. But before he could do much with his certificate, the Spanish-American War intervened. Lynch received a commission as an army paymaster from President William McKinley, whom Lynch knew from his service in Congress. Paymasters got to travel a lot, and since Lynch had recently divorced, he found much diverting pleasure in his job. He stayed in the service until 1911, when he retired and married again. This time Lynch moved to Chicago and lived a life of retirement. But he kept a hand in politics and became an advisor to Congressmen Oscar DePriest, one of the first blacks elected from a Northern district as a result of the African American migration northward during World War I.

Lynch also continued to write and speak on topics of interest to black Americans. He was highly critical of white history of Reconstruction and wrote his own book detailing his own perspective of what happened in Mississippi after the Civil War. He also wrote a powerful critique of the standard treatment of Reconstruction as presented by noted historians James Ford Rhodes (author of *History of the United States*) and James W. Garner (author of *Reconstruction in Mississippi*) and worked on an autobiography. Lynch attended meetings intended to assist blacks economically and socially, and he worked behind the scenes politically to enhance the role of blacks in American life. When John Lynch died in 1939, he had seen the United States grow from a nation whose main concern was the conquest of the American West to one whose main goal was its entrance upon the world stage as the most powerful nation on the globe. It was a big change, not all of it good for African Americans, but John Lynch did more than most to make the best he could of it.

John R. Lynch

See also African Americans and Reconstruction; Alcorn, James L.; Ames, Adelbert; Bruce, Blanche K.; Lynch, James; Revels, Hiram.

References Franklin, John Hope, "John Roy Lynch" (1982); Lynch, John R., *The Facts of Recon-struction* (1913), *Reminiscences of an Active Life* (1970), and "Some Historical Errors of James Ford Rhodes" (1917); McFarlin, Annjeannette Sophia, *Black Congressional Reconstruction Orators and Their Orations* (1976).

Military Reconstruction Acts

As a part of Radical Reconstruction, Congress passed four acts that put supervision of the Reconstruction process in the hands of the U.S. Army, which was occupying the South. Military commanders saw to  it that the individual Southern states, called military districts now, complied with congressional desires.

Passed the same day as the Command of the Army Act and the Tenure of Office Act (2 March 1867), the First Military Reconstruction Act divided the South into five military districts, each commanded by a major general appointed by the president. The First Military District was the old state of Virginia; the Second Military District was composed of the former states of North and South Carolina; the Third Military District comprised the prewar states of Georgia, Florida, and Alabama; the Fourth Military District had in its boundaries the one-time states of Arkansas and Mississippi; and the Fifth Military District included the old states of Louisiana and Texas. Tennessee was the only former Confederate state to be excluded because it had approved of the Fourteenth Amendment, which the rest of the South had rejected. The commanders of the military districts were to protect the civil and property rights of all persons; suppress all insurrection, disorder, and violence; and punish or cause to be punished all criminal actions. They could use existing civil and criminal courts, Freedmen's Bureau courts, or military tribunals as they felt necessary.

Existing state governments, established under the Andrew Johnson plan of Reconstruction, were declared to be provisional only and were warned not to interfere with the new reconstructing authorities. Each state was to call an election for delegates to a constitutional convention. The convention was to draw up a new state constitution and provide for universal male suffrage, bringing the state's organic laws into agreement with the results of the war in all respects. Once the acts of the convention were voted for by a majority of the registered voters, and a new state government elected, the state legislature would approve of the Fourteenth Amendment. Then the reconstructed states could send their duly elected representatives and two senators to Washington. Congress would review the process and, if satisfied, admit the new state back into the Union. Of all of the four Military Reconstruction Acts, only this one did not receive President Johnson's veto.

Because the first measure did not detail the procedure of registering state voters and the Southern governors dragged their feet in calling for the new convention election, the Second Military Reconstruction Act (23 March 1867) allowed the military commanders to go ahead without the approval of the governors. A general registration of all voters, including black males, was ordered. Voters had to take an oath of future loyalty and not fall into any of the categories of those whom Congress denied voting rights. The state conventions were to have the same number of delegates as represented in the lower house of the state legislature in 1860, and the commanding general would apportion these delegates according to the 1867 registration figures. The commanding general would appoint as many three-man registration boards as he thought necessary to accomplish the task in short order. The delegates were to assemble within 60 days of their election. The Second Military Reconstruction Act was passed over the president's veto.

The Third Military Reconstruction Act, passed on 13 July 1867, made district commanders, registrars, or any person appointed to office under military appointment free from obeying the orders or opinions of an executive official of the U.S. government. Registrars could disfranchise anybody, whether he could take the oath of future loyalty or not, for prior allegations of disloyal activities. Military commanders could remove from office any state official who obstructed the Reconstruction process and appoint loyal men in their stead. This law was brought about partly because conservative interpretations of the first two laws by Attorney General of the United States Henry Stanbery had declared that military officers had no power to deny registration or remove local officials; another reason was the inability of military commanders to replace obstructionists in office with loyal men. Congress told commanders and their appointees to be liberal in their interpretations under this law. The Third Military Reconstruction Act was passed over the president's veto.

The Fourth Military Reconstruction Act, passed on 11 March 1868, corrected a fault in the first act that stated that constitutions had to be approved by a majority of those registered. This act changed that to a majority of those voting. Whites in several Southern states had registered in large numbers and then refused to vote on the state constitutions, causing the one in Alabama to fail after several close calls in other states. This act marked the desire of Congress to get the Southern states back into the Union (unlike before, when keeping them out was the rule) so that black voters there could assist in electing a Republican president in 1868. The vote up North promised to be close, making Southern blacks critical to a Republican White House. By the time of the election only Virginia, Mississippi, and Texas had fallen behind because of local squabbles in the process and could not vote in the national elections.

See also Race Riots that Influenced the Reconstruction Acts; Radical Republicans and Reconstruction.

References Kincaid, Larry G., "The Legislative Origins of the Military Reconstruction Act" (1968); Sefton, James E., *Army and Reconstruction* (1967).

Mississippi Plan

There were two Mississippi Plans. The first was implemented in the mid-1870s and involved conservative white Southerners "redeeming" the state from the Republicans by force and intimidation. The second was implemented in 1890, when the state disfranchised black voters in its new constitution by circumventing the Fifteenth Amendment through such devices as literacy tests, understanding clauses, and poll taxes.

See also Disfranchisement; Redemption of the South since 1874; Shotgun Plan.

Mississippi Valley Experiment

As Union forces invaded the Mississippi Valley in late 1862, they encountered large numbers of slaves, who automatically became free under the provisions of the Second Confiscation Act. Aware of the promise of freedom, blacks flocked to the protection of Union army camps. By November 1862, the refugee situation threatened to get out of hand. Maj. Gen. Ulysses S. Grant, under whose jurisdiction the plantation areas of Northern Mississippi and West Tennessee lay, issued Special Orders No. 15, which authorized Chaplain John Eaton of the Twenty-seventh Ohio Volunteers to organize the African Americans into companies to be fed, clothed, and cared for. Eaton was to work the contrabands (the name given to slaves living behind Union lines during the Civil War) in abandoned fields at Corinth, Mississippi, and Grand Junction, Tennessee, where the largest camps of blacks were. Grant's main concerns were military ones, but he was also cognizant of other problems like competing interests among speculators, soldiers, and landowners; ideological concerns for the freedmen's futures; and the moral concern for racial justice.

Eaton was a good choice for Grant's trust. Appointed colonel of a new black regiment to give him the prestige and clout of military rank, he immediately applied to the Western Sanitary Commission (a benevolent society that had been created to look after soldiers' health, cleanliness, and morals in the cesspools that the initial Civil War camps were), as well as various other Northern associations (like the Freedmen's Aid Societies of the Middle West) interested in the cause of black liberation, to provide educators, food, and clothing. Meanwhile, Eaton put blacks under his charge to work gathering corn and cotton and chopping wood, and he introduced a wage labor system for all local plantations still occupied by their Southern owners.

Whatever profits that flowed from this labor went to the Department of the Treasury.

After the Emancipation Proclamation in January 1863, President Abraham Lincoln decided to affirm what had been done locally by several commanders and enroll black men into units that became the United States Colored Troops. Lincoln sent Brig. Gen. Lorenzo Thomas, the adjutant general of the Army to the Mississippi Valley, to handle the enlistments. (Eventually some 180,000 blacks served the Union war effort, with 134,000 from the slave states alone.) As he enlisted soldiers, Thomas looked into the possibility of creating a more general and permanent labor system than Eaton's. The Eaton plan relied on the government to be the employer through the army. But the army was always on the move and was unable to concentrate on both its military and free labor instruction goals. Like Eaton, Thomas decided to hire out all blacks for wages, but the farms would be managed by private investors rather than the government. Thomas's system led to much corruption—dishonest deductions for food and clothing, stolen wages, and physical abuse. Finding capable plantation managers was next to impossible (something Southern landowners could have told him about, as they had had to work with often-worthless overseers for years). Thomas did not help matters much by sending critics (mostly black) to the guardhouse.

In October 1863, General Thomas had had enough. He promulgated a whole new set of rules. All abandoned property owned by Rebels was to be seized and leased out to allegedly loyal men. Southerners still on their property were required to take on a loyal man as a business partner. Given the risks of planting when levees were broken, the seizure of all standing cotton until the owner was proved loyal, and Rebel retaliation, most landowners gladly leased their land to Yankees. But the army's real reason for leases was to create a loyal zone along the western rivers that would protect Union personnel from Rebel incursion. Each operator would receive a lease on land and labor good until

1 January 1865. The lessee had to register an oath of loyalty with the local provost marshal and agree to hire a specific number of African Americans (at $7 a month for able-bodied males, $5 for women, and $3.50 for children), care for the sick, provide provisions and shelter, and forego corporal punishment. The government was to receive a tax of $4 a bale for cotton sold and 5 cents a bushel for corn. Profits commonly were in the neighborhood of $100,000 per lease period. Any disloyal utterance (whatever that meant) could result in termination of the lease on the spot.

To protect the leased plantations from Rebel military incursions (Nathan Bedford Forrest's cavalry roamed the area regularly), local federal garrisons were to provide military aid and blacks were to be enrolled as home guards. If a loyal lessee were robbed by Confederate marauders, a like amount of goods or crops would be seized from the nearest disloyal person (one who had not or could not take the oath). If a loyal lessee were killed, an assessment of $10,000 would be levied on all disloyal plantation owners within 30 miles to defray costs to his family. Since the lease and labor area was so big, Thomas's loyal plantations were hard to protect. On the 95 safest loyal operations alone, the Rebels managed to carry off and reenslave 1,000 blacks and steal 2,300 horses and mules. The other operations were beyond help and statistics.

In the spring of 1864, after an adverse report by its agent, William Yeats, the Department of the Treasury came in to reform Thomas's system, which seemed to attract the corrupt, venal, and fraudulent, interested merely in profit rather than the well-being of the African American workers and their families. Yeats and another treasury man, William P. Mellon, instituted the Yeats-Mellon system, a collection of plantations (one per treasury district) where blacks could gather for mutual protection and negotiated wage employment as free laborers. Wages were to be at least $20 per month for males, $18 for women, and $15 for children. This would give black families a living wage and relieve the government of providing food supplies. But according to Thomas, employers refused to hire any but the best of hands, which actually increased the number of people on the dole. President Lincoln stepped in and ordered the army and the treasury to cooperate under one jointly developed plan.

The result was Special Orders No. 9 of 11 March 1864, issued through Thomas's headquarters. It created a three-tier system, with various levels of responsibility for the army (supervised by the provost marshals), employers (who had to pay overtime for Sunday work, not deduct more than $3 per month for clothing, and permit the freedmen to grow vegetables in their own small gardens), and freedmen (who had to stay on the plantation, be obedient laborers, and work "from day clean to first dark"). Wages were cut in half from the Yeats-Mellon plan, and one half of the reduced amount was held back until the crop was harvested and shipped, to cover any offenses against management.

The most famous agricultural experiment established under Gen. Lorenzo Thomas's Special Orders No. 9 of 11 March 1864 was at Davis Bend, south of Vicksburg, Mississippi, on the plantations of Joseph R. Davis (brother of the Confederate president). About 10,000 acres were isolated from the rest of the state by a canal cut across the neck of land that extended into the Mississippi River. Six separate plantations supervised by Provost Marshal Capt. Gaylord Norton employed blacks who farmed up to 100 acres, each plot resulting in profits of $500 to $1,000. The black laborers were organized into groups of 3 to 25 and provided with rations, implements, and animals at government expense, to be defrayed upon the harvest of the crop. The African Americans set up their own self-government, consisting of courts, juries, sheriffs, and judges. By the close of the war 1,400 blacks lived there in peace and prosperity, causing historians to wonder whether this is what ought to have happened everywhere in the South.

See also Davis Bend Experiment; Eaton, John; Port Royal Experiment; Virginia Experiment.

References Berlin, Ira, et al., *Slaves No More* (1992); Bigelow, Martha M., "Vicksburg" (1964) and "Freedmen of the Mississippi Valley" (1962); Currie, James T., *Enclave* (1980); Davis, Ronald L. F., *Good and Faithful Labor* (1982) and "The U.S. Army and the Origins of Sharecropping in the Natchez District" (1977); Gerteis, Louis S., *From Contraband to Freedman* (1973); Hermann, Janet S., *The Pursuit of a Dream* (1981) and "Reconstruction in Microcosm" (1980); May, J. Thomas, "Continuity and Change in the Labor Program of the Union Army and the Freedmen's Bureau" (1971); Wiley, Bell I., "Vicissitudes of Early Reconstruction Farming in the Lower Mississippi Valley" (1937).

Moderate Republicans and Reconstruction

In December 1865, after being out of session since March, Congress returned to Washington for its normal session according to the Constitution. It had been on the sidelines during the assassination of President Abraham Lincoln, the surrender of the Confederate armies, and the initiation of the Andrew Johnson Reconstruction. The South had largely completed President Johnson's program (with the exception of Texas, which was still forming a government) and had elected its new congressmen and senators, who arrived to be seated in their respective houses. But their seating was not guaranteed. The Constitution leaves it to Congress to rule on the admissibility of its own members. Congress can refuse to seat any elected representative or senator by simple majority vote. So it was not guaranteed that Johnson's Reconstruction, the Reconstruction of the South by itself, would be endorsed by the national legislature.

There was real reason to suspect that the Southern men would not be seated in either house of Congress. Congress still smarted because it had had little to say about Reconstruction, under either Lincoln or Johnson. Indeed, that was what the Wade-Davis Bill and the subsequent Wade-Davis Manifesto were all about. Many members of Congress, not just Radicals, believed that they should have a say in the Reconstruction program. They feared that Reconstruction so far had been too easy, was often based on undemocratic numbers, and ignored the needs of the recently freed slaves. Especially worrisome were the Black Codes. These laws existed in every state of the Union and restricted the participation of African Americans in all phases of American life. But Congress deemed the Southern versions too close to the old slave codes and considered them a sign that the South did not recognize that it had lost the war.

In addition to the conduct of the Southern state conventions and the laws of the allegedly reconstructed state legislatures were the personnel who made up the Southern representatives coming to Congress. They were familiar men. Most were not fiery secessionists, but they were nonetheless conservative men who had taken over the Southern governments from the 1861 revolutionaries after secession and had run the Confederate war effort. In the words of the popular press, they were the "Confederate brigadiers." Only eight months after the worst war in American history, the Southerners sent to represent their states in Washington included four Confederate generals, five colonels, six cabinet officers, and 58 Confederate congressmen, as well as the vice president of the Confederate government. Not one could have taken the oath of loyalty to the Union without a special pardon from President Johnson—who gave them such dispensation.

When the clerk read the roll call, the first order of business in any session of Congress, he passed over the names of the men from the South. This, in effect, refused them their seats. After denying the Southerners their seats, Congress then established a joint committee of 15 members from the House and Senate to examine the credentials of those passed over and to look into conditions in the Southern states. The chairman of the committee was William Pitt Fessenden of Maine, a moderate Republican of impeccable reputation for fairness. Under Fessenden's leadership, the Committee of Fifteen would then make recommendations to Congress, that is, create a Reconstruction program (the Second Congressional Plan) of their own. President Johnson's program

was dead (of course, in the meantime, that did not stop Texas from making the same mistakes as the other Confederate states—approving Black Codes and electing congressmen with Confederate backgrounds).

The committee called numerous witnesses to testify about what they had seen during recent trips to the South. Lt. Gen. U. S. Grant told the members that the South had been thoroughly whipped, would obey federal laws, and was ready to be readmitted to the Union. Grant's views were seconded by New York newspaper reporter Benjamin Truman, who felt the South was more loyal now than at any time before the war. But other witnesses were not so glowing in their observations south of the Mason-Dixon line. Maj. Gen. Carl Schurz, one-time German immigrant, volunteer Civil War soldier, and important Republican, feared that the use of Confederate politicians and the refusal of the Southern states to meet even Johnson's easy conditions of Reconstruction proved that the South had learned little from military defeat. J. T. Trowbridge, another newspaperman, charged that the South was as rebellious as ever, the dissent merely taking place in a more covert manner than before and during the war.

Because of the Black Codes and Southern reliance on compromised representatives (in Northern eyes, at least), Moderate Republicans believed that Congress ought to place more restrictions on Southern readmission to the Union. The Johnson state governments had been especially lax in providing basic civil rights for the freedmen (right to testify, participate on juries, use public facilities, and receive equal treatment under the laws). These Republicans wanted to work with the president and reach a compromise. So the committee appointed Illinois Senator Lyman Trumbull, a reasonable man, to be the congressional go-between to Johnson. Trumbull proved to be an unfortunate choice. He could not read Johnson, who had the nasty habit of shaking his head yes and being very accommodating in his conversations with Trumbull when he actually meant that he would think things over. Trumbull thought that Johnson agreed with Congress' ideas on expanding Reconstruction. At least, that is what he told the Committee of Fifteen.

Assured by Trumbull that Johnson would cooperate, the Committee of Fifteen reported two bills to the floor, both designed to put further conditions on the South before readmission. The first was the renewal of the Bureau of Refugees, Freedmen, and Abandoned Lands. Created in 1865 to last one year, the Freedmen's Bureau had done good service in helping black and loyal white refugees return to their homes after the war by providing rations and transportation. Because its administration was already in place, no new agency had to be established. The bureau could supervise white-black labor relations, giving some federal support and protection to African Americans in the first critical months of freedom. It was a reasonable compromise with the president. Johnson seemed to indicate the same to Trumbull.

Trumbull introduced the 1866 bill, backed by Fessenden and the Committee of Fifteen, under the impression that Johnson would accept it. The bureau would receive new powers under the new measure. It was to be extended indefinitely throughout the nation, not just in the South, with increased rights to try cases involving blacks and to act as a labor negotiator. Nowadays Americans are used to administrative law bodies like the Federal Trade Commission and the Interstate Commerce Committee, but in 1866 the bureau was seen by Americans North and South as an unprecedented interference in traditional local administration of law. Besides, the bureau was not without its critics. Its main problem was that those bureau men in the field who sincerely desired to help blacks tended not to get along with ex-Rebels, and vice versa. Field agents helped to organize the Union Loyal League (a Republican political front) among freedmen, and this angered Southern Democrats. There seemed no middle route among bureau personnel. All in all, the 1866 bill was not the type of measure that a strict constructionist (one who reads the Constitution literally) could accept without much

reservation. And Johnson was such a legal-minded person. So he vetoed the bill and Congress upheld his constitutional reservations by one vote.

Foiled in the expansion of the bureau, the committee still wished to compromise with the president and yet provide some protection to the former slaves. The committee sent Trumbull back to Johnson and explained their views. Congress wanted to pass a civil rights measure that would nullify the prewar *Dred Scott* decision (which denied blacks citizenship) and undercut the worst sections of the Black Codes. Again, Trumbull reported that the president seemed more than receptive. Congress created the Civil Rights Bill of 1866, which defined citizenship as being granted to anyone born or naturalized in the United States. All citizens received certain rights, including right to jury trial, to sue and be sued, to give evidence, to be on juries, and to receive full protection of the laws. No one could be denied these rights without due process of the law (a court proceeding), and the federal courts were to have sole jurisdiction in these cases.

The whole Republican party was for this measure. It seemed conservative, yet it protected black Americans as free people. But Johnson read Congress' position incorrectly. He saw that Congress had upheld his first veto, but he forgot that the veto was sustained by one slim vote. He vetoed the Civil Rights Bill of 1866 as a gross interference in state rights to legislate and adjudicate as preserved in the Constitution. He also gave a speech on George Washington's birthday in which he ridiculed key congressmen and their aides by name. This speech, along with Johnson's stubbornness and what Congress saw as his perfidy (given Trumbull's prior reports on his support) drove the Moderate Republicans over to the Radicals. Congress repassed the Civil Rights Act over Johnson's veto, and for good measure it brought up a modified version of the Freedmen's Bureau Bill. Johnson vetoed the new bureau measure, and Congress also repassed it over his veto.

But the Committee of Fifteen was not

pleased with the narrow margins that secured African American rights. The gains of the Civil War had to be thoroughly protected. The committee believed that a constitutional amendment was necessary, thus confirming their fear that Johnson might be correct in his interpretation. An amendment would prevent a future Congress not so interested in the position of blacks from easily repealing any protective measures. The result was the Fourteenth Amendment to the Constitution. This measure defined federal and state citizenship as in the Civil Rights Act of 1866; denied the states the right to abridge the privilege and immunities of citizenship, due process of the laws, and equal protection of the laws; permitted Congress to deny a state its full representation in the House of Representatives in the same proportion as the state did so to its population (indirectly granting blacks the right to vote, but allowing the states to deny this if they wished to lose seats accordingly); denied officeholding (not the vote) to anyone who had taken the oath to the federal government before secession and then taken an oath to support the Confederacy; and invalidated the Confederate debt and guaranteed payment of the federal war debt.

Congress approved the amendment by a two-thirds vote and sent it to the states, where three-fourths of them had to endorse it to make it part of the Constitution. Even though the Southern states had no representation, Congress sent the proposed Fourteenth Amendment to them, too. If the South accepted the measure, Congress reasoned, it would show some contrition for their past sins of war, slavery, and racial discrimination. There was also a fear that it would not be possible to obtain the support of three-fourths of the states, regardless of the South's not being seated in Congress. There were 36 states at that time. A no vote from 10 would negate the proposed Fourteenth Amendment, and the former Confederacy had been composed of 11. The way to disaster was open, especially since the 4 loyal border states had many of the seceded states' racial proclivities.

Congress asked Johnson to advocate approval of the proposed amendment. After all, an amendment would overcome the constitutional objections he had voiced earlier. Many historians believe that this was the final moment when the South, Congress, and the president could have gotten together and agreed on Reconstruction. But President Johnson advised the South, indeed all the states, that the proposed amendment be turned down. The South was more than happy to go along with rejection. The amendment would deny their leaders officeholding rights, others saw it as ill advised in the form of an amendment as it had been as a law, and still others refused to give the North any sign of compromise.

Of all the former Confederate states, only Tennessee, Johnson's home, approved the Fourteenth Amendment. "Parson" William G. Brownlow, the state's governor, a devout Union man, and a visceral hater of Andrew Johnson from before the war, led the forces for the amendment. When Democrats boycotted the state legislature, denying it a quorum, the speaker had four of them arrested. The detained men got writs of habeas corpus. The legislature impeached and removed the judge from office for issuing the writs and hauled two of the detained men into the legislature. A quorum was declared, though the two refused to speak or vote. When the speaker got a sudden belated attack of fairness and refused to sign he vote, he was impeached and removed from office. The president pro tem signed it for him. Brownlow sent the ratification to Congress: "We have fought the battle and won it,…two of Andrew Johnson's tools not voting. Give my respects to the dead dog of the White House!" For its astuteness and Brownlow's leadership, Tennessee was declared to be readmitted to the Union, the only Southern state so honored. But it all went for naught. Delaware and Kentucky sided with the former Confederacy to turn the amendment down.

By the fall of 1866 there were two plans—Johnson's and Congress'—before the American people as they prepared to vote in the off-year elections. Whoever won the electoral contest could declare a mandate from the people. But there were serious implications for President Johnson and his supporters—a president's party almost always loses seats in off-year elections. Johnson made an intense personal effort to get his supporters elected that fall. He went to the national Union convention, supposedly a gathering of Republicans and War Democrats, to rally his men. Delegates from North and South walked "arm in arm" down the aisle and pledged their fealty to the president. The only problem was that the Republicans who counted, those already in Congress, were notably conspicuous by their absence.

After the convention, Johnson hit the campaign trail, making a "Swing around the Circle" tour that replicated Lincoln's trip to Washington in 1861. Johnson was a great stump speaker, and he liked to take on hecklers in the style of the Southern backcountry from which he hailed. But this made him look unpresidential. Republican opponents sent special delegations to heckle the president and goad him into losing his temper and saying unwise things. Another committee followed Johnson a day or two later to make their own speeches against the president's Reconstruction policies. The result was an election that returned a veto-proof, hostile Republican Congress to Washington. Worst of all (for Johnson), it influenced the outgoing Congress to get tough in the lame duck session and compromise the president's ability to act between congressional sessions.

See also Black Codes; Bureau of Refugees, Freedmen, and Abandoned Lands; Civil Rights Acts; Confederate Brigadiers; Congressional Reconstruction; Fourteenth Amendment; Johnson and Reconstruction; Joint Committee of Fifteen on Reconstruction; Lincoln and Reconstruction; Race Riots that Influenced the Reconstruction Acts; Radical Republicans and Reconstruction; Swing around the Circle; Theories of Reconstruction; Washington Birthday Speech.

References Beale, Howard K., *The Critical Year [1866]* (1930); Burgess, John W., *Reconstruction and the Constitution* (1902); Carter, Dan T., *When the War Was Over* (1985); Castel, Albert, *The Presidency of Andrew Johnson* (1979); Cox, John, and LaWanda Cox, "Andrew Johnson and His Ghost Writers" (1961–1962) and *Politics, Principles, and Prejudice* (1963); Foner, Eric, *Reconstruction* (1988); Kendrick, Benjamin B., *The Journal of the Joint Committee of Fifteen on Reconstruction* (1914); Kincaid, Larry G., "The Legislative Origins of the Military Reconstruction Act" (1968); Lomask, Milton, *Andrew Johnson* (1960); McKitrick, Eric, *Andrew Johnson and Reconstruction* (1960); Milton, George F., *The Age of Hate* (1930); Nieman, Donald G., "Andrew Johnson, the Freedmen's Bureau, and the Problem of Equal Rights" (1978); Perman, Michael, *Reunion without Compromise* (1973); Rhodes, James Ford, *History of the United States from the Compromise of 1850 to the Final Restoration of Home Rule in the South* (1896–1906); Riddleberger, Patrick W., *1866* (1979); Sefton, James E., *Andrew Johnson and the Uses of Constitutional Power* (1980) and *The United States Army and Reconstruction* (1967); Stryker, Lloyd P., *Andrew Johnson* (1929); Thomas, Lately, *The First President Johnson* (1968); Trefousse, Hans, *Andrew Johnson* (1989); Winston, Hobert W., *Andrew Johnson* (1928).

Morgan, Albert T. (1842–1922)

Albert T. Morgan was a Mississippi Carpetbagger sheriff born in upstate New York. Morgan was a student preparing to enter Oberlin College in Ohio when the Civil War broke out. He returned to his family home, now in Wisconsin, where his father had done well in the wheat business, and enlisted in the Second Wisconsin Volunteer Infantry. He served in the eastern theater of the war, where his regiment made history as part of the famous Iron Brigade of the Army of the Potomac. Morgan rose from private to lieutenant colonel, was captured and exchanged, was severely wounded in the left thigh, and became sick with malaria. But he always returned to his post and finished up the war in his second enlistment. As a result of his injury, he walked with a limp and tired easily.

His brother Charles, also a Union war veteran, proposed that the two look around for a new start. They tried Kansas but disliked the plains and soon began to look south to the fertile soils of Mississippi. Landing at Vicksburg, they heard of land for sale at Yazoo City 100 miles northeast. Soon they were in the planting business in a big way. But Mississippi was one of the least friendly places in the South for Northern emigrants. Morgan was beaten up when he tried to collect a debt owed him. His problems were not eased any when he and his brother made known their ideas on race, which sprung from abolitionist fervor. They protested bad treatment of local African Americans, established a black school, and generally stood up for equal treatment. Meanwhile the planting went poorly. First came the floods and then the army worms. Had it not been for their sawmill, the brothers would have gone broke. But the people from whom they rented had the mill seized to guarantee the rent due, and without the mill functioning the Morgans folded.

Broke and needing a reason to go on, the Morgans took heart at the passage of the Reconstruction Acts and the emergence of the Republican party in Mississippi. Local blacks needed some candidates for their seat in the new state constitutional convention. So far only three Union army officers had announced. Morgan, another local Carpetbagger, and an African American blacksmith offered their names, too. All six men were running as Republicans, even though they acted as if they were from two different parties. No Democrats ran. Morgan's ticket won. He worked actively for black civil rights and for the disfranchisement of all who would not swear an oath to political and civil equality of all men. His massive disfranchisement carried the day and ensured a Republican victory in the first election in 1868. But Yazoo City remained in the Democratic column thanks to the inaction of Bvt. Maj. Gen. Alvin C. Gillem, commander of the District of Mississippi, and massive intimidation by local authorities.

Finally, with Bvt. Brig. Gen. Adelbert Ames in control of Mississippi as provisional governor and commanding general (replacing Gillem), Morgan managed to get himself elected to the county board of supervisors. He instituted Radical Republican policies, taxed property holders, and set up a system of public education and road repairs. His activity pleased black and Carpetbag voters, who sent him to the state legislature. At Jackson, Ames relied heavily on Morgan for advice on whom to appoint to local patronage positions. Morgan voted for the Fourteenth and Fifteenth amendments

and for Ames and Hiram Revels as U.S. senators. He also backed the repeal of the Black Codes and established a new court system and a public school system. He created new counties named for such prominent Yankees as martyred President Abraham Lincoln, Senator Charles Sumner, and Vice President Schuyler Colfax. But he opposed a public accommodations law because he feared that it would destroy Republicans as it had done in neighboring Louisiana. He also met a New York schoolteacher, a mulatto named Carrie Highgate. He married her in short order (which did not endear him at all to white Mississippi), and they went on a honeymoon to New York state. They returned to Yazoo City, where they set up housekeeping and Carrie gave birth to three children in as many years. Two more would come along later. Morgan, meanwhile, was elected county sheriff.

With marriage and family and a rousing political career ahead of him, Morgan thought that he had achieved heaven on earth. But he reckoned without white Mississippi. Even though Morgan had clearly won the election, his opponent, the incumbent (a Mississippi Union man during the war), refused to vacate the office. When the man left the room for an errand, Morgan and his deputies took possession. The ex-sheriff came back with his own posse and shooting erupted. Morgan returned fire and his opponent fell dead. A local judge appointed a new sheriff as Morgan was spirited away to Jackson under arrest. But Governor Ames removed the judge and his ersatz sheriff and put a new judge on the bench, who set Morgan free to resume office. Meanwhile the whites of Yazoo City had been organizing, arming, and training as unofficial militia companies. To reassure them, Morgan held a large political rally to which local white leaders were invited. At the meting Morgan and several black ministers spoke out for passive resistance rather than violence. They asked all to rely on the law and the electoral process.

But the whites were not about to be denied. They won the city elections that fall with a slight majority, although Morgan and his black and white allies carried the county. The only way Democrats could take the predominantly black county was through violence, and everyone knew it. Morgan had a perfect record of fair taxes, a new courthouse, and a public school system. At a rally for Republicans, however, a group known as the White Liners got a black man with a tax grievance against Morgan to interrupt the meeting. Shouting was followed by shooting. Morgan had to jump out a second-story window. Blacks warned him that a mounted force of an estimated 900 Ku Klux Klan members was searching for him. Hiding out at a friend's house, Morgan finally escaped to Jackson. But Governor Ames's administration was about to fall, too. Morgan gathered up his wife and children, who had been at a summer home in Holly Springs, and fled the state. Eventually Morgan got a federal job in Washington, D.C., as a second-class clerk in the pension office, thanks to Mississippi's second black senator, Blanche K. Bruce. He also wrote of his Mississippi experiences.

But the election of Grover Cleveland as president ended that phase of Morgan's life. He took his family to Kansas, then left them there as he toured the Colorado gold and silver fields as a prospector. He found little wealth. He took up the free silver crusade, changed political parties, campaigned for William Jennings Bryan, and wrote several pamphlets and magazines on behalf of the free silver cause. Meanwhile, Morgan's wife took their four girls (their son had become a railroad clerk) and went on a tour of the East as a singing family. With the exception of a few short meetings with his son, Morgan never saw his wife and family again. He died in Denver in 1922. His son brought his body to Indianapolis for burial. Mrs. Morgan applied for and received a pension, although officials could not believe that the Morgans had lived apart so long without formal separation or divorce. In the end, his son said that he believed that his father was too ashamed to come home, having been a failure so long.

See also Alcorn, James Lusk; Ames, Adelbert; Carpetbaggers; Redemption of the South from 1874.

References Current, Richard N., *Those Terrible Carpetbaggers* (1988); Harris, William C., *The Day of the Carpetbagger* (1979); Morgan, Albert T., *Yazoo* (1968 [1884]); Overy, David H., Jr., "The Wisconsin Carpetbagger" (1960).

Morrill, Justin M. (1810–1898)

Born in Vermont the eldest of ten children, Justin S. Morrill was educated in local schools and academies. He became a clerk in a local store and began a profitable life in merchandising that allowed him to retire to the life of gentleman farmer and scholar by 1848. Morrill married in 1851, and he and his wife had two sons. He learned much about politics from listening and taking part in discussions around his store's stove and front porch. He served in county and state committees and was elected to Congress as a antislavery Whig in 1854. He would serve 12 years in the House and 32 in the Senate, the longest unbroken tenure until the twentieth century. He soon changed over to the Republican party, where he continued to oppose slavery. However, Morrill's real talent lay in tariff and finance. He wrote the initials bills on the funding of the debt, the Civil War tariff designed to protect infant industry and raise revenue (the highest tariff in U.S. history at that point), and the Land Grant College Act (which gave land to public colleges offering education in agriculture and other practical subjects), his proudest achievement and one that was expanded in 1890. It is fair to say that Morrill had much to do with the passage of the Republicans' domestic economic program during the Civil War. During Reconstruction he came out as a hard money man against in favor of gold over silver or paper greenbacks and spoke in favor of beautifying the capitol grounds. Morrill was a literary man and wrote several books and articles on self-improvement. Because of his longevity in the Senate, he became known as the "grand old man of the Republican party" and a skillful legislator. Morrill had sharp features that were likened to a Roman statue; he had sideburns and a charming, modest manner that were liked by all he worked with. He died in Washington at the end of the century, having overwhelmingly won reelection each time he ran.

See also Moderate Republicans and Reconstruction.

References Fuess, Claude M., "Justin Smith Morrill" (1964–1981); Nevins, Allan, *The Origins of the Land-grant Colleges and Universities* (1962).

Moses, Franklin J., Jr. (1838–1906)

A South Carolina Scalawag, Franklin Moses, probably more than any other man, typified the stereotype of the socially prominent, pleasant, promising, young native white who sold his soul to corruption and turned on his race for personal profit. Moses's father, from a Spanish-Jewish family that had once fled the Inquisition, was a prominent Charleston attorney, a state legislator for 20 years before the war, and chief justice of the state supreme court afterward (a Scalawag, too). He was respected by friend and foe alike; not so the son. Born Franklin Israel Moses, Jr., Frank dropped his middle name (imitating his father) and substituted the initial "J." No one knows why; the Moseses were never discriminated against because of their ethnicity. Indeed, Charleston Jews were quick to point out that the younger Moses was raised as a Gentile and had married outside the faith. After his education Moses became personal secretary to Governor Francis W. Pickens. It was 1860, and South Carolina was in the process of seceding from the Union, the first Southern state to do so. Moses represented the governor in negotiations for the surrender of Fort Sumter, and after the battle he personally raised the Confederate flag over the captured installation. He later served as military enrolling officer with the rank of colonel—it looked respectable and it allowed him to avoid combat.

After the war Moses was admitted to the bar and joined the Episcopal Church. He edited a newspaper and endorsed President Andrew Johnson's Reconstruction policies. But with the passage of the Military Reconstruction Acts, Moses underwent a radical change. He grasped what was obvious to any ambitious politician: the key to control of the state would be the new black voters. He immediately began to organize Union Loyal Leagues among the former slaves. He criticized his social peers for their stupidity in refusing to submit to Radical Reconstruction. Thankful for his leadership, the blacks from his district sent him to the state constitutional convention, where he became an outspoken Radical Republican. He was elected to the state house of representatives, where he became speaker. Under the new administration Moses was appointed adjutant and inspector general of the state militia, trustee of the state university, and trustee of the state militia. In each office Moses made it clear that he could be bought. He took bribes in the house of representatives and dealt in bogus state pay vouchers. As head of the militia he diverted money raised for arms to his personal use.

In 1872 Moses became governor, again relying on the African American vote, by defeating a reform candidate, Daniel H. Chamberlain. As governor Moses sold pardons and political appointments, as well as his signature on all legislation. Backed up by his militia he defied court orders. He hobnobbed with his black constituents on a one-to-one level, wined and dined them all, and had affairs with many women, all of which offended conservative whites. He spent so much money that he could hardly steal fast enough to keep up with his bills. Even his corrupt colleagues became embarrassed by his raucous conduct. At the end of his two-year term, even the worst Republicans had deserted him for Chamberlain. The new governor began his reform administration by refusing to issue Moses his commission for circuit judge, a position to which he had been elected. With the triumph of the Red Shirts, a whites-only militia group, Moses managed to save himself from a prison term by ratting on all of his cronies.

In 1878 Moses lost his wife, who divorced him and left the state. Some of his kin changed their surnames so as not to be identified with his deeds. Moses himself wandered from one city to another, running small confidence games, operating as a petty thief, serving several prison terms, and winding up a drug addict. He died in Massachusetts of accidental asphyxiation from a poorly ventilated heater. Sadly, his death came just as he had finally seemed to show a desire to repent. He had cleaned up his body and soul and served briefly as moderator of the town meeting and editor of a local newspaper.

Moses spent the vast majority of his life as a moral weakling who gave in to every temptation that life had provided. Although he was not a typical Scalawag, he was perfect for the myths that followed Reconstruction that condemned the so-called Tragic Era as a time of unmitigated evil. Moses's shame is that he corrupted the idealism that the best in Reconstruction truly represented.

See also Chamberlain, Daniel H.; Scalawags; Scott, Robert K.

References Carter, Hodding, *The Angry Scar* (1959); Reynolds, John S., *Reconstruction in South Carolina* (1905); Simkins, Francis B., and Robert W. Woody, *South Carolina during Reconstruction* (1932).

New Departure Years after Reconstruction

With the accession of Rutherford B. Hayes to the presidency in 1877 through a shady mechanism of electoral compromise, Reconstruction was for all practical purposes over, at least as far as the North was concerned. But African Americans viewed the détente between Northern and Southern whites with alarm. Essentially what Hayes and his administration did was institute what came to be called the New Departure. Its central tenet was that the "better" classes in the South—those old Whigs who, though they had been slaveholders, had been reluctant to secede and were willing to be Scalawags during Reconstruction—would protect blacks as they had done in days of slavery. But Yankees either failed to realize the implications of their decision for black freedom or, in light of the struggle for the black vote in the North before and during Reconstruction, did not care.

Hayes himself seemed to have an inkling of the evil that the New Departure wrought but chose to look the other way for many reasons. To sway his opinion, Southern Bourbon Democrats, those who had "redeemed" the South (i.e., regained conservative political control) in the early 1870s and dealt with the Republicans in the Compromise of 1877, arranged a tour of the South for the president. Hayes became the first president since Lincoln (who went to Richmond in 1865) to actually go into the South Atlantic states to see for himself how "beneficial" the New Departure was. Instrumental in the selling job was Governor Wade Hampton of South Carolina, a Confederate Civil War cavalry general and the man put into power by the rifles of the Red Shirts militias. Hampton gave Hayes an artful treatment of the carrot and the stick—promising to watch out for violations of African Americans' freedoms as citizens and threatening a new race war if the Yankees ever again had the temerity to interfere with the South again. Hayes could trust the real "gentlemen" of the South, the message went. So blacks went from being wards of

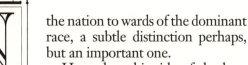

the nation to wards of the dominant race, a subtle distinction perhaps, but an important one.

Hayes kept his side of the bargain. He withdrew the troops, a policy essentially begun by President Ulysses S. Grant when he refused to interfere with elections in state after state as their inevitable Redemptions drew nigh. Hayes appointed Democrat David Key of Tennessee as postmaster general (this position not only affected a legion of political appointments nationwide but also had especially important implications in the South). But then the deal broke down. Hayes had great doubt that the "impoverished South," as he saw it, ought to get the internal improvements promised implicitly in the Compromise of 1877. The whole thing smacked of the crookedness that he had pledged to stop, North and South. The corruption, alleged or real, was one major reason that the country was tired of Reconstruction.

Besides, the Bourbons could not deliver the promised white vote, which was going for various Independent, Readjuster, and Greenback candidates in the by-elections of 1878. The New Departure relied on getting Southerners to support Republican economic programs that only the conservative, upper-class veneer in the South liked. The average Southern white yeoman was more prone to support radical farmer groups who promised debt relief and soft money (inflationary paper bills, rather than gold), ideas that Hayes and the old Southern Whigs found repugnant. Hayes's whole policy appalled many Northern Republicans, remnants of the Radicals who had lost their idealism in support of African Americans for the greed of office and were now called Stalwarts. These men were angry that Hayes allowed Postmaster General Key to appoint Democrats to lucrative positions in the South. Indeed, Hayes had honored only one Republican leader with higher office, Oliver P. Morton of Indiana, and then only indirectly by making Morton's crony, Richard W. Thompson, secretary of the Navy. One of the goals of Radical Reconstruction had been to expand Republican principles into the South through black voters. Stalwarts envisioned the Republican party in the South as largely black; they perceived the South as a perpetual rotten borough and told stories of Southern white political violence (i.e., they "waved the bloody shirt") to negate Democratic influence nationally. Hayes also hoped his policy would allow the Republican party to continue to extend into the South, but the New Departure envisioned this party as strong, white, and conservative. Hayes failed in his desire, as the off-year congressional elections and the South's vote against the Republican presidential candidate in 1880 showed, but he remained steadfast in pursuing his goal throughout his administration.

The odd thing about the New Departure was the equanimity with which African American leaders accepted it when it seemed so obviously against the best interests of their race. However, they saw it more as an experiment than as an etched-in-stone reality (and Frederick Douglass was among the leaders who spoke out in support of the plan). The catch was that, although the New Departure ignored blacks as a group, Hayes was careful to reward them as individuals with appointments to office. This allowed Hayes to maintain the illusion that he really was on the side of black America and to keep quiet those who accepted his appointments. And most influential black appointees did keep quiet. The result was the creation of a series of "Jim Crow" positions in every department of the government to which African American politicians might accede. But like all benefits of second-class citizenship, these positions were of the lower echelon. They continued to be filled with black Republicans until the turn of the century, when disfranchisement and the election of Woodrow Wilson eliminated even these positions.

Hayes's successor, James A. Garfield, was in office only six months by the time he was assassinated by a disappointed office-seeker. But Garfield had an importance for the New Departure that far outweighed his short tenure. He was an old Radical Repub-

lican who spoke out vigorously on behalf of black political rights in the "redeemed" South. Garfield also made much of the need for African Americans to receive a good education. Garfield's vice president, Chester A. Arthur, as a Stalwart and spoilsman, promised even more. But African Americans were doomed to disappointment again. Arthur and his advisors believed that Hayes had had the right idea (a white-supported Republican party in the South). Hayes had merely worked with the wrong whites, the upper-class minority. Arthur proposed to back the Readjusters, an independent group of lower- and middle-class Democrats who had captured control of Virginia under William Mahone, a man who wished to rescale Southern state debts. They and parties like them—variously labeled Independent Democrats, Greenbackers, and the like—had risen to oppose the Bourbon Redeemers during the economic panic of 1873 and its aftermath. Unlike the Bourbon conservatives with whom Hayes had dealt, the Independents represented a majority of Southern white voters. Many had been Scalawags early on in Reconstruction, before the race issue drove them into alliance with the Bourbons. They were the men who had been elected in 1878 and 1880 in opposition to the Redeemers.

Arthur used his appointive powers to support these Southerners. He also appointed so many former Confederates that even Hayes thought it to be a bit much. And he worked with the Redeemers in cases where the others were not in sufficient power to control their states. Put simply, Arthur appointed whites of all stripes to office and ignored the traditional black Republicans, except for the usual Jim Crow appointments in the executive departments in Washington. His goal was to elect a Republican Congress in 1882 and gain a renomination in 1884. This time, however, the African American leaders were not going to take it. If Hayes had instituted an experiment, then Arthur was about to make it permanent. Led by Frederick Douglass, among others, blacks met in the National Convention of Negroes at Louisville, Kentucky, and decided that if Arthur liked white Independents in the South so much, black Americans would become independent of the Republicans, too. Blacks largely blamed the U.S. Supreme Court's decisions against the Civil Rights Act of 1875 and other adverse decisions concerning the Fourteenth Amendment on the environment that Arthur created in Washington. T. Thomas Fortune, an important black opinion maker, spoke out against Arthur for two obvious faults: he refused to consult with traditional black Republicans in the South, and he was personally haughty and condescending in his attitude toward blacks in general. Fortune and Douglass warned Republicans that they could not rely on the black vote with impunity without the usual political rewards that must accompany any support.

Just how much influence the black intellectuals had with the rank and file is debatable (most blacks probably began to sit out presidential contests rather than vote Democratic), but the Republicans lost the 1884 race to Grover Cleveland, the only Democrat to win the presidency between James Buchanan (1856) and Woodrow Wilson (1914). But Cleveland's election revealed a horrible truth to black Americans—one they probably suspected all along. Though Cleveland was pretty liberal on race issues for a Democrat, and with notable exceptions (he fired Blanche K. Bruce and asked Frederick Douglass to resign) he kept the Jim Crow jobs in Washington black, he would support his party in the South, and home rule there became more brutal than ever.

The Cleveland administration became the age of the "Negrowump," an oblique reference to the normally Republican black intellectuals who thought much like the white Mugwumps (heirs of the Liberal Republicans of 1872) in supporting the reformist president of the opposite party. Cleveland did pledge to support black rights in the South; he refused to appoint the more blatant race-baiters to office and stood firmly behind the attempt of New Hampshire Representative Henry Blair to pass a federal bill to aid Southern public schools

(especially the black ones). But his administration was less concerned with the Southern question and race than any other that preceded it. Cleveland was more interested in reforming domestic politics in issues like civil service, greenbacks (soft money versus hard money), the tariff, creation of the Interstate Commerce Commission, and a change in how Indians were handled on the reservation system out West.

By 1888, African Americans were ready to return to the Republican fold, if indeed they had ever really left it. And Republicans were willing to give the usual pledge of support for black political aspirations, especially in the South. The Benjamin Harrison administration moved quickly to keep its promises. Harrison once again rewarded blacks with the Jim Crow jobs in Washington. He also began to turn away from the Civil War generation of black leaders and to recognize many young, new African American politicians in job appointments. The Henry Blair education bill was reintroduced. This time a greater share of the federal aid to public education would be apportioned to black schools (the allotment was structured on the number of illiterates over ten years of age in a state). After a lengthy debate, however, 17 Republican senators voted with a vast majority of Democrats to defeat the measure, to the outrage of blacks in the South.

But what was to come was worse. Senator Henry Cabot Lodge of Massachusetts proposed a new enforcement bill that would once again lead to federal elections being policed in the South. The House of Representative sent the bill through rapidly and it came to the Senate. There it met the doubts of senators from silver-mining states, disillusioned Mugwumps who now found their earlier idealism on behalf of blacks misplaced, and traditional business Republicans interested in working with the conservatives down South. The measure was delayed initially by tariff considerations. Then, despite Harrison's plea to support the measure, the bill fell to a deal between silver Republicans and Democrats. Human rights had given way to the needs of silver-inflated money.

With the failure of the Blair and Lodge bills, Congress gave the white South a green light to move ahead with restriction of the black vote. Mississippi met in convention and passed a new state constitution that effectively disfranchised voters on the basis of length of residence, literacy, poll taxes paid, and conviction of certain charges (petty larceny, vagrancy, and wife beating) that were known in the South as "Negro crimes." African Americans had been excluded from the political process, and it was all within the boundaries set by the Fifteenth Amendment—none of the restrictions the white South implemented mentioned race, color, or former condition of servitude. Economic concerns, recurring financial depressions, the jingoism (American imperialism) of the Spanish-American War, and a desire to create a "lily-white" Republican party in the South kept blacks out of politics until the New Deal of the 1930s and later. Reconstruction was over at last—only to return 60 years later in the form of the modern civil rights movement.

See also Disfranchisement; Economic Disfranchisement; Segregation (Jim Crow).

References Beatty, Bess, *A Revolution Gone Backward* (1987); DeSantis, Vincent P., "Negro Dissatisfaction with Republican Policy in the South" (1951), "President Hayes's Southern Policy" (1955), "The Republican Party and the Southern Negro" (1960), "President Arthur and the Independent Movements in the South" (1953), *Republicans Face the Southern Question* (1959), and "Rutherford B. Hayes and the Removal of the Troops and the End of Reconstruction" (1982); Fishel, Leslie H., Jr., "The Negro in Northern Politics" (1955–1956); Lewis, Elsie M., "The Political Mind of the Negro" (1955); Lewinson, Paul, *Race, Class, and Party* (1965); Logan, Rayford W., *The Betrayal of the Negro* (1965); Wesley, Charles H., "Negro Suffrage in the Period of Constitution-Making" (1947) and "The Participation of Negroes in Anti-slavery Political Parties" (1944); Woodward, C. Vann, "Seeds of Failure in Radical Race Policy" (1966).

Pardon, Amnesty, and Parole

As soon as the South had seceded from the Union, the problem arose of how to get it back in. Implicit in this concept was the notion of forgiveness; the Union could not be made whole once again without it. Forgiveness had several contexts: pardon is generally the forgiveness of an individual for certain acts, amnesty is pardon applied to a class of people, and parole (basically a promise) is reserved for soldiers. Until 1864, a captured enemy of either side was generally imprisoned briefly and exchanged. But in cases of mass surrender (there were three during the war, Ft. Donelson, Vicksburg, and Appomattox, all under Lt. Gen. Ulysses S. Grant), logistics demanded that the capturing force accept the solidiers' paroles to go home and not fight again until properly exchanged.

Abraham Lincoln was a pardoning president, perhaps because of his Southern background (he was born in Kentucky, was raised in southern Indiana, and became an adult in Illinois, where he had strong Southern connections, not the least of which were his wife and her family). His first public policy of pardon was his December 1863 Proclamation of Amnesty, which set into operation his wartime plan of Reconstruction. This policy was not a sign that Lincoln was weak. His pardon and amnesty powers were always tempered by restriction, although many Northerners thought him to be too lenient, as the 1864 Wade-Davis Bill demonstrated. According to Lincoln's plan, higher officials of the Confederate government or military could not participate in the initial formation of a loyal government in any Southern state.

Through his amnesty policy, Lincoln essentially sought out loyal persons, first those who had fought consistently against secession, then recanting Confederates. He also had a tendency to forgive minor infractions of military law, for example, by pardoning soldiers who fell asleep on sentry duty. He refused, however, to interfere in the death sentence of John Y. Beall, a prominent Marylander who got caught in civilian clothes in an attempt to release Confederate prisoners held at Johnson Island in Lake Erie. But he was against wholesale retribution, maintaining that "blood cannot restore blood, and government should not act for revenge." The surrender terms accorded Robert E. Lee's army at Appomattox are the best example of his attitude.

After Lincoln's murder, President Andrew Johnson seemed to have a harsher attitude toward forgiveness. He spoke of hanging traitors. Radical Republicans were pleased, but events showed the president not to be the man of retribution they wanted. Johnson's Proclamation of Amnesty and Reconstruction exempted 14 classes of citizens from being able to take the oath of future allegiance and accept amnesty. Most of these were common to all plans of Reconstruction: higher officials of the Confederate and state governments and staff officers of the military establishment. He also included a special class that exempted all persons worth $20,000 or more from amnesty. Instead they had to apply for individual pardon. These people were, of course, Johnson's old political enemies from the planting class, those who had opposed him early in his political career.

Johnson reserved particular venom for Confederate president Jefferson Davis, who was held at Fortress Monroe for two years, then set free on a writ of habeas corpus and admitted to bail while still under indictment. But Davis was included in the general Confederate amnesty that marked the final act of the Johnson administration (Christmas 1868). With the exception of Davis, who was never tried, the only other Confederate officials jailed were Vice President Alexander Stephens and Postmaster General John H. Regan. They were released in a matter of months. Most of those who had fled the United States in fear of their lives returned and lived unmolested, if often unreconstructed, lives.

Because Johnson proved to be almost as liberal as Lincoln in individual cases, those exempt from general amnesty applied in droves to regain their rights. This was essential for them to protect or regain their employment, property, patents, and copyrights because Johnson's exemptions included those who practiced 50 common occupations. The first step of the procedure was to apply to the provisional governor of the state (appointed by Johnson) for a recommendation. Then the application and letters of recommendation went to the U.S. attorney general's office, where the papers were reexamined for worthiness. Then everything was forwarded to the president, who, if he found the petition worthy, would issue a warrant for pardon, with the actual documents being filled out and signed by the U.S. secretary of state. Then the president's signature would be obtained and the documents returned to the state governor, who would convey the pardon to the original petitioner.

It was a long, involved process that had many points where bureaucratic snags might develop, so it became common to hire a pardon broker, an expert who would keep track of developments and push an application forward. (The government thought of creating a pardon bureau but never got around to it.) President Johnson thought the whole business unseemly, especially since several women were involved as pardon brokers, a fact considered rather daring in staid Victorian America. The pardon was free, but the services of a broker were not. And since the president granted 13,500 pardons (half of which were for persons in the $20,000 and above class) in short order, it was a lucrative, if short-lived, business. Johnson's harsh stance against the Confederate leaders soon evaporated. He had Lincoln's wartime example to live up to, Secretary of State William H. Seward was for a more lenient approach, and, most of all, the exempted Southerners groveled magnificently. Johnson's hostility soon became so beneficent that many Northerners, especially Republicans in Congress, began to question his motives. Too many old-time Democrats were being let off the hook.

Congress asked the Joint Committee of Fifteen to investigate the real behavior of the South; this committee found that the president's pardoning policy was moving too quickly (as Republicans had expected), excusing too many who ought to be proscribed from political participation for a much longer period, and not sufficiently taking into account the potential political and economic rights of African Americans. The result was the Civil Rights Act of 1866 and the officeholding proscription clause of the Fourteenth Amendment. Congress also repealed the clemency clause of the Second Confiscation Act, which had granted President Lincoln (and by extension President Johnson) the right to grant amnesty and pardon; many in Congress believed that the president did not have such powers without a specific grant from the legislative branch. The Military Reconstruction Act of 2 March 1867, then disfranchised anyone coming under the Fourteenth Amendment's proscription (anyone who took an oath to the United States and then subsequently to the Confederacy) until Reconstruction was completed.

Ever ready to take on Congress, Johnson drafted another amnesty, claiming that he had the power directly from the Constitution and needed no congressional sanction. On 7 September 1867, Johnson pardoned all former Confederates except executive officials of the Confederate government, governors of Confederate states, military officers above the army rank of brigadier general and naval rank of captain, anyone implicated in the assassination of President Lincoln, or anyone who had abused captured Union soldiers or officials. This left some 300 Southerners still without full citizenship. During his impeachment trial, Johnson decided to issue a third amnesty, but he wisely waited until he was acquitted before acting. On 4 July 1868, as the Democratic presidential nominating convention met in New York City and the rest of the nation celebrated Independence Day, Johnson extended amnesty to all former Confederates except anyone under indictment or conviction for treason or any other felony. Everyone pardoned was given back any seized property except slaves.

Finally, Johnson made a fourth amnesty on Christmas Day 1868, pardoning the few Confederate civil and military officials still under proscription, including people like Jefferson Davis, John C. Breckinridge (who had been vice president of the United States under James Buchanan and was widely hated), and Robert E. Lee. Johnson justified his action by saying that federal authority had been restored to all of the United States and that there was no need for any voting proscriptions of any kind. But unlike his other proclamations that had pardoned Southerners for "rebellion," this one used the term *treason*. The term was quite odious, to use one of Johnson's favorite adjectives, but it took care of Jefferson Davis, who was under indictment for treason, without having to mention his name specifically.

With President Johnson's departure from office in 1869 and the reluctance of President Ulysses S. Grant to argue over legislative prerogatives, the question of amnesty became pretty much a congressional one. Persons in the South had appealed to Congress for relief from the inception of Military Reconstruction, as soon as it became obvious that Johnson was not going to be able to do as he pleased on any question. Individual petitions had been received and some acted upon favorably. President Johnson had signed off on these, allowing Congress to act under its power according to the Fourteenth Amendment to remove officeholding disabilities. Congress approved a new oath especially designed for men who had held Confederate offices and wished to stand for election or had been elected after the war in July 1868.

By 1871, Congress had exempted some 4,600 from the officeholding proscription of the Fourteenth Amendment. President Grant, reflecting public sentiment, spoke in favor of an overall amnesty in 1871. In May 1872 Congress passed the General Amnesty Act, which removed officeholding proscriptions from all Confederates but those who had served in the two Congresses just before the Civil War or had been heads of federal executive departments, federal judges, foreign ministers for the United States, or officers in the army and navy. Although Congress denied an attempt to pass a general amnesty upon the death of Andrew Johnson in 1876, it continued to give those exempted from the General Amnesty Act individual consideration. Finally, in the shadow of the Spanish-American War, Congress restored everyone still exempted under the Fourteenth Amendment on 8 June 1898. Jefferson Davis, the main impediment to such a measure, had been dead for a decade. The Civil War was officially over at last.

See also Bureau of Refugees, Freedmen, and Abandoned Lands; Captured and Abandoned Property Act; Confiscation Acts; Disfranchisement; Fourteenth Amendment.

References Carter, Dan T., *When the War Was Over* (1985); Dorris, Jonathan Truman, *Pardon and Amnesty under Lincoln and Johnson* (1953), "Pardon Seekers and Brokers" (1935), and "Pardoning the Leaders of the Confederacy" (1928); Perman, Michael, *Reunion without Compromise* (1973); Rawley, James A., "The General Amnesty Act of 1872" (1960).

Pinchback, Pinckney Benton Stewart (1837–1921)

Born near Macon, Georgia, P. B. S. Pinchback was the eighth child of white planter William Pinchback and his slave Eliza Stewart. His mother had been released from slavery sometime around his birth, but she remained with her lover as he traveled from Virginia to Mississippi. P. B. S. Pinchback was born along the way. He was sent away to boarding school in Cincinnati, Ohio, returning to find his father near death. After he died, mother and children were hustled away to the North to prevent their being enslaved. His older brother became mentally incapacitated, so P. B. S. Pinchback went to work at age 12 as a cabin boy on canal boats in Ohio. There he learned all there was to know from some of the sharpest con men of the age. "Pinch," as he was appropriately called, later spoke of himself as legally being a quadroon, or one-fourth black. He advanced to a position of steward (the highest position that a black could have in slavery days) and augmented his income by taking advantage of the black roustabouts and deckhands along the way. In 1862, he slipped off a riverboat headed up the Yazoo and wended his way down to New Orleans to seek his fortune with the conquering Yankees.

Pinchback soon enlisted in the First Louisiana Volunteer Infantry. It was a white regiment, composed of loyal Union men who hoped to fight the secessionists with the North. But shortly thereafter, Bvt. Maj. Gen. Benjamin F. Butler issued a call for all blacks in the liberated sections of Louisiana to join up with the new Corps d'Afrique. Pinchback obtained authorization to raise his own company of African American volunteers, for which he was made captain. He spoke out freely in favor of equal opportunity and rights for black officers and men, which caused the whites above him to resent his presence. Clearly this was a man destined to go places—quite possibly higher than their own careers would take them. Faced with the barrier of racial prejudice, Pinchback resigned his commission. He raised a company of black cavalry, but this time the Yankees would not allow him to be its captain. He went North to get permission to raise a regiment of the U.S. Colored Volunteers, but the end of the war stopped that project before it fairly started.

Pinchback returned to the South, this time to Alabama, where he spoke to black assemblages in Montgomery and Mobile. He was an ardent supporter of the Radical Republican program of Reconstruction, and he made quite a mark with his fine oratorical delivery. With the passage of the Military Reconstruction Acts, Pinchback returned to New Orleans, a renowned mecca for any ambitious black man in the South. He organized the Fourth Ward Republican Club and entered politics. The ward sent him to the state constitutional convention. One-half of those attending the convention were African Americans, most of whom had been free men of color before the war, like Pinchback. Immediately he began to look on blacks of lesser ability than he with scorn. Pinchback called for all offices to be awarded on merit alone, claiming that racial apportionment would cause trouble later. He also spoke out against disfranchising whites for their Confederate activities. But he never forgot his race when it came to writing the constitution. He drafted the equal rights provision of the document, which also called for open access to public accommodations.

Pinchback's conduct at the convention brought him much notice among blacks and whites. He was immediately put up for state senator from the second district. The count showed that his white Democratic opponent won, but Pinchback filed for a recount. The state legislature took notice of the claim and upon investigation ruled favorably on Pinchback's behalf. Pinchback took his seat as a loyal member of the new Republican administration, with Illinois Carpetbagger Henry C. Warmoth as governor. Right away Pinchback became involved in a shootout with a black opponent of the administration. He then defended his conduct and pledged more violence if Democrats did not behave respectably toward elected Republicans. The result was that he was seen as a hothead, which continued to haunt him later. In 1868, Pinchback was elected delegate to the national Republican convention in Chicago. He took the time to become acquainted with party leaders, and it all paid off when, after the election, President Ulysses S. Grant made him registrar of the land office. Pinchback, however, declined the offer, preferring to stay in the state senate. Meanwhile he went into business as a cotton factor or broker and owner of a cross-river packet service that would carry blacks.

As Pinchback introduced civil rights measures opposed by white Republicans and refused to operate as a member of the administration (he saw himself as an independent senator), relations between him and Governor Warmoth grew tense. Warmoth was no fool. He knew that in Pinchback he had a clever potential rival. Pinchback had the same effect on black Lieutenant Governor Oscar J. Dunn. Worse yet, all three men were looking ahead to the U.S. Senate race in 1872. But Pinchback's relations with Warmoth were compounded by the governor's unwillingness to enforce civil rights in the state. He also vetoed a Pinchback bill that would have made it a crime to discriminate on the basis of race. In return, Pinchback and Dunn combined to defeat Warmoth as president of the party convention of 1870, with Dunn getting the job instead. Pinchback went about the state using his oratorical skills to advance the Republican cause and help elect a new legislature. He had a longer term as state senator, so he did not have to run himself.

In the new legislature, one of the more corrupt in Louisiana history, Pinchback took his share. Meanwhile, Warmoth went to the Mississippi Gulf Coast for rest from an injury and Lieutenant Governor Dunn tried to take over the party. Warmoth returned to keep control, but the move was indicative of much unrest by white and black factions alike. Already some thought that the governor ought to be impeached. This was very important to Pinchback, because just recently Lieutenant Governor Dunn had died of poisoning. Foul play was suspected and many wondered if Warmoth were behind it. Pinchback was also regarded suspiciously because Dunn's demise put Pinchback, as president pro tem of the state senate, next in line after Warmoth for the governorship, according to the constitution.

Pinchback, however, faced some problems with legislators in getting them to continue trying to remove the governor. Most saw Pinchback as a black version of Warmoth, slick and sticky-fingered, whereas Dunn had offered an honest choice. Pinchback and Warmoth split over the presidential election of 1872, Pinchback supporting Grant and Warmoth going for Greeley. The national Republican party called upon Pinchback, a popular orator among party faithful, to come up to New England to speak. There Pinchback consulted with party leaders and warned them that Warmoth was fouling up everything in Louisiana and that the state would probably go for Greeley unless changes could be made in the state's election laws to allow easier registration. The new law had been passed, but Warmoth was refusing to sign it. Then Pinchback discovered that Warmoth had

come North to explain his side of the impasse. No mean manipulators themselves, national Republican leaders wondered if Pinchback were willing to return to Louisiana ahead of Warmoth. Since the governor was out of the state, Pinchback would automatically become governor and could sign the registration reform law. Pinchback headed home posthaste. Warmoth caught on, seemingly too late to catch him.

But Pinchback was a victim of his own pride. As he reached Canton, Mississippi, he was awakened in his car and told there was a telegram for the governor of Louisiana. Pinchback had to see what it said. He stepped down and entered the room only to be locked in. Warmoth, meanwhile, had taken special trains by prior arrangement, and when he lumbered into Canton the next morning, Pinchback was let loose. The two men rode back to Louisiana together, affecting forced charm for each other's company. The Pinchback plot had been foiled. Meanwhile, to elect a Democrat as the next governor, Warmoth (who had switched parties) now signed one of the reform bills

P. B. S. Pinchback

and appointed a new returning board, which certified a Democratic victory. This act gave Pinchback the opening he needed to secure Warmoth's impeachment. Warmoth had called a special session of the state legislature, allegedly to secure his election as the next U.S. senator. But Pinchback turned it into an impeachment session that removed Warmoth from office. This allowed Pinchback to take office for just over a month before the new Republican administration under William P. Kellogg took over, with the support of both Pinchback and the Grant administration. Pinchback thus became the only black governor of a Southern state during Reconstruction. Not to be outdone, Warmoth installed the Democrats and their own legislature at the same time. Louisiana now had two governments, both claiming legality.

As part of the deal for supporting Kellogg, Pinchback went to Washington to claim his seat in the House. But after a lengthy investigation, his white Democratic opponent was seated. However, Pinchback had also since been elected to be a U.S. senator. He went over to the other side of Capitol Hill to complete his quest. But the Senate was unsure of what to do and tabled the motion to consider. Pinchback was reelected by the state legislature once again. This time, after lengthy debate and much delay, Pinchback's request to be seated was rejected. The Democrats had won the national elections in 1874, and Republicans did not wish to hurt their chances in 1876 by going with Pinchback. As consolation he was voted $16,000 in compensation and expenses.

When Pinchback got back to Louisiana, the 1876 national contest for president was on. Pinchback supported the national ticket, but he was less than enthusiastic for the state list, which contained too many of his old Republican enemies. Because the state had refused to support him adequately before the U.S. Senate, he transferred his allegiance to the Democrats after receiving their pledge to promote the educational and material interests of black Louisianans. Pinchback received a few federal appointments, as an internal revenue agent and as surveyor of customs. He switched parties again and went to several Republican national conventions. In 1879 he went to the state constitutional convention and worked hard for acceptance of a commitment to a black state college, which became today's Southern University. In 1886 he was admitted to the bar after studying law for one year, which gives some idea as to his acumen and the need he had to support his wife and six children with more regularity. In the mid-1890s, as the South fell under the Jim Crow laws, Pinchback went to New York and became a U.S. marshal. By the turn of the century he was in Washington, D.C., practicing law. He died in 1921 and was taken back to Metairie, Louisiana, where he was buried in the family tomb next to his mother.

P. B. S. Pinchback was fully a match for any of his white compatriots or opponents in Louisiana during his political career. (Of course, that is a curse as well as a compliment, because it puts him in with a pretty shady group.) But he joined the fray with the best and never lost sight of the need to provide for African Americans who were less fortunate and capable than he.

See also African Americans and Reconstruction; Dubuclet, Antoine; Dunn, Oscar J.; Warmoth, Henry Clay.

References Grosz, Agnes Smith, "The Political Career of Pinckney Benton Stewart Pinchback" (1944); Haskins, James, *Pinckney Benton Stewart Pinchback* (1973); Low, W. Augustus, and Virgil A. Clift, *Encyclopedia of Black America* (1981); Vincent, Charles, *Black Legislators in Louisiana during Reconstruction* (1976).

Port Royal Experiment

After a series of Union military disasters marred the opening summer of the Civil War, the North settled down to winning the war in a manner suggested by General-in-Chief Winfield Scott. The old lieutenant general (he had received his first star during the War of 1812) realized that the North's great advantage lay in the existence of its navy—the same advantage that had allowed Scott and others to conquer Mexico 15 years earlier. So Scott proposed that the North blockade the South, cut it into manageable sections by utilizing its numerous rivers, and sit back and watch it starve into submission. Scott's idea of Southern strangulation soon received the moniker "the Anaconda Plan," after the South American constrictor.

But the initial problem was that the North had too few ships and sailors to enforce a blockade (outside of the fact that one could not blockade one's own coast under international law, which raised the specter that such a move might implicitly recognize the independence of the Confederacy, which President Abraham Lincoln vehemently denied). But the Southern Atlantic area had a geographical feature that allowed the North to overcome its shortage in ships and men. These were the Sea Islands, a group of detached land masses of varying size in the tidal areas off the main coast of South Carolina and Georgia. Capturing these islands would allow the Union forces to create bases for land and sea operations against Charleston (the center of secession) and Savannah.

On 7 November 1861, the "day of the big gun-shoot" in the annals of the local slave population, the Union fleet arrived, opened fire, and landed a small brigade of infantry under Brig. Gen. Thomas Sherman (the "other Sherman" in Civil War terminology—i.e., no relation to William T. Sherman—who made his reputation in coastal operations) to seize Port Royal and Hilton Head Islands. It was hoped that this would be a cheap victory to counter the loss at First Manassas, cut off direct communication between Savannah and Charleston, close Savannah to the sea for the war's duration, and provide an anchorage for the Union blockade fleet and a base for future operations against Charleston.

At the first volley of naval gunfire, the entire white population fled the main town of Beaufort (pronounced "Bew' fert" in the local style) for the mainland, leaving behind their slaves. Although there was no policy of Northern liberation, these slaves became contraband of war and confiscable by the federal government. The problem now was what to do with this large black population of 10,000. As such, the Port Royal Island operations became a microcosm of the formal Reconstruction of the whole South that would follow the war.

Four governmental entities competed with each other for control of Port Royal, with the island's black residents caught in the middle. The first was the United States Army, which landed and secured the area against Confederate counterattack. The soldiers were not abolitionists and cared little about African Americans' problems as freed people. The soldiers were imbued with the racial prejudices of their day and saw blacks as pawns to be manipulated. Officers (those who cared) had a difficult time controlling their men. The troops robbed, raped, cheated, and fought the island's African Americans. Sherman's men compounded the problems when they told the local blacks that freedom meant they would not have to work, although that is exactly what the federal government expected freed blacks to do.

Sherman was soon replaced by Bvt. Maj. Gen. David Hunter, a full-fledged abolitionist who considered President Lincoln much too hesitant in freeing slaves in the South. So Hunter did it himself in the spring of 1862. He also enrolled all black males between the ages of 18 and 45 in self-defense units. Lincoln, worried about the possible loss of elections to Democrats in the North and the specter of black rebellion that Hunter's actions implied to race-conscious Northerners and border-state Southerners, canceled the general's orders and removed him from his post. By the summer of 1862, however, as Southern armies rolled over Yankee units in Kentucky and Virginia, Congress got tough and passed the Second Confiscation Act, permitting the emancipation of slaves whose owners were engaged in rebellion against the United States. Under Bvt. Brig. Gen. Rufus Saxton, the new commander at Port Royal, and with Lincoln's approval this time, the army enrolled the freedmen once again into self-defense units in August 1862.

The theory now was that blacks should fight to guarantee their own freedom. The army was not too nice about this concept either, using force to dragoon hesitant African Americans into regiments that became the nucleus of the United States Colored Troops later in the war.

The second federal agency that dealt with blacks at Port Royal was the Department of the Treasury. The treasury agents were interested in the high-quality Sea Island cotton, an especially fleecy, fine grade, that had been pledged to the Confederate war effort. The treasury men were to seize this as contraband of war. The treasury men rivaled the army in their rough treatment of the former slaves. Black work gangs were forcibly set up, and all of the 1861 cotton crop was harvested and taken to Beaufort for shipment. African Americans were supposed to be paid for their labor and receive free public education, but it all got lost in the shuffle to get the cotton crop in. The treasury men cheated blacks out of what money the latter received for work and stole their food and clothes to boot. Later audits showed that not only did the agents collect the cotton crop for shipment North, but that they sold substantial amounts to nearby Confederate agents, who smuggled it through the blockade for sale in Europe to further the Rebel war effort. Things were not going too well for the first Reconstruction, and the treasury men were recalled to Washington, D.C.

The next group to confront the particulars of Reconstruction at Port Royal at least had good intentions on their side. These were members of Northern missionary and benevolent associations out of Boston, New York, and Philadelphia who came down to "civilize" the wayward South. Led by Edward Pierce and the Reverend Mansfield French, the goal of these do-gooders was to remake the South in the style of New England, with public schools, Protestant Christianity, and a town-meeting style of self-government. They believed that if African Americans would act to ensure their own freedom, then all of the abolitionist agitation of the previous 30 years would be

justified. These reformers (both whites and Northern free blacks) became known as the Gideonites because, like the biblical Gideon's band, they were few in number bent on doing the Lord's work in a strange and savage land.

The Gideonites rejected hundreds of applicants to gain what they deemed to be the cream of their society, which put them one up on the army and the treasury. Once at Beaufort, they quarreled with both institutions over decent treatment of the ex-slaves, and they argued among themselves over the proper nature of their religion. The New Englanders tended to be intellectual in their approach to salvation, cold, disciplined, and austere. The missionaries from New York and Philadelphia preferred a more revivalistic, warmer style of worship, which was more like what the Sea Islanders had from their own African-based culture. Nonetheless, the Gideonites did establish churches and schools and administer to the physical needs of the already twice-picked-over freedmen. The do-gooders, however, were quite outraged when their black charges proved to be, on the one hand, good students with minds and preferences of their own, and, on the other, disappointing in how easily they lapsed into the "faults" of slavery such as lying, theft, and irresponsibility. Either way, the Gideonites unfairly perceived the freed blacks as ingrates.

The fourth group who exploited the capture of the Sea Islands included the private entrepreneurs, men who saw in the South an economic opportunity to get rich off of intensive agriculture. The most important of these was Edward Philbrick, who formed a "land company" with 14 others, as he put it to the chuckleheads in Washington, to carry on "free labor experiments under private auspices." The rules of Philbrick's land investors were awfully suggestive of slavery, especially to the Gideonites. Moreover, the African Americans hated cultivating the Sea Island cotton, especially refertilizing the fields, which involved putting fresh swamp mud on the crop, a back-breaking job. But Philbrick and his investors maintained that proper white leadership was necessary to transform the slave into a free person. Freedom meant more production, higher wages, and a market for Northern manufactured goods as the benighted South and its peoples were magnanimously brought into the mainstream of Americana—of course, the white overseers absorbed all of the profits from this service. The land companies bought Sea Island land at $1 per acre in 1863 (the land was put up for sale for lack of payment of Union wartime taxes on the part of its Confederate owners) and sold it to blacks at $5 per acre two years later. Philbrick and his cronies were sincere in their desire to help civilize the South through free agricultural labor practices, but their largess was strongly tinged with the profit motive.

Wartime Reconstruction in Port Royal had all of the elements of the process after the Civil War in the rest of the South: exploitation of the freedmen, benevolent assistance, good intentions. But it also had one element that the rest of the South did not witness. By the end of the war, the island's freed slaves owned three-fourths of the land and could support themselves as truck farmers independent of white overseers, Northern or Southern. This isolation allowed the development of a black community free from the nadir of turn-of-the-century American race relations. To have expected any postwar land distribution for the former slaves, an item many historians think was critical to Reconstruction's failure in the long run, was to overlook obvious constitutional limitations on the federal level and the lack of motivation and money for such purchases. But it was evident that freed blacks worked much harder until reality struck them during Andrew Johnson's pardon process, which returned land ownership to its prewar status; the freedmen realized that they would have no land for themselves beyond what they could ill afford to buy.

See also Confiscation Acts; Contrabands; Louisiana Experiment; Mississippi Valley Experiment; Virginia Experiment.

References Berlin, Ira, et al., *Slaves No More* (1992); Cimbala, Paul A., "The Freedmen's Bureau, the Freedmen, and Sherman's Grant in Reconstruction" (1989); Gerteis, Louis S., *From Contraband to Freedman* (1973); Johnson, Ludwell H., "Contraband Trade during the Last Year of the Civil War" (1963) and "Northern Profit and Profiteers" (1966); Pease, William H., "Three Years Among the Freedmen" (1957); Robinson, Armistead, "Reassessing the First Reconstruction" (1978); Rose, Willie Lee, *Rehearsal for Reconstruction* (1964).

Presidential Reconstruction

The concept that the president should make Reconstruction policy under the powers of executive proclamation led to two presidential plans of Reconstruction, one advanced by President Abraham Lincoln in 1863 and the other put forward by his successor, Andrew Johnson, in 1865. The period before the passage of the Military Reconstruction Act in March 1867 is generally referred to as Presidential Reconstruction, as opposed to the Congressional Reconstruction that followed and under which the South was readmitted to the Union.

See also Johnson and Reconstruction; Lincoln and Reconstruction; Moderate Republicans and Reconstruction; Radical Republicans and Reconstruction.

Race Riots That Influenced the Reconstruction Acts

Upon casual examination the bloodshed during Reconstruction seems pervasive and senseless, but a closer look reveals many patterns of political purpose. At first white Southerners appeared willing to accept any terms that the North might have for them after their loss of the Civil War. They even tried at first to court black voters, to no avail. Then, as reality hit, the white South became convinced that the Southern white loyalists (the infamous Scalawags, as much as a quarter of the white population in some states, such as Arkansas, North Carolina, Texas, and Tennessee), the Yankee newcomers (Carpetbaggers, in the jargon of the day), and the recently freed African Americans would control their states for a generation, just as many Republicans in Congress wished.

Their inability to regain political control peacefully led whites in the South to a standard American fallback position—violence. Regulator or vigilante-type movements were a constant theme in American history, particularly in the South, and the Southern propensity to be sensitive to alleged insult and respond personally in the form of the duel or street fight were themes of the region's social development for much of its history. The result was a violent counter-revolution—which gained its first momentum with race riots, the Ku Klux Klan, and then the White Leagues—that enabled conservative white Southerners to bulldoze their way back into power by 1876. This process was furthered by the inconsistency of Republican resistance on the national, state, and local levels, which made Redemption (as the process was called) possible.

The collapse of the Confederacy had produced an intense foreboding about the future of traditional native-born white power in the South. There had been much suffering during the war as the Yankee blockade cut off sources of trade and the advance of the armies ravaged the countryside. Hence the South greeted the minimal Lincoln and Johnson Reconstruction plans during and after the war as godsends. There was a real desire to make the old Union whole again. But this amity disappeared when Congress refused to seat the South's first postwar representatives in December 1865. For their inability to regain readmission into the Union, the Southern states blamed a perceived Radical Republican conspiracy to dominate the South through Negro-Carpetbag-Scalawag rule—through the very agents who had failed to support the cause of Southern independence. This travesty was imposed upon the white South, as they saw it, by the bayonets of the army and military government, reminiscent of what the British had tried to do to the Thirteen Colonies prior to the American Revolution. Worse now was the fact that Yankee military government had as its goal the imposition of black domination upon the South, the rule by social "inferiors," thereby upsetting a system of white racial domination that had endured for centuries and that the white South saw as "natural."

The result was an underground movement to restrain the liberating effects of Reconstruction on African Americans through violence. The outrages generally fell into one of four categories: spontaneous brawls, attacks by one race upon isolated members of the other, full-scale attacks of one race on the other, and random assaults (murders, stabbings, beatings). Although both races engaged in this activity, attacks by blacks on whites tended to be less effective and more isolated, except perhaps in South Carolina. In the words of one historian, it was pretty much a system of "white terror." In Southern eyes, African Americans came to symbolize the loss of the war, the turning of the white Confederate dream into the nightmare of Black Reconstruction. The goal was to prevent Yankee "meddlers" (Carpetbaggers, Freedmen's Bureau agents, soldiers) and their white and black brethren from turning Dixie into an 1865 version of Toussaint L'Ouverture's Haiti (or Saint Domingue, as it was called then) where whites were violently driven out of the

An 1866 engraving portrays the shooting of African Americans during the Memphis riot of 1 May 1866. The riot followed African American complaints of police brutality.

French colony to make room for a free black nation in 1802. The black revolution imposed by Congress was to be curbed by a white counterrevolution created by street mobs, the Ku Klux Klan, and the rifle clubs.

The first major explosion of racial tension occurred in Norfolk, Virginia, on 16 April 1866. The local African American population, which had been augmented by numerous ex-slaves looking for economic opportunity away from the plantation system in this busy port city, planned to march in support of the Civil Rights Act of 1866. Whites saw this march as rubbing their faces in a series of congressional humiliations and the loss of political majority to incoming black refugees. They decided that it was time to strike back. As the black marchers wended their way through rainy streets to a speaker's platform, local whites attacked them with rocks and bottles. The proverbial first shot rang out, and the riot was on, both sides returning fire. Both sides blamed the other for starting the incident. After the clash, one of the white ringleaders was killed, and white disciplinary squads re-

turned to the streets to exact vengeance. Only belated military intervention prevented another riot. It was a classic example of a riot to maintain the traditional white control that was being lost to the population shifts common during the early part of Reconstruction. It was also an indication that while the Civil War might be over on the battlefield, it had barely begun in the back alleys and byways of the former Confederacy.

The next major outbreak of violence was in Memphis, Tennessee, two weeks later on 1 May 1866. As with Norfolk, Memphis was a bustling port whose black population had increased dramatically, upsetting the traditional racial balance. Indeed, refugees, black and white, had nearly doubled the city's inhabitants during and right after the war. There was a large city bond debt that necessitated raising taxes, an economic recession, and a vigorous competition between African Americans and city whites, particularly Irish, for laboring jobs. There was also another issue. The city was garrisoned by black United States soldiers from a relatively ill-disciplined regiment, whom the

An 1867 Harper's Weekly *engraving depicts Andrew Johnson and his aides overlooking the 1866 New Orleans massacre. The caption reads "Amphitheatrum Johnsonianum Massacre of the innocents . . ."*

whites blamed for every disturbance. Local police, white only and predominantly Irish in membership, were neither understanding nor gentle in their treatment of alleged or real black lawbreakers. It was a situation ripe for trouble.

A riot came on the heels of African American complaints of police brutality. A crowd of protesters was met by police, who arrested certain ringleaders. Blacks fired weapons into the arresting officers, who returned fire. General volleys followed from both sides. The police retreated until later in the day, when they returned reinforced by a posse and the county sheriff. The demonstrators were gone, but the residents of a black shantytown were readily available. Revenge was exacted without mercy. Because local politicians had criticized the army, the local commandant refused to interfere with the 160 white soldiers in the garrison headquarters. He finally issued an order two days later for the mob to disperse after Freedmen's Bureau schools and per-

sonnel became mob targets. The mob dispersed in the face of threatened troop deployment, and the riot, dubbed the "Memphis Massacre" up North, subsided. All sides, including the army, protested their innocence during the ensuing investigation. The city newspapers justified the rioting as necessary to protect white civilization. But the violence boded ill for easy Southern readmission to the Union without more Yankee supervision and protection of blacks' rights. The tragedy of Memphis, however, disappeared in a real massacre at New Orleans two months later.

The riot in New Orleans, the bloodiest up to that point, took place on 30 July 1866. Unlike the Norfolk and Memphis scuffles, the motive behind the New Orleans Riot was not economic but political. The riot's political implications, as well as its long list of casualties, made it the story of the day during the ensuing Northern congressional political campaign of 1866 that doomed President Johnson and his plan of easy reunion; it led to the South being placed under congressional Military Reconstruction. Although New Orleans looked on the surface much like Norfolk and Memphis—a federal occupation early in the war, an increase of population caused by foreigners and blacks, economic competition between the groups, and a white population fearing the new order in which they had minimal participation—the rest was quite different.

Louisiana had been President Lincoln's Reconstruction showpiece. Under the Ten Percent Plan, Louisiana had called a constitutional convention in 1864 to create the first Free State government. The representation was based on whites alone, and for the first time New Orleans mechanics and small white farmers controlled Louisiana government. These whites had long resented the state version of a federal clause that counted slaves for purposes of representation and taxation, which kept rich sugar and cotton planters in control of the antebellum state. Thus, they refused to include black suffrage in the new Free State constitution. They allowed for the possibility of a future legislature supporting the black vote, but that was unlikely given that the legislature was under the control of these same whites. As the convention adjourned it took an unusual step. It passed an ordinance allowing the convention president or the state legislature to recall the delegates to rework the Free State constitution at some future unnamed date. It was wartime, after all, and the document was imperfect, especially with respect to the rights of blacks to vote. And New Orleans had some of the best-educated African Americans in the nation—mixed-blood men and women who were the sons and daughters of some of the state's most prominent families; these individuals had been sent to France for an education and were living and working in the Crescent City as free persons. These were not the kind of people who would be denied full rights as citizens very long.

The first government elected after the war's close under the Free State constitution was a white male, Democratic regime, complete with a governor who had led the early pro-Union government and now had switched sides, J. Madison Wells. He and his legislators passed the Black Codes and began to work to crush the nascent Republican party forever. But there was a forum that the Democrats still did not control—the constitutional convention that had met in 1864. So the Republicans decided to use the unusual, almost forgotten ordinance to reconvene this loyal body for their own purposes. Meanwhile Governor Wells changed sides again and spoke in favor of reconvening. He was the only major political figure who supported such a move. Since the legislature and the president of the convention refused to issue the call, the convention's president pro tem did it. This was stretching the mandate of the original law somewhat. Opponents of the convention asked the army to stop the new meeting, scheduled for 30 July at the New Orleans Mechanics Hall. Bvt. Maj. Gen. Absalom Baird refused to get involved. He said that the meeting of the old convention was part of the right to petition government and, legally binding or not, it had a right to meet and vote its wishes. Baird warned city officials, who were planning to arrest and indict the members for being part of an illegal assembly, to stay clear of the meeting.

Meanwhile the city officials decided to move on their own, despite the general's warnings. They were determined to prevent this "radical" body from interfering with the constitution and instituting black suffrage. They also felt forced to act when certain Republican speakers, especially Dr. A. P. Dostie, a dentist and former state auditor and a convention supporter, called for blacks to assist the convention members. Come ahead armed, Dostie said, and "if interfered with, the streets will run with blood." At least that is what the newspapers maintained. Some historians, however, wonder whether the press was a party to the conspiracy to attack the convention members and was simply establishing a defense for such action.

On the day of the convention it so happened that a quorum was not present, so the convention president pro tem sent the sergeant-at-arms to find the missing members. As they waited, a procession of black demonstrators marched up to the hall, waving banners and chanting in favor of a renewed convention. White bystanders, many of them underage and drunk, exchanged words and blows with the demonstrators. As usual, some unidentified person, black or white, fired the first shot. The police returned a volley into the crowd of demonstrators and the riot was on. The blacks fled into the hall for protection from the white mob that continued to grow in numbers and viciousness outside. The police joined the mob, and the whites assaulted the convention hall. Three times the attackers were driven back with losses before they took the hall. By the time United States troops arrived the riot was over. General Baird explained their tardiness by claiming that he thought the convention would meet at 6 p.m., not noon. The casualty list included 34 blacks killed, 4 whites killed (including Dr. Dostie, who was shot by rioters while in police protection), 119 blacks wounded, and 27 whites wounded.

Each side blamed the other for the riot, and local newspapers tended to play it down. But then the national press got the story and the North exploded in anger. Maj. Gen. Philip H. Sheridan (Baird's superior, who had been away in Texas during the riot) returned to defend the army and berate the police and local authorities. White New Orleans replied that the riot was obviously a Radical plot to force the African American vote upon the South. They pointed out that Washington officials, especially Secretary of War Edwin M. Stanton, who refused to answer General Baird's pleas for advice, seemed more intent on letting the riot get out of hand to make their point (a concept that more recent historians disbelieve as much as earlier historians agreed with it). But one thing was sure: the carnage in the streets of New Orleans did much to defeat what was left of President Johnson's plans for Reconstruction and to elect the Republican Congress that would enforce the Military Reconstruction Acts. It also showed the

white South that violence, when properly channeled, could be quite useful in the future. In their minds, the desire of Republicans to mold a new South based on a black-white loyal majority—resulting in the debasement of the traditional white ruling classes—made the use of such violence imperative.

See also Election of 1876 and Compromise of 1877; Enforcement Acts; Johnson and Reconstruction; Ku Klux Klan; Lincoln and Reconstruction; Redemption of the South before 1874; Swing around the Circle; Union Loyal Leagues.

References Carter, Dan T., *When the War Was Over* (1985); Edwards, John Carver, "Radical Reconstruction and the New Orleans Riot of 1866" (1973); Franklin, John Hope, *The Militant South* (1956); Holmes, Jack D. L., "The Underlying Causes of the Memphis Race Riot of 1866" (1958); Lovett, Bobby L., "Memphis Riots" (1979); Nieman, Donald G., ed., *Black Freedom/White Violence* (1994); Rabel, George C., *But There Was No Peace* (1984); Reynolds, Donald E., "The New Orleans Riot of 1866, Reconsidered" (1964); Riddleberger, Patrick W., *1866* (1979); Ryan, James Gilbert, "The Memphis Riot of 1866" (1977); Vandall, Gilles, *The New Orleans Riot of 1866* (1983) and "The Origins of the New Orleans Riot of 1866, Revisited" (1981); Waller, Altina L., "Community, Class and Race in the Memphis Riot of 1866" (1984); Wyatt-Brown, Bertram, *Southern Honor* (1982).

Radical Republicans

Standing in opposition to presidents Lincoln and Johnson and their notions of Reconstruction through executive action were the Radical Republicans. The term *radical* can mean different things at different times, but its use in this context is legitimate, despite historians' difficulty in defining it. Essentially, Radical Republicans were less racist, less scrupulous about constitutional restraints, and more vengeful than other Republicans.

Radical Republicans had several qualities in common. First, they believed that the full benefits of restoration should be withheld from the South for a period of time after the end of the Civil War. This attitude was considered vindictive by participants in Reconstruction; at the beginning of the twentieth century, historians popularized the idea that Reconstruction was a "tragic era" or "an era of hate." But in reality logic demanded that the South be made to show contrition over the war. The Southerners were, after all, traitors in the Northern mind. Moreover, the Republican party could not be expected to allow so many potential political opponents into Congress for free. No political party can be expected to commit suicide. All Republicans, however, not just the Radicals, held this viewpoint. Another idea the Radicals adhered to was the notion that Reconstruction ought to be determined by the legislative branch of government. The Radicals believed that they represented the people directly, contrary to the Jacksonian ideal that the president, as the single federal official elected by the whole population, did. Most did not deny the executive branch a contributory role, but they felt that role should be subordinate. Moderate and Conservative Republicans parted company with the Radicals here, reserving more of a role for the president.

But the most important factor that defined a Radical Republican was an interest in black rights. Other Republicans were also interested in black rights, but the Radicals made it a centerpiece of their Reconstruction ideology. The right of African Americans to vote—one Radical concern—could be perceived in terms of either principles or practical issues. Extending the vote was one way to ensure the Republican party would have a toehold in the South. It would also help African Americans retain their freedom. Another Radical issue was black civil rights, which included the right to a fair trial, to sue and be sued, to sit on juries, to own property, and to receive equal protection under the law—much of what the Civil Rights Law of 1866 promised. Once Congress passed this law, the Radicals theorized, the federal courts and the African American right to vote would secure the other rights forever.

Radicals also supported the right of African Americans to have an education. One cannot vote without knowledge, went the theory. One of the first acts of missionaries and secular benevolent associations was to establish black schools in the South. Southern whites resented these schools because their success disproved the myth of black inferiority. Disappointed whites retaliated by burning the schools and intimidating teachers and students. But in the end education was one of the most successful programs of Reconstruction, even though only a small number of the 4 million blacks in the South were reached.

Finally, Radical Republicans had an affinity for giving the ex-slaves land. Many wanted to seize all plantations and divide them up among the people who had worked them so long in bondage, hence the legendary Reconstruction slogan of "40 acres and a mule." Lincoln refused to allow any such land distribution until 1864, and Conservative Republicans and Democrats thwarted the Radicals by managing to block total confiscation amendments to the Freedmen's Bureau bills. Andrew Johnson then returned most of the seized properties to the original owners.

If the black vote, civil rights, education, and land grants were what defined Radical Republicans, what motivated them? Obviously some operated under the desire for revenge. White southerners were traitors and had to be punished for the sins of slavery and secession against America, God, and Constitution. This often was expressed by the slogan of "vote as you shot"; it also manifested itself through something called "waving the bloody shirt," which involved speaking in vivid and inflammatory terms about allegations of violent acts committed by conservative white Southerners. Another motivation for the Radicals was political. Freeing the slaves meant that the entire African American population would count toward statistics for congressional representation (whereas before the war, only three-fifths of slaves were so counted); thus the South actually would pick up seats in Congress when its states were readmitted. White Southerners hoped to prevent giving blacks the right to vote, but Radicals knew that would reduce Republican power. Radicals also operated to protect Republican domestic measures enacted during the war in the absence of Southern Democrats, including land grant colleges, the national banking system, internal improvements (especially the transcontinental railroad), contract labor, and a high protective tariff.

Important to a lot of Radicals (and many other Northerners) was the fear of a lost peace. This was a major cause of a hard Reconstruction policy. Radicals looked at the presidential Reconstruction plans and saw governments dominated by planters, Confederate military officers, and secessionists; discrimination against African Americans guaranteed through Black Codes; and a generally defiant attitude among Southern whites. Many feared that four years of bloody war had settled little, as demonstrated by the smashing Republican victory in the 1866 congressional elections, led by the Radicals.

Another thing that motivated Radicals was that they tended to have safe seats in Congress. No matter what their stand, they did not risk much in the way of political opposition back home, garnering 58 percent of the vote or more, a landslide in political terms. Indeed, historian David Donald ventures the thesis that the extent of Democratic opposition defined a winning Republican's stance on numerous Reconstruction issues. If the representative barely won (that is, received less than 50 percent of the votes in the last election), he was a Conservative Republican in favor of minimal or no black rights and a short, nonpunitive Reconstruction (i.e., he was sort of a warmed-over Democrat). Moderates were somewhere in the middle (working with a majority voter support from 50 to 58 percent); they were liable to face a hotly contested election but were likely to win. Because the Moderates were the largest group of Republicans, the Radicals needed to persuade them to risk all at the polls for Radical principles. Johnson's appeal to Southern intransigence cemented the alliance between the Moderates and the Radicals.

Other historians trace radicalism to rural New England constituencies or to a district elsewhere that had a New England cultural base. Radicals had certain things in common: an experience of poverty early in life,

self-education, law and business backgrounds, experience with immigrating westward, a former affiliation with Whigs or Anti-Nebraska Democrats (who were against the spread of slavery to the territories), and early enlistment in the Republican party. The motivating issues of their adult lives were the panic of 1837 (an economic depression), frustration over John Tyler's switch from the Whigs to the Democrats, the fervor of abolition, hatred over the annexation of Texas, opposition to the Mexican War, support of the Wilmot Proviso (which called for no slavery in territories gained from Mexico), and opposition to the Kansas-Nebraska Act (which extended slavery into the whole West). The only problem with this theory is that almost all congressional districts, Republican or Democratic, were rural (except in Pennsylvania), but Radicals came from the cities. So the safer the congressional seat, the more likely that a winning Republican would be a Radical on Reconstruction.

Finally, Radicals were motivated by idealism, a desire to help out the unfortunate who had suffered the vicissitudes of slavery. Assistance took the form of the right to vote, land grants, education opportunities, and civil rights. The prewar and wartime idealism of Republicans did not just die out when the Confederates surrendered at Appomattox. It continued throughout Reconstruction. Radicals had a compelling view of what the United States should be like, and they saw great logic and justice in their programs. They were also special kinds of politicians. They were men of principle who could not bear to compromise their ideals. They went to Washington and were not corrupted by the system like their peers. Their election was made possible by the revolutionary situation that the North-South controversy and the war brought on. Had times been more normal, their zeal may have been too much for voters. Their real obstacle during the war was Abraham Lincoln—a man who made numerous compromises to win the war. The Radicals feared that he would never free the slaves (he did) and that he would not punish the

South for secession (he died before that could be settled). Their real difference with Lincoln was timing. Radicals want to do it all, now. They were doctrinaire idealists who wanted to create a human paradise on earth.

There was a strong religious component to Radical thought. As one Radical said (paraphrasing Christ), it was better to be at one with God than to fall like Herod, listening to the shouts of the multitudes. The general definition of a radical individual given in Eric Hoffer's *True Believer* applies to the Radicals of the Reconstruction era: "The Radical has a passionate faith in the infinite perfectibility of human nature. He believes that by changing a man's environment and by perfecting a technique of soul-saving, a society can be wrought that is wholly new and unprecedented." The Radical Republicans believed that there was no truth beyond their own doctrine, and they shut their eyes and ears to contrary evidence. Not only were they in favor of a Reconstruction that would matter, they usually dabbled in their day's pursuits of human perfection, including such issues as African American rights, prohibition, women's rights, abolition of sweatshops, free land in the West, dietary reform (graham crackers), clothing reform (bloomers), and utopian socialist conceptions. They were the conscience of the society of their time.

See also Radical Republicans and Reconstruction.

References Benedict, Michael Les, *A Compromise of Principle* (1974); Blackburn, George M., "Radical Republican Motivation" (1969); Bogue, Allan G., *The Earnest Men* (1981); Donald, David H., "Devils Facing Zionwards" (1964), *The Politics of Reconstruction* (1965), and "The Radicals and Lincoln" (1956); Gambill, Edward L., "Who Were the Senate Radicals?" (1965); Hyman, Harold M., ed., *The Radical Republicans and Reconstruction* (1967); Kincaid, Larry G., "Victims of Circumstance"(1970); Linden, Glenn M., "'Radicals' and Economic Policies" (1966); Trefousse, Hans L., *The Radical Republicans* (1969); Williams, T. Harry, "Lincoln and the Radicals" (1964) and *Lincoln and the Radicals* (1941).

Radical Republicans and Reconstruction

Upon the Republican victory in the 1866 congressional elections, which returned a two-thirds majority for the upcoming Fortieth Congress, the Republicans in the outgoing Thirty-ninth Congress went to work in their lame duck session (December 1866 to March 1867) to clear the way for their new colleagues. Led by the Radical Republicans, the party imposed the measures that would become known as Radical Reconstruction. The first step was to make sure that the Fortieth Congress did not have to wait until December 1867 to meet, its traditional time to assemble. The congressional recesses were the periods presidents Abraham Lincoln and Andrew Johnson had used to impose executive proclamations of Reconstruction; these proclamations had done much to modify the influence of prior Congresses on Reconstruction. So the second session of the Thirty-ninth Congress called the Fortieth Congress into its first session the day after the former adjourned in March 1867. This would give the Fortieth Congress three sessions instead of the customary two. This was not a special session, because the Constitution reserves such calls for the president, so it became a new regular session, to be followed by the constitutionally called December sessions in 1867 and 1868.

The next order of business was to guarantee that the president could not easily get around congressional desires through other independent executive actions. The Command of the Army Act was added to the Army Appropriations Act. It ordered the commanding general of the United States Army (then Lt. Gen. Ulysses S. Grant) to have his headquarters in Washington, D.C. (Old Lt. Gen. Winfield Scott had had his in New York for years to avoid Washington politics.) The army in the field was not to obey any presidential order unless issued through the office of the commanding general. (Grant was a professional soldier who had the philosophy that Congress was the voice of the people and could not be disobeyed.) To safeguard the position of the commanding general, he was not to be replaced without the concurrence of the Republican-dominated Senate. There was another official who served as a spy inside the executive departments and the president's cabinet: Secretary of War Edwin M. Stanton. A Radical Republican and the source of many of the anti-Lincoln stories during the war, Stanton was keeping his Radical cronies informed of anything Johnson discussed behind closed doors in the executive offices. To protect him, Congress passed the Tenure of Office Act, which stated that any executive appointment made with the advice and consent of the Senate had to be removed in the same manner.

Finally, the last session of the Thirty-ninth Congress passed Radical Reconstruction, or the Military Reconstruction Act of 2 March 1867. This act created five military districts in the South under the command of a brigadier or major general of the regular army appointed by the president. Although martial law was not declared, it existed for all practical purposes. The boundary lines of the states had in effect been temporarily abrogated by army command boundaries. The district commanders were to assist the states (or were they now territories?) through the Reconstruction process. The state governors were still in power, but they were subordinate to the military commanders. State justice could be administered through state courts, Freedmen's Bureau courts, or military tribunals. The eventual clash between civil and military authority was inevitable.

The Military Reconstruction Act disfranchised all whites who could not hold office under the terms of the failed Fourteenth Amendment. Voter registrars were to enroll all remaining adult males in the Southern states, including blacks, to vote for delegates to a new state constitutional convention. Up to this point voting qualifications had been the exclusive prerogative of the states. Registrars, appointed by the military district commander in consultation with state officials, had to take the ironclad oath (one of never having given aid to the Confederacy), and all voters had to take an oath of future loyalty. Once a constitutional convention was elected, the new state constitution had to provide for black male suffrage (even though most Northern states did not do so). All unpardoned whites were

to be disfranchised, and the state could, at its discretion, disfranchise any other whites who had supported the Confederacy. (Actually, black delegates prevented this requirement from being implemented in all Southern states except Louisiana, Arkansas, and Alabama, which used the Fourteenth Amendment exclusions). The constitution then had to be ratified by a majority of registered voters and a new state legislature elected. Then the reconstructed state legislature had to approve of the Fourteenth Amendment. After this Congress would receive the states' representatives and U.S. senators, readmitting the state to the Union at last.

The Fortieth Congress inherited the task of enforcing the Military Reconstruction Act. The provision was really pretty vague and raised more questions than it answered. Who was really disfranchised? Did it include Union men who had had to take the Confederate oath under duress? How was the convention to be called? How could adequate governments be established if so few could take the ironclad oath? Could African Americans run for office or merely vote? Did disfranchisement apply to minor state officials like clerks of court, road supervisors, and sextons of cemeteries? If state governments refuse to cooperate, can the district military commanders act alone? It thus became imperative for the Fortieth Congress to clear matters up as they came to a head. In March 1867, Congress passed a Second Military Reconstruction Act that authorized all military commanders to act independent of state governments, which had refused to do anything to help the army reconstruct the South.

In July, Congress passed a Third Reconstruction Act, which declared the state governments to be illegal and authorized district military commanders to remove recalcitrant state officials from office and appoint substitutes. Voter registrars were allowed to determine whether oaths of allegiance were sworn to in good faith. If not, the suspect voter would be denied registration. There was no court appeal to this arbitrary action. (This method would be used by the South in the twentieth century against black voter applicants.) Because many whites refused to register and others were declared ineligible, black voters outnumbered whites in five states: Louisiana, South Carolina, Mississippi, Alabama, and Florida. (Only the first three states had a black population that equaled or outnumbered whites.) Of course, African Americans registered in large numbers to vote in all Southern states. The issues interested them, federal officials and the army encouraged them, and a Republican party organization, the Union Loyal League, organized them.

Then, in March 1868, a year after the process had begun, the Fourth Reconstruction Act passed Congress because a loophole had been discovered by many Southern states. Large numbers of whites would register to vote and then stay home on constitution approval day, denying the majority of registered voters needed to approve the document. Thus, the new measure declared that a majority of those voting could pass the new state constitution. Also, voters were required to reside in their precinct for only ten days prior to the election. Not only did this allow blacks who were still moving around a lot to vote, it also offered an easy way to stack the vote in close precincts. The measure was designed to speed up the Reconstruction process so that black Republicans might help the party elect a new president in 1868. By the election, all Southern states except Virginia, Mississippi, and Texas had completed the Reconstruction process and could participate fully in politics on the state and national levels. All that was left was to embarrass President Johnson completely through his impeachment and trial—then legislative government would be a reality.

See also Bureau of Refugees, Freedmen, and Abandoned Lands; Command of the Army Act; Congressional Reconstruction; Congressional Supremacy; Fortieth Congress Extra Session Act; Fourteenth Amendment; Impeachment; Johnson, Andrew, and Reconstruction; Lincoln and Reconstruction; Military Reconstruction Acts; Radical Republicans; Tenure of Office Act; Theories of Reconstruction.

References Benedict, Michael Les, *A Compromise of Principle* (1974); Kincaid, Larry G., "The Legislative Origins of the Military Reconstruction Act" (1968); Sefton, James E., *Army and Reconstruction* (1967).

Rainey, Joseph H. (1832–1887)

Born in Georgetown South Carolina, to a mulatto slave family, Joseph H. Rainey's father had purchased his whole family's freedom. Rainey received a rudimentary education through private instruction, and at the outbreak of the war he, like his father, was practicing barbering, a traditional position of leadership in America's black community. For a time he was a steward on a blockade runner, but when he was drafted to work on the military fortifications in Charleston Harbor, he fled to the West Indies, where he awaited the outcome of the war. He returned to South Carolina after the Yankee victory and with the passage of the Military Reconstruction Acts became a member of the newly constituted state Republican party. He was a delegate to the constitutional convention but played only a minor role. Nonetheless, he was elected to the state senate in 1868. He resigned his seat in 1870 to run for Congress. His victory made him the first African American ever to sit in Congress.

In Washington, Rainey was known as a

Congressman Joseph H. Rainey

quiet man who defended black rights with logic and forcefulness on the House floor. He did not attempt to humiliate the white South, but he insisted that the Enforcement Acts be properly executed, that the Ku Klux Klan be suppressed, and that the promises of the Fourteenth and Fifteenth amendments be upheld. He was also an advocate of black access to public accommodations and had to be forcibly ejected from a Virginia restaurant when he refused to leave. His most notable speech was a eulogy of Massachusetts Senator Charles Sumner in 1876. Rainey served in Congress until 1879, when he was replaced by a white Democrat. He was made special treasury agent for South Carolina until his resignation in 1881. He tried the banking and brokerage business in Washington, D.C., after his political career ended, but financial failure sent him back to his Georgetown home. He died there a few years later.

See also African Americans and Reconstruction.

References Low, W. Augustus, and Virgil A. Clift, *Encyclopedia of Black America* (1981); McFarlin, Annjeannette Sophia, *Black Congressional Reconstruction Orators and Their Orations* (1976); Simkins, Francis B., "Joseph Hayne Rainey" (1964–1981).

Red Shirts

The Red Shirts were a white Democratic party group of armed gunmen in South Carolina who intimidated black and white Republicans at elections in the mid-1870s, shot rival candidates and their supporters, and watched the polls to limit opposition voting.

See also Redemption of the South from 1874.

Redeemers

Those whites who overthrew the Reconstruction governments in the South in the 1870s were called Redeemers. They went on to rule their states during the New South movement of industrialization by coercing white and black agrarian radicals through voter fraud and racist appeals. But what exactly they stood for and really did has been a source of argument for historians ever since. That they were important cannot be denied. These Democrats controlled every former Confederate state in the last quarter of the nineteenth century and composed a voting bloc in Congress (about one-third of both houses) that rivaled Northeastern and Western Republicans in power and dominated the Democratic party's congressional and national party caucuses. Although it was fairly obvious that they would stand for home rule and undermine federal protection of blacks' civil rights (90 percent were veterans of the Confederate army or civil government), how they might vote on the paramount economic issues of the day would determine the fate of the nation. These issues were related to the economic legislation of the Civil War that made up the Republican party's domestic policy (as opposed to the policies of war and foreign affairs), such items as soft money (such as silver coins and paper bills), the national banking system, bond redemption, taxes and tariffs, and railroads and other internal improvements.

The premier historian of the Redeemers has been C. Vann Woodward. In his seminal study, *Origins of the New South, 1877–1913*, Woodward posits that the opposition to the Republican economic program arose in the "agrarian" West, while its support came from the "industrial" East. According to Woodward, during the disputed presidential election of 1876 and the Compromise of 1877 that followed, deals were made by Redeemers and Republicans who had been Whigs before the war or who sympathized with the Whig policy of national economic subsidies. Before this time, Southern Republicans (Scalawag, Carpetbag, and African American representatives in Washington of the Reconstructed state governments) had failed to deliver on such an economic program. Northern Republican power brokers had viewed the Southern Republicans with suspicion, had excluded them from meaningful councils, and had denied them the patronage that would have secured their power back home. Nor were the Southern Republicans helped by the burgeoning Liberal Republican movement dedicated to eradicating these economic programs as the epitome of corruption. Realizing that national Democrats would not grant these subsidies, and having missed out on their share of the graft of the period because of the Civil War and Reconstruction, the Redeemers made their own deal to elect Rutherford B. Hayes, gain removal of the federal troops (thus enabling home rule), and get in on the federal economic largess denied Southern Republicans. Woodward calls this the "Right Fork on the Road to Reunion," an agreement between conservatives of both sections.

But Woodward also perceives another branch in the road to reunion, the Left Fork. This one emphasized a more radical agrarian approach and cooperation with western elements in the Republican party. The program proposed by these elements was one of government reform, of replacing favoritism toward industry and business with assistance for the small farmers and laborers who dominated the American landscape in those years. It emphasized expanded credit through more paper money and the coinage of silver, a decentralized national banking system, and regulation of railroads. Because of the extended panic of 1873 (an economic depression that had lasted several years), the agrarian radicals swept into power in 1877. The Conservative Republicans managed to halt this reform trend by vigorously waving the bloody shirt (i.e., discrediting small Southern white farmers by telling tales of violence against black and white Republicans in the South), a process that disillusioned the Southern radicals and allowed the Redeemers to take over again. From there on out, the Southern states were the center of a quarrel between these two points of view. The struggle became more intense as the Redeemers sought to check their opponents by allying with blacks and cheating on the electoral returns to cut the agrarian radicals out of the process. Nationally, the Redeemers stood with the Grover Cleveland branch of the Democratic party, one that was as Republican in its economic policies as the Republicans themselves.

However, recent critics of Woodward are not convinced that he describes an accurate picture of what happened, at least on the national stage. Led by Carl V. Harris, these historians see the Redeemers in Washington as varying in their stand issue by issue and usually taking the left fork (the agrarian labor, or "radical," one), allying with western Republicans and western Democrats to support expanded silver coinage, redemption of bonds with greenbacks instead of gold, reduction of the tariff, restoration of the income tax, an expansive banking system to provide easier credit, and tough regulation of railroads. They voted with all Democrats to revise the revenue tax code to fall more heavily on the East and curtail African American civil rights. But this did not affect their desire to industrialize the South. Indeed, the Redeemers managed to attract nearly every economic group from business to agriculture (large and small landholders) to their banner. They put down the Populist revolt of the 1890s, which emphasized similar economic issues, not only by major election fraud, but by the viable political argument that the Democratic party promised more and had delivered more than the agrarian rebels could manage under a new party name and organization. Thus, the conservative coalition that manufactured the Compromise of 1877 did not carry over in the Redeemers' approach to congressional policies, which continued to the end of the century.

Reconstruction and the Gilded Age that followed caused the Redeemers to reexamine the fundamental premises of what it meant to be an American. In the process the redeemed South, more than any other section of America, came to have a social unity that was challenged only by the bravest or most foolhardy. When it came to race, the mind of the postbellum South was little different from the antebellum South—blacks had a definite place in society and were there to stay. The white South was a unique, separate part of the national whole, driven by racism, paternalism, a personal code of honor, and a Southern nationalism reinforced by a rigid concept of constitutionalism. Whatever the political stand of the Redeemers, whether they took the left fork or the right, they illustrated the persistence of Southern distinctiveness within the nation as a whole.

See also Disfranchisement; Grant and Domestic Policies; Redemption of the South before 1874; Redemption of the South from 1874; Scalawags; Segregation (Jim Crow).

References Benedict, Michael Les, "The Politics of Prosperity in the Reconstruction South" (1984); Degler, Carl N., *Place over Time* (1977); Harris, Carl V., "Right Fork or Left Fork?" (1976); Linden, Glenn M., "'Radicals' and Economic Policies" (1966); McDonald, Forrest, "Woodward's Strange Career" (1989); McPherson, James M., "Redemption or Counterrevolution?" (1985); O'Brien, Michael, "C. Vann Woodward and the Burden of Southern Liberalism" (1973–1974); Perman, Michael, *The Road to Redemption* (1984); Phillips, Ulrich B., "The Central Theme of Southern History" (1928–1929); Rabel, George C., "Bourbonism, Reconstruction, and the Persistence of Southern Distinctiveness" (1983); Roach, Hannah Grace, "Sectionalism in Congress" (1925); Seip, Terry L., *The South Returns to Congress* (1983); Summers, Mark W., *The Era of Good Stealings* (1993) and *Railroads, Reconstruction, and the Gospel of Prosperity* (1984); Woodward, C. Vann, *The Future of the Past* (1989), *Origins of the New South* (1951), and *Reunion and Reaction* (1951).

Redemption of the South before 1874

Redemption was the process by which whites, known as Redeemers, took back their state and local governments from the reconstructing Republicans elected by white and black loyalists. At first the Southern ruling classes tried to appeal to blacks to vote with their former masters, but African Americans knew where their true interests lay and refused to go along. This meant that Southern whites who lived in states that had a black majority, such as Louisiana, Mississippi, and South Carolina, were in deep trouble. So were select congressional districts and local county governments in any state. The federal elections of 1868 demonstrated that blacks could prove decisive in delivering Southern states' electoral votes to a Republican presidential candidate as well as to state and local contenders. Redemption also proved that Northern Democrats could not save the South from its fate. The result was the emergence of the Ku Klux Klan and its allied groups, the Knights of the White Camellia, the Knights of the Rising Sun, the Pale Faces, and others. These groups immediately made their influence felt in Georgia in the Camilla Massacre and in Louisiana in the St. Landry Riot and the New Orleans Riot of 1868.

The Camilla Massacre had its origins in Military Reconstruction and the election of a Republican government under the new state constitution. The Republican majority in the legislature was illusory. Many party members were Moderates whose ideas corresponded more with those of their Democratic opponents than they did with their Radical white and black colleagues. The Moderate Republicans and Democrats managed to combine and vote to expel 32 black Republicans by challenging their eligibility. This made Georgia whites more determined than ever to redeem their state at all levels during the fall 1868 elections. If fraud and violence had to be used, reasoned the non-Republican whites, so be it. The Second Congressional District, of which Camilla was a part, had white Carpetbaggers as Republican candidates for Congress and as its presidential elector. These individuals campaigned actively for office, an act of great courage in southwestern Georgia in those days.

Camilla, located in a small white farming area surrounded by former slave plantations, saw its black population double as African Americans looked for employment other than the backbreaking field work to which they had been restricted as slaves. The white town was not very happy with the increased numbers of black residents. The local Freedmen's Bureau agent was also uneasy. He had heard that cases of Henry repeating rifles had arrived at nearby Albany, and he feared that the election was going to be a hot one. He wondered if the target was supposed to be a planned Republican gathering at Camilla on 19 September. Contingents of African Americans gathered in neighboring communities and on friendly plantations (owned by Carpetbaggers) to march upon Camilla to hear the speeches. The white organizers told African

Americans that they would have no trouble if it were done quietly.

Meanwhile the news of the black "invasion" panicked white townspeople in Camilla. Rumors had the blacks armed to the teeth. White residents sent the local sheriff to meet with the marchers and ascertain their real intentions. The leaders of the march assured the sheriff that those with arms were not hostile but were merely carrying guns as was their habit when at home. But the marchers refused to leave their weapons outside town as the sheriff asked, because they had heard that an armed band of whites awaited them. Of course, any armed band was prohibited by gubernatorial proclamation, but all those with weapons claimed that they were individuals, not part of a real group. A proposed political meeting site at a plantation outside of town was rejected by the landowner.

When the blacks arrived in town to go to the courthouse, a lone white ran out and demanded that they stop their fife and drum music. The marchers refused and the man fired at the musicians. From the side of the street more armed whites appeared and joined in the shooting. The blacks panicked and fled to the woods and swamps outside town. The whites followed, firing their rifles and shotguns as they came. Several wounded blacks received a bullet in the head as they lay along the line of march. The shooting continued well into the night, lit up by a full moon. A dozen blacks died during the fray, with uncounted others being wounded.

As the fleeing marchers reached surrounding communities, blacks angrily decided to arm and go out to save the rest of the marchers and wreak what revenge they could on Camilla's white community. The Freedmen's Bureau agent tried to hold them back, but his work was made more difficult by the fact that night riders hit black labor camps on surrounding plantations. The raiders justified their actions as preempting a black insurrection that would threaten the lives of white women and children. The governor refused to send state troops, and the federal authorities denied

the use of the army. Republican candidates could not canvass their district. The Freedmen's Bureau was already preparing to go out of operation in Georgia and the rest of the South, so it did little to assist its agent at Albany. By election day the violence had accomplished its goal. Only two Republican votes were cast at Camilla. Fraud took care of the rest of the district. The whole area went to the Democrats, even though black and white Republicans outnumbered them in registration. A similar effect was seen throughout the state as the fallout from the Camilla Massacre spread statewide.

But the Camilla Massacre also had an adverse effect on the goals of conservative white Southerners. Congress, disturbed by the expulsion of the blacks from the state legislature and the riot at Camilla, decided that Georgia needed to be reconstructed again. Back came a reinvigorated army, and the old state legislature with its black members reassembled. Georgia now had to pass the pending Fifteenth Amendment, guaranteeing no discrimination on the basis of race, to return to the Union. However, the purge was only temporary. Within a year Georgia's readmission led to the same conditions as before the Camilla Massacre, and terror and fraud reappeared to help whites redeem the state government again by 1872.

Georgia was not alone in its early use of violence to redeem its local governments. Even though St. Landry Parish in central Louisiana west of Baton Rouge had a large black population (3 to 2 in favor of African Americans), the Republicans had not managed to upset the control of the local government, which remained in the hands of the white power structure before, during, and after the war. Military Reconstruction and the new state constitution had done little but unite whites as never before. It was true that blacks and their white Carpetbag leaders (only one white Scalawag was reported in the parish) had managed to elect many of the state legislative officials, but the parish itself was won narrowly by whites. The Republican party struggled to gain a base in St. Landry that had never before existed. Party members were assisted by several blacks who had been free before the war (and had been slaveholders, too, a not too uncommon Louisiana oddity), who acted as liaisons between the white Republicans and the black rank-and-file voters. White Democrats knew that they had to attract the African American vote to keep their hold on the parish—registration figures alone demonstrated this. So they organized barbecues and picnics and sent speakers into the black community to attract their support and counter Republican organizers. At the same time groups of whites rode at night to emphasize the alternative to those who would not come over.

The Republicans responded with armed guards to protect their political meetings, and by September 1868 the racial tensions in the parish were ready to explode. Whites threatened to shoot everyone who voted Republican. The Republicans, recognizing that they were outgunned, threatened arson against anyone who tried to shoot them. As the threat of racial war increased, a committee of five men from each side met to try to work out the terms for a peaceful presidential election in November. They agreed that members of both sides would be at all political meetings, firearms would not be allowed at gatherings, and the sheriff and his deputies were to guarantee order. But the move was too late. Whites were already convinced that African Americans were about to engage in an "insurrection" and moved to prevent it from happening.

The result was the St. Landry Riot on 28 September. It all started when a group of white regulators caned a Republican judge who was an organizer of black schools. Blacks organized to protect themselves and marched on Opelousas. They were met by a white mob and the shooting started. Total casualties on both sides amounted to five dead and six wounded, although Republicans claimed that nearly 300 died and Democrats asserted the number was around 30. The blacks quickly withdrew and the whites sent in a mounted contingent that pursued and "arrested" 29 blacks, whom they lodged in the parish jail. The next night all but two were taken by a mob and shot

dead, with the connivance of the sheriff and his deputies, who stepped aside.

The St. Landry Riot was a typical traditional response of white Southerners to the alleged threat of "Negro insurrection" common from slavery days, when Louisianans had crushed a slave rebellion in 1811 and posted the heads of the rebels along the river banks. But it had great political impact, too. The remaining leaders of the Republican party fled the parish for their lives. Black agricultural laborers, stuck in their homes, appealed to the Democrats for protection and withdrew from political participation. In November the parish, which had given the Republicans a 2,500-vote majority in the April statewide elections, reported not one vote for Ulysses S. Grant. A Republican effort to reorganize in the parish the following year also came to naught.

As in St. Landry Parish, violence visited New Orleans in 1868, as it had two years earlier. But this time the black and white Republicans were better prepared to resist, although the results were about the same. Riot had been a possibility throughout the fall of 1868. Black leaders were getting sick and tired of newspaper smears against their character, intelligence, and abilities. The first scuffle broke out when black Republican clubs took to the streets for Ulysses S. Grant on 22 September. White Democrats cheered for Horatio Seymour and a fight broke out, but it soon stopped. Whites were a bit testy in New Orleans. Although they had a slight majority of registered voters, victory was not guaranteed. Whites believed that Republicans imported blacks from surrounding parishes to vote and take the city (an old Louisiana ploy whites had use among themselves before the war, commonly called "Plaquemining," after the parish from which the ringers came). Whites also disliked the able leadership that blacks provided in the city, a result of the large educated free black population from before the war. Finally, there were numerous political clubs representing every possible faction of both parties. They did much to keep the pot boiling with their nightly parades and antics, designed to embarrass their opponents.

On Saturday, 24 October, two political clubs met by accident in Canal Street. They began to try to outshout each other. Then some white boys fired into the Republicans. Seven died as the blacks retreated. Infuriated, the blacks went home and armed themselves and began attacking every white in sight. Federal soldiers finally put an end to the rioting after two whites died and several were wounded. No bloodshed occurred the next day, though tensions ran high. But the next three days made up for the 24-hour respite, despite the appeals of leaders of both parties and the army command to cease political marches and fights. White Democrats gave the excuse that they were helping patrol the city in the absence of the Metropolitan Police, a largely black force. Gangs robbed and looted homes and businesses until Wednesday, when the army restored order again. Estimated casualties ranged from 63 in the state legislature investigation report down to a more realistic half-dozen whites and a dozen blacks. Uncounted others were wounded on both sides. But the results were felt during voting day, when the Democrats carried all polls. According to Democrats, blacks had been advised to stay home by their own Republican leaders. Republicans, on the other hand, claimed that their supporters were kept from the polls by force after the riot. In any case, as in St. Landry, violence had shown the white South how to defeat Republicanism and redeem white rule. It was the portent of things to come.

Although Georgians and Louisianans were the only white Southerners organized enough to make inroads on Republican votes in 1868, the impact of violence was felt in all of the states south of what one modern commentator aptly called "the Smith and Wesson line," roughly that part of the United States below the Ohio River. Whites pondered whether the campaign of terror could be coordinated, at least at the state level. Southerners realized that no matter what they did, nationally Republicans would "count in" the needed Republican vote for the presidential elections by dominating the returning boards that certi-

fied the electoral votes. Outside the traditional circles of power with no nonviolent channels through which to express their hostility, Southern whites exaggerated the power and corruption of Republican regimes and especially the hypocrisy of forcing the African American vote on the South while permitting state option in the North (a discrepancy eventually stopped by the Fifteenth Amendment).

So out came the stereotypes of the Scalawags (native Southern whites who sold out race and section), Carpetbaggers (Yankee corruptionists who came south to pluck the defenseless Southern pigeon), Negroes (illiterate ex-slaves one step removed from the jungle and under the influence of the Union Loyal Leagues), and the army (military men who interfered in the democratic process at the points of bayonets). Together these groups were said to represent unalloyed evil; their actions justified the acts of violence that became an election-time ritual in the South. A favorite tactic was to mob "visiting statesmen" like Pennsylvania congressman and ferrous metals magnate William D. "Pig Iron" Kelley. On a trip to Mobile, Kelley made the unwise decision to dare residents to misbehave because he had the army at his back. When the smoke cleared, the crowd had wrecked the dais and a shaken Kelley had to be kept hidden under military guard until he left the city.

Kelley was not the only supporter of Reconstruction to encounter a violent reception. At least he could go home to safety. Southern Reconstructionists were not so lucky. They had to remain behind and face the wrath of the Ku Klux Klan. Although dissatisfaction with the loss of the war, tougher Congressional Reconstruction, and just plain racism contributed to the Klan's growth, some of it was attributable to the poor economic climate in the agricultural South after the war. The two years before the Klan's entrance onto the scene as a covert political force were marked by crop failures and either too little or too much rain. Some modern researchers believe that the cotton crop, its size and price on the market, correlates directly with antiblack activities of white regulator groups like the Klan well into the twentieth century. It did not hurt any that important white Southerners, such as John B. Gordon in Georgia or Nathan Bedford Forrest in Tennessee, respected by the white community for their war records, led Klan activities, at least at first. Indeed, one might posit the thesis that the "better classes" (whatever that entails) of the South have always turned a blind eye to racial vigilante activities. The violence of night riders acted as a trump card for the powers that be. White ruling classes could discipline by vigilante justice those who cannot be touched by the law, yet turn in the perpetrators of violence if they get out of hand and appear to be liberal and forward-looking proponents of a New South. It was a win-win proposition.

In any case, the Klan directed its activities against black leaders, schoolteachers who taught black children, and federal and state authorities who backed the Reconstruction policy. Historians disagree on how united the Klans and other similar groups were. But Congress had no doubt; it entitled a 13-volume investigation and report *The Ku Klux Conspiracy*, implying a coordinated, centralized program of anti-Reconstruction violence in the South. Blacks fought back, but their inability to stop the raids was exacerbated by the ineffective efforts of the state and local Reconstruction governments to lend a hand. Southern Republicans wasted their party's energy arguing among themselves over mundane theoretical problems like whether all laws and contracts entered into under the rule of the Confederacy were null and void from their inception. Indeed, segments of the Southern Republican party seemed more intent on scoring political and mental victories over their black and white brethren than attacking real problems, like Klan violence, that affected the vote. In the end, the Republican party had a veneer of white Carpetbag and Scalawag leaders and a mass of black rank and file, divided among themselves by race as surely as were whites and blacks in the South in general. It did not make for an effective force against united white supremacists.

Republican governors in the South were faced with an impossible problem. They could not allow violence to cut the party's vote, but if they fought back they would have to rely on their own state militias, often staffed by black volunteers, and that would lead to a race war. It is significant that the more effective battles against vigilante-style violence occurred in states where there was a large element of loyal whites from the days of the war. This meant that an effective response to white violence was limited to parts of Texas, parts of Tennessee, and all of Arkansas. The latter state's governor, Powell Clayton, was able to defeat the Klan with a state militia composed of blacks from the Southern part of the state and whites from the pro-Union northern half; however, he was the exception. The more common situation left it up to the federal government to respond. The result was the three Enforcement Acts of the early 1870s. But even though these measures halted the Ku Klux Klan, primarily in South Carolina, the group was already starting to be disbanded by its own leaders, who were worried by the increase in criminal activities that were irrelevant to the original political goal.

The North's moral, psychological, economic, and political commitment against terrorism had been drained in the campaign against the Klan and kindred organizations. The white South criticized the Enforcement Acts as militarily enforced tyranny, protested the arrest and prosecution of key citizens on the word of black or white Republican "traitors," physically attacked marshals and district attorneys who carried out the laws, assassinated witnesses, dragged cases through endless litigation, and got the majority of cases dismissed as *nolle prosequi* (not pursued further than the initial indictment). The Congress refused to "waste" necessary amounts of money on the Southern question, and the army was unwilling to risk eventual prosecution by assisting civil authorities in their courses of action, which were more politically than criminally oriented.

The end of the Klan did not mark the end of racial violence in the Reconstruction South. In fact, violence now became more open. Slowly, conservatives began to get all whites on the side of the Democratic party by appealing to racial solidarity. Up to this point, some Southern whites had always been willing to cut deals with blacks. Now the Klan had destroyed the Union Loyal Leagues and isolated the Carpetbaggers and African Americans as the only supporters of Reconstruction. (It was at this time that the stereotypes of Carpetbaggers and Scalawags became so potent.) Tennessee, Virginia, North Carolina, and Georgia fell easily to the Redeemers, those whites who had joined together regardless of their political background to restore home rule to the South. Texas Republicans, having lost a recent election, appealed to President Grant for military support as they strove to maintain power by exploiting a technicality in state electoral law. Grant refused and that state went to the Redeemers, too.

The situation in Arkansas was a mite more complicated than that in Texas and the other states. There, Republicans broke into armed factions against themselves. The regular Republicans backed Powell Clayton's hand-picked successor, Elisha Baxter. Liberal Republicans stood behind Joseph Brooks in an effort to get rid of the political chicanery and corruption that Clayton represented. Both sides began shooting. The "Brooks-Baxter War" ended only when Grant backed the party regulars (probably as much to counteract what he had done in Texas as anything) and recognized the Baxter faction as the legitimate group to represent Republicans. But the Republicans were so divided that the Democrats easily took the upcoming state elections at the ballot box. Moderate Republicans and Democrats in Congress recognized the Democratic government, despite protests on the part of more radical Republicans concerning political violence.

As the situation in Arkansas indicated, more violence was to come. Alabama became the testing ground for Redemption by force and white racial solidarity. In 1870 there was a race riot in Eutaw, where the Scalawag county prosecutor was shot in the head several times by a Ku Klux Klan band;

this was followed a few months later by a street riot in which 2 blacks died and up to 50 were wounded. Violence erupted in 1874 in Mobile, where an election-day brawl marred proceedings, and in Eufala, where over a half dozen blacks died and nearly 80 were wounded. The stage was set for the final push. Key Union whites and black leaders faced assassination if they campaigned for the Republicans. Any black who voted Republican was threatened with loss of his job. The army refused to intervene in any disturbance that was not right at the polls, and even then recent orders prevented much interference. By reducing Republican strength in the black belt (a rich black-soil region that cut across the center of the state from east to west) and in Union counties just below the Tennessee River, Democrats took Alabama. In the few areas won by Republicans, Democrats prevented elected officials from obtaining bonds and forced them to relinquish their posts to Democratic contenders. Congress investigated and found the election to have been carried by fraud and intimidation; however, led by a Democratic insurgency that had repudiated Grantism in the North during the congressional elections of 1874, it refused to intervene. The way was now open for the rest of the unredeemed states of the Deep South to end Reconstruction within their borders.

See also Election of 1876 and Compromise of 1877; Grant and Reconstruction; Ku Klux Klan; Race Riots that Influenced the Reconstruction Acts; Redemption of the South from 1874.

References Baenzinger, Ann Patton, "The Texas State Police during Reconstruction" (1968–1969); Beck, E. M., and Stewart E. Tolnay, "The Killing Fields of the Deep South" (1990); Carter, Hodding, *The Angry Scar* (1959); DeLatte, Carolyn E., "The St. Landry Riot" (1976); Formwalt, Lee W., "The Camilla Massacre of 1868" (1987); Gillette, William, *Retreat from Reconstruction* (1979); Granade, Ray, "Violence" (1968); Hennessey, Melinda Meek, "Political Terrorism in the Black Belt" (1980), "Reconstruction Politics and the Military" (1976), and "To Live and Die in Dixie" (1978); Horn, Stanley, *Invisible Empire* (1939); Nieman, Donald G., ed., *Black Freedom/White Violence* (1994); Perman, Michael, *The Road to Redemption* (1984); Rabel, George C., *But There Was No Peace* (1984); Rogers, William Warren, "The Boyd Incident" (1975); Sefton,

James E., *Army and Reconstruction* (1967); Single-tary, Otis A., *Negro Militia and Reconstruction* (1957); Swinney, Everette, "United States v. Powell Clayton" (1967); Trelease, Allan W., *White Terror* (1971); Wiggins, Sarah Woolfolk, "The 'Pig Iron' Kelley Riot at Mobile, May 14, 1867" (1970).

Redemption of the South from 1874

By 1874, four states were still under control of the Reconstructionists (Florida, Mississippi, South Carolina, Louisiana). The first of these to attempt Redemption was Louisiana. There was nothing in the nation to compare to the political snakebed in the Bayou State. As many as five different political groups (to call them parties would be overly generous) were in the field at a time, all with shifting personnel. The state's infant Republican party was divided among (1) the Customs House faction, headed by U.S. Marshal Stephen B. Packard, which relied on federal patronage in New Orleans; (2) the African Americans (Louisiana had the best-educated black population in the South); and (3) a group controlled by Illinois Carpetbagger and power artist Henry Clay Warmoth. Because Warmoth had, by 1872, been impeached (though there is some debate on whether this occurred), he now favored working with conservative men of all stripes (Republicans, former Whigs, and Democrats) in what was called the Fusion Party. Bloodshed was always close at hand, and the active intervention of federal troops was all that kept the peace.

In the 1872 state elections, the Customs House had put up as its gubernatorial candidate a Vermont Carpetbagger, William Pitt Kellogg. This did not necessarily please die-hard Republicans, especially blacks, because Kellogg was rumored never to have shaken hands with an African American without first putting on a glove. Still, Kellogg received the support of the African American faction. Warmoth's people, knowing that Warmoth could not win, nominated Democrat John McEnery. He also had a burden: he was seen by many as an old prewar corruptionist. No one knows who really won the election. Warmoth controlled the process as outgoing governor

and declared for McEnery. But Louisiana had several other returning boards (which were supposed to consist of the governor, the lieutenant governor, the secretary of state, and two senators, or anyone who claimed to be acting for them) that claimed to be legitimate. One such board certified ballots that counted in Kellogg. One political grouping offered Warmoth a U.S. Senate seat if he and his returning board would abandon McEnery for Kellogg. Other bribes too numerous to mention made the rounds on all levels.

Kellogg then played the Customs House's usual trump card. He wrote the federal government through William E. Chandler, the national Republican party chairman, and asked for national support. The Grant administration ordered U.S. troops to stand by and told Marshal Packard to enforce federal court decrees. There was only one such decree—it ordered Kellogg to take over state government. It had been issued by a friend of his. Armed with this writ, Packard took over the statehouse with a military posse. The court also ordered Warmoth to turn over all of the official ballots. He refused. Kellogg's returning board declared their man elected governor and Republican candidates to be the new legislature. Meanwhile Warmoth's supporters did exactly the same for McEnery and the Democrats, and Louisiana had two legislatures and two governors, with Kellogg relying on federal troops and McEnery upon the state militia (organized earlier by Warmoth). Using federal soldiers and the New Orleans Metropolitan Police, Kellogg arrested McEnery's legislature and took over the government.

But the Republicans were in deep trouble in the outlying parishes (counties). Here dual governments also existed. But the weight of force lay with McEnery's people. When Kellogg's men took over the Grant Parish courthouse in central Louisiana and called in local blacks to help them defend it, four or five hundred armed men responded. Rumors of black rebellion brought in armed whites from miles around. The Fusion forces gathered outside and surrounded the courthouse. The black occupants and their Scalawag and Carpetbag allies refused a call to surrender. The whites assaulted the fortifications around the courthouse, breached the line, and brought up a cannon to shell the building. Mistakenly thinking that the Republican forces had surrendered, the whites moved forward to meet a new fusillade. Then everyone went berserk. The attackers set fire to the courthouse, and as the occupants fled a massacre ensued. Victims were chased into the surrounding countryside. Surrendering men were shot down. Forty blacks who had been taken were led out that night and summarily executed. Over 100 people died at Colfax, making it the bloodiest of Reconstruction race riots.

Federal troops arrived after the fact to restore order. Federal courts indicted 72 men, but on advice of the U.S. attorney general they tried only 9. Conflicting evidence (blacks swore the men had been leaders of the white attackers, but the accused produced witnesses who placed them far from the riot) led to hung juries and a second go-around. This time William Cruikshank and two others were found guilty of violating the Enforcement Acts. But Cruikshank appealed his case to the U.S. Supreme Court, which ruled that the Fourteenth and Fifteenth amendments prohibited states from interfering with a citizen's civil rights but could not be applied against the actions of individuals. Cruikshank and his pals beat the rap, and the Enforcement Acts were gutted. The significance of this case was not lost on potential Redeemers in Louisiana and the rest of the white South.

Although Kellogg actually turned out to be a conscientious reformer of Louisiana corruption, the Fusionists would not stop in their efforts to unseat him for McEnery. They even attempted assassination, but Kellogg led a charmed life. In the parishes the Fusionists began to organize a group called the White League. Just how cooperative the various parishes were is open to question, but, unlike the earlier Knights of the White Camellia, the White League operated openly and with full newspaper coverage. Usually the White Leaguers could

bluff Republicans into fleeing the former's area, but in 1874 Redemption took another turn to violence in Red River Parish. This parish, created recently by an earlier Warmoth state legislature, was the power base for a family of Vermont Carpetbaggers named Twitchell. Indeed, the whole extended male family had received political appointments and proceeded to make much money, allegedly from the construction cost overruns of the Coushatta courthouse. The Twitchells had the support of the black voters, who outnumbered whites by four to one, so their tenure looked unbeatable by ordinary electoral methods. The outvoted whites turned to the White League.

The excuse for violence was an explosive argument between whites and blacks at a nearby town. The whites killed their opponents, and the shooting spread to Coushatta. The Red River whites asked for reinforcement from neighboring parishes. Armed whites came in and arrested the local Republican officeholders, demanding they resign their positions and be escorted to Texas by a posse of their own choosing. After the Republicans left town, young White Leaguers voiced dissatisfaction with the results. They pursued the Republicans and caught up with them near Shreveport. There the six prisoners, one of whom was a Twitchell, with their chosen posse stepping aside, were murdered in what became known as the Coushatta Massacre. Governor Kellogg asked for federal help, and a battalion of the Seventh Cavalry arrived and restored the Republicans to power. The cavalry also arrested about 20 whites and charged them with murder and civil rights violations. But the charges were later dropped as McEnery's people screamed "military despotism."

By 1874, the White League had gained control of the countryside outside of New Orleans by using classic guerrilla tactics, thereby isolating Kellogg supporters to the city itself. The local Democratic Club rechristened itself the Crescent City White League, ordered rifles from New York, and awaited the yellow fever season, when U.S. troops would be sent to Holly Springs, Mississippi, for their health. The White League planned to arm, capture Kellogg, and exile him out of the state, installing McEnery as governor. When Kellogg refused to surrender, the White Leaguers threw up barricades and prepared to fight his black state militia and the Metropolitan Police. Led by noted Scalawag, former Confederate lieutenant general James Longstreet, the Republican forces attacked the White League position only to be driven back. The White Leaguers then charged and eventually cleared the streets. Longstreet's retreating men forted up in the Customs House, which the White League wisely decided not to attack (since it was federal property). But they took all of the state buildings and set up the McEnery people as the government. The Republican casualties were 11 killed and 60 wounded, while the White League had 21 killed and 19 wounded.

Meanwhile the federal soldiers came back from Mississippi. The White League actually cheered their arrival, never dreaming that the soldiers would overturn their victory. But under the demands of President Grant, that is exactly what happened. Refusing to fight federal troops, although some of the rank and file voted to do so, McEnery turned the government back to Kellogg and surrendered his men. But 1,500 stand of arms and two howitzers remained unaccounted for and presumably in White League hands for future trouble. This trouble came during the state election of 1874, in which the legality of the returns was once again hotly contested. Grant sent Maj. Gen. Philip Sheridan in to take charge, as only he could. After purging the state legislature of Democrats who had forcibly entered the chambers to claim power, Sheridan suggested that all opponents to Kellogg be declared "banditti" and arrested for trial by military commission. The result was more tumult as the shakiness of the Republican hold on the state was revealed. Finally, Congressman William Wheeler of New York and his congressional subcommittee on Louisiana worked out a deal. Kellogg was not to be impeached, and the lower house was to have a

Democratic majority. The senate would remain Republican.

The Wheeler Compromise, as the deal was called, left Louisiana in relative peace for two years, but other unredeemed states watched the Louisiana proceedings with trepidation. Grant appeared to be a military tyrant who would stop at nothing to subvert even those states that already had been redeemed. Yet the real significance was that even though Grant had given no other state as much federal aid as Republican Louisiana, the Reconstructionists had managed to hang on only by a precarious string. Grant had decided to back the Customs House Republicans and through a series of well-intentioned decisions had exhausted and confused support for Reconstruction in the North. Louisiana was now a Republican albatross for the upcoming presidential election in 1876. And Louisiana, although unredeemed, had shown the way for Mississippi, Florida, and South Carolina to combat successfully their own Republican administrations.

Building on the Louisiana example, Mississippi produced a more refined version of the White League process, known as the Mississippi Plan, or Shotgun Plan. The state Republican party was divided over the usual issues: whether the state ought to share the Carpetbag vision of a New England–style Radical Republican party based on black support or the Scalawag future of a Conservative Republican party that was a broad coalition of Southern whites who would protect African Americans in a select but secondary place in society. With a majority of voters being black, it was not hard to see in which direction Mississippi would go. The Carpetbag governor of the state was Adelbert Ames, a native of Maine who was married to the daughter of Gen. Benjamin F. Butler. Ames was a Yankee war hero, a wearer of the Congressional Medal of Honor, and—unlike his father-in-law, who was noted for his sticky fingers during the wartime occupation of the Gulf South— a scrupulously honest, upright man. The Scalawag was James L. Alcorn, who had preceded Ames as governor and represented the classic story of the Whig-turned-Republican for conservative, upper-class societal and economic values.

By the time Ames became governor in 1873, Mississippi was in an economic downturn, part of the nationwide panic of 1873. The following year, whites at Vicksburg organized the People's party and began to intimidate the all-black government and African American voters, who outnumbered them two to one. The black sheriff asked for military support to counter white military companies. Ames forwarded the request to the Grant administration, which refused to act. The resulting intimidation and vote fraud saw the People's party win some offices in Vicksburg and Warren County, a political disaster that Ames blamed upon President Grant's refusal to send in the army. But it was evident that the state itself had done little to police a local election. Ames's reluctance to act on his own merely encouraged more white violence, as did his refusal to disperse a black mob or call for federal military help in Tunica County near Memphis.

As yet Mississippi whites did not have anything comparable to Louisiana's White League. Once again the whites at Vicksburg led the way, demanding that their black sheriff resign and leave the area. The sheriff begged Governor Ames for assistance. Ames told him to form a posse to protect his job but did little more. When the sheriff organized his posse, whites appealed for help, and 160 volunteers crossed the river to show Mississippi how it was done in Louisiana. The result was a riot that extended well into the night as whites ransacked private homes and killed black residents. There were at least 36 dead or wounded as a result of the daytime riot, but the nighttime casualties remain unknown. The sheriff decided to resign and flee to Jackson. Governor Ames declared Warren County in insurrection and this time got federal troops to reinstate the sheriff, who resigned again when an assassination attempt was made against him after the U.S. soldiers withdrew.

As Congress investigated the "Vicksburg Insurrection," U.S. Senator James Alcorn "guided" his colleagues into looking at alleged corruption in Republican government, the sheriff's inability to control law and order, and Governor Ames's so-called complicity in intentionally provoking violence and backing a corrupt regime against the "will of the people." Yet whites in Mississippi remained divided over the need to destroy Ames's administration. The governor did his best to reform the state, but his program fell apart in the state legislature, once again revealing him to be a weak politician. When he raised a black state militia to protect his administration and local Republican officeholders, the whites in the state decided finally to get rid of Reconstruction at once by concerted white action. These White Liners maintained that they had nothing against black participation in politics but that the unity of African Americans behind the Radical regime and its corrupt programs forced them to engage in self-defense to protect themselves from being taxed out of existence. More cautious men, however, wondered whether racial strife might not lead to more federal intervention.

By 1875, renewed violence in Vicksburg set the tone for the state election campaign. Opponents to Ames organized a Conservative Democratic party and listened to the appeal of Senator Alcorn for racial harmony, acceptance of black suffrage, and the Fourteenth and Fifteenth amendments. The delegates responded by calling for civil and political equality and the redemption of the state—two contradictory notions, but it sounded good up North. Under the motto "peaceably if we can, forcibly if we must," the Conservatives went forth to take control of the legislature and capture the state treasurer's office, the only statewide contest that year. Gun dealers sold out several times over during the campaign. Ames pointed out that Conservatives made the color line the issue of the election despite their noble-sounding platform. Democratic U.S. Senator L. Q. C. Lamar preached peace in Washington to fool the nation while back home the night riders used the whip, rope, and gun to get the job done.

As in Louisiana, the fight was for the

county governments. At Yazoo City, Albert Morgan, a Wisconsin Carpetbagger, had engaged in planting, established black schools, married an African American woman, and become a dominant Republican. In 1873 he was elected sheriff, but his opponent, another Republican, refused to leave office until Morgan took it over at gunpoint. In the scuffle his opponent was killed. Democrats immediately accused him of murder. They wished to arrest him, but a posse of blacks prevented this. Morgan sought to allay white fears by holding a joint Republican-Democratic political meeting. It soon degenerated into a shooting fray, from which Morgan was lucky to emerge alive. Morgan hid out until the heat was off and fled to Jackson to plead for help. Ames did nothing, and the Republican party polled a total of seven votes in November. A similar riot occurred in Clinton outside of Jackson, but its proximity to the federal garrison meant the fighting could be stopped after three whites and four blacks died. Indictments were sought, but a grand jury found no true bill. Later, White Liners struck back by murdering black political and community leaders at night.

Governor Ames hoped that President Grant would see the political expediency in sending federal troops in to police the election. But Grant refused, saying, "The whole public are tired out with these annual autumnal outbreaks in the South, and the great majority are ready to condemn any interference on the part of the government." He told Ames to handle the problem himself. Ames came to understand the president's meaning when he considered sending the black militia into the field. He was roundly condemned for trying to settle the election by force (which overlooked the fact that his opponents were doing the same) and for bringing on a race war. The militia was not used. Instead the Democrats proposed a compromise. They warned the governor that if he refused the deal, the streets of Jackson would run red with blood. Ames agreed to keep the militia out of the election process, and the Democrats said that they would keep the peace for the rest of the contest.

The political agreement was of little consequence because the Democrats had already coerced most of the results. Mass meetings and torchlight parades, many complete with private white armies armed with cannons, as well as constant heckling of Republican candidates and voters, kept the heat on. The Conservative program rounded itself out with economic coercion (loss of jobs) and forcing local Republican officials to resign and go into exile. Men from Alabama and Louisiana "assisted" in keeping the peace with gunfire. Armed companies of whites policed the polls and permitted only those blacks with Democratic passes of good conduct to vote. The rest either stayed home or were hounded from the poll places. The "Rebel yell" went up often as voters passed between lines of white men to vote. The statewide Republican majority of 23,000 in 1873 became a Democratic majority of 30,000—this in a state with a large black majority of registered voters.

Although fraud, violence, and intimidation played a role, whites also mobilized their voters and united them in voting as a bloc for the first time since Reconstruction had begun. Democratic control of the legislature allowed them to impeach Governor Ames. In March 1876, the legislature dropped the charges (they had already convicted Ames's lieutenant governor), and Ames left the state, never to return. He retired to Massachusetts and died in Florida in 1933, bitter that his administration had been doomed because "the inferior race" had to "succumb to the superior race" even though the former had the support of the federal government. In his condescending reference to his supporters was a real truth—he did not have the support of the United States anymore. Florida, South Carolina, and Louisiana sat in the wings and took note. It would be their votes that determined the election of 1876 and the Compromise of 1877.

The easiest Democratic conquest occurred in Florida. There, blacks represented 49 percent of the vote, so the Republicans had to appeal for some white support. The

Republicans initially fielded two candidates, a prospect that boded well for the Democrats. Eventually the Republicans united behind their incumbent governor, Marcellus L. Stearns. The opposition put up a bland, conservative businessman, George F. Drew. Although there were some rifle clubs in the field and some intimidation, the Drew forces relied primarily on vote fraud to gain election. But their efforts did not ensure the presidential vote, which was later declared to be Republican.

Unlike Florida, there would have to be a real fight for South Carolina and Louisiana. South Carolina had experienced one of the more corrupt Reconstruction regimes in the South. In the end everyone was in on the take, a problem Republicans managed to overcome by nominating and electing Carpetbagger Daniel H. Chamberlain as governor in 1874. He had been a part of the previous administration, and many saw his election as a sign for business as usual. Chamberlain fooled them. He called for clean, economical government and a fair assessment of taxes; he acted to use the state patronage evenly, appointing some white conservatives to office. Whites, however, had little faith in Chamberlain's promises. They condemned all Republican-run governments as corrupt rule by ignorant blacks. Unfortunately, although Chamberlain lived in a state with a black majority, he never developed a good relationship with African American political leaders.

Because the majority of black voters in South Carolina was the greatest in the South, it became evident that mere fraud would not carry the day. The result was the adoption of the Mississippi Plan, which in South Carolina meant the organization of the Red Shirts, its own version of the White League. The movement got its biggest support in Edgefield County, which had been a hotbed of secession in 1860, the Ku Klux Klan after the war, and now the center of straight-out Democracy. The blacks in "Bloody Edgefield" had organized their own rifle clubs, so the scene was set for open hostility as soon as a triggering event could take place. Such an event occurred in nearby Hamburg. A black militia company paraded in the town's streets for the Fourth of July 1876. Two whites in a buggy told the commander to get his men out of the way. The soldier replied that there was plenty of room on either side of the column. The whites were about to remonstrate when a rain came up, dispersing the column to the porches on the side of the street; the whites drove on. A local court swore out an arrest warrant on the militia officer for blocking a public thoroughfare a couple of days later.

An armed group of two or three hundred whites showed up for the hearing. They demanded that the black militia surrender its weapons. The militia commander refused. Shooting soon erupted, and the blacks took refuge in a building, which the whites began to shell with a cannon. The blacks fled out the rear, 25 of their number being "arrested." One of the armed white companies, led by Benjamin R. Tillman, later a U.S. senator better known as "Pitchfork" Ben, refused to allow the black prisoners to be marched to jail and executed five men in its custody, an incident called the Hamburg Massacre. Although the murder was condemned by conservatives, they blamed the shootings on the evils flowing from Republican rule. At Chamberlain's request, President Grant sent federal soldiers to restore order. Then the Republicans instituted court proceedings, indicting 60 whites from the most prominent families of the area for the massacre. The trial, with the defendants appearing in their red shirts, was delayed until after the 1876 election so that passions might cool, at which time all of the accused were released.

The Hamburg Massacre scuttled all of the cooperation between Chamberlain and Conservative Democrats in the upcoming 1876 election. The Democrats, split between low-country conservatives who wanted a peaceful election and up-country fire-eaters who wanted more blood, cleverly concealed their differences by nominating Confederate war hero Maj. Gen. Wade Hampton. Their platform recognized the Civil War constitutional amendments and summoned all citizens regardless of color to join in reforming the corruption that had plagued the state. Although Hampton was a reasonable man, he lacked the power and possibly the will to stop the bloodletting that went on, especially upcountry (most of the fighting in the low country was initiated by black militia against their white opponents, a rarity in the Reconstruction history of most states). The Republicans stood with Chamberlain, their best chance of looking like honest reformers, too. Democrats condemned Chamberlain as "a carrion coward, a buzzard and a Puritanical seedy adventurer who came down here to steal our substance."

Unlike in Louisiana and Mississippi, where the Republicans dared not leave their capital cities, Chamberlain engaged in a vigorous campaign. But right behind him came the Red Shirts (there were nearly 300 white rifle clubs in the state), who intimidated, hanged, and shot potential Republican voters, mostly black. The Red Shirts were so active that a fear grew that they might even attack U.S. troops on election day. The worst violence of the campaign occurred in Ellenton in September 1876, in an area where whites had vowed to win the election or kill all the Republicans. A minor assault by two blacks, which Republicans claimed to be a trumped-up case, started the action. One of the suspects was captured, identified by a victim, and shot on the spot. The other had an arrest warrant filed against him. The rifle clubs broke up a Republican meeting the next day and chased the party members into a swamp. The Red Shirts demanded that the assault suspect be turned over. The blacks refused. After much talk, the two sides agreed to depart amicably, but some blacks shot one of the Red Shirts, and the whites went crazy, shooting up houses all over the county. The fighting spread into Ellenton, where a black state legislator was among the murdered. The arrival of federal troops finally restored the peace, just as the Red Shirts, many arriving by train, had cornered their opponents for the final kill. Over 100 blacks and a half-dozen whites died.

Governor Chamberlain responded with a proclamation to the rifle clubs to disperse. They promptly changed their names to things like the Allendale Mounted Baseball Club, Mother's Little Helpers, or the First Baptist Sewing Circle and rode on. Chamberlain complained to Grant, who ordered the Red Shirts to disband or face federal troops. The whites quickly drew back and election day passed quietly, barring a small riot put down by U.S. forces in Charleston. Hampton claimed victory, and in some respects he was right. It was amazing how little fight Chamberlain had put up—he never called up the black militia, for instance. Yet blacks in South Carolina had put up a better fight, especially in the area in and around Charleston, than Republicans in other states, but to no avail. Even though the state returning board awarded a majority of seats in the legislature to Republicans, it had to be done under the protection of federal troops. The state presidential electoral vote went to the Republicans and the governorship to Hampton in a sort of compromise that satisfied no one. Hampton warned Chamberlain that the latter's life and that of all other Republicans was in his own hands. Although the state's presidential vote went to Republican Rutherford B. Hayes, the lack of federal support meant that the government soon fell to the Red Shirts.

The same happened in Louisiana. As with all Southern states, the national election in 1876 was considered "small potatoes," in the words of a North Carolina politician, as Republicans and Democrats were pledged to end federal interference in the South. In Louisiana bands of regulators bulldozed blacks into voting Democratic. Republican ballots were unavailable outside New Orleans. Black voters were handed Democratic ballots instead and told to vote right. Parishes that had been the center of Republican strength before had not a single vote for the party ticket in 1876. To unite whites, the Democrats ran war hero Francis T. Nicholls, a man who had lost an eye, arm, and leg in defense of the Confederacy. The Republicans, reduced to the Customs House faction, nominated Stephen B. Packard, the U.S. marshal and its leader. Claiming victory, as did Nicholls, Packard held on until the presidential election was settled with Louisiana's electoral vote going to Hayes. Then he abandoned the government to the Democrats because he lost the support of the army.

Those historians who fault the lack of support for Reconstruction from the Grant administration overlook the tenacity of Southern white resistance to the process through violence. These Southerners were aided in their fight by the weariness of the North in enforcing Reconstruction and by the rise of a new philosophy, Social Darwinism, that precluded welfare or special assistance to any group that could not survive the struggle of life and emerge on top. Yet the Redeemers did not deliver on their promise of a better life for Southern whites. They continued to use the black vote to count out white agrarian radicals and keep the New South in the hands that ran the Old. It was not until the twentieth century that a man named Huey P. Long became the first Southern politician to really deliver on his promises to better the lives of those left behind as the South industrialized and tried to cope with the economic problems Reconstruction never solved.

See also Election of 1876 and Compromise of 1877; Grant and Reconstruction; Ku Klux Klan; Race Riots that Influenced the Reconstruction Acts; Redemption of the South before 1874.

References Beck, E. M., and Stewart E. Tolnay, "The Killing Fields of the Deep South" (1990); Carter, Hodding, *The Angry Scar* (1959); Gillette, William, *Retreat from Reconstruction* (1979); Hennessey, Melinda Meek, "Racial Violence during Reconstruction" (1985) and "To Live and Die in Dixie" (1978); Holmes, William F., "The Leflore County Massacre and the Demise of the Colored Farmers' Alliance" (1973); Johnson, Manie White, "The Colfax Riot of April 1873" (1930); Kousser, J. Morgan, *The Shaping of Southern Politics* (1970); Lestage, Oscar H., Jr., "The White League in Louisiana and Its Participation in Reconstruction Riots" (1935); Nieman, Donald G., ed., *Black Freedom/White Violence* (1994); Olsen, Otto H., ed., *Reconstruction and Redemption in the South* (1980); Perman, Michael, *The Road to Redemption* (1984); Rabel, George C., *But There Was No Peace* (1984) and "Republican Albatross" (1982); Sefton, James E., *Army and Reconstruction* (1967); Simkins, Francis B., "The Election of 1876 in South Carolina" (1922); Singletary, Otis A., *Negro Militia and Reconstruction* (1957); Trelease, Allan W., *White Terror* (1971); Woodward, C. Vann, *The Strange Career of Jim Crow* (1966).

Reed, Harrison (1813–1899)

Boston-born Harrison Reed was a Florida Carpetbag governor. He was short, slight, and unobtrusive in appearance. He showed little emotion. He was balding and wore thick glasses that made him look sort of like an owl and was much older than most Reconstruction participants. He had spent much of his life "in pursuit of the horizon," in the words of a biographer, moving into western Massachusetts, then Vermont, onto New York state, and finally winding up in Madison, Wisconsin. When the Civil War broke out he had gone to Washington, D.C., where he served as a nameless Treasury Department bureaucrat. He was a widower, and his daughter had also died young. In January 1863, Reed landed at Fernandina Island off the coast of Florida. His job was to follow federal forces into the mainland and collect the federal property tax owed the United States. To pay one had to take a loyalty oath. To refuse the oath meant that the property in question was liable to seizure and sale at an auction by the treasury men. He bought a great deal of seized property for himself and his two sons. He and the other commissioners also allowed blacks to bid on places where they were living before the lots opened up to public sale. But when Reed changed his mind and quarreled with one of his coagents over this practice, he lost his job.

Reed spent the next two years in Washington as a postal employee. President Andrew Johnson sent him back to Florida after the war as a postal supervisor for the whole state. He advised the president to appoint William Marvin as provisional governor and warned him of electioneering taking place on behalf of Salmon P. Chase (Lincoln's secretary of the treasury and now chief justice of the U.S. Supreme Court) among the treasury men who had run Reed off. Johnson had already heard of Marvin but was pleased to hear of the Chase election activities in Florida. Marvin sided with

Reed and had the treasury men relieved of their jobs, allowing Reed to get even for his 1863 firing. Reed went to Jacksonville and started a newspaper. He believed that this city would be a hot spot in Florida's postwar recovery. Reed was interested in developing Florida's economy, and he did not really care under which political banner it was done. He had no desire to take advantage of the Military Reconstruction Act, being a good Johnson man at heart, but by 1867 it was obvious that Republicanism was the wave of the future in the South. And to ride that wave he needed black votes. But Radical Republicans, known locally as the Mule Team, had a big jump on him. They had won the most seats at the state constitutional convention.

So Reed began by talking to individual delegates as they arrived at Tallahassee for the convention. He also won over Bvt. Maj. Gen. George Meade, military commander of the Third Military District (Georgia, Alabama, and Florida), and the Freedmen's Bureau assistant commissioner, Thomas W. Osborn. The latter had a good reputation among planters and freedmen alike for running a fair operation. But Reed could not defeat the Mule Team in the convention. So he pulled his delegates (who were almost all white) out and removed to Monticello to write his own constitution; it gave the governor large appointive powers for local offices and limited each county to just four seats in the legislature, which would offset the large Radical support in black counties, and it disfranchised no whites other than those specified the Fourteenth Amendment. The Radicals of the Mule Team, meanwhile, wrote their version of the state constitution, too. They wanted to make all offices elective and to apportion all seats by population. This would give blacks a big voice in what went on because they almost equaled whites when Confederate disfranchisement was taken into account. One night, as the Mule Team slept, the Reed delegates slipped back into the state capital and took over the convention hall. There they acted as the true convention and repassed their Monticello work. Outside an angry black mob, whipped up by the Mule Team, threatened to storm the hall.

Things looked bad until General Meade arrived from Atlanta. He deployed federal soldiers and forced the two conventions to meet together. Reed managed to persuade enough Mule Team delegates that his constitution was better and it passed. The convention also nominated Reed for governor on the Republican ticket. When the Mule Team complained to Congress, Reed went to Washington and convinced Congress that only he possessed the necessary majority to carry the day and complete Reconstruction. Back in Florida, Reed found that the Conservative Democrats had broken off their association with him to run their own candidate. But the Radicals also entered the fray as a third party. With the support of the Post Office Department, the Freedmen's Bureau, the U.S. Army, and Congress, Reed's ticket took the contest by a large majority.

But Reed had already reached the peak of his power. When he appointed his cabinet and local offices, he angered everyone. Radicals said that he appointed too many Democrats, and blacks were angry at receiving mostly menial jobs. White Democrats disliked the whole concept of blacks being able to vote because of outside Yankee meddling with their state. Federal patronage—which was so important because the associated jobs paid more—went into the hands of Reed's onetime ally, Thomas W. Osborn (who was now a U.S. senator). However, Reed had refused to go along with Osborn's scheme to fund state bonds at a profit (which Osborn offered to split with Reed). The legislature saw Reed veto bills to raise their pay and to open public accommodations to all races equally. And Democrats hated him for raising a "black and tan" (i.e., biracial) militia to put down the Ku Klux Klan. Mysteriously, the arms ordered for the militia were stolen en route from New York, making the troops ineffective.

At this point the legislature moved to impeach the governor after threats against his life failed to get his resignation. With the connivance of the secretary of state, the lieutenant governor stole the state seal and tried to run Reed out of office. Reed drove the usurper off at gunpoint. The lieutenant governor then set up shop in a hotel across from the capitol, claiming that Reed was already out of office. Reed pulled strings with a local judge he had appointed, got the seal back, and threw the lieutenant governor out of office on the technicality that he had not been in the state three years and was hence not a legal resident who could serve. He then removed the secretary of state, a onetime loyal appointee who had recently sided against him, and replaced the man with an African American Radical. Reed correctly surmised that this would cause black politicians to sit back and see what would develop. To give Reed a chance to act further on their behalf, the black legislators voted down the impeachment effort.

After this bout, Reed was still governor, but he was a man without a party. Nonetheless, he took a brief vacation to North Carolina, where he married Chloe Merrick, an organizer of black orphanages whom he had met back in his Fernandina days. He then returned to battle the legislature over civil rights and public finance. With the arms for his militia intercepted along the line somewhere, Reed decided to shift his appeal once again by refusing to use state forces to put down the Ku Klux Klan activities that plagued the Florida Panhandle. Murder and assassination of blacks, random or intentional, swept the state. Finally, legislators went over Reed's head and asked for federal troops. But so few came that the intimidation of blacks continued virtually unabated. Besides, the Grant administration was giving most of the attention to the bloodier Carolinas. When one of the Carpetbaggers who had survived an attempted murder threatened to have his fellow legislators impeach Reed once again, the governor grumbled, "Impeach and be damned!"

But there was an issue upon which impeachment could be based that did not concern race at all. It had to do with railroads, one of the governor's pet projects from the very beginning of his stay in Florida. Reed believed in public aid to private enterprise.

The financiers of the railroad projects were two men already on the lam from North Carolina for corruption there, Milton S. Littlefield and George W. Swepson. Reed knew the smooth-talking Littlefield from his Fernandina days and as a heavy campaign contributor. Littlefield had contributed heavily to Reed's gubernatorial campaign. And he and Swepson, with Reed's backing, persuaded the state legislature to trade $4 million in state bonds for railroad bonds. At first Reed held back on the exchange. Then, in 1870, Littlefield came into Tallahassee and had a long talk with him. A few days later the exchange was made. Rumor had it that Littlefield paid the governor $7,500 for his signature. Reed called it a personal loan, which he expected to repay. His connection with Littlefield remains unknown to this day, yet when he received an extradition request for Littlefield from North Carolina, Reed refused to honor it. By the end of his term in 1872, it is fair to say that Reed had little chance to be elected dogcatcher, much less something of importance. The legislature voted his impeachment unanimously and then adjourned indefinitely (as they had no evidence to hang on Reed), leaving the governor in limbo for the ten months left of his term.

Reed had to turn the office over to the lieutenant governor under the state constitution. He retired to his orange groves near Jacksonville. When he learned that the lieutenant governor had come to Jacksonville for a meeting, Reed took a quick train to Tallahassee and got the seal from a cooperative secretary of state. He asked the state supreme court to rule in his favor. The legislature had refused to try Reed, and he claimed this to be an acquittal. But the court ruled that only the senate could rule on this matter. The lieutenant governor then made a mistake. He called the senate into special session. Reed's Republican enemies moved to adjourn, but Democrats called for a trial. Reed's attorney then moved that the charges be dropped. The senate voted 10 to 7 in Reed's behalf, and he left office a free man, having outmaneuvered everyone again. Having beaten the impeachment,

Reed retired to raise oranges. He had made no money while governor. Indeed, he was in much debt. He and Chloe struggled on, raising oranges, promoting Florida real estate before it boomed. She died in 1897 and Reed followed in 1899, poor as ever, a conservative businessman to the end.

See also Carpetbaggers.

References Current, Richard N., *Those Terrible Carpetbaggers* (1988) and *Three Carpetbag Governors* (1967); Daniels, Jonathan, *Prince of Carpetbaggers* (1958); Fenlon, Paul E., "The Notorious Swepson-Littlefield Fraud" (1954); Overy, David H., Jr., "The Wisconsin Carpetbagger" (1960); Shofner, Jerrell H., "Florida" (1980); Smith, George Winston, "Carpetbag Imperialism in Florida" (1948–1949).

Reparations for Black Americans

In May 1969, James Foreman, a representative for the National Black Development Conference of Detroit, Michigan, stood during the service at Riverside Church in New York City and delivered a document known as the Black Manifesto. The manifesto, which advocated the total control by African Americans of their own economic future, presented a plea for $500 million dollars (roughly a cheap $15 dollars per person) as a beginning of reparations to be paid by white Americans and their "Racist Institutions" to blacks "as a people who have been exploited and degraded, brutalized, killed and persecuted" for the last 450 years.

The manifesto money would go not to individuals but to blacks as a race to finance a Southern land bank, publishing companies, television networks, research and training centers, an independent welfare organization, a black labor strike fund, a fundraising subsidiary, and a national black university. Others would prefer to see the reparation come in the form of increased government domestic spending, emphasizing employment, job training, housing facilities, health, education, and income support. But to the disappointment of many, and in line with the expectations of others, the manifesto received the usual treatment accorded black demands in the United States—a sympathetic hearing, vehement denial, much verbal self-flagellation, and in the end a failure to come to grips with the problem. As the *New York Times* put it, "There is neither wealth nor wisdom enough in the world to compensate in money for all the wrongs in history."

Proponents of reparations point out that had the time between slavery and the present truly been marked with equality in action and thought, the concept of payment for the past wrongs of slavery might be spurious. But such was not the case. Instead the constant discrimination in social, economic, and political areas has continued the effects of slavery in other guises, covered up by a legal doctrine of "separate but equal" that never really held true. Despite the changes since World War II, the legacy of Jim Crow (segregation) is still with us as a nation. The situation is compounded by recognition that blacks alone, of all U.S. immigrants, came as slaves. Many legal minds believe that African Americans could bring suit for the deprivation of equal treatment under Section 1983 of Title 42 of the U.S. Code, allowing a suit in equity by persons deprived of their rights under color of state law. The contention would be that "separate but equal" was never adequately followed by any state.

The concept of black reparations has lurked beneath the surface of much of American history since the end of the Civil War. One might see in the creation of the Freedmen's Bureau an attempt to deliver reparations in kind, through social services. In 1890, W. R. Vaughn proposed a Freedmen's Pension Bill to compensate "Old Slaves" for a lifetime of forced labor and the "past errors of the Government," for which Emancipation alone was inadequate. Vaughn's timing was poor, however, and even the three black representatives in Congress recognized the bill's futility in the face of imperialism abroad and the end of federal supervision of civil rights at home.

The recent payment of reparations to Japanese Americans incarcerated in concentration camps to remove their allegedly hostile presence from the Pacific coast in World War II and the government's willingness to pay selected Native Americans for past treaty violations have helped to keep the concept alive in the nation's psyche. Internationally, the examples of West Germany and Italy to compensate the victims of Nazism and Fascism are examples of how such a program might proceed. Yet many blacks oppose the concept of a cash payment, which would separate the black poor from others of different ethnic backgrounds in the same economic position and would be, in their view, a vain attempt to heal an "irreparable past" on purely a racial basis.

See also Bureau of Refugees, Freedmen, and Abandoned Lands.

References Bittker, Boris I., *The Case for Black Reparations* (1973); Foreman, James, *The Making of a Black Revolutionary* (1972); Vaughn, Walter R., *Vaughn's Freedmen's Pension Bill* (1971 [1891]).

Revels, Hiram R. (1822–1901)

Born a free man of color in Fayetteville County, North Carolina, Hiram Revels studied at a seminary and at Knox College in Galesburg, Illinois, becoming a preacher for the African Methodist Episcopal Church. He served congregations throughout the Old Northwest. When the war broke out, Revels recruited black soldiers for the Union cause and eventually became a chaplain in one regiment. After the war he settled in Mississippi and entered Republican politics as an alderman in Natchez. In 1870, as the state was readmitted to the Union, Revels was elected U.S. senator by the state legislature for the short-term seat, the one abandoned by Jefferson Davis in 1860. This made Revels the first black man to occupy a place in the U.S. Senate in American history.

The notion of a black man occupying the senatorial position once held by the president of the Confederacy caught the imagination of the nation. It became the subject of a famous Thomas Nast cartoon, which played upon a line in William Shakespeare's *Othello* ("For that I do suspect the lusty Moor hath leap'd into my seat: the thought whereof doth like a poisonous mineral gnaw at my inwards") and showed Davis as Iago gazing sinisterly upon Revels (Othello)

courting the Yankee Senators (the modern Desdemonas); the cartoon had the title "Time Works Wonders." Yet the extremely conservative Revels did little that Davis might not have done in the Senate beyond supporting an integrated school system in the District of Columbia. He spoke on behalf of the readmission of states like Mississippi into the Union and an increased federal levee system. After he stepped down (by prior agreement) at the end of his term, Revels became the editor of the *Southwestern Christian Advocate*, the president of Alcorn A&M College, and a district superintendent of the African Methodist Episcopal Church.

See also Ames, Adelbert; Alcorn, James L.; Bruce, Blanche K.; Lynch, John R.

References Low, W. Augustus, and Virgil A. Clift, *Encyclopedia of Black America* (1981); McFarlin, Annjeannette Sophia, *Black Congressional Reconstruction Orators and Their Orations* (1976).

Reynolds, Joseph J. (1822–1899)

A Kentuckian who grew up in Indiana, Joseph J. Reynolds graduated West Point in 1843. He served on the western frontier and in eastern garrison duty, with a stint as a mathematics instructor at the academy. In 1857, he resigned to teach at Washington University at St. Louis, then went home to assist in the family grocery business in Indiana. During the war he served with the Union in the Tenth Indiana Volunteer Infantry and soon rose to brigade and division command in the western theater of the conflict. He was breveted for bravery at Chickamauga and Missionary Ridge, where he was chief of staff to the Army of the Cumberland (succeeding future president Bvt. Maj. Gen. James A. Garfield), and wound up the war commanding the Seventh Corps in Arkansas. He decided to stay in the service after the war and received a post as colonel of the Twenty-sixth Infantry. By 1867 and the passage of the Military Reconstruction Acts he was in charge of the giant Subdistrict of the Rio Grande with headquarters at Brownsville.

As the senior officer behind the District of Texas commander, Bvt. Maj. Gen. Charles

Griffin, Reynolds was in line for the Texas command upon Griffin's death from yellow fever in September 1867. He proceeded to station his headquarters at Austin to be closer to the Texas state government (no general preceding him had ever met personally with former Texas Governor James W. Throckmorton, for example) and to be far from the yellow fever that regularly swept towns along the Gulf coast. There was much trepidation among the Texas Republicans about Reynolds's attitudes concerning Reconstruction and party necessities. Griffin had put one of their own men, Elisha M. Pease, in the governorship and had just begun to clean Democrats out of the state executive and courts before his untimely death. The big question was, what would Reynolds do? The prospects for Republicans did not look good: Reynolds had been a popular officer among the pro-Rebel civilians in Brownsville and that could only mean that he was not a Reconstruction advocate.

Republican leaders immediately contacted the general to find out his views. To their pleasant surprise Reynolds indicated he was willing to work with them on appointments. Of course, there was a price. Provisional Governor Pease (his detractors called him "Goober-Pease," indicating his alleged peanut-sized brain power) issued a unique proclamation declaring that the state government he represented was solely provisional and that its authority rested on the Military Reconstruction Acts and on any orders promulgated by General Reynolds. Reynolds recognized all persons in office as the current civil government. Most important, Pease agreed in writing to accept what would become the Shellabarger-Chase theory of Reconstruction; this theory became the basis for the U.S. Supreme Court decision *Texas v. White* (1869), which stated that all laws and contracts passed since 1861 not in conflict with the results of the war were valid. This was a denial of ab initio, a sacred tenet of the Radical Republicans that held just the opposite.

Pease had recognized the army as the supreme power in the state; this was some-thing all previous governors had denied, preferring to see the military men as adjuncts to the civil government. But Pease's action had opened more than a party schism. It had given him access to the man who could make all appointments and removals to state political positions at all levels. Pease had no time to waste in bickering over Reynolds's conditions for supporting the Republican party. The ideologues would simply have to accept the truth—Reynolds was king of the dung heap. And they had to move fast because the pending arrival of Maj. Gen. Winfield Scott Hancock at New Orleans—a known Democrat and opponent of Reconstruction and soon to be Reynolds's superior officer—would put an end to any political alteration of the Texas landscape for months to come. Reynolds did not let the party down. Using lists drawn up by loyalists since the end of the war and augmented by Griffin before he died, Reynolds removed 400 Democrats from office and appointed 436 Republicans (some positions had been vacant) to county offices. In several smaller orders (the big one ran over 13 pages in 9-point type) Reynolds appointed another 175 Republican candidates to office, including the city governments of Austin and San Antonio (he had taken care of Houston and Galveston in the big order), removing 99 more Democrats. Republicans had their miracle. They were ensconced in Texas local and state government as never before.

It had not occurred any too soon. General Hancock arrived in New Orleans and was met by letters and telegrams protesting Reynolds's partisan policies. But Lt. Gen. U. S. Grant refused to let him interfere with Reynolds's previous orders. So Hancock made sure that Reynolds could do no more harm. Hancock also ordered a reopening of registration for the upcoming convention election and liberalized the exclusionary rules for former Confederates. But in reality Reynolds was so far away that he could basically ignore any change in registration instructions. So long as Reynolds did not disobey any direct order, he could obstruct and delay, hoping that Grant would get the proud Hancock to resign by slighting him in military protocol. That occurred in March 1868, and Hancock's successor, Robert C. Buchanan (who was involved with completing Reconstruction in Louisiana), gave Reynolds a free hand once again.

Reynolds now turned to the Texas state constitutional convention. He escorted Governor Pease down the aisle to the rostrum, implying that Pease had the correct philosophy on a moderate, common-sense approach to Reconstruction. Though Reynolds was offered a seat on the floor, he declined to accept it. He did, however, have officers observe the proceedings and report back to him. Reynolds did not like what he heard. The convention was quickly deadlocked over ab initio; possible division of the state into loyal white, African American, and Rebel areas to guarantee Republican control in two of them; and disfranchisement of ex-Confederates. It soon became obvious that Reynolds was not going to be able to get a constitution out of the convention in time for the November 1868 presidential election.

Upon Grant's election under the Republican banner, President Andrew Johnson struck back by removing Reynolds, who was one of Grant's old West Point friends. Bvt. Maj. Gen. Edward R. S. Canby, an expert at getting constitutions out of recalcitrant state conventions in the Carolinas, replaced General Reynolds. Canby then forced the convention to hammer out a constitution in a second convention session. Reynolds, meanwhile, went to Washington to greet his old friend, now the incoming president of the United States. Texas Republicans petitioned Grant to remove Canby. They said they had noting against the general—he was imminently fair to all in Texas (which, of course, was his real liability—a lack of Republican partisanship), but they preferred Reynolds, to whom President Johnson had done an injustice. Grant happily complied.

Reynolds's return to Texas meant that Republican party building could continue as before. The Moderate Republicans had put forth an electoral ticket consisting of An-

drew J. Hamilton (President Johnson's provisional governor back in 1865), which was supported by Provisional Governor Pease. This ticket was opposed by a Radical Republican slate led by convention president Edmund J. Davis. The basic quarrel was over philosophical purity, that is, over which group was the real Republican party. Since Hamilton and Pease were appealing to "the thinking element" among the old Democrats, they looked suspicious. But General Reynolds might be able to make up for a lack of purity through his reports to Grant in Washington. He could also throw out of office any Davis supporters who used their positions to support Davis in the upcoming state elections. Reynolds indicated that he was more than happy to continue on as before, but that of course there would be a price for services rendered. He wanted to become one of the U.S. senators elected by the new state legislature. But there was a problem—Hamilton would not agree to the condition. Hamilton's cronies did their best to negotiate without him, but in the end they failed.

Reynolds was not to be put off. He went to Edmund J. Davis and the Radicals with the same deal. Davis knew that any election would be a close one, given the preponderant white voter registration in Texas. So he changed his party platform to ape the Moderates by dropping ab initio. Then Reynolds wrote to Grant that he had been forced to shift his support from Hamilton to Davis because the former was in bed with obstructionist Rebels. Reynolds began to throw Hamilton supporters out of office and replace them with Davis men. Provisional Governor Pease resigned in a huff. Reynolds assumed the governorship himself. Between April and December 1868, Reynolds issued 200 orders concerning political removals and almost 2,000 appointments before the state election. For the most part the general put Radical supporters in office. He also saw to it that Davis men got the federal patronage. Of course, not all of the appointees were guaranteed, die-hard Radicals, but the message was there—vote right or get out. When the election showed that the governor's contest hinged on the votes in two counties, Reynolds threw these votes out of the tally as tainted and Davis became governor. The Republicans also managed to win three of the four congressional seats.

But Reynolds was not done yet. With the approval of the Grant administration he appointed all elected men to office ahead of time. This meant that they would be federal employees rather that state elected officials until the actual reentry of Texas into the Union. All had to take the ironclad oath (promising they had never given aid to the Confederacy). The Hamilton men who slipped through the initial culling process before the election could be hit once again. Because of Hamilton's cooperation with the Democrats, many of his supporters locally who ran for office and won could not take the oath—too many had Confederate backgrounds. Reynolds appointed Davis-approved men to take their places, often times the very men who had lost the election to the Hamilton ticket in the first place. Then the state legislature met and finished the Reconstruction process by ratifying the Fourteenth and Fifteenth amendments. Next they considered electing U.S. senators. Reynolds was among the frontrunners. But newspapers castigated him statewide for running for office in a body he had largely manipulated into office. Ultimately he withdrew his name. Texas rejoined the Union in March 1870, nine years after leaving it.

General Reynolds remained behind in command of the army, which was now transferred to the frontier. He tried once more for the Senate seat in 1872 but failed to gain the support necessary to win. He followed the army out onto the Great Plains to fight the Sioux and Cheyenne. Locating one of their key villages on the Powder River in 1875, Reynolds's column launched an attack that was only partially successful, destroying the teepees and pony herd. Critics blamed him for leaving the dismounted warriors behind to fight again the following year at the Little Big Horn, Custer's last stand. A court-martial followed, and although the facts bore out Reynolds's tactics, he resigned from the army under a cloud.

Reynolds demonstrated that, despite the controls built into the American system of government, the sweeping powers of military rule contained in the Military Reconstruction Acts could easily lead to arbitrary righteousness and even wrongdoing. Although most officers did not wield those powers with his partisan skill, it took only a few to make such abuse a reality. And lost in the crass political struggle were African Americans, whose well-being had prompted Reconstruction in the first place.

See also Army and Reconstruction; Canby, Edward R. S.; Davis, Edmund J.; Griffin, Charles; Military Reconstruction Acts.

References Baggett, James Alex, "Birth of the Texas Republican Party" (1974–1975) and "Origins of Early Texas Republican Party Leadership" (1974); Boatner, Mark M., III, *The Civil War Dictionary* (1959); Carrier, John P., "A Political History of Texas during the Reconstruction" (1971); Crouch, Barry A., *The Freedmen's Bureau and Black Texans* (1992); Ramsdell, Charles W., *Reconstruction in Texas* (1910); Richter, William L., *The Army in Texas during Reconstruction* (1987), *Overreached on All Sides* (1991), and "'We Must Rubb Out and Begin Anew'" (1973); Robinson, Charles M., III, *A Good Year to Die* (1995); Sefton, James E., *The United States Army and Reconstruction* (1967); Self, Zenobia, "The Court Martial of J. J. Reynolds" (1973); Shook, Robert W., "Federal Occupation and Administration of Texas" (1970); Sinclair, O. Lonnie, "The Freedmen's Bureau in Texas" (1969); Vaughn, J. W., *The Reynolds's Campaign on Powder River* (1961).

Rifle Clubs

The rifle clubs were groups of armed white gunmen who intimidated black and white Republicans at elections in the mid-1870s, shot rival candidates and their supporters, and watched the polls to limit opposition voting. They often disguised their intentions by giving themselves ludicrous titles like the First Baptist Sewing Club, the Allendale Mounted Baseball Club, or Mother's Little Helpers, to stay within the bounds of federal and state law.

See also Redemption of the South from 1874; Shotgun Plan.

Ruby, George (1841–1882)

Born in New York City, George Ruby maintained that his father was a wealthy white man, but reality points to his parents as Ebenezer and Jemima Ruby; Ebenezer was a black clergyman and farmer who raised George in Portland, Maine. Ruby grew up receiving a fairly good local school education, but although racial discrimination was not a standard practice in Maine, there was enough to demonstrate to Ruby what being black in America could mean. In 1860 Ruby moved to Boston and became involved in a Haitian immigration project that was to show the world that blacks from the United States could manage on their own. Ruby went to Haiti to report on the group's progress, but the scheme turned out to be a failure. Throughout the rest of his life, Ruby was to display an interest in African American economic improvement (including education), believing that it would undercut political and social rights if it were not established first. When Ruby got back to the United States, the Union had occupied the southern third of Louisiana, so he joined hundreds of other Northerners and went there to educate the newly freed slaves on the necessities of citizenship. As the army began to expand into the backcountry, Ruby became a teacher in St. Bernard Parish. He then went over to the Freedmen's Bureau as the army turned educational activities over to it. As a bureau teacher Ruby was assaulted in East Feliciana Parish, thrown in a bayou, and told to get out of the area if he valued his life.

In September 1866, because Louisiana schools were plagued with financial problems, Ruby followed many other teachers to a new, more promising field in Texas. The superintendent there was Edwin Wheelock, who had served in the same capacity for the army in wartime Louisiana. Ruby worked in Galveston and the surrounding area. He soon established himself as a good teacher and a man of integrity, even among local whites. In 1867, Bvt. Maj. Gen. Charles Griffin hired Ruby as a Freedmen's Bureau inspector with a primary responsibility for education. Ruby also organized black temperance societies as he traveled about the state, extending his influence considerably. With the passage of the Military Recon-

struction Acts, however, Ruby decided to look for a better way to help his people—he would become a politician and help write the constitution and laws of the entire state. Ruby returned to Galveston to organize the local Union Loyal League, a Republican political front. At this time it seems that Ruby was still feeling his way along, mainly being used as an intermediary between white Republicans (mostly Scalawags) and black voters. But Ruby soon discovered that these men's declarations of support for blacks rights were merely theoretical; they had no intention of sharing power or socializing with any African American who thought for himself.

In the autumn of 1867 Ruby broke free from being a white man's lackey and announced his candidacy for a delegate's position at the state convention. The whites who had backed him as a political organizer now spoke out against his "divisive" move. Cut out of ordinary Republican circles, Ruby went out on his own. Black voters were controlled by the Union Loyal League, which he still managed. And there were so many black Republican voters in Galveston that Ruby could effectively deny election there to anyone. Nominated by the league, Ruby then demanded that the regular Republicans back him, too. Led by blacks, members overrode objections of the white party leaders and quickly endorsed Ruby's candidacy. His election was assured.

When Ruby arrived in Austin for the convention, he found that many knew him only as a Radical Republican, probably because he was in favor of equal rights and suffrage for African Americans. But Ruby was more—he was a skillful politician. He knew how to advance his goals through moderate speech, behind-the-scenes manipulation, and coalition building. He was elected convention vice president, the first recognition of his talents. After his election, Ruby worked to advance his program of black education, economic development, and legal protection through the curbing of violence. He faced an uphill battle because all but ten of the conventions delegates were whites. But the whites were divided among themselves. Republicans alone had three groups, plus the black delegates. Then there were Democrats, some of whom might co-operate on some issues and others who would oppose everything. By careful planning and a surprise announcement, Ruby scored his first victory by becoming the head of all Texas Union Loyal Leagues by one vote.

The convention stalled in its efforts to address other problems, such as declaring all laws in effect since secession as null and void, the splitting of Texas into more than one state to reflect black and white loyal support and isolate the former Confederates, and disfranchisement of higher-ranking Confederates. The failure of the convention to either divide the state or disfranchise whites meant that Ruby and black Texans in general were in for a long haul. The state had a majority of white voters, most of whom were quite hostile to black aspirations as free persons. Ruby went back to Galveston, where local Republican whites once again tried to limit his power. An altercation between him and a white Republican led to a riot that had to be put down by the police. This event, along with the decision to allow all men to vote without restriction, caused Ruby to side with 22 other delegates to defeat the constitution. As such he became allied with the Radical Republicans, led by E. J. Davis, although Ruby considered Davis less dedicated than Morgan Hamilton, a true Radical willing to adhere to principle to the end.

Ruby, meanwhile, asked Davis to delay the election to allow him to mobilize the Union Loyal League and announced his desire to run for state senator from Galveston and several cotton counties to the southwest. Davis quickly created a compromise platform that mimed the Moderate Republican version and appealed to the state military commander, Bvt. Maj. Gen. Joseph J. Reynolds, for backing with the Ulysses S. Grant administration. Reynolds, a personal friend and classmate of Grant at West Point, thought he had a deal with Davis in which he would be elected U.S. senator in exchange for his cooperation. He

got Grant to delay the election and to authorize numerous appointments to office that would assist the Davis ticket during the election. Ruby ran on the Davis ticket against a white Republican opponent. National Republican support proved crucial as the federal customs house collector backed Ruby and gave him a veto on all federal appointments in the area. Ruby won the election, but the closeness of the Republican election statewide, in which Davis was saved only by Reynolds's partisan counting of the vote, proved that Ruby would have to work closer with local whites to gain anything for his black constituents.

To solidify his African American voter support, Ruby still relied on the Union Loyal League in the countryside and on a union of black laborers on the Galveston Docks. This support would prove critical not so much for Ruby but for his protégé, Marcus Cuney, in the 1880s and 1890s. Ruby also built himself up as the intermediary between whites and the Davis administration. All local patronage and adjustments went through Ruby. He also voted on the many economic measures—railroads, banks, and insurance companies—that appealed to white businessmen and coincidentally provided jobs to local blacks. But he refused to compromise his stand in favor of equal rights. He stood in favor of measures to create the state militia (to guard the polls), the state police (to replace the Confederate-tainted Texas Rangers), public schools, and equal access to public accommodations. Because school administrators were patronage appointments, Ruby gained another way to influence voters on his behalf.

Meanwhile the whites were becoming more organized against the Davis regime and his backers like Ruby. Local elections proved that most whites had not voted in 1870 and that the Democrats were going to carry Ruby's district and eventually the whole state. Ruby supported Grant's reelection to keep the national administration in his corner. He also managed the renomination of Governor Davis in 1873, relying on his organization of black voters to provide the necessary clout. But it made little difference.

The Democrats took Texas that year, and an attempt to fight it out in the streets failed when Grant decided to live with the electoral results. There would be no help for Ruby from Washington or Austin—he would have to campaign against the power of Galveston's white Democrats alone. He decided to back a white Republican for his own senate seat, and although local blacks wanted him to run for the house seat from Galveston, Ruby recognized the inevitability of defeat and refused to enter the race. He received numerous write-in votes anyhow.

After the election, Ruby moved to New Orleans, where racial conditions were a bit more to his liking. He worked as editor of P. B. S. Pinchback's *State Register*. He campaigned on behalf of the exoduster movement that sought to move Southern blacks onto free land on the Kansas plains. Yet he never abandoned his original idea that African Americans would have to earn racial harmony by increasing their own economic power. He testified before a congressional hearing that blacks would stop migrating into Kansas only when they could make a living and have their civil rights respected where they lived. But Ruby's influence as a black leader of the late nineteenth century was cut short when he died in New Orleans of a malarial attack at age 41 in 1882.

See also African Americans and Reconstruction; Davis, Edmund J.; Reynolds, Joseph J.

References Barr, Alwyn, *Black Texans* (1973); Crouch, Barry A., "Self-Determination and Local Black Leaders in Texas" (1978); Moneyhon, Carl, "George T. Ruby and the Politics of Expediency in Texas" (1982); Pitre, Merline, "George T. Ruby" (1985); Smallwood, James, "G. T. Ruby" (1983); Woods, Randall B., "George T. Ruby" (1974).

Scalawags

Scalawags were native white Southerners who supported Reconstruction and the Republican party. Scalawags included obstructionist Union and Confederate deserter elements of the Civil War, as well as those former Confederates who for whatever reason believed that Reconstruction meant the dawn of a new day in the South. But the Scalawag label was the brand of a "traitor." According to the legend, these whites turned against those of their own race and background to support the Carpetbaggers, soldiers, and African Americans who brought about the changes implicit in the Military Reconstruction Acts—essentially the social, economic, and political equality of blacks. Scalawags were labeled low-born "white trash" who backed corrupt government, unprecedented self-aggrandizement, and Yankee military rule. While there might be some compassion for the position of newly freed African Americans and some understanding of the roles of Carpetbaggers as outsiders, the Scalawags received nothing but condemnation and hatred. In the end it would be shocking to see how much of Reconstruction relied on these native white Southerners.

The Scalawag stereotype has been etched into the American psyche by popular histories like Claude Bowers's *Tragic Era*, novels like Margaret Mitchell's *Gone with the Wind*, and scores of Hollywood motion pictures from D. W. Griffith's *The Birth of a Nation* through David O. Selznick's *Gone with the Wind* to a dozen lesser works very popular in the 1950s. It reached its epitome in popular treatment in the educational television production of Alistair Cooke's *America*, later brought out as a coffee-table book with the same title. The term is so ingrained in the tale of Reconstruction that even modern historians, who find it reprehensible, confess to being compelled to use it despite its pejorative context, the term "native white" not being powerful enough to replace it.

The appearance of slave-state Republicans in Congress and statehouses began during the Civil War in the unseceded border states. Unlike white Republicans from the seceded states, whose election would come from the support of enfranchised emancipated blacks under the *Military Reconstruction Acts*, these men were the product of loyalty oaths that restricted the political privileges of pro-Confederates. It was not unusual for state and federal authorities to interpret such oaths broadly, often equating Republicanism with loyalty. The army often stepped in to extend the oath from voters to officeholders, purging the border of all politicians suspected of having Southern sympathies.

The "purer" the state legislatures became in Missouri, Kentucky, Maryland, Delaware, and West Virginia, the more thorough the loyalty oaths were administered to keep Republicans in power, with the full acquiescence of the Abraham Lincoln administration and the president himself. The seceded state of Tennessee belongs with the border states on this matter; it was held back in its Republicanism until the end of the war only because the loyal area of eastern Tennessee was occupied continuously by the Confederate army for its strategic railroad line. The full impact of Union Republicanism and disfranchisement of Rebels through loyalty oaths came in Tennessee's ratification of the Fourteenth Amendment in 1867; Tennessee was the only ex-Confederate state to do so, the others still being dominated overtly or covertly by proto-Confederates. Nationally the Republicans from former slave states were decisive in the passage of Military Reconstruction and were supporters of its harshest provisions, many of which (like complete disfranchisement of ex-Rebels) were dropped from the final legislation, much to the party's disgust. It was only the rise of antiblack sentiment in these states that led to these oaths being repealed and Democrats coming back to power as the whole region, loyalist upper South and Confederate lower South, was "redeemed" in the 1870s.

Potential Scalawags could be found early on in the pro-Union areas of each Southern state. Unionism, however, could not account for the numerous white Republican voters present in all states during Reconstruction, particularly in the Deep South (where Scalawags accounted for as many as 30 percent of the voters in Mississippi alone). Who were these people? Were they "white trash," Confederate deserters, traditional ne'er-do-wells? Around the time of World War II, historians began to look deeper into the makeup of Scalawag ranks and came up with some surprising results. Led by David Donald, who was strongly seconded by C. Vann Woodward and Thomas B. Alexander, historians discovered that the Scalawags were not poorer whites but members of the respected prewar upper classes. The common thread among such men was their support of the antebellum Whig party—the nationalists led by Henry Clay of Kentucky—who were in favor of strong federal actions on behalf of business and agriculture, including high protective tariffs, internal improvements (building roads, canals, and railroads), and a national banking system. That is to say, they were adherents to a party that had contributed much to the philosophy of the Republican party's Civil War domestic program (both Abraham Lincoln and William H. Seward, among other Republicans, were former Whigs).

All things considered, Whigs were natural Republicans because they could tolerate the liberation of the slaves, had no fear of being socially "contaminated" (any more than they feared the common white socially), and liked the Republican notions of rebuilding America through federal aid and coordination. Donald asserted the Scalawags-as-Whigs notion first for Mississippi, and Woodward and Alexander extended the process into the rest of the South. Woodward made it central to his thesis of how the Compromise of 1877 was manufactured and who the rulers of the South after 1877 really were, although all whites by then called themselves Democrats.

Another wrinkle to the notion of upper-class Scalawags was T. Harry William's revelations about what was known as the Louisiana unification movement. As with the Whig proponents, Williams found business- and plantation-oriented whites who were disgusted by the excesses of the Carpetbag governments in the state, particularly the high property taxes that went into paying for what the rich saw as unnecessary governmental expenses. It was obvious that the major bloc of Reconstruction supporters were African Americans. The rich had little to fear from contact with blacks. These white Southerners had ruled over the former slaves and would never be economically, politically, or socially challenged by them. They knew how to "manage" blacks—at least, so they thought.

Williams posited that these men, led by ex-Confederate general and native Louisiana Creole Pierre G. T. Beauregard, made overtures to black Louisianans to unite with them to block the Reconstruction monetary excesses for which Louisiana was so infamous. Their platform, put forward in cooperation with upper-class black conservatives (so prominent in New Orleans from the prewar free black community), included complete political equality with blacks, an equal division of political offices by race, a plan whereby African Americans could become landowners, no discrimination in hiring, and integration of all public accommodations and services. But the movement failed. The unification leaders could not gain any other white support and could not convince backcountry blacks that the movement had any sincere basis beyond its desire for fewer taxes—there was no real equality to be forthcoming. Former slaves wanted more, like the public finding of social services, higher wages, shorter hours. All of this cost money, the very thing the white unifiers wanted to avoid. The Carpetbaggers could always outbid the conservatives when it came to such desires, so the black field hands refused to cooperated with the unifiers. The result was that the unifiers felt driven to become the leaders of the white counterrevolution of 1876. Although Williams did not make much of it, the Southern areas of Louisiana where the unifiers were strong also represented regions of former Whig control in the state.

By the 1960s the Whig thesis of Scalawag identification came under fire. Led by John V. Mering, the new historians saw more to Scalawag aspirations than a disguised Whig doctrine. Indeed, Mering thought that any yearning reminiscent of Whigs had disappeared in the postwar South or, if it existed at all, was one of many determining factors in Scalawags' motivations. The Whig thesis seemed most persuasive for North Carolina and Tennessee, but its application elsewhere was questionable. William C. Harris took on Donald's Mississippi analysis directly and in his reexamination of Mississippi Scalawags found that unionism was a more important factor than Whig philosophy. Other later Scalawags were mostly ex-Confederates who adhered to the Republican party because they believed that it was the only way to complete Reconstruction; because the election of Ulysses S. Grant marked the end of Radicalism in the national party, which was likely to move toward the "reasonable" center; and because of the party's program of public schools and internal development of the state after the adverse results of the war. These ideals were crushed when Grant refused to back the more moderate gubernatorial aspirations of his brother-in-law, Lewis Dent, the Scalawag favorite. James L. Alcorn was seen as too extreme in 1869, although he was a centrist relative to later Carpetbag candidates like Adelbert Ames.

The same criticism appeared in studies of Alabama and Louisiana Scalawags. Sarah Van V. Woolfolk found Alabama Scalawags to be upper-class men, well educated, varied in their political past, and highly experienced in the politics of state and nation. Frank Wetta questioned the political experience of Louisiana Scalawags, seeing them more as mid-level party functionaries. But he identified men who were relatively well educated for their time, experienced in political parties and with an unfortunate tendency to quarrel over personality as well as philosophy among themselves and with the Yankee Carpetbaggers. They were strong nationalists who were persistent in their unionism rather than sharing any Whig past and were not well disposed to blacks as free people; they were tough and cynical spoilsmen typical of the post–Civil War era and were few in number at any rate. Most of these studies saw Scalawag influence in Republican councils as strong at first, then declining markedly, during the Reconstruction period.

But there were others who looked at the Scalawags more in the light of famous black historian W. E. Burghardt DuBois—from a social or economic class perspective. DuBois reveled in a pseudo-Marxist analysis of Reconstruction, one that saw the white and black proletariat join to bring true reform to the South, only to be split apart by the bourgeoisie's appeal to racial differences. Williams was the first to attack this analysis directly in regard to Scalawags in his study of the Louisiana unification movement. But the argument for the Whig origins of Scalawags had the same economic criticism implicit within it. In the mid-1960s Allen W. Trelease and Otto H. Olsen took another look at Scalawags and found them, particularly as voters, to be more like what DuBois has theorized: small white farmers from Union areas who disliked the rich planters before, during, and after the war. Taking a look at the South as a whole, Trelease examined the voting records of 843 counties during the election of 1872. He made several assumptions: that all blacks voted Republican, that there were too few Carpetbaggers to skew the figures, and that wherever the Republican vote exceeded what might be expected in terms of the African American population it identified Scalawag strongholds. Trelease also admitted to the faults of the 1870 census in counting blacks in the South, that fraud might make figures inaccurate and that ex-Confederate disfranchisement might be a factor.

Nonetheless, despite difficulties with the census, Trelease found that there was a tendency for black counties to vote Republican and white counties to go Democratic (or whatever passed for Democratic in the various states). But in three places—western North Carolina, eastern Tennessee, and northwestern Arkansas—white Republicans were widespread. Every Southern state except Louisiana was represented by at least nine Scalawag-dominated counties. Texas had more, a fact attributed to the influence of Mexican and German immigrants. South Carolina showed up probably because Rebel whites refused to vote. Most of the Scalawags voters came from hilly, remote, and less prosperous areas of the South, but these areas were full of mineral and timber resources and the water power to utilize them if properly developed.

The states were too poor to undertake this development. It had to be a federal project, and that meant the Republican philosophy of government (there would be a shift in philosophies during the New Deal of the 1930s, during which the Democrats would absorb this concept of governmental development, with Republicans emphasizing private enterprise as the key). The plantation areas of East Texas, Louisiana, Mississippi, Alabama, Georgia, and Virginia had the fewest white Republicans. Scalawag voters were small farmers, who had little in common with slavery and slaveholders and could accept the black vote because it did not exist in their home counties. These people had been Jacksonian Democrats before the war. They believed in equality and reform, said Olsen, who studied North Carolina and supported Trelease's conclusions. The Whig counties from before the war went Republican only if they had Appalachian highlanders or numerous African Americans from slavery days who voted Republican. The Whigs/planters/businessmen of Donald, Woodward, and Alexander's analyses were conspicuous by their absence. Indeed, Olsen found them by and large to be mostly opposed to Reconstruction.

Using many of Trelease's methods and assumptions, Warren Ellem reexamined Mississippi in light of the criticism levied against Donald, Woodward, and Alexander; he concentrated on the 1871 congressional and state elections (the first actual elections since Mississippi had been readmitted to the Union under the Military Reconstruction Acts). He found that counties with black populations under 30 percent, generally white hill counties, did not support Republicanism as Trelease and Olsen theorized. Instead the Scalawag vote was among whites living in the predominantly black counties. This meant that the Scalawags were part and parcel of the old plantation system and came from counties that used to vote Whig before the Civil War. He maintained that Scalawags never accounted for more than 15 percent of all white voters or 6 percent of the total vote, white and black. Many left the party when Carpetbagger Adelbert Ames was elected in late 1873. Defection in Republican ranks was not accompanied by a corresponding rise in Democratic votes; hence the defectors did not participate in the 1876 contest that resulted in the white takeover of the state. Ellem, in effect, took the whole argument back to square one.

Were the Scalawags lower- or upper-class whites? The historians disagreed. But the work of Armistead Robinson on the state of Georgia offered a possible way out. The problem in Georgia was common to most Southern states. There were not enough Carpetbaggers and blacks to carry the day for Republicans. The party had to have a Scalawag vote of some proportions. As luck would have it, there was such a group available: the white, essentially non-slaveholding farmers of the Piedmont region in the foothills of the Appalachian Mountains. These people had for generations been angry with the way slaveholders dominated state politics. During the war many had dodged the draft, deserted the Confederate army, and even fought against the Confederacy. Now that the Civil War was over and the plantation aristocracy was defeated, these men, in debt from the vicissitudes of the war, entered commercial agriculture for the first time, eschewing their normal subsistence food production in favor of money crops. It was a rough gamble. The droughts following the war exacerbated their debt condition. They sought help from the Democratic state government (still dominated by planters, under Andrew Johnson's Reconstruction), but such help was not forthcoming. The Republicans, who entered politics with the ouster of the Democrats through the Military Reconstruction Acts, saw their opportunity, said Robinson, and acted. They promised debtor relief, homestead exemption to taxes, state social services, public education, and an eight-hour workday. The white farmers took it.

But Republicans were still not satisfied with the makeup of their party. They wanted to broaden it beyond the white and black working classes, continued Robinson. In seeking out white upper-class support—primarily from men like Joseph E. Brown, Georgia's obstreperous Civil War governor who had given exemptions to Confederate service to war opponents by enlisting them in the state militia with service at home—the Republicans set the stage for their own downfall. An antagonism broke out between Georgia's Scalawags, between Brown and the poor white farmers. Brown was an advocate of the "New South," a commercial-industrial state financed by the very men who held the small farm debt and hated delay in debt payments or repudiation of debts. He became a Republican to preempt the white and black lower classes in their populist economic program. The skills of Brown and people like him in Georgia and most other Southern states were sufficient to drive the yeoman farmer from the Republican party. Only after the economic policy split between the upper and lower classes within the Republican party did the racial equality problems arise, especially when black conservatives (black voters were as split among themselves as whites) experimented with, for example, Louisiana's unification movement, only to be turned down by their fellow field hands. Then whites joined forces to destroy biracial politics by getting rid of the African American voter who had a mind of his own. There were just too many interests to harmonize in Southern Republicanism, concluded Robinson.

If so many white Southerners were voting Republican by 1872, what in the world caused this vote to disappear and go over to the opposition within four short years? The black counties remained largely Republican in 1876. The loss of the Scalawag vote to Republicans throughout the South became a vital reason Reconstruction failed.

Olsen postulated in several of his writings that a major reason white Republicanism failed in the South was its moderation. Indeed, the period of the greatest Republican success in the South was under the Military Reconstruction Acts. Almost immediately the party leaders backed off any notion of further radical reform. The black vote had been won; nothing more seemed necessary to do. But the white farmers expected programs designed to help them. Moreover, when opponents launched their attacks on the Republicans through the Ku Klux Klan and its kindred organizations, only in Arkansas and to a lesser extent in parts of North Carolina did the Republicans defend the Scalawags from intimidation. Mostly the Republicans just yelled for the federal army, which was slow in coming, if it showed up at all. Moderation, said Olsen, led to impotence.

Another reason Scalawags deserted Republicanism for Redemption becomes evident from Mills Thornton's study of taxation. Thornton maintained that Republican fiscal policies caused a rise in property taxes that the small farmers—who were still in economic depression from the devastation of the war, especially in terms of access to markets, and were further ruined by persistent drought throughout the Reconstruction years—could ill afford. Before the war, it turned out, about two-thirds of the state taxes were paid by larger plantation owners. This gave the white lower and middle classes a free ride on the tax bill. But after the war, the increase in social services, not in the least more public education (the South had more public education than Yankees suspected before the war) expanded by the inclusion of the large free African American population for the first time, caused the Republicans to raise tax rates and include everyone in the deal. Add in the inflation of the panic of 1873, which caused higher prices for all goods and services, and one had a white farmer class that received fewer services at a higher cost than before the war.

Voting Republican had not paid off. The increase in taxes went to programs for blacks, who owned little land and paid hardly anything for their badly needed new public service benefits.

Finally, historian Peter Kolchin determined that Scalawags tended to be put on the Republican ticket in marginal districts of support, leaving Carpetbaggers and African Americans the safe seats. Using an analysis of congressional seats, Kolchin demonstrated that the South revealed three basic patterns of election to federal office. First there were the Scalawag states, Tennessee, North Carolina, and Georgia. Here Scalawags dominated their congressional delegations by three to one and only one black was elected. Then there were the non-Scalawag states of South Carolina, Mississippi, Louisiana, and Florida. The latter elected no Scalawags to its congressional seats. In Louisiana Carpetbaggers outnumbered Scalawags by four to one. In the congressional delegations of South Carolina and Mississippi, blacks and Carpetbaggers outnumbered Scalawags by two to one. Only in Louisiana were no blacks elected to Congress. Finally, there were the mixed states of Texas, Arkansas, Alabama, and Virginia. Here Scalawags and Carpetbaggers represented their states in Washington almost equally.

The differences among the Republicans parties in each state owed much to the parties' racial compositions. The greater the African American voter participation, the more likely it was that blacks and Carpetbaggers would be elected. Redemption also followed a similar course. The Scalawag states were all redeemed by 1871, the mixed states by 1874, and the non-Scalawag states by 1877; three of the latter (Louisiana, Florida, South Carolina) figured prominently in the election of 1876 and the Compromise of 1877. Further, Kolchin held that Carpetbaggers tended to be the driving force behind Republican leadership in the South. Northerners and blacks alike seemed to see that Southern whites were but temporary Republicans at best, ready to drift away from the party at the first sign of trouble,

especially when their opponents made an appeal to race. And Southern whites felt this distrust, especially when it resulted in adverse economic policy that favored the North. They considered it unmanly and unfair and eventually joined the other side, driven away by the complications of too many interests, few of which were their own. Reconstruction is the most difficult period of American history to understand, and nowhere is this fact better shown than in the ins and outs of being a Scalawag.

See also African Americans and Reconstruction; Alcorn, James Lusk; Army and Reconstruction; Brown, Joseph E.; Brownlow, William G.; Carpetbaggers; Davis, Edmund J.; Grant and Reconstruction; Holden, William W.; Ku Klux Klan; Longstreet, James; Moses, Franklin J., Jr.; Redemption of the South before 1874; Redemption of the South from 1874.

References Alexander, Thomas B., "Persistent Whiggery in Alabama and the Lower South" (1959), "Persistent Whiggery in Mississippi" (1961), "Persistent Whiggery in the Confederate South" (1961), and "Whiggery and Reconstruction in Tennessee" (1950); Bowers, Claude, *The Tragic Era* (1929); Carter, Hodding, *The Angry Scar* (1959); Coulter, E. Merton, *The South during Reconstruction* (1947); Donald, David H., "The Scalawag in Mississippi Reconstruction" (1944); DuBois, W. E. Burghardt, *Black Reconstruction* (1935); Ellem, Warren, "Who Were the Mississippi Scalawags?" (1972); Harris, William C., "A Reconsideration of the Mississippi Scalawag" (1970); Hume, Richard L., "The Arkansas Constitutional Convention of 1868" (1973); Kolchin, Peter, "Scalawags, Carpetbaggers, and Reconstruction" (1979); Mering, John Vollmer, "Persistent Whiggery in the Confederate South" (1970–1971); Olsen, Otto H., "Reconsidering the Scalawags" (1966); Robinson, Armistead L., "Beyond the Realm of Social Consensus" (1981); Sansing, David G., "The Role of the Scalawag in Mississippi Reconstruction" (1969); Seip, Terry L., *The South Returns to Congress* (1983); Stampp, Kenneth M., *The Era of Reconstruction* (1965); Thornton, J. Mills, III, "Fiscal Policy and the Failure of Radical Reconstruction in the Lower South" (1982); Trelease, Allen W., "Republican Reconstruction in North Carolina" (1976) and "Who Were the Scalawags" (1963); Wetta, Francis Joseph, "The Louisiana Scalawags" (1977); Wiggins, Sarah Woolfolk, "Alabama" (1980); Williams, T. Harry, "An Analysis of Some Reconstruction Attitudes" (1946) and "The Louisiana Unification Movement of 1873" (1945); Woodward, C. Vann, *Origins of the New South* (1951) and *Reunion and Reaction* (1951); Woolfolk, Sarah Van Voorhis, "Five Men Called Scalawags" (1964) and *The Scalawag in Alabama Politics* (1977).

Schofield, John M. (1831–1906)

Born in New York state, John M. Schofield graduated from West Point in 1853, seventh in a class of 52. He served in Florida and taught philosophy at West Point until 1860, when he received a leave to teach physics at Washington University in St. Louis. When the war began he became chief of staff to Brig. Gen. Nathaniel Lyon's small loyal army and fought at the Battle of Wilson's Creek. Schofield was elevated to brevet brigadier general of volunteers shortly afterward and was put in charge successively of the Military District of Missouri, the Military District of Southwest Missouri, and the Army of the Frontier. He was promoted to brevet major general, but the commission expired (a common occurrence in the Civil War command system); after some intense paper shuffling he received a new appointment as brevet major general and was assigned to the Army of the Cumberland, then in Tennessee. But the Missouri command beckoned him again, and by 1864 Schofield had served in numerous command areas but had managed to miss every major battle.

By the spring of 1864, however, with his return east of the Mississippi River to command the small Army of the Ohio (actually the Twenty-third Corps) in Bvt. Maj. Gen. William T. Sherman's advance on Atlanta, Schofield's battle history was to change. Schofield's corps was involved in every major fight on the road to Atlanta, often being used as the maneuver or reserve element as Sherman tried to pin down the Confederate army with rest of his force. After Atlanta was captured, Sherman began his March to the Sea, sending a large part of his force (including Schofield's units) back to Tennessee. There Schofield was nearly cut off from Nashville by a quick advance of the Confederates under Lt. Gen. John B. Hood. But Schofield managed to extricate his force by a quick march past the Rebels at Spring Hill into the fortified town of Franklin, where he stung Hood's attacking forces in a fight that cost the South five generals in an ill-advised charge across two miles of open ground. Schofield then withdrew to Nashville, fol-lowed by Hood. At Nashville Schofield was a part of the final attack that destroyed Hood's army in one of the truly decisive battles of the war. In 1865, Schofield was transferred to North Carolina and was in on the surrender of the Confederacy's second biggest force at Goldsboro to General Sherman. Schofield received a brigadier generalship in the regular army for his war service and later received the Congressional Medal of Honor for saving the Union army at Wilson's Creek.

After the Rebel surrender, Schofield was put in charge of the Military District of North Carolina. Having had much administrative and battlefield experience in the South, he was convinced that moderation was the only way in which a lasting peace might be constructed out of the throes of the war. Schofield expressed his feelings in a letter to Lt. Gen. Ulysses S. Grant in May 1865. He proposed that the South be placed under military rule and that all laws then in force and not in disagreement with the results of the war be declared in force. Persons who took an oath of future loyalty would be allowed to elect members to a state constitutional convention that would abolish slavery, repudiate secession, and restore the state to the Union. The people would then vote on the new constitution and elect new representatives to Congress. If Congress approved of the state's actions, the state would have its members seated and be fully restored. Schofield would not guarantee African Americans the vote (he condescendingly believed them unready for the franchise and in need of education and training in government) but would leave that up to the states as guaranteed in the U.S. Constitution.

Schofield never got a chance to put his plan in operation because he was sent to Europe to convince France to pull its troops out of Mexico and abandon the usurping government of Emperor Maximillian. When he returned he was assigned to command the Department of the Potomac, which included the state of Virginia. The importance of army commanders like Schofield in early Reconstruction cannot be overemphasized. They were the ones who influenced the policies of President Andrew Johnson's Reconstruction, not the other way around, a myth created by Radical Republicans and mouthed by historians ever since. Both sides, rebel and loyal, often preferred the protection that the army gave them from each other. Blacks, however, found that the army tended to side with their former masters and expected them to go back into the fields and work, whether they wanted to or not. The army often instituted a pass system as rigorous as before the war, and volunteer Union soldiers were quite racist in their assumptions about the black American's position in the new society. The army also succored refugees of both races, transported refugees and former Rebel soldiers to their homes (before the arrival of the Freedmen's Bureau), fixed the sharecrop system in place, and gave aid to transportation infrastructure repairs. It was also the army that spoke out on behalf of forgiving its enemies for the war.

For his part, Schofield fit in well with the army's approach to early Reconstruction. Although he was privately against the Fourteenth Amendment from a philosophical point of view (he thought it unjust and unwise, especially the punishment clause of section 3—the idea the federal government could interfere with a traditional state prerogative such as voter qualifications—and the fear that this would put blacks at the mercy of poorer whites who hated them), but he advised publicly that the state legislature accept the amendment as a peace offering. To refuse it, said Schofield, would merely lead to harsher conditions for readmission. Virginia failed to heed his advice. And the result was the Military Reconstruction Acts within a year. As President Johnson recognized when he vetoed these acts, the character of Reconstruction in each state and military district depended upon its commanders. Schofield took over the First Military District, which was composed solely of Virginia, on 13 March 1867. In some ways Virginia was lucky. It had no competing state in its military district. All policy would come from one man, and that man

John M. Schofield, *military director of Reconstruction in Virginia*

was Schofield, who ran a tight operation.

Schofield's first order as military district commander continued operation of the existing government. He would make such changes as circumstances demanded. Although the state objected to military rule philosophically, it accepted Schofield as better than most commanders. Schofield was not loathe to exercise his absolute power when necessary, but he tried to keep such cases to a minimum. When disarmed whites complained that blacks had weapons, Schofield organized a white militia to quell fears of racial violence. He also refused to let any armed group of any color patrol the roads and streets—that was a job for the army alone. He was willing to deploy force to guarantee African Americans the right to vote. He warned newspaper editors that he would not allow irresponsible baiting of the Reconstruction process. He refused to permit speeches by known crowd manipulators trying to incite riot and dissension. But in all cases he allowed the act to take place before moving against it. Whenever a civil office turned up vacant, Schofield appointed a new man in consultation with local leaders. He made few removals.

When it came to registration, Schofield made sure each three-man board was made up of one army or Freedmen's Bureau officer and two local loyal citizens. He preferred native whites or former Union army officers. Each board had a committee of three whites and three blacks to challenge the enrollment of any voter. Any challenge had to be for a real cause that was written down. Schofield saw to it that whites were disfranchised for participation in the rebellion, under the Fourteenth Amendment double-oath provision (this applied to anyone who had taken an oath to the Union before the war followed by another to the Confederacy during the war). Knowing that the political contests would be hot affairs, Schofield took extra precautions to protect campaigners and participants at political rallies. All civil authorities were warned to protect people and property. Should they fail to do so, Schofield divided Virginia into seven subdistricts, each with its own six or eight sitting military commissioners. Schofield granted the commissioners complete judicial authority to act when civil officials refused. Recalcitrant officials would be removed from office and replaced by a man who would act. But Schofield used the removal power sparingly, preferring to cajole cooperation.

Schofield then drew up new districts from which delegates would be selected to the state constitutional convention. The apportionment was partial to whites, but the election went to the Radical Republicans and their black allies only because whites refused to participate. In Richmond, Schofield kept the polls open an extra day. Democrats accused him of trying to build a Radical majority; Schofield countered that he wanted the fullest vote, regardless of party. Since Schofield was always an outspoken moderate, it seems unlikely that any fraud was intended. Shocked at the Radical nature of the convention delegates, whites called their own convention to rally those opposed to any constitution.

As expected, the Radical convention (the legal one) produced a constitution that disfranchised a large number of whites based on their support of the Confederacy after taking an oath to the United States before the war; one could not hold office without taking the ironclad oath. But it also provided for a statewide system of public schools and uniform taxes on property and all incomes over $600 a year. Schofield campaigned mightily, but in vain, to get the disfranchising clauses out of the document. He also objected to the popular election of county offices, an approach that he feared would place blacks in positions they could not handle. Schofield preferred that these positions be made appointive. Failing to get his ideas incorporated into the constitution, the general backed the defeat of the document at the polls. He wrote General Grant of his fear that a victory would brand the Republican party for decades as the party of the extreme. He hoped that a second convention might produce a more conservative constitution with full white participation this time. Meanwhile Schofield suspended all elections until Congress appropriated money for them. He believed that in this way Congress could indicate its approval or disapproval of Virginia's Reconstruction.

Schofield's cautious course got him in a lot of trouble from the state's Radical Republicans, who wanted the patronage that offices would offer. Elections for state, city, and county offices were due under the old constitution, and the Radicals wanted Schofield to declare the offices vacant and appoint men recommended by them. General Grant agreed with Schofield's desire to keep elected men in office past their term expiration dates to maintain a continuity of government. Then Schofield could fill vacancies from death or resignation and make whatever removals he might desire after finding more respectable people to fill them than the hack politicians who clamored for them. Schofield then acted to remove the one man he had wanted to throw out for almost a year: the governor, Francis Pierpont, who had been pardoning blacks convicted by state courts, which in turn had been supervised by Schofield's military commissions. Schofield once thought of taking over the office of governor himself but instead put Henry H. Wells, a Vermont Carpetbagger, in Pierpont's place. He rationalized this bit of philosophical inconsistency by stating that Pierpont was limited to one term by state law, whereas other continuing officials were not.

Pierpont raged about his removal, charging Schofield with favoring Carpetbaggers over native loyal white Virginians, but a military investigation ordered by Grant exonerated Schofield. Then Schofield exercised the right Grant gave him to clean out Virginia when he found conservative men to fill the offices. It was an arduous task. Schofield had removed incumbents and filled nearly 500 offices by May 1868, but he feared that approval of the Fourteenth Amendment nationally would force him to declare the rest open. He believed that he was running out of qualified men of a moderate to conservative turn of mind on Reconstruction. But he never had to solve that problem, since he was made secretary of war upon the failure to impeach President Johnson. After the expiration of Johnson's presidency, Schofield served in various departmental command slots and was superintendent at West Point. In 1896, the grade of lieutenant general, which had expired upon the death of Philip H. Sheridan in the late 1880s, was re-created for him as an honor for his faithful service. Virginia's representatives and senators spoke on his behalf during the hearings on his appointment, fondly remembering his moderate course during Reconstruction. He retired within the year and published his memoirs a year after that; he died nearly a decade later in St. Augustine, Florida.

See also Army and Reconstruction; Impeachment; Military Reconstruction Acts.

References Alderson, William T., "The Influence of Military Rule and the Freedmen's Bureau on Reconstruction in Virginia" (1952); Boatner, Mark M., III, *The Civil War Dictionary* (1959); Eckenrode, Hamilton J., *The Political History of Virginia during the Reconstruction* (1904); Gerteis, Louis S., *From Contraband to Freedmen* (1973); Lowe, Richard G., "Republicans, Rebellion, and Reconstruction" (1968); Maddex, Jack P., Jr., *The Virginia Conservatives* (1970) and "Virginia" (1980); Majeske, Penelope K., "Virginia after Appomattox" (1982); McDonough, James L., "John Schofield as Military Director of Reconstruction in Virginia" (1969); Schofield, John M., *Forty-six Years in the Army* (1897); Sefton, James E., "Aristotle in Blue and Braid" (1971) and *The United States Army and Reconstruction* (1967); Smith, James Douglas, "Virginia during Reconstruction" (1960); Taylor, Alrutheus A., *The Negro in the Reconstruction of Virginia* (1926).

Scott, Robert K. (1826–1900)

A Freedmen's Bureau agent and Carpetbag governor in South Carolina, Robert K. Scott was a Pennsylvanian by birth. He impressed observers as a typical self-made man—always looking for something better and using native wit to achieve it. At 16 he set out for Ohio, where he studied and practiced medicine. After fighting in the Mexican War, he followed the lure of gold to California, where he prospected and reestablished his practice. Upon failing to strike it rich, he returned to Ohio. Here he became quite prosperous as a physician and surgeon. With the advent of the Civil War he joined the Sixty-eighth Ohio Volunteers as a major. He fought in most of the campaigns in the western theater of the war and was promoted to brigade leader for his actions at Vicksburg. Captured outside of Atlanta, Scott tried to escape by jumping from a moving railroad prison car. He hurt his back and was recaptured. Later freed after a prisoner exchange, he made the campaign from Atlanta to the sea and through the Carolinas. He wound up the war with the rank of brevet major general and an opium drug habit (very common among injured Civil War soldiers and usually revealed by the use of laudanum, a morphine and whiskey mixture), courtesy of his everlasting back trouble.

After the Confederate surrender Scott received the assignment of assistant commissioner of the Freedmen's Bureau in South Carolina. His job was to reconcile the freedmen with their former masters and provide an equal place in U.S. society for African Americans. His worst task was to examine the land titles purchased by black families. Though 40,000 African American men, women, and children were affected by these deals, Scott and his agents could prove actual title for only 1,565. The remaining titles went back to their original Rebel owners under President Andrew Johnson's pardon policy or were fraudulent from the outset, having been sold by dishonest federal agents. Scott then proceeded to supervise the labor contract-making process for 1866. He was a fairly decent man in his approach, often liberalizing the terms that his agents agreed to and seeking the elusive ideals of black equality and freedom. He was most disturbed when freedom to whites seemed to mean abandoning the old, young, and infirm blacks, and killing off the intelligent, who were condemned as insolent. But the general opinion of most South Carolinians was that General Scott was a man of integrity and propriety in his bureau dealings.

As Military Reconstruction approached in 1867, Scott busied himself with his bureau responsibilities and the ordering of his large landholdings in Ohio and Michigan (he was worth over $300,000 at that time). He also sought loans and investments from Northerners to help alleviate the constant near-starvation among African Americans in South Carolina. But he achieved little on the last account. He did his best to keep the bureau and its agents out of Republican politics and Union Loyal League activities. When four of his agents won election to the state constitutional convention, he dismissed them to counter Democratic charges that the bureau was merely a political front for the congressional Reconstruction program. He received notice from Washington that the bureau was to be slowly shut down and that all independent assistant commissioners were to be mustered out in January 1868. This meant that he would lose his job and his commission at that time. Scott had already declined an attempt to put his name up on the Republican ticket for governor. But prominent South Carolinians of all colors and political philosophies urged him to reconsider. The convention nominated him over his protests. Once he decided to accept the nomination, he immediately changed his mind about bureau political meddling. He ex-

pected all of his agents to turn out a big black vote for him, and he easily won the election. And the heretofore friendly attitude of whites toward Scott began to change for the worse as the prospect of "Negro Rule" became evident.

Scott arrived in Columbia with a national reputation as the best among the Carpetbag governors elected in 1868's reconstructed South (Warmoth in Louisiana, Reed in Florida, and Clayton in Arkansas were the others; all other states had Scalawag governors or had not yet completed their conventions). He was viewed as well educated, a man of property, and reasonable in race matters. Scott began his administration by asking that all political disabilities against Confederates be removed. He approved of the end of the Freedmen's Bureau, asked that the federal government remove the occupying troops, and called for segregated public schools. He brought his wife and son to the state and bought a fine house for them to live in at Columbus (no mean task, as the city had not yet been rebuilt after being burned during the war). Friends, relatives, fellow politicians all begged him for position or loans—Scott was known as a generous man.

But Scott had bigger problems than those at Columbia. Throughout the state, reports flowed in that whites were organizing regulator clubs to attack loyal whites and blacks. This activity was not new but it was intensifying. Republican party officials were prime targets. Scott blamed the night riders on Democratic leadership in South Carolina (in the person of ex-Confederate hero Maj. Gen. Wade Hampton) and in Washington (in the person of Frank Blair, Jr., Scott's former superior in the army), who had pledged to overthrow Reconstruction. Scott managed to get Hampton, once one of the richest men in the South and now almost bankrupt, to issue a public message calling for peace and racial cooperation. As Scott would find out, Hampton was an expert at appearing reasonable on the surface while maintaining the attitude of a tough partisan underneath.

The Scott administration opened with

much hope for success, but it soon degenerated into a farce. Most of its failure had little to do with Hampton's opposition; instead the problems were internal and endemic to the Republican party. Scott himself had many personal liabilities. He was an opium addict, although few knew it. He also had an eyesight problem. He could see well enough to read, but he could not look at more than one word at a time. And to do this he had to read with a manuscript right up in his face. This meant that he worked slowly and could not speak in public from notes. He had to memorize any public oration. Hence he spoke little. His wife was an alcoholic, which meant that she had to be watched closely during all of the entertaining that a governor's wife had to do. This was difficult when every politician liked liquor and every whiskey drummer wanted to ply the statehouse with his finest offerings. Yet, as governor, Scott was more typically South Carolinian than might be expected. He shared a longtime dream of state politicians from the days of John C. Calhoun—the idea of a railroad from Charleston to Cincinnati and Memphis. Scott was a real estate agent himself, and along with several high-ranking Republicans he over-invested the state in rights of way and other lands, the latter of which were to be sold to freedmen. Some of the exorbitant prices paid were pocketed by politicians on the government boards that supervised these dealings. The Great Barbecue, as such corruption of the period was known, had arrived in South Carolina, and the governor and a lot of his friends cashed in.

The main impediment to the overthrow of Reconstruction was that black voters outnumbered white by some 30,000. In an honest election the Republicans would always win. This meant that white Democrats had to resort to other means that put a premium on fraud and violence. The result was a more methodical reorganization by the Ku Klux Klan. To face off against the Klan, Scott had the state militia, a poorly armed force of about 15,000 men. The rank and file were black, their officers white, mostly Carpetbaggers. It was a lousy way to catch the well-mounted, well-armed light

General Robert K. Scott

cavalry represented by the Klansmen, but the militia did offer some support as poll guards. Moreover, the Republican ranks were not unified. More radical blacks and more moderate whites threatened to splinter off from the party. This was balanced by the fact that many Democrats were willing to cooperate with Republicans if the party did not become too radical. These Democrats were led by James L. Orr, another Confederate war hero, who believed that the only way to appease blacks was to become a Republican. Orr's defection confused the Democrats greatly. The result was a sort of balancing act in which Scott stood with the blacks and managed to get himself reelected and send three of his four congressional candidates to Washington.

After the 1870 congressional election Scott faced two more problems. In the white upcountry the Klan, disgusted with Orr's compromising, began to ride again, taking revenge on those who had voted Republican or were members of the state militia. In the low country, led by state attorney general Daniel H. Chamberlain, planters and businessmen protested the higher taxes the spendthrift government cost them. Republican moderates and Fusion Democrats like Orr begged Scott to turn on his black backers, who could then unfairly be blamed for the fraud of Scott's cronies. In the midst of a shooting war with the Klan, Scott refused. He was investigated by a taxpayers' convention, but nothing could be proven against him personally. Meanwhile he worked with the federal government, which appointed special prosecutors and sent in the army to arrest the Klansmen and check their excesses. By the end of 1871, an uneasy peace reigned.

Still, the problem of corruption haunted the Republican party. Everyone knew it existed; the questions were, who was behind it and how much did Governor Scott know about it? In December 1871, Scott maintained his own innocence and shifted the blame to others in a message to the state legislature. He accused state Democrats of running up the debt before he took office and of now trying to unfairly destroy his administration through "Kukluxism applied to the state credit." But the legislature refused to buy Scott's assertions. Members of his own party, angry at political patronage snubs, joined with Democrats to introduce a resolution of impeachment. The goal was to filibuster for the rest of the session and then let Scott face the voters with the suspicion unanswered in 1872. But Scott managed to cancel a debt owed him by the speaker of the house, Franklin J. Moses, Jr., a Scalawag, and the filibuster failed when Moses refused to give the floor to the anti-Scott men. Rumors of bribery were everywhere. At the same time the railroad venture went broke, and disgusted stockholders took Scott and others to trial for the loss. This also made the Scott regime fodder for the national Liberal Republican revolt against the corruption of the Ulysses S. Grant administration.

With public criticism running high, the Republican party in South Carolina needed a new look. They found it, when Scott refused to seek another term, in Scalawag legislator Franklin J. Moses. Moses, however, nominated by heavy black support, turned out to be a truly corrupt Radical Republican. Scott announced that he would seek to be elected by the new state legislature to the U.S. Senate. A Republican victory at the polls elected Moses and produced a large majority in the state legislature, but that did not help Scott. His defeat was complete, and he retired to live the life of an ordinary citizen. In 1874 he put himself up as a possible gubernatorial candidate, after Moses's true excesses made Scott's indirect corruption minor by comparison. However, the nomination went to Moses, who was opposed by Daniel H. Chamberlain, attorney general under Scott and an honest man. Chamberlain eventually won the contest. But two years later, unable to shake the aura of corruption associated with the Republicans (built mostly by Moses and Scott's friends), Chamberlain and the Republicans lost out to a Democratic landslide, led by Wade Hampton (who was now governor) and his violent Red Shirt supporters.

Hampton did not waste much time in purging the state of what remained of Republicanism. He brought charges in criminal court against Chamberlain and Scott. Chamberlain had already left the state, and Scott decided it was a good time to take a prolonged "business" trip to Ohio. Scott's wife remained behind to wind up his affairs. Eventually she and their son went back to Ohio, too. The charges against Scott were continued in court for some time before being dropped. Scott continued to sell real estate in Ohio and Michigan, still a relatively wealthy man. He was, however, very protective of his son, because he and his wife had so many addictions to opiates and liquor. When he found that a neighbor had helped the 14-year-old get drunk, Scott shot the malefactor dead. In court he claimed that the whole shooting was an accident and that the victim had made a threatening move toward him. The jury bought the excuse and found him not guilty. Scott continued to live in Ohio, visiting South Carolina once again in 1896. He died from a cerebral hemorrhage in 1900, just after joining the Methodist church.

See also Carpetbaggers; Chamberlain, Daniel H.; Moses, Franklin J., Jr.

References Abbott, Martin, *The Freedmen's Bureau in South Carolina* (1967); Boatner, Mark M., III, *The Civil War Dictionary* (1959); Current, Richard N., *Those Terrible Carpetbaggers* (1988); Fowler, Wilton B., "A Carpetbagger's Conversion to White Supremacy" (1966); Holt, Thomas, *Black over White* (1977).

The Second Mississippi Plan

The Second Mississippi Plan was named after the 1890 Mississippi constitutional convention's idea of disfranchising blacks within the scope of the Fifteenth Amendment by using factors other than race. This approach proved more subtle and enduring than the violence of the First Mississippi Plan of 1876 (also known as the Shotgun Plan) in controlling the state for the white powers that be.

See also Disfranchisement.

Segregation (Jim Crow)

Historians differ as to the origins of racial segregation in the South, the so-called Jim Crow system. Many of the traditional white characterizations of African Americans had a condescending vaudevillian nature about them, stemming from the old minstrel shows so popular a century and a half ago; this image was originally an intentionally concocted racial stereotype designed to help relegate blacks to a second-class place in American society. These shows are forgotten now, but two classic minstrel roles were fated to be around longer than the rest of the minstrel genre: Zip Coon and Jim Crow. Zip Coon was the urbane, sophisticated city Negro who wore the latest fashion and perambulated about flashing a big grin and spinning his cane. His name endures in a derogatory term for African Americans. Jim Crow was his country cousin, poor, dressed in rags, lacking the streetwise demeanor and aggressiveness of Zip Coon. The more widely known term *Jim Crow* came to describe a system of seg-

regation (informal at first, legal later) that permeated American society from the days of slavery to the middle of the twentieth century, when the Reverend Martin Luther King, Jr., and others successfully attacked its legal and moral precepts.

Originating in the North, Jim Crow was designed as a system to replace slavery, which had gradually been eradicated there during and after the American Revolution. Segregation spread from the cities, because that is where traditional white control first broke down, in a gradual process that continued until the Civil War in the South. By 1865, the end of formal slavery under the new constitutional amendments meant that a new social, political, and economic provision had to be made for African Americans. Few whites considered complete equality as the answer. The result was segregation, disfranchisement, and peonage. The key to this process was the willingness of the North to assist or acquiesce in the result, as indicated by the failure of Congress to pass the Lodge Force Bill in 1890, which would have put teeth in the Fifteenth Amendment prohibition on using race as a condition of voting.

Historians argue whether there were "forgotten alternatives" existing during Reconstruction and the following Gilded Age that delayed the creation of the Jim Crow laws, or whether the system was so entrenched by popular convention that the laws merely formalized an existing tradition. According to historian C. Vann Woodward, the men who overthrew Reconstruction (the Redeemers) did so on the basis of race, but they did little to legalize their proscriptions into law. Indeed, until the disfranchising state conventions of the 1890s, blacks voted and actively participated in the Southern political process. African Americans still held political office in significant numbers, and formal segregation was not really needed because blacks were still adjusting to the different patterns, bearing, and nature between slavery and freedom.

Looking at legal segregation, Woodward best represents the view that Jim Crow was an afterthought, that there once existed at least three other possible solutions that competed well with the idea of separation between black and white society. The first of these was the liberal race philosophy, one that demanded complete racial equality, an end to segregated public schools, and complete participation of African Americans in the electoral process with open access to public accommodations. The two main white proponents of this concept were George Washington Cable of New Orleans and Lewis H. Blair of Richmond. Admittedly the two were not very influential, but their viewpoint was circulated and considered.

Another possible alternative to formal segregation that Woodward found was the conservative race philosophy. This was the view of the Redeemers and the Democratic party establishment. These men were largely former slaveholders who had little fear of African Americans socially, politically, or economically. Indeed, they feared the political power of poor whites more than that of blacks. The upper-class whites believed that each element of society had a natural place with its own responsibilities and obligations to others. An African American man's correct place was as a wage earner who had an obligation to vote for his white "betters." When blacks complied, the Bourbons (the name given to the Redeemers) had an obligation to rule with African Americans' interests in mind (provided they did not cost too much) and protect them from the lynch mobs of common white men that plagued the South during this era.

Should African Americans fail to meet their obligations (as the Redeemers envisioned them), they would be voted right anyhow and turned over to the lower-class whites for vengeance. Politically this philosophy worked on what was called the fusion principle. With blacks and lower-class whites splitting the vote nearly evenly, the Bourbons held the crucial swing vote. The Bourbons would fuse with the black Republicans, giving the latter a portion of the offices and what few state programs were available, and blacks would vote the Bourbons into office, negating the vote of the

white farmers and their radical ideas, like a fair vote and numerous social programs. The Bourbons kept formal segregation from happening and refused to isolate blacks from access to public accommodations. It was not exactly a perfect system from the African American point of view, but it did guarantee blacks some participation in a normally hostile system.

Woodward's final alternative to formal segregation was the radical race philosophy. The "radicals" in this context were not the Radical Republicans in Congress from the days of Reconstruction, but the poor white farmers of the South. These men had a visceral hatred of blacks because they competed economically, socially, and politically for the same crumbs of the societal table in the postwar South. They had favored the race separation of slavery, which kept blacks from openly competing with them for land, jobs, and social status. This explains why they and their fathers fought in the ranks to the bitter end for the Confederacy. But these whites also hated the Bourbons and anyone of their race who was rich. But their hatreds made them easy prey to the Bourbons' crass manipulation in the political arena. The Redeemers played on poor whites' hatred of blacks and glorified the "Lost Cause" of the Confederacy to blind them to an even bigger, more important reality—blacks and lower-class whites had essentially the same interests in government. Both groups wanted the large landowners to pay taxes to guarantee public schools, internal improvements to get their crops to market, and various social programs like debtor relief, lest everyone lose the family farm and have to go to work in the textile mills or become tenants on the land of others.

The Bourbons skillfully played the race card; they warned white farmers that if the ranks of racial solidarity were broken, blacks would rule as they had done during Reconstruction with national Republican patronage. Those whites who wished to challenge the Redeemers' control of the post-Reconstruction South had to bolt the Democratic party and form third parties like the Readjusters (who wanted to reassess taxes on the rich and gain debtor relief), Independents (anyone of any political philosophy who was not a Bourbon), and Greenbackers (those who wanted easier credit through inflated paper money). As the decade of the 1890s approached, the proliferation of these third parties made it evident that the usual system was about to fall apart. The new radical farmer's party—the People's party, or the Populists—began to flirt with a new concept of race. Southerner farmers, black and white, at last realized that they were being suckered by the Bourbons into a race war when they ought to be more cognizant of class differences. The Bourbons were in deep trouble, so they redoubled their efforts; they ridiculed those whites who would "desert" their race and forget all the whites who fought for the Confederacy, and they practiced racial intimidation and electoral fraud on a scale heretofore unimagined. Then they blamed the whole thing on African Americans.

Then the Bourbons turned to white farmers and promised them that if all whites could agree to remove the "evil" influence of blacks from Southern politics and society, whites could afford to disagree on political issues and have honest, competitive elections. Of course, the very things that disfranchised the black farmer also applied to the white farmer. To bar blacks from voting while allowing illiterate whites to do so, the disfranchising laws had exceptions; the grandfather clause enabled any man, literate or not, to vote if his grandfather had voted, and the understanding clause permitted the registrar alone to determine whether an applicant could understand a passage read to him and to substitute that understanding for a literacy test. Of course the registrar could arrange things so that whites "passed" and blacks "failed" this test. But the real effect was to disfranchise both black and white poor (no white in his right mind would admit to being unable to read or write or use the grandfather clause, which amounted to the same thing). So, historian Woodward concluded, the formal laws on segregation became reality for the first time, 30 years

after the end of the war and 20 years after the end of Reconstruction. They gave poor whites a feeling that no matter their actual place in the social, economic, and intellectual life of the region, they were different from blacks and were part of the "superior" white ruling class. It was not much, but it was something, and in time it became the only thing that counted.

Nowhere in the South does Woodward's thesis ring truer than in Louisiana, which has always been a bit different from other Southern states, partly because of the moderating Gallic influence on matters of race and the presence of the South's largest metropolis, New Orleans. The result was a trading center that exuded much influence beyond its boundaries and inspired much tolerance in ethnic, religious, economic, and racial diversity, in marked contrast to the rural South. City life tended to blur distinctions and undermine rigid controls. The Civil War merely increased these trends. While the city's white population grew one and a half times from the end of the war to the turn of the century, the black population tripled until it was 27 percent of the 287,000 people dwelling in New Orleans. Throughout the era, New Orleans saw two important developments: black protest and a wavering color line.

New Orleans blacks began their drive for racial equality when the city fell to Union troops in 1862. The ability of African Americans in the city to organize and articulate their views was assisted immeasurably by the presence of the South's largest population of free persons of color, many of whom were the sons and daughters of the state's most prominent white men and had been educated in the most reputed universities in Europe, especially France. The demand for racial equality in Louisiana, whatever it might have been in the rural South, was not an imported product. Demonstrations began immediately for access to all forms of public accommodation; however, without political rights (something President Abraham Lincoln had suggested with an eye on the New Orleans free black population), little had been achieved. Then came the Military Reconstruction Acts, and African Americans received the right to vote. Black Louisianans moved actively into the fray, winning some important victories. The 1868 state constitution provided for full rights to all citizens, including the vote, integrated public schools, and open public accommodations. Various laws and military edicts reinforced these concepts with local law, assisted by the Fourteenth and Fifteenth amendments federally.

Whenever the color line did not fall willingly, blacks protested its presence. The notorious "star cars," segregated streetcars, fell first. New Orleans' public schools were opened to those of all races, although this was the first institution to later revert back to separation in 1877. In a few notable cases, some facilities became segregated for the first time in the state's history. The Metairie Jockey Club excluded blacks and refused to bow to economic boycott. Under pressure from the White League (a Redeemer military organization), the French Opera House curtailed black attendance in 1874. Blacks went to court in several cases, but the results were not always satisfactory. One African American collected $1,000 in damages after being refused service in a saloon. But Josephine DeCuir lost her case against segregated steamboat accommodations, after winning in a lower court, when the company appealed to the United States Supreme Court (*Hall v. DeCuir* [1878]).

The DeCuir episode and the withdrawal of federal soldiers in 1877 signaled that Reconstruction was over, but blacks refused to back off in their quest for equal rights. Modest accomplishments were made. Streetcars, railroads, beach resorts on Lake Ponchartrain, some theaters, and all houses of prostitution opened up to blacks, with female and (in one case) male prostitutes. Hotels and restaurants generally denied service to all nonwhites. Very important was the ability of white and black labor to cooperate and divide up jobs. This cooperation continued until the depression of the 1890s became so severe that racial cooperation broke down in the face of joblessness. But the casual contact among races was in general harmonious. Grog shops, gambling dens, dance halls, Mardi Gras, and interracial baseball contests were biracial in their audiences. The 1884 Cotton Centennial Exposition was open to all races, and African Americans participated in "Louisiana Day" activities without regard to race, eliciting favorable comments from none other than Mississippi's ex-U.S. senator, Blanche K. Bruce, the chief commissioner of the "colored exhibit."

Admittedly race relations began to deteriorate in the 1880s, but many marveled that this process took so long. Several different reasons are given for the delay in the arrival of formalized Jim Crow in New Orleans. There was a fear of federal intervention until the Lodge Force Bill failed in 1890. Blacks remained a powerful voting bloc throughout the period and were not intimidated into voting crookedly by the Redeemers as in much of the South; they were actively independent and shifted their votes among white and black candidates on the basis of the candidates' stands on racial equality. But a new day was dawning, as racial separation swept the nation. New Orleans was no exception. Social distance became the rule unless the black was a servant of the white. A new state constitution and new state laws made the process legal for the first time. A race riot in 1900, the first since early Reconstruction, cemented race relations for the next 60 years.

Other historians, such as Howard N. Rabinowitz, believe that one must distinguish between exclusion (where blacks were kept out of a public accommodation) and segregation (where blacks were allowed into a public area but were restricted as to how, when, and where). Thus segregation becomes a forgotten alternative itself when compared to what else existed—namely, total exclusion. And by creating services for themselves upon being excluded from all-white facilities, blacks contributed to segregation's eventual triumph. After the end of the Civil War, Southern whites saw little need to change things racially from the way they were before the conflict. Blacks received no public services under the slave regime and few if any under the first governments during Presidential Reconstruction. Poorhouses, schools, orphanages, asylums, and institutions for the deaf, mute, and insane were for whites only. It was the army and the Freedmen's Bureau who introduced segregation to the South when they insisted that blacks must have their own copies of all services traditionally given to whites. But it was not until the Military Reconstruction Acts appeared in 1867 that the South was forced to truly grant new rights, privileges, and services to blacks. According to Rabinowitz, the difference between conservative white Southern policy and the Republican program can best be seen in three areas: militia service, education, and welfare facilities.

The Republicans were the first in the South to arm African Americans as members of the state militia (at least since the Louisiana example of using free black militia units in the 1814 Battle of New Orleans). But in deference to Scalawag racial mores, the rank and file were segregated by race, and black officers were permitted only in black units. Similar events took place in forming black fire companies (which often doubled as militia cadres in those days). The Republicans were the first to provide blacks with public education and opened separate schools in all states but Louisiana and South Carolina (states in which black politicians played decisive roles in Reconstruction governments). When it came to public welfare services, Republicans once again provided these to blacks for the first time, but facilities were segregated by building or by rooms or wings within a single building. In public conveyances, however, particularly railroads, the races were segregated by car. But the Jim Crow car often did double duty as a smoking car for males of both races. Except in New Orleans, streetcars were segregated by race, with blacks having cars of their own. Hence segregation replaced exclusion to the benefit of newly freed black citizens.

The theme of Reconstruction, according to Rabinowitz, was that Republicans provided public services for blacks but under a guise that later would be called "separate but equal." Few Republicans were truly egalitarian. The party as a whole, especially the Scalawag elements, had no desire to "Africanize" the South. Even party celebrations were often racially exclusive. Hence the South fairly bristled at the idea of Charles Sumner's Civil Rights Act of 1875, which would have guaranteed integrated public accommodations in all aspects of everyday life. The basic response of the Redeemers was to ignore the implications of the act until the U.S. Supreme Court declared it unconstitutional in the 1883 *Civil Rights Cases*. Instead the Redeemers continued the separate-but-equal notion brought South by the Republicans. Indeed, several states opened up institutions (like schools, orphanages, and asylums) that had never been opened before to blacks within their boundaries during the Gilded Age. But everything was segregated by race. Important here was the construction of separate waiting rooms at railroad stations. In restaurants, hotels, saloons, and prostitution houses, all services and facilities went from total exclusion of African Americans to segregation, epitomized by the Jim Crow Bible at the courthouse for use by black witnesses. As Frederick Douglass noted, an African American had more freedom on steamboats as a slave because "he could ride anywhere, side by side with his master.... As a freeman, he was not allowed a cabin abaft the wheel."

As whites persisted in exclusion or segregation of blacks, continues Rabinowitz, African Americans began to respond by opening their own places of services and amusement. They also began to drive whites out of teaching and sought to administer black colleges themselves. Part of this was a response to exclusion, but much of it represented a creation of their own group identity. Custom, then, had separated the races during and after Reconstruction. But there still remained some doubt among whites as to the permanency of the informal system. By the 1890s, this was resolved by laws that reinforced what had existed informally all along. The only real forgotten alternative, concludes Rabinowitz, was that segregation replaced total exclusion and thus represented an extension of public accommodations to blacks that had been denied before the war.

No instance came to typify the Jim Crow reality as of the 1890s better than the Louisiana case of *Homer A. Plessy v. Judge John H. Ferguson.* Louisiana had had a segregated system of streetcars, before and during the Civil War, that had been integrated by a concerted effort during Reconstruction. In 1890, prompted by Congress' failure to pass a new civil rights bill designed to enforce renewed Southern compliance in black rights of citizenship, Louisiana state passed a new law segregating railcars by race. Plessy himself was classified as an octoroon, one-eighth black; his participation in the case was no accident, but rather an intentional setup, under the theory that an almost white person might advance the cause with fewer racial hangups in the higher courts than an easily distinguished black person. Indeed, New Orleans blacks had tried to get an earlier case instituted by another light-skinned black, Daniel F. Desdunes, and won, but since his destination was outside the state, the Louisiana Supreme Court merely ruled that the law could not be applied to interstate travelers under the interstate commerce provisions of the U.S. Constitution, which left the law intact inside Louisiana. So Homer A. Plessy took a train ride from New Orleans to Covington, purchasing a first-class ticket and sitting in a "whites only" car. He was promptly arrested.

In the ensuing trial, Plessy's attorney was Albion W. Tourgée, a former Carpetbagger in North Carolina. Disillusioned with Reconstruction, Tourgée had gone to New York and written two novels on the subject, *A Fool's Errand* and *Bricks without Straw*; blacks had him brought to New Orleans specifically to plead Plessy's case. He maintained that the Louisiana law violated Plessy's rights under the Thirteenth and Fourteenth amendments. But Judge John H. Ferguson held that the case was a state matter and Plessy could be proscribed from riding in all but designated cars. Tourgée

appealed the case, eventually to the U.S. Supreme Court, as *Plessy v. Ferguson.* There, on 19 May 1896, the highest court in the land ruled that states could legally separate the races provided that "separate but equal" accommodations were provided for all those so proscribed. Technically the decision involved only transportation, but other decisions expanded this rule into all areas of American life. Custom had become enshrined in law; "separate but equal" had become a constitutional and legal reality as never before.

See also Abolitionists and Reconstruction; African American Education and Reconstruction; Disfranchisement; Economic Disfranchisement; Washington, Booker T.

References Bacote, Clarence A., "Negro Proscriptions, Protests, and Proposed Solutions in Georgia" (1959); Berlin, Ira, *Slaves without Masters* (1974); Bernstein, Barton J., "Case Law in Plessy *v.* Ferguson" (1962); Blassingame, John W., *Black New Orleans* (1973); Calcott, Margaret Law, *The Negro in Maryland Politics* (1969); Cartwright, Joseph H., *The Triumph of Jim Crow* (1976); Chesteen, Richard D., "Bibliographical Essay" (1971); Collins, Charles Wallace, "The Fourteenth Amendment and the Negro Race Question" (1911); Dethloff, Henry C., and Robert P. Jones, "Race Relations in Louisiana" (1968); Eaton, Clement, *The Waning of the Old South Civilization* (1968); Fischer, Roger A., "A Pioneer Protest" (1968), "The Post Civil War Segregation Struggle" (1968), "Racial Segregation in Antebellum New Orleans" (1969), and *The Segregation Struggle in Louisiana* (1974); Foster, Gaines M., *Ghosts of the Confederacy* (1987); Groves, Harry E., "Separate But Equal" (1951); Lemmons, Sarah M., "Transportation Segregation in the Federal Courts since 1865" (1953); Lewinson, Paul, *Race, Class, and Party* (1964); Litwack, Leon F., *North of Slavery* (1961); Logan, Frenise A., *The Negro in North Carolina* (1964); Logan, Rayford W., *The Betrayal of the Negro* (1965); McMillan, Neil R., *Dark Journey* (1989); Nathan, Hans, *Dan Emmett and the Rise of Early Negro Minstrelsy* (1962); Osterweis, Rollin G., *The Myth of the Lost Cause* (1973); Rabinowitz, Howard N., "From Exclusion to Segregation" (1974); Rice, Lawrence D., *The Negro in Texas* (1971); Roche, John P., "Plessy v. Ferguson" (1954); Somers, Dale A., "Black and White in New Orleans" (1974); Tindall, George B., *South Carolina Negroes* (1952); Wade, Richard C., *Slavery in the Cities* (1964); Wharton, Vernon L., *The Negro in Mississippi* (1947); Williamson, Joel, *After Slavery* (1965) and *The Crucible of Race* (1984); Woodman, Harold D., "Sequel to Slavery" (1977); Woodward, C. Vann, "The Birth of Jim Crow" (1964), *The Strange Career* *of Jim Crow* (1966), and "The Strange Case of a Historical Controversy" (1971); Wynes, Charles E., *Race Relations in Virginia* (1961).

Seward, William H. (1801–1872)

Born in Orange County, New York, William H. Seward studied law at Union College. Graduating in 1820, he soon left the legal practice and went into politics. Prompted by the mysterious death of William Morgan, who had betrayed the secrecy of the Masonic rituals by publishing accounts of them, Seward ran on the Anti-Masonic ticket for a seat in the state senate and won. From that time on he occupied influential elective and appointive offices, usually with the backing of influential upstate newspaper publisher and political king-maker Thurlow Weed. In 1838 (having changed parties) he became the first Whig governor of New York, initiating many reforms including the removal of political disabilities from foreigners and adjusting high rents that had caused much unrest in cities. He established the museum of natural history and a program of study and signed a law that provided for the trial of fugitive slaves by jury with counsel furnished by the state. During the 1840s he returned to the practice of law but kept his interest in politics up. By 1849 he was elected to the U.S. Senate and became an influential advisor to President Zachary Taylor. At this time Seward gave his "higher law" speech, in which he asserted that there was a law above statute and Constitution that demanded the exclusion of slavery from new states.

Seward's "higher law" speech became one of the battle cries in antislavery circles in the North. Seward continued in the Senate throughout the 1850s, speaking out against slavery as an institution. One of his more famous speeches was the one that expressed his "irrepressible conflict" doctrine, in which he stated his belief that the Union would have to solve the slavery issue and make the nation all free or all slave. His outspokenness made him a presidential candidate for the new Republican party in 1856 and 1860. But Seward was probably too well known, for his seemingly radical pronouncements scared many potential supporters, and he lost out to John Charles Frémont the first time and to Abraham Lincoln the second. Lincoln won the presidency in 1860 with Seward's support and appointed him secretary of state. At first Seward thought that Lincoln was a country bumpkin and incapable of handling the leadership of party and nation. He tried to help the new president out, even suggesting that the nation declare war on France and England to unite itself during the secession crisis. But Lincoln firmly yet kindly put Seward in his place, and Seward went on to become one of the best secretaries of state in American history and a valued advisor to presidents Lincoln and Andrew Johnson.

Seward completely reorganized the diplomatic service and sent brilliant instructions to wise men he recommended for foreign posts. Through his ability, Seward turned the fortunes of the Union around as many European countries were leaning strongly toward recognition of the Confederacy and a divided America. When a federal naval officer, without authorization, stopped a British ship to remove two Confederate ministers going to Europe, Seward and Lincoln cleverly released the men and praised England for her recognition of American shipping neutrality and exemption from search as announced in the War of 1812. He also asserted U.S. rights in what were known as the *Alabama* claims, eventually getting Great Britain to pay up millions in reparations for having built Confederate cruisers in violation of international neutrality law. Seward proved a vigorous defender of the Monroe Doctrine, supporting the Benito Juárez republican regime in Mexico against French incursion.

In domestic policy, Seward supported Lincoln's freeing the slaves by executive proclamation and suggested that the preliminary Emancipation Proclamation be delayed until a Union victory make it look like a forceful move rather than a gasp for salvation that could not be guaranteed on the battlefield. He also was most influential in getting the Thirteenth Amendment added to the Constitution to protect wartime liberation and make emancipation universal throughout the country. As the Union victory seemed assured in the spring of 1865, Seward was severely injured in a carriage accident. Thrown from his vehicle, the secretary suffered a broken arm and jaw. The splints and bandages on his wounds probably saved his life when he was attacked by John Wilkes Booth's co-conspirators intent on destroying the Lincoln government. His son and aide, Frederick, was badly cut as he intervened to protect his father from the knife assault of Lewis Paine. After Lincoln's death, Seward supported Andrew Johnson's Reconstruction policies and opposed the impeachment of the president late in his term. His support of the president led to many imputations and bitter censure in Republican circles, but he supported General U. S. Grant for president and the Republican ticket in 1868.

As secretary of state, Seward was one of the first real expansionists in the last half of the nineteenth century. He negotiated many treaties for annexing some new territories (the Dutch West Indies, the isthmus of Panama, and Samoa) that failed to gain Senate confirmation and one (Alaska) that was accepted. Because the secretary was ahead of his time by about 30 years in his expansionism, the new territory received the ungracious nicknames of "Seward's icebox" and "Seward's folly." But the discovery of gold in the 1890s and the vicissitudes of twentieth-century world politics showed the wisdom of his move. Seward retired in March 1869 and died a few years later at his Auburn, New York, home.

See also Emancipation; Impeachment; Johnson and Reconstruction; Seward and Reconstruction.

References Taylor, John M., *William Henry Seward* (1991); Van Deusen, Glyndon G., *William Henry Seward* (1967).

Seward, William H., and Reconstruction

Although historians traditionally blame Military Reconstruction upon the Radical Republicans, it is possible that as much (if not more) of the blame can be laid at the feet of Abraham Lincoln, Andrew Johnson, and William H. Seward. These men worked to create a new conservative political party, which led the South to resist Reconstruction excessively and resulted in a harsher Reconstruction program in the long run. By the end of the Civil War, Conservative Republicans were on a roll. They had backed and reelected Lincoln in 1864 and, through the person of Secretary of State Seward, had supported the president consistently since 1861. The Radical Republicans, however, had an image of party disloyalty. They had opposed Seward's candidacy for president in 1860, tried to oust him from the cabinet in 1862, threatened Lincoln's Reconstruction policy with the Wade-Davis Manifesto in 1864, bolted the party later that year for John Charles Frémont's so-called Radical Democracy, forced Union Democrat Frank Blair out of Lincoln's cabinet (despite the president's confidence in him) as the price of their reentry into the party, and tried to block Lincoln's renomination.

So by 1865 it was possible that new party coalitions might be in vogue. Democrats had opposed the war with their peace faction, and many War Democrats wanted to drop the party label, as they had done in 1864 by supporting the Lincoln-Johnson Union party ticket. Republicans were a minority party, capable of winning the presidency but not a majority in Congress with the return of the South. At stake was the political control of the United States for a generation or more, if the correct political moves were made. No one realized this more than Secretary of State Seward, who assumed a commanding position upon the death of Lincoln. He worked with the coalition he had assembled in 1864 and 1865 to garner passage of the Thirteenth Amendment through Congress (thus guaranteeing the liberty of the slaves nationwide).

Although the Republicans had managed to get the proposed constitutional amendment through the Senate, the House had proved to be another matter. A strong Democratic party led the opposition, operating under the party's slogan in the 1864 presidential election: "The Constitution as it is, and the Union as it was" (i.e., with slavery). Democrats disliked emancipation (especially through presidential decree) and abolitionists; believed the war was started intentionally to put the Republicans in a congressional majority and pass their domestic program (tariffs, taxes, national banking system, massive internal improvements); and were full of racial prejudice endemic in the North. The Democrats could deny the amendment the two-thirds vote necessary for passage.

Seward had warned Lincoln of the opposition in the House to the Thirteenth Amendment, but Lincoln was insistent that it had to pass. So Seward went to work to build a coalition that would do it. It would not be easy. Most Northern Democrats were from border areas, slave states that had remained loyal to the United States in 1861. But there were others, too, some from Seward's native state of New York. On 31 January 1865, Seward managed to cobble together a coalition that passed the amendment through the House by one vote. Sixteen Democrats had deserted their party, 14 of whom were lame ducks (i.e., were not reelected to office in the past November 1864 elections but were serving until March 1865) and 6 of whom were from New York state. Many suspected bribery carried the day, especially in the form of cash and political appointments. But there was more. Seward let it be known that if the Thirteenth Amendment lobby and cooperation among conservatives of all parties continued, Reconstruction would be short and sweet. Had Lincoln lived, it is possible that the coalition would not have lasted. But with his death, Seward was the conservative heir apparent in the Republican party.

The significance of Seward's manipulations to pass the Thirteenth Amendment is that had he failed it might have drastically altered American history. Lincoln had threatened to call a special session of Congress in the spring of 1865 to reconsider the amendment had it failed in January. Lincoln always doubted that his Emancipation Proclamation was legal since it stretched the limits of his war powers. He was not about to condemn blacks to a return to slavery under an adverse decision by the Supreme Court or some later, hostile Congress. (The South held their slaves who had not already run off well into 1866, just in case the amendment failed to be approved by the states.) He had to have an amendment one way or another. Lincoln's special session would have met in March and April 1865; that is, Congress would not have been out of session when Lincoln was killed, so Johnson would have been prevented from acting alone under presidential proclamation to institute his own Reconstruction program.

In any case, Johnson fell heir to Seward's conservative coalition and its form of Reconstruction: freedom for the slaves, generous terms to the defeated Confederates, quick return of Southern states to the Union, and cooperation among conservatives. However, Johnson saw the coalition differently from Seward (who saw it differently from Lincoln). To Johnson the coalition included all Democratic factions (he had to view the situation this way because the Democrats controlled the governments he established in the South) and excluded both Moderate and Radical Republicans—a critical mistake because the Moderate Republicans were the biggest group in both houses of Congress. Seward would have excluded the Radical Republicans (with whom Lincoln had desired to work) and the Southern secessionist and Northern peace Democrats. Seward would reorganize on the basis of all the middle-of-the-road politicians left over. All three men wanted to include the old Northern and Southern Whigs, the heart of pre–Civil War conservatism. Although Lincoln and Seward saw the coalition as Northern controlled, Johnson envisioned it as Southern controlled, as Democrats had been before the war. And Johnson had no desire to grant the freed African Americans any civil or political rights. Both Seward and Lincoln saw some black rights as essential to freedom. However, all conservative Reconstruction proposals had something in common: they all wanted a quick readmission of the South (to form a revitalized Whig party for Seward and Lincoln, or a greater Democratic party for Johnson). Essentially all the South had to do for the conservatives was free the slaves and forget the war.

See also Congressional Reconstruction; Johnson and Reconstruction; Lincoln and Reconstruction.

References Cox, John H., and LaWanda Cox, *Politics, Principles and Prejudice* (1963); Donald, David H., *Lincoln Reconsidered* (1956) and *The Politics of Reconstruction* (1965); Stampp, Kenneth M., *The Era of Reconstruction* (1965).

Sheridan, Philip H. (1831–1888)

Philip Sheridan is usually said to have been born in Albany, New York, but his family moved a lot and Massachusetts and Ohio have also claimed to be his birthplace. Appointed to West Point from Ohio, Sheridan took five years to complete the four-year program. His academic career was marred by a hot temper. He attacked a much bigger senior cadet with a bayonet for putting him on report. Reason took over before anyone got cut up, and Sheridan merely beat his antagonist with his fists. He managed to keep his appointment only because the review board decided that a willingness to fight was not exactly an unwanted quality in a future officer. After a one-year suspension he graduated in 1853 and was sent off to the Pacific Northwest, where he fought in several short, nasty Indian wars. At the beginning of the Civil War, Sheridan was a quartermaster lieutenant with few prospects. He soon faced a court-martial for improperly giving out vouchers for supplies, but he managed to get out of the command area and back to St. Louis in time to avoid trial. He was a roving horse buyer for the army when the chance for a combat command opened up; shortly afterward, Sheridan became the colonel of the Second Minnesota Cavalry.

Sheridan was a master of the battlefield. He had a brigade of cavalry within a week and a division of infantry in the Army of the Cumberland in just over a month. He played a prominent part in the Battle of Perryville and held on at Stone's River when the rest of the Union line ran in confusion (he probably saved the day). The army made him a brevet major general. Sheridan continued to lead his division at Chickamauga and Missionary Ridge, where he stormed the heights and very nearly captured Confederate general Braxton Bragg and his staff. As it was, only Sheridan's division had the cohesion left after the fight to make a credible pursuit. In the spring of 1864, Lt. Gen. Ulysses S. Grant, who had viewed Sheridan's masterful performance at Missionary Ridge, brought the young general east to put some spirit and organization into the cavalry of the Army of the Potomac.

In Virginia Sheridan bristled at the traditional role of the horsemen as guards and messengers; with Grant's approval he took the cavalry off on a raid to Richmond, hoping to entice the Confederate cavaliers of Maj. Gen. J. E. B. Stuart into a fight. Sheridan accomplished his goal and met Stuart at Yellow Tavern, where Sheridan's men slammed into the Rebel cavalry corps and killed Stuart in the process. Sheridan went on to lead the Union Army of the Shenandoah, where he defeated Maj. Gen. Jubal Early's greybacks in several battles, including one in which he saved his own men from a pending defeat at Cedar Creek and drove the enemy from the field in confusion. Returning to Grant and the Army of the Potomac in 1865, Sheridan took the cavalry corps on a ten-day campaign that finally cornered Robert E. Lee's Army of Virginia at Appomattox and forced the latter's surrender. At the end of the war he was, along with Grant and Maj. Gen. William T. Sherman, one of the best-known Northern generals of the conflict.

But Grant had one more assignment for Sheridan. He was to go to New Orleans and organize an expedition to conquer Texas, as yet unaffected by the war, and to overawe the French forces in Mexico under Maximillian. Sheridan accomplished the task with his usual aplomb, finding the rumors that Texas would fight the Union to be false; he actually opened up communications with Mexico's president, Benito

Juárez. Sheridan then proceeded to transfer numerous surplus arms to Juárez, which caused somewhat of a diplomatic scandal but gave France notice that the United States was not happy about the French incursion into Mexico.

After settling down to the more mundane occupation duties, Sheridan got a real surprise that disturbed the deep recesses of his orderly military soul. Southern politicians were sneaky, behind-the-scenes manipulators, friends one day and backstabbing traitors the next. No matter what reasonable request he might have, there were always complications, negotiations. These men never seemed to recognize an order when they received one. He especially believed that the elected governors of Louisiana (James Madison Wells) and Texas (James W. Throckmorton) were scoundrels. Louisiana particularly baffled him. There was always a second board, another committee that claimed to be more legal than the first. Both state legislatures passed discriminatory Black Codes and rejected the Fourteenth Amendment, and Texas even tried to raise its own militia composed of ex-Confederate soldiers, ostensibly to protect the state's western frontier. It was all highly "anomalous," to use the general's favorite word for describing anything he did not like (he used it a lot, too).

Sheridan had many anomalies to handle in 1866. He was constantly rushing from trouble spot to trouble spot, putting out political fires. First he was off to the Rio Grande, where black Union soldiers had crossed the river to attack a French garrison inside Mexico led by a former Confederate officer. Then it was back to New Orleans, where the city blew up in a race riot designed to prevent loyal men from having a political meeting to reconvene the wartime convention set up under the Abraham Lincoln's Ten Percent Plan. Then it was back to Texas to put down the hostile reaction to soldiers burning the business section in the small town of Brenham. Then it was back to Louisiana to supervise the registration of voters for the new state constitutional convention demanded by the Military Reconstruction Acts. Then he went off to Texas to do the same. It was all very frustrating.

Sheridan sat down and reexamined the congressional legislation to see if he might not clean out some of the political deadwood in Louisiana and Texas to lessen his chores. He targeted Louisiana's Governor Wells first, although General Charles Griffin, Sheridan's Texas subordinate, claimed the right to fire Texas Governor Throckmorton as quickly as possible. General Grant told Sheridan to hold off. He was not sure military commanders had the right to move against elected civil officials. But Grant also said that Sheridan might try removing some lower officials to see what good it did. Sheridan fired one registration officer in New Orleans for intimidating black voters. He reorganized the New Orleans police to require that half be former Union soldiers. Then he moved on the state levee board. In typical Louisiana style there were two boards, one appointed by the governor and another established by the state legislature. Sheridan fired both and set up a third made up of men of his own choosing. He integrated the streetcars in New Orleans. Finally, having weathered these storms, Sheridan fired Governor Wells as a "political trickster and dishonest man" and replaced him with Benjamin F. Flanders. When Wells refused to leave his office, Sheridan told him to leave or be dragged out by a squad of infantry. Wells left. The country went wild, both pro and con.

While Sheridan kept the public eye on his removal policy, he (along with Grant) secretly permitted voter registrars to contravene a decision of the U.S. attorney general that would have liberalized the process for ex-Confederates. Sheridan and Grant looked at the ruling as an opinion with which reasonable men could disagree. Sheridan believed that registrars as the government's representatives in the field ought to have wide discretion in registration. By summer, however, this policy could no longer be kept secret, and President Andrew Johnson ordered Grant to change it. Then, in July 1867, Congress vindicated Sheridan's desire to replace politicians who were "impediments to Reconstruction." Griffin had been pestering him to move against Throckmorton, who became the first official removed under the new act. In retaliation, President Johnson fired Sheridan and replaced him with a general known for his Democratic politics, Maj. Gen. Winfield Scott Hancock.

Although Wells had gone fairly quietly, Throckmorton did not. He published a 13-page address to the people of Texas in which he defended himself and his regime against charges of impeding Reconstruction. Sheridan had refused Throckmorton's request for a face-to-face meeting with him or Griffin; Throckmorton declared that Sheridan refused to allow any debate or disagreement as to policy and instead expected everyone to salute and say "yes, sir" like a boot second lieutenant. If anyone was an impediment to Reconstruction it was Sheridan and his subordinates, claimed Throckmorton. The governor charged Sheridan with covering up three military-civilian incidents in which guilty soldiers got off with no punishment: the Brenham fire, where troops burned the town in drunken response to not being allowed to attend a town dance while inebriated; the Lindley affair, in which a Waco man shot dead two alleged Rebels under military protection who could testify he was a horse thief; and the Walker affair, in which two black soldiers shot dead a deaf man for no apparent reason.

There was more, Throckmorton continued. Sheridan incorrectly ignored the ruling of the U.S. attorney general and forced all voters to take the ironclad oath (one of never having willingly aided the Confederacy) to register; he illegally set aside a state law allowing five judicial districts to disappear by reappointing two Union men and re-creating their districts; he permitted military commissions and Freedmen's Bureau courts to interfere with state courts contrary to a decision of the U.S. Supreme Court; he refused to permit the state to honor the remains of Confederate general Albert Sidney Johnston, an original "Texican," as the body moved from Galveston to Austin for burial; and he wrote a false report

in November 1866 that many blamed for providing Congress with the excuse to pass Military Reconstruction, alleging that "Pride in the Rebellion" was the motive for any attempt by a civil official to discuss a military order.

Actually, the whole argument boiled down to the charge that Griffin had made against Throckmorton: the latter had not violated any law, but he simply lacked the proper spirit for reconstructing the state. Throckmorton hurled the same charge back in the faces of the two officers; he claimed that Sheridan slurred the state's honor when the general supposedly said that if he owned Texas and Hell, he would rent out Texas and live in Hell. Sheridan's defenders, then and now, point out that the general really was not a dictator as charged but more of a man caught up in a situation never before contemplated in American government; if he had a fault, it was his dedication to the results of the war and his manner of dealing with second-rate politicians. But in the end Sheridan got caught up in his own web of half-truths. He had to get rid of Wells and Throckmorton or admit that he and Griffin were wrong. So the governors were removed and Sheridan became, in the words of Richard Taylor (son of one-time president Zachary Taylor and wartime Confederate commandant of Louisiana), "the General of the Radicals."

After his removal from the Fifth Military District, Sheridan was put in charge of subduing the Plains Indians. He went about the job with a ruthless efficiency, turning loose his chief weapon, the Seventh Cavalry under Bvt. Maj. Gen. George Armstrong Custer. The result was the Battle of the Washita, after which many of the Southern Cheyenne came in to surrender. Sheridan is reputed to have said, "The only good Indian is a dead one." Though it is uncertain whether he actually said these words, his deeds matched the words in his way of planning and executing a campaign, just as he had done against the Rebels during the Civil War.

In 1870 Sheridan went to Europe as an American observer for the Franco-Prussian

War. He traveled with the Prussian forces and admired their ability to mobilize soldiers using their railroad system. They in turn admired his ability to conduct campaigns in the no-quarter style of the Uhlans, the feared cavalry of the new German army.

In 1874 Sheridan was sent back to Louisiana as a special presidential emissary to make recommendations on suppressing the White League movement (Sherman had refused to go). It was not a wise choice, since Louisianans still remembered his first visit with hatred. They also knew that Sheridan would not be bluffed into making concessions. He was one of the few Radical generals left in the army. All of the others had retired or been transferred to posts out west. But Louisianans suspected correctly that the Northern public would have little stomach for any flashy show of Sheridan's noted grit. Bvt. Maj. Gen. William Emory quickly became aware that he no longer commanded in the state—all decisions would be up to Sheridan.

Sheridan immediately saw to it that five critical seats in the state legislature went to the Republican claimants. The army escorted the Democrats out of the house under threat of a bayonet point. Then Sheridan wrote Grant and suggested that the White Leaguers be declared "banditti" and arrested and tried by military commission. But Grant was not about to declare martial law because the Northern public would not stand for it. And Northern public criticism was mild compared to what Southern whites thought. All Grant could do was disown Sheridan's bluster and call him to Washington for consultation. The result was that General Emory lost his job as a concession to Sheridan's ego and inability to act. Sheridan would return during the crisis in 1876 but accomplish even less. Reconstruction was over and Sheridan's style of command no longer mattered.

After his trip to the South, Sheridan was once more placed in charge of the West. The 1876 Sioux campaign that resulted in the battles of the Rosebud and the Little Big Horn were accomplished under his tutelage. Although his men lost every battle, they won the war by forcing the Sioux and their northern Cheyenne allies to come into the reservations and sue for peace just to eat. Sheridan recognized that the slaughter of the buffalo by the hide hunters, which deprived Native Americans on the plains of their main food source, was probably the real factor that won the war. After Sherman's retirement, Sheridan took over command of the army. He was not hesitant to use armed force against any people who seemed to threaten the advance of American progress. Whether it was Southern whites challenging the Reconstruction of the South, Native Americans trying to protect their homelands, or Northern laborers trying to protect their jobs and wages through unionization and strikes, Sheridan was more than willing to act as their destroyer for the greed of the government, its politicians, contractors, and agents. He was the perfect military man of the nineteenth century.

See also Army and Reconstruction; Griffin, Charles; Hancock, Winfield Scott; Military Reconstruction Acts.

References Boatner, Mark M., III, *The Civil War Dictionary* (1959); Carrier, John P., "A Political History of Texas during the Reconstruction" (1971); Dawson, Joseph Green, III, *Army Generals and Reconstruction* (1982) and "General Phil Sheridan and Military Reconstruction in Louisiana" (1978); Gard, Wayne, *The Great Buffalo Hunt* (1960); Hutton, Paul Andrew, *Phil Sheridan and His Army* (1985); Ramsdell, Charles W., *Reconstruction in Texas* (1910); Richter, William L., *The Army in Texas during Reconstruction* (1987) and "General Phil Sheridan, the Historians, and Reconstruction" (1987); Robinson, Charles M., III, *A Good Year to Die* (1995); Sefton, James E., *The United States Army and Reconstruction* (1967); Sheridan, Philip H., *Personal Memoirs of Philip H. Sheridan* (1888); Shook, Robert W., "Federal Occupation and Administration of Texas" (1970); Taylor, Joe Gray, *Louisiana Reconstructed* (1974).

Sherman, John (1823–1900)

John Sherman, the brother of Maj. Gen. William T. Sherman, was born in Lancaster, Ohio. His father died early and his mother had to farm out her 11 children to relatives and friends to get by. John Sherman lived with one of his father's distant cousins, who saw to it the boy received an excellent education at schools in Lancaster and Mt. Vernon. Sherman developed a real talent for mathematics and surveying, and by age 14 he was working on various internal improvements that dotted the Ohio landscape. By age 16 he was a foreman of work on a canal. He was soon dismissed from the job because he was from a Whig family and the Democrats had just taken the state. It was sobering experience for the rabble-rousing John, who took a long look at his life and decided to mend his ways. He became a sober, cautious man, read law, and passed the bar by 1844. At the same time he engaged in lumbering and real estate and got married. The Shermans never had any children of their own, but they did adopt a daughter.

After entering the legal profession, Sherman became interested in Whig politics and worked in the party's state organization, attending the national conventions of 1848 and 1852. He held no public office until the wave of anti-Nebraska hysteria hit the North and carried Sherman into Republicanism and election to Congress. He served in the House (1855–1861); was elected to the Senate in place of Salmon P. Chase, who became Abraham Lincoln's secretary of the treasury, and served three terms (1861–1877); was secretary of the treasury under Rutherford B. Hayes (1877–1881); returned to the Senate for three more terms (1881–1897); and ended his long career as secretary of state under William McKinley (1897–1898).

Throughout his public career Sherman was a careful politician, not taking radical positions and instead becoming a student of money and government. Sherman was a hard-money man (in favor of gold and against silver coin and paper money), but he was tempered enough by the debtor psychology to understand the necessity of moderate inflation as a way of helping the poor get out of debt. He was against slavery and its expansion into the West, but he spoke against it conservatively. Later his name was attached to much economic legislation (the Specie Redemption Act, Sherman Silver Purchase Act, the Sherman Anti-trust Act, and much of the Interstate Commerce Act, although Senator Shelby M. Cullom of Illionis got the credit for the latter), and his ideas on promoting specie resumption (getting rid of paper bills and shrinking the money supply—the so-called Crime of '73) were blamed for causing the panic of 1873 (an economic depression). But he redeemed himself in 1878 as secretary of the treasury by allowing more inflation and the use of gold and silver coin. Sherman also had a desire to be president. He ran in 1880, 1884, and 1888, only to lose out to other men each time. He lacked an unscrupulous use of patronage, the hallmark of most successful politicians in that era; was devoid of a colorful personality that might attract the voter; had a disunited Ohio delegation that was more than willing to back sure winners like James A. Garfield; refused to manipulate fellow politicians; and was tainted by the Crime of '73.

However, Sherman was not totally naive

John Sherman

when it came to political reality, as his stand during Reconstruction showed. Although by nature Sherman was not a vindictive man when it came to the war and Reconstruction, he voted for the Radical program of rejecting Southern congressmen in 1866, for the imposition of Radical Military Reconstruction in 1867, and for the guilty verdict in President Andrew Johnson's impeachment trial in 1868. Why? Because it was dangerous not to do so if one wanted to be reelected. But Sherman was not shy in imposing his more conservative view on Reconstruction. It was he who wrote the initial Military Reconstruction Acts, removing much of their harshness while retaining civil rights for blacks. He also spoke out against impeaching the president over the Tenure of Office Act because, as he astutely pointed out, Johnson had never thrown Secretary of War Edwin M. Stanton out of office—the latter man still physically held the position. But Sherman voted to convict, partly because he did not have to vote to acquit to save the president—seven other Republicans by had by prior arrangement agreed to save Johnson. Thus, Sherman's career was saved for the future.

But Sherman was not without values. When he became William McKinley's secretary of state, Sherman was disturbed with the manner in which the president and the cabinet wanted to go to war, seemingly at any cost. By this time, Sherman had written his memoirs and was in the twilight of his career. He found that his mind wandered and that he was not physically able to withstand the rigors of public service. He spoke out forcefully against the expansionist sentiment of the time. By this time Sherman had little influence in a Senate dominated by such men as Nelson W. Aldrich, Eugene Hale, Oliver H. Platt, and John C. Spooner. So he made the most powerful statement that he could by resigning his cabinet post as a war protest. Within two years John Sherman was dead. It was just as well. The America that he once knew had died with him, and the nation was proceeding into a new century with a new program of involvement in world politics—something that

Sherman did not understand and reviled.

See also Impeachment; Moderate Republicans and Reconstruction; Radical Republicans and Reconstruction.

References Bridges, Roger D., "John Sherman and the Impeachment of Andrew Johnson" (1973); Burton, Theodore E., *John Sherman* (1906); Kerr, Winfield Scott, *John Sherman* (1906); Nichols, Jeannette P., "John Sherman" (1964–1981); Randall, James G., "John Sherman and Reconstruction" (1932–1933); Sherman, John, *Recollections of Forty Years in the House, Senate, and Cabinet* (1895).

Shotgun Plan

After the Force Acts dispersed the Klan, the First Mississippi Plan, or Shotgun Plan, came into vogue. Organizations like the Red Shirts and the White League were no longer secret and were generally referred to as rifle clubs; they were actually fielded armies with cannons, and they fought openly against loyalist blacks and whites of the pro-federal militia. The most spectacular example occurred in 1874, when the Louisiana White League defeated the pro-Republican Metropolitan Police and loyal militia led by none other than Gen. Robert E. Lee's former right-hand man, Lt. Gen. James Longstreet, now a Scalawag political appointee. This Battle of Canal Street, or the Third Battle of New Orleans, guaranteed the Redemption of Louisiana (i.e., the return of conservative white rule), as did the activities of similar groups in South Carolina and Mississippi. Recently there has been much political flak in New Orleans, now about 80 percent black in population, over the value of maintaining the monument that was raised on the battle site at the turn of the century.

See also Redemption of the South from 1874.

References Gillette, William, *Retreat from Reconstruction* (1979); Perman, Michael, *The Road to Redemption* (1984); Rabel, George, *But There Was No Peace* (1984).

Smalls, Robert (1839–1915)

Born into slavery in Beaufort, South Carolina, Robert Smalls was educated by his white owners and taken to Charleston, where they permitted him to hire out his

Robert Smalls

danger. For this act of courage he was made a captain in the navy and placed in command of the *Planter*, a post he held until September 1866, when the craft was decommissioned.

Returning ashore, Smalls was a natural as a politician. He was a hero to South Carolina blacks for his war record, and the fact that he harbored little animosity toward Southern whites, was good humored, intelligent, fluent in speech, and moderate in his views on Reconstruction made him the least objectionable African American in the state to whites. His modesty and lack of education alone kept him out of the state's Republican leadership at the beginning. But the black voters knew and respected him, and he served in the state constitutional convention (1868), both houses of the state legislature (1868–1870 in the house, 1871–1874 in the senate), and in the U.S. Congress (1875–1879, 1882–1887). He also served in the state militia and rose to the rank of major general (1865–1887).

He was not a flashy congressman, but he attacked South Carolina Democrats for their violent tactics at election time and supported increased access to public accommodations for his race. Smalls was convicted of accepting a bribe while state senator, but he was admired by so many of both races that South Carolina Democrats prevailed upon Governor William D. Simpson to pardon him without any jail time. He was a loyal Stalwart Republican, and he opposed civil service reform and favored increased pensions for Union veterans. He also tried to gain an extra $30,000 for his wartime heroism but failed to convince the rest of Congress. In 1889 Smalls was made port collector at Beaufort, a position he held until 1913, except during President Grover Cleveland's second term (1893–1897). In the interim he was one of six members to the state constitutional convention that disfranchised blacks within the scope of the Fifteenth Amendment, an action that he opposed. Smalls died shortly after Woodrow Wilson took office. Wilson was the first Southern-born man to be chief executive since Abraham Lincoln and was the man

own time as a waiter, hack driver, and a ship's rigger. In 1861, Smalls was impressed into Confederate service aboard the supply ship C.S.S. *Planter*, which plied the waters batween the various Charleston harbor fortifications. Aboard the ship, Smalls took special care to learn to navigate and pilot the boat. Then, on 13 May 1862, taking advantage of the fact that the white officers slept ashore, Smalls and other crew members smuggled their families on board and steamed out into the harbor. He gave the normal whistle signal to keep the Confederate batteries from firing on the boat, and as soon as he could he cut loose for the Union blockading fleet. Smalls became an instant hero. His name and fame spread throughout the North, and he was made a pilot in the Union navy and given a share of the *Planter's* prize money. When the *Planter* was placed in federal service, Smalls was sent along as pilot. On 1 December 1863, the ship came under fire from shore, and the white captain panicked; Smalls took command and brought the ship safely out of who completely segregated the federal government for the first time since the Civil War, depriving blacks of jobs that had been theirs by tradition since Smalls voted for Ulysses S. Grant 45 years earlier.

See also African Americans and Reconstruction.

References Bryant, Lawrence C., *South Carolina Negro Legislators* (1974); Gibbons, Tony, *Warships and Naval Battles of the US Civil War* (1989); Holt, Thomas, *Black over White* (1977); Low, W. Augustus, and Virgil A. Clift, *Encyclopedia of Black America* (1981); McFarlin, Annjeannette Sophia, *Black Congressional Reconstruction Orators and Their Orations* (1976); Quarles, Benjamin, "The Abduction of the *Planter*" (1958); Simkins, Francis B., "Robert Smalls" (1964–1981); Uya, Okun Edet, *From Slavery to Public Service* (1971).

Social Thought during and after Reconstruction

The last third of the nineteenth century is frequently referred to as the Gilded Age, a term popularized in the title of a novel by American writer Mark Twain. Through his character Col. Beriah Sellers, Twain explored a time of optimism, grandiose dreams, flexible ethical standards, and the idolization of that great American demigod, progress. The Gilded Age was influenced by two important events. The first was the Civil War, which had brought about not only a greater national unity but the corresponding disillusionment of Reconstruction, in which the prewar idealism was replaced by a crass seeking of wealth no matter the cost. The second event was the Industrial Revolution, which created major disruptions in American society, including the decline of the individual in favor of the group (labor unions, cartels, pools, agricultural societies, welfare groups, and the like).

Society had become more complex with the advent of Union, the machine, and big business, all of which had been accelerated by the need to defeat the Confederacy by any means possible. U.S. society was changing rapidly from a rural to an urban one, with all of the complexities that would become common to the twentieth century beginning to appear, like want and destitution, unemployment, wandering street people, noise, and pollution. There might have been poverty in the prewar agricultural society, but farmers could grow and consume their own food. Before the Civil War, events were seen as God's will. God had made the right life known to humankind through the Bible as a person strove to follow the divine plan and achieve eternal salvation. People were seen as a higher order of life, different from the animals because of the human abilities to talk and reason, to have a morality. Of course, one also had the free will to ignore the Scriptures, but one did so only at one's ultimate peril. Truth tended to be very absolute and empirical thought was limited in form.

However, during Reconstruction and accelerating in the eras that followed, all of this began to change. Everyone wanted in on what was known as the Great Barbecue—that is, everyone wanted to preempt, squander, and exploit. This vulgarity led one historian, Vernon L. Parrington, to call Reconstruction an age with a lot of brass but very little gilt. It was typified by late Victorian architecture, with its bulky buildings, poor aesthetic taste, ugly and useless ornamentation, and the adoption of turreted castles for homes. It was popularized by the exaggerations and lies of the dime novel and epitomized in the Horatio Alger tales, stories of the struggling boy who went from "rags to riches" through his inborn guile. And it was fed by the ideas of a British scientist, who had lived for a time on the Galapagos Islands off the coast of Equador, named Charles Darwin. In 1859, Darwin had published a book on his observations entitled *The Origin of Species*.

Before Darwin the story of the creation of the world was the biblical book of Genesis, which told of the seven days of God's creation of the world and all that lived in it. Darwin challenged biblical creation by theorizing that all species (he did not ever talk about humans specifically) evolved from a single act of creation. The theory of evolution was based on the earlier studies of the Austrian monk Gregor Mendel, fossil remains, and Darwin's own observations of the isolated unique life forms on the Galapagos. From the one act of creation, Darwin proposed that all life evolved from the simple to the complex through processes he called natural selection (adaptation of an organism to its environment) and survival of the fittest (in which the desire to live causes a struggle for survival that only the strongest can win). Of course, Darwin never specified who or what created the original cells, life itself. But he never attacked divine creation or biblical revelation. All he did was propose a theory that the animal world evolved from a single cell, as it were.

The problem was not Darwin but what others made of Darwin, people who carried his implications into the world of human beings and drew pseudoscientific conclusions about human society and used selected portions of Darwin's thesis for their own ends. The result was something called Social Darwinism, the foremost advocate of which was Englishman Herbert Spencer. In his volume *Synthetic Philosophy*, Spencer claimed that humans passed through evolutionary stages, just like Darwin's animal kingdom. He particularly saw human development passing through two eras. First came a military era during which individual people were governed by emotions that resulted in a continuous battle among themselves; there was also a fight between humans and their environment. In these struggles Spencer saw the fittest emerging to continue on. After this era, Spencer claimed, would follow the cooperative era, in which the individual was aided in survival through group efforts. As Spencer wrote during the Pax Britannica of the nineteenth century, when humans figured out that through industrialization and an enforced world peace those less fortunate could be helped by employment in the factories, and as he wrote in the vernacular rather than stilted academic prose, Spencer's ideas were an instant success. He offered a feeling of progress and scientific meaning to life beyond the religious. And the message was self-congratulatory. It made successful European nations appear as the fittest, following the so-called natural laws put forth in Darwin's work.

Of course, not all nations of European background were in the Old World. In the New World, Social Darwinism as revealed by Spencer was a natural. It put in pseudo-scientific terms something that the United States had believed in for a long time, Manifest Destiny. It gave meaning to the success of the nation and the need for other less fortunate peoples to make way for the superior white culture. It told Americans why the Native Americans and the Mexicans were being defeated in the West. And it gave new poignancy to the defeat of the Confederacy, the failure of Reconstruction, and the subordination of blacks in the East.

All that was needed was for an American scholar to apply Spencer to the United States directly. That man was William Graham Sumner, a Yale University professor. In his book *Folkways*, Sumner united three elements of intellectual interest in the nineteenth-century United States: the Protestant ethic (work was good for the soul and pacified and cleansed whoever did it), classical economics (the notion that a natural law, laissez-faire, ruled the wealth of nations), and natural selection (the Social Darwinist precept that a person who survived all challenges could manage without the aid or interference of government or other human cooperative groups). Sumner permitted the successful to assert that those who rose to the top of society were obviously superior to others. Indeed, one could extend the notion to its extreme and assert that the more ruthless one is in the pursuit of success, the better off the whole world would be. The more successful a business was, the more the unfortunate could be saved through the opportunities that expansion offered. Like Spencer, Sumner saw the staged development of humans, but he left unanswered how people came to be on the world in the first place. Essentially people developed from the primitive to the sophisticated through natural processes, which included economic scarcity, survival of the fittest, and learning an antagonistic cooperation through the development of governments. The role of the state was to guard the right of the individual to make choices. The individual was responsible for self-discipline and avoiding all excesses in life that might limit success. Humans would improve only if the weak were in effect culled out by failure, a human natural selective process. Equality was a false idea that made for mediocrity. Progress was a notion that made for human happiness and was obtained by following natural laws (which Sumner called by a more friendly term, *folkways*) without government interference.

Once Spencer and Sumner had handled the secular justification, it was necessary to join the concept with religion. After all, the Bible still had great potency, and in the Scriptures, God (particularly through Christ) seemed to speak out against great accumulations of wealth as corruption of the human soul. The result was the gospel of wealth. Most American millionaires at that time were Protestant, and a majority of those adhered to the Calvinist belief in predestination. Many were very involved with their denominations. They came to believe that God was only superficially against wealth. If one were to dig deeper in the Scriptures, ran the argument, one would find that godliness was in league with wealth and property rights; indeed, one had a duty to labor and become wealthy, for it revealed God's blessing. Wealth also promoted democracy by emphasizing individualism, liberty, and laissez-faire. Through hard work, sobriety, frugality, initiative, and a pietistic use of wealth to promote a Christian society, survival of the fittest became holy and the American way. Indeed, assisting others through God's great gift of personal wealth built one's own personal character.

No one did more to popularize the notion of wealth as stewardship than steel magnate Andrew Carnegie. He maintained that the accumulation of great wealth conveyed a social responsibility. The fortunate person who gained wealth was obligated to live modestly, shun ostentatious display, provide modestly for one's heirs (the less the better, as it would make them struggle to survive like everyone else) but give the rest back to the less fortunate. Wealth was allowed to accumulate, theorized Carnegie, so that one person might use its concentra-

tion more effectively with a greater impact than a thousand less wealthy could dream of doing. Carnegie maintained that to die rich was disgraceful and that it took more talent to give one's riches away than it did to earn them in the first place. Hence it was best to divest oneself of wealth during one's own lifetime to see that the job was properly done. If one failed to meet this obligation, Carnegie suggested that the government confiscate excess wealth upon the owner's death. Carnegie himself gave away a half billion dollars to build small town libraries and to the cause of world peace. But he did not give it away without a catch. For instance, he built the library buildings—but the townspeople had to provide their own books, lest they be spoiled and denied the opportunity to better themselves through their own work and public contribution.

Although many adopted Social Darwinism as their own, the concept was not without its critics. One conflicting notion was called the religion of humanity, a secular criticism that admitted to the efficacy of Social Darwinism but preferred to water down its excessive individualism by emphasizing group action. The concept's "humanist" proponents saw human society as developing through stages: a theological stage from the beginnings of life to the revelations of the Old Testament, a metaphysical stage that ran from the Old Testament to the rationalism of the Renaissance, and a scientific stage that replaced basic rationalism and religion with scientific principles or rules of life. Groups allowed those less fortunate to compete with the successful and cope with the problems of industrial technology.

Churches were not about to lose out to changes in the late nineteenth-century thought. Their response was the social gospel, an attack on the rampant individualism of Social Darwinism through a reorganization of traditional religion. It challenged Christians to respond to slums and wretched economic conditions brought on by industrialism and the development of the cities by walking in the steps of Christ in a united effort of all churches, regardless of denomination. It condemned the notion of applying Darwin's principles to people and spoke of the equality of all in the eyes of God. Essentially, it reattached a stigma to the unbridled accumulation of wealth at the expense of others and supported labor unions, strikes, and boycotts.

Other critics preferred relying on the government to counter the effects of Social Darwinism on society at large. Reasoning that the wealthy and the problems brought about by urbanization and industrialization could be curbed only by the power of the state, the biggest secular group of all, these new rationalists or new humanists (as they were called) issued the first calls for the welfare state that would be so common in the twentieth century. They hoped, by applying scientific principles of "dynamic sociology," to curb the excesses of wealth and the Industrial Revolution to create an earthly paradise.

Another concept to counter Social Darwinism was put forth by a group called pragmatists, who rejected the "straitjacket" of any one system of ideas as a single truth, preferring instead to think that truth was relative to existing experiences and conditions. In their view, the main way to achieve any reform of society was through education. If an idea worked to solve a problem, it had validity for that time and place but might not work on another problem (or the same problem) at another time and place. Human society had to be liberated from past traditions, and the best way to achieve that was through a free education that revealed the faults of the past and the possible solutions of the future.

The result of the interplay of all of these ideas created a breakdown of the rigid society that had existed in America before the Civil War. Nothing revealed the tremendous changes going on in American society and thought during Reconstruction better than the Beecher-Tilton affair, the most famous public scandal of its time, in which a married clergyman named Henry Ward Beecher was accused of carrying on a clandestine romance with the wife of his protégé, Theodore Tilton. The Beecher-Tilton affair forced the American people to take a realistic look at the changes in thought that were affecting postwar society: the breakdown of prewar absolute truths in religion and science and the changes wrought by increased immigration and social problems arising from a society that was converting itself from a rural base of the self-sufficient family farm to the uncertainties of wage-paying industrial jobs. Beecher helped define Victorian culture in America: a belief in fixed moral laws, emphasis on individual self-reliance, faith in education for self-improvement, and a stress on economic security and social control. But more than reassuring a nation that wanted to be loved by God and to love itself, he also revealed that nothing was sacrosanct except on the surface and helped convert the absolute truths of an earlier time to more relative truths based on conditions as they actually were. As such the Beecher-Tilton affair personified America's turning away from the usual moral issues that precipitated the war and Reconstruction to the varied truths that came to dominate the Gilded Age and the twentieth century that followed and the willingness to hide this change under a veneer of rectitude.

See also Beecher, Henry Ward; Corruption as a Problem in Reconstruction; Woodhull, Victoria Claflin.

References Abell, Aaron Ignatius, *Urban Impact on American Protestantism* (1943); Clark, Clifford E., *Henry Ward Beecher* (1978); Curti, Merle E., *The Growth of American Thought* (1943); Dombrowski, James A., *Early Days of Christian Socialism* (1966 [1936]); Gabriel, Ralph H., *The Course of American Democratic Thought* (1956); Hibben, Paxton, *Henry Ward Beecher* (1942); Higham, John, *From Boundlessness to Consolidation* (1969); Hopkins, C. H., *The Rise of Social Gospel in American Protestantism* (1940); Howe, Daniel W., "American Victorianism as a Culture" (1975); Knox, Thomas W., *Life and Work of Henry Ward Beecher* (1887); May, Henry Farnham, *Protestant Churches and Industrial America* (1949); McLoughlin, William G., *The Meaning of Henry Ward Beecher* (1970); Muraskin, William A., "The Social-Control Theory in American History" (1976); Parrington, V. L., *The Main Currents in American Thought* (1927–1930); Ryan, Halford R., *Henry Ward Beecher* (1990); Starr, Harris Elwood, "Henry Ward Beecher" (1964–1981); Waller, Altina L., *Reverend Beecher and Mrs. Tilton* (1982); Wish, Harvey A., *Society and Thought in America* (1950–1952).

Southern Carpetbaggers in the North

Although the story of Yankees who went South after the Civil War is well documented in the legend of the Carpetbaggers, the tale of Southerners who went North after the war is not. These "Southern Carpetbaggers" were part of an exodus of thousands from Dixie to many places in the North, the American West, Europe, Mexico, and Brazil. Most of the expatriates who went to Mexico during Maximilian's reign soon returned after the emperor's execution at the hands of Mexican Republicans under Benito Juárez. The others stayed in their places of exile, leading to a still-existing colony of Brazilians descended from Southern Americans near São Paulo. These Southerners left their homes for a multitude of reasons. Some feared Union military justice for alleged treason; others sought to leave a land where blacks were free people; others accurately foresaw the chaos that would follow the Union victory; and many of those who went to Brazil hoped to extend their lives as slaveholders (the institution was not abolished there until 1888).

Most of the Southerners who went North were under the age of 35. A slight majority were unmarried. Most sought a better economic situation and believed that they might find it in Northern cities, which were reputed to have better financial, social, and artistic opportunities than in the South at the end of the Civil War. A large number of the men who left went North to begin or resume their education. Others had property to sell. Many war widows tended to migrate to Northern resorts and cities looking for a male counterpart. Artists went to the cities because that is where the patrons were. And some were tired of rural life and wanted to experience the sights and sounds of the bustling Northern cities. Farmers were generally not among those who left—they seemed the most devoted to the Southern homestead and the "Lost Cause" of the Confederacy.

Of the men on whom there are records, about 60 percent had served in the Confederate armies, while the remainder had been in some governmental position. A third of

them sought careers in the world of finance (banking, real estate, insurance) or letters (journalism, writing), professions that had attracted only a small number of Southern men before the war. Another third entered the professions of law and medicine. About 30 percent had never held a job beyond military service and had been students when the war began. This gave them a mobility that their parents often lacked in starting over.

Of Northern cities, New York attracted the most Southerners. The city had always been pro-Southern. Before the war it had great contact with the South through cotton factorage and finance. It had been lukewarm in fighting secession and ardently opposed to the Union military draft. Longtime supporters of the Democratic party, many Southerners expected to find kindred spirits there speaking with Yankee accents. They were not disappointed. Although quite a few Southerners failed in business or grew homesick and returned to the South, most seemed to get along in moderate circumstances. The more successful ones, like Thomas F. Ryan, John H. Inman, Charles B. Rouss, Richard T. Wilson, and Joseph L. Robertson, became influential in business or on Wall Street and pumped millions of dollars in investment back into the South during and after Reconstruction. Roger A. Pryor was a big name in law, John A. Wyeth in medicine, William R. O'Donovan in art, and George C. Eggleston in literature, to name but a few of Southern successes in the North after the war.

About the only area that Southerners stayed out of was politics. Not that they avoided politics all together, but they seldom received patronage from political parties. They really had little chance in politics up North. They had no Military Reconstruction Act to get them going and no newly adopted state constitutions to disfranchise opponents and aid their political careers. This, more than anything else, differentiated them from Carpetbaggers in the South. Those who entered politics generally confined their activities to political clubs or a stray journalism career. Seven

Southern Carpetbaggers eventually held office in the North, but only two were elected before 1880.

The Southern expatriates tended to stick together in the North through clubs, societies, churches, and business and financial matters. They kept in touch with the folks back home, too. But they were not isolated from the rest of the community, and many owed their success to Yankee friends and business acquaintances. Indeed, Southerners in the North were out to exploit the Yankees as much as the real Carpetbaggers exploited those south of the Mason-Dixon line. Deep down it was not unheard of for Southerners in the North to have great scorn for all things Yankee. They were very proud of their service to the stars and bars and viewed the Northerners as devoid of honesty and honor. But they did admire the manner in which Northerners were so honest about their dishonesty, especially in business.

But in the end, these Southern Carpetbaggers would do much to assist in the sectional reconciliation that occurred in the latter part of the nineteenth century. They did much to make Rebels respectable up North through their wide contacts and their generally reserved and proper social bearing. Former Northern soldiers especially seemed to admire the courage of their former opponents; long before there were battlefield reunions, Yankees and Confederates got together in individual Northern cities and celebrated surviving the greatest war in American history. It is possible that in their sojourn north these Southern Carpetbaggers realized more than most Southerners what was required to obtain a lasting peace. Their integration into Northern society, their intermarriage with the onetime enemy, their contacts kept back home, all contributed to a healing of the nation by 1898 and an acceptance of the myth of the Lost Cause among whites nationwide.

See also Carpetbaggers.

Reference Buck, Paul H. *The Road to Reunion* (1937); Gaston, Paul M., *The New South Creed* (1970); Sutherland, Daniel E., "Former Confederates in the Post–Civil War North" (1981).

Southern Claims Commission

One of the oddities of the Civil War was that there was no "solid South" or "solid North." Over 300,000 Southerners served in Union blue. Major cities in the North were wracked by antidraft riots, while the countryside, especially in the Old Northwest along the Ohio River, teemed with citizens who belonged to movements that often gave comfort and even aid to the Rebels. Large geographical sections of the South had pro-Union populations, especially in the Appalachian region of Virginia, North Carolina, and Tennessee; the northern parts of Arkansas; the western parts of Texas; and a smattering of counties in other Confederate states. (One of the ironies of the war was that Maj. Gen. William T. Sherman had a personal escort from the First Alabama [Union] Volunteer Cavalry during his infamous March to the Sea.) The Southern Confederacy was not easy on what it determined to be traitorous activity. Actual military expeditions invaded these areas to enforce Confederate loyalty. Large numbers of white refugees fled from their lands to Yankee protection. The pro-Union areas were usually deep within the Confederacy and were freed very late in the war, if at all.

In the 50 years that followed the Civil War, Congress received a constant stream of appeals by loyal citizens for claims for goods taken, given, and used by the advancing Union armies. These claims represented one of the reasons the Freedmen's Bureau had departments for refugees and abandoned lands. The problem became so involved and proof was so often lacking in the form of proper vouchers that in 1871 Congress established the Southern Claims Commission to supervise the claims process. This commission's jurisdiction involved the legitimate claims held by loyal Southern whites against the government for services rendered during the war, a recognition that some of the white South had done the "right" thing and suffered unfairly for it. The North was correct to feel this obligation. It had sent agents into loyal areas to organize these people to assist the Union cause. Even the Emancipation Proclamation had taken these people into consideration when it exempted all loyal persons' slaves from its provisions, providing they were behind Union lines. These persons were the heart of Presidential Reconstruction and comprised the mass of early Scalawags, those willing to assist in the Reconstruction of the South.

As the Southern states came back into the Union, the numbers of claims against the federal government for loyal support during the war actually increased. Radical Republicans had to give in to a growing number of border-state, Deep South Scalawag, and Liberal Republican demands that the claims be dealt with in an orderly manner. A three-man commission was established to look into the validity of the claims. President Ulysses S. Grant appointed Judge Asa Owen Aldis of Vermont, Orange Ferris of New York (a former member of the U.S. House of Representatives), and former U.S. Senator James B. Howell of Iowa as the commission members. The board was intended to be in place for only two years, but it soon became evident from the number of claims filed in the first two days that it would have to be continued for many years. Eventually 22,298 claims worth over $60 million were considered.

Following the procedures used by the longtime federal court of claims, the board established a set of 22 rules under which all claimants would have to be measured. Information had to be as exact as possible: the name of the claimant, place of claim, circumstances of the claim, the Union soldiers involved (rank, company, and regiment), the commanding officer of the district, and the nature of the goods or services provided. The degree to which a claimant met these requirements often determined the recognition of the claim. The claimant's assertions were then checked against the pertinent records, if any, and a determination of validity made. Prices were determined from the time of the claim and a monetary value set. Of course, claimants made sure to specify that all fence rails were "brand new," all cattle were "fine and fat," all horses "ele-

gant," and all mules "the best." It would seem that the advancing Union armies traveled in style—which undoubtedly made the soldiers look back and wonder what happened to all that wonderful confiscated material they couldn't remember seeing.

One of the risks of filing a claim as a loyal Southern white was that lists of claimants were printed and distributed throughout their home area, making the filers liable to Ku Klux Klan revenge. It was not a business to be entered into lightly. And although one could file a claim for pasturage, crops, and animals actually taken (or "impressed," as the term was in those days), if one had a battle fought across one's fields and farm, the commission would recognize no claim. The rule was "stores and supplies" only. Of course, the determination of loyalty was a prime concern. No Rebels need apply for relief; they lost the war. It was easy to establish disloyalty, like enlistment in the Confederate army or service in national, state, and local government, but difficult to establish loyalty. Mere testimony by friends and neighbors had to be somehow substantiated by some kind of proof that aid had not been rendered to the enemy. Claimants could maintain, however, that they had been forced to assist the Confederacy and gain a claim against Union expropriations. But again some sort of proof was required.

To help investigate the truth of the claims, the board appointed 29 agents to go into the field and snoop about, looking into local records and interviewing people from the area in which the claim originated. These men had a list of 80 questions to get answered; the more questions answered, the better the chance of gaining consideration for monetary compensation. It was not uncommon to find that the claimant was a good Yankee when Union troops arrived and a good Rebel at other times. Hence a statement of loyalty from a prominent Union military officer or government agent was not looked upon with as much credibility as the statement of local witnesses and written records in a newspaper or courthouse. The investigators also looked into the economic condition of the claimant. A man who owned a ramshackle farm with a record of bad debt probably would not collect on 26,000 bushels of corn allegedly seized by a Union commissary officer.

The numbers of claims filed paralleled the course of the war. Tennessee had 3,168; Virginia, 2,930; Georgia, 2,151; Alabama, 1,958; Arkansas, 1,738; North Carolina, 1,645; Mississippi, 1,627; Louisiana, 517, South Carolina, 377; West Virginia, 140; Florida, 89; Texas, 61. The percentage of claims granted ran from a high of 40 percent in Tennessee, Virginia, Alabama, South Carolina, West Virginia, and Florida to a low of 25 percent in Mississippi and Louisiana, where large sugar plantations received the least and claimed the most. By 1880 the Southern Claims Commission had paid $4.6 million, compared to the nearly $10 million allowed by the federal court of claims that handled cotton and contraband confiscations. This would seem to indicate that the commission was careful with the government's money, but public newspapers nonetheless saw it as a vast boondoggle that aided people of dubious loyalty at best. In reality the careful work of the commission merely confirmed that many Southern whites had actively aided the Union cause.

See also Bureau of Refugees, Freedmen, and Abandoned Lands; Captured and Abandoned Property Act of 1863; Confiscation Acts; Pardon, Amnesty, and Parole.

References Klingberg, Frank Wysor, "The Southern Claims Commission" (1945–1946); Randall, James G., *The Confiscation of Property during the Civil War* (1913).

Southern Homestead Act of 1866

After the Civil War the South became a laboratory for experimentation in the sales of public lands. When the South seceded from the Union, there were nearly 48 million acres of public land in the states of Alabama, Arkansas, Florida, Mississippi, and Louisiana. All other Southern states had no federal lands within their boundaries. Generally it was believed that these southern lands were fairly worthless to individual farmers. They had been on the market since the 1830s at the standard $1.25 an acre, and in 1854, under the Graduated Land Act, prices had been reduced relative to time on the market to as low as 12.5 cents an acre with no appreciable increase in sales.

One of the staunchest Radical Republicans of his day was U.S. Senator George W. Julian of Indiana. He is noted for his abolitionist tendencies, but he ought to be better known for his opposition to land fraud against the federal government in the form of large corporate land grants, such as those made to the railroads before and during the war. Julian decided to put his love of black liberty and land for the average American together in the Southern Homestead Act of 1866. This was a measure designed to reserve the unused portions of the South in 80-acre plots to persons who could take the ironclad oath, that is, loyal whites and especially the freedmen. This meant that while the rest of the country was experiencing increases in plot sizes for agriculture and ranching of the plains, the South was going back to an older prewar system of smaller plots. Because such a plan was seen in Congress as an attempt to punish the large planters, even the advocates of land grants for business voted in favor of Julian's idea. It would be as close to the hoped-for "40 acres and a mule" as most ex-slaves would ever get.

The Southern Homestead Act lasted until the end of Reconstruction in 1876. By then it became obvious to the Redeemers (the conservative Southerners who regained political control of the South) that economic development of these marginal farm lands would depend on their use for lumber or railroads. So as Southern states gained more power in Congress, their senators and representatives begin to jockey for the repeal of Julian's program. They were assisted by the fact that Julian had retired in 1870 and was no longer present to wield his considerable influence, as well as by the end of Reconstruction fervor on behalf of the freedmen, upon whom the individual homesteads had been based. Hence the Southern Homestead Act was repealed and the federal lands opened up to speculators; that is, there was no limit as to the amount any one company or individual could buy. The result was that the lands were sold off to corporations that specialized in the timber business, most of which were Northern owned, particularly in Florida, Mississippi, and Louisiana. The chief benefactor of this process was Daniel F. Sullivan, "the timber king of Florida," a real wheeler-dealer of dubious character whose empire stretched from Mobile, through Pensacola, to the east.

In contrast with what Southern congressmen had hoped for, however, men like Sullivan kept their lands out of the business market and waited for them to appreciate as Northern timberlands became exhausted. This meant that after the initial purchase, little business activity resulted—the same thing that had happened under the Southern Homestead Act in 1866. Hence, by 1888, Southerners wanted to free up the large landholdings to get the timber cut, so they once again requested a change in the law. But the change came too late. By then the best stands of cypress and yellow pine were in the hands of nonresident speculators who took the biggest share of the profits, looting the South once more. These land purchases represent a seamy side of Reconstruction policy that one author cleverly described as the "Era of Good Stealings."

See also Bureau of Refugees, Freedmen, and Abandoned Lands; Captured and Abandoned Property Act of 1863; Confiscation Acts; Pardon, Amnesty, and Parole.

References Abbott, Martin, "Free Land, Free Labor, and the Freedmen's Bureau" (1956); Cox, LaWanda, "The Promise of Land for the Freedmen" (1958); Hoffman, Edwin D., "From Slavery to Self Reliance" (1956); Gates, Paul W., "Federal Land Policy in the South" (1940); Oubre, Claude F., *Forty Acres and a Mule* (1978); Randall, James G., *Constitutional Problems under Lincoln* (1964); Summers, Mark W., *The Era of Good Stealings* (1993).

Special Field Orders No. 15

Special Field Orders No. 15, issued by Maj. Gen. William T. Sherman on 16 January 1865, set aside all land between the St. Mary's River in northern Florida to Charleston, South Carolina, and 30 miles inland for the exclusive use of blacks, except for any land that had already been sold for nonpayment of taxes. Individual tracts were not to exceed 40 acres. This order was later canceled under President Andrew Johnson's pardon policies, but African Americans managed to purchase large amounts of this land, especially in coastal areas like that near Port Royal. These purchases gave former slaves a unique, independent economic base uncommon to the rest of the South.

See also Cox Plan of Reconstruction; Port Royal Experiment.

Reference Berlin, Ira, et al., *Slaves No More* (1992); Cimbala, Paul A., "The Freedmen's Bureau, the Freedmen, and Sherman's Grant in Reconstruction Georgia" (1989); Oubre, Claude F., *Forty Acres and a Mule* (1978); Rose, Willie Lee, *Rehearsal for Reconstruction* (1964).

Stanton, Edwin McMasters (1814–1869)

Edwin Stanton was the eldest son of a Steubenville, Ohio, Quaker physician. Stanton's father died when the boy was but 13 years old, forcing him to leave school and go to work at a bookstore. Continuing his studies when he could, he finally managed to work his way through Kenyon College and read law. He was admitted to the bar in 1836 and began a small private practice before becoming a partner with Ohio's U.S. Senator-elect Benjamin Tappan. Stanton showed great energy, ingenuity, and fidelity, which allowed him to make much money as an attorney. He moved from Steubenville to Pittsburgh and then Washington, D.C., and began to practice before the U.S. Supreme Court. He represented the state of Pennsylvania in the Wheeling & Belmont Bridge case (which dealt with a bridge that collapsed) and opponents to Cyrus McCormick in suits over the reaper patents. In the latter cases he worked with a relative unknown Illinois lawyer, Abraham Lincoln. In 1859, Stanton represented New York congressman Daniel Sickles in his trial for murdering his wife's lover, winning acquittal with a temporary insanity defense. He also worked on the prodigious cases of individuals who fraudulently claimed that they had been granted rich California lands; Stanton saved the public treasury some $150 million. Stanton's forte was the intense research and labor he put into each presentation, as well as the meticulous way in which he pursued the facts.

Because of Stanton's reputation, he was made attorney general during the waning days of the James Buchanan administration. Stanton had had little to do with politics before that, although he was a Jacksonian Democrat. He was against the spread of slavery into the Mexican Cession and disliked the domination of Democratic ruling circles by Southerners. Stanton was willing, however, to accept the Supreme Court's *Dred Scott* decision in 1857 (which declared the Missouri Compromise's restrictions on slavery unconstitutional and invalidated claims of African American citizenship) and to support 1860 presidential campaign of John Breckenridge (the proslavery candidate), believing that these measures offered the only hope of preventing secession. But when it came to war, Stanton was in favor of using force to hold on to federal property in

the South and to force the South back into the Union. Although he hated Lincoln and his Republican cohorts, Stanton came into the cabinet in January 1862 as secretary to clean up the poor administration in the Department of War. A stout man of medium height with thick glasses and a long stringy beard, Stanton's stern visage would become one of the best known in America by the end of the war. He was fierce in his appearance and attitude, leading one critic to label him the "black terrier."

As secretary of war, Stanton was controversial to say the least. He apparently was a pathological liar, playing all sides against the middle. But he was a meticulous administrator, honest in a monetary sense, and loyal to the Union cause, which was what Lincoln needed. Stanton reorganized the whole department, established assistant secretaries to whom he delegated specific tasks, cleaned up the corruption rampant in the procurement system, and railed against anyone in civilian and military positions who was disloyal or not pushing the war effort sufficiently. He was gruff and rude. Influential

An 1862 *Harper's Weekly political cartoon shows Edwin M. Stanton in a U.S. military shaving shop. The sign above him reads "E. M. Stanton: physiognomical hair cutter and ecstatic shaver."*

soldiers and civilians alike feared a penetrating interview by Stanton more than they did an attack by the Rebels. Stanton looked into the background and tactics of generals and cooperated with the powerful congressional joint committee on the conduct of the war, firing the slackers and fixing blame for all defeats. He ran the vast system of arrests and incarceration of suspected sympathizers in the so-called American Bastille, disregarding their constitutional rights at will. No modern secret police force has been more diligent in its work than Stanton's agents were.

In short, the pro–state rights, unionist Democrat became the most ultraradical of Radical Republicans. He turned on his friend Bvt. Maj. Gen. George B. McClellan, was the originator of many of the most uncomplimentary nicknames of President Lincoln ("the original gorilla"), and would stab anyone in the back to further what he saw as the proper carrying out of the Union cause. After the war, Stanton pursued Lincoln's assassins, apparently censored John Wilkes Booth's diary by deleting several important pages, saw to it that the conspirators were tried by a tough military commission rather than a possibly weak civilian jury, and hanged and jailed the guilty (and the innocent, some would say). Stanton always made quick decisions and, right or wrong, stuck to them. When Maj. Gen. William T. Sherman gave even milder terms to the Confederate army surrendering in North Carolina than Lt. Gen. Ulysses S. Grant had given Confederate general Robert E. Lee, Stanton nullified the act and made Sherman cut any implied political references to the legality of existing Southern state governments.

After Lincoln's death, President Andrew Johnson asked Stanton to stay on. As during the war, Stanton acted as a Radical Republican spy inside the cabinet, keeping important senators and representatives informed as to Johnson's planned course of action, kissing up to everyone in turn. He urged Johnson to accept Congress' version of Reconstruction, from the renewal of the Freedmen's Bureau Bill to the Civil Rights Act of 1866 to the Fourteenth Amendment to the Military Reconstruction Acts; then he helped Johnson write his vetoes of the same legislation. Aware of Stanton's importance, Congress responded with the Tenure of Office Act, designed to protect presidential appointments from easy removal, although there is some doubt as to whether the act really applied to Lincoln appointees like Stanton. Johnson's closest advisors warned him to get rid of Stanton, lest he threaten the whole administration. Stanton, determined to hold on for the good of the country, ignored Johnson's suggestions that he resign. This forced Johnson to fire Stanton outright, a process he initiated when Congress went out of session in late 1867 in hopes of having it all completed by the time Congress reassembled. But Stanton outmaneuvered the lackluster man Johnson sent to do the job and held on, fortified behind his office door, which was barricaded like the gate of a city under siege.

Stanton's sacrifice was well appreciated by the Radicals, who recognized it for what it was—a golden opportunity to impeach the president for interfering with congressional Reconstruction. But when the impeachment charges failed, Stanton accepted the inevitable and resigned on 26 May 1868. Stanton's vigor in prosecuting the Civil War and Reconstruction had cost him much of his health. He took a long rest and tried to resume his law practice. He also acted as a political advisor to the first Grant campaign, for which he was rewarded with a seat on the U.S. Supreme Court. But Stanton died shortly after the Senate confirmed his appointment.

See also Impeachment; Radical Republicans and Reconstruction; Tenure of Office Act.

References Meneely, A. Howard, "Edwin McMasters Stanton" (1964–1981); Pratt, Fletcher, *Stanton* (1970 [1953]); Thomas, Benjamin P., and Harold M. Hyman, *Stanton* (1962).

Stevens, Thaddeus (1792–1868)

Thaddeus Stevens was the last of four sons whose father either died or abandoned the family when Thaddeus was but a small boy (the record is uncertain). Stevens had a hard childhood that was made even more difficult by his poor health and a club foot. Early on he developed a dislike for the rich and aristocratic, although he aspired himself to become wealthy. He was born in Vermont and raised there and in Massachusetts, growing up on the frontier, being educated in local schools, and developing a very individualistic and democratic outlook common to America's backcountry. He entered Dartmouth as a sophomore and graduated in 1814. He also attended the University of Vermont briefly. He had the usual classic training from early American colleges but soon turned to reading law to pass the bar and make a living. He became a forceful public speaker with a great wit that was spiced with an often bitter invective. He moved to York, Pennsylvania, to teach at a local academy and complete his law studies.

After passing the bar examination in 1816, he set up practice at nearby Gettysburg. His law business grew slowly, but by the late 1820s Stevens had earned a reputation as an inventive and thorough attorney and began to pick up some of the biggest and most lucrative cases in the region. He was a hater of slavery, especially after he won a case to return a fugitive to her master in Maryland. Thereafter Stevens atoned for this moral slip by spending money he had saved for his law library to buy and liberate one slave and by gladly defending all fugitives brought before local courts for free. Yet he was also suspected in the mysterious murder of a young slave woman in Adams County, Pennsylvania. However, the charge was never proven and never adversely affected his later career.

As his legal practice grew, Stevens entered the iron business with partner James D. Paxton and bought a new forge he named Caledonia Furnace. The partners concentrated on producing "blooms," or iron ingots that were shipped to other companies to manufacturer into actual products. The iron forge was never really profitable, but Stevens insisted that it keep producing to keep its numerous employees at work. It was from his unproductive ironworks that Stevens became interested in both a high protective tariff to limit foreign competition and politics in general. Stevens was a Federalist at heart and very much an anti-Jackson man. But Stevens first sought to work with a truly egalitarian, leveling party, the Anti-Masons, and at their 1832 convention he spoke out against any secret meetings (such as those of the Masons) as being undemocratic and discriminatory against the average citizen. He served from 1833 to 1841 in the Pennsylvania assembly and became noted for his uncompromising stands on issues, particularly against the Masonic Lodge and slavery (especially in the District of Columbia as the seat of American democracy), as well as for free public schools, the protective tariff, the right of citizens to petition government, and a constitutional limit on the public debt. He excoriated his opponents regularly with his fiery rhetoric, by now one of his specialties.

Stevens's outspokenness caused him much trouble. Once he had to escape from an opposition mob in the Pennsylvania capitol by jumping from a second-story window. When a Democratic-controlled assembly declared his seat vacant, he was reelected immediately by his district. He also served in the 1837 state constitutional convention and railed against anything that smacked of privilege or class distinction. In 1841, although he was conceded to be "a giant among pigmy opponents," he retired from politics, probably angry that he did not receive what he saw as a well-deserved cabinet position in the William Henry Harrison administration. He returned to the law and made a small fortune in short order. But the rise of the slavery issue in connection with the Mexican Cession soon brought him back into the political fray. In 1848 he was elected to Congress as an antislavery Whig. He soon reestablished his uncompromising stand against slavery, the usual invective against his opponents, and a knack for parliamentary maneuver that set him apart from the run-of-the-mill free soil candidate. He wished to ring the slave states with free soil, believing that slavery would wither away in a quarter of a century under that pressure. He denounced slavery as a "curse, shame,

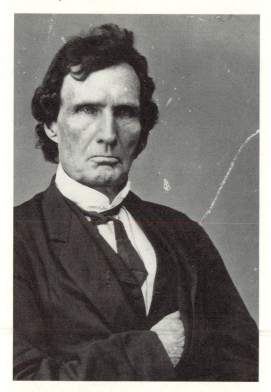

Thaddeus Stevens

He warned the South against secession, promising that "our next United States will contain no foot of ground on which a slave can tread, no breath of air which a slave can breathe." He spoke in favor of coercion of the South before secession in such a manner that friends in the House had to form a protective barrier around him on the floor to protect his life from harm.

Stevens again hoped for a cabinet seat, but Lincoln chose Cameron instead. In the end this turned out to be Stevens's good fortune, for he had too much power in Congress to accept a subordinate position in the executive branch. He took over the ways and means committee, which gave him control of the entire House legislation. And Stevens was a natural leader who assumed command by consent of all House Republicans. As party leader, Stevens disagreed mightily with Lincoln's approach to the war as too lukewarm on Southern rights. The only area in which he agreed with the administration was in finance. Stevens backed the funding of the war through greenbacks, the income tax, the direct tax on real estate, and the protective tariff. But when it came to the war, he was positively vindictive in his attitudes. He was one of two who in 1861 voted against the Crittenden Resolution, which declared that the war was not fought to subjugate the South or interfere with slavery. He urged total confiscation of Rebels' properties and later favored turning them over to the freedmen. He called for the arming and raising of black soldiers from the war's start. He bitterly criticized Lincoln for replacing generals John Charles Frémont and David Hunter and negating their military emancipations for Lincoln's go-slow emancipation policy, which Stevens dismissed as "diluted milk and water gruel."

Stevens did all he could to stiffen Northern resolve not only to restore the Union but to change its very core of meaning. He called on Lincoln to get rid of Republican compromisers in his administration like Secretary of State Seward and the Frank Blair family and other border-state politicos. He helped organize the joint commit-

and a crime." He accused slaveholders of "selecting and grooming the most lusty sires and the most fruitful wenches to supply the slave barracoons." And he attacked Northern compromisers as more immoral than the worst of the Southern slaveholders.

Stevens was looked upon as a reckless, foulmouthed, and irresponsible firebrand. Disgusted by what he saw as a weak-kneed stand of the Whigs on slavery, he quit Congress and he joined the infant Republican party, which he helped organize in Pennsylvania. In 1858, at age 68, he went back to Congress to enter the last debates on slavery before the Civil War. He spoke out for a high protective tariff and against the extension of slavery to the West. One debate with a Georgia congressman nearly caused a riot on the House floor. Stevens favored fellow Pennsylvanian Simon Cameron for president in 1860 but turned to Abraham Lincoln when the Cameron drive failed. After Lincoln's election, Stevens spoke out against compromise with the South as "the cowardly breath of servility and meanness."

tee on the conduct of the war, which had as its purpose the exposure and removal of "Democratic" generals (those who showed compassion to the occupied regions of the South and slavery) and the promotion of "Republican" ones (those who backed confiscation and emancipation). But the war did not go well despite Stevens's attempts to toughen Northern resolve. In 1863, it came home to Stevens personally, as Gen. Robert E. Lee's army invaded Stevens's home state of Pennsylvania. Confederate soldiers were well aware of Stevens's hostility and made a special trip to the outspoken congressman's ironworks, which they thoroughly wrecked and looted. Fortunately, Stevens was away in Washington, because Confederate Maj. Gen. Jubal Early, in charge of the expedition, had vowed to hang the old man, "divide his bones, and send them to the several states as curiosities."

As the war went on, Stevens theorized that the Constitution no longer applied to the South, that the South was but a conquered province because the Constitution had been so shattered by the force of the rebellion that it no longer had any application. Secession removed the Southern states' traditional rights and left the South susceptible to the will of the conqueror. A new basis of Union had to be drawn up, maintained Stevens, no holds barred. The entire South had to be remodeled in the proper manner to ensure that rebellion could never happen again. They had reverted to the territorial stage, such that they could have their very boundaries altered and had to do the bidding of the rest of the states through the federal administrators in the South. Part and parcel of this attitude was the enfranchising of African Americans as the only truly loyal group in the South. Of course, the whole process was to be congressional, not executive, in conception, and here Stevens ran head-on into Lincoln's Ten Percent Plan for Reconstruction (which Stevens considered pure nonsense). Stevens much preferred the harsher Wade-Davis Bill, and when the president gave it a pocket veto, Stevens characterized the action as "infamous."

It was only reluctantly that Steven supported Lincoln's second term, and he received the news of the chief executive's assassination with much equanimity. Stevens was quite thrilled with President Andrew Johnson's initial harsh statements on the content of Reconstruction but was greatly horrified when the new president announced his amnesty and pardon program. Stevens supported the renewal of the Freedmen's Bureau Bill and the passage of the Civil Rights Act of 1866 and got them passed over Johnson's vetoes; he exchanged bitter words with the president that led Johnson to deliver an ill-advised speech ridiculing particular congressmen by name. Stevens ran the whole Radical Republican program in the House, including the Fourteenth Amendment, the Military Reconstruction Acts, the Command of the Army Act, the Tenure of Office Act, and Johnson's impeachment.

When moderate elements of the party balked at Stevens's harsh program, he threatened, cajoled, taunted, and used his invective and sarcasm to the hilt to crack the party whip. But the drive to reconstruct the South took a toll on the old man, and his health began to fail him as the impeachment trial drew close. He took little part in the actual trial, even though he was one of the House managers. When Johnson survived the assault by one vote, it was too much for Stevens. His health sank so rapidly that he could not be carried home but died in Washington, with only his nephew and mulatto housekeeper, Lydia Smith (about whose actual relation with Stevens all sorts of prurient rumors had abounded), at his bedside. His funeral procession was second only to Lincoln's and attracted thousands of mourners. His self-penned epitaph was dedicated to the principle he had fought for all of his life: "Equality of Man before His Creator." And in tribute to his memory the voters of his Pennsylvania congressional district elected him posthumously one last time.

Stevens was ever the partisan whose career was marred by a harsh temper. His rare parliamentary talents made him a formidable force during Radical Reconstruction, but the vindictive nature of his assault on the South damaged many of his noblest ideals, including economic, social, and political equality for African Americans. He was well read and had a nimble mind and great courage. His sense of humor was a mite sardonic, as demonstrated by the time he handed his wig (he was completely bald) to a woman admirer who asked for a lock of his hair or, when after being praised on his healthy appearance, he remarked, "It's not my appearance but my disappearance that troubles me." He was a master of language and quick to cut to the point of any matter on which he spoke. To most historians (the most notable exception being W. E. Burghardt DuBois) he lacked the tolerance and magnanimity that would have made him a statesman, but he still remains one of the most important, colorful figures of the era, maligned by many, admired by some, and quoted by all. As biographer Fawn Brodie said, Stevens may have had indignation instead of love and a sense of injustice instead of hope, but he was the champion of the aspirations of African Americans as a free people. "It is sobering and disquieting to realize that if he had truly possessed both love and hope," Brodie concluded, "the Negro might well have had no such champion."

See also Johnson and Reconstruction; Lincoln and Reconstruction; Moderate Republicans and Reconstruction; Radical Republicans; Radical Republicans and Reconstruction.

References Bowers, Claude, *The Tragic Era* (1929); Brodie, Fawn, *Thaddeus Stevens* (1966); Bryant-Jones, Mildred, "The Political Program of Thaddeus Stevens" (1941); Callender, Edward B., *Thaddeus Stevens* (1972 [1882]); Current, Richard N., *Old Thad Stevens* (1942); DuBois, W. E. Burghardt, *Black Reconstruction* (1935); Korngold, Ralph, *Thaddeus Stevens* (1955); McCall, Samuel W., *Thaddeus Stevens* (1899); Morrill, George P., "The Best White Friend Black Americans Ever Had" (1971); Nevins, Allan, "Thaddeus Stevens" (1964–1981); Pickens, Donald K., "The Republican Synthesis and Thaddeus Stevens" (1985); Woodburn, James A., *The Life of Thaddeus Stevens* (1913); Woodley, Thomas Frederick, *Thaddeus Stevens* (1934).

Sumner, Charles (1811–1874)

Born in Boston of parents with all of the proper social credentials, Charles Sumner attended the prestigious Boston Latin School and Harvard College. He showed his greatest aptitude in history, literature, and forensics. He then attended Harvard Law School and was a student of Justice Joseph Story, who was a professor when he was not sitting on the U.S. Supreme Court. Through his acquaintanceship with Story, Sumner gained entry into Washington social and political circles; he attended the inner sessions of the Supreme Court when Chief Justice John Marshall was still presiding and heard Daniel Webster and Henry Clay speak on the floor of the U.S. Senate. Although Sumner professed at the time that he had nothing more than "any feeling but loathing" for politics, he had been fatally bitten by the political bug. But he was not fully aware of it yet. He went home to Massachusetts and found that the law held little attraction for him. He lectured at Harvard Law School only to find it boring. Sumner took a two-year trip to Europe, during which time he learned to speak Italian, German, and French with skill. He studied these countries' jurisprudence and governments and came home more weary than ever. Sumner applied for a court reporter's position only to be passed over. He tried to annotate the state law digest, which proved heartbreaking, as he was such a perfectionist.

Then in 1845 he got the opportunity that woke him up. Sumner was selected to give the annual Boston Independence Day address (which commemorated when General Thomas Gage left Boston in March 1776). It was a prestigious occasion, and Sumner rose to the challenge. His speech was that all peace was honorable and all war was dishonorable, a topic that did not appeal to the over 100 military guests present for the event. Although many believed that he had committed political suicide, it was a typical Sumner speech—taking the war to the enemy, so to speak, in his own lair. His controversial oration was perfectly delivered, however, and it made him the main attraction for years to come on the New England lyceum circuit. Sumner continued to plug away at the world's warmongers, making an appeal for a congress of nations that would arbitrate all disagreement among countries. And he attacked a local congressman and boyhood friend, John Winthrop, for voting in favor of the War with Mexico, which Sumner characterized as "the most wicked in our history."

But Sumner went even further. He called for the opposition of all good men to the traditional political parties (calling them an "alliance between the lords of the lash and lords of the loom") and issued a call for support for the Free Soil party. His outspokenness led a coalition of Free Soilers and Democrats to put his name up for the U.S. Senate. The call was so controversial that the state legislature was deadlocked. Finally several towns held special meetings and instructed their representatives to vote for Sumner. He took his seat in Washington in 1851. He would be there until his death 23 years later. Sumner immediately spoke out against the pro-slavery Compromise of 1850, a pact of laws that had nearly brought the nation to the verge of Civil War. For three hours he lambasted the Fugitive Slave Act, which guaranteed the return of escaped slaves to their Southern masters, and recommended that no money be appropriated for its enforcement. Sumner's amendment was rejected overwhelmingly, but his speech marked a turning point in the debate on slavery. The North had shifted from mere objection to the institution to an attack on its very existence.

But Sumner would become a household word in the debates over the Kansas-Nebraska Act. "With pleasure and pride" he led the fight against expanding the realm of slavery into the western territories through the repeal of the old Missouri Compromise of 1820, which had prohibited slavery in the Louisiana Purchase north of 36°30'. Sumner had dropped all other party affiliations and helped organize the Republicans. He pledged to uphold the U.S. Constitution only as he understood it, which meant without slavery. He asked the executive for all documents relating to the Kansas question.

Charles Sumner

Then he launched into his most famous speech, "The Crime against Kansas." He not only attacked slavery as an institution, but he named certain Southern senators by name—hitherto understood to be a no-no. He called Senator Andrew Butler of South Carolina slavery's Don Quixote, a man paying vows to his Desdemona of slavery, a harlot "polluted in the sight of the world, [but] chaste in his sight." Senator Stephen A. Douglas of Illinois, ever the compromiser with slavery, was labeled by Sumner as Sancho Panza, "the squire of slavery...ready to do its humiliating offices." Sumner accused Senator James Mason of Virginia, author of the Fugitive Slave Law, of representing another Virginia unknown to George Washington and Thomas Jefferson "where human beings are bred as cattle for the shambles." The speech horrified the whole Senate. Douglas believed that Sumner was trying to provoke a fight. Others called him a man without honor. He returned the insults with spite.

Several days later, when Sumner sat at his desk working on some papers, a man came up and called out his name. As Sumner looked up, the fellow introduced himself as Preston S. Brooks, a relative of Senator Butler. Brooks said that Butler had been absent during the "Crime against Kansas" speech and could not properly defend himself. Brooks then proceeded to "chastise" Sumner with his cane. He beat the Massachusetts man until the cane broke and then proceeded to hit him with the remnants until he was winded. Sumner, a big man (6'4" tall), was wedged in under his desk and could not rise. Then, in one burst of strength brought on by the pain of the beating, Sumner wrenched the desk up from the floor to which it had been attached and fainted from a loss of blood.

Brooks was an instant hero to the South. He resigned his congressional seat and was reelected by acclamation. People from all over the South sent him canes, some with the admonition "Hit him again!" The North was outraged. The incident seemed to personify the inability of the South to accept or answer a reasoned argument. Sumner was reelected to his seat, even though it would be three years before he could mount up the courage and well-being to attend another session. Meanwhile he went to Europe again to regain his health, submitting to the painful procedure of Moxa, a Japanese treatment in which the skin was burned by chemical treatment to relocate the pain, once described as "the greatest suffering than can be inflicted on mortal man." Publicists pointed to the "Empty Chair of Sumner" as evidence of the brutality brought on by slavery. When returned on the eve of the election of 1860, he delivered another tirade against slavery. Although many described it as rubbing salt in old wounds, Republicans republished it and distributed all over the North as an Abraham Lincoln campaign document.

As the South moved to secession, Sumner alone among the Massachusetts delegation to Washington urged no compromise. He ignored petitions from tens of thousands that he tone down the rhetoric and try to keep the nation whole. As the South left the Union and the Republican party finally took over Congress, Sumner received the chair of the committee on foreign relations. In this capacity he recognized the inevitability of having to free the Confederate commissioners to Europe—James Mason (author of the Fugitive Slave Act) and John Slidell—when an overzealous Union navy captain illegally took them from a British ship on the high seas. In October 1861, he was the first to move that slavery be completely ended throughout the nation, North and South. He continued to pressure the Lincoln administration to issue an emancipation proclamation. He was the first to call for equal rights, including the franchise, for all Americans regardless of color in early 1862.

At the same time, Sumner advanced his theory of Reconstruction, the state suicide theory. This concept argued that secession was impossible. Rather, by trying to leave the Union the states had committed a treasonous form of suicide. Although the United States retained control over these areas, the states had reverted to territorial status, under which they were at the mercy of Congress. This allowed state institutions (but not boundaries) to be altered at the pleasure of Congress with no constitutional guarantees to get in the way. Congress would decide what these suicidal brethren must do to return to the Union. And essentially what Sumner believed had to be done was to "civilize" and "Americanize" the South by making it over into an idealized version of New England.

Using his theory of Reconstruction, Sumner was instrumental in blocking any consideration of seating Lincoln's Louisiana Reconstruction government in Congress in 1864. Upon Lincoln's death, Sumner and Thaddeus Stevens in the House were brought into alliance by President Andrew Johnson's Reconstruction policies. Sumner was most interested in equal rights, while Stevens had a more political motivation—of not being voted out of the government by returning Southern Democrats and their Northern allies. Sumner fought for the recognition of African American political and social rights and suffrage. He also spoke in favor of free schools and homesteads for the freedmen. He was lukewarm on Johnson's impeachment, seeing it as a political rather than judicial proceeding. During the trial, however, he was more vindictive than he would have been in a real court proceedings and voted the party line to convict. Critics called it Sumner at his worst.

When the Ulysses S. Grant administration came into power, one might have expected Sumner and the chief executive to be in harmony at last. But Sumner and Grant never understood each other. Sumner rejected Grant's selection for secretary of the treasury on constitutional grounds. He prevented an early settlement of the *Alabama* claims, claiming that Great Britain owed the United States billions of dollars in claims from the destructive actions of Confederate cruisers built in Britain in violation of British laws. And Sumner was patently against the annexation of Santo Domingo, which he correctly saw as a corrupt action of Grant's inner circle. In retaliation Grant recalled Sumner's recommended appointment to Great Britain and had Sumner himself thrown off the Senate foreign relations committee. Despite this action Sumner continued to monitor foreign policy and spoke out in favor of the Treaty of Washington, which settled the *Alabama* claims in America's favor and recognized Sumner's hallowed principle of international arbitration.

About this time (1872) Sumner sponsored a bill that seemed out of character with his whole past. He asked that all Civil War battle names on federal regimental colors be obliterated as a gesture of reconciliation to the South. Opponents were outraged, and Sumner at first was verbally condemned and then censured (an act removed from the record two years later). But the act makes more sense when it is paired with the public accommodations bill Sumner introduced at the same time, a bill that became the Civil Rights Act of 1875 and was passed in his honor after his death. Sumner was willing to forgive and forget if the South was willing to do the same and truly free blacks. But Sumner never lived to see either measure become law. On 10 May 1874, he was felled by a heart attack. He died in Washington the next day. Many a Southern congressman took the opportunity to use his death for ending Reconstruction as they rose and spoke on his behalf. His funeral was held in Cambridge, Massachusetts.

Charles Sumner was a man who was hard to like, whether one stood for or against him. He was cold, austere, willing to argue any point to its fullest implication, and never one to compromise a principle. When a friend once accused him of being unwilling to see the other side of a question, Sumner replied with a booming finality, "There is no other side!" Sumner's genius was not in making laws. He was more like an ancient Hebrew prophet, a Jeremiah, who warned of God's vengeance if the world did not come over to his way of thinking. He felt he had a direct line to God. This made him quite smug and full of moral enthusiasm; he had a certain kind of intellectual courage and was a beacon of hope to the oppressed, and an assailer of injustice. But Sumner was more than a propagandizer. He diligently went through the everyday business of the Senate with care and took care of the claims of his constituents. He was an expert in foreign relations, money and finance, the tariff, postal regulations, and the copyright. His one goal was typified in the precepts of the Civil Right Act of 1875—absolute human equality to be secured and assured as invulnerable for all time.

See also Civil Rights Acts.

References Donald, David H., *Charles Sumner and the Coming of the Civil War* (1967) and *Charles Sumner and the Rights of Man* (1970); Freidel, Frank, "Francis Lieber, Charles Sumner, and Slavery" (1943); Haynes, George H., "Charles Sumner" (1964–1981); Hoar, G. F., ed., *Charles Sumner* (1900); Osofsky, Gilbert, "Cardboard Yankee" (1973); Ruchames, Louis, "Charles Sumner and American Historiography" (1953); Sefton, James E., "Charles Sumner for Our Time" (1971).

Supreme Court and Reconstruction

The third branch of government, the federal court system, theoretically posed as great a problem for Congressional Reconstruction as did the executive branch's proclamations and vetoes. Individual citizens and states had the right to appeal reconstructing policies of local civil jurisdictions and military commanders to the courts. White opponents to Reconstruction in the South immediately availed themselves of these remedies. So did Copperhead (antiwar) protesters in the North, who faced arrest and execution as a result of the same policies during the Civil War. Adverse opinions in the courts might undermine congressional authority to force the South to accept Republican Reconstruction policies as a condition of readmission to the Union.

During the Civil War the U.S. Supreme Court had essentially endorsed the Yankee war effort. The single exception was *ex parte Merryman*, in which Chief Justice Roger B. Taney railed against military arrest (outside the civilian court system) of nonmilitary personnel suspected of holding disloyal opinions. In the 1863 *Prize* cases, the Supreme Court had recognized a belligerent status for the Confederacy while denying it any more than de facto control of a specified land mass. It also endorsed in the same breath President Abraham Lincoln's numerous executive proclamations defining the war effort, proclamations that many in the North, including Republicans, believed lacked a constitutional mandate. The court would reaffirm its decision 15 years later in *Dow v. Johnson* (1879). In *ex parte Vallandigham* (1864) the court had gone along with a military trial of Clement L. Vallandigham, an outspoken anti-Lincoln agitator who was exiled to the Confederacy. And in *Miller v. United States* (1871) the court approved of the confiscation of property as a legitimate purpose of war. But many suspected that the court would rethink many of these issues (excepting confiscation, although the government would find it politic to return much seized property as part of its pardon policy) after the Rebel surrender.

The problem was fully revealed to Congress and the nation in a wartime case that concerned the activities of an Indiana Copperhead and Peace Democrat, Lamdin P. Milligan, who had been a member of the secret pro-Confederate Order of American Knights. As with most secret American orders, it seemed that the group had more government informants than actual members. In any case, tipped off as to Milligan's activities, the Union army arrested him and several compatriots for plotting to free Confederate soldiers being held as prisoners of war and spiriting them back into Confederate jurisdiction. Tried before a military tribunal, Milligan and two others were sentenced to hang. Naturally they appealed the decision, requesting a writ of habeas corpus and demanding a civilian trial. Because of the power of the Democratic party in Indiana, even the Republican governor who had spearheaded the drive for a military trial (the army was not happy to get involved) asked that the executions be deferred until the appeal was heard. In *ex parte Milligan et al.* (1866), the U.S. Supreme Court ruled that Milligan and his associates had been wrongfully convicted; the military court had no jurisdiction since civil courts were operating and available in Indiana despite the war. This also held true in the occupied South and threatened the jurisdictions of the Union army and Freedmen's Bureau, which regularly decided cases on behalf of blacks wronged by whites.

At the same time, the Supreme Court ruled on the use of test oaths. If loyalty oaths were administered as a part of punishment, they were unconstitutional bills of attainder or ex-post facto laws. But if they were drawn up as qualification requirements for public office, loyalty oaths were valid exercises of power by Congress or any state legislature. The problem was, of course, that during Reconstruction the test oaths were being administered as punishment for past actions. At least that is what the Supreme Court believed. In *Cummings v. Missouri* (1866) and *ex parte Garland* (1866), the court ruled that loyalty oaths like the ironclad oath (an oath of never having aided the Confederacy) were being used to punish white Southerners for past action rather than as qualifications for a future public position or voting.

Once again, Radical Republicans saw the court as a potential snag in their program for improving civilization in the South by introducing Yankee notions and institutions. The new federal appellate court for the District of Columbia defied the Supreme Court decisions in the *Cummings* and *Garland* cases with a bit of legal sleight of hand. They ruled that a member of the D.C. bar under the previous federal circuit court who had served with the Confederate army had to take the test oath because he was seeking membership anew under a court that had previously not existed under the same name (even though for all practical purposes it was the same body). Other institutions continued such foot-dragging (West Virginia refused to admit ex-Confederates to the bar even though the Supreme Court decisions implied that they should), but the problem eventually disappeared by the 1870s when pardons and new constitutions in the South eliminated the test oath as a requirement.

Congress, however, was not anxious to wait until the matter of Supreme Court reliability worked itself out. It proposed a measure that completely restructured the federal court system's circuits (which used to run east and west geographically but now ran north and south to negate any purely Southern jurisdiction) and reduced the number of justices on the Supreme Court from ten to seven. Modern historians excuse this measure by pointing out that it fit into Republican desires to attack the Slave Power Conspiracy, the undue Southern influence on all aspects of government (in Northern eyes, anyway). Older historians saw this as an attack on the integrity of the court through the person of President Andrew Johnson and appointments he might make. It would take four vacancies before the president could appoint one of his men to the court. This conspiracy thesis gained a lot of ground because Congress expanded the court to nine members as Johnson was going out of power and Ulysses S. Grant was coming in. But this can be seen as an attempt to keep the court Republican as much as a Radical attack on the court's independence.

Evidence of the court's independence was not long in coming after passage of the Military Reconstruction Acts. The provisional governors of the Southern states began a concentrated attack against the laws and asked that the executive branch be enjoined from carrying them out. Governor William L. Sharkey of Mississippi filed a suit asking that President Johnson refrain from carrying out the dictates of the Military Reconstruction Acts. But in *Mississippi v. Johnson* (1867), the Supreme Court refused to issue the order, claiming that the question was not a constitutional one that lay in the court's domain. The president had done his best to evade enforcement of the laws by using the constitutional remedy available to him, the veto. It was not the purpose of the court to tell a coequal branch of government how to carry out the laws of Congress.

Provisional Governor Charles J. Jenkins of Georgia took a slightly different tack with the same result. In *Georgia v. Stanton*, he sued Secretary of War Edwin M. Stanton, the man directly responsible for enforcing the Military Acts. Mississippi also filed a separate but similarly argued case against the secretary. They argued that the congressional laws interfered with an already constituted government by imposing an unconstitutional form of military rule. The court dismissed both suits, declaring that determining the republican form of government was properly a political question of sovereignty for the existence of a state and was reserved to Congress. (In this case, *republican* refers to a type of government, not a political party.) The court could rule only as to the rights of persons and property. If Congress seated or refused to seat a state government's representatives, the question was settled.

Temporarily foiled, Georgia refused to advance money from its state treasury to meet the expenses of Reconstruction (particularly in not paying for the state convention required by the Military Acts). Governor

Jenkins removed the state's money to New York and filed the suit *Georgia v. Grant et al.* (1868) to prevent the army from recovering it. In return, the army seized a state-owned railroad to get some money for the convention. But a key question arose as to whether Georgia was really a state with rights to sue, so the case was held off until this question was established under other pending suits.

But if the Georgia case involved investigating whether Georgia was actually a state and could bring suit, there was no such difficulty in the case of *ex parte McCardle*, which concerned the rights of an individual and was fully within the court's jurisdiction. William H. McCardle was a very vocal newspaper editor in Vicksburg, Mississippi. He was unalterably opposed to the Military Reconstruction Acts and editorialized against them to the point of vituperation. His basic contention was, do not obey these laws, boycott them. He published lists of those whites who cooperated with the federal authorities so that the town might properly ostracize them. Major General E. O. C. Ord, commanding the Fourth Military District (Mississippi and Arkansas), had him arrested and charged in front of a military tribunal with disturbing the peace and inciting insurrection. McCardle appealed his case to the U.S. Supreme Court, asking for a writ of habeas corpus. It looked a lot like the *Milligan* case except that there was no longer a Civil War. If McCardle's request were ruled upon based on the same principles, much of the impact of Reconstruction would be nullified, as arguments before the court on the comprehensiveness and unconstitutionality of a military commanders' civil powers under the Reconstruction Acts aptly showed.

Congress had gone through too much with President Johnson to allow a bunch of legal theorists sitting in isolation from the realities of the world to derail its intent in Reconstruction. After a few false starts that were definitely too radical for most members, Congress added an amendment on a simple bill allowing the court to review certain internal review laws. The amendment would negate the court's right to hear appeals under the Habeas Corpus Act of 1867, the measure McCardle had used to sue over the army's carrying out of the Reconstruction Acts. Ironically, the act had been passed to protect freedmen, army personnel, and Freedmen's Bureau officers from adverse action in hostile state courts. Now it would be used to protect one of their critics. This changed the case from one concerning Reconstruction and individual rights to one about the right of Congress to change the Supreme Court's appellate jurisdiction, a right guaranteed to Congress in the Constitution and something that the American Bar Association has repeatedly tried to change without success in the twentieth century through constitutional amendment (the court's original jurisdiction is unchangeable and also defined in the Constitution). The court immediately put off decision in the case until the following year, when it confirmed Congress' action without examining its motive and dropped the *McCardle* case completely without decision.

Meanwhile the problem of the constitutionality of the Military Reconstruction Acts arose once again in *ex parte Yerger*, another Mississippi newspaper editor's case, this one from Jackson. Edward M. Yerger had stabbed to death an army officer serving as the militarily appointed mayor of the Mississippi capital; the officer had seized a piano for nonpayment of taxes (Yerger was a bankrupt). Yerger was tried for murder before a military commission. As the trial proceeded he applied for a writ of habeas corpus from the circuit judge for Mississippi, Associate Justice Joseph Bradley. As the Supreme Court justice sitting on circuit, Bradley denied the plea. Yerger's attorneys applied directly to Chief Justice Salmon P. Chase, who at first refused to override Bradley, then acquiesced. The appeal, however, was brought under the Judiciary Act of 1789, not the Habeas Corpus Act of 1867. Thus Yerger would follow a different route to the Supreme Court, regardless of what would happen with McCardle.

When the Yerger case came up before the whole court, the judges ruled that they had jurisdiction through a writ of habeas corpus aided by a writ of certiorari. By now it was 1870 and Reconstruction was over in all states but Texas and Mississippi (and elections there would be held in a matter of months). So the court cut a deal whereby the federal government dropped the case and the Supreme Court remanded it to the Mississippi state courts as soon as the state was readmitted to the Union. There Yerger managed to escape authorities and flee to Maryland, where he dabbled in the Liberal Republican movement, published a Baltimore newspaper, and finally died in 1875 of natural causes. He was never brought to civilian trial for fear that it would constitute double jeopardy after the military trial.

But by the time Yerger's case was essentially dropped, the Supreme Court declared the nation to be a union of indestructible states in two other cases, *Texas v. White* (1869) and *Virginia v. West Virginia* (1871). The Texas case related to some state bonds sold during the war to finance the buying of military goods for the Confederacy. The problem in Texas and other Southern states was that Radical Republicans wanted the results of all laws passed between secession and surrender declared null and void ab initio (i.e., since their inception). This would include such mundane things as contracts and marriages made during the war. Of course, the Confederacy and the seceded states had done the same with debts owed to Yankees contracted from before the war. But an even more basic question had to be decided first. Was Texas a state, and could it bring suit before the Supreme Court? The court ruled yes on both counts. Once Texas had joined the Union it could not leave. Hence secession was null and void. But the court had to admit that, because of the attempted secession, Texas and the other Southern states were not in normal relations with the rest of the United States. These states had forfeited some rights because of the rebellion. It was the duty of Congress, under its mandate of securing a republican government for all states, to decide what conditions the South must meet to come back into normal relations with the rest of the country. Hence Military Recon-

struction, although unusual, was perfectly legal and constitutional.

Then the court moved on to the second issue, the bonds and ab initio. Texas did not have to pay off the bondholders, said the court. To decide the ab initio concerns, the court said that each particular situation had to be looked at. The bonds were designed to support the rebellion and were null and void ab initio. But normal relationships of everyday life were not connected to the war, and all of these issues handled during the war were entirely valid. Included were such items as criminal and civil trials and their results, normal business and personal contracts (like marriages, wills, deeds, and the like) "necessary to peace and good order among citizens." What the court finally did in *Texas v. White* was recognize the Chase-Shellabarger forfeited rights theory as being the basis of Reconstruction. It was a practical notion that made the deeds pertaining to the war invalid but allowed all other relationships to stand. It was, in effect, a Moderate Republican version of Reconstruction.

In *Commonwealth of Virginia v. State of West Virginia* (1871) the issue was whether two counties in the panhandle of West Virginia (Berkeley and Jefferson) had been truly admitted to the new state. West Virginia was something of an anomaly anyhow. When Virginia had seceded the western third of the state had refused to go along and had formed its own loyal government of Virginia still in the Union. Then, in 1862, this loyal Virginia had given the western counties permission to form a new state under the supervision and approval of Congress. For all practical purposes, since the loyal Virginia was actually the state of West Virginia, it had given itself permission to form. But two of the counties in West Virginia had not voted on inclusion in the new state constitution until after the new state had been created. After the war, secessionist Virginia wanted these counties back—actually it repealed the separation legislation and wanted all of the western counties back. When Congress reaffirmed what it had done during the war in 1866, Virginia went to court. On 6 March 1871, the court dismissed the case. It noted that the case had no relation to property or individuals but rested on assertions of sovereignty. These were political matters reserved for Congress under the Constitution, and Congress had taken note—albeit a bit late in the 1866 reaffirmation of West Virginia, but nonetheless valid and entirely within the forfeited rights theory of causing some actions of punishment for committing rebellion.

With the decision in *Virginia v. West Virginia* the Supreme Court had effectively disposed of the legal matters arising out of the Civil War and Reconstruction. But it would later take a look at other related matters on the enforcement of Reconstruction and the Civil War constitutional amendments that came up as the South was "redeemed" by conservative white rule.

See also Chase, Salmon P.; Johnson and Reconstruction; Lincoln and Reconstruction; Military Reconstruction Acts; Supreme Court and Redemption; Theories of Reconstruction.

References Fairman, Charles, *Reconstruction and Reunion* (1971–1987); Hyman, Harold, *A More Perfect Union* (1973); Johnson, Ludwell H., III, "Abraham Lincoln and the Development of Presidential War-Making Powers" (1989) and "The Confederacy" (1986); Kelly, Alfred H., and Wilfred A. Harbison, *The American Constitution* (1970); Kutler, Stanley I., "*Ex Parte McCardle*" (1967), *Judicial Power and Reconstruction Politics* (1968), and "Reconstruction and the Supreme Court" (1966); Lucie, Patricia M. L., "Confiscation" (1977); Pierson, William Wately, "Texas *Versus* White" (1914–1915, 1915–1916); Randall, James G., *Constitutional Problems under Lincoln* (1964); Warren, Charles, *The Supreme Court in United States History* (1922); Wiecek, William M., "The Great Writ and Reconstruction" (1970) and "The Reconstruction of Federal Judicial Power" (1969).

Supreme Court and Redemption

As the Southern states fell one by one to the Redeemers, the U.S. Supreme Court began to enunciate a series of decisions that essentially cut the heart out of the Fourteenth and Fifteenth amendments, which had epitomized the essence of Reconstruction. The result was that by 1900, with the assistance of the Supreme Court, Reconstruction was pretty well dead on all fronts.

The trend began quite early with the *Slaughter House* cases (1873). These cases, the first litigation under the Fourteenth Amendment, involved a Louisiana abattoir law that had been passed to regulate the slaughter of animals in the city of New Orleans. In an attempt to clean up the city's poor sanitation, the state legislature (after the usual bribes and payoffs) had decreed that all slaughtering had to take place at one location. Butchers had to pay to use the Crescent City Stock Landing and Slaughter House Company that had the monopoly. The city's butchers sued, in a series of cases finally combined into one, citing the measure as a form of involuntary servitude prohibited under the Thirteenth Amendment and a denial of their privileges and immunities as citizens guaranteed under the Fourteenth Amendment. The court dismissed the claims. It stated that the Thirteenth Amendment was related exclusively to black slavery. The court disposed of the Fourteenth Amendment's provisions in various ways: "privileges and immunities of citizenship" were declared to be state and federal, with the federal being limited to things like protection on the high seas and in foreign lands, use of domestic rivers and ports, and access to habeas corpus; "equal protection under the laws" was limited to African Americans and involved such illegal state matters such as the Black Codes; and "due process" was satisfied so long as the law in question had been correctly considered by the legislative body that passed it. Put bluntly, there were not many individual rights under the Fourteenth Amendment.

The Civil Rights Act of 1875, a lifelong project of Massachusetts Senator Charles Sumner, was the congressional answer to the court's curtailing of the wider implications of the Fourteenth Amendment. It was essentially the United States' first public accommodations law and guaranteed citizens of every race the "full and equal" enjoyment and use of inns, public conveyances, and theaters and other places of public amusement. It also had a section that race was not to be a factor in excluding persons from service on grand (indictment) and petit (trial) juries. But to the disappointment of many, it left out any mention of equal schools, cemeteries, and church attendance. These were politically inexpedient measures so far as Congress was concerned. Indeed, if the Civil Rights Act of 1875 had not been presented as a memorial to Senator Sumner, who had just died, it might not have been enacted at all. North and South, people thought the demands of the bill to be an invasion of individual personal prerogatives. But the bill went a long way toward correcting what blacks and their white allies saw as the shortcomings of the Fourteenth Amendment because of the *Slaughter House* cases. The courts would get to the Civil Rights Act's implications in due time after disposing of other matters first.

After weakening the Fourteenth Amendment in the *Slaughter House* cases, the court went on to consider the validity of convictions under the Enforcement Acts, which had been passed to enforce the Fifteenth Amendment. In *Minor v. Happersett* (1875) Virginia L. Minor had been refused the right to register to vote on grounds that she was a woman; in *United States v. Reese et al.* (1876), a state election official had been accused and convicted of not accepting and counting the vote of a black citizen who had not paid a required poll tax. But the court saw the provisions of the Enforcement Acts as being so broad as to punish any interference with the franchise even though the Fifteenth Amendment limited this to interference by race alone. Hence the Enforcement Acts lacked specific authority under the Constitution. Minor lost her bid to vote, while Hiram Reese and his two codefendants were sustained in their refusal to count votes.

In the *United States v. Cruikshank et al.* (1876), the defendants were among the attackers of blacks and white Republicans forted up in a Louisiana courthouse. A bloodbath known as the Colfax Massacre ensued. William Cruikshank and others were identified by victims, arrested, and convicted under the Enforcement Acts. The court found that Cruikshank and his codefendants had not violated the Fifteenth Amendment because no law in Louisiana prevented blacks from voting. Rather, Cruikshank and his companions were able to be tried under state laws concerning fraud, intimidation, murder, and assault. So long as a state did not interfere with the functioning of the Fourteenth or Fifteenth amendments formally, by law the illegal actions of individuals should be handled by a local authority. It was only when the state violated the amendment that federal law could apply directly to actions of individuals. In effect the Supreme Court put black and white Republicans at the mercy of roaming bands of armed gunmen, because no state could gain a conviction through the jury system for crimes considered by whites to be justifiable. And no state had acted to violate the terms of the Fifteenth Amendment.

This view was reemphasized a few years later in *United States v. Harris et al.* (1882), a case concerning a mob of 20 men who took four African Americans accused of various violations of Tennessee law from state authority and hanged them. The court ruled that the Fourteenth Amendment did not go into effect merely because the state had been overwhelmed in its enforcement of the law. Any effort, failed or otherwise, counted. Congress' inability to pass a proposed Fourth Enforcement Bill to tighten up the whole process left matters standing as the court declared.

But the court did not leave them for long. In the *Civil Rights* cases (1883), the court ruled that the Fourteenth Amendment did not in any way imbue Congress with the power to interfere in the domain of state legislation. The amendment instead provided a relief to people adversely affected by certain state legislation. This ruling attacked the equal accommodations section of the Civil Rights Act of 1875 as not operating on a specific state action but instead affecting the desires of private individuals. This was not the purpose of the Fourteenth Amendment, said the court, although the court had earlier (1880) upheld the parts of the Civil Rights Act of 1875 pertaining to the right of blacks to serve on juries (*Strauder v. West Virginia* and *Virginia v. Rives*), which the court saw as a valid exercise of the amendment. But the court stated its belief that at some point black Americans had to cease being objects of special treatment under the law and be dealt with the same as any other citizen. Again the gist of the court throughout this era was that the Fourteenth Amendment permitted Congress to enforce its provisions the moment the state failed to comply with those provisions. Absent the state's formal failure to act, however, Congress could do nothing to interfere with state prerogatives. A vigorous dissent by Associate Justice John Marshall Harlan of Kentucky, who said that these public accommodations were so basic that their absence violated not only the precepts of the Fourteenth Amendment but the Thirteenth Amendment against slavery as well, stood virtually alone.

The crowning decisions on the Fourteenth and Fifteenth amendments came at the end of the nineteenth century with Jim Crow (social and legal segregation) and black disfranchisement (political segregation). Originating in the North, the Jim Crow system had been designed to replace slavery, which was gradually being eradicated there by the first wave of the American Revolution. It spread from the cities because that is where traditional white control first broke down, a gradual process that continued until the Civil War in the South. By 1865, the end of formal slavery under the new constitutional amendments meant that a new social, political, and economic provision had to be made for African Americans. Few considered complete equality as the answer. The result was segregation, disfranchisement, and peonage. The key to this process was the willingness of the North to assist or acquiesce in the result. For this reason, it took 30 years after the Civil War ended to set Jim Crow in place, first by tradition, then by actual law. Lynching helped in the former, Congress and the Supreme Court in the latter.

No instance has come to typify the Jim Crow reality as of the 1890s better than the Louisiana case of *Homer A. Plessy v. Judge John H. Ferguson*. Louisiana had had a segregated system of streetcars before and during the Civil War (called "star cars" because they had five-pointed stars to indicate that black occupancy was allowed); these cars had been integrated by a concerted effort during Reconstruction. In 1890, prompted by Congress' failure to pass Henry Cabot Lodge's new Enforcement Bill designed to enforce renewed Southern compliance in black rights of citizenship, Louisiana passed a new law segregating railcars by race. Unlike most of the rest of the South, New Orleans had a highly articulate, well-educated population of blacks and people of mixed race. The state also had a Latin concept of race that allowed mixed-race relationships to be entered into more freely than anywhere else in the country. Plessy himself was classified as an octoroon, one-eighth black, and his participation in the case was no accident, but rather an intentional setup; it was felt that an almost white person might advance the cause with fewer racial hangups in the higher courts than an easily distinguished black person. So Homer A. Plessy took a train ride from New Orleans to Covington, purchasing a first-class ticket and sitting in a "whites only" car. He was promptly arrested.

In the ensuing trial, Plessy's attorney, Albion W. Tourgée, maintained that the Louisiana law violated Plessy's rights under the Thirteenth and Fourteenth amendments. But Judge John H. Ferguson held that the case was a state matter and Plessy could be proscribed from riding in all but designated cars. Tourgée appealed the case, eventually to the U.S. Supreme Court, as *Plessy v. Ferguson*. There, on 19 May 1896, the highest court in the land ruled that states could separate the races legally, provided that "separate but equal" accommodations were provided for all those so proscribed. Technically the decision involved only transportation, but other decisions soon expanded the "separate but equal" rule into all areas of American life. Judge Harlan again dissented to no avail.

Shortly after it decided the *Plessy* case, the U.S. Supreme Court validated the formal skirting of the Fifteenth Amendment in *Williams v. Mississippi* (1898). After Congress had dropped the Lodge Force Bill from consideration, Mississippi decided to take the final step and disfranchise African American within the limits set by the Fifteenth Amendment. Because of its negative wording, the amendment did not actually grant anyone the right to vote. It merely said that race could not be the sole determining factor. This left the states wide latitude to use any other method but race to achieve the same goal. Eventually two devices achieved the endorsement of the court: the literacy test and the poll tax. Two others, the grandfather clause and the white primary, would be declared unconstitutional because they excluded blacks on their skin color alone.

Mississippi led the way with the Second Mississippi Plan (the first plan had been the Shotgun Plan of 1876). The idea was simple: no one could vote without being able to read and write or understand the federal and state constitutions. Since these requirements on their face did not involve race, the court accepted them in 1898 as acceptable means to regulate elections. With the endorsement of disfranchisement on some other basis than race alone, *Williams v. Mississippi* gave the South the go-ahead to make disfranchisement of blacks an established fact. South Carolina and Louisiana quickly followed suit with new state constitutions imitating the Second Mississippi Plan. But the South could not keep away from overt racism. The real problem, of course, was that the tests were never given equally, and it was upon this fault that the exclusions would ultimately fail a half century later.

See also Redemption of the South before 1874; Redemption of the South after 1874; Supreme Court and Reconstruction; Tourgée, Albion W.

References Avins, Alfred, "Racial Segregation in Public Accommodations" (1967); Donald David H., *Charles Sumner and the Rights of Man* (1970); Emerson, Thomas I., et al., *Political and Civil Rights in the United States* (1967); Fairman, Charles, *Reconstruction and Reunion* (1971–1987); Fischer, Roger A., *The Segregation Struggle in Louisiana* (1974); Franklin, John Hope, "The Enforcement of the Civil Rights Act of 1875" (1989); Frantz, Laurent B., "Fourteenth Amendment Against Private Acts" (1964); Gaffney, Edward M., Jr., "History and Legal Interpretation" (1976); Gillette, William, *Retreat from Reconstruction* (1979); Kaczorowski, Robert J., *The Nationalization of Civil Rights* (1987); Kelly, Alfred H., "The Congressional Controversy over School Segregation" (1958–1959); Hyman, Harold, *A More Perfect Union* (1973); Kelly, Alfred H., and Wilfred A. Harbison, *The American Constitution* (1970); Kutler, Stanley I., *Judicial Power and Reconstruction Politics* (1968); Logan, Rayford W., *The Betrayal of the Negro* (1965); McPherson, James M., "Abolitionists and the Civil Rights Act of 1835" (1965); Murphy, L. E., "The Civil Rights Law of 1875" (1927); Nathan, Hans, *Dan Emmett and the Rise of Early Negro Minstrelsy* (1962); Olsen, Otto H., ed., *The Thin Disguise* (1967); Perman, Michael, *The Road to Redemption* (1984); Warren, Charles, *The Supreme Court in United States History* (1922); Weaver, Valerie W., "The Failure of Civil Rights 1875–1883 and Its Repercussions" (1969); Woodward, C. Vann, *The Strange Career of Jim Crow* (1966).

Swing around the Circle

In the fall of 1866, President Andrew Johnson took to the campaign trail to help elect Democrats to Congress. These Democrats would help him oppose Congressional Reconstruction, which was becoming more and more Radical (largely because of Johnson's own bad moves, such as a speech he gave on the anniversary of Washington's birthday, in which he lambasted certain congressmen by name). Ostensibly the purpose of the journey was to dedicate the tomb of former Illinois Senator Stephen A. Douglas, Abraham Lincoln's old debating partner from 1858. Johnson took along secretaries William H. Seward and Gideon Welles; Conservative Republican Senator James R. Doolittle; generals Ulysses S. Grant and George A. Custer; and Admiral David G. Farragut. Friends tried to convince the president not to go. Campaigning so openly for mere congressmen was deemed undignified in those days, and many feared a repeat of the Washington birthday speech would destroy what little claim Johnson had left to presidential solemnity.

As expected, the trip, which took place from 28 August to 15 September 1866, proved a disaster. Johnson was essentially a stump speaker in the rough-and-tumble style of the Southern backcountry, which did not go over in the urban cities of the

North. Stump speakers like to be challenged by the audience and reply with bitter invective, often with biting humor. In the days before radio, movies, and television, political speaking was a fine art of entertainment. But there was little entertainment in the "Swing around the Circle," as this presidential whistle-stop speaking tour from the back of a train (the first in American history) was called—unless one enjoyed watching the president commit political suicide. It became so embarrassing that one by one his entourage found reasons to cut their participation short.

Almost immediately hecklers hit Johnson right where it hurt. Although at New York City he received a banner from a soldier wounded at Antietam and imprisoned at Andersonville that read: "We who fought and gave our blood to perpetuate this Union, will not permit it to be severed by [Charles] Sumner, Thad Stevens, and other co-conspirators;" trouble began soon after. At Westfield, New York, Johnson began with his usual disclaimer that he was not going to make a speech—and then proceeded to make a speech. When a voice in the crowd persistently asked a question, the president shouted, "Keep quiet till I have concluded. Just such fellows as you have kicked up all the rows of the last five years." Radical reporters took note. In Ohio, Senator Ben Wade saw to it that professional hecklers were at every stop. Johnson compared himself to the crucified Christ and his opponents to Judas Iscariot. He wrapped his plan for the nation in the flag and Constitution.

"We advise loyal citizens to avoid him as they would any other convicted criminal," warned newspapers. At Terre Haute a crowd tried to derail the train. At Indianapolis a prearranged riot came off splendidly for the Republicans. Cries of "shoot the damned traitor" rang out. General Grant stepped up to the platform and shouted, "For the sake of your city, hear us all speak!" A spectator yelled back, "For the sake of our city, go to Hell!" (Grant left the convoy shortly afterward, disillusioned with Johnson and ripe for a Republican conversion.) At St. Louis, Johnson went back to biblical analogies again. "Stevens, Sumner, and [Wendell] Phillips liken themselves to Jesus Christ and call everybody else Judas," Johnson boomed out. "Hah! Well, if we must hang, thank God, they shall be crucified!" Local politicians of both parties began to call in sick at every stop.

Essentially the "Swing around the Circle" saw the president repudiate the party that elected him. It also failed to produce votes for the Democrats whom the president desperately needed to stop Congressional Reconstruction. It permitted the Moderate and Conservative Republicans of the Thirty-ninth Congress (still seated until March 1867), who had desperately worked for a Reconstruction compromise, to desert the president with clean consciences and join the Radicals to get tough on the South. And it produced a veto-proof majority for the Fortieth Congress to come in 1867. The whole revolutionary idea of presidential railroad campaigning to produce a Congress in league with him had blown up in Johnson's face.

See also Johnson and Reconstruction; Moderate Republicans and Reconstruction; Washington Birthday Speech.

Reference McKitrick, Eric, *Andrew Johnson and Reconstruction* (1960); Trefousse, Hans L., *Andrew Johnson* (1989).

Tax Laws

Under the Constitution, the federal government may raise a direct property tax. Such a tax was raised to finance the burden of fighting the Civil War. Because the North refused to consider the South as having seceded, the taxes were levied for all sections of the nation, including those in the Confederacy. This posed problems in terms of payment, with respect to both inconvenience and a belief in the South that the North had no jurisdiction. These problems were settled by the outcome of the war. Much Southern land was sold when the owner could not make the tax payment, although portions of this property were returned under the later pardon policies of President Andrew Johnson.

The Tax Law of 1861 was established by Congress to pay for the prosecution of the Civil War; it applied to land within the Confederacy as well as the rest of the nation. If this tax went unpaid, the law allowed the land in question to be sold for taxes owed. Usually Northern companies speculated on this land, often making large profits. Many of the effects of this confiscation were ameliorated by President Andrew Johnson's pardon policy.

The Tax Law of 1862, passed 22 June 1862, expanded the Tax Law of 1861 by creating special tax commissioners to collect revenues owed in insurrectionary sections of the United States. All assessments were made based on 1861 values; a 50 percent penalty was added to all accounts in arrears; and upon failure of the owner to pay the tax and any penalty, the land could be seized and sold to the highest bidder. Of course, this tax could be collected only in areas of the South occupied by the Union armies. These land sales differed from ordinary federal tax sales, in which the amount raised above the tax owed was given to the owner. Here it went to the federal treasury. The most famous case of property seizure under this law was the Arlington estate, home of the Robert E. Lees. For a tax owed of $92.07, which the commissioners insisted had to be paid in person rather than by legal representative as the Lees proposed, the estate was sold for $26,000 to the federal government, which turned it into the Arlington National Cemetery. Mrs. Lee's heirs (she actually owned the property) sued for its return. After a long and involved litigation, during which lower courts ruled that the estate was rightfully the Lees, the Supreme Court ruled that the tax commissioners in this particular case had overstepped their bounds. To retain the Arlington National Cemetery, the U.S. government settled with the Lees for $150,000 and a release to all claims in the 1880s.

See also Confiscation Acts.

Reference Randall, James G., *Constitutional Problems under Lincoln* (1964).

Ten Percent Plan

The Ten Percent Plan is a name given popularly to President Abraham Lincoln's plan of Reconstruction, which required 10 percent of the registered voters in any occupied Southern state to take an oath of future loyalty to the Union to begin the process of wartime Reconstruction.

See also Lincoln and Reconstruction; Wade-Davis Bill.

Reference Randall, James G., *Lincoln the President* (1945–1955)

Tenure of Office Act

The Tenure of Office Act, one of several measures designed to limit President Andrew Johnson's ability to interfere with congressional desires in Reconstruction, provided that executive branch officers appointed with the advice and consent of the Senate could be removed only through the same process. A presidential tenure was defined as the president's possession of office plus one month. By this act, along with the Command of the Army Act, Congress hoped to freeze in place a reliable power structure to control the actions of the army in occupying the South and enforcing Reconstruction. The key official here was the secretary of war, Edwin M. Stanton, a holdover from the Abraham Lincoln administration and a Radical Republican spy in the president's own cabinet. To keep up his charade as a loyal cabinet member, Stanton, a prewar lawyer of repute, even wrote up the president's veto message of the measure designed to protect him in office, knowing full well that Congress would override the veto. Johnson's intentional violation of this measure in order to create a legal case was one of the key parts of the impeachment charges leveled against him later.

See also Command of the Army Act; Impeachment; Johnson and Reconstruction; Moderate Republicans and Reconstruction; Radical Republicans and Reconstruction; Stanton, Edwin McMasters.

References Sefton, James E., *Army and Reconstruction* (1967); Thomas, Benjamin P., and Harold M. Hyman, *Stanton* (1962).

Theories of Reconstruction

There were almost a half dozen theories of Reconstruction's constitutional basis, each with variants of its own, and probably no one then or now can say that any one of them was entirely correct. Nowadays the constitutional theories are considered as important as they were early in the century, but for years few historians bothered to investigate them. Indeed, historians preferred to give Andrew Johnson the best of the argument by default. But others had their ideas, too.

THE PRESIDENTIAL THEORY

Applied by both President Abraham Lincoln and his successor, Andrew Johnson, the presidential theory arose from the executive proclamation, something that has great impact during a time of war. Lincoln put forth his Ten Percent Plan as a method to undermine the Southern will to fight. It permitted a small part of the population in any seceded state to apply for restoration if they (1) took an oath of future loyalty, (2) allowed themselves to be occupied by the federal army, and (3) recognized the wartime acts of Congress and the president. The centerpiece of this theory was an official refusal to accept that the states had ever really seceded. But Lincoln and Johnson saw the presidential plan as two different things. Lincoln envisioned it as a proposal, not excluding Congress from input, but nothing to be inflexibly tied to forever. Johnson thought of Reconstruction just the opposite. He expected Congress to go along with his plan and fought over modifications that Congress thought would make the South pay for the war, like freedmen's rights.

The real problem was that neither president could get his people seated in the Southern state governments without the concurrence of Congress. That body alone is charged in the Constitution with ensuring that each state has a republican form of government (in reference to the theory of government, not the party). Lincoln knew this would ultimately give Congress a voice in Reconstruction, but Johnson seemed to find this reprehensible (which was odd, given that Johnson was a constitutionalist). The result was that, after Lincoln's death, a bitter fight broke out between the legislative and executive branches over policy, with the Supreme Court caught in the middle. One suspects that Lincoln would have avoided this or at least handled it with more aplomb and skill than Johnson, who forgot that presidents have great power during the emergency of war but much less during the humdrum of peace.

THE SOUTHERN THEORY

One of the first doctrines of Reconstruction came from the South, and it naturally was one of the easiest to apply. The South was willing, after four years of bloody conflict, to admit that dissolution could not physically take place. Therefore it must submit at once to the Union and its Constitution. With the end of the war everything must revert to as it was in 1860, with the possible exception of the abolition of slavery. Individuals might be guilty of treason, but the states had the same rights and duties as before as described in the fundamental document. The governors ought to call their state legislatures into session and sue for peace. They certainly had nothing to lose by this gesture.

Oddly, the most famous proponent of the Southern theory of Reconstruction was none other than Maj. Gen. William T. Sherman, Lt. Gen. Ulysses S. Grant's right-hand man, the man who made Georgia howl as he cut a 60-mile wide swath of terror and destruction across its heart. Sherman's ideas were embodied in his terms to the surrender of the South's number two army, commanded by Gen. Joseph Johnston at Goldsboro, North Carolina. Unaware of Lincoln's explicit orders on the subject of surrender, but cognizant that Lincoln believed in a decent peace, Sherman allowed Johnston's army to disband with all of their equipment, which was to be restored to their state capitols. He also made a sweeping commitment on Reconstruction itself, something Grant did not do. He promised a general amnesty, that the people would be guaranteed their political and property rights (except with respect to slaves), and that no citizen would be molested because of the late war so long as they lived in peace and obeyed federal laws. He even recognized several Southern provisional state governments. The result was an uproar that even Grant and President Andrew Johnson could not bear. Sherman's peace was immediately repudiated and had to be renegotiated on the basis of Grant's offering at Appomattox. A simple return to the United States in 1860 would not suffice. Some kind of notice of the four years between Fort Sumter and Appomattox had to be made.

CONQUERED PROVINCES THEORY

Almost the exact opposite of the Southern theory, the conquered provinces theory asserted that the Constitution had been so shattered by the force of the rebellion that it no longer had any application to the South. The Southern states were no longer states in the Union; secession removed their traditional rights and left them conquered provinces, susceptible to the will of the victor. This theory, a favorite of Radical Republi-

can representative Thaddeus Stevens of Pennsylvania, maintained that the states had seceded and a new basis of union had to be drawn up, no holds barred. The entire South had to be remodeled in the proper manner to ensure that rebellion could never happen again. They had reverted to the territorial stage, where they could have their very boundaries altered and had to do the bidding of the rest of the states through the federal administrators in the South. Part and parcel of this was the enfranchising of African Americans as the only truly loyal group in the South. Of course, the whole process was to be congressional, not executive, in conception.

Oddly, more Southern whites admitted to this theory than Northerners. Yankees found it repugnant to the very idea of republican government, not the American way. Rebels admired its straightforwardness, its admission that they had seceded and created their own government and fought for four years to protect it. It also recognized that the South had altered the nation forever, for better or worse. Southerners, especially former Confederate soldiers, welcomed military government and occupation. These things promised law and order and conservative social stratification, which were sadly missing in the confusion that accompanied the fall of the Confederacy. However, this theory was too removed from the Constitution to suit most Americans and, like the Southern theory, it provided a starting point for discussion but little more.

STATE SUICIDE THEORY

A favorite of Massachusetts Senator Charles Sumner, the state suicide theory of Reconstruction argued that secession was impossible. Rather, by trying to leave the Union the states had committed a treasonous form of suicide. Although the United States retained control over these areas, they had reverted to territorial status, where they were at the mercy of Congress. This territorial status was important in both Sumner's and Steven's plans because it allowed state institutions (but not boundaries, according to Sumner) to be altered at the pleasure of Congress. There were no constitutional guarantees to get in the way. Congress would decide what these suicidal brethren must do to return to the Union. And for Sumner, as with Stevens, this included some recognition of African American rights, especially the vote.

SHELLABARGER-CHASE THEORY OF FORFEITED RIGHTS

First conceived by Republican representative Samuel Shellabarger of Ohio and later used by the U.S. Supreme Court under Chief Justice Salmon P. Chase, the forfeited rights theory of Reconstruction held secession to be null and void (no state could ever leave the Union) but admitted that the participant states had forfeited some of their rights by committing this form of treason. It worked under the Supreme Court case of *Luther v. Borden* from the 1840s Dorr War in Rhode Island. Then two warring factions had appealed to the court to settle their dispute. The court held that whichever representatives and senators Congress seated were the legal representatives of the state. Congress received this power directly from the Constitution under its responsibility to provide for a republican form of government in each state. In effect, the Supreme Court ruled that this was a political decision outside the court's boundaries to adjudicate. It would side with Congress' decision, and it did so in *Texas v. White* (1868), which held that all acts committed under the Confederate constitution that did not conflict with the results of the rebellion were valid (e.g., marriages, yes; canceling of debts owed to U.S. citizens, no). This approach was conservative, it made sense to all but ideologues, and it worked.

See also Johnson and Reconstruction; Lincoln and Reconstruction; Moderate Republicans and Reconstruction; Radical Republicans and Reconstruction; Supreme Court and Reconstruction.

References Benedict, Michael Les, *Fruits of Victory* (1986); McKitrick, Eric, *Andrew Johnson and Reconstruction* (1960).

Thirteenth Amendment
See Seward and Reconstruction

Tilden, Samuel J. (1814–1886)

Born in New Lebanon, New York, Samuel Tilden grew up in a political atmosphere. His father was a storekeeper and postmaster and member of the Albany Regency, the political machine that Martin Van Buren used to build up the Jacksonian Democratic political party. Politics was a constant topic of conversation at the Tilden home and business, and men like Van Buren, Silas Wright, William L. Marcy, and Edwin Crosswell, bigwigs in New York's Democratic machine, often visited. Tilden's father was a natural hypochondriac; his store sold drugs and patent medicines by the score, and the son soon developed similar tendencies. So Tilden grew up an American patriot devoted to the Democratic party and possessing a morbid interest in his health, which he always thought to be poor but really was not.

Samuel J. Tilden

Tilden's formal education was sporadic. He kept leaving school because he thought he was sick. He went to New York City to live with an aunt, both to continue his studies and to find better medical advice. Tilden was not yet out of his teens when he wrote a paper defending President Andrew's Jackson's removal of federal deposits from the Second Bank of the United States; this paper was so good that the Democratic party published it and had it distributed statewide. Tilden tried to go to Yale College, but the environment made him ill, as did the food. So he returned home and settled for an honorary degree, which he received in 1875. He returned to New York City, attended a local college, and spent much time writing on political matters. By 1841 he had studied enough to pass the bar and become a practicing lawyer.

Shortly after Tilden entered law practice, his father died. The removal of his father's influence, combined with a steady and purposeful life, led Tilden to greater health and well-being. He became a corporate lawyer (one of the first really good ones in the country) and entered Democratic politics. He quelled the tendency of New York Democrats to oppose the candidacy of James K. Polk in 1844 by pointing out that New York was such a critical state that its Democrats could obligate Polk as president to accede to their desires. The New York party was split between Hunkers (led by Marcy, who coined the phrase "to the victors belong the spoils of office" and served as Polk's secretary of war), who tended to side with the South over slavery to keep Democrats in power in Washington and take their share of patronage; and the Barnburners (led by Van Buren and Wright), who opposed the extension of slavery into the West after the Mexican War. Tilden belonged to the latter group but liked to mediate between them and Washington on matters in dispute. Tilden served in the state legislature (1846–1847) and on the state constitutional convention (1847), and he unsuccessfully ran for state attorney general in the mid-1850s. Meanwhile, his law business grew as he participated in many impor-

tant cases, particularly the organization and reorganization of railroads, that made him a very rich, well-known man.

Tilden did not take much interest in the Civil War. He opposed the election of Abraham Lincoln and believed the war to be a mistake. But he did go to Washington at the request of Secretary of War Edwin M. Stanton to advise him on the management of his department. Tilden told Stanton that he should crush the rebellion by massive force, the North's true advantage against the South. He then returned to New York and ignored the conflict, although he encouraged the Democrats to maintain a constitutional opposition to Lincoln's expansion of the executive branch. After the war, Tilden tended to support President Andrew Johnson's Reconstruction policies and advised the president often.

But his real reputation came from his prosecution of the William M. "Boss" Tweed Ring that was corrupting New York City during this period. This required some political courage in that Tweed and his henchmen delivered the massive New York City vote for the state Democrats regularly. But as chairman of the party, Tilden believed that it was his obligation to clean up the blatant corruption of the era, no matter who was involved. He got the state legislature to pass the necessary laws to combat Tweed and then worked to produce the mountain of evidence by which Tweed and his cronies were tried and convicted, after the public was informed by the *New York Times* and the famous cartoons of Thomas Nast. Tilden also led an investigation of the New York bar association into judges who had backed Tweed; this action ran them out of office. (Meanwhile Tilden kept his own involvement in the Crédit Mobilier payoffs an open secret.)

Tilden supported the Horatio Seymour campaign for president in 1868 and the Liberal Republican campaign against President Ulysses S. Grant in 1872. In 1874, Tilden ran for and won the governorship of New York. Here, too, he acted as a reformer, breaking up the so-called Canal Ring, which was composed of men of both parties who bilked the state out of millions. His cleanup of New York politics fired the imagination of the nation, and his nomination for president on the Democratic ticket in 1876 was inevitable. During the campaign the Republicans tried to make an issue of everything they could find: Tilden's health and general nuttiness in trying to preserve it, his status as a bachelor (which allegedly showed his lack of faith in American womanhood or the future of the country), and his alleged fraud in computing his wartime income tax returns. He ran literally no campaign, so much so that many thought him indifferent to the election's outcome. His unwillingness to buy one of the returning boards in the South condemned him to lose the disputed electoral count, although Tilden always maintained that he had been robbed unfairly of the post of chief executive (a view most historians agree with).

Tilden spent the rest of his years advising the inner circle of the Democratic party on an intermittent basis as a retired elder statesman. He bought a palatial home in Yonkers and traveled to Europe. He also had to fight the federal government because the Republicans pursued the unpaid income tax accusations for some years before they gave it up for lack of any real evidence. On his death, he established the Tilden fund from his $6 million estate and dedicated it to building a public library for New York City. His heirs managed to contest the will and retrieve about half of the money, but the rest went into the free public library, as Tilden wanted. Throughout his life, Tilden was a quiet man, unimpressive in looks or speech, but with a great intellect that allowed him to become one of the best lawyers of his time. His political influence came as a reform-minded politician, although he probably had a skeleton of corruption or two in his own closet, by today's standards at least. That he could keep out of the greatest conflict in American history is a wonder, as was his willingness to let the Republicans buy out the presidential election of 1876 through his own stinginess. It was the wrong time to emphasize the high morality of his reputation over the practicality of his victory. But maybe he really did not care who won—Rutherford B. Hayes was his double in every respect, politically speaking, and both were pledged to end Reconstruction in the South.

See also Election of 1876 and Compromise of 1877; Hayes, Rutherford B.

References Bigelow, John, *The Life of Samuel J. Tilden* (1895) and *The Writings and Speeches of Samuel J. Tilden* (1885); Flick, Alexander Clarence, *Samuel Jones Tilden* (1939); Ford, Amelia C., "Samuel Jones Tilden" (1964–1981).

Tourgée, Albion W. (1838–1905)

A North Carolina Carpetbagger, Albion W. Tourgée was born of French Huguenot parents in extreme northeastern Ohio. His mother died when he was five. He could not abide his stepmother and left for a relative's home in Massachusetts. There he lost the sight in his right eye when he and a friend were playing with percussion caps. He returned to Ohio to study and met Emma Kilbourne, whom he eventually married. He went off to study literature at Rochester, New York, where he and his classmates enlisted in a volunteer regiment for the war. He was run over by a gun carriage at First Bull Run and was paralyzed for a year because of the resulting back injury. He finally was able to walk with crutches and finished his college degree and studied for the law. Rejoining the war as a lieutenant in an Ohio regiment, Tourgée got hit in the hip at Perryville and was captured at Stone's River, spending four months in a Rebel prison before being exchanged. After marrying Kilbourne he returned to the army and served in the Chickamauga campaign, reinjuring his back at the Battle of Chattanooga. The injury cost him a promotion, so he resigned from the army in protest. Tourgée practiced law until he received a letter from Provisional Governor William W. Holden of North Carolina—actually it was an advertisement sent off to numerous soldiers in the North. It invited them to come to the Tar Heel State and try farming. Land was cheap and the loyal population happy to receive them. Holden did not emphasize that most of the state was Rebel and hostile even after surrender.

Albion W. Tourgée

A seasick Tourgée arrived in New Bern in the summer of 1865. He rode the train to Raleigh, where he met Holden, a Scalawag who had been a Whig, a Democrat, a Unionist, a secessionist, a war advocate, a pacifist, and now the "loyal" governor of the state. Holden's was a checkered past indeed. But he always tried to be on the side of the small white farmers against the aristocratic slaveholders, much like the man who appointed him to office, President Andrew Johnson. The people of the state were broke and willing to rent land cheaply, Holden said. Tourgée decided to go back north, get his wife and some friends, and come back to rent land in the Carolina upcountry to run a plant nursery. They would be pretty much alone there because most Yankees had stayed in the low country. But Tourgée found the climate more to his liking in Guilford County. However, try as he might to concentrate on farming, political events drew him in. He was disturbed by the Confederate nature of the first postwar election. Blacks, native Unionists, and Northern whites were roundly denounced. The new government was a far cry from the friendly

one Holden had run. Tourgée did his best to help local blacks by hiring them at fair wages and Unionists by representing them in court as they tried to collect for past damages. This did not improve his standing among locals.

But Tourgée went further in his political activities. He was part of a local Union convention that adopted his resolution for impartial suffrage. The convention then sent him to a Union Loyal League convention up at Philadelphia held to counter the "arm in arm" convention of Johnson supporters that met earlier. Here Tourgée met other North Carolina Scalawags and Carpetbaggers, who elected him chairman of the delegation. Tourgée made a credible speech on behalf of black suffrage. Then the loyalists decided to send out delegates to follow the president on his "Swing around the Circle" campaign to elect Democrats to Congress. They would speak a day or two later than the president to "clear up" anyone befuddled by Johnson's appeal. Tourgée was one of those selected to go to western Pennsylvania to campaign for Republicans. But a hasty letter from his wife back in North Carolina convinced him to return there. The whole state was up in arms over his convention speech and his electioneering up North. Governor Jonathan Worth, a Democrat, was making speeches and writing letters denouncing Tourgée as a Northern demagogue who hoped to interfere with the South's normal social structure. The nursery was failing because Tourgée and anyone associated with him faced social and economic boycott.

Tourgée and his associates had to sell out, but he refused to leave the state. He tried to sell real estate and he opened a loyal newspaper. Both enterprises failed. However, Congress had just passed the Military Reconstruction Acts in response to the rejection of the Fourteenth Amendment by Worth and men like him all over the South. Tourgée became one of the 19 Carpetbaggers, 88 Scalawags, and 13 African Americans elected to the new state constitutional convention. He had campaigned as a commoner, like his black and white constituents, opposed to the aristocrats. He carried an old horse pistol from Republican meeting to meeting and rode an old scrawny nag that, like him, was blind in one eye, as if to make a point. At the convention he had renewed his acquaintenceship with former governor Holden, now a delegate, too.

Tourgée's outspokenness at the convention made him one of the best-known and most notorious Carpetbaggers in the state. The convention was said to be made up of "Baboons, Monkeys, Mules, Tourgée, and other Jackasses." Tourgée backed the black vote, which he framed as democracy for all. He helped bring government to the people by standing against having local officials appointed from Raleigh. He even got the convention to allow the election of judges. He also spoke out against debt collection. For his trouble Tourgée was selected as one of three to recodify the state's laws. The pay was $200 a month (a good salary in those days, when Freedmen's Bureau officials made half that) and the appointment for three years. In the election that followed Tourgée was elected judge and Holden governor. Tourgée now had an annual salary from his two positions of $5,000 a year—really good money in those days. Holden also sent Tourgée north to try to raise money for poor North Carolinians starving from poor harvests that year. On the way he witnessed the acquittal of President Johnson, which he blamed on a senator from Kansas, E. A. Ross, getting a million-dollar payoff. Tourgée was disgusted.

For the next few years the Tourgées lived well. They bought a nice brick house at Greensboro that they named "Carpet Bag Lodge." Other parcels of land followed. Most of it was farm land, so they hired men to cultivate it. Tourgée invested in racehorses. He spent much and borrowed more from his friends Carpetbagger Milton S. Littlefield and Scalawag George W. Swepson. Both were as corrupt as one could be, but Tourgée was never in a position to help either in their schemes. Most of the time Tourgée rode circuit for his job on the bench. He regularly covered eight counties. The rest of the time he and his other two

code commissioners simplified the state's legal code, which drew the ire of those who had made a job of mastering its intricacies over the years. He became guardian for his black cook's child. And he began a lifelong hobby: he wrote novels set in the South that revealed the evils of slavery and the shortcomings of Reconstruction.

And there were proving to be a lot of shortcomings. One of these was the growing strength of the Ku Klux Klan. Even though North Carolina could never have a government dominated by African American voters like neighboring South Carolina, because its blacks were but about a third of the population, the specter of "Negro Rule" reigned nonetheless (one black voter seemed too many to some in those days). As judge, Tourgée was well aware that it was impossible to gain a conviction of a white man for any wrong done toward an African American or a Unionist white. In response to such incidents throughout the South, Congress passed the Enforcement Acts. It was up to the local government to carry out the provisions. But Holden proved to be somewhat less successful than Governor Powell Clayton was out in Arkansas. Holden authorized the state militia to take the field under George W. Kirk, who had commanded white loyalists during the Civil War. Kirk cleaned up a couple of counties and arrested numerous suspects, only to see them released by a friendly federal judge on writs of habeas corpus. That ended the so-called Kirk-Holden War. In the 1870 election the whole state went Democratic except for the two counties patrolled by Kirk's militia. The new Democratic legislature soon had the results in these counties thrown out and soon took control there, too. Reconstruction in North Carolina was over three years after it started.

Although Tourgée kept his judgeship, he felt obliged to resign from the code commission, which cost him half of his income. Tourgée hoped that his resignation would allow the commission to continue without its most controversial member. But the legislature had a better idea. They just let it languish, ignoring it and making it ineffective. Tourgée still rode circuit. He also opened a spoke-and-handle factory to employ Greensboro blacks. Litigants spoke of boycotting his court, but just as many respected his honest decisions and continued to use his court. The Democrats did attack Governor Holden, whom they impeached, removed from office, and stripped of all rights of North Carolina citizenship, making him a sort of pariah forever. Tourgée's friends Littlefield and Swepson were indicted for embezzlement. Both men proved unavailable to the court for further action. Tourgée continued the investigation against the Klansmen arrested during the Kirk-Holden War, and just as his efforts seemed ready to pay off, the state legislature repealed the law against masked men on public roads. After his second inaugural, President Ulysses S. Grant pardoned all of the Klansmen not yet free from charges.

In 1874 Tourgée's tenure as judge was up. He did not have to worry about reappointment. He once again turned to practicing law. But he did not do as well as he had hoped. Reluctantly he went to Washington, D.C., to seek a government job. He received a job as pension agent, which necessitated selling the home in Greensboro and moving to Raleigh. He ran for Congress in 1878 but was beaten by a Confederate veteran, Brig. Gen. Alfred M. Scales; Tourgée lost every county in the district. He continued his writing to keep from being too despondent. In 1879 he left North Carolina forever, going to New York City to see about the publication of his novels. His anonymous novel, *A Fool's Errand*, became a runaway best-seller. His next venture, under his own name, *Bricks without Straw*, did even better.

But bad investments soon drained his cash reserves, forcing him to write more. Tourgée continued to promote political civil and social rights for African Americans. In 1896 he penned his last great missive for black rights when he wrote a brief for the case *Plessy v. Ferguson*, which concerned the right of African Americans to use freely all public accommodations, in this case a whites-only railroad car. The U.S. Supreme court ignored Tourgée's appeal to enforce the Fourteenth Amendment and declared "separate but equal" to be the law of the land. Tourgée then accepted an appointment as U.S. consul at Bordeaux, France. He died there, still on duty, in 1905.

See also Carpetbaggers.

Reference Current, Richard N., *Those Terrible Carpetbaggers* (1988); Currie-McDaniel, Ruth, "The Wives of the Carpetbaggers" (1989); Daniels, Jonathan, *Prince of Carpetbaggers* (1958); Dibble, Roy F., *Albion W. Tourgée* (1968 [1921]); Gross, Theodore L., "The Fool's Errand of Albion W. Tourgée" (1963) and "The Negro in the Literature of Reconstruction" (1961); Harris, William C., *William Woods Holden* (1987); Olenick, Monte M., "Albion W. Tourgée" (1962); Olsen, Otto H., *Carpetbagger's Crusade* (1965) and "North Carolina" (1980); Weissbuch, Ted N., "Albion W. Tourgée" (1961).

Trumbull, Lyman (1813–1896)

Lyman Trumbull, the United States senator who acted as the congressional liaison to President Andrew Johnson in the early days of Reconstruction, was born in Colchester, Connecticut. He attended a local academy and went to Greenville, Georgia, to teach school for three years in 1833. He also read law in his spare time and was admitted to the bar in 1836; he began to practice law in Belleville, Illinois, near St. Louis, in 1837. Trumbull soon became interested in politics and was elected to the state legislature as a Democrat. He resigned his seat to become the secretary of state for two years before returning to his law practice. He ran for several offices but was not successful until he was elected judge of the state supreme court. He was reelected to the bench in 1852.

As Trumbull sat on the bench, the nation drifted to crisis over the extension of slavery into the West. Trumbull stepped down to run for a seat on the House of Representatives as an anti-Nebraska Democrat (i.e., against the extension of slavery into territory north of the old Missouri Compromise line). But before he could go to Washington, the Illinois legislature picked him to be the new U.S. senator. Trumbull won this seat with Whig support; Abraham Lincoln threw party support behind this

Democrat to get a free soil man to counter Democrat Senator Stephen A. Douglas already in Washington. Trumbull would be reelected two more times and would stay as senator until 1871.

In Washington, Trumbull soon deserted the Democrats for the new Republican party over the slavery issue. As Lincoln had hoped, Trumbull and Douglas opposed each other over the extension of slavery into the West. Trumbull opposed the admission of Kansas as a slave state under the Lecompton constitution; Douglas wanted the population of Kansas to vote on the issue through his doctrine of popular sovereignty, and Trumbull believed that until a territory actually became a state, Congress ought to have full authority. Trumbull refused to accept compromise over the secession movement, holding that the South had plenty of guarantees for its position under the U.S. Constitution as it stood. Trumbull acted as a Lincoln advisor during the president's administration, especially advising Lincoln on constitutional and legal matters. He proposed that Congress legalize acts of doubtful constitutionality that Lincoln performed while the legislature was out of session (expanding the army and navy, juggling appropriations from other departments into military expenses, suspending habeas corpus); at the same time he opposed granting Lincoln unlimited power to battle the rebellion. Trumbull backed confiscation of Rebel property, supported the admission of the Ten Percent government in Louisiana to Congress, and introduced the resolution that would become the Thirteenth Amendment (freeing the slaves nationwide).

After Lincoln's death, Trumbull acted as the congressional go-between to President Andrew Johnson and mistakenly thought he got the new president's agreement to sign the Freedmen's Bureau Renewal Bill and the Civil Rights Bill of 1866. Both measures were ones Trumbull had written and believed in as a moderate approach to Reconstruction. He warned Johnson that Congress was less inclined to permit presidential usurpation of its powers during peace than it had during the war. But Trumbull did not think that Radical Reconstruction (Military Reconstruction) was necessarily legal, constitutional, or wise. He said that he was "willing to be radical lawfully," but he would not "be radical rather than right." With this difference in mind, he was one of the seven who voted to acquit the president during the impeachment trial. This action was the last straw for the Republican leadership. They drove Trumbull out of their conferences and straight into the hands of the Liberal Republican movement that opposed Ulysses S. Grant's reelection in 1872. This move cost Trumbull any chance for reelection, and he retired after stumping the North for Horace Greeley and returned to the practice of law, this time in Chicago.

In 1876 he returned to the Democratic party and acted as a legal counsel for Samuel J. Tilden, the party's candidate in the disputed election of 1976. Trumbull ran for governor of Illinois in 1880 as a Democrat but lost the race. By the time of his death in 1896, he was flirting with the Populist movement. Trumbull was an admirable man of much importance during the Civil War and Reconstruction, but his devotion to conscience made him an unreliable politician who might bolt the party line at any time for what he saw as the good of the nation. This political unreliability created his influence in the 1850s and cost him his position in the 1870s. Hence he was an important but not spectacular man as senator, one who remains on the periphery of history.

See also Impeachment; Johnson and Reconstruction; Moderate Republicans and Reconstruction.

References Ellis, L. Ethan, "Lyman Trumbull" (1964–1981); Krug, Mark M., *Lyman Trumbull* (1965); White, Horace, *The Life of Lyman Trumbull* (1913).

Tweed Ring

The Tweed Ring, the first modern big city machine in American politics, had its origins in a New York City fire engine company, Americus No. 6. Organized in 1848 by William M. Tweed and others, the Americus company was a stepping-stone into city politics, like all other fire compa-

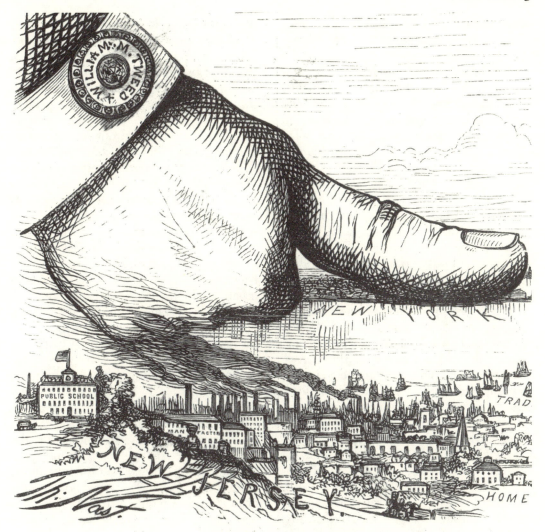

UNDER THE THUMB.

THE BOSS. "Well, what are you going to do about it?"

A political cartoon in Harper's Weekly *illustrates the power that the Tweed Ring, and William Tweed in particular, held over New York City during the mid-nineteenth century.*

nies of its day. Its symbol was the head of a Bengal tiger, which in time would become the sign of Tammany Hall, New York City's Democratic club. In 1850, William M. Tweed, a big, burly man with an ability to use his fists when reason failed to carry an argument, became the leader of the "Big 6," as city firemen fondly called the company. Tweed also ran for city alderman in his first grab at the strings of political power, but he lost by a small margin. The following year he ran again. This time he showed more of

the political acumen that he exercised the rest of his life. He had little chance to win in a two-way race, but he persuaded a friend to run as an independent Whig and thus split the Whigs' natural majority. Democrat Tweed was on his way to fame and infamy.

The common city council to which Tweed was elected was known as the "Forty Thieves." Its head, and the local political boss, was Fernando Wood. Tweed quickly fit into the system of graft for which the council was named, and in 1852 he was elected to a seat in the U.S. Congress. Tweed served only one term in Washington. He preferred municipal politics and the unbridled corruption for which it was renowned. But Tweed fell afoul of the anti-immigrant Know Nothing vote in 1856 and lost his alderman's position. In his years off he became fast friends with two other fallen Democrats, Peter B. "Brains" Sweeny and Richard B. "Slippery Dick" Connolly. Together the threesome formed the embryo of what became the biggest bunch of grafters and grifters in the country. Their first goal became to supplant Mayor Wood as the head of the party. In 1856 Tweed was reelected as a good government man (illustrative of how one should take that kind of claim with a grain of salt) to get rid of Wood and his corrupt cronies. It was a case of putting the fox in charge of the chicken coop. The new bipartisan board simply replaced the old grafters with themselves. Tweed soon engineered the election of Sweeny as city district attorney, Connolly as clerk of court, and another hanger-on, George G. Bernard, as recorder. The Tweed Ring was in power at last.

By this time Tweed had managed to supplant Wood as head of Tammany Hall, and he moved to put the last nail in Wood's political coffin by ousting the man as mayor in favor of John T. Hoffman, a Tweed ally. It cost Tweed $100,000 to do it, and in the process "Boss" (as Tweed came to be known) lost his own campaign for sheriff, but it was worth it. It took Tweed about two years to make up half of the monetary cost of defeating Wood, but his skillful manipulation of city favors as a county supervisor pulled in the requisite cash. Meanwhile he acted as head of the state Democratic party and got a new adherent in the form of A. Oakey Hall, who replaced Sweeny as district attorney and managed the field forces. Sweeny moved into the position of Tammany treasurer with Connolly as his creative auditor.

The Tweed Ring got its votes through its management of welfare for the poor, particularly the Irish immigrants. At that time there was no federal assistance, which did not really come into being until the New Deal, through which President Franklin D. Roosevelt took welfare out of the hands of the city bosses and nationalized it for his own use. In exchange for political loyalty, the ring handed out city jobs, housing, food, education, and citizenship papers. Tammany Hall would hold out its votes until upstate New York had voted and would then deliver the majorities required for the Democrats to win. Then Tammany men would vote the gravestones (i.e., cast ballots in the name of deceased individuals) and send in vote repeaters (they preferred men with full beards who would shave a little each time to look different) to pack the ballot boxes. The "adjusted" figures would usually keep the Democrats in power at Albany as well as in the city. Needless to say, Tweed and his henchmen were heroes to those in need, and New York City had many such people.

Tweed ran the ring out of his midtown law office. True, Tweed was not much of a lawyer, but he knew people and how they worked. He collected huge "legal fees" from every business that had an office inside the city. The Erie Railroad, for example, paid lawyer Tweed $100,000 for its rights to enter the city. In 1864, Tweed bought up a print shop and required that all businesses patronize it if they wished a license to operate. He also bought into a Massachusetts marble firm that provided building materials for public buildings at a nice markup. In 1868 Tweed and his men made another try at political musical chairs and sent Hoffman to the governor's chair while "Elegant Oakey" Hall (he was an especially sharp dresser) became mayor. Tweed himself was state senator from the city, and another henchman took over the state assembly speakership. Tweed had two mansions in which he lived during various political seasons, one in Albany (recognized as the Democratic headquarters for the whole state) and another up on Fifth Avenue in the city, the real mayor's office. Holding multiple offices was a Tweed specialty. He was also head of the state Democratic party, New York school commissioner, president of the county board of supervisors, and commissioner of public streets.

In 1869 the Tweed Ring decided that out of all bills paid by the city, 50 percent of the money would go to the ring. It soon appeared that the high standard of living for ring elders would suffer under such an arrangement, so the ante was raised to 85 percent. The cut was divided on the basis of 20 percent for Tweed, 20 percent for Sweeny, 20 percent for Hall, 20 percent for Connolly, and 20 percent for everyone else. Tweed went in with Jay Gould and Jim Fisk to plunder the Erie Railroad, and the Boss also became chairman of the board (without any investment on his part) of banks, gas companies, and street railways that operated in Manhattan. He also got the ball rolling on the Brooklyn Bridge for a mere $40,000 in stock (in this case, public interest seemed to override the usual massive take). But the true gem of the Tweed Ring was the New York City courthouse. Projected to be an $800,000 building of which the city could be proud, it turned into a $12 million boondoggle that was never finished during Tweed's tenure. It was a testament to his power that, when Tweed's daughter got married in 1870, she and her groom cleaned up with over $700,000 in gifts from "grateful" city business and social leaders.

But time was growing short for Tweed and his pals. *Harper's Weekly* magazine began its campaign against the ring, using the courthouse as its centerpiece. The campaign was reinforced not only by editorials and feature stories, but by the skillful drawings of cartoonist Thomas Nast. With a real penchant for hitting the ring and its members where it hurt, Nast illustrated the intricacies of government fraud for the uneducated and high society as well. It was not an easy job. At first people refused to believe that the kindly old man at city hall was anything but a near saint. Even leading citizens like Horace Greeley and Peter Cooper denied that Tweed could be anything but a good government man. Indeed, these men were part of the group that put in a new city charter that riveted the ring's power more firmly than ever. It took $600,000 from the

ring's coffers to pull off this stunt, with all of the leading chuckleheads of the city speaking out voluntarily on Tweed's behalf. But the Harper's campaign, illustrated by Nast's brilliant cartoon drawings, finally took its toll. Rumors of how much Tweed, Sweeny, Hall, and Connolly took got members of the last 20 percent share to question their rewards, and two dissatisfied politicos turned in Connolly's secret books—the real accounting—over to the *New York Times*.

The Tweed Ring offered to pay the *Times* $5 million not to publish. Nast over at *Harper's* received an offer of $500,000 to stop his drawings. Neither complied. The clincher was Nast's portrayal of a defiant Tweed, confronted by the evidence, saying, "Well, what are you going to do about it?" Tweed never really said this, but who cared? With the printing of the account books, it was all over. A public committee of 70 individuals formed to coordinate the prosecution, which was ably handled by Samuel J. Tilden and would raise him to presidential candidacy in 1876. Tweed was indicted on criminal charges and reelected to the state senate at about the same time. Injunctions prevented the ring from spending any more tax money. But Tweed managed to raise the requisite $2 million bail overnight, with the Erie's Jay Gould putting up half of it personally. A civil suit sought to reclaim the fraudulently spent public funds. Tweed's cronies did not wait to see if the Boss could beat the charges; men of little faith in the aroused public, they fled quickly to Canada and Europe. Tweed managed to get a hung jury on the first go-around in court. But a second trial brought in a verdict of guilty, and Tweed received a dozen years in prison and a $12,500 fine. Able attorneys appealed the verdict and got it reduced to a year and $250, and by 1875 Tweed was out of jail, having served his time and paid his fine.

But the civil suit had just begun. The prosecutors asked for a restitution of $6 million and a $3 million bail. Tweed could not raise either and went back to jail. But his treatment was quite lenient, as befitted a still-beloved and influential politician. Every afternoon he took carriage rides through town, and he was even allowed to visit his wife and family at home, accompanied by two guards. On one of these visits Tweed went through the front door and right on out the back. For two weeks friends kept him hidden in the city until, disguised as a seaman, he managed to get aboard a freighter and flee the country. Tweed went via Cuba to Spain, where Spanish police finally arrested him using one of Thomas Nast's cartoons as a wanted poster. Extradited to the United States, the Boss found that the civil suit had been decided against him in his absence, and in default of payment he went back to jail under close guard. His health had suffered greatly from the many years of this ordeal, and in an effort to save what was left of his life, Tweed turned state's evidence, detailing the many frauds he and his ring had perpetrated. But in 1878 he died alone in his cell, his wife and daughter having gone to Europe earlier at his request to spare them humiliation.

Tweed was never vindictive toward his enemies. He remained a friendly man to the end, endearing himself to his many supporters and opponents alike. But it is unlikely that he was really the innocent victim of political witch hunt, as historian Leo Hershkowitz has recently maintained. He asserts that real evidence against Tweed is nonexistent, that the Ring's activities were the fault of the second echelon of Tammany Hall politicians, and that Tweed's conviction was a product of a biased judge and a hand-picked jury. Even Tweed's confession is explained away as a lie in a vain effort to get out of jail before he died. Hershkowitz never convincingly explains what happened to the millions filched from the city.

The real significance of the Tweed Ring was that it was the first real big city machine in American political history, dwarfing all previous forays into this field. Modern urban politics was a phenomenon of the late nineteenth century, when cities and factories grew up as a part of the Industrial Revolution. The Tweed Ring marked the decline of the political influence of the upper and middle classes, the so-called respectable people, in favor of the "great unwashed" who were recently from Europe by way of the immigrant ship, looking for jobs, housing, education for their children, and citizenship. Tweed and his men provided these things for a price. The bad part was that it cost the city a fortune and Tweed's supporters their souls, since they were at the mercy of the ring's thugs, packed courts, and rigged juries.

Were it not for the general decay of morals that accompanied unchecked capitalism and the breakdown of society during the Civil War, Tweed would have had a harder time of it. But people were tired of causes, and this showed in the corruption rampant after the war during Reconstruction, North and South. It was an era in which everybody was trying to get ahead. Observers said that one could see this drive in people's faces, no matter their station in life. In their view, it was the force that made America great and the envy of the world. It was the same force that so repelled the good government people (the "goo-goos," in the parlance of the time).

Tweed was a first-rate political manager in an area that generally attracted third-rate people: municipal government. He built his ring around four bases of power: city hall, the state capitol, Tammany Hall, and the city justice system. Until he came along, Tammany Hall was just a political club like thousands of others. Tweed led the way for the disciplined political machines that became an art form in the first half of the twentieth century. He never had a majority of the voters in his pocket, but he was the one who counted all of the votes. He made up for the lack of voter control by a warm personal touch that was new in city politics, which was known to be run by cold bureaucrats. He was likable and approachable, even to his enemies. He gave the impression that he cared.

The Tweed Ring demonstrated that Reconstruction corruption was not merely a product of black-Scalawag-Carpetbagger Republican governments of the South. It was a nationwide malaise that infected a whole people regardless of political party for much of the last part of the nineteenth century. There were "robber barons," white and black, Republican and Democratic, North and South. Their methods might differ but the result was the same—a subversion of government for personal gain. Many took from government, most took from each other, but few if any took as much and as skillfully as William "Boss" Tweed. It was, in the words of one chronicler, "the Era of Good Stealings."

See also Grant and the Scandals; Tweed, William Marcy (Magear) "Boss."

References Bowen, Croswell, *The Elegant Oakey* (1956); Callow, Alexander B., *The Tweed Ring* (1966); Harlow, Alvin F., "William Marcy Tweed" (1964–1981); Hershkowitz, Leo, *Tweed's New York* (1977); Hoogenboom, Ari, and Olive Hoogenboom, "Was Boss Tweed Really Snow White?" (1977); Lewis, Alfred Henry, *Richard Croker* (1901); Mandelbaum, Seymour J., *Boss Tweed's New York* (1965); Summers, Mark W., *The Era of Good Stealings* (1993).

Tweed, William Marcy (Magear) "Boss" (1823–1878)

Born of parents of Scottish descent, William Marcy Tweed (Magear is his mother's name and believed today to be his real middle name) was born in New York City. His father was a chairmaker, and after a stint in public school young Tweed was apprenticed to his him to learn the trade. Two years later the boy went off to a saddler to learn that trade, too. He then went to a private academy in New Jersey to learn bookkeeping and became the accountant of a small brush factory that his father had recently bought. At age 19 he became a partner in the firm, and at 21 he married Mary Jane Skaden, with whom he had eight children. Tweed was known as a sober young man and a good husband and father. Outside the home, among men he was noted for being big in size and not adverse to using his fists to settle an argument. He became a volunteer fireman and helped create the Americus Fire Company No. 6, known as the "Big 6" in fire circles.

Tweed used the fire company as his stepping-stone into politics, a common path to power in the big cities of the nineteenth-century United States. He was New York City alderman (1852–1853), U.S. congressman (1853–1855), head of the board of supervisors (1856), school commissioner (1856–1857), street commissioner (1861–1870), commissioner of public works (1870–1871), and state senator (1867–1871). He ran the city with his cronies, basically from the street commissioner's office, with a political machine called the Tweed Ring. He increased the city payroll, giving jobs as a reward for loyalty and turning out the immigrant vote. He charged cost plus 85 percent on city contracts and through government regulations brought city business into line. His triumph was bilking the city of most of $12 million spent on the city courthouse building, constructed with granite from his own quarry. To keep his ring secure, Tweed managed to get a new city charter through in 1870 that placed all of the auditing into departments controlled by the ring, thereby allowing an increased pace of corruption.

Like all shakedown operations, books had to be kept of the money taken in and shares given out. Under attack from various city newspapers that suspected the worst but could not prove anything, Tweed was brought down when rumors of the lesser amounts given to underlings caused them to have a clerk copy the real accounts and release them through the *New York Times* to the public. With the truth out, the Tweed Ring began to fall apart. Most of the higher-ups in the organization fled the country, leaving Tweed to take the rap. He was sentenced to a dozen years in jail and a stiff fine, but appeals got both reduced. Stymied in the criminal proceedings, the good government "Committee of 70" filed a civil suit prosecuted by Samuel J. Tilden, a well-known corporate lawyer. Unable to make bail, Tweed languished in jail until he managed to escape while on a furlough home. He fled to Spain but was recognized by local authorities on the basis of one of Thomas Nast's cartoons, which had been instrumental in Tweed's original downfall. Returned to New York City, Tweed found himself convicted of the civil charges and unable to repay the money demanded by the court. He died shortly afterward in his jail cell at age 55.

See also Tilden, Samuel J.; Tweed Ring.

References Callow, Alexander B., *The Tweed Ring* (1966); Harlow, Alvin F., "William Marcy Tweed" (1964–1981); Hershkowitz, Leo, *Tweed's New York* (1977); Hoogenboom, Ari, and Olive Hoogenboom, "Was Boss Tweed Really Snow White?" (1977).

Union Loyal Leagues

With the granting of the vote to African Americans, it became important for the Republican party to organize and deliver that political power in elections locally and nationally. The vehicle for this task was the Union Leagues of America (also known as the Loyal Leagues or the Union Loyal Leagues). First founded in the North during the Civil War for white Republicans supporting the Lincoln administration after the Democrats' resurgence in the congressional elections of 1862, by the end of the war these organizations had spread to white Unionist areas of the South like the Appalachians, hills, and sandy pine barrens. Each organization was secret and had a pseudoreligious Masonic-like ritual (emphasizing chants involving the three L's: league, loyal, and Lincoln). Although their purpose was purely secular and political, the leagues often operated behind the front of the local black church or secular benevolent societies for protection.

Initially the white organizers of local Union Loyal Leagues had great power because of the political inexperience of African Americans. But it did not take long before blacks began to listen to their own natural leaders and become more attuned to advancing their own concerns. It was they who organized the informal militias to protect themselves against white marauders, the plantation boycotts that forced planters to get rid of the old gang labor system, the schools that educated its members in political realities along with basic learning, and the demand that political candidates deliver more (like desegregation of public services) than mere Republican party label to get elected. Frequently the point man for the leagues was the local Freedmen's Bureau agent. He had the contacts in the black community to get things rolling. He also had the power to sign off on labor contracts, and he knew what political rights the African Americans had coming. He was assisted in his supervision of his agency by league members informing on planters who operated in violation of fair labor standards.

By 1867 the leagues had incorporated the new black voters into its ranks and represented the vanguard of Republican Reconstruction support everywhere. As black representation among the leagues grew, the local white Union men (the original core of the leagues in the South), began to drop out. The transition between white and black control limited the effectiveness of Union Loyal Leagues in some areas during the elections of 1868, but soon afterward blacks began to move toward their own economic, social, and political goals with zeal. The leagues' tendencies were radical (which actually alarmed the Northern organizers, who were more interested in electing Republican congressmen of any stripe); their defense was through local "Negro militias"; and their power came through nomination of candidates and the mobilization of the vote, as well as strikes, boycotts (especially in the signing of contracts for the coming year), and social isolation.

The actual league meetings were secret for the security of the leaders and future programs, although Southern white opponents had a pretty good idea who was in charge. White economic intimidation proved ineffective because the whole black community rallied behind the victims and the planters could not fire everyone or they would lose their crop. After their states were readmitted into the Union and the army was withdrawn from protecting white and black Republicans, conservative whites turned toward their own secret military organization, the Ku Klux Klan. White violence was directed toward Republican officeholders and black leaders (ministers, suspected league leaders, and politicians) on the local level. The goal was to get blacks to vote Democratic or not vote at all.

First local newspapers asked for any "right-thinking" citizen to forward names for Ku Klux Klan attention. These names were printed as warnings. If nothing happened to lessen the league's influence, the disciplinary squads went into action. Results were especially dramatic in Alabama, where the Klans routed the leagues through a well-organized campaign of terrorism that led to a reassertion of planter wishes in agricultural matters by the 1870s. The Redemption of the South (the resumption of white political rule) did not kill off the leagues entirely. Indeed, when the Compromise of 1877 proved unworkable, Northern Republicans tried to reorganize the Union Loyal Leagues. But the rejection of the Lodge Force Bill and the disfranchisement movement of the 1890s did the leagues in permanently.

Historians of the early twentieth century envisioned the Union Loyal Leagues as among the most diabolical organizations in American history. They claimed that each league was held together by iron discipline, that backsliders were punished physically and socially, and that members did the bidding of the most malicious of the white Radical Republican interlopers in the South. More recent historians have tended to ignore the leagues, pointing out that they were not the black equivalent of the Ku Klux Klan but also denigrating their contribution to the reconstructing process. Yet the leagues did more than just get out the vote. They helped focus black resistance to traditional plantation organization, which blacks hated as a symbol of slavery (gang labor, white supervision, clustered cabins, and minimal personal freedom as emphasized in the Black Codes), and paved the way for the reorganization of the individual agricultural worker into a decentralized family farming system by 1868, whether the land was owned, rented, or sharecropped. Thus the Union Loyal Leagues were important in both a political and agricultural context and strengthened black resistance to complete white domination.

See also Black Codes; Bureau of Refugees, Freedmen, and Abandoned Lands; Enforcement Acts; Ku Klux Klan.

Reference Fitzgerald, Michael W., *The Union League Movement in the Deep South* (1989); Fleming, Walter Lynwood, "The Formation of the Union Leagues in Alabama" (1903); Owens, Susie Lee, *The Union League of America* (1947).

Urban Blacks during Reconstruction

In Southern cities before the Civil War lived a group of free blacks (as distinguished from freed blacks, or former slaves emancipated by the war) noted for their industriousness and independent social standing. The largest populations of free men and women of color lived in the South's two largest cities, Charleston, South Carolina, and New Orleans, Louisiana. Their different status was critical to their response to the conditions of Reconstruction. The Civil War changed more than the white South—it also changed the lives of the free blacks forever.

In Charleston the antebellum free blacks started Reconstruction with certain advantages over the freed men and women from the plantations of the countryside. The free men and women of color had accumulated property—not much, but a lot to the ex-slaves, who had nothing. Many of the free people of color came from liaisons between their mothers and the sons and fathers of the most prominent white families of the state's coastal plains. This lineage often allowed them access to good schools and an education that for some included attending colleges in the North and Europe. Those not as fortunate still learned to read and to a lesser degree to write. This gave them the ability to engage in all sorts of business, although most of them had trades, for example, as barbers, butchers, tailors, carpenters, and blacksmiths. Others were churchmen or teachers, and even a rare few were doctors of medicine.

Reconstruction brought these men a new opportunity to have a voice in the future of South Carolina through political activity. By examining these men and their backgrounds one can gain new insights into the black leadership of a select area, right down to the city ward heeler. Historian William C. Hine took such a look at Charleston's Reconstruction-era free blacks and found out several interesting points. Hine first identified 234 blacks through an examination of the census, tax records, and mention in newspaper articles. He excluded men who had influence in the black community but never stood for office, like Jonathan Gibbs, Martin Robison Delany, Macon B. Allen, and Samuel Dickerson. He preferred to isolate men who were nominated for office, were elected to a position in the party or city government, or attended the state convention. Political appointees were excluded.

Hine discovered that the average black politico in Charleston had a free background rather than having been a slave. Indeed, slavery in one's past tended to exclude one from leadership. The only ex-slaves who served in office represented rural counties, not the city. Most of these men were natives of Charleston or had dwelled in the city from before the war. Fewer than 7 percent had come from the North after the war. Their color was difficult to determine, but Hine believes that, even accounting for errors on the part of census takers, two-thirds of these men were black as opposed to being of discernible mixed race. Thus slavery was a greater hindrance to a leadership position in politics than color. Most were of middle age, but there was an active younger group on the way up and a few oldsters to leaven the age mix with experience. At least half were literate; that is, they could at least read if not write. But a few had as good an education as anyone could receive in nineteenth-century America, up to and including college. Two-fifths of the black politicians were skilled craftsmen, concentrated in the trades of tailor, carpenter, and butcher. Other trades like bricklayer and baker did not contribute very many to leadership councils. But one-fifth of the leaders were common laborers, draymen, stevedores, and chimney sweeps. It was not uncommon for a man to have held several different jobs, however, which was indicative of the economic fluctuation of the Reconstruction years.

Absent from the Charleston black political leadership were the professional men. There were few doctors, teachers, or ministers involved. But the most important local politicos, Francis Cardozo, Richard Cain, and Benjamin F. Randolph, were ministers. The politicians also tended to join a variety of social and benevolent societies, like the Brown Fellowship Society, the Humane and Friendly Society, the Veteran Republican Brotherhood, the Colored Young Men's Christian Association, various fire companies, and fraternal and literary guilds. Like the whites of South Carolina before them, blacks tended to develop family political influence, with the son following the father into political action.

Most interesting of all 39 of Hine's black politicians were the Democrats. These men, like their standard Republican counterparts, represented a broad cross section of the whole black community, but several had had the distinction of owning slaves of their own before the war. The very wealthy blacks did not take an active part in local politics. Most of the politicians were men of modest means. Indeed, Hine believes that political activity was an attempt by a black prewar middle class, thrown asunder by the economics of the war and Reconstruction, to earn a living that might promise more security than one of the usual trades. This interpretation might also explain the multitude of professions black leaders engaged in and their willingness to curry political favor. This led to much political divisiveness as the black leaders competed among themselves and their white Republican allies, who resented the blacks' assertiveness; it gave the more united conservative whites an edge in the battles for Redemption.

Nothing could be more different from the Charleston scene than those antebellum free blacks in Louisiana whose presence, particularly in New Orleans, formed such a critical part of Louisiana Reconstruction. An examination into the postbellum life of the antebellum free colored men and women of the Bayou State, like that made by historian David C. Rankin, illustrates the error of viewing black reaction to the forces of Civil War and Reconstruction as cohesive. When the Yankees in 1862 captured the southeastern third of Louisiana, the areas around and including New Orleans, they found three populations present: the whites, the slaves soon to be emancipated, and the free men and women of color, whose class had existed from the time of the French and was molded by Latin attitudes on race. Before the War of 1812, there had been an influx of many free blacks from

Saint Domingue (now Haiti), people of mixed race who were an active part of the island's slaveholding community, which was destroyed by a revolution led by Toussaint L'Ouverture. But by and large, Louisiana's free colored population was descended in part from the most prominent white families of the state. Such interracial births were encouraged by custom and by the relative lack of white women and black men in the region. Pairings between white men and black women were the result (indeed, New Orleans' renowned quadroon balls were the talk of the nation), and they lightened the free colored population until Louisiana's supreme court ruled in 1810 that the whiter the Negro, the greater the legal presumption of freedom.

But there was more than light color to the New Orleans free blacks, or "Creole colored people," as they were popularly called. These individuals adopted the lifestyle and culture of the Gallic society that created Louisiana in the first place. They were Catholic in religion, spoke flawless French, often attended local private academies, and were tradesmen of the highest skills. The first anthology of black verse published in this country, *Les Cenelles*, was penned by the teachers and students of free colored academies in New Orleans. It never mentioned slavery and was exclusively French in outlook, dominated by the philosophies of La Fontaine, Boileau, Fénelon, Racine, Corneille, and Victor Hugo. Indeed, the free colored population was decidedly not in league with their enslaved brothers and sisters; they were more than willing to turn over a runaway to the white slaveholders, inform on an insurrectionary plot, or help suppress a revolt. They had their own militia that was a part of the state system and had served with honor at the Battle of New Orleans in 1814. By the time of the Civil War they were among the finest of the city's tailors, carpenters, shoemakers, jewelers, and masons. They were also merchants, businessmen, and property owners. Almost half of the property, usually real estate, was owned by free women of color, inheritances from their white fathers. And they were

slaveholders; some were the biggest planters in the spate and were reputed to be the meanest of the mean when it came to treatment of bondsmen and women.

One of the oddities of the South was Louisiana's *Code Noire*, the state's law on slavery, which not only defined the "peculiar institution" but granted special distinctions normally reserved only for whites elsewhere on the basis of mixed blood. In the 1850s, when the rest of the South was tightening up on free African Americans and was trying to deport them or recommit them to slavery, the Louisiana supreme court once again stated that there was "all the difference between a free man of color and a slave, that there is between a white man and a slave." Truly the free persons of color of Louisiana were a class apart, without equal anywhere else in the nation. When the Civil War commenced they volunteered their service to defend the state against Yankee invasion. But as soon as the Union army and navy took New Orleans, the free colored people adapted readily to the new regime because there was something akin to the French Revolution in the Northern crusade—the possibility of the free colored men voting, a desire that topped everything in the Reconstruction agenda of free men of color.

But, in their quest for the vote, an aspiration that was shared by President Abraham Lincoln, the New Orleans free blacks found that they would actually lose status. The Union military commanders and even the Republicans in Congress did not understand their desire not to be included with the ex-slaves in any Reconstruction reforms. The free persons of color believed that the new state constitution drawn up under the Military Reconstruction Acts lessened their rights as individuals. Soldiers had seized their property for housing during the war, arbitrarily arrested them, demanded that they carry passes like any ordinary field hand, and excluded them from public transportation as if they were common "niggers." This loss of status hit them hard. They scorned being associated with the freedmen. Although some of the New Orleans free men of color, like newspaperman

Charles Louis Roudanez, tried to bridge the gap between themselves and the freed slaves, the nomination of Henry Clay Warmoth and his white Carpetbaggers to govern the state under the new state constitution of 1868 marked an end to free blacks' social and political influence. They now had to ride the Jim Crow streetcars and trains; they could not stand apart under law.

Reconstruction thus marked the death of the distinct class of free men and women of color in Louisiana. The wealth of these individuals declined with their prestige. They attempted to relocate in their desire to remain separate from ordinary blacks and whites alike. Many of them literally died or committed suicide under the stress. Others passed for white, usually moving out of the South where they would not be recognized for who they really were. Worse of all, the creative spark that had made them such a success in prewar Louisiana went out. They lived in abject depression and self-pity. They gave up social and political leadership to African Americans (as opposed to Creole Americans) like P. B. S. Pinchback, a man whom the free men and women of color always looked upon with distrust because he hobnobbed with those blacks "beneath" his station in life. They opposed the creation of all-black Southern University, believing that its establishment would actually retard the death of prejudice. Unlike the free blacks in Charleston, Reconstruction was not a liberating experience for the New Orleans people of mixed blood—it was an enslavement. It was the humiliation of being treated like any other black in the South. It resulted in their division, decline, and search for solace and seclusion. It was no wonder that the people who tried to break segregation by race in the 1890s case *Plessy v. Ferguson* were old Louisiana free persons of color, who felt that they were neither white or black, but superior to both, a class alone.

See also Louisiana Experiment; Pinchback, Pinckney Benton Stewart; Segregation (Jim Crow); Warmoth, Henry Clay.

References Berlin, Ira, *Slaves without Masters* (1974); Blassingame, John W., *Black New Orleans* (1973); Everett, Donald E., "Demands of the New Orleans Free Colored Population for Political Equality" (1955); Fitchett, E. Horace, "The Traditions of the Free Negro in Charleston, South Carolina" (1940); Harris, Robert L., Jr., "Charleston's Free Afro-American Elite" (1981); Hine, William C., "Black Politicians in Reconstruction Charleston, South Carolina" (1983) and "The 1867 Charleston Streetcar Sit-ins" (1976); Holt, Thomas, *Black over White* (1977); McCrary, Peyton, *Abraham Lincoln and Reconstruction* (1978); Rankin, David C., "The Impact of the Civil War on the Free Colored Community of New Orleans" (1977–1978), "The Origins of Black Leadership in New Orleans during Reconstruction" (1974), and "The Tannenbaum Thesis Reconsidered" (1979); Ripley, C. Peter, *Slaves and Freedmen in Civil War Louisiana* (1976); Somers, Dale A., "Black and White in New Orleans" (1974); Vincent, Charles, *Black Legislators in Louisiana during Reconstruction* (1976); Wade, Richard C., *Slavery in the Cities* (1964); Wikramanayake, Marina, *A World in Shadow* (1973).

Virginia Experiment

Whenever federal troops occupied the Confederacy, slavery as an institution collapsed. The first place where this happened was on the Virginia Peninsula at the massive stone fort of Fortress Monroe.  Never abandoned like other federal military installations and never attacked like forts Pickens and Sumter, Fortress Monroe was reinforced with Benjamin Butler's Massachusetts volunteers in May 1861. Other troops soon followed, and Butler became the fortress commander with the rank of major general.

Although Butler's post looked like a plum, the political general did not relish being exiled on the Atlantic coast so far from the seat of power in Washington. One could not advance in such isolation. So he moved to create his own fame by sending roving patrols into the hinterland. On 23 May 1861, three slaves followed a patrol back under the protection of the fort's massive guns. They sought protection from their masters and offered their services to the Union cause. Butler had initially sided with slaveowners as his men had moved southward through Maryland. His solicitude had caused Massachusetts Governor John A. Andrew to give him a severe rebuke. Butler replied that Maryland had yet to secede, so he could not rightly interfere with slavery there. But Virginia was another matter.

Soon a Virginia militia officer appeared as the representative of the slaveowners involved and asked for the return of the slaves under the Fugitive Slave Law of 1850. Butler refused. He said that he knew that similar slaves were erecting Confederate earthworks nearby, and he needed such labor, too. So he refused to return the slaves to their masters, preferring to declare them "contraband," liable to be confiscated under the rules of war. Ben Butler had taken the North's first hesitant step toward emancipation, and all slaves escaping to Union lines became "contrabands," in the parlance of the times. Although President Abraham Lincoln and his cabinet endorsed Butler's action, it would take Congress almost a year to forbid the return of fugitive slaves. However, Congress did pass the First Confiscation Act in August 1861, which allowed Southern slaves used in a military capacity to be seized (not freed) for the duration of the conflict. Soon afterward Butler was transferred to the Gulf.

News spread quickly throughout the immediate area, and slaves began to come in in droves. Now the Yankees were faced with a problem they had not anticipated—how to care for these black refugees. Many suggested that the contrabands, as all fugitive slaves were called, be collected and sent North to labor. Others—including Butler and his successor, Bvt. Maj. Gen. John Wool—thought that putting them to work on abandoned plantations and fortifications, paying them a small wage ($8 a month for men, $4 for women) on paper, which could be confiscated and used to feed and house those who could not work, was a better idea. Wool also turned to the American Missionary Association and other similar benevolent societies for aid. These missionaries and other secular do-gooders set up schools, regulated contraband camps, and suggested that the army increase contraband salaries to $15 a month for men and $5 for women. He also urged Wool to permit contrabands not employed by the army to care for themselves by farming garden plots. A similar policy was established at Roanoke Island in North Carolina, another federal base in the Atlantic South.

Wool was soon replaced by a younger man, Bvt. Maj. Gen. John Dix. This bothered the benevolent and religious societies because Dix had associated himself with the preservation of slavery at Baltimore, his last posting. Dix wished to exclude all contrabands from his jurisdiction, but the existence of 15,000 fugitive blacks within his lines and a new more aggressive congressional policy under the Second Confiscation Act that even hinted at arming the contrabands soon changed the general's philosophy. Still, Dix tried to protect loyal Virginians in their property rights, a policy that was confirmed in Lincoln's 1863 Emancipation

Contrabands follow a railroad track to work in this 1862 engraving. Contrabands, slaves liberated during the war, were paid a small wage to work for the Union army.

Proclamation, which freed only slaves behind Confederate lines. On the other hand, Dix allowed the benevolent societies to pursue their own policies based on those announced by General Wool, so long as Dix was not bothered by details. He did, however, set up a giant contraband camp at Newport News to isolate African Americans from the often malevolent influence of his condescending, racist white troops, who made a sport of harassing African Americans whenever they were encountered. Those blacks who did not move voluntarily to the new camp were chased down by whooping soldiers and relocated by force.

At the new camp, the religious and benevolent societies quarreled over the amount of aid to be given and in what form. Many preferred, for example, to give cloth to be sewn into clothing rather than the actual articles, reasoning that the contrabands would be taught self-reliance as well as succored. By the middle of 1863, the federal government had decided that its "Negro policy" would be to institute managed work forces on abandoned plantations

owned or managed by loyal men; this arrangement would place blacks in a state of pseudo-freedom for the rest of the war. They would be free to work as they were told; no more, no less. In the midst of this policy change, General Butler returned from his controversial administration of Reconstruction in Louisiana. Butler was more interested in raising the new U.S. Colored Troops than in agricultural endeavors. He declared all males between 18 and 45 to be eligible for enlistment. He promised each recruit $10 a month and subsistence rations for his family. Those who refused to go along with the program would be declared unemployed and liable to arrest for idleness and forced labor on fortifications (General U. S. Grant was about to embark on his Richmond campaign, so the need was great) with no rations to their families.

Despite Butler's policies, most blacks worked on leased plantations during the rest of the war. Yet as hard as the benevolent societies tried, only a small proportion of contrabands were fully employed. And as the war ended the slaves' owners reappeared and demanded their lands back, dispossessing the blacks of their livelihood. Butler proved to be less than brilliant as a military commander and was replaced by Bvt. Maj. Gen. E. O. C. Ord, a man noted for his lack of sympathy for freedmen. He sought to make blacks independent of government aid as quickly as possible, arresting and putting to hard labor all those who refused to seek an outside job. Others were signed over to landowners for the remainder of the 1865 season. Similar policies prevailed in North Carolina. And here matters stood until the arrival of the Freedmen's Bureau administrators later that year.

See also Louisiana Experiment; Mississippi Valley Experiment; Port Royal Experiment.

Reference Berlin, Ira, et al., *Slaves No More* (1992); Gerteis, Louis, *From Contraband to Freedman* (1973).

Wade, Benjamin F.
(1800–1878)

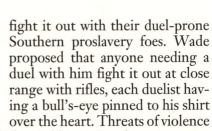

Born in Massachusetts, the ninth of ten children, Benjamin F. Wade received little formal education during his childhood, save what his mother and a small local school provided. In 1821, his parents took the family to Andover, Ohio, where Ben Wade went to work as a farmer, drover, and common laborer. He also studied medicine and taught school. Five years later he took up the study of law and by 1828 was in practice, having been admitted to the bar. He had trouble speaking in public at first but kept at it until he had mastered the art. He was in partnerships with Joshua R. Giddings and Rufus P. Ranney and by 1838 was quite established in northeastern Ohio. In 1841 he married Caroline Rosekrans, with whom he had two sons. They set up a home in Jefferson.

Already interested in politics, Wade was an antislavery man who had served as local prosecutor and spent a term in the state senate. He was defeated on his second try for the senate but returned to that body in 1841 and was made a circuit judge in 1847. He was a forceful man whose businesslike methods and increasingly popular decisions led the Whig party to nominate him, apparently with no effort on his own part, for the U.S. Senate. He won the seat in 1851 and remained there until 1869, changing his party allegiance to Republican before his second term.

Wade was an unusual man for the antislavery forces in the Senate. He was rough, coarse, and vituperative in an arena that thrived on the suave and soft-spoken. He denounced the Fugitive Slave Law of 1850 and opposed the extension of slavery represented by the Kansas-Nebraska Act. He favored the Homestead Bill, which he characterized as "land to the landless," and opposed the suggestion of the acquisition of Cuba. Along with two other rough fellows, Zachariah Chandler of Michigan and Simon Cameron of Pennsylvania, Wade became the protector of less rugged antislave senators who feared to physically

fight it out with their duel-prone Southern proslavery foes. Wade proposed that anyone needing a duel with him fight it out at close range with rifles, each duelist having a bull's-eye pinned to his shirt over the heart. Threats of violence subsided quickly as Southerners complained of the "unmanly" style of Wade's methods.

As the South moved to secede, Wade became more and more intransigent against compromise. During the war he was among the most belligerent of Northern senators. He went down to Virginia to watch the Battle of First Bull Run and played a prominent role in stemming the panicked retreat. He badgered ever-cautious Maj. Gen. George B. McClellan to get moving and attack the Confederate armies. He acted as chairman of the joint committee on the conduct of the war and became the terror of all called before its prying eye. He labeled all who dissented from his desires as disloyal to the Union. He was temperamentally incapable of understanding the subtleties of President Abraham Lincoln's war policies (which nearly cost Wade reelection in 1863 because of opposition within the Union party, a coalition of Republicans and War Democrats), all of which seemed too weak and slow to him. He introduced a more stringent plan of Reconstruction along with Winter Davis of the House (the Wade-Davis Bill) to counter Lincoln's Ten Percent Plan, and he raged at the rationale for the president's pocket veto in the Wade-Davis Manifesto. He tried to get Lincoln replaced by Secretary of the Treasury Salmon P. Chase in the 1864 election, only to be rebuffed by his own supporters back in Ohio.

Wade welcomed the change at the presidential helm occasioned by Lincoln's assassination but soon realized that President Andrew Johnson was far worse than Lincoln ever had been. Along with Thaddeus Stevens, Charles Sumner, and others, Wade worked to make Reconstruction tougher. He championed the enfranchisement of blacks in the District of Columbia in 1865 and in the election of 1866 called for it to be a national commitment to freedmen everywhere. Although he was willing to readmit the South if it ratified the Fourteenth Amendment, he was in the vanguard in proposing the Military Reconstruction that followed. In March 1867 he succeeded to the office of president pro tem of the Senate, next in line to Johnson should the latter die or be removed from office. But Wade's willingness to push everything to its fullest extreme made him as many enemies as friends. Many commentators believe that the picture of Ben Wade as chief executive in place of an impeached President Johnson actually harmed the final impeachment vote. Wade had no reservations at all about the impeachment and, instead of excusing himself as having a conflict of interest in the outcome, voted to convict the president. Indeed, he had already begun to choose his cabinet, so confident was he of ultimate victory. He failed in his presidential ambitions by one vote.

Evidently the party and voters back home were not amused by Wade's antics in Washington. They refused to send him back for a fourth term in the Senate. Wade attempted to gain the vice presidency under a Ulysses S. Grant ticket, but the party convention went for the more amiable "Smilin'" Schuyler Colfax instead. Wade returned to Ohio to practice law until his death ten years later. Meanwhile he had no lack of political things to do. He served as a lawyer for the Northern Pacific Railroad, on the board of directors of the Union Pacific Railroad, and as a commissioner to look into the annexation of Santo Domingo.

See also Johnson and Reconstruction; Lincoln and Reconstruction; Moderate Republicans and Reconstruction; Radical Republicans; Radical Republicans and Reconstruction; Wade-Davis Bill; Wade-Davis Manifesto and the Elections of 1864.

References Meneely, A. Howard, "Benjamin Franklin Wade" (1964–1981); Shover, Kenneth B., "Maverick at Bay" (1966); Trefousse, Hans L., "Ben Wade and the Failure of the Impeachment of Andrew Johnson" (1960) and *Benjamin Franklin Wade* (1963).

Wade-Davis Bill

The Wade-Davis Bill, also known as the First Congressional Plan of Reconstruction, was a response to President Abraham Lincoln's Ten Percent Plan, then in use in the South to establish loyal governments in the reconquered states of Louisiana, Arkansas, and Tennessee. Although it is now believed that Senator Ira Harris of New York wrote the original measure, it was sponsored by Representative Henry Winter Davis of Maryland and Senator Ben Wade of Ohio (both Radical Republicans). Working from an earlier theory put forth by representatives James M. Ashley and John A. Bingham of Ohio, the bill assumed that if the South was not out of the Union (something the president claimed to be true) it was so far gone that conditions for reentry, like the end of slavery, could be imposed by Congress, much as if that body were handling the admission of a territory to statehood for the first time. The Wade-Davis plan called for 50 percent of the 1860 registered voters of a reoccupied Southern state to take an oath of future loyalty to the Union. It had the appearance of democracy in its reliance on a majority of registrants, but it would be difficult to achieve, since most Southern states had been only partially occupied by Yankee troops; it would also tend to delay Reconstruction after the war's end, when a more thought-out, truly radical plan might be introduced. As with the Lincoln plan, certain high-ranking Confederate civil and military men were excluded from political participation.

Once a majority of 1860 voters had pledged their future loyalty, the state could elect delegates to a state convention. However, only some of the oath-takers could vote. These were the men who could take a second oath, known as the ironclad oath, that they had never willingly given aid, directly or indirectly, to the Confederate cause. That is to say, the Wade-Davis plan relied on the Union men of the South to reform their states without interference from the seceders. The state convention elected by these truly loyal individuals had to abolish slavery (Davis assumed that Lincoln's Emancipation Proclamation, as a wartime military edict, was too radical and that abolition had to be formally accomplished not by soldiers but by the elected politicians of individual Southern states in convention). The convention also had to disfranchise certain Confederate civil and military leaders (to allow the loyal government to start off without Rebel obstructionists) and repudiate the Confederate war debt (making secession and the Confederacy illegal). This meant that the convention attenders would invalidate all aspects of Confederate thought. Once the state constitution was drawn up, everyone who took the original oath of future loyalty could elect a state government and their national representatives. These men could then apply for congressional consideration and be seated if the whole Congress agreed.

The Wade-Davis Bill did little for the former slaves except insist on freedom. Seventeen Republicans abstained from voting on it for this or other reasons, but it received enough votes to pass both houses of Congress on 2 July 1864. When Lincoln came down to the presidential office to sign bills, he refused to ink the Wade-Davis measure. Since Congress had already adjourned for the summer, he pocket vetoed it—that is, he let it lie on the table for ten days, whereupon it automatically expired (had Congress been in session, ignoring the bill would have led to its automatic passage). Although a president need not say why he pocket vetoed any bill, Lincoln chose to speak out on the Wade-Davis proposal. He claimed that he did not wish to be committed to any single course of action at that time. He also professed not to be against anything in the bill and said that if any Southern state wished to come in under its provisions, he would be happy to acquiesce in that decision.

See also Lincoln and Reconstruction; Wade-Davis Manifesto and the Elections of 1864.

References Belz, Herman, *Reconstructing the Union* (1969); Benedict, Michael Les, *A Compromise of Principle* (1974); Cox, LaWanda, *Lincoln and Black Freedom* (1981); Foner, Eric, *Reconstruction* (1988); Hesseltine, William B., "Lincoln and the Politicians" (1960) and *Lincoln's Plan of Reconstruction* (1960); McCrary, Peyton, *Abraham Lincoln and Reconstruction* (1978).

Wade-Davis Manifesto and the Elections of 1864

Although President Abraham Lincoln said he was amenable to any seceded Southern state that wanted to apply for readmission to the Union under the Wade-Davis Bill, his pocket veto of the bill angered many of the Radical Republicans, who thought his statement a bit flippant. The Wade-Davis Manifesto accused the president of interfering with Congress' prerogative to reconstruct the South under the constitutional guarantee of ensuring republican state governments (*republican* in this sense refers to a type of government, not the political party). The Radical Republicans were dissatisfied with failed attempts to compromise on the Reconstruction issue after the pocket veto, and they were angered by what they viewed as the president's hesitant attempts to end slavery, win the war by scourging the South, and punish the traitors who had rebelled. Thus the Radicals turned to a more "reliable" candidate for the party's nomination as president in 1864, John Charles Frémont. "The Pathfinder," as he was popularly known from his western trails experiences, had tried to free the slaves in his military command at St. Louis in the early days of the war, only to suffer Lincoln's rebuff and removal. He had also been the party's first nominee in 1856 and although he lost the election, the results demonstrated that the Republicans could win the presidency with only Northern electoral votes.

But by the fall of 1864, Lincoln's field commanders had finally destroyed the Confederate armies enough to make winning the war a matter of time. It was obvious that Lincoln would receive the approval of the Republican convention and a large popular and electoral majority. The Radicals needed to get back in with the Lincoln supporters in order to have a say in future policy, but they did not wish to crawl too much. Lincoln threw them a sop by removing Frank Blair as postmaster general. Blair was from an important Democratic family and was considered soft on the place of freed blacks in American society. Upon Blair's removal (he agreed to step down for the good of the party at Lincoln's request) Frémont withdrew as an independent Republican candidate and the Radicals came back to the fold.

Lincoln's electoral victory in 1864, the Radicals' return to the party ranks, and Congress' refusal to seat the representatives sent to Washington from the Southern states that had followed Lincoln's Reconstruction plan meant that everything was up for grabs in 1865. There was no Reconstruction plan all could agree on. There were indications that Lincoln was considering some compromise with Congress at the time of his death—maybe a proposal that Congress would recognize his governments in Virginia, Louisiana, Tennessee, and Arkansas—and that he would reorganize the rest of the South on another basis with congressional input. But his death prevented anyone from knowing what exactly he had in mind. Whatever it was, it was not the approach of his successor, Andrew Johnson, who took on Congress with no compromise.

See also Johnson and Reconstruction; Lincoln and Reconstruction; Wade-Davis Bill.

References Belz, Herman, *Reconstructing the Union* (1969); Benedict, Michael Les, *A Compromise of Principle* (1974); Cox, LaWanda, *Lincoln and Black Freedom* (1981); Foner, Eric, *Reconstruction* (1988); Hesseltine, William B., "Lincoln and the Politicians" (1960) and *Lincoln's Plan of Reconstruction* (1960); McCrary, Peyton, *Abraham Lincoln and Reconstruction* (1978).

Waite, Morrison R. (1816–1888)

Born in Lyme, Connecticut, Morrison R. Waite came from an old New England lineage. His father was a local judge who advanced to the state supreme court as chief justice. Inspired by his father's example, Waite graduated from Yale College in 1837 with top grades. After reading law with his father for a year, Waite moved to Ohio, where he set up practice as a business attorney in Maumee and then Toledo. In 1840 he married his second cousin, Amelia Warner. An active member of the Whig party, Waite was elected to the Ohio state legislature in 1849.

When the question of the expansion of slavery into the western territories arose, Waite helped form the Ohio Republican party. He supported Abraham Lincoln's nomination over that of home state candidate Salmon P. Chase. In 1862 he stood for Congress but was defeated in the Republican primary by James Ashley, a more radical Republican. He worked to elect War Democrat John Brough as governor of Ohio over Peace Democrat Clement L. Vallandigham (the latter had recently returned from Confederate exile). His national reputation came during the *Alabama* claims, a dispute with Great Britain over allowing Confederate cruisers to be built, armed, and supplied in British ports. Waite represented the United States along with Caleb Cushing and his old classmate, William M. Evarts. Waite's appointment was partly accidental, a prior candidate having refused the nomination. It was Waite's reply to Lord Rondell Palmerston that clinched the American claim to Britain's liability.

Waite returned to Ohio somewhat of a hero and received an honorary doctor of laws from Yale. In 1873 he was chosen by both parties to be a representative in the Ohio state convention to modify its state constitution. He also served as president of the convention. Later that same year President Ulysses S. Grant nominated him to be chief justice of the U.S. Supreme Court, for which he received the unanimous approval of the Senate. During his term the court decided on numerous issues of import including the constitutionality of the Enforcement Acts, the rights of states to regulate railroads (the *Granger* cases), federal control of elections, the Tenure of Office Act, repudiation of state debts, the rights of labor unions, Chinese exclusion, and the patent of the telephone. He was a man who liked details and paid the strictest attention to the docket of the court and the nature of upcoming cases. He had a reputation for fairness above party considerations. Waite fell sick while reading an opinion, stepped down from the bench, and went home and collapsed. He died three weeks later from pneumonia.

See also Chase, Salmon P.; Supreme Court and Redemption.

References Fairman, Charles, *Reconstruction and Reunion* (1971–1987); McGrath, C. Peter, *Morrison R. Waite* (1963).

Warmoth, Henry Clay (1842–1931)

Born in Illinois, Henry Clay Warmoth was a Carpetbag governor of Louisiana during Reconstruction. He grew up with a modicum of education, mostly gleaned from books that his father (a justice of the peace and a harness maker) had lying around and from setting type in a local print shop. When he was almost 18 he left home for Missouri, where he put up a sign and practiced law, having learned a bit of it from his father's law books. As soon as the war broke out, Warmoth went off with the Thirty-second Missouri Regiment to fight for the Union. He rose to the rank of lieutenant colonel until Maj. Gen. Ulysses S. Grant removed him from command, claiming Warmoth had been away without leave and had given vital information to the enemy in a newspaper interview. Warmoth went to Washington to defend himself successfully in front of President Abraham Lincoln. He was restored to his position with all back pay. He fought with the regiment at Vicksburg and Chattanooga and as a staff officer in the Red River campaign. Warmoth went to Washington to view Lincoln's second inaugural ball and toured Richmond a few days after the Confederates fled on the road to Appomattox. At the end of the war he went to St. Louis to visit his sisters, and he and his father took a steamboat south to New Orleans for a sightseeing trip.

Warmoth was impressed with the big plantation culture he found in Louisiana. He promised himself one day that such luxury would be his. He reacquainted himself with Bvt. Maj. Gen. Nathaniel Banks and his wife; Banks insisted on making his young friend a military judge. Warmoth began hearing cases the very next day. After a few months he left the army and opened up shop as a lawyer, representing those who had had property seized by the War or Treasury departments. Business was very good in occupied Louisiana, but disturbing things were happening as far as loyal Northerners were concerned. Provisional Governor J. Madison Wells, once a cotton planter with four plantations and numerous slaves, a secessionist in 1861, a Unionist in 1864, and now a Rebel sympathizer promoting Andrew Johnson's lenient Reconstruction, got General Banks sent home. Warmoth decided that he should organize a Republican party to oppose such ideas. He took as his example the Jacobin Robespierre from the French Revolution, a man who could mold others and events to fit his scheme of things. Of course, Warmoth would not follow his idol to the guillotine, but there was a lot of intriguing ground to cross before that kind of disaster would come up.

Warmoth constructed his Louisiana Republican party from three elements. First were the native whites who had engaged in Lincoln's wartime Reconstruction and drawn up the 1864 Free State constitution. The second group would be the numerous Northerners who came South during and after the war. The third group was to be African Americans, who in Louisiana included a large number of educated blacks who had never been slaves (indeed, in that oddest of Southern states, they had owned a few slaves themselves). For the time being, Warmoth avoided the use of the word *party* and called his organization a club or association. Immediately he ran into opposition from New Orleans blacks, who had been free before the war and were able to articulate their own cause. They wanted to know just who this Warmoth fellow was to come in and tell them what they wanted and how to achieve it. But Warmoth managed to join his groups into a tenuous alliance with the help of Thomas J. Durant, a leader of the wartime free state movement. In a convention they adopted the name of Republican party for the first time.

The convention, with black delegates participating, voted to send a territorial representative to Congress. Durant declined, but Warmoth accepted the nomination.

Congress actually gave him a seat (but no vote), as his presence played right into the prejudices of the more radical Republicans, since Warmoth came from a body that did not claim statehood. Louisiana's regularly elected congressmen under the Lincoln Reconstruction, whom the House refused to recognize, had to watch the charade from the gallery. Warmoth returned to New Orleans in time to witness the New Orleans Riot, which he characterized as "a dark day for the city of New Orleans." Then Warmoth attended the convention of Southern loyalists held in Philadelphia; he toured the North following President Johnson's "Swing around the Circle" campaign to negate Johnson's efforts and help elect Republicans. By the time of the passage of the Military Reconstruction Acts he was back in Louisiana enrolling black and white Union veterans in the Grand Army of the Republic, a Republican veterans organization. He was by now the best-known Republican in the state.

Warmoth was a rather noteworthy young man by anyone's standard. Over six feet tall and weighing in at 140 pounds, he had dark hair and eyes and a full mustache in the style of the day. He smoked and drank way too much and was an incurable womanizer. His friends in Missouri wrote him that they all missed his stories and the young ladies his presence. Another wrote him from Great Salt Lake City that Warmoth ought to come out to Utah. Gentile (non-Mormon) men were all the rage, claimed the informant, warning, "You would kill yourself here in about one year." When he entered a room he attracted the attention of everyone with his "lordly air." Women, young and old, married and single, black and white, Northern and Southern, flirted with him outrageously. After he became governor he received many anonymous love letters, one which referred to his "grand physical beauty"—not bad for a lady writing in normally staid Victorian America. Eventually, years later, he would marry a Louisiana woman, Sally Durand, who was well educated and from a very wealthy family.

Meanwhile Warmoth accompanied Freedmen's Bureau agents into the hinterland to encourage black voters to register. Although he was not a delegate to the constitutional convention, he played a major role. He got himself and a few others admitted with full privileges on the floor. He got the convention to lower the age requirement for governor from 35 to 25 so that the 25-year-old Warmoth could run for the office. But by now the Republicans had split into two factions, the Pure Radicals and the White Republicans. When Warmoth beat out the Radicals' candidate for the gubernatorial slot on the ticket, the Radicals put their own man, a Union white, up against him. The Democrats decided not to participate in the election, leaving the field to the split Republicans. During the election Warmoth complained mightily that the army under Maj. Gen. Winfield Scott Hancock and then Bvt. Maj. Gen. Robert C. Buchanan were too pro-Democrat. But in April 1868, the election passed peacefully, the constitution carried, and Warmoth won the governorship.

When the legislature met, black Lieutenant Governor Oscar J. Dunn refused to admit any white-elected state senator who could not take the ironclad oath (of never having given aid to the Confederate cause). His African American counterpart in the house of representatives did the same. The result was a near riot that was calmed down by federal troops. But Warmoth and the Republicans knew they would not have the army to help them forever. Already the Knights of the White Camellia (Louisiana's version of the Ku Klux Klan, with a lot less disguise and ritual) were beginning to ride in the backcountry. Violence was spreading from parish to parish (Louisiana's name for counties). Under Warmoth's guiding hand the legislature passed laws creating a metropolitan police, a parish constabulary, and a state militia. He also saw to it that the governor was a member of the returning board that validated all votes, in order to make up for the violence and intimidation that the police could never totally eliminate.

In the beginning, Warmoth worked smoothly with his fellow Republican legislators and got them to elect William Pitt Kellogg, a personal friend and Illinois Carpetbagger, to one of the U.S. Senate seats. The Republican vote had already dropped by half as a result of intimidation, and Warmoth could not hold Louisiana in the Republican column for Ulysses S. Grant or elect any Republicans to Congress in November 1868. But since most local parish jobs were appointive through the governor, Warmoth kept the party in power through his own actions. And all appointees received their commissions only after they submitted a signed, undated letter of resignation to the governor as a guarantee of their loyalty.

In time many of the legislators grew to resent Warmoth's concentration of all appointive power for local patronage in his own hands. The governor seemed to give more than the fair share of offices to his Carpetbag friends. The resentment spread from Scalawags to blacks. Both resented being shortchanged on patronage decisions. African Americans were even more incensed when Warmoth vetoed a public accommodations bill. Worse yet, Warmoth began to alienate some of his Carpetbag friends, especially Kellogg. It seems that President Grant's wife had a favorite sister whose husband had received a presidential appointment as collector of customs in New Orleans. Kellogg and others of the congressional delegation had opposed the man, but Warmoth knew Louisiana Republicans needed Grant's aid in appointments and military interference at elections, so he sent in a letter agreeing with the president. But he failed to tell Kellogg and the Washington delegation. This made their stand look foolish. They never forgave Warmoth for going behind their backs. After other state Republicans accepted Grant's relative as one of their own, Grant hinted that he wanted the man to stand for the U.S. Senate from Louisiana. The Louisiana delegation agreed, but Warmoth would have none of this (he made local patronage decisions, no one else) and put up his own man, who won. Now Warmoth had alienated the president.

Then Warmoth had an accident aboard a steamboat that lamed him severely. Rather than healing, the wound grew worse, and Warmoth took off to the Mississippi Gulf Coast to heal. In his absence, Lieutenant Governor Oscar Dunn, a former slave and now a plasterer by trade, took over the governor's post. Warmoth thought this would be a formality, but Dunn was in for keeps. Not only that, he plotted the removal of Warmoth's appointees and their replacement by his own men. On crutches, Warmoth returned to New Orleans and confronted Dunn before any real damage could be done. He also took the opportunity to dress down all of his opponents (a lengthy process by then) at the so-called Gatling Gun Convention, where rival Republicans hoped to reorganize the party without him. Warmoth was stopped from entering the hall by U.S. troops and a Gatling gun. So he stood on a chair and railed against the federal presence until the soldiers escorted him away. Warmoth repaired to another hall with the party faithful and delivered a speech that harangued everyone he could think of who questioned his conduct as governor. Charges and countercharges were exchanged in local newspapers, and eventually Warmoth was challenged to a duel. He refused to fight, saying it was beneath his dignity as governor to engage in an illegal act.

Warmoth made enemies for other reasons, too, many of them monetary. His opponents accused him of every kind of crooked political deal from pocketing bribes, to overcharging for state printing (20 times too much, according to one story), to collecting fees from his appointees for the right to continue in office. He also bought depreciated state bonds and got the legislature to fund them, not to mention what his influence cost railroad companies and levee builders. According to one story, Warmoth, when offered $50,000 for signing a pavement contract, made a counterproposal for $75,000 and a percentage of company profits. When questioned by a naive Yankee newspaper correspondent if Louisiana were corrupt, he replied, "I don't pretend to be honest." State politicians "are as good as the people they represent," he continued. "Corruption is the fashion down here." Then

Warmoth coyly implied that he could have taken more and was more honest than his political enemies, who did not know when to stop. In 1872, a congressional committee came down to Louisiana to investigate Reconstruction corruption. Warmoth's testimony—full of all sorts of vagaries—lasted three days and filled 135 pages. At the end of the session, the chairman stated privately to Warmoth that the committee members did not know whether he was a "angel from Heaven or a devil from Hell." As one perceptive historian remarked since, "Warmoth liked that."

Warmoth ran into a bit of luck when Lieutenant Governor Dunn died of a suspected poisoning. Warmoth convinced the legislature to elect P. B. S. Pinchback as president pro tem of the state senate, in effect lieutenant governor. Pinchback, a sort of darker-skinned version of Warmoth, had been one of the governor's constant supporters until now. By 1872 it was obvious that if Warmoth expected to gain anything by the end of his term, like a U.S. Senate seat, he would have to appeal to the Democrats. Oddly enough, there was a fairly easy way to do this. Since he and Grant were on the outs, Warmoth turned down Pinchback's offer of help in getting reelected (and becoming Pinchback's pawn) and declared himself to be a Liberal Republican in favor of Horace Greeley's election as president. Besides, there were actually five parties contesting the upcoming state elections: Custom House Republicans (mostly white Grant men), Pinchback Republicans (mostly black Grant men), Liberal Republicans (white Greeley men), Reform Democrats (ardent white Greeley men), and Regular Democrats (reluctant white Greeley men). It was going to be a very interesting election, to say the least.

By the end of August 1872, Warmoth had worked out a deal to combine the Liberal Republicans with both Democratic factions behind the candidacy of John McEnery for governor. For his political acumen, Warmoth was promised election to the U.S. Senate by what he hoped would be the Democratic legislature. Their real opponent was Kellogg, backed by the Customs House faction led by Stephen B. Packard (the U.S. marshal) and state senator Pinchback. The latter went off to New England for a vacation of campaigning for the national ticket. Warmoth followed soon after to New York City on state business. By an odd quirk, the two men bumped into each other on the street and agreed to a dinner date. Pinchback never showed. Warmoth assumed that he had had a better offer in the meantime and went to bed.

Suddenly he woke up with a start. The first man back to Louisiana would be the acting governor! There were several pieces of key civil rights legislation that Warmoth had been holding ransom to keep Radical Republicans in line. If Pinchback signed them, he would become a Radical hero, undercut Warmoth, and be stronger than ever. Warmoth raced to the train station. Yes, he was told, a flashy dresser like Pinchback was hard to forget; he had left on the night train, hours ago. Warmoth telegraphed ahead to a friend who worked on the Illinois Central Railroad to have a special car ready. He hurried out on the Pennsylvania Railroad, the fastest in the nation, to catch his train for the Deep South in Kentucky. The South's railroads (on which Pinchback rode) lived up to their reputation for slowness. At Warmoth's request, the Canton, Mississippi, station master locked Pinchback up in a storeroom, causing him to miss his connection for Baton Rouge. Warmoth caught up to Pinchback at Canton. Together they rode back to Louisiana, Warmoth still governor.

Warmoth's Fusion party won the state by 10,000 votes; at least, that is what his returning board said. But the Regular Republicans got a federal judge to declare their own returning board as the correct one and to enjoin Warmoth from having anything to do with validating the returns. The U.S. Army took over the statehouse in New Orleans and refused to admit anyone to the legislature who was not on the judge's approved list. Pinchback got up before the senate and announced that Warmoth had approached him with a $50,000 bribe the preceding midnight to let his people be seated. Of course, Pinchback said he was above all monetary considerations as leader of the senate; he had refused the money. The house was informed and quickly impeached Warmoth, suspending him as governor until he could be tried. Pinchback broke into the governor's office and took over. As president pro tem of the senate, he was next in line to be governor.

The only problem was that Pinchback's senate term technically had already expired. Warmoth, as the only legitimate governor, issued an order to the citizens to disregard Pinchback. The latter man ordered the militia to report to him to defend the statehouse. The militia refused and indicated they would stand by Warmoth. Pinchback then called on the Metropolitan Police to assist him. They came forward. War seemed imminent. Then a contingent of federal soldiers came forward with a telegraphed order from Washington. Pinchback was to be governor for the rest of Warmoth's term, said President Grant. On 13 January 1873, both Kellogg and McEnery took the oath of office as governor of Louisiana, each guarded by their adherents. But Kellogg had an ace up his sleeve: he had the support of President Grant. The Fusionists would have to wait for 1876 and the removal of the federal troops by President Rutherford B. Hayes.

Meanwhile Warmoth had killed a man in a streetfight over a political quarrel. Because the other had attacked him with a revolver and Warmoth had a knife, the case was ruled to be one of self-defense. Warmoth retired to a sugar plantation in the bayou country west of New Orleans that he had bought with some of his political proceeds. He got married and lived out a long and fruitful life in a style that he had always dreamed of. He remained a power in Louisiana Republican circles, once running for governor in 1888. He wrote his memoirs. He seemed forgotten when he died in 1931, but he was not. He had an unknown admirer who used all of Warmoth's political tricks to attain power in the state. This man instructed the legislature on how to vote, se-

questered all patronage in the governor's office, and required undated resignations from all appointees. His name was Huey P. Long.

See also Carpetbaggers; Longstreet, James; Redemption of the South before 1874; Redemption of the South from 1874.

References Binning, Francis W., "Henry Clay Warmoth and Louisiana Reconstruction" (1969); Current, Richard N., *Those Terrible Carpetbaggers* (1988) and *Three Carpetbag Governors* (1967); Dufour, Charles L., "The Age of Warmoth" (1965); Harris, Francis B., "Henry Clay Warmoth" (1947); Taylor, Joe Gray, "Louisiana" (1980); Warmoth, Henry Clay, *War Politics and Reconstruction* (1930).

Washington, Booker T. (1856–1915)

Booker T. Washington was born in bondage in what is now West Virginia of a liaison between his mother and a local white, whom he never knew. At birth he was called only "Booker," but he added the rest of his name later in his childhood, when he noticed other children had surnames. His mother married and his new stepfather put him to work at salt works and coal mines early in life. Encouraged by his mother, the young man went to school and tried to find a better station in life. He finally got a job as a house servant at the home of Lewis Ruffner. Mrs. Ruffner began his education in cleanliness, efficiency, and order, which became the hallmarks of any decent life in Washington's eyes. His praise for the Ruffners and his ability to "know his place" led later critics to assert that Washington never lost the attitude of being "a favorite slave."

In 1871, Washington went Hampton, Virginia, to enroll in the school for blacks founded by Samuel C. Armstrong, a Union Civil War veteran who had commanded African American troops. At Armstrong's Hampton Institute, Washington learned his lessons well—to avoid politics, learn a trade, and work one's way up the ladder of life from a lowly position to a higher one. Again, the emphasis was on morality, discipline, and character molded by cleanliness, thrift, abstinence, and dignity. Once again Washington was in the presence of a white man who greatly moved him. After graduation, Washington went back home to teach, convinced that there was more to education than mere book work, primarily the bath and the proper and frequent use of a toothbrush. His belief in character building along with practical industrial education was reaffirmed when he took time off to attend Wayland Seminary at Washington, D.C. Here he saw students well versed in Greek and Latin who were little inclined to go into the countryside to help the majority of blacks still laboring in the fields.

Shortly after beginning the course at Wayland, Washington was invited to come back to Hampton Institute as an instructor. He accepted readily and took over the institute's program for Native American children, as well as its night school for blacks, where students worked by day to earn their tuition as they studied. Impressed by Washington's talent, Armstrong recommended him as principal for a new version of Hampton Institute envisioned for the town of Tuskegee, Alabama. In 1881, Washington went South to begin what became his life's work, the creation of Tuskegee Normal and Industrial Institute in Alabama. His goal became to teach African American students the Protestant ethic of hard work and discipline, to impart a useful trade, and to do all of this without making them a threat to the existing white sociopolitical order. Indeed, Washington maintained that filling a black student with "a blind discontent" was worse than providing no education at all. Since he had to start from scratch, Washington quickly became an expert fund-raiser for his school. He worked mostly among Northern philanthropists but also appealed to Southern whites to help out. He emphasized how his school turned out self-made people, conservative producers of a better society through hard work.

By 1895, Washington and Tuskegee were vibrant symbols of the place of African Americans in the New South. It was a time of immense crisis, one in which segregation and disfranchisement were the more civilized aspects of a life that was marked by lynchings and abuses of the convict lease (by which the labor of convicts was sold to individuals outside the prison system). It was also a time when black America lost most of its Reconstruction leaders to old age, people like Frederick Douglass, Blanche K. Bruce, and John M. Langston. Someone needed to step into the void left by the loss of these men, and that person became Booker T. Washington. But Washington was of a different personality than the old leaders, people like Douglass who attacked the white power structure head on. Washington was a devious, behind-the-scenes manipulator who often presented more than one face to the public—black statesman to Northern whites, safe Negro to Southern whites, stepfather to Northern blacks, father to Southern blacks, artful political boss to politicians, and yet another role in his letters and private life. He had a tendency to tell white America what it wanted to hear and then to work to change whites into being more receptive to Washington's true goal of equal rights, privileges, and responsibilities in American society for all people. It was the same purpose as those "moral giants" who preceded him and those who would come later, but Washington was much subtler in his means.

The vehicle by which Washington became the new black leader was the Cotton States Exposition at Atlanta, seven months after Douglass's death. Atlanta represented the New South, a region of businessmen and entrepreneurs who sought to build the industrial base needed to overcome the economic losses represented by the defeat of the Confederacy. The audience, racially mixed, listened for 20 minutes as Washington addressed them on racial harmony and how it was to be achieved. He carefully walked the razor's edge as he emphasized means rather than ends, opportunities instead of grievances, mutuality of interests rather than disparity. Essentially Washington asked the audience to rise above prejudice by focusing on economic initiative and self-help. He talked against black political involvement, scoffed at those who would leave the South, and repudiated any need for social equality. He spoke of how the two races could be as separate as the five fingers but as united as the whole hand. His approach came to be known as the Atlanta Compromise.

Washington was not for a base submission to Southern whites but rather for bearing everyday wrongs that could not be righted and going on to the greater good of personal and economic improvement. He was, however, depending upon the ultimate kindness and justice of whites, and in this he may have been too idealistic, as the case of Homer Plessy showed. Plessy was a successful Louisiana businessman, nearly white in color, who could not ride on any but the Jim Crow car in a passenger train. At least that is what Louisiana law, backed up by the U.S. Supreme Court, said. Economic success had its limits. But to his credit Washington worked to try to get "separate but equal" to really mean equality in treatment. He did ask that disfranchising laws be applied the same against blacks and whites. He did not eschew all forms of protest. He maintained that any group that could not vote by law was at a disadvantage in the American form of government. Somehow he never lost the hope that if African Americans would only emulate him they too could cross the color line in civil rights, public accommodations, and social acceptance. He always believed that whites could not hold blacks in a ditch without getting in that ditch themselves.

Whites all over the nation lauded Washington for his Atlanta Compromise. Overnight he became viewed as the most important black man in America. It was a position and title that he guarded jealously. Skillfully he moved to grab the power implicit in his being a spokesman for his race. He was a master of secrecy and deviousness. Though he was outwardly an accommodationist, he moved quietly to combat peonage, segregation, disfranchisement, and "lily white" Republican parties in the South, as well as to gain appointment of judges who were sympathetic to blacks' problems. He became the confidant of presidents, especially Theodore Roosevelt and William Howard Taft. He was the African American political boss of his age, called the "black Warwick" (a

reference to the fifteenth-century English aristocrat known as Warwick the Kingmaker) in charge of what was known as the "Tuskegee machine." He put out a continuous flow of propaganda in the form of syndicated newspaper columns, editorials, articles, and books, usually penned by ghost writers. His autobiographical *Up from Slavery*, which he wrote himself, became a worldwide best-seller. He worked to stifle any criticism of him being the "white man's nigger." Washington also worked to persuade, boycott, or buy out the opposition press. He extended his influence into religious denominations and fraternal orders. He founded the Negro Business League to extend his power into Northern cities. And he spied on anyone or any group that might undermine his coveted position in the white community.

His power, however, was based on the image of him that whites saw, not on what blacks envisioned. African American critics like W. E. Burghardt DuBois and Monroe Trotter challenged his contention that blacks ought to back off from alienating whites in their demands for equal citizenship. DuBois spoke of a "talented tenth," a group of blacks not fit for manual labor alone, but mentally ready to take full part in the intellectual life of the nation. These critics complained that Washington's philosophy perpetuated a racial caste system in America, consigning African Americans to a subservient role in perpetuity. They resented his condescending retelling of "darkey jokes" to white audiences and his self-effacing, obsequious manner in the presence of Southern whites. They accused Washington of bargaining away the rights of a whole race for a "mess of pottage." DuBois especially criticized how Washington expected black Americans to become businessmen and property owners while giving up the political rights that would defend these interests. And like everyone else, Washington's critics disliked his very slipperiness, his unwillingness to commit to anything, and his secretive, behind-the-scenes flitting among his alleged white friends.

As the twentieth century broke, Washington was placed on the defensive. Especially embarrassing to him was his inability to prevent President Roosevelt from discharging a battalion of black soldiers accused of rioting in Brownsville, Texas, in 1906. This helped his opponents organize what eventually became the National Association for the Advancement of Colored People (NAACP), which was dedicated to doing everything that Washington stood against: agitating for equal rights in all aspects of American life. With the fall of the Republicans and the election of the Woodrow Wilson administration, full of Southern Progressives who believed that good, clean government was for whites only, Washington's influence in the capital city's circles of political power came to a dismaying crash. In October of 1915, he collapsed during a speaking tour up North and asked to be taken home to the South to die. He died less than a month later on the Tuskegee campus that had been such an important part of his life. One cannot question the importance of Washington's influence in turn-of-the-century America. But controversy still rages over whether he could have done more, given the temper of the times in which he lived, or should have done more, given the importance of the task, than having presided over or seemingly acceded to the final act of Reconstruction—the subordination of African Americans to second-class citizenship.

See also African American Education and Reconstruction; African American Leadership and Reconstruction; African Americans and Reconstruction; Disfranchisement; Economic Disfranchisement; Segregation (Jim Crow).

References Bond, Horace Mann, *Negro Education in Alabama* (1939); Broderick, Francis L., *W. E. B. DuBois* (1959); Cox, LaWanda, "From Emancipation to Segregation" (1987); Cox, Oliver C., "The Leadership of Booker T. Washington" (1851); DuBois, W. E. Burghardt, *The Souls of Black Folk* (1903); Friedman, Lawrence J., "Life 'in the Lion's Mouth'" (1974); Harlan, Louis R., *Booker T. Washington* (1972–1983), "Booker T. Washington and the White Man's Burden" (1966), and "Booker T. Washington in Biographical Perspective" (1970); Harlan, Louis R., et al., eds., *The Booker T. Washington Papers* (1972–1989); Hawkins, Hugh, ed., *Booker T. Washington and His Critics* (1962); Logan, Rayford W., *The Betrayal of the Negro* (1965); Low, W. Augustus, and Virgil A. Clift, *Encyclopedia of Black America* (1981); Meier, August, "Booker T. Washington and the Rise of the NAACP" (1954) and *Negro Thought in America* (1966); Scott, Emmett, and Lyman B. Stowe, *Booker T. Washington* (1916); Spencer, Samuel R., Jr., *Booker T. Washington and the Negro's Place in American Life* (1955); Strickland, Avrah E., "Booker T. Washington" (1973); Washington, Booker T., *My Larger Education* (1900), "My Views on the Segregation Laws" (1915), *Up from Slavery* (1901), and *Working with the Hands* (1904); Woodward, C. Vann, *Origins of the New South* (1951).

Washington Birthday Speech

Right after President Andrew Johnson had his veto of the renewal of the Freedmen's Bureau sustained by Congress, he spoke to an impromptu audience at the White House. It was the first time the public had really seen the president since he was sworn in as vice president at Abraham Lincoln's second inaugural, almost a year earlier. It was a very important event because, amid an appeal to the Constitution and the invocation of George Washington's example, Johnson crossed the invisible line between good politics and decency by insulting his opponents personally. This meant that any future compromise between the executive and legislative branches over Reconstruction would be next to impossible.

Johnson was preoccupied with himself as a martyr. He used the word "I" 152 times and accused unnamed congressmen of conspiring against him and his plan of Reconstruction, which he pronounced only just as the war had ended. Johnson pointed to his pardons and maintained that the Rebels had repented their sins of secession and rebellion. He even compared his plan to the type of approach Jesus Christ would have taken had he been there—kind, just, forgiving. He then went on to say that there were men in the North whose disunionist designs were fully as evil as anything put forward by Jefferson Davis, Robert Toombs, John Slidell, and "a long list of others."

"Give us their names," came an anonymous voice from the crowd.

Johnson rose to the occasion. "A gentle-man calls for their names," he began. "Well, I suppose I should give them....I say Thaddeus Stevens of Pennsylvania [tremendous applause followed, according to a witness]. I say Charles Sumner [great applause]. I say Wendell Phillips [a prominent abolitionist] and others of the same stripe are among them," the president continued.

"Give it to Forney," came the voice, referring to John W. Forney, editor of the *Philadelphia Press* and now clerk of the U.S. Senate—the one who would not seat the senators from the South elected under Johnson's "Christ-like" plan of Reconstruction.

Johnson bellowed, "Some gentleman in the crowd says 'Give it to Forney.' I have only just to say that I do not waste my ammunition on dead ducks" [laughter and applause].

All Republicans were mortified by Johnson's hasty speaking. "Was he drunk?" inquired a friend of Senator John Sherman. Tragically, no. What the president had done was publicize a breach between him and Congress. This made it official in the eyes of the public and hard to heal. He also conferred a great power on Pennsylvania representative Thad Stevens, something the congressman had lacked up to that moment. A lot of influential people who disliked the president up to now came to hate him and saw in his Reconstruction program the potential loss of the peace. His vetoes would no longer hold up in disagreements over future congressional measures, and it was the first step on the long road to impeachment.

See also Johnson and Reconstruction; Moderate Republicans and Reconstruction; Radical Republicans and Reconstruction.

Reference McKitrick, Eric, *Andrew Johnson and Reconstruction* (1960).

Waving the Bloody Shirt

"Waving the bloody shirt" was a colorful phrase of post–Civil War politics that essentially accused white Southern Democrats of wholesale slaughter of white Unionists and black Republicans in the South and Northern Democrats of wholehearted complicity in these deeds by opposing Republican congressional programs in Washington. The phrase came from cross-eyed Benjamin Franklin Butler, a Massachusetts politician better known as the "Beast of New Orleans" for his tough occupation policies and heavy-handed larceny. After the war Butler supported a harsh Reconstruction and helped manage the impeachment of President Andrew Johnson. During one debate on violence in the South, Butler waved a bloody shirt over his head, asserting that the scourged victim was an Ohio Carpetbagger who had merely tried to obtain justice for African Americans in Mississippi. The antic was so successful in demonstrating Southern white retaliations on loyal people that the term came to be applied to any attack on the Democrats that emphasized their support of Southern violence and subordination of legitimate black social and political aspirations as free persons.

See also Blaine, James G.; Butler, Benjamin F.; Greeley, Horace.

Reference Carter, Hodding, *The Angry Scar* (1959).

White League

The White League was a Louisiana Democratic party group of armed white gunmen who intimidated black and white Republicans at elections in the mid-1870s, shot rival candidates and their supporters, and watched the polls to limit opposition voting.

See also Redemption of the South before 1874; Redemption of the South from 1874.

White Liners

The White Liners were a Mississippi Democratic party group of armed white gunmen who intimidated black and white Republicans at elections in the mid-1870s, shot rival candidates and their supporters, and watched the polls to limit opposition voting.

See also Redemption of the South before 1874; Redemption of the South from 1874.

"HALT!"

"This is not the way 'to repress corruption and to initiate the Negroes into the ways of honest and orderly government.'"

Lady Justice wields her sword against a member of the White Men's League to keep him from stepping on the back of an African American in this 1874 illustration. The White League used intimidation and violence to limit Republican opposition at the polls.

Women's Rights and Reconstruction

Along with increased rights for black males, Reconstruction witnessed a rise in women's rights, especially when it came to property. In every Southern state except Virginia that had to rewrite its state constitution under the Military Reconstruction Acts, the guarantee of the property rights of women, independent of their husbands, was recognized. South Carolina also gave women the right to file for divorce, and Texas even seriously considered granting the right to vote (as did Arkansas and South Carolina to a lesser extent), but that proposal was shelved in a raucous convention that had trouble turning out a normal fundamental law, much less one reformed beyond congressional demands.

Contrary to the picture many Americans hold of antebellum Dixie, the South had actually led the nation in reforms in women's rights before the Civil War. In Alabama, Arkansas, Florida, Louisiana, Mississippi, and Texas, the Reconstruction constitutions merely reconfirmed what laws those states had in place before the war. Reconstruction, then, was but one stage in an ongoing reform that had its inception in Mississippi in 1839. This reform was so successful because men had a real stake in the outcome and because it had little to do with feminism directly. The equality that flowed from these laws was a by-product of the laws themselves, not their actual intent. Under the common law a single woman had the same right as a man in property as a matter of tradition. Marriage, however, changed this; after marriage a woman's possessions and the woman herself became part of the property of her husband. She could make no independent contracts, sue or be sued, or execute a valid will.

The "gallant" Southern men who dominated Reconstruction constitutional conventions feared that a woman could be taken advantage of by unscrupulous men. So they wrote laws to allow her these property rights, and the result was an equality not dreamed of. Another consideration during the Reconstruction period was the vast indebtedness of the South. Indeed, this prob- ably was the reason the states first enacted these laws beginning in 1839. They were a response to another bad economic period, marked by the intense economic panic of 1837. These laws protected a woman from losing her property to the collection of debts owed by her husband. And so it was during Reconstruction, except that the earlier laws were now elevated to constitutional status. Three states, Alabama, Florida, and Texas, went even further. They did not allow a husband to sell the family homestead without his wife's permission.

The real problem was that these grants of power to women were done in a fairly vague manner, which left it to the courts to round them out with specific decisions. The first state to do this was Georgia, and it did so with a vengeance. In *Huff v. Wright* (1869) the state ruled on a case involving a woman who claimed not to have to pay a debt incurred in 1866; she claimed the promissory note was null and void because she was married at the time. The court held that the state constitution confirmed that the law before the war was valid and that the new constitution went so far as to make two separate entities of a husband and wife. The wife was no longer subordinate to her husband but free to purchase, hold, and convey property, contract and be contracted with, and sue or be sued, just as if she were a single woman. It would take several decades for case law in all states to catch up with Georgia's, but the rights of women in property had been changed forever throughout the South (as well as the rest of the nation) by the actions of the Reconstruction conventions. Admittedly there were inconsistencies among the various states and sometimes within the states themselves, but the trend toward equality in property rights between the sexes was certain.

See also Radical Republicans.

References Beard, Mary R., *Woman as a Force in History* (1946); Boatwright, Eleanor M., "The Political and Civil Status of Women in Georgia" (1941); Brown, Elizabeth G., "Husband and Wife" (1944); Johnston, John D., Jr., "Sex and Property" (1972); Lebsock, Suzanne D., "Radical Reconstruction and the Property Rights of Southern Women" (1977); Rabkin, Peggy, "The Origins of Law Reform" (1975).

Woodhull, Victoria Claflin
(1838–1927)

Victoria Claflin Woodhull, the first woman to run for the presidency of the United States (during the election of 1872), was born the seventh of ten children to a one-eyed con artist and his wife. At age three Victoria claimed that she saw spirits come for the soul of the family's recently deceased housekeeper. As a child she constantly spoke to spirits in much the same way that most young girls spoke to dolls. Though she was brilliant, she had only three years of formal education. Her real schooling was in the mysteries of life itself, and she earned a veritable doctorate in such lessons over the years, as did her younger sister, Tennessee (1846–1923), with whom Victoria spent much of her time as a child and an adult.

At age 16 she married Dr. Canning Woodhull, with whom she had two children. Marriage did not stop her various con games. She and her husband moved to California, where she gave "psychic demonstrations." Later, Victoria and Tennessee worked the sucker circuit between Cincinnati, St. Louis, and Chicago as "Tennessee Claflin and Victoria Woodhull, Clairvoyants." They engaged in spirit conjuring, fortune telling, magnetic healing (the laying on of hands), and prostitution (which they covered up by calling it "closer communication with the spirits"). They also tried their hand at extortion but were caught and had to pay off the police in Ohio to get away.

The two sisters met up with Cornelius Vanderbilt, a 74-year-old multimillionaire who enjoyed having affairs with younger women. They made a fortune by getting Vanderbilt to back them with cash and insider information in a brokerage house. Woodhull, Claflin & Company made a $700,000 profit in three years, which they invested in various stocks that they managed to sell before Black Friday in 1869. The company was one of the only successful truly female-owned and -managed businesses in the country until Vanderbilt's wife put an end to the proceedings.

But by now Woodhull was pulling in a salary of $50,000 a year and no longer needed Vanderbilt anyhow. She wanted more than mere money. She decided to go for power. In 1870 she announced through her own recently begun newspaper, *Woodhull and Claflin's Weekly*, that she would stand for the presidency in 1872. "While others argued the equality of woman with man, I proved it," said Woodhull. "I therefore claim the right to speak for unfranchised women of the country." The only place where women could vote in the United States at that time was Wyoming Territory. Her candidacy was treated as a joke by most and probably would have faltered quickly had it not been for the literary talents of members of her entourage. She adopted as her political platform the concept of pantarchy—the governmental care of children and property, which she felt allowed adults the maximum freedom to explore religion, morality, free love, and spiritualism. To publicize the campaign Woodhull and her associates used *Woodhull and Claflin's Weekly*, which sold for a nickel a copy and was "devoted to the interests of the people," pledging to its readers they were "breaking the way for future generations" to enjoy "progress, free thought, [and] untrammeled lives." But by the end of 1870, the campaign was faltering. The newspaper cost a lot to print and gave such meager returns. So Woodhull entered the contest in person. She came out for free love, abolition of the death penalty, short skirts, vegetarianism, excess profit taxes, spiritualism, world government, better public housing, birth control, magnetic healing, easier divorce laws, legalized prostitution, exposés of Wall Street scandals, classes in anatomy for women, self-help articles on abortion, the minimum wage, pantarchy, and anarchy; she published the first English translation of Karl Marx's *Communist Manifesto*. The platform included everything Woodhull knew or experienced and was about 100 years before her time. She paid no heed to the raised eyebrows of the critics and put all her views in a one-page flyer that flooded the nation.

Meanwhile Woodhull studied the records of congressmen to see who might

Victoria Woodhull, the first woman to run for president, sparked controversy with a platform that called for women's rights and birth control.

bella Beecher Hooker. Woodhull stammered because it was her first public address, but she recovered and launched into a brilliant speech that attacked the inability of women to vote. The delegates went wild. But behind the scenes Lucretia Mott and others questioned the idea of tying their efforts to one with so "infamous" a record. Stanton reassured her that Woodhull could make a go of it, and Anthony stated that she would "welcome all the infamous women in New York if they would make speeches for freedom" like Woodhull.

While the public support from women nationwide was appreciated, Woodhull did not stop there. She let it be known that her opponents would be exposed in her *Weekly* for their past indiscretions. In May 1871, she spoke before another gathering of suffragettes at New York City. She spoke for a new Constitution for the United States with a woman's vote guaranteed. If her demands were not met, she threatened secession and treason to obtain that lofty goal. She wound up her talk with a plea for a revolution of righteousness to sweep the nation.

Then Woodhull became involved in a dispute over the legality of her second marriage. The press had a field day with the story. The idea of Woodhull being served by two or more "husbands" made for a lot of sales. Woodhull was furious. She threatened to expose the hypocrisy of the "respectable people" of the city. She said she was being pilloried by men who held a double standard. "I advocate free love in its highest, purest sense, as the only cure for immorality....My judges preach against free love openly, practice it secretly," she went on. "For example, I know of one man, a public teacher of eminence, who lives in concubinage with the wife of another. All three concur in denouncing offenses against morality."

The "Victoria League," as her devoted backers were called, met in a convention and organized the Equal Rights party. Woodhull spoke out for world revolution on her already announced platform. A voice from the delegates called for her nomination for president. All in favor shouted "aye." Then

prove amenable to standing up for women's rights and her presidential campaign. She came up with Benjamin Butler of Massachusetts, a Civil War general. It was an interesting choice. Butler was still reviled for his so-called woman order, which declared any ladies of New Orleans who spat upon and cursed federal soldiers to be prostitutes plying their trade and liable to arrest as such. Butler agreed to read a manifesto on women's rights before the house judiciary committee. But the House voted not to print the memorial, with only Butler and one other congressman opposing.

Next Woodhull went to the existing women's rights groups and presented her case. Her first presentation was before the National Women's Suffrage Association at their third annual meeting at the nation's capital. This organization included some of the biggest names in nineteenth-century reform and women's causes, like Elizabeth Cady Stanton, Susan B. Anthony, and Isathe convention nominated Tennessee as their candidate for Congress from New York. When the question of the vice presidency came up several names reached the podium, but the delegates chose Frederick Douglass, noted black author and speaker, reformer, abolitionist, and escaped slave. The party slogan was "We have the oppressed Sex represented by Woodhull, we have the oppressed Race represented by Douglass." Unfortunately, Douglass was not at the convention and knew nothing about what had transpired until he read it the next morning in the newspapers, much to his amazement and embarrassment. He wrote an open letter that appeared in the next editions declining the nomination.

Woodhull's candidacy was treated with scorn by the male-dominated political establishment and horror by all "right-thinking" men and women everywhere. She was banned in towns. No one would rent her rooms, serve her food, or allow her to rent a public hall. She lost her brokerage business to the expenses of the campaign. Landlords raised her rents in her New York City home office. Horace Greeley, later nominated as the Liberal Republican candidate in the same presidential race, wrote a little doggerel that went "Gibbery, gibbery, gab, the women had a confab, and demanded the rights to wear the tights, gibbery, gibbery, gab." The governor of Massachusetts refused to allow her to speak in Boston, declaring that she "might as well have the undressed women of North Street on the stage there!" Fed up with the discrimination she had suffered, Woodhull spoke anyhow. It was quite a speech. She revealed that she had been having a six-month-long affair with Theodore Tilton, a New York City religious publisher and close friend of Henry Ward Beecher. But that was not all. Woodhull also revealed that she had had liaisons with Beecher, too, and she knew that Beecher and Tilton had been sharing Tilton's wife Elizabeth for years. The regular press refused to print the story, so she brought it out in *Woodhull and Claflin's Weekly*. The edition sold 100,000 copies overnight. It became so popular that

single issues went for as much as $10 each and then, as they became really scarce, for $40 each. If Woodhull could not win a legitimate race, she vowed to take the "moralistic socialist camp," as she called them, down with her.

Because of the Beecher-Tilton exposé, Woodhull was arrested for dispensing pornography to the public, in violation of a federal postal law because she mailed her newspaper throughout the nation. She spent election night in jail, in the company of Ben Butler, who dropped by to commiserate with her. "If Jesus Christ had been running against this man, he'd have been defeated," was Woodhull's glum assessment of Grant's reelection. Beating the pornography charge (the law applied to magazines but not newspapers), she went free. As the Beecher-Tilton affair wound its slow way through the courts, she was blamed for revealing it to the public and ruining the lives of two respectable families.

Woodhull eventually adopted a Christian approach to life and moved to Great Britain, where she married again. She took to London society, even if society had some reservations about her. But her conduct was immaculate, except for a fake family tree she invented that made her a descendant (remote, of course) of the Scottish Stuarts. She also set up her daughter as the publisher of an innocuous magazine, *The Humanitarian*. At the turn of the century, her husband died and left a substantial sum to his devoted wife. Victoria spent the rest of her life in England, the perfect converted immigrant. She wrote a hot letter to President Woodrow Wilson complaining about America's hesitancy to enter the World War I but generally lived in seclusion with her daughter and Tennessee. She died in 1927 as she slept in her rocking chair, three months short of her ninetieth birthday.

See also Beecher, Henry Ward; Corruption as a Problem in Reconstruction; Election of 1872; Grant and the Scandals; Social Thought during and after Reconstruction.

References Harlow, Alvin F., "Victoria Claflin Woodhull" (1964–1981); Stern, Madeleine B., *The Victoria Woodhull Reader* (1974); Wallace, Irving, *The Nympho and Other Maniacs* (1971).

Chronology

1861 (2 April) Morrill Tariff Act passes Congress; it is amended to create a higher tariff in 1862 and 1864.

(29 April) Lincoln issues an executive proclamation creating martial law in Maryland.

(25 May) Major General Benjamin F. Butler declares escaped slaves to be contraband of war.

(28 May) In *ex parte Merryman*, Chief Justice Roger B. Taney issues his circuit court opinion challenging President Abraham Lincoln's arbitrary arrest policy toward suspected Confederate sympathizers.

(5 August) Tax Law passes Congress and is levied on the seceded South, too.

(6 August) First Confiscation Act passes Congress.

(7 November) Reconstruction begins in the Confederate South with a Union invasion of the South Carolina Sea Islands.

(18 November) Hatteras Convention of loyalists meets in North Carolina and elects Unionist Marble Nash Taylor as congressional representative, but he is refused a seat in Congress.

1862 (3 March) Lincoln appoints Andrew Johnson military governor of Tennessee.

(16 April) Congress abolishes slavery in the District of Columbia and all federal territories.

(24 April) Union fleet under Rear Adm. David G. Farragut takes New Orleans.

(1 May) Bvt. Maj. Gen. Benjamin F. Butler begins the occupation and Reconstruction of the southeast third of Louisiana and other sites along the Gulf.

(19 May) President Lincoln appoints Unionist Edward Stanley as provisional governor of North Carolina.

(20 May) Homestead Act passes.

(19 June) President Lincoln appoints John S. Phelps provisional governor of Arkansas.

(22 June) Tax Law passes Congress, creating special tax commissioners to collect sums owed in arrears in the seceded South.

(1 July) Pacific Railroad Act passes Congress; it is amended in 1864.

(17 July) Second Confiscation Act passes Congress.

(31 July) President Lincoln stresses that Louisiana be brought back into the Union as soon as possible.

(20 August) Horace Greeley claims that abolition of slavery is the "Prayer of Twenty Millions."

(22 September) Lincoln issues the preliminary Emancipation Proclamation, giving the South until New Year to surrender or lose its right to slavery.

(3 December) Louisiana elects its first loyal congressmen, B. F. Flanders and Michael Hahn, who are seated in Congress until its adjournment in March 1863.

(16 December) Bvt. Maj. Gen. Nathaniel P. Banks becomes commander of the Department of the Gulf, including Louisiana, to move Reconstruction forward.

1863 (1 January) Emancipation Proclamation frees all slaves in Confederate territory.

(15 January) Provisional Governor Stanley of North Carolina resigns because of his lack of sympathy with emancipation.

(25 February) Congress creates national banking system, which is amended in 1864.

(3 March) Captured and Abandoned Property Act passes Congress.

(10 March) Supreme Court decides *Prize* cases, in which the court recognizes Lincoln's right to deal with the Confederacy as belligerent without legitimizing the Rebel government.

(24 April) Adjutant General's Office issues General Orders No. 100 promulgating the Lieber code, the American rules of war.

(20 June) President Lincoln appoints Unionist Francis S. Pierpont provisional governor of Virginia upon creation of West Virginia as a state.

(2 July) Morrill Land Grant College Act passes Congress; it is amended in 1890.

(19 July) President Lincoln revokes appointment of John S. Phelps as provisional governor of Arkansas.

(5 November) Free Colored Men of New Orleans petition for the right to vote as the Union Radical Association.

(9 November) Confederate General E. W. Gantt switches to Union side in Arkansas and calls for an elected convention under Lincoln's Ten Percent Plan.

(7 December) Virginia legislature calls for members of constitutional convention to be elected on 21 January 1864.

(8 December) Abraham Lincoln issues Proclamation of Amnesty and Reconstruction.

1864 (4 January) Arkansas state constitutional convention under Presidential Reconstruction begins.

(20 January) State convention elects Unionist Isaac Murphy provisional governor of Arkansas.

(15 February) In *ex parte Vallandigham*, the U.S. Supreme Court upholds a Confederate sympathizer's arrest, military trial, and exile to the Confederacy.

(4 March) Unionist Michael Hahn is inaugurated as first Free State governor of Louisiana.

(11 March) In Special Orders No. 9, Adjutant General Lorenzo Thomas codifies employment practices with respect to contrabands in the Mississippi Valley.

(28 March) Louisiana elects delegates to a constitutional convention under Lincoln's Ten Percent Plan.

(11 April) Free State of Arkansas elects Isaac Murphy governor.

(21 May) Arkansas' U.S. senators and representatives present credentials to Congress and are put off in prolonged debate.

(8 July) Wade-Davis Bill, the first congressional plan of Reconstruction, passes but is pocket vetoed by President Lincoln.

(5 August) Wade-Davis Manifesto denounces Lincoln's veto of first congressional plan of Reconstruction.

(6 October) Louisiana state constitutional convention meets under the Lincoln Ten Percent Plan.

(6 December) Salmon P. Chase becomes chief justice of the U.S. Supreme Court.

1865 (16 January) Maj. Gen. William T. Sherman issues Special Orders No. 15 creating a 30-mile-wide land zone set aside exclusively for the use of freedmen and their families along the South Atlantic coast.

(13 February) Virginia state constitutional convention meets under Lincoln's Ten Percent Plan.

(3 March) Charter of Freedmen's Savings and Trust Company is issued.

(3 March) Bureau of Refugees, Freedmen, and Abandoned Lands is created.

(4 March) Governor Michael Hahn of Louisiana accepts election to the U.S. Senate, turning the governorship over to James M. Wells.

(11 March) General Orders No. 23 of the Department of the Gulf codify employment practices for contrabands in Louisiana.

(5 April) William G. "Parson" Brownlow is elected first loyal governor of a seceded state, Tennessee.

(11 April) President Lincoln speaks on behalf of seating the Free State government of Louisiana in Congress.

(15 April) Lincoln dies and is succeeded by Andrew Johnson as president.

(9 May) President Johnson recognizes the Pierpont Virginia government.

(29 May) President Johnson appoints Unionist William W. Holden provisional governor of North Carolina.

(13 June) President Johnson appoints Unionist Benjamin F. Perry provisional governor of South Carolina.

(13 June) President Johnson appoints Unionist William H. Sharkey governor of Mississippi.

(17 June) President Johnson appoints Andrew Jackson Hamilton provisional governor of Texas.

(17 June) President Johnson appoints James Johnson provisional governor of Georgia.

(19 June) Pierpont government moves from Alexandria to Richmond, Virginia.

(21 June) President Johnson appoints Conservative Lewis Parsons provisional governor of Alabama.

(13 July) President Johnson appoints Unionist William Marvin as provisional governor of Florida.

(14 August) Mississippi state constitutional convention begins under Presidential Reconstruction.

(12 September) Alabama state constitutional convention begins under Presidential Reconstruction.

(13 September) South Carolina state constitutional convention begins under Presidential Reconstruction.

(27 September) Radicals meet in Louisiana and elect Carpetbagger Henry Clay Warmoth as territorial delegate to Congress (Warmoth is seated in December when the real Louisiana delegation is refused its seats).

(2 October) Georgia state constitutional convention begins under Presidential Reconstruction.

(2 October) North Carolina state constitutional convention begins under Presidential Reconstruction.

(2 October) Conservative Benjamin G. Humphries is elected governor of Mississippi.

(18 October) Conservative James L. Orr is elected governor of South Carolina.

(25 October) Florida state constitutional convention begins under Presidential Reconstruction.

(6 November) Unionist J. Madison Wells is elected governor of Louisiana under President Johnson's Reconstruction plan on both Union and Democratic tickets and switches his party affiliation to Democrat.

(9 November) Conservative Jonathan Worth is elected governor of North Carolina.

(15 November) Conservative Charles M. Jenkins is elected governor of Georgia.

(29 November) Conservative David S. Walker is elected governor of Florida.

(December) Ku Klux Klan founded in Pulaski, Tennessee.

(2 December) Mississippi legislature enacts Black Code.

(4 December) Congress rejects the Confederate Brigadiers as the South's federal representatives and senators.

(13 December) Conservative Robert M. Patton is inaugurated governor of Alabama.

(15 December) Alabama legislature enacts Black Code.

(18 December) Thirteenth Amendment is ratified.

(20 December) Louisiana legislature enacts Black Code.

(21 December) South Carolina legislature enacts Black Code.

1866 (15 Janurary) Florida legislature enacts Black Code.

(7 February) Texas state constitutional convention begins under Presidential Reconstruction.

(8 February) Congress passes Southern Homestead Act.

(19 February) Johnson vetoes Freedmen's Bill renewal.

(22 February) Johnson delivers his Washington's birthday speech and announces an open breach with Congress over Reconstruction.

(28 February) Virginia legislature enacts Black Code.

(10 March) North Carolina legislature enacts Black Code.

(17 March) Georgia legislature enacts Black Code.

(9 April) Civil Rights Act of 1866 passes over Johnson's veto.

(16 April) Race riot occurs in Norfolk.

(26 April) President Johnson officially ends the Civil War.

(1 May) Race riot occurs in Memphis.

(13 June) Fourteenth Amendment passes Congress and is sent to the states for ratification.

(20 June) Report of the Joint Committee of Fifteen on Reconstruction is issued.

(8 July) Judge R. K. Howell (probably illegally) recalls the Louisiana State Convention of 1864 to meet on July 30 to amend the state constitution so as to allow African American suffrage and to adopt the Fourteenth Amendment.

(16 July) Freedmen's Bureau Renewal Act passes over Johnson's veto.

(24 July) Tennessee ratifies Fourteenth Amendment and is restored to the Union.

(30 July) Race riot occurs in New Orleans.

(13 August) Conservative James W. Throckmorton is sworn in as governor of Texas.

(14 August) "Arm-in-Arm" Convention is held, in which the National Union political coalition meets to support Andrew Johnson's Reconstruction policy.

(28 August) Johnson's "Swing around the Circle" tour begins and alienates Northern voters.

(8 November) Texas legislature enacts Black Code.

(17 December) In *ex parte Milligan*, U.S. Supreme Court rules that suspension of civil courts is unconstitutional unless an area is under actual enemy attack.

1867 (7 January) Congress begins investigation designed to impeach Johnson.

(8 January) Blacks receive right to vote in District of Columbia.

(14 January) In *ex parte Garland*, U.S. Supreme Court limits the use of the test oath for practitioners in federal courts.

(14 January) In *Cummings v. Missouri*, U.S. Supreme Court limits the use of the test oath for clergymen.

(2 March) Command of the Army Act passes Congress.

(2 March) First Military Reconstruction Act passes Congress.

(2 March) Fortieth Congress Extra Session Act keeps Congress in session to negate any chance that President Johnson would interfere with Military Reconstruction.

(2 March) Tenure of Office Act passes Congress.

(11 March) President Johnson appoints commanders of the military districts: First Military District (Virginia), Bvt. Maj. Gen. John Schofield; Second Military District (North and South Carolina), Bvt. Maj. Gen. Daniel Sickles; Third Military District (Georgia, Alabama, and Florida), Bvt. Maj. Gen. John Pope; Fourth Military District (Arkansas and Mississippi), Bvt. Maj. Gen. E. O. C. Ord; Fifth Military District (Louisiana and Texas), Maj. Gen. Philip H. Sheridan

(Spring) Union Loyal Leagues organize white and black Republican voters in South.

(15 April) In *Mississippi v. Johnson*, U.S. Supreme Court upholds the president's enforcement of the Military Reconstruction Acts.

(22 April) Bvt. Maj. Gen. John Pope tries to replace Governor Jenkins of Georgia without success.

(23 April) Congress passes Second Military Reconstruction Act.

(30 April) Alaska is purchased from Russia.

(13 May) In *Georgia v. Stanton*, Supreme Court upholds the secretary of war's enforcement of the Military Reconstruction Acts.

(3 June) Maj. Gen. Philip H. Sheridan appoints Scalawag Republican B. F. Flanders provisional governor of Louisiana in place of Democratic Governor J. Madison Wells.

(19 July) Congress passes Third Military Reconstruction Act.

(30 July) Maj. Gen. Philip H. Sheridan appoints Scalawag Republican Elisha M. Pease provisional governor of Texas; Conservative James W. Throckmorton is removed.

(19 August) President Johnson appoints Bvt. Maj. Gen. Charles Griffin commander of Fifth Military District; General Sheridan is removed.

(5 September) President Johnson appoints Bvt. Maj. Gen. E. R. S. Canby commander of Second Military District.

(16 September) General Griffin dies of yellow fever; President Johnson appoints Bvt. Maj. Gen. Joseph Mower commander of Fifth Military District.

(23 September) Louisiana state constitutional convention begins under the Military Reconstruction Acts.

(5 November) Alabama state constitutional convention begins under the Military Reconstruction Acts.

(29 November) Maj. Gen. Winfield Scott Hancock replaces General Mower as commander of Fifth Military District and issues his General Orders No. 40, which limit the effect of military government in his command area.

(9 December) Georgia state constitutional convention begins under the Military Reconstruction Acts.

(28 December) Bvt. Maj. Gen. George G. Meade replaces General Pope in charge of Third Military District.

1868 (7 January) Arkansas state constitutional convention begins under the Military Reconstruction Acts.

(9 January) Mississippi state constitutional convention begins under the Military Reconstruction Acts.

(9 January) President Johnson appoints Bvt. Maj. Gen. Alvan C. Gillem commander of the Fourth Military District; General Ord is removed.

(13 January) General Meade appoints Bvt. Brig. Gen. Thomas H. Ruger provisional governor of Georgia; Charles M. Jenkins is removed.

(14 January) South Carolina state constitutional convention begins under the Military Reconstruction Acts.

(20 January) Florida state constitutional convention begins under the Military Reconstruction Acts.

(4 February) Scalawag Republican William H. Smith is elected governor of Alabama.

(10 February) In *Georgia v. Grant et al.*, Supreme Court upholds the army's enforcement of the Military Reconstruction Acts.

(17 February) In *ex parte McCardle*, Supreme Court upholds the Congress's right to alter the court's appellate jurisdiction.

(24 February) Congress impeaches President Johnson.

(4 March) Johnson impeachment trial begins.

(11 March) Congress passes Fourth Military Reconstruction Act.

(25 March) President Johnson appoints Bvt. Maj. Gen. Robert C. Buchanan commander of Fifth Military District; General Hancock resigns.

(4 April) Bvt. Maj. Gen. John Schofield appoints Carpetbag Republican Henry H. Wells governor of Virginia; Francis S. Pierpont is removed.

(16 April) Carpetbag Republican Robert K. Scott is elected governor of South Carolina for a first term.

(20 April) Carpetbag Republican Rufus Bullock is elected governor of Georgia.

(23 April) Scalawag Republican William W. Holden is elected governor of North Carolina

(23 April) President Johnson appoints Bvt. Maj. Gen. George Stoneman commander of First Military District to replace General Schofield, who replaced Edwin M. Stanton as secretary of war.

(16 May) Johnson is found not guilty in impeachment trial.

(1 June) Texas state constitutional convention begins under the Military Reconstruction Acts.

(4 June) President Johnson appoints Bvt. Maj. Gen. Irvin McDowell commander of the Fourth Military District; General Gillem is removed.

(15 June) General Irvin McDowell appoints Bvt. Maj. Gen. Adelbert Ames governor of Mississippi; Benjamin G. Humphries is removed.

(22 June) Arkansas becomes first state to be readmitted to Union under Military Reconstruction Acts.

(22 June) Mississippi rejects its constitution drawn up under the Military Reconstruction Acts.

(24 June) General Meade appoints Scalawag Republican William H. Smith governor-elect; Conservative Governor Robert M. Patton of Alabama is removed.

(25 June) Florida is readmitted to the Union under the Reconstruction Acts.

(25 June) Omnibus Bill readmits North Carolina, South Carolina, Florida, Georgia, Alabama, and Louisiana under Military Reconstruction Acts.

(30 June) Bvt. Maj. Gen. E. R. S. Canby appoints Scalawag Republican William W. Holden governor; Jonathan Worth is removed.

(1 July) Carpetbag Republican Harrison Reed is inaugurated governor of Florida.

(2 July) Carpetbag Republican Powell Clayton is inaugurated governor of Arkansas.

(4 July) North Carolina is readmitted to the Union under the Reconstruction Acts.

(6 July) Congress extends Freedmen's Bureau for one more year.

(9 July) Louisiana is readmitted to the Union under the Reconstruction Acts.

(9 July) South Carolina is readmitted to the Union under the Reconstruction Acts.

(10 July) President Johnson reappoints Bvt. Maj. Gen. Alvan C. Gillem commander of Fourth Military District; General McDowell is removed.

(13 July) Alabama is readmitted to the Union under the Reconstruction Acts.

(13 July) Carpetbag Republican Henry Clay Warmoth is inaugurated governor of Louisiana.

(25 July) Congress closes down all Freedmen's Bureau operations—except those connected with education—as of 1 January 1869, Bvt. Maj. Gen. Oliver O. Howard is confirmed as head of bureau for its duration or until he chooses to resign.

(28 July) Fourteenth Amendment is ratified.

(28 July) President Johnson appoints Bvt. Maj. Gen. Joseph J. Reynolds commander of Fifth Military District, now consisting of Texas alone.

(11 August) Thaddeus Stevens dies.

(3 September) Georgia legislature expels black members.

(19 September) Race riot occurs in Camilla, Georgia.

(4 November) Bvt. Maj. Gen. E. R. S. Canby appointed commander of Fifth Military District; General Reynolds is removed.

(4 November) Governor Powell Clayton of Arkansas declares martial law for four months to fight the Ku Klux Klan, the Knights of the White Camellia, and assorted lawbreakers.

(6 November) First impeachment attempt of Governor Harrison Reed of Florida fails.

(1 December) Georgia is kicked out of the Union again for violating Military Reconstruction Acts.

(8 December) Second session of Texas state constitutional convention begins under Military Reconstruction Acts.

(9 December) Virginia state constitutional convention meets under Military Reconstruction Acts.

(24 December) Johnson issues a general amnesty of Confederate soldiers and civil officials.

1869 (26 January) Second impeachment attempt of Governor Harrison Reed of Florida fails.

(7 February) Civilian-military committee assembles Military Reconstruction constitution in Texas.

(25 February) Parson Brownlow resigns as governor of Tennessee to become U.S. senator, appointing Scalawag Republican DeWitt C. Senter to succeed him as governor.

(4 March) Ulysses S. Grant is inaugurated as president.

(5 March) President Grant appoints Bvt. Maj. Gen. Thomas Ruger commander of Third Military District.

(5 March) President Grant appoints Bvt. Maj. Gen. Joseph J. Reynolds commander of Fifth Military District; Bvt. Maj. Gen E. R. S. Canby is removed.

(18 March) Public Credit Act guarantees the payment of the U.S. debt in gold or its equivalent.

(27 March) Bvt. Maj. Gen. George Stoneman tries to remove Governor Wells of Virginia but is replaced by Bvt. Maj. Gen. E. R. S. Canby; Wells is reinstated.

(12 April) In *Texas v. White*, Supreme Court upholds the Military Reconstruction Acts.

(10 May) Transcontinental railroad is completed at Promontory Point, Utah.

(31 May) President Grant appoints Bvt. Maj. Gen. Alfred Terry commander of Third Military District.

(6 July) Conservative Fusionist Gilbert C. Walker is elected governor of Virginia on platform of "universal suffrage and universal amnesty."

(21 September) Bvt. Maj. Gen. E. R .S. Canby appoints Governor-elect Walker to office in Virginia.

(24 September) "Black Friday" crash on New York Stock Exchange as Jay Gould and Jim Fisk attempt to corner gold market.

(30 September) Bvt. Maj. Gen. Joseph J. Reynolds assumes governorship of Texas upon resignation of Elisha M. Pease.

(4 October) Tennessee is "redeemed"; after Republicans nominate a different man, Scalawag Republican DeWitt C. Senter changes parties to join the Conservative Democrats and wins the election.

(5 October) Virginia is "redeemed," the only Southern state where this happens before readmission to the Union under the Military Reconstruction Acts.

(25 October) In *ex parte Yerger*, Supreme Court upholds its jurisdiction in habeas corpus cases under the Judiciary Act of 1789 regardless of the intent of Congress during more recent Reconstruction measures.

(30 November) Mississippi votes for its constitution and against disfranchisement of whites of Confederate background, electing Scalawag Republican James L. Alcorn as governor.

(22 December) Congress tells Georgia to reassemble the legislature under which it had been readmitted in 1868.

(24 December) Bvt. Maj. Gen. Alfred Terry is sent to purge Georgia of rebellious elements.

1870 (18 January) Scalawag Republican Edmund J. Davis is sworn in as governor of Texas.

(26 January) Virginia is readmitted to Union under Military Reconstruction Acts.

(7 February) In *Hepburn v. Griswold*, U.S. Supreme Court rules that greenbacks are legal for debts contracted only after 1862.

(23 February) Mississippi is readmitted to the Union under the Military Reconstruction Acts.

(25 February) Hiram R. Revels becomes first African American U.S. senator.

(30 April) Fifteenth Amendment is ratified.

(30 April) Texas is readmitted to Union under Military Reconstruction Acts.

(31 May) Congress passes First Enforcement Act.

(20 June) Five-month Kirk-Holden War against the Ku Klux Klan in North Carolina begins.

(14 July) Funding Act allows bondholders to exchange bonds issued in wartime and bought with inflated greenbacks for new ones redeemable in gold.

(15 July) Georgia is readmitted to Union for second time under Military Reconstruction Acts.

(4 August) Conservatives win control of North Carolina legislature.

(19 October) Carpetbag Republican Robert K. Scott is elected governor of South Carolina for a second term.

(23 October) Race riot occurs in Eutaw, Alabama.

(3 November) North Carolina is essentially "redeemed" with seating of conservative legislature.

(4 November) Conservative Democrat Robert B. Lindsay is elected governor of Alabama, but a legislative split (Democratic house, Republican senate) stalemates the regime.

(12 December) Joseph H. Rainey becomes first African American to sit in U.S. House of Representatives.

(15 December) North Carolina state legislature impeaches Governor William W. Holden, finds him guilty, and removes him from office.

1871   (10 January) Brooks-Baxter War between rival Republicans in Arkansas begins as Powell Clayton goes to U.S. Senate.

(28 February) Congress passes Second Enforcement Act.

(3 March) Congress creates Southern Claims Commission.

(6 March) Ku Klux Klan starts riot in Meridian, Mississippi.

(6 March) In *Virginia v. West Virginia*, U.S. Supreme Court upholds the creation of the new state from the old, alleging Virginia's loyal government had agreed to the separation.

(3 April) In *Miller v. United States*, U.S. Supreme Court rules that the Confiscation Acts had been passed against traitors as individuals, not against belligerents, and thus they have to follow due process of the laws.

(20 April) Congress passes Third Enforcement (Ku Klux Klan) Act.

(1 May) In *Knox v. Lee*, U.S. Supreme Court rules that greenbacks are legal for all debts, reversing *Hepburn v. Griswold*.

(24 May) *Alabama* claims settled as Treaty of Washington is ratified.

(8 July) Tweed Ring is exposed in New York City.

(9 August) Gatling Gun Convention takes place in Louisiana; Radical Republicans read Governor Henry Clay Warmoth out of the party for being too conservative.

(4 September) Crédit Mobilier scandal breaks, revealing corrupt financing of the transcontinental railroad.

(17 October) President Grant declares suspension of the writ of habeas corpus in select counties of South Carolina to suppress the Ku Klux Klan.

(1 November) Georgia is "redeemed" for second time; Conservative Democrat James M. Smith becomes governor.

(22 November) African American Republican Lieutenant Governor Oscar Dunn of Louisiana is poisoned under mysterious circumstances and is succeeded by African American Republican and Carpetbagger P. B. S. Pinchback.

1872   (10 February) Third impeachment of Governor Harrison Reed of Florida succeeds, but he is never brought to trial.

(22 May) Congress passes a general amnesty act removing officeholding proscriptions from most (all but 500) Confederate soldiers and civil officials.

(1 August) Scalawag Republican Tod R. Caldwell is elected governor of North Carolina with a Conservative state legislature.

(16 October) Scalawag Republican Franklin J. Moses, Jr., is elected governor of South Carolina.

(5 November) Carpetbag Republican Marcellus L. Stearns is elected governor of Florida.

(5 November) Grant defeats Horace Greeley for president.

(7 November) Scalawag Republican David P. Lewis is elected governor of Alabama, but both political parties seat their own legislatures.

(30 November) Presidential candidate Horace Greeley dies before the electoral votes are counted.

(9 December) Governor Henry Clay Warmoth is impeached by extra session of Louisiana state legislature and is succeeded by African American Republican Carpetbagger P. B. S. Pinchback.

1873 (9 January) Carpetbag Republican William Pitt Kellogg is inaugurated governor of Louisiana and backed by federal troops; Conservative Democrat John McEnery is also inaugurated with his own shadow government.

(14 January) Texas is "redeemed"; Conservative Democrat Richard Coke becomes governor.

(12 February) Silver Coinage Act is passed by Congress and takes silver out of circulation, called the "Crime of '73."

(11 April) Bvt. Maj. Gen. E. R. S. Canby becomes the first American general officer to die in an Indian war.

(13 April) Colfax Massacre in Louisiana occurs (Easter Sunday).

(14 April) In *Slaughter House* cases, U.S. Supreme Court begins the process of limiting remedies under the Fourteenth Amendment.

(1 July) Confederate General Pierre G. T. Beauregard begins the Louisiana unification movement, a political alliance between black voters and upper-class white leaders for honest, conservative government.

(18 September) Failure of Jay Cooke & Company precipitates the panic of 1873.

(8 October) After prolonged street fighting, court action, and federal intervention, Scalawag Republican Elisha Baxter becomes governor of Arkansas over Carpetbag Republican Joseph Brooks.

1874 (21 January) Morrison R. Waite becomes chief justice of the U.S. Supreme Court.

(22 January) Carpetbag Republican Adelbert Ames is inaugurated governor of Mississippi.

(30 August) White League initiates Coushatta Massacre in Louisiana.

(14 September) White League initiates Third Battle of New Orleans.

(17 September) President Grant puts down the September White League Rebellion in Louisiana with threat of federal troops restoring Republicans to control.

(15 October) Carpetbag Republican Daniel H. Chamberlain is elected governor of South Carolina.

(10 November) Arkansas is "redeemed"; Conservative Democrat Augustus H. Garland is elected governor.

(11 November) Alabama is "redeemed"; Conservative Democrat George S. Houston is elected governor with race riots at Eufala and Mobile.

(7 December) Race riots in Vicksburg, Mississippi, mark the rise of the First Mississippi Plan's violence in favor of Redemption.

1875 (6 January) Maj. Gen. Philip H. Sheridan sends a telegram recommending that Louisiana White Leaguers be declared "banditti."

(14 January) Special Resumption Act expands the amount of greenbacks in circulation as well as the amount of silver to ease the economic depression caused by the panic of 1873, pledging to return solely to gold in 1879.

(1 March) Congress passes Civil Rights Act of 1875.

(29 March) In *Minor v. Happersett*, U.S. Supreme Court rules that Fifteenth Amendment right to vote does not apply to women because it refers to race alone.

(17 April) Congressman William A. Wheeler of New York establishes Wheeler Compromise in Louisiana, which leaves Republican Carpetbag Governor William P. Kellogg in power but splits the state legislature between Democrats (lower house) and Republicans (upper house).

(1 September) White Liners riot at Yazoo City, Mississippi, driving Carpetbag Republican Albert Morgan from power.

(4 September) White Liners riot at Clinton, Mississippi.

(5 September) North Carolina conventioners meet to rewrite its state constitution.

(13 October) The so-called peace agreement between Republicans and Conservative Democrats quells violence in Mississippi state elections.

(2 November) Conservative Democrats win the Mississippi state legislature, thereby "redeeming" the state.

1876 (2 March) Mississippi state legislature impeaches Governor Adelbert Ames and replaces him with Scalawag Republican John M. Stone.

(27 March) In *United States v. Cruikshank*, U.S. Supreme Court limits the effect of the Enforcement Acts to curb election violence.

(27 March) In *United States v. Reese*, U.S. Supreme Court limits the effect of the Enforcement Acts, which had been implemented to curb election fraud.

(28 March) Pryor Compromise is implemented, by which Governor Adelbert Ames of Mississippi steps down as governor and impeachment charges are dropped.

(7 July) Hamburg Massacre in South Carolina occurs.

(6 September) Charleston race riot in South Carolina occurs.

(15 September) Three-day Ellenton race riot in South Carolina occurs.

(16 October) Cainhoy race riot in South Carolina occurs.

(7 November) Conservative Democrat Wade Hampton is elected governor of South Carolina but is prevented from taking power by the presence of federal troops.

(7 November) Presidential election is deadlocked between Rutherford B. Hayes and Samuel J. Tilden over disputed electoral vote; "visiting statesmen" go South to try to clear up the count with bribes.

(11 November) South Carolina is "redeemed" by Red Shirts.

1877 (1 January) Conservative Democrat Zebulon Vance is inaugurated governor of North Carolina.

(2 January) Florida is "redeemed"; Conservative Democrat George F. Drew is elected governor of Florida.

(8 January) Both Conservative Democrat Francis T. Nicholls and Carpetbag Republican Stephen B. Packard are inaugurated governor of Louisiana, though Packard has federal troop support.

(8 February) Electoral commission awards all disputed electoral votes to Hayes.

(26 February) Wormley House bargain permits Congress to agree that Hayes is the new president.

(10 April) Federal troops begin final withdrawal from South Carolina; Conservative Democrat Wade Hampton becomes governor.

(24 April) Federal troops begin final withdrawal from Louisiana, and Conservative Democrat Francis T. Nicholls becomes governor.

1878 (14 January) In *Hall v. DeCuir*, U.S. Supreme Court declares that segregated accommodations on steamboats are permissible.

(28 February) Congress passes Bland-Allison Act, leading to a ratio of silver coins to gold of 16 to 1.

(31 May) Congress passes Fort Act, returning the United States to the gold standard but keeping all silver and greenbacks then in circulation.

(18 June) Congress passes Posse Comitatus Act.

1880 (1 March) In *Strauder v. West Virginia*, U.S. Supreme Court upholds parts of the Fourteenth Amendment as guaranteeing the right of blacks to serve on juries, failing which the case can be transferred to a federal court.

(1 March) In *Virginia v. Rives*, the U.S. Supreme Court upholds parts of the Fourteenth Amendment guaranteeing the right of African Americans to serve on juries in the states; failing this, cases could be transferred to federal court.

1882 (22 January) In *United States v. Harris*, U.S. Supreme Court limits the ability of the Enforcement Acts to curb violence.

1883 (15 October) In *Civil Rights* cases, U.S. Supreme Court rules that public accommodations can be segregated, as can any act or service initiated by an individual rather than a government entity.

1890 (20 March) Blair Federal Aid to Education Bill fails to pass Congress.

(2 July) Lodge Enforcement Act passes House but fails in Senate.

(1 November) Mississippi state constitutional convention disfranchises black voters within the terms of the Fifteenth Amendment.

1895 (10 September) South Carolina constitutional convention disfranchises black voters within terms of the Fifteenth Amendment.

(18 September) Booker T. Washington delivers an Atlanta Cotton States Exposition address endorsing development of the races in America in a manner as separate as the five fingers but as united as the hand.

1896 (18 May) In *Plessy v. Ferguson*, U.S. Supreme Court rules "separate but equal" public accommodations acceptable under Fourteenth Amendment.

1898 (11 January) Louisiana elects a constitutional convention that disfranchises black voters within terms of the Fifteenth Amendment.

(25 April) In *Williams v. Mississippi*, the U.S. Supreme Court upholds Mississippi's disfranchisement of black voters so long as it is done without direct reference to race.

(8 June) Congress removes proscriptions from all Confederate soldiers and civil officials without exception.

1899 (18 December) In *Cumming v. Georgia*, U.S. Supreme Court rules "separate but equal" education for races is acceptable under Fourteenth Amendment.

Bibliography

Abbott, Martin. "Free Land, Free Labor, and the Freedmen's Bureau," *Agricultural History* 30 (1956): 150–56.

———. "The Freedmen's Bureau and Negro Schooling in South Carolina," *South Carolina Historical Magazine* 57 (1956): 65–81.

———. *The Freedmen's Bureau in South Carolina, 1865–1872.* Chapel Hill: University of North Carolina Press, 1967.

———. "Freedom's Cry: Negroes and Their Meetings in South Carolina, 1865–1869," *Phylon* 20 (1959): 263–72.

Abbott, Richard H. *The Republican Party and the South, 1855–1877.* Chapel Hill: University of North Carolina Press, 1986.

Abell, Aaron Ignatius. *Urban Impact on American Protestantism.* Cambridge, MA: Harvard University Press, 1943.

Adams, James Truslow. "Our Lawless Heritage," *Atlantic Monthly* 142 (1928): 732–40.

Ahern, Wilbert H. "The Cox Plan of Reconstruction: A Case Study in Ideology and Race Relations," *Civil War History* 16 (1970): 293–308.

———. "Laissez Faire vs. Equal Rights: Liberal Republicanism and Limits to Reconstruction," *Phylon* 40 (1979): 52–65.

Aitken, Hugh G. J., ed. *Did Slavery Pay?* Boston: Houghton Mifflin, 1971.

Albrecht, Winnell. "The Black Codes of Texas." M.A. thesis, Southwest Texas State University, 1969.

Alderson, William T. "The Freedmen's Bureau and Negro Education in Virginia," *North Carolina Historical Review* 29 (1952): 64–90.

———. "The Influence of Military Rule and the Freedmen's Bureau on Reconstruction in Virginia, 1865–1870." Ph.D. dissertation, Vanderbilt University, 1952.

Alexander, Roberta Sue. "Hostility and Hope: Black Education in North Carolina during Presidential Reconstruction, 1865–1867," *North Carolina Historical Review* 53 (1976): 113–32.

Alexander, Thomas B. "Persistent Whiggery in Alabama and the Lower South, 1860–1867," *Alabama Review* 12 (1959): 35–52.

———. "Persistent Whiggery in the Confederate South, 1860–1877," *Journal of Southern History* 27 (1961): 305–29.

———. "Persistent Whiggery in Mississippi: The Hinds County Gazette," *Journal of Mississippi History* 23 (1961): 71–93.

———. "Strange Bedfellows: The Interlocking Careers of T. A. R. Nelson, Andrew Johnson, and William G. (Parson) Brownlow," *East Tennessee Historical Society Papers* 24 (1952): 68–91.

Bibliography

———. "Whiggery and Reconstruction in Tennessee," *Journal of Southern History* 16 (1950): 291–305.

Allen, James. *Reconstruction: The Battle for Democracy.* New York: International Publishers, 1937.

Ambrose, Stephen E. *Halleck: Lincoln's Chief of Staff.* Baton Rouge: Louisiana State University Press, 1962.

Ames, Blanch. *Adelbert Ames, 1835–1933: General, Senator, Governor.* New York: Argosy-Antiquarian, 1964.

Aptheker, Herbert. *American Negro Slave Revolts.* New York: Columbia University Press, 1943.

———. *The Negro in the Civil War.* New York: International Publishers, 1938.

Argersinger, Peter H. "The Southern Search for Order," *Reviews in American History* 3 (1975): 236–41.

Armstrong, Warren B. "Union Chaplains and the Education of Freedmen," *Journal of Negro History* 52 (1967): 104–15.

Ashcraft, Alan C. "Role of the Confederate Provost Marshals in Texas," *Texana* 6 (1968): 390–92.

Avins, Alfred. "The Ku Klux Klan Act of 1871: Some Reflected Light on State Action and the Fourteenth Amendment," *St. Louis University Law Journal* 11 (1967): 331–81.

———. "Racial Segregation in Public Accommodations: Some Reflected Light on the Fourteenth Amendment from the Civil Rights Act of 1875," *Case Western Law Review* 18 (1967): 1251–83.

Ayers, Edward L. *Vengeance and Justice: Crime and Punishment in the Nineteenth Century American South.* New York: Oxford University Press, 1984.

Bacote, Clarence A. "Negro Proscriptions, Protests, and Proposed Solutions in Georgia, 1880–1908," *Journal of Southern History* 25 (1959): 471–98.

Baenziger, Ann Patton. "The Texas State Police during Reconstruction: A Reexamination," *Southwestern Historical Quarterly* 72 (1968–69): 470–91.

Baggett, James Alex. "Birth of the Texas Republican Party," *Southwestern Historical Quarterly* 78 (1974–75): 1–20.

———. "Origins of Early Texas Republican Party Leadership," *Journal of Southern History* 40 (1974): 441–50.

———. "The Rise and Fall of the Texas Radicals, 1867–1883." Ph.D. dissertation, North Texas State University, 1972.

Bailyn, Bernard. *Ideological Origins of the American Revolution.* Cambridge, MA: Harvard University Press, 1967.

Baker, George T. "Mexico City and the War with the United States: A Study of the Politics of Military Occupation." Ph.D. dissertation, Duke University, 1970.

Ballantine, Henry W. "Martial Law," *Columbia Law Review* 12 (1912): 529–38.

———. "Unconstitutional Claims of Military Authority," *Yale Law Journal* 24 (1914–15): 201–202.

Barnard, Harry. *Rutherford B. Hayes and His America.* Indianapolis: Bobbs-Merrill, 1954.

Barney, William L. *Flawed Victory: A New Perspective on the Civil War.* New York: Praeger Publishers, 1975.

Barr, Alwyn. "Black Legislators of Reconstruction Texas," *Civil War History* 32 (1986): 340–52.

———. *Black Texans: A History of Negroes in Texas, 1528–1971.* Austin: Jenkins Book Publishing Co., 1973.

———. *Reconstruction to Reform: Texas Politics, 1876–1906.* Austin: University of Texas Press, 1971.

———. "Records of the Confederate Military Commission in San Antonio, July 2–October 10, 1862," *Southwestern Historical Quarterly* 70 (1966–67): 93–109, 289–313, 623–44; 71 (1967–68): 247–78.

———. "The Texas 'Black Uprising' Scare of 1883," *Phylon* 41 (1980): 179–87.

Barrett, Don C. *The Greenbacks and the Resumption of Specie Payments, 1862–1879.* Cambridge, MA: Harvard University Press, 1931.

Beale, Howard K. *The Critical Year [1866]: A Study of Andrew Johnson and Reconstruction.* New York: Harcourt, Brace & Co., 1930.

———. "On Rewriting Reconstruction History," *American Historical Review* 45 (1939–1940): 807–27.

———. "The Tariff and Reconstruction," *American Historical Review* 35 (1929–1930): 276–94.

Beard, Charles A., and Mary Beard. *The Rise of American Civilization.* 2 vols. New York: Macmillan, 1927.

Beard, Mary R. *Woman as a Force in History: A Study in Traditions and Realities.* New York: Macmillan, 1946.

Beatty, Bess. *A Revolution Gone Backward: The Black Response to National Politics, 1876–1896.* New York: Greenwood Press, 1987.

Beck, E. M., and Stewart E. Tolnay. "The Killing Fields of the Deep South: The Market for Cotton and the Lynching of Blacks, 1882–1930," *American Sociological Review* 55 (1990): 526–39.

Beisner, Robert L. *From the Old Diplomacy to the New, 1865–1900.* New York: Thomas Y. Crowell, 1975.

Belz, Herman. *Emancipation and Equal Rights: Politics and Constitutionalism in the Civil War Era.* New York: W. W. Norton, 1978.

———. "The Ethridge Conspiracy of 1863: A Projected Conservative Coup," *Journal of Southern History* 36 (1970): 549–67.

———. "The Freedmen's Bureau Act of 1865 and the Principle of No Discrimination According to Color," *Civil War History* 21 (1975): 197–217.

———. "Henry Winter Davis and the Origins of Congressional Reconstruction," *Maryland Historical Magazine* 67 (1972): 129–43.

———. *A New Birth of Freedom: The Republican Party and Freedmen's Rights, 1861–1866.* Westport, CT: Greenwood Press, 1976.

———. "The New Orthodoxy in Reconstruction Historiography," *Reviews in American History* 1 (1973): 106–13.

———. *Reconstructing the Union: Theory and Practice during the Civil War.* Ithaca, NY: Cornell University Press, 1969.

Benedict, Michael Les. *A Compromise of Principle: Congressional Republicans and Reconstruction, 1863–1869.* New York: W. W. Norton, 1974.

———. "Equality and Expediency in the Reconstruction Era: A Review Essay," *Civil War History* 23 (1977): 322–35.

———. *Fruits of Victory: Alternatives in Restoring the Union, 1865–1877.* Lanham, MD: University Presses of America, 1986.

———. *The Impeachment Trial of Andrew Johnson.* New York: W. W. Norton, 1973.

———. "The Politics of Prosperity in the Reconstruction South," *Reviews in American History* 12 (1984): 507–14.

———. "Preserving Federalism: Reconstruction and the [Chief Justice Morrison R.] Waite Court," *Supreme Court Review* (1978): 39–79.

———. "Preserving the Constitution: The Conservative Basis of Radical Reconstruction," *Journal of American History* 61 (1974): 65–90.

———. "The Rout of Radicalism: Republicans and the Elections of 1867," *Civil War History* 18 (1972): 334–44.

———. "Southern Democrats and the Crisis of 1876–1877: A Reconsideration of *Reunion and Reaction,*" *Journal of Southern History* 46 (1980): 489–524.

Benet, Stephen Vincent. *Treatise on Military Law and the Practice of Courts Martial.* 2d ed. New York: D. Van Nostrand, 1868.

Bennett, Lerone, Jr. *Black Power, U.S.A.: The Human Side of Reconstruction.* Chicago: Johnson Publishing Company, 1967.

———. "Was Abe Lincoln a White Supremacist?" *Ebony* 23 (1968): 35–38, 40, 42.

Bentley, George R. *A History of the Freedmen's Bureau.* Philadelphia: University of Pennsylvania Press, 1955.

Berger, Raul. *Impeachment: The Constitutional Problems.* Cambridge, MA: Harvard University Press, 1973.

Bibliography

Bergeron, Paul H. *Antebellum Politics in Tennessee*. Lexington: University of Kentucky Press, 1982.

Berlin, Ira. *Slaves without Masters: The Free Negro in the Antebellum South*. New York: Pantheon, 1974.

———. *Slaves No More: Three Essays on Emancipation and the Civil War*. New York: Cambridge University Press, 1992.

Bernstein, Barton J. "Case Law in Plessy *v.* Ferguson," *Journal of Negro History* 47 (1962): 192–98.

Berry, Mary Frances, and John W. Blassingame. *Long Memory: The Black Experience in America*. New York: Oxford University Press, 1982.

Berwanger, Eugene H. *The West and Reconstruction*. Urbana: University of Illinois Press, 1981.

Bethel, Elizabeth. "The Freedmen's Bureau in Alabama," *Journal of Southern History* 14 (1948): 49–92.

Bigelow, John. *The Life of Samuel J. Tilden*. 2 vols. New York: Harper & Brothers, 1895.

———, ed. *The Writings and Speeches of Samuel J. Tilden*. 2 vols. New York: Harper & Brothers, 1885.

Bigelow, Martha M. "Freedmen of the Mississippi Valley, 1862–1865," *Civil War History* 8 (1962): 38–47.

———. "Vicksburg: Experiment in Freedom," *Journal of Mississippi History* 26 (1964): 28–44.

Billington, Ray Allen, ed. *The Journal of Charlotte L. Forten*. New York: Norton, 1981[1953].

Binning, Francis W. "Henry Clay Warmoth and Louisiana Reconstruction." Ph.D. dissertation, University of North Carolina, 1969.

Birkhimer, William E. *Military Government and Martial Law*. 2d ed. Kansas City: F. Hudson Publishing Company, 1904.

Bittker, Boris I. *The Case for Black Reparations*. New York: Random House, 1973.

Blackburn, George M. "Radical Republican Motivation: A Case Study," *Journal of Negro History* 54 (1969): 109–28.

Blackiston, Harry S. "Lincoln's Emancipation Plan," *Journal of Negro History* 7 (1922): 257–77.

Blassingame, John W. *Black New Orleans, 1860–1880*. Chicago: University of Chicago Press, 1973.

———. "The Union Army as an Educational Institution for Negroes, 1861–1865," *Journal of Negro Education* 34 (1965): 152–59.

Blight, David W. "'For Something beyond the Battlefield': Frederick Douglass and the Struggle for the Memory of the Civil War," *Journal of American History* 75 (1989): 1156–78.

Blue, Frederick J. *The Free Soilers: Third Party Politics, 1848–1854*. Urbana: University of Illinois Press, 1973.

Bluntschli, Johann Kaspar. *Das Moderne Kriegsrecht der Civilisierten Staaten als Rechtsbuch Dargestellt*. Noerdlingen: C. H. Beck, 1866.

Boatner, Mark M., III. *The Civil War Dictionary*. New York: D. McKay and Company, 1959.

Boatwright, Eleanor M. "The Political and Civil Status of Women in Georgia, 1783–1860," *Georgia Historical Quarterly* 25 (1941): 301–24.

Bogue, Allan G. *The Earnest Men: Republicans of the Civil War Senate*. Ithaca, NY: Cornell University Press, 1981.

Bonadio, Felice A. *North of Reconstruction*. New York: New York University Press, 1970.

Bond, Horace Mann. *Negro Education in Alabama: A Study in Cotton and Steel*. Washington, DC: Associated Publishers, 1939.

———. "Social and Economic Forces in Alabama Reconstruction," *Journal of Negro History* 23 (1938): 290–348.

Boritt, Gabor S. "The Voyage to the Colony of Lincolniana: The Sixteenth President, Black Colonization, and the Defense Mechanism of Avoidance," *Historian* 37 (1975): 619–32.

Bowen, Croswell. *The Elegant Oakey*. New York: Oxford University Press, 1956.

Bowers, Claude. *The Tragic Era: The Revolution after Lincoln*. Boston: Houghton Mifflin, 1929.

Boyd, William K. "William W. Holden," *Trinity College Historical Society Papers*, Series III (1899): 38–78, 90–133.

Boynton, H. V. "The Whiskey Ring," *North American Review* 123 (1876): 280–327.

Bradford, M. E. "Against Lincoln: A Speech at Gettysburg." In *The Reactionary Imperative: Essays Literary and Political*, edited by M. E. Bradford. Peru, IL: Sherwood Sudgen, 1990, 219–27.

———. *Founding Fathers: Brief Lives of the Framers of the United States Constitution*. 2d rev. ed. Lawrence: University Press of Kansas, 1994.

———. "The Lincoln Legacy: A Long View." In M. E. Bradford, *Remembering Who We Are: Observations of a Southern Conservative*. Athens: University of Georgia Press, 1985, 143–56.

Brandt, Irving. *Impeachment: Trials and Errors*. New York: Alfred A. Knopf, 1973.

Bratcher, John V., ed. and trans. "A Soviet Historian [A. V. Efimov] Looks at Reconstruction," *Civil War History* 15 (1969): 257–64.

Braxton, Allen Caperton. *The Fifteenth Amendment: An Account of Its Enactment*. Lynchburg, VA: N. Pub., ca. 1903.

Bremner, Robert H. *American Philanthropy*. 2d ed. Chicago: University of Chicago Press, 1988.

Bridges, Roger D. "John Sherman and the Impeachment of Andrew Johnson," *Ohio Historical Quarterly* 82 (1973): 176–91.

Brock, Eugene W. "Thomas W. Cardozo: Fallible Black Reconstruction Leader," *Journal of Southern History* 47 (1981): 183–206.

Brock, William R. *An American Crisis: Congress and Reconstruction, 1865–1867*. New York: St. Martins Press, 1969.

———. "Reconstruction and the American Party System." In *A Nation Divided: Problems and Issues of the Civil War and Reconstruction*, edited by George M. Frederickson. Minneapolis: Burgess Publishing Company, 1975, 81–112.

Broderick, Francis L. *W. E. B. DuBois: Negro Leader in a Time of Crisis*. Palo Alto, CA: Stanford University Press, 1959.

Brodie, Fawn. *Thaddeus Stevens: Scourge of the South*. New York: W. W. Norton, 1966.

———. "Who Won the Civil War, Anyway?" *New York Times Book Review*, August 5, 1962, 7, 1.

Bronson, Louis Henry. "The Freedmen's Bureau: A Public Policy Analysis." Ph.D. dissertation, University of Southern California, 1970.

Brown, Elizabeth G. "Husband and Wife—A Memorandum on the Mississippi Woman's Law of 1839," *Michigan Law Review* 42 (1944): 1110–21.

Brown, Ira V. "Lyman Abbott and Freedmen's Aid, 1865–1869," *Journal of Southern History* 15 (1949), 49–92.

Bryant, Lawrence C. *South Carolina Negro Legislators: State and Local Officeholders, Biographies of Negro Representatives, 1868–1902*. Orangeburg, SC: L. C. Bryant, 1974.

Bryant-Jones, Mildred. "The Political Program of Thaddeus Stevens," *Phylon* 2 (1941): 147–54.

Buck, Paul H. *The Road to Reunion, 1865–1890*. Boston: J. B. Lippincott, 1937.

Buenger, Walter L. *Secession and the Union in Texas*. Austin: University of Texas Press, 1984.

Buley, R. Carlyle. *The Old Northwest: Pioneer Period, 1815–1840*. 2 vols. Bloomington: Indiana University Press, 1950.

Bullock, Henry Allen. *A History of Negro Education in the South from 1619 to the Present*. Cambridge, MA: Harvard University Press, 1967.

Burgess, John W. *Reconstruction and the Constitution, 1866–1876*. New York: Charles Scribner's Sons, 1902.

Bibliography

Burton, Theodore E. *John Sherman*. Boston: Houghton Mifflin, 1906.

Butchart, Ronald E. *Northern Schools, Southern Blacks, and Reconstruction: Freedmen's Education, 1862–1875*. Westport, CT: Greenwood Press, 1980.

Butler, Benjamin F. *Autobiography and Personal Reminiscences of Major-General Benjamin F. Butler: Butler's Book*. Boston: A. M. Thayer, 1892.

Byrne, Frank L. "'A Terrible Machine': General Neal Dow's Military Government on the Gulf Coast," *Civil War History* 12 (1966): 5–22.

Cable, George W. "The Convict Lease System in the Southern States," *Century*, n.s., 5 (1884): 582–99.

Calcott, Margaret Law. *The Negro in Maryland Politics, 1870–1912*. Baltimore: Johns Hopkins University Press, 1969.

Callender, Edward B. *Thaddeus Stevens: Commoner*. New York: AMS Press, 1972 [1882].

Callow, Alexander B. *The Tweed Ring*. New York: Oxford University Press, 1966.

Campbell, Charles S. *The Transformation of American Foreign Relations: 1865–1900*. New York: Harper & Row, 1976.

Campbell, Clarice T. "Exploring the Roots of Tougaloo College," *Journal of Mississippi History* 35 (1973): 15–27.

Campbell, Randolph. *A Southern Community in Crisis: Marshall, Texas, 1850–1880*. Austin: Texas State Historical Association, 1983.

———. "Carpetbagger Rule in Reconstruction Texas: An Enduring Myth," *Southwestern Historical Quarterly* 97 (1993–94): 586–96.

Carleton, Mark T. *Politics and Punishment: The Story of the Louisiana Penal System*. Baton Rouge: Louisiana State University Press, 1971.

Carpenter, A. H. "Military Government of Southern Territory, 1861–1865," *American Historical Association Annual Report* 1 (1900): 465–98.

Carpenter, John A. "Atrocities during the Reconstruction Period," *Journal of Negro History* 47 (1962): 234–47.

———. *Sword and Olive Branch: Oliver Otis Howard*. Pittsburgh: University of Pittsburgh Press, 1964.

———. *Ulysses S. Grant*. New York: Twayne Publishers, 1970.

Carper, N. Gordon. "Slavery Revisited: Peonage in the South," *Phylon* 37 (1976): 85–99.

Carrier, John P. "A Political History of Texas during the Reconstruction, 1865–1874." Ph.D. dissertation, Vanderbilt University, 1971.

Carter, Clarence E. "James Mitchell Ashley." In *Dictionary of American Biography*, edited by Allen Johnson et al. New York: Charles Scribner's Sons, 10 double vols. + 9 supplements, 1964–1981, 1: 389–90.

Carter, Dan T. "Anatomy of Fear: The Christmas Day Insurrection Scare of 1865," *Journal of Southern History* 42 (1976): 345–64.

———. "Moonlight, Magnolias, and Collard Greens: Black History and the New Romanticism," *Reviews in American History* 5 (1977): 167–73.

———. *When the War Was Over: The Failure of Self-Reconstruction in the South, 1865–1867*. Baton Rouge: Louisiana State University Press, 1985.

Carter, Hodding. *The Angry Scar: The Story of Reconstruction*. Garden City, NY: Doubleday & Company, 1959.

Cartwright, Joseph H. *The Triumph of Jim Crow: Tennessee Race Relations in the 1880s*. Knoxville: University of Tennessee Press, 1976.

Casdorph, Paul D. *A History of the Republican Party in Texas, 1865–1965*. Austin, TX: Pemberton Press, 1965.

Cash, William M. "Alabama Republicans during Reconstruction: Personal Characteristics, Motivations, and Political Activity of Party Activists, 1867–1880." Ph.D. dissertation, University of Alabama, 1973.

Caskey, William M. *Secession and Restoration of Louisiana*. Baton Rouge: Louisiana State University Press, 1938.

Castel, Albert. *The Presidency of Andrew Johnson*. Lawrence: University of Kansas Press, 1979.

Catton, Bruce. *The Army of the Potomac*. 3 vols. New York: Doubleday & Co., 1951–53.

———. "The Generalship of U. S. Grant." In *Grant, Lee, Lincoln and the Radicals*, edited by Grady McWhiney. Evanston, IL: Northwestern University Press, 1964, 3–31.

———. *Grant Moves South*. Boston: Little, Brown, 1960.

———. *Grant Takes Command*. Boston: Little, Brown, 1969.

———. *U. S. Grant and the American Military Tradition*. Boston: Little, Brown, 1954.

Chalmers, David M. *Hooded Americanism: The History of the Ku Klux Klan*. Chicago: Quadrangle Books, 1968.

Charnwood, Godfrey Rathbone Benson, Lord. *Abraham Lincoln*. New York: Henry Holt, 1916.

Chesnut, Charles Haddell. *Frederick Douglass*. Boston: Small, Maynard, 1899.

Chesteen, Richard D. "Bibliographical Essay: The Legal Validity of Jim Crow," *Journal of Negro History* 56 (1971): 284–93.

Chidsey, Donald Barr. *The Gentleman from New York: A Life of Roscoe Conkling*. New Haven, CT: Yale University Press, 1935.

Christian, Marcus B. "The Theory of the Poisoning of Oscar J. Dunn," *Phylon* 6 (1945): 254–66.

Cimbala, Paul A. "The Freedmen's Bureau, the Freedmen, and Sherman's Grant in Reconstruction Georgia, 1865–1867," *Journal of Southern History* 55 (1989): 597–632.

———. "The 'Talisman of Power': Davis Tillson, the Freedmen's Bureau, and Free Labor in Reconstruction Georgia," *Civil War History* 28 (1982): 153–71.

Cimprich, John. "The Beginning of the Black Suffrage Movement in Tennessee, 1864–1865," *Journal of Negro History* 65 (1980): 185–95.

———. *Slavery's End in Tennessee, 1861–1865*. University: University of Alabama Press, 1985.

Clark, Clifford E. *Henry Ward Beecher: Spokesman for a Middle-Class America*. Urbana: University of Illinois Press, 1978.

Clark, John G. "Historians and the Joint Committee of Reconstruction," *Historian* 23 (1961): 348–61.

———. "Radicals and Moderates in the Joint Committee on Reconstruction," *Mid America* 45 (1963): 79–98.

Clarke, Grace Julian. *George W. Julian*. Indianapolis: Carlon & Hollenbeck, 1889.

Clayton, Powell. *The Aftermath of the Civil War in Arkansas*. New York: Neal Publishing, 1915.

Coben, Stanley. "Northeastern Business and Radical Reconstruction," *Mississippi Valley Historical Review* 46 (1959–1960): 69–90.

Cochran, Thomas. "Did the Civil War Retard Industrialization?" *Mississippi Valley Historical Review* 43 (1961): 197–210.

Cochran, Thomas, and William Miller, *The Age of Enterprise: A Social History of Industrial America*. New York: Macmillan, 1942.

Cohen, William. *At Freedom's Edge: Black Mobility and the Southern White Quest for Racial Control, 1861–1915*. Baton Rouge: Louisiana State University Press, 1991.

———. "Negro Involuntary Servitude in the South, 1865–1940: A Preliminary Analysis," *Journal of Southern History* 42 (1976): 31–60.

Cohen-Lack, Nancy. "A Struggle for Sovereignty: National Consolidation, Emancipation, and Free Labor in Texas, 1865," *Journal of Southern History* 58 (1992): 57–98.

Colby, Ira C. "The Freedmen's Bureau: From Social Welfare to Segregation," *Phylon* 46 (1985): 219–30.

Coleman, Charles H. *The Election of 1868: The Democratic Effort To Regain Control*. New York: Columbia University Press, 1933.

Coleman, Peter J. "The Dorr War and the Emergence of the Leviathan State," *Reviews in American History* 4 (1976): 533–38.

Bibliography

Collins, Charles Wallace. "The Fourteenth Amendment and the Negro Race Question," *American Law Review* 45 (1911): 830–56.

———. *The Fourteenth Amendment and the States: A Study of the Operation of the Restraint Clauses of Section One of the Fourteenth Amendment to the Constitution of the United States.* Boston: Little, Brown, 1912.

Connelly, Thomas L., and Barbara L. Bellows. *God and General Longstreet: The Lost Cause and the Southern Mind.* Baton Rouge: Louisiana State University Press, 1982.

Conway, Alan. *The Reconstruction of Georgia.* Minneapolis: University of Minnesota Press, 1966.

Cook, Samuel Dubois. "A Tragic Conception of Negro History," *Journal of Negro History* 45 (1960): 219–40.

Cooper, William J., Jr. "A Reassessment of Jefferson Davis as War Leader: The Case from Atlanta to Nashville," *Journal of Southern History* 36 (1970): 189–204.

Cornish, Dudley T. *The Sable Arm: Negro Troops in the Union Army.* New York: W. W. Norton, 1966.

———. "The Union Army as a School for Negroes," *Journal of Negro History* 37 (1952): 368–82.

Coulter, E. Merton. *The Civil War and Readjustment in Kentucky.* Chapel Hill: University of North Carolina Press, 1926.

———. *The South during Reconstruction, 1865–1877.* Baton Rouge: Louisiana State University Press, 1947.

———. *William G. Brownlow: Fighting Parson of the Southern Highlands.* Knoxville: University of Tennessee Press, 1937.

Cox, John, and LaWanda Cox. "Andrew Johnson and His Ghost Writers: An Analysis of the Freedmen's Bureau and Civil Rights Veto Messages," *Mississippi Valley Historical Review* 48 (1961–1962): 460–79.

———. "General O. O. Howard and the 'Misrepresented Bureau,'" *Journal of Southern History* 19 (1953): 427–56.

———. "Negro Suffrage and Republican Politics," *Journal of Southern History* 33 (1967): 303–30.

———. *Politics, Principles and Prejudice, 1865–1866: Dilemma of Reconstruction America.* New York: Atheneum, 1963.

Cox, LaWanda. "From Emancipation to Segregation: National Policy and Southern Blacks." In *Interpreting Southern History: Essays in Honor of Sanford W. Higgenbotham,* edited by John Boles and Evelyn Thomas Nolan. Baton Rouge: Louisiana State University Press, 1987, 199–253.

———. *Lincoln and Black Freedom: A Study in Presidential Leadership.* Columbia: University of South Carolina Press, 1981.

———. "The Promise of Land for the Freedmen," *Mississippi Valley Historical Review* 49 (1958): 413–40.

Cox, LaWanda, and John H. Cox. "Negro Suffrage and Republican Politics: The Problem of Motivation in Reconstruction Historiography," *Journal of Southern History* 33 (1967): 303–30.

Cox, Merlin G. "Military Reconstruction of Florida," *Florida Historical Quarterly* 46 (1967–68): 219–33.

Cox, Oliver C. "The Leadership of Booker T. Washington," *Social Forces* 30 (1951): 91–97.

Craven, Avery O. *Reconstruction: The Ending of the Civil War.* New York: Holt, Rinehart, and Winston, 1969.

Cresswell, Stephen. "Enforcing the Enforcement Acts: The Department of Justice in Northern Mississippi, 1870–1890," *Journal of Southern History* 53 (1987): 421–40.

Crouch, Barry A. "'All the Vile Passions': The Texas Black Code of 1866," *Southwestern Historical Quarterly* 97 (1993): 13–34.

———. *The Freedmen's Bureau and Black Texans.* Austin: University of Texas, 1992.

———. "Self-Determination and Local Black Leaders in Texas," *Phylon* 39 (1978): 344–55.

———. "'Unmanacling' Texas Reconstruction: A Twenty Year Perspective," *Southwestern Historical Quarterly* 93 (1989–1990): 275–302.

Cruden, Robert. *James Ford Rhodes: The Man, the Historian, and His Work, with a Complete Bibliography of the Writings of James Ford Rhodes*. Cleveland: Press of the Case Western Reserve University, 1961.

———. *The Negro in Reconstruction*. Englewood Cliffs, NJ: Prentice-Hall, 1969.

Current, Richard N. "Carpetbaggers Reconsidered." In *A Festschrift for Frederick B. Artz*, edited by David H. Pinckney and Theodore Ropp. Durham: Duke University Press, 1964, 139–57.

———. "Grant without Greatness," *Reviews in American History* 9 (1981): 507–509.

———. *The Lincoln Nobody Knows*. New York: McGraw-Hill, 1958.

———. "President Grant and the Continuing Civil War." In *Ulysses S. Grant: Essays and Documents*, edited by David L. Wilson and John Y. Simon. Carbondale: Southern Illinois University Press, 1981, 1–8.

———. *Old Thad Stevens: A Story of Ambition*. Madison: University of Wisconsin Press, 1942.

———. *Those Terrible Carpetbaggers: A Reinterpretation*. New York: Oxford University Press, 1988.

———. *Three Carpetbag Governors*. Baton Rouge: Louisiana State University Press, 1967.

Currie, James T. *Enclave: Vicksburg and Her Plantations, 1863–1870*. Jackson: University Press of Mississippi, 1980.

———. "From Slavery to Freedom in Mississippi's Legal System," *Journal of Negro History* 65 (1980): 112–25.

Currie-McDaniel, Ruth. "The Wives of the Carpetbaggers." In *Race, Class, and Politics in Southern History*, edited by Jeffrey J. Crow et al. Baton Rouge: Louisiana State University Press, 1989, 35–78.

Curry, Leonard P. "Congressional Democrats, 1861–1863," *Civil War History* 12 (1966): 213–29.

Curry, Richard O. "The Abolitionists and Reconstruction: A Critical Appraisal," *Journal of Southern History* 34 (1968): 527–45.

———. "The Civil War and Reconstruction: A Critical Overlook of Recent Trends and Interpretations," *Civil War History* 20 (1974): 215–38.

———. "Copperheadism and Ideological Continuity: Anatomy of a Stereotype," *Journal of Negro History* 57 (1972): 29–36.

———. *Radicalism, Racism, and Party Realignment: The Border States during Reconstruction*. Baltimore: Johns Hopkins University Press, 1969.

———. "The Union as It Was: A Critique of Recent Interpretations of the 'Copperheads,'" *Civil War History* 13 (1967): 25–39.

Curti, Merle E., *The Growth of American Thought*. New York: Harper & Brothers, 1943.

Daniel, Pete. "The Metamorphosis of Slavery, 1865–1900," *Journal of American History* 66 (1979): 88–99.

———. *The Shadow of Slavery: Peonage in the South*. New York: Oxford University Press, 1973.

Daniels, Jonathan. *Prince of Carpetbaggers*. Philadelphia: J. B. Lippincott, 1958.

Davis, David Brion. "Abolitionists and the Freedmen: An Essay Review," *Journal of Southern History* 31 (1965): 164–70.

———. *The Slave Power Conspiracy and the Paranoid Style*. Baton Rouge: Louisiana State University Press, 1969.

Davis, Ronald L. F. *Good and Faithful Labor: From Slavery to Sharecropping in the Natchez District, 1860–1890*. Westport, CT: Greenwood Press, 1982.

———. "The U.S. Army and the Origins of Sharecropping in the Natchez District: A Case Study," *Journal of Negro History* 62 (1977): 60–80.

Davis, Susan Lawrence. *Authentic History: Ku Klux Klan, 1865–1877*. New York: Susan Lawrence Davis, 1924.

Davis, Varina Howell. *Jefferson Davis*. New York: Belford, 1890.

Davis, William W. *Civil War and Reconstruction in Florida*. New York: Columbia University, 1913.

Bibliography

Dawson, Joseph Green, III. *Army Generals and Reconstruction: Louisiana, 1862–1877.* Baton Rouge: Louisiana State University Press, 1982.

———. "Army Generals and Reconstruction: Mower and Hancock as Case Studies," *Southern Studies: An Interdisciplinary Journal of the South* 17 (1978): 255–72.

———. "General Phil Sheridan and Military Reconstruction in Louisiana," *Civil War History* 24 (1978): 133–51.

Degler, Carl N. *The Other South: Southern Dissenters in the Nineteenth Century.* New York: Harper & Row, 1974.

———. *Place over Time: The Continuity of Southern Distinctiveness.* Baton Rouge: Louisiana State University Press, 1977.

———. "Rethinking Post–Civil War History," *Virginia Quarterly Review* 57 (1981): 255–56.

———. "The South in Southern History Textbooks," *Journal of Southern History* 30 (1964): 48–57.

DeLatte, Carolyn E. "The St. Landry Riot: A Forgotten Incident of Reconstruction Violence," *Louisiana History* 17 (1976): 41–49.

Dennison, George M. *The Dorr War: Republicanism on Trial.* Lexington: University of Kentucky Press, 1976.

Dennison, George W. "Martial Law: The Development of a Theory of Emergency Power, 1776–1861," *American Journal of Legal History* 18 (1974): 52–95.

DeSantis, Vincent P. "Negro Dissatisfaction with Republican Policy in the South," *Journal of Negro History* 36 (1951): 148–59.

———. "President Arthur and the Independent Movements in the South," *Journal of Southern History* 19 (1953): 346–63.

———. "President Hayes's Southern Policy," *Journal of Southern History* 21 (1955): 476–94.

———. "The Republican Party and the Southern Negro, 1877–1897," *Journal of Negro History* 45 (1960): 71–87.

———. *Republicans Face the Southern Question: The New Departure Years, 1877–1897.* Baltimore: Johns Hopkins University Press, 1959.

———. "Rutherford B. Hayes and the Removal of the Troops and the End of Reconstruction." In *Region, Race, and Reconstruction: Essays in Honor of C. Vann Woodward,* edited by J. Morgan Kousser and James M. McPherson. New York: Oxford University Press, 1982, 417–50.

Dethloff, Henry C., and Robert P. Jones. "Race Relations in Louisiana, 1877–1898," *Louisiana History* 9 (1968): 301–23.

Dew, Charles B. "Disciplining Salve Ironworkers in the Antebellum South: Coercion, Conciliation, and Accommodation," *American Historical Review* 79 (1974): 393–418.

———. *Ironmaker to the Confederacy: Joseph R. Anderson and the Tredegar Iron Works.* New Haven, CT: Yale University Press, 1966.

Dibble, Roy F. *Albion W. Tourgée.* Port Washington, NY: Kennikat Press, 1968 [1921].

Dillon, Merton L. "The Failure of American Abolitionists," *Journal of Southern History* 25 (1959): 159–77.

Dobson, John M. *Politics in the Gilded Age: A New Perspective on Reform.* New York: Praeger, 1972.

Dodd, William E. *Jefferson Davis.* Philadelphia: G. W. Jacobs, 1907.

Dombrowski, James. *Early Days of Christian Socialism in America.* New York: Octagon, 1966 [1936].

Donald, David H. *Charles Sumner and the Coming of the Civil War.* New York: Alfred A. Knopf, 1968.

———. *Charles Sumner and the Rights of Man.* New York: Alfred A. Knopf, 1970.

———. "Devils Facing Zionwards." In *Grant, Lee, Lincoln and the Radicals,* edited by Grady McWhiney. Evanston, IL: Northwestern University Press, 1964, 72–91.

———. *Lincoln.* New York: Simon & Schuster, 1995.

———. *The Politics of Reconstruction, 1863–1867.* Baton Rouge: Louisiana State University Press, 1965.

———. "The Radicals and Lincoln." In *Lincoln Reconsidered,* by David H. Donald. 2d ed. New York: Vintage Books, 1956, 103–27.

———. "Reconstruction." In *Interpreting American History: Conversations with Historians,* edited by John A. Garraty. New York: Oxford University Press, 1970, 363–64.

———. "The Scalawag in Mississippi Reconsidered," *Journal of Southern History* 10 (1944): 447–60.

———. "Towards a Reconsideration of the Abolitionists." In *Lincoln Reconsidered: Essays on the Civil War Era,* edited by David H. Donald. 2d ed. New York: Vintage, 1956.

———, ed. *Inside Lincoln's Cabinet: The Civil War Diaries of Salmon P. Chase.* New York: Longmans, Green, 1954.

———. *Lincoln Reconsidered: Essays on the Civil War Era.* 2d ed. New York: Vintage Books, 1956.

Donald, Henderson H. *The Negro Freedman: Life Conditions of the American Negro in the Early Years after Emancipation.* New York: Abelard-Schumann, 1971.

Dorris, Jonathan Truman. *Pardon and Amnesty under Lincoln and Johnson: The Restoration of Confederates to Their Rights and Privileges, 1861–1898.* Chapel Hill: University of North Carolina Press, 1953.

———. "Pardon Seekers and Brokers: A Sequel to Appomattox," *Journal of Southern History* 1 (1935): 276–92.

———. "Pardoning the Leaders of the Confederacy," *Mississippi Valley Historical Review* 15 (1928): 3–21.

Douglass, Frederick. *The Life and Times of Frederick Douglass Written by Himself.* Hartford, CT: Parker Publishing, 1881.

———. *Narrative of the Life of Frederick Douglass.* Boston: Anti-slavery Office, 1845.

Downey, Matthew T. "Horace Greeley and the Politicians: The Liberal Republican Convention in 1872," *Journal of American History* 53 (1966–67): 727–50.

Drago, Edmund L. "Black Georgia during Reconstruction." Ph.D. dissertation, University of California–Berkeley, 1975.

———. *Black Politicians and Reconstruction Georgia: A Splendid Failure.* Baton Rouge: Louisiana State University Press, 1982.

Drake, Richard B. "The American Missionary Association and the Southern Negro, 1861–1888." Ph.D. dissertation, Emory University, 1957.

———. "Freedmen's Aid and Sectional Compromise," *Journal of Southern History* 29 (1963): 175–86.

Driggs, Orval T. "The Issues of the Powell Clayton Regime, 1868–1871," *Arkansas Historical Quarterly* 8 (1949): 1–76.

Duberman, Martin, ed. *The Antislavery Vanguard: New Essays on the Abolitionists.* Princeton, NJ: Princeton University Press, 1965.

DuBois, W. E. Burghardt. *Black Reconstruction: An Essay toward a History of the Part Which Black Folk Played in the Attempt to Reconstruct Democracy, 1860–1888.* New York: Harcourt, Brace, 1935.

———. "Frederick Douglass." In *Dictionary of American Biography,* edited by Allen Johnson et al. New York: Charles Scribner's Sons, 10 double vols. + 9 supplements, 1964–1981, 5: 406–407.

———. "The Freedmen's Bureau," *Atlantic Monthly* 87 (1901): 254–65.

———. "Reconstruction and Its Benefits," *American Historical Review* 15 (1909–10): 781–99.

———. "Reconstruction, Seventy Five Years After," *Phylon* 4 (1943): 205–212.

———. *The Souls of Black Folk: Essays and Sketches.* Chicago: A. C. McClurg, 1903.

Dufour, Charles L. "The Age of Warmoth," *Louisiana History* 6 (1965): 335–64.

Duncan, Russell. *Entrepreneur for Equality: Governor Rufus Bullock, Commerce, and Race in Post–Civil War Georgia.* Athens: University of Georgia Press, 1994.

Dunning, William A. *Essays on the Civil War and Reconstruction.* New York: Macmillan, 1897.

Bibliography

———. "More Light on Andrew Johnson," *American Historical Review* 2 (1905–1906): 574–94.

———. *Reconstruction, Political and Economic, 1865–1877*. New York: Harper Brothers, 1907.

Durden, Robert F. *The Gray and the Black: The Confederate Debate on Emancipation.* Baton Rouge: Louisiana State University Press, 1972.

Eaton, Clement. *The Freedom of Thought Struggle in the Old South.* Enlarged ed. New York: Harper & Row, 1964.

———. *Jefferson Davis.* New York: Free Press, 1977.

———. *The Waning of the Old South Civilization, 1860s–1880s.* Athens: University of Georgia Press, 1968.

Eaton, John. *Grant, Lincoln, and the Freedmen.* New York: Negro Universities Press, 1969 [1907].

Eberstadt, Charles. "Lincoln's Emancipation Proclamation," *New Colophon* 3 (1950): 312–55.

Eckenrode, Hamilton J. *Jefferson Davis: President of the South.* New York: Macmillan, 1923.

———. *Political History of Virginia during the Reconstruction.* Baltimore: Johns Hopkins University Press, 1904.

———. *Rutherford B. Hayes: Statesman of Reunion.* New York: Dodd, Mead, 1930.

Eckenrode, Hamilton J., and Bryan Conrad. *James Longstreet: Lee's War Horse.* Chapel Hill: University of North Carolina Press, 1936.

Eckert, Edward K. "Contract Labor in Florida during Reconstruction," *Florida Historical Quarterly* 47 (1968): 34–50.

Eckert, Ralph Lowell. *John Brown Gordon: Soldier, Southerner, Statesman.* Baton Rouge: Louisiana State University Press, 1989.

Edwards, John Carver. "Radical Reconstruction and the New Orleans Riot of 1866," *Journal of History and Politics* 11 (1973): 48–64.

Elkins, Stanley M. *Slavery: A Problem in American Institutional and Intellectual Life.* Chicago: University of Chicago Press, 1959.

Ellem, Warren A. "Who Were the Mississippi Scalawags?" *Journal of Southern History* 48 (1982): 349–72.

Elliott, Claude. "The Freedmen's Bureau in Texas," *Southwestern Historical Quarterly* (1952–53): 1–24.

Ellis, L. Ethan. "Lyman Trumbull." In *Dictionary of American Biography*, edited by Allen Johnson et al. New York: Charles Scribner's Sons, 10 double vols. + 9 supplements, 1964–1981, 19: 19–20.

Emerson, Thomas I., et al. *Political and Civil Rights in the United States.* 3d ed. Boston: Little, Brown, 1967.

Engdahl, David E. "Soldiers, Riots, and Revolutions: The Law of Military Troops in Civil Disorders," *Iowa Law Review* 57 (1971): 1–70.

Englesman, John C. "The Freedmen's Bureau in Louisiana," *Louisiana Historical Quarterly* 32 (1949): 145–224.

Escott, Paul D. "White Republicanism and Ku Klux Klan Terror: The North Carolina Piedmont during Reconstruction." In *Race, Class, and Politics in Southern History*, edited by Jeffrey J. Crow et al. Baton Rouge: Louisiana State University Press, 1989, 3–34.

Evans, W. McKee. *Ballots and Fence Rails: Reconstruction on the Lower Cape Fear.* Chapel Hill: University of North Carolina Press, 1967.

Everett, Donald E. "Demands of the New Orleans Free Colored Population for Political Equality, 1862–1865," *Louisiana Historical Quarterly* 38 (1955): 43–64.

Everly, Elaine C. "The Freedmen's Bureau in the National Capital." Ph.D. dissertation, George Washington University, 1972.

Ewing, Cortez A. M. "Two Reconstruction Impeachments," *North Carolina Historical Review* 15 (1938): 197–230.

Fairman, Charles. "Does the Fourteenth Amendment Incorporate the Bill of Rights?" *Stanford Law Review* 2 (1952–53): 5–139.

―――. *Five Justices and the Electoral Commission of 1877*. New York: Macmillan, 1988.

―――. *Reconstruction and Reunion, 1864–1888*. 2 pts. New York: Macmillan, 1971–1987.

Farnham, Wallace D. "'The Weakened Spring of Government': A Study in Nineteenth Century American History," *American Historical Review* 68 (1963): 662–80.

Farnum, Henry W. *Chapters in the History of Social Legislation in the United States to 1860*. New York: AMS Press, 1970.

Fast, Howard. *Freedom Road*. New York: Duell, Sloan & Pearce, 1944.

Faulkner, Harold U. *Politics, Reform, and Expansion, 1890–1900*. New York: Harper & Row, 1959.

Fehrenbacher, Don E. *The Dred Scott Case: Its Significance in American Law and Politics*. New York: Oxford University Press, 1978.

Fenlon, Paul E. "The Notorious Swepson-Littlefield Fraud: Railroad Financing in Florida, 1868–1871," *Florida Historical Quarterly* 32 (1954): 231–61.

Ferrell, Robert H. *American Diplomacy: A History*. New York: W. W. Norton, 1969.

Ficklen, John. *History of Reconstruction in Louisiana (through 1868)*. Baltimore: Johns Hopkins University Press, 1910.

Field, William T., Jr. "The Texas State Police, 1870–1873," *Texas Military History* 5 (1965): 131–41.

Fields, Barbara Jane. *Slavery and Freedom on the Middle Ground: Maryland during the Nineteenth Century*. New Haven, CT: Yale University Press, 1985.

Filler, Louis. *The Crusade against Slavery, 1830–1860*. New York: Harper & Row, 1960.

Fischer, Roger A. "A Pioneer Protest: The New Orleans Street-Car Controversy of 1867," *Journal of Negro History* 53 (1968): 219–33.

―――. "The Post Civil War Segregation Struggle." In *The Past as Prelude: New Orleans, 1718–1968*, edited by Hodding Carter et al. New Orleans: Tulane University Press, 1968, 288–304.

―――. "Racial Segregation in Antebellum New Orleans," *American Historical Review* 74 (1969): 926–37.

―――. *The Segregation Struggle in Louisiana, 1862–1877*. Urbana: University of Illinois Press, 1974.

Fish, Carl Russell. "James Gillespie Blaine." In *Dictionary of American Biography*, edited by Allen Johnson et al. New York: Charles Scribner's Sons, 10 double vols. + 9 supplements, 1964–1981, 2: 322–29.

Fishel, Leslie H., Jr. "The Negro in Northern Politics, 1870–1900," *Mississippi Valley Historical Review* 42 (1955–56): 466–89.

―――. "Repercussions of Reconstruction: The Northern Negro, 1870–1883," *Civil War History* 14 (1968): 325–45.

Fitchett, E. Horace. "The Traditions of the Free Negro in Charleston, South Carolina," *Journal of Negro History* 25 (1940): 139–52.

Fitzgerald, Michael W. *The Union League Movement in the Deep South: Politics and Agricultural Change during Reconstruction*. Baton Rouge: Louisiana State University Press, 1989.

FitzSimmons, Theodore B. "The Camilla Riot," *Georgia Historical Quarterly* 35 (1951): 116–25.

Flack, Horace E. *The Adoption of the Fourteenth Amendment*. Baltimore: Johns Hopkins University Press, 1908.

Fladeland, Betty L. "Compensated Emancipation: A Rejected Alternative," *Journal of Southern History* 42 (1976): 169–86.

Flannigan, Daniel. "The Criminal Law of Slavery and Freedom, 1800–1868." Ph.D. dissertation, Rice University, 1973.

Fleming, Thomas. "Lincoln's Tragic Heroism," *National Review* 41 (December 8, 1989): 38–40.

Bibliography

Fleming, Walter Lynwood. *Civil War and Reconstruction in Alabama*. New York: Columbia University Press, 1905.

———, ed. *Documentary History of Reconstruction: Political, Military, Social, Religious, Educational & Industrial, 1865 to the Present Time*. 2 vols. Cleveland: Arthur H. Clark Co., 1906–1907.

———. "The Formation of the Union Leagues in Alabama," *Gulf States Historical Magazine* 2 (1903): 73–89.

———. *The Freedmen's Savings Bank: A Chapter in the History of the Negro Race*. Chapel Hill: University of North Carolina Press, 1927.

———. *The Sequel to Appomattox*. New Haven, CT: Yale University Press, 1921.

Flick, Alexander Clarence. *Samuel Jones Tilden: A Study in Political Sagacity*. New York: Dodd, Mead, 1939.

Folk, Edgar Estes. "W. W. Holden and the Election of 1858," *North Carolina Historical Review* 21 (1944): 294–318.

———. "W. W. Holden and the North Carolina Standard, 1843–1848," *North Carolina Historical Review* 19 (1942): 22–47.

Folk, Edgar Estes, and Bynum Shaw. *W. W. Holden: A Political Biography*. Winston-Salem, NC: John F. Blair, 1982.

Foner, Eric. *Free Soil, Free Labor, Free Men: The Ideology of the Republican Party before the Civil War*. New York: Oxford University Press, 1970.

———. "The Meaning of Freedom in the Age of Emancipation," *Journal of American History* 81 (1994): 435–60.

———. *Politics and Ideology in the Age of the Civil War*. New York: Oxford University Press, 1980.

———. *Reconstruction: America's Unfinished Revolution, 1863–1877*. New York: Harper & Row, 1988.

———. "Reconstruction Revisited," *Reviews in American History* 10 (1982): 82–100.

Ford, Amelia C. "Samuel Jones Tilden." In *Dictionary of American Biography*, edited by Allen Johnson et al. New York: Charles Scribner's Sons, 10 double vols. + 9 supplements, 1964–1981, 18: 537–41.

Foreman, James. *The Making of a Black Revolutionary*. New York: Macmillan, 1972.

Formwalt, Lee W. "Antebellum Planter Persistence in Southwest Georgia—A Case Study," *Plantation Society in the Americas* 1 (1981): 410–29.

———. "The Camilla Massacre of 1868: Racial Violence as Political Propaganda," *Georgia Historical Quarterly* 71 (1987): 399–426.

Forten, Charlotte L. "Life on the Sea Islands," *Atlantic Monthly* 13 (1864): 587–96.

Fortune, T. Thomas. *Black and White: Land, Labor, and Politics in the South*. New York: Fords, Howard, Hulbert, 1884.

Foster, Gaines M. *Ghosts of the Confederacy: Defeat, the Lost Cause, and the Emergence of the New South, 1865 to 1913*. New York: Oxford University Press, 1987.

———. "The Limitations of Federal Health Care for Freedmen, 1862–1868," *Journal of Southern History* 48 (1982): 349–72.

Fowler, Wilton B. "A Carpetbagger's Conversion to White Supremacy," *North Carolina Historical Review* 43 (1966): 286–304.

Frankfurter, Felix. "Memorandum on 'Incorporation' of the Bill of Rights into the Due Process Clause of the Fourteeenth Amendment," *Harvard Law Review* 78 (1964–1965): 746–67.

Franklin, John Hope. *The Emancipation Proclamation*. Garden City, NY: Doubleday, 1963.

———. "The Enforcement of the Civil Rights Act of 1875." In *Race and History*, by John Hope Franklin. Baton Rouge: Louisiana State University, 1989.

———. "History—Weapon of War and Peace," *Phylon* 5 (1944): 249–59, quotes from 249, 250, 257.

———. "Jim Crow Goes to School: The Genesis of Legal Segregation in Southern Schools," *South Atlantic Quarterly* 58 (1959): 225–35.

———. "John Roy Lynch: Republican Stalwart from Mississippi." In *Southern Black Leaders of the Reconstruction Era*, edited by Howard N. Rabinowitz. Urbana: University of Illinois Press, 1982, 39–58.

———. *The Militant South*. Cambridge, MA: Harvard University Press, 1956.

———. "Mirror for Americans: A Century of Reconstruction History," *American Historical Review* 86 (1980–1981): 1–14.

———. *Race and History: Selected Essays, 1938–1988*. Baton Rouge: Louisiana State University, 1989.

———. *Reconstruction: After the Civil War*. Chicago: University of Chicago Press, 1961.

———. "Whither Reconstruction Historiography," *Journal of Negro Education* 17 (1947): 446–61.

Franklin, John Hope, and Alfred A. Moss, Jr. *From Slavery to Freedom: A History of the African American*. New York: Alfred A. Knopf, 1994.

Frantz, Laurent B., "Fourteenth Amendment against Private Acts," *Yale Law Journal* 73 (1964): 1353–84.

Frederickson, George M. *The Black Image in the White Mind: The Debate on Afro-American Character and Destiny, 1817–1914*. New York: Harper & Row, 1971.

———. *The Inner Civil War: Northern Intellectuals and the Crisis of the Union*. New York: Harper & Row, 1965.

———. "A Man But Not a Brother: Abraham Lincoln and Racial Equality," *Journal of Southern History* 41 (1975): 39–58.

Fredman, L. E. *The Australian Ballot: The Story of an American Reform*. Lansing: Michigan State University Press, 1969.

Freidel, Frank. "Francis Lieber, Charles Sumner, and Slavery," *Journal of Southern History* 9 (1943): 75–93.

———. "General Orders No. 100 and Military Government," *Mississippi Valley Historical Review* 32 (1945–46): 541–56.

Friedman, Lawrence J. "Life 'in the Lion's Mouth': Another Look at Booker T. Washington," *Journal of Negro History* 59 (1974): 337–51.

———. "The Search for Docility: Racial Thought in the White South, 1861–1917," *Phylon* 31 (1970): 313–23.

Friedman, Milton, and Anna Jacobson Schwartz. *A Monetary History of the United States, 1867–1960*. Princeton, NJ: Princeton University Press, 1963.

Fuess, Claude M. "Justin Smith Morrill." In *Dictionary of American Biography*, edited by Allen Johnson et al. New York: Charles Scribner's Sons, 10 double vols. + 9 supplements, 1964–1981, 12: 198–99.

Fuke, Richard Paul. "A Reform Mentality: Federal Policy toward Black Marylanders, 1864–1868," *Civil War History* 22 (1976): 214–35.

Fuller, J. F. C. *The Generalship of U. S. Grant*. 2d ed. Bloomington: Indiana University Press, 1958.

Fuller, Joseph V. "Hamilton Fish." In *Dictionary of American Biography*, edited by Allen Johnson et al. New York: Charles Scribner's Sons, 10 double vols. + 9 supplements, 1964–1981, 7: 145–50.

Furman, H. W. C. "Restrictions upon the Use of the Army Imposed by the Posse Comitatus Act," *Military Law Review* 7 (1959): 85–129.

Futrell, Robert F. "Federal Military Government in the South, 1861–1865," *Military Affairs* 15 (1951): 181–91.

Gabriel, Ralph H. "The American Experience with Military Government," *American Historical Review* 49 (1944): 632–37.

———. *The Course of American Democratic Thought*. 2d ed. New York: Rondell Press, 1956.

Gaffney, Edward M., Jr. "History and Legal Interpretation: The Early Distortion of the Fourteenth Amendment by the Gilded Age Courts," *Catholic University Law Review* 25 (1976): 207–49.

Gambill, Edward L. "Who Were the Senate Radicals?" *Civil War History* 11 (1965): 237–44.

Ganus, Clifton L., Jr. "The Freedmen's Bureau in Mississippi." Ph.D. dissertation, Tulane University, 1953.

Gara, Larry. "Slavery and the Slave Power: A Crucial Distinction," *Civil War History* 15 (1969): 5–18.

Gard, Wayne. *The Great Buffalo Hunt.* New York: Alfred A. Knopf, 1960.

Garner, James W. "General Orders 100 Revisited," *Military Law Review* 27 (1965): 1–48.

———. *Reconstruction in Mississippi.* New York: Macmillan, 1901.

Gaston, Paul M. *The New South Creed: A Study in Southern Mythmaking.* New York: Alfred A. Knopf, 1970.

Gates, Paul W. "Federal Land Policy in the South, 1866–1880," *Journal of Southern History* 6 (1940): 303–60.

Genovese, Eugene D. "On Southern History and Its Historians: A Review Article," *Civil War History* 13 (1967): 170–82, especially 178–79.

———. *Roll Jordan Roll: The World the Slaves Made.* New York: Pantheon Books, 1974.

———. *The Slaveholders' Dilemma: Freedom and Progress in Southern Conservative Thought.* Columbia: University of South Carolina Press, 1992.

———. *The World the Slaveholders Made: Two Essays in Interpretation.* New York: Random House, 1969.

George, Joseph, Jr. "Black Flag Warfare: Lincoln and the Raid against Richmond and Jefferson Davis," *Pennsylvania Magazine of History and Biography* 115 (1991): 291–318.

Gerteis, Louis S. *From Contraband to Freedman: Federal Policy toward Southern Blacks, 1861–1865.* Westport, CT: Greenwood Press, 1973.

———. "Salmon P. Chase, Radicalism, and the Politics of Emancipation, 1861–1864," *Journal of American History* 60 (1973–1974): 42–62.

Gibbons, Tony. *Warships and Naval Battles of the US Civil War.* Limpsfield, Surrey, UK: Dragon's World, 1989.

Gilbert, Abby L. "The Comptroller of the Currency and the Freedmen's Savings Bank," *Journal of Negro History* 57 (1972): 125–43.

Gilchrest, David T., and W. David Lewis, eds. *Economic Change in the Civil War Era.* Greenville, DE: Eleutherian Mills–Hagley Foundation, 1965.

Gillette, William. *Retreat from Reconstruction, 1869–1879.* Baton Rouge: Louisiana State University Press, 1979.

———. *The Right to Vote: Politics and the Passage of the Fifteenth Amendment.* Baltimore: Johns Hopkins University Press, 1965, 1969.

Gipson, Lawrence H. "The Statesmanship of President Johnson: A Study of the Presidential Reconstruction Policy," *Mississippi Valley Historical Review* 2 (1914–1915): 363–83.

Glatthaar, Joseph T. *Forged in Battle: The Civil War Alliance of Black Soldiers and White Officers.* New York: Free Press, 1989.

Goff, Patrick J. "The Abolitionist Movement in High School Texts," *Journal of Negro Education* 32 (1963): 43–51

Gold, Robert L. "Negro Colonization Schemes in Equador, 1861," *Phylon* 30 (1969): 306–16.

Goldhurst, Richard. *Many Are the Hearts: The Agony and the Triumph of Ulysses S. Grant.* New York: Crowell, 1975.

Govan, Gilbert E., and James W. Livingood. "Chattanooga under Military Occupation," *Journal of Southern History* 17 (1951): 23–47.

Graebner, Norman A., ed. *The Enduring Lincoln.* Urbana: University of Illinois Press, 1959.

Graglia, Lino A. "Does Constitutional Law Exist?" *National Review* 47 (1995): 31–34.

Graham, Frank D. "International Trade under Depreciated Paper: The United States, 1862–1879," *Quarterly Journal of Economics* 36 (1922): 220–73.

Graham, Howard J. "The 'Conspiracy Theory' of the Fourteenth Amendment," *Yale Law Journal* 47 (1938): 371–403.

———. "Procedure to Substance—Extra-Judicial Rise of Due Process," *California Law Review* 40 (1952–1953): 483–500.

Granade, Ray. "Violence: An Instrument of Policy in Reconstruction Alabama," *Alabama Historical Quarterly* 30 (1968): 181–202.

Grant, Ulysses S. *Personal Memoirs of U. S. Grant.* 2 vols. New York: Charles L. Webster, 1886.

Grant, Ulysses S., III. *Ulysses S. Grant: Warrior and Statesman.* New York: William Morrow, 1969.

Gray, Daniel Savage. "Bibliographic Essay: Black Views on Reconstruction," *Journal of Negro History* 58 (1973): 73–85.

Gray, Ronald N. "Edmund J. Davis: Radical Republican and Reconstruction Governor of Texas." Ph.D. dissertation, Texas Tech University, 1976.

Grimshaw, Alan. "Lawlessness and Violence in America and Their Special Manifestations in Changing Negro-White Relationships," *Journal of Negro History* 44 (1959): 52–72.

Groff, Patrick. "The Freedmen's Bureau in High School History Texts," *Journal of Negro Education* 51 (1982): 425–33.

Gross, Theodore L. "The Fool's Errand of Albion W. Tourgée," *Phylon* 24 (1963): 240–54.

———. "The Negro in the Literature of Reconstruction," *Phylon* 22 (1961): 5–14.

Grosz, Agnes Smith. "The Political Career of Pinckney Benton Stewart Pinchback," *Louisiana Historical Quarterly* 27 (1944): 527–612.

Groves, Harry E. "Separate But Equal—The Doctrine of Plessy v. Ferguson," *Phylon* 12 (1951): 66–72.

Gunderson, Robert Gray. *Old Gentlemen's Convention: The Washington Peace Conference of 1861.* Madison: University of Wisconsin Press, 1961.

Gutman, Herbert G. *The Black Family in Slavery and Freedom, 1750–1925.* New York: Pantheon Books, 1976.

———. "The Slave Family and Its Legacies," *Historical Reflections* 6 (1979): 183–211.

Hacker, Louis. *Triumph of American Capitalism: The Development of Forces in American History to the End of the Nineteenth Century.* New York: Simon & Schuster, 1940.

Hackney, Sheldon. "Southern Violence," *American Historical Review* 74 (1969): 906–25.

Hagerman, Edward. *The American Civil War and the Origins of Modern Warfare: Ideas, Organization, and Field Command.* Bloomington: Indiana University Press, 1988.

Hair, William Ivy. *Bourbonism and Agrarian Protest: Louisiana Politics, 1877–1900.* Baton Rouge: Louisiana State University Press, 1969.

Hale, William Harlan. *Horace Greeley: Voice of the People.* New York: Collier Books, 1950.

Hall, Kermit L., ed. *Civil Rights in American History: Major Historical Interpretations.* New York: Garland Publishing, 1987.

———. "Political Power and Constitutional Legitimacy: The South Carolina Ku Klux Klan Trials, 1871–1872," *Emory Law Journal* 33 (1984): 921–51.

———, ed. *Race Relations and the Law in American History: Major Historical Interpretations.* New York: Garland Publishing, 1987.

Hall, Kermit L., and Lou Falkner Williams. "Constitutional Tradition amid Social Change: Hugh Lennox Bond and the Ku Klux Klan in South Carolina," *Maryland Historian* 16 (1985): 43–58.

Halstead, Jacqueline J. "The Delaware Association for the Moral Improvement and Education of the Colored People: 'Practical Christianity,'" *Delaware History* 15 (1972): 19–40.

Hamilton, Joseph G. de Roulhac. *Reconstruction in North Carolina.* New York: Columbia University Press, 1914.

Hammond, Bray. *Sovereignty and an Empty Purse: Banks and Politics in the Civil War*. Princeton, NJ: Princeton University Press, 1970.

Hanchett, William. *The Lincoln Murder Conspiracies*. Urbana: University of Illinois Press, 1983.

———. "Lincoln's Murder: The Single Conspiracy Theory," *Civil War Times Illustrated* 30 (November/December): 28–35, 70–71.

———. "Reconstruction and the Rehabilitation of Jefferson Davis: Charles G. Halpine's *Prison Life*," *Journal of American History* 56 (1969–1970): 280–89.

Hancock, Almira R. *Reminiscences of Winfield Scott Hancock*. New York: Charles L. Webster, 1887.

Harding, Vincent. *There Is a River: The Black Struggle for Freedom in America*. New York: Harcourt Brace Jovanovich, 1981.

Harlan, Louis R. *Booker T. Washington*. 2 vols. New York: Oxford University Press, 1972–1983.

———. "Booker T. Washington and the White Man's Burden," *American Historical Review* 71 (1966): 446–67.

———. "Booker T. Washington in Biographical Perspective," *American Historical Review* 75 (1970): 1581–99.

———. "Desegregation in New Orleans Public Schools during Reconstruction," *American Historical Review* 67 (1961): 663–75.

Harlan, Louis R., et al., eds. *The Booker T. Washington Papers*. 14 vols. Urbana: University of Illinois Press, 1972–1989.

Harlow, Alvin F. "Victoria Claflin Woodhull." In *Dictionary of American Biography*, edited by Allen Johnson et al. New York: Charles Scribner's Sons, 10 double vols. + 9 supplements, 1964–1981, 20: 494–95.

———. "William Marcy Tweed." In *Dictionary of American Biography*, edited by Allen Johnson et al. New York: Charles Scribner's Sons, 10 double vols. + 9 supplements, 1964–1981, 19: 79–82.

Harper, Alan D. "William A. Dunning: The Historian as Nemesis," *Civil War History* 10 (1964): 54–66.

Harrell, John M. *The Brooks and Baxter War: A History of the Reconstruction Period in Arkansas*. St. Louis: Slawson Printing, 1893.

Harris, Carl V. "Right Fork or Left Fork? The Section-Party Alignments of Southern Democrats in Congress, 1873–1897," *Journal of Southern History* 42 (1976): 471–506.

Harris, Francis B. "Henry Clay Warmoth, Reconstruction Governor of Louisiana," *Louisiana Historical Quarterly* 30 (1947): 523–652.

Harris, Robert L., Jr. "Charleston's Free Afro-American Elite: The Brown Fellowship Society and the Humane Brotherhood," *South Carolina Historical Magazine* 82 (1981): 289–310.

———. "Coming of Age: The Transformation of Afro-American Historiography," *Journal of Negro History* 67 (1982): 107–21.

Harris, William C. "Blanche K. Bruce of Mississippi: Conservative Assimilationist." In *Southern Black Leaders of the Reconstruction Era*, edited by Howard N. Rabinowitz. Urbana: University of Illinois Press, 1982, 3–38.

———. "The Creed of the Carpetbaggers: The Case of Mississippi," *Journal of Southern History* 40 (1974): 199–224.

———. *The Day of the Carpetbagger*. Baton Rouge: Louisiana State University Press, 1979.

———. "James Lynch: Black Leader in Southern Reconstruction," *Historian* 34 (1971): 40–61.

———. "Mississippi: Republican Factionalism and Mismanagement." In *Reconstruction and Redemption in the South*, edited by Otto H. Olsen. Baton Rouge: Louisiana State University Press, 1980, 78–112.

———. *Presidential Reconstruction in Mississippi*. Baton Rouge: Louisiana State University Press, 1967.

———. "A Reconsideration of the Mississippi Scalawag," *Journal of Mississippi History* 32 (1970): 3–42.

———. *William Woods Holden: Firebrand of North Carolina Politics.* Baton Rouge: Louisiana State University Press, 1987.

———. "William Woods Holden: In Search of Vindication," *North Carolina Historical Review* 59 (1982): 354–72.

Haskins, James. *Pinckney Benton Stewart Pinchback.* New York: Macmillan, 1973.

Haskins, Ralph W. "Internecine Strife in Tennessee: Andrew Johnson vs. Parson Brownlow," *Tennessee Historical Quarterly* 24 (1965): 321–40.

Hasson, Gail S. "Health and Welfare of Freedmen in Reconstruction Alabama," *Alabama Review* 35 (1982): 94–110.

Hattaway, Herman, and Archer Jones. *How the North Won: A Military History of the Civil War.* Urbana: University of Illinois Press, 1983.

Hawkins, Hugh, ed. *Booker T. Washington and His Critics.* Lexington, MA: D. C. Heath, 1962.

Haworth, Paul L. "George Washington Julian." In *Dictionary of American Biography,* edited by Allen Johnson et al. New York: Charles Scribner's Sons, 10 double vols. + 9 supplements, 9 (1964–1981): 245–46.

———. *The Hayes-Tilden Disputed Presidential Election of 1876.* Cleveland: Arthur H. Clark, 1906.

Haynes, George H. "Charles Sumner." In *Dictionary of American Biography,* edited by Allen Johnson et al. New York: Charles Scribner's Sons, 10 double vols. + 9 supplements, 1964–1981, 18: 208–14.

Hennessey, Melinda Meek. "Political Terrorism in the Black Belt: The Eutaw Riot," *Alabama Review* 33 (1980): 35–48.

———. "Race and Violence in New Orleans: The 1868 Riot," *Louisiana History* 20 (1979): 77–91.

———. "Racial Violence during Reconstruction: The 1876 Riots in Charleston and Cainhoy," *South Carolina Historical Magazine* 86 (1985): 100–12.

———. "Reconstruction Politics and the Military: The Eufala Riot of 1874," *Alabama Historical Quarterly* 38 (1976): 112–25.

———. "To Live and Die in Dixie: Reconstruction Race Riots in the South." Ph.D. dissertation, Kent State University, 1978.

Henry, Robert Self. *The Story of Reconstruction.* Indianapolis: Bobbs-Merrill, 1938.

Hentig, Gerald S. "Henry Winter Davis and the Speakership Contest of 1859–1860," *Maryland Historical Magazine* 68 (1973): 1–19.

———. *Henry Winter Davis: Antebellum and Civil War Congressman from Maryland.* New York: Twayne Publishers, 1973.

Hermann, Janet S. *The Pursuit of a Dream.* New York: Oxford University Press, 1981.

———. "Reconstruction in Microcosm: Three Men and a Gin," *Journal of Negro History* 65 (1980): 312–35.

Herrnstein, Richard J., and Charles Murray. *The Bell Curve: Intelligence and Class Structure in American Life.* New York: Free Press, 1994.

Hershkowitz, Leo. *Tweed's New York: Another Look.* Garden City, NY: Doubleday, 1977.

Hesseltine, William B. "Economic Factors in the Abandonment of Reconstruction," *Mississippi Valley Historical Review* 22 (1935–1936): 191–210.

———. "Lincoln and the Politicians, *Civil War History* 6 (1960): 43–55.

———. *Lincoln's Plan of Reconstruction.* Tuscaloosa, AL: Confederate Publishing Company, 1960.

———. *Ulysses S. Grant: Politician.* New York: Dodd, Mead, 1935.

Hesseltine, William B., and Larry Gara. "Georgia's Confederate Leaders after Appomattox," *Georgia Historical Quarterly* 35 (1951): 1–15.

Heyman, Max L., Jr. "'The Great Reconstructor': General E. R. S. Canby and the Second Military District," *North Carolina Historical Review* 32 (1955): 52–80.

————. *Prudent Soldier: A Biography of Major General E. R. S. Canby, 1817–1873.* Glendale, CA: A. H. Clark, 1959.

Hibben, Paxton. *Henry Ward Beecher: An American Portrait.* New York: Press of the Readers Club, 1942.

Higham, John. *From Boundlessness to Consolidation: The Transformation of American Culture, 1848–1860.* Ann Arbor: University of Michigan Press, 1969.

Higham, Robin D. S., ed. *Bayonets in the Streets: Use of Troops in Civil Disturbances.* Manhattan: Kansas State University Press, 1969.

Hine, William C. "Black Politicians in Reconstruction Charleston, South Carolina: A Collective Study," *Journal of Southern History* 49 (1983): 555–84.

————. "The 1867 Charleston Streetcar Sit-ins: A Case of Successful Black Protest," *South Carolina Historical Magazine* 78 (1976): 110–14.

Hirshon, Stanley P. *Farewell to the Bloody Shirt: Northern Republicans and the Southern Negro.* Bloomington: Indiana University Press, 1962.

Hoar, G. F., ed. *Charles Sumner: His Complete Works.* 20 vols. Boston: Lee & Sheppard, 1900.

Hoeveler, J. David, Jr. "Reconstruction and the Federal Courts: The Civil Rights Act of 1875," *Historian* 31 (1969): 604–17.

Hoffman, Edwin D. "From Slavery to Self-Reliance," *Journal of Negro History* 41 (1956): 8–42.

Hoffnagel, Warren. "The Southern Homestead Act: Its Origins and Operation," *Historian* 32 (1970): 612–29.

Hofstadter, Richard. *The Age of Reform.* New York: Vintage Books, 1955.

————. *The American Political Tradition and the Men Who Made It.* New York: Alfred A. Knopf, 1948.

Holdsworth, W. S. "Martial Law Historically Considered," *Law Quarterly Review* 18 (1902): 117–32.

Holladay, Florence Elizabeth. "The Extraordinary Powers and Functions of the General Commanding the Trans-Mississippi Department of the Southern Confederacy." M.A. thesis, University of Texas, 1914.

Holmes, Jack D. L. "The Underlying Causes of the Memphis Race Riot of 1866," *Tennessee Historical Quarterly* 17 (1958): 195–225.

Holmes, William F. "The Leflore County Massacre and the Demise of the Colored Farmers' Alliance," *Phylon* 34 (1973): 267–74.

Holt, Thomas. *Black over White: Negro Political Leadership in South Carolina during Reconstruction.* Urbana: University of Illinois Press, 1977.

Holzman, Robert S. *Stormy Ben Butler.* New York: Macmillan, 1954.

Hoogenboom, Ari A. *Outlawing the Spoils: A History of the Civil Reform Movement.* Urbana: University of Illinois Press, 1961.

————. *The Presidency of Rutherford B. Hayes.* Lawrence: University Press of Kansas, 1988.

————. *Rutherford B. Hayes: Warrior and President.* Lawrence: University Press of Kansas, 1995.

Hoogenboom, Ari, and Olive Hoogenboom. "Was Boss Tweed Really Snow White?" *Reviews in American History* 5 (1977): 360–66.

Hopkins, C. H. *The Rise of Social Gospel in American Protestantism.* New Haven, CT: Yale University Press, 1940.

Horn, Stanley. *Invisible Empire: The Story of the Ku Klux Klan, 1866–1871.* Boston: Houghton Mifflin, 1939.

Hornsby, Alton, Jr. "The Freedmen's Bureau Schools in Texas, 1865–1870," *Southwestern Historical Quarterly* 76 (1972–73): 397–417.

Horowitz, Robert F. "James M. Ashley and the Presidential Election of 1856," *Ohio Historical Quarterly* 83 (1974): 4–16.

————. "Land to the Freedmen: A Vision of Reconstruction," *Ohio Historical Quarterly* 85 (1977): 187–99.

Hosmer, John, and Joseph Fineman. "Black Congressmen in Reconstruction Historiography," *Phylon* 39 (1978): 97–107.

House, Albert V. "The Speakership Contest of 1875: Democratic Response to Power," *Journal of American History* 52 (1965): 252–74.

Houston, G. David. "A Negro Senator," *Journal of Negro History* 7 (1922): 243–256.

Howard, Oliver Otis. *Autobiography of Oliver Otis Howard.* 2 vols. New York: Baker and Taylor Company, 1908.

Howard, Victor B. *Black Liberation in Kentucky: Emancipation and Freedom, 1862–1884.* Lexington: University of Kentucky Press, 1983.

———. "The Black Testimony Controversy in Kentucky, 1866–1872," *Journal of Negro History* 58 (1973): 140–65.

———. "The Kentucky Press and the Negro Testimony Controversy, 1866–1872," *Register of the Kentucky Historical Society* 71 (1973): 29–50.

Howe, Daniel W. "American Victorianism as a Culture," *American Quarterly* 27 (1975): 507–32.

Hume, Richard L. "The Arkansas Constitutional Convention of 1868: A Case Study in the Politics of Reconstruction," *Journal of Southern History* 39 (1973): 183–206.

———. "Carpetbaggers in the Reconstruction South: A Group Portrait of Outside Whites in the 'Black and Tan' Constitutional Conventions," *Journal of American History* 64 (1977–78): 313–30.

Humphrey, George D. "Failure of the Mississippi Freedmen's Bureau in Black Labor Relations, 1865–1867," *Journal of Mississippi History* 45 (1983): 23–37.

Hurst, James Willard. *A Legal History of Money in the United States, 1774–1970.* Lincoln: University of Nebraska Press, 1973.

Hutton, Paul Andrew. *Phil Sheridan and His Army.* Lincoln: University of Nebraska Press, 1985.

Hyman, Harold M. "Deceit in Dixie," *Civil War History* 3 (1957): 65–82.

———. *The Era of the Oath: Northern Loyalty Tests during the Civil War and Reconstruction.* Philadelphia: University of Pennsylvania Press, 1954.

———. "Johnson, Stanton, and Grant: A Reconsideration of the Army's Role in the Events Leading to Impeachment," *American Historical Review* 66 (1960): 85–100.

———. "Law and the Impact of the Civil War: A Review Essay," *Civil War History* 14 (1968): 51–59.

———. "Lincoln and Equal Rights for Negroes," *Civil War History* 12 (1966): 258–66.

———. *A More Perfect Union: The Impact of the Civil War and Reconstruction on the Constitution.* New York: Alfred A. Knopf, 1973.

———, ed. *The Radical Republicans and Reconstruction.* Indianapolis: Bobbs-Merrill, 1967.

———. "Reconstruction and Political-Constitutional Institutions: The Popular Expression." In *New Frontiers of the American Reconstruction*, edited by Harold Hyman. Urbana: University of Illinois Press, 1959, 1–39.

Jackson, Luther P. "The Educational Efforts of the Freedmen's Bureau and Freedmen's Aid Societies in South Carolina, 1862–1872," *Journal of Negro History* 8 (1923): 1–40.

Jaffa, Harry V. "Lincoln's Character Assassins," *National Review* 42 (January 22, 1990): 34–38.

James, Joseph B. *The Framing of the Fourteenth Amendment.* Urbana: University of Illinois Press, 1956.

———. "Southern Reaction to the Proposal of the Fourteenth Amendment," *Journal of Southern History* 22 (1956): 477–97.

Jellison, Charles A. *Fessenden of Maine, Civil War Senator.* Syracuse, NY: Syracuse University Press, 1962.

Johnson, Allen, et al., eds. *Dictionary of American Biography.* 10 double vols. + 9 supplements. New York: Charles Scribner's Sons, 1964–1981.

Bibliography

Johnson, Ludwell H., III. "Abraham Lincoln and the Development of Presidential War-Making Powers: Prize Cases (1863) Revisited," *Civil War History* 35 (1989): 208–24.

———. "The Confederacy: What Was It? The View from the Federal Courts," *Civil War History* 32 (1986): 5–22.

———. "Contraband Trade during the Last Year of the Civil War," *Mississippi Valley Historical Review* 49 (1963): 635–41.

———. "Lincoln and Equal Rights," *Journal of Southern History* 32 (1966): 83–87.

———. "Northern Profit and Profiteers: The Cotton Rings of 1864–1865," *Civil War History* 12 (1966): 101–15.

———. *Red River Campaign: Politics and Cotton in the Civil War.* Baltimore: Johns Hopkins University Press, 1958.

Johnson, Manie White. "The Colfax Riot of April 1873," *Louisiana Historical Quarterly* 13 (1930): 391–427.

Johnston, John D., Jr. "Sex and Property: The Common Law Tradition, the Law School Curriculum, and Developments toward Equality," *New York University Law Review* 47 (1972): 1033–92.

Jones, Howard James. "Images of State Legislative Reconstruction Participants in Fiction," *Journal of Negro History* 67 (1982): 318–27.

Jones, Jacqueline. *Soldiers of Light and Love: Northern Teachers and Georgia Blacks, 1865–1873.* Chapel Hill: University of North Carolina Press, 1980.

Jones, Robert R. "James L. Kemper and the Virginia Redeemers Face the Race Question: A Reconsideration," *Journal of Southern History* 38 (1972): 393–414.

Jordan, David M. *Roscoe Conkling of New York: Voice in the Senate.* Ithaca, NY: Cornell University Press, 1971.

Josephson, Matthew. *The Politicos, 1865–1896.* New York: Harcourt, Brace & World, 1938.

———. *The Robber Barons: The Great American Capitalists.* New York: Harcourt, Brace, 1934.

Julian, George W. *Political Recollections.* Miami, FL: Mnemosgne Press, 1884, 1969 repr.

Kaczorowski, Robert J. *The Nationalization of Civil Rights: Constitutional Theory and Practice in a Racist Society, 1866–1883.* New York: Garland Publishing, 1987.

———. "Searching for the Intent of the Framers of the Fourteenth Amendment," *Connecticut Law Review* 5 (1972–73): 369–98.

———. "To Begin the Nation Anew: Congress, Citizenship and Civil Rights after the Civil War," *American Historical Review* 90 (1987): 45–68.

Keener, Charles V. "Racial Turmoil in Texas, 1865–1874." M.A. thesis, North Texas State University, 1971.

Kelly, Alfred H. "The Congressional Controversy over School Segregation, 1867–1875," *American Historical Review* 64 (1958–1959): 537–63.

Kelly, Alfred H., and Wilfred A. Harbison. *The American Constitution: Its Origins and Development.* 4th ed. New York: W. W. Norton, 1970.

Kendrick, Benjamin B. *The Journal of the Joint Committee of Fifteen on Reconstruction, 39th Congress, 1865–1867.* New York: Columbia University Press, 1914.

Kennedy, John F. *Profiles in Courage.* New York: Harper & Row, 1956.

Kerr, Winfield Scott. *John Sherman: His Life and Public Services.* 2 vols. Boston: Sherman, French & Co., 1906.

Key, V. O., Jr. *Southern Politics in State and Nation.* New York: Alfred A. Knopf, 1949.

Kimball, Philip Clyde. "Freedom's Harvest: Freedmen's Schools in Kentucky after the Civil War," *Filson Club Historical Quarterly* 54 (1980): 272–88.

Kincaid, Larry G. "The Legislative Origins of the Military Reconstruction Act, 1865–1867." Ph.D. dissertation, Johns Hopkins University, 1968.

———. "Victims of Circumstance: An Interpretation of Changing Attitudes toward Republican Policy Makers and Reconstruction," *Journal of American History* 57 (1970): 48–66.

Kirby, Jack Temple. *Darkness at the Dawning: Race and Reform in the Progressive Era*. Philadelphia: J. B. Lippincott, 1972.

———. "D. W. Griffith's Racial Portraiture," *Phylon* 39 (1978): 118–127.

Klement, Frank L. "Midwestern Opposition to Lincoln's Emancipation Policy," *Journal of Negro History* 49 (1964): 169–83.

Klingberg, Frank Wysor, "The Southern Claims Commission: A Postwar Agency in Operation," *Mississippi Valley Historical Review* 32 (1945–1946): 195–214.

Knauss, James O. "Jacob Meritt Howard." In *Dictionary of American Biography*, edited by Allen Johnson et al. New York: Charles Scribner's Sons, 10 double vols. + 9 supplements, 1964–1981, 9: 278–79.

Knox, Thomas W. *Life and Work of Henry Ward Beecher*. Hartford, CT: Hartford Publishing, 1887.

Kolchin, Peter. "Class Consciousness," *Reviews in American History* 20 (1992): 85–90.

———. *First Freedom: The Responses of Alabama's Blacks to Emancipation and Reconstruction*. Westport, CT: Greenwood Press, 1972.

———. "The Myth of Radical Reconstruction," *Reviews in American History* 3 (1975): 228–36.

———. "Race, Class, and Poverty in the Post–Civil War South," *Reviews in American History* 6 (1979): 515–26.

———. "Scalawags, Carpetbaggers, and Reconstruction: A Quantitative Look at Southern Congressional Politics, 1868–1872," *Journal of Southern History* 45 (1979): 63–76.

Korngold, Ralph. *Thaddeus Stevens: A Being Darkly Wise and Rudely Great*. New York: Harcourt, Brace & Co., 1955.

Kousser, J. Morgan. *Dead End: The Development of Nineteenth Century Litigation on Discrimination in Schools*. New York: Oxford University Press, 1985.

———. "Ecological Regression and the Analysis of Past Politics," *Journal of Interdisciplinary History* 4 (1973): 237–62.

———. "Separate But Not Equal: The Supreme Court's First Decision on Racial Discrimination in Schools," *Journal of Southern History* 46 (1980): 17–44.

———. *The Shaping of Southern Politics: Suffrage Restriction and the Establishment of the One Party South, 1880–1910*. New Haven, CT: Yale University Press, 1970.

Krebs, Sylvia. "Will the Freedmen Work? White Alabamians Adjust to Free Black Labor," *Alabama Historical Quarterly* 36 (1974): 151–63.

Krug, Mark M. *Lyman Trumbull: Conservative Radical*. New York: A. S. Barnes, 1965.

———. "On Rewriting of the Story of Reconstruction in the U.S. History Textbooks," *Journal of Negro History* 46 (1961): 133–53.

Kutler, Stanley I. "*Ex Parte McCardle*: Judicial Impotency? The Supreme Court and Reconstruction Reconsidered," *American Historical Review* 72 (1967): 835–51.

———. "Impeachment Reconsidered," *Reviews in American History* 1 (1973): 480–87.

———. *Judicial Power and Reconstruction Politics*. Chicago: University of Chicago Press, 1968.

———. "Reconstruction and the Supreme Court: The Numbers Game Reconsidered," *Journal of Southern History* 32 (1966): 42–58.

Lacy, Alex B., Jr. "The Bill of Rights and the Fourteenth Amendment," *Washington and Lee Law Review* 23 (1966): 37–64.

LaFeber, Walter. *The New Empire: An Interpretation of American Expansion, 1860–1898*. Ithaca, NY: Cornell University Press, 1963.

Lancaster, James L. "The Scalawags of North Carolina, 1850–1868." Ph.D. dissertation, Princeton University, 1974.

Lane, Ann J., ed. *The Debate over Slavery: Stanley Elkins and His Critics*. Urbana: University of Illinois Press, 1971.

Lebsock, Suzanne D. "Radical Reconstruction and the Property Rights of Southern Women," *Journal of Southern History* 43 (1977): 195–215.

Bibliography

Ledbetter, Billy D. "White over Black in Texas: Racial Attitudes in the Antebellum Period," *Phylon* 34 (1973): 406–18.

Lee, Anne S., and Everett S. Lee. "The Health of Slaves and Freedmen: A Savannah Study," *Phylon* 38 (1977): 170–80.

Legan, Marshall S. "Disease and the Freedmen in Mississippi during Reconstruction," *Journal of the History of Medicine and Allied Sciences* 28 (1973): 257–67.

———. "Southern Democrats in the Crisis of 1876–1877: A Reconsideration of *Reunion and Reaction*," *Journal of Southern History* 46 (1980): 489–524.

Lemmons, Sarah M. "Transportation Segregation in the Federal Courts since 1865," *Journal of Negro History* 38 (1953): 174–93.

Lerner, Eugene M. "Money, Prices, and Wages in the Confederacy, 1861–1865." In *The Economic Impact of the American Civil War*, edited by Ralph Andreano. Cambridge, MA: Schenkman Publishing, 1962, 31–60.

———. "Southern Output and Agricultural Income, 1860–1880," *Agricultural History* 33 (1959): 117–25.

Lestage, Oscar H., Jr. "The White League in Louisiana and Its Participation in Reconstruction Riots," *Louisiana Historical Quarterly* 18 (1935): 617–95.

Lewinson, Paul. *Race, Class, and Party: A History of Negro Suffrage and White Politics in the South*. New York: Grosset & Dunlap, 1965.

Lewis, Alfred Henry. *Richard Croker*. New York: Life Publishing Company, 1901.

Lewis, Elsie M. "The Political Mind of the Negro, 1865–1900," *Journal of Southern History* 21 (1955): 189–202.

Lewis, Lloyd. *Captain Sam Grant*. Boston: Little, Brown, 1950.

Lien, Arnold J. *Concurring Opinion: The Privileges and Immunity Clause of the Fourteenth Amendment*. St. Louis: Washington University Press, 1957.

Linden, Glenn M. *Politics or Principle: Congressional Voting on the Civil War Amendments and Pro–Negro Measures, 1838–1869*. Seattle: University of Washington Press, 1976.

———. "'Radicals' and Economic Policies: The Senate, 1862–1873," *Journal of Southern History* 32 (1966): 189–99.

Lindsay, Arnett G. "The Negro in Banking," *Journal of Negro History* 14 (1929): 156–201.

Lindsey, David. *Americans in Conflict: The Civil War and Reconstruction*. Boston: Houghton Mifflin, 1974.

Link, Arthur S., and Rembert W. Patrick, eds. *Writing Southern History: Essays in Historiography in Honor of Fletcher M. Green*. Baton Rouge: Louisiana State University Press, 1965.

Linn, William Alexander. *Horace Greeley: Founder of the New York Tribune*. Indianapolis: Bobbs-Merrill, 1926.

Little, Monroe H. "Making a Way out of No Way," *Reviews in American History* 5 (1977): 524–28.

Litwack, Leon F. *Been in the Storm So Long: The Aftermath of Slavery*. New York: Alfred A. Knopf, 1979.

———. *North of Slavery: The Negro in the Free States, 1790–1860*. Chicago: University of Chicago Press, 1961.

Lochhead, Carolyn. "The Yoke of Preferential Politics," *Insight on the News* 6 (June 25, 1990): 22–24.

Lockett, James D. "Abraham Lincoln and Colonization: An Episode That Ends in Tragedy at L'Isle à Vache, Haiti, 1863–1864," *Journal of Black Studies* 21 (1991): 428–44.

Logan, Frenise A. *The Negro in North Carolina, 1876–1894*. Chapel Hill: University of North Carolina Press, 1964.

Logan, Rayford W. *The Betrayal of the Negro: From Rutherford B. Hayes to Woodrow Wilson*. New York: Collier Books, 1965.

Logsdon, Joseph. "Black Reconstruction Revisited," *Reviews in American History* 1 (1973): 553–58.

Lomask, Milton. *Andrew Johnson: President on Trial.* New York: Farrar, Straus & Cudahy, 1960.

Longstreet, Helen D. *Lee and Longstreet at High Tide.* Gainesville, GA: Helen D. Longstreet, 1904.

Longstreet, James. *From Manassas to Appomattox: Memoirs of the Civil War in America.* Philadelphia: J. B. Lippincott, 1896.

Lonn, Ella. *Reconstruction in Louisiana after 1868.* New York: George Putnam's Sons, 1918.

Lovett, Bobby L. "Memphis Riots: White Reactions to Blacks in Memphis, May 1865–July 1866," *Tennessee Historical Quarterly* 38 (1979): 9–33.

Low, W. Augustus. "The Freedmen's Bureau and Civil Rights in Maryland," *Journal of Negro History* 37 (1952): 221–47.

———. "The Freedmen's Bureau in the Border States." In *Radicalism, Racism, and Party Alignment: The Border States during Reconstruction,* edited by Richard O. Curry. Baltimore: Johns Hopkins Press, 1969, 245–64.

Low, W. Augustus, and Virgil A. Clift. *Encyclopedia of Black America.* New York: McGraw-Hill, 1981.

Lowe, Richard G. "The Joint Committee on Reconstruction: Some Clarifications," *Southern Studies,* n.s., 3 (1992): 55–66.

———. "Republicans, Rebellion, and Reconstruction: The Republican Party in Virginia, 1856–1870." Ph.D. dissertation, University of Virginia, 1968.

Lucie, Patricia M. L. "Confiscation: Constitutional Crossroads," *Civil War History* 23 (1977): 307–21.

Lunde, Erik S. *Horace Greeley.* Boston: Twayne, 1981.

Lynch, John R. *The Facts of Reconstruction.* New York: Neale Publishing, 1913.

———. *Reminiscences of an Active Life: The Autobiography of John Roy Lynch.* Edited by John Hope Franklin. Chicago: University of Chicago Press, 1970.

———. "Some Historical Errors of James Ford Rhodes," *Journal of Negro History* 2 (1917): 345–67.

———. *Some Historical Errors of James Ford Rhodes.* Boston: Cornhill Publishing, 1922.

Lynd, Staughton. "Rethinking Slavery and Reconstruction," *Journal of Negro History* 50 (1965): 198–209.

Mabry, William Alexander. "Disfranchisement of the Negro in Mississippi," *Journal of Southern History* 4 (1938): 318–33.

MacDonald, William. "Schuyler Colfax." In *Dictionary of American Biography,* edited by Allen Johnson et al. New York: Charles Scribner's Sons, 10 double vols. + 9 supplements, 1964–1981, 4: 297–98.

———. "Zachariah Chandler." In *Dictionary of American Biography,* edited by Allen Johnson et al. New York: Charles Scribner's Sons, 10 double vols. + 9 supplements, 1964–1981, 3: 618.

Maddex, Jack P., Jr. *The Virginia Conservatives.* Chapel Hill: University of North Carolina Press, 1970.

———. "Virginia: The Persistence of Centrist Hegemony." In *Reconstruction and Redemption in the South,* edited by Otto H. Olsen. Baton Rouge: Louisiana State University Press, 1980, 113–55.

Magdol, Edward. *A Right to the Land: Essays on the Freedmen's Community.* Westport, CT: Greenwood Press, 1977.

———. "Local Black Leaders in the South, 1867–1875: An Essay toward the Reconstruction of Reconstruction History," *Societas* 4 (1974): 81–110.

Main, Jackson Turner. *The Anti-Federalists: Critics of the Constitution, 1781–1788.* Chicago: Quadrangle Books, 1964.

———. *The Sovereign States, 1775–1783.* New York: New Viewpoints, 1973.

Maizlish, Stephen E. "A Look inside the Carpetbag," *Reviews in American History* 17 (1989): 79–84.

Bibliography

Majeske, Penelope K. "Virginia after Appomattox: The United States Army and the Formation of Presidential Reconstruction Policy," *West Virginia History* 43 (1982): 95–117.

Mallin, William D. "Lincoln and the Conservatives," *Journal of Southern History* 28 (1962): 31–45.

Mandelbaum, Seymour J. *Boss Tweed's New York*. New York: John Wiley & Sons, 1965.

Mandle, Jay R. *The Roots of Black Poverty: The Southern Plantation Economy after the Civil War*. Durham, NC: Duke University Press, 1978.

Mann, Kenneth Eugene. "Blanche Kelso Bruce: United States Senator without a Constituency," *Journal of Mississippi History* 38 (1976): 183–98.

Mantell, Martin E. *Johnson, Grant, and the Politics of Reconstruction*. New York: Columbia University Press, 1973.

Maslowski, Peter. "'*Treason Must Be Made Odious*': Military Occupation and Reconstruction in Nashville, Tennessee, 1862–1865." Ph.D. dissertation, Ohio State University, 1972.

Mathews, John M. *Legislative and Judicial History of the Fifteenth Amendment*. Baltimore: Johns Hopkins University Press, 1909.

Matthews, Clifford. "Special Military Tribunals, 1775–1865." M.A. thesis, Emory University, 1951.

May, Henry Farnham. *Protestant Churches and Industrial America*. New York: Harper & Brothers, 1949.

May, J. Thomas. "Continuity and Change in the Labor Program of the Union Army and the Freedmen's Bureau," *Civil War History* 17 (1971): 245–54.

———. "Medical Care of Blacks in Louisiana during Occupation and Reconstruction, 1862–1868: Its Social and Political Background." Ph.D. dissertation, Tulane University, 1970.

———. "A Nineteenth Century Medical Care Program for Blacks: The Case of the Freedmen's Bureau," *Anthropological Quarterly* 46 (1973): 160–71.

Mayer, George H. *The Republican Party, 1854–1866*. 2d ed. New York: Oxford University Press, 1967.

McCall, Samuel W. *Thaddeus Stevens*. Boston: Houghton Mifflin, 1899.

McCormick, Richard P. *The Second American Party System: Party Formation in the Jacksonian Era*. Chapel Hill: University of North Carolina Press, 1966.

McCormick, Thomas D. "John Armor Bingham." In *Dictionary of American Biography*, edited by Allen Johnson et al. New York: Charles Scribner's Sons, 10 double vols. + 9 supplements, 1964–1981, 2: 277–78.

McCrary, Peyton. *Abraham Lincoln and Reconstruction: The Louisiana Experiment*. Princeton, NJ: Princeton University Press, 1978.

———. "The Political Dynamics of Black Reconstruction," *Reviews in American History* 12 (1984): 51–58, especially 57–58.

McCurdy, Charles W. "Legal Institutions, Constitutional Theory, and the Tragedy of Reconstruction," *Reviews in American History* 4 (1976): 203–11.

McDonald, Forrest. "Woodward's Strange Career," *National Review* 41 (27 October 1989): 46–47.

McDonald, Forrest, and Grady McWhiney. "The South from Self-Sufficiency to Peonage: An Interpretation," *American Historical Review* 85 (1980): 1095–1118.

McDonald, John. *Secrets of the Great Whiskey Ring*. St. Louis: W. S. Bryan, 1880.

McDonough, James L. "John Schofield as Military Director of Reconstruction in Virginia," *Civil War History* 15 (1969): 237–56.

McFarland, Gerald W. "Another Perspective on the Compromise of 1877," *Reviews in American History* 2 (1974): 257–61.

McFarlin, Annjeannette Sophia. *Black Congressional Reconstruction Orators and Their Orations*. Metuchen, NJ: Scarecrow Press, 1976.

McFeely, William S. *Frederick Douglass*. New York: W. W. Norton, 1991.

———. *Grant: A Biography*. New York: W. W. Norton, 1981.

———. *Yankee Stepfather: General O. O. Howard and the Freedmen*. New Haven, CT: Yale University Press, 1968.

McGinty, Garnie W. *Louisiana Redeemed: The Overthrow of Carpet-bag Rule, 1876–1880*. New Orleans: Tulane University Press, 1941.

McGrath, C. Peter. *Morrison R. Waite: The Triumph of Character*. New York: Macmillan, 1963.

McKelvey, Blake. "Penal Slavery and Southern Reconstruction," *Journal of Negro History* 20 (1963): 153–79.

McKenzie, Robert H. "The Shelby Iron Company: A Note on Slave Personality after the Civil War," *Journal of Negro History* 58 (1973): 341–48.

McKitrick, Eric. *Andrew Johnson and Reconstruction*. Chicago: University of Chicago Press, 1960.

McLoughlin, William G. *The Meaning of Henry Ward Beecher*. New York: Alfred A. Knopf, 1970

McMillan, Neil R. *Dark Journey: Black Mississippians in the Age of Jim Crow*. Urbana: University of Illinois Press, 1989.

McPherson, James M. *The Abolitionist Legacy: From Reconstruction to the NAACP*. Princeton, NJ: Princeton University Press, 1975.

———. "Abolitionists and the Civil Rights Act of 1875," *Journal of American History* 52 (1965): 493–510.

———. *Abraham Lincoln and the Second American Revolution*. New York: Oxford University Press, 1990.

———. "Antebellum Southern Exceptionalism: A New Look at an Old Question," *Civil War History* 29 (1983): 230–44.

———. "Grant or Greeley? The Abolitionist Dilemma in the Election of 1872," *American Historical Review* 71 (1965–1966): 43–61.

———. "The Hidden Freedmen: Five Myths in the Reconstruction Era." In *The Black Experience in America: Selected Essays*, edited by James C. Curtis and Lewis L. Gould. Austin: University of Texas Press, 1970, 68–86.

———. "Redemption or Counterrevolution? The South in the 1870s," *Reviews in American History* 13 (1985): 545–50.

———. *The Struggle for Equality: Abolitionists and the Negro in the Civil War and Reconstruction*. Princeton, NJ: Princeton University Press, 1964.

———. "White Liberals and Black Power in Negro Education, 1865–1915," *American Historical Review* 75 (1970): 1357–86.

Mechelke, Eugene R. "Some Observations on Mississippi's Reconstruction Historiography," *Journal of Mississippi History* 33 (1971): 21–38.

Mecklin, John W. "The Black Codes," *South Atlantic Quarterly* 16 (1917): 248–59.

Meek, Clarence I., III. "Illegal Law Enforcement: Aiding Civil Authorities in Violation of the Posse Comitatus Act," *Military Law Review* 70 (1975): 83–126.

Meier, August. "Booker T. Washington and the Rise of the NAACP," *The Crisis* 61 (February 1954): 69–76, 117–123.

———. "Negroes in the First and Second Reconstructions of the South," *Civil War History* 13 (1967): 114–30.

———. *Negro Thought in America, 1880–1915*. Ann Arbor: University of Michigan Press, 1966.

Mendelson, Wallace. "A Note on the Cause and Cure of the Fourteenth Amendment," *Journal of Politics* 43 (1981): 152–58.

Meneely, A. Howard. "Benjamin Franklin Wade." In *Dictionary of American Biography*, edited by Allen Johnson et al. New York: Charles Scribner's Sons, 10 double vols. + 9 supplements, 1964–1981, 19: 303–305.

———. "Edwin McMasters Stanton." In *Dictionary of American Biography*, edited by Allen Johnson et al. New York: Charles Scribner's Sons, 10 double vols. + 9 supplements, 1964–1981, 17: 517–21.

Bibliography

Mering, John Vollmer. "Persistent Whiggery in the Confederate South: A Reconsideration," *South Atlantic Quarterly* 69 (1970–1971): 124–34.

Messner, William F. "Black Education in Louisiana, 1863–1865," *Civil War History* 22 (1976): 41–59.

———. "Black Violence and White Response: Louisiana, 1862," *Journal of Southern History* 41 (1975): 19–38.

———. "The Federal Army and Blacks in the Gulf Department." Ph.D. dissertation, University of Wisconsin, 1972.

———. *Freedmen and the Ideology of Free Labor: Louisiana, 1862–1865.* Lafayette: Center for Louisiana Studies, 1978.

Miller, Perry. *The New England Mind: From Colony to Province.* Cambridge, MA: Harvard University Press, 1952.

———. "The Religious Impulse in the Founding of Virginia: Religion and Society in the Early Literature," *William and Mary Quarterly*, 3d series, 5 (1948): 492–522.

Milton, George F. *The Age of Hate: Andrew Johnson and the Radicals.* New York: Howard-McCann, 1930.

Mitgang, Herbert. "Was Lincoln Just a Honkie?" *New York Times Magazine*, 11 February 1968, 34–35, 100–107.

Mohr, Clarence L. *On the Threshold of Freedom: Masters and Slaves in Civil War Georgia.* Athens: University of Georgia Press, 1986.

———. "Southern Blacks in the Civil War: A Century of Historiography," *Journal of Negro History* 59 (1974): 177–85.

Mohr, James C., ed. *Radical Republicans in the North: State Politics during Reconstruction.* Baltimore: Johns Hopkins University Press, 1976.

———. *The Radical Republicans and Reform in New York during Reconstruction.* Ithaca, NY: Cornell University Press, 1973.

Moneyhon, Carl. "George T. Ruby and the Politics of Expediency in Texas." In *Southern Black Leaders of the Reconstruction Era*, edited by Howard N. Rabinowitz. Urbana: University of Illinois Press, 1982, 363–92.

———. *Republicanism in Reconstruction Texas.* Austin: University of Texas Press, 1980.

Moore, A. B. "One Hundred Years of Reconstruction of the South," *Journal of Southern History* 9 (1943): 153–80.

Moore, James T. "Black Militancy in Readjuster Virginia, 1879–1883," *Journal of Southern History* 41 (1975): 167–86.

Moore, Richard. "Radical Reconstruction: The Texas Choice," *East Texas Historical Journal* 16 (1978): 15–23.

Moore, Wilton P. "The Provost Marshal Goes to War," *Civil War History* 5 (1959): 62–71.

———. "Union Provost Marshals in the Eastern Theater," *Military Affairs* 26 (1962): 120–21.

Moran, Robert E. "The Negro Dependent Child in Louisiana, 1800–1935," *Social Service Review* 45 (1971): 53–61.

Morgan, Albert T. *Yazoo; or, On the Picket Line of Freedom in the South.* New York: Russell & Russell, 1968 [1884].

Morgan, H. Wayne. *From Hayes to McKinley: National Party Politics, 1877–1896.* Syracuse, NY: Syracuse University Press, 1968.

Morrill, George P. "The Best White Friend Black Americans Ever Had," *Reader's Digest* 99 (July 1971): 169–74.

Morris, Robert C. *Reading, 'Riting, and Reconstruction.* Chicago: University of Chicago Press, 1981.

Morris, Thomas D. "Equality, 'Extraordinary Law,' and Criminal Justice: The South Carolina Experience, 1865–1866," *South Carolina Historical Magazine* 83 (1982): 15–33.

Morrison, Stanley. "The Fourteenth Amendment Challenged," *Georgetown Law Journal* 36 (1948): 398–411.

Muller, Philip D. "Look Back without Anger: A Reappraisal of William A. Dunning," *Journal of American History* 61 (1974): 325–38.

Muraskin, William A. "The Social–Control Theory in American History: A Critique," *Journal of Social History* 9 (1976): 559–69.

Murphy, L. E. "The Civil Rights Law of 1875," *Journal of Negro History* 12 (1927): 110–27.

Murray, Pauline. *Proud Shoes: The Story of an American Family.* New York: Harper & Row, 1956.

Muzzey, David S. *James G. Blaine: A Political Idol of Other Days.* New York: Dodd, Mead, 1934.

Myrdal, Gunnar. *An American Dilemma.* 2 vols. New ed. New York: McGraw-Hill, 1964.

Nathan, Hans. *Dan Emmett and the Rise of Early Negro Minstrelsy.* Norman: University of Oklahoma Press, 1962.

Nathans, Elizabeth Studley. *Losing the Peace: Georgia Republicans and Reconstruction.* Baton Rouge: Louisiana State University Press, 1968.

Neely, Mark E., Jr. "Abraham Lincoln and Black Colonization: Benjamin Butler's Spurious Testimony," *Civil War History* 25 (1979): 77–83.

Nevins, Allan. *Hamilton Fish: The Inner History of the Grant Administration.* 2 vols. New York: Dodd, Mead, 1936.

———. "Horace Greeley." In *Dictionary of American Biography*, edited by Allen Johnson et al. New York: Charles Scribner's Sons, 10 double vols. + 9 supplements, 1964–1981, 7: 528–34.

———. *The Origins of the Land-grant Colleges and Universities: A Brief Account of the Morrill Act of 1862 and Its Results.* Washington, DC: Civil War Centennial Commission, 1962.

———. "Rutherford Birchard Hayes." In *Dictionary of American Biography*, edited by Allen Johnson et al. New York: Charles Scribner's Sons, 10 double vols. + 9 supplements, 1964–1981, 8: 446–51.

———. "Thaddeus Stevens." In *Dictionary of American Biography*, edited by Allen Johnson et al. New York: Charles Scribner's Sons, 10 double vols. + 9 supplements, 1964–1981, 17: 620–25.

———. *The War for the Union.* 4 vols. New York: Charles Scribner's Sons, 1959–1971.

Newby, I. A. "Historians and Negroes," *Journal of Negro History* 54 (1969): 34–47.

Newby, Robert G., and David B. Tyack. "Victims without Crimes: Some Historical Perspectives on Black Education," *Journal of Negro Education* 40 (1971): 192–206.

Nichols, Jeannette P. "John Sherman." In *Dictionary of American Biography*, edited by Allen Johnson et al. New York: Charles Scribner's Sons, 10 double vols. + 9 supplements, 1964–1981, 17: 84–88.

Nichols, Roy Franklin. "United States vs. Jefferson Davis," *American Historical Review* 31 (1925–1926): 266–84.

Nieman, Donald G. "Andrew Johnson, the Freedmen's Bureau, and the Problem of Equal Rights, 1865–1866," *Journal of Southern History* 44 (1978): 399–420.

———, ed. *Black Freedom/White Violence, 1865–1900.* New York: Garland Publishing, 1994.

———. "Black Political Power and Criminal Justice: Washington County, Texas, 1868–1884," *Journal of Southern History* 55 (1983): 391–420.

———. "The Freedmen's Bureau and the Mississippi Black Code," *Journal of Mississippi History* 40 (1978): 91–118.

———. *To Set the Law in Motion: The Freedmen's Bureau and the Legal Rights of Blacks, 1865–1868.* Millwood, NY: Kraus International, 1979.

Nolan, Claude H. *The Negro's Image in the South: The Anatomy of White Supremacy.* Lexington: University of Kentucky Press, 1967.

North, Douglass C. *Economic Growth of the United States, 1790–1860.* Englewood Cliffs, NJ: Prentice-Hall, 1960.

Notaro, Carmen Anthony. "History of the Biographic Treatment of Andrew Johnson in the Twentieth Century," *Tennessee Historical Quarterly* 24 (1965): 143–55.

Novak, Daniel A. *The Wheel of Servitude: Black Forced Labor after Slavery.* Lexington: University of Kentucky Press, 1978.

Nugent, Walter T. K. *The Money Question during Reconstruction.* New York: W. W. Norton, 1967.

Bibliography

Nunn, W. C. *Escape from Reconstruction.* Fort Worth: Texas Christian University Press, 1962.

———. *Texas under the Carpetbaggers.* Austin: University of Texas Press, 1962.

Oakes, James. "A Failure of Vision: The Collapse of Freedmen's Bureau Courts," *Civil War History* 25 (1979): 66–76.

Oates, Stephen B. *Abraham Lincoln: The Man behind the Myths.* New York: Harper & Row, 1984.

———. *With Malice toward None: The Life of Abraham Lincoln.* New York: Harper & Row, 1977.

O'Brien, John T. "Reconstruction in Richmond: White Restoration and Black Protest, April–June 1865," *Virginia Magazine of History and Biography* 89 (1981): 259–81.

O'Brien, Michael. "C. Vann Woodward and the Burden of Southern Liberalism," *American Historical Review* 78 (1973–1974): 589–604.

O'Connor, Richard. *Sheridan the Invincible.* Indianapolis: Bobbs-Merrill, 1953.

Olds, Victoria Marcus. "The Freedmen's Bureau as a Social Agency." Ph.D. dissertation, Columbia University, 1966.

Olenick, Monte M. "Albion W. Tourgée: Radical Republican Spokesman of the Civil War Crusade," *Phylon* 23 (1962): 332–45.

Olsen, Otto H. "Abraham Lincoln as Revolutionary," *Civil War History* 24 (1978): 213–24.

———. *Carpetbagger's Crusade: The Life of Albion W. Tourgée.* Baltimore: Johns Hopkins University Press, 1965.

———. "The Ku Klux Klan: A Study in Reconstruction Politics and Propaganda," *North Carolina Historical Quarterly* 39 (1962): 340–62.

———. "North Carolina: An Incongruous Presence." In *Reconstruction and Redemption in the South,* edited by Otto H. Olsen. Baton Rouge: Louisiana State University Press, 1980, 156–201.

———. "Reconsidering the Scalawags," *Civil War History* 12 (1966): 304–20.

———. "Southern Reconstruction and the Question of Self-Determination." In *A Nation Divided: Problems and Issues of the Civil War and Reconstruction,* edited by George M. Frederickson. Minneapolis: Burgess Publishing, 1975, 113–14.

———, ed. *Reconstruction and Redemption in the South.* Baton Rouge: Louisiana State University Press, 1980.

Olsen, Otto H., ed. *The Thin Disguise: Turning Point in Negro History—Plessy v. Ferguson, a Documentary Presentation, 1864–1896.* New York: Humanities Press, 1967.

Osofsky, Gilbert. "Cardboard Yankee: How Not To Study the Mind of Charles Sumner," *Reviews in American History* 1 (1973): 595–605.

Osterweis, Rollin G. *The Myth of the Lost Cause, 1865–1900.* Hamden, CT: Archon Books, 1973.

Osthaus, Carl L. *Freedmen, Philanthropy, and Fraud: A History of the Freedmen's Savings Bank.* Urbana: University of Illinois Press, 1976.

Oubre, Claude F. *Forty Acres and a Mule: The Freedmen's Bureau and Black Land Ownership.* Baton Rouge: Louisiana State University Press, 1978.

Overy, David H., Jr. "The Wisconsin Carpetbagger: A Group Portrait," *Wisconsin Magazine of History* 44 (1960): 15–49.

Owen, James L. "The Negro in Georgia during Reconstruction, 1864–1872: A Social History." Ph.D. dissertation, University of Georgia, 1975.

Owens, Susie Lee. *The Union League of America: Political Activities in Tennessee, the Carolinas, and Virginia.* Ann Arbor: University of Michigan Press, 1947.

Painter, Nell Irvin. *Exodusters: Black Migration to Kansas after Reconstruction.* New York: Alfred A. Knopf, 1976.

Paludan, Phillip S. "The American Civil War: Triumph through Tragedy," *Civil War History* 20 (1974): 239–50.

———. *A Covenant with Death: The Constitution, Law, and Equality in the Civil War Era.* Urbana: University of Illinois Press, 1975.

———. *The Presidency of Abraham Lincoln.* Lawrence: University Press of Kansas, 1994.

Parks, Joseph H. "A Confederate Trade Center under Federal Occupation: Memphis, 1862 to 1865," *Journal of Southern History* 7 (1941): 289–314.

———. *Joseph E. Brown of Georgia.* Baton Rouge: Louisiana State University Press, 1977.

Parmet, Robert D. "Schools for the Freedmen," *Negro History Bulletin* 34 (1971): 128–32.

Parrington, V. L. *The Main Currents in American Thought.* 3 vols. New York: Harcourt, Brace, 1927–1930.

Parrish, William E., ed. *The Civil War: A Second American Revolution?* New York: Holt, Rinehart & Winston, 1970.

Patrick, Rembert W. *The Reconstruction of the Nation.* New York: Oxford University Press, 1967.

Patton, James Welch. *Unionism and Reconstruction in Tennessee, 1860–1869.* Chapel Hill: University of North Carolina Press, 1934.

Paxon, Frederic L. "James Abram Garfield." In *Dictionary of American Biography*, edited by Allen Johnson et al. New York: Charles Scribner's Sons, 10 double vols. + 9 supplements, 1964–1981, 7: 145–50.

———. "Roscoe Conkling." In *Dictionary of American Biography*, edited by Allen Johnson et al. New York: Charles Scribner's Sons, 10 double vols. + 9 supplements, 1964–1981, 4: 346–47.

Payne, Walter A. "Lincoln's Caribbean Colonization Plan," *Pacific Historian* 7 (1963): 65–72.

Pearce, Haywood J., Jr. "Longstreet's Responsibility on the Second Day at Gettysburg," *Georgia Historical Quarterly* 10 (1926): 26–45.

Pearce, Larry W. "The American Missionary Association and the Freedmen's Bureau in Arkansas, 1868–1878," *Arkansas Historical Quarterly* 30 (1971): 123–44; 31 (1972): 246–61.

Pease, Jane H., and William H. Pease. *They Who Would Be Free: Blacks' Search for Freedom.* New York: Atheneum, 1974.

Pease, William H. "Three Years among the Freedmen: William C. Gannett and the Port Royal Experiment," *Journal of Negro History* 42 (1957): 98–117.

Peek, Ralph L. "Lawlessness in Florida, 1868–1871," *Florida Historical Quarterly* 40 (1961–62): 164–85.

———. "Military Reconstruction and the Growth of Anti-Negro Sentiment in Florida, 1867," *Florida Historical Quarterly* 47 (1968–69): 380–400.

Pereyra, Lillian A. *James Lusk Alcorn: Persistent Whig.* Baton Rouge: Louisiana State University, 1966.

Perkins, Archie E. "Oscar James Dunn," *Phylon* 4 (1943): 105–21.

Perman, Michael. "Eric Foner's Reconstruction: A Finished Revolution," *Reviews in American History* 17 (1989): 73–78.

———. *Reunion without Compromise: The South and Reconstruction, 1865–1868.* New York: Cambridge University Press, 1973.

———. *The Road to Redemption: Southern Politics, 1869–1879.* Chapel Hill: University of North Carolina Press, 1984.

Perry, Ralph Barton. *Puritanism and Democracy.* New York: Vanguard Press, 1944.

Peskin, Allan. *Garfield: A Biography.* Kent, Ohio: Kent State University Press, 1978.

———. "Was There a Compromise in 1877?" *Journal of American History* 60 (1973): 63–75.

Pessen, Edward. "How Different from Each Other Were the Antebellum North and South?" *American Historical Review* 85 (1980): 1119–49.

Bibliography

Pfanz, Harry W. "The Surrender Negotiations between General Johnston and General Sherman, April 1865," *Military Affairs* 16 (1952): 61–70.

Phillips, Paul D. "White Reaction to the Freedmen's Bureau in Tennessee," *Tennessee Historical Quarterly* 25 (1966): 50–62.

Phillips, Ulrich B. *American Negro Slavery*. New York: D. Appleton, 1918.

———. "The Central Theme of Southern History," *American Historical Review* 34 (1928–29): 30–43.

———. *Life and Labor in the Old South*. Boston: Little, Brown, 1930.

Pickens, Donald K. "The Republican Synthesis and Thaddeus Stevens," *Civil War History* 31 (1985): 57–73.

Pierce, Paul Skeels. *The Freedmen's Bureau: A Chapter in the History of Reconstruction*. Iowa City: State University of Iowa Press, 1904.

Pierson, William Wately. "Texas *Versus* White," *Southwestern Historical Quarterly* 18 (1914–15): 341–67; 19 (1915–16): 1–36, 142–58.

Piston, William G. *Lee's Tarnished Lieutenant: James Longstreet and His Place in Southern History*. Athens: University of Georgia Press, 1987.

Pitre, Merline. "The Evolution of Black Political Participation in Reconstruction Texas," *East Texas Historical Journal* 26 (No. 1, 1988): 36–45.

———. "The Party Loyalist." In *Through Many Dangers, Toils, and Snares: The Black Leadership of Texas, 1868-1900*, by Merline Pitre. Austin, TX: Eakin Press, 1985.

———. *Through Many Dangers, Toils, and Snares: The Black Leadership of Texas, 1868-1900*. Austin, TX: Eakin Press, 1985.

Plesur, Milton. *America's Outward Thrust: Approaches to Foreign Affairs, 1865–1890*. DeKalb: Northern Illinois University Press, 1971.

Polakoff, Keith Ian. *The Politics of Inertia: The Election of 1876 and the End of Reconstruction*. Baton Rouge: Louisiana State University Press, 1973.

Pomerantz, Sidney I. "Election of 1876." In *History of American Presidential Elections, 1789–1968*, edited by Arthur M. Schlesinger, Jr., and Fred L. Israel. 4 vols. New York: Chelsea House, 1971, 2: 1379–1435.

Potter, David. "Explicit Data and Implicit Assumptions in Historical Study." In *Generalizations in Writing History: A Report of the Committee on Historical Analysis of the Social Science Research Council*, edited by Louis Gottschalk. Chicago: University of Chicago Press, 1963, 184–85.

———. "Jefferson Davis and the Political Factors of Confederate Defeat." In *Why the North Won the Civil War*, edited by David Donald. Baton Rouge: Louisiana State University Press, 1960, 91–114.

———. *The South and the Concurrent Majority*. Edited by Don E. Fehrenbacher and Carl N. Degler. Baton Rouge: Louisiana State University Press, 1972.

Powell, Lawrence N. *New Masters: Northern Planters in the Civil War and Reconstruction*. New Haven, CT: Yale University Press, 1980.

———. "The Politics of Livelihood: Carpetbaggers in the Deep South." In *Region, Race, and Reconstruction: Essays in Honor of C. Vann Woodward*, edited by J. Morgan Lousser and James M. McPherson. New York: Oxford University Press, 1982, 315–47.

Pratt, Fletcher. *Stanton: Lincoln's Secretary of War*. Westport, CT: Greenwood Press, 1953, reprint 1970.

Pressley, Thomas J. *Americans Interpret Their Civil War*. New York: Free Press, 1965.

———. "Racial Attitudes, Scholarship, and Reconstruction: A Review History," *Journal of Southern History* 32 (1966): 88–93.

Prickett, Robert C. "The Malfeasance of William Worth Belknap, Secretary of War, October 13, 1869, to March 2, 1876," *North Dakota History* 17 (1950): 5–51.

Proctor, Samuel. "Yankee 'Schoolmarms' in Post-war Florida," *Journal of Negro History* 44 (1959): 275–77.

Quarles, Benjamin. "The Abduction of the Planter," *Civil War History* 4 (1958): 5–10.

———. *Frederick Douglass*. Washington, DC: Associated Publishers, 1948.

———. "Frederick Douglass: Challenge and Response." In *Encyclopedia of Black America*, edited by W. Augustus and Virgil A. Clift. New York: McGraw-Hill, 1981, 319–25.

———. *Lincoln and the Negro*. New York: Oxford University Press, 1962.

———. *The Negro in the Civil War*. Boston: Little, Brown, 1953.

Rabel, George C. "Bourbonism, Reconstruction, and the Persistence of Southern Distinctiveness," *Civil War History* 29 (1983): 135–53.

———. *But There Was No Peace: The Role of Violence in the Politics of Reconstruction*. Athens: University of Georgia Press, 1984.

———. "Republican Albatross: The Louisiana Question, National Politics, and the Failure of Reconstruction," *Louisiana History* 23 (1982): 109–30.

———. "Southern Interests and the Election of 1876: A Reappraisal," *Civil War History* 26 (1980): 347–61.

Rabinowitz, Howard N. "From Exclusion to Segregation: Health and Welfare Services for Southern Blacks, 1865–1890," *Social Service Review* 48 (1974): 327–54.

———. "From Exclusion to Segregation: Southern Race Relations, 1865–1890," *Journal of American History* 325–50.

———. "Half a Loaf: The Shift from White to Black Teachers in the Negro Schools of the Urban South, 1865–1890," *Journal of Southern History* 40 (1974): 565–94.

———, ed. *Southern Black Leaders of the Reconstruction Era*. Urbana: University of Illinois Press, 1982.

Rabkin, Peggy. "The Origins of Law Reform: The Social Significance of the Nineteenth-Century Codification Movement and Its Contribution to the Passage of the Early Woman's Property Acts," *Buffalo Law Review* 24 (1975): 683–760.

Ramsdell, Charles W. *Reconstruction in Texas*. New York: Columbia University Press, 1910.

Randall, James G. *The Civil War and Reconstruction*. Boston: D. C. Heath, 1937.

———. *The Confiscation of Property during the Civil War*. Indianapolis: Bobbs-Merrill, 1913.

———. *Constitutional Problems under Lincoln*. Rev. ed. Urbana: University of Illinois Press, 1964.

———. "John Sherman and Reconstruction," *Mississippi Valley Historical Review* 19 (1932–1933): 382–93.

———. *Lincoln the President*. 4 vols. New York: Dodd, Mead, 1945–1955.

Randall, James G., and David Donald. *The Civil War and Reconstruction*. 2d ed. Boston: D. C. Heath, 1961.

Randall, Ruth Painter, *Mary Lincoln: Biography of a Marriage*. Boston: Little, Brown, 1953.

Rankin, David C. "The Impact of the Civil War on the Free Colored Community of New Orleans," *Perspectives in History* II (1977–1978): 377–416.

———. "The Origins of Black Leadership in New Orleans during Reconstruction," *Journal of Southern History* 40 (1974): 417–40.

———. "The Tannenbaum Thesis Reconsidered: Slavery and Race Relations in Antebellum Louisiana," *Southern Studies* 18 (1979): 5–31.

Ransom, Roger L., and Richard Sutch. *One Kind of Freedom: The Economic Consequences of Emancipation*. Cambridge: Cambridge University Press, 1977.

Raper, Horace W. *William W. Holden: North Carolina's Political Enigma*. Chapel Hill: University of North Carolina Press, 1985.

Raphael, Alan. "Health and Social Welfare of Kentucky Black People, 1865–1870," *Societas* 2 (1972): 143–57.

Rawley, James A. "The General Amnesty Act of 1872: A Note," *Mississippi Valley Historical Review* 47 (1960): 480–84.

Reddick, Lawrence J. "Racial Attitudes in American History Textbooks of the South," *Mississippi Valley Historical Review* 19 (1934): 225–65.

Bibliography

Reid, George W. "Four in Black: North Carolina's Black Congressmen, 1874–1901," *Journal of Negro History* 64 (1979): 229–43.

Reid, John Philip. *In Defiance of the Law.* Chapel Hill: University of North Carolina Press, 1981.

Reid, Joseph D., Jr. "Sharecropping as an Understandable Market Response—The Postbellum South," *Journal of Economic History* 33 (1973): 106–30.

———. "White Land, Black Labor, and Agricultural Stagnation: The Causes and Effects of Sharecropping in the Postbellum South," *Explorations in Economic History* 16 (1979): 31–55.

Reynolds, Donald E. "The New Orleans Riot of 1866, Reconsidered," *Louisiana History* 5 (1964): 5–27.

Reynolds, John S. *Reconstruction in South Carolina.* Columbia: University of South Carolina Press, 1905.

Rhodes, James Ford. *History of the United States from the Compromise of 1850 to the Final Restoration of Home Rule at the South in 1877.* 7 vols. New York: Macmillan, 1896–1906.

Rice, Lawrence D. *Negroes in Texas, 1874–1900.* Baton Rouge: Louisiana State University Press, 1971.

Rice, Paul Jackson. "New Laws and Insights Encircle the Posse Comitatus Act," *Military Law Review* 104 (1984): 109–38.

Richardson, Joe M. "An Evaluation of the Freedmen's Bureau in Florida," *Florida Historical Quarterly* 41 (1963): 223–38.

———. "The Florida Black Codes," *Florida Historical Quarterly* 47 (1968–69): 365–79.

———. "Francis L. Cardozo: Black Educator during Reconstruction," *Journal of Negro Education* 48 (Winter 1979): 73–83.

———. "The Freedmen's Bureau and Negro Education in Florida," *Journal of Negro Education* 31 (1962): 460–67.

———. "The Freedmen's Bureau and Negro Labor in Florida," *Florida Historical Quarterly* 39 (1960): 176–84.

———. *The Negro in the Reconstruction of Florida, 1865–1877.* Tallahassee: Florida State University, 1965.

Richter, William L. *The Army in Texas during Reconstruction, 1865–1870.* College Station: Texas A&M University Press, 1987.

———. "'Devil Take Them All': Military Rule in Texas, 1862–1865," *Southern Studies* 25 (1986): 5–30

———. "General Phil Sheridan, the Historians, and Reconstruction," *Civil War History* 33 (1987): 131–54.

———. "James Longstreet: From Rebel to Scalawag," *Louisiana History* 11 (1970): 215–29.

———. "One Hundred Years of Controversy: The Fourteenth Amendment and the Bill of Rights," *Loyola [New Orleans] Law Review* 15 (1968–1969): 281–95.

———. *Overreached on All Sides: The Freedmen's Bureau Administrators in Texas, 1865–1868.* College Station: Texas A&M University Press, 1991.

———. "The Papers of U. S. Grant: A Review Essay," *Civil War History* 36 (1990): 149–66; 38 (1992): 342–48.

———. "Tyrant and Reformer: General Charles Griffin Reconstructs Texas, 1866–1867," *Prologue: The Journal of the National Archives* 10 (1978): 255–41.

———. "'We Must Rubb Out and Begin Anew': The Army and the Republican Party in Texas Reconstruction, 1867–1870," *Civil War History* 19 (December 1973): 334–52.

———. "Who Was the Real Head of the Texas Freedmen's Bureau?: The Role of Brevet Colonel William H. Sinclair as Acting Assistant Inspector General," *Military History of the Southwest* 20 (1990): 121–56.

Riddleberger, Patrick W. "The Break in the Radical Ranks: Liberals vs. Stalwarts in the Election of 1872," *Journal of Negro History* 44 (1959): 136–57.

———. *1866: The Critical Year Revisited.* Carbondale: Southern Illinois University Press, 1979.

————. "The Radicals' Abandonment of the Negro during Reconstruction," *Journal of Negro History* 45 (1960): 88–102.

Ripley, C. Peter, "The Black Family in Transition: Louisiana, 1860–1865," *Journal of Southern History* 41 (1975): 369–80.

————. *Slaves and Freedmen in Civil War Louisiana.* Baton Rouge: Louisiana State University Press, 1978.

Roach, Hannah Grace. "Sectionalism in Congress (1870–1890)," *American Political Science Review* 19 (1925): 500–26.

Roark, James L. *Masters without Slaves: Southern Planters in the Civil War and Reconstruction.* New York: W. W. Norton, 1977.

Roberts, Derrell C. *Joseph E. Brown and the Politics of Reconstruction.* University: University of Alabama Press, 1973.

Robinson, Armistead L. "Beyond the Realm of Social Consensus: New Meanings of Reconstruction for American History," *Journal of American History* 68 (1981): 276–97.

————. "Explaining the Failure of Democratic Reform in Reconstruction South Carolina," *Reviews in American History* 8 (1980): 521–30.

————. "Reassessing the First Reconstruction: Lost Opportunity or Tragic Era?" *Reviews in American History* 6 (1978): 80–86.

Robinson, Charles M., III. *A Good Year to Die: The Story of the Great Sioux War.* New York: Random House, 1995.

Robinson, William A. "William Pitt Fessenden." In *Dictionary of American Biography*, edited by Allen Johnson et al. New York: Charles Scribner's Sons, 10 double vols. + 9 supplements, 1964–1981, 6: 348–49.

Roche, John P. "Plessy *v.* Ferguson: *Requiescat in Pace?*" *University of Pennsylvania Law Review* 103 (1954): 44–58.

Rogers, William Warren. "The Boyd Incident: Black Belt Violence during Reconstruction," *Civil War History* 21 (1975): 309–29.

Rose, Willie Lee. *Rehearsal for Reconstruction: The Port Royal Experiment.* Indianapolis: Bobbs-Merrill, 1964.

Rosen, F. Bruce. "The Influence of the Peabody Fund on Education in Reconstruction Florida," *Florida Historical Quarterly* 55 (1977): 310–20.

Rosenberg, John S. "Toward a New Civil War Revisionism," *American Scholar* 38 (1969): 250–72.

Ross, Stephen Joseph. "Freed Soil, Freed Labor, Freed Men: John Eaton and the Davis Bend Experiment," *Journal of Southern History* 44 (1978): 213–32.

Rostow, Walt W. *Stages of Economic Growth.* 3d ed. Cambridge: Cambridge University Press, 1990.

Ruchames, Louis. "Charles Sumner and American Historiography," *Journal of Negro History* 38 (1953): 139–60.

Russ, William A., Jr. "Disfranchisement in Louisiana (1862–1870)," *Louisiana Historical Quarterly* 18 (1935): 557–80.

————. "The Negro and White Disfranchisement during Radical Reconstruction," *Journal of Negro History* 19 (1934): 171–92.

————. "Radical Disfranchisement in North Carolina," *North Carolina Historical Review* 11 (1934): 271–83.

————. "Radical Disfranchisement in Texas, 1867–1870," *Southwestern Historical Quarterly* 38 (1934–35): 40–52.

————. "Registration and Disfranchisement under Radical Reconstruction," *Mississippi Valley Historical Review* 21 (1935): 163–80.

Russell, Charles Edward. *Blaine of Maine: His Life and Times.* New York: Cosmopolitan, 1931.

Russell, James F. S. "Railroads in the 'Conspiracy Theory' of the Fourteenth Amendment," *Mississippi Valley Historical Review* 41 (1955): 601–22.

Ryan, Halford R. *Henry Ward Beecher: Peripatetic Preacher.* New York: Greenwood Press, 1990.

Bibliography

Ryan, James Gilbert. "The Memphis Riot of 1866: Terror in a Black Community during Reconstruction," *Journal of Negro History* 62 (1977), 243-57.

Safire, William. *Freedom: A Novel of Abraham Lincoln and the Civil War.* Garden City, NY: Doubleday & Co., 1987.

Sandburg, Carl. *Abraham Lincoln.* 6 vols. New York: Harcourt, Brace & Co., 1926-1939.

Sandlin, Betty Jeffus. "The Texas Reconstruction Constitutional Convention of 1868-1869." Ph.D. dissertation, Texas Tech University, 1970.

Sanger, Donald B., and Thomas R. Hay. *James Longstreet.* 2 vols. Baton Rouge: Louisiana State University Press, 1952.

Sansing, David G. "The Role of the Scalawag in Mississippi Reconstruction." Ph.D. dissertation, University of Southern Mississippi, 1969.

Savitt, Todd L. "Politics and Medicine: The Georgia Freedmen's Bureau and the Organization of Health Care, 1865–1866," *Civil War History* 28 (1982): 45–64.

———. "The Use of Blacks for Medical Experimentation and Demonstration in the Old South," *Journal of Southern History* 48 (1982): 331–48.

Sawrey, Robert D. *The Dubious Victory: The Reconstruction Debate in Ohio.* Lexington: University Press of Kentucky, 1992.

Schafer, Joseph. "James Rood Doolittle." In *Dictionary of American Biography*, edited by Allen Johnson et al. New York: Charles Scribner's Sons, 10 double vols. + 9 supplements, 1964–1981, 5: 374–75.

Scheiber, Harry N. "Economic Change in the Civil War: An Analysis of Recent Studies," *Civil War History* 11 (1965): 396–411.

Scheips, Paul J. "Lincoln and the Chiriqui Colonization Project," *Journal of Negro History* 37 (1952): 418–53.

Schell, Herbert S. "Hugh McCulloch and the Treasury Department, 1865–1869," *Mississippi Valley Historical Review* 17 (1931): 404–23.

Schofield, John M. *Forty-Six Years in the Army.* New York: Century, 1897.

Schultz, John H. "Thomas Pownall and His Negro Commonwealth," *Journal of Negro History* 30 (1945): 400–404.

Schwarz, Benjamin. "The Diversity Myth: America's Leading Export," *Atlantic Monthly* 275 (May 1995): 57–67.

Schweninger, Loren. "The American Missionary Association and Northern Philanthropy in Reconstruction Alabama," *Alabama Historical Quarterly* 32 (1970): 129–56.

———. "Prosperous Blacks in the South, 1790–1880," *American Historical Review* 95 (1990): 31–56.

Scott, Emmett, and Lyman B. Stowe. *Booker T. Washington: Builder of a Civilization.* Garden City, NY: Doubleday, Page, 1916.

Scott, Rebecca. "The Battle over the Child: Child Apprenticeship and the Freedmen's Bureau in North Carolina," *Prologue* 10 (1978): 101–13.

Scroggs, Jack B. "Carpetbagger Constitutional Reform in the South Atlantic States, 1867–1868," *Journal of Southern History* 27 (1961): 475–93.

———. "Southern Reconstruction: A Southern View," *Journal of Southern History* 24 (1958): 407–29.

Sefton, James E. *Andrew Johnson and the Uses of Constitutional Power.* Boston: Little, Brown, 1980.

———. "Aristotle in Blue and Braid: General John Schofield's Essays on Reconstruction," *Civil War History* 17 (1971): 45–57.

———. "Charles Sumner for Our Time: An Essay Review," *Maryland Historical Magazine* 66 (1971): 456–61.

———. "Chief Justice Chase as an Advisor on Presidential Reconstruction," *Civil War History* 13 (1967): 242–64.

———. "The Impeachment of Andrew Johnson: A Century of Writing," *Civil War History* 14 (1968): 120–47.

———. *The United States Army and Reconstruction, 1865–1877.* Baton Rouge: Louisiana State University Press, 1967.

ro in Tennessee, 1865–1880.
DC: Association for the Study
and History, 1934.

ro in the Reconstruction of
hington, DC: Association for
Negro Life and History, 1926.

y. "Louisiana: An Impossible
nstruction and Redemption in
ted by Otto H. Olsen. Baton
iana State University Press,
.

ua Reconstructed, 1863–1877.
: Louisiana State University

. Garfield of Ohio: The Available
ork: Norton, 1970.

n Henry Seward: Lincoln's Right
York: HarperCollins, 1991.

l. Destruction and Reconstruction:
riences of the Late War. New
pleton, 1879.

obus. Equal under Law: The
rigins of the Fourteenth
New York: Collier Books,

min. Abraham Lincoln. New
A. Knopf, 1953.

min P., and Harold M.
nton: The Life and Times of
etary of War. New York: Alfred
62.

d Y. A History of Military
in Newly Acquired Territories of
ates. New York: Columbia
ress, 1904.

sas in Civil War and
n, 1861–1874. Little Rock:
ghters of the Confederacy,
apter, 1923.

ory of Military Government in
red Territories of the United
York: Columbia University

ry M. The Confederacy as a
y Experience. Englewood Cliffs,
e-Hall, 1971.

Seip, Terry L. The South Returns to Congress: Men, Economic Measures, and International Relationships. Baton Rouge: Louisiana State University Press, 1983.

Self, Zenobia. "The Court Martial of J. J. Reynolds," Military Affairs 37 (1973): 52–56.

Sellers, James L. "An Interpretation of Civil War Finance," American Historical Review 30 (1925): 282–97.

———. "The Economic Incidence of the Civil War in the South," Mississippi Valley Historical Review 14 (1927): 179–90.

Shapiro, Herbert. "Afro-American Responses to Race Violence during Reconstruction," Science and Society 36 (1972): 158–70.

———. "The Ku Klux Klan during Reconstruction: The South Carolina Episode," Journal of Negro History 19 (1964): 34–55.

———. White Violence and Black Response: From Reconstruction to Montgomery. Amherst: University of Massachusetts Press, 1988.

Shapiro, Samuel. "A Black Senator from Mississippi: Blanche K. Bruce," Review of Politics 44 (1982): 83–109.

Sharkey, Robert P. Money, Class, and Party: An Economic Study of the Civil War and Reconstruction. Baltimore: Johns Hopkins University Press, 1959.

Sheppard, William A. Red Shirts Remembered: Southern Brigadiers of the Reconstruction Period. Atlanta: Ruralist Press, 1940.

Sherer, Robert G. Subordination or Liberation? The Developing Theories of Black Education in Nineteenth Century Alabama. University: University of Alabama Press, 1977.

Sheridan, Philip H. Personal Memoirs of Philip H. Sheridan. 2 vols. New York: D. Appleton, 1888.

Sherman, John. Recollections of Forty Years in the House, Senate, and Cabinet: An Autobiography. Chicago: Herner, 1895.

Shlomowitz, Ralph. "'Bound' or 'Free'? Black Labor in Cotton and Sugarcane Farming, 1865–1880," Civil War History 50 (1984): 569–96.

———. "The Origins of Southern Sharecropping," Agricultural History 53 (1979): 557–75.

Shofner, Jerrell H. "Custom, Law, and History: The Enduring Effect of Florida's 'Black Code,'" Florida Historical Quarterly 55 (1977): 277–98.

———. "Florida: A Failure of Moderate Republicanism." In Reconstruction and Redemption in the South, edited by Otto H. Olsen. Baton Rouge: Louisiana State University Press, 1980, 13–47.

———. "Militant Negro Laborers in Reconstruction Florida," Journal of Southern History 39 (1973): 397–408.

———. Nor Is the Day Over Yet. Gainesville: University Presses of Florida, 1974.

Shook, Robert W. "Federal Occupation and Administration of Texas, 1865–1870." Ph.D. dissertation, North Texas State University, 1970.

———. "Toward a List of Reconstruction Loyalists," Southwestern Historical Quarterly 76 (1972–73): 315–20.

Shouler, James. History of the United States of America under the Constitution. 7 vols. New York: Dodd, Mead, 1880–1913.

Shover, Kenneth B. "Maverick at Bay: Ben Wade's Senate Re-election Campaign, 1862–1863," Civil War History 12 (1966): 23–42.

Shy, John. Toward Lexington: The Role of the British Army in the Coming of the Revolution. Princeton, NJ: Princeton University Press, 1965.

Silver, David M. Lincoln's Supreme Court. Urbana: University of Illinois Press, 1956.

Simkins, Francis B. "The Election of 1876 in South Carolina," South Atlantic Quarterly 21 (1922): 225–41, 335–51.

———. "Joseph Hayne Rainey." In Dictionary of American Biography, edited by Allen Johnson et al. New York: Charles Scribner's Sons, 10 double vols. + 9 supplements, 1964–1981, 15: 327–28.

———. "The Ku Klux Klan in South Carolina, 1868–1871," Journal of Negro History 12 (1927): 606–47.

Bibliography

————. "New Viewpoints of Southern Reconstruction," *Journal of Southern History* 5 (1939): 46–61.

————. *Pitchfork Ben Tillman: South Carolinian*. Baton Rouge: Louisiana State University Press, 1944.

————. "Robert Smalls." In *Dictionary of American Biography*, edited by Allen Johnson et al. New York: Charles Scribner's Sons, 10 double vols. + 9 supplements, 1964–1981, 18: 224–25.

Simkins, Francis B., and Robert W. Woody. *South Carolina during Reconstruction*. Chapel Hill: University of North Carolina Press, 1932.

Simon, John Y., et al., eds. *The Papers of Ulysses S. Grant*. 20 vols. to date. Carbondale: Southern Illinois University Press, 1963– .

Simpson, Brooks D. "Butcher? Racist? An Examination of William S. McFeely's *Grant: A Biography*," *Civil War History* 33 (1987): 62–83.

————. *Let Us Have Peace: Ulysses S. Grant and the Politics of War and Reconstruction*. Chapel Hill: University of North Carolina Press, 1991.

Sinclair, O. Lonnie. "The Freedmen's Bureau in Texas: The Assistant Commissioners and the Negro." Unpublished paper submitted to the Institute of Southern History, Johns Hopkins University, July 22, 1969.

Singletary, Otis A. *Negro Militia and Reconstruction*. Austin: University of Texas Press, 1957.

Small, Sandra E. "The Yankee Schoolmarm in Freedmen's Schools: An Analysis of Attitudes," *Journal of Southern History* 45 (1979): 381–402.

Smallwood, James. "Black Texans during Reconstruction: First Freedom," *East Texas Historical Journal* 14 (No. 1, 1976): 9–23.

————. "Emancipation and the Black Family: A Case Study in Texas," *Social Science Quarterly* 57 (1977): 849–57.

————. "G. T. Ruby: Galveston's Black Carpetbagger in Reconstruction Texas," *Houston Review* 6 (1983): 24–33.

————. "Perpetuati[ng] Agricultural Wor[...] Texas," *Mid-Ame[...]*

————. *Time of Hop[...] Texans during Rec[...]* Washington, NY: [...] Publications, 198[...]

Smith, George Win[...] Imperialism in Flo[...] *Historical Quarterl[...]* 99–130, 268–99.

Smith, James Dougla[...] Reconstruction, 1[8...] Economic, and So[...] dissertation, Unive[...]

Smith, Ronald D., ar[...] *Fascinating People a[...] from American Hist[...]* ABC-CLIO, 1993.

Smith, Samuel Denn[...] *1870–1901*. Chape[...] North Carolina Pr[...]

Smith, Theodore C. [...] *Parties in the North[...]* Longmans, Green, [...]

————. *The Life and [...] Garfield*. 2 vols. Ne[...] University Press, 19[...]

Smith, Thomas H. "[...] Mississippi Freedm[...] *Ohio History* 78 (19[...]

Smith, Willard H. *Sch[...] Changing Fortune of [...]* Indianapolis: Indian[...] 1952.

Sneed, Edgar P. "A H[...] Reconstruction in T[...] Problems," *Southwe[...]* 72 (1968–69): 435–[...]

Somers, Dale A. "Blac[...] Orleans: A Study in [...] *Journal of Southern H[...]*

Spence, Clark C. "Rob[...] Emma Mine Affair,"[...] *Quarterly* 68 (1959): [...]

Spencer, Samuel R., Jr. [...] *and the Negro's Place [...]* Boston: Little, Brow[...]

Bibliography

Suthron, W. J. "Dubious Origins of the Fourteenth Amendment," *Tulane Law Review* 28 (1953–1954): 22–44.

Sweat, Edward F. "Francis L. Cardozo—Profile of Integrity in Reconstruction Politics," *Journal of Negro History* 46 (1961): 217–32.

————. "Some Notes on the Role of Negroes in the Establishment of Public Schools in South Carolina," *Phylon* 22 (1961): 160–66.

Swift, Donald. "John Bingham and Reconstruction: The Dilemma of a Moderate," *Ohio Historical Quarterly* 77 (1968): 76–94.

Swinney, Everette. "Enforcing the Fifteenth Amendment, 1870–1877," *Journal of Southern History* 28 (1962): 202–18.

————. "United States v. Powell Clayton: Use of the Enforcement Acts in Arkansas," *Arkansas Historical Quarterly* 26 (1967): 143–54.

Swint, Henry Lee. *The Northern Teacher in the South, 1862–1870*. Nashville, TN: Vanderbilt University Press, 1941.

Tannenbaum, Frank. *Slave and Citizen: Slavery in the Americas*. New York: Alfred A. Knopf, 1947.

Tansill, Charles C. *The United States and Santo Domingo, 1798–1873: A Chapter in Caribbean Diplomacy*. Baltimore: Johns Hopkins Press, 1938.

Tarbell, Ida M. "How the Union Army Was Disbanded," *Civil War Times Illustrated* 6 (1967–68): 1–9, 44–47.

Taylor, Alrutheus A. "Historians of Reconstruction," *Journal of Negro History* 23 (1938): 16–34.

————. "Making West Virginia a Free State," *Journal of Negro History* 6 (1921): 131–73.

————. "Negro Congressmen a Generation After," *Journal of Negro History* 7 (1922): 127–71.

————. *The Negro in South Carolina during Reconstruction*. Washington, DC: Association for the Study of Negro Life and History, 1924.

————. *The N[...]* Washingto[...] of Negro L[...]

————. *The N[...] Virginia*. W[...] the Study o[...]

Taylor, Joe G[...] Task." In *[...] the South*, e[...] Rouge: Lo[...] 1980, 202–[...]

————. *Louis[...]* Baton Rou[...] Press, 197[...]

Taylor, John [...] *Man*. New [...]

————. *Willi[...] Hand*. New [...]

Taylor, Richa[...] *Personal Ex[...]* York: D. A[...]

Ten Broek, J[...] *Antislavery [...] Amendmen[...]* 1965 [195[...]

Thomas, Ben[...] York: Alfre[...]

Thomas, Ben[...] Hyman. *St[...] Lincoln's Se[...]* A. Knopf, [...]

Thomas, Da[...] *Governmen[...] the United [...]* University [...]

————. *Arka[...] Reconstruct[...]* United Da[...] Arkansas C[...]

————. *A H[...] Newly Acq[...] States*. Ne[...] Press, 190[...]

Thomas, Em[...] *Revolutiona[...]* NJ: Prenti[...]

———. "Lost Cause Alive: Queries and Confederates," *Reviews in American History* 16 (1988): 403–409.

Thomas, Lately. *The First President Johnson: The Three Lives of the Seventeenth President of the United States of America*. New York: William Morrow, 1968.

Thompson, C. Mildred. "The Freedmen's Bureau in Georgia in 1865–1866: An Instrument of Reconstruction," *Georgia Historical Quarterly* 5 (1921): 40–49.

———. *Reconstruction in Georgia, Economic, Social, Political, 1865–1872*. New York: Columbia University Press, 1915.

Thompson, George H. *Arkansas and Reconstruction: The Influence of Geography, Economics, and Personality*. Port Washington, NY: National University Publications, 1976.

Thompson, Henry T. *Ousting the Carpetbagger from South Carolina*. Columbia: University of South Carolina Press, 1926.

Thompson, Jerry Don. *Vaqueros in Blue and Gray*. Austin, TX: Presidial Press, 1976.

Thornberry, Jerry. "Northerns and the Atlanta Freedmen, 1865–1869," *Prologue* 6 (1974): 236–51.

Thornbrough, Emma Lou, ed. *Black Reconstructionists*. Englewood Cliffs, NJ: Prentice-Hall, 1972.

Thornton, J. Mills, III. "Fiscal Policy and the Failure of Radical Reconstruction in the Lower South." In *Region, Race, and Reconstruction: Essays in Honor of C. Vann Woodward*, edited by J. Morgan Kousser and James M. McPherson. New York: Oxford University Press, 1982, 349–94.

Thorpe, Earl E. *Black Historians: A Critique*. New York: Morrow, 1971.

Tidwell, William A. *April '65: Confederate Covert Action in the American Civil War*. Kent, OH: Kent State University Press, 1995.

Tidwell, William A., with James O. Hall and David Winfred Gaddy. *Come Retribution: The Confederate Secret Service and the Assassination of Lincoln*. Jackson: University of Mississippi Press, 1988.

Tindall, George B. *The Disruption of the Solid South*. Athens: University of Georgia Press, 1972.

———. *South Carolina Negroes, 1977–1900*. Columbia: University of South Carolina Press, 1952.

Toll, William. "Free Men, Freedmen, and Race: Black Social Theory in the Gilded Age," *Journal of Southern History* 44 (1978): 571–96.

Townes, A. Jane. "The Effect of Emancipation in Large Landholdings: Nelson and Goochland Counties, Virginia," *Journal of Southern History* 45 (1979): 403–12.

Treagle, Joseph G., Jr. "Thomas J. Durant, Utopian Socialism and the Failure of Presidential Reconstruction in Louisiana," *Journal of Southern History* 45 (1979): 485–512.

Trefousse, Hans L. "The Acquittal of Andrew Johnson and the Decline of the Radicals," *Civil War History* 14 (1969): 148–61.

———. *Andrew Johnson: A Biography*. New York: W. W. Norton, 1989.

———. *Ben Butler: The South Called Him BEAST!* New York: Twayne Publishers, 1957.

———. *Benjamin Franklin Wade: Radical Republican from Ohio*. New York: Twayne Publishers, 1963.

———. "Ben Wade and the Failure of the Impeachment of Andrew Johnson," Historical and Philosophical Society of Ohio *Bulletin*, 18 (1960): 241–52.

———. *Impeachment of a President*. Knoxville: University of Tennessee Press, 1975.

———. *Lincoln's Decision for Emancipation*. Philadelphia: J. B. Lippincott Co., 1975.

———. *The Radical Republicans: Lincoln's Vanguard for Racial Justice*. New York: Alfred A. Knopf, 1969.

Trelease, Allan W. *Reconstruction: The Great Experiment*. New York: Harper & Row, 1971.

———. "Republican Reconstruction in North Carolina: A Roll-Call Analysis of the State House of Representatives," *Journal of Southern History* 42 (1976): 319–44.

———. *White Terror: The Ku Klux Klan Conspiracy and Southern Reconstruction.* New York: Harper and Row, 1971.

———. "Who Were the Scalawags?" *Journal of Southern History* 29 (1963): 445–68.

Tucker, Glenn. *Hancock, the Superb.* Indianapolis: Bobbs-Merrill, 1960.

———. *Lee and Longstreet at Gettysburg.* Indianapolis: Bobbs-Merrill, 1968.

———. *Zeb Vance: Champion of Personal Freedom.* Indianapolis: Bobbs-Merrill, 1965.

Turner, Thomas R. *Beware the People Weeping: Public Opinion and the Assassination of President Lincoln.* Baton Rouge: Louisiana State University Press, 1982.

Turnier, William J. "George W. Julian." M.A. thesis, Pennsylvania State University, 1967.

Tyson, Raymond W. "Henry Winter Davis: Orator for the Union," *Maryland Historical Magazine* 58 (1963): 1–19.

Ulrich, John William. "The Northern Military Mind in Regard to Reconstruction, 1865–1872: The Attitudes of Ten Leading Union Generals." Ph.D. dissertation, Ohio State University, 1959.

Unger, Irwin. "Businessmen and Specie Resumption," *Political Science Quarterly* 74 (1959): 46–70.

———. *The Greenback Era: A Social and Political History of American Finance.* Princeton, NJ: Princeton University Press, 1964.

Urofsky, Melvin I. "Blanche K. Bruce: United States Senator," *Journal of Mississippi History* 29 (1967): 118–41.

U.S. Congress. House. *House Reports*, No. 22. "Condition of Affairs in the Late Insurrectionary States." 42d Cong., 2d sess., 1873. Washington, DC: Government Printing Office.

———. *House Reports*, No. 30. "Report of the Joint Committee on Reconstruction." 39th Cong., 1st sess., 1866; reprinted, New York: Negro Universities Press, 1969.

Uya, Okun Edet. *From Slavery to Public Service, Robert Smalls, 1839–1915.* New York: Oxford University Press, 1971.

Vandall, Gilles. *The New Orleans Riot of 1866.* Lafayette: University of Southwestern Louisiana Press, 1983.

———. "The Origins of the New Orleans Riot of 1866, Revisited," *Louisiana History* 22 (1981): 135–65.

Van Deusen, Glyndon G. *Horace Greeley: Nineteenth Century Crusader.* Philadelphia: University of Pennsylvania Press, 1957.

———. *William Henry Seward.* New York: Oxford University Press, 1967.

Vandiver, Frank E. "Jefferson Davis—Leader without a Legend," *Journal of Southern History* 43 (1977): 3–18.

Vaughn, J. W. *The Reynolds's Campaign on Powder River.* Norman: University of Oklahoma Press, 1961.

Vaughn, Walter R. *Vaughn's Freedmen's Pension Bill.* Freeport, NY: Books for Libraries Press, 1971 [1891].

Vaughn, William P. "Partners in Segregation: Barnas Sears and the Peabody Fund," *Civil War History* 10 (1964): 260–74.

———. "Separate and Unequal: The Civil Rights Act of 1875 and Defeat of the School Integration Clause," *Southwestern Social Science Quarterly* 48 (1967): 146–54.

Veysey, Lawrence. "The Autonomy of American History Reconsidered," *American Quarterly* 31 (1979): 455–77.

Vincent, Charles. "Aspects of the Family and Public Life of Antoine Dubuclet: Louisiana's Black State Treasurer, 1868–1878," *Journal of Negro History* 66 (1981): 26–36.

———. *Black Legislators in Louisiana during Reconstruction.* Baton Rouge: Louisiana State University Press, 1976.

———. "Louisiana's Black Legislators and Their Efforts To Pass a Blue Law during Reconstruction," *Journal of Black Studies* 7 (1976–77): 47–56.

Vogeli, V. Jacque. *Free But Not Equal: The Midwest and the Negro during the Civil War.* Chicago: University of Chicago Press, 1967.

Volz, Harry A., III. "The Administration of Justice by the Freedmen's Bureau in Kentucky, South Carolina, and Virginia." Ph.D. dissertation, University of Virginia, 1975.

Wade, Richard C. *Slavery in the Cities: The South, 1820–1860.* New York: Oxford University Press, 1964.

Wagandt, Charles L. "The Army Versus Maryland Slavery, 1862–1864," *Civil War History* 10 (1964): 141–48.

———. *The Mighty Revolution: Negro Emancipation in Maryland, 1862–1864.* Baltimore: Johns Hopkins Press, 1964.

Wagstaff, Thomas. "The Arm-in-Arm Convention," *Civil War History* 14 (1968): 101–19.

———. "Call Your Old Master—'Master'": Southern Political Leaders and Negro Labor during Presidential Reconstruction," *Labor History* 10 (1969): 323–45.

Wakelyn, Jon L. *Biographical Dictionary of the Confederacy.* Westport, CT: Greenwood Press, 1977.

Walker, Clarence E. *Deromanticizing Black History: Critical Essays and Reappraisals.* Knoxville: University of Tennessee Press, 1991.

Walker, Jacqueline Baldwin. "Blacks in North Carolina during Reconstruction." Ph.D. dissertation, Duke University, 1979.

Wall, Joseph F. *Henry Watterson: Reconstructed Rebel.* New York: Oxford University Press, 1957.

Wallace, Ernest. *The Howling of the Coyotes: Reconstruction Efforts To Divide Texas.* College Station: Texas A&M University Press, 1979.

———. *The Nympho and Other Maniacs: The Lives, the Loves, and the Sexual Adventures of Some Scandalous and Liberated Ladies.* New York: Simon & Schuster, 1971.

———. *Texas in Turmoil.* Austin, TX: Steck-Vaughn, 1965.

Wallace, John. *Carpetbag Rule in Florida: The Inside Workings of the Reconstruction of Civil Government in Florida after the Close of the Civil War.* Gainesville: University of Florida Press, 1964.

Waller, Altina L. "Community, Class, and Race in the Memphis Riot of 1866," *Journal of Social History* 18 (1984): 233–46.

———. *Reverend Beecher and Mrs. Tilton: Sex and Class in Victorian America.* Amherst: University of Massachusetts Press, 1982.

Waller, John L. *Colossal Hamilton of Texas: A Biography of Andrew Jackson Hamilton.* El Paso, TX: Western Press, 1968.

Warmoth, Henry Clay. *War Politics and Reconstruction: Stormy Days in Louisiana.* New York: Macmillan, 1930.

Warner, Ezra J. *Generals in Blue: Lives of the Union Commanders.* Baton Rouge: Louisiana State University Press, 1964.

Warren, Charles. *The Supreme Court in United States History.* 2 vols. Boston: Little, Brown, 1922.

Washington, Booker T. *Frederick Douglass.* Philadelphia: G. W. Jacobs, 1906.

———. *My Larger Education.* Garden City, NY: Doubleday, Page, 1900.

———. "My Views on the Segregation Laws," *New Republic* 5 (December 4, 1915): 113–15.

———. *Up from Slavery.* New York: Doubleday, Page, 1901.

———. *Working with the Hands.* New York: Doubleday, Page, 1904.

Weaver, Herbert. *Mississippi Farmers, 1850–1860.* Nashville, TN: Vanderbilt University Press, 1945.

Weaver, Valerie W. "The Failure of Civil Rights 1875–1883 and Its Repercussions," *Journal of Negro History* 54 (1969): 368–82.

Webb, Ross A. *Benjamin Helm Bristow: Border State Politician.* Lexington: University of Kentucky Press, 1969.

Bibliography

Webb, Walter Prescott. *The Texas Rangers: A Century of Frontier Defense*. Austin: University of Texas Press, 1965.

Weigley, Russell F. *The American Way of War: A History of the United States Military and Strategic Policy*. New York: Macmillan, 1973.

———. *History of the United States Army*. New York: Macmillan, 1967.

Weinstein, Allen. "Was There a Crime of '73: The Case of the Demonetized Dollar," *Journal of American History* 54 (1967): 307–26.

Weisberger, Bernard A. "The Dark and Bloody Ground of Reconstruction Historiography," *Journal of Southern History* 25 (1959): 427–44.

Weissbuch, Ted N. "Albion W. Tourgée: Propagandist and Critic of Reconstruction," *Ohio Historical Quarterly* 71 (1961): 27–44.

Welch, Richard E., Jr. "The Federal Elections Bill of 1890: Postscripts and Prelude," *Journal of American History* 52 (1965): 511–26.

Welles, Gideon. *Diary of Gideon Welles*. Edited by Howard K. Beale. 3 vols. New York: Houghton Mifflin, 1911.

Wellman, Manly Wade. *Giant in Gray: A Biography of Wade Hampton of South Carolina*. New York: Charles Scribner's Sons, 1949.

Wert, Jeffrey D. *General James Longstreet: The Confederacy's Most Controversial Soldier—A Biography*. New York: Simon & Schuster, 1993.

Wesley, Charles H. "Lincoln's Plan for Colonizing the Emancipated Negroes," *Journal of Negro History* 4 (1919): 7–21.

———. "Negro Suffrage in the Period of Constitution-Making, 1787–1865," *Journal of Negro History* 32 (1947): 143–86.

———. "The Participation of Negroes in Anti-slavery Political Parties," *Journal of Negro History* 29 (1944): 32–74.

Wesley, Edgar B. "Forty Acres and a Mule and a Speller," *History of Education Journal* 8 (1957): 113–27.

West, Earle H. "The Peabody Fund and Negro Education, 1867–1880," *History of Education Quarterly* 6 (1966): 3–21.

Wetta, Francis Joseph. "The Louisiana Scalawags." Ph.D. dissertation, Louisiana State University, 1977.

Wharton, Vernon L. *The Negro in Mississippi, 1865–1890*. Chapel Hill: University of North Carolina Press, 1947.

———. "Reconstruction." In *Writing Southern History: Essays in Historiography in Honor of Fletcher M. Green*, edited by Arthur S. Link and Rembert W. Patrick. Baton Rouge: Louisiana State University Press, 1965, 295–315.

White, Horace. *The Life of Lyman Trumbull*. Boston: Houghton Mifflin, 1913.

White, Howard A. *The Freedmen's Bureau in Louisiana*. Baton Rouge: Louisiana State University Press, 1970.

White, Kenneth B. "The Alabama Freedmen's Bureau and Black Education: The Myth of Opportunity," *Alabama Review* 34 (1981): 107–24.

———. "Black Lives, Red Tape: The Alabama Freedmen's Bureau," *Alabama Historical Quarterly* 43 (1981): 241–58.

———. "Wager Swayne: Racist or Realist?" *Alabama Review* 31 (1978): 92–109.

White, Leonard D. *The Jacksonians: A Study in Administrative History, 1829–1861*. New York: Macmillan, 1954.

———. *The Republican Era: A Study in Administrative History, 1869–1901*. New York: Macmillan, 1958.

Whiting, William. *War Powers under the Constitution*. New York: Lee, Shepard and Dillingham, 1871.

Wiecek, William M. "The Great Writ and Reconstruction: The Habeas Corpus Act of 1867," *Journal of Southern History* 36 (1970): 530–48.

———. "The Reconstruction of the Constitution," *Reviews in American History* 1 (1973): 548–53.

———. "The Reconstruction of the Federal Judicial Power, 1863–1875," *American Journal of Legal History* 13 (1969): 333–59.

Wiener, Jonathan M. "Class Structure and Economic Development in the American South, 1865–1955," *American Historical Review* 84 (1979): 970–92.

Wiggins, Sarah Woolfolk. "Alabama: Democratic Bulldozing and Republican Folly." In *Reconstruction and Redemption in the South*, edited by Otto H. Olsen. Baton Rouge: Louisiana State University Press, 1980, 48–77.

———. "The 'Pig Iron' Kelley Riot at Mobile, May 14, 1867," *Alabama Review* 23 (1970): 45–55.

Wikramanayake, Marina. *A World in Shadow: The Free Negro in Antebellum South Carolina*. Columbia: University of South Carolina Press, 1973.

Wiley, Bell I. *Southern Negroes, 1861–1865*. New Haven, CT: Yale University Press, 1938.

———. "Vicissitudes of Early Reconstruction Farming in the Lower Mississippi Valley," *Journal of Southern History* 3 (1937): 441–52.

Williams, Alfred B. *Hampton and His Red Shirts: South Carolina's Deliverance in 1876*. Charleston, SC: Evans & Cogswell, 1935.

Williams, Frank B. "The Poll Tax as a Suffrage Requirement in the South, 1870–1901," *Journal of Southern History* 18 (1952): 469–96.

Williams, George Washington. *History of the Negro Race in America from 1619 to 1880*. New York: G. P. Putnam's Sons, 1883.

Williams, Lou Falkner. "The South Carolina Ku Klux Klan Trials and Enforcement of Federal Rights, 1871–1872," *Civil War History* 39 (1993): 47–66.

Williams, T. Harry. "An Analysis of Some Reconstruction Attitudes," *Journal of Southern History* 12 (1946): 469–86.

———. "General Banks and Radical Republicans in the Civil War," *New England Quarterly* 12 (1939): 268–80.

———. *Hayes of the Twenty-Third: The Life of a Volunteer Officer*. New York: Alfred A. Knopf, 1965.

———, ed. *Hayes: The Diary of a President, 1875–1881, Covering the Disputed Election, the End of Reconstruction, and the Beginning of Civil Service*. New York: D. McKay, 1964.

———. *Lincoln and His Generals*. New York: Alfred A. Knopf, 1952.

———. "Lincoln and the Radicals." In *Grant, Lee, Lincoln and the Radicals*, edited by Grady McWhiney. Evanston, IL: Northwestern University Press, 1964, 92–117.

———. *Lincoln and the Radicals*. Madison: University of Wisconsin Press, 1941.

———. "The Louisiana Unification Movement of 1873," *Journal of Southern History* 11 (1945): 349–69.

Williamson, Joel. *After Slavery: The Negro in South Carolina during Reconstruction*. Chapel Hill: University of North Carolina Press, 1965.

———. *The Crucible of Race: Black-White Relations in the American South Since Emancipation*. New York: Oxford University Press, 1984.

Wilson, David L., and John Y. Simon, eds. *Ulysses S. Grant: Essays and Documents*. Carbondale: Southern Illinois University Press, 1981.

Wilson, Theodore B. *The Black Codes of the South*. University: University of Alabama Press, 1965.

Wilson, Woodrow. *A History of the American People*. 10 vols. Harper & Brothers, 1902.

Winston, Hobert W. *Andrew Johnson: Plebeian and Patriot*. New York: Henry Holt, 1928.

Wish, Harvey A. "Slave Disloyalty under the Confederacy," *Journal of Negro History* 23 (1938): 435–50.

———. *Society and Thought in America*. 2 vols. New York: Longmans, Green, 1950–1952.

Wood, Forrest G. *Black Scare: The Racist Response to Emancipation and Reconstruction*. Berkeley: University of California Press, 1968.

———. *The Era of Reconstruction, 1863–1877*. New York: Thomas Y. Crowell, 1975.

———. "On Revising Reconstruction History: Negro Suffrage, White Disfranchisement, and Common Sense," *Journal of Negro History* 51 (1966): 98–113.

Wood, George A. "The Black Codes of Alabama," *South Atlantic Quarterly* 13 (1914): 350–60.

Wood, W. D. "The Ku Klux Klan," *Quarterly of the Texas State Historical Association* 9 (1905–1906): 262–68.

Woodburn, James A. *The Life of Thaddeus Stevens*. Indianapolis: Bobbs-Merrill, 1913.

Woodley, Thomas Frederick. *Thaddeus Stevens*. Harrisburg, PA: Telegraph Press, 1934.

Woodman, Harold D. *King Cotton and His Retainers: Financing and Marketing the Cotton Crop of the South, 1800–1925*. Lexington: University of Kentucky Press, 1968.

———. "Post Civil War Agriculture and the Law," *Agricultural History* 53 (1979): 319–37.

———. "Sequel to Slavery: The New History Views the Postbellum South," *Journal of Southern History* 43 (1977): 523–54.

Woods, Randall B. "George T. Ruby: A Black Militant in the White Business Community," *Red River Valley Historical Review* 1 (1974): 269–80.

Woodson, Carter G., and Charles H. Wesley. *The Negro in Our History*. 10th ed. Washington, DC: Association for the Study of Negro Life and History, 1962.

Woodward, C. Vann. "The Birth of Jim Crow," *American Heritage* 15 (1964): 52–55, 100–103.

———. "Clio with Soul," *Journal of American History* 56 (1969): 5–20.

———. "Emancipations and Reconstructions: A Comparative Study." In *The Future of the Past*, by C. Vann Woodward. New York: Oxford University Press, 1989, 145–66.

———. "Equality: The Deferred Commitment," *American Scholar* 27 (1958): 459–72.

———. "Flight from History—The Heritage of the Negro," *Nation* 201 (1965): 142–46.

———. *The Future of the Past*. New York: Oxford University Press, 1989.

———. "The Irony of Southern History," *Journal of Southern History* 19 (1953): 3–19.

———. *Origins of the New South, 1877–1913*. Baton Rouge: Louisiana State University Press, 1951.

———. "Our Past Isn't What It Used To Be," *New York Times Book Review*, July 28, 1963, 1 ff.

———. "Reconstruction: A Counterfactual Playback." In *The Future of the Past*, by C. Vann Woodward. New York: Oxford University Press, 1989, 183–200.

———. *Reunion and Reaction: The Compromise of 1877 and the End of Reconstruction*. Boston: Little, Brown, 1951.

———. "Seeds of Failure in Radical Race Policy." In *New Frontiers of the American Reconstruction*, edited by Harold M. Hyman. Urbana: University of Illinois Press, 1966, 125–47.

———. *The Strange Career of Jim Crow*. 2d rev. ed. New York: Oxford University Press, 1966.

———. "The Strange Case of a Historical Controversy." In C. Vann Woodward, *American Counterpoint: Slavery and Racism in the North-South Dialogue*. Boston: Little, Brown, 1971, 234–60.

———. *Tom Watson: Agrarian Rebel*. New York: Oxford University Press, 1938.

———. "Yes, There Was a Compromise of 1877," *Journal of American History* 60 (1973): 215–19.

Woody, Robert H. "The Labor and Immigration Problem of South Carolina during Reconstruction," *Mississippi Valley Historical Review* 18 (1931): 195–212.

———. "The South Carolina Election of 1870," *North Carolina Historical Review* 8 (1931): 168–86.

Woolfolk, Sarah Van Voorhis. "Five Men Called Scalawags," *Alabama Review* 17 (1964): 45–55.

———. *The Scalawag in Alabama Politics, 1865–1881*. University: University of Alabama Press, 1977.

Wyatt-Brown, Bertram. *Southern Honor: Ethics and Behavior in the Old South*. New York: Oxford University Press, 1982 (abridged version, *Honor and Violence in the Old South*. New York: Oxford University Press, 1986).

Wyne, Charles E. *Race Relations in Virginia, 1870–1902*. Charlottesville: University of Virginia Press, 1961.

Wynne, Lewis N. "The Role of Freedmen in the Post Bellum Cotton Economy of Georgia," *Phylon* 42 (1981): 309–21.

Yates, Richard E. *The Confederacy and Zeb Vance*. Tuscaloosa, AL: Confederate Publishing, 1958.

Zilversmit, Arthur. *The First Emancipation: The Abolition of Slavery in the North*. Chicago: University of Chicago Press, 1967.

———. "Grant and the Freedmen." In *New Perspectives on Race and Slavery in America: Essays in Honor of Kenneth M. Stampp*, edited by Robert H. Abzug and Stephen E. Maizlish. Lexington: University of Kentucky Press, 1986, 128–45.

Zilversmit, Arthur, ed. *Lincoln on Black and White: A Documentary History*. Belmont, CA: Wadsworth Publishing Company, 1971.

Zuber, Richard L. *Jonathan Worth: A Biography of a Southern Unionist*. Chapel Hill: University of North Carolina Press, 1965.

Index

Index

Index

Index